The Economics of Regulation
Principles and Institutions

The Economics of Regulation
Principles and Institutions

Volume I   Economic Principles
Volume II   Institutional Issues

Alfred E. Kahn

The MIT Press
Cambridge, Massachusetts
London, England

© 1988 Massachusetts Institute of Technology

First published in two volumes in 1970–1971 under the title *The Economics of Regulation: Principles and Institutions* (volume I: *Economic Principles*, 1970; volume II: *Institutional Issues*, 1971) by John Wiley & Sons Inc., New York, copyright © 1970 and 1971 John Wiley & Sons Inc.

This book was printed and bound in the United States of America.

Library of Congress Cataloging-in-Publication Data

Kahn, Alfred E. (Alfred Edward)
  The economics of regulation.

  Bibliography: p.
  Includes index.
  Contents: v. 1. Economic principles—v. 2. Institutional issues.
  1. Industry and state—United States.   2. Trade regulation—United States.   3. Monopolies—United States.
I. Title.
HD3616.U47K28   1988   338.973   87-32484
ISBN 0-262-11129-2
ISBN 0-262-61052-3 (pbk.)

To Mary

Contents

Volume II   Institutional Issues

Foreword

Paul L. Joskow

I am pleased that The MIT Press has decided to reprint Alfred Kahn's *The Economics of Regulation: Principles and Institutions*. Not only is this two-volume treatise a classic in the literature on the economics of regulation, but a great deal of the analysis that it contains continues to be of contemporary interest from both an intellectual and a public policy perspective. The seventeen years that have passed since the publication of these volumes have witnessed a renaissance of academic interest in the economics of regulation. An enormous technical literature has accompanied this renaissance. Many changes in public policies toward regulated industries have taken place during this period of time as well. Nevertheless, it is still often the case that the most thoughtful and intuitive discussions of difficult contemporary regulatory problems are "in Kahn."

It is a special pleasure for me to have been given the opportunity to provide a brief foreword to these volumes. I took my first courses in the economics of regulation from Alfred Kahn when I was an undergraduate at Cornell at just about the time he began writing volume I. Many of my interests in economics are a direct result of the exciting ideas that were presented in those courses and that have been incorporated in these volumes. My career as a professional economist spans almost exactly the time period that has elapsed since their publication. As a co-editor and associate editor of the *Bell Journal of Economics*—now the *Rand Journal of Economics*—for almost ten years, I had an opportunity to have a first-hand view of the rapid growth of academic interest in the economics of regulation. As a professional economist I have seen the important impact that this book and its author have had on public policy. As a teacher, I have made extensive use of the book in both undergraduate and graduate courses and have been disappointed that it has been difficult to assign it since it has been out of print. There is a great deal of wisdom in these volumes and we should be grateful that students of economic regulation will now be able to gain access to them more easily.

The Economics of Regulation is divided into two volumes. The first focuses on "economic principles" and the second on "institutional issues." This division is somewhat artificial. Although volume I is devoted primarily to the development of the economic principles that should guide the economic regulation of monopolies to promote consumer welfare, it also contains extensive discussions of how these economic principles have and can be applied in practice. It includes numerous examples of the problems that arise in the regulation of firms in many different industries and how the principles of economics can be applied to them. These examples are essential for understanding the prospects and problems associated with putting these principles to use in the regulatory arena. Similarly, while volume II focuses on institutional issues, it develops many important economic principles that are not included in the first volume. This marriage of neoclassical economic theory with institutional considerations and empirical evidence is an important strength of the treatise and a model for sound analysis of problems in applied economics generally.

The voluminous literature that has emerged since these volumes were written has of course expanded our understanding of the underlying problems of economic regulation and how we should deal with them. There have been many papers written on peak load pricing and on optimal pricing for an enterprise characterized by economies of scale. A substantial amount of work has been devoted to developing pricing principles for multiproduct natural monopolies. Recently, there has been a renewed interest in the incentive properties of different systems for setting prices and profits for regulated firms; and the problems associated with price regulation in industries characterized by a mixture of competition and regulation have become of central concern.

This literature is generally more technical mathematically than is the treatment here. It is striking, however, to see how many of the insights provided by more recent theoretical work can in fact be found in these volumes. The central role of marginal cost in any regulatory regime has not changed. The problems associated with pricing different products produced with joint and common costs have not really changed. The issues associated with optimal pricing for natural monopolies faced with a revenue constraint have not changed. The difficult task of finding pricing rules to use in industries in which regulation and competition are permitted to coexist has grown in importance. We have become even more concerned about the potential for regulation to dull incentives to minimize costs and to innovate and about the search for mechanisms to provide better incentives in these dimensions.

The Economics of Regulation continues to provide an extremely clear and intuitive treatment of the basic economic principles that apply to these issues. These principles are, at the very least, a necessary foundation for fully understanding the contribution and applicability of more recent theoretical developments. This may be unfair, but in some cases I believe that the more recent theoretical developments are little more than a very useful mathematical appendix to the fundamental principles developed here. I continue frequently to find it useful to go back to the original text, not only for a clear understanding of the principles of economic regulation, but also to learn more about the intellectual and institutional foundations of the problems and competing solutions that are attracting so much attention today. Especially in an age when our educational system no longer requires students to learn the social, political, economic, and intellectual history of various theoretical and public policy controversies, Kahn's treatment of the economic

and institutional foundations of economic regulation is an essential component of the education of any serious student of the subject.

Developments in the economics of regulation in the past seventeen years
have, of course, extended well beyond the pages of scholarly journals. There
have also been profound changes in the nature and extent of economic
regulation in practice. Several industries have been fully or partially deregulated. In other industries we are in the process of increasing the role
of market forces and reducing the role of administrative regulation. In
still others regulatory rules and procedures have changed considerably
in response to economic and political pressures and new intellectual
developments.

A student of economic regulation cannot expect to rely on this treatise to
obtain a complete understanding of these changes. The new introduction
does a good job of giving us a taste for the kinds of changes that have taken
place and the kinds of questions that they have raised. The promised volume
III will be a welcome addition to the treatise since it will explore them in
more detail. However, the institutional changes that have taken place have
not significantly diminished the value of the historical discussion of regulatory institutions and the relationship between economic priniples and institutional structure and behavior presented here. We find, especially in volume II, very useful and surprisingly contemporary discussions of the
underlying economic forces and regulatory problems that have led to significant changes in institutional arrangements in industries such as telecommunications, transportation, airlines, and natural gas. These portions of the
book provide useful background for understanding both how we got to
where we are today and also the nature of the controversies that these institutional changes continue to cause.

Despite all of the talk about deregulation, many of the industries that were
subject to pervasive economic regulation seventeen years ago continue, at
least to some extent, to be regulated today. These include electric power,
natural gas transmission and distribution, telephone, and the railroads. In
those cases where the public utility concept continues to provide the primary
intellectual foundation for economic governance, many of the principles for
sound economic regulation developed here have, over the last two decades,
gradually been adopted as standard components of actual regulatory rules
and procedures. In the case of electric power, for example, the fundamental
role of marginal cost has been recognized by many regulatory agencies. The
discounted cash flow model presented in volume I is used by virtually all
regulatory agencies to estimate the cost of capital. The controversy over the
use of an original cost or a fair value rate base has been implicitly resurrected
through the application of phase-in plans and renewed interest in the used-
and-useful concept. The incentive issues and the application of specific incentive plans discussed in volume II have been of growing concern to regulators. The contribution to regulatory reform of the economic principles
discussed so lucidly in this volume cannot be underestimated. For those in
the trenches who have the responsibility to regulate well, these pages have
been and continue to be an important source of ideas and practical
guidance.

The introduction to the first edition of volume II (p. xiii) identified the "central institutional issue of public utility regulation" as finding the proper mix between competition and regulation. This challenge is even more important today than it was seventeen years ago. Clearly, the problems associated with mixing competition and regulation have become much more important and much more evident in recent years. Different mixtures of competition and regulation are emerging in the railroad, telephone, natural gas, and electric power industries. They have led to ongoing controversies about ratemaking in the presence of competition and ongoing debates about the proper mix of these two very different mechanisms of economic control. And it is here that these volumes provide extraordinarily contemporary theoretical and institutional guidance that is simply unavailable elsewhere. I believe that our actual experience with mixing competition and regulation over the past several years must lead to a less optimistic appraisal of our ability to do so well than is suggested in these volumes. (This conclusion is consistent with Kahn's extensive discussion of these issues in the new introduction.) Nevertheless, the analysis of the issues associated with regulating prices in the presence of competition contained here is of great value for understanding and resolving such current issues as have arisen over the regulation of railroad rates for captive customers, the pricing of telephone, electricity, and natural gas service for customers with competitive alternatives, a public utility's obligation to serve, and the proper mix of regulation and competition in industries with diverse economic characteristics. The new introduction makes it clear just how relevant these principles are today.

The value of *The Economics of Regulation* goes beyond the coverage of specific theoretical and institutional topics. It represents a general approach to economic analysis of public policy questions that I believe is very appealing and all too rare. By mixing theoretical, institutional, and empirical analysis it shows how economics can be applied scientifically to public policy problems. Regulation, deregulation, competition, and various combinations of them are not good or bad in the abstract as some ideologues would have us believe. They are merely different ways of organizing economic activity to achieve certain ends. They are all imperfect. Whether we should regulate or not, how we should regulate, and what mixture of competition and regulation will be most effective in promoting consumer welfare depend on the specific characteristics of individual products and markets. To make the right choice requires that we carefully balance the advantages and disadvantages of different institutional arrangements in light of the characteristics of the products and firms to which these institutions will apply. *The Economics of Regulation* shows us how economic analysis can be used to help us choose the best match between economic institutions and industry characteristics to promote consumer welfare. I am pleased that another generation of economists will now be able easily to obtain these volumes and have the opportunity to learn as much from them as I have.

Cambridge, MA
September 1987

Introduction: A Postscript, Seventeen Years After

"Introductory Postscript" is, I suppose, an oxymoron. It would be incongruous, however, to reprint these two volumes without some reference to the seventeen years since their original publication; but if that reference were to go into the text at the end, where it belongs chronologically, it would demand the proportions of a third volume—a project on which I am in fact separately engaged. The resulting compromise is this prefatory postscript.

The context in which I embarked on these volumes had two principal features. The first was that economists had only recently begun to apply the familiar principles of microeconomics in comprehensive fashion to the subject; most of the preceding treatises were very largely historical, descriptive, and legal.[1] The other was a general acceptance of the institution of regulated monopoly, at least for the traditional public utilities, not for lack of recognition of its limitations but, by general consensus (with the notable exception of the Chicago School and Marxists), as the only available institution of control in situations in which competition seemed infeasible (see volume II, chapters 1 and 7, and especially pp. 327–329).

In the intervening years, the economics of regulation—the first of these phenomena—has burgeoned: consider the single fact, for example, that the first issue of the *Bell Journal of Economics and Management Science*—now the *Rand Journal of Economics*—whose pages have been the vehicle for a goodly part of this renaissance, appeared in 1970.

The second phenomenon, in contrast—the general consensus—has been shattered, and it would not be hyperbolic today to characterize Horace Gray's negative eulogy, "The Passing of the Public Utility Concept," as prophetic—prematurely so, by some forty years, but prophetic nevertheless.

The Deregulation Revolution

The most dramatic manifestations of the deregulation revolution have, of course, been not in the traditional public utilities but in such structurally

---

[1] It will be unjust to the people unwittingly omitted from the following list, but it would be even more unjust to fail to mention, among the pioneers, Bonbright, Brown, Vickrey, Baumol, and, mainly in the application of those principles to transportation, Friedlaender, Meyer and colleagues, the two Nelsons, and George Wilson.

competitive industries as the airlines, trucking, stock exchange brokerage services, railroads, buses, cable television, oil, and natural gas. In most of these cases the original rationale for regulation was not natural monopoly, but the conception that unregulated competition would be destructive of the quality, continuity, reliability, and safety of service, and unacceptably discriminatory among various groups of customers. (What made some of these industries "structurally competitive" was inter- rather than intraindustry competition—between railroads and other transport modes, between cable and off-the-air broadcasting, for example.) About most of these something of a consensus was already emerging in the early 1970s among disinterested students that regulation had suppressed innovation, sheltered inefficiency, encouraged a wage/price spiral, promoted severe misallocation of resources by throwing prices out of alignment with marginal costs, encouraged competition in wasteful, cost-inflating ways, and denied the public the variety of price and quality choices that a competitive market would have provided.[2]

No such consensus has emerged about the more conventionally defined public utilities—telephone, electric, gas transmission and distribution—or about financial markets generally. All of these industries, however, have likewise been subjected to very substantial deregulations of entry and price, and the result has been a serious erosion of that historic institution.

The reasons for this dramatic change were of course not the same for all these industries. But particularly for the structurally competitive ones, the major common element was the change in the general economic climate between the period of the Great Depression, when many of these controls were imposed, and the 1970s. The Depression, understandably, gave rise to a widespread and thoroughgoing skepticism of unregulated markets. In his famous dissent in *New State Ice* v. *Liebman*,[3] Justice Brandeis expounded the view that unregulated competition was responsible for the business cycle— that is, for cycles of overly exuberant investment, leading in turn to excess capacity and destructive price-cutting, which he saw as the mechanism of economy-wide deflation. (Recall that this was before the distinction between micro- and macroeconomics came into vogue, in both economic thinking and government policymaking.) And it was this attitude, as well as the depth of the Depression itself, that inspired the attempt to cartelize the entire economy under the National Industrial Recovery Act, as well as the specific regulatory statutes more recently overturned.

---

[2]See volume II, chapters 1 and 5; Paul L. Joskow and Roger C. Noll, "Regulation in Theory and Practice: An Overview," in Gary Fromm, ed., *Studies in Public Regulation,* Cambridge, MA: MIT Press, 1981, pp. 4–10; and the excellent survey of the literature in Paul L. Joskow and Nancy L. Rose, "The Effects of Economic Regulation," MIT Working Paper No. 447, April 1987, in Richard Schmalensee and Robert Willig, eds., *Handbook on Industrial Organization,* North-Holland Press (forthcoming). As that survey demonstrates, this broad summary gives inadequate recognition to differences among these industries. In particular, the cases of oil and natural gas (like the control of hous-ing rents) were really quite different from the others: while regulation in these cases, like the others, promoted severe resource misallocation, it was motivated primarily by income-distributional considerations rather than a fear of destructive competition, consisted therefore primarily in the setting of price ceilings rather than floors, and imposed no restrictions on entry—in short, did not involve competition-suppressing cartelization. See, e.g., Stephen Breyer, *Regulation and Its Reform,* Cambridge, MA: Harvard University Press, 1982, chapters 1 and 13.

[3]285 U.S.262 (1932), especially at 292 and 307–308.

The conditioning circumstances and public attitudes of the 1970s were in many ways the mirror image of those of the '30s: the remarkable resurgence of Western capitalism in the intervening decades, the rediscovery of the virtues of a market economy all over the world—in countries both developed and underdeveloped, behind and in front of the Iron Curtain—and a mounting public concern with inflation.[4]

These changes in external economic circumstances and prevailing opinion have no doubt contributed to the erosion of public utility regulation as well, but their general influence was powerfully reinforced by even more dramatic developments specifically affecting these industries.

In the case of telecommunications, the preponderant factor has been the explosion of technology. It has obliterated the always-dubious technological basis for the previous impenetrable regulatory barriers between record and voice communications, satellite and terrestrial transmission, video and audio, and computers and computing, on the one side, and communications on the other: to take only the most dramatic example, the modern electronic telephone switch *is* a computer. It has also enormously increased the number and variety of potential suppliers of telecommunications services. The development of microwave radio transmission, for example, made it almost inevitable that large users would insist successfully on setting up their own facilities, for their own internal needs, in large measure in order to escape the regulatorily inflated charges for long-distance calling.[5] More broadly, it is difficult to believe that it would have been either possible or desirable for us to have continued to entrust to a single monopoly, no matter how efficient, the exploitation of modern telecommunications and computing technologies, with their dazzling versatility and the exploding diversity of services that they make possible.

In the cases of the electric and gas utilities, in contrast, at least one villain of the piece was technological *failure*; the other was double-digit inflation and the fuel crises with which it was closely associated. It had been above all else technological progress and the progressive achievement of economies of scale during the preceding decades that accounted for the very successful performance of the public utility industries, which seemed in turn to justify a reasonably favorable appraisal of the institution itself (volume II, pp. 95–100). After that date, it was the abrupt cessation of those trends, on the one side, and exploding fuel and capital costs, on the other, the most extreme manifestations of both of which developments was the (at least temporarily) failed promise of nuclear power, that have come close to destroying the public utility institution.

---

[4]See my "The Political Feasibility of Regulatory Reform: How Did We Do It?" in LeRoy Graymer and Frederick Thompson, eds., *Reforming Social Regulation*, Beverly Hills: Sage Publications, 1982, pp. 247–263, and Martha Derthick and Paul J. Quirk, *The Politics of Deregulation*, Washington, DC: Brookings Institution, 1985.
[5]See volume I, pp. 152–54. At their peak, these overcharges generated an estimated $11 billion annual net revenue contribution to holding down the basic monthly charge. For a fuller appraisal, see A. E. Kahn and W. B. Shew, "Current Issues In Telecommunications Regulation: Pricing," *Yale Journal on Regulation* (Spring 1987), IV:191–256.

The Results of Deregulation in the Structurally Competitive Industries

Any brief description of the results of deregulation will inevitably do inadequate justice to the many differences in that experience from one industry to another, and to the continuing differences of opinion over the wisdom of that radical change in policy. At the same time—as to the first of these complications—the explicit, central assumption of these two volumes is that there are relevant general principles and common institutional tendencies, and that regulation itself has certain inherent or common characteristics from one context to another (preface to volume I and introduction to volume II); it would be surprising if that were not true of the consequences of deregulation as well. As to the second, I believe it is possible to speak of and summarize something approaching an academic and professional consensus (to which both proponents and critics of deregulation would presumably attach the adjective "respectable," with its correspondingly differing connotations).

The one effect about which there can be no quarrel is that deregulation set off an explosion of competition. One manifestation was a flood of entry, both by new firms—thousands of new truckers and bus companies; entry into telecommunications by public utility companies, railroads, industrials, real estate developers, and banks—and market interpenetrations by incumbents—airline companies on to one another's routes, AT&T into computers and IBM into telecommunications, retail chains and investment houses into banking, and banks into brokerage and underwriting. Initially, this produced marked declines in market concentration; it also set off price wars, business failures and consolidations, and labor unrest, along with other rapid changes in accustomed ways of doing business.

But of course the fact that competitive markets—and especially markets suddenly opened to competition after decades of close regulation—tend to be more turbulent than regulated ones is in itself neither surprising nor dispositive of the comparative merits of the two institutions (volume II, pp. 12–13). What generalizations are possible about the consequent changes in the performance of these industries?

1. In some cases—notably airlines, stock exchange brokerage commissions, and, apparently, trucking—the sharply intensified competition resulted in substantial price reductions, in real terms. Long-distance telephone rates have dropped on the order of 30 percent in real terms, as well.[6]

2. In telecommunications, financial services, and the railroads, the effects of deregulation on the structure of rates have been far more dramatic than on their average levels. In the first two cases, competition forced individual rates into much closer alignment with marginal costs. The decline in long-distance telephone rates has been accompanied by a roughly corresponding increase in the basic monthly charge to subscribers. No longer insulated from competition in the interest rates they pay for deposits, financial institutions have been forced to relate their vari-

---

[6]This last change was effected not so much directly by competition, since most of these rates continue to be regulated, as by a recognition on the part of the Federal Communications Commission that competition at the local level was undermining the ability of the local telephone companies to overcharge the long-distance carriers for access to subscribers placing and receiving calls. See Kahn and Shew, op cit., pp. 196–197.

ous service fees more closely to the respective costs of providing them. Brokerage houses have, under pressure of competition, abandoned the previous absurd flat percentage commission rates, regardless of the size of the transaction (volume II, p. 196).

Similarly, airline fares have come more closely to reflect the tendency of costs per mile to decline with both distance and density of traffic (the latter because of economies of scale in the size of planes) and also the very wide differences in marginal costs of carriage on and off peak; truckers and railroads are apparently offering discounts for back-hauls on an increased scale, similarly reflecting the lower marginal cost of that off-peak service. The tendency has of course by no means been universal in the airlines case: experienced travelers can readily cite examples of seemingly outrageous geographic price discriminations against relatively thin routes. These doubtless reflect the lesser effectiveness of competition in thin than in dense markets. On the other hand, the differences are not entirely discriminatory: it costs more per passenger to provide service on thin routes, other things being equal. Similarly, most discount fares are typically made available only discriminatorily, to travelers with the more elastic demands—for example, by attaching a requirement of staying over a weekend. Still, standby fares are not discriminatory at all, because they impose no capacity costs; and the familiar discount fares are in effect anticipatory standbys, because their availability is limited, flight by flight, to the number of seats that are estimated as likely otherwise to go out empty. Moreover, all travelers continue to have the protection—admittedly in varying degrees of effectiveness—of the relatively high degree of contestability of airline markets, and of the ability of many travelers to drive to larger towns, where a greater variety of fares is typically available.

Readers of these two volumes—indeed, students of elementary economics—will need no explanation of why realignments of rates with marginal costs, with some rates going up and others going down, are by no means a "zero sum game": other considerations aside, bringing rates previously below marginal costs up to that level improves economic efficiency and social welfare just as much as (elasticities of demand being equal) reducing previously inflated rates down to that level.

One central purpose of deregulating the railroads, in contrast, was to give them greater freedom to *vary* their markups above out-of-pocket costs, as a reflection of the widespread belief that rates set at the latter levels (or, more strictly, at incremental cost) would not produce adequate total revenues. This newly conferred freedom—like the earlier controversies over the desirability of the FCC permitting AT&T greater flexibility to reduce rates for competitive services toward incremental costs (volume I, pp. 156–158, 173–174)—stimulated a great deal of discussion and testimony by economists about the proper limits of such price discriminations, and, in particular, the standards for residual regulation of rates to "captive shippers."[7] In general, the upshot of this literature is that so long as rates to demand-elastic customers cover incremental

---

[7]William J. Baumol and Robert D. Willig, *Verified Statements*, Interstate Commerce Commission Ex Parte No. 347 (Sub-No. 1), and *Coal Rates Guidelines—Nationwide*, May 11, 1981, and April 13, 1982; A. E. Kahn, *Verified Statement*, ibid., September 1981.

costs, on the one hand, and rates to demand-inelastic customers do not exceed the costs of supplying them on a stand-alone basis, the latter cannot be said to be subsidizing the former (volume I, pp. 142–143).[8]

3. Competition is offering consumers a greatly increased variety of price/quality options: a proliferation of telecommunications services and equipment; a kaleidoscopic profusion of air fares, with correspondingly diverse conditions and associated degrees of comfort;[9] discount brokerage—simple transaction-consummation; a variety of new financial instruments—NOW accounts, money market funds, certificates of deposit; and an expanded availability of intermodal transport services and contractual rail rates—the latter, previously impermissible, offering valuable protection to shippers undertaking long-term investments.

4. Freed of pervasive regulatory restrictions, and subjected to the greatly accentuated pressures of competition, the deregulated industries generally have greatly improved the efficiency of their operations. The airlines, railroads, and telephone companies sharply reduced their work forces;[10] the Teamsters, railway unions, and pilots have been forced to surrender historic featherbedding practices; all the transportation industries have experienced a more efficient adaptation of type of equipment to type of market; a dramatic move to hub-and-spoke operations has resulted in a fuller utilization of aircraft, the ability to use larger, more efficient planes, and the provision of a wider range of destinations from all originating points, by virtue of the confluence at the hub of traffic from the various spokes; and (thanks largely to the widespread adoption of peak/off-peak fare differentials and under pressure of price competition) airline load factors have been consistently above pre-deregulation levels.

5. In several of these industries, especially in the airlines and trucking, competition has exerted powerful downward pressure on egregiously inflated wages—painful for the workers affected but healthy for the economy at large.

6. The effects of deregulation on the quality of service are difficult to summarize briefly.

The frequently asserted contributions of trucking regulation to the

---

[8]Gerald R. Faulhaber, "Cross-Subsidization: Pricing in Public Enterprises," *American Economic Review* (December 1975), LXV:966–977; William W. Sharkey, *The Theory of Natural Monopoly*, New York: Cambridge University Press, 1982, pp. 40–42; Steven J. Brown and David S. Sibley, *The Theory of Public Utility Pricing*, New York: Cambridge University Press, 1986, pp. 52–53.

The residual issues in the railroad captive shippers cases have revolved around the sufficiency of these limitations, along with a restraint on overall returns, and the definition of the stand-alone shipper or groups of shippers for calculation of the stand-alone cost limit. See the references in note 7 and the Verified Statements by the same witnesses in *Omaha Public Power District* v. *Burlington Northern Railroad Co.*, ICC Docket No. 38783, November 1984 and April 30, 1986 (Kahn), and February 24, 1986 (Baumol and Willig).

[9]The complexity and constant change in these offerings, far beyond the ability of the traveler fully to grasp, has been a source of confusion and vexation. The fact remains that fully 90 percent of all travel in 1986 was at discount fares, averaging 61 percent below regular coach levels: Air Transport Association of America, *Air Transport 1987*, Washington, DC, 1987, p. 5.

[10]American Airlines and United Airlines reported work force reductions of 17 and 24 percent, respectively, in the first few years after deregulation. Total industry employment, however, was 39 percent higher in 1986 than a decade earlier, while total revenue passenger miles had increased 105 percent (ibid., p. 3).

service of small communities proved upon examination to be totally fraudulent: the Interstate Commerce Commission had never in its memory denied any carrier the right to abandon service to any community and, indeed, had no record of what carriers were serving which communities; surveys by the Department of Transportation at the time the deregulation statute was pending demonstrated that small communities were served preponderantly by exempt truckers, United Parcel Service, and specialized common carriers, and virtually not at all by carriers in a position to cross-subsidize that service with protected profits on more lucrative routes.[11]

In the case of the airlines, small communities as a group have experienced very substantial increases in weekly departures; and many more communities have gained service than have lost it. Thanks partly to the subsidized Essential Air Service Program, no community that received a minimum level of certificated—i.e., regulated—service at the time of deregulation has lost it.

The accident rates (on a per flight basis) of the US scheduled carriers have dropped dramatically—on the order of 40 percent between the averages for the five or ten preregulation years and 1979–1986. This is not to deny the possibility, widely asserted, that the pressures of competition have induced or forced the carriers to operate on a narrower safety margin—skimping maintenance, for example—or that the number of near misses may have increased, because of the increased volume of traffic stimulated by price competition and inadequately matched by expanded airport and air traffic control capacity. It is only to say that the record offers no support for the proposition that economic regulation is necessary in order to ensure whatever level of safety society is willing to pay for.

The same is true of trucking: fatal accidents and fatalities per vehicle mile averaged about 20 percent lower in 1981–1986 than in the preregulation period 1976–1979; total accident rates show a similar decline, once the minimum property damage threshhold for reporting them is adjusted for inflation.[12] Moreover, the finding in a report by the California Public Utilities Commission and Highway Patrol of a remarkably close inverse correlation, over the 1976–1986 period, between the number of on-road inspections and accident rates[13] demonstrates that the way to ensure safe practices by truckers is, indeed, simply to police the highways (volume II, pp. 185–186, 192–193).

The quality and safety of rail service has unequivocally improved, with drastic declines in "standing derailments" and in accidents and enforced slowdowns attributable to track defects, largely because the greatly improved financial condition of the railroads has enabled them to make up years of maintenance arrearages. In the case of telecommunications, apart from the disruptions created by the breakup of AT&T—which was neither synonymous with nor absolutely required by deregulation—services have clearly improved in variety and adaptation to customers' needs; the same has been true of financial services.

---

[11]Dorothy Robyn, *Braking the Special Interests, Trucking Deregulation and the Politics of Regulatory Reform,* Chicago: University of Chicago Press, 1987, pp. 69–72.

[12]Information from the U.S. Department of Transportation.

[13]Joint Legislative Report, AB 2678, June 30, 1987.

The quality of the air travel experience has, however, clearly deteriorated—congestion, delays, and customer complaints have increased sharply in recent years—and deregulation bears a large part of the responsibility. Whether this has involved a net social welfare loss is far less obvious: the low fares to which travelers have responded in such profusion necessarily entail lower-quality service—tighter seating, longer lines, fewer amenities, and higher load factors. The enormous response of travelers to the availability of these new options has been, in itself, a vindication of deregulation, not a condemnation of it.[14]

Moreover, the upsurge of traffic need not have entailed the great increase in congestion that we have actually experienced. Responsibility properly rests, instead, with major failures of government policy—inadequate staffing of the Federal Aviation Administration with safety inspectors and flight controllers; failure to expand airport and air corridor capacity sufficiently; inefficient pricing of airport takeoff and landing "slots" at the congested airports. A reader of these two volumes would be astounded to discover that these last rights, instead of being either auctioned off or priced at marginal opportunity costs (volume I, pp. 79–80, 87–88), through variable landing fees, are instead typically priced on the basis of the weight of the planes, without differentiation between peak and off-peak, at levels intended merely to cover the historic costs of construction. The simple market solution would be for the airport authorities to price their services efficiently (volume I, p. 100).[15]

It is necessary to confront the possibility, finally, that the benefits of the competition unleashed by deregulation will prove only temporary—that, as many opponents of deregulation have consistently predicted, competition will ultimately kill itself off. The discovery by the large incumbent airlines of effective ways of blunting the competition of the low-cost, aggressively price-cutting new-entrant carriers—by control of computerized reservations

[14]This is by no means to dismiss the increasingly frequent complaints about lost baggage, misleading scheduling, last minute cancellations of flights with few bookings, involuntary bumping of passengers on overbooked flights, and severe delays. Travelers had no reason to believe these were part of the service package they were buying. There is no necessary incompatibility between economic deregulation—dropping comprehensive governmental restraints on competition—and vigilant governmental protection of consumers from the misrepresentations and violations of implicit contracts that such practices involve. On the response to bumping, see note 15.

[15]In principle, the rules adopted by the Civil Aeronautics Board in 1977, still essentially in effect, prohibiting involuntary bumping of passengers on overbooked flights and requiring the airlines instead to offer compensation sufficient to induce the requisite number of passengers to give up their seats voluntarily, accomplishes exactly the same result. No traveler for whom the value of remaining on the flight is greater than the value of the bribe has to give

up a seat; only passengers for whom the cost of the time lost waiting for a later flight is less than the value of the bribe volunteer. Similarly, landing fees set at marginal opportunity costs (the value of taking off or landing at that particular time and place to the first excluded flight and passenger) would have the effect of offering travelers to whom it is important to take off and land at those particular times and places the high-value service they require, delay free, at its correspondingly high marginal cost, and travelers for whom money is more valuable than those conveniences could be offered corresponding bargains to travel off-peak or to use less convenient airports.

In principle, incidentally, the bumping rules could be expected also to produce the economically optimal amount of overbooking, with airlines equating the (rising) marginal costs of the requisite bribes (reflecting the real cost to consumers of giving up their seats) at successively higher percentages of seats of flights overbooked with the (declining) anticipated marginal revenue—in the form of increasing assurance that every seat will be sold.

systems, by getting their own costs under control, and by developing such successful marketing devices as frequent flyer programs and deeply discounted fares confined to seats expected otherwise to be unfilled; the domination of hubs, and, therefore, of traffic originating and terminating there, by one or two carriers; the failures of most of the new entrants; and the wave of mergers that has reconcentrated the industry on a national level—all these make the question both legitimate and important. It must suffice for our purposes to observe that competition has not killed itself off in American industry generally, even where oligopoly has become typical; that even though concentration at the national level has, after an initial sharp decline, now surpassed preregulation levels, the average number of carriers serving individual markets has apparently increased, as the removal of regulatory restrictions has made each an active or potential competitor of the other; that competition remains extremely intense; and that, in any event, the possibility in this or any other industry that competition might ultimately prove unviable was hardly a justification for having comprehensively restricted it in the first place.[16]

The verdict of the great majority of economists would, I believe, be that deregulation has been a success—bearing in mind, as always, the central argument of these two volumes that society's choices are always between or among imperfect systems, but that, wherever it seems likely to be effective, even very imperfect competition is preferable to regulation (volume II, pp. 112, 328–329, and passim).

Changes in Utility Regulatory Practices—Aggregate Revenue Requirements

Among the public utilities proper, the principal initial response to the acceleration of inflation and explosion of fuel prices in the 1970s was not deregulation but refinements of traditional regulatory practices, aimed mainly at making rate awards more responsive to rapidly rising costs. After two decades of relative quiescence, during which regulators were comparatively complaisant about costs falling faster than rates and earned rates of return tending systematically to exceed levels determined previously to be "just and reasonable," requests for rate increases began suddenly to press hard one upon another, as each award proved to be inadequate even before it went into effect, and achieved returns fell systematically short of the cost of capital.[17]

---

[16]These concerns about the viability of airline competition may have been vindicated unnecessarily by the failure of the federal government vigorously to enforce the antitrust laws' proscriptions of competition-suppressing mergers, predatory pricing, and exercise of control over bottleneck facilities such as computerized reservations systems and airport slots in such a way as to deny competitors a fair opportunity to compete on the basis of their comparative efficiency in serving the public. Here, as in antitrust enforcement generally, all of these possibilities raise the familiar and difficult problem of distinguishing interventions that on balance preserve competition from interventions that on balance

suppress it, by protecting competitors from deserved extinction.

[17]See Paul L. Joskow, "Inflation and Environmental Concern: Structural Change in the Process of Public Utility Price Regulation," *Journal of Law and Economics* (October 1974), XVII:291–314. Market-to-book ratios of electric companies, in consequence, which had run at something like a comfortable 2.0, dropped well below 1.0 after 1973. See, for example, the table in my "Utility Regulation Revisited," an address before the New England Conference of Public Utility Commissioners Annual Symposium, June 15, 1981 (National Economic Research Associates: White Plains), p. 14.

Considering the extremity of the change, it is surprising that, for several years, comparatively little attention was paid to the ancient issue of reproduction versus original cost rate bases (volume I, pp. 35–41). Instead, while continuing preponderantly to set permissible revenues on the basis of original or book capital costs, commissions attempted in various ways to make their rate awards more realistic—adjusting the costs and revenues in the historic "test year" for known changes, determining aggregate revenue requirements on the basis of forecasted test years, incorporating "attrition allowances" in the form of a supplement to the allowed rate of return, allowing for the automatic passing through of changes in fuel and purchased gas prices, and other such automatic escalations or indexations. While evidently falling far short of moving average rates up to marginal or replacement costs, all of these expedients had the essential virtue in economic efficiency terms of bringing them closer to those levels.

A separate consideration that became increasingly important in motivating these various departures from traditional practice was a perceived need to permit the companies an increased cash flow to finance capacity expansions. The most important and intensely controverted method of achieving that end was one that, I think it worth pointing out, I had not even mentioned in these volumes—the incorporation of construction work in progress (CWIP) in company rate bases. Regulation (and I) had tended previously to assume that both the incentive and the ability of public utility companies to finance construction could be taken for granted, if the allowed return exceeded the marginal cost of capital. The assumption was not incorrect. The particularly severe inflation of the costs of constructing new utility facilities (including the cost of capital), however, along with the persistent failure of utility companies to earn their allowed returns, had the effect of drastically reducing their cash flows relative to the requirements for new construction.[18] In these circumstances, the traditional regulatory practice of keeping the accruing expenditures on plant under construction (including the accruing returns on that investment—the "allowance for funds used during construction," or AFUDC) out of rate base until the plant came into service confronted commissions with the prospect of downratings of bonds, sharply increased cost of both debt and equity, and in extreme cases a simple inability to finance.

One solution, which commissions understandably resisted, was simply to allow much higher returns on equity, reflecting the apparently increased marginal cost of capital—sufficiently also to offset the growing suspicion among investors that the companies would not in fact earn the "allowed" return.[19]

The other, which came increasingly into usage (and has now greatly diminished in importance, as both inflation and construction have fallen off

---

[18]Another contributing factor was the introduction of accelerated depreciation and investment tax credits into the Internal Revenue Code, which, in the absence of normalization—see volume I, pp. 33–34—narrowed the gap between before-tax and after-tax income. This, along with the other adverse developments, sharply depressed interest coverages, which are calculated as the ratio between *pretax* earnings and interest obligations.

[19]One manifestation of this suspicion was their increasing tendency to discount reported earnings that consisted in very large measure (50 and even 100 percent in the case of companies with unusually large construction programs) of AFUDC—in effect, regulatory promises to pay by eventually admitting those accumulations into rate base.

and average market-to-book ratios risen well above 1.0), was to admit some portion of the accruing, capitalized CWIP into rate base, there to earn a return from ratepayers currently in the form of cash rather than accrue in the form of AFUDC.

Needless to say, this practice, typically involving much larger rate increases than would otherwise have been necessary, generated extremely bitter, often demagogic, criticism. The most frequent complaint, that ratepayers were being forced to supply capital interest-free to the companies, was simply wrong: since the traditional alternative was to let the return on the invested capital accumulate in the form of AFUDC, on which, once it entered the rate base, customers would ultimately have to pay carrying charges, putting CWIP in rate base spared customers those carrying charges, inflated by the passage of time. In short, when ratepayers supply the capital in advance in this way, they earn a return on those additional up-front payments equivalent to the companies' own allowed rate. Moreover, to the extent that the resulting conversion of company earnings from AFUDC to cash and improved interest coverage ratios reduced the companies' cost of capital (and such other future costs as property taxes on the plant, because of its reduced book value), the return to investors would actually have exceeded the regulatorily allowed return on rate base.

At the same time, this kind of forced levy on present ratepayers—regardless of their own, varying rates of time preference—could in itself be an economically inefficient way of raising capital. Moreover, since the benefit to customers—in the form of reduced future carrying charges on rate base—would accrue only over the life of the investment, it raised inescapable questions of intergenerational equity. Hostile intervenors argued also, not entirely unreasonably, that practices like these merely encouraged the companies (still, perhaps, subject to the Averch-Johnson-Wellicz distortion—however anomalous that would be in a period in which market-to-book ratios below unity suggested investors were expecting returns to fall short of the cost of capital) to construct more capacity than would in fact prove to be needed.[20]

Severe as these problems were, and much as they challenged traditional regulatory practice, they might well have worked themselves out—indeed, the recovery of electric company market-to-book ratios to levels in excess of 1.0 by the early '80s suggests that was indeed occurring—had it not been for (1) the piling on of a second outburst of double-digit inflation, with an even more painful inflation of capital costs, (2) another trebling of world oil prices—both of these in the 1979–1981 period—(3) the explosion in the costs of nuclear plants into the multibillion dollar range, and (4) a dramatic

---

[20]For a survey of the literature since 1970 assessing the AJW model (see volume II, pp. 49–59, and both volumes, passim) and attempting to test it empirically, see Joskow and Rose, op. cit., pp. 42–44. Joskow himself has supplied one of the most telling criticisms—namely, that the model assumes incorrectly that the central goal of regulation is to hold the realized rate of return to the allowed level (op. cit., *Journal of Law and Economics*, 1974). For a preview of his more realistic model—according to which regulators are far less concerned about the returns companies achieve in the context of stable or declining rates than when confronted with requests for rate increases—which he documents persuasively, see volume II, pp. 66–67. This suggests, Joskow observes, that the AJW effect is more likely to be observed in periods of rising than of declining costs (op. cit., p. 304). At such times, however, the resistance of regulators and the public to rate increases could well be an at least equally powerful deterrent to excessive employment of capital.

deceleration in the growth of demand, so that completion of plants left the industry with a large amount of excess capacity. This combination of developments raised problems of a magnitude that our traditional regulatory institutions proved ill-equipped to handle.

The problems took two principal forms: The first was the threat of rate shock as these huge lumps of investment came or threatened to come into the rate base (or were canceled and part or all of the costs recovered from ratepayers). One result was the exploration of ways to introduce these investments more gradually into rate base, in some cases beginning at the CWIP stage, but in any event continuing after the plants actually came into service. This had the virtue not only of being less unattractive politically but also of being more equitable to the various generations of ratepayers, by producing a somewhat better synchronization between the opposing effects on rates of heavy capital costs, on the one side, and fuel savings, on the other. It also made economic sense: after 50 years of dormancy, the old controversies over original versus reproduction cost regulation came alive again, and it became necessary to confront the economic as well as political irrationality of an original cost regulatory system that (a) held rates totally stable until a plant came in (indeed, caused them to decline, as depreciation eroded the original-cost rate base), even though marginal costs were probably increasing, then (b) would have increased them as much as 40 to 70 percent when that plant came into rate base and had applied to it a current cost of equity capital that incorporated a compensation for anticipated *future* inflation (at a time when, with a large lump of capacity coming into service, marginal costs were presumably dropping), only then (c) to decline over the ensuing 20 or 30 years as that cost of capital was applied to a declining rate base, even though marginal costs would presumably once again be rising (cf. volume I, pp. 103–109).

Increasingly, therefore, economists began to advocate either a return to some kind of reproduction cost (or inflation-indexed original cost) rate base, on the principle that this would cause rates more closely to track current costs, or some form of economic depreciation that would cause the rate base to reflect the actual change in the economic value of a plant (and could well therefore be negative during a period of inflation).[21] No regulatory commission has to my knowledge actually adopted either of these formal techniques, but phasing in of the costs of these lumpy investments became very widespread.

The other, even more dramatic challenge was to the concept, fundamental to original cost regulation, that utility companies are entitled to a fair opportunity to earn a "reasonable" return on all dollars prudently invested in fulfilling their service responsibilities. Regulatory commissions have of course both the authority and responsibility, under that system, to disallow imprudent expenditures. But judgments of prudence can, in principle—and

[21]Myron J. Gordon, "Comparison of Historical Cost and General Price Level Adjusted Cost Rate Base Regulation," *Journal of Finance* (December 1977), XXXII:1501–1512; Sally Hunt Streiter, "Trending the Rate Base," *Public Utilities Fortnightly* (May 13, 1982), CIV (No. 10):32–37, "Indexed Bonds and Other Issues," ibid. (June 10, 1982), CIV (No. 12):40–47, and "Avoiding the 'Money-Saving' Rate Increase," ibid. (June 24, 1982), CIV (No. 13):18–22; Stewart C. Myers, A. Lawrence Kolbe, and William B. Tye, "Inflation and Rate of Return Regulation," *Research in Transportation Economics* (1985), II:83–119; Peter Novarro, Bruce C. Petersen, and Thomas R. Stauffer, "A Critical Comparison of Utility-Type Ratemaking Methodologies in Oil Pipeline Regulation," *Bell Journal of Economics* (Autumn 1981), XII:392–412.

in fairness—be made only as of the time when the pertinent commitments and expenditures were made.

These doctrines proved totally inadequate to the inescapable task of distributing the burdens of multibillion dollar investments that turned out (or appeared to have turned out) catastrophic mistakes.[22] It was very difficult to demonstrate honestly that the pertinent decisions along the way had been imprudent: nuclear plants already in operation were producing power at very low cost, and while the costs of plants under construction were escalating from the $300 to $400 range originally estimated to many thousands of dollars per kW, under the impact of inflation and the multiplying safety requirements imposed after the 1979 Three Mile Island accident, the price of oil was likewise going up, from approximately $12 to $35–40 a barrel, and it constantly appeared, even to disinterested observers, that the *incremental* costs of completing plants already in process of construction would be smaller than the cost of alternative supply sources.

On the other hand, the political process simply could not tolerate making ratepayers bear the entire cost of hundred million or even multibillion dollar mistakes. The modal treatment of abandoned nuclear plants has been to permit the amortization of the accumulated capital costs over periods of 10 years, while denying the companies a return on the unamortized balance—which involves a very substantial disallowance in present value terms and could totally eradicate the stockholder equity in those plants.[23] And in the case of completed plants, commissions have found one ground or another for major disallowances, often departing explicitly from original cost valuation in favor of one version or another of minimum incremental cost.[24]

What made these departures particularly violative of the principles of original-cost regulation was not so much that the valuations were based on hindsight—in effect holding utility managements to a standard of perfect foresight—as that they were selectively and asymmetrically so. Regulators,

---

[22]In the case of nuclear plants abandoned in mid-construction, the conclusion was of course unequivocal that those investments were not "used and useful." In the case of plants completed, however, even at costs two and three times either the national nuclear average or the costs of newly constructed coal plants, and in many cases leaving the companies with grossly excessive capacity, the possibility can not be excluded of external circumstances changing so radically over their productive lives—another multiplication of the price of oil, or an upsurge in demand—as to vindicate even those investments. The foresight of regulatory commissions judging the value of such plants upon their completion could of course prove to be just as faulty as the foresight of the company managements in having previously undertaken their construction or deciding to complete them.

[23]A study commissioned by the Department of Energy estimated that this modal treatment would, depending on the pertinent discount rate, impose some 30 percent of the burden each on investors and ratepayers, with the

Treasury bearing the remainder, because of the ability of the company to take an immediate write-off of the investment for tax purposes (*Nuclear Plant Cancellations: Causes, Costs, and Consequences*, Washington, DC: Energy Information Administration, U.S. Department of Energy, April 1983, pp. 35–57).

If, then, that investment had been financed 70 percent or more with senior securities, the equity in the plant would have been wiped out entirely: that is, the dollar returns annually to the company would suffice to cover only interest on the debt and dividends on the preferred stock.

[24]An unpublished study by Lewis Perl, of National Economic Research Associates (White Plains, NY), in 1986, estimated, on the basis of the experience to date, that total disallowances for both canceled and completed nuclear plants would total $35 billion. This would amount to almost 54 percent of the industry's total equity in those plants, and 16 percent of the entire equity of all privately owned electric utilities in the country.

continuing to hold the rate bases associated with the other plants to original cost, were in effect opting for original or replacement cost, depending upon which produced the lower result, and in so doing denied investors a reasonable opportunity to earn the cost of capital on the sum total of their prudent investments. And yet, to repeat, strict application of the prudence test alone would have struck regulators and ratepayers as at least equally unfair.

It was precisely the unbridgeability of that gap between what appeared to be fair to the company under original cost principles and what appeared to be fair to consumers in these circumstances that produced institutional breakdown, and opened up the possibility of a true "passing of the public utility concept."[25]

Changes in Utility Regulatory Practices—Rate Structures

Well before these radical developments of the 1980s, regulatory commissions had responded to the 1973–1974 fuel crisis and outburst of inflation, as well as to the intensified national concerns about energy conservation and environmental preservation, with a sharply increased attention to utility rate structures. This shift in emphasis was in itself one that an economist would applaud (volume I, pp. 54–57). In addition, regulatory commissions were, in so doing, increasingly motivated explicitly by considerations of economic efficiency: the conviction became increasingly widespread that more efficient rate structures could, by discouraging inefficient consumption, contribute to conservation and, by relieving pressures to expand capacity at a time of rising capital costs, hold down rates and mitigate environmental degradation.[26]

One sign of this development was the resolution of the National Association of Regulatory Utility Commissioners in 1974 calling on the Edison Electric Institute and Electric Power Research Institute to undertake a far-reaching "study of the technology and costs of time-of-day metering and electronic methods of controlling peak-period usage of electricity, and also a study of the feasibility and cost of shifting various types of usage from peak to off-peak periods." This eventuated in a mammoth *Electric Utility Rate Design Study*, which ultimately ran to some 95 reports.[27] Another similar sign was the Public Utility Regulatory Policies Act of 1978 (PURPA), which, among many other provisions, requires the state commissions to consider and make explicit determinations of the cost effectiveness (measured by comparisons of incremental savings and incremental costs) of rates to the various classes of customers (a) based on the respective costs of serving them, (b) reflecting variations in costs by time of day and season, (c) eliminating non-cost-justified declining blocks, and (d) offering industrial and com-

---

[25]In considering the implications of these developments, below, we shall allude also to evidences of a similar breakdown in natural gas transmission and distribution, where long-term commitments to purchase high-cost gas, quite possibly prudently incurred, provide the analogy to the sunk costs of nuclear electric generating stations.

[26]See the very interesting account of these developments, particularly in New York State and California, in Douglas D. Anderson, *Regulatory Policies and Electric Utilities*, Boston: Auburn House, 1981.

[27]See the *EPRI Guide, Technical Reports Published 1972–1981*, Palo Alto: Electric Power Research Institute, September 1986.

mercial customers interruptible rates reflecting the lower costs of such service.[28]

The change in state regulatory practice has apparently been dramatic. A survey by Parmesano, Bridgman, and Perry-Failor found that electric utilities in 25 states were in 1987 using marginal costs explicitly in setting retail rates (see the bibliography). In further illustration, New York State instituted

- separate charges for telephone directory assistance; the institution of a 10 cent per call charge, with all customers beginning each month with three free calls and a 30 cent rebate, produced within the first two months a reduction of 40 to 45 percent in the volume of these calls and the full rebate for 85 percent of the residential customers—a $25 million rate reduction;

- an order to the New York Telephone Company to offer all customers the option of measured local service, with timing of messages and a cost-based charge per minute, accompanied by what purported to be a correspondingly cost-justified reduction in either the basic monthly charge or in the rate for individual messages;[29]

- a reduction in the minimum charging time for intrastate toll calls from three to two minutes, in recognition of the fact that the third minute imposes a separate marginal cost, which had the additional attraction of avoiding a rate increase (for calls of two minutes or less);

- an insistence that the Telephone Company raise its charges for customer premises equipment up to current costs (which exceeded embedded or book costs);

- a reduction in intrastate toll charges, in explicit recognition of the fact that they far exceeded marginal cost and that demand for this service was relatively elastic;

- a prohibition of the inclusion of utility services in the rents on new residental buildings,[30] accompanied by

- relaxations in the previous prohibitions of commercial landlords and co-operatives submetering both new and existing premises—in both cases in order to confront users of those services with a measure (however rough) of the positive incremental costs that their use imposes on society;

- requirements that water companies, particularly ones facing supply shortages and the prospect of markedly increasing costs, install meters;

- an order to all major electric companies of the state to propose marginal-cost-based, time-of-day electric rate schedules to customers large enough to be equipped economically with the requisite meters, and to develop promotional rates for customers willing to have their appliances—particularly water heaters—"rippled off" during peak periods, and, similarly,

---

[28]Public Law 95-617, 95th Congress, November 8, 1978, 92 Stat. 3117, Title I, Subtitle B. While the term "marginal cost" nowhere appears among the standards stipulated, the concept is implicit—for example, in instructions to commissions to determine the extent to which total costs would change with additions to capacity and additional consumption of energy: ibid., Sec. 115(a)(2). While most of the debate over PURPA concentrated on this provision and

very little on Title II, the former appears to have had very little effect, while Title II has turned out to be very important. See note 38.

[29]For a survey of more recent studies casting doubt on the cost effectiveness of local measured service, see Kahn and Shaw, op. cit., pp. 234–239.

[30]PURPA later incorporated a similar prohibition of master metering, subject to a cost effectiveness test: loc. cit., Sec. 113(b)(1).

- encouragement to companies to institute especially low rates for interruptible (and, therefore, zero marginal capacity cost) usage.

The circumstance responsible for the most innovative developments in both theory and practice was the abrupt change—shortly after these two volumes appeared—from a situation in which it appeared generally marginal costs were below to one in which they were above average costs (i.e., average revenue requirements, as determined under traditional regulatory practice).[31] This produced a radical shift in the attitude of regulators toward promotional rate structures as well as toward active promotion of sales by the companies, from permissiveness and encouragement to hostility. Whereas growth—in the economy at large and in the consumption of utility services particularly—seemed as recently as the early 1970s to be the universal lubricant of all social and economic frictions, commissions became painfully aware shortly thereafter that growth meant increasing, not decreasing, rates:

"The fact is that in most public utility industries today, growth means increasing, not decreasing, unit costs, in real terms. It is the high costs of new plant and of capital that, in these heavily capital-intensive industries, has inflated rate bases, produced ridiculous ratios of allowances for funds during construction to real cash income, and depressed interest coverage ratios, all of which have been forcing us to provide allowances for capital attrition, raise returns on equity, put sizeable fractions of construction work in progress in rate bases, and give serious consideration to normalization of income taxes, all of which are now accounting for the *major* portion of the rate increases we have recently been forced to grant."[32]

Economists had during the 1960s and '70s been rediscovering and propounding the now-familiar Ramsey prescription for reconciling marginal costs and aggregate revenue constraints for the then-typical situation of marginal costs falling short of average: for services with independent demands, markups above marginal cost inversely proportional to elasticities of demand.[33] Both they and regulatory commissions all over the country became increasingly aware that the principle applied, symmetrically, in the opposite situation: what was called for were mark*downs* from marginal cost inversely proportional to demand elasticities.

In any event, these altered circumstances, along with interventions by conservation-minded organizations and consumer advocates, suspicious of the

---

[31]Because the two are so easily confused, it is worth reemphasizing (see volume I, pp. 124–130, and especially p. 134) that "average revenue requirements" under original cost regulation are not the same as the economist's conception of "average costs," and the difference between the former of these and marginal cost is therefore not necessarily a reflection of economies or diseconomies of scale, or, therefore, of the presence of increasing or decreasing costs, in the economic sense. The economist's conception refers to the slope of the static short- or long-run average cost curve; the difference between marginal cost and average revenue requirements, in contrast, reflects also the effects of changes over time in technology and price

levels, since the latter contains a large component of historic or book investment costs, which are irrelevant to either marginal or average costs, in the economic sense.
[32]A. E. Kahn, "Recent Developments in Cost Analysis and Rate Design," address to the Third Annual Symposium on Problems of Regulated Industries, Kansas City, MO, February 14, 1977.
[33]Volume I, p. 144. See also Frank P. Ramsey, "A Contribution to the Theory of Taxation," *Economic Journal* (1927), XXXVII:47; William J. Baumol and David F. Bradford, "Optimal Departures from Marginal Cost Pricing," *American Economic Review* (June 1970), LX:265–283.

effect of expanding demand on average prices, forcibly directed regulators' critical attention to the traditional declining block rate structure of electric and gas prices. Since these rates, introduced in important measure to forestall self-supply by large customers, seemed to encourage expanded usage, and since the marginal costs associated with supplying large customers were (other conditions equal) no lower than for small customers, regulators moved to eliminate the declining blocks.

At that point, conservationists began to urge regulators to go even further and invert the blocks—that is, charge progressively higher rates for higher blocks of usage. This proposal—like the proposals of "lifeline rates," current at the time—had the additional attractiveness on political grounds of seeming to favor the smaller residential users—even though rates of electricity consumption are only very imperfectly correlated with family income; the intention was in many instances quite explicitly to subsidize residential at the expense of business customers.[34] It also seemed plausibly to satisfy Ramsey principles: demand in the smallest blocks of consumption (which, in typical residential tariffs, are intended to cover the customer costs that do not vary with the levels of consumption—volume I, pp. 95–96, 152—and represent minimal needs for lighting, refrigeration, and perhaps water-heating) is probably highly inelastic; and so rates in those blocks below marginal cost would do the least damage by way of inefficiently stimulating consumption.

These developments were accompanied by a fuller development of the theory of such multipart or nonlinear tariffs. This literature demonstrated that these tariffs could be more efficient than Ramsey prices, because the latter would presumably have to be uniform (or "linear") for particular services or classes of service, whereas the former permit *marginal consumption* to be priced closer to marginal cost, with the revenue deficiency (or surplus) made up in the inframarginal price—the fixed fee or the price for the initial usage block or blocks.[35]

By the mid-1980s, the relationship between marginal and average costs of electricity in many areas of the country, and in natural gas transmission and distribution generally, had come full cycle back to the circumstances generally posited in these two volumes. In the case of electricity, the combination of a sharply decelerated rate of growth in demand after around 1973, the completion of large generating plants that had been predicated in considerable measure on the expectation of continued growth in demand, and the entry into ratebase of very costly nuclear and coal plants had, in many areas of the country, once again driven average revenue requirements far above marginal costs. In natural gas, the combination of the severe shortages in the 1970s and declining domestic production—both exacerbated by continued regulation of the field price—the resulting frantic acquisition of new supplies by pipeline and distribution companies at very high cost, under long-term contracts with take-or-pay-for-obligations, followed by the col-

---

[34]See Anderson, op. cit., especially chapters 5 and 6.

[35]Brown and Sibley, op. cit., chapter 4; Robert D. Willig, "Pareto-Superior Nonlinear Outlay Schedules," *Bell Journal of Economics* (Spring 1978), IX:56–69; M. Barry Goldman, Hayne E. Leland, and David S. Sibley, "Optimal Nonuniform Pricing," *Review of Economic Studies* (April 1984), LI:305–319. In this way, nonlinear tariffs come closer than Ramsey tariffs to perfect price discrimination—a separate price for every sale—which achieves the same efficient results as pure marginal cost pricing: see volume I, pp. 131–132.

lapse of open-market fuel prices in 1985 to 1987 had the same result: marginal costs far below average revenue requirements.

The economic principles, as we have observed, are symmetrical. The result in these altered circumstances should have been a reversal of the regulatory practices of the 1970s: receptivity to—indeed, active encouragement of—sales promotion, and a reversion to declining block rates or their equivalent, with a disproportionately large recovery of revenue requirements in the flat customer charge and initial blocks of consumption. One important political difference, of course, was that the requirements of economic efficiency were now far less attractive to emotional conservationists and consumerists. (To an economist, of course, "conservation" is synonymous with economic efficiency, and is violated just as much by rates above as rates below marginal cost.)

The concept of two-part or multipart tariffs has proved attractive also as a possible means of reconciling the more efficient pricing of telephone services with the historic reasons for overcharging long-distance calling in order to hold down the basic residential charge—the desire to promote universality of service and generally held conceptions of distributional equity.[36] Telephone companies have expanded their offerings of a variety of two-part or multipart options—offering impecunious users who might otherwise drop off the system the option of service at a very low fixed monthly charge along with high charges per call (perhaps beyond some "basic" minimum number), while giving larger users with a considerably more elastic demand for usage—even threatening perhaps to bypass the telephone companies entirely and supply their own needs in order to escape inflated usage charges—the choice of a more fully compensatory flat charge along with usage charges closer to marginal costs.[37]

The Anomalies and Distortions of Partial Deregulation

The experiences of the early 1980s with nuclear plants—traumatic for investors, companies, their customers, and utility commissions alike—contributed in various ways to the dissolution of the public utility institution. On the part of the companies, it bred a widespread disinclination to undertake new investments in capital-intensive facilities with long-lead construction times, for fear that it would expose them once again to major disallowances in the future on the basis of hindsight. On the part of regulators and legislators, it inspired a quest for alternative regulatory or deregulatory arrangements that would transfer a greater share of the investment risks from customers to investors. If these efforts were in some measure opportunistic—even unprincipled—they were motivated also by a suspicion that the companies would never have persevered in completing some of these plants had they not hoped for the usual cost-plus treatment, and by a recognition of the superior reward and incentive properties of competition.

And so the last decade has witnessed some genuine tendencies toward the admission of competition into public utility markets:

- Under PURPA, electric companies are required to purchase the output of "qualifying facilities"—independent small-scale hydro, solar, and in-

[36]Kahn and Shew, op. cit., pp. 241–242, 253–255.
[37]Gerald R. Faulhaber and John C. Panzar,

"Optimal Two Part Tariffs with Self-Selection," Bell Laboratories Economic Discussion Paper No. 74, 1977.

dustrial cogenerating facilities—at rates no lower than their own incremental costs, i.e., the costs they avoid by such purchases, and supply them power on nondiscriminatory terms.[38]

- Electric companies and natural gas producers and pipelines, finding themselves with excess capacity, have been offering bargain supplies to large industrial customers and wholesale distributors outside their franchise territories, and large customers, correspondingly, have been shopping around on an increasing scale—purchasing their gas at bargain prices directly in the field and their gas and electricity from suppliers outside their franchise territories, then presenting these supplies to the pipelines and local gas or electric companies for carriage to the point of consumption.

- The Federal Energy Regulatory Commission, in its historic order 436,[39] encourages gas transmission companies to hold themselves out as common carriers (instead of, as under the historic practice, carrying only gas that they purchase themselves and sell directly to industrial customers and local distributors) and proposes to permit distribution companies served by such pipelines to opt out of their contractual purchase obligations over a five year period.[40]

- Utility commissions have been considering setting rates for all power issuing from facilities henceforward constructed at incremental or avoided costs, and have in some states considered requiring electric distribution companies to acquire their future power through auctioning—putting their requirements out for competitive bidding.

- Independent enterprises have been proposing to construct generating facilities to supply power on a competitive basis to any and all nonaffiliated distribution companies.

All these steps, however, add up to something far short of full deregulation. The overwhelming majority of transactions in all of the three major historic public utilities continue to be regulated; and there is no consensus about how far along the deregulatory path it is desirable to go, or, indeed, whether the steps taken so far have been in the right direction.

The reasons for these uncertainties are rather obvious, and closely interrelated:

- The overwhelming majority of customers still have no easy alternative to receiving their local telephone, electric, and gas service from franchised monopolists.

- Regulators and the public alike have been unwilling to permit the realignment of their rate structures with marginal costs that unregulated competition would enforce, to the extent this would entail increases in the politically most sensitive charges—basic residential rates.

---

[38]Title II Sec. 201 and 210, 92 Stat. 3134–3135, 3144–3145.

[39]FERC Order No. 436, *Regulation of Natural Gas Pipelines After Partial Wellhead Decontrol*, Final Rule and Statement of Policy—Dkt. No. RM85-1-000, 50 F.R. 42408, issued October 9, 1985.

[40]This decision was returned to the Commission by a Circuit Court of Appeals with instructions to give further consideration to the effect on the long-term take-or-pay commitments of the pipeline companies of this proposed loosening of contractual obligations of their customers: US Court of the District of Columbia, Circuit Court of Appeals No. 85-1811, *Associated Gas Distributors* v. *Federal Energy Regulatory Commission*, decided June 23, 1987.

In any event, natural gas transmission lines in 1986 for the first time carried more gas for others than for their own account.

- Some of the markets into which competition has actually entered—long-distance telephone service, local telephone service within large industrial and commercial establishments, the connections between large users and long-distance carriers, some of the competitive generation and acquisition of gas and electricity—may well be naturally monopolistic, with competition having been feasible only because of distortions in the regulated rates charged by the franchised incumbent suppliers—as we shall more fully explain below.[41]

- Finally, there is the pervasive concern that the regulated monopolists may use their control over bottleneck facilities—the local telephone networks, the electric and gas transmission and local distribution systems—to deny rivals a fair access to customers. This was the rationale for breaking up AT&T, separating the putatively monopolistic local service from the assumedly competitive or potentially competitive long-distance business. Closely associated have been concerns about the possibility of cross-subsidization: however much the revenue contributions have in fact flowed in the opposite direction, the possibility that the incumbents, regulated on the basis of their aggregate costs and revenues, might price their competitive services at unfairly low levels and recoup the resultant revenue deficiencies, with the permission of their regulators, from captive customers (volume I, pp. 171, 176; volume II, p. 54).

It would ordinarily not be seemly to quote from oneself, in an introduction to one's own book; that rule would presumably not apply, however, to a confession of partial error:

"The two principal institutions of social control in a private enterprise economy are competition and direct regulation. Rarely do we rely on either one of these exclusively. . . . The proper object of search in each instance is the best possible mixture of the two. . . .

"The marriage (perhaps the better term would be miscegenation) of these two approaches in the public utility context is inevitably an uneasy one, but the almost universal conception is that the mixed marriage is better than none; that such competition as can be permitted, consistent with efficiency, can contribute to improved performance . . ." (Volume II, pp. xiii, 115).

---

[41]For an explication of this possibility in the telephone case, see volume II, pp. 146–152: "If Competitors Want to Enter, How Natural Can Monopoly Be?" Economists—most of them originally associated in one way or other with AT&T—have since 1970 very thoroughly developed the conception that (1) long-run increasing returns within the relevant range are not a necessary condition of natural monopoly: an industry might be naturally monopolistic because of economies of scope or integration— i.e., the ability to produce a combination of services at lower cost than could separate suppliers—and (2) a natural monopoly springing from such economies might not be sustainable against selective, competitive entry. What these expositions have not convincingly demonstrated is the extent to which the conditions for nonsustainable natural monopolies are in fact encountered in the real world, in the absence of regulatory limitations on the competitive responses of the incumbent; and they fall far short of justifying regulatory restrictions on entry, in order to preserve such otherwise nonsustainable natural monopolies. See, e.g., John C. Panzar and Robert D. Willig, "Free Entry and the Sustainability of Natural Monopoly," *Bell Journal of Economics* (Spring 1977), VIII:1–22; Paul L. Joskow and Roger C. Noll, op. cit., pp. 14–17; David S. Evans and James J. Heckman, "Natural Monopoly," in David S. Evans, ed., *Breaking Up Bell*, New York: North-Holland, 1983, pp. 127–156; Sharkey, op. cit.; William G. Shepherd, "Competition and Sustainability," in Thomas G. Gies and Werner Sichel, eds., *Deregulation: Appraisal before the Fact*, Ann Arbor, MI: University of Michigan, 1982, pp. 13–34.

Recent experience clearly suggests, instead, that the mixed system may be the worst of both possible worlds.[42]

The problem is that continued regulation of the incumbent companies in the presence of freedom of entry of essentially unregulated competitors introduces a host of distortions. The most troublesome of the restraints on the former are the requirements that they

- set prices on the basis of average system-wide costs—which means in some markets above cost, and therefore subject to competitive invasion, and in others below, in a continuing effort to practice internal subsidization;
- sell both old and new services only under preapproved, posted tariffs, from which they are forbidden to depart except with permission of the regulatory agency, while their competitors are subject to no such constraints;
- price on the basis of original or book costs that often far exceed the short- and long-run marginal costs of both the regulated companies themselves and their unregulated rivals, because they contain a very large component of capital carrying charges on investments grossly overvalued on their books—whether because of inadequate past depreciation rates (volume I, pp. 117–121; volume II, pp. 146, 150) or because of the recent entry into rate base of generating stations whose costs far exceed the minimum cost of duplicating the service and/or that have saddled the companies with excess capacity, or—in the natural gas case—because the companies have incurred heavy contractual obligations to take or pay for very high cost supplies;
- price their competitive services on the basis of full cost distributions or allocations that have nothing to do with their marginal costs; and, finally,
- are obliged to incur the sunk costs of installing capacity necessary to fulfill their continuing obligation to serve, while customers in a position to seek supplies elsewhere are free to slough off the corresponding obligation to pay carrying charges on those investments, and to return and demand a resumption of service, without penalty, whenever that alternative is the more attractive one.

In these circumstances, we cannot know to what extent the competition that has sprung up is competition on the basis of efficiency, to what extent instead it has been made possible only by the continued artificial restrictions on the prices and activities of the regulated companies. A good deal of the transferring of patronage by big customers from one supplier to another and recourse to acquiring or generating supplies directly is inevitably impelled by comparisons of alternatives severely distorted by the sunk costs covered by regulated rates. Large customers have attempted to shift from one electric utility to another, in order to obtain lower rates, in situations in which the two belonged to the same power pool, and the respective marginal costs were therefore identical. Industrial users of gas have made purchases at competitive prices in the field and proffered the gas to a pipeline for carriage in order to stop buying from pipelines or local distribution companies with lower marginal costs but higher regulated rates, reflecting heavy sunk costs. Some industrial companies are undoubtedly generating their

---

[42]See A. E. Kahn, "The Uneasy Marriage of Regulation and Competition," *Telematics* (September 1984), p. 2, quoting a perceptive paper by Herman Roseman and Irwin Stelzer suggesting a similar conclusion.

own power at costs lower than the *rates* but higher than the *incremental costs* of their utility company suppliers. And many of these shifts are economic from the standpoint of the customers only because of their ability to continue to depend upon the utility supplier for backup service (volume II, pp. 149, 229, 238–240) either in the event that the competitive alternatives fail or when such supplies are no longer available on more favorable terms.

In short, a great deal of the competition we are witnessing in the public utility industries merely represents an evasion of sunk costs—or, in effect, their transfer to captive customers, service to whom continues to be regulated on the traditional basis.[43] And there is, in these circumstances, no assurance that it is socially rational or conducive to economic efficiency.

While regulation in these circumstances—in particular, the setting of *floors* under the prices charged in competitive markets—is often motivated by a desire to protect captive customers from such unjustified discriminations, it also inevitably takes on the characteristic of protecting *competitors* from competition, to which tendency regulators are in any event prone (volume II, chapter 2). This tendency is directly related to the continuing uncertainties about whether some parts of these businesses may really be natural monopolies: so long as we limit the competitive responses of the incumbent companies, we have no way of knowing the answer to that question.[44]

This introduction is an inadequate vehicle for attempting to resolve these dilemmas. It would seem, however, that their resolution would have to be based on the following propositions:

1. The logic of opening any industry to free entry ultimately demands deregulation of the incumbent companies as well: wherever we decide we can safely rely on competition, we must, logically, abandon public utility-type regulation. The only way to find out where competition is feasible and where it is not, ultimately, is to permit it to take place and let the market tell us the answer; and the longer we postpone that determination the greater the cost to the public.

2. The only way of reconciling full deregulation of competitive markets with continued protection of captive customers is to find ways of breaking the link between the prices to the monopoly customers and the revenues and costs ascribed to the competitive operations. As long, instead, as the regulated prices continue to be set, directly or indirectly, on the basis of total company costs and revenues, or on the basis of some continuing process of allocation of costs between regulated and unregulated operations, there will always be the danger, in principle, of subsidization of the latter by the former. In those circumstances, conscientious regulators will not be able to refrain from setting floors under the competitive prices as well as ceilings over the putatively monopolistic ones.

How is that separation to be effected? So far as I can see, there is no possible method that will not be essentially pragmatic, indeed arbitrary. Some states, for example, are attempting thoroughly to separate the accounts of the two operations. While that is probably better than the present situation, it is not likely to suffice, not merely because it will inevitably involve all sorts of arbitrary allocations (that might be a small price to pay if it permitted the

---

[43]See, e.g., volume II, pp. 167–170.
[44]See John R. Haring, "Implications of Asymmetric Regulation for Competitive Policy Analysis," Federal Communications Commission, Office of Plans and Policy, Working Paper No. 14, 1984.

regulators thereafter to keep their hands entirely off the competitive pricing and investment decisions) but because, so long as the two sets of services continue to be provided for largely from common facilities, regulators will never be able to get out of the business of making those arbitrary allocations on a continuing basis—the very process that makes partial deregulation so unsatisfactory.

It seems likely, therefore, that we shall see increasing recourse, instead, to schemes that permit changes in the monopoly prices only in step with some external index—whether the Consumer Price Index or an index of cost of inputs to the industry—or freezes of one kind or another such as have recently been introduced in states like Vermont and New York. As an example of the former, the privatized British Telecommunications is constrained during its first five years (1984–1989) to raise the average of its prices no more than the retail price index minus three points, and no subcategory of prices—for example, the basic residental charge—more than the RPI plus two points.

None of these reservations about the effects of partial deregulation of the traditional public utilities is intended to minimize the positive contributions of competition. The foregoing suggestions for resolving the dilemmas and distortions of a mixed regime, indeed, implicitly assume that continued deregulation is the proper way to go, to the extent feasible.

The conclusion today, seventeen years later, is essentially the same as the conclusion of these two volumes: industries differ one from the other, and the optimal mix of institutional arrangements for any one of them cannot be decided on the basis of ideology alone. The "central institutional issue of public utility regulation" remains the one that I identified at that time—finding the best possible mix of inevitably imperfect regulation and inevitably imperfect competition.

The Economics of Regulation
Principles and Institutions

Preface

The purpose of these volumes is to explore the contribution that economics can make to government regulation of business.

When governments try to influence the performance of particular industries, they must first define the purposes of that regulation. Second, they must devise the social arrangements best suited to those purposes.

The economics of regulation has two corresponding aspects. First, traditional theory provides guiding *principles*: these define the goal of economic efficiency and provide rules for achieving it. The development and the application of these principles are the subject of Volume I. Second, there exists a branch of economics dealing with the relations between various *institutional* arrangements—market structures, systems of incentives, laws and administrative procedures—and economic performance. Volume II examines the major institutional issues in the field of regulation, in relation to the goal of economic efficiency. Together, the two volumes are an attempt to join neoclassical theory with "institutional economics." The latter is aimless if it is not informed by theory. And a normative theory of public policy is not of much use if it cannot be related to the selection of the best set of social arrangements for achieving those norms. Therefore, each volume is written with continuous reference to the other.

As this dichotomy suggests, I see validity in both the quest for generalizations about the economic process *and* the view that every actual market or industry is unique—in its technology, in the nature of the service involved, and in the package of social and political goals that the institutions of economic control are supposed to promote. In order to make the informed judgments necessary for understanding and for prescribing public policies, we must bring to each problem a knowledge and understanding of the relevant general principles, and we must assess and apply them in terms of the particular circumstances of each case.

This study attempts to develop the tools and the general guidelines, and to analyze the common institutional considerations and tendencies. The numerous references to specific regulatory problems and particular regulated industries are intended only as illustrations of generalizations, not as solutions of the policy issues raised. I regard with equanimity the probability that the specific policy judgments I offer may be good or bad; the generalizations, I trust, are always relevant, valid, and useful.

Since understanding requires not only a grasp of the common principles but also the experience of trying to apply them to particular cases, I suggest, if these volumes are to be used successfully in teaching, that each student be required to do the second kind of exercise on his own: to dig deeply into the facts and issues relating to a specific case or policy problem and to try to apply to it the principles developed here. The numerous footnotes and illustrations provide suggested topics for this type of individual study. But an hour's perusal of several *Wall Street Journals* would serve the same purpose.

Over the years I have incurred so many debts in connection with the preparation of this book it is difficult to know where to begin or end my acknowledgments. First, let me express thanks for the many profitable discussions of these problems that I have had with Herman Roseman, Peter Boone, Rachel Simmons, David Kadane, Anna Holmberg, Lynn Silverman, Jules Joskow, and Caleb Rossiter. Then there are people who have supplied very useful criticisms of particular portions of the manuscript: among them it is a pleasure to acknowledge Daniel Gray, George Cook, Thomas Simmons, Joel Dirlam, J. David Mann, Lisa Pollack, William Freund, Jane Bryant, and Lippman Bodoff. Just as I did her namesake twenty-five years ago, so now I gratefully acknowledge the editorial help of Hannah Kahn, who taught me among many other things never to say "literally" unless I meant it, literally.

My special thanks to Agnes Sasaki Stelzer, who took a thousand IBM belts and with care, patience, and unbelievable efficiency converted them into drafts whose only fault was that they were physically so beautiful it was painful to lay pencil to them, and to Mertie Decker, who has somehow kept me from flying off in a hundred directions during the first year of a new and demanding job and in so doing made it possible for me to finish the book.

Throughout the volumes are reflections of the help and suggestions of my present and former graduate students, notably Irwin Stelzer, Douglas Greer, John Landon, Kenneth Fraundorf, and Keith Anderson—and of my research assistants, Rachel Kahn and Sharon Morris.

It would take another entire preface to acknowledge adequately my debt to Irwin Stelzer. The imprint of our discussions of these subjects appears throughout the two volumes. And it is the simple truth—literally—that I could not possibly have written them without his continuous advice, encouragement, assistance, stimulus, and support.

Ithaca, New York   ALFRED E. KAHN
January 1970

VOLUME I
Economic Principles

PART I
The Institution of Regulated Monopoly

CHAPTER 1

Introduction: The Rationale of Regulation and the Proper Role of Economics

Economics emerged in the eighteenth and nineteenth centuries as an attempt to *explain* and to *justify* a market system. This is an oversimplification, but it is a broadly accurate characterization of the mainstream of Western economic thought. The purpose has been to describe how an essentially uncontrolled economy, in which the critical economic decisions are made by individuals, each separately pursuing his own interest, can nonetheless orderly and efficiently do society's work. The coordinating and controlling mechanism is the competitive market and the system of prices that emerges out of the bargains between freely contracting buyers and sellers. The competitive market guides and controls the self-seeking activities of each individual, so that, as Adam Smith stated in 1776, while "he intends only his own gain . . . he is . . . led by an invisible hand to promote an end which was no part of his intention"[1]—that is, to maximize the wealth of the nation.

This rationalization and description of the competitive market is still in large measure relevant to Western economies today. The economic reforms initiated in the 1960s by many Communist countries were short steps in the same direction. For all the great modifications to which market economies have been subjected in practice during the last century, and for all the qualifications that must be attached to the case for such an economy, the competitive market model is still in important measure (some economists would even say essentially) descriptive both of reality and of the community's conception of what an ideal economic system would look like.[2]

[1] *An Inquiry into the Nature and Causes of The Wealth of Nations*, Edwin Cannan, ed., 4th ed. (London: Methuen & Co. Ltd., 1925), I: 421.
[2] Apart from the fact that no two economists could agree on its precise formulation, it is impossible for even a single, nonschizophrenic, informed observer to make any brief statement that would adequately characterize the extent to which the model remains descriptively or analytically valid. There are large segments of the economy to which the model applies only peripherally—the governmental, public utility,

and nonprofit sectors, including in the latter the entire household economy. See, for example, Eli Ginzberg, Dale L. Hiestand, and Beatrice G. Reubens, *The Pluralistic Economy* (New York: McGraw-Hill Book Co., 1965). Even where it does apply, the competition that actually prevails is highly imperfect at best. It may be agreed that even when the model does roughly characterize the functioning of the economy from some perspectives—for example, explaining how resources are allocated—it is almost entirely silent about other essential aspects—for example,

THE REGULATED SECTOR

There are at least two large chunks of the economy that the competitive market model obviously does not describe or even purport to describe. These are the huge and growing public sector, the allocation of resources to which is determined not by the autonomous market but by political decisions, and the public utilities, in which the organization and management is for the most part (in the United States—not in most other countries) private but the central economic decisions are subject to direct governmental regulation.[3]

To be sure, the government influences the functioning of the private, competitive sectors of the economy as well in many ways—for example, by regulating the supply and availability of money, enforcing contracts, protecting property, providing subsidies or tariff protection, prohibiting unfair competition, providing market information, imposing standards for packaging and product content, and insisting on the right of employees to join unions and bargain collectively. In principle, these influences, however pervasive, are intended to operate essentially at the periphery of the markets affected. Their role is generally conceived as one of maintaining the institutions *within* whose framework the free market can continue to function, of enforcing, supplementing, and removing the imperfections of competition—not supplanting it.[4] In these sectors the government does not, or is not supposed to, decide what should be produced and how or by whom; it does not fix prices itself, nor does it control investment or entry on the basis of its own calculations of how much is economically desirable; the government does not specifically control who should be permitted to do what jobs, nor does it specify the permissible dimensions and characteristics of the product.[5]

---

how the decisions of the assumedly "sovereign consumer" are really made. See Thorstein Veblen, *The Theory of the Leisure Class; an Economic Study of Institutions* (New York: The Macmillan Company, 1912) and John Kenneth Galbraith, *The New Industrial State* (Boston: Houghton Mifflin, 1967), Chapter 19 and *passim*.

[3] See the reference in note 2 to the large private nonprofit sector, also.

[4] Professor Hayek greatly stresses the distinction between governmental interventions consistent and inconsistent with the preservation of competition as the central economic regulator. It is the latter, not the former, he argues, that pose a threat to political and social freedom. Friedrich A. Hayek, *The Road to Serfdom* (Chicago: University of Chicago Press, 1944), 88–100.

Professor Clair Wilcox organizes his excellent text, *Public Policies Toward Business*, 3rd ed. (Homewood: Richard D. Irwin, 1966), under a similar set of headings. See also Lee Loevinger, "Regulation and Competition as Alternatives," *The Antitrust Bulletin* (January–April 1966), XI: 104–108.

[5] It is important even in a general introduction not to leave the reader with the misleading impression that government policy is more logical, consistent, or clear-cut than it really is. We shall point out the fuzzy and frequently inconsistent shifting line that various governments have drawn between the essentially competitive and the regulated sectors of the economy. The Food and Drug Administration has determined that bread baked according to a formula developed by Cornell University may not be sold as white bread because it contains 6% soya flour. And that a perfectly healthful confection cannot be labeled as "jam" or even, clearly, as "imitation jam" unless it has at least 45% by weight of the purported fruit ingredient. See *62 Cases, More or Less, Each Containing Six Jars of Jam et al. v. U.S.*, 340 U.S. 593 (1951). In this instance the Supreme Court overturned the FDA. Heavyweight champions may be denied the right to defend their titles if they have had the temerity to make unpopular statements to the press. In many states professional wrestlers, veterinarians, and undertakers may not practice their trade without taking loyalty oaths. And we shall have occasion to note the many ways in which government restrictions on entry into supposedly competitive trades do in fact have major economic consequences, consequences often intended by those who administer them. On the other hand, the rationale or justification of such interventions, of which the foregoing

In contrast, the government does do all these things with the public utilities. Here the primary guarantor of acceptable performance is conceived to be (whatever it is in truth) not competition or self-restraint but direct governmental prescription of major aspects of their structure and economic performance. There are four principal components of this regulation that in combination distinguish the public utility from other sectors of the economy: control of entry, price fixing, prescription of quality and conditions of service, and the imposition of an obligation to serve all applicants under reasonable conditions. This book is an analysis of the economics of that regulation—its characteristics and consequences, the principles that govern it, and the principles that ought to govern it.

THE LEGAL RATIONALE

For some 67 years, roughly in the period 1877–1934, the United States Supreme Court took the position that there were certain more or less readily identifiable industries, peculiarly and sufficiently "clothed" or "affected with a public interest" to justify legislatures subjecting them to regulation despite the Fourteenth Amendment's injunction that "No State shall . . . deprive any person of life, liberty, or property, without due process of law." In a series of landmark decisions in the field of constitutional law, it drew tight boundaries around that group of industries, holding that outside those boundaries the Fourteenth Amendment prohibited any such drastic interferences with the freedom of contract. It admitted into the select circle grain elevators,[6] banks,[7] fire insurance companies,[8] and insurance agents.[9] In so doing it recognized also the long-accepted right of legislatures similarly to regulate the suppliers of gas, electricity, water, and transport services on the ground that these companies operated under governmental franchises giving them the right to make use of public streets or to condemn private property; these, being contracts freely entered into, could legitimately impose various regulatory conditions on the franchisee. And, typically over the vigorous dissents of such justices as Oliver Wendell Holmes, Louis D. Brandeis, and Harlan Fiske Stone, the Supreme Court declared "essentially private in nature"[10] and therefore beyond the reach of state regulation the manufacture of food, clothing, and fuels,[11] and the operations of theater ticket brokers,[12] employment agencies,[13] gasoline service stations,[14] and ice plants.[15]

represent an almost infinitesimally small sample, is not the direct control over economic performance. The purported and often real purpose is either a political one—harassment of the "disloyal"—or to see to it that consumers are not misled in making their free choices, that is, to assure that competition itself functions more effectively.

[6] *Munn v. Illinois*, 94 U.S. 113 (1877).

[7] *Noble State Bank v. Haskell*, 219 U.S. 104 (1911).

[8] *German Alliance Insurance Company v. Lewis, Superintendent of Insurance of the State of Kansas*, 233 U.S. 389 (1913).

[9] *O'Gorman & Young, Inc., v. Hartford Fire Insurance Co.*, 282 U.S. 251 (1931).

[10] *New State Ice Co. v. Liebmann*, 285 U.S. 262, 277 (1932).

[11] *Chas. Wolff Packing Co. v. Court of Industrial Relations of The State of Kansas*, 262 U.S. 522 (1923).

[12] *Tyson & Brother—United Theatre Ticket Officers v. Banton, District Attorney*, 273 U.S. 418 (1927).

[13] *Ribnik v. McBride, Commissioner of Labor of the State of New Jersey*, 277 U.S. 350 (1928).

[14] *Williams, Commissioner of Finance, et al. v. Standard Oil Co. of Louisiana*, 278 U.S. 235 (1929).

[15] See note 10. In a way it is ironic and somewhat misleading to trace the restrictiveness of this doctrine back to *Munn v. Illinois*, since in that decision the Supreme Court deferred to the judgment of the legislature in finding in the strategic position of the grain elevators (their importance to the public and purported power) a sufficient justification for regulation. It

Since that fascinating chapter in constitutional history was completed in 1934 and since the story has in any event been well told in other places, there is no need to reproduce it here.[16] Suffice it to point out that the varying views of the court and its members seem to have hinged on the following closely interrelated factors:

1. The extent to which they adhered to the precepts of judicial restraint, of which Holmes was the principal proponent—restraint in substituting their judgments for those of the legislature about what might be construed by some as essentially legislative, by others as essentially constitutional issues.[17]

2. The extent to which they interpreted the "due process" requirement of the Fourteenth Amendment as subjecting legislation only to a procedural test as against calling for a determination of its substantive merits or imposing a substantive commitment to a policy of *laissez faire*.[18]

3. The degree to which they identified freedom from government regulation of *economic* activities as inseparable from or essential to the preservation of the basic human freedoms protected by the Bill of Rights.[19]

---

adopted from the common law the notion that "property does become clothed with a public interest when used in a manner to make it of public consequence, and affect the community at large" (94 U.S. 113, 126, 1877) in order to support this extension of regulation to companies that were not franchised or given monopolistic privileges by the state. It was only later Courts, notably in the 1920s, that converted the doctrine into a straightjacket.

[16] See, for example, Dexter Merriam Keezer and Stacy May, *The Public Control of Business* (New York: Harper & Brothers, 1930), Chapter 5; Emery Troxel, *Economics of Public Utilities* (New York: Rinehart & Company, 1947), Chapter 1; Charles F. Phillips, Jr., *The Economics of Regulation*, rev. ed. (Homewood: Richard D. Irwin, 1969), Chapter 3. See also the useful compendium by Irston R. Barnes, *Cases on Public Utility Regulation* (New York: F. S. Crofts & Co., 1938), Chapter 1.

[17] "For protection against abuses by legislatures the people must resort to the polls, not to the courts." Chief Justice Waite, speaking for the majority in *Munn v. Illinois*, 94 U.S. 113, 134 (1877).

"We have no right to revise the wisdom or the expediency of the law . . . we would not be justified in imputing an improper exercise of discretion to the legislature of North Dakota." Shiras, for the majority, in *Brass v. North Dakota*, 153 U.S. 391, 403 (1894).

"I think the proper course is to recognize that a state legislature can do whatever it sees fit to do unless it is restrained by some express prohibition in the Constitution . . . and that the Courts should be careful not to extend such prohibitions beyond their obvious meaning by reading into them conceptions of public policy that the parti-

cular Court may happen to entertain. . . .

"I am far from saying that I think this particular law a wise and rational provision. That is not my affair. But if the people of the State of New York speaking by their authorized voice say that they want it, I see nothing in the Constitution of the United States to prevent their having their will." Holmes, dissenting in *Tyson v. Banton*, 273 U.S. 418, 446–447 (1927).

[18] "The Fifth Amendment, in the field of Federal activity, and the Fourteenth, as respects state action, do not prohibit governmental regulation for the public welfare. They merely condition the exertion of the admitted power, by securing that the end shall be accomplished by methods consistent with due process. And the guaranty of due process . . . demands only that the law shall not be unreasonable, arbitrary, or capricious, and that the means selected shall have a real and substantial relation to the object sought to be attained." Roberts, for the majority, in *Nebbia v. New York*, 291 U.S. 502, 525 (1934).

"The Fourteenth Amendment does not enact Mr. Herbert Spencer's Social Statics. . . . a constitution is not intended to embody a particular economic theory, whether of paternalism and the organic relation of the citizen to the state or of laissez faire." Holmes, dissenting in *Lochner v. New York*, 198 U.S. 45, 75 (1905), involving a law fixing the maximum permissible workweek for bakers at 60 hours.

[19] "If this be sound law, if there be no protection, either in the principles upon which our republican government is founded, or in the prohibitions of the Constitution against such invasion of private rights, all property and all business in the State are held at the mercy of a majority of its legislature." Field, dissenting in *Munn v. Illinois*, 94 U.S. 113, 140 (1877).

4. The extent to which they were prepared (a) to confine the powers of the state to regulate price—"the heart of the contract"[20]—or entry, or to impose an obligation to serve, to situations in which the very ability of the firm to do business required that it obtain a franchise from the state, which admittedly gave the latter the contractual right to insist on such regulatory provisions as it saw fit;[21] or (b) to extend it to specific businesses that had been recognized as "public" in character under the common law because, similar to inns, ferries, hackmen, grist mills, and other "common callings," they "held themselves out to serve the public" anyhow or for some other reason had been held "clothed with a public interest"; or (c) to extend the category even farther by analogy to other businesses that had for one reason or another "risen" to a "public" character because the owner had "devoted his business to a public use" or "to a use in which the public has an interest," whatever that meant;[22] or (d) to permit or to confine

---

"This is not regulation, but management, control, dictation—it amounts to the deprivation of the fundamental right which one has to conduct his own affairs honestly and along customary lines. . . . if it be now ruled that one dedicates his property to public use whenever he embarks on an enterprise which the Legislature may think is desirable to bring under control, this is but to declare that rights guaranteed by the Constitution exist only so long as supposed public interest does not require their extinction. To adopt such a view, of course, would put an end to liberty under the Constitution." McReynolds, dissenting in *Nebbia v. New York*, 291 U.S. 502, 554–555 (1934).

[20] *Adkins v. Children's Hospital*, 261 U.S. 525, 554 (1923), voiding a minimum wage law. See note 1, Chapter 2.

[21] "It is only where some right or privilege is conferred by the government or municipality upon the owner, which he can use in connection with his property, or by means of which the use of his property is rendered more valuable to him, or he thereby enjoys an advantage over others, that the compensation to be received by him becomes a legitimate matter of regulation. Submission to the regulation of compensation in such cases is an implied condition of the grant, and the State . . . only determines the conditions upon which its concession shall be enjoyed." Field, dissenting in *Munn v. Illinois*, 94 U.S. 113, 146–147 (1877).

"It is suggested that there is a monopoly, and that that justifies legislative interference. There are two kinds of monopoly; one of law, the other of fact. The one exists when exclusive privileges are granted. Such a monopoly, the law which creates alone can break; and being the creation of law, justifies legislative control. A monopoly of fact anyone can break, and there is no necessity for legislative interference. . . . If the business is profitable, anyone can build another; the field is open for all the elevators, and all the com-

petition that may be desired. If there be a monopoly, it is one of fact and not of law, and one which an individual can break."

Brewer, dissenting in *Budd v. New York*, 143 U.S. 517, 550–551 (1892), also involving grain elevators. Note that this view embodies not only a legal principle but an economic conclusion: that the only monopoly that can be great and enduring enough to justify regulation is one conferred or protected by governmental grant of exclusive privilege.

[22] These various rationalizations (listed as b and c) are so closely intertwined that it is awkward to document them separately.

"Businesses said to be clothed with a public interest justifying some public regulation may be divided into three classes:

(1) Those which are carried on under the authority of a public grant of privileges which either expressly or impliedly imposes the affirmative duty of rendering a public service demanded by any member of the public. Such are the railroads, other common carriers and public utilities.

(2) Certain occupations, regarded as exceptional, the public interest attaching to which, recognized from earliest times, has survived. . . . Such are those of the keepers of inns, cabs, and grist mills. . . .

(3) Businesses which though not public at their inception may be fairly said to have risen to be such and have become subject in consequence to some government regulation. . . . In the language of the cases, the owner by devoting his business to the public use, in effect grants the public an interest in that use and subjects himself to public regulation to the extent of that interest. . . .

"It has never been supposed, since the adoption of the Constitution, that the business of the butcher, or the baker, the tailor, the wood chopper, the mining operator, or the miner was clothed with such a public interest that the price of his product or his wages could be fixed by State regulation. . . .

"An ordinary producer, manufacturer or shopkeeper may sell or not sell as he likes. . . ." Chief Justice Taft, for the unanimous court in *Wolff Packing Company v. Kansas*, 262 U.S. 522, 535–537 (1923).

"Property does become clothed with a public interest when used in a manner to make it of public consequence, and affect the community at large. When, therefore, one devotes his property to a use in which the public has an interest, he, in effect, grants to the public an interest in that use, and must submit to be controlled by the public for the common good. . . ." C. J. Waite, for the majority, in *Munn v. Illinois*, 94 U.S. 113, 126 (1877).

"The public has no greater interest in the use of buildings for the storage of grain than it has in the use of buildings for the residences of families. . . . The public is interested in the manufacture of cotton, woolen, and silken fabrics, in the construction of machinery, in the printing and publication of books and periodicals, and in the making of utensils of every variety . . . indeed, there is hardly an enterprise or business . . . in which the public has not an interest in the sense in which the term is used by the court in its opinion. . . ." Field, dissenting *ibid.*, pp. 140–41.

"Is the business of insurance so far affected with a public interest as to justify legislative regulation of its rates? . . . We have shown that the business of insurance has very definite characteristics, with a reach of influence and consequence beyond and different from that of the ordinary business. . . ." McKenna, for the majority, in *German Alliance Insurance Co. v. Kansas*, 233 U.S. 389, 406, 414 (1914).

For majority opinions excluding from these categories businesses supplying various "ordinary commodities of trade" (*Williams v. Standard Oil*, 278 U.S. 235, 240, 1929) and services, see notes 10–15.

Holmes argued against the meaningfulness of these closed categories:

"The notion that a business is clothed with a public interest and has been devoted to the public use is little more than a fiction intended to beautify what is disagreeable to the sufferers. The truth seems to me to be that, subject to compensation when compensation is due, the legislature may forbid or restrict any business when it has a sufficient force of public opinion behind it. Lotteries were thought useful adjuncts of the State a century or so ago; now they are believed to be immoral and they have been stopped. Wine has been thought good for man from the time of the Apostles until recent years. . . . What has happened to lotteries and wine might happen to theatres in some moral storm of the future, not because theatres were devoted to a public use, but because people had come to think that way." Holmes, dissenting in *Tyson v. Banton*, 273 U.S. 418, 446 (1927).

"The phrase 'business affected with a public interest' seems to me to be too vague and illusory to carry us very far on the way to a solution. It tends in use to become only a convenient expression for describing those businesses, regulation of which has been permitted in the past. To say that only those businesses affected with a public interest may be regulated is but another way of stating that all those businesses which may be regulated are affected with a public interest." Stone, dissenting *ibid.*, p. 451.

"The business of supplying to others, for compensation, any article or service whatsoever may become a matter of public concern. Whether it is, or is not, depends upon the conditions existing in the community affected. If it is a matter of public concern, it may be regulated, whatever the business. . . .

"The notion of a distinct category of business 'affected with a public interest,' employing property 'devoted to a public use,' rests upon historical error. . . . In my opinion, the true principle is that the State's power extends to every regulation of any business reasonably required and appropriate for the public protection." Brandeis, dissenting in *New State Ice Company v. Liebmann*, 285 U.S. 262, 301–303 (1932).

It was these views, of Holmes, Stone, and Brandeis, that ultimately prevailed, in *Nebbia*:

"Obviously Munn and Scott had not voluntarily dedicated their business to a public use. They intended only to conduct it as private citizens, and they insisted that they had done nothing which gave the public an interest in their transactions or conferred any right of regulation. The statement that one has dedicated his property to a public use is, therefore, merely another way of saying that if one embarks in a business which public interest demands shall be regulated, he must know regulation will ensue." *Nebbia v. New York*, 291 U.S. 502, 533–534 (1934).

Although the latter decision eliminated the constitutional requirement, in some situations exposure to public utility regulation continues to turn in practice or under the governing statutes on whether the company "held itself out" to serve the general public. On the case of petroleum (and petroleum product) pipelines, for example, see George S. Wolbert, Jr., *American Pipe Lines* (Norman: University of Oklahoma Press, 1952), 111–132. The decision in 1969 by the public utilities commission of New Jersey to subject to regulation a business that had been set up to distribute fuel oil by pipeline from central storage to the individual residents in a real estate develop-

regulation to businesses enjoying "monopolies in fact," as contrasted with legally-conferred grants of exclusive privilege;[23] or, at the other extreme, (e) to permit legislatures to intervene in whatever manner required and in whatever situations a case could be made that the uncontrolled market worked badly. In principle this last view could prove to be just as restrictive as the first, depending on how its proponent answered the question: to whom did that sufficiently convincing case have to be made? But, of course, in practice proponents of that view were proponents also of judicial restraint or of more active state intervention in the economic field.

5. The extent to which they themselves believed in the efficacy of the unregulated market, competitive or otherwise.[24]

One view, which convinced the Court majority in *Munn v. Illinois*, in 1877, was that regulation might properly be introduced to protect customers from exploitation by private monopolists. Quite a different view, of which Brandeis was a leading exponent, was that unregulated competition could be excessively strong—injurious not just to the businessmen involved but to the public at large as well.[25]

In any event, it was over 36 years ago that the Supreme Court abandoned this historic distinction. In *Nebbia v. New York* it held, in effect, that there was no longer any constitutional barrier to legislatures imposing any type of economic regulation on any industries within their jurisdictions, where in their judgment it would serve the public interest, provided only that they did not do so in an utterly capricious or discriminatory manner:

"It is clear that there is no closed class or category of businesses affected with a public interest, and the function of courts in the application of the Fifth and Fourteenth Amendments is to determine in each case whether the circumstances vindicate the challenged regulation as a reasonable exertion of governmental authority or condemn it as arbitrary or discriminatory. . . . The phrase 'affected with a public interest' can, in the nature of things, mean no more than that an industry, for adequate reason, is subject to control for the public good. . . .

"So far as the requirement of due process is concerned, and in the absence of other constitutional restriction, a state is free to adopt whatever economic policy may reasonably be deemed to promote public welfare, and to enforce that policy by legislation adapted to its purpose. . . . If the laws passed are

---

ment project turned in part on the issue of whether the operation was a "service for public use," in part on whether they were operating under special grant of privilege from the state. *Public Utilities Fortnightly* (April 10, 1969), LXXXIII: 51–52. For other instances in which this criterion has been employed—for example in rejecting regulation over publication of the yellow pages of a telephone book—see A. J. G. Priest, *Principles of Public Utility Regulation* (Charlottesville: Michie Co. 1969), Chapter 1.

[23] This was one basis for the majority opinion upholding regulation of grain elevators in *Munn v. Illinois* and rejecting it for ice companies in *New State Ice*. See the opposing view of the dissenters in *Budd v. New York*, note 21, who refused to admit either the constitutional validity or the possible economic necessity of regulating

"monopolists in fact," on the one hand and, for a refusal to *confine* regulation to monopolies, see the famous dissenting opinion of Brandeis, in *New State Ice*, arguing that regulation was both permissible and desirable because competition frequently proved to be *excessive*. 285 U.S. 262, 280–311 (1932). The latter view prevailed in *Nebbia*.

[24] See note 23 contrasting the extreme views of Brewer, in the *Budd* dissent, and Brandeis, in *New State Ice*.

[25] Brandeis believed that competition was not just wasteful at the level of the individual industry but also responsible for the wide swings of the business cycle, for the succession of periods of speculative, overinvestment followed by long periods of excess capacity and deeply depressed prices and incomes. See *ibid*.

seen to have a reasonable relation to a proper legislative purpose, and are neither arbitrary nor discriminatory, the requirements of due process are satisfied. . . . With the wisdom of the policy adopted, with the adequacy or practicability of the law enacted to forward it, the courts are both incompetent and unauthorized to deal."[26]

As far as the United States Constitution is concerned, there is no longer any distinction between the public utilities and other industries.

THE DISTINCTION IN PRACTICE

The distinction has become progressively blurred in practice as well. The government in one way or another regulates price and/or quality of product and/or entry in many industries that are not properly regarded as public utilities in most essential respects. Consider, for example, the application of the wage-price guideposts to particular pricing decisions by the steel and aluminum industries, among others, during the Kennedy and Johnson administrations;[27] the use of stockpiling of strategic materials (and releases from stockpiles), purportedly for national security but also, clearly, to raise (and, later, to hold in check) the prices and incomes of the producers;[28] the complicated government policies affecting the prices of agricultural products, the level of oil production, the quantity of sugar, oil and textile imports, the quality of drugs, and the number and identity of doctors, liquor stores, and tree surgeons permitted to practice their trades. The list could be extended almost indefinitely; the exercise would shed interesting light on the truly mixed character of the American economy.

In principle, as we have already suggested, many of these interventions are not intended to constitute economic regulation. The avowed purpose of licensing doctors, barbers, prize fighters and drugs is not usually to have the government substitute its judgment for that of the market in determining, on economic grounds, how many or who should be permitted to enter the market, but only to assure that those who do enter are qualified—on professional, scientific, or technical grounds.[29] But in point of fact, as we shall see, the licensure *is* often economic, in motivation or effect, and does effect-

---

[26] 291 U.S. 502, 536–537 (1934).

[27] John Sheahan, *The Wage-Price Guideposts* (Washington: Brookings Institution, 1967); George P. Shultz and Robert Z. Aliber, eds., *Guidelines, Informal Controls, and the Market Place* (Chicago: University of Chicago Press, 1966); Grant McConnell, *Steel and the Presidency* (New York: W. W. Norton & Co., 1962); Roy Hoopes, *The Steel Crisis* (New York: John Day Co., 1963); Gilbert Burck, "Aluminum: the Classic Rollback," *Fortune* (February 1966), LXXIII: 107–111 and ff.

[28] Walter Adams, "The Military-Industrial Complex and The New Industrial State," *Amer. Econ. Rev.*, *Papers and Proceedings* (May 1968), LVIII: 659–661, summarizing U.S. Senate, Committee on Armed Services, National Stockpile and Naval Petroleum Reserves Subcommittee, 88th Cong., 1st Sess., *Inquiry into the Strategic and Critical Material Stockpiles of the United States, Draft Report*, Washington, 1963.

[29] Similarly, the encroachments that antitrust decisions in the 1950s and 1960s made on the right of businessmen outside the public utility industries to choose their customers did not in principle represent a substitution of economic regulation for competition. In principle it is only the public utilities that have an obligation to serve; other businessmen supposedly are free to refuse to sell, for reasons sufficient to themselves, unless that refusal is part of or incident to the imposition of an illegal restraint on price competition (for example, is a way of enforcing resale price maintenance) or to illegal monopolization. In practice, the result of the above-mentioned decisions has been to come much closer to imposing a positive obligation to sell (instead of, for example, exclusively to lease, as in *U.S. v. United Shoe Machinery Corp.*, 110 F. Supp. 295, 1953) on companies with market power. Still, the justification in these instances was the preservation of competition, not its replacement.

ively limit the force of the competitive market. Even in principle it is clear that many of the other instances of governmental intervention just mentioned represent policies of direct economic regulation, no more and no less, whatever their public rationalizations.

The period of the 1920s and 1930s, the very time when the constitutional issue was most strenuously contested and ultimately resolved, were especially propitious for this extension and blurring of the edges of the public utility concept, that is, of the boundaries between the industries appropriately regulated and those left to the regime of competition. Economists and lawmakers were pointing with increasing emphasis to the pervasiveness of monopoly elements throughout the economy,[30] and this suggested at least to some that direct regulation of performance might be required to protect the consumer over a far wider range of industry than the public utilities proper.[31] In other contexts, these and other observers were pointing out that some of the same factors that made competition infeasible and potentially destructive among public utility companies—notably economies of scale and heavy overhead costs—were widespread in unregulated industry as well.[32] This led some of them to call for the introduction of comprehensive regulation as a means of eliminating the wastes, instabilities, and social costs imposed by

---

See *U.S. v. Parke, Davis and Co.*, 362 U.S. 29 (1960); *U.S. v. General Motors Corp. et al.*, 384 U.S. 127 (1966); *U.S. v. Arnold, Schwinn & Co. et al.*, 388 U.S. 365 (1967); and *U.S. v. International Business Machines Corp.*, Civil Action No. 69, filed January 17, 1969, U.S. Dist. Ct., S.D.N.Y., *CCH Trade Regulation Reporter*, ¶ 45,069 (Case 2039).

[30] See, for example, Edward H. Chamberlin, *The Theory of Monopolistic Competition* (Cambridge: Harvard University Press, 1933), and Joan Robinson, *The Economics of Imperfect Competition* (London: Macmillan and Co., Ltd., 1933), both giving formal recognition in their theoretical models to the fact that all real markets lie somewhere between the polar extremes of perfect competition and pure monopoly.

[31] See Arthur Robert Burns, *The Decline of Competition* (New York: McGraw-Hill Book Co., 1936), especially Chapters 11 and 12. See also the dissenting opinions of Justice Stone in *Tyson v. Banton*, 273 U.S. 418, 447–454 (1927) and *Ribnik v. McBride*, 277 U.S. 350, 361–375 (1928), contending that the presence of substantial monopoly power and the necessity of protecting the unemployed from extreme exploitation justified these attempts by the states to regulate the fees of ticket brokers and employment exchanges. Of course, not all economists concluded that widespread imperfections of competition made it necessary to abandon antitrust policy generally and turn to regulation. See, for example, J. M. Clark, "Toward a Concept of Workable Competition," in American Economic Association, *Readings in the Social Control of Industry* (Philadelphia: The Blakiston Co., 1942), pp. 452–475.

[32] J. M. Clark was a leading and perhaps most profound exponent of this view:

"It soon became evident that railroads were not the only industry using large fixed capital and subject to the 'peculiarities' of constant and variable costs. It also became evident that discrimination was not the only untoward result. . . . It became evident that economic law did not insure prices that would yield 'normal' returns on invested capital. . . . The business cycle had become a recognized part of the order of things, with its recurrent periods of excess producing capacity, during which active competition tended to lower prices until even efficient concerns could make little or no return on their investment. . . .

"Here we have an array of problems, primarily relating to the economist's search for the laws governing normal and market price and to the question whether competition is natural and can endure. . . .

"Other important developments have occurred in connection with public utilities. . . . Here, for the first time, organized technical attention is paid to the recurrent ebb and flow of output and the daily and seasonal 'peaks' of demand. . . . [But] Restaurants, theaters, golf clubs, garment-making industries, railroads and street cars, building, and other trades—all have their peaks, daily or seasonal. And all industries suffer in common from the unpredictable irregularities of the business cycle." *Studies in the Economics of Overhead Costs* (Chicago: University of Chicago Press, 1923), 11–15. Copyright 1923 by the University of Chicago. All rights reserved.

competition,[33] an argument that reinforced the movement, increasingly popular among businessmen, for "rationalization" of industry by industry-wide cooperation and cartelization.[34] Not surprisingly, it was in the middle of the Great Depression that these views ultimately prevailed—in the *Nebbia* decision, which involved *minimum* price fixing for milk, and more generally in the National Recovery Program, which, in quest of general economic recovery, introduced industry-wide 'codes of fair competition.'"[35] That these codes were used to involve much more self-regulation of industry and cartelization than effective governmental controls does not alter the fact that the National Recovery Administration represented during its short lifetime a further blurring of the distinction between the competitive and public utility sectors; and many of its policies continue to be applied today.

And yet there *is* such a thing as a public utility. The line between these and other types of industries is a shadowy area; and it shifts over time. But there remains a core of industries, privately owned and operated in this country, in which, at least in principle, the primary guarantor of acceptable performance is *conceived* to be (whatever it is in truth) not competition or self-restraint but direct government controls—over entry (and in many instances exit), *and* price, *and* conditions of service—exercised by adminis-trative commissions constituted for this specific purpose.[36] In this respect, the public utilities remain a fairly distinct group, comprising the same industries that 60 to 80 years ago would have been given essentially the same designation and regulatory treatment—the generation, transmission, and distribution of electric power; the manufacture and distribution of gas; telephone, telegraph, and cable communications; common-carrier trans-portation, urban and interurban, passenger and freight; local water and sewerage supply (to the extent at least that these continue to be provided by privately-owned companies); and, in a sense at the periphery, banking. The list could well embrace, also, warehouses, docks, wharves, stockyards, taxis, ticket brokers, employment exchanges, ice plants, steam heating companies, cotton gins, grist mills, irrigation companies, stock exchanges, and express

---

[33] See, for example, the analysis and proposals by Walton H. Hamilton and Helen R. Wright, *The Case of Bituminous Coal* (New York: The Macmillan Co., 1925), and Walton H. Hamilton, *A Way of Order for Bituminous Coal* (New York: The Macmillan Co., 1928); and A. R. Burns, *loc. cit.*

[34] See, for example, Robert A. Brady, *Business as a System of Power* (New York: Columbia Univer-sity Press, 1943), Chapters 7 and 8; George W. Stocking and Myron W. Watkins, *Cartels or Competition?* (New York: Twentieth Century Fund, 1948), Chapter 2; and *Monopoly and Free Enterprise* (New York: Twentieth Century Fund, 1951), Chapter 8.

[35] See A. R. Burns, *op. cit.*, Chapter 10; and Clair Wilcox, *op. cit.*, 677–687.

[36] Every state, including the District of Columbia, Puerto Rico, and the Virgin Islands, has such a commission, although the powers vested in them vary. For example, the Minnesota and Nebraska state commissions do not regulate either the retail or the wholesale rates, and those of Texas and South Dakota control only the

wholesale rates charged by private electric companies. But the Nebraska exception is easily explained: there are no private electric utilities in that state. In all four states the municipalities have jurisdiction over the retail rates. All the other state commissions regulate at least the retail rates. No less than nine states have not given their commissions authority to require certificates of convenience and necessity before companies may begin service in a new area or to control abandonments; but in many, if not all of them, the municipalities do have these powers. The situation in natural gas distribution is similar. All states except Texas regulate telephone rates. For a survey, see U.S. Senate, Committee on Government Operations, Subcommittee on Intergovernmental Relations, 90th Cong. 1st Sess., *State Utility Commissions: Summary and Tabulation of Information Submitted by the Commissions*, Washington, 1967. See also Federal Power Commission, *Federal and State Commission Jurisdiction and Regulation: Electric, Gas, and Telephone Utilities*, Washington, 1967.

companies.[37] There have been some new entrants that would have been recognized barely or not at all in, for example, 1900—the production and field sale of natural gas, common carrier pipeline transmission of hydrocarbons, commercial aviation and trucking. But the principles underlying the extension of direct regulation to most of them were the traditional ones: they were new common carriers, or required franchises or certifications carrying with them the right of eminent domain, or were conceived of as so intimately affecting the prices or service of the traditional utilities as to require regulation themselves (as in the case of trucking and the field sales of natural gas).

THE ECONOMIC RATIONALE

It would be tidy to include in this introduction an exposition of the economic logic of the institution of regulated monopoly. The list of economic justifications would have to involve the following:

1. The importance of these industries, as measured not merely by their own sizeable share in total national output, but also by their very great influence, as suppliers of essential inputs to other industries, on the size and growth of the entire economy. These industries constitute a large part of the "infrastructure" uniquely prerequisite to economic development. On the one hand they condition the possibilities of growth (as Adam Smith recognized, the division of labor is limited by the extent of the market, and the latter depends in turn on the availability and price of transportation).[38] On the other hand, because many of these industries are characterized by great economies of scale, their own costs and prices depend in turn on the rate at which the economy and its demand for their services grows. As general economic growth proceeds, the contribution of these industries to further expansion is thus enhanced by their own progressive realization of those economies of scale, in a cumulative and self-reinforcing process.

2. That many of them are "natural monopolies": their costs will be lower if they consist in a single supplier. This creates the efficiency case for monopolistic organization and, along with the importance of the service and the consequent inelasticity of demand, the need for regulation to protect the consuming public.

3. That for one or another of many possible reasons, competition simply does not work well.

But this would be a terribly superficial statement. And it will take many chapters to make it less so. The reason is that every part of the rationalization involves an issue or series of issues instead of a settled conclusion. For instance, the public utilities are important; but do they make a greater contribution to national product or economic growth than the provision of food, medical

---

[37] See, for example, Paul J. Garfield and Wallace F. Lovejoy, *Public Utility Economics* (Englewood Cliffs: Prentice-Hall, 1964), Chapters 1, 3, 13, and for specific industries *passim;* Martin G. Glaeser, *Public Utilities in American Capitalism* (New York: The Macmillan Co., 1957), Chapters 1–9. While entry into banking is restricted by the issuance of charters, and the operations of individual banks are subjected to complicated restrictions and detailed inspection and supervision, and certain restrictions are placed on their pricing—notably limitations on the interest charges they may pay to depositors—the rates banks actually pay and charge and the profits they may earn are not explicitly set by the regulatory authorities.

[38] Adam Smith, *op. cit.*, I: 19–22.

care, housing or education, none of which is regulated in the same fashion? Their importance, clearly, is not a sufficient explanation or economic justification for their subjection to regulation. Nor is it a *necessary* condition—one could find economic justification for regulating "unimportant" industries such as ticket brokers, except that since it uses resources to regulate, there would be no economic point in doing so for industries so unimportant that the benefits of regulation could not possibly outweigh the costs of administration.

There is no room for doubt that at least *some* of the public utility industries are in *some* respects "natural monopolies." But the interesting economic questions are: What makes them so? Is natural monopoly synonymous with long-run decreasing cost tendencies? If so, what about the public utilities, such as the supply of water, that *seem* to be characterized by long-run tendencies to increasing costs? Does a tendency for costs to decline over time constitute an evidence of natural monopoly?[39] What parts of these industries are natural monopolies, what parts not? Might they be natural monopolies in some static, efficiency sense but "unnatural" ones in terms of the prerequisites for innovation and growth? And how then do we handle, in theory and in practice, the growing competition between "natural monopolists," such as electric and gas distribution companies for the home heating and cooking market, or between international cable and satellite communications? And how do we cope with the historical fact that the prime historic exemplars of the extension of public utility regulation in the United States in the last quarter of the nineteenth century—railroads and grain elevators—were not really natural monopolists?[40]

As we have already suggested, part of the case for regulation and the inappropriateness of competition inheres in the heavy fixed costs that characterize most of these industries. But do heavy fixed costs make monopoly "natural"? Or competition unreliable? What then of agriculture or even the practice of medicine, most of whose costs are likewise fixed? Or trucking, whose fixed costs are only a small proportion of the total, yet which is regulated like a public utility? And does it make any difference whether the fixed costs that must be recovered from the sale of a number of services are mainly *common* to those various services, or *joint*?

In short, we have here not a description but a series of complicated analytical questions concerning the proper roles of competition and monopoly in these industries—questions that will concern us throughout this entire book, and especially in its second volume.

THE ECONOMICS OF REGULATION

In any event, the subject of this study is not the "economics of public utilities," but the "economics of regulation." Reflecting and encouraged by

---

[39] There is no reason to keep the reader in suspense or confusion on this point: the answer is "not necessarily." For an example of confusing decreasing costs *over time*, attributable to technological progress, with the "long-run decreasing costs" that are the condition of natural monopoly, see Charles F. Phillips, Jr., *op. cit.*, 23, note 8. The enormous decline of real costs in, for instance, agriculture over the last several decades obviously does not signify that this is a "natural monopoly." See on this point pp. 127–129, Chapter 5.

[40] See James R. Nelson, "The Role of Competition in the Regulated Industries," *Antitrust Bulletin* (January–April 1966), XI: 7–8, 17–21. The natural monopoly concept is the subject of Chapter 4 of our Volume 2.

the *Nebbia* decision, as we have already seen, the government regulates many industries that are not really public utilities. Conversely, even among the "public utility" industries or at least at their periphery the regulation is often incomplete—control over price but not entry (for example, in insurance), over entry but not price (for example, in radio and television) or quality of service (for example, in banking), and so on. And even over those industries most thoroughly regulated and most clearly identifiable as public utilities, issues abound concerning the appropriate definition and role of regulated monopoly as the principal institution of social control. These issues must of course be examined—but not in a first chapter, in *a priori* fashion, as though they represented settled and generally accepted principles. Instead we shall analyze them in detail *after* a detailed exposition of the relevant economic principles, in a series of chapters that examine this institution of regulated monopoly, its strengths, limitations, and the principles for delineating its proper scope.

This is not to deny that, even after *Nebbia*, there is a more or less distinctive core of public utility industries. It is to emphasize instead that it is the phenomenon of economic regulation itself, wherever practiced, whose economics we study here—not the public utility industries as such. Licensure of entry has certain implications and tendencies wherever it is practiced, whether over gas pipelines, radio and TV stations, community antenna television (CATV), doctors, or barbers. Government price-fixing has similar consequences whether it is for electricity, post office services, farm products, or air travel; and so has governmentally-enforced divisions of the market, whether by licensing motor carriers or assigning output quotas to individual oil wells. Private, collective price-fixing and market-sharing are subject to similar tensions and tendencies, whether by maritime shipping conferences, boards of fire insurance underwriters, stock exchange members, or real estate boards—although these implications and consequences will vary with the circumstances of the industry to which they are applied. Our purpose is to expose the unifying economic principles and tendencies, the common problems, rather than to describe or analyze the particular characteristics or regulatory problems of specific industries.

This purpose must not be interpreted as reflecting a belief that any simple set of rules can answer all problems of regulatory policy. On the contrary, each regulated industry (in fact, each unregulated one, too) is in essential respects unique and must be so treated.[41] This book springs from a conviction that valid scientific generalizations can be drawn and useful general guides to regulatory policies can be developed. Their intelligent application in particular situations, like the decision to regulate in the first place, can only be done on the basis of full consideration of the special characteristics of the industry in question—its technology and other conditions of supply, the nature of its market—and of the varying mix of public purposes, economic and

[41] Probably the outstanding proponent of this view was Walton H. Hamilton:

"an industry, like an individual, is part of all that it has met; it has a character, a structure, a system of habits of its own. Its pattern is out of accord with a normative design; its activities conform very imperfectly with a chartered course of industrial events." *Price and Price Policies* (New York: McGraw-Hill, 1938), 4.

"A policy for the operation of an economy is one thing; the ordering of the affairs of an industry quite another. . . . As the economy which fails to perform needs its general remedy, so the industry out of order requires its specific." "Coal and the Economy—A Demurrer," *Yale Law Journal* (February 1941), L: 595.

other, that regulation is supposed to serve. But the job is likely to be very badly done if it is not informed by a clear grasp of the common economic principles and considerations.

ECONOMICS AND NONECONOMICS, SCIENCE AND PRESCRIPTION

We have stated that we are interested in the principles that govern regulation and "the principles that ought to govern it." What policy *ought* to be is a topic about which the politician and political scientist, sociologist, philosopher and clergyman, and indeed, in a democracy, anyone who votes has important and relevant things to say. Public economic policies are not, cannot and should not be framed on the basis of "purely economic" considerations alone. Economic institutions and policies are in the last analysis only means to ultimately noneconomic ends—such ends as a good life, justice, the fuller development of the potentialities of the individual, national strength, or the glory of God. They can therefore be formulated and judged only in terms of some conception of the proper definition and weight to be placed on these various noneconomic goals. We shall try throughout our discussions to take into account the ways in which different social, political, and ethical considerations might and do properly influence the political process out of which public economic policies emerge.

At the same time, our main focus is on economic principles. Our central question is: What guidance can economics provide legislators, administrators, and judges in framing, applying, and enforcing policies involving the direct regulation of private industry?

The answer to this question combines the two quite distinct purposes of economics—science and prescription.[42] There is nothing unusual about this double motivation; it involves ambivalence only when we fail to keep clearly in mind which of the two purposes we are at any time serving, and in which of our two roles, physician or scientist, we are acting. As for the first, there must be very few professional economists who were not moved to enter that gloomy profession (no matter how far they may later have gone astray) by a belief that economic problems bulk large among the many vexations of human existence in society, and by a hope that the application of goodwill, intelligence, and professional expertise to the formulation of public policy could make an important contribution to the improvement of the human condition. The title of Adam Smith's master work, *An Inquiry Into the Nature and Causes of the Wealth of Nations*, suggests that his was essentially a scientific treatise. But Smith's work

"was, in fact as in intention, a system of political economy. . . . By a system of political economy I mean an exposition of a comprehensive set of economic *policies* that its author advocates on the strength of certain unifying (normative) principles such as the principles of economic liberalism, of socialism, and so on."[43]

The "principle of Natural Liberty" that Smith professed to have discovered was, as Schumpeter observed,

---

[42] The two currently fashionable adjectives for characterizing these two types of economics are "positive" and "normative," respectively.

[43] Stress supplied. Joseph A. Schumpeter, *History of Economic Analysis* (New York: Oxford University Press, 1954), 38.

"both a canon of policy—the removal of all restraints except those imposed by 'justice'—and the analytic proposition that free interaction of individuals produces not chaos but an orderly pattern that is logically determined: he never distinguishes the two quite clearly."[44]

This book is an essay in "political economy"—"the economic life of the nation and what we can do about it"[45]—which is what economics used to be called in the eighteenth and nineteenth centuries.

But if such an inquiry is to be conscientious, its scope and method must be rigidly scientific as well. The economist who asks a politician "Won't you let me advise you on your legislative program?" deserves only another question in response: "What do you *know*?" And only the economist who can answer "Well, I can tell you that if you pass a law that says such-and-such, these are the things that will probably happen," or, "If you do nothing about such-and-such, this is what will probably happen," deserves to have his offer taken seriously.

This is not to argue that economists have no other function in government than to serve as technical assistants to politicians. As we have already suggested, formulating public policy can never be a job for the scientist alone. In the last analysis, deciding what *should* be done can never be accomplished only with the help of the type of information that says "If you do A then B will follow." And if it follows from this truth that economists cannot, *as scientists*, presume to settle the ultimate issues of public policy, it also follows that there are no *other* scientists who can presume to do so either. If framing public policy requires in the last analysis the *art* of the politician or philosopher, this is an art that the economist may be better equipped than anyone else to acquire and to practice within his own domain: who can have given more thought than he to the ultimate ethical and political implications of alternative public economic policies?

Economists have a particular advantage when it comes to taking a direct role in the regulatory process. The job is an extremely technical one and becomes more so each year. It used to be done almost exclusively by lawyers and politicians, with accountants and engineers as assistants. But for decades there has been great and increasing dissatisfaction with their performance. One important criticism has been that they were behaving too much like lawyers and bookkeepers—excessively concerned with proper administrative procedures, the balancing of equities, and the measurement and covering of accounting costs—and too little like economists—paying practically no attention to things such as marginal cost, elasticities of demand, or to the dynamic conditions of innovation and growth. For these and other reasons that will appear later, economists have been drawn more and more into the process, bringing with them their own esoteric terminology and tools; the lawyers that have failed to seek their direct cooperation find they cannot understand what their opponents' witnesses are saying.

WHAT CAN ECONOMICS CONTRIBUTE? PRINCIPLES AND INSTITUTIONS

The unique set of tools that economics can contribute to the regulatory process is the familiar body of microeconomic theory, which purports to

[44] *Ibid.*, 185.
[45] Ben W. Lewis, "It's Political (Repeat Political)   Economy," *The Antioch Review* (September 1949), IX: 372.

explain and predict the behavior of the individual consumer, investor, worker, firm, and industry under various circumstances.[46] Like all other scientific models and the generalizations that emerge from them, the models of microeconomic theory are simplified, describing causal relationships involving a limited number of variables. Therefore, the relationships it predicts will prevail only under the condition of *ceteris paribus*—"all other things remaining equal." Observations or predictions such as that under pure competition price will be set at marginal cost; that with monopoly and blocked entry, an industry will (tend to) earn supernormal profits; that customers will buy more of most products or services if their prices are reduced; that firms will continue to operate at subnormal or even negative profits so long as they cannot withdraw their capital and their revenues cover their variable costs; that prices will fluctuate more in response to changes in supply and demand if those functions are price-inelastic than if they are elastic—generalizations such as these are valid only subject to certain rather strict behavioral assumptions and only *ceteris paribus*.

The hypothesized causal relationships are based partly on deductive reasoning, partly on observation, partly on more rigorous empirical verification. The question of how relevant these traditional models are to the real world, and, therefore, how useful either as explanations of how the economy really works or as predictive tools is an open one. The belief underlying this

---

[46] Microeconomics is a study of the behavior of the *individual* decision-making unit, or, at succeeding levels of aggregation, the individual market, industry, or geographic region in an interdependent world of several regions. It is concerned with the way in which these transacting units or groupings make their economic decisions, and the way in which their several activities are coordinated by economic institutions to make the basic choices dictated by the universal economic problem of scarcity—what to produce, how and by whom to produce it, and how the product is to be distributed. In Western economies, the coordination is effected through the market system. Therefore microeconomics is concerned with the operation of individual markets—how prices, outputs, and distributive shares are determined—and their interrelationships. The criteria of effective performance consist in the desirability of the resulting allocation of resources, the physical efficiency (both statically and dynamically) with which scarce resources are used, and the acceptability of the resulting distribution of income.

Macroeconomics, in contrast, is concerned with the behavior of the major economic aggregates, not with prices in individual markets relative to prices elsewhere (affecting the allocation of resources and the distribution of benefits) but with the "general price level"; not with employment and output in this or that industry relative to others, but with total employment and output in the economy—its stability, adequacy, and growth.

The reason that two largely (and probably

excessively) distinct bodies of economic theory have been developed to explain and predict these separate types of phenomena is that their determinants are largely distinct. For example, the causes of the often unsatisfactory performance of aggregate employment are not to be sought principally in correctable decisions by individual householders, businessmen, investors or workers, or in the defective structure of individual markets (although one must emphasize the qualification "principally" in that statement). When the general price level or aggregate employment moves up or down, the pattern of changes in prices and employment in individual markets and industries exhibits two familiar characteristics: dispersion and central tendency. Microeconomics supplies the explanation of the first characteristic. It can explain why prices in individual markets rise or fall relative to those in other markets: something obviously has happened to demand or supply functions in individual markets relative to those in other markets that explains the divergent results. But it takes macroeconomics to explain the central tendency: the proximate cause must be found in a change in aggregate spending in the economy at large and the remedy must be found principally in public policies aimed at regulating the flow of aggregate demand. Individual transactors, markets, and industries are essentially powerless to react to deficiencies or excesses or instabilities in economy-wide demand in such a way as to prevent or remedy their unfortunate macroeconomic consequences, and public policies attempting to improve matters by regulating

book is that they are or can be useful in both ways; the reader will have to judge for himself whether that belief has proved justified.

As our earlier characterization of Adam Smith's grand design suggested, the elaboration of these theoretical models of a market or price system had a dual purpose: not just to describe and to explain, scientifically, but also to justify and to advocate. The main body of microeconomic theory can be interpreted as describing how, under proper conditions—for example, of economic rationality, competition, and laissez-faire—an unregulated market economy will produce optimum economic results. We will at a later point briefly examine the underlying value judgments on which this conclusion is based. We merely emphasize here that such a conclusion is meaningless except if stated in terms of specified political or ethical criteria or definitions of what constitutes a "good" or a "bad" result; and that the choice of criteria is not one that the economist as such is any more qualified to make than anyone else.[47]

It remains true that the particular standards or values that underlie this favorable appraisal of a market economy are still widely accepted in Western society; and that there is a wide consensus among liberals and conservatives alike that such an economy, regulated principally by the constraints of competition, would at least in some respects be ideal. (The major differences of political opinion in Western society therefore consist largely of differing judgments about the extent to which the conditions necessary for the market to work "ideally" do in fact prevail or can be made to prevail.) So that, for example, the single most widely accepted rule for the governance of the regulated industries is regulate them in such a way as to produce the same results as would be produced by effective competition, if it were feasible.

Microeconomic theory provides regulators with a set of principles that, if followed, will produce optimum results, by widely accepted criteria of optimality. The principles are at one and the same time *behavioral rules*, describing how prices should be set, investment decisions guided and so forth, and descriptions of the *ideal results* that these rules are supposed to produce—notably the use of society's limited resources in such a way as to maximize consumer satisfactions.

Part II of this volume is an attempt to expose those principles and to apply them to the task of regulation.

Even if we regarded the above body of economic theory as a complete and adequate description of the type of performance we would wish to elicit from the economy, its principles alone do not provide a sufficient set of policy rules

---

individual prices, businesses, or markets will be similarly ineffective.

[47] The economic historian could shed light, however, on why it was that Western economists chose to develop a scientific explanation of a market economy instead of another type—for example, one that was centrally planned; why it was that that specific economy emerged; and why the mainstream of Western economic thought chose to justify instead of to condemn that economy. The historical explanations would have to run in terms of (1) the configuration of economic groups, notably the emergent mercantile and industrial capitalists, that thought their interests would be best served by such an economy; (2) the emergent ideals of Western society—for example, of economic liberalism and improved material welfare instead of, for instance, of a more nearly equal distribution of income or the enhanced power of the national state or church; (3) the intellectual currents of the "Age of Reason," which looked in the social as well as the physical universe for the "natural laws" that maintained order without the need for human or governmental intervention; and (4) the scientific and technological developments that conditioned all the others.

for regulated industries. They do not answer the questions of *how* and *by what institutional arrangements* those ideal results are to be achieved. For unregulated industries, economic theory provides at least a large part of the answer: leave it to self-interest, constrained in turn by the "invisible hand" of competition. Competition will weed out the inefficient and concentrate production in the efficient; it will determine, by the objective test of market survival, who should be permitted to produce; it will force producers to be progressive and to offer customers the services they want and for which they are willing to pay; it will assure the allocation of labor and other inputs into the lines of production in which they will make the maximum contribution to total output.[48]

What institutional incentives, compulsions, and arrangements will play the same role where "the invisible hand" of competition is for one reason or another infeasible? "The visible hand of regulation" is not a sufficient answer. The reason, as we shall see more fully below, is that in a society that profoundly respects the institution of private property, the initiative, operating control, and responsibility for economic performance continue, even under regulation, to rest primarily with private management. The role of the government remains essentially negative—setting *maximum* prices, supervising expenditures, specifying *minimum* standards of service, in short, contravening the decisions of private persons only after the fact, only when their performance has been or would otherwise be obviously bad. In these circumstances regulation cannot supply the same assurances as competition that performance will be *positively good*—efficient, progressive, risk-taking, innovative. Its most important task is to define and develop institutional arrangements that will provide correspondingly powerful incentives and pressures on regulated monopolists.

Volume 2 is devoted to a survey and analysis of these critical institutional questions. In view of the historic controversies in economics between the "theorists" or, more precisely, "classical economists," on the one hand, and "institutionalists" on the other, it is important to emphasize that we intend to imply no such dichotomy by this distinction between these two major divisions of this study. On the contrary, the micro theory that is divorced from institutional realities is sterile. The essential task of useful theory is precisely to identify the important institutional determinants of economic behavior—such as number of sellers, barriers to entry, complexity of product, shape and character of the production cost function, or the presence of regulation—and to formulate hypotheses about their impacts on the various aspects of performance. Conversely, the "institutional economics" that is

---

[48] This is not to suggest that the ability of society to rely on competition to serve these ends solves all the institutional problems in the "unregulated" sectors of the economy. In a sense it merely restates the problem: there remain an almost unlimited number of difficult questions about the kinds of institutional arrangements and government policies best suited to preserve competition and make it most effective. What number of sellers best preserves the likelihood of strong interfirm rivalry consistent with achievement of economies of scale in production and innovation? What degree of patent protec- tion strikes the optimum balance between the encouragement of competitive innovation and avoidance of excessive, patent-based monopoly? To what extent can government licensing or prescription of product standards make com- petition more effective by overcoming consumer ignorance? A student of the antitrust laws will recognize how difficult it is to determine either in general or in specific cases what types of policies respecting mergers, integration, various kinds of interfirm collaboration, price discrimina- tion, or exclusive dealing will be best suited to preserve the most effective competition possible.

informed by no theory about which institutional variables are important and which unimportant, that begins with no testable hypotheses about how these variables are likely to operate, that attempts to develop no models of the relation between the various structural and performance variables is no science at all.

The distinction between our two volumes is, instead, that the first is essentially deductive and the second inductive. The former sets forth and develops the formal *rules* for achieving economic efficiency, rules inherent in the normative model of the competitive market system, and shows how they would apply to regulated industries. The latter analyzes the institutional arrangements in the regulated industries that determine how closely those norms are in fact achieved; it is a study of how regulated monopoly does in fact work and how it might be improved. Both make use of the main corpus of microeconomic theory to build the bridge between what we know or think we know and what we think policy ought to be.

CHAPTER 2

The Traditional Issues in the Pricing of Public Utility Services

The essence of regulation is the explicit replacement of competition with governmental orders as the principal institutional device for assuring good performance. The regulatory agency determines specifically who shall be permitted to serve; and when it licenses more than one supplier, it typically imposes rigid limitations on their freedom to compete. So the two prime requirements of competition as the governing market institution—freedom of entry and independence of action—are deliberately replaced. Instead the government determines price, quality and conditions of service, and imposes an obligation to serve.

The licensure of entry in most public utility industries tends to be an infrequent, once-and-for-all or almost-all determination. Franchises legally may have to be renewed, and new firms may seek to be licensed; in radio and television, and trucking this is a frequent occurrence. But even in those cases, and even more so in others, the tendency is to rely on the same chosen instruments, year after year and decade after decade; the structure of the market and identity of the firms selected to serve remain essentially unchanging. And what public utility commissions mainly *do* (though not in broadcasting) is to fix the prices the chosen instruments may charge—not just a ceiling, as in the case of permissible interest rates paid on time deposits or as prescribed in usury laws, or a floor, such as a minimum wage—but a set of specific prices. It is through the regulation of price that the limitation of profits is purportedly achieved; it is incident to the regulation of price that the levels and permissible kinds of cost are controlled, by allowing or disallowing payments for various inputs, by supervising methods of financing and controlling financial structures. Price regulation is the heart of public utility regulation.

This assertion might strike a constitutional lawyer or anyone who has read Chapter 1 as strangely old-fashioned. It sounds like something the United States Supreme Court would have said 40 to 50 years ago, when it was systematically striking down legislative attempts to regulate prices or wages outside the traditional "industries affected with a public interest" on the ground that the right to set prices free of public control was at the heart of the freedom of contract protected by the Fourteenth Amendment.[1] In 1934, in *Nebbia v. New York*, the Supreme Court finally rejected the notion that there was anything constitutionally sacrosanct about private price-determination, and declared that if any industry could, for good and sufficient reasons, be subjected to public regulation, there was no constitutional bar to its being subjected to price regulation in particular.[2]

Our assertion may seem irrational also to the economist. And to some extent it is. One purpose of regulation is to protect buyers from monopolistic exploitation—but buyers can be exploited just as effectively by giving them poor or unsafe service as by charging them excessive prices. Another purpose is to prevent destructive competition—but it would seem that sellers can compete just as destructively by offering better or more service for the same price as by offering the same service at lower prices. Price really has no meaning except in terms of an assumed quality of service; price is a ratio, with money in the numerator and some physical unit of given or assumed quantity and quality in the denominator. Price regulation alone is economically meaningless. Moreover, the nature of our dependence on public utility services is typically such that customers may correctly be *more* interested in the denominator than in the numerator—in the reliability, continuity, and safety of the service than in the price they have to pay.[3]

This relatively greater concentration on price than on quality of service is one reflection of the severe limitations of regulation as an institution of social control of industry. In this chapter we examine the major traditional components of that effort. In addition to laying the necessary factual foundation for our subsequent analysis, the purpose of this preliminary survey is to suggest (1) the limited resemblance between what regulation, as traditionally practiced, tries to do and the principles of normative microeconomic theory, thus providing the justification for our alternative approach, in Part II, and (2) the severe limitations of this institutional device for achieving optimal economic results, which provides the background for Volume 2.

THE LIMITED ATTENTION TO QUALITY OF SERVICE

The regulatory process devotes considerable attention to the denominator of the money-quantum-of-service ratio.[4] The governing statutes generally empower commissions to investigate and issue findings on whether the service offered under their jurisdiction is "unjust, unsafe, improper, inadequate or insufficient," and to promulgate rules for its improvement. The rules adopted

---

[1] See notes 11–20, Chapter 1. In *Adkins v. Children's Hospital*, the Court struck down a law fixing minimum wages for women in the District of Columbia in these terms:

"The essential characteristics of the statute now under consideration, which differentiate it from the laws fixing hours of labor. . . . [are] that the latter . . . deal with incidents of the employment having no necessary effect upon the heart of the contract; that is, the amount of wages. . . .

"If now, in the light furnished by the foregoing exceptions to the general rule forbidding legislative interference with freedom of contract, we examine and analyze the statute in question, we

shall see that it differs from them in every material respect. It is not a law dealing with any business charged with a public interest. . . . It has nothing to do with the character, methods, or periods of wage payments. It does not prescribe hours of labor or conditions under which labor is to be done. . . . It is simply and exclusively a price-fixing law. . . ." 261 U.S. 525, 553–554 (1923).

[2] 291 U.S. 502, 531–532, 536–537 (1934).

[3] See Irston R. Barnes, *The Economics of Public Utility Regulation* (New York: Appleton-Century-Crofts, 1942), 742–743.

[4] For a useful survey, see Charles F. Phillips, Jr., *op. cit.*, 400–438.

cover matters such as safety standards, minimum physical specifications (accuracy of meters, voltage of electricity, heating value of gas), the requirements of prompt meeting of customer demands, extension of service to new customers, controls on abandonment of service, provision of special facilities and arrangements, and certification of new entrants.[5]

But it is far more true of quality of service than of price that the primary responsibility remains with the supplying company instead of with the regulatory agency, and that the agencies, in turn, have devoted much more attention to the latter than to the former. The reasons for this are fairly clear. Service standards are often much more difficult to specify by the promulgation of rules. Where they can be specified, they are often essentially uncontroversial. Where they cannot—and this is particularly the case when it comes to innovations, to the dynamic improvement of service—in a system in which the private companies do the managing and the government the supervision, there is no choice but to leave the initiative with the company itself. The only role the regulatory commission can typically play is a negative one—formulating minimum standards and using periodic inspections to see that they are met; investigating customer complaints and issuing orders when service has been obviously poor, when management or subordinates have been blatantly inefficient or unfair, or when it wishes to insist that the companies take on or retain unremunerative business.[6]

This authority is by no means negligible. The aggressive commission has available to it the ability to penalize offending companies by holding permissible rates at less remunerative levels than it would otherwise be prepared to allow—subject to the constraint, however, that it would be self-defeating to punish them so severely as to impair their financial capacity to institute the desired improvements. And commissions frequently do use this weapon.[7]

Still, their role is essentially a negative one and this raises fundamental questions about the efficacy of the entire process. If, as far as quality of service is concerned, the principal responsibility rests with the private monopolist,

[5] "Public utility commissions are constantly passing upon questions of service. The determination of a rate without a determination of the quality of the service rendered would be similar to an individual's agreeing to pay a stipulated sum of money for a commodity without specifying the kind or grade of commodity he expects to receive in return for his outlay. A very large portion of the commissions' time is, then, necessarily devoted to the determination of the quality of service rendered by the utilities under their jurisdiction. Most states which have active commissions now have state-wide service standards. . . . Where there are departures from these standards the utility is obviously derelict in the performance of its duties, and unless excused by the commission because of unusual circumstances is subject to its disapproval." Charles Stillman Morgan, *Regulation and the Management of Public Utilities* (Boston: Houghton Mifflin, 1923), 270–271.

[6] The question of whether and in what circumstances a utility company may be required to

extend service to new customers and areas, or be forbidden to discontinue services may of course be regarded as an aspect of the regulation of service and is usually so treated. But the issue here is usually quite explicitly one of price or of the relation of revenues to costs, present or prospective: to what extent may utilities be required to take on new, or continue to serve old markets that they think are or will be unremunerative; to what extent should profitable business subsidize unprofitable extensions or continuations? These issues are thus embraced (sometimes explicitly, sometimes implicitly) in our later discussions of cost-price relationships. Of course, as we have already suggested, all regulations of service quality are in economic effect also regulations of price.

[7] For example,

"The testimony given in the gas service case hearing at Neenah was conclusive that the quality of service rendered is totally inadequate. . . . The Commission finds therefore that no increase in rates for gas should be given consideration until the service rendered in the gas department shall conform in a reasonable manner to the standard laid down by the Commission. . . . That no increase in rates for the electric and street railway departments of this utility should be granted until the service in each of them shall be shown to be reasonably satisfactory, and the burden of proof of so doing shall be put on the company. . . ." Morgan, *op. cit.*, 272.

Or, to turn to more recent examples:

"We are receiving numerous complaints from portions of the territory served by Southern Bell. In some areas . . . installation intervals, or the time required to install service, fall well below a reasonable standard. Operator answering time consistently meets Bell's requirements but does not meet the standards recently adopted by this commission. By far the biggest complaint . . . is the length of time required to obtain service. . . . These are problems that can and must be resolved. We have recently adopted uniform standards for telephone service, and have prescribed administrative rules requiring periodic reports which, together with field inspections, will keep the commission fully advised concerning the quality and sufficiency of telephone service being provided. . . . Any rate adjustments, including the one in this docket, will be on a temporary basis for a reasonable period of time pending any necessary improvements in the quality and sufficiency of service. . . .

"Southern Bell will be required to furnish a good and sufficient surety bond conditioned on the prompt and full refund of the difference, if any, between the rates collected by it on a temporary basis pursuant to this order, and the rates ultimately prescribed or approved . . . . as a result of any further order that may be entered in this docket reducing such temporary rates because of service deficiencies."

Re Southern Bell Telephone and Telegraph Company, Florida Public Service Commission, Order No. 4462, November 26, 1968, 76 *Public Utility Reports* 3rd, 412–413.

"We make the following findings:

1. The present earnings of United Telephone Company of Florida are far below a reasonable level and said utility is entitled to some relief on a temporary and emergency basis.
2. United Telephone's present earnings of 3.15 per cent will not support the additional financing that is necessary to enable it to complete its improvement program.
3. The telephone service presently being rendered . . . by United Telephone has improved substantially during the past several months, but is not sufficiently adequate and efficient to justify the full increases requested. . . .

4. The company has virtually completed 64 per cent of its current 3-year (1967–1969) improvement program and, thus, has been able to bring about substantial improvement in service. On that basis, it is fair and reasonable to allow the utility 64 per cent of the requested increases in local exchange rates. . . .
5. The emergency increases authorized by this order will not result at this time in a fair and reasonable return for United Telephone Company, but will improve its financial position so that it should be able to finance the remainder of its improvement program. . . ."

Re United Telephone Company of Florida, Florida Public Service Commission, Order No. 4451, November 12, 1968, 76 PUR 3rd, 471. For other examples, see *ibid.*, 441–451 and 461.

"After years of deliberation, the Federal Communications Commission has decided to tackle the controversial question of how fast Western Union Telegraph Co. should be required to deliver telegrams. . . .

"Communications experts say the commission's involvement could lead to the first Government-mandated standards regulating the speed of domestic telegram deliveries. . . .

"Western Union Telegraph has come under increasing fire in recent years from critics who complain that the cost of telegrams keeps going up while the quality of service declines. . . .

"The FCC's decision to consider the speed-of-service issue cropped up as a little-noticed part of the FCC's current investigation of telegram rate increases proposed by Western Union Telegraph. In announcing the inquiry, the FCC said it would consider not only the rate boosts, but also the 'speed, quality and adequacy' of the company's telegram service.

"FCC officials say this phrase means the commission probably will deal with a number of service-related telegram issues in its investigation, such as how many telegraph offices Western Union Telegraph should maintain, and whether it should be investing more money in its telegram service. But a key question, these sources maintain, is whether the FCC should force Western Union to meet certain speed requirements in its telegram deliveries. . . ." *Wall Street Journal,* October 18, 1968.

Again, in 1969 the New York State Public Service Commission ordered the Penn Central Company to take more than a dozen specific steps to provide "safe, adequate, just and reasonable service" on its Harlem and Hudson commuter lines, including the purchase or lease of at least 80 new cars and 24 new engines, assuring that each of its 340 weekday trains runs on time at lest 80% of the time each month, and providing enough telephone lines and employees

and the government supervisor can intervene only where objective standards can be set or, after the event, when the monopolist's performance has been *obviously bad*,[8] do we have an adequate assurance—comparable to the assurance provided by competition in other sectors of the economy—that his performance will be *positively good* and continuously as good as possible? If poor service is economically the equivalent of high price, why is there not just as great a danger that monopoly power will involve the one as the other? If monopoly carries the danger of sluggishness with respect both to efficiency and to dynamic cost-reduction, is there not the danger of sluggishness as well in improving the quality and extending the scope of service?

These problems are real. Although, as we shall see later, they can never be wholly solved within the regulatory framework, they deserve more creative and active attention from commissions than they now receive.[9] But there is another reason why public utility commissions have been willing, and to some extent justified, to leave the quality of service, far more than price, to the companies themselves—the latter will typically have a strong interest in providing good, ample, and expanding service, as long as they can recoup its costs in the prices they charge. In this respect, far more than in the matter of price, the interest of the monopolist on the one hand and the consumer on the other are more nearly coincident than in conflict.[10] Why so?

1. Maintaining and improving the quality and quantity of service typically is costly. Any regulated monopolist who is prevented by regulation from fully exploiting the inelasticity of his demand but assured (albeit with a regulatory lag) of his ability to incorporate these additional costs in his cost-of-service and hence of recouping them in his price, will presumably be less hesitant than a nonregulated monopolist to incur them.[11]

2. Improvement and extension of service will often involve an expansion of the company's invested capital—that is, its "rate base"—on which it is entitled to a return. The regulated monopolist therefore will have some

---

so that passengers phoning to check on train schedules "receive a prompt response." *The New York Times*, June 6, 1969, 1. In response, the company petitioned for a rehearing. *Ibid.*, July 4, 1969, 1.

For a more general discussion of the way in which service standards and orders may be enforced and particularly of the authority of commissions to condition rate increases on specified improvements or extensions of service, see "The Duty of a Public Utility to Render Adequate Service: Its Scope and Enforcement," *Columbia Law Rev.* (Feb. 1962), LXII: 312, 327–331.

[8] See the astonishing intention of Senator Pastore, chairman of the U.S. Senate Subcommittee on Communications, explicitly to confine the powers of the Federal Communications Commission in precisely this manner in deciding whether or not to renew broadcasting station licenses. He would prohibit challenges to renewals unless the FCC first determines that the station has violated the "public interest." Daniel Zwerdling, "FCC Impropriety," *The New Republic*, June 21, 1969, 10–11. See also

note 134, Chapter 2, Volume 2.

[9] For the case of radio and television, and for a novel case involving the quality of passenger rail service, see Chapter 2 of Volume 2.

[10] Indeed, the greater danger might be that the companies place excessive instead of inadequate emphasis on providing high-quality service, at the expense of economy, for reasons that follow. See also the discussion in Chapter 5, Volume 2, of whether the public utilities reflect a general tendency for limitations on price competition to be associated with an intensification of quality competition.

[11] The unregulated monopolist also will have an incentive to improve his product or diversify his product offerings, to the extent that his demand is sufficiently responsive to offset the additional costs of his so doing. But if he is a profit maximizer presumably he will have set his price-quality combination at the profit-maximizing point, beyond which superior service will add more to costs than to revenues. A public utility, in contrast, if prevented from fixing its price at the profit-maximizing level, has a reserve of incompletely exploited monopoly power; in the

temptation to err in the direction of expanding and improving his services, and thus increasing his rate base beyond the point of economic optimality instead of the reverse.[12]

3. A public utility company is peculiarly exposed to public criticism if its service is inadequate. This exposure is increased by the possibility of customers complaining to regulatory commissions. Possibly associated with this consideration may be a tendency for managers of such companies to assume a quasi-professional responsibility for giving the best possible service, even at the expense of profit maximization.[13] Although customers may have very definite opinions about whether the prices they pay are too high, the determination of whether in fact they are doing so is a complicated matter, as we shall see. But they need no complex investigative and adjudicatory processes to tell them when they are suffering from a power failure, or a refusal of a railroad to make freight cars available to them, or when they keep getting busy signals or wrong numbers on the telephone.[14] Adequate levels of service can be guaranteed more satisfactorily than price by customer complaints, on the one hand, and the "conscience of the corporation," on the other.[15]

It is doubtful that these pressures are as reliable as those exerted by competition; and an unregulated monopolist will surely be subject to similar influences. Still, motivations such as these do to some extent take the place of competition in inducing the franchised monopolist to have a favorable attitude toward providing good and ever-improving service to his captive customers.

The customer may have a fair notion of whether the service he gets is satisfactory. He is likely to find it much more difficult to judge whether its quality and variety are *improving* at a satisfactory rate, because in making such a judgment it would not be pertinent to compare the quality of what he is receiving with what he has been accustomed to expect. But it is precisely these questions about dynamic performance, with respect not only to the quality of service but also to costs and price, that the regulatory commission also is least competent to answer decisively. Although it is in this respect that there may be the greatest danger of inadequate monopoly performance—or *excessive* performance, for the reason suggested under (2), above—this danger is not one to which the commissions have typically been able to devote effective attention.

REGULATING THE RATE LEVEL

Public utility commissions spend the major part of their time, by far, directly or indirectly regulating price. This task has two major aspects and the commissions have tended typically to treat them quite distinctly. The first has to do with the level of rates, taken as a group. The second has to do with the structure of rates—the specific charges on different categories of

---

same circumstances it will therefore have less disincentive to improve service, since any additional costs involved can serve as the justification for raising price correspondingly.

[12] On this particular distortion, see the section on the "A–J–W Effect," in Chapter 2, Volume 2.

[13] See, for example, Troxel, *Economics of Public Utilities*, 464–465, 557–560.

[14] See the flurry of complaints in New York City in July of 1969 over the annoying frequency of busy signals in the New York Telephone Company's Plaza 8 exchange. See, for instance, *New York Times*, July 14, 1969, 22.

[15] But see Glaeser, *op cit.*, 115, emphasizing the need for regulation, to overcome consumer ignorance and managerial inertia.

service and the relationship between them. Outside of the transportation field, the former task has claimed much the greater share of commission attention.

"The rate level," like "the general price level," is a statistical abstraction. It could be expressed only as some sort of index number, summarizing the numerous individual rates for the various classifications of service provided by each company: there are some 43 trillion railroad rates on file with the Interstate Commerce Commission![16] Its real economic meaning is disclosed when these separate prices are translated into total company revenues or into total profits expressed as a percent of owners' investments. Actually the regulatory process works the other way around. The commissions decide what total revenues the companies are entitled to take in, then adjust permitted "rate levels," either selectively or across the board, to yield these totals.

They typically do this by undertaking a thorough examination and appraisal of total company costs in a recent, "test" year.[17] In this way, item by item, they build up an estimate of total permissible "revenue requirements." On the basis of this total, adjusted as much as possible for known or readily predictable changes between the test year and the period for which rates are to be ascertained, the company is ordered or permitted to propose the required adjustments in its rate schedules. Therefore, discussions of rate levels are really discussions of total revenues.

The process of determining permissible revenues falls traditionally into the following three parts or steps, each of them involving an enormous variety of problems and boasting a correspondingly rich history of legal and economic controversy.

Supervision and Control of Operating Costs and Capital Outlays

Just as competition is supposed to hold prices down to the cost of production (ignore for a moment the question of precisely what that means) so regulation takes cost as its standard of the "revenue requirements" of public utility companies, hence the "just and reasonable" rates that the typical controlling statute enjoins them to maintain. It became clear that if the commissions were to be something more than rubber stamps they had to exercise their own judgment about the propriety of the items presented to them as the major components of the cost of service. To do so, first, they had to require the companies to keep uniform systems of accounts, according to procedures and rules stipulated by the commissions, and subject to their audit.[18] Then they needed to make determinations about which costs they were prepared

[16] C. F. Phillips, *op. cit.*, 314.

[17] They may do so regularly or only once in a long while, in a major general rate investigation, or never. If only occasionally, they may employ more limited checks in the intervening years, possibly permitting rate changes on the basis of estimates of cost changes since the "test year." For an illuminating case study of "The General Passenger Fare Investigation," the first undertaken by the Civil Aeronautics Board, about 15 years after passage of its enabling act (a delay for which it was criticized), see the case

study of that title by Emmette S. Redford, in Edwin A. Bock, ed., *Government Regulation of Business: A Casebook* (Englewood Cliffs: Prentice-Hall, 1962), 336–411. On the Federal Communications Commission's "continuous surveillance" over the telephone industry, see Chapter 2, Volume 2, at note 37.

[18] Commissions cannot review costs unless the regulated companies keep their records in some uniform and prescribed fashion. Accounting regulations become necessary also to prescribe those elements of outlay that are to be charged

to authorize for inclusion in the computed company cost-of-service; and, of these, which could be charged directly as operating expenses and thus included in annual revenue requirements dollar for dollar, and which capitalized, thus entering the cost of service in the form of annual allowances for depreciation and return on the undepreciated portion of the investment. Since mere disallowance of certain outlays after the fact could have the effect of reducing excessively the companies' rates of return, and hence of threatening their ability to attract additional capital, commissions came to insist also on the authority to control company expenditure in advance, supervising and passing on their budgets.

Why should it be necessary for commissions to involve themselves in passing on the operating costs of public utility companies? Presumably even an unregulated profit-maximizing monopolist would wish to hold his costs to a minimum, entirely on his own initiative. Could not the commissions then leave such matters to the self-interest of the company managers themselves? Answers can be framed at several levels.

First, there is the simple danger of concealment of profits by exaggeration of costs. Whatever his *actual* level of costs, it obviously pays a regulated monopolist to exaggerate his estimated cost of service. As long as regulation is effective in holding his profits lower than they otherwise could be, he can more completely exploit his monopoly power by fooling the commission into permitting him higher rates than his actual costs justify. Such exaggerations might be expected to show up, after the event, in excessive rates of earnings. But profits can be computed only from accounting records; if there are no understandings about how costs are to be computed and recorded, expenditures to be audited, and the capital value of the stockholders' investment to be measured, there is no way of appraising those records, and supernormal rates of profit can be concealed in padded expense figures and inflated capital accounts.

Second, the charge for depreciation represents not an objective datum but an imputation, an attribution to the production in any given accounting period of responsibility for the using up or obsolescence of capital assets. Similar to the cost of capital itself—that is, the requisite return on invested capital that must likewise be included in the cost of production—there is room for differences of judgment about its proper level. It is obviously in the interest of the regulated company to exaggerate its gross cost of capital—depreciation plus return on investment—and for the commission to hold it to the minimum, as we shall see more fully presently.

Third, it might be in the interest of the company—always assuming that regulation is effective in holding its profits below the levels that the market would otherwise permit—to incur actually greater costs than is in the best interest of the consumer, provided it is then permitted to incorporate those costs in the regulated price. One example would be heavy expenditures for advertising and public relations, since the companies might receive numerous

---

directly to income and those that are to be capitalized. The appropriate charges for depreciation cannot be determined and reviewed unless the depreciable property accounts are kept in some comprehensible fashion. Accounting rules are also necessary with respect to the valuation of property, which plays an extremely important role in determining the final cost of service, as we shall see. They are similarly necessary if the utility company itself or the commission is to use cost intelligently in the devising of rate structures.

benefits therefrom while passing the costs on to the consuming public. Public utility companies advertise in the hope of influencing regulatory commissions to treat them generously, and electric companies have financed expensive propaganda campaigns in opposition to competing public power projects.[19] Similar purposes might be served by large charitable contributions; with these, as with advertising outlays, commissions have had to decide how much, if any, is properly charged to the consumer and how much should be borne by the stockholders. A similar need for regulatory supervision could be created by the possible temptation of utility companies—to which we have already alluded, and which we will analyze more fully below—to use capital wastefully in order to inflate their rate bases and hence their total permissible profits.

Fourth, the regulated companies—even more, their promoters and managers—have extracted some of these potential monopoly profits by paying excessive prices to affiliated, unregulated companies for equipment, supplies, financial advice and underwriting, engineering, and managerial services—charges included in the cost of service and recovered from customers.[20]

Fifth, since the public utilities are typically not subject to intensive price competition, they are probably not under the same pressures as firms in more competitive industries to hold their costs down. It is understandable, therefore, that regulatory commissions, charged with taking the place of competition, should make some efforts in the same direction. The necessity for their doing so is accentuated, finally, by the unusually high degree of

---

[19] See Ernest Gruening, *The Public Pays: A Study of Power Propaganda*, rev. ed. (New York: Vanguard, 1964), *passim*. Gruening includes (xxix-xliii) the *Memorandum Opinion* of the Federal Power Commission, *In the Matter of Northwestern Electric Company et al.*, Docket No. IT–5647, Opinion No. 59, 1941, reporting on its investigation of the accounting disposition of expenditures for political purposes by five electric companies. Merle Fainsod and Lincoln Gordon report an estimate that the costs of the "educational" campaign by utility companies after World War I "to 'sell' their industry to the public and to convince the American people of the adequacy of existing regulatory techniques and of the dangers of further penetration of government into the utility business" ran $25–30 millions a year, "all charged off as proper advertising expenses . . . and computed in the rates which the public was required to pay." *Government and The American Economy* (New York: Norton, 1941), 308. And those were Coolidge and Hoover, not Nixon, dollars. The problem, although ancient, has not disappeared: "Five Manhattan State Senators protested yesterday what they called the Consolidated Edison Company's 'gigantic' advertising and promotion campaigns in connection with its request for higher electricity charges." According to the Company's own estimate, its expenditures for institutional advertising would have come to some $2.1

millions in 1965. *New York Times*, August 23, 1966, 27.

Utility companies engage in commercial as well as political and "institutional" advertising, and the former expenditures may well be economically legitimate (see, for example, note 16, Chapter 4). American Telephone and Telegraph (AT&T) and its affiliated companies ranked fourteenth among the nation's advertisers in 1965 with total expenditures of $70 million. But this was a relatively modest 0.6% of the system's total revenues, of $11.3 billion. *Advertising Age*, August 29, 1966, 44, 61.

For a summary of the regulatory treatment of such expenditures, see A. J. G. Priest, *Principles of Public Utility Regulation*, 59–65; also "Trends and Topics, Promotional Programs," *Public Utilities Fortnightly* (June 23, 1966), LXXVII: 65.

[20] See, for example, Louis D. Brandeis, *Other People's Money and How the Bankers Use It* (Washington: The McClure Publications, 1913); James C. Bonbright and Gardner C. Means, *The Holding Company: Its Public Significance and its Regulation* (New York: McGraw-Hill, 1932), esp. Chapter 6. The holding company in some ways has contributed to greater efficiency; but it was also used as a device for milking the (controlled) operating companies, and through them the rate-payers. The relation of the various Bell System companies to their parent, AT&T, and to its wholly-owned subsidiary and equipment

separation of ownership and managerial control in these companies.[21] This fact, taken in conjunction with the lesser pressures of price competition and the possibility of recouping higher costs in higher prices along an inelastic demand curve, creates a particular danger that, in the absence of regulatory scrutiny, managements may vote themselves unusually large salaries, expense accounts and other perquisites, as well as engage in other methods of exploiting their position for their own personal profit or nonpecuniary advantage, as in fact they have from time to time in the past.[22]

Manifestly, the operating expenses and capital outlays of public utility companies are by far the most important component of their rate levels, on the one hand, and the efficiency with which they make use of society's resources on the other. Therefore, in terms of their quantitative importance, it would be reasonable to expect regulatory commissions to give these costs the major part of their attention. But in fact they have not done so; they have given their principal attention instead to the limitation of profits.

The reasons for this perverse distribution of effort illustrate once again the inherent limitations of regulation as an institution of effective social control of industry. Effective regulation of operating expenses and capital outlays

---

supplier, Western Electric Company, has thus been a subject of continuing regulatory concern. In one of the landmark United States Supreme Court decisions in the 1920s the Court refused to permit the Public Service Commission of Missouri to disallow certain payments by the local Bell company to AT&T for rentals and services. *Southwestern Bell Telephone Company v. Public Service Commission of Missouri*, 262 U.S. 276, 288–289 (1923). The Court reversed itself on this matter in *Smith v. Illinois Bell Telephone Co.*, 282 U.S. 133, 152–153 (1930), and the general rule is that these charges must be justified in terms of the costs to AT&T of performing the services. Similarly, numerous state commissions check on the payments by their various Bell companies for Western Electric equipment and supplies, and the *Smith v. Illinois Bell* decision required that this scrutiny take into account Western's profits from these sales. The Michigan Commission has in the past scaled down the payments when it found that the rate of return on Western Electric's capital exceeded the rate of return that it permitted the Michigan Bell Company to earn. C. Emery Troxel, "Telephone Regulation in Michigan," in William G. Shepherd and Thomas G. Gies, ed., *Utility Regulation: New Directions in Theory and Policy* (New York: Random House, 1966), 168–169. But the overwhelming majority of commissions have found Western's charges reasonable and have permitted them to enter the operating companies' cost of service without adjustment. For a fuller discussion, see Chapter 6, Volume 2.

[21] Distribution of 176 large corporations, according to the proportion of voting stock owned by managements, September 30, 1939, by industrial classes:

Percent of Stock Outstanding	Industrial	Public Utility	Railroad
0–1	66	33	21
1–5	29	3	1
5–10	7	2	1
10–20	6	—	—
20–30	2	—	—
30–40	—	—	—
40–50	1	—	—
50 plus	4	—	—
Total	115	38	23

Source. Robert Aaron Gordon, *Business Leadership in the Large Corporation* (Washington: The Brookings Institution, 1945), 27.

A later study of the 200 largest nonfinancial corporations found that in 1963 18% of the industrial corporations were controlled by owners of more than 10% of their stock; the corresponding figures for public utility and railroad corporations were 2% and 4% respectively. At the other extreme, management-controlled companies were 78% of the industrial and 98% of the public utility group. In the case of railroads the percentage was 83, but if one adds in the corporations found to be controlled by a legal device such as pyramiding or the use of voting trusts, that figure rises to 97%, while the ratio for industrials rises only to 82%. Robert J. Larner, "Ownership and Control in the 200 Largest Nonfinancial Corporations, 1929 and 1963," *Amer. Econ. Rev.* (September 1966), LVI: 781.

[22] See Barnes, *Economics of Public Utility Regulation*, 618–619 and the cases cited there. Following up a finding by Gary S. Becker that monopolistic

would require a detailed, day-by-day, transaction-by-transaction, and decision-by-decision review of every aspect of the company's operation. Commissions could do so only if they were prepared completely to duplicate the role of management itself. This society has never been willing to have commissions fill the role of management and doubtless with good reason: it is difficult to see how any company could function under two separate, coequal managements, each with an equally pervasive role in its operations. Therefore, when the controlling decisions are made, they are made in the first instance by private management itself. Regulation can do little more than review the major decisions after the fact, permitting here and disallowing there. In these circumstances they have been unable as a general practice to substitute their judgments for those of management; and often when they have tried, the courts have denied them the authority to do so, except in cases of obvious and gross mismanagement.[23] Profits, in contrast, are merely a markup, something added to the sum total of expenses. This does not mean that profit control is noncontroversial—quite the contrary. But their regulation does not involve the same type of detailed and pervasive supervision as would a comparable control of the decisions that determine a company's efficiency.

---

enterprises discriminate against blacks more frequently than competitive ones, Armen A. Alchian and Reuben A. Kessel developed the more general hypothesis that the managements of companies whose pecuniary profits are limited by regulation (or similar pressures) will be under strong temptation to take out any possibilities of monopoly profit that remain unexploited in the form of "nonpecuniary gains," one category of which is "the indulgence of one's tastes in the kind of people with whom one prefers to associate. Specifically, this may take the form of pretty secretaries, pleasant, well-dressed congenial people who never say anything annoying, of lavish offices, of large expense accounts, of shorter working hours, of costly administrative procedures that reduce the wear and tear on executives . . . having secretaries available on a moment's notice . . . and of many others." "Competition, Monopoly, and the Pursuit of Pecuniary Gain," in Universities-National Bureau Committee for Economic Research, *Aspects of Labor Economics* (Princeton University Press: Princeton, 1962), 163. The likelihood of this managerial behavior may not be significantly greater for regulated public utility companies than in the case of unregulated companies with market power. See Oliver E. Williamson, "Managerial Discretion and Business Behavior," *Amer. Econ. Rev.* (December 1963), LIII: 1032–1057, and William G. Shepherd, "Market Power and Racial Discrimination in White-Collar Employment," *Antitrust Bulletin* (Spring 1969), XIV: 141–161 and, with particular reference to regulated companies, 155–157.

[23] See, for example, William K. Jones, *Cases and Materials on Regulated Industries* (Brooklyn: The Foundation Press, 1967), 175–186.

"Good faith is to be presumed on the part of the managers of a business. . . . In the absence of a showing of inefficiency or improvidence, a court will not substitute its judgment for theirs as to the measure of a prudent outlay." *West Ohio Gas Co. v. Public Utilities Commission* 294 U.S. 63, 72 (1935). See the exhaustive summary of the case law in Priest, *Principles of Public Utility Regulation*, I, Chapter 3.

On the other hand:

"The Alaska commission upheld disallowance of $50,000 of expenses to compensate for inefficiencies in an electric company's operation. Comparison of the company's expense with that of automated companies . . . showed the cost to be one and one-half to seven times that of the other companies designated as comparable. . . .

"[According to the hearing officer:] It was not out of place for the commission to disallow expenses claimed to be excessive because available advances in technology had been ignored and the capacity and efficiency of the plant had been eroded through years of inadequate maintenance. . . .

"It was not so much a matter of how the company stacked up in relation to the efficiency of other companies, but a measurement of how it operated at present compared to how it would have operated if suggested recommendations had been put into effect. . . .

"The company had adequate notice and opportunity to institute procedures recommended by engineers it had hired as consultants, which it had neglected to do."

"Expense Reduction to Compensate for Inefficiencies Upheld," *Public Utilities Fortnightly*, March 27, 1969, 60–61.

The process has focused primarily on profits, also, because these are politically the most visible—excessive profits the most obvious danger and sign of consumer exploitation, in the absence of effective competition, regulated profits the most obvious and comforting evidence that regulation can be "effective."[24]

And in those numerous, though comparatively unimportant instances in which commissions do in fact decide whether or not to disallow some item of expenditure, the governing consideration turns out to be what policy would be most "fair" to stockholders on the one hand and consumers on the other—a constantly recurring theme in the regulatory process.[25] It is certainly not suggested here that considerations such as these are irrelevant in what is, inescapably, a political determination—that is, a determination of who gets what and how much (and the "who" may include not just stockholders, managers, and customers but, for example, the colleges, churches, or minority groups that might benefit from contributions or other such expenditures that the corporation may be unable to justify on a purely economic basis).[26] But it is important to recognize that criteria such as these may or may not coincide with the type of results competition would produce, or with what would be economically optimal.[27]

---

[24] The analogous situation prevails with respect to weapons acquisition by the Department of Defense:

"a workable definition of efficiency requires considering all of the costs generated in a weapons program, profit . . . being just one special form of cost. Herein lies the second reason for the emphasis on minimum profits as an indicator of weapons acquisition efficiency. It is usually much easier for government negotiators or auditors to say that profits are too high than to claim that the cost of developing some technically complex item of equipment is excessive. Government personnel recognize that if any item in the weapons bill can be attacked and perhaps reduced, it is the profit item. However, this Machiavellian realism ignores the 90% or more of the bill in which a much greater potential for efficiency improvements typically exists." Merton J. Peck and Frederic M. Scherer, *The Weapons Acquisition Process: An Economic Analysis*, Division of Research, Graduate School of Business Administration (Boston: Harvard University, 1962), 509.

[25] It frequently recurs outside the regulatory area as well. A striking example is to be found in the field of antitrust policy, where precisely the same issues arise about the compatibility of "fair competition" and economic efficiency. See, for example, Joel B. Dirlam and Alfred E. Kahn, *Fair Competition, The Law and Economics of Antitrust Policy* (Ithaca: Cornell University Press, 1954), which is addressed to this issue.

[26] This means that the process, being essentially political, is capable of generating violent emotions or at least rhetoric, on the part both of the industry, in its efforts to reduce the load of regulation, to justify its managements' compensation and its own performance against the threat of government competition, and of its critics, who see regulation as ineffective and the consumer subjected to merciless gouging. For a fine example of the latter, see Lee Metcalf and Vic Reinemer, *Overcharge* (New York: David McKay Company, 1967), *passim*, and, specifically on cost items such as charitable contributions, managerial compensation, and political advertising, Chapters 6, 8, and 9. It is no condescension to point out that the book's economic analysis and appraisals are neither objective nor thorough; but its argument cannot be ignored.

[27] See, for example, the survey of the policies of regulatory commissions with respect to the allowance or disallowance of promotional, public relations, or charitable expenditures in C. F. Phillips, *op. cit.*, 186–188. Or see the very interesting conflicting majority, concurring, and dissenting opinions on the subject of contributions in *Pacific Telephone and Telegraph Co. v. Public Utilities Commission of the State of California et al.*, 401 P. 2d 353, 374–375, 379–382 (1965). It is very difficult to detect any consistent consideration, let alone application, of economic criteria, of the kind to be developed in Part II. Instead there is a mushy mixture of questions such as: Do these outlays benefit the company? Or the community at large? Or the stockholders, mainly? Are they properly part of the utility business? What would be fair? These observations are by no means intended to suggest that application of "strictly economic" criteria would provide any simple answers to these problems either.

Therefore, although efficient operation and continuous improvement therein are, quantitatively, the most important aspects of industrial performance, the principal reliance for securing these results cannot, in the nature of the case, be placed on the regulatory process itself. The major contribution that regulation can make, and it is a modest one, can only be the providing of incentives—or taking care not to remove incentives—for private managements to exert themselves continuously in this direction. Whether such incentives can ever be sufficient, once the spur of competition has been drastically attenuated, is the fundamental question with which we deal in Volume 2.

The allowance for depreciation expenses is of quite a different character. Operating expenses involve actual money outlays, which can be automatically recorded in company accounts and transferred into the computed cost of service. Depreciation, too, goes into cost of service and price; but it is not a money outlay in the year it is charged. It is an imputed cost, introduced to take account of the fact that the economic life of capital assets is limited; to distribute the decline in their value—which is a genuine cost of production— over their economic life, in order to assure its recoupment from customers. So the portion of total revenues it permits the company to earn does not, as is the case with normal operating expenses, go out in payments to outside parties—suppliers of raw materials, workers and so on. It belongs to the owners; it is part of the gross return they are permitted to earn on their investment.

The return to capital, in other words, has two parts: the return *of* the money capital invested over the estimated economic life of the investment and the return (interest and net profit) *on* the portion of investment that remains outstanding. The two are arithmetically linked, since according to the usual (but not universal) regulatory practice the size of the net investment, on which a return is permitted, depends at any given time on the aggregate amount of depreciation expense allowed in the previous years—that is, the amount of investment that remains depends on how much of it has been recouped by annual depreciation charges previously. And the two are linked economically, since the rate at which owners are permitted to get their capital out helps determine the true rate of return that they earn on their original investment. To the extent—as happens in some jurisdictions—that accrued depreciation is not fully deducted from the rate base, the regulated companies in effect are being permitted a higher rate of profit; and the same result could be achieved by allowing a higher nominal rate on original investment cost less full depreciation.

Any economic discussion of depreciation should really consider it along with the return on investment. In many contexts it must take into account also the changing provisions of the corporation income tax law concerning allowable rates of depreciation for tax purposes. Consider, for instance, the three-fold effect on the cost of service, hence on allowable rates of return, of provisions for accelerated depreciation in the income tax laws, such as were enacted in 1964, via (1) what it may do to the appropriate level of annual depreciation expense allowed by the regulatory commission, (2) the effect of different rates of annual depreciation on the net remaining investment, on which the net return is permitted, and (3) the amount of income taxes that ought to be included in the cost of service. That requires some explanation.

The effect of accelerated tax depreciation is not to reduce total taxes paid over the life of any particular piece of capital equipment, but only to change its timing. Only the original cost of the equipment can be charged off, in total, over its life. When a company charges a disproportionately large part of the total in the earlier years for tax purposes—which has the effect of reducing taxable income, hence taxes—this means it will be able to charge off correspondingly less, hence will be forced to pay equivalently higher taxes, in later years. Assuming no change in tax rates in the interim, the taxes saved in the early years have to be paid back in full in the later years. But the postponement is beneficial to the taxpayer; in effect, accelerated depreciation means the Treasury Department is giving him an interest-free loan, during the period of the postponement. It increases the real rate (after tax) of return on investment, if one is permitted to keep more of his profits for a while, before having to hand them over to the government.

So regulatory commissions have had to decide whether the taxes to be incorporated in price should be only those actually paid—in which event the benefits of accelerated depreciation are passed on entirely to customers in the years of tax saving—or "normalized" over the life of the investment (higher than actual taxes in the early years, lower in the later)—in which event the interest-free loan is retained by the company. If the latter is chosen, commissions have had to decide also what treatment should be given to the revenues recouped from consumers in excess of the taxes actually paid in the earlier years. These "phantom taxes" are typically segregated in a special reserve for deferred taxes, in recognition of the fact that taxes will in later years exceed these "normalized" recoupments from customers. But the controversial question is whether the amount of that reserve should be deducted from the company's net investment or rate base, on the ground that, as with depreciation, these monies have been retrieved from customers and that it would be double recoupment to permit the company also to earn a return on that portion of its undepreciated investment; or whether it should be left in the rate base, because Congress intended the tax savings to benefit investors and by so doing to encourage additional investment. The more frequent practice is to permit the company no return on the assets represented by the tax reserve; but many commissions permit a small return (for example, 1.5%, in contrast with 6.5% on the normal rate base), and some allow the full return—that is, they do not reduce the rate base by the accumulations of deferred taxes at all.[28]

Advocates of including in the cost of service only the taxes actually paid, which involves "flowing through" the benefits of accelerated depreciation to the customers, argue that the benefits are likely to be permanent—that is, that the amount of taxes saved is not really postponed but is, in effect, forgiven. And they are more right than wrong, *provided* the company's total investments grow over time at a sufficiently rapid rate. In that event, the tax postponements on its newer (and ever larger) investments will always exceed the higher taxes continually coming due on the older (and smaller) investments. Indeed, as long as total company assets grow at all, taxes will always be lower under accelerated amortization than they would be otherwise. Opponents of flow-through, assuming instead that the tax is merely postponed, maintain that this method confers a windfall of rate reductions on

---

[28] See Eugene F. Brigham, "Public Utility Depreciation Practices and Policies," *National* *Tax J.* (June 1966), XIX: 149.

current customers at the expense of future customers. And, indeed, under almost any assumption about future growth of the company, rates under flow-through *will* have to be increased at some time in the future—although, as long as growth is positive, not to the levels that would have to be charged all the way along by a company that failed to take advantage of this tax privilege.

Rate-payers benefit from normalization also, as long as the accumulated tax reserve is deducted in whole or in part from the rate base, since they no longer have to pay a return on that part of the company's total assets represented by those accumulated tax-savings. Flow-through gives them the greatest immediate benefit. Whether in the long run rates end up lower under flow-through than normalization depends, for the reasons already indicated, on how rapidly the company's total assets grow.[29]

Not surprisingly, there has been continuous controversy and litigation over which of these methods, if either, utility commissions ought to adopt; and, if they adopt flow-through, whether regulated companies can be required to avail themselves of the tax privileges, although they retain none of the benefits and run the risk of having to ask for rate increases in the future.[30] These are really questions of the appropriate return to be permitted on capital investment. When company spokesmen argue against flowing-through or deducting the deferred-tax reserves from their allowable rate base, they are in effect arguing for a larger return on investment. When consumer representatives argue on the other side, their contention, at least implicitly, is that regulation must in any case provide a sufficient rate of return—in which event these additional incentives are unnecessary and ought to be passed on in lower rates.

Another issue associated with the determination of depreciation expense is whether the number of dollars that investors are permitted in this fashion to recoup from customers should be the amounts originally invested, or whether that total should be adjusted over time to reflect the changing purchasing power of those dollars. Here, again, the question is really one of what type of return investors ought to be permitted; in economic essence, it is the same issue in another form as whether the rate base, on which the

---

[29] For a general survey of the issues, see Garfield and Lovejoy, *Public Utility Economics*, 109–114. For a very lucid account and analysis of the pattern of rates over time under the various possible systems and under different growth rate assumptions, see Eugene F. Brigham, "The Effects of Alternative Tax Depreciation Policies on Public Utility Rate Structures," *National Tax J.* (June 1967), XX: 204–218.

[30] A survey at the outset of 1970 showed that commissions in 20 states required normalization, in 17 flowing-through, and in 12 had taken no action at all. Both the Federal Power Commission and the Interstate Commerce Commission have ordered flow-through; the Civil Aeronautics Board, normalization; and the Federal Communications Commission has taken no stand, except to declare that the failure of a regulated company to take advantage of accelerated depreciation for tax purposes would be

taken into account in fixing the rate of return. "States Split on Accelerated Depreciation," *Electrical World*, January 20, 1969, 73, and *ibid.*, January 12, 1970, 12. FPC decisions requiring flow-through and computing company costs of service *as though* the companies had availed themselves of the tax privileges even though they had ceased to do so, have been sustained in the courts. See *Alabama-Tennessee Natural Gas Co. v. Federal Power Commission*, 359 F. 2d 318 (1966), cert. denied, 385 U.S. 847 (1967); *Natural Gas Pipeline Co. of America v. Federal Power Commission*, 385 F. 2d 629 (1967); and *Midwestern Gas Transmission et al. v. Federal Power Commission*, 388 F. 2d 444 (1968), cert. denied 392 U.S. 928 (1968). But the ability of commissions to require flowing-through was severely curtailed by the 1969 income tax law revision. Public Law 91–172, 91st Congress, December 30, 1969, 83 Stat. 487, 625–628.

allowable return is to be computed, should be similarly adjusted—to which we turn shortly.

The treatment of depreciation expense under public utility regulation provides an early illustration of the respects in which pricing here departs from the norms of microeconomic theory. It is an elementary proposition of that model and one aspect of its central rule, as we shall see more fully in Chapter 3, that price ideally should be set at marginal cost—that is, at short-run marginal cost. But that marginal cost is a measure of changes in *variable* costs alone; it does not include (most of) depreciation, or any part of the net return on investment, as such. Nor do monopolists, who are supposed to equate marginal cost to marginal revenue, take depreciation into account either in their pricing decisions—again according to the traditional theory of the firm, which assumes continuous, short-run profit maximization. In both cases this means, roughly, that the businessman must cover his variable costs, if he is to continue to operate at all; and so far as gross return on investment is concerned, he takes as much as he can get, over and above the variable costs—sometimes much, sometimes little—whatever the market will bear. It is only in the long run, over the life of investments, that prices, thus set, are expected to be high enough on the average to cover fixed costs. Therefore, when regulatory commissions include fixed costs such as depreciation and return on investment in their cost of service computations, and hence in the permissible rates, they are in effect requiring not marginal-cost but average-cost or full-cost pricing—a practice widely followed in unregulated industries as well. How serious this departure from optimum pricing is in practice is a major topic of Part II.

Determination of the "Rate Base"

Since the production of public utility services typically is unusually capital-intensive,[31] the element of cost represented by the return on invested capital necessarily bulks larger in their final selling price than in unregulated

---

[31] Garfield and Lovejoy offer as typical the following capital turnover ratios (gross revenues divided by capital investment).

Electric utilities	0.30
Natural gas utilities	0.60
Natural gas pipelines	0.40
Bell Telephone System	0.40
Water utilities	0.20
Total manufacturing	2.00

Source. *Op. cit.*, 23.

A clearer impression of the unusually heavy utilization of capital in the public utility industries is provided by the following skeletal financial data taken from the Annual Reports of a public utility, a steel, and a grocery retailing company. Note the wide range in the ratios of their capital to sales, whether the former is measured by total assets, fixed assets —land, plant, and equipment—or, on the liability side, by total invested capital—that is, long-term debt and owners' equity. Or, to describe the same relationship by its reciprocal, note the differences in the number of times their capital "turns over" each year in the form of sales.

	Pacific Gas and Electric Co.	United States Steel Corp.	The Great Atlantic & Pacific Tea Co. (A&P)
Current assets	236	2,091	558
Land, plant, and equipment, net	3,551	3,446	326
Other assets	28	854	—
Total assets	3,815	6,391	884

industries generally.[32] And since it is this element in the cost of service that determines the size of the company's profit, it is not surprising that its determination has been by far the most hotly contested aspect of regulation,[33] consuming by far the greatest amount of time of both commissions and courts.

The number of dollars of investment return are, of course, a product of the aggregate investment, on which some return is to be allowed, and the percentage rate permitted. Arithmetically, the two factors are of equal importance; the result can be changed by increasing or decreasing one just as well as the other. But, largely for constitutional reasons, the traditional emphasis and focus of most of the litigation in the American regulatory experience has been on the former, the "rate base."

It was not always so. In its historic *Munn v. Illinois* decision, the Supreme Court addressed itself to the contention of the appellants that it was up to the courts to determine whether the rates prescribed—in this case by the legislature itself—were reasonable or unreasonable. It specifically declined to do so:

"It is insisted, however, that the owner of property is entitled to a reason-

	Pacific Gas and Electric Co.	United States Steel Corp.	The Great Atlantic & Pacific Tea Co. (A&P)
Long term debt	1,830	—	—
Owners equity	1,625	3,344	627
Total invested capital	3,456	3,344	627
Sales	1,005	4,609	5,459
Ratios to sales:			
Total assets	3.8	1.4	0.16
Fixed assets	3.5	0.7	0.06
Invested capital	3.4	0.7	0.11

Source. The P.G.&E. and U.S. Steel figures are for 1968, the A&P for the fiscal year 1967–68; balance sheet items are for the end of those years. From their *Annual Reports*.

[32] Capital costs as a percentage of sales, 1965.

	Net Income After Taxes Plus Interest Paid %[a]	Depreciation Plus Income Taxes %[b]
Transportation	5.9	9.7
Communications	13.4	18.6
Electric, gas, and sanitary services	15.4	19.3
Total manufacturing	5.1	6.3

Source. Computed from U.S. Treasury Department, Internal Revenue Service, *Statistics of Income, 1965, Corporation Income Tax Returns*, Washington, 1969, 17, 20.

[a] This column presents net return on investment (equity plus borrowed capital) as a percentage of total business receipts. Interest alone represented the following portions of the total return in the four industry groups: 41, 21, 38 and 14%, respectively.

[b] These are shown additionally in consideration of the fact, already noted, that they are also part of the gross costs of capital. The percentages in the two columns should therefore be added to obtain a fuller indication of the relative importance of all capital costs in these various industries.

[33] This generalization, along with the generalization that commissions have devoted their major attention to the general level of rates, does not apply to transportation, where, for more than four decades, profits (at least of railroads) have typically been below levels that regulatory commissions would have regarded as reasonable, and primary attention has gone instead to rate structures and the conditions of inter-carrier competition. See p. 170, below.

able compensation for its use, even though it be clothed with a public interest, and that what is reasonable is a judicial and not a legislative question.

". . . the practice has been otherwise. In countries where the common law prevails, it has been customary from time immemorial for the legislature to declare what shall be a reasonable compensation under such circumstances, or, perhaps more properly speaking, to fix a maximum beyond which any charge made would be unreasonable. . . .

"We know that this is a power which may be abused; but that is no argument against its existence. For protection against abuses by legislatures the people must resort to the polls, not to the courts."[34]

Thirteen years later, however, the Court took the opposite position:

"The question of the reasonableness of a rate of charge for transportation by a railroad company, involving as it does the element of reasonableness both as regards the company and as regards the public, is eminently a question for judicial investigation, requiring due process of law for its determination."[35]

Finally, in *Smyth v. Ames*, in 1898, the Court not only strongly reaffirmed its responsibility under the Fourteenth Amendment's due process clause to review the reasonableness of rates set by state commissions, but it proceeded to specify its criteria of reasonableness:

"We hold . . . that the basis of all calculations as to the reasonableness of rates to be charged by a corporation maintaining a highway under legislative sanction [the case in question involved a railroad] must be the *fair value* of the property being used by it for the convenience of the public. And in order to ascertain that value, the original cost of construction, the amount expended in permanent improvements, the amount and market value of its bonds and stock, *the present as compared with the original cost of construction*, the probable earning capacity of the property under particular rates prescribed by statute, and the sum required to meet operating expenses, are all matters for consideration, and are to be given such weight as may be just and right in each case. We do not say that there may not be other matters to be regarded in estimating the value of the property. What the company is entitled to ask is a fair return upon the value of that which it employs for the public convenience."[36]

The "specification" was hardly precise; several of the listed "matters for consideration" were distressingly vague, and the Court was also vague about how it wanted all of them, along with the "other matters," combined into a composite "fair value" figure. Nor were regulatory commissions thereafter much clearer about how they were following those instructions, as Ben W. Lewis has caustically observed:

"A word should be said at this point with reference to the hybrid 'fair value' ('trance') method. . . . The 'fair value' method consists of an examination by the commission of evidence relating to reproduction cost and prudent investment, together with evidence of intangible values and observed condition of the property, the application of judgment whose processes defy

---

34 94 U.S. 113, 133–134 (1877).
35 *Chicago, Milwaukee & St. Paul Railway Company v. Minnesota*, 134 U.S. 418, 458 (1890). For a compendium of the leading cases concerning the judicial review of utility regulation, see Barnes, *Cases on Public Utility Regulation*, Chapter 3.
36 Stress supplied. 169 U.S. 466, 546–547 (1898).

analysis or description, and the selection of a final value figure which bears no derivative relation to any figures in evidence and no ascertainable relation to any functional purpose of rate making. The determination is typically accompanied by explicit denials that a formula was employed or that the result is a compromise, together with a statement that the commission is quite incapable of retracing and setting forth the processes by which the value figure was reached."[37]

It was not only its lack of precision that made *Smyth v. Ames* the bane of public utility regulation for the next 50 years, embroiling commissions and courts in endless controversies about the definition and measurement of fair value. It was also its specific insistence that stockholders were entitled to a return not on the dollars they had actually invested—a quantity easily recorded in the company accounts, hence readily ascertainable—or "prudently invested," but on the current value of their investment. The first thing wrong with such a standard is its possible circularity. As the Supreme Court pointed out 46 years later, in overturning *Smyth v. Ames*, "fair value" cannot serve as the basis for rate regulation if it is taken to mean market value, since the market value of any enterprise or of its common stock depends on its earnings or anticipated earnings, which in turn depend on the rates that are allowed it: "'fair value' is the end product of the process of rate-making not the starting point . . . ."[38] This objection is sound, however, only if "fair value" is to be measured in terms of the market value of the enterprise. It is incorrect if applied to the customary interpretation that measured fair value (at least in part) with reference to the cost of reproducing the company's assets, as *Smyth v. Ames* likewise instructed commissions to do. Whatever the problems of applying the reproduction cost standard, and they were great, circularity was not one of them. The current cost of duplicating the existing facilities or others capable of giving the same service does not move up or down so as to validate whatever levels of rates and earnings are permitted.[39]

---

[37] In Leverett S. Lyon and Victor Abramson, *Government and Economic Life: Development and Current Issues of American Public Policy* (Washington: The Brookings Institution, 1940), 2: 692.

[38] "The heart of the matter is that rates cannot be made to depend upon 'fair value' when the value of the going enterprise depends on earnings under whatever rates may be anticipated." *Federal Power Commission v. Hope Natural Gas Co.*, 320 U.S. 591, 601 (1944).

The "market value of its bonds and stock" was one of the considerations that the Supreme Court said had to go into the determination of "fair value" in *Smyth v. Ames.*

[39] There *is* some causal connection between rates and reproduction costs. Higher or lower rates will mean a greater or lesser volume of sales, hence a need for greater or lesser production capacity. To the extent that capacity is supplied under conditions of increasing or decreasing cost, its reproduction cost will vary depending on whether a greater or lesser volume is demanded, hence on the level of rates. In principle, this relationship does not preclude a single determinate solution, with a level of rates set in order to permit the desired return on the current cost of producing the capacity required to satisfy the demand elicited by that rate level (and structure). In contrast, there are any number of possible rate levels compatible with earning that return on the *market value* of investment, since—if demand is sufficiently inelastic —higher rates will mean a correspondingly higher market value, low rates a lower market value. Indeed, in perfectly functioning capital markets the market value of the company will move up and down, whatever the level of rates set, sufficiently to keep the rate of return earned on that market value at a constant level. (If investors are satisfied with a 10% return on investment, the market value of any company or of its securities will be ten times its permitted earnings, no matter what the rates it is permitted to charge; so its earnings will always be equal to 10% on its "fair value," thus defined, no matter what their absolute level.)

As we shall see, a strong economic case can be made for basing rate levels on "the present as compared with the original cost of construction," as *Smyth v. Ames* suggested. But as it developed in practice it had a fatal flaw: it invited endless controversy over the proper valuation of sunk capital, in direct contradiction of the economic principle that sunk investment costs are prominent among the "bygones" that ought to be ignored in price making.[40]

"It is not too much to say that in terms of cost, delay, uncertainty, and the arousing of animosity and contention, the performance of the reproduction cost method falls little short of a public scandal; by far the greater part of the grotesque and costly ponderosity which characterizes modern rate regulation is to be attributed directly and solely to the reproduction cost approach. There is no occasion here to recite details of the maneuvering in a typical rate proceeding. The months and years spent by contending parties, commissions, and courts over such hypothetical factors as pricing, conditions of construction, labor performance, overheads, intangibles; the huge sums paid to engineers and accountants and other professional experts, directed in their claims and counter-claims by high-priced attorneys skilled in the art of rate case strategy; the highly charged, politico-legal-mystic character of the whole performance—this is all accepted practice under the reproduction cost method, yet it seems far removed from the essential business of setting the price of a single service in a single community under conditions of simple monopoly."[41]

It is ironic that when the Supreme Court insisted on the relevance of current or reproduction cost, in *Smyth v. Ames*, it did so in the interest of effective regulation, and specifically in order to preserve "the right of the public to be exempt from unreasonable exactions."[42] For obvious reasons, the respective enthusiasms for original and reproduction cost on the part of regulatory commissions and regulated companies has varied depending on the trend of prices and construction costs. *Smyth v. Ames* came at a time when the general price level had fallen to its secular low point as a result of the deflations following the Civil War and the extended Depressions of the 1870s and the 1890s. It was the state of Nebraska that argued for the use of present value, as measured by (the lower) reproduction cost, and the railroads that argued for book or historical cost. In supporting the position of the former, the Court had in mind not only the long-term decline of construction costs, hence of fair value relative to original investment, but also the common complaint that railroad capital structures, on the liability side, and property valuations, on the asset side, were vastly inflated because of excessive payments to contractors and promoters and inadequate accounting for depreciation.[43]

---

[40] This does not mean that the returns permitted on past investments are irrelevant to the optimal pricing of public utility services. It means that endless controversies over the proper valuation and continual revaluation of capital investments made in the past are a deplorably inefficient and indirect way of approaching the task of devising economically efficient rates. (See the discussion on pp. 109–117, Chapter 4).
[41] Lyon and Abramson, *op. cit.*, 2: 691. For a more recent appraisal, see Lewis' "Emphasis and Misemphasis in Regulatory Policy," in Shepherd and Gies, *op. cit.*, 229–236. A place of high honor in these evaluations must be accorded also to Justice Louis D. Brandeis, who made many of the same observations as long ago as 1923; see his famous dissenting opinion in the *Southwestern Bell Telephone* case, 262 U.S. 276, 289–312 (1923).
[42] 169 U.S. 466, 544 (1898).
[43] See *ibid.*, 544–545, and Justice Brandeis, in *Southwestern Bell Telephone, op. cit.*, 298.

During and after World Wars I and II, the positions of the contending agencies were reversed: inflation and the introduction of more effective controls over book (historical) property valuations and company capitalizations converted regulated companies into enthusiasts for reproduction cost, and most commissions and advocates of effective regulation the other way—into proponents of a rate or earnings base measured by "prudent investment"—the number of dollars originally, prudently invested in the property used and usable in public service, less accumulated depreciation.[44]

It was not until 1944, in the *Hope Natural Gas* case,[45] that the Supreme Court at last decided, in the immortal words of Lord Mountararat, to "withhold its legislative hand," when it explicitly declined to tie the Federal Power Commission to any particular prescribed formula for the fixing of reasonable public utility rates. Rejecting fair value on grounds of circularity, the Court asserted that it would no longer insist on commissions taking reproduction cost into account in fixing permissible rates, either.

"Under the statutory standard of 'just and reasonable' it is the result reached not the method employed which is controlling."[46]

What "end results" were relevant? The tests would henceforth be economic and pragmatic:

"Rates which enable the company to operate successfully, to maintain its financial integrity, to attract capital, and to compensate its investors for the risks assumed certainly cannot be condemned as invalid, even though they might produce only a meager return on the so-called 'fair value' rate base."[47]

As long as regulation treats investors sufficiently well, by the acid test of the competitive capital-market place, to enable the regulated companies to raise whatever funds they need to provide acceptable service, the Court seemed to say, it would pose no additional tests or obstacles.[48]

The Court has been true to its promise. Outside of the novel area of natural gas production, it has entertained no public-utility rate-level case of the traditional kind since *Hope*.[49] State regulatory commissions have responded,

---

[44] See, among others, John Bauer and Nathaniel Gold, *Public Utility Valuation for Purposes of Rate Control* (New York: The Macmillan Co., 1934), Chapter 3; Barnes, *The Economics of Public Utility Regulation*, Chapters 11–17, an especially thorough analysis; Troxel, *Economics of Public Utilities*, Chapter 13; Eli Winston Clemens, *Economics and Public Utilities* (New York: Appleton Century-Crofts, 1950), 157–158; Wilcox, *Public Policies Toward Business*, 311–314; James C. Bonbright, *Principles of Public Utility Rates* (New York: Columbia University Press, 1961), Chapters 11–12; C. F. Phillips, *op. cit.*, 231–240.

[45] *Federal Power Commission v. Hope Natural Gas Co.*, 320 U.S. 591 (1944).

[46] *Ibid.*, 602.

[47] *Ibid.*, 605.

[48] Even in applying that primary test, it indicated it would give heavy weight to the "expert judgment" of the regulatory commission:

"Moreover, the Commission's order. . . . is the product of expert judgment which carries a presumption of validity." *Ibid.*, 602.

[49] Information by courtesy of Edward M. Barrett. In the natural gas cases, the Federal Power Commission was attempting to evolve some system for fixing the field prices of a commodity produced at widely varying costs by a large number of producers. The Supreme Court had to decide a number of issues, the most important of which was whether the Commission had to make the traditional type of cost of service determinations, company by company, or might instead shift, as it wished to do, to setting area-wide rates applicable to all companies regardless of their individual costs. In general, following the philosophy of *Hope*, the Court sustained the Commission's exercise of its own "expertise." See *Wisconsin v. Federal Power Commission*, 373 U.S. 294 (1962) and *Permian Basin Area Rate Cases*, 390 U.S. 747 (1968). For a similar decision in a case involving the ICC's use of multi-company costs in determining the proper division

in varying degree, by shifting their attention from a preoccupation with the rate base to the more manageable question of the appropriate rate of return.[50] In a sense, the change is completely insubstantial: the substantive question of how much return on investment should be incorporated in the total cost of service is the same whether it focuses on one or the other of the two factors by which it is determined. And, as for administrative practicability, since it is the aggregate of dollar profits that concerns the parties to regulatory proceedings, it would seem there would be just as much opportunity for controversy over the percentage rate as there was in the past over the principal sum to which that rate was to be applied. The battle has not abated but merely shifted ground. As regulatory attention has turned from the rate base to the rate of return, and the latter has become less and less an essentially conventional 6% or so, the litigants have become increasingly skilled and assiduous in developing prolonged, complex, and inconclusive testimony about its proper measurement.[51]

Nevertheless the transformation of the rate base by most state commissions from a hypothetical or imaginary to an actual book figure,[52] representing actual money outlays, introduced a strong element of stability and predictability into the regulatory process. While the question of what constitutes a "fair" rate of return, as an ethical or political matter, would seem to be just as potentially productive of controversy as the question of what constitutes "fair value," the economic question, though in a sense unchanged and no easier to solve than before, is at least subject to the pragmatic test suggested by the Supreme Court itself—are the regulated companies succeeding in attracting the capital they require?[53]

---

of revenues for multi-line freight service, see *Chicago & North Western Railway Co. et al. v. Atchison, Topeka & Santa Fe Railway Co. et al.*, 387 U.S. 326 (1966).

[50] This does not mean that they have been permitted to ignore the rate base. On the contrary, as long as the courts continue to review commission rate orders at all, it is difficult to see how they can avoid insisting on some evaluation of the property on which a reasonable return must be permitted. This has been the continuing practice of such courts as have spoken since *Hope*. See Francis X. Welch, "The Rate Base is Here to Stay!" *Public Utilities Fortnightly* (October 22, 1953), LII: 635–641.

[51] See, for example, the possibly jaundiced view of Ben Lewis:

"as we begin in sheer disgust to move away from the debacle of valuation, we will probably substitute a new form of Roman holiday—long-drawn-out, costly, confusing, expert-contrived presentations, in which the simple directions of the *Hope* and *Bluefield* cases are turned into veritable witches' brews of statistical elaboration and manipulation. . . . We do not need to do this sort of thing to regulation; we do not need to do it to ourselves. The behavior of investors will tell us, day by day, all we need to know about 'comparability.'" In Shepherd and Gies, *op. cit.*,

242–243. Copyright, 1966, by Random House, Inc.

[52] On the imaginary character of the reproduction cost calculation, see Wilcox, *op. cit.*, 317.

[53] Controversy over the rate base has by no means disappeared. With price levels increasing secularly since the *Hope* decision, it has paid regulated companies to argue for some incorporation of reproduction cost in their rate bases. The state commissions have to some extent acceded: as of 1967, 31 of them (including the District of Columbia) used original cost (or "prudent investment") in regulating electric and gas utilities, 12 used fair value—a compromise between original and reproduction cost—one called its method "average net investment," and one used reproduction cost specifically. Of the remaining six states, four had no state commissions to regulate gas and electric utilities (see note 36, chapter 1) and two commissions had no established procedures. U.S. Senate, Committee on Government Operations, Subcommittee on Inter-governmental Relations, *State Utility Commissions, op. cit.*, 37–40. See also Federal Power Commission, *Federal and State Commission Jurisdiction and Regulation: Electric, Gas, and Telephone Utilities, op. cit.*, 11–12, which gives a slightly different tabulation; and Joseph R. Rose on "Confusion in Valuation for Public Utility Rate Making," *Minnesota Law Review* (1962),

Selection of the Permitted Rate of Return

In essence, every part of the regulatory price making exercise involves determining the proper level of earnings to be permitted the regulated companies. This is obviously true of the explicit determination of return, whether concentrating, as it traditionally has, on the valuation of the property on which a more or less conventional rate of return is to be allowed, or, as has become the practice in the majority of jurisdictions, on the rate of return to be permitted on the dollars actually invested in the enterprise. It is also the consequence of a commission's deciding whether or not to include items such as public relations expenditures in the cost of service, or how to measure depreciation, or how to treat income tax costs when accelerated depreciation is available. The process has inevitably reflected a complex mixture of political and economic considerations. Governmental price-fixing is an act of political economy. And, it bears repeating, this means that it necessarily and quite properly involves the striking of a balance between conflicting economic interests, influenced by political considerations in both the crassest and the broadest possible senses, and informed by community standards of fairness. Therefore, from time to time, the courts and commissions have characterized the entire task of setting ''just and reasonable rates,'' and particularly that portion representing return to shareholders, in terms of reaching an acceptable compromise between the interests of investors on the one hand and consumers on the other.[54] The conception is that there is no single, scientifically correct rate of return, but a ''zone of reasonableness,'' within which judgment must be exercised.

What are the limits of this zone? The bottom limit is an economic one, set by the necessity of continuing to attract capital; but, as we shall see, even that limit is an elastic one, depending on how much capital is required and how well one wishes to treat the company's existing stockholders.[55] The upper

---

XLVII: 1, whose analysis demonstrates that the foregoing simple designations conceal considerable differences in application. In a few instances, for example, "original cost" states have applied the permissible rate of return to an *undepreciated* rate base. For a thorough survey of actual valuation practices and rates of return allowed, see *Return Allowed in Public Utility Rate Cases, 1915–54* and *1955–61*, 2 vols., Arthur Andersen & Co. (place and date of publication not indicated); also A. J. G. Priest, "The Public Utility Rate Base," *Iowa Law Review* (Winter 1966), LI: 283–303, yielding a count of 31 original cost, and 19 fair value jurisdictions.

This continued emphasis on the rate base might seem irrational: inflation can be taken into account just as effectively by varying the permissible rate of return as by continuing to fight the old valuation controversies. To some extent this is what has happened. State commissions continuing to employ original cost have tended to compensate by allowing higher rates of return than the states that have either continued to use or have turned to fair value. But the compensation has been only partial. There continues to be a strong element of convention

and tradition in the allowable rates of return; confined to something like a 5.5 to 8% interval, their variation has not been a complete substitute for alterations in the rate base as well. See C. F. Phillips, Jr., *op. cit.*, 268–271, Garfield and Lovejoy, *op. cit.*, 133–134, and the sources cited by both.

[54] See, for example, the words of Justice Douglas, speaking for the Supreme Court majority in the *Hope* case, 320 U.S. 591, 603 (1944).

[55] A firm can continue to attract outside capital, within limits, even though its overall rate of return is held well below the rate that new investors will require if they are to make funds available to it. If it does so, it will be at the expense of its present stockholders. See note 64, p. 46. Its managers will therefore be reluctant to do so in those circumstances, to the extent that they are interested in the welfare of their stockholders. The bottom limit can be lower if it is defined as how much the firm must be permitted to earn on its total investment in order for it to be *able* to pay new investors enough to have them willingly supply the firm with additional funds than if it is defined as the rate that will make a company *willing*, without

limit has been either what it was estimated capital was obtaining in investments of similar risk elsewhere or, even higher, at whatever it was deemed the traffic would bear. As Justice Holmes once commented, rate regulation

". . . has to steer between Scylla and Charybdis. On the one side, if the franchise is taken to mean that the most profitable return that could be got, free from competition, is protected by the Fourteenth Amendment, then the power to regulate is null. On the other hand, if the power to regulate withdraws the protection of the Amendment altogether, then the property is nought. *This is not a matter of economic theory, but of fair interpretation of a bargain.* Neither extreme can have been meant. A midway between them must be hit."[56]

Such a view of regulation, as a sort of collective bargaining process, with the commission mediating between investors and consumers, may be justified on two quite distinct bases. The first is that there really *is* such a thing as the correct rate of return, but that it is impossible to *measure* it precisely. The economist, taking as his model the equating of price and marginal cost, would ordinarily begin[57] by identifying as the "correct" return the one that covers the costs of (incremental) capital.[58] But as we shall see there is no objective, unequivocal method of ascertaining the cost of capital, even for a particular regulated company at a particular time and place; the process requires the exercise of a good deal of judgment, and judgments will inevitably differ as to the result.

---

coercion by the regulatory authorities, to seek outside capital. And it can be lower, still, if the company does not need *outside* capital. The point in either case is that, by virtue of their power to control the distribution of dividends and both to prohibit the discontinuance and to require extensions of service, commissions can compel public utility companies to reinvest internally generated funds or to seek outside funds despite the fact that allowed returns are less than sufficient to induce such investment on a voluntary basis. If the supply of capital thus obtained sufficed to provide the desired quantity and quality of service, it would not be necessary to give shareholders a return as high as would be demanded by suppliers of new capital. This is merely a recognition of the fact that capital irretrievably sunk in an enterprise has a lower opportunity cost than incremental capital. See pp. 70–73, 118.

This was one consideration underlying the decision of the Federal Power Commission in 1965 to introduce a two-price system for natural gas, with a lower price for gas discovered in the past and already committed under existing contracts, and a higher price for new, additional supplies of gas committed in new interstate contracts. The differentiation in this case took the form not of allowing different nominal rates of return but of using different cost computations for old and new gas, with the price for the latter being set at the estimated full current cost of new, additional supplies. The justification,

proffered by this writer and accepted by the Commission, was that it was both undesirable and unnecessary to extend that higher price to the old gas—undesirable because to do so would confer windfalls on the owners of reserves discovered and developed at lower costs in the past (a noneconomic argument), and unnecessary because the investments in the old gas had already been made (an economic consideration). *Area Rate Proceeding, Claude E. Aikman, et al.,* 34 FPC 159, 185–192 and *passim* (1965), sustained in *Permian Basin Area Rate Cases,* 390 U.S. 747 (1968).

[56] Stress supplied. *Cedar Rapids Gas Light Co. v. Cedar Rapids,* 223 U.S. 655, 669 (1912).

[57] On the reasons why he will not necessarily stop there, see pp. 44 and 69–70.

[58] This was one of the criteria listed by the Supreme Court in its leading decision in the *Bluefield* case, back in 1923:

"The return should be reasonably sufficient to assure confidence in the financial soundness of the utility and should be adequate, under efficient and economical management, to maintain and support its credit and enable it to raise the money necessary for the proper discharge of its public duties." *Bluefield Water Works & Improv. Co. v. Public Service Commission of West Virginia,* 262 U.S. 679, 693 (1923).

It was also one of the standards set forth by the Supreme Court majority in the *Hope* decision. See p. 40.

The other view would be that the proper return that the regulatory process seeks and should seek to ascertain is not itself an objective phenomenon: what is a "just" or "fair and reasonable" return is a political, not a scientific question. This view is certainly not incorrect, either as a description of the rate making process or as prescription. A model of the price system in the modern, impurely competitive economy constructed in terms of the interplay of various organized groups, each with some degree of market power, with the results determined by the equilibrium of power relations, on the one hand, and influenced by considerations of "just price," on the other, is in some ways more relevant than one in which the transacting parties are conceived of as individuals, each a pecuniary profit-maximizer whose actions are entirely dictated by the objective constraints of the impersonal market. In any event, the economist cannot claim that such a vision of regulation as an essentially political process is "wrong;" all he can do is point out the costs to society of departing from purely economic standards.

Economists could make such an argument with better grace and greater forcefulness if they could themselves declare unequivocally what rate of return those purely economic standards dictate. The problem is that even if we confine ourselves to economic criteria we find that the very *idea* of the "correct" rate is elusive. The cost of capital is only the beginning point, for two reasons, both of which we will be explaining and exploring at a later point. (1) If perfect competition does not prevail in the real world, nonregulated industries generally may earn more (or less) than that minimum return. If so, it would produce misallocation to hold the prices of regulated services down (or up) to that level: this is the problem of the so-called "second best."[59] (2) The microeconomic model that calls for equating all prices to (marginal) cost and profits to the (marginal) cost of capital, which we describe in Chapter 3, is a static one. It tells us how to make the most satisfactory use of our limited resources with given tastes and a given technology. But it does not necessarily tell us how best to promote economic progress. The provision of incentives and the wherewithal for dynamic improvements in efficiency and innovations in service may require allowing returns to exceed that level: this was the essence of Joseph A. Schumpeter's classic defense of monopoly.[60] Thus, the rate of return must fulfill what we may term an *institutional* function: it somehow must provide the incentives to private management that competition and profit-maximization are supposed to provide in the nonregulated private economy generally. We have already identified this as a central problem of regulation.[61] There is as yet no scientific way even of defining the rate of return arrangements that would achieve this more complex definition of economic optimality, not to mention measuring them.

In keeping with the purpose of this entire chapter, the following survey of

[59] See pp. 69–70, Chapter 3 and p. 195, Chapter 7.

[60] See his *Capitalism, Socialism and Democracy* (New York: Harper & Brothers, 1942), Chapters 7–9.

[61] This is not to suggest that it is only through the rate of return that the necessary incentives are best provided. Given the divorce between ownership and management, the rewards might better be offered to, and penalties assessed against, the managers themselves, for example, in the form of variable bonuses proportioned to some measure of performance. See the section on "Incentive Plans," Chapter 2, Volume 2.

the major problems and issues in determining the proper rate of return (we assume, for simplicity, that the investment to which it is to be applied is valued at original cost less depreciation) is intended principally to illustrate the foregoing observations. While summarizing the major traditional issues in price regulation, as background for our own, alternative approach in Part II, it should demonstrate also (1) the problems in measuring the minimum cost to which prices would be held by effective competition, which regulation is supposed to emulate; (2) the important influence of noneconomic considerations, and especially of conceptions of what is "fair;" and (3) the elusiveness of the proper economic standards, for the reasons just identified— the problem of "second best" and the institutional function of the rate of return.

Problems in Measuring the Cost of Capital. The public utility company competes with all other companies in the economy for the various inputs of its production process—for labor, materials, and capital. To the extent that these are supplied in open markets (instead of, for example, under negotiated bids), in principle there ought to be readily available objective measures of the prices of these inputs that have to be incorporated in the cost of service. This is clearly true of the capital input: since the regulated company must go to the open capital market and sell its securities in competition with every other would-be issuer, there clearly is a market price (a rate of interest on borrowed funds, an expected return on equity) that it must be permitted and enabled to pay for the capital it requires. Of course, the costs that go into its price (or rate levels) are a function not only of the unit prices of its inputs (for example, the price of a ton of coal, delivered to the generating plant, or the interest rate on its bonds) but also of the efficiency with which they are employed (for example, the number of tons of coal or the number of dollars of capital investment required to generate a kilowatt hour of electricity); and we have already alluded to the problem of assuring maximum efficiency under regulation and to the important role that the allowable rate of return may play in providing an incentive for managers to run their companies as efficiently as possible. But the proper starting point is clearly the competitive price—in this case, the so-called "cost of capital."

1. But whose cost of capital? Should it be the cost to the individual company under consideration? Or of a representative group of companies? If the latter, what constitutes a representative group? The concept of regulation as seeking to keep prices at the lowest possible level consistent with the company's supplying the amount and quality of service demanded at that price—which is surely the competitive ideal, also—would argue for measuring the actual cost of capital to that company alone. But suppose one company is so well run (or promises to become so much more so) that investors, having particularly great confidence in it (or in the stability or growth of its future earnings) are willing to make capital available to it at a price (for example, at current or promised rates of return) less than the average for other regulated companies? If the unusually efficient company's resultant lower cost of capital is automatically translated into lower permitted profits per dollar of invested capital—something that would *not* automatically happen under pure competition—will it not have been deprived of the incentive to be efficient, or to become more so? Its owners, and therefore conceivably its managers, would have been deprived

of the supernormal rewards (quasi-rents) that constitute in nonregulated markets a prime spur to efficiency.[62]

2. Should it be the cost of capital at a particular moment in time, or an average over some period in the past? If the former, what moment? If the latter, how long a period? Is what is sought the *historical* cost of capital, as of the time when it was raised? Or the current cost? The reader will recognize the relatedness of these questions to the question of whether the rate base and depreciation should likewise be measured at original or at current cost.[63] The usual practice is to combine the actual or historical interest cost, as far as debt capital and preferred stock are concerned, with the (estimated) current cost of raising money by sale of common stock. Does this make economic sense? Is it fair? How do these various possible approaches compare with the results that would be produced by competition? And, in such a comparison, *what* "competition" is relevant— "ideal" pure or perfect competition? Or the highly imperfect mixtures of competition and monopoly that actually prevail in unregulated markets?

3. The usual starting point for measuring the cost of equity capital is the ratio of earnings to market prices of the common stocks of the company or companies selected. The logic of this procedure—and it is persuasive— is that the price investors are willing to pay in the open securities markets for shares of stock with known levels of earnings provides an objective measure of the terms on which they are willing to make their money available to the companies in question. If, for example, the common stock sells at 10 times annual earnings, the earnings/price ratio is 10% and that may (subject to the very serious qualifications to be noted) be taken as the cost of capital—the rate of return that the companies must be able to earn on any additional dollars invested in them if they are going to be willing and able to raise those dollars in the capital markets.[64]

However, the principal difficulty is that what investors are capitalizing in the purchase price of the securities they buy is not current but antici-

---

[62] Of course, some diminution of the incentive to efficiency is inherent in any system of regulation that holds rates of return to some prescribed level, regardless of how or where that level is set. Still, if the more efficient and progressive company is permitted some sort of higher, industry-average rate of return, instead of its own, low cost of capital, it is on this account rewarded for its own, deserved, above-average attractiveness to investors, and retains an incentive to improve its efficiency in hope of increasing that reward.

[63] He is reminded, too, that we consider the economics of these interrelated choices in the following chapters—in particular, Chapter 4.

[64] As we have already suggested, a company *can* raise capital even if it is allowed a rate of return

below the cost of capital, but only at the expense of its existing stockholders. The common sense of this should be apparent: if a company sells its new stock on terms that give the new stockholders, for instance, a 10% return on their investment—the cost of capital being 10%, they will pay only ten times the prospective earnings for each share—and invests the funds in assets on which it is permitted to earn only 7 1/2%, clearly the other 2 1/2% must be coming out of earnings previously available to its existing stockholders. This is what is known as dilution—dilution of the share in equity (that is, in the claim on net assets of the firm) of existing stockholders.

Suppose, for example, the firm had the following skeleton balance sheet before the new stock issue:

Assets		Liabilities	
Net plant	$100	Net worth	
		Common stock (10 shares)	$50
		Surplus	50

And suppose its permitted rate of return (r) and cost of equity capital (k) were, as above, 7½% and

10%, respectively. In this event, its permitted earnings would be $0.75 per share, and investors

pated earnings;[65] and there is no objective measure of what their antici-pations were or are. Thus, computed contemporaneous earnings/price ratios will either underestimate or overestimate the actual cost of capital, depending on the extent to which investors were expecting earnings to rise or fall from current levels when they paid those prices. From the late 1940s on, for example, security prices in the United States soared relative to earnings; this sharp drop in earnings/price ratios continued all through the 1950s, leveling off during 1960–1965 at the 5 to 6% level, which was well below the average of the preceding half-century.[66] There can be little doubt that these trends partly reflected the anticipation of increasing earnings and future appreciation of security values; those anticipations were an important consideration in the high and rising prices investors were willing to pay for each dollar of current earnings.[67] If so, the contemporaneous earnings/price ratios must have understated the true cost of equity capital: investors *thought* they were getting a better return

would pay only $7.50 for a share. (The market value would thus be below the book value of $10 per share, precisely because r is less than k; see note 69.) Now suppose the company sought to raise another $100 to invest in plant. It would be permitted to earn an additional $7.50 on this investment, or a total of $15. How many shares would it have to sell and at what price would they sell? Let x be the required additional number of shares. Then earnings per share will end at $15/(10+x)$. These earnings would be capitalized at 10%—that is, investors would pay 10 times those earnings for each new share of stock, assuming they expected per share earnings to remain thenceforth at that level. So the price of each share would be $(10)\,(\$15)/(10+x)$ and x shares would have to be sold at that price to raise the required $100:

$$\frac{(10)\,(\$15)}{10+x}\,x = \$100$$

$$x = 20$$

Therefore 20 additional shares would have to be sold to raise the added $100, at a price of $5. The price per share would thus have dropped from $7.50 to $5; the total permitted earnings of $15 would now be distributed among 30 shares, yielding $0.50 per share, capitalized at 10%. Assuming they predicted accurately the trend in earnings per share, the new investors would be in a position to demand the 10% k—they would pay only $5 for a share promising earnings of $0.50. But sale of the stock in these circumstances would *dilute* the share in ownership of the holders of the 10 original shares of stock: their share in book equity would decline from the original $10 per share to $6.67, the new total equity of $200 being distributed now among 30 shares. The $33\frac{1}{3}$% decline in the market value of their stock would reflect this corresponding dilution of their equity.

A company *can*, thus, raise more capital when r is below k (within limits—try to work out the above example if r is only 5%) but only at the expense of its existing stockholders. This is something its management would ordinarily be unwilling to do.

[65] It is uncertain to what extent and in what direction investors' appraisal of earnings is altered by variations of the proportions respectively distributed in dividends and reinvested in the business. The weight of informed opinion since the early 1950s seems to be that it is total earnings instead of dividends alone that investors value in purchasing securities; that pay-out ratios have little if any effect—that is, that investors are essentially indifferent to what percentage of earnings is distributed in dividends. See Fred P. Morrisey, "Current Aspects of the Cost of Capital to Utilities," *Public Utilities Fortnightly* (August 14, 1958), LXII: 217–227; Merton H. Miller and Franco Modigliani, "Some Estimates of the Cost of Capital to the Electric Utility Industry," *Amer. Econ. Rev.* (June 1966), LVI: 368–370; Irwin Friend and Marshall Puckett, "Dividends and Stock Prices," *ibid.* (September 1964), LIV: 656–682; cf. E. W. Clemens, "Some Aspects of the Rate-of-Return Problem," *Land Econ.* (February 1954), XXX: 32–43.

[66] Dividend/price ratios showed a similar trend, and between 1955 and 1965 were lower relative to levels of the preceding half-century than were earnings/price ratios. Board of Governors of the Federal Reserve System, *Historical Chart Book, 1967*, Washington, 37.

[67] It can be demonstrated that, under not un-reasonable assumptions, the market price of a share of stock (P) will be equal to current dividends (D) divided by (the cost of capital, k, minus the anticipated annual percentage growth in dividends, g): $P = D/(k-g)$. Or, in other words, that the cost of capital is equal to the

than would be indicated by that ratio.[68] Any successful effort by utility commissions to hold earnings on the companies' rate bases thereafter to the low rates suggested by those ratios would surely have resulted in a deflation of security prices, and, by thus increasing earnings/price ratios, have demonstrated that the true cost of capital was higher than they had originally inferred.[69] But how much higher, it is impossible to say with any precision.[70]

4. Is there need for consistency between the basis on which the cost of equity capital is determined and the rate base to which it is then applied? If the

---

current dividend/price ratio plus that anticipated percentage growth: $k = D/P + g$. For a fuller explanation, see the Appendix to this chapter, which reproduces a very lucid account by Herman G. Roseman.

To some extent, g results merely from the reinvestment of earnings. If a company earns 9% on book equity, distributes 2/3 and reinvests 1/3 (that is, 6% and 3% of book equity, respectively), the book value of each share of stock will grow 3% a year and dividends may therefore be expected to do the same on this account, *ceteris paribus*. If 9% is also the cost of capital, the market value of the stock will be equal to book (see footnote 69, below) and $(D/P) + g$ (in this case $6\% + 3\%$) will, as far as this source of growth is concerned, be the same as the earnings/price ratio, E/P (9%). The problem arises when g is expected to be greater or less than what would result merely from the reinvestment of earnings. See for example the estimates referred to in note 70.

[68] That certainly had been their experience during the preceding years. An investment of equal amounts in every stock traded on the New York Stock Exchange in December 1950 would have yielded an investor 15.0% compounded annually, in dividends and capital appreciation, by December 1960; a similar investment in December 1955 would have yielded 11.1% by

the later date. See L. Fisher and J. H. Lorie, "Rates of Return on Investments in Common Stocks," *Jour. of Bus.* (January 1964), XXXVII: 5. During the first period E/P ratios dropped continuously from over 15 to less than 5%, during the second its range was from about 8 to 5%. Board of Governors, *op. cit.*, note 66. Obviously what dropped E/P ratios was investor expectations that they would continue to see this kind of growth in earnings and market value of their investments.

[69] On the other hand, the sharp appreciation in the prices of public utility stocks, to one and a half and then two times their book value during this period, reflected also a growing recognition that the companies in question were in fact being permitted to earn considerably more than their cost of capital. Perhaps, indeed, the discrepancy was growing over time: as the data in note 76 demonstrate, the return on equity among the public utilities increased markedly relative to manufacturing in the two decades after World War II. See Miller and Modigliani, *op. cit.*, *Amer. Econ. Rev.* (June 1966), LVI: 386; David A. Kosh, "Recent Trends in the Cost of Capital," *Public Utilities Fortnightly* (September 26, 1963), LXXII: 19–26. Suppose, for example, the following skeletal balance sheet of a regulated company:

Net plant	100	Equity	
		Common stock (10 shares)	50
		Surplus	50

And suppose the true cost of capital is 10%. If the regulatory commission permits the company to earn 10% on its net plant, valued at original cost, the profits will be $1 a share, and, *ceteris paribus*, investors will buy those shares for $10: market value and book value will coincide. But the market value will exceed book value if the commission permits a return in excess of the cost of capital: if, for example, it allows 15%, this will yield $1.50 a share, for which investors will bid $15.

But suppose, to illustrate the point in the text, the commission had been allowing only the true cost of capital, 10% or $1 a share, but investors had bid share prices up to $15, yielding currently

only $6\frac{2}{3}\%$, because they expected to get the other $3\frac{1}{3}\%$ from future increases in earnings and appreciation of the securities' prices. If in this event the commission took the $6\frac{2}{3}\%$ earnings/price ratio to represent the cost of capital, it would permit earnings of only $0.67 per share, and the market price of the securities would collapse either to the book value of $10, if investor confidence in future trends continued unshaken, or down to $6.67, if those favorable anticipations were now destroyed.

[70] Since the true cost of capital (k) may be taken as equal to $(D/P) + g$ (see note 67), some company witnesses in regulatory proceedings have attempted in various ways to make plausible

cost of equity capital is determined on the basis of the ratio of earnings to the *market price* of the company's common stock, is there not some inconsistency in applying that rate of return to a rate base as valued in the company's *books*—that is, at original or historic cost—when, as has been true for well over a decade, the market value of most public utility shares has far exceeded their book value? If, for example, earnings per share were $5, the market price $100, and the book value $50, the E/P ratio would suggest a 5% cost of capital; if that 5% were applied to the book value of (the equity portion of) the rate base, this would produce a return of only $2.50—thus eliminating the justification for the $100 market price.

The answer is that there would be an inconsistency in this case, but only because it involves inconsistent assumptions about regulatory policy.

---

estimates of the g investors had in mind in purchasing the company stock, in order to come up with an estimate of k (since D and P are of course known). See, for instance, the testimony of Irwin Friend, May 26, 1966, in Federal Communications Commission, *In the Matter of American Telephone and Telegraph Company*, Docket 16258, and of Roseman before the Pennsylvania Public Utility Commission, Re: *The Peoples Natural Gas Company*, Docket No. 18527, Exhibit No. 16, 1968. Roseman's basic approach, for example, is to determine statistically which measure of growth (average annual growth in earnings, in dividends, in book equity, in revenue, or in net plant, all over various time periods up to the present) correlates most closely with the current evaluation placed by the market on dividends—that is, with the D/P ratios—of 21 gas distribution companies. The correlation is negative: the higher the anticipated g, the higher the price investors will pay for a dollar of current dividends, so the lower is the D/P ratio. Then, having in this way identified the measure of actual past growth with the highest negative correlation with D/P, he proposes that for his measure of the (anticipated) g component of k. Applying this method for each of the 20 companies (in addition to the one for which he was testifying), he obtained an average estimate for k of 9.8%, compared with an *earnings*/price ratio of 7.6%. Roseman describes this method also in "Measuring the Cost of Equity Capital for Public Utilities," ABA, *Annual Report, Section of Public Utility Law*, 1969, 54–67.

Two other writers have suggested an alternative solution that would permit the use of E/P ratios alone as the measure of k. Their reasoning is that whenever regulated companies purchase their inputs in competitive markets, regulatory commissions correctly accept the prices thus determined for incorporation in the cost of service. Capital markets are highly competitive; they, too, therefore, should be able to provide commissions with a very accurate measure of the competitive, minimum necessary cost of capital. The problem at present is that commissions have no way of telling what are the terms of the equity share contract. That is, when investors pay x dollars for a share of stock, they are buying not just current earnings but some unmeasurable amount of growth over and above the growth that occurs because of the mere reinvestment of earnings. (As we have already seen, if dividends are expected to grow only because of reinvestment of earnings, $(D/P) + g$ is the same as E/P, and the latter is a correct measure of k. See note 67, above. It is the expectation of greater— or lesser—growth than this that renders E/P an inaccurate measure of k.) The first key to a solution to this problem is to be found in the fact that when earnings are expected to grow over time merely because of reinvestment of earnings, the market and book values of a share of company stock will grow together; there is no reason for such growth to produce any discrepancy between them. It is the expectation of a capital gain resulting from a *discrepancy* between market and book values, thus, that makes E/P an inaccurate measure of k, and so makes the latter so difficult to measure. The second key to the solution is that if the allowed rate of return (r) is held at the cost of capital (k), market value will tend to equal book value (see note 69), and the possibility of a discrepancy between them is greatly diminished.

Therefore, the authors suggest, if regulatory commissions were to put investors on notice that henceforth they would allow a return equal only to whatever earnings/price ratio the securities markets set when the market value of the common stock equaled its book value (at which point presumably r equals k), they could greatly diminish, if not eradicate, the expectation of capital gains or losses arising from divergencies of market and book value and thereby cause the current earnings/price ratios to give them a much more accurate reflection of the true cost of

That is, it assumes at one and the same time that the commission allows returns on equity (*r*) in *excess* of and equal to the cost of capital (*k*). The source of the discrepancy between market and book value has been that commissions have been allowing *r*'s in excess of *k*; if instead they had set *r* equal to *k*, or proceeded at some point to do so, both the discrepancy between market and book value and the inconsistency would have disappeared, or would never have arisen.[71] The fact that market value has remained above book value indicates that in most jurisdictions *r* has been high enough, relative to *k*, so that its application to the lower book value, in determining allowable earnings, has not destroyed the willingness of investors to continue to pay above book value for public utility company shares.[72]

5. To what extent does the cost of capital, which is a weighted average of the separate costs of obtaining funds by sale of bonds, preferred stock, and common stock, depend on the particular mixture of sources of financing selected? There is general agreement that up to a point the composite cost will be reduced by resorting to borrowing, because the interest costs of borrowed capital may be deducted from taxable income, whereas the return on equity capital—which is no less a genuine economic cost of production—is subject to the corporation income tax.[73] But some commentators have maintained that, apart from this tax aspect, the capital structure has no effect on the composite cost of capital; that the more a company resorts to borrowing, typically at lower contractual interest rates than the rates of return it has to promise to common stockholders, the correspondingly higher is its true cost of equity capital, in reflection of the greater risks to stockholders of having a larger and larger share of aggregate earnings subject to the prior, contractual claim of the bond holders.[74] The more traditional view is that up to some point

---

capital. Thereafter, when investors purchased the stock they would be buying only current earnings plus such anticipated growth as would result from reinvestment of profits, which would raise book and market value per share simultaneously. They would no longer be paying also for the expectation that the market value per share might rise relative to the number of stockholder dollars actually invested in the enterprise. Regulatory commissions could presumably obtain successive approximations to the true cost of capital by reducing permitted rates of return (*r*) sufficiently to bring market prices down to book value per share, and then adjusting *r* to the earnings/price ratios that emerged on announcement of the policy that destroyed anticipations of market price diverging from book.

In brief, what the commissions would be doing in this way would be specifying the terms of the equity share contract. If they succeeded in doing so, the capital market would then provide them with an accurate measure of the true competitive cost of capital. See Robert J. Gelhaus and Gary D. Wilson, "An Earnings-Price Approach to Fair Rate of Return in Regulated Industries," *Stanford Law Rev.* (January 1968),

XX: 287–317.

[71] In the foregoing example, once market value per share was reduced to book value—that is, to $50—because *r* was set at *k*, here assumed to be 5%, there would no longer be any inconsistency, provided, of course, the commission had correctly estimated *k* at 5%. Return per share would be $2.50, and this would be 5% of both market and book value.

[72] See note 69.

[73] If the cost of debt capital to a company is 5% and the cost of equity capital is 10%, and it raises $100 by borrowing, this will add $5 a year to its costs; if it raises it by issuing new stock, it will add not $10 but, with the corporation income tax rate at 48%, $19.23 a year to what it must recover in rates—$9.23 for the Internal Revenue Service, $10 for the new stockholders.

[74] Actually the cost of debt capital would likewise rise, reflecting growing risk to bond holders as well, as a larger and larger share of company income was pledged to them. The Grand Inquisitor's observation in *The Gondoliers*,

"When every one is somebodee, Then no one's anybody!"

clearly applies to bondholders: when everyone

trading on equity has the effect of reducing the average cost of capital, even apart from the tax advantage. Some commissions, in consequence, have based their allowances for rate of return not on the actual capital structure of the regulated company but on their conception of a preferable one, with a lower inferred composite cost.[75]

Should the Rate Be Adjusted for Changes in Prices? What allowance, if any, should be made for changes in the purchasing power of the investor's dollar, measured in terms of its changing ability either to buy consumer goods and services or to replace capital equipment? In particular, should the owners of the business be offered some sort of protection against inflation, whether by introducing some reflection of (presumably rising) replacement costs in the rate base and/or in allowable depreciation expenses, or in a higher rate of return? On grounds of fairness? Of economic efficiency? *Ought* or *need* the same protections be offered to existing shareholders as to future suppliers of capital? If to stockholders, why not also to creditors? We consider these questions at length in Chapter 4.

The Standard of Comparable Earnings. During the early 1960s, when price/earnings ratios ran around 5 to 6%, manufacturing corporations were earning 10 to 13% on their book equity.[76] *Ought* or *need* public utility

---

who supplies capital is at the head of the line in his claim on income, no one is at the head of the line—there is no line. See the considerably more complex argument of Modigliani and Miller, "The Cost of Capital, Corporation Finance and the Theory of Investment," *Amer. Econ. Rev.* (June 1958), XLVIII: 261–297, and "Some Estimates of the Cost of Capital," *Amer. Econ. Rev.* (June 1966), LVI: 338–343, 364–367; the comments on the former article by Joseph R. Rose and David Durand and the Modigliani-Miller reply, *ibid.* (September 1959), XLIX: 638–669; Haim Ben-Shahar, "The Capital Structure and the Cost of Capital: A Suggested Exposition," *Jour. of Finance* (September 1968), XXIII: 639–653.

[75] See C. F. Phillips, Jr., *op. cit.*, 169–171, 280–283; Troxel, in Shepherd and Gies, *op. cit.*, 166–168.

"On oral argument, Respondents' counsel stated:

'. . . I think the Commission's function here is to examine a debt policy that we follow . . . but unless you find that we have abused our discretion or have been imprudent, I don't believe you should disturb it. . . .'

"We agree that this Commission is not the manager of Respondents' business. It is neither our obligation or duty to dictate the business policies and practices to be followed by management. On the other hand, we have the statutory responsibility for the establishment and maintenance of just and reasonable rates. . . . If we are to discharge this responsibility . . . we must be free to examine fully all matters affecting the future level of rates. . . . We are not limited to acting in situations in which we have first found abuse, imprudence or indiscretion on the part of management in the past. . . .

"At the 10-percent return on equity sought by respondents herein, each dollar of equity financing requires nearly five times as much gross revenue as a dollar of debt financing. Thus, the rate payer is penalized if more of the financing is by equity than is required. . . .

"We find, therefore, that a continuation by respondents of their past policies with respect to capital structure will not be conducive to the raising of future required capital in a reasonably economical fashion. . . .

"Accordingly, in fixing the rate of return to be allowed, we shall take into account this 'additional' and extraordinary amount of risk insurance respondents have given its [sic] stockholders by its low debt ratio policy. . . . respondents are in a position to improve equity earnings by increasing their debt ratio. . . ." FCC, *In the Matter of American Telephone and Telegraph Company*, Docket No. 16258, Interim Decision and Order, 9 FCC 2d. 30 (1967), sec. 86, 89, 216, 220, 222.

[76] See note 66, Chapter 2. During these same years (1960–1964, inclusive), the returns on book equity of the "electric power, gas, etc." companies surveyed by the First National City Bank of New York ranged between 10.0 and 11.0%, of telephone and telegraph companies between 9.7 and 10.3% and of transportation companies between 2.3 and 5.5%, as the following table shows. All returns are after tax.

companies be permitted earnings comparable to those received by companies in nonregulated industries, under conditions of comparable risk?[77] This question involves a number of issues, conceptual and factual.

1. Is the comparable earnings standard merely another measure of the cost of capital, reflecting what public utility companies themselves or purchasers of their stocks could obtain on their dollars elsewhere? Or may it be higher: may not returns in industry generally contain some monopoly component, for example? In point of fact, the owners or purchasers of public utility and industrial common stocks might well not be able to obtain that type of rate of return if they were to go into the market and buy those securities.[78] The cost of capital, which is what a utility company must match if it is to attract funds, is what investors could obtain by buying the *securities* of other companies in the open market—not what the companies themselves earn on a dollar of additional investment.[79]

2. If "comparable earnings" exceed the cost of capital, then, would an attempt to hold public utility earnings to the lower, competitive level reduce the prices of their services excessively, relative to the prices of other goods and services?[80]

Net Returns on Net Assets

Year	Total Mfg	Electric Power, Gas, etc.	Telephone and Telegraph	Total Transportation
1947–54	15.4	9.3	7.8	...
1959	11.7	10.1	9.9	3.9
1960	10.6	10.0	9.9	2.9
1961	9.9	10.0	9.9	2.3
1962	10.9	10.4	9.5	3.9
1963	11.6	10.6	9.7	4.6
1964	12.6	11.0	10.3	5.5
1965	13.9	11.3	9.9	6.9
1966	14.2	11.5	10.4	7.4
1967	12.6	11.6	10.2	5.4
1968	13.1	11.2	9.7	4.9
No. of Companies				
1968	2,250	237	19	176

Source. First National City Bank of New York, *Monthly Economic Letter*, April issues. 1947-54 compilation from Shepherd and Gies, *op. cit.*, 103.

[77] The Supreme Court specified such a comparable earnings standard in both its *Bluefield* and *Hope* decisions. 262 U.S. 679, 692 (1923); 320 U.S. 591, 603 (1944).

[78] See for example, Calvin B. Hoover, "On the Inequality of the Rate of Profit and the Rate of Interest," *The South. Econ. Jour.* (July 1961), XXVIII: 1–12; James Tobin, "Economic Growth as an Objective of Government Policy," *Amer. Econ. Rev., Papers and Proceedings* (May 1964), LIV: 13–14. This discrepancy is suggested by the far lower earnings to market price ratios of both industrial and public utility common stocks than those companies earn on book equity. However, as we have seen, investors have been earning more than the contemporaneous earnings/price ratios. (See note 68.) Whether what they have in fact earned in this way was the same as the cost of capital—that is, the rates

that they would have been *willing* to take to make their funds available—is highly uncertain.

[79] If the cost of capital is lower, any attempt of a regulatory commission, persuaded by the comparable earnings argument, to permit investors the higher return would only be self-defeating. Investors would respond to the higher earnings per share by bidding up the prices of the securities to the point at which new purchasers would earn only the old cost of capital on their investments. The only beneficiaries would be those who happened to own the stock at the time the policy change was announced or anticipated. There is no way of giving new purchasers of stock more than the cost of capital, except by changing the rules after they have made their purchases. See the same argument in another context, p. 116, Chapter 4.

[80] This is the "problem of the second best,"

3. In applying this standard, how does one select nonregulated industries of comparable risk? How *do* risks in public utilities compare with those of other industries, and to the extent they do differ how would this difference be allowed for in translating comparable earnings elsewhere into permissible rates of return here?[81]

The Problem of Rewards and Incentives. How, if at all, can rates of return be varied in order to reward, and hence to provide an incentive for efficiency and innovation? What standards of performance are available that will separate results attributable to good or bad management from those attributable to other factors? How can such rewards be related to performance, and how much in the way of rewards is required? In particular, is there any way of punishing poorly managed companies with a reduced rate of return without jeopardizing their ability to attract the very capital they may need to do a better job?

It has been urged by defenders of the comparable earnings standard and by others that public utilities be allowed returns markedly above the bare cost of capital, in order to provide them with both the financial means and the incentive to engage in risky innovation, both technological and commercial. That regulatory commissions have in fact allowed earnings well in excess of k is suggested not just by the behavior of the market prices of public utility securities but also by the apparent ease with which such companies have been able, since World War II, to raise the huge amounts of capital required to meet growing demands. It is suggested also by their aggressiveness in seeking such capital and expanding capacity, something that they would obviously have been reluctant to do if allowable returns were less than k.[82]

But this does not necessarily prove that these companies have been offered the optimum amount of incentive for undertaking risky investments.[83] The defining characteristic of such investments is that they offer a wide range of possible outcomes; those that are nevertheless economically worthwhile are so because the possibilities of very large pay-offs balance the possibilities of failure. Any restriction on aggregate earnings, by threatening to cut off the opportunities for the great successes, will therefore have some immeasurable effect of discouraging risky investments that otherwise would be made. How important this effect may be in public utility regulation is very difficult to determine, but it is probably slight. For one thing, there are mitigating or countervailing considerations, among them the slowness of regulation in

---

to which we have already referred. As Shepherd has observed, the problem of the second best is the core of economic validity in the comparable earnings standard. "Regulatory Constraints and Public Utility Investment," *Land Econ.* (August 1966), XLII: 353. See pp. 195–198, Chapter 7.
[81] See, for example, Shepherd, "Utility Growth and Profits Under Regulation," in Shepherd and Gies, *op. cit.*, 35–45. "if utility stocks are compared with those of non-utility corporations of comparable size, utilities which are protected from many forms of competition will be compared with the winners in other areas with no such . . . protection. . . . Somehow, in strict logic, the shadow losses of long defunct automobile companies would have to be subtracted from the profits of General Motors, after these

in turn had been adjusted downward for the hypothetical competition—and then, following this trip through the looking-glass, the result would be comparable earnings. . . ."

James R. Nelson, "Reassessment of Economic Standards for the Rate of Return Under Regulation," in Harry M. Trebing and R. Hayden Howard, *Rate of Return under Regulation: New Directions and Perspectives* (Institute of Public Utilities, Michigan State University: East Lansing, 1969), 16.
[82] See Troxel and Lewis, in Shepherd and Gies, *op. cit.*, 170–175 and 237–239 and note 64, above
[83] See Thomas G. Gies, "The Need for New Concepts in Public Utility Regulation," *ibid.*, 105–107.

reducing earnings that prove *ex post* to be "excessive"—this is the familiar "regulatory lag"—and the ability of regulated companies to seek any rate increases that may be required to keep their overall rates of return at satisfactory levels, and hence to compensate for some of their failures. More important is the fact that the regulatory restriction is on total earnings, not the returns from individual investments. It would only be if the latter were so overwhelmingly large as to threaten to push the total above permissible levels that regulation might discourage it. To the extent all these offsets and qualifications are insufficient, there is no easy solution to the incentive problem. Merely permitting all regulated companies as a matter of course to earn rates in excess of the cost of capital does not supply the answer; there has to be some means of seeing to it that those supernormal returns are *earned*, some means, for example, of identifying the companies that have been unusually enterprising or efficient and offering the higher profits to them while denying them to others. We return to these institutional problems in Chapter 2 of Volume 2.

REGULATING RATE STRUCTURES

With respect to the second major aspect of public utility price regulation—the regulation of rate patterns or structures—the typical statutory or judicial injunction is that rates be not "unduly discriminatory," that differences in the rates charged various customers or classes of service be likewise "just and reasonable." At this point we need make only two general observations about the way in which most regulatory commissions have carried out this mandate. First, outside of the transportation field, they have given far less attention to this subject than to determining general rate levels and especially the rate base and rate of return.[84] The height of particular rates and the differences between them have been from the very outset a very important consideration in the regulation of railroads: the feeling of different customers and localities that they were being subjected to unfair discrimination played a vital role

---

[84] The managements of public utility companies have been at least equally delinquent. See the following acid comments by the Public Utilities Commission of California on the apparent lack of interest of the Pacific Telephone Company in the various individual components of its aggregate cost of service and unwillingness to supply information about them:

"Pacific adheres to a concept of setting basic telephone rates in relation to the availability of main stations and on a statewide pattern. . . . By this scheme Pacific, as in all prior rate proposals, ignores the costs of providing service and from the present record it is apparent that it isn't even interested in knowing what its costs are for any given existing service. It is content to rely on broad and loosely-made estimates first put together at the time an initial or innovative service offering is proposed, no matter how long ago such estimates may have been made. . . . That the executives of Pacific have developed no means by which the actual costs of any of

Pacific's existing basic tariff offerings may be determined or measured seems incomprehensible but this record clearly establishes that such is the fact. Equally incomprehensible is the fact that Pacific does not even know, nor can it readily determine, what revenues its individual tariff offerings produce. . . . [F]or example, Pacific cannot even tell the Commission what revenues it actually receives from its charges for colored telephones without making a special 'study' of the situation."

"[I]t has been repeatedly pointed out that Pacific has not supplied actual revenue, cost or plant data in support of its tariffs. When specifically requested to do so . . . its Counsel argued in opposition to the request. . . .

"The arguments of Pacific's counsel and the comments of its witnesses make it abundantly clear that the whole subject is distasteful to Pacific. It desires, apparently, to forever rely on estimates made prior to the setting of rates on

in the passage and enforcement of the Interstate Commerce Act, from the very beginning.[85] In the other utilities, the major issue has usually revolved around the adequacy of total or net revenues; and the solution has usually been a more or less across-the-board increase or decrease of the entire structure.[86] Second, to the extent regulatory laws and commissions have considered the pattern of prices set, they have been guided by the same sort of mixture of essentially economic and political-social considerations as have influenced their determinations of the proper returns on investment.

The relative neglect of individual prices most clearly epitomizes the difference between the traditional approach to public utility price regulation and the one the economist would recommend. In this area, the commissions typically proceed only in response to specific complaints: businessmen in locality A complain that the freight rates charged them are higher than those charged their competitors; railroads point out that they are losing particular classes of business to trucks or barges and ask permission to reduce the relevant rates to meet competition; the affected trucking and navigation companies intervene to prevent the proposed reductions. Commercial customers assert that they are paying a higher price than residential users for electricity; local utility commissions complain that high rates for local service are subsidizing unduly low rates on long-distance calls; oil jobbers argue that gas distribution companies are offering uneconomically low promotional rates on home heating; the latter maintain that too large a proportion of the capacity costs of the interstate pipelines that supply them are incorporated in the demand charges that they pay and too little is imposed on the lines' direct industrial customers; and representatives of the bituminous coal industry join in these protestations, because the low-priced gas sold for use as boiler fuel for electricity generation takes business away from them. And all too often, from the economist's standpoint, the commissions resolve such controversies on bases other than economic efficiency, seeking to protect offended competitors from excessive losses of business, to preserve a "fair share" of the

---

new services as justification for continuing rate forms and relative rate levels whether or not the services are in reality today properly priced. One of its witnesses is 'hopeful' that the original estimates will so price new services that they will not be a burden on basic service. While this Commission may share or even applaud such 'hopes,' it has the duty to see to it that rates are fair and reasonable. . . ." *In the Matter of . . . the Pacific Telephone and Telegraph Company et al.*, Decision No. 74917, November 6, 1968, mimeo., 30–31, 60–61.

[85] In describing what was to become the Act to Regulate Commerce, in 1887, the Cullom Committee said: "the provisions of the bill are based upon the theory that the paramount evil chargeable against the operation of the transportation system of the United States as now conducted is unjust discrimination between persons, places, commodities, or particular descriptions of traffic." U.S. Senate, Select Committee on Interstate Commerce, 49th Cong., 1st Sess., Sen. Report 46, Part I, Washington,

1886, 215. Correspondingly, "it would be possible to write an extensive history of railroad regulation without mentioning cost of capital or rate of return." James R. Nelson, "Pricing and Resource Allocation: The Public Utility Sector," in Shepherd and Gies, *op. cit.*, 83. Since 1922, the Interstate Commerce Commission "has not found it necessary to specify a fair rate of return for the roads." Phillips, *op. cit.*, 271.

[86] See, for example, Troxel, in Shepherd and Gies, *op. cit.*, 150–151, 175–176. Regulatory commissions and courts alike have tended to leave the designing of rate structures to the discretion of managements. Even in transportation, both company managements and the Interstate Commerce Commission for much too long neglected the much-needed reconsideration of common-carrier rate structures in the light of the intensified competition of newer transport media and of private and contract carriers. See the section on "Transportation," Chapter 1, Volume 2.

market for each, to strike some equitable or politically acceptable distribution of common costs among the various classes of patrons. We will see numerous illustrations of this kind of behavior in Chapters 1 and 2 of Volume 2.

Microeconomics, in contrast, is interested first and foremost in the determination of individual prices. Its normative models also include certain notions about the appropriate relation between an industry's average prices or total revenues on the one hand and its average or total costs on the other; but that optimum is conceived to be the result or *end product* of a competitive process that operates directly and in the first instance in individual markets, in the fixing of individual prices.[87]

With respect to those individual markets, the rules of microeconomics are in principle simple and grounded in objective facts: subject to important qualifications that we shall elaborate at a later point, prices should be equated to marginal costs. In this scheme, there is no room for separate considerations of "fairness." Or, to put it another way, fairness is defined in strictly economic terms: those prices are fair that are equal to marginal costs, those unfair that are not equal.

"As in so many other policy areas, the lawyers and engineers (and increasingly the accountants)—*not* the economists—have largely dominated regulatory policy."[88] This does not mean that economists have not written at length and incisively about public utility regulation. But until recently, their analyses have been directed mainly toward the traditional issues, and organized within the framework formulated by administrative commissions and courts and by *Smyth v. Ames* in particular. Our next chapters, following

---

[87] These comments may seem arbitrarily to suggest that short-run equilibrium is somehow more important than long-run, and in so doing to reflect the essentially static character of traditional economic theory, or its tendency simply to assume mobility of resources sufficient to ensure the achievement of long-run equilibrium. In a dynamic world and in the presence of resource immobilities, competition sufficiently pure to hold prices constantly at short-run marginal cost may prove destructive and violently unstable; and much of the pricing in impurely competitive or oligopolistic markets can often be understood as seeking to achieve the long-run competitive result—which in a perfectly competitive market could safely be left to instantaneous inflows and outflows of labor and capital—at the possible expense of the constant equation of price with short-run marginal cost. The student of industrial organization may be as much concerned with the process that holds an industry's total profits, averaged over some period of time, at the competitive level as that its individual prices be instantaneously equated with short-term marginal cost.

The fact remains that the welfare ideal is constructed on the basis of the equation of price to marginal cost in individual markets and in the short-run. That is where the process starts. Departures from that standard must be individually justified. The mere control of overall

rates of return does not in itself ensure that the pattern of individual prices is economically efficient:

"A great many *different* patterns, efficient and inefficient, within the firm may be perfectly consistent with a *given* over-all rate of return. So, whatever the rates of return may actually have been, they cannot by themselves demonstrate whether resource allocation (to and within the utilities) has been efficient." Shepherd, in Shepherd and Gies, *op. cit.*, 20. See also Nelson, *ibid.*, 66.

Moreover—and this is a point critically important with respect to the public utility industries—even long-run equilibrium price is not the same thing as a price that covers current operating expenses plus some acceptable average rate of return on investment, which is what has principally concerned regulatory commissions. On the contrary, it involves the equation of price with long-run marginal cost. Correspondingly, the investment policy that produces long-run equilibrium in the competitive ideal is one that equates with the cost of capital the rate of return on incremental investment, not the *average* rate of return on historical investment, however the latter is valued. We shall explore these similarities and differences in the ensuing chapters.

[88] Shepherd, "Conclusion," in Shepherd and Gies, *op. cit.*, 266.

the lead of some of the recent economic literature[89] and accepting the implied invitation of the *Hope Natural Gas* decision, returns to the economic principles and attempts to apply them to the problems of public utility regulation. In so doing we will try not to neglect the traditional regulatory issues set forth in this chapter, but will instead analyze them in economic terms, while continuing, as throughout this study, to assess the limitations as well as the possible contributions of economics to their resolution.[90]

---

[89] See, for example, the works cited *ibid.*, 267 and throughout this chapter and those that follow.
[90] There is no intention here to exaggerate the novelty of this approach, as compared with current regulatory thinking and practice. On the contrary, the traditional approaches that we have been describing in this chapter have certainly been modified in recent years. Regulated companies and commissions alike have been paying increasing attention to the design of economically efficient rate structures; and, in this task and in others, as we have already observed, they have made dramatically increasing use of the tools and perspectives of the economist. This book is in a sense a survey, summary, and critique of this emergent practice.

Explanation of Mathematical Derivation of Cost of Capital Formula

The price the investor will be willing to pay for a stock will be equal to what he estimates to be its present worth. This present worth is the discounted value of what he expects to receive as a result of being a stockholder, namely the dividends he will be paid plus the price at which he will eventually sell the stock. As we shall see, this boils down to the present worth of all expected future dividend payments.

Let us suppose that the investor buys the stock at the beginning of Year 0. He expects to receive dividends of D_0 at the end of Year 0, D_1 at the end of Year 1, D_2 at the end of Year 2, etc. He expects to sell the stock at the price P_n at the end of Year n. If the investor is using a discount rate of 10%, then the present worth of a dividend D_0 received one year from now is:

$$P.W. = \frac{D_0}{1.10}$$

For any discount rate, k,

$$P.W. = \frac{D_0}{1+k}$$

The present worth of a dividend D_1 received *two* years from now is:

$$P.W. = \frac{D_1}{(1+k)^2}$$

Thus, if the investor has a discount rate of k, the present worth of all the expected future receipts will be:

$$P.W. = \frac{D_0}{1+k} + \frac{D_1}{(1+k)^2} + \frac{D_2}{(1+k)^3} + \cdots \frac{P_n}{(1+k)^{n+1}}$$

---

*This appendix is taken unchanged from the testimony of Herman G. Roseman before the Pennsylvania Public Utility Commission, in cases involving The Peoples Natural Gas Co., C. 18527 et al., Exhibit No. 16, Appendix B, 1968, and is reproduced here by courtesy of National Economic Research Associates.

The following numerical example may be helpful in understanding this formula.

Year	Receipts	Discount Factor	Present Worth of Receipts
1	1.00	1.100	0.91
2	1.05	1.210	0.87
3	1.10	1.332	0.83
4	1.15	1.464	0.79
5	1.20	1.610	0.75
5	$25.00	1.610	15.53
			$19.68

In this example, the investor expects to receive dividends of $1.00, $1.05, $1.10, $1.15, and $1.20 at the end of each of the first five years and also to seel the stock for $25.00 at the end of the fifth year. The second column shows the applicable discount factor for each of the years; the discount rate is 0.10, or 10%, and the discounting gets progressively greater by the law of compound interest, with each year. The final column is derived by dividing the receipts in each year by the discount factor for that year. This column represents the present worth of these future receipts; for example, the present worth of a $1.05 dividend received two years from now is $0.87. The total present worth of these receipts, including the price at which the stock is later sold, is $19.68. Thus, the investor will only be willing to pay $19.68 for this stock.

Let us now consider what basis the investor might have for estimating the future price at which he will be able to sell the stock. Obviously, some other investor at that future date will be willing to buy the stock at a price based on *his* estimate of dividends to be received at a still later date and the price at which *he* will be able to sell the stock. The third buyer must envisage still a later buyer, etc. Thus, as we push the analysis further and further into the future, we find that the value of the stock is equal to the present worth of all the dividends to be paid to stockholders over the entire future. This makes a certain amount of ordinary sense, once you brush away the technicalities, because all that the stockholders as a group will ever be able to get out of the company are dividends, so that the true value of a company to its stockholders must depend on the value of the dividends it will pay out over its life.

The present worth of a stream of annual dividends extending indefinitely into the future is:

$$P.W. = \frac{D_0}{1+k} + \frac{D_1}{(1+k)^2} + \frac{D_2}{(1+k)^3} + \cdots \frac{D_n}{(1+k)^{n+1}}$$

Now, if we suppose that the dividends grow at a constant annual percentage rate of growth, g per cent per year, the equation becomes:

$$P.W. = \frac{D_0}{1+k} + \frac{D_0(1+g)}{(1+k)^2} + \frac{D_0(1+g)^2}{(1+k)^3} + \cdots \frac{D_0(1+g)^n}{(1+k)^{n+1}}$$

As is shown in the Mathematical Appendix,* if the current price, P_0, is equal to the present worth of the stock, then it follows that:

$$P_0 = \frac{D_0}{k-g}$$

That is, the price the investor is willing to pay for the stock will depend on (1) D_0, the first year's dividend, (2) g, the expected long-term growth rate, and (3) k, the investor's discount rate, which is the company's cost of equity capital. Thus, if we know what the current price and dividend are, and if we can make a reasonable estimate of growth, we can infer what k, the cost of equity capital must be. By simple algebra,

$$k = \frac{D}{P} + g$$

This is the basic formula for measuring the company's cost of equity capital.

---

*This is Appendix A of Roseman's testimony. It explains the solution of the preceding equation, which can (like the familiar multiplier in macroeconomics) be reduced to a constant term $(D_0/1+k)$ times the sum of an infinite geometric progression

$$\left(1/1-\frac{1+g}{1+k}\right),$$

the latter term of which can be reduced to $1+k/k-g$. So

$$P_0 = \frac{D_0}{1+k} \cdot \frac{1+k}{k-g} = \frac{D_0}{k-g}$$

This solution is possible only if k exceeds g; but actually any persistent excess of g over k is economically inconceivable.

PART II
Economic Principles of Rate Making

CHAPTER 3

Marginal Cost Pricing

The traditional legal criteria of proper public utility rates have always borne a strong resemblance to the criteria of the competitive market in long-run equilibrium. The principal benchmark for "just and reasonable" rate levels has been cost of production, including, as the economist would include, the necessary return to capital. The rule that individual rates not be unduly discriminatory similarly has been defined in terms of the respective costs of the various services. Rates that produce widely divergent profits on different parts of the business are suspect.[1] The famous prohibition of "long versus short haul" discrimination in the original Interstate Commerce Commission Act of 1887 was grounded in a recognition that it could not cost more to transport passengers or the same commodity "for a shorter than for a longer distance over the same line or route in the same direction, the shorter being included within the longer distance. . . ."[2] Correspondingly, rates may differ if costs differ: this is the justification of higher monthly charges for one-party than for multi-party line telephone service or for basing railroad rates for carload shipments partially on weight.[3]

Actually, from the very beginning, regulated companies have also been permitted to discriminate in the economic sense, charging different rates for various services even when the costs were not correspondingly different. In particular, rates have been adjusted to the respective "value of service" to different classes of customers; what this means, in effect, is that they have in

---

[1] In its comprehensive examination of the reasonableness of the rates charged by the American Telephone & Telegraph Company (and its associated companies), initiated in 1965 —the first in 33 years—the Federal Communications Commission instructed AT&T as follows:

"In connection with respondents' presentations as to the appropriate ratemaking principles and factors which should govern the proper relationships among the rate levels for each of their principal services, respondents shall take into consideration the wide variations in levels of earnings revealed by the . . . seven-way cost study." *In the Matter of American Telephone and*

Telegraph Company and the Associated Bell System Companies, Docket No. 16258, Memorandum Opinion and Order, 2 FCC 2d 143 (1965).

See also *Atlantic Coast Line Railroad Co. v. North Carolina Corporation Commission*, 206 U.S. 1 (1907), at 25–26, and Isaak B. Lake, *Discrimination by Railroads and Other Public Utilities* (Raleigh: Edwards and Broughton), 153–188.

[2] *U.S. Code*, 1964 ed. (Washington, 1965), Title 49, Sec. 4.

[3] C. F. Phillips, Jr., *The Economics of Regulation*, 311–312, 358; D. Philip Locklin, *Economics of Transportation*, 6th ed. (Homewood: Richard D. Irwin, 1966), 159.

part been patterned on the basis of the respective elasticities of demand. The railroads have been the leading practitioners of this type of pricing, typically charging higher rates for more valuable than for less valuable commodities, on the assumption (not always justified, as we shall see) that these differences reflect what the respective traffics will bear. A similar justification underlies the typically higher monthly flat-rate telephone service charges for commercial than for residential customers. Of course, price discrimination would be impossible under pure competition. But the traditional rationalization—not typically stated in these terms, to be sure—was that it could permit a closer approximation to optimum use of resources in situations in which pure competition was infeasible.[4] In principle this argument is correct, as we shall see.

Various developments of recent decades have encouraged an even more explicitly economic approach to public utility pricing. One was the open invitation of the *Hope* decision to regulatory commissions to break out of the fair return on fair value of property box within which *Smyth v. Ames* had them confined for so long. A second has been the tendency of business management to adopt increasingly sophisticated economic criteria and techniques in formulating investment and price policies.

Finally, the march of technology has made most of the traditional public utilities, even the most "naturally monopolistic" among them, increasingly subject to competition. The share of total intercity ton-miles of the nation's freight traffic carried by the railroads dropped from 74.9% in 1929 to 61.3% in 1940 and to 41.6% by 1967.[5] The decline in their share of total freight *revenues* was even greater, as competitive carriers made deep inroads into their higher-priced business (whose demand the railroads for too long continued to assume was inelastic), leaving them with the carriage of bulky, heavy commodities, at comparatively low-ton mile rates.[6] The rapid spread throughout the country of interstate natural gas transmission lines since World War II has enormously accentuated the competition of local natural gas distribution companies with the unregulated distributors of distillate oils and coal in the home heating market, of residual fuel oils and coal for industrial uses such as boiler fuel, with electric companies in the fields of residential and hot water heating, cooking, and air-conditioning.[7] Electric companies responded with special promotional rates for the all-electric home, using electricity for air-conditioning in the summer and home heating in the

---

[4] See, for example, Arthur T. Hadley, *Railroad Transportation, Its History and Its Laws* (New York: Putnam's, 1895), Chapter 6.

[5] James C. Nelson, *Railroad Transportation and Public Policy* (Brookings: Washington, 1959), 10, and Interstate Commerce Commission, *82nd Annual Report, 1968* (Washington, 1968), 86. The rate of decline slowed down considerably after 1960.

[6] For example, the participation of the railroads in the combined tonnage of intercity freight carried by them and by trucks dropped only from 86 to 74% between 1940 and 1955; but the share of Class I railroads in the estimated freight revenues of themselves and all intercity motor carriers of property fell from 67.4 to 38.7% in

the same period. Partially computed from J. C. Nelson, *op. cit.*, 10, 439, and 445.

[7] There were 218,000 miles of natural gas pipelines and utility main in the United States in 1945 and 816,000 in 1967. *Statistical Abstract of the United States, 1968*, 521. Approximately 10% of the occupied dwelling units in the United States were heated by utility-supplied gas in 1940; in 1960 the figure was 43%. The proportion of those heated by fuel oils and kerosene also rose in this period from 10 to 32%, while the share heated by coal dropped from 55 to 12%. U.S. Department of Commerce, Bureau of the Census, *Census of Housing, 1960*, Washington, U.S. Government Printing Office, 1963, Vol. I, Part 1, XL.

winter;[8] and oil and gas companies have in turn made major efforts to develop and market total energy, which enables large users to generate their own electric power, while using the by-product heat for heating purposes.[9] In the communications field, reduced long-distance telephone rates have made sharp inroads into Western Union's telegraph business; and the spreading use of private microwave systems by businesses and governments has offered growing direct competition with the regulated common carriers. The latter have in turn responded by offering their own special communication and data-transmission services, in competition with both the private systems and each other. And communications satellite systems compete with overland wire and microwave communications and undersea cables.

This intensification of competition has forced these companies into fundamental reexaminations of their pricing policies. Both they and their regulators have found themselves groping for criteria by which to develop and to test competitive rates, where the regulated company itself is interested in knowing to what extent it is in its own interest to reduce prices in order to compete for business, and commissions have to decide under what circumstances these competitive rates may be unduly or destructively discriminatory. Among the most important and challenging developments in utility ratemaking in recent decades have been the efforts of railroads to free themselves from their own conservative pricing practices and regulatory restrictions, in order to regain some of their lost business; the increasing attention paid by electricity and gas distributors to the possibilities of promotional rates and by regulatory commissions to the complaints that such rates have elicited from competitors; and the various investigations by the Federal Communications Commission of the rate structures of the Bell System and of the proper method of integrating the costs of transmission-by-satellite into communications rates.[10]

These various developments have compelled a reexamination of the economics of public utility pricemaking. They make particularly appropriate the attempt to develop and apply economic standards to the assessment of both the private and the public interests in that process.

THE CENTRAL ECONOMIC PRINCIPLE: MARGINAL COST PRICING

The central policy prescription of microeconomics is the equation of price and marginal cost. If economic theory is to have any relevance to public utility pricing, that is the point at which the inquiry must begin.

As almost any student of elementary economics will recall, marginal cost is the cost of producing one more unit; it can equally be envisaged as the cost that would be saved by producing one less unit. Looked at the first way, it

---

[8] In 1965, over 20% of new houses were equipped with electric heating, thus cutting into a market long dominated by gas and oil. Lee C. White, "Growth Prospects for the Natural Gas Industry," *Public Utilities Fortnightly* (October 13, 1966), LXXVIII: 38.

[9] See Irwin M. Stelzer and Bruce C. Netschert, "Hot War in the Energy Industry," *Harv. Bus. Rev.* (November–December, 1967), XLV: 14–19.

[10] We will be discussing these various developments below. Another similar development, this one stimulated in part by financial adversity, was the economic analysis of the airline fare structure by the staff of the Civil Aeronautics Board, published in 1968, and the Board's proposals for revising that structure so as to relate individual fares much more closely to their respective costs. See *Wall Street Journal*, June 16, 1969, 34.

may be termed incremental cost—the added cost of (a small amount of) incremental output. Observed in the second way, it is synonymous with avoidable cost—the cost that would be saved by (slightly) reducing output. (Although these three terms are often used synonymously, marginal cost, strictly speaking, refers to the additional cost of supplying a single, infinitesimally small additional unit, while "incremental" and "avoidable" are sometimes used to refer to the *average* additional cost of a finite and possibly a large change in production or sales.) Why does the economist argue that, ideally, *every buyer* ought to pay a price equal to the cost of supplying one incremental unit?

At any given time, every economy has a fixed bundle of productive resources, a finite total potential productive capacity. Of course, that total can grow over time; but at any given time the basic economic problem is to make the best or most efficient use of that limited capacity. The basic economic problem, in short, is the problem of choice. A decision to produce more of any one good or service is, in these circumstances, *ipso facto* a decision to produce less of all other goods and services taken as a bunch. It follows that the cost to society of producing anything consists, really, in the other things that must be sacrificed in order to produce it: in the last analysis, "cost" is opportunity cost—the alternatives that must be foregone. In our economy, we leave the final decision about what shall be produced and what not to the voluntary decisions of purchasers,[11] guided by prices on the one hand and their own wants or preferences on the other.

If consumers are to make the choices that will yield them the greatest possible satisfaction from society's limited aggregate productive capacity, the prices that they pay for the various goods and services available to them must accurately reflect their respective opportunity costs; only then will buyers be judging, in deciding what to buy and what not, whether the satisfaction they get from the purchase of any particular product is worth the sacrifice of other goods and services that its production entails. If their judgments are correctly informed in this way, they will, by their independent purchase decisions, guide our scarce resources into those lines of production that yield more satisfaction than all available alternatives—which means that total satisfaction will be maximized.

But why does economic efficiency require prices equal to marginal, instead of, for example, average total costs? The reason is that the demand for all goods and services is in some degree, at some point, responsive to price. Then, if consumers are to decide intelligently whether to take somewhat *more* or somewhat *less* of any particular item, the price they have to pay for it (and the prices of all other goods and services with which they compare it) must reflect the cost of supplying somewhat more or somewhat less—in short, *marginal* opportunity cost. If buyers are charged more than marginal cost for a particular commodity, for example because the seller has monopoly power, they will buy less than the optimum quantity; consumers who would willingly have had society allocate to its production the incremental resources

---

[11] We briefly summarize the familiar rationalization of a market system, in which the consumer is supposed to be sovereign. How "voluntary," or "free" consumer decisions actually are in any such economy is an interesting and important question. To the extent that an economic system influences consumer tastes, it is no longer possible for an economist to describe its functioning as "optimal" or "efficient" on the ground that it gives consumers what they want, since the system itself helps determine what they want. See note 2, Chapter 1, and pp. 67–69, below.

required, willingly sacrificing the alternative goods and services that those resources could have produced, will refrain from making those additional purchases because the price to them exaggerates the sacrifices. Conversely, if price is below incremental costs, perhaps because the suppliers are being subsidized, production of the products in question will be higher (and of all other products taken together lower) than it ought to be: society is sacrificing more of other goods and services to produce the additional quantities of the subsidized service than customers would willingly have authorized, had the price to them fully reflected that marginal opportunity cost.

The corollary of the social rule that price should equal marginal cost is the rule of thumb for the businessman—it pays him to continue to produce and sell as long as his incremental revenues cover his incremental costs. Since under pure competition incremental revenues to the businessman are simply the market price times the additional quantities sold, we have the elementary proposition that under pure competition businessmen will increase production and sales up to the point where their marginal costs are equated to price. Therefore, competitive behavior assures the equation of price and marginal cost that is required if free consumer choices are to result in the optimum allocation of resources.

It is impossible here to provide an adequate survey of all the assumptions, definitions, and value judgments implicit in the foregoing sketchy summary, or of all qualifications to which the marginal cost equals price rule must be subjected. Many will be introduced, where appropriate, as we go along: recall our initial statement that marginal cost is (only) the place to *begin*.[12] But we must point out at once that the allocation of resources that the rule produces can be described as "optimal" only on the basis of two essentially unprovable assumptions or value judgments: that the "best" economy is the one that gives consumers what they individually want; and that income is either distributed optimally or can best be redistributed without departing from marginal cost pricing.

1. One need accept the allocation of resources the rule produces in a market economy only to the extent that one approves of the choices consumers make or would make. The economist has no scientific basis for objecting if, instead, society decides to improve on the result, either by trying to influence consumer choices (for example by education or by taxing or prohibiting sale of goods whose consumption it wishes to discourage) or by subsidizing the production of goods it thinks would otherwise be consumed in inadequate quantities. The question of what is the best measure or definition of social welfare, which it is the function of the economy to serve, is a political or philosophical, not an economic, one. Economics as such is the science of means, not ends.

2. One need accept the result as optimal only if one is willing to place a similar evaluation on the distribution of income—either the preexisting distribution of income, which decides how many dollar votes each buyer has in deciding what to order the economy to produce,[13] or the

---

12 The reader will recognize that we have already raised such questions (see pp. 25, 29–31, 44–45, 53), about which the rule is silent, as the proper level of cost, to which price is to be equated, the proper rate of service or process innovation, and

the problems of achieving these ends in the public utility industries. We return to these extremely important questions in Volume 2.

13 It reasonably could be argued that satisfactions are not being maximized in an economy

distribution of income that results from equating price to marginal cost.[14] This, too, is an ethical judgment, not an economic one.

The pricing rule does suggest that if one disapproves of the distribution of income, one might better correct it by lump-sum taxes (for example, on rents, income, or inheritance) and money transfers than by departing from the requirements of economically efficient pricing: equating price to marginal cost remains a necessary condition if the best choices are to be made, *however* income is distributed or redistributed. Unfortunately, however, there are few taxes that are completely neutral—that is, that may not themselves distort marginal choices and thereby thwart the maximizing of satisfactions.[15] In practice, as Graaff puts it, "tinkering with the price mechanism is one of the more feasible and generally satisfactory ways of securing whatever distribution of wealth is desired."[16]

For example, the government may feel that a particular service is so

---

that produces yachts for some while providing inadequate food and medical care for others. The quarrel here would be with the distribution of income, about which the economic rules for the efficient making of choices are silent. The assumption underlying such a criticism is that a dollar spent by a poor man yields more satisfaction than one spent by a rich man (or simply that some noneconomic value such as justice requires a reordering of our economic priorities in the suggested direction). See, for example, A. C. Pigou, *The Economics of Welfare* (London: Macmillan and Co., 1920), Chapter 8, and Abba P. Lerner, *The Economics of Control* (New York: The Macmillan Co., 1944), Chapter 2. Economists have been typically unwilling, *as economists*, to make judgments involving interpersonal utility comparisons.

[14] For example, equating price to marginal cost produces economic rents—scarcity returns to nonreproducible factors of production of supermarginal quality, such as well situated land or some scarce natural resources. One may object to the earning of such "unearned income," and be prepared to sacrifice some of the benefits of an efficient price system for what one conceives to be a better distribution of income. This was an important consideration underlying the decision by the Federal Power Commission to adopt a two-price system for regulating the field price of natural gas, in which only newly committed gas would receive the higher price corresponding to (current) marginal cost. The reason for departing from the economic rule that the price of *all* units sold be set at marginal cost was a reluctance to permit the consequent large transfer of income from consumers to companies that had discovered their gas many years earlier, at far lower cost, and committed it under longterm contracts at much lower prices. Area Rate Proceeding, Claude E. Aikman, *et. al.*, 34 FPC 159, 185–194 (1965), sustained, 390 U.S. 747 (1968). Compare Joel B. Dirlam, "Natural Gas: Cost, Conserva-

tion and Pricing," *Amer. Econ. Rev., Papers and Proceedings* (May 1958), XLVIII: 491–495 and Kahn, "Economic Issues in Regulating the Field Price of Natural Gas," *ibid.* (May 1960), L: 506–510, with Paul W. MacAvoy, *Price Formation in Natural Gas Fields* (New Haven: Yale University Press, 1962), 252–263. Or, like Henry George (and most other economists), one may prefer to keep prices equal to marginal costs, and tax away the unearned increment. *Progress and Poverty* (San Francisco: W. M. Hinton & Company, 1879). See also note 55, Chapter 2; James C. Laughlin, "The Case Against Dual Pricing in Southern Louisiana," *Land Econ.* (February 1967), XLIII: 56—64; Kahn, "Comment" on that article and Laughlin, "Reply," *ibid.*, forthcoming.

Again, equating price to marginal cost under conditions of decreasing costs would require public subsidies to make up the difference between marginal and average total costs. (See pp. 130.) This means an income transfer from taxpayers to consumers of the service in question. For a strong statement that economists are incompetent to evaluate such results of marginal cost pricing, with particular application to public utilities, see J. Wiseman, "The Theory of Public Utility Price—An Empty Box," *Oxford Economic Papers*, (February 1957), n.s. IX: 58–59, 62–68.

[15] Excise taxes obviously cause relative prices to diverge from marginal costs. But the income tax too *may* distort the choice between work and leisure, by reducing the individual's return from marginal effort below the social value of his product. (See note 15 Chapter 5.)

[16] J. de V. Graaff, *Theoretical Welfare Economics* (Cambridge: Cambridge University Press, 1957), 171. Graaff's point here is that the economist cannot say that such tinkering is "wrong"; all he can do is "make clear . . . the probable consequences of setting it [price] at various different

important to welfare generally that it may wish to subsidize its consumption by holding its price below marginal cost, either generally or selectively (for instance, for poor families); and it may be unwilling to achieve this purpose instead by merely making cash grants to poor families, for fear they may spend the cash instead for other, less socially approved purposes.

There are two corollaries of the marginal cost pricing principle:

1. Prices must reflect all the (marginal) costs of production and consumption—not only those borne directly by the transacting parties but also those that may be foisted on outsiders. (A familiar case of an external cost is the air or stream pollution that may be caused by a particular production process or a particular act of consumption. If it is not borne by the responsible party, his marginal cost will understate the true opportunity cost of the transaction in question—the true sacrifice involved in making it possible—and the result will be overproduction of the good or service in question.) All the social benefits of particular acts of production or consumption must similarly accrue to or otherwise be brought to bear in (positively) influencing the decisions of the buyers, who alone will determine whether the production is undertaken. (If, for example, I would benefit if my neighbor undertook the expense of keeping mosquitoes from breeding on his land, that benefit must somehow be added into his calculus of costs and satisfactions if the proper amount of resources is to be devoted to this endeavor: I might, for instance, offer to pay part of the costs. Where external benefits of a particular economic activity are not appropriated by or do not accrue to the transacting parties, the effect will be an underallocation of resources to that activity.)

2. The rule does not necessarily produce optimal results if it is applied only partially: it does not necessarily provide a correct guide for pricing in individual markets or industries if it is not being followed uniformly throughout the economy. If, for example, the price of good A is held above marginal cost, perhaps by monopoly or by disproportionately heavy taxation, then it may produce a worse instead of a better allocation of resources to push the price of its substitute, B, down to marginal cost. This "problem of the second best" is obviously a very serious one in an economy shot through with imperfections of competition, monopoly power, and government taxes and subsidies, causing all prices to diverge in varying directions and degrees from marginal costs. The "first best" solution, in the foregoing example, would be to reduce the prices of both A and B (and of all other goods and services in the economy) to marginal costs; the "second best" *might* be to keep the price of B above its marginal cost, perhaps by means of an excise tax, in order to avoid distorting buyers' choices between it and A.[17]

levels." *Ibid.* For a general argument against "tinkering with price" for such purposes, see Bonbright, *Principles of Public Utility Rates*, 58–62 and chapter 7.

[17] On the other hand one cannot be certain, strictly speaking, that this is the proper solution without taking into account all other distortions in the economy as well. The pioneering demonstration of this is by R. G. Lipsey and Kelvin Lancaster, "The General Theory of Second Best," *Rev. Econ. Studies* (1956), XXIV: 11–32; they in turn cite the earlier analyses of J. E. Meade. Lipsey and Lancaster show that

". . . in general, nothing can be said about the direction or the magnitude of the secondary departures from optimum conditions made necessary by the original non-fulfillment of one condition. . . . In particular it is *not* true that a situation in which all departures from the

The existence of pervasive imperfections in the economy greatly complicates the problem of efficient pricing. In the author's view in principle it does not make solution impossible in specific situations, nor does it make it practically impossible in such instances to make the type of informed piecemeal decisions policymakers must inevitably make about how far and in what directions to qualify the basic rule of marginal-cost pricing:

"Over the whole of the discussions . . . there looms most menacingly the injunction of the theorem of the second best: Thou shalt not optimize piecemeal. But I would argue that in practice this admonition must be softened lest otherwise all effective policy be stultified. I would propose, instead, that one should shun piecemeal ameliorative measures that have not been sanctioned by careful analysis and the liberal use of common sense. Many policies may plausibly be expected to yield improvements even though things elsewhere are not organized optimally."[18]

PROBLEMS OF DEFINING MARGINAL COST

It is no simple matter to measure marginal costs—that is probably the understatement of the year. But even before one turns to that task, a number of difficult questions have to be answered about what it is, precisely, that one is trying to measure.

Specifying the Time Perspective

It is a familiar and elementary proposition in economics that sunk costs are and should be irrelevant to short-run pricing and output decisions. The only costs relevant in deciding how much to produce in plants already constructed, with production capacity already installed, are the variable costs of operating that plant, farm, or service establishment already equipped.

The longer the time perspective of the costing process, the greater the proportion of costs that become variable. As existing plant and equipment continue to be operated over time, they will ordinarily involve higher and

---

optimum conditions are of the same direction and magnitude is necessarily superior to one in which the deviations vary in direction and magnitude. For example, there is no reason to believe that a situation in which there is the same degree of monopoly in all industries will necessarily be in any sense superior to a situation in which the degree of monopoly varies as between industries." *Ibid.*, 12.

Their article has stimulated extensive discussion in literature about whether and under what circumstances the problem they elucidate means that it is impossible to tell *even in individual instances* whether efficiency is served by bringing a *particular* price closer to marginal cost. See M. J. Farrell, "In Defense of Public-Utility Price Theory," *Oxford Econ. Papers* (February 1958), n.s. X: 112–113; J. Wiseman, "The Theory of Public Utility Price: A Further Note," *Ibid.* (February 1959), XI: 92–93; Otto A. Davis and Andrew B. Whinston, "Welfare Economics and the Theory of Second Best," *Rev. Econ. Studies* (January 1965), XXXII: 1–14; and the articles by P. Bohm, Takashi Negishi,

M. McManus, and Davis and Whinston, *Ibid.* (July 1967), XXXIV: 301–331.

[18] William J. Baumol, *Welfare Economics and the Theory of the State*, 2d ed. (Cambridge: Harvard University Press, 1965), 30. As Baumol points out elsewhere, the problem of piecemeal solutions demonstrated by the theory of second-best is one of interdependencies: the proper price for *A* depends on the price-to-marginal-cost relationships of all other commodities the production of which is in any way, however remotely, related to that of *A*. But some interrelationships are more remote and therefore more safely ignored than others. "It may, then, be possible to partition the economy more effectively than some might have expected." "Informed Judgment, Rigorous Theory and Public Policy," *South Econ. Jour.* (October 1965), XXXII: 144. Similarly I.M.D. Little, who regards the general P = MC rule as both useless and wrong in an imperfect economy, nonetheless urges not only the possibility but the necessity for making informed judgments in individual cases about the proper relationship of prices and marginal cost. *A*

higher variable costs—of shutdowns, repair and maintenance, and wastage of labor and materials. Meanwhile, the progress of technology will ordinarily make increasingly attractive alternatives available. Eventually, therefore, the question of replacement will arise. At some time, the businessman, in determining whether or not to continue to produce and if so on what scale, will be able to decide once again whether to incur some or all of the capital costs of production. He will find, that is, that these costs—fixed in the short run—are variable in the long-run. The doctor can and should ignore the costs he incurred in the past for his training, in deciding whether it is worthwhile for him to keep practicing; but each prospective medical student makes the calculation afresh in deciding whether to embark on that profession. When the competitive model prescribes prices equated to marginal costs, does it mean the incremental short-run, variable cost of operating existing capacity, or intermediate-run cost, which will include also the prospectively mounting costs of repair, maintenance and operation, or the long-run costs of ultimately renewing, replacing, or adding to capacity? Are the optimum medical fees what it takes to induce doctors already trained to continue offering their services, or what it takes to bring in a fresh supply of new doctors?

When we turn to the practical problems of price making we will find that there is no single answer to these questions. But the economic principles are clear-cut. They are two. First, the essential criterion of what belongs in marginal cost and what not, and of which marginal costs should be reflected in price, is causal responsibility. All the purchasers of any commodity or service should be made to bear such additional costs—*only* such, but also *all* such—as are imposed on the economy by the provision of one additional unit.[19] And second, it is short-run marginal cost to which price should at any given time—*hence always*—be equated, because it is short-run marginal cost that reflects the social opportunity cost of providing the additional unit that buyers are at any given time trying to decide whether to buy.

It might appear that these two principles are in conflict. The first one surely implies that price must include *all* the costs that production of an additional unit imposes, regardless of when those costs are actually realized. If, for example, taking on additional business will for a time involve only the hiring of additional workers, the use of additional raw materials and fuels, but in time will necessitate also higher expenditures than otherwise for maintenance and repairs; if it will cause capital equipment to wear out faster and therefore need to be replaced sooner than otherwise—then the principle of causal responsibility would clearly require that these longer-run marginal costs be reflected in price. The second rule would seem to state, in contrast, that if some of these additional costs, for which present production is causally responsible, will in fact be felt only at some time in the future, then present purchasers should not have to bear them. But this latter interpretation would be incorrect. Variable costs include any sacrifice of future value or any future realization of higher costs that are causally attributable to present production.[20] Short-run marginal cost is simply the change in total variable cost

Critique of Welfare Economics, 2d ed. (Oxford: Clarendon Press, 1957), compare 161, 194 and 201–202.

[19] We set aside the possibility that different purchasers of the same service may be charged different prices. Economic efficiency calls for a uniform price to all buyers of an identical service at any given time (unless there can be perfect price discrimination: see pp. 131–132).

[20] This element in variable cost is called user cost: it is the loss in the net value of a firm's assets attributable to its having engaged in

caused by producing an additional unit: to the extent wear and tear of equipment varies with use—and it certainly does—depreciation *is* a variable cost, although it is typically most convenient for accounting purposes to lump physical wear-and-tear together with provision for obsolescence, label the package "depreciation," and charge it off per unit of time instead of output.[21] If price does not cover such variable costs, it is not doing its job, which is to reflect the marginal opportunity costs to society of providing the service. The second principle remains valid: ideally, price should reflect *only* those ("short-run") costs that do vary with output (regardless of when they are actually felt or give rise to additional cash outlays), because production of an additional unit is causally responsible for only those costs.

It then follows that to the extent that maintenance, depreciation, cost of capital, and various other overhead expenses are *not* a function of use, they do not belong in short-run marginal cost or, *as such*, in the ideal price. (Whether the ideal price will nevertheless cover these fixed costs is a question we shall consider presently.) Depreciation, for example, is in large measure a provision for obsolescence and not just for physical deterioration as a result of production; to this extent, it, along with the minimum necessary return on capital, is a function of time instead of the rate of utilization. To the extent that such costs are truly fixed, so far as the continued provision of service is concerned, they do not belong in the computation of marginal cost, for purposes of economically efficient pricing.[22] Moreover, even to the extent

---

production instead of not engaging in production at any particular time period. See John Maynard Keynes, *The General Theory of Employment Interest and Money* (New York: Harcourt Brace & Co., 1936), 52–55, 66–73. It may be measured as the discounted, present value of the additional prospective yield that could be obtained from the facilities if they were not used now. We encounter it most frequently as an important determinant of the proper rate of producing stock natural resources: part of the social cost of producing a ton of copper today is the (discounted) future value of that copper if it were instead sold next year; but the concept of user cost applies equally to any depreciation of capital equipment attributable to current use. Or it could be conceived as the (discounted) additional future costs of repair or earlier replacement attributable to current use.

[21] The source of confusion is the economist's use of the unfortunate terms "short-run" and "long-run." They seem to correspond to time in some chronological sense—short-run to costs that are incurred today and long-run to those incurred next year, or some such. But in fact they do not. Most firms are at any given time making both short-run and long-run decisions—determining the daily level of output, on the one hand, buying new equipment or hiring a new office secretary, on the other—and incurring the corresponding costs. The difference is that the former relates to output decisions with given capacity and to costs that vary with such decisions, while the latter relates to investment

decisions, broadly defined—to the acquisition of fixed factors of production—and give rise to costs that will not then vary as the capacity thus created is more or less fully utilized. Thus, the distinction is between costs that are fixed and those that are variable with output during some arbitrary period of time.

These variable costs, which is what we mean by short-run costs, may be not only incurred but realized instantly (for instance, the cost of the power required to turn a lathe, or the materials on which it operates) or only eventually (for example, the additional wear and tear, hence higher maintenance expense or earlier scrapping, of equipment). P. J. D. Wiles, on whose *Price, Cost and Output*, 2d. ed. (Oxford: Blackwell, 1961), 8–11, this discussion draws heavily, suggests we abandon the short- and long-run distinction, and substitute two others: partial vs. total adaptation (which corresponds to what economists mean by the rejected terms) and immediate vs. ultimate costs (depending on when the costs are actually realized). So there could be both immediate and ultimate marginal costs under "partial adaptation" (that is, in the short-run). User cost belongs in the category "ultimate marginal cost under partial adaptation."

[22] If the capacity can be used to provide other services, its use for any particular service does involve an opportunity cost—the value of the other services foregone. Therefore, that cost should be reflected in price. Also, if it has scrap or salvage value, the variable costs of continued

that depreciation does vary with use, what belongs in the marginal cost calculation is not the book cost, the writing off of investment costs historically incurred, but the amount by which this and other capital costs will be higher than they would otherwise be *in the future* by virtue of the incremental production in question. It is for the higher future costs or the decline in future values—not for fixed, historically sunk costs—that the marginal production is causally responsible; it is only the future, not the past, costs that will be saved if the production is not undertaken. Notice how, at once, the traditional practices of public utility price regulation diverge from economic principles.

It follows also that these additional repair and replacement costs belong in marginal cost and in price only if (there is a likelihood that) they will in fact be incurred; and this will depend, in turn, on whether there is likely to be sufficient demand to justify those additional expenditures. Suppose, as is probably true of much railway plant,[23] production of the additional service is the only possible use of the equipment in question, present or future, and that output cannot now or in the foreseeable future be sold for a price that covers the additional depreciation, or the cost of the eventual additional repairs, attributable to operating instead of not operating.[24] As long as users *will* pay a price covering the immediate, variable costs of operation—including the current value equivalent of whatever salvage value the equipment may have—it would be better from the standpoint both of society and the stockholders to charge them such a price (the stockholders will be indifferent unless the price includes something extra for them, however little) and continue to operate, than to refuse the business. Operations should continue until the time when either higher operating costs on the increasingly dilapidated equipment or the impossibility of further postponing the required repair, maintenance, or replacement expenditures finally drive immediate, short-run marginal costs above price and force a shutdown. In this case, the buyers will have been subsidized by the stockholders who made the mistake of financing the capacity in the first place. But from the point of view both of society and the stockholder, those costs are bygones and best forgotten as far as efficient pricing is concerned. For a continuing or expanding operation, in contrast, no business should be taken on that does not cover all the costs causally attributable to it, immediate and ultimate.

The second principle of efficient pricing might seem to raise yet another difficulty. If the ideal is to set price at marginal short-run variable cost, and if only a part of the firm's costs is variable in the short run, it would seem that these ideal prices would never cover fixed costs—notably the minimum gross return on invested capital (depreciation and return and income taxes) that must be earned if internally generated funds are to continue to be reinvested in the business and outside capital to be attracted. It is important to see clearly that this is not necessarily the case. As a glance at the familiar Figure 1 will quickly disclose, while short-run variable costs per unit of output

---

operation must include a return above direct costs equivalent to what the owners could earn on their investment if they scrapped the plant and invested the money elsewhere: this is also a marginal opportunity cost of continued production. This is a variant of the principle that we shall encounter below, that when the absolute limits of capacity are reached, price should be equated to marginal social opportunity cost. But this is still not the same as incorporating capital costs like depreciation, as such, in price.

23 See James R. Nelson, *op. cit.*, *The Antitrust Bulletin* (January–April 1966), XI: 23.

24 In this event, to use the concept of note 20, the marginal user cost—which should always be incorporated in price—is zero.

(*AVC*) can never be as large as total costs (*ATC*), short-run marginal costs (*SRMC*) can be lower, equal to (at *Pe*), or higher than average total costs, depending on the relation of market demand to plant or industry capacity. As that diagram demonstrates there will usually be some point, with any given plant, beyond which the rate of output can be expanded only at rising unit variable costs. If the average total cost curve turns up at any point along the output scale, it will be because marginal costs beyond that point exceed total unit costs. Marginal-cost pricing at or beyond this point will therefore cover or more than cover average total costs as well. Therefore pricing at short-run marginal cost need not be unremunerative in the long run or inconsistent with long-run equilibrium: the price need never explicitly be formulated to cover long-run or fixed costs, yet at certain times, when demand is sufficient, it will do so or more than do so.[25]

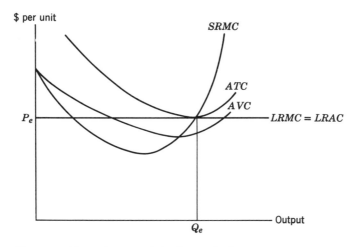

Figure 1. The unit costs of the firm under long-run constant returns.

Whether in fact prices set at SRMC will cover ATC with sufficient reliability and without involving intolerably great fluctuation over time, is a question we consider below (pp. 84–86, 103–109).

---

[25] In long-run competitive equilibrium, as Figure 1 shows, price will be at precisely the point (*Pe*) where short-run marginal costs (*SRMC*) and average total costs (*ATC*) are equal. This demonstration is simplified by the assumption in Figure 1 that the industry operates under conditions of long-run constant costs—that is, if a firm were to plan to produce much more or much less than *Qe*, it could best do so in plants with the same lowest cost (*Pe*) as the one shown. So the long-run marginal cost (*LRMC*)—that is, the total additional costs per unit of additional blocks of output, when capacity is altered so as to produce the larger output at minimum cost—is at *Pe*, and coincides with long-run average costs. A similar coincidence of *SRMC*, *LRMC*, and *ATC* would be achieved by perfect competition in industries subject to increasing costs as well. But if the industry were instead subject to long-run decreasing costs, as some public utilities are in important respects, pricing at the ideal point where both *SRMC* and *LRMC* were equal would be inconsistent with long-run equilibrium, because *ATC* would not be covered (as we shall see, pp. 130–133). On these matters, see F. H. Knight, "Some Fallacies in the Interpretation of Social Cost," *Q. Jour. Econ.* (1924), XXXVIII: 582–606; Jacob Viner, "Cost Curves and Supply Curves," *Zeitschrift Für Nationalökonomie* (1931), III: 23–46; Howard S. Ellis and William Fellner, "External Economies and Diseconomies," *The Amer. Econ. Rev.* (1943), XXXIII: 493–511, all three as reproduced in the American Economic Association, *Readings in Price Theory* (Selection Committee, George J. Stigler and Kenneth E. Boulding) (Chicago: Richard D. Irwin, 1952), 160–179, 198–232, and 242–263, respectively.

In sum: the economic ideal would be to set all public utility rates at short-run marginal costs (with appropriate adjustments for problems of second-best);[26] and these must cover all sacrifices, present or future[27] and external as well as internal to the company, for which production is at the margin causally responsible. The ideal is worth emphasizing, because in certain circumstances it can and should be embodied in rates. But, in the real world, it is not usually feasible or even desirable to do so, for a variety of reasons that will become clear as we consider two other related aspects of the problem of defining marginal costs.

Specifying the Incremental Block of Output

The level of incremental cost per unit depends, also, on the size of the increment. Consider the passenger airplane flight already scheduled, with the plane on the runway, fueled up and ready to depart, but with its seats not completely filled. The incremental unit of service in this case might be defined as the carrying of an extra passenger on that flight—in which case, the marginal cost would be practically zero. It was just such a marginal cost calculation, involving the smallest possible number of additional units and the shortest-possible run, that underlay the introduction of standby youth-fares by some American airlines in 1966—half-price for young people willing to come out to the airport and take their chances of finding an empty seat on their flight ten minutes before departure time.

Or is the incremental unit in question the particular scheduled flight, taken as a whole, involving the carrying of 50 or 100 passengers between a particular pair of cities at a particular time? If the plane must fly anyhow, as long as the flight is scheduled, the additional cost of taking on all the passengers is still practically zero. But schedules can be changed in the comparatively short run, in which event the relevant marginal costs of a particular flight include all the costs of flying the plane as compared with not flying it. Or is the incremental unit of sales the provision of regular service between a pair of cities, involving an entire schedule of flights? In this case, still more costs enter into the marginal calculation—airport rentals, ticket offices, the cost of advertising in local newspapers, indeed the cost of the planes themselves, which need not be acquired or can be used in other service. The larger the incremental unit of service under consideration, the more costs become variable.

As in the choice between short- and long-run marginal cost, so the choice of the proper unit of sale for purposes of pricing necessarily involves a balancing of the practicable and the economic ideal. This topic is the subject of the concluding section of this chapter. The nature of the possible conflict between these two considerations and the need for compromise should already be clear.

Ideally, if the flight is going anyhow, it is economically inefficient to turn away any passenger willing to pay the marginal opportunity cost of his trip —which is virtually zero as long as there are empty seats. In short, the ideal remains pricing at the shortest-run marginal cost for the smallest possible

---

[26] We shall ignore the second-best qualification during the subsequent discussions, returning to it at a later point—though only briefly, because it is impossible to set forth general rules, in *a priori* terms, about how and to what extent to take it into account.

[27] Strictly speaking, any postponed cost incurrences should be incorporated in price only at present, discounted value.

increment of output. That is why the youth fare plan was an inspiration, at least for the (young) flying public: it offered them the option of traveling at greatly reduced fares on seats that would otherwise go unused. But the airlines were able to move closer to short-run marginal cost pricing in this instance only because and to the extent that (1) they could offer a genuinely inferior service—the travelers had to take the risk that any particular flights for which they might stand by would have no space for them and (2) they could do so selectively—the youth fare was an ingenious form of price discrimination, the principles of which we discuss more fully in Chapter 5. In fact, the airlines found it difficult to preserve the necessary separation of the two markets.[28] Moreover, being discriminatory, the plan was still not economically "ideal": that would have required offering a zero price to all potential customers, as long as there were empty seats—something that would have been very difficult for an airline company to arrange, while still collecting fares high enough to cover the common costs of the entire flight.

In fact, as we shall see, the ideal would be for the airlines to determine the proper level of capacity—number and scheduling of flights—and then to auction off the seats on each flight nondiscriminately, at prices down to marginal cost, in such a way as to assure that as many seats as possible were sold. Such a procedure would indeed produce prices for each flight equal to the marginal opportunity cost of a single passage, that is, to short-run marginal cost, while also enabling the airlines to cover total costs, provided their decisions with respect to capacity were correct.[29]

Of course, the proper size of the incremental unit of output depends on the perspective of the decision under consideration. From the standpoint of the supplier, the decision to add an extra section to a flight already scheduled will involve a different marginal cost, which is to be compared with marginal revenues, than the decision to add another flight or route to its schedules. When the decision is one to extend or withdraw an entire service to some particular block of customers—as in the abandonments of railroad passenger service that have become increasingly frequent since 1958—the relevant unit

---

[28] This experience also illustrates both the necessity and the difficulty, familiar in the economics of price discrimination, of keeping the various markets or classes of customers separate. The differentiation was on the basis of (1) age and (2) willingness to take a service that was inferior because it carried no assurance of space on any particular flight. However, the airlines found that youths were telephoning and making reservations under fictitious names—thus foreclosing the sale of those spaces at full fare to regular customers—which they then neglected to claim at the regular price. In this way, they increased their assurance that there would be an empty seat available for them at half-fare, while causing the airlines to lose full-fare business. For example, Braniff Airways pointed out that during the period the youth fare was in effect, the ratio of its cancellations to boardings rose from 1.8 to 4.8%. *Brief* in Civil Aeronautics Board, *Standby Youth Fares Young Adult Fares*, Docket 18936, Exhibit BI-10, November 14, 1968. Several companies found that the marginal

costs of the program were well above zero: they encountered a greater demand on the time of agents in answering questions about the possibilities of finding standby space, greater congestion at ticket counters, and increased annoyance to regular passengers, who were often offended by the sartorial, hirsute and ablutional state, and the comportment of some of their new fellow travelers.

[29] See notes 49, 51, this chapter, and pp. 87–93, 103–104. The market for seats on each flight could be further differentiated, without discrimination, by letting passengers bid and pay varying prices, depending on the amount of advance assurance they required with respect to their having a reserved seat. See the ingenious proposal along these lines by William Vickrey for transoceanic flights, with tickets going at varying prices as the time of departure approaches, "Some Objections to Marginal-Cost Pricing," *Jour. Pol. Econ.* (June 1948), LVI: 232–234.

of output is clearly the entire service in question. And the relevant economic question is: What additional costs would be imposed if that service were to be extended, what total costs saved or avoided by its withdrawal?[30]

Identifying Marginal Cost When a Large Proportion of Costs Are Common

The problem of specifying the size of the incremental block of output, the unit cost of which is to determine the ideal price, is itself a reflection of a more general phenomenon, that of common costs. The costs of carrying 50 passengers on a scheduled plane flight constitute a single lump of common costs: they are incurred not on a passenger-by-passenger basis but all together or not at all. Another way of saying this is that the unit of production (the single flight), which is the basis of cost incurrence, is larger than the unit of sale (a single ticket to a single passenger).[31] In consequence, the marginal cost of each sale, considered alone, is practically zero; whereas the cost of the unit of production comes to very much more than zero per passenger.

No public utility company (and precious few others) sells a single product or service to all customers. A single railroad company carries passengers for trips of varied lengths, and an enormous variety of freight for equally varied distances. Virtually no part of its plant provides only a single one of these services, at a single price. The gas company sells fuel during the day and at night, in winter and in summer; to some customers it guarantees a firm supply at all times; to others it sells on an interruptible basis, which means that it can decline to meet the buyer's needs when its capacity is being fully employed in meeting the demands of its firm customers; the same mains carry gas to numerous customers for heating, cooking, clothes-drying, and suicide. River valley development projects supply electric power, water for irrigation, flood control, and navigation services, largely with the same facilities. By far the largest part of the interstate plant of the Bell System is used to furnish message toll telephone, day and night, telephotograph, teletypewriter services, television program transmission, and various business data transmission services.[32]

To the extent that multiple products or services are supplied by the same plant or productive operation, their costs are either common or joint (we will distinguish the two presently). Individual services or sales do of course typically have their own clearly identifiable specific costs: the turbines employed in a multiple-purpose river development project serve only to generate electricity; and every purchaser of a thousand cubic feet of natural gas at the terminus of a pipeline specifically imposes on that line the necessity for buying one thousand cubic feet of gas in the field. But most costs are common: the same interstate pipeline carries gas for sale to customers A, B . . . Z under different conditions and at various times during the year. Since costs must be recovered over periods of time instead of instantaneously —even wages are paid on a weekly basis—the costs of serving customer A

[30] See pp. 154–155.
[31] See George W. Wilson, *Essays on Some Unsettled Questions in the Economics of Transportation*, Foundation for Economic and Business Studies (Indiana Univ., 1962), 14–20, 69–78. This would be even more clear if one regarded the unit of production as the provision of regular service between two cities.

[32] For an interesting illustration of the pervasiveness of common costs in satellite communications, see Leland L. Johnson, "Joint Cost and Price Discrimination: The Case of Communications Satellites," in Shepherd and Gies, *op. cit.*, 118–121.

today and customer A tomorrow are likewise in a sense common, even if the service is physically the same. The same theatrical performance may be witnessed from row B or row Z, on Wednesday afternoon or Saturday night; the services are different, most of the costs are joint. Indeed, what constitutes a separate product or service depends in a sense on what it pays the businessman to price or to cost separately.[33]

The fact that most services are typically provided in combinations, using the same facilities, does not mean that definable shares of the common costs can not in principle be causally attributed to each. When the same equipment may be used to make products A and B, and when producing A uses capacity that could otherwise be used to supply B, then we may speak of their costs as common instead of joint: and in this event, the marginal cost of A *may* include an identifiable part of these common costs. This situation is widespread in the public utilities, and in industry generally. The same railway plant can be used for passenger or freight service, and for any number of kinds of freight, over any number of routes.[34] The same coaxial cable may transmit telephone messages, business data, or TV programs. The same warehouse may be used to store a variety of products. If any one of these products or services uses freight cars, circuits, or warehouse space that would in fact otherwise be used for one of the others, or if it requires the construction of greater capacity than would otherwise be necessary, then it *does* bear a causal responsibility for a share of the common capacity costs.[35] The cost allocation formulae actually employed may achieve only a rough, rule-of-thumb approximation to the actual costs for which each product or service is responsible, but those costs have objective reality.[36]

---

[33] The producer of a play may sell each seat for a separate price, or may differentiate them by blocks. He may vary his prices from day to day, depending on what the traffic will bear. The airline may have a single per passenger charge between any two points, or may sell separately the carriage of infants, wives, adults, with or without free champagne, with wider or narrower spacing between seats, and with varying charges from one day to the next.

[34] See the reference, note 11, Chapter 4, to the famous Taussig-Pigou controversy, which hinged on the question of whether rail costs were mainly joint or common, and whether therefore individual rail services might be said to have separate costs.

[35] Whether A's marginal cost includes a portion of the capacity costs (for example, depreciation and return on investment) *as such*, depends, strictly speaking, on whether one is thinking of short-run or long-run marginal costs. As we have already seen (see pp. 71–74, above), short-run marginal cost does not include them. But if as a matter of economic (that is, not merely technological) fact, the capacity could indeed be used to make either A or B, then even short-run marginal cost of A includes as an opportunity cost the value of B that has been sacrificed. See note 22, and pp. 83, 85.

Here again we see the relevance of the other

dimensions of costing already mentioned. If the plant or warehouse has excess capacity sufficient to produce or store A without cutting down service B—and this will depend, too, on how much equipment or room A takes, and that will depend in turn on how the incremental service "A" is defined—the relevant marginal costs of A could be zero or considerably more, depending on whether it is long- or short-run costs that are being measured, and whether the excess capacity is short-lived or permanent.

[36] Companies often allocate various common overhead costs in proportion to the variable costs that can be directly attributed to the individual products. The assumption presumably is that the greater the quantity and the higher the cost of labor and materials used in fabricating a product, the greater also will be the quantity and value of equipment employed in its production, the draft on the time and attention of inspectors, superintendents, purchasing agents, salesmen, and so forth. Less tenuous would be the practice of distributing the expenses of a personnel department among operating divisions on the basis of the relative number of employees; or the practice of sawmills allocating the joint costs of production among the numerous grades of lumber on the basis of the relative number of board feet of the various types and grades— on the assumption that a board-foot of low-grade

If services produced in common are to have separate marginal production costs it must be possible to vary their proportions. At least in the long run, this is true of almost all such products. As Marshall pointed out, sheep can be bred to give more or less mutton per pound of wool;[37] crude oil, which used to be subjected only to a physical separation of its components in whatever proportions they were found in the original state, is now cracked in order to increase the yields of the higher-value and decrease those of the lower-value fractions. A system of dams can be constructed or, once constructed, operated to yield varying proportions of electric power, flood control, water for irrigation, navigation benefits, and so on. But for this possibility to yield economically relevant, separate costs, the physical variability must fall within the range of economic feasibility—and this depends on the respective demands for the individual services. If, for example, it is physically possible to increase the production of A, while holding the quantities of B constant, but the cost of doing so is more than buyers are willing to pay, or need pay as long as the output produced in invariant proportions meets their requirements, then the services are still being produced in fixed proportions, and have no separate economic costs.[38] If then the proportions are effectively (that is, economically) variable, one can unequivocally identify as the marginal cost of any one product the addition to the total cost of the joint production process occasioned by increasing the output of that one product, while leaving the output of the others unchanged.[39]

When instead the products are truly joint, in that they can be economically produced only in fixed proportions, neither of them has a genuine, separate incremental cost function, as far as the joint part of their production process is concerned. (They will each typically have separate additional costs of processing, shipping, and marketing, but these need not concern us here.) If producing a bale of cotton fiber invariably involves producing also the seeds from which can be extracted ten gallons of cottonseed oil, there is no objective way—if one looks at the cost of production alone—of attributing causal responsibility for some part of the joint production costs to one of the products and the remainder to the other. The economic product is the composite unit; the only economically definable cost of production, marginal or average, and "price" or "marginal revenue" are those of the composite unit.

However, each of a number of joint products does have a competitive supply function. The intersection of these with the respective demand functions yields an economically optimal set of separate prices for the joint products—a set that would be achieved by perfect competition—that will not only equate the total of their prices with their composite marginal *production* cost but will also equate the price of *each* with its own separate

---

lumber has fabricating, handling and storage costs comparable to a board-foot of high quality lumber. On the use of this technique, see Theodore Lang, ed., *Cost Accountants' Handbook* (New York: Ronald, 1947), 526.

[37] *Principles of Economics*, 9th ed., I: 389–390; see also his discussion of this entire subject in *Industry and Trade* (London: Macmillan, 1932), 190–194.
[38] See National Bureau of Economic Research, Committee on Price Determination, *Cost Behavior and Price Policy* (New York: N.B.E.R., 1943),

177–179. Also J. M. Clark, *Studies in the Economics of Overhead Costs*, 99.
[39] Such a calculation can then be made not only for the short run—what would it add to total costs to increase the output of product A, holding the output of the other products constant, with existing capacity?—but also for the long run—what will it add to total costs to build additional capacity to produce A, while holding constant the capacity available to produce B?

marginal *opportunity* cost. These separate marginal opportunity costs can not be determined from production costs alone; what makes them determinate is the joint supply function, on the one hand, and the separate demand functions on the other. Since joint supply is pervasive in the public utility industries, it is important to explain these propositions in some detail.

In Figures 2 and 3, we posit the joint production of cotton fiber and cotton seeds in any fixed proportion—the ratio of one bale to enough seeds to make ten gallons of cottonseed oil is purely illustrative. The relevant marginal production costs are the same in the two figures. They are assumed for simplicity to be constant (that is, horizontal) within the relevant range, and may be taken to stand for either short- or long-run marginal costs. MC_{c+cso} is the joint cost of producing the combination; MC_{cso} is the cost for the separate production process of extracting cottonseed oil from the seeds. (In reality the fiber will also have its own processing costs, but here we assume it has none; introducing them would add nothing to the demonstration.)

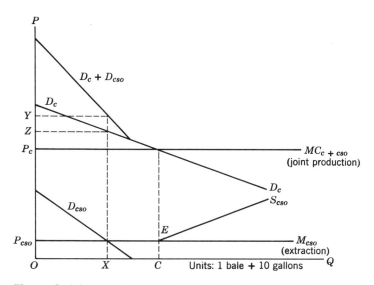

Figure 2. Joint production, cotton and cottonseed oil; cotton seeds a free good.

The only difference between the two figures is the relationship between the separate demands for fiber and oil (D_c and D_{cso}). For simplicity, D_c is held the same; only D_{cso} is altered. The demands can be summed vertically to show the combined "prices" or average revenues at which various quantities of the composite unit of fiber and oil can be sold ($D_c + D_{cso}$). For example, OX composite units in Figure 2 (for example, 2 million bales of fiber plus 20 million gallons of oil) would bring in an average revenue of OY, composed of a price of OP_{cso} for each 10 gallons of oil and OZ for each bale of fiber.

There is no way of defining individual production costs for the separate products, except for MC_{cso}, which is distinct from the joint production process. But note that it *is* possible to define a competitive supply function for each, given the cost data and demand *for the other*. For simplicity we do it in Figure 2 only for the oil; since the demand for cotton *fiber* is the same in both figures, the supply curve for *oil* is likewise the same in both. Producers of the oil must always obtain a price at least as high as MC_{cso}. How much more will they require? Up to the quantity OC, nothing more; the demand for cotton is so strong that quantities of fiber offered up to OC will bring a price (P_c or better) that covers all the joint costs. However, beyond OC additional offerings of fiber will force prices below MC_{c+cso}; for additional supplies of oil to be forthcoming, its price will have to make a contribution to the joint costs sufficient to fill the gap. Therefore, the separate processing costs, the joint costs, and the demand for cotton fiber together define a competitive supply curve for oil (S_{cso}) that runs along the MC_{cso} curve to E, then rises, as indicated in both figures. The supply function for cotton fiber (S_c) in Figure 3 is constructed in the same way, by determining from the demand for oil how much of a contribution purchasers of that product would make (over and above MC_{cso}) to the joint costs (MC_{c+cso}) when different quantities are offered for sale: when OC is offered, for example, the price of (10 gallons of) oil will contribute only EF to the joint costs; therefore, if OC bales of fiber are to be forthcoming, buyers will have to pay CG (CG plus EF equals CH).[40]

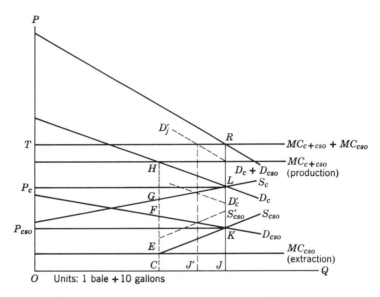

Figure 3. Joint production, cotton and cottonseed oil.

We are now in a position to determine how much of each product would be produced and at what price they would sell under perfect competition. The equilibrium outcome requires that the combined prices cover joint marginal cost, that the price of each cover any separate marginal costs, and that prices clear the market—that is, that all who are willing to buy and sell at the price are in fact able to do so. In Figure 2, the demand for cotton alone is so strong relative to the demand for oil that it alone determines how much fiber and seeds are produced: adding the demand for oil to the demand for cotton does not change the equilibrium output, OC bales. Each bale will sell

[40] The derivation may be easier to see if the reader will look to the top cost curve in Figure 3, $MC_{c+cso} + MC_{cso}$, which tells for how much the composite units must sell if they are to cover all relevant costs—the costs both of joint production and of extracting the oil. OJ units of oil will bring a price that contributes JK to this total; cotton will have to pay JL: the supply curve for cotton, S_c, is derived as the difference between the composite cost and the contribution made by purchasers of oil, D_{cso}, so that $RL = JK$, and JL plus $JK = JR$.

at OP_c; fiber will bear all the joint costs. Only OX gallons of oil will in fact be extracted—that is where D_{cso} intersects the supply curve—and they will sell at OP_{cso}. Any additional quantities of oil offered would only depress the price below the marginal costs of extracting the oil. If their only use is as a source of oil, oil *seeds* are a free good in this case; they will sell for a zero price and some of them will still go unsold and unused.[41]

In Figure 3, the solution is easier to see when we introduce the cost function $MC_{c+cso} + MC_{cso}$, because in this case the relation of the demands is such that all components of the composite unit produced will be sold, and each such unit will have to return a price sufficient to cover both the marginal joint production cost and MC_{cso}. Here the perfectly competitive output will be OJ for both end products, produced in the fixed ratio of one bale to ten gallons. The fiber will sell at OP_c, the oil at OP_{cso}; together these prices will cover total costs, and at those prices the quantities of each product demanded and supplied will be equated.

This result could be read off Figure 3 merely by noting that the intersection of the combined demands $(D_c + D_{cso})$ and the combined marginal cost $(MC_{c+cso} + MC_{cso})$ establishes the equilibrium output OJ, and the separate demands then indicate the separate prices at which OJ cotton and OJ cottonseed oil will sell. Or the separate results could be read directly as determined by the intersection of the individual demands *with their respective individual supply functions*. As far as the joint production process is concerned, joint products do not have separate production cost functions. Each does have a definite competitive supply function, indicating how much of the joint costs its purchasers must pay for various quantities.

Are these respective supply curves true cost functions? Little purpose would be served by semantic argument. But the Figure 2 situation definitely embodies objectively separate marginal costs of production, in the only economically important sense—which is that they reflect incremental, causal cost responsibility. For all outputs beyond OX—that is to say, *within the range in which the sales ratios will in fact vary*—all the joint costs are unequivocally attributable to cotton fiber. Any joint costs that society incurs for production beyond OX are incurred solely in order to serve the fiber customers; added costs of MC_{c+cso} will be incurred if they ask for more, and saved if they ask for less. Increases in the demand for cottonseed oil will, up to OC, impose no additional joint production costs on society; decreases in the demand for oil will reduce joint production outlays not one whit. Therefore, economic efficiency requires that the price of cotton reflect 100% of the joint costs, in the Figure 2 situation.

In the Figure 3 situation, it is not true in the same sense that each product has a separate production cost function. Within its entire range, sales will be in fixed proportions. An increase or decrease in the demand for one of the

[41] In the case of joint products it might appear that if either product is produced at all, the cost of the other is in a sense zero—and conversely. But actually this will be true only if the "one" (this would be the cotton, in Figure 2) is produced in sufficient quantities to supply all of the "other" that will be demanded at a zero price. In that event, the marginal cost of the latter (cotton seeds, in Figure 2) is zero. Consumption of an additional cotton seed would impose no additional production cost on society and would deprive no one of desired cotton seeds. But whether that condition prevails will depend, then, on the respective levels of demand for the two products; it does *not* prevail in the circumstances depicted in Figure 3; and it cannot be true of both products simultaneously.

joint products will *not*, unless that range is exceeded,[42] increase or decrease society's production costs by the amount of the competitive price it had been paying (or by the area under its competitive supply curve). It will change the distribution of the joint burden borne by itself and the other product, and how much of society's resources will be drawn into additional output or saved will depend on the elasticity of the two demands.[43]

Whether the separate supply functions do represent corresponding marginal *production* costs, the equilibrium prices of the several joint products, derived as indicated in Figure 3, do equal their respective marginal opportunity costs. What is the measure of the marginal opportunity cost of supplying some customer the OJth unit of cotton and cottonseed oil? It is what the next customer, the first one *not* served, would have been willing to pay for that last bale or gallon, auctioned off at their respective market-clearing prices: and in Figure 3, that would be (infinitesimally less than) OP_c and OP_{cso}. Therefore, the economically efficient solution does involve equating the price of each joint product to its marginal opportunity cost.[44]

TEMPERING PRINCIPLE WITH PRACTICALITY— OR ONE PRINCIPLE WITH ANOTHER

The outcome of this entire discussion about the problems of defining (as contrasted with actually measuring and applying) marginal cost is that neither the choice between short and long-run, nor the problem of defining the incremental unit of sale, nor the prevalence of common and joint costs raises any difficulties in principle about the economically efficient price. It is set at the short-run marginal cost of the smallest possible additional unit of sale. Common costs do not preclude separable marginal production costs, and joint products have separate marginal opportunity costs.

But, as we have already suggested, short-run marginal costs (SRMC) are the place to begin. There are situations in which it is both efficient and practical to base rates on them, as we shall see. Typically, this is not the case; principle must be compromised in various ways in the interest of practicality, for a number of interrelated reasons:

1. It is often infeasible, or prohibitively expensive, for businesses to make the

---

[42] If either demand shifted far enough relative to the other to restore a Figure 2 situation, we would once again have separate production costs. This would be so in Figure 3 if, for example, D_{cso} shifted sufficiently to the left to intersect S_{cso} short of point E.

[43] A change of this type is depicted in Figure 3, in dashed lines. D_c declines to D'_c. This means that the combined demand (D_{c+cso}) falls by the same amount, to D'_j. (It is unnecessary, but perhaps helpful, to draw in the new supply curve for oil, S'_{cso}, reflecting the diminished contributions fiber purchasers are now prepared to make toward joint costs at various levels of output.) Joint output falls to OJ'. Society's resource savings are not measured by the area between J and J' under the cotton fiber supply curve, S_c, as they would be if this were a true marginal production cost curve; instead they are measured by the entire area between J and J' under the

combined cost curve $(MC_{c+cso} + MC_{cso})$.

[44] See Jack Hirshleifer, "Peak Loads and Efficient Pricing: Comment," *Q. Jour. Econ.* (August 1958), LXXII: 458–459. On the application of this reasoning to public utility pricing, see pp. 87–88 and pp. 91–93, Chapter 4.

On the general theory of joint products, their costing and pricing under competitive and monopolistic conditions, see the very lucid discussion in Mary Jean Bowman and George Leland Bach, *Economic Analysis and Public Policy: An Introduction* (New York: Prentice-Hall, 1943), Chapter 18. Also see Kenneth E. Boulding, *Economic Analysis, Microeconomics* (New York: Harper & Row, 1966), I: 579–584; Joel Dean, *Managerial Economics* (New York: Prentice-Hall, 1951), 317–319; T. J. Kreps, "Joint Costs in the Chemical Industry," *Q. Jour. Econ.* (May 1930), XLIV: 416–461.

necessary fine calculations of marginal cost for each of their numerous categories of service.

2. Marginal costs will vary from one moment to the next, in a world of perpetually changing demand, as firms operate at perpetually changing points on their SRMC functions (unless marginal costs happen to be constant, that is, horizontal), and between far wider extremes than either average variable or average total costs (see Figure 1). It will vary also because cost functions themselves are constantly shifting. Thus, it would be prohibitively costly to the seller to put into effect the highly refined and constantly changing pricing schedules, reflecting in minute detail the different short-run marginal costs of different sales. It would also be highly vexatious to buyers, who would be quick to find discrimination in departures from uniform prices, who would be put to great expense to be informed about prices that were constantly changing, and whose ability to make rational choices and plan intelligently for the future would be seriously impaired.

3. For these reasons the practically-achievable version of SRMC pricing is often likely to be pricing at *average* variable costs (AVC), themselves averaged over some period of time in the past and assumed to remain constant over some period in the future—until there occurs some clear, discrete shift caused by an event such as a change in wage rates. But since short-term AVC (in contrast with SRMC) are never as large as average total costs (see Figure 1), universal adoption of this type of pricing is infeasible if sellers are to cover total costs, including (as always) a minimum required return on investment. This in turn produces a strong tendency in industry to price on a "full cost" basis—usually computed at AVC (really *average* AVC over some period of time) plus some percentage mark-up judged sufficient to cover total costs on the average over some time period[45]—a far cry, indeed, from marginal cost pricing.[46]

4. SRMC can be above or below ATC, as we have seen; but whether it is above often enough for businesses pricing on that basis to cover total costs on the average depends on the average relationship over time between demand and production capacity. As J. M. Clark has often pointed out, excess capacity is the typical condition of modern industry;[47] and we would probably want this to be the case in public utilities, which we tend to insist be perpetually in a position to supply whatever demands are placed on them. In these circumstances, firms could far more often be operating at the point where SRMC is less than ATC than the reverse,[48] and if they based their prices exclusively on the former they would have to find some other means of making up the difference. Partly for this reason, and partly because of the infeasibility of

---

[45] See the survey article by Richard B. Heflebower, "Full Costs, Cost Changes, and Prices," in National Bureau of Economic Research, *Business Concentration and Price Policy* (Princeton: Princeton Univ. Press, 1955), 361–392.

[46] Recall that to the extent that depreciation, taxes, and return on capital are a function not of use but of time—as is preponderantly the case—they do not belong in SRMC, hence in price, at all.

[47] *Overhead Costs*, 437–439, 448–449; *Competition as a Dynamic Process* (Washington: Brookings Institution, 1961), 59, 81, 120–121, 133, 140.

[48] This does not follow inevitably from the perpetual presence of surplus capacity. Most of the standby capacity probably has high variable costs—that, indeed, is why it is selected for the standby function. In consequence, even if an industry operates on the average at, for example, 80% of physical capacity, it might find its

permitting prices to fluctuate widely along the SRMC function, depending on the immediate relation of demand to capacity,[49] the practically achievable benchmark for efficient pricing is more likely to be a type of average long-run incremental cost, computed for a large, expected incremental block of sales, instead of SRMC, estimated for a single additional sale. This long-run incremental cost (which we shall loosely refer to as long-run marginal cost as well) would be based on (1) the average incremental variable costs of those added sales and (2) estimated additional capital costs per unit, for the additional capacity that will have to be constructed if sales at that price are expected to continue over time or to grow.[50] Both of these components would be estimated as averages over some period of years extending into the future.

5. The prevalence of common costs has similar implications. Service A bears a causal responsibility for a share of common costs only if there is an economically realistic alternative use of the capacity now used to provide it, or if production of A requires the building of additional capacity. The marginal opportunity cost of serving A depends on how much the alternative users would be willing to pay for devoting the capacity to serving them instead. The sum of the separable marginal costs will therefore cover the common costs only if at separate prices less than this the claims on the capacity exceed the available supply.[51]

6. Long-run marginal costs are likely to be the preferred criterion also in competitive situations. Permitting rate reductions to a lower level of SRMC, which would prove to be unremunerative if the business thus attracted were to continue over time, might constitute predatory competition—driving out of business rivals whose *long-run* costs of production might well be lower than those of the price-cutter.

SRMC on the average equal to its composite ATC—running far above ATC when operations exceeded the 80% level and correspondingly below at other times. See pp. 94–97, Chapter 4, below.

[49] If SRMC pricing did not cover ATC over time, capital would eventually be withdrawn and new capital, needed to meet the rising demand, repelled, until a recovering demand, moving up along a steeply rising MC curve, pushed prices up high enough and held them there long enough to attract new capital into the industry—with the possibility of a return of depressed prices with any temporary reemergence of excess capacity. In the case of the partly-empty airplane (see pp. 75–76), the "efficient price" would be zero as long as the response of travelers remained insufficient to fill the plane; then it would have to jump the moment the empty spaces fell one short of demand, possibly to the full cost of an added flight but in any case to whatever level necessary to equate the number of available seats with the number of would-be passengers. On each flight, the available seats would have to be auctioned, with the uniform price settling at the point required to clear the market.

[50] See W. Arthur Lewis, *Overhead Costs* (New York: Rinehart, 1949), 15–20; Marcel Boiteux, "Peak-Load Pricing" in James R. Nelson, *Marginal Cost Pricing in Practice* (Englewood Cliffs: Prentice-Hall, 1964), 70–72.

[51] As we have just seen in another connection (pp. 82–83), the marginal opportunity cost of providing a cubic foot of warehouse space to any particular user, A, is the most valuable alternative use of that space excluded by serving A—what the most insistent excluded customer would have been willing to pay for it. If at any price per foot less than the proportionate share of the common costs (that is, less than ATC) of the warehouse, there are or would be unsatisfied customers—that is, more cubic feet demanded than were available—then clearly the marginal opportunity cost of each cubic foot would be at least equal to average total costs, and prices correctly set at SRMC would cover total costs. If, instead, at a price equal to ATC there is excess capacity, this demonstrates that price exceeds marginal opportunity costs: serving A is not preventing anyone else willing to pay that much from getting all the space he wants. In this circumstance, prices set lower, at true SRMC, would not provide enough revenue to cover total costs.

It is important to recognize that all these reasons for compromising principle with practicality make sense even in purely economic terms—hence the equivocal subtitle of this section. Consider the fact, for example, that it is costly—that is, it uses resources—to measure and base prices on SRMC. (This will be easier to see at a later point: see pp. 182–187.) If these costs exceed the efficiency advantages of moving to such a pricing system, clearly considerations of economic efficiency alone would dictate refraining from doing so. Therefore, it is not a matter merely of compromising an economic principle; it is a question of correctly applying the relevant principle or of balancing one principle with another.

The limitations of trying to base prices solely on SRMC may be stated more generally. The theory of efficient pricing that we sketched earlier in this chapter is a static theory. It describes the conditions for optimum choosing, given some preexisting technology and pattern of consumer desires. It describes the optimum, equilibrium outcome that will prevail after all adjustments have been made to those two fundamental determinants of supply and demand functions. It makes no calculation of the costs or likelihood of achieving that result in a dynamic economy, in which demand and costs are constantly changing. Or, alternatively, it may be said to describe how that result will be achieved effortlessly, costlessly, and instantaneously under perfect competition—where buyers and sellers of every good and service are infinitely numerous, have perfect knowledge and foresight and act rationally on it, and where resources are perfectly mobile and fully employed. But obviously these conditions do not and cannot prevail in the real world. Only, then, if we can compare the efficiency gains of each proposed movement toward SRMC pricing, on the one hand, with its possible costs and drawbacks in a world of imperfect competition, knowledge, rationality, and resource mobility can we decide whether that move is indeed optimal even in purely economic terms. We have just suggested several reasons why it might not always be optimal.

This list of considerations is by no means exhaustive. Since the best probable compromise of offsetting considerations will clearly vary from one pricing context to another, it is impossible to set forth an integrated, general set of conclusions. Instead what we have is really a set of hypotheses, of relevant considerations. We proceed now to apply them to the most important public utility pricing problems: to the proper distribution of capacity costs; to the optimum pattern of rates over time (these two in Chapter 4); to decreasing cost situations, where MC is less than ATC, and the proper design of a rate structure in these circumstances (Chapter 5); and to situations in which competition is involved—competition involving public utility companies themselves and competition among their customers (Chapter 6).

CHAPTER 4

The Application of Long- and Short-Run Marginal Costs

Having established in Chapter 3 that economically efficient prices of public utility services would be based on some *a priori* unspecifiable mixture of short and long-run marginal costs, in this chapter we consider two major contexts in which the best mixture needs to be discovered and applied: in determining which customers should pay the capital costs, and in deciding how and to what extent rates ought to be changed over time, as marginal costs change.

THE DISTRIBUTION OF CAPACITY COSTS

In industries as capital-intensive as public utilities, the costs of providing the capacity to serve—depreciation, property, income taxes, and return on investment—are very large. Yet, we have asserted, capacity costs are not part of SRMC and therefore, in principle, should not be reflected in price (except to the limited extent that they are in fact variable).

However, what if a price that covers only the variable operating costs elicits a demand for the service so great that it cannot be supplied with existing capacity? Economists have long been bemused by Dupuit's and Hotelling's historic example of the bridge and the strong case they made against charging tolls, on the ground that operating, maintenance, and capital costs do not vary significantly with the rate of utilization.[1] But what if charging a zero toll would, at least at certain hours of the day, produce such an increase in traffic that cars lined up for miles at the bridge entrance and a crossing took an hour instead of a few minutes? In that event, the SRMC of bridge crossings, at those times, is not zero. It can be envisaged in terms of congestion: the cost of every bridge crossing at the peak hour is the cost of the delays it imposes on all other crossers. Or it can be defined in terms of opportunity cost: if A uses the bridge at that time, he is taking up

---

[1] Jules Dupuit, "On The Measurement of the Utility of Public Works," *Annales des Ponts et Chaussées*, 2nd series, VIII (1844), and reprinted in *International Economic Papers*, No. 2 (New York: Macmillan, 1952), 83–110; Harold Hotelling, "The General Welfare in Relation to Problems of Taxation and of Railway and Utility Rates," *Econometrica* (July 1938), VI: 242–269.

space that someone else could use; therefore, the cost of serving him is the value of that space or capacity to others who would use it if he did not.[2]

The Shift to Long-Run Marginal Costs

Suppose now that for any one or more of the following reasons, we decide that it is either infeasible or undesirable to base tolls on SRMC

1. It would mean an unacceptable fluctuation in rates over time, depending on the changing relation of demand to capacity;
2. It would be too difficult, annoying, or expensive to compute the changing marginal congestion or opportunity costs just described and to base price on them;
3. Pricing on this basis might not cover ATC over the life of the bridge, and therefore might require public subsidy.[3]

Suppose, therefore, we decided to base tolls on long-run marginal costs. Then we would have to recognize that satisfying additional demand at times of congestion may sooner or later call for construction of additional capacity. In these circumstances, LRMC includes capital or capacity costs: and efficiency (of a kind of "second-best," however[4]) requires that each potential bridge-crosser be confronted with the price that reflects those marginal opportunity costs of serving him.

But notice that a shift from SRMC to LRMC does *not* mean that prices should be set on the basis of current variable costs plus a gross return (including depreciation) on past investment, however valued. Marginal costs look to the future, not to the past: it is only future costs for which additional production can be causally responsible; it is only future costs that can be saved if that production is not undertaken. If capital costs are to be included in price, the capital costs in question are those that will have to be covered over time in the future if service is to continue to be rendered. These would be the depreciation and return (including taxes) of the future invest-ments that will have to be made. These incremental capital costs per unit of output will be the same as average capital costs of *existing* plant only in a completely static world and under conditions of long-run constant cost. As for the former and by far the more important qualification, in a dynamic economy, with changing technology as well as changing factor prices, there is every reason to believe that future capital costs per unit of output will not be the same as the capital costs historically incurred in installing present capacity.

Here, then, we encounter a major discrepancy between the economist's

[2] See our discussion for the separability of joint costs on this basis, pp. 79–83, above. For an interesting example in the case of communications satellites, see Johnson, in Shepherd and Gies, *Utility Regulation*, 119, note 5 and 120. And for a strong demonstration of the inefficiencies caused by our failure to impose charges for the use of the radio spectrum reflecting these opportunity costs—measured by the value of any particular allotted channel to the next-excluded potential user—see Harvey J. Levin, "The Radio Spectrum Resource," *Jour. Law & Econ.* (October 1968), XI: 433–501.
[3] On the first two problems see pp. 83–86 and

103–109; the third is the subject of Chapter 5.
[4] "First-best" rates would equal LRMC only by chance at some instant of time: at certain times (when capacity is ample—for example, right after the new or additional bridge has been built) they would be far below, then (as demand grew) they would rise gradually to and above it, as congestion increased, to whatever point necessary to cover congestion costs and ration the limited capacity, until construction of yet more facilities was justified. LRMC would instead represent an average over time of estimated total additional costs. (See pp. 107–108.)

prescription for optimal pricing and the traditional and still generally followed approach of public utility regulation. The latter, preoccupied with assuring a reasonable gross return on the existing investment, cannot possibly, except by accident, be basing its permitted rates on marginal costs, long-run or short-run.[5] The one conceptual merit—in contrast with its crippling administrative infeasibility—of the use of the reproduction cost instead of the original cost rate base was that it sought to bring the computation of capital costs closer to current, and away from historic costs. But, as we shall see later in this chapter, its manner of doing so was defective.

Does the shift to LRMC mean that all users of the bridge should pay a price that includes capacity costs? No. The off-peak users impose no such costs on society, *provided* their demand is sufficiently slight and inelastic that even at a zero toll no congestion occurs at the time they cross over. The incremental costs of serving them—in the long-run, not just the short—are still zero, and may remain so indefinitely. This is the case even if the off-peak demand grows over time and continues to be satisfied without congestion only because the bridge's capacity is being expanded. The necessity for expansion is imposed by the customers at the peak hours. It remains true that if one or all of the off-peak users ceased to cross the bridge, briefly or permanently, society would be saved no costs whatever.

Notice how the intensity and elasticity of demand help determine the level of marginal costs. For those hours of the day at which demand is insufficiently strong or responsive to a toll covering only operating expenses, long-run marginal costs include only those operating expenses; for those times of day at which demand is strong or so responsive to a lower toll as to cause congestion, LRMC necessarily includes capital costs as well.[6]

Peak Responsibility

The economic principle here is absolutely clear: if the same type of capacity serves all users, capacity costs *as such* should be levied only on utilization at the peak. Every purchase at that time makes its proportionate contribution in the long-run to the incurrence of those capacity costs and should therefore have that responsibility reflected in its price. No part of those costs as such should be levied on off-peak users.

The principle is clear, but it is more complicated than might appear at first reading. Notice, first, the qualification: "if the same type of capacity serves all users." In fact it does not always; in consequence, as we shall see, off-peak users may properly be charged explicitly for some capacity costs. Second, the principle applies to the explicit charging of capacity costs, "as such." Off-peak users, properly paying *short-run* marginal costs, will be making a contribution to the covering of capital costs also, if and when SRMC exceeds average variable costs. Third, the principle is framed on the assumption that all rates will be set at marginal cost (including marginal capacity costs). Under conditions of decreasing costs, uniform marginal-cost

---

[5] See, for example, Troxel, *Economics of Public Utilities*, 305–306, and in Shepherd and Gies, *op. cit.*, 150:

"Like other state commissions, the Michigan Commission relies mainly on legal and accounting ways of thought. In a general-rate case, for instance, attention is focused primarily on past revenues, past costs, and the value of an existing plant."

[6] This should not be surprising. Except when marginal costs are constant, it has to be the intersection of the demand and the cost functions that determines the equilibrium level of MC.

pricing will not cover total costs. Lacking a government subsidy to make up the difference, privately owned utilities have to charge more than MC on some of their business. In these "second-best" circumstances, some (of the difference between average and marginal) capacity costs might better be recovered from off-peak than from peak users. We will illustrate all these facets of the principle presently though reserving systematic consideration of the decreasing costs situation for Chapter 5.

First, to establish the basic principle, it is wisest to simplify. Consider only a uniform type of capacity, serving both peak and off-peak users; assume that marginal costs, both short- and long-run, are constant, so that SRMC cannot ever exceed AVC and there can be no difference between marginal and average capacity cost; and assume, finally, that the peak is fixed—that is, that demand at one fixed time or period always presses hard on capacity (after making allowance for reserve capacity held in standby for emergency)[7] and at "the" other period never does so even if the former bears all and the latter none of the capacity costs.

The problem of apportioning capacity costs between these two classes of customers is, precisely, the problem of costing joint products—the solution for which we have already described, using the example of cotton fiber and cottonseed oil. In the present instance, the same production capacity is available to provide two separate services, in fixed proportions: every kilowatt of electricity capacity, every cubic inch of natural gas pipeline space, every telephone circuit available for service in January is available also in July. As we have already seen, the respective supply prices of the joint services (as far as the joint portion of the production process—in this case, the provision of capacity—is concerned) depend on the relative elasticities and intensities of the two demands. The competitive solution requires, first, that the combined prices of the two services add up to no more than the marginal cost of producing the two together, and, second, that the price of each be set at a level at which the quantities demanded and the quantities supplied will be equated.

The case of the fixed and unchanging peak is the case illustrated in our Figure 2. The peak demand there is for cotton; the demand for cottonseed oil is irrevocably "off-peak" and must bear none of the capacity costs. Any attempt to shift capacity costs to the off-peak demands, by raising prices for that service above its own separate, incremental cost (MC_{cso}), will cause available production capacity at that time (cottonseeds) to be wasted, and would cut off purchasers willing to pay the additional cost of serving them. Any reduction of the peak (cotton) price below the full joint cost, P_c, would stimulate additional purchases at the peak, requiring additions to capacity that would not be made if buyers had to pay the full opportunity costs of the additional resources required to supply them. Similar to the cotton seeds in Figure 2, the capacity available off-peak is a free good and should be priced that way: it has a zero marginal cost at the point of intersection of competitive supply and demand.

---

[7] Actually a utility has some discretion about the times and seasons when it will close down various units of capacity for repair and maintenance, and will try to concentrate those shutdowns in off-peak periods. It will have identifiable peak and off-peak uses, then, only if the fluctuations of demand are wider than the fluctuations in plant availability due to maintenance. See Ralph Turvey, "Peak-Load Pricing," *Jour. Pol. Econ.* (January–February 1968), LXXVI: 103.

In the real world, demand peaks do not necessarily stay fixed: their location may shift for two reasons. First, if the elasticities of the separate demands are great enough, imposing all of the capacity costs on the peak customers and none on the off-peak may give rise to excess capacity at the former time (the previous peak) and congestion or shortages at the latter. And, second, the pattern of demand may change over time. The first phenomenon is static: it exists because the relationship between the demand functions is such that the proportion of total capacity costs imposed on each will determine at which time demand presses on capacity. An example would be the way in which public utility promotion of residential air-conditioning has apparently contributed in some areas to a shift in the peak demand for electricity from winter to summer. The second source of the shift is dynamic: it occurs as a result of changes over time in the respective demand functions. The increased use of electricity for summer air-conditioning has almost certainly reflected, above all else, dynamic factors such as the general rise in incomes, the perfection and reduced prices of air-conditioning equipment and the inclusion of air-conditioned summer comfort in the American standard of living. We confine our attention in this section to the static phenomenon; the second clearly belongs in our discussion, below, of what utility companies should do if long-run marginal costs change over time.

The demand situation in Figure 3 is the one that corresponds to the shifting peak. We reproduce it in Figure 4 with captions relevant to a public utility situation—for example, the demand and supply of natural gas in January and in July[8]—with the added complications of (1) recognizing that each of these services will have its own, separate set of variable costs (AVC), (2) introducing (in a dashed line, $SRMC_b$) an alternative short-term marginal cost, embodying the assumption of short-run increasing costs (for simplicity, we do so for a plant designed to produce OB units at lowest possible cost), (3) adding a line (AQ) that enables us to show how the competitive norm would apply in a situation of long-run disequilibrium, and (4) introducing a third, much weaker demand—for April.[9] Let us begin with the assumption that the variable costs are constant—that is, that the $SRMC_b$ does not apply. In this event we can ignore the April customers: their demand is unchangeably off-peak; they should pay MC_1, consume OM, and contribute nothing to the joint costs.

Suppose, initially, that capacity is OA. Clearly, it would be wrong at this point to levy all the capacity costs on the January customers: at such a price (LRMC separate), which includes the total joint capacity costs plus the

---

[8] In this event the x-axis would represent cubic feet, the y-axis cents per cubic foot; MC and $LRMC$ would be the marginal costs of supplying various quantities of cubic feet *per month*. The assumption here is that those costs would not differ from one month to another; it is not a necessary assumption but it simplifies the presentation. And it is assumed that only January and July are potential peaks, depending on the allocation of the joint capacity costs between them.

[9] The figure and exposition are based on Hirschleifer, *op. cit.*, *Q. Jour. Econ.* (August 1958), LXXII: 452, slightly reformulating those of

Peter O. Steiner, "Peak Loads and Efficient Pricing," *Q. Jour. Econ.* (November 1957), LXXI: 588. For a slightly different presentation of these same solutions see Ronald L. Meek, "An Application of Marginal Cost Pricing: The 'Green Tariff' in Theory and Practice," Part I, *Jour. Ind. Econ.* (July 1963), XI: 224–230 and the famous article by Marcel Boiteux, *op. cit.*, in Nelson, *Marginal Cost Pricing in Practice*. For an elegant, more generalized statement of the solution, see Oliver E. Williamson, "Peak-Load Pricing and Optimal Capacity under Indivisibility Constraints," *Amer. Econ. Rev.* (September 1966), LVI: 810–827.

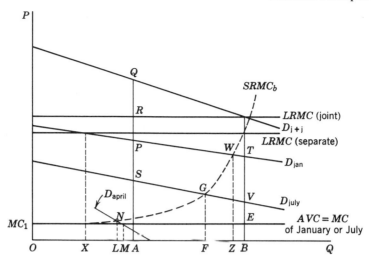

LRMC (joint) includes long-run capacity costs plus two long-run variable costs, one for January, one for July. Both are assumed constant. This is the amount that the sum of January and July prices must cover, in long-run equilibrium.

LRMC (separate) includes long-run capacity cost plus one long-term variable cost, representing the long-run costs of serving January or July.

AVC: the long-run variable costs of serving January or April or July.

SRMC_b: an alternative short-run marginal cost of producing from a plant of OB capacity.

Figure 4. Allocation of capacity costs, shifting peak.

variable costs of serving the January customers, they would demand only the quantity OX; XA capacity would remain idle in January. And the July users, being charged only their own separate variable costs (MC_1), would experience shortages. For the limited available supplies to be effectively rationed, while fullest economic use is made of capacity, the July users would have to be charged AS and the January customers AP. At such prices, the supplier would be earning excess profits: a combined price of AQ for one unit of sales in each month (remember that the demand curve D_{j+j} represents a summation of D_{july} and $D_{january}$)[10] compared with a combined unit cost of AR. The long-run competitive solution would be to increase capacity to OB, which is at the juncture of the combined demands and the joint long-run marginal costs of supplying both (capacity costs plus one set of long-run average variable

---

[10] The addition of the two demands (and the entire discussion in the text) assumes that they are independent of one another. This was a reasonable assumption for cotton fiber and cottonseed oil. But as between peak and off-peak power, gas or telephone service, there is likely to be some cross-elasticity of demand: a reduction in the rate on night long-distance telephone calls, for example, is likely to induce some users to shift their telephoning from day to night. To this extent, adding together the separate demand curves as though they were independent will exaggerate the elasticity of the joint demand curve. (In Figure 4, for example, $D_{january}$ shows how the quantities of power purchased in

January would vary if the January price *alone* were changed and correspondingly for D_{july}. But if their prices were reduced simultaneously, from AP to BT and AS to BV, respectively, and if the elasticity of each was in part a reflection of cross-elasticity, the combined quantities purchased would not increase by the full AB indicated.) Rate cuts on either of the two services would take some business away from the other, and would therefore not increase total sales by the amount indicated by the separate curves. (An attempt to sell the additional quantities AB both in January and July would thus depress the respective prices below BT and BV.)

In practice, public utility companies will, of

costs for each), charging the January users BT, the July users BV. At this point, both efficiency requirements are met: the combined prices do not exceed the marginal cost of producing the two services, and the price of each is set at a level that clears the market. There is no other set of prices at which these equilibrium conditions would be satisfied.

The introduction of the shifting peak does not alter the fundamental principle of peak-responsibility. The point is, simply, the January and July users both represent the peak, and they must therefore share the costs. On what basis? On the basis of the respective intensities and elasticities of the two demands.[11] It remains true that the long-run marginal cost of supplying purchasers in, for example, April and October includes no capacity costs as such; nor, ideally, should their prices.

Whether confronting a fixed or a shifting peak, the principle of peak responsibility is a relatively simple one in the presence of simplifying assumptions. One of these assumptions is that variable costs are constant to

---

course, have to take into account the impact of changes in some of their rates on revenues from other parts of their business in planning both their price structures and their decisions with respect to capacity. But this consideration in no way vitiates the conclusions we have reached with respect to socially optimal pricing; it merely suggests that in our Figure 4, the presence of cross-elasticities of demand will produce a long-run equilibrium capacity of something less than OB and rates for January and July sales somewhat higher than BT and BV, respectively.

[11] Steiner concluded for this reason that his solution to the problem of apportioning capacity costs in the case of the shifting peak involved price discrimination: the separate marginal costs of serving the January and the July customers are the same (AVC in Figure 4), yet the prices charged them differ. Hirschleifer contends, correctly I believe, that the solution is not discriminatory. His exposition follows two alternative lines.

1. The fact that the correct solution would involve the nondiscriminatory result of carrying on production in each market to the point where short-run marginal cost equaled price is obscured, in Figure 4, by the convenient, simplifying assumption of constant short-run marginal costs up to the limit of physical capacity. If the more conventional costs were assumed, increasing before the limit of producing capacity is reached (as in $SRMC_b$), it would be clear, as we point out in the text immediately following, that the efficient solution would involve producing in each market up to the point (F and Z respectively) where that short-run marginal cost was equated with demand price.

2. But even if the short-run marginal cost were indeed horizontal, then discontinuous, as at EVT, in Figure 4, so that in both January and July production was carried on to the physical limit of capacity, the efficient prices would still be equated with the respective marginal opportunity costs. As we have already pointed out in discussing the separate costing of joint products (pp. 82–83), the economic cost of supplying an additional unit to any single customer in each of the two markets is measured by what the next customer, the first one not served, would have been willing to pay for that service: and, in Figure 4, that would be (infinitesimally less than) BV and BT in the respective markets. Therefore, according to this conception of cost as well, the correct solution involves equating price in each market to $SRMC$, and hence no discrimination.

This second line of argument, as Steiner points out, does seem to obscure the difference between the demand function and the cost function, which are supposedly equated at the margin in each market if there is to be no discrimination: the "marginal opportunity *cost*" is defined as equal to the market price at *whatever* level the latter happens to be set. It might seem therefore to define away the possibility of discrimination. "Reply," *Q. Jour. Econ.* (August 1958), LXXII: 467–468. But in fact it does not. The critical consideration, Hirschleifer responds, is that when markets are artificially separated, in the familiar price discrimination model, the marginal opportunity costs in the two markets are really the same—namely the price that the next-unsatisfied customer *in the higher price market* would be willing to pay: so, since their MC's are the same and their prices differ, genuine discrimination is practiced in that case. In the January–July model, instead, the joint products are not the same; the marginal cost of supplying the July customer is the lost opportunity of supplying the next-unsatisfied purchaser in *July*, not in

the physical limit of capacity, as in the horizontal *AVC* of Figure 4.[12] But in point of fact the production of public utility services is at times subject to short-run increasing costs. This is particularly clear of the generation of electricity. At any given time, generating plant will vary widely in age, type, location, and efficiency—hence in the level and slope of its *SRMC*. The common—and entirely rational—practice of electric companies, therefore, is to hold the less efficient generating units in reserve and phase them into operation from one moment to the next, according to the level of demand, in ascending order of their marginal costs.[13]

In this event some such alternative as *SRMC_b* of Figure 4 becomes the relevant marginal cost function. How does its introduction alter the solution? Now, ideally, production in July should not exceed *OF*, and July users should pay not *BV* but *FG*.[14] Clearly the July users, though charged only the *SRMC* of serving them, will end up paying a much larger contribution to joint costs than before in each MCF of gas they buy. Even more interesting, note what happens to the April customers. They ought now to be charged *LN*. But this price exceeds the average variable costs. Therefore, although they pay only *SRMC*, consume far less gas than the January and July customers, and their purchases are certainly off-peak, they make some contribution (over and above *AVC*) to joint capacity costs—and correctly so.[15]

January; and correspondingly for the January customer. So *their* marginal opportunity costs do differ, and, if so, their prices *should*; and, if they do, there need be no price discrimination. *Ibid.*, 459. The classic discussion of this very issue was that of Frank W. Taussig and A. C. Pigou, on the subject of "Railway Rates and Joint Costs", *Q. Jour. Econ.* (February, May, and August 1913), XXVII: 378–384, 535–538, and 687–694. A central issue in their debate was whether railway services to different customers are in fact homogeneous, in which event it would be proper to characterize rate differences as discriminatory. Their underlying difference of opinion was whether the costs of serving different railroad customers may properly be regarded as joint, as we have used the term (in which event the rate differences, they agreed, would not be discriminatory), or common.

However, in practice, for reasons we have already suggested, it has usually been infeasible for utility companies to differentiate and to vary their rates with the ever-shifting balances of capacity and demand at various times of day, year, and planning period in such a way as to equate price at each moment to short-run marginal opportunity costs. Therefore, they typically—in wholesale and large industrial sales—charge separately for variable and for capacity costs (as in the two-part tariff, discussed below), and do engage in considerable price discrimination in distributing the latter burden among various classes of customers on the basis of their respective elasticities of demand (see pp. 95–98, on the 2-part tariff, and Chapter 5).

[12] Another simplifying assumption that we make in this chapter is that LRMC are constant. We turn to the decreasing cost situation in Chapter 5. For the solution to the problem of apportioning capacity costs in the case of the shifting peak under conditions of decreasing costs, a case that unequivocally requires price discrimination if revenues are to cover total costs, see Johnson, in Shepherd and Gies, *op. cit.*, 131–132.

[13] For a more precise statement see the discussion of integration and power pooling, at note 51, Chapter 2, Volume 2. Also Meek, *op. cit.*, Part II, *Jour. Ind. Econ.* (November 1963), XII: 46–47; Bonbright, *Principles of Public Utility Rates*, 320–322.

[14] January users would now pay *ZW*, instead of *BT*, and consume correspondingly less. We make no effort here to relate the case of rising SRMC to determining the correct size of plant or ascertaining at what level of capacity total revenues collected at the new January and July prices (equated to the *SRMC* of that plant) would cover total costs. See the sources cited in note 9. It might appear that *OB* was still the proper size, since the combined demand prices just suffice to cover total *LRMC* at that point. But the *LRMC* curves represent the costs *per unit* of output, on the assumption that whatever plants are built are operated to capacity in January and July. If in fact, with rising *SRMC*, only *OF* and *OZ* are now consumed, the *LRMC* per unit for a plant of *OB* capacity will be higher than those shown on the diagram.

[15] See, for example, Meek, *op. cit.*, Part II, *Jour. Ind. Econ.* (November 1963), XII: 47–48.

Public utility companies do employ peak-responsibility pricing to some degree. The telephone companies charge lower rates for night than for daytime long-distance calls; electric companies frequently have low night rates for hot-water heating; both they and natural gas companies—local distributors and interstate pipelines alike—offer at lower rates service that the customer will agree may be interrupted if capacity is being taxed by other users and try to promote off-peak sales in numerous ways;[16] railroads charge lower rates for return-hauls of freight, when the greater flow is in the opposite direction; airlines offer special discount fares—family plans, youth fares, and so forth—for travel on unfilled planes or in slack seasons or days of the week.[17]

The two-part tariff, generally credited to John Hopkinson, an English engineer, and almost universally used by electric and gas utilities for large-volume sales at wholesale and to industrial users, represents an effort to apply just such a principle. The first part—the energy, commodity or "running" charge—embodies the variable costs, properly charged to all customers, and is levied on a per unit of consumption basis (per kwh or per MCF of gas). The second part—the demand or capacity charge—is a charge for the utility's readiness to serve, on demand. This readiness to serve is made possible by the installation of *capacity*: the demand charge, therefore, distributes the costs of providing the capacity—the fixed, capital costs—on the basis of the respective causal responsibilities of various buyers for them. And the proper measure of that responsibility is the proportionate share of each customer in the total demand placed on the system at its peak. (Sometimes the tariff will have three instead of two parts—the third, "customer" charge reflecting the costs of services such as meter-reading and billing that vary on a per customer basis instead of with different amounts purchased.)[18]

Unfortunately, the principle has usually been badly applied, in several important ways. First, if the demand charge were correctly to reflect peak responsibility it would impose on each customer a share of capacity costs equivalent to his share of total purchases at the time coinciding with the

[16] A particularly illuminating example is provided by the case of a combination company—that is, one distributing both electricity and gas—the two major portions of whose business had noncoincident peaks. The Chairman of the Board of Directors of the Public Service Electric and Gas Co. reported to his stockholders:

"In our sales promotion programs we are stressing the selling of 'off-peak loads', such as electric heating, to increase the winter use of electricity, thus helping to offset the summer air-conditioning peak; and gas air-conditioning and interruptible gas service to induce greater use of gas in the off-peak summer period." Annual Meeting of Stockholders, April 18, 1966.

Note that the company was competing with itself—pushing the off-peak sales of each product in competition with the other in periods of the latter's peak demand.

Our discussion of peak-responsibility has run entirely in terms of pricing policies. As the

Public Service example suggests, the same considerations would justify public utility companies using various other sales promotional devices, such as intensive advertising or the sale of the relevant appliances at cost, or less, to increase off-peak sales. On the general question of the proper treatment of selective promotional expenditures, see pp. 149 and 164, note 10.

[17] For a decision sustaining reduced railroad rates for coal shipped during the slack season, provided those rates were available nondiscriminatorily to all shippers, see *ICC v. Louisville & N.R. Co.*, 73 F. 409 (1896) and another disallowing a similar seasonal reduction by a motor carrier on household goods because it did not meet the condition of nondiscrimination, ICC, *Reduced Seasonal Household Goods Rates*, Report and Order, 332 ICC 512 (1968).

[18] More often the customer costs will be recovered by specifying a minimum bill, or in sufficiently high per unit charges for the first block of electricity or gas purchased.

system's peak (a "coincident peak" demand charge). Instead, the typical two-part tariff bases that rate on each customer's *own* peak consumption over some measured time period, regardless of whether *his* peak coincides with that of the system (hence the designation "noncoincident" demand charge). That is, the peak (for example, half-hour) consumption of all customers, regardless of the time of day or year in which each falls, is added up, and each then is charged a share of total system capital costs equivalent to the percentage share that his peak consumption constitutes of that total. The noncoincident demand method does have some virtue: it encourages customers to level out their consumption over time, in order to minimize their peak taking, hence their share of capacity costs. This, in turn, tends to improve the system's load factor—the ratio of average sales over the year to capacity—that is, the degree of capacity utilization. But it is basically illogical. It is each user's proportion of consumption at the *system's* peak that measures the share of capacity costs for which each is causally responsible;[19] it is consumption at *that* time that determines how much capacity the utility must have available. The system's load factor might well be improved by inducing individual customers to cut down their consumption to a deep trough at the *system* peak and enormously increase *their* peak utilization at the system's off-peak time: yet the noncoincident demand system would discourage them from doing so.[20]

Second, the charges have typically been based on average instead of marginal costs. Therefore, the energy charge has generally ignored the fact that electricity is produced under conditions of short-run increasing cost; and the demand charge has tended to embody the opposite error.

Third, the two-part tariff has applied only to bulk sales. Retail sales of gas and electricity to households typically contain no such differentials based on time of consumption (with specific exceptions such as special night rates for water-heating). Instead, they usually carry block rates, with diminishing charges for larger blocks of consumption: for instance, 6¢ for the first 30 kwh, 4¢ for the next 50, 3¢ for the next 100, 2¢ for the next 570 and 1½¢ for anything above 750 kwh—regardless of the time of taking.[21] Since household utilization typically has a marked peak that coincides roughly with that of the system (whether because of air-conditioning on hot summer days, or for home heating, lighting, and cooking in the early evenings of short and cold winter days), the use of diminishing block rates has a strong perverse tendency to underprice marginal sales at the peak.[22] Against this distortion, however, one must weigh the tendency of such declining block rates correctly to reflect the declining unit costs of electricity and gas distribution with increased intensity of use.

---

[19] This entire discussion continues under the assumption that capacity costs are constant, so that *average* capacity costs (which is what are measured by both coincident and noncoincident demand methods) are the same as marginal capacity costs. If instead the system is subject to decreasing costs (see Chapter 5), each user will be *marginally* responsible for less than his percentage of coincident peak demands multiplied by total capacity costs, because marginal cost is less than average.

[20] See W. Arthur Lewis, *op. cit.*, 50–53; Ralph

K. Davidson, *Price Discrimination in Selling Gas and Electricity* (Baltimore: Johns Hopkins Press, 1955), 84–88, 133–134, 192–193.

[21] This schedule is taken from C. F. Phillips, *op. cit.*, 352, who identifies the preponderant uses of the successive blocks as lighting; refrigeration, washer, and dryer; cooking; water-heating and air-conditioning; and electric house heating, respectively.

[22] See Shepherd, "Marginal-Cost Pricing in American Utilities," *South. Econ. Jour.* (July 1966), XXXIII: 62.

In recent years, both England and France have taken important steps toward remedying some of these deficiencies of the Hopkinson tariff. The famous French "Tarif Vert," put into effect in 1956 (only for bulk and industrial sales), instituted rates varying with the time of day and season of the year in order to base demand charges on the system peak. The change recognized that energy charges too should vary with the level of demand because variable costs are not constant.[23] The British Central Electricity Generating Board (CEGB) went over in 1962–63 to the coincident peak for determining demand charges on its (wholesale) sales to the regional Area Boards and introduced a differential day-night "running" (that is, energy) charge.[24] In 1967–68, explicitly recognizing that the latter charges were erroneously based on average (day and night) instead of marginal operating costs, it introduced differential time-of-day, -week and -year energy charges reflecting the increasing SRMC function.[25]

The 1967–68 reforms reacted to another, even more interesting problem already alluded to briefly above: how should the principle of peak responsibility be applied if the same capacity does not serve all users? If capacity is not interchangeable, so that the same type of plant or equipment does not necessarily serve both peak and off-peak users, it is no longer true that peak consumption alone should bear all capacity costs. In electricity generation, it is economical for short periods of time to use gas turbine generating units, which have low capital costs but high operating costs. These are inefficient for continuous utilization, but are less costly than installing regular capacity for just the extreme peak demands.[26] In consequence, when the CEGB tried to incorporate the entire capacity costs in the demand charges, at about £10 a year per kw, it found that some of its Area Board customers began to install their own gas turbines, at a cost of about £4 per kw, and therefore cut down their peak purchases. The Board correctly recognized that the true incremental or avoidable costs of supplying capacity that would be used for peaks of comparatively short duration (it estimated this type of capacity would be economic if operated no longer than 250 hours of the year) were not £10 but £4 per kw, and that the £11 now estimated to be the capital costs per kw of basic capacity, such as would be economic for longer periods of operation (because of its far lower variable costs) should therefore be borne by

---

[23] The demand charge to industrial customers in the Paris region provides discounts ranging from 0% in winter peak hours to 98% in summer "empty" hours. Eli W. Clemens, "Marginal Cost Pricing: A Comparison of French and American Industrial Power Rates," *Land Econ.* (November 1964), XL: 391. See also Meek, *op. cit.*, Part II, *Jour. Ind. Econ.* (November 1963), XII: 45–63, and the articles by Marcel Boiteux and Pierre Massé in J. R. Nelson, *Marginal Cost Pricing in Practice*, 134–156.
[24] R. L. Meek, "The Bulk Supply for Electricity," *Oxford Econ. Papers* (July 1963), n.s. XV: 107–123.
[25] The Board settled for three running or energy rates:

". . . one for *peak units*—now defined as those used between 8 and 12 A.M. and for 4:30 and

6:30 P.M. from Mondays to Fridays in December and January, except for Christmas and Boxing Days . . .;
". . . a second rate for *day units* used between 7:30 A.M. and 11 P.M. daily, but outside the peak . . .;
". . . a third rate for *night units* used between 11 P.M. and 7.30 A.M. . . ." "Puncturing the Power Peak," *The Economist*, May 14, 1966, 734.

The consequence of moving to increasing marginal charges for operating costs was to cause the operating charges to make some contribution to capacity costs as in our model, p. 94, above; the French Green Tariff has the same effect.
[26] For a general, diagrammatic statement of the conditions for such a choice, see M. A. Crew, "Peak Load Pricing and Optimal Capacity: Comment," *Amer. Econ. Rev.* (March 1968), LVIII: 168–170.

consumption during the longer-period, "winter plateau" of demand.[27] Similar qualifications of simple-minded peak responsibility pricing would clearly be appropriate to the extent storage capacity instead of basic pipeline capacity served the peak needs of natural gas consumers.[28]

Although most public utility executives and regulators recognize that peak responsibility pricing has some validity, probably most would also vigorously resist its wholehearted acceptance. William G. Shepherd's survey disclosed that the majority of American electric utilities practice little or no explicit marginal cost pricing, and among those that do, the main emphasis is on raising off-peak sales, by charging them something less than average capacity costs, instead of purposefully imposing all the capacity charges on the peak users.[29] He found, moreover, that publicly-owned companies, if anything, follow marginalist and peak responsibility principles even less than private;[30] and that electric utilities in states with "tough" regulatory commissions, such as New York and California, similarly incorporate little marginalism in their rate structures.

An outstanding illustration of the resistance of strong regulatory commissions is provided by the Federal Power Commission's formula for natural gas pipeline rate-making specified in its famous *Atlantic Seaboard* decision of 1952.[31] The distinctive feature of the Atlantic Seaboard formula is that it requires that capacity costs be distributed 50–50 between the demand and commodity charges instead of incorporated exclusively in the former. Since the demand costs are distributed among customers in proportion to their shares in the volume of sales at the system's (three-day) peak, while the commodity costs are borne in proportion to their annual volume of purchases, the consequence of the 50–50 formula is to shift a large proportion[32] of capacity costs to off-peak users. This produces an uneconomic encouragement to sales at the peak (whose price falls short of the true marginal costs of peak

---

[27] Accordingly, it introduced two demand rates: an £11 "basic capacity charge" for consumption during the winter plateau, when it estimated that demand would be on the average no more than 90% of the maximum system demand, and a "peaking capacity charge" of £4 for the period, estimated not to exceed 250 hours a year, when demand would exceed the 90% plateau. See R. L. Meek, "The New Bulk Supply Tariff for Electricity," *Econ. Jour.* (March 1968), LXXVIII: 48–53 and *passim;* "Puncturing the Power Peak," *The Economist,* May 14, 1966, 734.

This complicating factor in peak responsibility pricing was pointed out by Melvin G. de Chazeau, "Reply," *Q. Jour. Econ.* (February 1938), LII: 357 and recognized—along with most other problems—by Bonbright, *op. cit.,* 354 note.

[28] For an analysis of the ways in which the introduction of gas storage requires a modification of the simple charging of all capacity costs to peak users, see R. K. Davidson, *op. cit.,* 138–147.

[29] *Op. cit., South Econ. Jour.* (July 1966), XXXIII: 61–65. Effective earlier critics of the failure of

electricity as well as gas distribution companies to employ marginal costing, in particular with respect to the allocation of capacity costs, were I. M. D. Little, *The Price of Fuel* (Oxford: Clarendon Press, 1953), 54–76 and R. K. Davidson, *op. cit.,* especially 81–97, 111–147.

[30] See also Richard L. Wallace, "Cost and Revenue Associated with Increased Sales of TVA Power," *South. Econ. Jour.* (April 1967), XXIII: 526–534; and, for an Australian example, H. M. Kolsen, "The Economics of Electricity Pricing in N. S. W.," *Economic Record* (December 1966), XLII: 564–565.

[31] *In the Matters of Atlantic Seaboard Corporation and Virginia Gas Transmission Corporation,* Opinion No. 225, 11 FPC 43 (1952).

[32] This is not wholly 50%, because peak users also pay their proportionate share of the commodity charge, which includes half of the capacity costs. But the point is that in deciding to what extent to cut their purchases at the peak relative to off-peak, peak customers are influenced by only the 50% of capacity costs incorporated in the demand charge; the other 50% does not affect that calculation because they pay it equally whenever they take the gas.

service[33]) and an uneconomic discouragement of off-peak.[34] (In fairness, it should be pointed out that the FPC has permitted departures from this strict formula when it appeared that the pipelines would suffer large losses of interruptible, off-peak sales at the inflated commodity charges it produced—permitting them instead to "tilt" the rate schedule downward on the commodity side of the balance.[35] Among other alleged harmful consequences of *Atlantic Seaboard* has been a tendency to discourage distribution companies from installing storage capacity: demand and commodity charges more fully reflecting the true respective marginal costs of peak and off-peak purchases would have increased their incentive to "shave" their purchases at the former

---

[33] This is so, as we have already pointed out, only to the extent that the pipeline function is subject to constant costs. Since pipelines do have some tendencies to long-run decreasing costs (see the section on "Natural Gas Transmission, Economies of Scale," Chapter 4, Volume 2), so that LRMC may be lower than ATC, the arbitrary 50–50 allocation tends to produce a less harmful result, that is, less of an understatement of the true *marginal* costs of peak service, than would otherwise be the case. Laurence C. Rosenberg concludes, however, that some considerable distortion remains. See his *Natural Gas Pipeline Rate-Making Problems*, unpublished Ph.D. dissertation, Cornell University, June 1963, 176–184 and *passim*. See also Stanislaw H. Wellisz, "Regulation of Natural Gas Pipeline Companies: An Economic Analysis," *Jour. Pol. Econ.* (February 1963), LXXI: 33, who contends that the constant cost assumption is not unreasonable.

It should be reemphasized, too, that the fact of gas storage may justify imposition of some capacity costs on off-peak customers—to the extent that, by using pipeline space that could otherwise be used to pump gas into storage, they create a need for more capacity than would otherwise be required. (See p. 98.)

[34] The formula discourages off-peak sales not only by the pipeline companies but also by their distribution company-customers, since *their* variable costs are inescapably inflated - by the 50% allotment of fixed costs to the commodity charge. Wellisz demonstrates that the pipeline companies would in any event have an incentive to exploit their off-peak customers, charging them a monopoly price and using the supernormal profits thereby earned to subsidize peak sales, in this way "justifying" an uneconomic expansion of capacity. See *op. cit.*, 35–36. This tendency is discussed at greater length in Chapter 2, Volume 2.

[35] See, for example, C. F. Phillips, *op. cit.*, 624–628 on this and for a description of the Atlantic Seaboard formula; also Garfield and Lovejoy, *Public Utility Economics*, 181–185 and Wellicz, *op. cit.*, 30–43. The difference between the two rates is large: in 1968 the demand

charges of one pipeline company on one schedule ranged between $2.79 and $4.28 per MCF, while its commodity charges ran from 22.1¢ to 26.2¢.

A later decision, interestingly enough involving the Atlantic Seaboard Company itself, demonstrates how far the "tilting" process has gone, under the pressures of competitive necessity. The case involved a protest by the Lynchburg Gas Company against special "partial requirements" rates that the FPC had permitted Atlantic Seaboard and other subsidiaries of the Columbia Gas Company to institute—higher, penalty rates imposed on those customers that purchased their supplies in part from suppliers other than the Columbia companies. In justification of these rates, the Commission had accepted the pipeline companies' justification that any losses of sales that they suffered by virtue of such diversions made it necessary for them to raise the rates that they charged their more loyal, full requirements customers. The Circuit Court of Appeals sent the case back to the Federal Power Commission, holding that these special rates had been inadequately supported in the record. See *Lynchburg Gas Co. v. FPC*, 336 F. 2d. 942 (1964). Upon rehearing, the FPC Presiding Examiner found that the Columbia System companies had so drastically departed from the original Atlantic Seaboard formula as to undermine their previous justification of the partial requirements rates. As the Circuit Court of Appeals explained in 1968, after the case had returned to it for a decision, one reason for the alleged necessity of protecting the full requirements customers from any loss of sales by their suppliers was that "not all of Columbia's fixed costs are recovered by the demand charges." At the time of the original *Lynchburg* decision, roughly half of Seaboard's fixed costs were recovered by the commodity rate. Thereafter, the Columbia companies had departed drastically from the original formula, in order to be better able to compete for off-peak business, with the result that only 6% of the company's fixed costs were now being recovered in the commodity rate. *Atlantic Seaboard Corporation et al. v. Federal Power Commission et al.*, 404 F. 2d. 1268, at 1270–1271 (1968).

by installing storage, which they could fill by low-cost purchases off-peak and draw on at the peak.[36]

We present two last examples of the pervasive uneconomic departure from peak responsibility pricing. First, commutation books and other such devices that give commuters quantity discounts on passenger trains and toll bridges have the consequence that occasional travelers, who usually travel off-peak, pay a higher rate than commuters, who concentrate their traveling in the rush hours.[37] Second, airplane landing fees do not reflect the enormous variations in airport congestion, from one time of day, day of the week, or one airport to another. These variations themselves doubtless tend to induce air travelers and airplane companies to rearrange their traveling plans and schedules to avoid peak hours and locations and make fuller use of off-peak time; equivalently varying landing fees could make a further contribution.[38]

There are often very good reasons of expediency and practicality for these widespread departures from economically efficient pricing, to some of which we shall allude below. But objections are sometimes made to the principle itself. Prominent among these are:

1. It is unfair and discriminatory to charge peak-utilization alone with the fixed costs, since the capacity obviously serves all users at all times;[39]
2. The utilities or regulators have a special responsibility to protect the ordinary, unorganized householder, and should try to keep down his rates;

---

[36] See Homer Ross, "How Practical Is The Seaboard Formula?" *Public Utilities Fortnightly* (January 3, 1963), LXXI: 32 and Wellisz, *op. cit.*, 41. For (1) a reminder that the Commission's methods are defective also because the capital charges they allocate are historic instead of future costs, (2) an interesting and persuasive application of the peak responsibility principle to the problem of allocating the demand costs among customers located in different geographic markets, and (3) a clear demonstration that the Commission's methods of doing so fail by a wide margin to reflect customers' respective marginal responsibilities for the capacity of the various segments of the pipeline, see Laurence C. Rosenberg, "Natural-Gas-Pipeline Rate Regulation," *Jour. Pol. Econ.* (April 1967), LXXV: 159–168.

[37] See William Vickrey, "Some Implications of Marginal Cost Pricing for Public Utilities," *Amer. Econ. Rev., Papers and Proceedings* (May 1955), XLV: 619.

[38] See William D. Grampp, "An Economic Remedy for Airport Congestion: the Case For Flexible Pricing," *Business Horizons* (October 1968), XI: 21–30.

[39] As Garfield and Lovejoy state, "The fact that the [Atlantic Seaboard] formula permits no free ride on the line is its greatest strength. . . ." *Op. cit.*, 183. Here is the Commission's justification, in that decision:

"A pipeline would not normally be built to

supply peak service, that is to say, service on the peak days only. We know . . . that pipelines are built to supply service not only on the few peak days but on all days throughout the year. In proving the economic feasibility of the project in certificate proceedings, reliance is placed upon the annual as well as the peak deliveries. Stated another way, the capital outlay for the pipeline facility is made—and justified—not only for service on the peak days but for service throughout the year. Both capacity and annual use are important considerations in the conception of the project and in the issuance of certificates of public convenience and necessity. Both capacity and volume, therefore, are what are known as cost factors or incidences in respect to the capital outlay for a pipeline project. It follows that reasonably accurate results can be achieved only by allocating the fixed expenses flowing from the capital outlay to both operating functions, viz., capacity and volume " *Atlantic Seaboard*, Opinion No. 225, 11 FPC 43, (1952).

A similar, further illuminating example of this argument was offered by the National Association of Railroad and Utilities Commissioners (NARUC) in support of a procedure, adopted by the Federal Communications Commission in 1967, for allocating the interexchange plant of the Bell System between interstate and intrastate service—a necessary procedure for FCC rate regulation since it has jurisdiction only over the former. The issue was whether it was appropriate

3. The utilities should promote the maximum extension of their services, subject only to the condition that aggregate revenues cover aggregate costs—goals that may well conflict with peak responsibility pricing.[40]

Justifications such as these are for the most part not susceptible to scientific refutation, since basically they involve nonscientific value judgments.[41] An economist can only cite the following counterconsiderations:

1. In economic terms, peak-responsibility pricing is not discriminatory between peak and off-peak users. Discrimination consists in price differences not corresponding to cost differences. It is an objective fact that it costs more to supply users at the peak than off-peak, and the proposal is to reflect that cost difference in the respective prices. Every peak user actually *imposes* on society, in the long run, the incremental cost of the capacity on which he draws. There is no such causal connection between off-peak utilization and capacity costs: the capacity would be there whether or not the off-peak user made demands on it. It would be discriminatory to levy any of these costs on the off-peak user.[42]

---

to lump together plant of AT&T's Long Lines Department, which is used exclusively for interstate service, with other facilities used for both inter- and intrastate service, before allocating the total between the two services on the basis of the number of message-minute-miles of each type. NARUC argued for lumping the two on the ground that "The toll network has been designed as an entity and every portion benefits every other portion. . . ." *In the Matter of American Telephone and Telegraph Co.,* Interim Decision and Order, 9 FCC 2d 30, 71 (1967). AT&T argued, correctly, that the costs of any facilities used exclusively by one of the services (in this case the Long Lines plant) should be assigned directly to that service, and only the common plant be allocated between the services. It also pointed out that combining the two discriminated against long-distance messages, since it obscured the fact that the (average) investment cost (per circuit mile) of the Long Lines Department is markedly less than that of the Associated Company plant (*Ibid.,* 96–97). Indeed, since it is the Long Lines Department that has the greater tendency to long-run decreasing costs, the marginal costs diverge even more than the average. Here again, an argument that all users *benefit* from the presence of capacity was used to obscure the markedly different *costs* of the two services, which should have been reflected in their respective rates. NARUC and the Commission were later persuaded to accept the AT&T position. *In the Matter of Prescription of procedures for separating and allocating plant investment etc.,* Docket No. 17975, Report and Order, January 29, 1969, pars. 6–19. For further discussion of these separations procedures, see pp. 152–153, Chapter 5.

[40] This is the implicit assumption of G. J. Ponsonby, when he seems willing to see off-peak

users of city buses charged more than the LRMC of serving them, in order to permit a greater improvement of service at the peak than what that traffic would itself be willing to pay for. "The Problem of the Peak, with Special Reference to Road Passenger Transport," *Econ. Jour.* (March 1958), LXVIII: 78–82, 87. For a suggestion that these goals may also be in the interest of the public utility companies themselves, see note 34.

[41] However, Wellisz does point out that the *Atlantic Seaboard* formula is of dubious efficacy even as a means of achieving the goal of subsidizing household consumption (much of which is at the peak). The householder buys his gas from the distribution company. The latter, he points out, will have an incentive, for the reason just suggested (note 34), to maximize profits on its off-peak sales, because this will enable it to subsidize peak sales. But when its own marginal costs of supplying off-peak gas are inflated by the incorporation of capital costs in the commodity charge, it will be forced in turn to price such sales above the point that would maximize their contribution to the overhead costs of the system as a whole, hence to the subsidization of on-peak sales. *Op. cit.,* 37–38. When seller B buys some of his inputs from producer A at prices in excess of marginal costs, B's own profit-maximizing price will in turn exceed the price that would maximize the profits of A and B together. On the reason for this, see the section "Financial Integration," Chapter 6, Volume 2.

[42] It might be argued that peak-responsibility pricing involves no discrimination, also, because peak and off-peak power are not the same service, in economic terms, any more than are Tuesday and Saturday evening tickets to the same theatrical performance; and price discrimination occurs only when different prices are charged for

2. In this sense, it is inequitable to make off-peak users pay some share of capacity costs, for which they are not themselves causally responsible.[43]

3. Moreover, such a policy would be economically inefficient. To the extent that off-peak demand has any elasticity at all, a charge to these users that incorporates any capacity costs will cause them to give up satisfactions, the true social costs of which they would be perfectly willing to pay. And some productive capacity is left wastefully idle. Conversely, and subject to the same condition, if peak users do not have to pay the full (marginal) costs of being supplied, they will induce society to provide them with a capacity that uses resources that would have given greater satisfaction if directed to other employments.

4. In these circumstances, off-peak users would be subsidizing peak users. Now this may be something that society is willing to do; but such a policy will make sense only if the membership of each group is clearly identified, so that the decision in effect to transfer income from the one to the other is a conscious one. The mere identification of the subsidizing group as consisting of commercial and industrial customers and of the subsidized group as householders, for example, does not in itself demonstrate that the abandonment of economically efficient pricing is justified as a means of promoting a more equal distribution of income. The higher-than-marginal costs imposed on business and industrial customers must ultimately be paid by *their* customers or the customers of their customers: and these, too, are people, who may or may not, on the average, have higher incomes than the direct household customers of the utilities.[44]

---

the same service. As students of the Robinson-Patman Act will recognize, this argument is a treacherous one. What makes the Tuesday and the Saturday evening tickets of "unlike grade and quality," in the terms of that Act, is not just the physical difference in the service, but also the fact that buyers are willing to pay more for the latter than for the former. Since discrimination always requires that some customers be willing to pay more than others, if that difference in willingness to pay is then used in turn to prove that the services are economically different, there never can be any discrimination. However, the fact remains that the two services are in this case objectively separate: the use of capacity to supply gas in July for cooking could not be transferred to January and used instead to cut the costs of home-heating; the two markets are not artificially, but physically and inescapably separate. See note 11.

[43] It might appear that peak users are responsible not for the entire capacity, but only for that portion by which their consumption exceeds off-peak consumption—that is, that efficiency requires that they pay the entire costs only of the "peak" or protuberance of the mountain above the surrounding plateau, not of the entire mountain. The answer is to be found in the case for equating price to *marginal* cost. *Every* peak kilowatt hour consumed is marginal in the sense that capacity costs would be less in its absence.

The purchaser of every kilowatt hour at the peak must therefore be confronted with a price that, by including its share of incremental capacity cost, makes him decide whether it is worthwhile to him to impose on society the cost of constructing his share of the entire mountain. *No* off-peak use is marginal in this sense.

[44] The *Atlantic Seaboard* formula, for example, has the effect of imposing higher-than-marginal cost rates on, among others, electricity generating companies that purchase natural gas on an interruptible basis for their steam generating plants; in effect, therefore, it tends to impose lower-than-economic costs on residential purchasers of natural gas (who buy heavily at the peak) and higher-than-economic costs on residential purchasers of electricity. It would be difficult to demonstrate that the formula produces a more acceptable distribution of income than would full peak-responsibility pricing. Again, the Federal Communications Commission is often urged to exercise its regulatory authority over interstate telephone rates to give particular protection to the householder instead of the business subscriber. But the average income of the (weighted) average household user of interstate (that is, long distance) telephone service could well be considerably higher than that of the customers of most of the commercial and industrial users of Bell System services.

5. Even if society were to make a conscious decision to transfer income from off-peak to peak users, such a policy would not be an intelligent one if it did not take into account the fact that departures from efficient pricing are an economically inefficient way of effecting such a transfer. The "proof" of this, which depends only on peak demand having some elasticity, is that if the transfer were made as a money grant to those users, instead of in the form of prices below cost, they would not use all that money to purchase the public utility service in question, but would spend some of it for a variety of other goods and services.[45]

THE APPROPRIATE TIME PATTERN OF RATES

Efficient pricing of public utility services calls for as fine a differentiation as practical of rates for the various services provided, in various locations, so as to reflect the different marginal costs of each. To the extent that differences in marginal cost can be ascribed also to the particular times at which service is taken, rate schedules should incorporate time-differentials as well. All this would be true even in a purely static situation, with unchanging cost and demand functions.

In the real world, costs and demands are constantly changing over time. These dynamic changes give rise to at least three major types of problems of efficient pricing. First, the ever-changing relationship of capacity to demand raises the question of whether it is feasible to price on the basis of short-run marginal cost, and what mixture of SRMC and LRMC would provide the optimum combination of feasibility and efficiency. Second, how should prices be varied over time in reflection of the changes in cost functions, because of ever-changing input prices, productivity, and technology? Third, if one departs from pricing on the basis of SRMC, what is the proper time pattern for the recovery of fixed costs such as depreciation, in the face of fluctuating demand on the one hand and unpredictably changing technology on the other?

Changing Relationship of Capacity to Demand

System demand peaks shift not merely because the quantities demanded respond to different prices—a static, elasticity phenomenon; they shift also because demands at any given price change over time. Promotional pricing of air-conditioning equipment by electric companies, like the pusher's free distribution of addictive drugs, may have played a role in spreading the habit; but the habit spread for other reasons as well, moving demand sufficiently to the right and making it sufficiently price-inelastic to give rise in some areas to a fixed, summer peak. If the peak shifts, or becomes shiftable, or *may* shift five, ten, or fifteen years in the future, how should that shift or shiftability be reflected in peak responsibility pricing today?

---

[45] For a more formal demonstration, see pp. 190–191, Chapter 7. This "proof" is of course no better than the assumptions underlying the economic model whose conclusions it adopts: notably that the subsidized purchasers would be the best judges of what most satisfies them and that society *ought* therefore to be more willing to give them cash grants than, for example, cheap electricity. See pp. 67–69, Chapter 3. Even if a governmental body rejects the second precept, the economist could still observe that the social decision is more likely to be rational and the economic costs less if the subsidized service is paid for openly by appropriation of taxpayer funds instead of covertly in charges levied on off-peak users.

Apart from peak shifts, changes in demand from one moment, month, or year to the next will involve movements along existing SRMC functions—and unless those costs are constant (horizontal), this will mean corresponding changes in marginal costs. We have already seen how volatile the SRMC of individual airplane trips must be—ranging between zero and levels far in excess of average total costs, depending on what price it takes to ration the fixed number of places—that is, to fill the plane while turning away no traveler willing to pay the price.

Similarly, on the supply side, capacity is constantly changing. Typically, public utility companies must build in advance of demand in order to be in a position to meet unexpected peak requirements and simply because the investment process is a lumpy one: additions to capacity are most economically made in large units. Therefore, at any given time, there is almost certain to be excess capacity,[46] which will remain idle if customers are charged long-run marginal costs. What, in these circumstances, is the proper measure of marginal costs? Or, to put the question another way, how far into the future should the calculation of long-run marginal costs extend?

As we have already seen, there is a strong economic case for letting price rise and fall as demand shifts along the rising SRMC curve. If SRMC is at times zero and at other times discontinuous (because an absolute physical limit of capacity has been reached), the price should fluctuate—down to zero, if necessary, because in the presence of excess capacity, no matter how temporary, no business should be turned away that covers the SRMC of supplying it; and up in periods of shortage to whatever level is necessary to ration limited supplies among customers. Once the new bridge is built, it is wasteful to keep people from crossing it; the time to charge for crossings is when congestion sets in.[47]

But, we have also pointed out, this is a counsel of perfection. It may well require modification in a world where (1) buyers and sellers make mistakes, (2) perpetual price fluctuation can be expensive for sellers to administer and buyers to keep track of and respond to intelligently, (3) capital and labor are incompletely mobile, (4) many other prices are highly inflexible, and (5) there is a business cycle.[48]

---

[46] For a demonstration that economies of scale make it rational to have excess capacity see Hollis B. Chenery, "Overcapacity and the Acceleration Principle," *Econometrica* (January 1952), XX: 1–10. Chenery shows that the optimum amount of the excess is comparatively insensitive to the interest rate, which determines how costly it is to build capacity in advance of the time it is utilized.

[47] It might appear that no customer whose continued patronage would eventually require additions to capacity should ever be charged a price that completely excludes those capital costs; the economic ideal, it might appear, would be to include them, but discounted back to present value, to reflect the fact that continued service of the customer in question would require their incurrence only sometime in the future. Such a prescription ignores the fact that buyers whose continued patronage *could* require the

incurrence of additional capacity costs are not in fact responsible for them if they drop out of the market when the time comes for the supplying company to make the decision whether to make the additional investment. It is only at *that* time, when there is a possibility of resources being used to expand capacity, that *all* (peak) customers should be confronted with a price that once again incorporates those costs, forcing them (as before) to decide whether the benefit to them of continued service justifies society's incurring the marginal opportunity costs of serving them.

[48] See pp. 83–86, Chapter 3. Consider how vexatious it would be to price each airplane flight at *SRMC* by auctioning seats off at whatever price it takes to clear the market—how difficult and costly to administer, how much time of passengers and airplane employees (and computers) would be used in the auctioning process itself, how difficult it would make it for

Consider what it means, for example, about the proper method of recovering the gross cost of capital—depreciation, interest, profits, income and property taxes—over the business cycle.

Except for the portion of depreciation that varies with the extent to which the facilities are used (that is, that represents user cost), these costs are a function of time—so much per dollar of investment per year—instead of a function of the rate of output from given facilities. There are three possible ways in which they might be recovered from customers:

1. In equal amounts for equal periods of time—for example, a certain amount per year. This method would seem to be recommended by the fact that these costs are a function of time. This means they would be recovered in prices that fluctuated inversely with the fluctuations in demand—capital charges per unit being low in years of large sales and high in years of low sales.

2. In equal amounts per unit of sales, on the theory that no purchase or purchaser should pay more than any other, per unit of purchase, over the life of the investment. This would mean recovery in constant prices over the cycle, which is the tendency under regulation. Depreciation, taxes, and return are calculated at a particular amount of money per year.[49] Usually, the companies are then instructed to propose a schedule of rates that will cover the total charges on the average over some period of years in the future. This means that in practice the capital costs will be recovered unequally over the cycle—in larger amounts when sales exceed the average, in smaller amounts when they fall below the average.[50]

3. In prices that fluctuate directly with the business cycle. This would be the tendency of pricing at SRMC: prices would be low and revenues would tend to cover only variable costs in periods of weak demand in recognition of the fact that the demand at such times puts no burden on capacity. Price would have to move up far enough above that level and remain there long enough in periods of recovering and strong demand not only to cover ATC at that time but to make good the losses of previous periods.

There is no settled economic theory of the ideal behavior of the general price level over the cycle (Indeed, cyclical fluctuations have become so much more modest since World War II that the subject itself is of reduced interest.) Economists would almost certainly reject the first as a general rule. In view of the general tendency of prices in the economy to move up and down with the cycle (although the latter tendency especially has become faint in recent

---

passengers to plan their travel. Or suppose the same free pricing system were used for taxicabs: consider how their rates would have to fluctuate from sunny to rainy days, from one time of day and from one section of the city to another, and with what costs of time and annoyance to passengers and drivers.

[49] Straight-line depreciation—writing off an investment in equal amounts over its estimated life—remains the usual procedure. When accelerated depreciation is taken for purposes of calculating income tax liability, the taxes incorporated in the cost of service are often "normalized," that is, set at a stable annual figure over the life of the asset, although actual taxes will be below that normalized level in the earlier years and above it in later years. See pp. 32–34.

[50] This is only a tendency. It may be offset by a tendency of *variable* costs to fluctuate directly with the level of operations—for example, because the utility puts inefficient plant into service only when necessary—while the variable component of the cost of service is an average estimated for a period of years.

decades), it would probably result in uneconomic distortions to have public utility prices going the other way. Moreover, it would tend to have precisely the wrong effect in rationing consumption—discouraging utilization when demand is low relative to capacity and encouraging it when marginal (congestion) costs are high.[51] Economists would be less clear in their response to the third way of recovering costs. It would probably be fair to say that most believe it serves no useful purpose to have the general price level fluctuate widely with the cycle, either. In view of the comparative rigidity of the general price level it would probably do more harm than good to have the prices of public utility services alone fluctuate as widely as the third rule would dictate.[52]

Therefore, the usual practice of charging capital costs on a per unit of sales basis and recouping them *on the average* over the cycle—that is, the second rule—is probably the best available general rule as far as the determination of general rate *levels* is concerned.[53] The rate stability that it provides is not just a pragmatic compromise between the extremes produced by rules 1 and 3: it also has the positive virtue of making it easier for customers to make the type of long-run commitments that consumption of a utility service usually involves (to install a certain furnace, to locate industry in a particular area), on the basis of reasonably stable expectations about the prices they are likely to have to pay.

This does not mean that SRMC, or fluctuations in the relationship of demand to capacity, should be ignored. The key is the necessity for reasonable predictability on the part of supplier or customer. Where not only *differences* but *changes* in the SRMC of supply at different times can be predicted with reasonable assurance, it is economically efficient to embody corresponding differentials in rate *structures*. In the presence of excess capacity, utility companies ought to make every effort to design rates, down to SRMC, to put it to use. We have recognized that the "ideal" of rates fluctuating with SRMC could have highly inefficient consequences on the buyers' side of the market. Household customers induced to shift to electricity or natural gas or industrial users persuaded to locate somewhere by rates approximating short-term marginal costs in periods of excess capacity would have a legitimate complaint if, having made the switch, they were then faced unpredictably with steadily rising rates as SRMC came increasingly to cover capacity costs as well. Therefore, the essential proviso would have to be attached that the proffer of any such temporarily low rates be accompanied with the warning that service would be interrupted as demand caught up, or rates increased to whatever extent necessary to ration demand until additional capacity was once again constructed.

---

[51] See the same observation in an analogous context, by Seymour Smidt, "Flexible Pricing of Computer Services," *Management Science* (June 1968), XIV: B–582.

[52] However, see the reference to J. R. Nelson, note 67. Additionally, Bonbright points out that if public utility rates were free to fluctuate like purely competitive prices over the cycle, it would in principle be necessary for regulatory commissions to play a much more active role than they now need to in the investment decision process—specifically, to compel companies to expand capacity when necessary. Private managements would have a strong temptation to delay capacity expansion in time of strong demand, hoping instead to enjoy the high profits resulting from the high prices required to ration customers. *Op. cit.*, 99.

[53] The Civil Aeronautics Board has explicitly recognized that it would be futile to try to iron out year-by-year fluctuations in rate of return in an industry so subject to fluctuation in its financial fortunes. See its *General Passenger Fare Investigation*, 32 CAB 291, 294–309 (1960).

Such a notice would protect the utility against charging customers less than the true and full eventual MC of serving them, while also giving the latter the predictability of future rates necessary if they are to avoid making irrational commitments.

The same sort of warnings are necessary with peak responsibility pricing. The ideal, once again, would be to price on the basis of *current* MC: this means that currently off-peak users would pay zero capacity costs today and full capacity costs in the event of a shift to a new fixed peak at their time of consumption tomorrow. But fluctuations of this kind would be impractical, for the reasons already given. The key once again must be reasonable predictability. Therefore, capacity costs ought to be shared in varying proportions, from 100% down to zero, by purchasers in periods that have correspondingly varying likelihoods of being or becoming peaks in the foreseeable future. The farther ahead the utility can see with reasonable assurance that certain sales will remain off-peak, the greater is the justification for offering this service on a firm (noninterruptible) basis at rates that incorporate no capacity costs. Conversely, if there is a strong possibility that within a very few years the service that is now off-peak will in fact put a strain on capacity, the off-peak tariffs are justified only if they are interruptible[54] and/or the buyers are put clearly on notice that the rates may in time have to be sharply increased.[55]

On the other hand, customers have no absolute right to perpetual protection against drastic rate changes if cost changes counsel such measures. Considerations of fairness will join with considerations of efficiency in calling for reasonable compromises between the interests of different classes of customers: offering moderate assurances of rate stability in the face of unanticipated cost changes unfavorable to certain customers, yet refusing indefinitely to burden other customers with the necessity of paying prices disproportionately *above* the MC of serving them in order to shelter the former group permanently against the consequences of change or of errors, their own or the company's.[56]

We return to some of these practical considerations in Chapter 7. But there is no simple solution available. The proper balance will ordinarily have to make very large concessions in the direction of rate stability: the efficiency advantages of having rates vary over the life-cycles of particular increments to capacity are typically outweighed by the numerous disadvantages.[57] And even the advantages are probably diminishing over time: as the electricity generating industry and natural gas pipelines (the latter far more slowly than the former) approach participation in regional or national grid systems, in which additions to capacity in the various regions of the country are synchronized over time, the problem of temporary excesses of capacity on the one hand, and the efficiency advantages of varying prices over time because of them, will become correspondingly less important.

For these various reasons, growing public utility industries that are constantly adding to capacity generally must attempt to set their rates, as

---

[54] Standby, no-reservation airplane service, to which the youth fares apply, is by definition this type of service.
[55] On most of these problems, see Bonbright, *op. cit.*, 360–366.
[56] See *ibid.*, 129.

[57] For examples of electricity rates remaining absolutely unchanged for 10 and 15 year periods and a consideration of the reasons for this, see Raymond Jackson, "What Others Think, Rigidity in Electric Rates," *Pub. Util. Fort.* (June 20, 1968), LXXXI: 42–44.

stably as possible, on the basis of some estimated average cost level over some more or less arbitrarily selected planning period—of perhaps five years.[58] In this event, the appropriate benchmark must be some estimated average level of long-run, not short-run marginal costs[59]—and closer approximations to SRMC must be confined largely to (1) incorporation in rate schedules, insofar as prediction is possible,[60] (2) the offer of special rates for interruptible service, and (3) exemption of clearly off-peak pricing from capacity charges.[61]

Yet there all sorts of possible situations in which stability and predictability may be less important than the efficiency advantages of flexible SRMC pricing. With sufficient ingenuity, it is often possible to find ways of practicing it. For example, Smidt has proposed that computers be programmed so as to vary the price of their own service from one five-minute interval to the next, as well as over the life of the equipment, depending on the balance of demand and capacity, with users given considerable choice in specifying in advance

---

[58] An indirect confirmation of the reasonableness of an offer of stability over a more or less arbitrary planning period is provided by the special, short-term arrangements under which the Tennessee Valley Authority and the Bonneville Power Commission sold surplus power to private utilities, in one case under a five-year contract, in the other subject to cancellation on five-year notice if the power were required by municipal distributors and co-ops. See Glaeser, *Public Utilities in American Capitalism*, 499–500, 557. According to officials of AT&T's Long Lines Department, they build capacity when and where needed in the expectation that it will come to be fully used within four to six years. They base prices on average estimated costs for such a period, and on a nationwide basis, because they feel it is entirely infeasible to price flexibly within that period or with reference to local differences in excess capacity. Their system is national in the sense that communications are automatically switched from one route to another depending on which circuits are busy and where there is excess capacity. (See the section on "the national telecommunications network," Chapter 4, Volume 2.) For a finding of ten- and twenty-year (or more) planning horizons for capital budgeting by electric power companies—projections over which are "not . . . taken very seriously"—with five years being "the standard long-term forecast in the industry," and three years "the point at which important practical consequences follow from projections of demand," see Michael Gort, "The Planning of Investment: A Study of Capital Budgeting in the Electric-Power Industry," Part I, *Jour. of Bus.* (April 1951), XXIV: 81–82.

Vickrey defines the proper planning period for which marginal costs are appropriately measured as being determined by the period during which it is anticipated rates will be stable: "The proper time horizon for the cost determination is the

probable interval between rate adjustments." And he would solve the question of the proper size of the incremental block of output, for which LRMC are to be estimated, in a similarly pragmatic way:

"The increment in traffic for which the cost increment is to be estimated should have a composition similar to the increment induced by the rate change under consideration. . . . Thus unless a policy is being contemplated of suppressing a class of service entirely, the traffic increment for which the cost is being ascertained should never be an entire class of traffic, but only a final increment in that traffic corresponding to a realistically contemplated rate change." Testimony in FCC Dockets 16258 and 15011, *In the Matter of American Telephone and Telegraph Company*, Networks Exhibit No. 5, July 22, 1968, mimeo., 23–24.

[59] See Bonbright, *op. cit.*, 331–336.

[60] See some of the challenging suggestions of William Vickrey in Lyle Fitch and Associates, *Urban Transportation and Public Policy* (San Francisco: Chandler Publishing Co., 1964), esp. pp. 146–156; "Pricing in Urban and Surburban Transport," *Amer. Econ. Rev.*, Papers and Proceedings (May 1963), LIII: 452–460; and "Pricing Policies," *International Encyclopedia of the Social Sciences* (New York: The Macmillan Co. and The Free Press, 1968), XII: 457–463.

[61] The second and third examples are really only one illustration of the first. Moreover, they are equally examples of LR as of SRMC pricing: the LRMC of definitely off-peak business (and interruptible service is by definition off-peak) includes no capacity costs either. And, it should be noted, (2) and (3) both are aspects of given rate schedules instead of examples of rate *changes* over time. (It is not really the long-distance telephone rate that "changes" at 6:00 P.M.: it is time that changes, moving subscribers from one prescribed rate schedule to another.)

the priority they wish assigned to their jobs and for which they are willing to pay.[62] William Vickrey, one of the most assiduous and ingenious proponents of "reactive pricing," has suggested it could feasibly be applied to long-distance telephoning, tickets for theatrical performances, sporting events, long-distance airplane travel, and electricity. For the first, he would have computers programmed to inform subscribers, immediately on dialing, how much—depending upon the availability of circuits—it would cost them to place that particular call at that particular time, giving them the opportunity then to decide whether the call should be completed. He has proposed that the prices of the theater and airplane tickets might be gradually reduced as the time of performance or departure nears, depending on how much of the space has been sold to customers willing to pay the premium for advance reservation. For electricity, he observes,

". . . the same load signal used by Électricité de France to switch rates according to time of day could be used to vary rates on a reactive basis, simultaneously encouraging the switching on and off of deferrable demands such as water heaters and refrigerators."[63]

He is certainly correct in pointing out that there is no reason in logic or fairness for public authorities to impose tolls on bridges immediately on their completion and take them off when the investment is fully paid off—a practice likely to produce a time pattern of rates just the opposite of what the relation of demand to capacity requires.[64]

Changing Cost Levels: Reproduction versus Original Capital Costs

Most of the time and energy expended in regulatory proceedings is taken up with recomputing aggregate company revenue requirements, with a view toward adjusting the general rate level to changes in total costs.[65] There is no question of economic principle about the necessity for these efforts: ideally, prices should reflect marginal cost at the time of sale—not at some time in the past.

This consideration constitutes the strongest economic argument for the use of reproduction instead of original cost as the basis for computing capital charges. As proponents of that method of valuation point out, prices in competitive markets will tend to be set at the level that covers current, not past, capital costs. This is a statement of long-run tendency only, to be sure; in periods of rising reproduction costs, it will be achieved only as demand presses to the limits of existing capacity and new investments need to be attracted or old capacity replaced. Still, it represents the competitive ideal, and departures from it in periods of long-run inflation or deflation involve inefficiencies, to the extent that there is any elasticity in demand. These

[62] *Op. cit.*, B–581–600.

[63] *Op. cit.*, *International Encyclopedia of the Social Sciences*, XII: 460. See also his "The Pricing of Tomorrow's Utility Services," paper presented at Occidental College, June 1966, processed, and note 29, Chapter 3.

[64] As a result, he observes, in New York City a great deal of traffic over the East River is diverted from the new toll bridges, with comparatively large capacities and ample access

facilities, to the clogged, ancient bridges that no longer carry tolls, and dump traffic right in the middle of the most congested areas of the city. *Op. cit.*, *Amer. Econ. Rev.*, *Papers and Proceedings* (May 1963), LIII: 455.

[65] To some extent this is accomplished automatically, as in the purchased-gas and fuel-adjustment clauses incorporated in the tariffs of many distributors of gas and electricity. See Garfield and Lovejoy, *op. cit.*, 146.

distortions may take various possible forms (for simplicity, we assume the situation is one in which reproduction costs exceed book costs):

1. Current costs reflect marginal social opportunity costs. Since under original cost valuation the buyers pay not these, but some lower average as the cost of new, increasingly expensive plant is blended in with that of the old, the result is excessively large purchases of the public utility service and correspondingly excessive flow of resources into its supply.

    This tendency is accentuated when the service competes with unregulated commodities whose prices may behave more nearly according to the competitive norm—railroads with trucks, buses, and private cars, electricity and gas with oil, common carrier transportation and communication with private microwave. Since the competition of these substitutes increases the elasticity of demand for the regulated services, this is only another way of saying that the greater the elasticity of demand, the greater the waste consequent on holding price below marginal cost.

    It might appear that basing prices on historic capital costs would cause offsetting distortions in investment incentives—for example, in periods of rising capital costs discouraging capital expenditures that would otherwise be made. If this were true there would be an underallocation instead of overallocation of resources into regulated industries in periods of inflation. But, as long as the permitted rate of return covers the cost of capital, neither management nor investors need be deterred from making whatever additional investments are required to satisfy the artificially inflated demand. Whatever current dollars are required for the incremental investment enter the original cost rate base, on which the required rate of return is then permitted: as long as additional investments bring in enough additional net revenue to cover the cost of capital, it is in the interest of the company and of its existing stockholders to make the additional investments.[66] The distortion is on the demand, not the supply side.

2. When customers have a choice to buy from one utility company or another, that choice will be determined not solely, as it should be, by their respective marginal costs, but, quixotically, by differences in the average age of their plants, which will produce different average rates. Thus, industry may be impelled to locate where the suppliers of electricity or transportation have a rate base of comparatively old vintage, even though long-run marginal supply costs may actually be higher there than elsewhere.

3. Original rate-base costing tends to produce a perverse cyclical behavior of prices, holding down the charges for utility services when commodity prices generally are rising, and holding them up in periods of general

---

[66] Walter A. Morton, who supports reproduction cost valuation on grounds of fairness, concedes that an original cost earning base need not involve economic inefficiency on this score. "Rate of Return and the Value of Money in Public Utilities," *Land Econ.* (May 1952), XXVIII: 117–118. The statements by M. J. Peck and J. R. Meyer to the contrary in "The Determination of a Fair Return on Investment for Regulated Industries," in *Transportation Economics,* A Conference of the Universities—National Bureau Committee for Economic Research (New York: National Bureau of Economic Research, 1965), 202–203 seem to be incorrect. Actually a company could raise additional capital, within limits, even if the permitted rate of return were below the cost of capital. But since this would dilute the equity of existing stockholders, the company presumably would be reluctant to do so. See note 64, Chapter 2.

price decline. In addition to the inefficient substitution effects of the resulting relative price movements already mentioned, there are adverse macroeconomic consequences because of the high capital-intensity of these industries: holding down their prices and encouraging consumption of their services in periods of general inflation forces them to expand their disproportionately large investment outlays, thus contributing to the excessive levels of aggregate demand. The opposite happens on the downturn.[67]

Although arguments such as these have traditionally been directed toward the question of the proper valuation of the rate base, the same economic principles apply to the computation of depreciation expense and rate of return. What gross cost of capital (depreciation plus return) should be entered into the economically efficient price? Is it the historic cost of the dollars invested in the enterprise at various times in the past? Or the current or future cost of capital? Setting aside the consideration that capital costs as such do not enter at all into the computation of short-run marginal costs, clearly, it is an average of future costs of capital over the planning period that properly belongs in LRMC. Yet the usual formula for capital cost calls for a heterogeneous mixture—composed of depreciation computed by applying some conventional length of time based roughly on past experience to historic investment; a current cost of equity capital, usually estimated over some period in the recent past, and applied to an original-cost rate base; and an actual, historic cost of debt capital, as embodied in existing bond obligations, adjusted to include the cost of any debt planned for incurrence in the near future—all of these plus an inescapable element of "judgment."

This practice is rationalized essentially on the ground that it is the function of regulation to permit companies simply to cover their revenue requirements—to recover the money capital actually invested in the service of the public, to earn a return on investment sufficient to meet their actual debt service obligations, and to attract new equity capital. And it does do these things. It avoids conferring windfall gains on stockholders, such as they would earn in a period of inflation and high interest rates under a system that incorporated in the cost of service the current instead of the (lower) historic cost of debt capital; and it protects them in turn from the windfall losses they would otherwise suffer when interest rates turn down. In so doing, it also protects the credit standing of the company and its ability therefore to serve the public, both of which could be impaired under a reproduction cost system, when current interest rates were much lower than those the company had actually incurred in the past.[68]

But it is precisely the characteristic of competitive markets that they expose stockholders to the possibilities of earning unanticipated, windfall gains and losses, of getting back much more or much less than the dollars they originally invested, or earning much more and much less than the cost of capital on

---

[67] See James R. Nelson, in Shepherd and Gies, op. cit., 71–76. See the classic statement of these various arguments by Harry Gunnison Brown, "Railroad Valuation and Rate Regulation," Jour. Pol. Econ. (October 1925), XXXIII: 505–530 and "Railroad Valuation Again: A Reply," ibid (August 1926), XXXIV: 500–508; also Willard J. Graham, Public Utility Valuation,

Studies in Business Administration, Vol. 4 (Chicago: Univ. of Chicago Press, 1934).
[68] See Bonbright, op. cit., 186–187, 245, 248–249, 278–280. We consider below the opposing argument that such a system does not really treat stockholders fairly for the very opposite reason: that it fails to take into account the changing purchasing power of the dollar.

those dollars. Such markets necessarily expose buyers to prices that vary and fluctuate correspondingly.

These arguments against the use of historic costs can be appraised at various levels. Some of the opposing considerations concede the theoretical validity of the criticisms but deprecate their practical importance; others strike at their theoretical validity as well. Some responses (in addition to the very important considerations of administrative feasibility, already suggested in Chapter 2) argue for the superiority of an original-cost rate base; others emphasize that to fix prices principally by applying a gross cost of capital to a rate base, however valued, is economically unsound and in any case constitutes the minor part of the task of efficient rate making:

1. The actual importance of the case for reproduction costs depends not on principle but on fact. How serious a distortion is created by the lag of prices behind reproduction costs depends on (a) the size of the lag and (b) the elasticity of the demand for public utility services. As for the first, all utility company rate bases are a mixture of vintages; all of them, in growing industies, are heavily weighted by recent expenditures.[69] The difference between the prices produced by original and reproduction cost valuation therefore can easily be exaggerated. As for the second, defenders of original costing have tended to argue that demand is comparatively price-inelastic.[70]

2. The seriousness of the distorting effect also depends on how promptly prices in unregulated markets, and particularly of substitute services, adjust to the long-run competitive equilibrium level. The pervasiveness of market imperfections in the nonpublic utility sectors of the economy (consider for example the cyclical price behavior of such competitors as trucks, cars, buses, and petroleum) suggests that any attempt to fix public utility rates at the purely competitive equilibrium level would produce distortions in the opposite direction. This observation, the reader will recognize, raises once more the problem of the "second best." It suggests the necessity of looking to the prices of specific public utility services in the light of the elasticities of their particular demands, which necessitates in turn a consideration of the price of substitutes and the relationship of those prices to *their* costs, before deciding whether to try to move any of the former closer to the purely competitive level. Since this is an argument as much against marginal-cost pricing in general as against reproduction cost rate bases, we return to it briefly in Chapter 7. But most economists would almost certainly reject any general attempt to make prices in only one sector of the economy highly flexible cyclically.

3. As Justice Brandeis pointed out decades ago, the "reproduction cost" to which prices in purely competitive markets tend to correspond is not the current cost of reproducing the existing plant, brick by brick, but the current cost of producing the *service* with the most modern technology available. It has been the former, not the latter, that public utility

[69] See B. W. Lewis, in Lyon, Abramson and Associates, *op. cit.*, II : 689, including the reference in note 134 to Bernstein, *Public Utility Rate Making.*

"For instance, the 1963 A.T.&T. Annual Report shows a net telephone plant investment of more than 23½ billion dollars in 1963 . . . as against a mere 7¼ billion in 1950. All of the difference, as well as a considerable part of the 7¼ billions, consists of warm *new* dollars. . . ." Lewis, in Shepherd and Gies, *op. cit.*, 237.

[70] See Bauer and Gold, *op. cit.*, 405–413.

commissions have typically been involved in laboriously estimating in reproduction-cost proceedings.[71] In view of the rapid technological progress that has characterized some public utility industries and their tendencies toward long-run decreasing costs (see pp. 124–130), it is by no means clear that reproduction costs correctly defined are typically higher than original costs in periods of moderate inflation.

4. If the reproduction-cost rate base were correctly defined to embody the most recent technology, it would still be anomalous to add together, as is the typical regulatory procedure, capital costs for such a hypothetical new plant and operating expenses actually incurred in some test year in the plant that actually did the producing. If the competitive norm is conceived to be the average total cost of a new plant, using new technology, it is the operating cost of *that* plant that would have to be incorporated in the cost of service.[72]

5. Of course, the proper economic standard is not current average total cost but either short- or long-run marginal cost. The entire concept of determining rates by incorporating some average necessary rate of return on *total investment*, however valued, is a misleading one except in the circumstance that the industry operates under conditions of long-run constant cost. Under any other conditions, the level of cost depends on the level of output, and the latter in turn depends on the price that is set, if demand has any elasticity at all. In these circumstances, the typical method of basing average prices on average current *or* past costs of producing current or past levels of output in some test year[73] becomes

[71] See, for example, the listing of the typical methods of estimating reproduction costs in C. F. Phillips, *op. cit.*, 241–242, all of which ,it will be noted, ignore technological progress. For the Brandeis observation, see his famous dissent in *Southwestern Bell Telephone Company of Missouri v. Public Service Commission*, 262 U. S. 276, at 312 (1923); see also J. M. Clark, *Social Control of Business*, 2d ed. (Chicago: Univ. of Chicago Press, 1939), 306–308; and compare H. G. Brown, *op. cit.*, *Jour. Pol. Econ.* (October 1925), XXXIII: 505–530 with John Bauer, "Rate Base for Effective and Non-Speculative Railroad and Utility Regulation," *Jour. Pol. Econ.* (1926), XXXIV: 494–495. As J. R. Nelson aptly observes, "if particular assets are really to be replaced in kind, there must be something wrong with allowing for *any* obsolescence in the annual depreciation charge." Shepherd and Gies, *op. cit.*, 72.

[72] See Charles W. Smith, "Public Utility Depreciation," *Pub. Util. Fort.* (October 23, 1952), L: 630. However, this defect in the application of reproduction cost would disappear if the allowance for depreciation deducted were just sufficient to reflect the obsolescence of the old plant and hence to offset its excessive (by new plant standards) operating costs. See Bonbright, *op. cit.*, 229 and our fuller discussion in the next section of this chapter.

[73] An interesting departure from reliance on a single past test-year has been the informal acceptance by the Federal Communications Commission staff of an accounting system for the Communications Satellite Corporation in which revenue requirements are estimated on the basis of *anticipated* cost experience over a five-year period in the future. This innovation was dictated by the fact that Comsat's rate schedules had to be developed before the company had accumulated any operating experience with its revolutionary new method of communication, and—of particular significance at this point— the elasticities of demand and the prospective future behavior of unit costs made it evident that the company would suffer high operating losses during its initial period of operations under any conceivable system of rates. Congress had instructed the FCC to develop a global system of space communications as rapidly as possible. Had Comsat attempted to set rates high enough to cover the high initial costs of doing so, it would have found itself without customers. Therefore, it and the Commission properly decided that some of these high initial costs were chargeable to later users. (On this principle, see pp. 121–122.) They agreed to amortize some of the developmental costs and preoperating expenses over a ten-year period, using the *reverse* sum-of-the-digits method—that is to say, with heavier depreciation allowances taken in later years than in earlier—in order better to match

hopelessly circular: it offers no indication of what average costs *would be* if some other level of rates were set, leading to some other volume of sales.[74]

Of course, competitive prices do move up and down in correspondence with costs. But they are not determined solely by costs, and certainly not by average total costs, reproduction or historic.[75]

---

depreciation expenses with the anticipated sharply rising flow of revenues. They envisaged, similarly, that the annual rate of return would be substantially below the ordinary range of reasonableness in the early years of service, and substantially above it in later years. These various understandings, they believed, would permit Comsat to charge rates low enough to induce a rapidly increasing utilization of its large initially installed capacity, thus drastically reducing unit costs over the life of the satellite. See the interesting paper by A. Bruce Matthews, "Problems Posed by Current Regulatory Practices to the Rapid Introduction of Communications Satellite Technology," delivered at a Symposium on the Rate Base Approach to Regulation at the Brookings Institution, June 7, 1968.

[74] In a survey of 90 public utility commission decisions over the period from 1937 to 1946, Troxel found that only two indicated any allowance for buyer responses to price changes. "Demand Elasticity and Control of Public Utility Earnings," *Amer. Econ. Rev.* (June 1948), XXXVIII: 372–373. "To achieve better regulatory effects, commissions need studies of demand behavior—any studies." *Ibid.*, 382.

Troxel and, following him, Phillips both argue also that regulation should pay closer attention to the marginal instead of the average return on investment—pointing out that efficiency requires firms to invest up to the point at which the return on *incremental*, not average, investment is equated with the cost of capital (k). See Troxel, *Economics of Public Utilities*, 391–395 and C. R. Phillips, *op. cit.*, 300–302. (On the possibility of firms being faced with an increasing cost of capital, where the MC of capital exceeds the average, and the implications of profit-maximizers equating the marginal return with the former instead of the latter, see note 30, Chapter 2, Volume 2.) I confess to great difficulty in following their argument.

I can think of three tendencies (in addition to those suggested in the text, above) to which they may be referring when they imply, as they seem to do, that the concentration of regulatory attention on the average return on total investment (however valued) may produce inefficiencies. First, there are times when permitting regulated companies to earn an average return equal at least to k may result in excessively high prices and underutilization of capacity. This would be so in a period of inadequate demand,

when the prospective marginal return on investment is in any event below k, so that the companies would not be making any investments anyhow and would therefore have no economic need or justification (on SRMC-grounds) for earning such returns. This may be what Troxel has in mind when he says:

". . . the marginal rate of return is not the same thing as the cost of capital. Yet utility commissions use current costs of capital to determine the fair rate of return. Either the utility companies pay these borrowing costs, the commissioners say, or no borrowing can be done. True; but the utility company does not borrow unless the marginal rate of return is above the market rates of interest." *loc. cit.*, 392.

The second possible resulting distortion is that regulated companies may undertake investments the marginal return on which is *less* than k— investments that are, therefore, socially undesirable—where they have reason to believe regulation will permit them to recoup the difference in other markets, in order to keep their average rate of return at the legally permissible level. To prevent such investments, regulatory commissions might have to investigate the return on each investment, in order to disallow those that fell short of k. (We discuss this "A–J–W" tendency at length in Chapter 2, Volume 2.)

The third possibility is that the traditional policy may discourage regulated companies from undertaking very risky investments—risky because they offer a strong possibility of heavy losses, but worth undertaking because they offer the possibility also of very high returns—by threatening to take away the gains from a successful venture if it raises the company-wide average return too high. (See pp. 53–54.)

Apart from these three possibilities (and it is by no means clear that these are what they intend) I do not see what the authors have in mind. It is certainly *not* true that regulation prevents companies from attracting whatever additional capital they need for investments on which the marginal return exceeds the cost of capital. See our discussion of this point, p. 110.

[75] For an argument that rate base calculations are irrelevant to efficient pricing in the cases of railroads, natural gas, and urban transport, as well as an excellent analysis of the entire reproduction cost rate base issue, see Bonbright, *op. cit.*, 224–237.

Quasi-competitive pricing can be achieved for public utilities only by an explicit and separate consideration of the short- and long-run marginal costs on the one hand, and the intensities and elasticities of demand on the other for each one of their services in each of their markets. The economic and constitutional requirement that investors be given some assurances of a sufficient average return on their investment must, to be sure, exert some influence on these individual pricing decisions, and especially on the level of the entire structure. But, as Melvin de Chazeau has eloquently argued, the valuation of property, which is an essential part of the process of determining an "*earnings* base" for purposes of regulating the return to investors, is of very little use as a "*rate* base"—that is, for the determination of rational individual prices.[76]

This much remains valid in the economic case for a reproduction cost rate base and gross rate of return as an approach to price making: that unless second-best considerations dictate otherwise, and to the extent that prices are to be based on LR instead of SRMC, it is definitely the current and future—not the historic—capital costs that are relevant. But the use of reproduction cost valuation itself makes small contribution to efficient pricing compared with the immense resources that have gone into its support and application. Indeed, to the extent that LRMC are below ATC, because of economies of scale, its contribution could well be negative, even in a period of long-run inflation. The reason for this is that both original and reproduction cost rate base valuation are relevant only to average-cost pricing. If average costs are higher on the latter than on the former rate base, because of inflation, moving to reproduction costs may compound the inefficiency inherent in such pricing, and prices based on average historic costs may therefore come closer to the proper level.[77]

It should be emphasized that the case for reproduction cost does not rest on economic considerations alone. At least equally influential, particularly as a result of the general inflation since 1940, has been the noneconomic argument that reproduction cost valuation is much fairer to utility company stockholders than original cost. To base depreciation charges and return on investment on historic costs during or after a period of inflation is to return to the investors dollars of much lower purchasing power (measured in terms of the cost either of consumer goods and services or of replacing the old capital goods with new, that is, of keeping their capital investment intact in real terms) than the dollars they originally invested.[78]

The consensus of most economists in this matter would seen to be the following:

1. As Ben Lewis has put it, "any scheme of compensation is fair provided only that it was reasonably anticipated at the time of investment."[79] The

[76] *Op. cit. Q. Econ. Jour.* (February 1938), LII: 346–359; see, also, essentially in agreement, Bryan and Lewis, *ibid.*, 342–345.

[77] That is, efficiency could require two corrections of prices based on average historic costs in these circumstances—upward because of inflation and downward because LRMC are below ATC. Reproduction cost valuation does only the first of these. In so doing it may push prices far above LRMC; whereas prices based on average historic costs may come much closer to that level.

[78] See the excellent survey of the arguments on both sides of this issue in Glaeser, *op. cit.*, 315–331, 393–402; and for a strong presentation of the view just summarized, see Morton, *op. cit.*, pp. 91–131.

[79] In Lyon, Abramson and Associates, *op. cit.*, II: 688.

argument here is that as long as investors are informed in advance of whether they will be explicitly protected against inflation (or, by use of an original cost rate base, against deflation), they can in fairness be left to take that fact into account in the prices they pay for the stock at the time of purchase. If, for example, they anticipate inflation, they will presumably pay a lower price per dollar of current earnings for the stock of company A, which promises them no protection, than for company B, whose rate base and/or depreciation are determined on the basis of reproduction cost. In this way they will demand—and get—a percentage yield on their actual investment in A sufficiently higher to compensate for their poorer treatment.

2. By this reasoning, it is *impossible* to compensate *future* stock purchasers for past inflation—they will simply bid up the price of the stock and thereby offset that compensation; or to protect them against future inflation: they will simply compete to pay a higher price for the stock when they buy it, in reflection of this better treatment. And to change the regulatory rules in order to give such compensation to *existing* stockholders would be simply to confer on them a windfall, a higher return on their investment than they had reason to expect when they made it.[80]

3. If the desire is, rather, to compensate existing stockholders because such inflation as has occurred or may occur in the future has exceeded or may exceed their expectations—protecting them against their mistakes—what ethical reason is there to do so for stockholders and not for bondholders? It is only the former who would benefit by increasing the total number of dollars allowed for depreciation or included in the rate base. This seems particularly anomalous when it is stockholders who typically demand and receive the higher return, precisely in order to compensate them for the greater risks they are supposed to bear.

4. If, nonetheless, the government does want to adjust stockholder returns, in the interest of fairness, it can do so just as well and with far less damage to the efficiency of the regulatory process by varying (their part of) the permissible rate of return, or by applying some sort of price index number to the total dollars of permitted net income.[81]

5. Finally, to return to our main theme of whether revaluation of property or investment is necessary in order to assure fair *earnings* to existing stockholders, it makes economic sense as the basis for fixing *prices* only as some sort of average for all services taken together and over a number of years.[82]

---

[80] "The yield on securities cannot be determined [that is, fixed or set] by regulatory fiat in the same manner as the rate of return on invested capital or equity. The best commissions can do with the market is arbitrarily influence the prices of the securities by altering investor expectations and generating windfall gains or losses to those who hold the stock coincidentally with the effectuation of those influences." Morris Mendelson, "The Comparable Earnings Standard: A New Approach," paper presented to the Bell Telephone Co. of Pennsylvania Seminar on the Economics of Public Utilities, June 9, 1967, mimeo., 4–5.

[81] It is difficult to quarrel with Bonbright's observation that employing a reproduction cost rate base is "an absurdly crude device" for remedying this situation, if indeed it calls for a remedy. *Op. cit.*, 189–191.

[82] See de Chazeau, "The Nature of the 'Rate Base' in the Regulation of Public Utilities," *Q. Jour. Econ.* (February 1937), LI: 298–316, the illuminating comment by Robert F. Bryan and Ben W. Lewis, "The 'Earning Base' as a 'Rate Base,'" and the "Reply" by de Chazeau, *ibid.* (February 1938), LII: 335–359. Also see Bonbright, *op. cit.*, 266–276.

Depreciation Policy and Technological Progress

One of the most difficult and interesting problems of rate making in the face of cost changes over time has to do with the appropriate reflection of technological change in determining the depreciation component of cost of service.[83] In view of the immense importance of technological progress for economic welfare it becomes especially important to see to it that cost-of-service determinations are compatible with the optimum adoption of new technology.

The purpose of including an allowance for depreciation in price is to ensure recovery of invested funds over the economic life of the physical capital in which they have been embodied; and of course to see to it that price reflects this authentic economic cost. (We assume, as is the case in most jurisdictions, that the original vs. reproduction cost issue has been resolved in favor of returning the dollars originally invested, no more and no less.) The principal limits on that economic life are wear-and-tear (a user cost) and obsolescence; we confine our attention here to the latter, since, in principle, the former obviously should be included among the other variable costs of production.[84]

It is equally correct to say that the *total* of depreciation charges is supposed to reflect the total decline in the value of the physical asset, from original cost to scrap value—that is to the point where it is just as valuable in the form of scrap as installed production capacity. A familiar question in the public utility literature has been whether the *periodic*—for example, annual—depreciation charges should have the same function—that is, whether they should also reflect as closely as possible the year-by-year decline in that economic value; or whether, instead, they can be nothing more than a conventional and arbitrary mechanism for prorating the total amount to be recovered over the total estimated economic life. We make no effort to resolve that controversy, although it is clear that the latter is surely more accurate than the former as a description of actual practice, considering that (1) rate bases are now typically stated in original costs instead of "fair value,"[85] (2) straight-line depreciation is the method almost universally used,[86] and (3) the rate of decline in economic or market value depends primarily on trends in replacement cost[87] and technological change, whose year-by-year rates are surely irregular and unpredictable. However, some of the most interesting economic questions arise when the rate of decline in market value differs significantly from the depreciation rate actually employed.

What happens if technological change has been unexpectedly rapid? (It is

[83] Is it unbearably repetitious to remind the reader again that rate making on the basis of SRMC can ignore the depreciation that is not part of variable cost, but that pricing on the basis of LRMC or ATC must take it explicitly into account?

[84] See pp. 71–73, Chapter 3.

[85] As Bonbright points out, it is anomalous to think of depreciation as measuring decline in market value when one uses an original cost rate base, making no effort to adjust it up or down with the current value of the asset. *Principles of Public Utility Rates*, 194–201.

[86] Eugene F. Brigham, *op cit.*, *National Tax J.* (June 1967), XX: 210.

[87] In a period of inflation the market value of the asset may remain stable or actually rise, despite wear and tear and obsolescence: presumably "economic depreciation" would have to take this offsetting factor into account, so that the book value of the asset (original value less depreciation) would correctly reflect market value at the end of each accounting period. For simplicity we assume constant price levels in this discussion.

this possibility instead of the opposite one that most troubles economists and public utility companies, partly because regulatory commissions have typically been very conservative in the depreciation rates they allow[88] and partly because the discrepancy of inadequate depreciation can have a more seriously distorting effect on pricing and replacement policy.) There is a real danger in this event that replacement of old plant and equipment with new will be uneconomically discouraged. To understand this danger, we must have a brief and simplified look at the economics of replacement.

The way for a company to decide whether to replace a piece of machinery (or plant or other equipment) is to compare the average *variable* cost of producing with it (AVC_0) with the average *total* cost of production with new equipment (ATC_n). Only the variable costs of the old can be saved by turning to the new; the choice therefore is between continuing to incur those AVC, on the one hand, or incurring the ATC—including the capital costs as well—involved in purchasing a new machine. If the AVC_0 are smaller than the ATC_n it is economical to continue to use the old capital goods. But if, *regardless* of the fixed costs on the old, the AVC_0 are the greater, it is foolish not to scrap; every moment of continued production with the old means a greater drain on the company's resources, a greater avoidable cost of production, than would be involved in replacement.[89]

In either event, the continuing, fixed costs on the old equipment—the depreciation that may not yet have been fully recovered, the return on the net investment not yet fully written off, interest on the debt already incurred —are irrelevant to the decision. Sunk costs such as these are bygones, unchangeable past history, and best forgotten. The way to maximize profit is to minimize the variable, or incremental, or avoidable costs of production (since the others are fixed anyway); and that means the variable costs for existing plant and the total costs for new. This is just as true for a monopolist as for a firm operating under pure competition.

But it need not be true for a regulated company. That company cannot ignore the fixed costs on existing assets, because the regulatory commission may or may not choose to include them in its cost of service once the assets have been replaced. Suppose, for example, that the average variable costs under the old process are a constant $7 per unit, the average fixed costs (depreciation and return on the unamortized part of the investment) $3, and the regulated price is $10. Suppose then a new process becomes available with the same capacity as the old, with average variable costs of $4.50 and average fixed costs of $2. Such an investment would be economically efficient; every unit that continued to be produced under the old process (at an avoidable cost of $7) would be involving society as well as the firm in the unnecessary expenditure of 50 cents worth of resources (since the *total* unit

[88] In 1964, depreciation expense for large privately owned electric utilities seems to have run at 2 to $2\frac{1}{2}\%$ of gross book investment. Federal Power Commission, *Statistics of Electric Utilities in The U. S., 1964, Privately Owned*, March 1966. The typical depreciation rate for interstate gas pipelines is 3 to $3\frac{1}{2}\%$. Richard W. Hooley, *Financing the Natural Gas Industry* (New York: Columbia Univ. Press, 1961), 66. The FCC prescribed an increase in the rate for the telephone industry from 5.1 to 5.4% effective

January 1, 1968.
[89] This statement ignores the effect on these calculations of the expectation that in the future some even more efficient plant or machine may become available. Such an expectation might justify a company practicing what Fellner has termed "anticipatory retardation"—stalling the replacement of an old machine with a new, in order to await the next, even lower ATC_n that will be available. See note 91.

costs under the new are only $6.50). In an unregulated industry, even a monopolist would make the investment: at the very least, he could produce at the same rate and sell his product at the same price as before, and simply pocket the 50-cent per unit cost saving. Suppose, however, that the company was a regulated utility and that its regulatory commission insisted that the cost savings be more or less promptly translated into price reductions. A price cut to $9.50 would raise no difficulty, apart from possible considerations of risk: the company could continue to obtain the $3 of capital costs on the old equipment plus the $6.50 full unit cost of the new. But the commission might well insist that the old assets be removed from the rate base, once they had been replaced, even though depreciation on them had not yet been fully recovered. It might insist, that is, that the price be reduced to $6.50, the new unit cost of service, thus forcing the stockholders to bear the loss of the unamortized portion of their investment in the old equipment. In this event the company would find itself in a position of having incurred *additional* capital costs of $2 a unit, and yet had its gross return on capital (depreciation and profit) reduced from $3 a unit to $2 a unit. It obviously would have been better for the company to postpone the new investment and continue to take in the $3 per unit of depreciation and return on the old assets until the latter had been completely written off.

What happened in this example was that technological progress had outrun the allowances for depreciation: it reduced the economic value of the old plant to zero (or to its value as scrap) before those assets were wholly written off in the books and the original investment fully recovered from customers. And the moral would seem to be that when this occurs, a regulated company will be deterred from replacing old assets with economically more efficient new ones unless it is permitted to continue to charge customers the capital costs of the unamortized portion of previous investments.[90] These customers may complain, with justice, that they are being made to pay more than the marginal, or indeed the total cost of serving them; that the company is being permitted to recoup from them sunk costs that should have been charged against customers in the past. But they are still better off than if the company refused to install the new, lower-cost equipment for serving them.[91]

---

[90] See Troxel, *Economics of Public Utilities*, 356–369.

[91] There is no well-developed "economics of error"; in the present instance there is no perfect solution of a problem that arises because mistakes have been made in the past. But it should also be emphasized that price will not instantaneously fall to the ATC of the newest and lowest-cost available processes even under perfect competition. As William Fellner has pointed out, rational firms will practice "anticipatory retardation" in the face of a continuous flow of cost-reducing innovations over time. Even pure competitors will not instantly adopt a new technology as soon as the ATC of the latest available process falls below market price. With correct anticipations they will recognize that, since technological progress is continuous, such an investment policy would produce continual disappointment; with further improvements in technology, price would be perpetually slipping below (or, to the extent that the gains of improved productivity are passed on in higher incomes to the factors of production, costs would be perpetually rising above) the levels at which the calculations were made, and investors would therefore continuously fail to make the anticipated return on investment incorporated in the ATC_n. They will therefore systematically delay the introduction of new processes, introducing not the first improvement whose ATC is below current market price but one later on in the flow of improvements, waiting until the return from cost savings promises to be sufficiently high in the early years of life of the new equipment to offset the eroding away of those gains as still later techniques become available—until, that is, it appears they will be able to earn the anticipated depreciation and return over the life of the new plant. So purely competitive price remains on

It could be argued, instead, that the costs of mistakes such as these ought to be borne by the stockholders. It is their function, not that of consumers, to bear the risks of unanticipatedly rapid obsolescence; their rate of return ought to be high enough to compensate for such risks. The argument would not be wrong, in principle. But by the same reasoning the allowable rate of return of public utilities is kept typically below that in industry generally precisely because stockholders share these risks with consumers; what consumers would gain by a different treatment of depreciation in these circumstances they would lose by having to pay a higher return.[92] Moreover, allowable depreciation is usually determined by the regulatory authorities: if it proves *ex post* to have been inadequate, it is not clear that the burden is properly borne by stockholders.[93] Here again is reflected the conception that regulation should in the face of change and uncertainty permit public utility companies to cover their authorized revenue requirements—not more and not less—rather than treat them as they would be treated by a competitive market. Finally, there remains the basic problem that putting the burden on stockholders would discourage economically efficient replacement of obsolete assets.[94]

---

the average sufficiently above the total unit costs under the latest available technique to permit investors on the average to write off old plant and earn the required return on its undepreciated portion. William Fellner, "The Influence of Market Structure on Technological Progress," in Amer. Econ. Ass'n, *Readings in Industrial Organization and Public Policy* (Homewood: Richard D. Irwin, 1958), 287–291. This is precisely what the recommended public utility commission treatment of depreciation and return on undepreciated, replaced equipment would accomplish: by holding price above ATC_n it would permit recovery of the fixed costs of the old. The danger, then, would not be that utility companies would be unduly discouraged from introducing new techniques but that they would be encouraged in this manner to inflate their rate bases, being permitted by their commissions to recover investment in the old and to earn a return on the new even though the latter was unneeded. On this "A–J–W" danger, see Chapter 2, Volume 2.

[92] This consideration does not fully dispose of the argument. It might still be that efficiency would be better served by having risks of this kind borne in the overall rate of return than in continued amortizations of incompletely depreciated, obsolete assets: the incidence of these two methods would almost certainly differ, depending on how precisely the amortization was effected.

[93] But see note 94. "In a non-regulated competitive industry, market forces will punish those investors who select managers who have incorrectly foreseen the rate of technological advance....

"In a regulated industry with only one or two suppliers, however, society can not afford the

disruptive effects on supply which the market discipline enforces for inevitable errors of foresight....

"Regulation should not, of course, provide an umbrella for all errors of managerial judgment; however, it appears to me that a consistently used current cost base might reduce the willingness of investors to provide capital funds . . . *unless* management slows down the rate of technological change to one that is more readily predictable and is in line with past investment decisions embedded in existing durable equipment." Testimony of Paul Davidson, in FCC, *In the Matter of American Telephone and Telegraph Co.*, Docket 16258, Western Union Exhibit 4, 1968, mimeo., 71–76.

[94] It is very largely the fear of unanticipatedly rapid technological obsolescence that apparently explains the recent tendency of regulated companies to press for higher allowable rates of depreciation—a tendency that might otherwise be difficult to understand, since higher depreciation expense means a more rapid diminution of the rate base. (See note 32, Chapter 2, Volume 2.) This fear is intensified where the utility companies face the competition of companies that have access to the newer technology and are unencumbered by the costs of older, incompletely amortized plant—a situation that has prevailed in communications in recent years. See the discussion in Chapter 4 of Volume 2, especially around notes 94–96.

On the other hand, the utilities are themselves responsible in part for these difficulties. Many of them have resisted the adoption of more rapid depreciation, with its attendant income tax advantages, precisely in order to avoid the more rapid decline in rate base that this would have

Therefore, if technological progress outstrips depreciation, and regulated companies are permitted to recover their as-yet unamortized investment in obsolete facilities, prices will exceed LRMC. This will be true even under conditions of constant costs, when LRMC equals ATC_n. The source of the discrepancy is the difference between ATC computed so as to include gross return on a historic rate base and ATC_n. If the rate of depreciation accurately reflects the year-by-year decline in the economic value of existing assets no such discrepancy can occur: ATC on a historic rate base will be the same as ATC_n. The reason for this is that the economic value of existing assets at any given time is, precisely, the current value of the differences between AVC_o and ATC_n over their remaining life (or their value as scrap, whichever is larger). As long as AVC_o is less than ATC_n, the plant clearly has positive value, measured by the cost-saving that continued use makes possible. Once those two are equal, the old plant has zero value (for purposes of production; it may have positive scrap value). If the economic value were correctly stated on the books, the addition of gross return on that net book value to the variable costs of operating the old plant would produce a cost of service exactly equal to that of a new plant.[95]

The same end would be achieved by using a true current value rate base. But it is not the calculation of a reproduction cost rate base, as such—with all the administrative travail and expense that this has traditionally involved—that is the goal. Instead the goal is to estimate the cost of reproducing the service, with current technology. In principle, this can be achieved just as well by following an economically realistic depreciation policy, applied to original cost. In practice, the task of predicting obsolescence is likely to be a difficult one: but so has been the use of reproduction cost.

Clearly the charging of depreciation raises interesting and difficult questions of who should pay what share of capital costs over time. We have already posed the question of the proper rate when a plant is built far in advance of total need—perhaps because there are great economies of scale. To charge depreciation in equal annual installments would be to impose a disproportionately heavy burden on customers in earlier years, when much of the capacity lies idle. Considerations of fairness—the idle capacity is really for the benefit of future, not present customers—and economic efficiency present a case for something similar to SRMC pricing, which would have the effect of concentrating the capital charges in later years.[96]

Precisely the opposite course is suggested with respect to an investment required to meet current needs, but which may be expected to become rapidly

---

entailed. They did so feeling secure in their monopoly positions and their ability to continue earning an acceptable return on the larger investment. They have resisted also for fear of being forced by regulatory commissions to flow through the resulting tax benefits in the form of lower rates—a practice that does expose them to the possibility of higher tax liabilities and consequently reduced earnings in the future, and the necessity of asking for rate increases at that time. See pp. 32–34, above, and the excellent "Comment" by William H. Melody in Trebing and Howard, *op. cit.*, pp. 164–175,

which concludes: "The long-run viability of utilities in some markets that are subject to external competitive pressures may well depend upon the maintenance of a depreciation policy that properly reflects the rate of economic depreciation in an environment of rapid technological change."

[95] The preceding discussion draws heavily on the testimony of Vickrey in FCC, *In the Matter of American Telephone and Telegraph Co.*, Docket 16258, mimeo., esp. 53–56.

[96] See the example of Comsat, note 73, p. 113, note 4, p. 88, and p. 104.

outmoded by new technology already on the horizon.[97] In this instance, the investment should be written off rapidly, however long its physical life is likely to be, in reflection of the early anticipated decline in its economic value. The effect would be to put the heaviest capital charges on customers now and in the immediate future—and properly so, since it is for their benefit that the capacity is being built now instead of later, when it could embody the lower cost technology. Such higher charges might well restrict demand sufficiently to demonstrate that the investment in question would better be postponed until the new technology was perfected. The opposite course—to charge depreciation only at the modest rate dictated by average historic experience— would result in charging future users much more than LRMC: they would be stuck with the costs of writing off the inadequately depreciated and obsolete older equipment. And the effect in this event would be to discourage the introduction of the new technology, because demand at that later time would be restrained by the inefficiently high price for the services, "rolling-in" the excessive ATC of the old, inadequately depreciated assets with the much lower ATC of the new.[98]

Manifestly, the rate at which depreciation is charged can have important effects on technological progress. And although it is an impossible task to estimate the proper rate in advance, as Vickrey states,

". . . even a rough approximation to the inclusion of such an analysis in the rate making process is to be preferred to sticking to a fundamentally erroneous approach."[99]

---

[97] This example also depends heavily on the Vickrey testimony, *ibid.*, 27 and 56–60.

[98] Considerations of this type were apparently central to the controversy within the FCC that eventuated in 1968 in its authorizing AT&T to lay a submarine cable between the United States and Spain. In the dissenting opinion of Commissioner Johnson the cable project played the role of supplying the additional capacity (questionably) required in the near future, with current technology, and the satellite the role of the superior technology of the future (indeed, he felt, of the present). Commissioners Cox and Loevinger asserted, in support of the FCC decision, that:

". . . satellites are not now, and will not for at least the next 5 to 7 years be, the most economic means of providing international communications service."

But, Johnson asserted:

"Of course, by depreciating the cable over *twenty* years it appears that the per-year cost of the cable is lower than the per-year additional satellite cost over its projected *five*-year life. The point is that . . . neither will be needed as insurance for more than five years." FCC 68–212, 12514, letter from Rosel H. Hyde, Chairman, to Richard R. Hough, Vice President, American Telephone and Telegraph Company, and accompanying Concurring Statement of Commissioners Cox and Loevinger and Dissenting Opinion of Commissioner Johnson, February 16, 1968.

[99] *Op. cit.*, FCC Docket 16258, 59.

CHAPTER 5

Decreasing Costs and Price Discrimination

The marginal cost pricing principle justifies, at the extreme, a separate price for every sale. The marginal costs of serving no two customers are identical, except by chance; and those costs will fluctuate from one instant to the next as output moves up and down along the SRMC production curve and as the price necessary to clear the market fluctuates similarly with the changing balance of demand and capacity. Or, tempering that principle with the others we have already discussed, it justifies an elaborate system of rate *differentials* for the various categories of service, corresponding to their different (approximate) marginal costs, even if the entire structure is held constant for substantial periods of time. But it does not justify rate *discrimination*—that is, charging different purchasers prices that differ by varying proportions from the respective marginal costs of serving them. On the contrary, charging any customer more or less than the marginal cost of serving him violates the dictates of economic efficiency, for reasons we have already set forth.

THE OCCASIONS FOR DISCRIMINATION

One of the virtues of pure competition is that it eliminates the possibility of price discrimination. The more necessitous buyer does not have to pay more than the less, the rich more or less than the poor; no one, however inelastic his demand, can be exploited by sellers with monopoly power— which is, precisely, the power to hold price above marginal cost. And in long-run equilibrium, the seller can have no *need* to discriminate in price, although he would find it profitable to do so if he could: when capacity is properly adjusted to the level of demand, the price to all buyers can be at SRMC and at the same time cover ATC, as our Figure 1 (p. 74) illustrates.

But this coincidence of SRMC and ATC is possible only if the firm is not operating on the declining portion of its ATC curve. Only when ATC is at its lowest point are the two equal. In fact, the public utility industries are preeminently characterized in important respects by decreasing unit costs— or increasing returns—with increasing levels of output. That is indeed one important reason why they are organized as regulated monopolies: a "natural monopoly" is an industry in which the economies of scale—that is, the tendency for average costs to decrease the larger the producing firm—are continuous up to the point that one company supplies the entire demand. It is a reason, also, why competition is not supposed to work well in these industries.[1]

The Nature and Prevalence of Decreasing Costs

The phenomenon of decreasing costs, or increasing returns, has three possible aspects that must be kept quite distinct, in principle. The first is short-run decreasing costs, which reflects the familiar fact that once an investment has been made to provide a productive capacity (recall our definition of the short run as the period in which the firm operates with a given capacity already in being), total unit costs of production decline as output increases up to or almost up to the physical limits of capacity operation. Any plant and equipment will be designed for some level of production at which total unit costs will be at their lowest point. As output increases to that point, the fixed costs are spread over a larger and larger number of units. (Up to a point variable costs per unit will probably decline also, as the number of workers and the amount of raw material and other variable inputs approximate the level for which the operation was designed.) In view of the heavy fixed costs of most public utility operations and the tendency for companies to build capacity in advance of demand—partly because of the economies of building in large units and partly because of their obligation to supply a service that cannot in most cases be stored but can only be produced on demand—excess capacity and short-run decreasing costs as output expands, at least in certain dimensions,[2] are pervasive.

The second is long-run decreasing costs (LRDC). In many aspects of public utility operations, there are great economies of scale, in the sense that the larger the plant constructed or the larger the unit of additional capacity put into operation, the lower will be its unit costs if operated to the capacity for which it has been designed. Long-run, like short-run decreasing costs, as the economist uses the term, is a static phenomenon: with *given* technology, at any *given* point in time, the utility has before it the possibility of constructing larger or smaller capacities or additions thereto;[3] and, at least in certain aspects of production or distribution, its engineers will tell it that the unit costs of the larger capacities will be less than of the smaller, if operated at optimum rates. It is LRDC that constitute the justification for considering some public utility operations "natural monopolies."

We make no effort here to summarize the evidence of the extent to which the various public utility industries do operate under long-run decreasing

---

[1] See the fuller analysis of these two rationalizations of the public utility institution in Chapters 4 and 5, Volume 2.

[2] One source of confusion in characterizing the cost tendencies in any industry is that "output" is not unidimensional. As we shall see, increased sales of electricity, gas, and telephone services to existing customers will almost certainly be subject to at least short-run decreasing costs, whereas extension of service to additional customers (another possible "expansion of output") might well exhibit the opposite tendency. See the discussion along the same lines with respect to long-run costs, immediately following.

[3] The purest case of LRDC prevails when a firm begins with an absolutely clean slate and faces a "planning curve" demonstrating the unit costs of different planned levels of output, each in a plant constructed in order to produce *that* output at minimum cost. But most firms carry with them into new investment decisions the consequences of investment decisions made in the past. They also will face an LRDC situation when and if additional output would reduce ATC (entirely apart from changes in technology) or involve lower unit costs the greater the addition to output.

costs, other than to observe that the phenomenon is widespread and important. It should be emphasized that they may in certain respects but not in
others. For example, the telephone business is said to be subject to long-run
increasing costs, when the dimension of output is taken to be the number of
subscribers, because as that number increases the number of required
connections in the central exchange increases more than proportionately.[4]

On the other hand, telephone capacity costs *per message* almost certainly
decline within very wide limits as the number of messages per subscriber are
increased. In the same way electricity distribution costs per customer may
well increase with increased urban sprawl, that is, with increased average
distance between customers; the same is probably true of the distribution of
gas and water and the supply of urban transit. But electric generating costs,
and electric and gas distribution costs and the costs per passenger over
existing routes decline sharply per customer and per unit of sales in any given
area.[5] The distribution cost of serving an all-electric house is said to be
probably no more than 10 to 15% higher than for the average residence,
though its average electricity consumption may run five or six times as much.

The long-distance telephone business provides striking illustrations of these
static economies of scale. Table 1 summarizes the estimated costs of providing

table 1 Illustrative Costs for TD2 Radio Relay Systems per Repeater Station

Voice Grade Circuit Capacity	Total Costs	Average Costs per Circuit	Additional Circuits	Incremental Costs per Circuit
600	$368,000	614	600	614
3,600	$492,000	137	3,000	41
6,000	$574,000	96	2,400	34

Source. Testimony of Albert M. Froggatt, FCC Docket No. 16258, *op. cit.*, Bell Exhibit 24.
May 31, 1966, Table I.

a particular facility for transmitting various types of messages via microwave
radio, with varying alternative capacities, supplied by an AT&T vice-
president testifying before the FCC. There are certain common, starting-up
costs totaling $368,000 that must be incurred whether the planned capacity
is 600 or 6,000 circuits—the costs of the land, tower, building and access
roads, maintenance equipment, and so forth. If capacity is planned for only
the 600 channels, the average cost per circuit is $614; if 6,000 circuits, the
average cost falls to $96. If the average cost falls in this fashion, it must be
that the incremental costs of adding circuits fall even more sharply, or at
least remain below the average within this range of output. The first increment of 600 costs $614. The cost is only $124,000 to add the next 3,000
circuits: this gives an incremental cost of $41 per circuit. To move from 3,600
to 6,000 circuits adds another $82,000, for an incremental cost of $34.

---

[4] David G. Tyndall, "The Relative Merits of
Average Cost Pricing, Marginal Cost Pricing and
Price Discrimination," *Q. Jour. Econ.* (August
1951), LXV: 369. But see the section "Cases of
apparently increasing costs," in Chapter 4,
Volume 2.
[5] See, for example, Ralph Turvey, *Optimal
Pricing and Investment in Electricity Supply* (London:
George Allen and Unwin, Ltd., 1968), 70–72.

William Iulo finds that consumption per residential customer is the single most important
determinant of intercompany cost differences.
Its sign is negative: the greater the former the
lower the costs per unit. *Electric Utilities—Costs
and Performance* (Pullman: Washington State
Univ. School of Economics and Business, 1961),
102–107.

This example illustrates also some of the ambiguities of the concept of long-run decreasing costs. Although what it describes is a long-run, planning phenomenon—the costs of supplying varying capacities—the increasing returns within the 600 to 6,000 range may be construed instead as illustrating only short-run decreasing costs. ATC declines because certain investment outlays have to be made merely to provide the 600 circuits. These outlays create capacity that can then be spread over the next 5,400. Since the average utilization of these repeater stations was said to be only 3,500 circuits or so, as of 1967, do we not have here a mere illustration of the (short-run) tendency of ATC to decline in the presence of excess capacity? The point is that tendencies to increasing returns, of both varieties, are created basically by the presence of indivisibilities. The cost of clearing land, digging trenches (for gas or water mains and oil or gas pipelines), putting up telephone and electric poles, putting a telephone and a gas, electricity, or telephone line and a meter into a customer's home or place of business are an inescapable, indivisible burden of installing any capacity at all. What creates economies of scale is that these indivisible outlays then can be used to provide greater or lesser capacities and a greater amount of service by supplementary investments and variable expenses that will increase total cost less than proportionately. That is what makes it inefficient to have more than one supplier. As long as the market demand is less than the ultimate total that can be provided in this way, the firm is operating on the declining portion of its long-run as well as its short-run average cost curve; LRMC are below LRAC.[6]

---

[6] Moreover, according to Froggatt, the economies of scale are not exhausted at the 6,000-circuit capacity. If it became necessary to add successive increments of circuits, the average total cost would rise as the company passed each multiple of 6,000, but each time to a level below the ATC of the preceding 6,000, because, once again, some of the same facilities could be used for the larger number of messages.

For other attempts to determine over how wide a range of plant or firm size static economies of scale prevail in various regulated industries, see George H. Borts, "The Estimation of Rail Cost Functions," *Econometrica* (January 1960), XXVIII: 108–131 (LRAC increasing in the Eastern U.S., decreasing or constant in the West and South); Kent T. Healy, *The Effects of Scale in the Railroad Industry*, Committee on Transportation (New Haven: Yale Univ. Press, 1961), 3 (costs turn up beyond a range of 10,000–19,000 employees); Zvi Griliches, "Notes on Railroad Cost Studies," University of Chicago, Center for Mathematical Studies in Business and Economics, Report 6918, June 1969 (few economies of scale once the very small roads are eliminated); J. Johnston, *Statistical Cost Analysis* (New York: McGraw-Hill, 1960), 44–73 (LRAC for electricity generation in U.K. plants in 1946–1947 was L-shaped—that is, beyond a point, there were no more economies of scale); Marc Nerlove, "Returns to Scale in Electricity Supply," in Carl

Christ et al., *Measurement in Economics* (Stanford: Stanford Univ. Press, 1963), 167–198 (LRAC for the firm first declines, then shows a mixed picture at the upper reaches of firm size); Ryutano Komiya, "Technical Progress and the Production Function in the U.S. Steam Power Industry," *Rev. Econ. Stat.* (May 1962), XLIV: 156–166 (continuously increasing returns to scale within the observed range); Yoram Barzel, "Productivity in the Electric Power Industry," *ibid.* (November 1963), XLV: 401–403 (strong economies of scale in generating plant size and consumption per customer); Phoebus J. Dhrymes and Mordecai Kurz, "Technology and Scale in Electricity Generation," *Econometrica* (June 1964), XXXII: 287–315 (LRAC decreasing); Leslie Cookenboo, Jr., *Crude Oil Pipelines and Competition in the Oil Industry* (Cambridge: Harvard Univ. Press, 1955), 8–32 (LRAC declining up to pipelines carrying 400,000 barrels per day); Johnson in Shepherd and Gies, *op. cit.*, 121–124 (economies of scale in communications satellites); and, on natural gas pipelines, see note 33, Chapter 4. The statistical findings are inevitably dependent on the particular dimension of output selected. As Griliches points out, his negative findings do not exclude the likelihood of decreasing average costs

". . . for some types of traffic, at some times, in some areas. But all the studies examined ask the

The third aspect of decreasing costs in public utilities must be handled with special care because as usually conceived it is not a phenomenon of decreasing costs at all. This is the decline in ATC *over time* as a result of technological progress. Most public utilities can be sure that unit costs will decline over time, unless the tendency is offset by inflation in the economy at large; a plant constructed ten years from now will be much more efficient than a plant constructed today. In most utility operations, the technology is so dynamic that it is highly probable real costs fall more rapidly than in most other sectors of the economy.[7]

In principle, dynamically decreasing costs, in consequence of technological progress, are clearly distinguishable from statically decreasing costs, both long- and short-run. Technological progress does not in itself mean that a larger output can be produced at lower ATC than a smaller output; that there are economies of scale; or, therefore, that MC are less than ATC. It could simply lower the ATC function at all levels of output, for all sizes of firm, and still leave the relation of MC to ATC unchanged. But in practice, the two phenomena may be causally intertwined.[8] Technological progress may either *involve* or *reflect* genuine increasing returns in one of two possible ways. First, the technological advance may be of a type that embodies or gives rise to static economies of scale. (Or it may do the opposite.) Second, the technological advance may itself be *induced* by the higher levels of demand or output—that is, it may not be truly independent of the increase in output. If the need for higher levels of output either *calls forth* or makes it economical *to put into practice* technological advances *that would not otherwise be induced or feasible*, then it is reasonable to consider that the reduction in cost (over time) was in fact a consequence of the higher level of output, hence reflected increasing returns in the strict sense of the term.

Because the relationship of technological change to the level of output is far more difficult to specify, predict, or prove than static relationships of cost to different levels of planned output with a given, known technology or set of technical alternatives, this type of "economy of scale" is not usually embraced within the economist's conception of increasing returns. But it is in principle identical, and in the real, dynamic world may be even more important than the others.

Two illustrations will dramatically demonstrate the possible gains from rapid technological progress in the public utilities and indicate its possible

---

question what will happen to average costs if total traffic is expanded on the *average* in the same proportions and having exactly the same distribution over the various commodities, types, routes and seasons as the previously handled traffic. There may be very little return to scale from a *proportionate* increase in all kinds of traffic." *Op. cit.*, 30.

For a strong argument that the railroad cost studies measure economies of scale "in a manner that is totally irrelevant to the special economics of the transportation industry," and in no sense undermine the presence of substantial economies of scale for increases in "the volume of traffic in a given area or along a given corridor," see William Vickrey, "Current Issues in Trans-

portation," unpublished manuscript, undated. See also note 87, Chapter 6, Volume 2.

[7] See Chapter 3, Volume 2. This means that if input prices rise only in proportion to the rise in average productivity in the economy at large—a general condition of average price-level stability implied in the wage-price guidelines (note 27, Chapter 1)—money unit costs in public utilities would be expected to fall over time.

[8] The classic statement on the difficulty (he would have said meaninglessness) of distinguishing the two is J. H. Clapham, "Of Empty Economic Boxes," *Econ. Jour.* (1922), XXXII: 305–314, reprinted in American Economic Association, *Readings in Price Theory*, 119–130.

causal connection with decreasing costs, strictly defined. The size of electrical generating units commissioned in Great Britain rose from 30 megawatts in 1950 to 550 megawatts in 1963. And the capital costs per kilowatt sent out declined from £67 to £37 in the same period—and this in the face of a very substantial increase in the general price level.[9] In the United States, the largest generating unit in operation in 1930 had a capacity of 208,000 kw; in 1956, the largest was 260,000 kw; and by 1965, only nine years later, a 1,000,000 kw unit was placed in service. Transmission voltages have shown a similar growth curve, with correspondingly dramatic effects on the distances over which it is feasible to transport power and on the opportunities for economies from large-scale generation and power pooling.[10] A reflection of these developments has been the decline in annual operating expenses of privately owned companies from a peak of 8.95 mills per kwh in 1948 to 6.56 in 1966—in the face of a 17% increase in the wholesale price index.[11] The electricity case seems clearly to be one in which dramatic technological advances have greatly increased the economies of large and geographically coordinated operations.[12]

A different example, in which the expansion of demand has clearly played an important causal role in inducing technological advance, is provided by long-distance communication in the last few decades. The same AT&T testimony that provided the basis for Table 1 supplied a chart showing the book costs per circuit route mile of the company's Long Lines Department between 1930 and 1965: the figure starts at $217 and drops continuously—to $158 in 1940, $78 in 1945, $40 in 1955 and $25 in 1965.[13] These unit cost figures, observed as the circuit route mile capacity of the system grew, almost certainly do not reflect simply a static, unchanging LRAC $_{'30-'65?}$ curve as shown in our purely illustrative Figure 5—in which event plants built at any time during that period would have had ATC's like $SRAC_1$ and $SRAC_2$, depending solely on their size. All we have is a series of observations, at different points in time, of various book costs associated with various levels of capacity and output (marked with X's). This historical experience reflected a mixture of causal influences.

1. To some extent the decline in costs could have had nothing to do with the scale of operations. That is, costs might have declined whatever the level of output: the 1930 observation might have been a point on the $LRAC_{'30?}$ indicated in the figure, the 1940 observation on a lower $LRAC_{'40?}$ and so on. If this horizontal set of hypothetical cost curves is the true one, the net book cost could have been $25 per circuit route mile in 1965 for a company $\frac{1}{2}$, $\frac{1}{10}$, or $\frac{1}{100}$ the size of AT&T, as suggested by the alternative $SRAC_a$ and $SRAC_b$.

[9] Andrew Shonfield, *Modern Capitalism: The Changing Balance of Public and Private Power* (New York: Oxford Univ. Press, 1965), 49 note.
[10] Federal Power Commission, *National Power Survey*, Washington, 1964, Part I, 14, and *Steam Electric Plant Construction Costs and Annual Production Expenses* (annual).
[11] The expenses are for all departments combined —production, transmission and distribution, customer accounting and collecting, sales and administrative. Derived from Edison Electric Institute, *Historical Statistics of the Electric Utility Industry* (New York, 1963) and id., *Statistical Yearbook of the Electric Utility Industry* for 1966 (New York, 1967); and (for the WPI) *Statistical Abstract of the United States, 1968* (Washington, 1968), 341.
[12] See also the studies referred to in note 6, and, for a discussion of the institutional implications of these developments, the section "The imperfect adaptation of business structure: electric power," in Chapter 2, Volume 2.
[13] A. M. Froggatt, *op. cit.*, Chart 4. The backup table provided by the company.

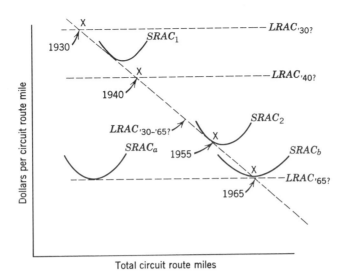

Figure 5. Alternative hypothetical explanations of the decline in book costs of circuit route miles.

2. To some extent it probably reflected *SRDC*—simply a fuller use of capacity, particularly in the first 15 years. During World War II this fuller use also involved some degradation of the quality of service, so that the decline in money costs shown for that period is in some degree misleading.

3. To an important extent it also reflected genuine static economies of scale of the familiar kind: that is, the static *LRAC* functions in 1930, 1945, and 1965 all were undoubtedly negatively sloped, for reasons we have already suggested, though certainly not over the entire range suggested by the *LRAC* $_{30-'65?}$ curve depicted in Figure 5. The 1930 system used poles with open wire: once the poles were up, added wires could be attached with a less than proportionate increase in costs. Then the company used cables; the cost of a cable with 100 pairs of wires is less than twice as much as one with 50. Similar economies of scale were available in the subsequent systems, using successively coaxial cable, microwave radio, and larger coaxial cables.

4. It involved static economies of scale in yet another sense: with higher levels of demand, it became economically feasible to use preexisting technology whose *ATC* would be lower only if the market were large enough to justify its emplacement.

5. The preceding aspect merges with the dynamic one: higher levels of demand *stimulated* the company to develop the new technologies in order to meet the burgeoning needs. When telephone company officials point out that coaxial cable, costing $100,000 a mile, would have been prohibitively expensive in the past and became economical only when hundreds of thousands of circuits were required, they are talking about a mixture of 4 and 5, probably more the latter than the former. But in any event they are describing a genuine phenomenon of decreasing cost—a larger output involving lower unit costs than a smaller one.

Therefore, we have three types of decreasing cost situations in the public utility industries: SRDC, in the presence of excess capacity; LRDC, or static economies of scale; and that part of technological progress that is causally attributable to the increase in volume. All three mean that the more rapidly output expands, the lower unit costs will be. And this means in turn that incremental or marginal costs, both short- and long-run, to the extent that these tendencies prevail, will be less than average total costs. (See, for example, Figure 1, in which this condition prevails at all outputs less than Q_e. Or see Figure 6.)

Implications and Solutions

The consequence is that in all such situations we encounter a flat contradiction between these two fundamental rules: one, that price *to all buyers* be equated with marginal costs and two, that total revenues cover total costs. (If marginal cost is less than the average total cost per unit, and prices are set at the former level, total revenues will be less than total costs.)

Some economists have resolved this conflict by preferring the first to the second principle. If following the rule of equating price to marginal cost means that total revenues fall short of total costs, their solution would be to make up the difference out of taxpayer-financed subsidies. Governments have in fact adopted this solution with respect to numerous "public goods" —the technical definition of which is that the marginal cost of making them available to an additional user is zero.[14] They have also subsidized the provision of public utility services in various ways. But these subsidies are not usually explicitly justified or justifiable by, or systematically related to, the discrepancy between marginal and average costs. Consider, for example, the fact that commercial barge and shipping lines are not charged for the costs of maintaining the inland waterways or that large, diesel-burning trucks apparently do not pay the *marginal* highway costs for which they are causally responsible. On the other hand, the subsidized interest rate for rural electricity cooperatives might have some such justification, in whole or in part. But since governments do not usually follow this practice with respect to privately owned utilities, we devote no more attention to this way out of the conflict.[15]

---

[14] See note 102, Chapter 1, Volume 2.

[15] Economists have long been arguing the theoretical correctness and the practicability of marginal-cost pricing plus public subsidies in circumstances such as these, a debate we make no effort to summarize or resolve here. Our failure to pursue this possibility is grounded mainly on the practical considerations that governments in the United States at least do not follow it with respect to privately owned utilities and that there would be considerable political objection to having taxpayers subsidize users of the service as a general practice. This latter consideration illustrates the limited qualifications of economists for advocating schemes of this sort; the resort to taxpayer-financed subsidies inevitably involves in practice some redistribution of income, from taxpayers to users of the services. As we have already indicated, economic theory alone cannot state in such circumstances that the one result is

"better" than the other. (And this of course raises also the noneconomic consideration that it may strike voters and legislators as unfair.)

Even if we confine our attention to considerations of economic efficiency, our advocacy of tax-financed subsidies to permit marginal-cost pricing must confront the anomaly of

"reliance on the tax system to adjust divergences between average cost and marginal cost despite the fact that the tax system itself is the greatest example of nonmarginal cost pricing." Eli W. Clemens, "Discussion," *Amer. Econ. Rev., Papers and Proceedings* (May 1963), LIII: 482.

Except for levies on pure economic rents, there are practically no neutral taxes, no taxes, that is, that do not in one way or another distort the functioning of a price system. Individual excise taxes alter the relationship between price and cost, hence artificially discourage the con-

There is another solution, even more acceptable in principle (for the reasons indicated in note 15) that comes closer to the one that is feasible for unsubsidized, privately owned utility companies: perfect price discrimination. The entire justification for marginal cost pricing lies in the elasticity of demand—the fact that customers will buy more or less than the optimum amount if price is lower or higher than marginal cost. More satisfactions are conferred on buyers than are taken away from sellers when prices are reduced to marginal cost; producers can be spared losses greater than the buyer satisfactions sacrificed if prices that are below marginal costs are raised to that level.[16] What if, then, the seller could segregate each purchase by each customer, charging him for that particular purchase as much as he is willing to pay, charging less and less as necessary to bring in additional purchasers or to induce existing buyers to take additional units, finally down to marginal costs for those purchases that will not be made at any higher

sumption of the taxed commodities compared with others; and general excise taxes affect the decisions of households to spend on consumption or to save. Income taxes are taxes on work, saving, and investing; so they too introduce an extraneous consideration into those decisions.

See Richard A. Musgrave, *The Theory of Public Finance, A Study In Public Economy* (New York: McGraw-Hill, 1959), 140–159, and for a survey of some of the literature, Nancy Ruggles, "Recent Developments in the Theory of Marginal Cost Pricing," *Rev. Econ. Studies* (1949–1950), XVII: 110–111, 119; also Robert W. Harbeson, "A Critique of Marginal Cost Pricing," *Land Econ.* (February 1955), XXXI: 54–74. In short, the problem would be one of weighing the benefits of a closer approach to economically efficient pricing made possible by these subsidies against the possible departure therefrom involved in the taxes required to finance them.

This consideration obviously weakens the *general* economic case for marginal-cost pricing plus tax-financed subsidy of utility services, but it does not destroy it, as many economic theorists sometimes suggest. It calls instead for a factual judgment of benefits and costs in each individual case. See, for example, the very useful survey in Little, *A Critique of Welfare Economics*, Chapter 11, which begins with a general rejection of marginal-cost pricing and then proceeds to indicate a wide range of services for which it may be desirable. It has yet to be shown, for example, that income or inheritance taxes do, *in fact*, significantly affect the choice between work and leisure (see George F. Break, "The Effect of Taxation on Work Incentives," in Edmund S. Phelps (ed.), *Private Wants and Public Needs, Issues Surrounding the Size and Scope of Government Expenditure*, rev. ed. (W. W. Norton and Company, Inc., 1965), 55–65 and the Brookings study by Robin Barlow, et al., *Economic Behavior of the Affluent* (Washington: The Brookings Institution, 1966). Where economic rents have been inflated by the subsidized

investment (for instance, property values around a newly constructed bridge) they could well be tapped to finance the subsidies without involving either economic distortion or unfairness.

[16] In other words, both moves would maximize total "transactions surplus"—the sum of consumer surplus and producer (or seller) surplus. Consumer surplus is the difference between what buyers would be willing to pay for any given quantity of output and what they actually do pay: so it is represented by the entire area under the demand curve above price. Seller surplus is the difference between the revenues necessary to elicit any given quantity of output (that is, the sum total of marginal costs) and the revenues actually received: so it is represented by the entire area between the marginal cost curve and price. Consider the following simple example:

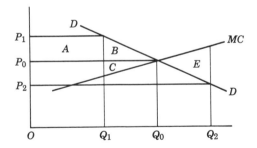

A reduction of price to *MC*, from P_1 to P_0, will increase consumer surplus by the sum of areas *A* and *B*. Area *A* will not represent a net increase in transaction surplus, since it is a mere transfer from seller surplus to buyers. But area *B* represents a net addition to both consumer and transaction surplus, since it reflects the difference between what buyers would have been willing to pay for the additional output, Q_1Q_0, and what they actually have to pay, and does not come out of the pockets of producers. Similarly, area *C* represents a net addition to both seller and transactions surplus, since that added output

price? Suppose, for example, that the toll-collector on the (zero marginal-cost) bridge that we referred to at the beginning of Chapter 4 were omniscient and could charge for each crossing just what the traffic would bear—$1.50, perhaps, to those for whom the particular crossing was very important, down to zero to those who would be deterred by any toll at all. The correct number of crossings would take place; no one would be deterred from buying as much as he would if price were at marginal cost; and no crossing would occur whose value was less than the additional cost to society of making it possible. If production were justified in the first place, total revenue could be made to cover total costs. Instead of collecting only the price equal to marginal cost on the total volume of sales, the seller would collect that low price only on the marginal ones, and take in progressively more on the intramarginal sales.[17]

Perfect price discrimination involves fashioning charges according to what each unit of traffic will bear. Its basis is differences not in cost but in demand, in the value of each unit of service to each purchaser. Of course, it is not achievable in actual practice. In rough approximation, it is how private businesses, natural monopolies and others, determine their differential

---

costs them only the area under the MC curve between Q_1 and Q_0 whereas they receive a price of P_0 for those added sales. Therefore, total transaction surplus is increased by B plus C.

By the same reasoning, raising the price *to MC* from P_2 (which is below MC for the output OQ_2) would produce a net increase in seller plus buyer surplus measured by area E—the difference between what supplying Q_0Q_2 adds to producer costs and consumer satisfaction (the areas under the MC and DD curves, respectively, between Q_0 and Q_2).

[17] See the articles by Dupuit and Hotelling, cited in note 1, Chapter 4; also H. T. Koplin, "A Note on Price Discrimination," *Land Econ.* (February 1958), XXXIV: 92–95. In the extreme case, price discrimination might make it economical for a private firm to construct facilities that would not otherwise be feasible because, as illustrated by the accompanying diagram, at no single price (AR) would revenues be large enough to cover total costs. The socially

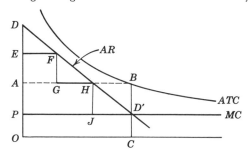

optimum price would be OP, output OC, but the resulting revenue, $OPD'C$ would fall short of total cost. Perfect discrimination could achieve the same output but capture revenues equal to the entire area under the demand curve $ODD'C$. As

long as this exceeded total costs, $OABC$, the investment would be justified in private terms. Pricing successive blocks of sales at lower prices —for example, $EFGHJD'$ in the diagram— could approximate the same result. A take-it-or-leave-it offer of OC quantity at an OA unit price would work also but would be feasible only if there were a single buyer or buying group.

Would the investment be socially justified? Since the total benefits, as measured by the total amount consumers would be willing to pay, would exceed the total costs, the proximate answer is yes. It must be qualified by a recognition that there are many alternative uses to which society's resources might be put that would be equally justified in terms of the size of the consumers' surplus but are not because of the impracticality of sufficient price discrimination; to apply this more generous test in some areas and not in others could therefore lead to misallocation. See Bonbright, *Principles of Public Utility Rates*, 397–398; and J. R. Meyer, J. F. Kain, and M. Wohl, *The Urban Transportation Problem* (Cambridge: Harvard Univ. Press, 1965), 344–345. For an analogous argument see Robert M. Dunn, "A Problem of Bias in Benefit-Cost Analysis: Consumer Surplus Reconsidered," *South. Econ. Jour.* (January 1967), XXXIII: 337–342.

There is special justification in decreasing cost situations that does not apply in others: under conditions of constant or increasing cost, price can be equated to marginal cost and also cover total costs without the need for discrimination. The welfare loss from failing to discriminate and failing to take advantage of the possibilities of increasing returns to scale are therefore greater in the former than in the latter situation. See on this also p. 197, below.

charges—on the basis of the respective elasticities of demand in their various markets, where they can be separated.

The practice of price discrimination is to some extent suspect in industry generally. Charging customers on the basis of value of service, ability to pay or benefits derived instead of on the basis of cost is like levying taxes; these criteria are in fact familiar principles or rationalizations of taxation. Therefore, in private industry the practice can serve as an effective method of monopolistic exploitation, as we have already suggested. Nor is it as frequently necessary for economic efficiency in competitive industries, where the phenomenon of decreasing costs is in normal times less pervasive, and where, therefore, price can be at marginal and average cost at one and the same time.[18] But in public utility situations, where the possibilities of monopolistic exploitation are subject to stringent controls, price discrimination is an often essential way of dealing with the pervasive phenomenon of marginal cost below average total cost.[19]

Price discrimination then becomes the means by which public utility companies can (1) cover (or come closer to covering) average total costs, while (2) making fuller use of existing capacity and/or (3) taking fuller advantage of long-run decreasing costs, by (4) permitting as many purchases as possible to be made as long as buyers are willing to pay the incremental costs of supplying them.[20]

---

[18] This is an oversimplification, to be sure. Imperfectly competitive industries are frequently burdened by excess capacity, hence subject to SRDC; and all in varying degree have economies of scale or LRDC, within limits. *Given* pervasive monopoly pricing in unregulated markets, price discrimination (in particular, reducing price closer to MC in markets with greater elasticity of demand) may more often than not bring output closer to the optimum level. See J. Robinson, *The Economics of Imperfect Competition*, 188–195. The fact remains that in industries in which competition is feasible—that is, in which internal economies of scale are exhausted well before the point at which a single firm supplies the entire market—price discrimination is less necessary for achieving optimal results.

The welfare case for price discrimination is that by enabling a firm, in the presence of short- or long-run decreasing costs, to charge some buyers something closer to marginal costs than would be possible if charges to all buyers had to be uniform, it permits either a fuller use of capacity or a fuller achievement of economies of scale. In the competitive situation, any additional sales that a firm obtains in this way are likely to be obtained mainly by taking customers away from other sellers or by buying off potential buyer-entrants. This fact inevitably raises the question of the possible deleterious effects on the preservation of effective competition, a question of less significance in the public utility area outside of transportation. (See our Chapter 6.) Moreover, in this case the "marginal-cost pricing" is far less

likely to lead to fuller utilization of *total industry* capacity than in the case of a public utility company—which is more likely to *be* the entire industry in itself. Similarly, to the extent public utilities are more "naturally monopolistic," with long-run marginal cost below average total cost throughout the entire relevant range, the justification in terms of the fuller achievement of economies of scale is more persuasive for these companies than in the competitive sector. With respect to the latter, it is proper to pose the question: if there are economies of scale to be achieved, why do they require *selective* price cuts?

[19] This does not deny that *inadequately regulated* price discrimination is probably more dangerous in public utility than in unregulated industries, precisely because of the greater monopoly power of the former. There is always the possibility of customers shifting to other suppliers and of competitive entry, outside the public utility arena. The subscriber hooked up to the only gas, electric, water or telephone company in the area typically has no such alternatives. It was mainly because competition in the public utility industries, and particularly in transportation, tended to be highly selective and discriminatory that they were subjected to regulation.

[20] See especially E. W. Clemens, "Price Discrimination in Decreasing Cost Industries," *Amer. Econ. Rev.* (December 1941), XXXI: 794–802; also the extremely clear graphical presentation by D. A. Worcester, Jr., "Justifiable Price 'Discrimination' Under Conditions of National Monopoly: A Diagrammatic Representation," *ibid.* (June 1948), XXXVIII: 382–388.

Technological Progress and Overhead Costs

There are two other possible occasions for price discrimination that remain to be considered. One is decreasing cost in the popular—not the economic—sense: that is, the tendency of costs to decline over time, without reference to economies of scale. As long as the capital component of average total costs —depreciation, return, income and property taxes—is computed in part on the basis of historic, book values, the average total cost of producing with new plant and equipment (ATC_n) may fall below the utility's unit cost of service (ATC_o). This will occur, we saw in Chapter 4, only if the rate of technological progress outruns the effects both of price inflation (which tends to inflate ATC_n) and the gradual erosion of the historical rate base by the application of (in this case unrealistically low) depreciation allowances. We have already discussed the merits of permitting utilities in these circumstances to recover their uneconomically high ATC_o, when economically efficient prices should be based on ATC_n: marginal cost looks to future instead of past cost responsibility. The fact remains that if utilities *are* permitted to do so, marginal costs will on this account be below ATC, and price discrimination is a possible way out of the dilemma, permitting the companies to recover these fixed, sunk costs from some markets while pricing closer to marginal costs in others.

The other is the pervasive joint and common costs described in Chapter 3. May not price discrimination be justified or necessary as a means of distributing and recovering these overhead costs among the various services jointly produced? In principle, no, except in the presence of decreasing costs. The presence of common or joint costs does not itself justify or necessitate price discrimination; it is only the fact that joint output may be subject to increasing returns that does so, for reasons we have already fully explored. But in practice (as our "in principle" qualification suggests) discrimination may indeed be the only, or the most, feasible method of recovering some part of the costs.

Consider, first, the case of joint costs, that is, where the proportions of the several services cannot be varied. In public utilities the same capacity is available to produce the same volume of service at different times of the day, week, or year, or because every trip of a railroad train in one direction inevitably creates the equivalent capacity for a return haul. Joint services do not have separable production costs. And, as Figure 4 in Chapter 4 illustrates, the joint costs *must* be distributed between them in a manner *akin* to price discrimination—that is, on the basis of the relative intensities and elasticities of the separate demands. But such pricing is *not* discriminatory. The markets are not artificially but physically and inevitably separate and distinct. There is no way of selling more in the high-price market by diverting capacity or product from the low-price market, as would be the competitive solution in the case of genuine discrimination. The capacity is in each market being rationed among the only customers who could possibly compete for it, in such a way as to clear that market; and each customer that continues to be served is in fact forced to pay the marginal opportunity cost of doing so— which is what the first-excluded customer in that market would have been willing to pay.[21]

---

[21] See pp. 87–88 and esp. note 11, Chapter 4,   380–381.
and Bonbright, *Principles of Public Utility Rates,*

Consider next the case of common costs. As long as the proportions of the common services and the capacity planned or used for each can be varied, the marginal cost of each can be determined. The marginal cost would be either the cost of producing an additional unit of the one while holding output of the others constant or the value of the other that could be produced with common facilities, or for whose production the facilities could otherwise have been designed. And there is no reason why these marginal costs (multiplied by their respective quantities) should not add up to total costs—unless, that is, production is subject to increasing returns.[22] In these circumstances price discrimination is in principle not necessarily justified: no service should sell at less than its marginal costs, and none need sell for more, since the sum total of marginal costs could well cover total revenue requirements.[23]

Common costs might well be subject to increasing returns, of the two familiar varieties. Every board-foot of lumber has a proportional cost responsibility for its share of the total warehouse space. But the marginal cost of storing it will be equal to the average total cost only: (1) if the warehouse is full or would be filled even if the particular board-feet being costed were not there and (2) if there are no economies of scale in the provision of additional cubic feet of warehouse space. As for the first, if excess capacity prevails, the short-run marginal opportunity cost of storing the lumber could be anything down to zero, depending on what price it would take to fill the warehouse.[24] That would be the value of the space to the first-excluded user. In reference to the second possibility, if the cost of providing an additional cubic foot is less than the average, here again there arises the problem that the sum total of marginal costs will fall short of total costs. If either SRDC (1) or LRDC (2) prevails, discrimination becomes possibly justifiable as a way of more closely approaching economically efficient pricing while covering total costs.[25]

---

[22] Bonbright's discussion of the reasons for the "failure of the sum of differential costs to equate with total costs" seems at one point to suggest that such a failure is inevitable in all common cost situations:

"These differential or incremental or marginal costs are nonadditive except under special conditions. For the determination of the cost of any particular type and amount of output assumes the continued production of the rest of the output, an assumption which is shifted when the costs of other types and amounts of output are under inquiry," *Ibid.* 297, 299.

However, at other times Bonbright attributes this failure only to one of the following circumstances: (1) decreasing costs, in the static sense, (2) differences between historical and current costs, or (3) the enormous practical difficulties of making the fine distinction necessary to break down all the common costs among all the categories of services and customers, taking into account the enormous variety of independent factors determining the variation in cost from one unit of sale to another, and incorporating all these variations in differential rates. The third

set of considerations, which Bonbright lucidly and persuasively expounds, does not conflict in principle with the statement in the text, above, but constitutes a powerful practical reason for price discrimination to recover a large portion of the common costs. See *ibid.* 296–301, 346 note, 348 note, 351 note (to miss Bonbright's footnotes is to miss some of the most interesting parts of the book), 355–356, 361–362, 383.

[23] For a strong statement of this position, see Donald H. Wallace, "Joint and Overhead Cost and Railway Rate Policy," *Q. Jour. Econ.* (August 1934), XLVIII: 583–619.

[24] Wallace's conclusions are subject always to the proviso "when the state of demands is such that best utilization can be obtained with uniform rates to all customers," *ibid.*, 585. That is to say, when there is excess capacity, he points out, the situation will resemble that of joint costs, in which rates may appropriately be varied in relation to the different elasticities and intensities of demand for the various services.

[25] Apart from the true joint-cost case (the solution to which he improperly terms discriminatory, *ibid.*), Wallace maintains that price discrimination is not economically justified

Finally, there are the practical considerations. In the presence of pervasive common costs, it is simply infeasible to make exhaustive computations of the ever-changing and infinitely differing marginal costs of each unit of service and to embody them in charges. To this extent, it is impossible for public utility companies to escape basing charges first on ascertainable, separate

except in the presence of excess capacity, a situation that is ordinarily only temporary. Since this view denies that the presence of *long-run* decreasing costs justifies continuing discrimination, the argument must be set forth and confronted.

The (static) concept of long-run costs refers to a planning situation, one in which a firm is in a position to build new or additional capacity of various possible sizes. If these potential plant sizes fall within the range of decreasing long-run costs, a situation described in the accompanying figure, the long-run marginal cost curve will fall below the long-run average cost curve, reflecting the fact that output can be expanded with a less than proportionate increase in total cost. Now, whatever the slope of its planning curve (*LRAC*), the firm sooner or later must construct a particular plant. If it is planning for some particular output—setting aside expectations that demand

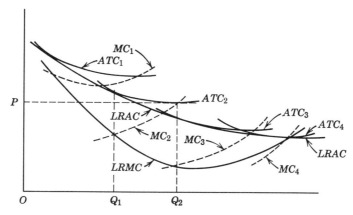

LRAC, LRMC, ATC, and SRMC for four different plants, under conditions of long-run increasing returns. Taken from E. W. Clemens, *op. cit., Amer. Econ. Rev.* (December 1941), XXXI: 799.

may change over time—it would pick the lowest-cost plant for that level of output. In the figure, the appropriate plant for output OQ_1, for example, would be the one with the *ATC* denoted by the subscript 2. There are three things to note about that choice. First, at that level of output the *SRMC* of the particular plant selected (MC_2) and the *LRMC* are equal. If they were not equal, the firm must have built the wrong-sized plant: it could have achieved its output at lower cost by operating farther along whichever of the two marginal cost curves was the lower—the short- or the long-run. See E. W. Clemens, *op. cit., Amer. Econ. Rev.* (December 1941), XXXI: 799–800, and *Economics and Public Utilities*, 262–265. It is precisely the comparison between the costs of producing at a higher rate in a given plant with the costs of producing with an expanded plant that plays an important role in the decision to build additional capacity. The

point of indifference is where *SRMC* and *LRMC* are equal. See Fellner, *op. cit.*, 277–287. Another way of seeing this necessary equality is to recognize that when a firm is producing its output in the lowest-cost plant for that level of production, it is operating at the point at which the *ATC* of that plant is tangent to the long-run average cost or envelope curve; their slopes are equal, and so are the slopes of the total cost curves of which they represent the respective averages. Since *SRMC is* the slope of the former total cost function, and *LRMC* of the latter, *SRMC* and *LRMC* must likewise be equal at this point.

The second observation is that the plant selected is not necessarily the one with the lowest of all possible costs. Larger plants (for example, ATC_3 and ATC_4 in the figure) might have potentially lower average total costs but not be justified by the level of demand. Finally, the plant selected will not itself be operated at its

average variable costs and using price discrimination to recoup from their customers the additional revenues needed to cover unassignable common costs.[26]

PRINCIPLES OF DISCRIMINATION

The various possible occasions for price discrimination all involve the same common elements: (1) the relevant, ascertainable, or chargeable marginal costs are below average total costs, (2) there may or may not be a single, uniform price at which total costs could be covered by total revenues;

---

lowest cost point (that is, where its *SRMC* and *ATC* are equal), which would be at an output of OQ_2 instead of OQ_1. Whatever the planned level of output (in this illustration OQ_1), the rational firm would have selected the particular plant to build whose short-run *ATC* was tangent to *LRAC* at that output: that would give it the OQ_1 production at the lowest possible cost. The firm would have *planned* to have some excess capacity (Q_1Q_2, in the figure). Actually, to the extent that public utility companies expect that demand for their services will increase over time, they will typically construct plants (perhaps ATC_3 in the figure) that will be lowest-cost for an output that they expect to achieve not instantly but several years in the future. In either event, as long as these plants, once constructed, are operating short of their lowest-cost point (for example, at Q_1), their short-run marginal costs will be below their average total costs and price discrimination may be justified, as long as the incremental business taken on covers those marginal costs. But *if and as demand expands* over time, the excess capacity will disappear, the plant will come closer and closer to operating at its optimum point (Q_2 in our example), where marginal costs and average total costs are equal (at P). At this point, Wallace observes, *price discrimination is no longer necessary or desirable*: no class of service *should* pay less than its marginal costs and none *need* pay more than average total costs for total costs to be covered out of total revenues; and *MC* and *ATC* are equal. Therefore, although price discrimination might initially have been justified by the discrepancy between both marginal costs and ATC_2, the range of permissible price differences should thereafter be narrowed, as the quantities demanded increase toward OQ_2 and the firm moves up along the $SRMC_2$ curve until, finally, all customers are served at a uniform P.

According to this model, price discrimination depends on the presence, size, and duration of discontinuities in additions to capacity. And against this must be weighed the degree to which it is impractical to vary rates over time to reflect changing levels of capacity utilization. To justify discrimination, there are classic examples of building ahead in large lumps such as the case of

a railroad shifting from a single to a double track and examples of chronic excess capacity such as persist in that industry. On the other hand, there is argument to the contrary, that even for railroads, once the basic line has been constructed, "investment in railroad plant is for all intents and purposes continuous . . . ," and that railroad average costs probably do not decrease over the normal operating range. Merton H. Miller, "Decreasing Average Cost and the Theory of Railroad Rates," *South. Econ. Jour.* (April 1955), XXI: 395 note, also the studies cited at 390 note; Wallace, *op. cit.*, 608. See, on the other hand, the estimate of Vickrey that long-run marginal costs for railroad freight transport are on the order of only 80% of average costs. *Op. cit.*, *Amer. Econ. Rev.*, *Papers and Proceedings* (May 1955), XLV: 614. This demonstration seems to minimize unduly the role of long-run decreasing costs in justifying continuing price discrimination. First it slights the fact that public utility firms may be more or less constantly "facing their planning curves," that is, almost constantly making decisions with respect to expansions of capacity. Although this fact may reduce the significance of the discontinuities and short-term excess capacities, it confronts them constantly with the discrepancy between their long-run marginal and long-run average costs. Instead of being confronted, principally, with a steady upward creep of production along a rising *SRMC*, requiring the gradual elimination of rate differentials, their principal decisions would in these circumstances be relating to what size of plant to build—and such a decision must perpetually evoke the possible contributions of price discrimination in enabling them to build the more instead of the less efficient plant. Second, it ignores the possible discrepancy between long-run average and long-run marginal costs consequent on technological progress, inadequately reflected in depreciation allowances. Third, the practical difficulties of pricing constantly at a changing *SRMC* level, which Wallace cites as arguing against discrimination, typically cuts the other way, as we point out in the text immediately following.

[26] See the references to Bonbright, note 22.

but (3) the latter condition could still be met while permitting a level of output closer to the optimum by charging different prices to different classes of customers. In Figure 6 we have chosen to use the case of static, long-run decreasing costs as our example for illustrating the principles common to all. The choice seems appropriate in light of the general case for basing utility prices on long-run instead of short-run marginal cost.[27]

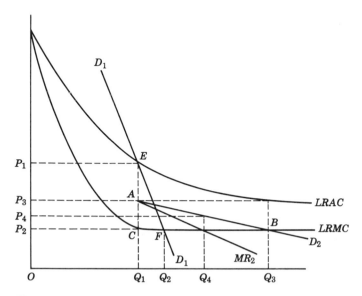

Figure 6. Decreasing costs and price discrimination.

So we assume, in Figure 6, that the firm is in the planning stage, attempting to choose between the various possible sizes of plants tangent to the *LRAC* curve, each with its own *MC* function, as in the figure in note 25. There are assumed to be two potentially separable classes of customers, with the respective demands D_1 and D_2. The D_1 customers could be served alone at a uniform price. That price would be P_1, and their demand would justify the construction of the size of plant appropriate for producing an output of Q_1.[28] But such a uniform price would fall considerably short of optimality. There are some D_1 buyers and an entire class of D_2 willing to buy a great deal more, $Q_1 Q_2$ and $Q_1 Q_3$, respectively, at prices covering the long-run

---

[27] To use Figure 6, instead, to exemplify the case of short-run decreasing costs, we would need only to interpret *LRAC* and *LRMC* as representing the short-run functions with existing capacity.

The model is simplified in that it excludes the possibility of separate, identifiable marginal costs of serving the different classes of customers; in effect, it assumes the provision of a uniform service. Separable marginal costs could easily be incorporated, by interpreting the respective demand curves D_1 and D_2 as representing the demands not for the separate final products or services but only for the common or joint portion of the production process—derived by subtracting from each of the demands for the final

services its separate marginal costs. In this way, the diagram could be modified also to illustrate the third possible case for discrimination, the presence of common or overhead costs that cannot practically be either identified or charged to the separate classes of service. Steiner uses this device in treating the problem of the proper distribution of (joint) capacity costs. *Op. cit.,* *Q. Jour. Econ.* (November 1957), LXXI: 585–610.

[28] Since in note 25 we have already illustrated the process of choosing the right size of plant, we omit from Figure 6 the *SRAC* functions for the individual plants of various sizes.

incremental costs of that additional output, Q_3B. (For simplicity, we have drawn the D_2 demand curve as though its vertical axis were at Q_1 instead of at the origin; therefore, the quantities taken at various prices by the D_2 customers should be read as beginning at Q_1.) The ideal price (setting aside the problem of financing the resultant deficit) would clearly be P_2, uniformly for all customers; or a system of perfect price discrimination that gave all D_1 and D_2 customers that price for their marginal purchases; or a lump charge to all customers giving them, then, the right to buy all they want at the P_2 price—provided that lump-sum charge did not exclude from the market any customers willing to buy some at the P_2 price.

Suppose, at the other extreme, that the only price discrimination possible is a crude separation of the D_1 and D_2 markets. Clearly, this would still be an improvement over the uniform P_1 price to all. If a lower price were set for the D_2 customers—the ideal one from their standpoint would be P_2—it would be possible to pick up their business and earn from it revenues sufficient to cover the full additional costs of supplying them. This means that neither the company nor the D_1 customers would be injured because of this additional business taken on at discriminatorily low prices: the unchanged P_1 price to the latter, on their OQ_1 sales, and the P_2 for the Q_1Q_3 sales to the D_2 market will still together cover ATC. Another way of saying this is that, by virtue of picking up the added Q_1Q_3 sales, the company has been enabled to choose the more efficient plant size appropriate for the larger output OQ_3, reducing its ATC from OP_1 to OP_3; as a glance at the figure will indicate, that new average cost is covered by the P_1 and P_2 prices, on the OQ_1 and Q_1Q_3 sales respectively.[29] The gain in social welfare is indicated by the

---

[29] We have simplified this demonstration by conveniently assuming that the $LRMC$ is constant (that is, horizontal) over the entire range of the incremental Q_1Q_3 output. A price set at $LRMC$ at the point of intersection with the D_2 demand happens, conveniently, to cover the total costs of that added increment of sales, CBQ_3Q_1. Whether the ideal price for the D_2 customers, set at that point of intersection, will in fact cover the total additional costs of their added sales—which is measured by the total area under the $LRMC$ curve—depends on the shape and slope of the $LRMC$ curve within the Q_1Q_3 range. If, for example, the D_2 intersects $LRMC$ while the latter is still declining, charging the D_2 customers only $LRMC$ at the margin will produce a deficit, denoted by the shaded area.

If instead D_2 intersects $LRMC$ in a rising range, the P price can produce a surplus (the next fig.).

Yet, in both cases the additional output is in a sense desirable (see note 17), since the area

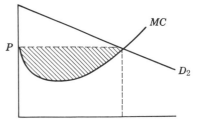

under the demand curve exceeds the area under the MC curve. In the first case, taking on the D_2 business at OP_2 would necessitate raising the price to the D_1 buyers above P_1 if total costs were to be covered; in the latter, the surplus can be applied to reducing P_1 as well.

The reader also should be reminded that price discrimination will not in all circumstances, even in correctly regulated industries, result in a larger volume of sales. Figure 6 illustrates a particularly easy case: where only one class of customers would have been served under a single-pricing scheme and discrimination enables the class of customers with the more elastic demand also to be served, the result will always be a higher output. See Miller, *op. cit.*, 397, and

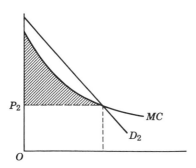

triangle ABC—the difference between what the D_2 customers would have been willing to pay for the Q_1Q_3 purchases that they are enabled by the price discrimination to make and the added costs to society of supplying them.[30]

Who Deserves the MC Price?

As the antitrust laws recognize, price discrimination can be injurious to competitors of the discriminating seller and to the customers discriminated against; and it may accomplish a more effective monopolistic exploitation of the latter. The idea that it is economically desirable to reduce rates down to marginal cost for "marginal buyers" is all very well; but how is one to decide which buyers are marginal and which are not?

In (impurely) competitive markets the "marginal business" is the business you either do not yet have or that you are in danger of losing. As the Robinson–Patman Act recognizes, a justification of selective price reduction on marginal business thus defined could be entirely circular: if it is all right to discriminate in favor of marginal buyers, and marginal buyers are all those whom the seller feels he has to favor in this way, all price discrimination is permissible. As far as causal cost responsibility is concerned, however, all customers are marginal.

Suppose, for example, the utility has two groups of customers, one, A, whose demand is stable, another, B, whose demand is increasing. And suppose expansion of the latter demand finally requires expansion of capacity. Does that mean, following our rules of peak responsibility pricing, that B are the marginal buyers on whom capacity costs alone should be imposed? Obviously not. True, it is the increase in B's purchases that precipitates the additional investment; but the additional costs could just as well be saved if A reduced their purchases as if B refrained from increasing theirs. So A's *continuing* to take service is just as responsible, in proportion to the amount they take, for the need to expand investment as B's increasing needs, and A should therefore be forced just as much as B to weigh the marginal benefits of the capacity to them against the marginal costs they impose on society by continuing to make demands. This reasoning clearly applies even when incremental investment costs per unit of capacity are rising and where, again, it might appear on first consideration that since it is the expansion of the B demands that is responsible for the supplier's incurring the higher costs, it is that group that ought to bear the additional burden. Even though B's demand is "marginal" in the temporal sense, both groups are marginal in the economic sense. Both should be forced to match those higher capacity costs against the satisfaction they derive from continuing to use the service.[31]

But what if, to come to the case closer at hand, long-run incremental costs are less than average total costs? Ideally, both A and B should be confronted with the low marginal opportunity costs to society of supplying the additional capacity. A might demand more capacity if offered the lower price, just as might B. But the ideal is unachievable: it is impossible to reduce the rates to

---

R. K. Davidson, *op. cit.*, 173–179. Our purpose has been merely to show that discrimination *can* improve welfare all around.

[30] By the same criterion, society continues to lose the potential addition to welfare CEF that it could have enjoyed had it found ways of extending the ideal price of P_2 to the D_1 customers as well.

[31] Suppose that A is the user of a piece of city land, acquired a long time ago, when land in the center of the city was plentiful and cheap. A would be irrational if he did not, as the demand and price for land rose, consider as the cost of continuing to hold on to what he has, not the historic price that was paid but the opportunity cost to society of his holding the land. As

the lower level for both buyer groups, because in that event total revenues would be inadequate. How then does one choose between the claims of A and B to the lower incremental cost?

The only generally acceptable answer would have to be on the basis of the comparative elasticities of the respective demands within the relevant range (between ATC and the relevant MC). Suppose, for example, that B's demand, though growing over time, is comparatively independent of price—this might well be the case, we have suggested, with respect to the demand for electricity for air conditioning—whereas A's, though not growing over time, would respond very sharply to a reduced price. In these circumstances, the intelligent decision would ordinarily be to lower the price not to B but to A.[32]

Why so? We know that it will pay any company, if it can separate the markets in which it sells, to discriminate between them on the basis of their respective elasticities of demand. A profit-maximizing company will equalize the marginal revenues it receives from the respective markets in which it sells (assuming variable costs are the same). If it could add more to its revenues by selling more in one than in the other, it would increase its sales efforts in the former and decrease them in the latter until the incremental revenues were once again equated. Since the difference between marginal and average revenue will be greater the less elastic is demand, the company will charge a higher price in the market with the less elastic and a lower price in the market with the more elastic demand.[33] This is merely an explicit version of the common sense notion that sellers will price in different markets on the basis of what the respective traffics will bear;[34] the more inelastic the demand, the higher the price a market will bear.

Public utility companies should, in certain circumstances, be encouraged to adopt the same type of system, forcing different customers to contribute to common costs (over and above the identifiable costs of serving them separately) on the basis of their respective abilities and willingness to pay or the value of the service to them. (See Figure 6.) At all levels of price at which there are customers in both categories, the demand D_1 is less elastic than D_2: the same price reduction or increase will bring a greater reaction by the D_2 than by the D_1 buyers. A price below P_1 is *necessary* to pick up the D_2 customers. They are willing and able to pay the full additional costs of serving them; so production on their behalf is economically justified.[35]

---

prices rose, he might at a certain point decide he was better off selling out and moving elsewhere. It would be economically inefficient for society as well if A were not forced to make such a calculation. From the point of view of the marginal opportunity costs of his using the land, he is just as much a marginal buyer as the new purchaser, B, even though he is not overtly in the market.
[32] The reason these statements are qualified ("the only generally acceptable answer," "the intelligent decision would ordinarily be"), as will be indicated, is that the problem requires a choice among different distributions of the benefits of decreasing costs among different classes of customers, a choice that cannot be proved right or wrong by economic reasoning alone.

[33] See, for example, George J. Stigler, *The Theory of Price*, 3rd ed. (New York: Macmillan, 1966), 209–213.
[34] This widely used expression is a very imprecise statement of the profit-maximizing condition. Most markets will "bear" prices much higher than a profit-maximizing monopolist would charge, in the sense that *some* sales would continue to be made at that price, but not enough to maximize the difference between total revenues and total costs. The economist will interpret the phrase as implying the equation of marginal cost and revenue.
[35] This is indicated by the fact that for at least some of its range, their demand, D_2, lies above the $LRMC$: note this is true also in the more complicated cases described in note 29. Perfect

This means that the D_1 customers, who are being discriminated *against*, need not be injured by the discrimination; instead, they can actually be benefited. If (in the case of short-run increasing returns) the rate reduction permits the fuller use of existing capacity, and the additional business taken on by the preferentially low rate covers anything more than the variable costs it entails, then the D_2 customers are making some contribution to the common costs that the D_1 customers would otherwise have to bear entirely by themselves. If instead, the question is one of permitting the construction of a larger plant than would otherwise be feasible, the lower rates to the D_2 customers make it possible for the firm to achieve economies of scale that would not otherwise be available. Once again, if the D_2 customers are made to pay anything in excess of the long-run incremental cost for which they are responsible, it would be possible for the company to reduce its rates to the D_1 customers below P_1 and still cover total costs. And it will of course be the function of effective regulation to require it to do so.[36]

Therefore, discriminatory rate reductions are not only justifiable but economically desirable, if the following possibilities exist.

1. The relevant cost of taking on the incremental business is less than the average cost of the total company operation without it.
2. The lower rates are required to elicit the additional business.
3. The elasticity of the demand in question is sufficiently in excess of unity that selective rate reductions could increase the system's total revenues by at least the additional costs incurred. Whether rates *should* be reduced to this end is a question we shall consider presently.

   To these three conditions, there should be attached a warning.
4. Additional restrictions may have to be imposed in the event that the supplying company is competing with other suppliers or that the customers charged the different prices are in competition with each other— circumstances that we study in Chapter 6.

The Proper Limits of Discrimination

Figure 6 implies that the proper limits of discrimination are the prices P_1 and P_2: a price to the inelastic demand customers no higher than the *ATC* of serving them in the absence of discrimination; a price to the elastic demand customers no lower than the full additional costs of taking on that additional business. These are the rules that most authorities have adopted, and with which we concur.[37] One implies the other: as long as the favored customers pay their full additional costs, the others cannot on this account be

---

(and possibly even highly imperfect) price discrimination could theoretically extract more revenues than serving them would add to costs. However, see note 17.

[36] If the utility as a whole is not earning its permissible rate of return, then of course the customers paying the higher rates will receive no direct benefit, since any additions to revenues over costs consequent on extending the preferential rates to markets with elastic demand will serve only to bring the company's rate of return closer to the permissible level. It remains true in this case that D_1 customers need not be injured by the lower rates extended to the others (unless

they themselves compete with the D_2 buyers, a possibility we consider in the following chapter). Even if their rates are not actually reduced at once, they can benefit by the better financial condition of the company and its consequent superior ability to maintain and improve service over time.

[37] See, for example, Harry Gunnison Brown, *Principles of Commerce: A Study of the Mechanism, the Advantages, and the Transportation Costs of Foreign and Domestic Trade* (New York: Macmillan, 1916), Part III, 123–124, 172; Tyndall, *op. cit.*, 343, 347–348; Clemens, *Economics and Public Utilities*, 256; and the following pronouncement

led to pay more than the costs of serving them in the absence of discrimination. And both together imply the condition that discrimination be permitted only as long as it imposes no burden on the customers being discriminated against.

Such a rule would prohibit *internal subsidization*. Regulatory commissions, particularly in the transportation field, often consider it one of their responsibilities to assure the provision of maximum service, as long as the system's total revenues cover total costs. Under considerable political pressure from the affected localities or groups of customers, they interpret the public utility franchise as imposing an obligation on the company to maintain service in markets that are sparse and costly to serve, according to time schedules that are convenient to customers, at prices that do not cover even the avoidable, incremental cost of provision. This obligation is often used as a justification for limiting competition and restricting entry into the more remunerative markets, on the ground that if the profitability of the latter portion of the business were reduced, the common carriers would no longer be financially able to fulfill their less remunerative responsibilities. In the long run this must involve charging other customers more than the average total cost of serving them alone. Of course, society may choose to tax certain of its members in order to subsidize the provision of electricity, telephone, railroad, or air service to other classes of customers; all the economist can do is to underline the direct and indirect costs of providing the subsidy in this manner, that is, by setting certain prices above and others below the respective marginal social costs, instead of by direct monetary grants.[38]

But, in fact, an economic case could be made for extending the permissible limits at both ends. The ideal price would be at MC—the cost of the single last unit demanded. A price to the D_2 customers at that level might well not cover the full additional cost of serving them—that is, the cost of their entire, added increment. This could be so if the MC itself (and not just the ATC) were declining over some portion of that incremental output.[39] If, then, the

---

of the U. S. Supreme Court:

"Let it be conceded that if a scheme of maximum rates was imposed by state authority, as a whole adequately remunerative, and yet that some of such rates were so unequal as to exceed the flexible limit of judgment which belongs to the power to fix rates, that is, transcended the limits of just classification and amounted to the creation of favored class or classes whom the carrier was compelled to serve at a loss, to the detriment of other class or classes upon whom the burden of such loss would fall, that such legislation would be . . . inherently unreasonable. . . ." *Atlantic Coast Line Railroad v. North Carolina Corporation Commission* 206 U. S. 1, 25–26 (1907).
[38] For an illustration of the case against such a practice, see pp. 190–191, Chapter 7. There is no doubt that widespread internal subsidization of this type does prevail; we shall supply some examples, particularly in our discussion of "cream skimming," in Chapters 1 and 5, Vol. 2. But whether the alleged subsidization is real depends, of course, on whether the costs of the respective services cited have been computed

according to the economically correct, marginal principles. The mere fact of price discrimination does not in itself demonstrate internal subsidization. Although in the long run it may well be that the disproportionate contribution to overheads by the customers being discriminated against—the D_1 market in our Figure 6—alone makes it possible for service to continue to flow to those paying a price closer to marginal costs, it seems anomalous to characterize their contribution as subsidization when (1) the favored customers do over the long-run, cover the incremental costs of serving them and (2) the disfavored—a graceless word—pay no more, and possibly pay less, than they would if the discrimination were not practiced. But, as we shall see when the question is raised of where the respective rates ought actually to be set *within* the upper and lower limits just described, subsidization may be said to occur if the rates in the price-elastic market are set below the level that would *maximize* their net contribution (that is, over and above $LRMC$) to company overheads—because in this event the rates to the price-inelastic market could have been lower, while the company still covered total costs.

rules were altered to set the lower limit at marginal instead of full additional cost—and that *would* have to be the bottom limit, as far as economic considerations prevail—the upper limit could, indeed, would have to, exceed the ATC (P_1 in Figure 6) of serving the high-price market alone.

Whichever set of limits is adopted, the question remains of where the actual discriminatory prices should be set within those limits.

According to one standard of welfare economics, the prices of the various services should be marked up above MC in inverse proportion to their elasticities of demand. This prescription stems from the idea that the optimal pricing scheme will be the one that maximizes the surplus of all consumers taken as a group, subject to the constraint of raising sufficient revenue to cover total costs. Since total well-being, and hence total consumer surplus, is maximized when all goods are priced at marginal cost,[40] the solution, in situations where pricing above that level is unavoidable, is to minimize the amount of surplus sacrificed in this way. This will be achieved when the loss of consumer surplus that would result from a price increase sufficient to contribute one added dollar to overhead costs is equalized for all classes of service. If they were not equal, total consumer surplus could be increased by raising price in the market where the loss of surplus per dollar of net additional revenue was low and by reducing it where the ratio was high, since the surplus lost by the price increase in the former market would be smaller than the surplus gained by the reduction in the latter. If we begin from a situation where all prices are equated to *average* total cost, prices will go up in the inelastic demand markets and down in the elastic until the respective ratios to marginal costs for the various services, $(P - MC)/P$, are inversely proportional to their respective elasticities of demand.[41] Such prices will have the effect of reducing sales in all markets by the same percentage below what their respective levels would be if all prices were equal to marginal cost. Clearly, to achieve equiproportionate reductions in sales from that ideal level, prices will have to be raised much more above marginal cost for services with inelastic than with elastic demands.

But following such a rule would have the effect of favoring the D_2 over the D_1 customers. The ones with the less elastic demands, also, would be interested in taking additional quantities of service if the price to them were reduced below P_1. A decision to set the prices at the limits would in effect represent a decision to distribute the major part of the benefits of the increasing returns to the D_2 customers. Such an action could be justified on the ground that, since the surplus or welfare gain that the D_2 customers obtain from a reduction in price to MC exceeds what the D_1 customers lose, the former could compensate the latter. But without any arrangements for such compensation, this discriminatory pricing pattern would in effect distribute more income to the D_2 than to the D_1 group. As we have already seen, economics cannot provide a decisive answer to distributional questions such

[39] This possibility is illustrated in the first of the figures in note 29.
[40] See note 16.
[41] See William J. Baumol, "Reasonable Rules for Rate Regulation: Plausible Policies for an Imperfect World," in Almarin Phillips and Oliver E. Williamson, eds., *Prices: Issues in Theory, Practice, and Public Policy* (Philadelphia:

Univ. of Pennsylvania Press, 1967), 122–123, citing previous formulations by Alan S. Manne, Marcus Flemming, and Marcel Boiteux. Also the testimony of Baumol and of William S. Vickrey in FCC, *In the Matter of American Telephone and Telegraph Co. et al.*, Docket 16258, 1968; the latter's Appendix A is a particularly lucid explanation.

as these. It can supply no common denominator for comparing or adding up the psychic satisfactions that the D_1 patrons would get from their additional purchases with the corresponding satisfactions that would be enjoyed by the D_2 customers if the price to them were reduced to its lower limit—except to observe that compensation would be possible.[42]

Mainly for this reason—and also because of the difficulty of measuring demand elasticities—some economists have opposed the use of price discrimination in public utility rate making, advocating instead that the long-run marginal costs of as many classes of service as possible be identified and rates be set uniformly above those respective costs by whatever percentage required to bring in the necessary aggregate revenues. That is, instead of the various rates being set discriminatorily at varying percentages of marginal costs, in (inverse) dependence on the respective elasticities of demand, the price to marginal cost ratios would be constant for all classes of service.[43] Most economists would probably permit discriminatory departures from the rule for those categories of business that, by virtue of their high elasticity of demand, would be completely excluded by it from the market.[44]

Finally, some commentators, aware of the possible benefits of price discrimination to all parties but unwilling to sanction transfers of benefit from one group of customers to another, have proposed that discriminatory reductions be permitted *only* to the point of maximizing the benefit to customers discriminated *against*. By this rule, rates would be lowered in markets with elastic demand only if elasticity is great enough so that the discriminatory reduction results in those markets making an increased net contribution to common costs; and rates would be reduced only to the point

---

[42] That is, "maximizing the total consumer surplus" in the manner indicated involves equating a dollar of area under A's demand curve with a dollar under B's demand curve, and, where it will increase the total number of dollars of surplus, conferring benefits on consumer A and not on consumer B. It is impossible to add together incommensurable quantities in this way. How can we decide that the worth of a dollar to A is the same as to B? Even if we do so decide, by what right do we as economists decide it is proper to transfer income from one to the other?

[43] This is the arrangement of the French *tarif vert*. See James R. Nelson, "Practical Applications of Marginal Cost Pricing in the Public Utility Field," *Amer. Econ. Rev., Papers and Proceedings* (May 1963), LIII: 480.

[44] See the discussion by Baumol, in Phillips and Williamson, *op. cit.*, 120–121, and Vickrey, in his supplementary testimony in FCC, Docket 16258, 1969. The question of whether "ideal output" can be achieved equally well with prices proportional instead of equal to marginal cost has been extensively debated in the literature. The concensus seems to be negative, but that proportionality should produce tolerably good results with one major qualification: that for all primary and intermediate goods and services—

that is, for all inputs in the production process—severe distortions will result unless prices are equal to marginal costs. The reason for this exception is that if all inputs and intermediate goods were priced at some ratio in excess of marginal cost, that excess would be subjected to geometric expansion each time one of those inputs or one of the products in which it was then embodied was sold to the next level of production or distribution. The reader may recognize here the opposite side of the general case for vertical integration: that it eliminates this progressive cumulation of interstitial mark-ups. (See the discussion of Figure 1, Chapter 6, Volume 2.)

Apart from this problem, the general opinion is that because setting prices in proportion to rather than equal to marginal costs leaves unchanged the (proportional) relationship between them, "the Proportionality Rule is likely to prove adequate." Lionel W. McKenzie, "Ideal Output and the Interdependence of Firms," *Econ. Jour.* (December 1951), LXI: 788; see also 785–803. See Ruggles, *op. cit.*, 110–111, 119 and the literature cited there; E. J. Mishan, *Welfare Economics*, Five Introductory Essays (New York: Random House, 1964), 20–22; Tibor Scitovsky, *Welfare and Competition, The Economics of a Fully Employed Economy* (Chicago: Richard D. Irwin, 1951), 356–362.

and refraining from imposing all their capacity charges on peak users.[53]

This particular distortion provides another illustration of the inadequacy of regulation that concentrates only on rate levels, in order to assure that the regulated companies earn no more than a specified average return on investment. As Troxel has pointed out, economic efficiency requires that the cost of capital be equated with not the *average* but the marginal rate of return on investment.[54] To prevent excessive *aggregate* investment, regulatory commissions must see to it not only that the *average* return permitted on total investment does not *exceed* the cost of capital, but also that no individual investments are made that earn *less* than the cost of capital.[55] This requires, among other things, that all discriminatory rate reductions be limited by the floor of long-run incremental costs (including the required return on incremental investment).

The kind of rate making that would be permissible under even these restrictive rules would almost certainly still strike the reader, the rate-payer, and most regulatory commissions as outrageously discriminatory. Consider the following illustration of the kinds of problems that face commissions today in passing on selective rate reductions proposed by electric companies in their increasingly avid competition for the home heating market, where, because of the competition of gas and oil, their demand is apparently highly elastic. (We reserve for Chapter 6 consideration of the relevance of the fact that it is the presence of competition that creates this elasticity.) Suppose the company has two groups of customers that it proposes to put in separate classes for purposes of rate making: A and B. Suppose their incomes and all other relevant economic characteristics are identical, and the only difference between them is that A customers heat their houses with electricity and B customers do not. Suppose also that the electric company proposes a lower rate to B, even though once those customers accept the offer the amount and timing of their purchases will be identical with that of A. The proposal is to give different treatment to customer classes identical in all ways, including the cost of serving them, except for the fact that A are already tied to the electric company and B are not.[56]

It is entirely conceivable, considering the long-run decreasing cost characteristics of the electricity industry, that a lower rate to class B would be defensible under the rules we have set forth; and that the consequence would be not only not to injure A but to benefit them. Such a differential could obviously not be justified under the cost-saving justification of the

---

[53] See pp. 24–25 and note 33, Chapter 4.

[54] See the discussion in note 74, Chapter 4.

[55] Troxel believes that the practice of telephone companies imposing a flat and uniform charge for all local telephone calls within a wide urban area, even though unit costs rise as service is extended to less densely settled outlying regions of the city, does create the possibility of "a marginal return at the suburban fringes below the cost of capital. That is, deficient returns to capital may occur at the extensive urban margin of telephone operations rather than in a whole metropolitan network." In *Shepherd and Gies, op. cit.*, 184.

[56] A "Request for Investigation" presented to the Federal Trade Commission by the Virginia Petroleum Jobbers Association, *In the Matter of Promotional Payments by Electric Companies*, December 14, 1965, referring specifically to alleged practices by the Virginia Electric & Power Company, claimed:

"VEPCO will provide free underground wiring to builders of all-electric subdivisions and apartment houses. In contrast, where electricity is used only for lighting and for appliances, then *even though the amount of electricity used may be as great* as in an all-electric subdivision, underground wiring will be provided only at a prohibitive charge." Par. I, Sec. 3.

Robinson-Patman Act,[57] which would require that the difference in prices charged A and B be itself justified by differences in the respective costs of serving them—that is, that the rates not be discriminatory. Yet, the discrimination would be defensible in terms of the discrepancy between average and long-run marginal cost of the industry. The discrepancy might be politically objectionable or regarded as morally repugnant; but (apart from any possible deleterious effect on competition, which we consider below) it could be economically justified.

As in most of these discussions, we have concentrated our attention on pricing. The same principles would apply to nonprice methods of soliciting business.[58] Commissions have long grappled with the question, for example, of how to treat the appliance-selling activities of electric and gas companies. The general practice has been to require separate accounting for such activities in order to exclude their expenses or net losses from the utility cost-of-service and their revenues or profits from utility earnings.[59] Discussion of the merits of this procedure has run largely in terms of whether nominal losses on such sales are, like routine business advertising, an acceptable means of promoting sales of gas or electricity, hence a reasonable charge on the public utility part of the business; or really an unrelated activity that ought not to be permitted to burden rate-payers.[60] The correct economic approach, it would seem, would be to treat the costs of cut-rate appliance sales and advertising directed at particular kinds of customers as a form of rate making. The relevant questions would be: Are they discriminatory? If so do they meet our other tests—are they justified by the presence of decreasing costs, that is, by MC being less than ATC? Do the additional sales that they promote cover their long-run incremental costs, including the costs of promoting them? The purpose of asking these questions would be to decide not whether to segregate the appliance-selling business for purposes of rate regulation but whether, just as with the offering of straightforward promotional rates, such methods of sales promotion should be permitted at all.[61]

In concluding, it is important to reemphasize the basic prerequisite: the presence of decreasing costs. Where it is not present, rate discrimination becomes very questionable. Consider, for example, the various promotional airline fares to which we have already alluded. As long as reduced fares are for standby service or travel on off-peak days or seasons they are not discriminatory; they merely reflect (perhaps even inadequately) the lower marginal costs of travel that makes no marginal demand on capacity. To the extent that they are offered only to select groups—young people under 21, wives and children accompanying husbands—they are discriminatory but the discrimination may be justified because (1) of the presence of short-run decreasing costs at times when capacity is in excess and (2) the demand by these classes of travelers may well be more elastic than by single unaccompanied adults, many of them traveling on business.[62] But to the extent that

[57] 15 U.S.C. 13(a) (1964 ed.).

[58] See the same observation applied to the appraisal of selective promotional expenditures in light of the principle of peak-responsibility pricing, note 16, Chapter 4.

[59] C. F. Phillips, *op. cit.*, 189.

[60] See for example, Troxel, *Economics of Public Utilities*, 241–245.

[61] An additional consideration that has been raised in many of these cases is whether such practices constitute unfair competition with local appliance dealers. We treat problems of rate making in the presence of competition in Chapter 6.

[62] The Civil Aeronautics Board allowed these tariffs to become effective in 1966. *American*

the purpose of such fares, or of the subsidies paid to the airlines that serve smaller towns, or the discriminatorily low rates on short-hop trips[63] is merely to "promote air travel" or the habit of using airplanes, without reference to whether the travel promoted is on peak or off peak, it seems to lack economic justification, in view of the apparent absence of economies of scale in the air transport business in the relevant range.[64] In short, there seems to be much uneconomic internal subsidization in this industry.

FULLY DISTRIBUTED COSTS

When public utility commissions or companies attempt systematically to construct or to appraise a rate structure, they do not ordinarily do so by calculating long-run marginal costs and demand elasticities. More often they use various methods of distributing or allocating total revenue requirements (including, as always, return on investment) among the several services or categories of service. The costs of electric companies will be fully distributed between residential, commercial, industrial, street lighting uses and the like; the costs of railroads will be divided between passenger and freight business; of telephone common carriers between message toll and their various business service offerings; of telephone and gas pipeline companies subject to both federal and state regulation between jurisdictional and nonjurisdictional business by the respective regulatory agencies. These totals are then reduced to costs per unit on the basis of some measure of the physical quantities taken by each group of customers—ton-miles, revenue passenger miles, kilowatt hours, MCF's, telephone message minutes or message-minute-miles—whatever seems appropriate. To the extent that the rates for these respective classes of customers are then based on or conform to such fully distributed costs, all services, by definition, will earn the same rate of return on the investment allocated to them; and the rates thus determined or justified are "completely nondiscriminatory," by definition.

Space does not permit any systematic summary of the various, often extraordinarily complex methods employed to distribute costs in this

---

Airlines, Standby Youth Fares, Order E-23137, January 20, 1966. A number of bus companies succeeded, however, in getting a Circuit Court of Appeals decision ordering the Board to hold hearings on the subject. *Transcontinental Bus System, Inc. v. Civil Aeronautics Board*, 383 F.2d 466 (1967). Also, a Federal Circuit Court of Appeals in 1969 ordered the CAB to hold hearings on the complaint of bus companies that the family fares are unjust and discriminatory. *Wall Street Journal*, June 17, 1969.

In 1969 the Board tentatively decided that neither the standby youth fare (which offers a 50% reduction for standby service) nor the "young adult" fares (a $33\frac{1}{3}\%$ discount on reserved-seat service) was "unjustly discriminatory." *Standby Youth Fares—"Young Adult" Fares*, Docket 18936, Opinion, August 25, 1969.

[63] See note 69, p. 153.

[64] See the discussion on this point at note 180, Chapter 5, Volume 2. The Board did, however,

offer in justification the alleged presence of an interesting type of dynamic long-run decreasing cost. The fares were justified, it argued, because the growing traffic volume that they promoted in turn made possible the more rapid development and adoption of new, more efficient, speedier and more commodious equipment and scheduling, providing "service at an increasing level of speed, comfort and convenience." *Loc. cit.*, note 62, above. As we have suggested, if the expansion of demand is causally related to the development of cost-reducing technology, this may properly be regarded as the kind of LRDC that could justify discrimination. In principle the same would be true of technological progress that provided improved service at constant cost. But the CAB's emphasis on service improvements intead of cost reduction may itself reflect an uneconomic bias. See our discussion of this point in the section on "The Regulation of Non-Price Competition: Air Transport," in Chapter 5 of Volume 2.

fashion.[65] In general, some costs can be directly assigned exclusively to one service or other—for example, railroad passenger agents to passenger service, box cars and freight terminals to freight. But most costs must be allocated at least in part because they are incurred in serving more than one class of customers—maintenance, depreciation, return, operating costs of loco-motives, roundhouses, track and right of way, and so on. These common or joint costs may be distributed on the basis of some common physical measure of utilization, such as minutes, circuit-miles, message-minute-miles, gross ton-miles, MCF, or kwh employed or consumed by each. Or they may be distributed in proportion to the costs that can be directly assigned to the various services.[66] An ingenious variant of the latter was the "alternative justifiable expenditures" method devised by the Tennessee Valley Authority, which in general allocated the common costs of multipurpose river develop-ment schemes among the various services supplied (electric power, navigation, flood control) in proportion to what it *would* have cost to provide each of those services in the same quantity in single-purpose projects set up exclu-sively for them.[67]

Quite simply, the basic defect of fully distributed costs as a basis for rate making is that they do not necessarily measure marginal cost responsibility in a causal sense. They do not measure by what amount costs would be increased if additional quantities of any particular service were taken, or by what amount costs would be reduced if the service were correspondingly curtailed. They are average costs: the allocations among the various services

---

[65] For an excellent discussion and appraisal, see Bonbright, *Principles of Public Utility Rates*, Chapter 18.

[66] See for instance, Howard W. Nicholson, "Motor Carrier Costs and Minimum Rate Regulation," *Q. Jour. Econ.* (February 1958), LXXII: 142. For an example of a combination of these two methods, the ICC prorates running track maintenance on the basis of the gross ton-miles of passenger and freight service, common equipment repairs on the basis of the relative use in each service, and some other expenses in proportion to solely related expenses. ICC *Investigation of Costs of Intercity Rail Passenger Service*, Report transmitted to the Senate Com-mittee on Commerce and House Committee on Interstate and Foreign Commerce, Washington, July 16, 1969, 15. See also *Separation of Operating Expenses between Freight and Passenger Service*, 302 ICC 735 (1958) and *Railroad Passenger Train Deficit*, 306 ICC 417 (1959). For other examples of plausible methods of allocating common costs, see note 36, Chapter 3.

[67] The method was actually slightly more compli-cated, in that those investment costs specifically attributable to the individual services were deducted both from the aggregate investment costs of the multipurpose project and from the estimated costs of the individual, single-purpose projects, with the residue of the former being distributed in proportion to the residues of the latter. See the Federal Power Commission,

Report on Review of Allocations of Costs of the Multiple-Purpose Water Control System in the Tennessee River Basin, Washington, March 23, 1949, 21–22. The FPC was later prevailed on to accept a similar method, the "relative cost method," for allocating the costs of production on joint-product leases between natural gas, on the one hand, and oil and various natural gas liquids, on the other, in order to ascertain a "just and reasonable" field price for the natural gas. The method involved distributing the joint costs of producing those same quantities in proportion to the actual costs of producing that same number of barrels of crude oil on leases in which oil was produced in the absence or virtual absence of natural gas, on the one hand, and that number of cubic feet of natural gas from virtually dry gas leases on the other. See *Phillips Petroleum Co.*, 24 FPC 537, 553, 623–625 (1960) and *Opinion and Order Determining Just and Reasonable Rates for Natural Gas Producers in the Permian Basin*, 34 FPC 159, 214–215 (1965). In advocating this method, at a later stage only for pricing gas that had already been discovered and committed to pipe-line purchasers, the present writer emphasized that while it might be deemed to provide a just or a fair distribution of the joint costs, it did not provide an economic measure of the separate costs. Testimony in the *Permian Basin* proceeding, FPC Docket No. AR 61–1, 1962, tr. 7212–17, 7346–47. See also my *op. cit.*, *Amer. Econ. Rev.*, *Papers and Proceedings* (May 1960), L: 510–514.

are often made in part on the basis of the relative number of physical units of consumption or utilization by each, and the total allocated dollars are then divided by those physical units to get the unit costs. Also, being apportionments of historical costs, even when they do accurately reflect historical responsibility for the incurrence of these costs among the respective users, they do not provide a reliable measure of what will happen to costs in the future if particular portions of the business are expanded or dropped. Therefore, they do not tell whether a particular service is really profitable or unprofitable, in the sense that its continued provision at existing rates makes a net contribution to company revenues over and above the costs for which it is responsible, or whether, instead, it is a burden on the other subscribers.

This is a defect, of course, only to the extent that marginal costs diverge from average. The full distribution of costs that underlies the familiar two-or three-part tariff for gas and electricity, for example, with its separate customer, commodity (or energy) and demand charges, is in part along lines that reflect true causal responsibility: costs such as meter reading and billing do in fact depend on the number of customers, others (such as fuel) on the mere quantity taken, and others (capacity costs) on the amount the supplier may be called on to provide on demand at the time of the system's peak. Note that the distribution is not among classes of customers, as such, but along functional lines that recognize the various genuine determinants of cost. But the unit costs so determined are average, not marginal. They give no recognition, therefore, to the fact that some of the capacity is provided under LRDC conditions; and that the generation of electricity is subject to short-run increasing costs, with the result (see pp. 94–97, Chapter 4) that those charges ought properly to be high enough at times to make a contribution to overheads. The functional distribution itself may conceal interesting discrepancies between marginal and average costs. In the case of gas pipeline companies, for example, the costs of their own gas producing operations are placed among commodity costs, presumably on the ground that the cost of the gas itself obviously must vary with the number of cubic feet taken. But pipelines obtain most even of their *purchased* gas under long-term contracts that promise a certain maximum daily deliverability and often oblige the line to pay for certain minimum specified daily quantities of gas whether or not they take that much. Even though they pay a certain price per MCF, therefore, some part of the costs of the purchased gas is fixed, not variable, and is a function of the capacity required at the peak. Similarly, many of the costs of the pipelines' own production are fixed, representing the investment required to provide a certain production capacity. Therefore, the cost of the gas itself that the pipelines transport and sell is only partly variable with quantities taken, and hence belongs only partly in the commodity charge; part of it really belongs in the demand charge.

Again, one important component of the "separations procedures" used by the Federal Communications Commission to (fully) distribute Bell System investment costs between interstate and intrastate service (since it regulates only the former) is the allocation of those costs on the basis of relative minute-miles or relative minutes of use for the two purposes.[68] To the extent that capacity costs incurred do indeed depend on the number of minutes taken up

---

[68] See, for example, FCC, *In the Matter of American Telephone and Telegraph Co. et al.*, Docket Nos. 15011 and 16258, Interim Decision and Order, 9 FCC 2d 30, 93 and *passim* (1967).

and miles covered by individual messages, this allocation method does reflect the respective average cost responsibilities of the two services. But since this procedure treats all minutes the same, peak and off-peak, it fails to recognize the varying capacity cost responsibilities of calls made at different times. Moreover, being a measure of average historical instead of marginal cost, it ignores the very marked tendencies to decreasing cost in long-distance telephonic communication, which we have already described. Finally, it is simply not the case that all the costs thus allocated do in fact vary with minutes or miles of use.[69]

A particularly clear example of the lack of correspondence between average, fully distributed and marginal costs and of the irrationality of basing rates on the former is provided by the FCC's distribution between intra- and inter-state jurisdictions of the costs of telephone "subscriber plant"—the equipment on the customer's premises and between those premises and the local office or exchange. (Net investment in Bell System subscriber plant amounted to $15.4 billion in 1966.) It decided in 1967 to do so on the basis of (1) the relative minutes of use of that equipment for interstate and intrastate service, which measure produced an allocation of only 4% to the former, (2) with a judgmental adjustment for the greater average *value* of a minute's use for interstate than for intrastate messages—producing a final allocation of 12% to the former.[70] But subscriber plant is in fact idle most of the time: it was used an average of only 29 minutes a day in the test period. It is simply available at all times for any and all calls. A doubling of any of these utilizations would cause the company no additional cost incurrence for subscriber plant: the marginal cost is therefore zero.[71] The FCC's adjustment for the different value of the different uses was a recognition that since neither the 4% nor any other allocation could produce a measure of relative marginal cost responsibility, the allocation would have to be based on demand considerations. But in so doing it failed entirely to recognize that the economically relevant demand characteristic in these circumstances would have been demand elasticity, as Commissioner Johnson implied in his concurring opinion,[72] and that the upward adjustment of the allocation to

[69] On these separation procedures, see also note 39, p. 100, Chapter 4 and Richard Gabel, *Development of Separations Principles in the Telephone Industry* (East Lansing: Institute of Public Utilities, Michigan State Univ., 1967). AT&T has pointed out, for example, that it was irrational of the FCC to allocate all the costs of inter-exchange plant on the basis of message-minute-miles, since some of that plant consists in terminals, the costs of using which have nothing whatever to do with the miles over which the messages travel. *Ibid.*, 9 FCC 2d 30, 100.

The CAB and the airlines have in recent years come to recognize the same serious defect in a passenger fare structure that was originally based on a uniform rate per mile. Since the costs at the terminal—ticket sales, baggage check-in, loading and unloading, landing and take-off—are essentially the same per passenger or per flight, regardless of the length of the trip, these costs are fixed when the dimension of output is the number of miles traveled. On the other hand,

obviously the costs of the flight itself will vary with the length of the trip. Combining the fixed and variable costs produces a "tapered" cost structure, one in which costs per mile decline the longer the journey. The CAB has pointed out and the airlines have come increasingly to recognize that at a uniform rate per mile the long trips have been subsidizing the short runs, and both parties have therefore been moving toward a more tapered fare structure. See, for example, *Wall Street Journal*, June 16, 1969, 34; *New York Times*, August 10, 1969, Sec. 3, 1; and the CAB Rates Division, Bureau of Economics, Staff Report, *A Study of the Domestic Passenger Air Fare Structure* (Washington, January 1968).

[70] *In the Matter of American Telephone and Telegraph Co. et al.*, Docket Nos. 15011 and 16258, 9 FCC 2d 30, 101–110.

[71] We set aside the increased possibility of busy signals, that is, of congestion costs.

[72] *Ibid.*, 128–129, 135–137.

long-run distance calls was, by this criterion, probably an adjustment in the wrong direction.[73]

A final illustration of the discrepancy between fully distributed and marginal costs is provided by the efforts of the ICC over the years to determine the separate costs of rail passenger and freight business, particularly in connection with the accelerating efforts of the roads to drop almost all their passenger service. The passenger business, taken as a whole, clearly no longer covers its long-run marginal costs. But the size of this deficit is greatly exaggerated if one compares passenger revenues with the fully distributed costs allotted to it by the Interstate Commerce Commission: as the commission has itself estimated, only about 75% of the cost thus determined would definitely be saved if the service were abandoned, the remaining 25% representing a distribution of common costs of freight and passenger traffic.[74]

In August of 1968, the ICC's Bureau of Economics pointed out that although the deficit of the pasenger operations for all Class I railroads on a fully allocated basis was $485 million in 1967, the extent to which passenger service revenues fell short of operating expenses related solely to those services was only $72 million; and whereas the former figures showed comparably large deficits all through the 1960s (and, indeed, deficits in every year since World War II), the latter showed annual surpluses from 1959 through 1966.[75] This is not to say that these "solely related operating expenses" are a full or correct measure of the avoidable costs of passenger operations. For example, passenger equipment has salvage value, the return on which is a genuine opportunity cost of continuing that service, and undoubtedly some portion of such common costs as track maintenance,

---

[73] In so doing, the FCC mystifyingly compounded what it recognized was already an inefficient discouragement of toll telephone calls, resulting from the fact that all the costs allocated to that service are recovered in toll charges, which exceed the marginal costs of (additional) calls, whereas the capital costs of local, intrastate calls are recovered largely in a monthly rental charge, which produces a zero price for additional calls. *Ibid.*, par. 301. It clung to the same logic in its later modification of these separations procedures. *In the Matter of Prescription of Procedures for Separating and Allocating,* . . . [etc.], Docket No. 17975, Report and Order, January 29, 1969 (16 FCC 2d 332), pars. 20–33.

In practice, the devising of separations procedures has been mostly a political process, involving a balancing of the interests of state and federal regulatory agencies. See the dissenting opinion of Commissioner Johnson, *ibid.* In particular, the modifications described both here and in Chapter 4 (p. 100, note 39), both of which had the effect of shifting costs—uneconomically, we have suggested—from the intrastate to the interstate level were apparently in response to the marked tendencies after World War II for their respective costs to move in the opposite directions. The state commissions, anxious to avoid the embarrassment of having to permit

continuous increases in local rates, pressed for separations that would tend to offset these divergent trends and, conceivably, the Bell System was willing to go along in order to diminish correspondingly the necessity of asking for such increases at the state level and of accepting reductions in interstate toll rates. According to a private estimate made in 1969 the overall effect of the change in separations was to keep interstate toll cost of service 12% higher, and state rates 10% lower (on a 1968 basis) than they would otherwise have been. AT&T's efforts to correct some of these distortions in recent years must have reflected the company's growing competition on the interstate part of its business, and its difficulties in meeting that competition as long as its interstate rate base was inflated in this way. See, for example, pp. 173–174, and the section on the national telecommunications network in Chapter 4, Volume 2.

[74] See ICC, *Investigation of Costs of Intercity Rail Passenger Service*, 1969, 48. See also the summary of the evidence in C. F. Phillips, *op. cit.*, 154–157; also J. C. Nelson, *op. cit.*, 284–296; and our discussion of the *Southern Pacific* decision, Chapter 2, Volume 2.

[75] *Transport Economics, Monthly Comment*, August 1968, 2–3.

repairs, and general administrative expenses could well be eliminated if passenger service were dropped.[76]

Therefore, in 1968 the ICC undertook an intensive study of the true avoidable costs of passenger service. Its analysis of the passenger operations of eight major intercity railroads concluded that these roads would eventually have saved $118 million more in expenses than they would have lost in revenues if they had not operated any passenger service in that year. In addition, they could have earned approximately $5 million on the salvage value of the facilities and equipment that would no longer be needed. On the other hand the $118 million includes some allowance for depreciation—evidently about $14,500,000—on the ground that this "is a properly assignable expense under generally accepted accounting procedures"[77]; but this is clearly not a real marginal cost that would have been avoided in an economic sense. (What would have been "avoided" would be the periodic accounting recording of depreciation, not any use of cash or real resources.[78]) The $118 million figure may be compared with the full ICC deficits of these roads measured with fully allocated costs, of $214 million.[79]

The basic defect of full cost distributions as the basis for pricing is, then, that they ignore the pervasive discrepancies between marginal and average cost. And, as this chapter has demonstrated, those discrepancies may require prices that take into account not just the costs but also the elasticities of demand of the various categories of service if the company is to recover its total costs. Whenever there is some separable portion of the demand sufficiently elastic that a rate below fully-distributed costs for it would add more to total revenue than to total costs, any insistence that each service or group of patrons pay their fully allocated costs would be self-defeating. It would force the firm to charge a price that would result in its turning away business that would have covered its marginal costs—in other words, would prevent it from obtaining from customers with an elastic demand the maximum possible contribution to overheads. Thus, under the guise of ensuring a fair distribution of common costs and preventing undue discrimination, it would be serving the interests neither of the patrons who would be prepared to take additional quantities if prices were closer to marginal costs, nor of the customers with the more inelastic demands.[80]

---

[76] On the other hand, not all solely related expenses are avoidable: for example, some of the expenses of passenger car and road locomotive repairs could not be eliminated. ICC *Investigation of Costs of Intercity Rail Passenger Service*, 1969, 49–52.

[77] *Ibid.*, 20; see also 37–38.

[78] A similar question might be raised about its inclusion of property taxes. These, in contrast with depreciation, are a genuine avoidable expense from the standpoint of the railroads; the question is whether they are a true social cost, representing a use of resources. To the extent that property—for example, passenger terminals in cities—could be used for other purposes, on which such taxes could in fact be paid out of commercial revenues, the taxes are properly included, as a reflection of the opportunity cost to society of using the property for the passenger

service. On the other hand, by this measure, railroad property is probably overtaxed. (See note 34, Chapter 7.)

[79] The biggest explanation of the difference is that only 74.4% of the expenses charged to passenger operations by the ICC separation rules could actually have been avoided by cessation of that service. See *ibid.*, i–iii, 47–48 and *passim*.

[80] See the testimony of Bonbright, Baumol and Froggatt, Bell Exhibits (in FCC Docket No. 16258, *op. cit.*, 1966). See, also, the testimony of Baumol in Verified Statement No. 67, January 20, 1966, *Canned Goods Between Pacific Coast and the East et al.*, Interstate Commerce Commission, Docket No. 34573 *et al.*; de Chazeau, *op. cit.*, *Q. Jour. Econ.* (February 1938), LII: 349–350, 355–356.

For an analysis and criticism of the "cost ascertainment system" of fully allocating costs

The most venerable and familiar illustration of this defect is provided by the historic inability of the railroads to charge uniform freight rates per ton-mile. What was the economic basis for charging higher rates per ton-mile for furniture than coal, or for watches than furniture—entirely apart from possible differences in the respective costs of carrying them? Or for charging lower rates to carry coal into towns with their own possible sources of supply than into towns with no potential local sources of production? The basis was that if the railroads charged uniform rates, all of them equal to the average total cost per ton-mile of traffic, they might have succeeded in getting the higher-value business, the watches and possibly the furniture and the coal delivered into towns with no local supply, but would have gotten very little if any of the lower-value business. The traffic in bulky, low-value per ton commodities, they discovered, was highly responsive to the rates charged. In contrast, the traffic in commodities with a high value per ton, for which the same rate per ton-mile would amount to a much lower proportion of their final sales price, was correspondingly price-inelastic. The former traffic would bear only a comparatively low rate, the latter a high rate at least before the truck offered a feasible alternative.[81] The consequences of a uniform, nondiscriminatory rate would have been an underutilization of rail capacity and a loss of traffic that could easily have covered incremental costs and made a contribution to common costs.[82]

A fully distributed cost analysis of the interstate and foreign communications services of the Bell System played a leading role in the FCC's comprehensive investigation of the rates and the rate structures of AT&T and its associated companies, initiated late in 1965. Following the directions of the Commission, the respondent companies prepared a Seven-Way Cost Study, which distributed the interstate and foreign costs of the System among seven major services mainly on the basis of their relative use of the common facilities: message toll telephone, teletypewriter exchange, wide-area telephone, telephone grade private-line, telegraph grade private-line, TELPAK, and all others. A comparison of these costs with the corresponding revenues produced calculations of the "profitability" of each of these services. The ratios of their net operating earnings to (allocated) net investments ranged for the 12-month period, September 1, 1963 to August 31, 1964, from 0.3% (on TELPAK) to 10.1% (on wide-area telephone service). Calling to the attention of the respondents the wide variation in earnings revealed by this analysis, the Commission instructed them:

---

employed by the U.S. Post Office and argument that it is irrelevant for rate making, or for deciding which services do or do not pay their way, along similar lines, see *Towards Postal Excellence*, Report of the President's Commission on Postal Organization, Washington, June 1968, 30–31, 130–135 and Annex, Vol. 2, Report on *Rates and Rate Making*.

[81] See section on transportation in Chapter 1, Volume 2.

[82] See the lucid statement by Ford K. Edwards, before the ICC, *Rules to Govern the Assembling and Presenting of Cost Evidence*, Docket No. 34013, Reply to the Report and Order Recommended

by Jair S. Kaplan, Hearing Examiner, February 28, 1967; and his "The Proper Function of Incremental Costs in Rate Making," a paper presented before the Federal Bar Association Twenty-second Annual Meeting, May 3, 1967; and George W. Wilson, "Value of Service Pricing for the Railroads," *Business Horizons* (Fall 1958), I: 88–97. As Edwards points out elsewhere, not only did 65% of railroad freight tonnage move in 1960 at rates below fully distributed costs, but some of the freight with the lowest *percentage* markup over out-of-pocket cost made the largest *aggregate* contribution to overheads. Testimony before the ICC, *Ingot*

"Respondents shall indicate the specific rate adjustments, if any, which they consider should be made on an interim basis in the light of such study results and the rate-making principles and factors advocated by them."[83]

The following table provides a truncated summary of the results. It combines the figures for the six business services, since the principal controversy is related to the low apparent earnings on these as compared with the 10.0% computed return on message toll telephone service.[84] It was the complaint by Western Union that AT&T's low rates on the former services, in the offer of some of which the two companies were competitors, were subsidized by the high profits in the monopoly MTT market that precipitated the inquiry.

table 2 Bell System Interstate Services (Total Day) for 12-Month Period September 1, 1963 to August 31, 1964 Earnings Statement Summary

	Message Toll Telephone	All Other Services	Total
Total revenues	$2,137,522	$ 562,352	$2,699,874
Total expenses, income charges and operating taxes	$1,710,799	$ 496,486	$2,207,285
Net operating earnings	$ 426,723	$ 65,866	$ 492,589
Net investment	$4,286,702	$2,271,704	$6,588,406
Ratio of net operating earnings to net investment	10.0%	2.9%	7.5%

Source. FCC *Special Interstate Cost Study*, Docket No. 14650, AT&T Exhibit 81, Attachment A, 4.

The interpretation of these data by Western Union and some of the FCC staff was, of course, that the various business services were not earning the 7.5% legal allowable return on investment, that the users of message toll telephone service were being overcharged in order to subsidize the business services and that Western was indeed being subjected to unfair, subsidized competition.

The FCC never did finally decide whether the data justified these conclusions.[85] We need observe only that they do not necessarily. The fundamental test of whether the MTT customers were subsidizing the rates on the business services is whether the latter covered their long-run marginal costs, including the 7.5% return on the *incremental* investment causally attributable to them. *If* (setting aside the allocations of the various expense items) the investment required for the Bell companies to provide message toll telephone service alone would have been not $4.3 but some $5.7 billion, and *if* the incremental investment costs necessary to introduce the various business services were not $2.3 billion but just short of $900 million, then the net operating earnings shown in table 2 would have represented a 7.5% return on the investments in both categories. In fact, the business services would have

Molds—Pennsylvania to Steelton, Kentucky, Docket 8038, April 21, 1964.

[83] *In the Matter of American Telephone and Telegraph Co. et al.*, Docket No. 16258, Memorandum Opinion and Order, 2 FCC 2d 142, 143 (1965). See also note 1, Chapter 3.

[84] Apart from WATS, returns on the business services ranged between 0.3 and 4.7%.

[85] See the inconclusive "Statement of Rate-Making Principles and Factors" that ultimately emerged from this phase of the investigation. *In the Matter of American Telephone and Telegraph Co.*, Dockets 16258, 15011 and 18128, Memorandum Opinion and Order, July 29, 1969.

been remunerative and imposed no burden on ordinary long-distance telephone callers.

But cost considerations alone could not determine whether the MTT customers might or might not have had a legitimate complaint about who was getting the LRMC price and who was being forced to make a disproportionately large contribution to overheads. Why, it must still be asked, should the former have attributed to them the full average costs of serving them alone and the latter only the requisite incremental investment? Justification for this kind of discrimination must be found in the comparative elasticities of demand for the two services. If demand for the various business services was the more elastic of the two, and if rates on those services had been set at a point that maximized their net contribution to aggregate system revenues, no rearrangement of the rates could have improved the situation for the patrons of the message toll telephone service.

If these various conditions existed, Western Union might still have claimed to be the victim of subsidized competition, in the sense that the prices with which it was having to compete were discriminatorily low. But if they were lowered only to the point of maximizing the benefit to the MTT customers, whose rates under any other system of pricing could only have been *higher*, it is difficult to see that the "subsidized" characterization could have any economic substance.[86] In any event, the presence of competition introduces a whole new set of considerations that we reserve for treatment in Chapter 6.

The Seven-Way Cost Study served to raise the question of whether these necessary conditions were in fact present in the telephone industry. But the study could not answer the question.

The other side of the coin is that where these conditions are *not* present— for example, for those segments of demand that do not have the requisite high elasticity—prices based on fully distributed costs have much to recommend them. This is so, at least in so far as they consist of identifiable, separate costs for the various classes of service plus a proportionate contribution to joint or otherwise inallocable costs. To the extent that the relation of marginal to average costs is the same for these different categories, this type of full-cost pricing amounts to fixing rates in proportion to marginal costs and, hence, retaining the same relative price relationships as would prevail under strict marginal cost pricing. We have seen that this comes tolerably close to avoiding any distortion of consumer choices among the various services. It may also have attractiveness on distributional grounds, since economics provides no assurance that there is any better way of distributing the advantages of joint operation and decreasing cost among the various classes of rate-payers.[87] Moreover, the respective average historic cost responsibilities of the various classes of service plus proportionate contributions to overhead will most likely strike the various rate-payers as equitable and nondiscriminatory. Where none of these categories of demand is sufficiently elastic for discriminatory rate reductions to confer advantages on all, any other pattern of rate making would involve making some customers better off at the expense of others.

---

[86] See notes 38 and 45, p. 143 and p. 145.   [87] See p. 145.

CHAPTER 6

Rate-Making in the Presence of Competition

We began Chapter 3 with the observation that some of the most challenging developments in public utility rate making in recent years have been the efforts of regulated companies to revise their rate structures in the face of competition. Our exposition of economic principles has thus far given no explicit recognition to this consideration. Yet it could not have been far beneath the surface: one of the two fundamental criteria for rate making in the presence of decreasing costs is elasticity of demand; and the most powerful determinant of the elasticity of demand for the services of any *single* company is the presence or absence of competing suppliers. In practice, therefore, the principal impetus to discriminatory price reductions is likely to be the desire of the public utility company to hold or to attract certain categories of customers from competitors. In addition, price discrimination raises the most serious questions when the customers being discriminated among are themselves in competition with one another, the danger being that the differences in the terms on which they are able to acquire public utility services—differences, being discriminatory, that are not explained by the relative costs of serving them—may distort that competition. How may the presence of competition, at the level either of the discriminating seller or his customers qualify the various principles set forth in our preceding chapters?

In a way these problems are more intense in the public utility arena than in competitive industry generally. It takes monopoly power to hold price above marginal cost in the price-inelastic market. The fact that most public utility companies are physically linked to their customers in the supply of an essential service—the very fact that makes monopoly "natural" because it is usually inefficient to have more than one company linked in this way to customers in a particular area and because increasingly intensive use of that link involves decreasing unit costs—ties customers to them and makes those customers potentially victims of exploitatively high prices. Except for transportation, competitive pressures are typically confined to particular branches of business or particular locations. Even in transportation, where the pervasiveness of competition permits one legitimately to raise the question of whether the scope of regulatory supervision might not appropriately be sharply diminished and competitive forces given freer play, there can be little doubt that such competition would remain highly selective, with particular customers or classes of business, in particular locations, potentially well protected by competitive forces and others subject to the danger of considerable monopolistic exploitation.

Our examples will come mainly from the field of transportation, where we have had a rich history of regulation, extending back almost a century. From the outset, an important aspect of transportation regulation was aimed at controlling competition instead of merely regulating a monopolist. Indeed, it has been the prevalence and growth of this competition that has made it questionable to refer to the railroads as "public utilities" at all, or to attempt to apply to them the principles appropriate to "natural monopolists." Still, the competitive considerations in transportation, although different in degree and pervasiveness, are not different in kind from those applicable to rate making by electricity and gas distribution companies or communications common carriers.

The lessons to be learned from our long experience with intercarrier competition would seem to be these:

1. Long-run marginal costs are still the place to begin in assessing the validity of competitive rate reductions, and, particularly where the cost structures of the competing suppliers are widely divergent, LRMC will in most instances constitute a complete and sufficient test.

2. Not all rates will be set as low as long-run marginal costs, because competitive pressures will differ between different customers, classes of service, and localities; nor can all rates be set as low as LRMC and still cover average total costs. When the customers being discriminated between are in competition with one another, selective rate reductions down to marginal costs give rise to a danger that competition at the buyer level will be distorted. When this danger arises, competitive rate reductions must be further scrutinized, to consider on the one hand whether they are conducive to a more efficient conduct of the business at the primary level, that is, on the suppliers' side, and, on the other hand, whether they contribute to an uneconomic diversion of business at the secondary level, that is, between competing buyers. The merits of discriminatory reductions are most likely to be questionable when the competitors have similar cost levels and structures.

3. Special consideration may have to be given to the institutional implications and consequences of discriminatory price competition. This would include the following: (a) the important stimulus that price competition imparts to keeping companies on their toes, energetic in cutting costs, enterprising in experimenting with price reductions, innovative in service, and (b) the possibility that competition will be predatory or destructive.

THE CENTRAL ROLE OF LONG-RUN MARGINAL COSTS

Apart from possible noneconomic considerations, society's interest is in having transportation, energy, or communications provided at the lowest possible cost, with due allowance for possible differences in the quality of services supplied or the costs imposed on the users.[1] And economic efficiency requires, additionally, that no business be turned away that covers the cost

---

[1] Trucks give door-to-door, and often speedier service than do railroads. The proper test of the desirability of these added services is whether customers are willing to pay the incremental cost

to society of providing that service. These basic goals are served by permitting rates to be set at long-run marginal costs. The consequence will be that, after consumers have made allowance in their choices for possible differences in the quality of the service, the competing company with the lowest long-run marginal costs will get the business; and the services will thus be provided by those companies which, in so doing, will impose the minimum opportunity costs on the economy at large.

This criterion is especially relevant in assessing proposed rate reductions by railroads in order to compete more effectively with trucks or barges. Railroads have heavy fixed costs, chronic excess capacity, and the widest discrepancy between marginal and average total or fully allocated costs. The other transport media, to a much greater extent, use variable factors: trucks are shorter-lived and both they and barges travel on roadways and rivers for which they pay on a variable basis, whether year-to-year in license fees or mile-by-mile in excise taxes on fuel and tires, in tolls, and so forth.[2] Moreover, both trucks and barges can more readily be taken off particular routes or branches of service (locomotives and freight cars can as well, but terminals and road beds cannot), so that for any particular market their entire cost is more nearly variable. And to a much greater extent than in the case of railroads their total costs vary in proportion with the mileage of each trip. This is true of the costs of drivers, fuel, and the depreciation of the trucks themselves.[3] Therefore, it is roughly true that the long-run marginal costs for the railroad carriage of particular commodities over particular routes, on the one hand, and the average total costs of trucks and barges, on the other,[4] represent the marginal opportunity costs to society of using these respective modes of transportation. In these circumstances, if railroad rates, set no lower than long-run marginal costs, succeed in taking business away from trucks and barges, it follows that it is efficient for society to permit them to do so.

---

of providing them. The market solution would be for the competing services to be priced at their respective long-run marginal costs, leaving the choice to customers, considering both the different rates and different qualities.

[2] The particular arrangements devised to recover these costs make them variable from the users' standpoint. The costs might be fixed from the standpoint of society, which is really what counts. But society is constantly adding to its highway capacity and is therefore in a position to alter promptly the size of those increments depending on the amount of traffic. Also, depreciation of the roads and the need for maintenance is in considerable measure a user cost; to the extent that trucks (particularly heavy trucks) curtail their use of highways, much of these costs can be avoided. These considerations apply much less to water transport. The principal distortion there, however, is that the users do not pay the full costs, fixed or variable, of maintaining and improving the waterways. This constitutes an even stronger argument for letting the choice be between the *marginal* costs of rails and the *total* costs of the barges. It would be even more conducive to efficiency if the latter were adjusted even higher to include the full

costs of providing these "road beds."

[3] Terminal and other overhead costs, which are fixed for a particular shipment, are higher for railroads. This combination of circumstances gives a competitive advantage to the trucks for shorter trips—up to about 300 miles—and to the rails for longer trips. The ATC of the rails decline as the length of trip increases, whereas the ATC of the trucks is more nearly constant. See George W. Wilson, "Effects of Value-of-Service Pricing upon Motor Common Carriers," *Jour. Pol. Econ.* (August 1955), LXIII: 341; Dudley F. Pegrum, *Transportation: Economics and Public Policy* (Homewood: Richard D. Irwin, 1963), 189–190 and Chapter 8; F. K. Edwards, "Cost Analysis in Transportation," *Amer. Econ. Rev., Papers and Proceedings* (May 1947), XXXVII: 449–452; and Merrill J. Roberts, "Transport Costs, Pricing and Regulation," in Universities-National Bureau Committee for Economic Research, *Transportation Economics*, esp. 3–12.

[4] Indeed, in as much as heavy diesel trucks and barges do not pay the full long-run marginal costs of the provision of roads or waterways, even their average total costs underestimate the real costs of transportation by these media.

This was roughly the comparison offered to the ICC and the U.S. Supreme Court in the famous *Ingot Molds* case.[5] The case involved a proposed reduction in a joint all-rail rate from $11.86 to $5.11 per ton, which would have taken all the business away from trucks and barges. The contesting parties essentially agreed that the fully distributed and long-run marginal costs for the railroads were on the order of $7.59 and $4.69 per ton, respectively, whereas for the barge-truck service both cost figures were approximately the same figure, $5.19 per ton.[6]

It should be emphasized that the foregoing reasoning applies not just to general but also to selective rate reductions. As long as a public utility company can take business away from its competitors at rates that cover long-run incremental costs for that business, both efficiency in the performance of the public utility function and the interest of all rate-payers recommend its being permitted to do so, all other things being equal. The competitive advantage may spring from simple differences in the efficiencies of firms in essentially similar industries, using essentially similar technology, or—as is much more likely and common in the public utility situation—differences in the respective technologies and cost structures, which have the effect of producing markedly lower long-run incremental cost for certain companies than for others. It is sometimes contended by trucking or barge companies, or by oil jobbers facing this discriminatory rate making, that the competition to which they are being subjected is unfair: their competitors are quoting discriminatorily low prices on those portions of the business in which they meet in competition, relying on the sheltered portions of their business for the greater contribution to overhead costs. However, the inequality of such competition resides in objective differences in the cost behavior and structure of the two industries. If following the rules outlined above results in business being taken away from the complaining companies, it is simply because the successful competitor is able to fulfill the function with a lesser expenditure of society's resources, not because it is subsidizing that competition out of high profits earned on its sheltered business. The consequence of its getting the competitive business is not to require recoupment from the higher-margin business but instead to permit reduction of that margin.

Some of the justices of the U.S. Supreme Court evidently found it difficult to understand or to accept this elementary proposition in the *Ingot Molds* case, as the following report of some of their colloquies on oral argument shows:

"Justice Byron R. White, and to a lesser extent, Chief Justice Earl Warren expressed concern that using out-of-pocket costs as a standard where competition exists might result in the rails' saddling shippers with higher rates, where there is no competition, so that overall costs could be met. . . .

"Justice White hammered at the theme that money lost by cutting rates below full costs 'must be recovered by some other traffic.'

---

[5] *American Commercial Lines, Inc., et al. v. Louisville & Nashville Railroad Co. et al.*, 392 U.S. 571 (1968).
[6] *Ibid.*, 575–576. The $4.69 figure for the rails, which was the ICC's estimate of "long-term out-of-pocket" costs, still included a 4% return on the portion of total investment allocated to this service under the Commission's method for full distribution of costs.

For a similar example, suggesting that the long-run marginal costs of communication by satellite might be below those of microwave radio but the average costs above, with the same conclusion—that the business should go to the former, see Johnson in Shepherd and Gies, *op. cit.*, 125–126.

". . . Justice Warren . . . remarked: 'If they [the railroads] don't get full costs in this situation where they had competition, don't they have to make that up where there are no competitors?'

"Mr. Friedman replied that 'obviously total operations must be borne by all customers.' But, he said, in this case since the rate is compensatory, the customers would be better off in the long run. He reasoned that through the rate cut the rails obtained traffic that it would not have otherwise and that the revenue acquired above out-of-pocket costs would go toward general overhead. . . .

"Later, Justice Fortas pointed out that the fixed costs of railroads are much greater than those of barge lines.

"'So if out-of-pocket costs are the standard, the railroads would always have an advantage. There is an enormous spread between fixed and out-of-pocket costs.

"'What you are saying,' he told Mr. Friedman, 'is that in every case the Commission has to allow the railroads to cut their rates within a marginal area and take business from barge lines.'"[7]

The point that the justices failed to see was that it was not a simple matter of one medium of transport having a lower ratio of variable to total costs than the other: there would be no logic in letting the business go to a firm merely because some portion of its total costs was lower than its competitors'. The advantage of the rails was that their long-run *marginal* costs—*including* fixed costs on any incremental investment that might have been required to handle the additional traffic—were lower than the long-run marginal costs of their competitors.

Clearly, the possibilities of this kind of competitive displacement are greatest where the technologies of the competing suppliers are sharply different, as in the case of railroads and trucks. It may similarly be true between electric companies and home heating oil distributors. But if the electric companies have a cost advantage in this competition, it does not lie in the mere fact that a much smaller proportion of their costs are variable than is the case of the oil jobbers, the major part of whose costs consist of the cost of purchased fuel oil. In fact, the latter companies receive their supplies preponderantly from highly integrated companies, which would presumably be prepared, if need be, to reduce the prices they charge for the oil down to *their own* variable costs. The relevant comparison of variable to total cost ratios would thus be between electric companies and vertically integrated oil producer-refiners. In any event, the principal possible advantage of the electric companies would not be that their *average*, short-term variable costs set a lower floor under their prices than is the case with the oil companies. It would be that they employ a technology with strong tendencies toward long-run decreasing cost; and they compete with an essentially extractive industry, whose inherent, static tendencies toward long-run increasing costs can be offset only by continuous technological progress. In these circumstances the former have a much lower ratio of *long-run marginal* to average cost than the latter. And to the extent that their LRMC are lower than for the oil companies, it is better for *all* their customers and for society as well if they get the business.[8]

---

[7] *Transport Topics*, April 29, 1968, 1.

[8] The lower marginal costs may be the result not of a difference in technology but of the presence of joint costs, in situations where the competitive

The marginal costs against which competitive rates should be judged are the costs of the company quoting or proposing to quote those rates, *not the costs of their competitors*.[9] Effective competition and economic efficiency alike require that lower-cost firms be encouraged, because of their own lower costs, to reduce their prices to take business away from their higher-cost competitors.[10] The basic economic objection to cartels and cartel-like arrangements is that they impede this process by forcing the lower-cost firms to price instead in consideration of average industry costs or the costs of their less efficient competitors. The same objection applies to the historic reluctance of the ICC to permit railroad companies to reduce rates to long-run marginal costs in situations where these are below the average total costs of trucks and barges.[11] The purpose has been the same—to preserve a fair share of the con-

---

business is "off-peak." For example, in one striking case, the ICC correctly approved sharply reduced rail rates on the carriage of coal from Kentucky to points in Florida on the ground that the rail cars would in any event be returning empty after having hauled phosphate rock from Florida to points northward of the Kentucky mines and that the reductions were required if the railroads were to get the business in competition with water carriers. The coal rates were judged compensatory because they were above the slight additional costs involved in hauling the cars back with coal in them *instead of empty*:

"The omission by the respondents of a proportionate share of the round-trip line-haul costs results in a short-term variable cost and the reduced rate based thereon is essentially a 'back haul' rate. Normally, the proper level of cost by which to judge a rate is the long-term out-of-pocket cost, which includes a proportionate share of the joint round-trip cost." *Coal—Southern Mines to Tampa and Sutton, Fla.*, 318 ICC 371, 382 (1962).

Although the reduction on the coal was clearly selective it was not discriminatory in economic terms: the rate resulted in effect from auctioning off the joint (return haul) capacity—like the cotton seeds in Figure 2, Chapter 3—at whatever price was required to clear the market. And despite the ICC's characterization, it truly covered long-run, not just short-run incremental cost, since the costs of the round trip would have been incurred whether or not the coal was carried. But there was an element of discrimination in that the roads asked and received permission to cut the coal rate on hauls only to Florida, not to intermediate points that did not enjoy the barge alternative. The justification for this type of discrimination is further analyzed in our discussion relative to Figure 7.

[9] See William Baumol *et al.*, "The Role of Cost in the Minimum Pricing of Railroad Service," *Jour. of Bus.* (October 1962), XXXV: 365. An earlier version of the Transportation Act of 1958, attempting to give force to this economic principle, provided that in passing on proposed railroad rate reductions in competition with some other mode of transport, the ICC should "consider the facts and circumstances attending the movement of the traffic by railroad and *not by such other mode*." See *American Commercial Lines v. Louisville & Nashville Railroad*, 392 U.S. 571, 580 (1968); also note 12, below.

[10] As we have already pointed out in this connection (see pp. 148–149, Chapter 5), the same type of economic rationale might justify the use of advertising or promotional allowances of one kind or another by the company with the cost advantage. Gas, oil, and electric companies have been offering various inducements to builders— outright gifts of money or offers to pay the costs of laying lines underground, for example—to induce them to install cooking and heating equipment using their respective services. The costs of these various nonprice inducements must be added to the long-run marginal costs of providing the public utility service, in determining whether the proposed rates are compensatory.

On the other hand, there could be institutional reasons for regulatory commissions insisting that all such interfuel competition be confined to the price of the fuel or energy itself to the ultimate user instead of being permitted to focus on the builder's decision about the kind of equipment to install. Any such decision would properly turn on the effectiveness of competition in the construction industry as a mechanism for getting the proper decisions made. This would include a consideration of whether the buyers of homes and commercial establishments whose builders had been influenced by such inducements are able to take intelligent account of the probable fuel or energy costs of the edifices they buy, when they come equipped to use one fuel or energy source rather than another. See the discussion of this problem on pp. 177–180.

[11] For a recent example see the ingot molds decision, *American Commercial Lines v. Louisville & Nashville Railroad*, 392 U. S. 571 (1968). See, also,

tested business for the latter carriers.[12] And so have the results; this anti-competitive and protectionist policy has contributed to inefficiency in our

the Commission's earlier decision, *New Automobiles in Interstate Commerce*, 259 ICC 475 (1945).
[12] See the discussion of these policies in the section on transportation, Chapter 1, Volume 2. The Interstate Commerce Act was amended in 1958 to instruct the Commission not to hold up the rates of a carrier to a particular level in order to protect the traffic of any competing transport medium. This might have justified its looking only at rail costs to test the validity of proposed railroad rate cuts. But the 1958 amendment still enjoined the ICC to give "due consideration to the objectives of national transportation policy," which includes recognizing and preserving "the inherent advantage of each" mode of transport. In so doing, the Commission therefore continues to look at the costs of all the carriers involved in the contested traffic, in order to assess their respective "inherent advantages."

The ICC would deny that its purpose in so doing is anticompetitive. Its avowed purpose is to prevent predatory competition by the carrier that happens to have lower out-of-pocket costs from taking the business away from the carrier with the "inherent cost advantage." But its method of determining that balance of advantage is by comparison of fully distributed costs. It was on this basis that it refused to permit the Louisville and Nashville and Pennsylvania Railroads to reduce rates on ingot molds in the direction of their own incremental costs in order to take the traffic away from the truck-barge combination. (See the relative cost data on p. 162.)

"We do not agree with respondents' arguments that fully distributed costs are an inappropriate or inadequate measure of the inherent cost advantages of competing regulated carriers . . . . [M]erely because a carrier is able, without incurring an out-of-pocket loss, to handle certain traffic at rates below fully distributed costs, and perhaps . . . to maximize thereby the contribution that such traffic would make to its overhead, does not necessarily mean that the carrier is the more efficient of the two. Carriers, such as the railroad respondents, do not, in the circumstances here present, possess an inherent cost advantage within the context of the national transportation policy. . . .

"In short, by reducing its rate below the level of the barge-truck full costs, the respondent railroads have unlawfully impinged upon the ability of the barge-truck mode competitively to assert its inherent cost advantage." *Ingot Molds, Pa. to Steelton, Ky.*, 326 ICC 77, 82, 85 (1965).

In fact, it is precisely the comparison of long-run marginal costs that, on grounds of economic efficiency, ought to determine which carrier has

the "inherent advantage." For a powerful argument to the same end, see the *Brief for the United States* in this case, *Louisville and Nashville v. U.S. and the ICC*, U. S. District Court, Western District of Ky., Civil Action No. 5227, Sept. 6, 1966, in which the Department of Justice, "confessing error," asked the Court to overturn the ICC. Interestingly, the Commission was perfectly willing to use out-of-pocket rail costs as its test of the compensatory character of reduced rail rates when the target of those reductions was the competition of unregulated truckers instead of other regulated carriers. *Grain in Multiple-Car Shipments—River Crossings to the South*, 325 ICC 752, 758–759, 770–776 (1965).

This comparison of carrier costs by the ICC has raised another interesting question in cases of rail-barge competition, where the latter carrier is subsidized: which measure of the barge costs ought the ICC to take into account in determining its "inherent advantage"—the (higher) real social costs of carriage or the (lower) monetary costs of the private carrier itself, the difference between the two being made up by government subsidy? If barge costs are to be considered at all in such cases, economic efficiency would surely require use of the first criterion—a comparison of the real, social long-run marginal costs of the two competing media. This question figured prominently in an important case in which the Southern Railway Company, using in part the justification of its having introduced "Big John" freight cars, proposed a reduction of approximately 60% in rates for grain shipped in multiple-car lots to a point in the southeast, principally in order to meet the competition of unregulated truckers. In consideration of the protests raised by competing barge-lines, the Commission approved instead a cut of only 53.5% in order to "preserve for the barge line the cost advantage they enjoy with respect to certain port-to-port movements." "Big John: ICC Cuts Against the Grain," *Railway Age*, July 22, 1963, 32. See 321 ICC 582 (1963) 616. The Commission's own Division 2 had recommended that the costs borne by the taxpayer be considered in determining which was the lower-cost mode, and had on that basis approved the 60% rail rate reduction. *Grain in Multiple-Car Shipments—River Crossings to the South*, 318 ICC 641, 683 (1963). But the full Commission reasoned that such a test would flout the will of Congress, which, in subsidizing water transportation, could logically be presumed to have expressed a wish that the mode of transportation obtain a larger share of the business than it could obtain in the open market. *Ibid.*, 321 ICC 582, 599 (1963).

transportation industry,[13] to the preservation of unnecessarily high rates, and to the chronic financial weakness of the railroads.[14]

But this statement of the continued validity of the long-run marginal cost test is only the beginning, not the end of the task of appraising competitive rate reductions. Against their possible contribution to a more efficient performance of the public utility function must be weighed their possibly deleterious impact on competition.

THE IMPACT ON COMPETITION AT THE SECONDARY LEVEL

As in competitive industry generally, price discrimination by public utility companies may have undesirable consequences either at the primary level —that is, on competition between the discriminating seller and rival suppliers —or at the secondary level—that is, on competition among customers of the discriminating monopolist. Once the principle is accepted that rates may not be reduced below long-run marginal costs, the first danger becomes of considerably less significance than the second, since this rule goes far toward preventing the cutting of rates to unremunerative levels. It also assures, therefore, that if competitors are displaced by the selective rate cuts, it will be because their marginal costs are higher and they deserve to be supplanted.[15] But distortions at the secondary level are inescapable in any system of price discrimination: not all customers will be charged the long-run marginal costs of serving them. In certain circumstances, the resultant inefficiencies at the buyers' level will outweigh the economic advantages at the primary level.

To begin with a fairly simple example, suppose we have the railroad depicted in Figure 7, which serves the localities A, B, C, and D and suppose, also, that the terrain from A to D is in all respects similar to that between A and C, so that there is no physical reason why the costs of carrying freight along one route are greater or less than along the other. However, suppose that both A and C are coal-producing centers, with the mines in A being lower cost than those in C: that, for example, the costs at C are $6 a ton and at

---

Commissioner Freas, dissenting, argued:

"Certainly it is no usurpation of Congressional power to say that in providing for fair competition under the mandate of the National Transportation Policy the true cost of providing a given service is properly the necessary criterion by which to judge a contention of cost advantage." *Ibid.*, 620. See references in this footnote above and Chapter 1, Volume 2, for the subsequent history of this case, and p. 197, Chapter 7 for a more general consideration of the problems raised by differential taxes and subsidies.

[13] For estimates that the annual excess costs run to billions of dollars see the Presidential Advisory Committee on Transport Policy and Organization, *Revision of Federal Transportation Policy*, in U.S. Department of Commerce, *Modern Transport Policy*, Washington, June 1956, 2. Merton J. Peck, "Competitive Policy for Transportation?" in Almarin Phillips ed., *Perspectives on Antitrust Policy* (Princeton: Princeton Univ. Press, 1965), 246.

[14] See, for example, the comparative profits data in note 76, p. 51, Chapter 2.
[15] The danger is not completely eliminated, first, because long-run marginal costs are difficult to compute and require the application of judgment —something each of the contesting parties is likely to do in the manner best suited to its own interest. In consequence, rates might well be cut below LRMC either unknowingly or in an excess of competitive zeal, with the regulatory commission unable to prove, decisively, that this had in fact occurred. This is the burden of a large part of the testimony of Harold H. Wein in the FCC's investigation of AT&T's rates, *op. cit.*, Docket 16258, where he emphasizes the threat to Western Union implicit in AT&T's discriminatory rates on competing business services. And second, as long as the LRMC of two or more competitors fall short of their ATC, there is the danger that competition between them might become destructive—a possibility that we consider at length in Chapter 5 of Volume 2.

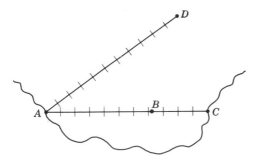

Figure 7. Rail-water carrier competition.

A $4.20 a ton, so that if the railroad is to get the business of carrying coal from *A* to *C* it cannot charge more than $1.80 for the trip.[16] Finally, suppose that the road's average cost for carrying a ton of freight from *A* to *C* exceeds $1.80, but that the incremental cost is below that figure. Would the roads be justified in reducing its rates selectively on coal from *A* to *C* in order, in effect, to compete successfully with *C*'s local mines? The competition in this case would be not with some other freight carrier but with local self-sufficiency.

The first answer is that since it is necessary for the railroad to reduce the *AC* rate below $1.80 in order to obtain the coal traffic, and since that business does cover its marginal costs, the reduction is justified. Is it justified however, even if the coal carried from *A* to the equidistant *D* and even to the less-distant *B*, neither of which has effective alternative sources of supply, continues to be charged an *ATC* of, for example, $2.20 and $2.00 a ton, respectively? The mine owners at *C* have no legitimate economic complaint: as long as the marginal costs to society of producing the coal at *A* and carrying it to *C* are less than the $6 a ton it costs to produce at *C*, efficiency requires that the coal business be taken over by the *A* firms. Nor, it would seem from our discussion of the proper limits of price discrimination in Chapter 5, do the customers at locations *B* and *D* have a legitimate complaint: the rates they are charged do not exceed the average total costs of serving them alone; the lower *AC* coal rates cover all the incremental costs of that traffic and possibly even contribute to the overhead costs that the *B* and *D* customers would otherwise have to bear entirely on their own.

But suppose the purchasers at *B*, *D*, and *C* are in some way or other in competition. Suppose, for example, that they are competing producers of coke. It costs just as much to mine a ton of coal at *A* and sell it at *C* as it does to mine and sell it at *D*, and more than to sell it at *B*; yet efficient use of the railroad has resulted in a delivered price of $6 a ton at *C*, compared with $6.20 at *B* and $6.40 at *D*. The coke plants will tend therefore to locate at *C* in preference to the other locations, despite the fact that the social costs, as far as coal production and transportation are concerned, are lower at *B*

---

[16] In most of these examples, it will be unnecessary to specify whether it is short-run or long-run marginal costs that are under consideration, since we have already discussed the circumstances under which the one or the other becomes the appropriate criterion. In this example, in addition, it is simplest to assume that the coal is produced under conditions of constant cost. This particular example is a modification of one that appears in Brown, *Principles of Commerce*, Part III, 64–65, 144–145, 166. In the various illustrations that follow, we draw heavily on the examples and discussion in Brown's book, Part III, Chapters 2, 4, 5, and 6.

and no higher at D than at C. Still, the railroad's discrimination confers no greater competitive advantage on customers at C than they would have enjoyed anyhow: the lower price of coal delivered in C merely reflects that location's natural advantage resulting from the fact that it has local mines capable of producing at $6 a ton. The railroad merely permits A's coal mines to match that price.

The fact remains that the ultimate result is not perfect; there will be some incremental resources of society devoted to carrying coal from A to C because of the lower rail rate that would otherwise be required to carry it only from A to B. It is important to see the precise cause of the difficulty: it is that *not all customers can be charged* only marginal costs, because MC is less than ATC and no public subsidy is available to make good the deficiency. Given the requirement that total revenues cover total costs, the victims of the price discrimination, B and D, pay no higher transportation rates than they would otherwise have to pay, even if there were no traffic between A and C; but to the extent that they compete with C, they *are* injured in that competition, and some misallocation of society's resources occurs, as some coal-using industries are diverted from them to C that would not leave if they too could get coal carried at MC.

Suppose, now, that the competition that necessitates a lower rate from A to C than to the other locations is competition not with local production at C but with a water carrier able to carry the coal along the rippling stream marked in Figure 7 at a long-run marginal cost (and average total cost) of $1.80 a ton.[17] The answer is the same. As long as the railroad can do the job at an LRMC less than $1.80, it is more efficient to let the railroad reduce its rates enough to the C customers to take over the traffic. As before, any advantages that the C customers thereby achieve over their B and D competitors are merely a reflection of their favorable location along a river; they could get their coal at $6 a ton, by water, even if the railroad did not quote the $1.80 rate to them. The fact remains that, in the ultimate solution, some coal will be carried by rail from A to C that would otherwise be carried, at lower social opportunity costs, to users who would have located at B. The solution, once again, is not ideal, because not all customers can be charged marginal costs.[18]

Our examples in this chapter so far have been of situations in which the competitors had markedly different cost structures—in particular where one of them and not the other had marginal costs markedly below average costs. The issue becomes much more difficult when the competition is between suppliers with similar cost structures. As we shall see, the main historical rationalization of railroad regulation and one important rationalization of the whole institution of regulated monopoly has been that

---

[17] This and other representative examples are briefly but clearly presented by Wilcox, *op. cit.*, 352–353, though without explicit consideration of the problems arising from the failure of all rates to be set at marginal costs.

[18] Not all the using industries will be driven, uneconomically, from B to C. Depending on the size of the rate differential, coal-using companies located at B may still have a competitive advantage over those at C when selling in markets west of B. But in markets east of B, the discriminatorily lower AC coal rates will tip the competitive balance progressively toward companies located at C, with the result that service of some customers between the two locations will involve hauling coal from A to C and then coke back westward towards B, when, at nondiscriminatory rail rates, the coal would go only to B and the coke on eastward toward C.

competition among *like* suppliers—two railroads, two gas, or two electricity distribution companies—is likely to become destructive and undesirably discriminatory, precisely because all of them have a similar wide gap between marginal and average costs.[19]

Suppose, then, that the competition in question is between two railroads. Assume, first, that one railroad runs directly from A to C, the other circuitously, as illustrated in Figure 8, where the respective terrains are such

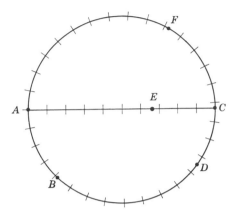

Figure 8. Rail-rail carrier competition.

that there is no reason to assume any physical difference in the costs per ton-mile over the one route as compared with the other. Competition might have the effect of depressing rates between A and C below the levels charged from between either of those points and the intermediate points on the circuitous line, B and D, or on the direct line E.

Under certain circumstances, a case could be made for permitting the circuitous route $ABDC$ to reduce its rates between the terminal points in order to meet the competition of the direct route AEC. This would be so if the direct route had not yet been built, or were already fully utilized and therefore confronted with the decision of whether to add to its capacity, whereas the roundabout road was capable of carrying the AC business without additional capital expenditure or with less additional expenditure. In this case, the latter road might legitimately be permitted to reduce its rates between A and C sufficiently to handle or share the business, reflecting the fact that the cost to society of permitting it to do so, even though over a longer distance, would be less than having that incremental business taken on by the direct line. The customers at B and D would not be burdened by higher rates because of the reductions between A and C as long as the latter covered the long-run incremental costs of the business. Competition between them and the A and C customers might be distorted; as before, however, the favored customers might legitimately claim that the lower rates to them were a reflection of the fact that their business was sufficiently great to justify their being served by a direct route and that the roundaboutness of the $ABDC$ route was properly attributable to the necessity for serving B and D—provided, that is, that the rates between A and those intermediate points did not exceed the average total costs of serving them alone.

---

[19] See Chapters 1 and 4, Volume 2.

It is difficult to imagine circumstances in which the presence of such competition would justify the direct route reducing *its* rates discriminatorily between *A* and *C* relative to those charged between *A* and *E*. The customers at *A* and *C* could point to no physical aspect of their location justifying their getting lower rates relative to marginal costs than the intermediate point, *E*. The resulting distortion in competition at the buyers' level, between *C* and *E*, would have no offsetting efficiency justification at the transportation end, since the lower rates between *A* and *C* would have as their purpose only some redistribution of the total business between the direct and the circuitous lines.[20]

Similarly, if competition between the two roundabout lines, *AFC* and *ABDC*, threatened to reduce the *AC* rates below those between intermediate points, there would seem to be no economic justification for permitting this arbitrary identification of the latter customers as marginal merely because they alone have competitive alternatives. From the point of view of the individual roads competing with one another, the *A* to *C* demand is clearly the more elastic. But the consequence of those selective rate reductions would not be a better use of the aggregate railway plant or performance of the transportation function at lower social costs. The distorting effect at the buyer end would have no offsetting social advantage.[21]

In the case of the railroads, the danger of selective, discriminatory competition is not, principally, that the customers or localities served by only a single road will have their rates increased to recoup revenue deficiencies on competitive business since the railroads as a group have not earned as much as 5% on investment in any five-year period since 1921—in contrast with the 5.75% that the ICC fixed as reasonable—and have exceeded 6% in only one year (1942) in that time.[22] Presumably, they have not been seriously restrained from charging the profit-maximizing price on noncompetitive business anyhow—in which event there is nothing left to recoup.[22a] In these circumstances, it would not seem rational for them to reduce competitive rates below LRMC in the hope of making good the resultant losses in those sheltered markets.[23] The main danger is that choices will be distorted at the buyer or customer level by virtue of the fact that some rates are set at

[20] On these cases, see Brown, *Principles of Commerce*, Part III, 40–49, 120–126.

[21] See *ibid.*, 97–103; also Baumol, et al., "Statement of Clarification," *Jour. of Bus.* (July 1963), XXXVI: 351 note. George Wilson points out that where the traffic in question has a low elasticity of demand for transportation service generally, the ICC will step in to "prevent the unraveling of the rate structure" caused by competition between two regulated carriers: "It will force a kind of compulsory cartel and . . . will generally maintain rate levels well above any measure of ATC." *Op. cit., Amer. Econ. Rev., Papers and Proceedings* (May 1964), LIV: 165.

[22] James C. Nelson, *op. cit.*, 199, 228 and note 76, Chapter 2.

[22a] But see Chapter 1, Volume 2, at note 27.

[23] This is not to suggest that there can have been no recoupment by railroads from monopolistic traffic of losses suffered on competitive traffic during these years. First of all, not all companies have failed consistently throughout this period to earn the allowable rate of return. (*Ibid.*, 215, 460, 464.) The successful companies could have had an incentive to fight for unremunerative competitive business, with the expectation of being permitted then to make up revenue deficiencies in other markets. Second, we must allow for the inevitability of ignorance, uncertainty, and irrationality. Long-run marginal costs are difficult even to define in workable terms, not to mention to measure incontrovertibly. In these circumstances, it is entirely possible that railroads might have been induced by competition to reduce certain rates below incrementally remunerative levels; and when, as occurred regularly during the period 1946 to 1952, they turned to the ICC to request general rate increases—freight rates were raised 78.9% in this period (*ibid.*, 125 note)—they might have justified

marginal cost and others above—a danger that is particularly extreme when the favored and nonfavored customers are in competition with one another.

In the other public utility industries there is the first danger as well: that in competing for residential heating, cooking, industrial power, or communications customers the companies may be willing to set rates below long-run marginal costs—in expectation, conscious or otherwise, of being enabled in this fashion to expand their rate base and to recoup on the portions of their business in which they do not encounter such competition.[24]

Even if no rate is permitted to go below LRMC, and even if the several companies genuinely try to follow the rule of cutting rates on price-elastic business only to the point of maximizing the benefit to the other customers, competition still creates a genuine danger of selective reduction that will be a burden on the customers not so favored. The key to this paradox is the difference between what constitutes profit (or net revenue) maximization from the standpoint of the individual firm, acting independently, and of the industry, acting as a single entity. Each individual competitive price cut may be wholly compatible with the above-outlined rules, if regarded narrowly from the point of view of the individual firm making the proposal. Each competitor, individually, may be able to point out that, taking the prices of his rivals as given, he must be permitted to cut his rates in order to get or keep the business in question and to maximize its net contribution to overheads; and that his other customers would only be injured if he were denied the opportunity of doing so. And he would be right, *ceteris paribus*. But each rate reduction by one firm, justified in this manner, creates the opportunity, indeed the necessity, for a corresponding reduction, similarly justified, on the part of his rivals; and so on, until the bottom limit of marginal cost is reached. From the standpoint of all competing firms, taken as a group, the total effect of the successive reductions may well be mutual frustration. Their *combined* net revenue (over and above incremental costs) from the competitive markets probably will have been sharply reduced; if the competition is pure, it will have fallen to zero.

This is of course precisely the way in which competition is supposed to work: demand for the product of each individual competitor being highly elastic, price is driven down to marginal cost and supernormal profits are eliminated. But where marginal costs are below average total costs and the competition is between regulated companies—two or more railroads, gas and electric companies, AT&T and Western Union—one or more of which is capable of recouping any losses in net revenue from certain markets by higher rates in others, the result will be absolutely higher charges in the noncompetitive markets than would otherwise have been necessary.

greater increases on the noncompetitive portions of their business than they would have been able to do otherwise.

Conversely, a major explanation for the increasing financial difficulties and loss of business by the railroads to competing carriers has been their continued, irrational adherence to value-of-service pricing (using rate structures inherited from the days when they enjoyed something close to a national transportation monopoly) in situations where, because of the increasing intrusions of trucks, the markets would no longer bear those rates. (See Chapter 1, Volume 2.) In the face of this widespread evidence of their failure to behave like intelligent profit-maximizers, it would surely be an extreme example of the economist's confusing his deductive models with the real world if he were to deny the possibility of unremunerative rate reduction and recoupment on the ground that this is something no intelligent profit-maximizer would do.

[24] See Chapter 2, Volume 2, for the fuller appraisal of this danger.

Whether or not recoupment takes place, distortions will have been introduced at the buying end by the fact that some rates exceed marginal costs by more than others, without economic justification or compensating advantage.

It is impossible to lay down general economic rules telling regulatory commissions how heavily to weigh the possible efficiency advantages of price discrimination at the sellers' level against the possible inefficiencies or distortions thereby introduced at the buyers' level—a problem, enormously accentuated by the uneven incidence of competition among public utilities. However, the following guidelines seem reasonable.

1. Discriminatory, competitive rate reductions should not be permitted unless they make for a more efficient performance of the supplying function. This means that competition (or some other device) should be permitted to allot the business to the medium with the lowest long-run marginal costs, when there are substantial differences in the respective levels of those costs. But it also means that selective rate reductions are suspect where they have no justification other than the fact that the favored customers happen to have competitive alternatives that other customers do not enjoy. In that event the only effect is to introduce distortion at the buying level.

This generalization does not answer the question of what commissions are to do when both of the foregoing circumstances are present (as may frequently be the case): (a) one competitor does have lower marginal costs than another and (b) because competition prevails only in some markets and not in others, it will tend to drive certain rates all the way down to those marginal costs, which will mean lower net revenues from this particular business and, hence, a possibly objectionable burden on the customers who have no such protection. The problem becomes one of devising arrangements that will achieve the efficient redistribution of the business at the supply end while minimizing the injury (more precisely, maximizing the benefit) to those other customers. Since the question of whether competition ought to be restricted and some other device used to achieve this end is essentially an institutional one, we reserve the major part of its consideration for Volume 2. In principle, it would seem that the ideal result could be achieved by keeping the rates of the competing suppliers above their respective marginal costs by the same absolute amounts[25] and reducing them toward those respective marginal costs only to the extent justified by the elasticity of their *combined* demand—that is, only as long as marginal revenue to all competitors taken together exceeded marginal cost.[26]

---

[25] Competitive rates should differ by the absolute difference in marginal supply cost instead of in proportion to those marginal costs because of the reason provided in our third rule.

[26] I am indebted to H. Roseman for this suggestion. Suppose, to take a very simple example, the LRMC of supplying a particular residential heating market with natural gas is $1.20 per therm, and with electricity $1.00. The efficient distribution of the business could just as well be effected at respective rates of $2.20 and $2.00 as at $1.20 and $1.00. If the total demand for therms (for natural gas and electricity, together)

is inelastic, there would seem to be no justification for permitting competition to drive promotional rates on new business to the lower levels, forcing an increase in the rates to other customers (let us say, those with heating equipment already installed, for whom no promotional rate reductions are proposed). So a regulatory commission could impose the nondiscriminatory $2.20 and $2.00 pattern.

This example assumes, of course, that only regulated companies are involved in the competition. Where the gas and electric companies are competing also with unregulated heating oil

The problem in cases of discriminatory rate making in competitive situations is to decide whether we are confronting a "rail–water carrier" or a "roundabout-rail–roundabout-rail" competition, of the types described in Figures 7 and 8. In both situations, conceivably, it is only the presence of competition between points A and C that makes the demand elastic for the individual, competing carrier. But in the first case, because of the differences in the cost *structures* of the competitors *and* the fact that the AC traffic would have been served at lower costs than the AB and AD even in the absence of discrimination, we concluded that economic efficiency would be served by permitting the discrimination. In the second, the absence of these two conditions called for a prohibition of the discriminatory rate cutting.

This has been the unrecognized issue in the FCC's lengthy investigation of the rate structure of AT&T, in its Docket No. 16258. The development of microwave radio resulted in the 1960s in many large business and governmental bodies setting up their own, private communications systems. AT&T responded by reducing its rates on certain business services discriminatorily, in the direction of its long-run marginal costs, and this in turn brought objections not only by its own competitors, such as Western Union, but also by Motorola, Inc., a manufacturer that had been supplying equipment for the private systems. In defense of these rate reductions, AT&T argued that in view of (a) its great economies of scale and (b) the elasticity of the demand of these business users— consequent on their ability, now, to serve some of their own needs—it would be in the interest of both efficiency in the performance of the communications function and of AT&T's *other* customers to permit it to reduce these particular rates down toward LRMC. This defense fails explicitly to recognize that if this was a "rail-rail" situation, the mere fact that the business demand was elastic from the standpoint of any single, competing supplier did not justify the competitive rate reductions.[27]

However, the situation could well be of the "rail–water carrier" variety. What made the entry of competitors into the provision of private microwave service economically feasible was the fact that their average total

---

distributors, there may be no alternative to permitting whatever rate reductions are required, down to marginal costs, to achieve the efficient distribution of the business.

It is important to qualify these observations by pointing out that they take no account of the institutional case for free price competition, which we consider at length in Volume 2. Given the institutional weaknesses of regulation, price competition, although discriminatory, may be the most effective mechanism for producing efficient results.

[27] Bonbright alone of the AT&T witnesses explicitly recognizes that this problem may arise in reference to the competition between that company and Western Union.

"What here gives rise to such difficulty is . . . that both enterprises are presumed . . . to be supplying their services under conditions of declining unit costs. . . .

"Under these special conditions . . . a plausible case can be made for the establishment by regulation of a floor of minimum rates higher than mere incremental . . . costs. . . . Unless this were done, both companies might feel constrained to hold or lower their competitive rates down close to, or right at, barely incremental cost levels. If this should be the actual experience, the revenues from the competitive services would yield little or no contribution to the coverage of the unallocable corporate overhead costs. . . .

". . . serious consideration should be given to the proposal . . . that actual rates be set at levels reasonably designed to maximize *the combined net earnings* of the two regulated telecommunications systems on their directly competitive business." Stress supplied. Testimony in FCC Docket No. 14650, AT&T Exhibit 89, mimeo., 27–29, December 8, 1965. Note the similarity to our suggestion in note 26.

costs were less than the rates that they had been charged by AT&T, which were based on the latter company's ATC. Whereas the ATC of the private microwave facilities were for all practical purposes the same as their LRMC,[28] the LRMC of AT&T, because of its enormous economies of scale, were far below its ATC—precisely the rail–water carrier situation. In these circumstances, if AT&T could obtain some or most of the business by reducing its rates toward its own LRMC, it would seem that it should be permitted to do so, because (a) the result would be to have the communications function performed at lower marginal cost to society and (b) as long as the rates were reduced only to the extent necessary to get the business, other customers would not only not be injured—since the large private users had the alternative (corresponding to the availability of water transport to AC in Figure 7) of getting their communications at lower costs anyhow—but would be positively benefited by the contribution that the price-elastic business would make to the common costs of the system.

2. Where the competitive necessity for the selective rate reductions to particular customers merely reflects the latter's "natural advantages," the reductions should be permitted, even though customers less well situated may have to pay higher rates relative to the marginal costs of serving them and some inefficiency may be introduced. Examples of such natural advantages would be those enjoyed by customers located on a river route, where the average total costs of water transportation are less than the average total costs of rail; or by customers supplied by a local producer (for example, of brick) whose costs of production can be successfully competed with by distant suppliers (for instance, of building stone) if the latter are charged transport rates below average total but above LRMC; or perhaps by homeowners in the process of deciding on a new heating system, who have the opportunity to install oil at favorable rates; or by large users of communications services who have a choice of installing their own, private microwave systems.[29]

3. Where the customers are in direct competition with one another *and* the favored buyers enjoy no such "natural entitlement" to the lower rates, the rates charged them should differ only by the absolute amount of the differences in the incremental costs of serving them.[30] Other things being

---

[28] There are apparently great economies of scale in microwave ccmmunications (see pp. 125–126, Chapter 5), but in as much as the private users were confined to supplying their own needs, the costs relevant to their decision of whether to do so themselves would have been the average total costs of that operation. Whether it was desirable for the FCC to have so confined them depends on whether the provision of common-carrier communications service is a "natural monopoly," a question that we consider in Chapter 4, Volume 2.

[29] It is sometimes easier to state this principle than to apply it in particular situations. The question of what is a "natural" advantage and what is the consequence of defective institutions —like the mere availability of competitive alternatives to some customers and not to others—

is one to which we shall return in our discussion of institutional issues in regulation. See in particular the discussion of "the discrimination problem" in the cream-skimming section of Chapter 5, Volume 2.

[30] "Even if a utility company, by the skillful practice of discrimination, could and would thereby reduce *all* of its rates, including the rates which it charges to those customers who are discriminated against, the practice should nevertheless be forbidden if it would seriously prejudice the competitive business relationships between these consumers and those other consumers who would receive a preference." Bonbright, *Principles of Public Utility Rates*, 384.

See *ibid.*, 374–377 for a fuller discussion of whether rate differentials should be proportional or equal to the absolute differences in marginal costs.

equal, the rates charged by the same railway or by competing railways for carrying brick and stone should differ only by the difference in the long-run marginal costs of carrying each: only then would the purchasers receive the correct signals about their choice between the two. The same would be true of the respective rates charged for raw materials and the finished products into which they are converted. If rates differ by more than this amount, the processing industry will tend to be inefficiently located, too near either to the source of raw material or the market.[31] This does not mean that identical charges per ton are appropriate. If the road carrying the brick has chronic excess capacity, possibly because the greater portion of the traffic is in the opposite direction and it has many freight cars that would otherwise return empty, whereas the road carrying the stone would have to expand capacity to supply the entire demand, their respective long-run marginal costs will differ, and so should their rates.

This third rule would apply whenever there is a high cross-elasticity of demand between services: direct competition between two customers is only one possible source of this.[32] Bonbright offers another example: if a commercial customer has the choice between buying low- or high-voltage power, the former of which imposes on the supplier the extra costs of stepping down the voltage of its distribution network, the difference in the rates for the two should reflect, as accurately as possible, the absolute costs of making the transformation.[33]

IMPACT AT THE PRIMARY LEVEL AND OTHER INSTITUTIONAL CONSIDERATIONS

We should also consider the danger that discriminatory rate reductions may be predatory in intent or effect: that they will eliminate competition at the level of the discriminating seller. We shall not devote much attention to this possibility in the present chapter, because here we are concerned with the principles of efficient public utility pricing, not with the institutional arrangements for following those principles. Whether competition, regulated or unregulated, is likely to prove destructive or predatory is one of the many operational questions that must be confronted whenever one undertakes to translate the *a priori* rules into functioning social institutions; and these institutional problems form the subject matter of Volume 2.[34] We confine our present discussion to enunciating and briefly illustrating the relevant principles and governing considerations.

1. Reducing rates to marginal costs is exactly the way in which competition is supposed to achieve an efficient allocation of business at the primary level. It would be a confusion of means and ends to forbid rate reductions to that level merely in order to protect individual competitors against

---

[31] See the discussion in Brown, *Principles of Commerce*, Part III, 160–169.

[32] Cross-elasticity of demand is a measure of the sensitivity of purchases of product A to changes in the same direction in prices of product B. If two users of transportation service are in direct competition, a discriminatory reduction in the price of transportation to the one will tend

to result in a transfer of business to him and therefore a reduction in purchases of transportation service by the other.

[33] Testimony in FCC, *In the Matter of American Telephone and Telegraph Co. et al.*, Docket No. 16258, Bell Exhibit 25, May 31, 1966, mimeo., 33–34.

[34] See especially Chapters 4–6.

displacement, when displacement of higher (marginal) cost suppliers is the very result competition is supposed to produce.

2. The presence of competition does, however, increase the desirability of setting the lower limit at long-run instead of short-run marginal costs. Whereas it might be desirable to permit a regulated monopolist to reduce rates temporarily to the latter level when it has excess capacity, the possibility that such reductions might be predatory or destructive makes this kind of pricing much more objectionable in a competitive situation. This still does not mean that rail rates need to cover the capital costs of such quasipermanent installations as road beds, rails, and terminals, except insofar as taking on additional business will indeed entail additional maintenance or investment costs for these facilities.

3. The possibilities of selective, predatory rate-cutting might conceivably be controlled, as some writers have suggested,[35] by permitting the regulated companies to reduce such rates as they chose, subject to the condition that they might not raise them again in the future unless it could be demonstrated that their costs had somehow changed in the interim.[36] Such a provision might deter a railroad, for example, from cutting its rates temporarily to unremunerative levels, in expectation of raising them once it had succeeded in driving out competition. But it would not necessarily be effective in preventing such unremunerative pricing as long as the regulated companies were not fully exploiting their monopoly power elsewhere, because in one of their subsequent general rate investigations, a general revenue deficiency—which, given the variety of circumstances that would almost certainly have changed in the interim, could hardly be traced to any particular rate reductions on any particular business—could serve as the basis for regulatory permission to raise the general rate structure.

4. There remains the possibility that although it may be more efficient for society, in the static sense, to permit a public utility company to take the business away from its rivals by reducing rates on competitive services to marginal costs, there may be some dynamic loss if the result is the elimination of those competitors. If it were true, for example, that because of the Bell System's superior size or integration Western Union were incapable of competing with it in providing business communications services, at rates fully covering AT&T's long-run marginal costs, efficiency would seem to require that Western Union go out of that business. It would seem anomalous to try to retain the protection that competition affords *customers* by protecting Western Union *against* competition, by holding up the Bell System rates. Yet it remains a possibility that preserving the competitor and the stimulus to Bell's performance of its continued presence might in the long run contribute

---

[35] See, for example, Baumol, in Phillips and Williamson, *op. cit.*, 118–119.

[36] The 1910 amendment of the Interstate Commerce Act contained such a provision:

"Whenever a carrier by railroad shall in competition with a water route or routes reduce the rates on the carriage of any species of freight to or from competitive points, it shall not be permitted to increase such rates unless after hearing by the commission it shall be found that such proposed increase rests upon changed conditions other than the elimination of water competition." The Act to Regulate Commerce, Section 4, as amended by the Act of June 18, 1910, c. 309, par. 8, 36 Stat. 547.

See, however, *Skinner & Eddy Corp. v. U.S., et al.*, 249 US 557 (1919), which placed a very narrow construction on this provision.

sufficiently to a greater and more varied innovation, to continual improvements in the industry's service and efficiency to outweigh the static welfare loss involved in keeping it alive. This assessment could only be made in each particular instance, considering all the alternatives available to customers—including, in this particular case, their own private microwave relay systems—and the presence of other sources of competitive pressures and innovation. However, economists would probably agree that anyone arguing merely to protect a competitor from extinction would have to sustain a very heavy burden of proof before they would be convinced that the way to preserve competition and its advantages is to restrict it.

5. The determination of whether unregulated competition is the best device for achieving economically efficient pricing and, if not, what controls ought to be imposed can be made only on the basis of an appraisal of the particular technological and economic circumstances of each individual case. Central to any such inquiry must be a consideration of how perfectly competition would work or could be made to work in the situation under examination.

The way in which serious market imperfections or the presence of important externalities might require regulatory intervention is interestingly illustrated by the increasingly intense competition between electric, gas, and fuel oil companies for the residential and commercial heating market that developed in the 1960s. This competition, apparently increasingly, took the form of offering developers and builders inducements of one sort or another to influence the type of equipment they installed—loans, cash payments, free or cut-rate undergrounding of electricity lines, insulation, installation of appliances and equipment, advertising allowances and so on.[37] The reason for this is obvious: once the house has been built, the choice of *kind* of fuel or energy is essentially determined, and the costs of converting equipment already installed usually preclude a shift to an alternative fuel at that point. We have already suggested that advertising or promotional payments might well be justified as a means of getting business distributed to the lowest-cost supplier, provided the costs of these various outlays are incorporated in the LRMC floor below which price should not be permitted to go.[38] But a question remains of whether this type of competition, focusing on influencing the decision of the builder or developer instead of the home-owner or business man concerning the kind of fuel that will be used in his completed house or store is likely to get the proper economic choices made.

This depends in turn on the effectiveness of competition in the construction market, which would determine whether these promotional payments get translated into lower prices of the buildings sold and

---

[37] A survey by a subcommittee of the House of Representatives Committee on Small Business of the promotional payments by public utility companies in the 1963 to 1966 period disclosed that about one-half went to builders, developers, or owners of tracts of homes or apartments, another 8% to appliance or equipment dealers, about 17% to trade associations, and probably only slightly more than one-quarter directly to the ultimate customer. *Promotional Practices by Public Utilities and Their Effect upon Small Business*, House Report No. 1984, 90th Cong. 2d Sess., Washington, December 31, 1968, 106, 109 and Wallace F. Lovejoy, "The Impact of Competition Among Public Utilities: Gas Versus Electricity," paper presented at the Public Utilities Institute, Michigan State Univ., March 25, 1969, 6–13.

[38] See note 10.

whether buyers have a sufficiently wide choice among buildings in desired locations with various types of equipment and appliances already installed. It would depend also on whether the buyers are able intelligently to weigh the respective merits of buildings with different purchase prices on the one hand and different prospective fuel or energy costs on the other. The more imperfect the market, the greater the danger that competition in bribing builders may result in the latter making installation decisions that are not in the interest of the prospective buyer, hence of society.

It has been claimed, for example, that these subsidies are less likely than direct reductions in the prices of gas, electricity, or heating oils to be passed on to the person who ultimately buys the house or store; and that inducements of this sort may lead builders to install equipment that saddles the ultimate buyer with higher heating costs than he would otherwise care to incur. It is difficult to accept such claims without careful investigation. If competition among builders is ineffective and buyer ignorance creates additional opportunities for exploitation, it is not clear why builders would not have been fully exploiting those opportunities before any promotional allowances were offered. They would in any event be under systematic temptation to put in the equipment that was least expensive to install, since this would minimize their own outlays, saddling the ignorant buyer with the burden of unnecessarily high maintenance and operating costs in the future. To contend that the introduction of the promotional allowances would result in even greater exploitation, with builders merely pocketing the monetary payments, would be tantamount to arguing that any competition among suppliers of building materials or other inputs is not only fruitless but possibly injurious to the ultimate buyer. Such a position would not be tenable, as a general proposition. The general assumption must be that any reductions in production cost, whether of competitors or monopolists, will tend in the short or long run to be passed on.

On the other hand, the introduction of promotional allowances to the builders does create a new incentive and opportunity, a possibility of builders increasing their profits by installing less efficient equipment and leaving the ultimate buyer stuck with higher heating bills. It does introduce a new possible source of distortion of the builder's decision. One cannot prove by purely deductive reasoning that there may not be serious lags in the transmission of these benefits into the price of the house, or that the ultimate purchaser has either sufficient knowledge and ability to make the necessary comparisons of initial outlays and operating costs, or a sufficient number of alternatives of roughly comparable quality and attractiveness to him among which to choose, so as to protect him from exploitation by this sort of competition. Whether the introduction of this new element in the builder's calculus has the desirable effect of offsetting the preexisting distortion (inducing builders now to install the more efficient equipment by making it comparatively less costly to them), or accentuates the distortion, or merely introduces an alternative method of exploiting buyer ignorance is a question that is impossible to resolve in *a priori* terms. The generalization remains valid: the more effective is competition in the construction market and the information available to buyers, the greater is the likelihood that promotional rivalry among public utility companies will be beneficial. It must be recognized that it *is* a form of competition and a form that tends to push effective price closer to long-run marginal cost.

However, there is another possible source of distortion. To an electric or gas company, it is essentially a matter of indifference whether it competes in the home-heating markets by the offer of various promotional allowances to builders, or via rate reductions to homeowners, except for the fact that the former method permits the finer degree of price discrimination, with the inducements being extended only to those with the elastic demands—that is, the customers in process of making up their minds. In either case, if an allowance to a builder induces him to install electric heating equipment, the public utility can be certain, because of its monopoly, that the current or gas will thereafter be purchased from it. The benefits of its promotional allowances, in brief, are internal to it.

Consider the case of the individual fuel oil dealer, in contrast. If he offers a promotional allowance to a dealer to install oil-burning equipment, he has far less assurance that the homeowner will buy the oil from him. The benefits of this promotional device will be largely external—that is, they will tend to flow in large measure to his competitors. Only if all the fuel oil dealers could organize themselves, as a monopoly, would they be as certain as the electric company that the benefits of promotional allowances to builders would all flow to them. Such an organization would encounter the institutional obstacle of the antitrust laws. But, apart from those laws, there would always be the temptation for the individual dealer to stay outside of the organization, refusing to bear his proportionate share of the burden of the promotional allowances, because he could not in any event be prevented from reaping some of the benefits.[39]

We make no effort to resolve these various conflicting considerations. Since we are in any event dealing with regulated monopolies, the question is not ordinarily one of removing all controls. If regulation of rate structures is required in order to prevent injurious discrimination, regulation of promotional competition is equally required and for the same reason.[40] It is conceivable that a decision by regulatory commissions to confine interfuel or energy competition to competing quotations in the price of the gas or electricity itself might be the most effective institutional device for achieving the benefits of competition while avoiding the dangers and distortions of unregulated discrimination.[41] Conceivably, alterations of published rates afford inadequate play for the strong competitive forces that have emerged

[39] This point, essentially, was made by the Virginia Petroleum Jobbers Association, in its request of the FTC for investigation of the promotional practices of the Virginia Electric & Power Company and the Appalachian Power Company, *In the Matter of Promotional Payments by Electric Companies, Request for Investigation*, December 14, 1964, Par. III, sec. B. 2. However, to the extent that these promotions are heavily financed by a relatively small number of major integrated oil companies, the force of this consideration is diminished.

[40] We must also consider the legitimate complaints of independent appliance dealers and plumbing and heating contractors, who have had to face the competition of sales-below-cost by public utility companies that have been willing to take these nominal losses on appliance sales and installations in order to increase their sales of gas and electricity at rates that afford a margin of return on investment well in excess of the cost of capital. See *Promotional Practices by Public Utilities and Their Effect on Small Business, op. cit., passim*.

[41] For an interesting example of the use of a direct promotional rate in the gas–electricity

in these industries; and to confine competition to those rates would diminish its effectiveness in forcing costs down and in probing the great opportunities for improved consumer welfare inherent in elasticity of demand and the tendency of unit costs to decrease with increased output.[42]

Once one moves from the rules of statically efficient pricing to the prerequisites for dynamic improvement of industry performance, it becomes essential to ask what degree of price competition is most conducive to the alert, aggressive extension and improvement of service. In general, this consideration probably argues for more instead of less freedom to compete in price, particularly in industries such as these, which, by virtue of the prevalence of long-established, government-protected monopoly, might tend to fall easily into conservative and unimaginative ways of doing business. Increasing returns to scale afford opportunities for improvements in welfare; but they must be aggressively explored if the benefits are to be realized. Yet there must also be attached the condition that regulators remain alert to the danger of utility companies using their monopoly profits in sheltered markets to squeeze enterprising rivals out of competitive areas. This is the basic paradox of the institution of regulated monopoly.

CONCLUSIONS

The testing of competitive rates must begin with marginal costs; other things being equal, rates equal to incremental cost are compensatory and are not a burden on other customers. In the presence of competition, long-run, not short-run, marginal costs should set the floor.

The costs that are relevant in applying this test are the costs of the company proposing to cut its rates, not those of its competitors.

Not all rates would tend to be driven by competition to marginal costs because the intensity of competitive pressures will differ between different customers, classes of service, and markets; nor can they be equal to marginal costs and still cover average total costs. Price discrimination becomes inevitable, then. When the customers being discriminated between are in competition with one another, directly or indirectly, such discrimination raises the danger of distortion and inefficiency in the distribution of business. In these circumstances, the possible contribution of selective rate reduction to greater efficiency on the supply side must be weighed against their possible undesirable effects at the buying end.

---

competition, a special rate offered by a natural gas company for total-energy installations, see Federal Power Commission, *Northern Natural Gas Co.*, Docket No. RP69-5. A Presiding Examiner, citing other cases in which the Commission had approved promotional rates for space heating and to facilitate competitive sales for industrial uses, recommended approval of the offering, although it allegedly would not cover fully distributed costs, on the ground that "The proposed rate offers better than a fair chance of providing an increase in the use of natural gas, and an excess of revenues over incremental costs, and will impose no undue financial burden on other customers on Northern's system." *Initial Decision*, issued February 11, 1969.

[42] For an excellent review of the economic arguments for and against this method of competition, see the testimony of Irwin M. Stelzer, William J. Baumol, and James W. McKie, the comments by the first two on the testimony of the third and the latter's response, House of Representatives, Subcommittee on Activities of Regulatory Agencies, Select Committee on Small Business, 90th Cong. 2d Sess., *Promotional Practices by Public Utilities and Their Impact upon Small Business*, Hearings, Washington 1968, 589–645, 677–695 and, for a broad survey of the case for competitive rate making in the same context, Irwin M. Stelzer, Bruce C. Netschert, and Abraham Gerber, "Competitive Rates and Practices by Electric Utilities," *ibid.*, A 171–289.

The justification at the selling end depends on a contribution being made to the fuller use of existing plant or a fuller achievement of economies of scale in the entire supplying industry, considering both the company that obtains and the company that loses the business as a result. Where the resources displaced are readily shiftable in the comparatively short run, efficiency in the entire industry can be enhanced. Where, instead, the competition is between suppliers with essentially similar cost structures, it is not necessarily true that the transfer of business from one supplier to the other contributes to greater efficiency; in these circumstances, and particularly when there is some danger of distortion at the buying end, price discrimination may be unjustifiable.

Special provisions must also be made against the possibility that the selective price cuts may eliminate competition—not in order to protect competitors automatically regardless of their respective long-run marginal costs, but in order to prevent predatory competition, to guard also against the possibilities of recoupment of the losses by the surviving firm either in charges to other customers or by raising rates in the competitive market once the competition has been eliminated, and also to preserve the dynamic advantages of continuing competition.

CHAPTER 7

Qualifications: Practicability, Externalities, Second-Best and Noneconomic Considerations

These are the principles of economically efficient public utility pricing. Formulating them was the easy part of the job. Most public utility executives and regulators would probably acknowledge their validity, while taking pains at the same time to point out that economic efficiency is not the sole test or purpose of their performance. But they would also hasten to emphasize that these principles fall far short of providing workable rules for the guidance of their accountants or engineers. The task of translating these principles into actual price schedules is so extraordinarily difficult that it is entirely possible to accept their validity while at the same time concluding that the task of following them is an impossible one. Few would go as far as to abandon the effort entirely. But all would point out, and correctly so, that even the most sophisticated and conscientious effort to apply these principles inevitably involves large doses of subjective judgment and, at the very best, can achieve only the roughest possible approximation of the desired results. The uncertainty of the resulting estimates and the impossibility of devising and enforcing rate structures that fully embody them counsel a rounding of the edges, a tempering of the principles themselves. Such a tempering is not necessarily objectionable even on purely economic grounds: as we have already pointed out, the economic costs of ascertaining and enforcing economically efficient rates, in particular circumstances, can well outweigh the efficiency advantages that such rates are supposed to achieve.[1]

This is additionally, and most troublesomely, the case in the presence of competition, particularly competition between sellers of widely divergent size and financial staying power. Permitting selective rate reductions down to

---

[1] For an illuminating example of the enormous effort and expense required to measure the costs of handling particular kinds of railway freight in Western Canada, see W. J. Stenason and R. A. Bandeen, "Transportation Costs and Their Implications: An Empirical Study of Railway Costs in Canada," in Universities-National Bureau Committee for Economic Research, *Transportation Economics*, 125.

LRMC is the basic economic rule for intermodal competition. In view of the possible incentives of regulated companies to reach out for business at rates below LRMC and the uncertainty and arbitrariness about the precise definition, measurement, and enforceability of that minimum, one cannot ignore the danger of predatory competition that attempts to apply the principle may in practice involve.

Noneconomic goals usually require similar modifications of these principles. The desire to distribute the business "fairly" among competing suppliers and the difficulty of estimating marginal cost both argue against permitting one rival or the other to cut prices below fully-distributed costs in competitive situations. Considerations of national security might similarly call for preserving a variety of alternative modes of supply, even though only one of them deserves to survive on the basis of efficiency calculations alone. National security may also join with uncertainty about the location and stability of peak demands in counseling against strict adherence to peak responsibility pricing because the national interest may call for construction of a larger capacity than would be supported by the market demand of peak users alone. Considerations of fairness or the desire to protect the small user against discrimination combine with the impossibility of accurately measuring relative demand elasticities in counseling compromises with the principle of constructing rate structures on the basis of value of service.

Even if we stick to purely economic criteria, there are two other hurdles that have to be confronted: externalities and the problem of second best. First, if the supply of a public utility service involves social costs in addition to those reflected in the books of the supplying company, or benefits to the community at large in addition to those that accrue to the individual purchaser, those costs and benefits somehow must be brought to bear on the process of deciding how much shall be produced, how, and by whom. Second, if prices in the economy generally are not uniformly set at social marginal cost, if output decisions outside the public utility arena are influenced by monopoly, taxes, and subsidies that fall with different weight on different services, then the efficient price for the utility service must no longer necessarily be set at marginal cost either.[2]

We must therefore examine these four new sets of considerations that must be brought to bear on the pricing, hence on the investment and output, decisions of public utility companies:

1. Administrative considerations, having to do with the practicability of measuring the relevant private parameters of efficient price and embodying them in rates;

2. The necessity of adjusting private costs and output decisions to reflect external costs and benefits;

3. Second-best: what prices will produce the efficient allocation of resources in a world of imperfect competition and differential taxes and subsidies; and

4. How society twists the market process and outcome to serve social goals other than those embodied in the market system's concept of economic efficiency.

---

[2] See the general discussion of these principles at pp. 69–70, Chapter 3.

All four considerations are so closely intertwined in practice that we shall find it impossible in most cases to discuss one without alluding to one or more of the others.

ADMINISTRATIVE CONSIDERATIONS

It is extraordinarily difficult to convert economic principles into actual rates. There are two types of practical problems: estimation and application. In practice these are interrelated—there is no point in trying to estimate the different marginal costs of different units of service (different customers, in different geographic locations, or at different times, or services of different specifications) if it is infeasible to embody those differences in rates; conversely, there is no point in attempting to set up fine distinctions in rates where differences in the respective costs cannot be estimated with tolerable accuracy or reliability.

The simplest way to illustrate the principles is to assume production of a standardized service, as in Figure 6 or note 25, Chapter 5, where the unit costs depend on the level of output. Or two standardized services, as in Figure 4 of Chapter 4. But public utility companies supply an enormous variety of services and the behavior of the unit costs of each in relation to the volume of output will vary enormously depending on the particular *dimension* along which output is being expanded. A major source of the tendency toward long-run decreasing costs, for example, is increasing *intensity* of use—when customers within a given geographic area consume additional electricity or gas or make more telephone calls. The behavior of unit cost is very different when the expansion of service occurs, instead, by taking on additional customers. Here again it will vary depending on whether those additional customers are in regions already served, in which case their incremental patronage may also entail a greater intensity of use, or in outlying geographic areas, in which event the opposite tendency might be involved. If it is impractical to vary charges from city block to city block, depending on the concentration of purchases, or from customer to customer, depending on whether his patronage involves a more or less intensive use, it is not clear *which* marginal cost should govern rates.

Therefore, it makes sense for an electricity or gas company, following the familiar classifications of the three-part tariff, to compute separately marginal energy, customer, and capacity costs involved respectively in supplying additional kwh or cubic feet to existing customers, serving additional customers, and meeting additional demands at the peak. But these three dimensions of cost are far from exhaustive. Marginal customer and capacity costs will both vary also from customer to customer, subject to, for example, the distance between them, the consequent differences in the time required to read their meters, and in the amount of sales per mile of distribution line or pipe.[3]

---

[3] See the proposal of Vickrey to levy the costs of electric, gas, and telephone mains, ducts, and poles against landowners on the basis of their frontage-feet or area, regardless of how much or even whether they use the service. He points out that this dimension is often reflected in charges for water or sewer service, but rarely for other services. A tennis court, even one that might have no telephone or use no electricity or gas itself, would be levied a charge reflecting the additional distribution capacity required to get past it to other customers. The effect, Vickrey recognizes, is similar to that of a tax on land itself. *Op. cit.*, *International Encyclopedia of the Social Sciences*, XII: 463.

Transportation and communication common carriers are in a better position to reflect some of these dimensions of cost-incurrence in price because they can vary their charges for carriage between different pairs of localities or for different commodities. But, here again, there is no single dimension of output that influences the behavior of cost in a single direction. Cost per ton-mile will vary with increasing volumes of business for different routes with varying gradients and other cost-influencing physical characteristics and will also respond differently to an increase in tonnage, with distance constant, than to distance, with tonnage constant. The variation in costs per message-minute-mile will vary similarly depending on whether the increase is in the number of messages, minutes, or miles, on the type of information transmitted (different kinds of messages—voice, data, television video, audio—use different numbers of circuits), and on whether the additional sales are on peak or off peak. The marginal cost of carrying a ton will change with reference to the density of the commodities carried—a ton can take up part of a boxcar or many boxcars. The marginal cost will be greater if the freight is to be carried (or messages transmitted or computer results provided) rapidly and with a high priority on crowded track (or circuits or computers), and it will be less if it is to be carried slowly. It will be slight if the bulk of the traffic is in the opposite direction, so that the particular business in question is in a sense off peak, and it will include the total capacity costs if it is in the direction of the major flow of traffic. It also will include varying proportions of the joint costs of the round trip depending on which direction's demand will press on the limits of capacity with varying distributions of the joint costs between the two.[4] The cost will be different depending on whether the traffic is regular and can be planned for in advance, or sporadic.[5]

These considerations bring us to the second major problem in estimating marginal costs: their height will depend on the elasticity of demand. Marginal costs that are continuously low in the presence of excess capacity will jump to a much higher level if rates set on the basis of them elicit an expansion in the volume of traffic sufficient to give rise to congestion. Of course, the costs that are relevant are future, not past costs. Therefore, all the accounting and statistical records in the world can do no more than hint at their level, except in the unlikely event that the industry operates under constant costs, in both the static and dynamic sense. Even where separate production costs are conceptually measurable, because the proportions of the various services can be altered, and *a fortiori* where they are not—that is to say, in the presence of joint costs—the estimation of demand elasticities becomes an inescapable part of the task. And that, as we shall see, is a very difficult exercise, the results of which will always be subject to considerable uncertainty.

The difficulties in estimating demand weigh heavily against any cut-and-

[4] This is the case of the shifting peak, illustrated in Figure 4, Chapter 4.

[5] For an excellent survey of the problems of estimating costs in transportation, by an author who recognizes the economic necessity of attempting to base rates on them, see Wilson, *Essays on Some Unsettled Questions in the Economics of Transportation*, Chapter 2 and especially 40 and 77, on which many of these observations are based; for the same with respect to electricity, see Turvey, "Practical Problems of Marginal-Cost Pricing in Public Enterprise: England," in Phillips and Williamson, *op. cit.*, 124–132. For a brief reference to the six parameters selected by Vickrey to approximate the response of operating costs on the New York subways to various changes in service and traffic, see Bonbright, *Principles of Public Utility Rates*, 346 note.

dried application of peak-responsibility pricing. Peaks shift over time, in response to relative rates, changes in consumer habits, technology, and so forth. In view of the political difficulty of sharply increasing off-peak rates when the demand in question turns out instead to fall at the peak, and the inefficiencies that may be introduced at the buyer level by rates set excessively low on the mistaken assumption that they ought to bear no portion of capacity costs, public utility executives and regulators alike are understandably reluctant to follow the rule of imposing all of the capacity costs on peak consumption if there is the slightest possibility that in five or ten years the pattern may change.[6] This reluctance is reinforced by the feeling that it is "only fair" for all users who benefit from the existence of capacity to pay part of the costs.

The practical problems of converting marginal cost calculations for different items of service into different rates are equally complex. We have already suggested the difficulties of basing rates on short-run marginal costs, which are particularly volatile. Whether they can be employed is almost entirely a matter of whether particular portions of business sufficiently small so as not to produce congestion can be, if necessary only temporarily, singled out for this particular kind of treatment; and whether the inconvenience to customers of fluctuations in rates outweighs the efficiency advantages of basing rates on SRMC.

Whether peak-responsibility pricing can be consistently applied depends on the ability to enforce separate peak and off-peak rates so that each applies to the appropriate portion of the service. Most residential and commercial customers in the United States have only watt-hour meters, measuring simply their total consumption of electricity during the period in question. Introduction of pricing that would encourage them to cut down their consumption during the peak portions of the day and increase it correspondingly during off-peak hours must wait until meters capable of recording these separate purchases can be installed.[7] This immediately raises a question of whether the costs of more elaborate metering would be justified by the benefits.[8] But

---

[6] Originally, when the peak traffic was westward, the railroads set low rates for the eastward movement of Pacific Coast lumber. It took 15 years for them to obtain permission to raise those rates, after the lumber traffic had the effect of shifting the peak to the eastward direction. See Marvin L. Fair and Ernest W. Williams, *Economics of Transportation*, 1st ed. (New York: Harper & Brothers, 1950), 430–432.

Apparently AT&T similarly underestimated the elasticity of demand for long-distance telephone calls when it instituted its famous $1.00 rate for calls after 9 P.M. and all day Sunday. Considerable congestion resulted and it appears that additions to capacity were required. *Wall St. Journal*, April 16, 1964, 32.

[7] According to Vickrey, Électricité de France now implements its Tarif Vert by use of "a small relay sensitive to signals at a nonstandard frequency emitted from the central station," which permits time-of-day tariffs to "relatively small customers at very little cost." "The Pricing of Tomorrow's Utility Services," paper presented

at Occidental College, June 19–24, 1966, processed. For discussion of this and other metering devices in use or under development, see Melvin Mandell, "Inside Industry," *Dun's Review and Modern Industry* (November 1961), LXXVIII: 97–102E, and H. S. Houthakker, "Electricity Tariffs in Theory and Practice," *Econ. Jour.* (March 1951), LXI: 22, 24 note 1.

Industrial customers will usually have meters that measure their maximum consumption, as the basis for assessing a demand or capacity charge; but most of them measure only the non-coincident demand—that is, they measure the maximum consumption at the time of the user's peak, without regard to whether it coincides with the peak of the system. Bonbright, *Principles of Public Utility Rates*, 361; see also pp. 96–97, Chapter 4.

[8] See Turvey, "Peak-Load Pricing," *Jour. Pol. Econ.* (January–February 1968), LXXVI: 104–107. The entire article provides convincing support for Turvey's argument that "the theoretical 'solutions' to the peak-load problem are a

in the absence of such devices, the familiar pattern of charges for residential and commercial use—with a minimum, high per kwh charge for the first block of consumption, to cover the customer costs, and with progressively lower per unit charges for subsequent blocks—though making sense as a rough device to reflect the decreasing average costs of more intensive utilization,[9] also has the opposite, inefficient consequence of encouraging additional consumption at low marginal rates without regard to whether those increments are taken on or off the system peak.[10] Obviously, there are immense problems in fashioning separate rates for separate classes of patronage, where the marginal costs differ. The problem is not simply one of classifying customers into different groups and charging varying rates to them, but also of varying the charges to *each* customer depending on the type of service he takes and the cost of the service. On the other hand, it would not be impossible to vary fares on the New York City subway system or commuter railroads with the length of the trip—as in the London underground—and with the time of day,[11] just as is done with toll telephone calls.

The discussion of practical problems so far has concentrated on the difficulties of measuring the marginal costs of different categories of service and equating rates to them. Additional problems of estimation and administration are introduced by value-of-service pricing, that is, by price discrimination, the outstanding one of which is the uncertainty that attaches to all estimates of demand elasticity. All the econometrician or statistician has to work with is historical data showing volumes of sales of various kinds at various prices; from these he must infer a causal relationship between price and quantity that will enable him to predict the effect on the latter of a change in the former. But consider the many difficulties. First, price is rarely a unique single number. Most public utility services are sold under complex tariffs, in which the charge depends on the number of uses, type of equipment employed, length of the use (for example, minutes or miles or both), time of use, and so on. One can combine these various dimensions of price into an index number, but if that index changes over time, it could be because specific prices had changed or because the mix of uses had changed, and ordinarily it will be both. Second, and closely related, quantity of sales is not a unique number either, for the same reasons. Third, if the analysis is to be of time series, there has to be a record of experience of substantial price change over time, so that the associated volume changes may be measured. Or, if

---

beginning, not an end. . . . While the matters which then have to be examined are less suited to the tools of the armchair economist, they are both important and fascinating." *Ibid.*, 113.

[9]This is an imperfect way, however, of offering each customer a price that reflects the marginal costs of the system. Impecunious customers, who might willingly take more power at the marginal rate, may be dissuaded from ever reaching those lower brackets by the higher rates which they must pay for their initial, smaller blocks of consumption. See, for example, Tyndall, *op. cit., Q. Jour. Econ.* (August 1951), LXV: 348, 357–358; also Davidson, *Price Discrimination in Selling Gas and Electricity, passim.*

[10] For a finding of a similar tendency in Australia, see H. M. Kolsen, *op. cit., Econ. Record*, XLII

(December 1966), 562–565, 570–571. Kolsen singles out for special criticism the promotional rates for all-electric homes. On the other hand, the installation of special water-heating rates, when the water heater is equipped to go on principally during the night and is separately metered, conforms much more directly to correct, marginal-pricing principles. See the brief descriptions of current practice on pp. 96–100, Chapter 4.

[11] Vickrey, *op. cit., Amer. Econ. Rev., Papers and Proceedings* (May 1963), LIII: 453–454; also his "A Flexible Change-Free Collection System for Buses and Subways," processed, May 10, 1966. See, also, references to some of his other suggestions, note 60, Chapter 4.

the analysis is cross-sectional (with comparisons of different markets or companies with varying price-quantity relationships), there must be significant price differences to which volume differences may be associated. Fourth, and most important, volume of sales will always be affected by a vast number of other determinants that can never be anything but very imperfectly separated out in order to ascertain the effect of price alone. This difficulty is particularly severe in the analysis of time series, when so many determining factors will have been changing simultaneously. And fifth, the statistical measures are inevitably measures of past relationships, or of relationships that have developed over the past. These cannot provide decisive answers to the crucial question, which is how quantities purchased will change *in the future* if rates are varied from wherever they are now set.[12]

In addition, since perfect discrimination (the pricing of each individual sale separately) is impossible, there are the problems of distinguishing and enforcing classifications of business and groupings of customers for purposes of discrimination. The groupings can be based on location, time, volume, type of use, income, age, or some other attribute of users. All raise problems of enforcement; all involve complex distributional effects; all will be economically imperfect; and all will inevitably raise noneconomic questions about what is fair, politically acceptable, and so on.

As might be expected, problems such as these appear with particular frequency in competitive situations, for it is (imperfect) competition, above all, that drives sellers into devising more and more ingenious (and discriminatory) forms of promotion to attract business away from rivals. When an electric or gas company instructs its salesmen to obtain a fixed percentage of the house heating market, by whatever means necessary, and the latter respond by offering all sorts of special deals and allowances to individual builders of new homes, the notion of a separate effective price for each customer, such as is involved in perfect discrimination, begins to seem not entirely unrealistic. Competitive suppliers of fuel or energy, building contractors and appliance dealers, small builders who feel they receive less favorable treatment than large ones, and customers with furnaces already installed—who are less likely to be wooed in this way—will all complain that this type of competition is unfair to them.[13]

Similarly, airline companies have developed a great variety of promotional fares in their competition, with special rates for young persons between the ages of 12 and 22, reductions up to 50% for servicemen in uniform, varying discounts for family members travelling together, and excursion fares, with the precise discounts varying between airlines and depending on the day of the flight and whether the passenger is guaranteed a seat or takes the risk of "standing by." It may well be, as we have already suggested, that young people have a sufficient elasticity of demand for travel on a standby basis to justify offering them special rates for this type of travel; but there may well be wealthy young people whose demand is not sufficiently elastic, and, on the other hand, poor people over 21 years of age who justifiably might be accorded a similar privilege on the economic grounds enunciated in our

---

[12] This summary of problems draws heavily on the account by Irwin M. Stelzer and Jules Joskow, *Utility Rate-Making in the Competitive Era* (New York: National Economic Research Associates, 1966).

[13] See the reference to these complaints on pp. 177–180, above.

Chapter 5. Therefore, the designation of the group on the basis of age or family status of travelers is, at best, only a rough and arbitrary approximation to the kind of discrimination that would be economically justified. Even if plans such as family discounts did represent the closest possible approximation of devices for separating various parts of the market on the basis of their respective elasticities of demand, they too would inevitably be imperfect unless they were confined to situations in which marginal costs were less than average total costs. Senator Monroney has commented in these circumstances,

> "The promotional fare structure is 'getting so crazy . . . that you have to travel at 3:02½ in the morning, in the dark of the moon with six children, two of whom have to be blondes . . . . it seems to me that the regular travelers are entitled to some consideration.' "[14]

And he is not necessarily wrong, even on economic grounds.

NONECONOMIC CONSIDERATIONS

The foregoing discussion has already illustrated how noneconomic considerations inevitably intrude in the very practical process of devising and administering economically efficient rate structures. They influence the decision of which customers or groups of customers should receive the benefit of rates closer to marginal costs, where price discrimination is justified because of the presence of decreasing unit costs. Consider, for example, the following court decision justifying a city's supplying water free of charge to a school while charging other users on the basis of their consumption:

> "It is urged . . . that the court must necessarily conclude . . . that in delivering free water to the Normal School there would be a cost to the city which the plaintiff . . . and water consumers, would be compelled to pay. . . . [S]o far as appears from this record, there may be a surplus of water in the city which may be disposed of without any extra expenditure in the operation of the water plant."[15]

The fact that the marginal cost might have been zero (the water was delivered by gravity flow) did not explain why the school in particular was singled out for the benefit of marginal-cost pricing, in preference to other users.

Noneconomic considerations intrude even when the intention is to charge all customers rates equal to marginal cost. In principle, each individual electricity customer could be charged according to his own complex individual structure of rates and lump sum charges, reflecting precisely the costs of serving him—the capital cost of hooking him up and providing him with generation, transmission and distribution capacity, and the variable costs of reading his meter, mailing his bills and generating, transmitting, and distributing power to him. But the system would be excessively complex and expensive to administer. Therefore it becomes necessary to group customers for purposes of pricing even in the absence of increasing returns.[16] But all such groupings, departing from individual cost responsibility, involve

---

[14] *Wall Street Journal*, October 9, 1967, 32.
[15] *Fretz v. City of Edmond et. al.*, 66 Okla. 262, 263; 168 Pac. 800, 801 (1916).

[16] See Turvey, *Optimal Pricing and Investment in Electricity Supply*, 98–106.

averaging; and the application of average group costs to individual buyers is inevitably to some extent arbitrary and unfair. Different groupings would produce different averages and no one individual's cost responsibility will, except by accident, be the same as the average. They therefore raise both administrative questions—what kinds of cost groupings can be developed, measured, and enforced and at what cost—and distributional issues—what kinds of customer classifications are fair or politically acceptable?

Social or political objectives are especially obvious in the practice of internal subsidization—where some services or markets pay less than their marginal costs, thus clearly imposing a burden on other users. The practice is often rationalized on distributional grounds, the desire being to make the service more widely available to people who could not otherwise afford it. Internal subsidization of service to rural areas may be justified also on the ground that by helping to keep the population dispersed, it contributes to reduced social and psychological tensions. There is also a possible economic justification—in the event that the particular use subsidized confers economic benefits on others besides the individual purchaser. Making telephone service and electricity available on the farm benefits city dwellers as well because it holds down urban congestion. Since a good deal of governmental economic activity and collective consumption involves precisely the provision of services that are believed to confer large external benefits— outstanding examples are public education and public health[17]—it is not surprising that the social or political objectives that are brought to bear on public utility rates often involve, explicitly or implicitly, a purely economic judgment that the private market provides insufficient consumption because the external benefits are large.

Internal subsidization provides an apt opportunity for demonstrating how an economist would go about explaining or measuring the costs of such departures, on political or social grounds, from the norm of economic efficiency. Ralph Turvey does so, using the familiar example of uniform electricity rates to rural and urban customers, where the marginal costs of serving the former greatly exceed the latter, in the manner shown in Figure 9.[18] At a uniform price equal to the weighted average of their marginal costs, C_a, the rural customers will take OR, the urban OU kwh. If instead the rates were differentiated according to their respective marginal costs, the rural customers would buy none, the urban OU'.

Ignoring the problem of interpersonal comparisons—that is, setting aside for the moment the possibility that a dollar may be worth more to rural than to urban customers—it is possible to show that society would be better off with the differential prices, by the total of areas A and B. That is to say moving the price in each market to its marginal cost would increase total transactions surplus by this amount, following the demonstration of our note 16 in Chapter 5. B represents the difference between the added costs imposed on producers by the UU' output for the urban market (the area

[17] See Francis M. Bator, *The Question of Government Spending* (New York: Harper & Brothers, 1960), Chapters 6 and 7.

[18] *Optimal Pricing and Investment in Electricity Supply*, 97–98. Actually the relative positions of the three marginal cost curves is simplified. When the quantities taken in the two markets are the same, the weighted average MC would presumably be halfway between the other two. The particular weighted average shown in Figure 9 might be construed as the one that would prevail when the rural customers take OR and the urban OU, as they would at the uniform price equal to that average cost, C_a.

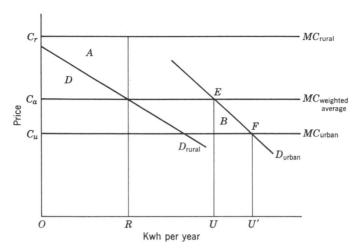

Figure 9. Hypothetical illustration of the welfare costs of internal subsidization.

under MC_{urban}) and the value of that additional output to urban customers (the area under D_{urban}). Area A represents the difference between the cost saving from eliminating the OR sales in the rural market (the area under MC_{rural}) and the value of those sales to the rural customers (the area under D_{rural}).

This also means that the urban buyers could give the rural ones monetary compensation sufficient to offset the latter's loss of consumer surplus from those purchases (measured by the area of triangle D) and still remain better off themselves—they benefit not only by B but also from the C_a to C_u price cut on the OU they had been buying. The producers are by assumption indifferent between the two pricing schemes, since they in either case recover only their incremental costs.

Of course, society might still decide that the internal subsidization is a worthwhile device for transferring income from urban to rural customers; and the economist can not say it is wrong. He can only point out that this is an inefficient way of making the transfer, since it involves taking away the entire area C_uC_aEF from the former in order to confer a benefit of only the area D upon the latter. He might also question whether society really thinks the result is an improved distribution of income. Internal subsidization is a very crude device for promoting egalitarian objectives. Uniform subway fares, regardless of distance, subsidize commuters who live in outlying districts of cities at the expense of commuters in the central city; uniform electricity and telephone rates for metropolitan areas ignore the lower costs of the more intensive consumption in the center city and benefit suburbanites.[19]

There are many extraeconomic considerations that may seem to society to dictate departures from marginal-cost pricing and the allocation of resources that it would produce (for example, the national pride that played so large a role in inducing us to devote tens of billions of dollars to landing a man on the moon and the far more meager appropriations for the deplorably pacific "War on Poverty"). These considerations and the ways in which they

---

[19] See our discussion along similar lines of the purportedly egalitarian argument for departing from peak responsibility pricing, pp. 102–103, Chapter 4.

may qualify the principles of economic efficiency are so obvious that little purpose would be served by an extended listing or appraisal of them.[20]

Most of the cases are mixed. As we have already observed, most qualifications of purely efficient pricing on so-called social or political grounds can be rationalized by the presence of external costs or benefits, which must be taken into account on grounds of economic efficiency as well. When the ICC refused to permit railroad abandonments of passenger service, it did so on the basis of a variety of considerations: the national interest in preserving different transport media for possible emergency; a desire to maintain the quality of life in out-of-the-way communities; a feeling that the external benefits of continued passenger service to such communities may have justified the continuation even though private revenues fell short of private costs; recognition of the fact that railway property has traditionally been disproportionately heavily taxed. The ICC believed that such distortions should not drive out a railway service that might otherwise be privately remunerative. They also hoped that state and local governments might be persuaded to change those policies and supply subsidies instead.[21]

The flat charge for local telephone service in most cities supplies an interesting final illustration of the complicated mixture of administrative, economic, and extraeconomic considerations that impinge on utility rate making. In a sense, the flat charge is inefficient because it involves a zero price for additional local calls, whereas their MC is certainly not zero: in 1969, New York City telephone subscribers witnessed the costs of congestion and the New York Telephone Company was made aware of the consequences of its failure to have provided sufficient capacity to meet the unanticipatedly large increase in demand in the years immediately preceding. On the other hand, (1) most customers apparently prefer the flat charge because it gives them the freedom to make local calls freely, without having to worry about their bills; (2) a flat rate is also preferred by the phone companies because when they charge on a per call basis they incur additional costs—of equipment to count the calls, employees to handle customer complaints about their bills, and so forth; (3) also, the incremental costs of local calls are well below average costs because of economies of scale when the dimension along which output is expanded is the number of calls made per subscriber.

---

[20] They would explain, for example, the 1956 amendment to the Federal Aviation Act (eliminated in 1960) that authorized reduced-fare air transportation on a standby basis to "ministers of religion," 49 USC 1958 and 1964 eds., Sec. 1373 (b); the fact that reduced fares for military personnel were upheld on national security grounds by the same Circuit Court that sent the standby youth and young adult fares back to the CAB for further examination (see note 62, Chapter 5); the below-cost postal rates on newspapers and magazines; the FCC's authorization of special low communication rates for newspapers (*In The Matter of AT&T*, 34 FCC 1094, 1098–99, 1963) (an FCC examiner recommended in 1969 that this discount on telegraph, telephotograph, and other private-line services be eliminated, *Wall Street Journal*, June 18, 1969,

21); and AT&T's offer of interconnection service to the Corporation for Public Broadcasting on an interruptible basis at about 15% of normal commercial rates, *Wall Street Journal*, March 19, 1969, 16. According to Turvey:

"Greek members of parliament do not pay for their telephone calls and telegrams (with the result that their constituents visiting Athens frequently ask to use their telephone), the parents of large families in France pay extra low rail fares and Swedish university students pay concessionary prices at the state opera. In none of these cases, so far as I know, is the motive that of a monopolist seeking to exploit different elasticities of demand." In Phillips and Williamson, *op. cit.*, 133.

[21] See our discussion of some of the problems in Chapter 2, Volume 2.

These are all strictly economic considerations. Customers prefer to buy one service (the privilege of making unlimited local calls) instead of another (the privilege of making local calls at some positive price per call). And if they are willing to pay the higher marginal costs of the former service in preference to the latter—to pay, that is, whatever it adds to the costs of a telephone company to let subscribers have unlimited local calling at a zero price per call—then giving them the more costly service is unobjectionable on economic grounds. For the telephone companies, the difference in the marginal costs of the two services is narrowed when the greater costs of administering the latter are taken into account.[22] Point (3) suggests that the distortion introduced by the zero marginal price for individual local calls would be exaggerated if we compared it with the average cost of making such calls. In any event, point (1) should be decisive: provided the prices accurately reflect their respective marginal costs (which would take points 2 and 3 into account), customers should have the service they prefer.

As long as it is infeasible for the telephone company to offer *each* individual subscriber his choice of service, at prices clearly reflecting the marginal costs he individually would impose on the system by taking the one or the other, distributional considerations are inescapably introduced. The choice of service then becomes a collective one and all subscribers are forced to take the only one that is available or go without, and to pay some sort of average cost instead of what they individually impose. Specifically, the flat monthly charge, based inevitably on average company cost experience, presumably transfers income from those who use their phones sparingly to those who use it freely for local calls. Internal subsidization is inherent in any averaging or customer grouping system, and society could conceivably decide that this sort of income transfer is unjust, for example, that it involved the poor subsidizing the wealthy. If it did so, the economist might reasonably question its underlying factual assumption; but if its facts were right he could not, on grounds of economic efficiency, say it was wrong to have reached such a decision.

EXTERNALITIES

We have emphasized the "public" character of the public utility industries as consisting partly in the unique relationship between the supply of transportation, communication and energy and the process of economic growth. Everyone's economic activities indirectly affect the welfare of others—effects that do not enter into his own decisions. (Your very presence on this planet takes up space that could otherwise be empty, blocks my view and, through your demand for food, induces farmers to use just a little more insecticide that helps pollute my lakes.) Externalities are ubiquitous. The external effects of public utility company operations are particularly great.

---

[22] James R. Nelson includes "the less metering the better" as one aspect of the desire for rate simplification that, on the one hand, consumers seem to desire and, on the other, is basically hostile to marginal cost pricing. He is right, of course. "Practical Problems of Marginal-Cost Pricing in Public Enterprise: the United States," in Phillips and Williamson, *op. cit.*, 139. But the *costs* of metering are properly weighed in deciding to what extent rate differentiation on the basis of marginal costs is in fact economically efficient; and if consumers strongly dislike metering, this too must be considered in deciding what is the efficient outcome.

On the cost side, their possible contributions to air pollution, to thermal and nuclear pollution of lakes and rivers, to the hazard of leakages and explosions (in the case of gas pipelines), to "visual pollution," to destruction of the wilderness and scenic beauty with their poles, transmission lines, dams, and reservoirs have all been the subject of intense and mounting concern and controversy in recent years. On the external benefit side are their afore-mentioned contributions to economic growth (with its own full measure of external costs!)[23] and, along with, for example, water and sewerage systems, to the general welfare. (It is in *my* interest to have you use water freely—perhaps more freely than you would if you had to pay the MC of supplying it to you—especially if I ride on the subway next to you.) Commuter train and local air service benefit not only commuters and air travelers but people who own real estate in the communities they serve.

As we have already suggested, almost every case in which public utility prices and output decisions are influenced by social or political considerations also can be rationalized on the basis of external economic benefits. The reduced air fares for clergymen no doubt contributed indirectly to the enhanced spiritual satisfaction of the community at large, as perhaps its later withdrawal made happier the staunch anticommunists who have objected to clerical expressions of opposition to the Vietnam war. The reduced telegraph, telephoto, and postal rates for newspapers undoubtedly reflect the external benefit to society (over and above the benefit to buyers, advertisers, and subscribers) of the wider transmission of news and comic strips to which they contribute. And so on.

Perhaps the most important observation to make about the implications of externalities for public utility pricing is that they really have nothing to do with the economics of regulation. In principle, there is no difference between the way society should handle the location of an electric generating plant, or dam, or gas pipeline[24] and that of a steel mill or a ski resort,[25] or the possible contributions to air or visual pollution of an oil refinery or private automobile on the one hand or a coal or oil-burning power station on the other. On the benefit side, every time any businessman hires and trains an unskilled worker or provides opportunities on equal terms for the member of a minority group he is probably generating an external benefit by contributing also to the diminution of social and political tensions. (A member of the Students for a Democratic Society might for this reason regard it as an external *dis*economy, if he ever attended his economics classes. Economic values like any others are inherently subjective.) There is nothing inherent in the economics of the public utility industries or their regulation that makes it appropriate for them to do more or less along these lines than unregulated

---

[23] E. J. Mishan, *The Costs of Economic Growth* (London: Staples Press, 1967).

[24] "Report on Power Plants Urges Planning to Control Pollution," *New York Times*, January 5, 1969, reporting the submission of a study to the President by the energy policy staff of his Office of Science and Technology:

"If placed indiscriminately and without built-in controls, they will pollute our air and water and despoil our land. Areas of great natural beauty will become ugly eyesores. Opportunities for healthy recreational activities will be lost forever." *Ibid.*

"FPC Plans Rules to Protect Environment in Path of Gas Pipelines; Opposition Seen," *Wall St. Journal*, June 9, 1969, 12, reporting the formulation of proposed aesthetic guidelines.

[25] On the latter see the *New York Times Magazine*, August 17, 1969, Sec. 6, 24 and ff.

companies.[26] The decision to subsidize the provision of electricity or telephone service to particular members of the populace or areas of the country is in principle no different from the decision to provide them with a decent diet, medical care, housing and education. None of this is to deprecate the importance of these things being done in fuller measure; but it is an argument against doing so in the former case by internal subsidization and in the latter by other devices, merely because the former industries happen to be regulated anyway.

The second general observation is that the mere identification of external benefits does not suffice to justify unlimited, or, indeed, any, subsidies to consumption. It does not create an unlimited case, for example, for the internal or external subsidization of passenger railroad service that the passengers themselves have deserted.[27] Since external benefits are ubiquitous, the conclusion that each calls for a subsidy involves concluding that more of almost everything should be produced—hardly a solution to the problem of the optimum allocation of scarce resources. Nor do they lessen the force of the case for using a price equated to marginal cost for the strictly economic purpose of restricting wasteful consumption. (My interest in your liberal use of water does not extend to putting you in a position where it does not pay you to hire a plumber to repair your leaky faucet, as is said to contribute to immense wastage in cities that do not charge users directly for their water; and it must be tempered by a recognition of the social costs imposed whenever the City of New York buries another upstate town under water to give itself an additional reservoir.[28])

There is no substitute for the application of judgment in cases such as these. And, the economist must admit, his own criteria are not necessarily decisive. But this does not justify his criteria being ignored; an intelligent regulatory decision cannot be made without assessing costs and benefits.

THE PROBLEM OF SECOND BEST

The final problem in translating principle into policy is that of the "second best." Deviations *anywhere* else in the economy from optimal pricing and resource allocation make it impossible to conclude *as a general proposition* that application in any single sector of the normative rules that we have been developing will be desirable. No single policy decision can be determined to be optimal except on the basis of a general equilibrium analysis of the situation in the entire economy, which takes into account all the ways in which that equilibrium will be altered by the adoption of any particular policy for any particular part of the economy—manifestly an impossible task.

[26] Because public utility companies have an unusually close link and identification with their local communities, they may be expected to take the leadership in attacking the problems of urban poverty and decay. We can use all the leadership, talent, and money possible directed to the solution of problems such as these. But this has nothing to do with the economics of regulation. For a summary of the problems along with a strong argument that it is desirable for public utility companies and regulation to pursue "externality-solving policies and programs" and social goals, see Warren J. Samuels, "Externalities, Rate Structure, and the Theory of Public Utility Regulation," a paper presented at a conference of the Institute of Public Utilities, Michigan State University, 1969. For an argument closer to the one made here, see Bonbright, *Principles of Public Utility Rates*, Chapters 7 and 8.

[27] See, for example, Ward Bowman, "The New Haven, a Passenger Railroad for Nonriders," *Jour. Law and Econ.* (October 1966), IX: 49–59.

[28] Noel Perrin, "New York Drowns Another Valley," *Harpers Magazine* (August 1963), CCXXVII: 76–83.

This general proposition means that, as a matter of pure economics, adoption of any particular economic policy on the basis of the rules we have expounded could well end up doing more harm than good in practice. But the observation applies equally to the policy of having *no* policy. Most economists would draw the conclusion, from this dilemma, that a conscious policy is better than an unconscious one; that, therefore, the important contribution of the theory of the second best is not that it recommends a policy of no policy but that it emphasizes the need for considering, as best as one can, the implications for any particular policy of the presence of suboptimal conditions elsewhere in the economy; and that as a practical matter it is not impossible to make informed judgments about the ways in which *the most directly relevant* imperfections elsewhere might suggest modification of the rules.[29] In short, here as elsewhere, there is no substitute for judgment when one comes to the job of applying our principles—judgment in identifying the imperfections elsewhere that bear most directly on the wisdom of the policy under consideration and in deciding in what way those imperfections counsel modification of that policy.[30]

The first task, then, is to decide what relationships elsewhere in the economy are sufficiently close and important to require consideration.[31] The most obvious relationships would be between prices and marginal social costs of close substitutes, complementary products, or products using the public utility service as input. Turvey lists four major possible reasons for pricing electricity above its nominal marginal costs:

"(a) Important close substitutes sell at significantly above marginal cost or generate external economies

"(b) Products in whose production electricity constitutes a major input sell at significantly below marginal cost or involve large external diseconomies

"(c) Important close complements sell at significantly below marginal cost or generate large external diseconomies

"(d) Major inputs of the electricity industry are bought at significantly below marginal cost or involve large external diseconomies."[32]

The second, and probably even more delicate, exercise of judgment involves a decision of how to modify the rules to take account of any particular deviations from first-best conditions elsewhere. The answer will depend

[29] The reader will have to make his own allowances for the possibility that most economists expressing such an opinion—including this one—may not be unbiased. It is very difficult for any one but a pure theorist—"pure" in more than one meaning of the word—to admit that he simply does not know enough to be able to give useful advice, for which he is often well paid.

[30] See note 18, Chapter 3. See also E. J. Mishan, "Second Thoughts on Second Best," *Oxford Econ. Papers* (October 1962), n.s. XIV: 205–217 and Turvey, *Optimal Pricing and Investment in Electricity Supply*, 87–88.

[31] "The sort of non-optimality which has to be disregarded can be illustrated by two extreme examples. Take first, the existence of a large excess of the price of shaving cream over its marginal cost. This will make the use of electric razors larger than it would be in a 'first-best' situation, but it would nevertheless be absurd to suggest adjusting the price of electricity to compensate for it. The non-optimality is, by assumption, known but it is totally insignificant. Second, consider the point that income taxation may cause labour inputs to be non-optimal. [On this, see note 15, Chapter 5.] Since this affects the whole economy the effect is not trivial, but as its implications for electricity are wholly unknowable there is no point in fretting about it." *Ibid.*, 88.

[32] *Ibid.*

largely on whether those deviations must be taken as given and ineradicable. But they may themselves be influenced by whatever decision is taken about the utility price. For example, the fact that the price of oil in the United States is held considerably above marginal cost by the domestic system of production and import control might be taken as an argument on allocational grounds for holding the regulated price of natural gas similarly high. On the other hand, a price of gas held closer to its marginal cost will undoubtedly help hold in check the cartel-controlled price of oil.[33]

The solution will depend also on the net effect of *all* relevant deviations from first best. Probably the most important distortion is created by the unusually severe weight of taxation on public utility companies.[34] This is true, first, even of taxes such as those on corporate profits and property, which are taxes on capital. Since production of public utility services is unusually capital-intensive, if such taxes are shifted forward at all they will raise these prices by a greater percentage than the prices of products that use less capital relative to other inputs. Second, property and excise taxes are evidently levied discriminatorily heavily on utility services. Consider, for example, the special excise taxes on common carriers, which confer an advantage on the many private carriers that compete with them. The subsidies that important competing carriers enjoy[35] operate in the same direction, effecting an uneconomic underutilization of railway services. Common carrier commuter transit media, similarly, are exposed to the competition of the private automobile, which does not pay the full external costs of the congestion it imposes on the central city in rush hours.[36]

All of these factors, if they are indeed the most important ones, strengthen the general case for adopting first-best pricing of public utility services— permitting at least marginal cost pricing below average total cost (and perhaps even prices below marginal cost) for those services whose demand is elastic. In these circumstances so does the phenomenon of decreasing average cost. A tax that is shifted forward gives rise to a greater increase in price and reduction in output, hence a greater departure from optimality, in a decreasing than in an increasing cost situation. This is because the price in the former case has to be raised to cover not just the tax but also the higher average cost attributable to the lower level of output, whereas in the latter case the price can rise by less than the tax, because reduced output entails reduced unit costs.[37]

---

[33] See my "Economic Issues in Regulating the Field Price of Natural Gas," *Amer. Econ. Rev., Papers and Proceedings* (May 1960), L: 514–517, in which I try to assess these offsetting considerations, including also the effects of the tax preferences that affect the supply and price of natural gas and oil alike. Also R. Rees, "Second-Best Rules for Public Enterprise Pricing," *Economica* (August 1968), n.s. XXXV: 269–270 and Turvey, *Optimal Pricing and Investment,* 88–89.

[34] See Clemens, *Economics and Public Utilities,* 523–526; Dick Netzer, *Economics of the Property Tax* (Washington: Brookings Inst., 1966), 23–27; Garfield and Lovejoy, *op. cit.,* 385–390. For the documentation of these and other distortions that uneconomically discourage use of the railroads,

see Chapter 2, Volume 2; also Haskel Benishay and Gilbert R. Whitaker, Jr., "Tax Burden Ratios in Transportation," *Land Econ.* (February 1967), XLIII: 44–55, which concludes that rails bear four to twelve times the tax burdens of motor carriers.

[35] See note 12, Chapter 6 and Ann F. Friedlaender, *The Dilemma of Freight Transport Regulation* (Washington, D.C.: The Brookings Institution, 1969), 103–11.

[36] See notes 60, 64, Chapter 4. Also Bonbright, *Principles of Public Utility Rates,* 402–405.

[37] See C. Lowell Harriss, "Taxation of Public Utilities: Considerations for the Long Run," *Taxes* (October 1965), XLIII: 663–664; and Clemens, *Economics and Public Utilities,* 542–543.

The above-marginal cost prices of such major competitors as petroleum and automobiles are the principal factors operating in the opposite direction. We have already pointed out that second-best considerations constitute the main economic case for allowing public utility companies a rate of return equated to comparable earnings instead of the cost of capital.[38] It is possible, on the basis of the foregoing considerations, to show that the argument is a tricky one and probably more wrong than right. Since public utility companies are highly capital-intensive, a one percentage point increase in their rate of return on capital will mean a greater percentage increase in their total costs and final sales prices than in industry generally. Thus the attempt to raise their returns to a level comparable with that of industry generally, in order to prevent a distortion in consumer choices between their services and others, will instead produce a distortion in the opposite direction —excessively discouraging their purchase. Once considerations of second-best are introduced, it becomes necessary to consider *all* possible distortions. On balance second-best considerations probably argue more often for pricing utility services below marginal cost than above.

To this conclusion must be added the institutional consideration that we treat at greater length in Volume 2: that the principal virtue of setting rates at marginal cost is the virtue of competition; it exerts the maximum pressure on competitors to improve their own efficiency and service offerings. Competition is particularly important where reduced prices make possible the fuller exploitation of static economies of scale; it also exerts pressures to bring the prices of substitute products closer to first-best levels; and it is a powerful stimulus to dynamic improvement in industry performance.

CONCLUSION

The decision about what kinds of modifications second-best considerations recommend can be made only by looking at the facts in each individual case.

No set of economic principles can substitute for the use of judgment in their application. There is no point in attempting to make estimates of marginal cost for categories of service more refined than can in fact be distinguished for purposes of rate making. There is no point in attempting greater precision in the design of rates, in decreasing-cost situations, than can be justified in terms of *probable* differences in costs or in demand elasticity. If the prices of substitutes are markedly above or below their respective marginal costs, or if the burden of taxes differs markedly from one product to another, or if one or the other involves major externalities, a public utility company or regulatory commission ought to take such discrepancies into account in setting the rates under its own jurisdiction.

In view of the pervasive uncertainties with respect to the measurement of marginal costs and elasticities of demand, certain dangers are introduced by following the economic principles we have enunciated. It becomes difficult to be sure whether rates reduced below fully distributed costs really do cover their long-run marginal costs and are compensatory. It becomes less clear whether such rates constitute a burden on other customers.

But any system of pricing involves the exercise of judgment. The question is whether that judgment should be employed in order best to apply economic-

---

[38] See note 80, Chapter 2.

ally efficient principles or irrational principles.[39] The fact that the elasticity of demand is difficult to estimate does not make it more sensible to assume that demand has no elasticity at all. The anxiety to avoid burdening certain customers by charging others less than fully distributed costs does not justify burdening them even more by refusing a utility permission to reach out for additional business, when a discriminatory rate is necessary to get it and where it seems reasonably probable that it will cover its full additional costs. The fact that off-peak consumption at certain times of the day or year is close enough to the peak to make it reasonably probable that the peak might shift is no excuse for forcing customers also to bear capacity costs at times that are unlikely to become peaks.[40] The fact that future costs are difficult to estimate does not make it rational to cling to past costs, when there is clear reason to believe they are wrong. The use of correct principles is still far from solving all the problems of intelligent public utility pricing; but it is the correct place to begin.

---

[39] "An approximation, even one subject to a wide margin of error, to the correct answer is better than the wrong answer worked out to seven decimal places." Vickrey testimony in FCC Docket 16258, 7.

[40] See Bonbright, *Principles of Public Utility Rates*, 358, 360, 365–366; also Little, *The Price of Fuel*, 146, who proposes that the demand charge be distributed among time periods in accordance with their respective probabilities of coinciding with the peak.

VOLUME II
Institutional Issues

Introduction

Most of our Volume 1 was devoted to developing rules for the efficient pricing of public utility services. The length of that treatment is itself instructive: the economist, like anyone else, spends most of his time doing the things that he is trained to do. In this, he is like the man who, having dropped a coin on the sidewalk on a dark night, looks for it under the street-light, not necessarily because he thinks that is where it probably has come to rest but because that is the only place he has any hope of finding it. The rules for efficient pricing flow out of the main stream of microeconomics as it has developed during the last century or two; that is our street-light, and we make such use of it as we can. We urge society to make use of it, too, because we are convinced of its usefulness.

But there is also a long tradition in economics of dissent from the "conventional wisdom" of normative microeconomic theory and a recognition of its limitations even as a purely economic guide to policy—although to read Mr. Galbraith one would think that his was the first and only pair of hands trying to strike matches over some of the darker parts of the sidewalk.[1]

These limitations are of two quite different kinds. First, there are the limitations of the rules and of the goals they are intended to achieve, even as statements of economic rules and goals. We obviously want our industries to achieve a lot more than such allocational efficiency and distributional equity as can be achieved by the mere equating of prices and marginal costs; and we are prepared, if need be, to make very large sacrifices of static allocational efficiency to the extent necessary to serve these other purposes. Specifically, we want industry:

1. To be efficient in the technical sense, that is, to keep the costs (social as well as private) to which price is to be equated as low as possible.

2. To improve its efficiency as rapidly as is economical—perpetually to devote efforts to improvements in efficiency so long as the incremental costs of those efforts are exceeded by the (discounted current) value of the cost savings thus achieved.

---

[1] Compare his *The Affluent Society* (Boston: Houghton Mifflin, 1958) and *The New Industrial State* (Boston: Houghton Mifflin, 1967) with almost any book by Thorstein Veblen or J. M. Clark.

3. To engage in product or service innovation with an intensity subject to the same economic test.

The listing of these additional goals suggests the second major limitation of any mere exposition of the normative rules of economic behavior and performance: they tell us absolutely nothing about *how to achieve* these results. This is what we mean by the *institutional* problems of regulation or of the ordering of the economy generally: by what kinds of institutional arrangements can we obtain the maximum assurance (compatible with such noneconomic values as security, freedom, due process of law, and so on) that the goals will in fact be achieved? How do we *get* prices down to marginal cost, services extended as widely, and the efficiency of production and quality of service kept as high and improved as rapidly as the pure theory of markets tells us is economically desirable? When we turn from the normative question of *what we want* to the institutional question of *how we get it*, we find ourselves launched into the baffling arena of social and political as well as economic behavior and organization, into the real world of ignorance, error and corruption, where all institutions are in varying degrees imperfect.

In that world, compromise and balance must be embodied in all the plans that are formulated. Entirely apart from the need for compromising economic and noneconomic objectives, there is an inescapable problem of choice and trade-offs even among the economic goals, and no simple blueprint can point the way to maximizing along all fronts simultaneously. Economies of scale create an immediate necessity for balancing off the requirements of the smaller number of sellers compatible with efficiency, on the one hand, and necessary for pure competition, on the other. The optimum rate of innovation requires a balance of pressures of competition on the one hand and protections against immediate competitive replication and appropriation of the fruits of innovation on the other, of maximum profit incentives for innovating, on the one hand, and maximum speed in passing on its benefits, on the other. The patent system and infant industry protection are two illustrations of the kinds of imperfect compromises that have to be made.

Problems like these are far less tractable to economic or indeed any other kind of analysis than the ones that concerned us in Volume 1. There are no clear-cut principles or proofs, no answers that are demonstrably right or wrong; the only available analytical tool is judgment informed by economic theory and experience.

And to even this modest statement of qualifications, the economist must attach a caveat. Experience is useful in forming judgment only to the extent that it is transferable. But the very decision to regulate, to withdraw an industry from the general rules that govern most markets, reflects a determination that the industry is in some essential respect peculiar. To the extent that determination is justified, the experience of unregulated industry, generally, or of other regulated industries is less applicable to any particular regulatory situation than it is within the more or less competitive and unregulated sectors of the economy. This consideration suggests that this part of our study, which addresses itself to institutional problems in the public utility industries taken as a group. is seeking a level of generalization broader than the varying and peculiar characteristics of the individual industries falling within this group would justify. In view of this great diversity of the regulated industries, we obviously cannot hope to supply authoritative solutions to any of the numerous specific issues to which we shall allude in these chapters.

But there are major features general to the regulatory experience; there are common problems, even though the socially appropriate answers may differ from one context to the next. The various combinations of institutional arrangements—for example, market structures and regulatory policies—tend to yield predictable economic results. It is these common problems, these generally observable causal relationships that we attempt to expose and to illustrate in this volume, as they bear on the formulation of regulatory policy.

The two principal institutions of social control in a private enterprise economy are competition and direct regulation. Rarely do we rely on either of these exclusively: no competitive markets are totally unregulated, and no public utilities are free of some elements of rivalry. The proper object of search, in each instance, is the best possible mixture of the two. This is the central institutional issue of public utility regulation, and it is therefore the central theme of our remaining chapters. The theme has three separate, though closely interrelated aspects. First, there is the multifaceted question of how much competition it is appropriate to continue to permit, encourage, and rely on in the regulated sectors of the economy. The second concerns the kinds of policies—for example, with respect to integration, mergers, entry, price discrimination, and interfirm collaboration—that will be promotive of workable competition, to the extent that this is a feasible goal. These are the subjects of our Chapters 4 to 6. But if the search for the proper mix of competition and regulation is to be made intelligently, it can only be in full recognition of the inherent characteristics and problems of the regulatory device itself, as such. It is to the latter that we turn first: What are the competencies and incompetencies of the regulatory device? What kinds of incentives and distortions does it introduce? What are the main institutional influences on public utility performance? These are the subjects of Chapters 1–3.

In searching for answers to these questions, it is useful to remind ourselves that the scope of government regulation extends far beyond what we have, with some degree of arbitrariness, defined as the public utility area. If this technique has certain inherent or common characteristics, we should expect to find them exhibited also, therefore, in such disparate ventures as the framing of building codes, the licensing of doctors, electricians, and television stations, setting production quotas for oil or sugar; and we should not hesitate to draw on these experiences as well. Good reasons can be adduced for and against each of these policies. What will differ from one case to the next is the particular *balance* of need for regulation on the one hand and limitations and dangers on the other.

CHAPTER 1

Monopoly and Protectionism

If the decision to regulate were nothing more than a decision that competition was in some way or other inadequate to serve the public interest, and if regulation itself merely *supplemented* such competition as prevailed, there would still be problems of making those decisions but there would be no general regulatory dilemma. The general dilemma arises from the fact that the decision to regulate is, typically, a decision also to restrict competition, not just to supplement it in one way or another, but to *supplant* it. Whether this essentially competitive rather than complementary relationship between these two alternative systems of social control is inescapable or is the result of bad policy, the fact remains that as it has evolved historically, regulation has consisted largely in the imposition and administration of restrictions on entry and on what might otherwise have been independent and competitive price and output decisions.

THE ASSOCIATION OF REGULATION WITH MONOPOLY

There are several interrelated reasons for this association of regulation with restrictions on competition;[1] all of them help to define the major institutional issues in this field.[2]

---

[1] We alluded briefly to some of these in the first chapter of Volume 1.

[2] The word "reasons" has two, quite distinct meanings. In one sense, it refers to the *reasoning* by which particular courses of action are supported, the rationalization of policies. In its other meaning, it refers to the "real" reasons, the historical *forces* explaining why particular courses of action have been adopted. The former meaning embraces arguments and justifications; the latter, such operative factors as group interests and pressures in the political arena. There is no need to distinguish the two explicitly in this discussion. For one thing, the two categories are not mutually exclusive: surely most professors must believe, for example, that "ideas are weapons"

(see the book of this title by Max Lerner, Viking Press, New York, 1940) that is, that arguments do have real historical efficacy. Public policies usually are enacted in response partly to pressures of interested parties and partly because some more or less disinterested people become convinced by arguments that the policies will serve the public interest. That such arguments are typically proffered by privately interested parties does not make them wrong any more than the fact that "public interest" considerations likewise motivate some disinterested legislative decisions necessarily makes them right.

Our principal concern, of course, will be with the arguments and their merits, rather than the real historical reasons. But it is often impossible

One reason is the conception of *"natural monopoly"*: that the technology of certain industries or the character of the service is such that the customer can be served at least cost or greatest net benefit only by a single firm (in the extreme case) or by a limited number of "chosen instruments." In such circumstances, so the argument runs, unrestricted entry will be wasteful and productive of poorer service, with cycles of excessive investment followed by destructive rivalry (spurred by the wide spread between marginal and average costs). If the pressure of excessive capacity leads to rate wars—as are said to have characterized United States railway history periodically in the nineteenth century, or the maritime shipping industry in the absence of effective government regulation or collusive price-fixing—the effect may be to push rates down so close to short-run marginal costs as to impair the ability of the surviving companies to maintain their plant in good working order, to introduce needed renovations, or to continue to give good service. If, on the other hand, as may well occur when sellers are few, the parties refrain from vigorous price rivalry, customers continue to be poorly served because there exists no reliable mechanism for driving out the excessive number of firms, concentrating production in the hands of the "natural monopolist," and bringing costs and prices down to the minimum, technologically feasible level. In either event, the required policy is, allegedly, one of licensing only such entrants as are required by the "public convenience and necessity."

The character and applicability of the natural monopoly rationalization will, of course, vary from industry to industry. A particularly specialized version applies to the case of radio and television. The natural monopoly in this instance is the width of the radio-frequency band required for effective transmission of signals and the geographic area to which those signals reach, encroachment on which by competitors results in excessive interference and deterioration of signal quality.

We reserve for Chapters 4 and 5 all assessments of these rationalizations for regulatory restrictions on competition. It is worth pointing out, however, that some economists and historians have taken violent exception to the concept of natural monopoly, whether as an explanation of the way in which public utility monopolies have actually emerged or as a justification of the "unnatural" acts that conferred monopoly on them. An outstanding critic has been Horace M. Gray:

"The public utility status was to be the haven of refuge for all aspiring monopolists who found it too difficult, too costly, or too precarious to secure and maintain monopoly by private action alone. Their future prosperity would be assured if only they could induce government to grant them monopoly power and to protect them against interlopers. . . .

"The obvious conflict between the traditional ideology and the public utility concept was resolved by resort to rationalization. It was said that enterprises supplying gas, electricity, street transportation, water, and telephonic communication were 'inherently' or 'naturally' monopolistic;

to assess the arguments for a particular course of regulatory action without understanding also the political forces that will help to determine how the proposed policy will work out in actual practice. And it is precisely such inherent tendencies that regulation may exhibit in the real world that must be understood if one is to evaluate the institution itself. The same, obviously, can be said for such institutions as "competition," "private enterprise," or "socialism."

that they had certain 'natural characteristics' which distinguished them from other enterprises . . . that, because of this 'natural' force, they tended 'inevitably to become monopolies. . . . Thus, the fiction of "natural monopoly" was invented to explain the centripetal tendencies then observable. . . .

" 'Franchises, way-leaves, contracts, charters, patents, secret agreements, injunctions, dummy corporations, cut-throat competition, newspaper and banking influences, and political corruption are the institutional ingredients from which monopoly was forged by skillful and unscrupulous manipulators. A critical evaluation of these elements might have shed considerable doubt upon the "naturalness" of this and similar monopolies.' "[3]

A second reason has been *the need for franchises*: in most of the public utility industries it would be infeasible for companies to operate without government permission. Railways, turnpike companies, electric companies, and pipelines have ordinarily (some more consistently than others) required access to the right of eminent domain in order to construct their various facilities. Distributors of gas, water, and steam have to have the right to dig up city streets; telephone and electric companies to put up poles and wires along the sidewalks, highways and across the country. That governments have been unwilling to dispense these privileges freely to all applicants is a reflection in part of natural monopoly—why let several companies tear up the streets to lay competing gas or water mains or build their own telephone or electricity poles when one would suffice? To these technical considerations must be added the political influences dictating a restrictive policy—the possibility of *selling* exclusive franchises as a means of rewarding favorites or raising money, whether for the government itself or for the officials dispensing these favors; and the self-interest of the applicants, anxious to enlist the support of the government in ensconcing them in monopolistic positions.[4]

Governments have exercised this licensing authority in a restrictive manner also for *promotional reasons*. As our patent system itself recognizes, one way of

---

[3] "The Passing of the Public Utility Concept," reprinted in American Economic Association, *Readings in the Social Control of Industry* (Philadelphia: The Blakiston Company, 1942), 283–284.

"One of the most unfortunate phrases ever introduced into law or economics was the phrase 'natural monopoly.' Every monopoly is a product of public policy. No present monopoly, public or private, can be traced back through history in a pure form." James R. Nelson, "The Role of Competition in the Regulated Industries," *The Antitrust Bulletin* (Jan.–Apr. 1966), XI: 3.

The historical fact, if it is a fact, that none of our present so-called public utilities would have enjoyed a monopoly had it not been for the intervention of government does not, of course, necessarily invalidate the natural monopoly thesis as a rationalization for that intervention, as Nelson's own ensuing analysis makes clear (see his pp. 5–10). See also pp. 117–126, Chapter 4, below. On the other hand, even where the

natural monopoly argument is valid, governmental licensure of entry is not necessarily called for. With respect even to the seemingly irrefutable case for licensure of radio stations, Coase argues that the courts were already well on the way to establishing property rights in the radio spectrum, which could have been bought and sold in such a way as (a) to avoid excessive interference and (b) to ensure the most economical allocation and utilization of that scarce resource, before Congress intervened and imposed the system of administrative allocation that we have today. R. H. Coase, "The Federal Communications Commission," *Jour. Law and Econ.* (October 1959), II: 25–35. See also note 2, Chapter 4 of Volume 1.

[4] "As for monopoly in general: to this day, clues must be sought in the nature of Charles I as well as in the nature of things." Nelson, *op. cit., The Antitrust Bulletin* (Jan.–Apr. 1966), XI: 3. The same is true of the origins of our modern patent system. On the franchise as the legal basis for regulation, see note 21, Chapter 1 of Volume 1.

inducing private investment in unusually risky fields—the East India trade at the end of the sixteenth century, the building of turnpikes or railroads into as-yet insufficiently settled areas in the nineteenth century, or the development of commercial air transport in the twentieth century[5]—is to offer the investors some protection against subsequent competition. Again as in the case of the patent, the exclusive franchise may, by assuring to the initial investors the opportunity to reap the full rewards of their innovational or promotional endeavors, internalize benefits that would otherwise be external from their standpoint; without such assurances economically desirable investments (whose benefits exceed total costs) might in fact not be made. Where, as in the case of the American airlines, the promotional purposes are achieved in part, as well, by the grant of subsidies, an additional consideration inducing governments to restrict entry is the desire to minimize the burden on taxpayers, by limiting the number of potential recipients and assuring to each the maximum opportunity to cover costs with ordinary revenues. Restrictive licensing might, of course, discourage development of the industry more than the subsidies might encourage it; we are not at this point assessing the wisdom of these policies.[6]

The all-embracing reason for the close association of regulation with monopolization or cartelization is, of course, the fact that society invokes the former process whenever and wherever it believes that unregulated competition produces unsatisfactory results. In the natural monopoly cases it takes the view that competition conflicts with the technological requirements for maximum efficiency. But in many other instances in which competition is

---

[5] According to Edgar Gorrell, president of the Air Transport Association of America,

"Hitherto, when we have approached questions of government regulation, we have thought largely in terms of protecting the public from abuse of economic power in private hands. . . . [But] the need for [aviation] legislation springs . . . rather from the need to assure the industry itself opportunity for vigorous growth."

"The Civil Aeronautics Act of 1938 and Democratic Government," *Jour. Air Law* (October, 1938), IX: 705, 708. See also Lucile S. Keyes, *Federal Control of Entry into Air Transportation* (Cambridge: Harvard Univ. Press, 1951), 59–105.

[6] On the possibility that methods of subsidization could have been devised that would have permitted more competition without necessarily imposing a greater burden on the American taxpayer, see note 182, Chapter 5, below. See also pp. 233–235, on the promotional case for restricting competition.

The historic link between subsidies and restriction of competition is an ancient one. In 1690 Louis XIV officially adopted and began to subsidize the theatrical company that he named the *Comédie Française*. He gave it the exclusive right to perform all plays by authors no longer living. Many independent ventures were formed,

but as they expanded their offerings, the *Comédie* complained and induced the Crown to impose various restrictions on them:

"Some could let their characters faint or bleed, but not die. Some could let their performers do only acrobatics or pantomime. Two small establishments . . . were forced to hang a gauze curtain between actors and audience. One amateur theater . . . could open only at seven, over an hour after the others, and so on."

All the familiar criticisms were heaped on the favored company—excessive admissions charges, conservatism in its productions.

Not surprisingly, the onset of the French Revolution was accompanied by attacks on the royal monopolist. At the news of the storming of the Bastille, the director of one of the aforementioned restricted theaters, "[t]earing down the curtain of gauze the police had required on his stage . . . threw himself onto the forestage, shouting, 'Long live Liberty!' The battle for freedom was launched." The ascendancy of Napoleon brought a return of licensing, censorship, and a reservation of the repertoire of the Comédie to that subsidized company; the same favored treatment was accorded the Opéra and the Opéra-Comique. See Marvin A. W. Carlson, *The Theater of the French Revolution* (Ithaca: Cornell Univ. Press, 1966), Chapter 1 and especially pp. 12, 16.

technologically entirely feasible, regulation is invoked because it is believed that competition would be characterized by intolerable imperfections.

One such imperfection is *buyer ignorance*—the inability of buyers readily to judge the quality of what they purchase. In one trade after another, entry is controlled and methods of doing business subjected to a variety of restrictions in the belief that unregulated competition leads to serious deterioration of the quality of service. Building codes and the licensing of doctors, tree surgeons, public accountants, barbers, undertakers, and plumbers are only a few of the almost limitless reflections of this kind of reasoning. In principle, we have already observed, regulation of this kind need not substitute governmental fiat for the competitive process in making the basic economic decisions, about what shall be produced and sold, by whom, of what dimensions, at what price. It might be confined, for example, to requiring disclosure of the ingredients of the product or the qualifications of the supplier. As others have observed, mere registration or certification could conceivably, in most cases, provide customers with the necessary information and the government with sufficient means of enforcing ethical behavior, without being as subject to monopolistic abuse as licensure. On the other hand, the belief that customers are unable to judge quality in advance and could therefore suffer irreparable damage from poor service has resulted in much more direct regulation—minimum product specifications, standards of cleanliness or safety, and admitting into the field only those with specified qualifications. Such considerations provide a conceivable justification for licensing plumbers, tree surgeons, veterinarians, and even beauticians, not to mention drug manufacturers. By means of licensing, applicants can be forced to meet tests of qualification; and if they face the penalty of forfeiting the right to practice if they prove unworthy of their trust, they can perhaps be held more effectively than otherwise to high standards of performance.

Even licensing could in principle be compatible with reliance on competition as the prime economic regulator, in determining the number of sellers, price, and even the quality of service over and above the legally prescribed minima. But in practice these controls, and particularly occupational licensure, have all too often been perverted into an instrument for raising barriers to entry and brazenly protecting practitioners in a wide variety of trades from unwanted competition.[7]

Moreover, in some industries believed to be inherently subject to *destructive*

---

[7] See note 5 of Chapter 1, Volume 1. For elaborations and documentation, see Milton Friedman, *Capitalism and Freedom* (Chicago: Univ. of Chicago Press, 1962), Chapter 9; Walter Gellhorn, *Individual Freedom and Governmental Restraints* (Baton Rouge: Louisiana State Univ. Press, 1956), Chapter 3; Thomas G. Moore, "The Purpose of Licensing," *Jour. Law and Econ.* (October 1961), IV: 93–117; and, for a specific instance, Reuben A. Kessel, "Price Discrimination in Medicine," *Jour. Law and Econ.* (October 1958), I: 20–53. According to Gellhorn's survey, 75 percent of the occupational licensing boards were composed exclusively of practitioners with a direct economic interest in the decisions made. *Op. cit.*, 140.

"GOTTA LICENSE? A growing number of jobs require you to have one.

"Occupational licensing by Federal, state and local bodies increases sharply. The Labor Department estimates that 550 occupations are licensed by at least one governmental jurisdiction, double the number 25 years ago. Recent additions to the list: Pest-control experts, nuclear materials handlers and fund-raisers. Licensing often results from public outcries against unqualified or dishonest practitioners.

"But Labor Department officials worry that the licensing power is sometimes used to keep qualified workers out of certain occupations. In one small community, a licensing board dominated by plumbing contractors rejected seven of

competition, the asserted purpose of maintaining the quality of service has been used to justify quite explicit substitution of thoroughgoing public utility regulation for competition. In these situations, competition is believed to be infeasible because it tends to be excessively keen and ultimately destructive of the ability of the industry to offer good service. In common carrier trucking, for example, restrictive licensing was imposed on entry not merely into the industry but, with some specific exceptions, into every single one of its submarkets—each individual route, each kind of freight—with the Interstate Commerce Commission deciding in the case of each applicant whether his proposed service is *economically* justifiable, on the ground that excessively easy entry had produced unreliability of service, unacceptable instability and unreliability of published rates, inadequate protection of shippers against damage, loss or disappearance of their cargoes and a breakdown in the ability of the regulatory authorities to enforce standards of safety and financial responsibility on the carriers.[8]

A similar argument has been offered by the Bell companies to justify their historic policy of prohibiting "foreign attachments" to telephones—independently produced accessories and equipment of one kind or another, like devices to muffle conversations or to permit conversations between the telephone instrument and parties at the other end of private communications systems. To permit independent equipment manufacturers this free competitive access and subscribers such free choice would, they have asserted, lead to deterioration in the quality of the telephone service. That this rationalization, like the others that we have been listing thus far, must be taken seriously becomes quite clear when it is recognized that the alleged threat is not merely to the quality of the service enjoyed by the customer who chooses to install the equipment—in which event there would seem little justification to abandon the protection of *caveat emptor*—but also to the service of innocent, third parties, whose reception might be subjected to all sorts of obscure interference. What we really have in this case is a variant of the natural monopoly rationalization, and we therefore consider it in Chapter 4.[9]

---

eight applicants for a license required to set up a plumbing business. Despite its large Spanish-speaking population, New York City gives its licensing exams only in English.

"Prostitutes, rainmakers, tatoo artists, beekeepers and lightning-rod dealers are among today's licensed practitioners." *Wall Street Journal*, August 5, 1969, 1.

[8] See, for example, U. S. House of Representatives, Committee on Interstate and Foreign Commerce, 74th Cong. 1st Sess., *Report of the Federal Coordinator of Transportation, 1934*, House Document No. 89, Washington, January 30, 1935, 113–114, 119–120. For a similar rationalization underlying the Civil Aeronautics Act of 1938, see W. K. Jones, *Cases and Materials on Regulated Industries* (Brooklyn: Foundation Press, 1967), 735–738. For a brief historical summary of the main judicial and economic contributions to this general line of argument for regulation, see pp. 7–10, Volume 1; for a fuller evaluation of it, see Chapter 5, below.

An interesting variant on this rationalization for limiting competition is applied mainly in various financial markets, where it is felt that excessive competition can have harmful effects on the operation of the economy at large. It is on grounds such as these that limitations are imposed on the ability of banks to compete with one another, for example by offering higher interest rates on deposits—the fear being that this kind of competition will, via its effect on credit policies, contribute to macroeconomic instability. A similar rationale is offered to justify self-regulation by the stock exchanges, including the right to prevent competition among their members in the commissions they charge for effecting security transactions (see pp. 199–200, Chapter 5, below). Analogous justifications apply in the field of insurance.

[9] One interesting example of the possible deterioration in service consequent on unrestricted entry and unregulated rivalry is provided by the electricity supply industry in

A related justification is the fact that even within individual industries the degree of monopoly power will differ greatly from one market to another. In consequence, competition tends to be highly selective and *discriminatory*, hence not merely unfair but injurious to the disadvantaged customers. This case is strengthened in the public utility industries, as we have already seen, by the fact that in many, perhaps most of their markets, suppliers have no direct competition at all; that effectively regulated monopolists have strong incentives to expand their markets and rate bases, even by taking on unremunerative business; and that this combination of circumstances creates the possibility of certain customers being forced to subsidize their supplier's competition for the patronage of others. This was the prime original justification for the institution of railroad rate regulation at the federal level. It remains the central issue today, after several decades of increasingly intensive and pervasive intercarrier competition have cast doubt on the continued necessity for any residual regulation of competition in the transportation field at all: the question remains whether a sufficient percentage of shippers, of particular commodities and between particular points, enjoy a sufficient range of competitive alternatives to prevent excessive discrimination among them. Considerations such as these constitute a case for the regulatory fixing of specific prices—both maximum rates, to protect customers inadequately protected by competition, and minimum rates, to prevent either undue preference to particular shippers or destruction or predation at the primary level.[10]

Regulatory agencies frequently intervene also to prevent the practice known as *cream-skimming*. The contention is that if entry is free, competitors will naturally choose to come into only the lucrative markets, "skimming the cream" of the business, negligently leaving to the established common carriers the burden of providing continuing service to the poorer and thinner markets—the isolated communities generating only small volumes of traffic, the off-peak business, and the like. The same kind of reasoning is used to oppose free price competition, which would likewise be expected to focus on the creamy markets. The alleged threat is that the common carriers, finding themselves either losing or suffering reduced returns on the profitable part of the business, forced increasingly to subsist on a diet of skimmed milk, will be unable to carry on in the thinner geographic and seasonal markets, with consequent destruction of service to large areas of the country and bodies of customers.

The phenomenon and the corollary case for restricting competition are not confined to the public utility arena. All businesses are in some measure and in some respect conglomerates: they operate in more than one market, supply more than one service, or supply a given service at more than one point in time. And, because the conditions of supply and demand, and particularly

---

Great Britain, where the profusion of separate companies resulted in a corresponding profusion of qualities and specifications of service. The result was that the institution of a national interconnecting grid was seriously delayed by the incompatibilities of the various separate systems. The development of the electrical manufacturing industries was similarly retarded: since it was necessary to produce appliances and equipment of varying specifications for use with different frequencies and voltages, it was impossible to standardize products sufficiently to exploit fully the potential economies of large-scale production. See *Statist*, Supplement (Dec. 17, 1938), 1–2, 4, 7.

[10] See note 85, Chapter 2, and Chapter 6 in Volume 1; also note 64, pp. 26–27, below.

the intensity of competition, will inevitably vary from one of these markets to the other, all companies will find, inevitably, that the profitability of these various operations (by *some* meaningful measure) will vary correspondingly. If competition prevails, it will tend naturally to concentrate on the lucrative markets. That is how it is supposed to operate—to erode away supernormal returns, to equalize returns in various markets except for differences in risk. But here again objection may be raised and legal restrictions on competition advocated, if in some way the creamy business was "carrying" the others, with the result that intensified competition in the former threatens curtailment of supply to the latter. This kind of case has been made, for example, for resale price maintenance: that unrestricted price competition on popular, fast-moving brands (best-selling books, whiskeys, toothpastes, or appliances) would drive out of business the small, conveniently situated, low-volume retailer, the merchandiser who offers service, the diversified bookstore, the neighborhood pharmacist, all of whom, it is alleged, survive in part because of the protected margins on the former items.[11]

But it is in the public utility arena that the issues are most sharply posed. Public utility companies have, typically, been given exclusive or partially exclusive public franchises, in return for which they are asked to assume the obligations of common carriers or of public callings; and implicit in these obligations is, usually, at least a general conception that the company has a responsibility to extend supply as broadly as possible, and to continue to provide service even where it may not be economical for it to do so. This view clearly reflects extraeconomic considerations—notably the possible benefit to national security of preserving financially strong common carrier transportation and communications systems, with greater and more widespread capacity to serve than would be justified by purely market tests; and the desire to assure service even to segments of the country unable to pay the long-run marginal costs of serving them. But there are possible economic arguments of an institutional character as well, as we shall see. In these circumstances, it could well be considered the function of public policy to protect firms that assume such obligations, against the competition that might impair their abilities to continue service in good seasons and in bad, in thick markets and in thin.

The cream-skimming argument was an important part of the rationale for the Motor Carrier Act of 1935, which imposed on the industry the pervasive controls briefly described above.

"The contract carrier may differ from the common carrier only in the fact that he undertakes to skim the cream of the traffic and leave the portion which lacks the butterfats to his common-carrier competitor. Obviously such operations can have very unfortunate and undesirable results."[12]

"Prior to regulation, a very important factor in railroad rates was 'what

[11] See my "The Tyranny of Small Decisions: Market Failures, Imperfections, and the Limits of Economics," *Kyklos* (1966), XIX: 34–39. The reader may recognize that the case for restricting competitive cream skimming thus far presented is a case for preserving a pattern of internal subsidization, a practice that we demonstrated was economically indefensible in Volume 1 (pp. 143, 190–191). And so it is, in the usual presentation. But, in fact, some defenses can be erected on economic grounds. We analyze and appraise the issue more systematically on pp. 223–243, below.

[12] *Report of the Federal Coordinator of Transportation, 1934, op. cit.*, 17.

the traffic will bear.' . . . The result of this . . . has been that in general the higher-valued commodities and the shorter hauls pay higher rates, relatively, than the lower-valued commodities and the longer hauls. . . .

"It will be readily seen . . . that this deviation from cost of service favored truck competition, since it made the traffic vulnerable on which the relatively higher rates are charged. This is what the railroads mean when they say that the trucks are taking the 'cream of the traffic' . . . ."[13]

"A broader aspect of responsibility also deserves mention. This relates to the maintenance of truck or bus service on which the shipper or traveler has come, perhaps entirely, to depend. Certainly no responsibility is felt by the motor-transport industry today to maintain unprofitable or relatively unprofitable service, such as the railroads have maintained, frequently voluntarily, although sometimes by order of public authorities. The highway operator assumes a lesser degree of responsibility for a complete coverage of the transportation needs of the area he sets out to serve. Truck and bus operators tend commonly to concentrate their efforts on the profitable avenues of traffic."[14]

Similar arguments have been used to justify the limitations on entry imposed by the Civil Aeronautics Board.

"It is clear that, if there had been no regulation, the quantity of service and the extent to which service has been provided to different and less populated areas of the United States would have been curtailed substantially. Or, to put it differently, an overwhelming majority of the cities to which the airlines provide service just do not generate enough traffic to warrant operations if air transport were not regulated and was subject only to the rules of the 'free' market place. . . .

"It is surprising to some that trunk carriers as well as local service carriers provide service to the smaller cities in the United States. The trunklines are able to do this because the losses sustained at these marginal cities, *which also deserve the advantages of air transportation*, are compensated for by the revenues developed at the greater traffic-producing areas. . . . [Stress supplied.]

"A most effective way to illustrate the specious nature of this doctrine of freedom of entry is to imagine the situation which would doubtless result if there were no regulatory limitation on entry. . . .

"On the day that concept was introduced, every airline would tear up its timetables, disregard its certificates, forget that it has franchise responsibilities, and do what business it pleased in the interest of greater profits and not public convenience. . . . The industry, in such a chaotic struggle for survival, would then have to abandon service to roughly some 500 of the cities to which it is now certificated, and operate only between the 50 most profitable pairs of points."[15]

[13] *Ibid.*, 114–115.
[14] *Ibid.*, 120. See also Ernest W. Williams, Jr., *The Regulation of Rail-Motor Rate Competition* (New York: Harper & Brothers, 1958), 8–9.
[15] Stuart G. Tipton and Stanley Gewirtz, "The Effect of Regulated Competition on the Air Transport Industry," reprinted from the *Jour. Air Law and Commerce* (1955), XXII, No. 2 in U. S. Senate Select Committee on Small Business,

84th Cong. 2d Sess., *Materials Relative to Competition in the Regulated Civil Aviation Industry, 1956*, April 18, 1956, 204, 217.

Similar supports for this position may be found in D. Philip Locklin, *Economics of Transportation*, 6th ed. (Homewood: Richard D. Irwin, 1966), 827–828 and Daniel Marx, Jr., *International Shipping Cartels: A Study of Industrial Self-Regulation by Shipping Conferences* (Princeton:

As we shall see in Chapter 4, the issue has come to be keenly contested in the field of communications as well, where such technological developments as microwave radio and communications satellites have opened up the possibility of large users bypassing the major common carriers. The latter have in turn sought to induce Congress and the Federal Communications Commission to block this emergent competition on cream-skimming grounds.

Another rationalization for regulation of competition in industries that could not, by any stretch of the imagination, be termed natural monopolies is interestingly related to some of the ones mentioned so far. This is the argument that, at least in certain circumstances, there is a danger of *excessive nonprice rivalry*, producing not deterioration but unduly costly inflation of the quality of service. The phenomenon has been encountered in recent years in air passenger transportation, where the International Air Transport Association and the American Civil Aeronautics Board have found it necessary to specify maximum distances between seats and maximum quality of free meals and beverages served on tourist flights, to require a charge for motion pictures, and to consider restricting the competitive scheduling of flights. As we shall point out more fully in Chapter 5, this kind of regulation is or ought to be the inescapable consequence and counterpart of restrictions on price rivalry. If members of a cartel agree on minimum prices, they may well find it necessary, if there remains any spark of independence and rivalry among them, to enforce corresponding ceilings on quality of service.[16] Restrictions of this type cannot be lightly dismissed; the possibility must be confronted that in some circumstances competition may take on a destructive character not only in price cutting but in service inflating, to the ultimate detriment of customers.

The reader will recognize here the counterpart of the case we set forth in Chapter 2 of Volume 1 for regulating the quality of service provided by public utility companies. If a monopolist can exploit buyers by charging excessively high prices, he may do so also by providing excessively poor service. If competitors may compete "destructively" by cutting prices they may do so also by improving the quality of service. In each case if the government wants to prevent the first practice it may well have to try to prevent the second.

Two concluding words: What we have done so far is merely to list some of the outstanding historical reasons and theoretical justifications for the association of regulation with the imposition of restraints on competition. We have not yet appraised them, either in general terms or in specific contexts. That is the first word. The second is that the merits of the policies implied must, in the nature of the case, be constantly changing over time. For example, technology is perpetually developing: so the natural monopoly of yesterday may no longer be natural today.[17] Again, the economic case for

---

Princeton Univ. Press, 1953), 4, 56–57, 187–198. In the case of ocean shipping, it should be noted, the argument is used to justify not governmental licensure or entry, but shipping conferences— private organizations of shipping companies setting minimum rates. Many conferences also give shippers substantial discounts if they use the services of conference members exclusively. These exclusive patronage refunds have the same tendency to restrict the entry of price-cutting

independents, who, it is alleged, skim only the heavily traveled routes in the busy seasons, leaving it to the "reputable" conference members to maintain reliable schedules, in thin markets as well as thick, in and out of season.

[16] See pp. 209–220, Chapter 5, below.

[17] The converse may also be true: technology may spawn new "natural monopolies." But it seems to be in the nature of modern technology that it tends on balance to increase rather than

promotional policies, like patent protection, is inherently self-limiting in time, as far as specific applications are concerned: either the infants grow up to a point where they no longer need protection or they ought to be permitted to die. Again, market structures that are conducive to destructive competition in periods of depression may not be so in periods of general economic expansion. When we come to examine some of the issues raised in this section, we will want particularly to do so in the context of the technology and the general economic environment of the 1970s, not that of the 1930s or the 1890s.

PROTECTIONISM AND CONSERVATISM

The close two-way causal association of regulation and restraint of competition is in turn closely linked to another set of characteristics that the regulatory process exhibits in practice—protectionism and conservatism. Generalizations of this kind are of course always dangerous when applied to such a variegated set of social and political institutions. There have been wide differences between commissions and in their legislative mandates, and changes over time in the political environment in which they operate. Both the differences and changes on the one hand and the common core are illustrated, for example, in the oversimplified but illuminating generalization that regulatory commissions tend to go through a life cycle, setting out as vigorous, imaginative, and enthusiastic protagonists of the public interest, reflecting the public concern and ferment that had to be mobilized to legislate them into existence in the first place, defining their responsibilities broadly and creatively, then gradually becoming devitalized, limited in their perspective, routinized and bureaucratized in their policies and procedures, and increasingly solicitous and protective of the interests of the companies they are supposed to regulate, resistant to change, wedded to the *status quo*.[18]

We leave to historians and political scientists the task of deciding to what extent developments such as these are reflections of a tendency for regulatory agents to be "captured" by the industries they were set up to govern. There are certainly many factors that tend to have this effect—the disparity in the quality of personnel and the amount of financial resources available to each side; corruption, including the subtle corruption that may affect administrators whose hope for future advancement may lie in working for the private companies they are supposed currently to be regulating; the fact that

---

decrease the range of alternatives, developing additional ways of satisfying old needs, and new wants to compete with old ones. The connection between technological progress and monopoly is of course a complex one, particularly when one turns to the question of what is the best form of market organization for the generation of such progress. But if one looks only to the results, one must conclude that—at least in the dynamic sense and probably statically as well—technology is far more often the enemy than the promoter of monopoly. If the invention of the automobile resulted in the displacement of a competitive carriage industry with a monopolistic automobile industry, in one dynamic sense the invention

could be said to have introduced additional competition—added choices for consumers. But by producing a change in consumer tastes, it would in this event have left the economy, statically, with more possibility of monopolistic exploitation than before. On the other hand, clearly, even if automobile manufacturers have a great deal of monopoly power, they have increased competition in the interurban transport of people and commodities.

[18] See, for example, Marver H. Bernstein, *Regulating Business by Independent Commission* (Princeton: Princeton Univ. Press, 1955), especially Chapter 3, "The Life Cycle of Regulatory Commissions."

producing interests are typically better organized than consumer interests to exert pressure, either directly on commissions or indirectly on legislatures, when it comes to public policies that bear directly on them. All of these factors have undoubtedly been influential.[19]

More subtle and, the economist might say—betraying his parochialism— more fundamental, is the inherent consequence of substituting regulation for competition as the prime instrument of social control. When an administrative commission is invested with authority over the central economic decisions of an industry, it finds itself invested also with a heavy responsibility. The decision to regulate usually takes for granted the strength and financial health of the industry and seeks to introduce a counterpoise, to control abuses and protect the public. But the regulatory commission soon finds, in framing its policies, that it cannot take the health on the supply side of the market for granted. For one thing, it has to reckon with legislative injunctions on it to be fair to investors, and with judicial warnings that it cannot, consistent with the Fourteenth Amendment (and corresponding injunctions in state constitutions), deprive them of a fair return on the fair value of their investment. Then there are the wearily predictable protestations of company witnesses and lawyers that any regulation will immediately dam up the flow of capital into the industry and thereby bring down on the commissioners' heads the wrath of the consuming public, Congress, and the courts. But the commission cannot in any event escape recognizing its responsibility for contentment on *both* sides of the market. Responsible for the continued provision and improvement of service, it comes increasingly and understandably to identify the interest of the public with that of the existing companies on whom it must rely to deliver these goods.

The virtues of the competitive market are many. One major one is that no one company or coherent, identifiable group of companies can be said to bear direct responsibility for industry performance.[20] Another, and related one, is that each individual investor or businessman can therefore afford to be irresponsible, to take the risk of large losses in the hope of large gains, to experiment, to upset the status quo, to destroy existing equities. Indeed, competition *forces* businessmen to behave in this "irresponsible" fashion if they are to prosper, even to survive.[21]

---

[19] See, in addition to the above, James M. Landis' excellent *Report on Regulatory Agencies to the President-Elect*, December 1960, published as a Committee Print by the U. S. Senate Committee on the Judiciary, 86th Cong. 2d Sess., Washington, 1960, 13–15 and 71.

[20] "It is because of this basic dissimilarity between the automobile industry and the natural gas industry, for example, that regulation must be 'protectionist' to the extent that it must assure the continued financial integrity of the industry in order that the consumer will have continued reliable, adequate utility service. If an automobile dealer goes out of business there are others to sell automobiles; but if an interstate pipeline goes out of business, many of its customers will have no source of supply. Because of this basic distinction, regulation must as a

matter of social policy intrude at some point to stifle the impersonal forces of competition and perform the role of a 'protector' of the regulated industry." Carl E. Bagge, Federal Power Commissioner, "Regulated Competition: An Alternative to Anti-trust," an address before· the Independent Natural Gas Association of America, San Francisco, September 4, 1967, mimeo., 3.

[21] This picture of competition is of course an idealized one. The reader might have difficulty recognizing in it any resemblance to, let us say, the American steel industry. The implied contrasting picture of the functioning of regulation is, in the author's opinion, at least equally overdrawn. But there remains an important difference in the impact of these two alternative systems of organization.

But these very virtues of competition are its defects from the regulatory standpoint. If the commission is responsible for the proper performance of industry, how can it permit that responsibility to be diluted by the independent, competitive maneuvering of a bunch of irresponsible firms, known and unknown, which are not subject to its control? If it is responsible for the financial health of the regulated companies, from whom it is thereby enabled in turn to exact certain guarantees with respect to the continued provision and quality of service and on whom it can force a reduced return on investment, reflective of the security that regulated monopoly conveys, how can it afford to have that security subject to the vagaries of unregulated competition? [22] Regulation necessarily places a high value on predictability and continuity: how else can the commission proceed on the basis of evidence respecting some past, test year to set rates or pass on investment plans that look to the future—especially in view of the legal restraints, the complicated rules and procedures that govern administrative proceedings, enacted to assure fair treatment of all contesting parties, which often stretch the decision-making process over hundreds of volumes of testimony, exhibits, and "briefs," and many years? Competition introduces strong elements of unpredictability—unpredictability about prices, instabilities of market shares. Industry planning is one thing, competition quite another, and there are strong incompatibilities between the two.

It is extremely difficult to *plan* for *change*, for the kind of flux and disruption that competition entails, for one supervising agency to program the types of results that are produced when the sources of initiative and responsibility are dispersed.[23]

It is for reasons such as these, apart from the more obvious political influences, that regulation itself tends to be conservative. This conservatism is enhanced when, as is typically the case, regulators cannot themselves initiate or force the companies under their supervision to undertake risky investments, to embark on new and unproven ventures, because they too are dealing with "other people's money."[24] Because planning requires stability, regulators are apt to be tolerant if not positively enthusiastic about rate bureaus and similar devices by which potential competitors post prices and agree to adhere to them. They are likely to be hostile to new entrants and prone to adopt policies that assure a "fair sharing" of contested business among the inside parties rather than to leave its determination to the warfare of competition.

This is not to conclude—at this point, at least—that the purposes of improving service and protecting competitors, or the interests of consumers and the owners of regulated companies, are necessarily in conflict. The point is, only, that regulation typically chooses to serve the one by serving the other. That the companies pressing for the legislation and for a protectionist interpretation of it are doubtless interested primarily in the latter goals is relevant as a historical fact, but does not resolve the question of whether the methods chosen are socially the best ones available.

---

[22] For an interesting illustration of this attitude, in which the "chosen instrument," insulated from competition, is given direct responsibility for regulation as well, see the case of the organized stock exchanges, in Chapter 5, pp. 194–200, below.

[23] See, for example, David McCord Wright, *Democracy and Progress* (New York: The Macmillan Company, 1948), Chap. 1.

[24] See note 20, Chapter 2, Volume 1.

The evidences of this conservatism and protectionism on the part of regulatory agencies are so numerous that it would be impossible to cite even a small fraction of them; we postpone the detailed appraisal of these tendencies and of the specific decisions in which they have been manifested for later chapters. We set forth some major examples in considerable detail at this point, however, partly because concrete illustrations are always more informative than broad generalizations, partly to demonstrate the wide variety of regulatory circumstances in which these tendencies manifest themselves, and partly to describe a few of the major regulatory issues and policies that we shall more fully analyze at a later point.

Transportation

It should not be surprising that the leading examples of these tendencies can be found in the transportation field; it is there, above all the so-called public utilities, that the possibilities of competition are so great and the consequent necessity for the choice between regulation and competition so pervasive.

The Motor Carrier Act of 1935. The two principal operative provisions of this statute extended the authority of the Interstate Commerce Commission to include licensure of entry and regulation of rates charged in intercity operations by common and contract carriers by truck (the former offer their services to the public at large, the latter limit themselves to serving the needs of particular, individual shippers.) We have already cited the major consideration motivating the imposition of this comprehensive set of public utility-type controls on a highly dispersed and competitive industry—the belief that unregulated entry and price competition had resulted in poor service. The other side of the coin is that the Act was passed and has been enforced with the explicit purpose and effect of protecting railroads against the intensified competition of motor carriers and protecting motor carriers from one another.[25]

It is not a contradiction but a fuller explanation of this protectionism that it was in turn motivated largely by a desire to protect the discriminatory pricing structure of the railroads from being undermined by competition. Indeed, one important reason for the deep inroads of trucking into the freight business was that the rails had clung unimaginatively for decades to a "value of service" rate structure that involved extreme price discrimination against more valuable commodities, on the theory that their demand for transportation was inelastic. This assumption may well have been appropriate when railroads had a virtual monopoly. It became irrelevant once trucks were available to compete for that business. The common carrier truckers, in general, merely matched the rail rates; and because of the superiority of their service (greater speed and door-to-door delivery, without need for intermediate loading and unloading) they were able in this way to take away the bulk of this more valuable business.[26]

---

[25] See, for example, U. S. Senate, Committee on Interstate Commerce, 74th Cong. 1st Sess., *Report to Accompany S. 1629*, Senate Report No. 482, Washington, April 11, 1935, 2–3; *Report of the Federal Coordinator of Transportation, 1934, op. cit.*, 127.

[26] See pp. 64, 155, and 171 (note 23) of Volume 1, and especially Wilson, "Effects of Value-of-Service Pricing Upon Motor Common Carriers," *Jour. Pol. Econ.* (Aug. 1955), LXIII: 337–344. Once the trucking alternative was available, defining value of service (or demand inelasticity)

One consistent thread that runs throughout the entire history of the Interstate Commerce Act is the desire on the part of Congress and the ICC to keep freight rates low on the large-volume, low-valued agricultural commodities—a preferential treatment made possible in part by the traditional discrimination against the high-valued manufactured products. If this pricing pattern was to be preserved, the railroads clearly had to have some protection against the competition by trucks for the latter traffic. The Motor Carrier Act of 1935 filled this need.[27]

In its licensing provisions, the Act places on the applicant for common carrier authorization the burden of proof that the service he proposes to offer is "required by the present or future public convenience and necessity. . . ."[28] It does not suffice that a trucker is willing to take the risks of going into the business himself; he must convince the Commission that his services are required. When the service he proposes would compete, directly or indirectly, with that offered by an existing carrier, the latter may enter a protest. And in any event the Commission has pursued an extremely restrictive policy with regard to the issuance of new licenses. The possibility that the applicants would take business away from existing carriers has been an important consideration in inducing it to refuse them. Time and again, it has turned down applications that enjoyed the support of shippers, on the ground that the service provided by existing carriers either was in its judgment sufficient *or could become so.* In short, even an admittedly poor performance by existing carriers is not necessarily a sufficient justification for permitting more competition.[29] Moreover, the licenses that the ICC does

---

in terms of the value of the commodities being shipped became highly illogical. As Joel Dean has pointed out:

"If the value of commodities should be recognized by the rate structure at all, exactly the opposite treatment would be the most effective in competing against trucks. This is because trucks reduce the time merchandise is tied up in transit. The higher the value of the merchandise, the larger the cost saving from fast delivery; hence, to compensate for the railroads' slower and more erratic service, rail rates per 100 pounds should be lower, relative to trucks, on high-value commodities than on low-value commodities. . . ." As quoted in U. S. Senate, Committee on Interstate and Foreign Commerce, 87th Cong. 1st Sess., *National Transportation Policy*, Preliminary Draft of a Report prepared by the Special Study Group on Transportation Policies in the United States (John P. Doyle, Staff Director), Washington, January 1961 (hereinafter referred to as the *Doyle Report*), 662–663.

See also pp. 8–7, above, and 97, below.

[27] For a challenging documentation of this argument, describing the especially great opposition during the depression to the rails' effort to make good some of their revenue losses on high-valued commodity freight by increasing rates on agricultural products, see Robert A. Nelson and

William R. Greiner, "The Relevance of the Common Carrier Under Modern Economic Conditions," in Universities–National Bureau Committee for Economic Research, *Transportation Economics* (New York: National Bureau of Economic Research, 1965), 352–374. This means that the purpose of the restriction was to preserve a pattern of internal subsidization—holding rates to some customers above the ATC of serving them alone (by truck) in order to hold the rates to others closer to marginal costs. Contrast this purpose with the rules for acceptable price discrimination set forth at pp. 142–143, Volume 1, above; see also the discussion of this alleged cream-skimming by the trucks at note 154, p. 226, below.

The exemption of the carriage of agricultural commodities from the provisions of the 1935 Act was of course entirely consistent with this basic purpose. See also Ann F. Friedlaender, *The Dilemma of Freight Transport Regulation* (Washington: The Brookings Institution, 1969), 10–27.

[28] 49 U. S. Code 307 (a), 1964 ed.

[29] It is always hazardous to attempt general characterizations of Commission policy, when that policy is laid down over a great number of years in thousands of individual cases. When faced with an application for permission to extend service to areas or for the carriage of products in which, according both to shipper

complaints and its own findings, existing service was inadequate, the Commission has insisted on first giving existing carriers the opportunity to improve their service. It has done so with sufficient frequency to lead a District Court to find, in 1967, that this was its "invariable rule":

"The invariable rule of the Commission is and has been for a long time that no certificate affecting the area of another carrier will be issued until that other carrier has been furnished an opportunity either to improve or to correct his service to such route or decide whether he wishes to or can furnish the added service sought by the applicant carrier." *Dixie Highway Express, Inc. v. United States*, 268 F. Supp. 239, 241 (1967).

In support of this finding, the same District Court referred to the following declaration by the Commission itself, issued in 1965.

"'We have repeatedly stated that existing carriers normally should be accorded an opportunity to transport all of the traffic they can handle in an adequate and efficient manner without the added competition of a new operation.'" *Dixie Express Inc. et al. v. U. S.*, 242 F. Supp. 1016, 1021 (1965).

The ICC attitude on this specific point contrasts interestingly with the policy of the CAB.

"There is still another way in which the Board's handling of route cases tends to furnish a continuous incentive for carriers to maintain the quality of service, even in monopoly market segments or those where the number of carriers has not changed recently. Decisions in route cases often note that existing carriers have moved to rectify the inadequacies in their service after a route proceeding has been opened. If the Board would accept such improvements as a basis for not adding competitors, the carriers would have a relatively easy time of neutralizing the Board's efforts to promote the quality of service through point-to-point competition. However, the Board does not operate in this way. Rectifying service inadequacies to deter a competitive route award has in no significant case caused the Board to stay its decision to add competing service. A carrier which fears that one of its markets may attract would-be competitors cannot skimp on service until the threat is actually in sight." Richard E. Caves, *Air Transport and Its Regulators* (Cambridge: Harvard University Press, 1962), 240.

On the other hand, in the *Dixie Express* case itself—and in others, as well, in recent years (*Wall Street Journal*, December 19, 1967)—the Commission obviously had departed from that rule, finding,

"in considerable detail . . . . that shippers and receivers were hampered by the inadequacy of existing service, and . . . that, despite numerous complaints, existing carriers had not demonstrated that they could be depended upon to furnish adequate service,"

and therefore authorizing another carrier to extend service to the points in question. On complaint by competing motor carriers, the District Court twice returned the case to the Commission, the second time on the ground of the alleged "invariable rule" and on the ground too "that carriers have a property right to such opportunity [that is, to improve their service] before a new certificate may be issued. . . ." *United States et al v. Dixie Highway Express, Inc., et al.*, 389 U.S. 409, 410, 411 (1967).

The Supreme Court concluded that "no such limitation has been established by the Commission's own decisions or by judicial determinations," holding, instead, that:

"'the Commission may authorize the certificate even though the existing carriers might arrange to furnish successfully the projected service.' *ICC v. Parker*, 326 U.S. 60, 70 (1945); see *Schaffer Transportation Co. v. United States*, 355 U.S. 83, 90–91 (1957)." *Ibid.*, 411–412.

No doubt the Supreme Court itself deserves considerable credit for this partial relaxation of ICC policy in recent years. In the *Schaffer* case, just cited, the Commission had refused to issue a license to a trucker to provide service between points previously served only by rail, on the ground that:

"The evidence indicates that the witnesses' main purpose in supporting the application is to obtain lower rates rather than improved service. It is well established that this is not a proper basis for a grant of authority. . . ." As quoted 355 U.S. 83, 89 (1957).

But the Supreme Court pointed out, in overruling the Commission, the ICC itself had found that the lower truck rates on less-than-carload service would permit shippers to avoid the delays and expense of accumulating full carload shipments, as they had hitherto done because of the much lower rail rates on that service; and that shippers had asserted they were at a disadvantage in competing with suppliers from other areas who did enjoy the benefit of truck service.

"The ability of one mode of transportation to operate with a rate lower than competing types of transportation is precisely the sort of 'inherent advantage' that the congressional policy requires the Commission to recognize." *Ibid.*, 91.

So it quoted with approval the statement of the ICC's own Division 5 that:

"no carrier is entitled to protection from competition in the continuance of a service that

grant are extraordinarily detailed in their limitations,[30] permitting carriage of only specified commodities over only specified routes, in specified directions: licenses that permit carriers to offer service between points A and B

fails to meet a public need, nor, by the same token, should the public be deprived of a new and improved service because it may divert some traffic to other carriers." *Ibid.*, 91.

The U. S. Senate Select Committee on Small Business held hearings in 1955 in order

"to examine the validity of the many and bitter complaints received from small truckers and small shippers directed at the policies and practices of the Interstate Commerce Commission. No better summary statement of the charges . . . has come to the attention of your committee than those contained in a letter from an attorney accustomed to representing small trucking clients in proceedings before the Commission. This concise yet comprehensive summary of allegations is as follows:

"'It seems to me and to my clients that the basic problem confronting Congress and the country with respect to the ICC is not simply that the decisions are long delayed and expensive. The basic problem is that the ICC takes such a narrow and restrictive view of the motor carrier authority that should be authorized that even when a small carrier is willing to run the gantlet [sic] of an ICC procedure, it has very little hope of being able to secure any significant extension or addition of authority. The ICC seems to take the same view of the economy that is taken by reactionary business and labor unions when they seek to prevent the entry of any new enterprises into their respective fields. This view seems to be based on the assumption that there is only a limited amount of business and that it is to be the interest of those in the business to get the biggest slices of the pie that they can by keeping everyone else out of the field.

"'When such conduct is engaged in by private business or by labor unions, it is prosecuted as a violation of the antitrust laws and regarded as highly improper. It seems to me that the effects are just as baneful and antisocial when they are caused by a Government agency. . . .

"'It is respectfully submitted that any careful analysis of an examination into the ICC administration of the Motor Carrier Act will indicate that the Commission has acted principally to prevent the entry of new enterprises or the expansion of old ones and that this is an unwise, unreasonable, and improper method of administering the transportation policy of this Nation and is an extremely poor method of encouraging the economic growth and expansion of the

Nation.' " *Competition, Regulation, and the Public Interest in the Motor Carrier Industry, Report*, 84th Congress, 2d Session, Senate Report No. 1693, March 19, 1956, 2.

As the Committee itself concluded,

"the Commission tends to ignore shipper needs and to show an inordinate concern for the protection of truckers already possessing operating authority. . . .

"The Commission's own testimony in this regard is both revealing and alarming. Commissioner Mitchell, chairman of Division 1, stated the Commission's views on 'public convenience and necessity' as follows:

"'If I was convinced that one carrier was capable of giving good service to a shipper, I do not believe I would authorize another one. . . .

"'All I am interested in is the evidence of the proof of the need. I believe that if you put a lot of transportation companies in a certain territory that we are going to destroy many of them and the public is not going to get the kind of service they should. . . .'

"Given this economic orientation, the Commission is not likely to approve operating authority for a potential competitor over a specified route, even though the applicant may demonstrate that he can provide cheaper, more efficient, or more effective service to the shipping public. Under the circumstances, public convenience tends to be subordinated to public necessity, and public necessity interpreted in a narrow, physical sense rather than a meaningful, economic sense. . . . As long as service over a given route is physically adequate, the Commission seems satisfied, even though such service could be improved and costs reduced through the certification of additional competitors." *Ibid.*, 9–10.

See, also, the illuminating case study, David M. Welborn, "Trucking Service for Pittsburgh Plate Glass," in Edwin A. Bock, ed., *Government Regulation of Business, a Casebook* (Englewood Cliffs: Prentice–Hall, 1965), 412–448; also Jones, *op. cit.*, 505–558.

[30] This is true also of the ones it issued, after proceedings involving some 90,000 applications and over a decade of litigation, under the Act's "grandfather clause"—that is, to carriers already conducting operations at the time the law was enacted. See John B. Lansing, *Transportation and Economic Policy* (New York: The Free Press, 1966), 254.

and B and C do not necessarily convey the privilege of going directly between A and C, when all three are not on a straight line, or of picking up cargo for the return hauls.[31]

The important point is not that the ICC is typically right or wrong in its determinations of whether there is a "need" for additional service in these cases. It is that it is the *Commission* that decides whether existing service is so *inadequate* as to justify granting competitive authorizations; that *it* has to be convinced of their desirability; that in so deciding it feels it must give heavy weight to the interests of existing carriers; that it understandably places a heavy burden of proof on those who wish to compete, even when potential customers actively support those efforts; and that it places little value on competition as such as a force for providing a performance that is more than "adequate."[32]

As for the rate-making authority, it is perhaps a sufficient indication of the legislative intention that it is schedules of *minimum* rates that contract carriers are required to file and adhere to. And, as to its application in practice, of the 173,248 tariffs filed with the ICC in 1962, the Suspension Board considered 5,170; of the latter, approximately 95% involved rate *decreases*.[33]

The Motor Carrier Act was passed in the middle of the Great Depression. We shall have occasion, below, in assessing the feasibility of freer competition in trucking, to ask to what extent the apparent evils of excessive competition during that period, which played an important role in inducing Congress to cartelize the industry, were a temporary phenomenon, reflecting the general state of the economy. We have already remarked, in Volume 1, on some of the other, similarly anticompetitive regulatory policies introduced during the same period—NRA, farm price supports, production control in crude oil, the Civil Aeronautics Act of 1938, a federal fair trade law and so on; recall, too, that the Supreme Court's *Nebbia* decision was handed down in 1934.[34]

The Problems Created by Exempt Carriers. The difficulties of the railroads, however, persisted and intensified during the extremely prosperous

---

[31] See for example the case described in the Senate Small Business Committee Report, *op. cit.*, 7; Jones, *op. cit.*, 559–576. For a survey of these restrictions and of ICC policy in this regard see Charles A. Taff, *Operating Rights of Motor Carriers* (Dubuque, Iowa: Wm. C. Brown Company, 1953); also Carl H. Fulda, *Competition in the Regulated Industries, Transportation* (Boston: Little, Brown and Co., 1961), 71–105 and Alexander Volotta, *The Impact of Federal Entry Controls on Motor Carrier Operations* (University Park, Pa.: Pennsylvania State Univ., 1967). Lansing cites evidence developed by James C. Nelson indicating that many motor carriers have as many as 200 certificates covering specific permissible kinds of business, and a statement by an Interstate Commerce Commissioner pointing out that the 244 grants of operating authority held by one carrier filled a 124-page volume, and reporting also that the Commission receives "upwards of 30,000 requests each year as to whether or not a particular carrier holds the right to transport a particular shipment." *Op. cit.*, 256. See also

pp. 187–188, below.

[32] "We are of the opinion that applicant has failed to establish any substantial inadequacy in the service which Dugan is authorized to provide from Sioux Falls. . . . As for applicant's contention that protestant's service is monopolistic in character, the mere existence of monopoly, standing alone, is not a sufficient justification for the establishment of a new operation in the absence of a showing of some inferiority or inadequacy in the transportation service of the existing carrier." *Transport, Inc., Extension—Sioux Falls, S. Dak.*, 81 M.C.C. 751 (1959), as excerpted in Jones, *op. cit.*, p. 552.

The question is: without competition to show the way, how can it be determined whether existing service is as good as it could possibly be?

[33] Merton J. Peck, "Competitive Policy for Transportation?" in Almarin Phillips, ed. *Perspectives on Antitrust Policy* (Princeton: Princeton Univ. Press, 1965), 257.

[34] See pp. 8–10, Volume 1, and 180–182, below.

fifteen years or so after the end of World War II.[35] And the common carrier trucks, too, continued having their competitive problems. Although the ICC's policy of restrictive licensing and discouragement of price competition (see the following section of this chapter) under the Motor Carrier Act helped to preserve the value-of-service rate structure, it also had the effect of leaving the door wide open for the growth of exempt motor carriage. The 1935 Act had established two major exemptions from regulation—carriers of agricultural commodities and private carriage (that is, in trucks owned and operated by the shipper). Shippers could therefore escape from the noncompetitive common-carrier rates by using their own trucks; and farmers applied sufficient political pressure to keep the truckers serving them similarly free of ICC-enforced operating limitations and rate minima. Moreover, the exempt carriers were under strong temptation to invade the common carriage market. Agricultural, private, or contract carriers with a preponderance of freight in one direction—from the farm or company plant, for example—solicited customers for the return trip at cut rates, reflecting its negligible incremental cost.[36] And when, as it consistently did, the Commission sought to close these loopholes,[37] the exempt carriers sought various ways of escaping. They would lease out their trucks at cut rates to common carriers for the return trip, often by highly circuitous routes—wherever the business took them; or engage in the fiction of nominally purchasing the goods at the point of origin and reselling them at the destination.

All of these moves and countermoves provide illuminating case studies in the economics and politics of cartellike restrictions on competition, illustrating these inherent tendencies: (1) a tendency of the cartels themselves to hold prices above the marginal costs of at least some producers; (2) a tendency for such producers to try in one way or another to take advantage of the profit opportunities thereby created—by entering the cartelized market, if they are outside it, by soliciting business at cut rates, if at all possible; (3) a consequent pressure on the cartel managers or regulators to limit or control these competitive incursions; and (4) the exertion of political and economic pressures by the various parties affected, the "spoilers" to keep free of cartel controls, the companies already regulated to extend the controls to the intruders and price cutters.[38]

---

[35] See pp. 52 note 76, 64, and 170, Volume 1.

[36] See the similar situation involving railroads in note 8, p. 164 of Volume 1. And for an appraisal of the economics of competition in these circumstances, see pp. 182–184, Chapter 5, below.

[37] For example, by attempting to deny the agricultural exemption to farm products that had been subjected to any processing at all; by imposing strict limitations on the practice of trip-leasing; by limiting what agricultural cooperatives could bring back to the farm on return hauls; and by vigilant efforts to keep contract carriers from soliciting business generally and thereby encroaching on the common-carriage market. These attempts were sometimes overturned by the Courts, then sometimes later confirmed by Congress. See Louis B. Schwartz, "Legal Restriction of Competition in the

Regulated Industries: An Abdication of Judicial Responsibility," *Harvard Law Rev.* (January 1954), LXVII: 456–460; Jones, *op. cit.*, 507–520, 535–540; Walter Adams, "The Role of Competition in the Regulated Industries," *Amer. Econ. Rev., Papers & Proceedings* (May 1958), XLVIII: 535–537. See also the footnote immediately following.

[38] See the section of this chapter, "The tendency of regulation to spread," below. Consider, for example, the history of the agricultural cooperatives exemption—49 U.S.C. 303 (b) (5), 1964 ed.—itself, obviously, the consequence of successful political pressure by the farm block in Congress and one that is estimated to have saved farmers one-fifth to one-third in their trucking costs (see note 58, pp. 190–191, below). In principle, the purpose of none of the farm-related exemp-

tions was to permit the carriers thus favored to engage without restriction in common carrier trucking. The exemption (from all but the Act's safety provisions) of a farmer's own trucks was specifically confined to their use "in the transportation of his agricultural . . . commodities . . . or in the transportation of supplies to his farm"; the exemption of "motor vehicles used in carrying . . . agricultural . . . commodities" explicitly applied only "if such motor vehicles are not used in carrying any other property, or passengers, for compensation. . . ." But the exemption of "motor vehicles controlled and operated by a cooperative association," in contrast, contained no such limitation. 49 U.S.C. 303 (b), 1964 ed.

In consequence, farm cooperatives began extensively to haul nonfarm-related products for the account of nonmembers. The ICC complained, in 1964:

"the number of groups and organizations claiming exemptions as agricultural cooperatives . . . has grown considerably in the last 10 to 15 years . . . . these exemptions are being used by various groups and organizations as a guise to perform general transportation services and to divert substantial amounts of tonnage from regulated motor carriers and freight forwarders." *Annual Report, 1964*, 76–77.

Confronted with the unqualified exemption in the Motor Carrier Act, the Commission sought redress in an interpretation of the Agricultural Marketing Act, which provides that cooperatives not deal in *farm* products, supplies, or business services with or for nonmembers in amounts greater in value than with or for members. 12 U.S.C. 1141j (a), 1964 ed. This provision, the ICC asserted, implied that cooperatives could not deal in *nonfarm* products or services at all; and in a leading case it sought to apply this interpretation to the Northwest Agricultural Cooperative Association's haulage of nonexempt commodities for nonmembers.

This, the Circuit Court of Appeals held, was an unreasonably and unjustifiably strict interpretation. The obvious purpose of the provision, it said, was simply to require that cooperatives do at least half of their business with members. As long as the carriage of nonfarm commodities was necessary and incidental to the essential business of buying, selling and transporting farm and farm-related commodities on behalf of their farmer members, the defendants retained the essential character of a cooperative and were thus entitled to complete exemption from the route and rate regulation of the ICC.

"On the uncontradicted facts, Northwest's transportation of nonfarm products and supplies was incidental and necessary to its farm-related transportation . . . incidental because limited to otherwise empty trucks returning from hauling member farm products to market, and producing a small return in proportion to Northwest's income from trucking farm products and farm supplies; necessary because it is not economically feasible to operate the trucks empty on return trips and because the additional income obtained is no more than that required to render performance of the cooperative's primary farm transportation service financially practicable."

The Court therefore concluded that the

"trucking operation, viewed as a whole, is a farm service performed jointly by Northwest's members 'for themselves.' The return hauls enjoined are 'connected with farm operations,' for they are incidental and necessary to the effective performance of Northwest's trucking operation." *Northwest Agricultural Cooperative Association, Inc. v. Interstate Commerce Commission*, 350 F. 2d 252, 255, 257 (1965).

As a result of this decision, advertisements soon appeared in various business journals, in which agricultural cooperatives offered their services to haul goods of all kinds at reduced rates; several actually signed contracts with the Department of Defense. The ICC, in turn, went to Congress, with the support of representatives of the common carriers, to close the flood gates. See the United States Senate, Committee on Commerce, Subcommittee on Surface Transportation, 90th Cong. 1st Sess., *Agricultural Cooperative Transportation Exemption*, Hearings, July 1967 and Senate Report 1152, May 28, 1968. The outcome was, understandably, a compromise: PL 90–433, signed by the President July 26, 1968 (82 Stat. 448) provided that a cooperative might carry nonfarm-related commodities for the account of nonmembers only insofar as this was "incidental to its primary transportation operation and necessary for its effective performance," only in tonnages up to 15 percent of the total and subject to full access by the Commission to the records of such operations. This account is in large measure a summary of a paper prepared for me by my student William C. Van Dam.

Similarly, the statute exempting from ICC regulation the carriage of commodities in bulk by barges sets three commodities as the maximum number that barge lines may carry on a single tow, and forbids the mixing of exempt and nonexempt cargo. Following the lure of economic opportunity created by the development of increasingly powerful towboats, barge operators petitioned the ICC to permit them to put together large convoys mixing exempt cargo with freight subject to ICC route and rate authority. The Commission ruled against them, and its prohibition was sustained in the courts.

In any event, the consequence was a continuing competitive handicap imposed on the common carriers. It was estimated that in 1964 only 33 percent of all intercity truck ton-miles were carried by holders of ICC operating licenses; the other two-thirds were handled by exempt motor carriers.[39]

Price Cutting by the Railroads. The railroads and common carrier truckers were understandably unhappy at this competition. They argued with some justification that they were unfairly disadvantaged by the ICC controls, which limited their ability to reduce rates while leaving the exempt carriers free to quote whatever charges they pleased. The rails, in particular, began, belatedly and with widely varying degrees of aggressiveness,[40] an attempt to regain some of the lost traffic, by introducing modern equipment and proposing sharp rate reductions. They showed a salutary disposition to abandon the discriminatory and increasingly unrealistic value-of-service rate schedules and to bring prices down more nearly to long-run incremental costs.

It is excessively easy to oversimplify in characterizing the ICC's response to these efforts.[41] Perhaps the most important characterization is, as Ernest

---

Gulf Canal Lines, Inc. v. United States, 386 U.S. 348 (1967). In 1967, however, recognizing the immense cost-savings of long, mixed tows, the ICC granted the barge companies a temporary exemption and both parties asked Congress to relax the restrictions. The companies estimated that the temporary exemption had produced cost-savings of about 30 percent. But the railroads opposed the requested liberalization, and as of January 1970 Congress had not acted. *Wall Street Journal*, October 11, 1967, 2, and *Business Week*, January 10, 1970, 104, 106.

[39] Lansing, *op. cit.*, 254. According to the 1963 *Census of Transportation*, U. S. Department of Commerce, Bureau of the Census, Vol. IV, 3, 42,986 of the 57,800 motor carriers in the U. S. in that year were exempt from ICC regulation. It is not clear that regulated motor carriers have suffered a persistently declining share of the business. The percentage of total intercity *truck* traffic (ton-miles) handled by regulated carriers was 37.2 percent in 1939 and fluctuated roughly around that level for the next 25 years; their share was 36.1 percent in 1965. Jones, *op. cit.*, 521 and ICC, *81st Annual Report*, 1967, 57. See also *Business Week*, November 10, 1962, 82, reporting a study by the Northwestern University Transportation Center that showed no appreciable difference in the rates of growth of regulated and unregulated motor carriers between 1939 and 1959.

But, of course, the continued decline during these years in the share of total traffic carried by the rails resulted in a corresponding decline in the market share of all regulated as compared with all unregulated carriers. See Friedlaender, *op. cit.*, 100–103.

In the United Kingdom, railroad freight traffic declined from 22 to 15 billion ton-miles between

1952 and 1965, while licensed motor carriage rose from 10 to 16 billion, and private road carriage from 9 to 25 billion ton-miles. A. A. Walters, "Subsidies for Transport?" *Lloyd's Bank Rev.* (January 1967), 22.

[40] "The traffic downturn of 1954 . . . may some day be recorded as the beginning of a series of events which may perhaps bring the rail carriers to a reluctant recognition that their industry has been bankrupt in the matter of effective policy for coping with intercarrier competition.

"The Commission's exercise of its regulatory powers must bear a share of the responsibility, but the result has been shaped more, perhaps, by carrier policies than by any policies generated by the Commission. For the Commission has played its essentially passive role case by case. . . . Meanwhile, if there has been any railroad policy, other than sheer expediency, we have been unable to detect it. That railroads have fought a delaying action against motor-carrier competition is clear, but they have not developed and put forward a plan for reshaping the vulnerable areas of their rate structure in a way designed to prevent diversion where the cost advantage is with the railroads.

". . . railroads appear to have lost one opportunity after another to establish under regulation a basis for rates in the competitive area which would give scope to their cost advantage." Williams, *op. cit.*, 219–222. For a similar verdict, see Edward T. Thompson, "What Hope for the Railroads?" *Fortune* (February 1958), 137–139 and ff., especially 148.

[41] "One of the difficulties in generalizing in this field is that ICC decisions are like the Bible; textual support can be found for any position." Peck, *op. cit.*, 251 note 11.

Williams makes quite clear in his study, that it never did formulate a general policy. The only reasonably consistent pattern discernible is one of conservatism and protectionism. As far as rate competition between regulated carriers is concerned, this attitude is reflected in a fairly consistent resistance by the Commission to reductions that would threaten the general principle of "rate parity"—the principle that the rates ought to be either equal or unequal only to the extent necessary to reflect differences in the quality of service. The general tendency is to eliminate rates as a factor in competition, with the ultimate purpose of preserving for all existing regulated carriers a "fair share" of the business. Both the operating rule and the goal are, of course, in flat contradiction to the economic principles enunciated in our Chapter 6, which would require that the rates of competing carriers reflect their own respective long-run marginal costs and that the business be apportioned purely on the basis of those costs. As Williams observes:

"With respect to the relationship of rail to motor-carrier rates the Commission seemingly has been moved by a desire to preserve both types of transportation in virtually the whole range of service they had come to occupy at the time its jurisdiction was broadened. Consequently it has given large emphasis to the preservation of the opportunity to compete and to secure a 'fair' share of the traffic. . . . [P]roposed rail rates which the Commission feared would impair motor-carrier service have been disapproved, and the Commission's concept of meeting competition through rate parity has left the motor carriers in possession of advantages of lower minimum weights, lower costs to shippers for packaging, loading, and unloading, and faster, more complete and flexible service. . . .

"In contrast to this indirect effect of rate relationships, the principle of rate parity can and does, immediately and directly, deprive one type of carrier of its cost advantage over the other in so far as its bid to the market is concerned, in apparent disregard of the national transportation policy . . . . It is difficult to avoid the conclusion that regulation has consistently, over the twenty years since the Motor Carrier Act, deprived the low-cost carrier of its cost advantage, a result often tantamount to depriving it of all opportunity to compete for traffic. . . .

"This result is consistent with a point of view which concerns itself primarily with what must be done 'in fairness' to the carriers which have actually been competing for the particular traffic in issue. . . . It does not, however, contribute to the development of a more economic division of the traffic, to coordination of the services, or to the development of economy in the handling of the available business. And it extends great encouragement to the growth of private and exempt trucking to the detriment of all common carriers. . . ."[42]

---

[42] *Op. cit.*, 210–215. For other, similar assessments, see James C. Nelson, *Railroad Transportation and Public Policy* (Washington: The Brookings Institution, 1959), Chapter 5 and pp. 431–435; Jervis Langdon, Jr., "The Regulation of Competitive Business Forces: The Obstacle Race in Transportation," *Cornell Law Q.* (Fall 1955), XLI: 57–92; Presidential Advisory Committee on Transport Policy and Organization, *Revision of Federal Transportation Policy* (Washington, June 1956: "carriers, notwithstanding demonstrated lower costs, are permitted to do no more than to meet the competition facing them which, with some exceptions, means to name the same rate regardless of cost relationships." 5); David Boies, Jr., "Experiment in Mercantilism: Minimum Rate Regulation by the Interstate Commerce Commission," *Columbia Law Rev.* (April 1968), LXVIII: 599–663.

In fairness to the Commission, it should be pointed out, as we shall presently observe more fully, that the laws under which it operates contain the same bias. On the other hand, it has had an important role in writing those laws and in their interpretation. The persistence of the financial difficulties of the railroads during the 1950s and the growing recognition of the unfairness and economic irrationality of the ICC's cartellike policies[43] finally led Congress in 1958 to amend the law in order to permit freer rate competition on the basis of the respective costs of the competing transport media. But the ICC exerted its influence to soften the amendment and interpreted it thereafter as enjoining it to continue protecting the trucks and water carriers from rail competition. We have already told part of this story in Chapter 6: how the proposed amendment would have enjoined the Commission to look only to the costs and traffic of the railroads proposing rate reductions; how, in its final version, it contained the added, qualifying clause, "giving due consideration to the objectives of national transportation policy," and how the ICC thereafter, on the basis of that qualification, continued not only to weigh the costs of all carriers concerned but to apply the test of fully distributed rather than long-run marginal cost in determining which carrier had the "inherent advantage" and whether therefore the proposed rate reduction should be permitted.[44] What remains to be added is that it was the Commission, along with the carriers with which the rails compete, that "objected strongly" to the original formulation of the amendment, precisely on the ground that "the ICC would be unable to protect the 'inherent advantages' enjoyed by the competing carriers on the traffic to which a rate reduction was to be applied"[45] and that the altered language was specifically introduced to cover cases in which railroads might establish rates below their own fully distributed costs.[46]

So, not surprisingly, the ICC continued its protectionist policies after 1958 as far as regulated carriers were concerned. In its *New Haven* decision of 1960, subsequently overturned by the Supreme Court, it refused to permit railroads to set a rate that was above even their fully distributed costs on half of the traffic simply because, it decided, the proposed rates would in time destroy the coastal shipping industry.[47] In its first *Southern Railway* decision, in 1963, the ICC rescinded part of a 60 percent rail reduction that still left the rates above incremental costs, in order to protect competing barge lines.[48] Ironically, the railway had spent $13 million for more than 500 new, oversize aluminum cars to carry the grain, precisely in order to get its costs down, an innovation that the Commission itself hailed as a "major break-through in the control of costs and a notable advance in the art of railroading."[49] This decision was reversed by the courts and on reconsideration the Commission permitted the full cut.[50]

But its reasoning on reconsideration was instructive. It justified its willing-

---

[43] See, in addition to the authorities already cited, the 1957 *Economic Report of the President* (Washington, 1957), 51.

[44] See notes 9 and 12, pp. 164 and 165, Volume 1.

[45] *American Commercial Lines, Inc., et al. v. Louisville & Nashville R. Co. et al.*, 392 U.S. 571, 580 (1968).

[46] *Ibid.*, 581–582, 585–586.

[47] *Interstate Commerce Commission v. New York, New Haven & Hartford Railroad Co. et al.*, 372 U.S.

744 (1963). For a more defensible aspect of this decision, however, see p. 249, Chapter 5, below.

[48] See note 12, Chapter 6, Volume 1.

[49] *Grain in Multiple-Car Shipments—River Crossings to the South*, Second Report and Order of the Commission on Reconsideration, 325 ICC 752, 759–760 (1965).

[50] *Ibid.*

ness in this instance to use "long term out-of-pocket costs"[51] as a test of whether the proposed rates were compensatory only because the competition in question was primarily with *unregulated* truckers—for the preservation of whose "inherent advantages" it had no statutory responsibility. Nor, obviously, did it feel any other kind of responsibility. The Commission made it perfectly clear that it proposed still to use fully distributed costs if the competition were with another regulated carrier.[52] And so it did, just a few months later, in the *Ingot Molds* case, as we have already seen. In this instance, the Supreme Court sustained the Commission's refusal to permit the railroads to reduce their rates to a point above their estimated long-term out-of-pocket costs, in order to save the business for the trucks and barges. The statutory language and legislative intent, the Court reasoned, clearly gave the ICC authority to use fully distributed costs as its measure of "the inherent advantages" of the various carriers; and the Courts were obliged in those circumstances to defer to the expert judgment of the regulatory agency. The only ray of hope was the Court's observation that the ICC then had under way a broad examination of the cost standards to be used in making intermodal comparisons; that it was not itself insisting that the Commission cling to fully distributed costs, but that it was particularly reluctant in these circumstances to prejudge the outcome of those deliberations.[53]

The Orientation of Regulatory Policy. At least the Commission was reasonably consistent in its policies—on the one hand suppressing price competition and protecting "fair shares" in the business, on the other interpreting the exemptions from its authority narrowly and attempting continuously to bring more exempt carriage under its cartel umbrella.[54] The Report issued in April 1955 by the Presidential Advisory Committee on Transport Policy and Organization, which President Eisenhower had constituted in recognition of the growing plight of the railroads,[55] provides an amusing illustration of a more schizophrenic attitude.

The principal emphasis of the Committee's report was on the enormous increase in competition that had occurred in transportation during the preceding thirty years and the desirability of giving much freer play to these competitive forces, in order to assure the most efficient distribution of the business. On the other hand, another strong underlying theme was the desirability of protecting the common carriers, with a corollary hostility to unregulated competition:

"regulated common carriers today encounter large and growing competition by exempt for-hire carriers or pseudo carriers whose operations are

---

[51] As we have already pointed out, this measure includes a return on a portion of allocated investment, and therefore exceeds true long-run marginal costs. See note 6, p. 162, Volume 1.
[52] 325 ICC 752, 772; see also 758–759—where it identifies this as the controlling consideration— 770, 773–776. It seems reasonable to conclude that the willingness of the Commission in 1962 to sanction railroad rates close to extremely low, incremental backhaul costs on the carriage of coal from Kentucky to Florida—see note 8, p. 164, Volume 1—was attributable to the fact

that the competition was with unregulated water carriers, as it specifically pointed out.
[53] 392 U.S. 571, 578, 590–591 (1968). Justice Harlan concurred only with this explicit understanding and, obviously, only with great reluctance. *Ibid.*, 594–597.
[54] The Commission's *Annual Reports* provide a convenient summary of these efforts. See especially the reports of 1967, 95–96; the report of 1968, 110–114 and 129.
[55] *Revision of Federal Transportation Policy, op. cit.*

largely opportunistic in character. These operations are conducted without the necessity to publish rates[,] with freedom to discriminate in rates and service, and with no obligation to serve the general public. The continuing growth of this exempt for-hire carriage would seriously impair the maintenance of a strong and healthy common carrier industry, which by contrast is generally obliged to serve all of the public without discrimination."[56]

Along, then, with strong recommendations

"to reduce economic regulation of the transportation industry to the minimum consistent with the public interest to the end that the inherent economic advantages, including cost and service advantages, of each mode of transportation, may be realized in such a manner so as to reflect its full competitive capabilities,"[57]

the Report asks also for a tightening of exemptions: for example.

"Redefine a private carrier by motor vehicle as any person not included in definition of a common or a contract carrier who transports property of which he is the owner, provided that the property was not acquired for the purpose of such transportation. . . .

"A primary problem in transportation at present concerns the infringement of private carriers upon the field of common carriage and the need for remedial action in the form of more effective regulation of private carriers. . . .

"Redefine motor and water contract carriage as being that transportation providing services for hire but otherwise equivalent to *bona fide* private carriage and require that actual, rather than minimum, charges be filed.

"The definition of contract carrier by motor vehicle and contract carrier by water . . . should be sharpened to make clear that such carriers are of a specialized nature, and that they should be so regarded only if they clearly substitute for a feasible private carrier operation and do not perform common carrier services which would ordinarily be undertaken by common carriers."[58]

The Kennedy administration made a conscious attempt to achieve a greater degree of consistency. The *Presidential Message on Transportation* to Congress, dated April 4, 1962, took as its major theme the desirability of freeing management from the "excessive, cumbersome, and time-consuming regulatory supervision that shackles and distorts managerial initiative," and of leaving the allocation of transportation business to "reliance on unsubsidized privately-owned facilities, operating under the incentives of private profit and the checks of competition to the maximum extent practicable."[59] As to the problem of exempt carriage:

---

[56] *Ibid.*, 3.

[57] *Ibid.*, 4.

[58] *Ibid.*, 7–8. There were other recommendations along similar lines, including a request that Congress reexamine and limit the agricultural commodity exemptions. See the review of the Committee's report by James C. Nelson, "Revision of National Transport Regulatory Policy," *Amer. Econ. Rev.* (Dec. 1955), XLV: 910–918. Nelson specifically underlines the inconsistency between these two aspects of the

report, pointing out that, for all its references to the feasibility and desirability of enhanced competition, the Committee has no criticisms to offer of the tight restrictions on entry into the common-carrier business by road and waterway, and asking

"Why do common carriers need protection from competition of private, contract or unregulated transportation if common-carrier organization is inherently more efficient?" *Ibid.*, 917.

[59] Mimeo. version, 2–3.

"the transportation of bulk commodities by water carriers is exempt from all rate regulation under the Interstate Commerce Act, including the approval of minimum rates; but this exemption is denied to all other modes of transportation. This is clearly inequitable both to the latter and to shippers—and it is an inequity which should be removed. *Extending to all other carriers the exemption from the approval or prescription of minimum rates* would permit the forces of competition and equal opportunity to replace cumbersome regulation for these commodities. . . . While this would be the preferable way to eliminate the existing inequality, Congress could elect to place all carriers on an equal footing by repealing the existing exemption—although this would result in more, instead of less, regulation and very likely in higher though more stable rates."[60]

Similarly, with respect to the exemption of the carriage of agricultural and fishery products by motor carriers, the President recommended:

"*This exemption from minimum rates should also be extended to all carriers.*"[61]

These two proposals would have exempted from ICC minimum rate control freight accounting for 44 percent of total rail revenues and 70 percent of total tonnage.[62]

It should be noted, parenthetically, that the President did not recommend elimination of ICC regulation even over these commodities. The burden of his recommendations was to free competition by taking away the Commission's authority to fix *minimum* rates,

"while protecting the public interest by leaving intact the ICC's control over maximum railroad rates and other safeguards (such as the prohibition against discrimination, and requirements on car service and common carrier responsibility)."[63]

It is an interesting question, which we need not however try to settle here, whether the continuous concern of the ICC with protecting the common carriers has been the result of an administrative hardening of the arteries (as is suggested by the "life cycle of the administrative commission" theory, mentioned above), a historical shift in the thrust of its policy, or has been reflective of the legislative intent from the very outset—that is, back in 1887.[64] But it would, in any event, be a misreading of that history to see the

---

[60] *Ibid.*, 3–4.

[61] *Ibid.*, 4.

[62] Peck, *op. cit.*, 252.

[63] *Ibid.*, 4. See the general argument along lines similar to those of the Kennedy *Message* in the 1970 *Economic Report of the President* (Washington, February 1970), 108–109.

[64] The traditional view has been that the entire corpus of railroad legislation, beginning with the state granger laws of the 1870s, was the response above all else to public outrage at the monopolistic exploitations by the railroads; that the roads themselves bitterly opposed this legislation and exerted themselves continuously and with almost complete success during the first twenty years of the Commission's life to hamstringing its regulatory efforts; and that it was the combined

pressures by shippers, the public at large, and the ICC that finally produced the Hepburn Act of 1906 and Mann–Elkins Act of 1910, which gave the Commission the authority it needed to protect the public. See, for example, the monumental study by I. L. Sharfman, *The Interstate Commerce Commission, A Study in Administrative Law and Procedure* (New York: The Commonwealth Fund, four volumes, 1931–1937), Vol. I, 14, 23–24, 39–40, 71–72. According to this view, the Commission emerged from these struggles "almost universally accepted as an essential arm of the government," with "its many fruitful accomplishments . . . generally accorded unstinted recognition," (*Ibid.*, Vol. I, 12) and it was only many decades, indeed almost a half-century, later that the Commission became the great cartelizer. See, for example, Clair Wilcox, *Public Policies toward Business*, 3rd ed. (Homewood: Richard D. Irwin, 1966), 401.

Recently, Gabriel Kolko has presented a great deal of convincing historical evidence in many respects fundamentally contradicting the traditional conception.

"the railroads, not the farmers and shippers, were the most important single advocates of federal regulation from 1877 to 1916. . . .

"From the 1870's until the end of the century. . . . railroad freight rates, taken as a whole, declined almost continuously. . . . In their desire to establish stability and control over rates and competition, the railroad executives often resorted to voluntary, cooperative efforts involving rate agreements and the division of traffic. When these efforts failed, as they inevitably did, the railroad men turned to political solutions to rationalize their increasingly chaotic industry. . . .

"The crucial point is that the railroads, for the most part, consistently accepted the basic premises of federal regulation since only through the positive intervention of the national political structure could the destabilizing, costly effects of cutthroat competition, predatory speculators, and greedy shippers be overcome." *Railroads and Regulation, 1877–1916* (Princeton: Princeton Univ. Press, 1965) 3–6. Copyright 1965 by Princeton Univ. Press.

It is not feasible here to summarize the evidence that Kolko adduces. The interested reader should consult also the empirical study by Paul W. MacAvoy, demonstrating that:

"The regulation of the structure of rates . . . tended to make more effective the cartel's control of the level of long-distance rates. . . . Rates were 'stabilized,' and 'increased,' for long-distance transport of bulk commodities [in the carriage of which competition would otherwise have prevailed]. Rates were 'destabilized' when regulation was weakened by the Supreme Court in the later 1890's." Reprinted from *The Economic Effects of Regulation, The Trunk-Line Railroad Cartels and the Interstate Commerce Commission before 1900*, 1965, v, by permission of The M.I.T. Press, Cambridge, Massachusetts. See also George W. Hilton, "The Consistency of the Interstate Commerce Act," *Jour. Law & Econ.* (October 1966), IX: 87–114.

So far as the legislative *intent* is concerned, there is evidence also on the other side. For example, many of the original state granger laws fixed *maximum*, not minimum rates; contrary to the interest of the railroads, the original Interstate Commerce Act did explicitly forbid pooling; the Commission began by specifying rate *reductions*; the Hepburn Act finally gave it specific authorization to fix *maximum* rates; and it was not until the Transportation Act of 1920 that the Commission was given explicit authority to fix minimum rates and to encourage combinations, pooling, and consolidations of railroads. See, for example, Wilcox, *op. cit.*, 388–395. Also see the review of the Kolko book by Louis Galambos, *Econ. Hist. Rev.* (April 1967), XX: 200.

The one thing we can be sure of is that, while there are important differences between these two interpretations, the conflict can easily be overdrawn. The farmer and shipper interests who most loudly emphasized the necessity for protection placed heavy emphasis on the evils "of destructive competitive warfare, of fluctuating and discriminating rate adjustments" (Sharfman, *op. cit.*, Vol. I, 14), which the railroads were equally interested in stopping. One of their central complaints was that the intense rivalry among railroads, under the pressures of big shippers, proved to be highly discriminatory; it is not surprising, therefore, that the interests of both smaller shippers and the railroads to some extent converged. Nor does the fact, noted by Sharfman and Kolko alike, that the Elkins Act of 1903, which greatly strengthened the power of the Commission to prohibit rate rebates to powerful shippers, "was enacted on the initiative of the railroads themselves, as a means of conserving their revenues" (*ibid.*, Vol. I, 36; compare Kolko, *op. cit.*, 94–101) necessarily vitiate the former's further observation that the measure

"was generally regarded, from the public standpoint, quite as much a necessary instrument for curbing the unconscionable tactics of the so-called trusts in extorting special favors from the carriers as a desirable extension of federal authority over the railroads. . . .

"The Elkins Act . . . proved from the very beginning to be 'a wise and salutary enactment.'" (Vol. I, 36–37.)

The more important point, for us, is that it is unnecessary and perhaps not even sensible to try to choose between these conflicting interpretations. What we would emphasize, instead, is the inherent tendency for even a predominantly "public-minded" commission to betray a hostility toward intense price rivalry, which tends— inevitably, in highly imperfect markets—to produce instability and discrimination among buyers. This is a consequence of neither stupidity nor venality, but of the resort to regulation, the case for which can not be lightly dismissed merely by pointing to the virtues of an unattainable perfect competition. On the other hand, it does not follow that this tendency should not be resisted.

Commission's philosophy as resulting from either historical accident, perversity or a subversion of the regulatory process. It is not a matter of the ICC having become excessively "railroad-minded," or untrue to its legislative mandate; these policies are just as protective of the interests of existing regulated motor carriers (and of the Teamsters Union) as of the railroads[65]; and they have been applied at a later date just as much to discourage competitive rate reductions *by* railroads, in an effort to retrieve their lost business, as to insulate the rails from truck competition. Rather, these developments reflect the inherent thrust of regulation itself, which confides to the expertise of an administrative agency the responsibility for ordering the affairs of industry; to such a planning venture, competition is troublesome and disruptive.[66]

The Tendency of Regulation to Spread

The story of the ICC illustrates another kind of historical principle as well: the necessity for limitations on competition to become ever more extensive and thorough if they are to succeed. So long as regulation imposes restraints on competition, it will have continuously to widen and deepen its scope. The economics of this is quite simple. If regulation limits competition, it must be because some competition would otherwise be feasible: the ability and will to compete are therefore present. And, if the regulation is effective, price will be held above at least some producers' or potential producers' marginal costs. In these circumstances, controls over price competition are subject to evasion by accentuated quality and service rivalry, limited only by the ingenuity of businessmen in seeking new methods of enticing customers. They will be impelled to exercise such ingenuity so long as price is held above marginal cost. Similarly, the elevation of price—above the marginal cost of insider firms, above the average total cost of potential entrants, using the newest possible technology—sets up persistent temptations for new businessmen to come into the market, in turn creating the necessity for regulatory limitations on entry, and for extension of controls to unregulated firms.[67]

---

[65] See Robert D. Leiter, *The Teamsters Union* (New York: Bookman Associates, 1957), 135–139. Of the contested applications for rate reductions, many more are proposed by motor carriers than by railroads—probably reflecting the potentially more competitive nature of trucking. Merrill J. Roberts, "Transport Costs, Pricing and Regulation" in *Transportation Economics, op. cit.*, 18–20.

[66] See the violent attack by Samuel P. Huntington, "The Marasmus of the ICC: The Commission, The Railroads, and The Public Interest," *Yale Law Jour.* (April 1952), LXI: 467–509; the response by Charles S. Morgan, "A Critique of 'The Marasmus of the ICC: The Commission, The Railroads, and The Public Interest,'" *ibid.* (December 1952), LXII: 171–225; "The ICC Re-examined: A Colloquy," *ibid.* (November 1953), LXIII: 44–63; and the comment in Louis L. Jaffe, "The Effective Limits of the Administrative Process: A Reevaluation," *Harvard Law Rev.* (May 1954),

LVII: 1107–1108.

[67] See Kahn, "Cartels and Trade Associations," *International Encyclopedia of the Social Sciences* (The Macmillan Co. and The Free Press, 1968), II: 321–322. Also, for example, our discussion at pp. 194–197, Chapter 5, below, of some of the consequences of the fixed minimum brokerage commission schedule imposed by the securities exchanges: a tendency for the protected brokers to bid for the business by "give-ups"—surrenders of large portions of their commissions by one subterfuge or other—and various reciprocal deals, all to get round the exchanges' prohibitions of rebates. This in turn led the New York Stock Exchange to attempt to prohibit such deals; and this in turn subjected it to demands by institutional investors for the right to membership on the exchange in order to get around the monopolistically high commission rates they were being charged. "Both exchanges have asked the SEC to declare a moratorium on such further memberships until the commission produces a

These tendencies are clearly illustrated by the history of the American oil industry. Under the rule of capture, every landowner is entitled to whatever oil or gas he can draw up from the reservoir that lies under his own land and that of his neighbors. The result has been an irresistible temptation to terrible waste; no one landowner can afford to hold underground oil that his neighbor can suck up from under him. As a result, the several major producing states have instituted systems of direct production control, assigning specific quotas to each individual well (though exempting the majority of wells, which produce in relatively small volume). In addition, the provisions of the federal income tax law provide various special stimuli to encourage the exploration for and production of oil. The combination of these two circumstances has been to hold price far above the marginal cost of the large-capacity wells, whose output has been curtailed in the manner just-described. It has also apparently been for long periods of time below the ATC of new, successful explorers.

As a result, for ten to fifteen years after World War II, exploration continued apace and—until 1956—expanded rapidly. In addition, the sustained price gave rise to an artificially enhanced incentive to drill additional wells, on which one could then demand a production quota. The resultant expansion of capacity required a continuous tightening of production controls: wells were held to a lower and lower rate of production. The higher costs thus imposed on producers—with more and more investment in wells, with lower and lower production quotas—then clearly forced the extension of regulation to the control of well-drilling also. Finally, the resulting high costs and diminished profitability of domestic production encouraged producers to go into the foreign field. In time this—along with the natural expansion of low-cost foreign output—in conjunction with the artificially sustained domestic price threatened to drown the domestic market with a flood of imports. So once again the scope of regulation had to be extended: in 1959 mandatory controls were imposed on imports. And so it goes: one interference with competition necessitates another and yet another, and an industry of "rugged individualists" becomes more and more tightly enmeshed with the government to which they originally turned in hope of protecting themselves from competition.[68]

Technological progress—which may itself be stimulated by the monopoly pricing of the regulated service—tends likewise to break down cartels. And it confronts regulatory commissions with the dilemma of seeing their charges

set of guidelines." *Wall Street Journal*, June 10, 1969, 4. Fortunately for the economy, the cartelman's lot is not a nappy one, as Gilbert and Sullivan almost put it.

For a general explanation of the tendency of regulation to spread, see Lee Loevinger, "Regulation and Competition as Alternatives," *Antitrust Bull.* (Jan.–April 1966), XI: especially 117–123.

[68] This account is of course extremely sketchy. See, for a fuller analysis, Melvin G. de Chazeau and Alfred E. Kahn, *Integration and Competition in the Petroleum Industry* (New Haven: Yale Univ. Press, 1959), Chapters 6–10; Kahn, "The Depletion Allowance in the Context of Carteliza-

tion," *Amer. Econ. Rev.* (June 1964), LIV: 286–314, and "The Combined Effects of Prorationing, the Depletion Allowance and Import Quotas on the Cost of Producing Crude Oil in the United States," U.S. Senate, Committee on the Judiciary, Subcommittee on Antitrust and Monopoly, 91st Cong., 1st Sess., *Government Intervention in the Market Mechanism*, Hearings, *The Petroleum Industry*, Part 1 (Washington, 1969), 132–140; Paul T. Homan and Wallace F. Lovejoy, *Economic Aspects of Oil Conservation Regulation*, published for Resources for the Future by Johns Hopkins Press, Baltimore, 1967, and the forthcoming volume by Stephen L. McDonald on this subject.

lose business and the regulated price structure threatened with undermining —or trying to bring the new suppliers as well under the regulatory tent. The case of trucking is an obvious illustration; so, as we have seen, has been the development of new technology by the railroads—the unit train, the "Big John," piggybacking—in their effort to regain business from their competitors. This impact of new technology and the dilemmas it creates for a protectionist regulatory commission are nowhere more clearly illustrated than in the field of communications.[69]

But before we turn to that field, it is necessary to observe that cartelization is not the only reason legislatures and commissions find it necessary to spread the regulatory net wider and wider over time. A quite different but equally pervasive occasion, and one that has no necessary connection with protecting the interest of the regulated companies themselves, is to be found in the ingenuity of businessmen in seeking new and alternative ways of exploiting their monopoly power, when regulation has blocked certain paths to that goal.

For example, as the progress of technology in the 1920s and 1930s made increasingly feasible the interstate transmission of electricity and natural gas, local and state commissions found an increasingly large component of the cost of service of the companies under their jurisdiction—namely, the electric current or the gas imported from out of state—falling outside their reach.[70] This growing gap was filled by the Federal Power Act of 1935 and the Natural Gas Act of 1938, which conferred on the Federal Power Commission regulatory authority over those wholesale rates.[71]

The Public Utility Holding Company Act of 1935 represented a regulatory response to a similar kind of problem. As, during the 1920s, local gas and electricity distribution companies came under the control of the rapidly spreading network of holding companies, the local regulatory authorities found themselves, once again, unable to exercise jurisdiction over a large portion of the cost of service—in this case, the prices paid by the operating companies to their holding company affiliates, not only for power and gas but also for various technical, managerial, and financial services. The 1935 Act met this difficulty by vesting in the Securities and Exchange Commission authority to break up and to simplify the structure of the holding company

---

[69] See Walter Adams and Joel B. Dirlam, "Market Structure, Regulation, and Dynamic Change," in Harry Trebing, ed., *Performance under Regulation* (East Lansing, Mich.: MSU Public Utilities Studies, 1968), 131–144.

[70] See *State of Missouri v. Kansas Natural Gas Company*, 265 U.S. 298 (1924).

[71] See Chapter 17, "'Gaps' in the Regulatory Process and the Federal Dentist," in A. J. G. Priest, *Principles of Public Utility Regulation, Theory and Application* (Charlottesville: Michie Co., 1969), II: 523–556. On the important extensions of the FPC's authority over virtually all wholesale sales of electricity after 1961, on the ground that electricity generated and sold intrastate is "comingled" with electricity sold interstate— increasingly the case as the nation's electric utilities become more and more interconnected

(see pp. 64–65 and 314–323, Chapter 2 and 6 below)—see the leading *City of Colton* case, *FPC v. Southern California Edison Company*, 376 U.S. 205 (1964) and Louis Lister and Paul T. Homan, *Energy Industries and Public Policies in the United States*, draft ms. (Washington: Resources for the Future, 1968), Part IV, Chap. 2, 20–23. On the great importance of the *Colton* decision in safeguarding the competitive opportunities of publicly owned distributing companies, see pp. 322–323, Chapter 6, below. For similar developments in gas, see *FPC v. East Ohio Gas Co. et al.*, 338 U.S. 464 (1950), retracted by the so-called Hinshaw Amendment of 1954 to the Natural Gas Act (15 U.S.C. 717c, 1964) and the extension of the comingling doctrine in *California et al. v. Lo–Vaca Gathering Co. et al.*, 379 U.S. 366 (1965).

systems, reorganizing companies on functional and geographic lines, and also to regulate the charges made by parents to subsidiaries.[72]

Since these extensions of regulation were clearly necessary to close off newly developed avenues for the monopolistic exploitation of consumers, their necessity has not seriously been questioned by impartial observers. For the same reasons, they are, at least in retrospect, far less controversial than the extensions of regulation whose purpose has been to forestall or to restrict newly emergent *competition*.

This observation can certainly not be made, however, about the extension of the FPC's authority from control over the rates charged by interstate natural gas transmission lines to the prices those lines are charged for the natural gas that they purchase in the field from producing companies. The rationalization of this step was similar to the ones just described. The Natural Gas Act of 1938 had given the Commission jurisdiction over "the transportation of natural gas in interstate commerce" and "the sale in interstate commerce of natural gas for resale for ultimate public consumption," and had explicitly stated that its provisions were not to apply "to any other transportation or sale of natural gas or to the local distribution of natural gas or . . . to the production or gathering of natural gas."[73] Until 1954, the Commission had assumed, though not without dissent, that the explicit exemption of the "production or gathering of natural gas" was intended to deny it authority over the prices charged by producers or gatherers *to* pipelines, even though these too were "sales in interstate commerce for resale." Then, in its controversial *Phillips* decision of 1954, the Supreme Court instructed the FPC to see to it that the prices paid for natural gas in the field by pipeline companies were likewise "just and reasonable," holding that the statutory exemption of "production and gathering" did not extend to *sales* of gas by producers and gatherers. The Court justified this finding on the ground that it had been precisely the purpose of the 1938 Act to close the gap in regulation created by the inability of the local and state regulatory commissions to control the prices paid by local distribution companies for supplies purchased interstate, and that the price paid by interstate pipelines for gas purchased in the field was an important component that could not be neglected if regulation were to be effective.[74]

This particular extension of regulation has been much more controversial than those contemplated originally in the 1935 and 1938 Acts cited above, not only because it was by no means clear that this was the original intent of Congress but also because it was not established that the producers of natural gas had the kind and degree of monopoly power sufficient to justify extension of public-utility-type regulation to them. Effective regulation of local electricity rates has not typically been construed, for example, to require public-utility regulation of the prices charged electricity generating companies by sellers of residual fuel oil or coal, even though these constitute an important part of their total cost of service. The assumption has been that the industries supplying these important inputs have been sufficiently competitive to protect the consumer; and that as long as they remained financially independent, the regulated monopolists had no incentive to pay more than

---

[72] See also, on this topic, pp. 70–73, Chapter 2, below.

[73] 15 U.S.C. 717b, 1964 ed.

[74] *Phillips Petroleum Company v. Wisconsin et al.*, 347 U.S. 672, 681–685 (1954).

the competitive price. Whether the same is true of the field market for natural gas has been the subject of intense controversy.[75] In any event, the purpose and economic effects of this extension of regulation, like those involved in the Federal Power, Public Utility Holding Company and Natural Gas Acts of 1935 and 1938, were quite different from the cartellike, widening restrictions on competition that we have traced in the field of transportation.

Community Antenna Television

The Federal Communications Commission has the responsibility of licensing radio and television stations, as well as other users of the limited radio spectrum.[76] For television, there is room for only 12 channels on the very high-frequency (VHF) band, and the Commission had set aside 552 channels in this range for commercial stations in the contiguous 48 states as of June 1, 1967; 518 of those channels were actually occupied by authorized stations as of June 30, 1968.[77] In consequence principally of the physical limitation but partly also for economic reasons, approximately two-thirds of the country's communities receive only two or fewer signals.[78]

Into this breach stepped a new industry in the 1950s, community antenna television (CATV). These systems, by use of large receiving antennae, pick television signals directly off the air, amplify them and transmit them directly to subscribers by cable; they may also use microwave radio relay to bring the signals into the wire distribution system. Their contribution is to bring as many as twelve (and it may soon be twenty) signals, of high quality, into homes that could otherwise receive only one or two; their original success was therefore mainly in small towns.[79] In the 1960s, however, CATV entrepreneurs began to tap a much richer market in large cities, where their principal contribution is to offer signals of a far superior quality, free of interference from airplanes, electric motors, and reflection off buildings and other obstacles; but here, too, they have been able to offer the possibility of bringing in additional programs from the outside. In either event, CATV systems are direct competitors of local stations, which had theretofore

---

[75] See, for example, the masterly summary and survey in Lister and Homan, op. cit., Part II, Chap. 6, 3–20; also the discussions in our Volume 1, at pp. 40 note 49, 42 note 55, and 68 note 14.

[76] The relevant legislation has been the Radio Act of 1912 (37 Stat. 302), conferring limited regulatory authority on the Department of Commerce, the Radio Act of 1927 (44 Stat. 1162), and the Communications Act of 1934 (48 Stat. 1064). See 47 U.S.C. 151–609, 1964 ed.

[77] FCC, 34th Annual Report, Fiscal Year 1968 (Washington, 1969), 110.

[78] According to a 1965 study, only 95 of the 265 television markets in the continental United States had three or more stations, 172 had one or two—more than half of the latter only one. Martin H. Seiden, An Economic Analysis of Community Antenna Television Stations and the Television Broadcasting Industry, a Report to the Federal Communications Commission, Washing-

ton, February 12, 1965, 82. The total number of stations authorized increased from 668 to 835 between mid-1964 and mid-1968 (FCC, Annual Reports). But since by far the greater number of the entrants were in the UHF band and most of them in the larger cities, the situation in the smaller markets remains essentially the same, as far as the presence of local stations is concerned. FCC, Annual Reports, 1968, 110; 1964, 78. Also Leland L. Johnson, The Future of Cable Television: Some Problems of Federal Regulation (Santa Monica: The Rand Corporation, Memorandum RM–6199–FF, January 1970), 1–7.

[79] Of the 377 CATV systems established or franchised in the period from January 1960 through August 1964, 77 percent were located in areas that were not within 40 miles of two network signals and 91 percent in areas more than 40 miles away from three network signals; the majority of the remainder were in places with special terrain problems. Seiden, op. cit., 82.

enjoyed virtual monopolies (or oligopolies) in their receiving areas.[80]

Set up to prevent physical interference between competing users of the radio spectrum, the FCC now found its wards subject to *economic* competition. Its response was to extend its authority over the CATV systems—regardless of whether they actually used the limited spectrum.[81]

These initial regulations, promulgated in 1965 and 1966, have since been largely superseded. But they remain instructive, as illustrations of the protectionist bias of the regulatory institution. In its 1966 ruling, the Commission required, first, that all[82] CATV systems carry the signals of all local television stations in their vicinity. Although this rule, like the others,

---

[80] Between January 1, 1960 and January 1, 1969, the number of CATV systems increased from 640 to 2260, their subscribers from 650,000 to 3,600,000. Annual data from Television Digest, Inc., *Television Factbook*, reproduced in Johnson, *The Future of Cable Television*, 11. For a summary of a study concluding that:

"(1) CATV's economic impact on station revenues is substantial. (2) A significant percentage of existing stations, particularly in small markets, cannot withstand a relatively small increase in CATV penetration in their audience area without concomitant cost reduction. (3) A substantial percentage of potential new station entrants, particularly UHF, are likely to be discouraged from entry by a relatively small increase in CATV penetration in their potential audience area," see Franklin M. Fisher and Victor E. Ferrall, Jr., in association with David Belsley and Bridger M. Mitchell, "Community Antenna Television Systems and Local Television Station Audience," *Q. Jour. Econ.* (May 1966), LXXX: 250.

On the other hand, both Seiden (*op. cit.*, 5, 84–86) and the President's Task Force on Communications Policy (*Final Report*, Washington, 1968, Chapter VII, 10–11) have deprecated this competitive impact on existing stations and potential entrants. And while Johnson persuasively argues that unregulated CATV does indeed pose a serious threat to marginal broadcasters, he also emphasizes that, with proper safeguards, the relationship between the two can be complementary and mutually supportive. *The Future of Cable Television*, 68–73; see also note 111, below.

Although the immediate impact of CATV has been to introduce direct competition with television broadcasters, it offers the opportunity also for an exciting variety of quite different communications services—fire and burglary alarm systems, facsimile duplication of newspapers in the home, facsimile mail, linkage to computers, to video tape libraries, in short providing the communications link for a broad

spectrum of a city's mercantile and banking operations. Jack Gould, *New York Times*, October 15, 1967, Section 2, 25; and FCC, *In the Matter of Amendment of Part 74, Subpart K, of the Commission's Rules and Regulations Relative to Community Antenna Television Systems etc.*, Docket No. 18397 (hereinafter referred to by the docket number), Notice of Proposed Rule Making and Notice of Inquiry, December 12, 1968, par. 8–9, 60. See also the analysis by H. J. Barnett and E. Greenberg, "On the Economics of Wired City Television," *Amer. Econ. Rev.* (June 1968), LVIII: 503–508 and the proposal for community use of CATV advanced by Stephen White in "Toward a Modest Experiment in Cable Television," *The Public Interest*, Number 12 (Summer 1968), 52–66.

[81] The Commission had, as far back as 1956, successfully asserted its authority to impose certain engineering standards on CATV systems, in order to eliminate electrical interference between their signals and those of the regular broadcasters. FCC, *22nd Annual Report, for the Fiscal Year 1956*, Washington, 1956, 99–100. In its first attempt to assert economic jurisdiction, in 1965, the FCC confined its attention to the smaller portion of the industry that employed microwave relay service from communications common carriers to carry signals from their master antennae to their local cable distribution systems. *In the Matter of Amendment of Subpart L, Part II, To Adopt Rules and Regulations to Govern the Grant of Authorization . . . for Microwave Stations to Relay Television Signals to Community Antenna Systems*, First Report and Order, 38 FCC 683 (1965) (hereinafter referred to as *Microwave CATV*). In 1966, the Commission promulgated general rules covering all CATV systems, whether microwave-served or operated exclusively via antennae and cable. *Microwave CATV*, Second Report and Order, 2 FCC 2d 725 (1966). This final assertion of authority was upheld by the Supreme Court in *U.S. et al. v. Southwestern Cable Co. et al.*, 392 U.S. 157 (1968).

[82] Specifically exempted were systems serving less than fifty customers, or serving only as apartment house master antennae.

illustrates a tendency to protect the regulated companies from competition, it is difficult to take exception to it. A CATV system is itself a natural monopolist, within any given geographic region, subject to the familiar increasing returns with increasing intensity of use; it would obviously be inefficient to have more than one antenna and system of cables serving any particular locality. Moreover, the quality of the signal and service it provides is typically superior to that received by the set that takes its programs directly off the air; where cable service is available, therefore, many or most households attach themselves to it, and most of them give up their own antennae. If, then, this franchised monopolist were to refuse to carry the programs of local stations over its facilities, it could well deprive them of a market and drive them out of business. This would be in its own interest because it would deprive householders of their one alternative source of television programs and thereby force anyone who wished to enjoy television at all to enter the lists of its subscribers. It would enhance its monopoly power in dealing with local advertisers as well.[83] Finally, it would have the indirect effect of completely depriving of television service people in nearby rural areas too sparsely inhabited to justify extension of the cable. Here is an example of a situation in which it may be necessary to compel regulated companies to cooperate.[84] It illustrates the fact, also, that none of the institutional issues we confront in these chapters can intelligently be posed as a simple, once-and-for-all choice between competition and regulation, since either system is subject to imperfections of varying intensity and mischievousness.

Second, the Commission forbade CATV operators to duplicate programs broadcast by local stations during the same day. The earlier version of this rule, adopted in April, 1965, had forbidden duplication of local broadcasts within a much greater period—15 days before and 15 days after. This second restriction on competition was clearly more questionable than the first, as is indicated by its considerable modification in the 1966 as compared with the 1965 order. A rule prohibiting precisely simultaneous duplication, it would seem, would have been unobjectionable: for a CATV system, required in any event to carry the programs of the local stations, to bring the identical programs to their subscribers on more than one channel at the same time would serve no purpose but diversion, with a consequent threat to the continued viability of the local station. But it clearly limits viewers' choices to deny them the opportunity of seeing the same program at some other time during the same broadcast day.

Still, there was some justification in principle for this protectionist policy as well, tracing back to the fact that the fundamental conditions for effective

---

[83] Station operators had, in fact, complained to the FCC that their CATV competitors were refusing to carry their programs. FCC, *32nd Annual Report for the Fiscal Year 1966*, Washington, 1967, 85.

[84] CATV carriage of the programs of a local station is not costless; it would ordinarily have to be at the expense of carrying the programs of some other, outlying station. In most instances, however, it would appear that the programs in question would be those of one of the three national networks, and the choice would therefore merely be one of bringing in identical programs from the local or from the outlying station. It would appear in such instances that forcing the CATV operator to transmit the programs of the local station would have no cost to the viewer—since the programs sacrificed would be identical—and would preserve an important alternative source of broadcasts and possible program origination.

competition, large numbers of sellers and freedom of entry, are physically impossible in this industry.[85] Since the justification is a rather complicated one, it will be helpful to outline its major components, before proceeding to explain each. They are:

1. Unregulated competition in these circumstances can not produce economically optimal results;
2. One possible cure is to impose on broadcast licensees certain obligations with respect to programming that may conflict with their self interest;
3. In return, it may be necessary to protect them from the competition of CATV companies that merely import programs originated by others without paying for them.

The competition among the limited number of stations and networks that can reach homes in any one locality is competition for an audience that does not, as such, pay for the programs it views. The goal of each competitor is to deliver the attention of a maximum number of viewers to advertisers, who are the ones who foot the bills and whose interest is, of course, in getting the largest and most receptive audience possible for their commercial messages. Where broadcasters compete in this way for audience, they necessarily aim their programs at the "least common denominator," at the mass market; this produces a high degree of similarity in their programming. And this has the result that commercial broadcasters make less than optimum use of the limited channels available *even in the purely economic sense*—that is, taking as the test of optimality whether the limited spectrum is employed to generate the maximum of viewer satisfaction over cost of production and transmission, taking consumer or viewer preferences as they are, not as they would be if consumers had better taste.

With free entry, no block of demand for a particular variety of product that is willing to pay the costs of serving it need or will go unsatisfied. When, instead, the number of sellers is limited, there may be a conflict between the self-interest of each on the one hand and the interest of all their customers, taken together, on the other. Each one may feel himself forced to come as close as possible to duplicating the service of the other, in hope of getting a share of the mass market, even though most of the sales he gains in this manner are merely diverted from his competitors.[86] What happens in television, thus, is that the mass audience is spread among all competing stations by minor differences in the programs they offer, while other viewers with more specialized tastes go unsatisfied entirely. If, instead, the firms were jointly owned or pooled their revenues, it would be in their collective interest to make a composite offering of greater variety, in order to maximize their

---

[85] This limitation was particularly intense until at least the late 1960s, when commercial broadcasting was virtually confined to the very-high frequency (VHF) range. The technical progress that opened up the ultrahigh-frequency range (UHF), coupled with the passage of the all-channel television receiver law in 1962 (76 Stat. 150)—which required that all television sets manufactured thereafter be equipped to receive UHF and so promised in time to eliminate the principal obstacle to entry of new UHF stations, the fact that very few receivers were equipped to receive their signals—opened up the possibility of a substantial expansion in the number of competitive stations in any given place.

[86] On this general tendency of competing sellers to cluster, with the result that "buyers are confronted everywhere with an excessive sameness," see the historic article of Harold Hotelling, "Stability in Competition," *Econ. Jour.* (March 1929), XXXIX: 54.

aggregate audience. The latter course could well produce more total viewer satisfaction than the former. The mass audience, that is to say, might still be retained with little loss in satisfaction by an offering that contained one fewer typical commercial program at any given time, leaving the single, released station free, then, to program for a very different kind of audience. But this is something that the individual commercial station would be unwilling to do as long as it could hope by conventional programming to attract away from other commercial competitors a larger number of viewers than it could obtain by radically different programming.[87]

The FCC's historic response to these problems was certainly not illogical. It has placed its major emphasis on encouraging the entry of additional stations, particularly in the still largely vacant UHF spectrum: the major step in this program was passage of the all-channel receiver law, which promised in a few years to assure that almost all sets would be equipped to receive UHF programs.[88] And it has proclaimed—though unfortunately hardly enforced[89]—a policy of pressing local stations to generate their own local, public service programs, as a condition of keeping their valuable franchises. Given this orientation, its desire to keep local stations alive in the face of CATV competitors importing mainly national commercial programs was understandable. (On the other hand, it is difficult to reconcile this reasoning with the Commission's historic hostility to program origination by the CATV companies themselves—a theme of FCC policy to which we shall turn presently.)

The Commission's protectionist policy may be justified, also, on grounds of externalities. We have already had one example of this—the loss of television service to inhabitants of rural areas, which cannot economically be reached by CATV, if competition by the cable in town drives the local station out of business or discourages the entry of another. The CATV customers, naturally, do not take this external cost into account in deciding whether to subscribe. In fact, those customers might, by subscribing to an unrestricted CATV service, be imposing a similar external cost *on themselves*: they too might place considerable value on the continued operation of the local station, as the sole possible source of locally originated programming, even though each willingly subscribes to the cable service when it is offered to him. The effect of a general acceptance of that service in forcing the local station out of business would be an external cost of those individual subscription decisions; it would pay no one viewer to refuse to subscribe in hope of keeping the local station alive, because the effect of his individual abstention in this respect would be miniscule; it would take collective action or

[87] See, for example, Peter O. Steiner, "Program Patterns and Preferences, and the Workability of Competition in Radio Broadcasting," *Q. Jour. Econ.* (May 1952), LXVI: 194–223; Jerome Rothenberg, "Consumer Sovereignty and the Economics of TV Programming," *Studies in Public Communication*, No. 4 (Autumn 1962), 45–49; and Joel B. Dirlam and Alfred E. Kahn, "The Merits of Reserving the Cost-Savings from Domestic Communications Satellites for Support of Educational Television," *Yale Law Jour.* (January 1968), LXXVII: 514–518. See on the

other hand the argument by John J. McGowan, "Competition, Regulation, and Performance in Television Broadcasting," *Washington Univ. Law Q.*, Fall 1967, 499–520, especially 507–513, to the effect that the individual broadcasters are under considerable pressure to differentiate their offerings during any programming period and will therefore come closer to maximizing their aggregate audience and profits than is suggested by the foregoing exposition.

[88] See note 85, above.

[89] See pp. 89–90, Chapter 2, below.

regulation to prevent the disappearance of this alternative source of supply. The market does not give viewers a separate, effective opportunity to express the intensity of their desire to keep this alternative option available.[90]

The fact remains that the FCC adopted a protectionist approach to ensuring optimal use of the limited airways; it sought to encourage the entry of new, commercially marginal stations (particularly in the opening-up UHF spectrum) *by protecting them as well as existing local stations from competition.*[91] Its reaction to CATV was clearly affected by the threat that this innovation posed to its own regulatory program, as well as to the survival of the many local stations who hastened to complain about this new competition. The fact remains, moreover, that CATV, too, offered viewers increased alternatives, though in a manner different from the one envisaged by the Commission. It was obviously providing a new service that subscribers were anxious to have. The FCC reaction, therefore, though moderate and measured, was a typical regulatory reaction. When considered in conjunction with its almost complete failure in practice to hold local stations to its proclaimed standards of performance, as we shall see in Chapter 2, the essentially protectionist character of its policies becomes even more manifest.

It would be impossible on economic grounds to quarrel with the Commission's purpose of encouraging the maximum number of economically viable stations and sources of programming, consistent with physically good signals. But if that effort was limited by the economically marginal character of many stations (both those in existence and those on the margin of entry), the better solution, it would seem, would have been not to impose restraints on the CATV alternative, but to broaden the geographic coverage of the

---

[90] Much of this reasoning is developed by Franklin M. Fisher, "Community Antenna Television Systems and the Regulation of Television Broadcasting," *Amer. Econ. Rev., Papers and Proceedings* (May 1966), LVI: 320–329. For a general analysis of this particular kind of market failure, in which the disappearance of facilities available to satisfy "option demand"—the desire to have certain services *available* for use, even though one does not necessarily use them sufficiently to keep them economically alive—is exposed as an external cost, see Burton A. Weisbrod, "Collective-Consumption Services of Individual-Consumption Goods," *Q. Jour. Econ.* (August 1964), LXXVIII: 471–477.

I have characterized these market failures as issuing from the "tyranny of small decisions": the decision by each subscriber whether to take CATV service is a "small" decision; neither individually nor collectively do subscribers and rural nonsubscribers ever have the opportunity to cast their dollar votes with respect to the "large decision" of whether the local stations should be kept alive. *Op. cit., Kyklos* (1966), XIX: 23–47.

[91] This protective attitude is in interesting contrast to the Commission's traditional position with respect to radio that "under the Communications Act economic injury to a competitor

is not a ground for refusing a broadcasting license," *FCC v. Sanders Brothers Radio Station*, 309 U.S. 470, 472 (1940), a view upheld by the Supreme Court:

"We hold that resulting economic injury to a rival station is not in and of itself, and apart from considerations of public convenience, interest, or necessity, an element the petitioner [the FCC] must weigh, and as to which it must make findings, in passing on an application for a broadcasting license. . . .

"The sections dealing with broadcasting [in the Communications Act] demonstrate that Congress has not, in its regulatory scheme, abandoned the principle of free competition, as it has done in the case of railroads. . . .

"the broadcasting field is open to anyone, provided there be an available frequency over which he can broadcast without interference to others, if he shows his competency, the adequacy of his equipment, and financial ability to make good use of the assigned channel.

"The policy of the Act is clear that no person is to have anything in the nature of a property right as a result of the granting of a license. . . .

"Plainly it is not the purpose of the Act to protect a licensee against competition but to protect the public." *Ibid.*, 473–475. For other examples, see Jones, *op. cit.*, pp. 1094–1105.

television markets each is licensed to serve.[92] Such a course of action, too, would have diminished the competitive attractiveness of CATV, whose primary appeal was that it brought into markets theretofore served by less than three stations the additional signals available from a distance; but it would have done so by loosening the restrictions on existing suppliers rather than tightening the controls over the threatening competitors. If the Commission's purpose was merely to encourage local programming it could have imposed requirements to this effect on the CATV operators as well—rather than restricting their right to originate their own programs and to sell advertising.[93] And if the still necessarily few stations serving any particular area do not provide optimum program variety, far more effective than the restriction on CATV and the exertion of feeble pressures on every small community in the United States to generate it own programs would be direct public subsidies to public television,[94] the exertion of powerful pressures on the major networks to expand their efforts in this direction, and, above all, a far more strenuous insistence that the local franchise holders accept more of the excellent public service programs that the networks already make available to them.[95]

The core of monopoly power in this industry is in the local, franchised station. It has the exclusive right to a portion of the spectrum, which it sells off to the highest bidder. Not surprisingly, it is here that the highest profits[96]

---

[92] This was the recommendation of Seiden, *op. cit.*, 7, 89–90.

[93] For reference to some relatively limited local programming by CATV operators and their promise in this regard, see Edward Greenberg, "Wire Television and the FCC's Second Report and Order on CATV Systems," *Jour. Law and Econ.* (October 1967), X: 185–186. As of 1968 or so, about 10 percent of the CATV systems originated some of their own programs. *Fortnightly Corporation v. United Artists Television, Inc.* 392 U.S. 390, 392, note 6 (1968). On the later shift of FCC policy in these respects, see pp. 43–45, below.

[94] See, for example, Carnegie Commission on Educational Television, *Public Television: A Program for Action*, New York, 1967; Sidney S. Alexander, "Public Television and the 'Ought' of Public Policy," *Washington Univ. Law Q.*, Winter 1968, 35–70.

[95] It is my impression that the local network affiliates exercise their rights of program selection far more often to refuse the public service than the commercial programs proffered by the networks, precisely because this is what it would be in their financial interest to do. In his justly famous "vast wasteland" speech, Newton M. Minow, then chairman of the FCC, referred to this practice and expressed the opinion that local stations should be required to explain all such refusals. *The New York Times*, May 10, 1961, 79. The failure of the Commission to adopt such a policy, imposing entirely proper conditions on its free gift of valuable franchises to broadcaster applicants, provides yet another illustration of pusillanimous regulation.

For this failure Congress must share a large portion of the blame: the speed with which it responds to the complaints of broadcasters when the Commission moves to regulate them more effectively, accompanied by irrelevant outcries against "public censorship," borders on the scandalous—particularly when it is recognized that many Congressmen themselves have financial interests in broadcasting stations. For a particularly flagrant example, as well as a discussion of the censorship issue, see pp. 91–92, and note 129, p. 90, below.

[96] Strictly speaking, these represent not monopoly profits but economic rents, the scarcity value of the nonreproducible natural resource the disposition of which the franchisee controls. As we have suggested in Volume 1 (p. 88, notes 2 and 4), if this resource were sold off at auction, bidders would have to pay a price that reflected the marginal opportunity cost of their having it—that is, the value of that portion of the spectrum to the next-highest bidder. If this were done, it would have not only the attraction on distributional grounds that the rents would accrue to the taxpayer rather than to private parties, but also that the spectrum would be allocated in the most efficient fashion (that is, to those to whom it was the most valuable, by the test of the competitive market) and users would be under strong pressure to use it economically. See Coase, *op. cit.* On the other hand, as Harvey J. Levin has suggested (most thoroughly in a manuscript

are earned: in the four-year period 1964–1967, the VHF stations as a group earned an extraordinary average of 75.3 percent before taxes on the depreciated value of their investment in tangible broadcasting property. (True, the three major networks earned even more—148.9 percent; but this figure represents a lumping together of the much higher returns from their own stations and the much lower return on their networking operations as such.)[97]

The third restraint that the FCC imposed on CATV in its 1966 order was the most flagrantly protectionist of all. We have already referred to the tendency of the cable systems to move into the larger television markets, in part because of their ability to bring in sharper signals, in part because subscribers have appreciated their ability to bring in additional "foreign" programs not otherwise available locally. Because the Commission has its highest hopes of inducing the entry of UHF stations in these relatively rich markets it was particularly anxious to prevent the spread of CATV there. It was also, apparently, concerned lest the CATV systems begin to provide for pay-television—something that is most likely to be feasible in concentrated urban areas. Accordingly, it proclaimed that

"Parties who obtain state or local franchises to operate CATV systems in the 100 highest ranked television markets . . . will be required to obtain FCC approval before CATV service to subscribers may be commenced. . . .

"An evidentiary hearing will be held as to all such requests for FCC approval. . . . These hearings will be concerned primarily with (a) the potential effects of the proposed CATV operation on the full development of off-the-air television outlets (particularly UHF) for that market, and (b) the relationship, if any, of proposed CATV operations and the development of pay television in that market. . . .

"the Commission will entertain petitions objecting [also] to the geographical extension to new areas of CATV systems already in operation in the top 100 television markets."[98]

---

on spectrum management, to be published around 1970 by Resources for the Future), society might instead choose to demand those rents "in kind"—demanding from the broadcasters standards of performance—that is, of programming—that would, because of their external benefits, otherwise justify taxpayer subsidization. An outstanding example would be the provision of free air time for political candidates.

[97] Computed from figures in FCC, *Annual Reports*. For figures for the period 1958–1966 and supporting references for these conclusions, see Dirlam and Kahn, *op. cit.*, *Yale Law Jour.* (January 1968), LXXVII: Table 1 and 497–499. Of course, the high *average* profits of television stations conceal an extremely wide spread. The UHF stations as a group have lost money every year since 1965 (*ibid.*, 509n and FCC, *Annual Reports*; the 1968 figures are the latest ones available as of this writing).

So the FCC's concern that CATV might discourage the entry of new UHF stations was not necessarily groundless— see notes 80, above, and 98,

below—though it may have been misguided.

[98] FCC, Public Notice, "FCC Announces Plan for Regulation of all CATV Systems," Washington, February 15, 1966, mimeo., 2. No such hearing was to be required for proposed CATV systems or operations in markets ranking below the top 100. "However, the Commission will entertain, on an *ad hoc* basis, petitions from interested parties concerning the carriage of distant signals by CATV systems located in such smaller markets." *Ibid.*

In 1968, by a 4–3 vote, the FCC overturned the opinion of its hearing examiner and found in the experience of CATV companies bringing Los Angeles signals into San Diego a competitive threat to local UHF stations great enough to justify its imposing limitations on the former companies. *In the Matter of the Petition of Midwest Television, Inc. et al.*, Decision, Docket No. 16786, 13 FCC 2d 478 (1968). These findings in turn provided the justification for its proposals later that year to continue restrictions on CATV entry into the top 100 markets. See p. 44, below.

When the Commission requires CATV systems to carry the signals of local stations and forbids their duplicating those programs within a short time period it does not subject viewers to appreciable deprivation. But when, in its zeal to protect local stations, it forbade the cable systems bringing in entirely different programs, indicated that it would subject any such applications to the test of whether they might impede the entry of new stations, and announced that it would ask Congress for a "prohibition of the origination of programs or other materials by a CATV system with such limitations or exceptions, if any, as are deemed appropriate,"[99] it unmistakably set out on the same well-marked path as the ICC has been following for at least the preceding thirty years.

One theme that runs through the FCC's 1966 opinion and order is a suspicion if not outright hostility toward pay or subscription TV; the Commission was at least tentatively aligning itself with the other interested parties battling to "save free TV."[100] First of all, "free TV" is hardly free. Viewers themselves buy their seats and pay for repairs and electricity; advertisers pay billions of dollars to television networks and stations and no one has suggested that this comes out of the profits of their stockholders; and the industry makes free use of a crowded spectrum from which other potential users are excluded—and we have already seen that the opportunity cost of using a congested facility is certainly not zero.[101] True, the viewer as such does not pay for the costs of programming and transmission. But it is not clear what virtue there is in having this particular price held to zero—rather than, say, the price of food or medicine—particularly when poor people pay it, willy-nilly, when they buy the products that are advertised on television.

The present system of financing television programming has the one, major economic virtue of conforming to the fact that, as Samuelson has pointed out,[102] television is in one important respect a public good—that is, one whose marginal cost is zero. This is the case when the dimension of output is taken to be the supply of programs to additional viewers: it adds nothing to aggregate costs if more rather than fewer people turn on their sets. It makes economic sense from this standpoint, therefore, that the price is zero: other than the costs of electricity and a more rapid wearing out of the receiver (both of which are, of course, incremental costs and quite properly borne by the viewer), the viewer pays no charge for tuning in a program.

On the other hand, when the dimension of output is the production of programs, there are very definite, positive marginal costs: it is obviously possible to expend fewer or more resources on program quality. And in as

---

[99] *Ibid.*, 3.

[100] "CATV is a form of pay-TV. . . . there are substantial numbers of people who either cannot afford to or do not wish to pay for television. If then the CATV blocks development of UHF broadcasting, it would again mean that some people would be getting additional service at the expense of those who cannot afford or are unwilling to pay for such service." 2 FCC 2d 725, 775 (1966); see also 787, where the Commission recommends that Congress prohibit program-origination by CATV systems.

[101] See the references in note 96, above, and especially Levin, "The Radio Spectrum Resource," *Jour. Law and Econ.* (October 1968), XI: 433–501.

[102] Paul A. Samuelson, "A Pure Theory of Public Expenditure," *Rev. Econ. Stat.* (November 1954), XXXVI: 387–389; "Diagrammatic Exposition of a Theory of Public Expenditure," *ibid.* (November 1955), XXXVII: pp. 350–356, and "Aspects of Public Expenditure Theories," *ibid.* (November 1958), XL: 332–338.

much as viewers do not have to pay prices for programs of varying qualities reflecting those varying incremental costs, the economic propriety of those production outlays is not subjected to the familiar market test. There *is* a market test, of sorts, which does to some extent serve as a proxy for the market's directly ascertaining what viewers would be willing to pay for programs of varying qualities: the charges are borne by advertisers, and they undoubtedly do compare marginal costs of more expensive programming with the value of the additional audiences that it is expected to attract. But since much of the advertising conducted in a monopolistically competitive economy is not informational but hortatory and mutually offsetting —with advertiser A forced to devote resources to this purpose merely in order to prevent diversion of sales to advertiser B, and B operating under a similar pressure, but with both able in imperfect markets to pass on all or part of the costs to buyers of their products—it seems a fair conclusion that this particular method results in an overallocation of resources into television transmission and programming—more, that is, than would be justified if the viewers themselves were confronted with prices correctly reflecting the marginal costs of increasing output along these dimensions.[103]

Moreover, the interests of advertisers must be a very imperfect representative of the tastes and desires of viewers. The former are interested in maximizing the net monetary value (over cost) of the television programming they sponsor measured in terms of the response of viewers as purchasers of their products, rather than the maximum net satisfaction of their audience as viewers of the programs.

"To take a simple-minded example, suppose that the more intelligent (or better-educated) the viewer the more impervious he is to advertising messages. Then, to the extent advertisers are rational, the interests and tastes of the more intelligent potential viewers will carry less weight in program selection than those of the more gullible purchasers of the advertised product."[104]

"In the 'Golden Age' of television drama, the advertisers believed that the ideal play for television must not be too boring or the viewer would switch to another channel, nor too interesting or the viewer would resent the commercial break."[105]

Pay or subscription television is, in a sense, the other side of this coin. It has the disadvantage of imposing a positive charge, with the result that some families are deterred from viewing from which they would derive positive satisfaction, even though the marginal costs of supplying them are zero. On

---

[103] On the tendency toward an excessive allocation of resources to advertising, see Nicholas Kaldor, "The Economic Aspects of Advertising," *Rev. Econ. Studies* (1949–1950), XVIII: 1–27; compare Lester G. Telser, "Supply and Demand for Advertising Messages," *Amer. Econ. Rev., Papers and Proceedings* (May 1966), LVI: 457–466, and especially the comments by Harold J. Barnett and Peter O. Steiner, *ibid.*, 467 and 472–474.

My student, Keith Anderson, has pointed to an offsetting consideration. The marginal revenue (to the advertiser) of (additional) expenditures on programming is probably a function predominantly of the additional viewers it will attract. But the marginal satisfaction thereby generated from the social standpoint is the additional enjoyment thus conferred on *all* viewers, including those who would have tuned in even to less expensive programs. This consideration suggests a tendency to *under*allocation of resources to programming, since the benefit to the advertiser (who pays for it) is less than the total social benefit.

[104] Dirlam and Kahn, *op. cit.*, *Yale Law Jour.* (January 1968), LXXVII: 517–518.

[105] Gore Vidal, "Classy TV," *New York Review of Books*, December 7, 1967, 25.

the other hand, it has the major advantage of affording a market test with respect to both the appropriate quantity of resources to put into television and their proper distribution between different kinds of programs.[106] Neither system, therefore, is ideal; but it would seem that the closest approach to the ideal would be to permit both to coexist, in competition.[107]

Another consideration influencing the FCC's decision to impose restrictions on CATV systems was its feeling that their competition with regular broadcasters is unfair, since the CATV operators do not have to pay for the programs that they pick out of the air and transmit, at a rental, to their subscribers.[108] This issue was raised in an intriguing manner in 1966, when on the complaint by a company that owned copyrights to motion pictures, a U. S. District Court held that such CATV operations involve "performing" the works in question and therefore infringe the copyright if done without a license.[109] In consequence of this unfavorable decision, CATV operators began negotiations with the broadcasting industry, and it appeared that a compromise settlement might emerge in which the broadcasters would waive their claim for royalties in exchange for an agreement by CATV companies not to originate any programs of their own.[110] Like the FCC's own 1966 decision, this would surely have protected the regular broadcasters from competition.

This particular threat to competition was at least temporarily forestalled in 1968 when the Supreme Court reversed the lower court opinion, holding that the operations of the CATV systems were analogous not to performance of the copyrighted works but to the mere viewing of them.[111] But, as will

---

[106] See the exchange between Jora R. Minasian, "Television Pricing and the Theory of Public Goods," and Paul A. Samuelson, "Public Goods and Subscription TV: Correction of the Record," *Jour. Law and Econ.* (October 1964), VII: 71–83. Minasian, ignoring the tendency for an excessive allocation of resources to advertising, concludes that more rather than fewer resources would probably be drawn into the industry under a system of pay-television. It is not necessary, for our purposes, to decide whether his prediction or ours is correct, although it is difficult to imagine the average American family being willing to have its television set going five or six hours a day if it had to pay more than the present zero charge. More important is our agreement that the present system does not produce the appropriate allocation.

[107] On the presence or absence of an unsatisfied demand for pay-television, see David M. Blank, "The Quest for Quantity and Diversity in Television Programming," *Amer. Econ. Rev., Papers and Proceedings* (May 1966), LVI: 452–454, and the comments by Harold J. Barnett, Hyman H. Goldin and Peter O. Steiner, *ibid.*, 467–475.

[108] *Microwave CATV*, First Report and Order, 38 FCC 683, 704–705 (1965).

[109] *United Artists Television, Inc. v. Fortnightly Corporation*, 255 F. Supp. 177 (1966).

[110] *New York Times*, June 18, 1968, 96.

[111] "Essentially, a CATV system no more than enhances the viewer's capacity to receive the broadcaster's signals; it provides a well-located antenna with an efficient connection to the viewer's television set. It is true that a CATV system plays an 'active' role in making reception possible . . . but so do ordinary television sets and antennas." *Fortnightly Corp. v. United Artists Television*, 392 U.S. 390, 399 (1968).

The economic merits of the issue are complicated. As far as network programming is concerned, it is difficult to see that the claim for copyright protection has any validity. Broadcasters sell the attention of viewers to advertisers. Anything that increases their audience increases the value of their service. So it is the networks that pay the local stations to induce them to carry their programs—not the other way around —by sharing advertising revenues with them. By the same token, the networks justify their expenditures on programming in terms of the audiences that the programs promise to attract. The larger the audience, the greater the value to them of such programs—and the larger a price a copyright owner of a program could expect to get from them. When CATV operators pick up the broadcast signals and bring them to a larger number of viewers, they are obviously increasing the value of what the networks sell to advertisers

appear presently, the FCC promptly demonstrated once again that it was not dependent on the copyright laws to protect stations from CATV competition.

Fortunately, the persuasive power of a rapidly developing technology is extremely difficult to resist. Within two and one-half years of its 1966 order, the FCC issued a proposed notice of rule making for CATV that was practically ecstatic about its vast and versatile potential for offering a previously undreamt-of variety of communication services, while saving on use of the limited radio spectrum.[112] In this statement, the Commission seemed also to recognize how much more richly CATV promised to achieve the very goals it had previously sought by protecting local stations from its competition—to increase the number of alternative programs offered to the householder and, in particular, the possibility of catering to minority tastes and the opportunities for local and public service programming.[113] Accordingly, it now proposed actually to *require* CATV operators to originate their own programming as a condition of being permitted to operate at all, and to encourage them also to lease channels to others for the same purpose.[114]

---

and the value of the films and programs sold to the networks. It is difficult to see any justification, therefore, for charging them royalties. In a competitive market, it would seem, they too, like the local stations, might successfully claim compensation from the network for their contribution; broadcasters would compete to induce them to accept and retransmit their programs.

To some extent these same considerations should apply to programming that originates with the local station. It too can charge advertisers more or less—and afford to pay more or less for the films or other programs it rents—depending on the size of its audience; and CATV increases the number of viewers it can reach. But much of the local station's revenue comes from the sale of time to local advertisers, who may not find it any more valuable because CATV systems carry their messages into other localities: to this extent CATV does the station no favor; but neither does it do it any injury.

None of this is to deny that CATV competes with the local station into whose territory it carries programs from the outside—the very competition that the FCC was trying to curb. What it denies is that the stations whose signals it carries have any legitimate economic complaint against them worth honoring.

On the other hand, the independent program producer may actually be injured in these circumstances, in such a way as to diminish the value of his copyright. He obtains a large part of his revenues by selling programs to individual stations for subsequent runs, after the network showing. Here it is the station that pays, receiving its reimbursement directly from national and local spot advertisers. Many of these, as just suggested, are interested only in the local audiences. To the extent this is the case, the

CATV systems increase neither what the advertiser is willing to pay to the originating station nor what the latter is willing to pay the copyright owner, when they carry those programs into other cities. But in so doing, they reduce what local stations in those other cities will either at that time or thereafter be willing to pay for the program: they have reduced its value for those showings in the other cities. (I am indebted to A. Frank Reel for pointing this out to me.)

So in effect CATV does diminish the ability of a copyright owner to parcel out the privilege of showing his property in separate markets in such a way as to maximize his return. But that is what competition does, too.

For a careful analysis of the merits of requiring cable systems to pay for the programs they import, concluding that on balance such a requirement would provide a desirable stimulus to additional and more diversified programming, see Johnson, *The Future of Cable Television*, 14–40.
[112] See the reference to its discussion of this potential at note 80, this chapter, above.
[113] Docket No. 18937, Notice of Proposed Rule Making and Notice of Inquiry, December 12, 1968, pars. 4–10.
[114] *Ibid.*, par. 15.

"We believe that the public interest would be served by encouraging CATV to operate as a common carrier on any remaining channels not utilized for carriage of broadcast signals and CATV origination. This would provide an outlet for others to present programs of their own choosing. . . . It might also provide a low cost outlet for political candidates, possibly advertisers, programs on a subscription basis, and various modestly funded organizations and entities in the community who may be unable to afford time on or obtain access to broadcast

It expressed a willingness also to consider wider use of CATV as an instrument for introducing pay-TV, that is, by a per program or a higher monthly charge (Par. 17). In late 1969, it put the first of these proposals into effect, ordering all CATV systems with 3500 or more subscribers, as a condition of being permitted to carry the signals broadcast by others, to operate "also to a significant extent as a local outlet by cablecasting," and it encouraged smaller systems to do the same.[115]

But the FCC was not prepared, as of December 1968, entirely to give up its protectionist policies. In the *Notice of Proposed Rule-Making*, issued that month, it announced that it was ready to consider prohibiting CATV stations from selling time to advertisers, giving no justification other than that otherwise CATV competition might impair the viability of competing stations (pars. 17–18). Still concerned that the "unfair" competition by CATV operators importing signals into the largest (100) markets[116] could discourage the entry of new UHF stations there, it proposed not, as before, to deny licenses in these cases but to require the CATV operator to obtain the consent of the originating stations for that retransmission (pars. 32–43).[117] In this way, the Commission in effect proposed to hand back to the broadcasters the opportunity that the Supreme Court had taken away from them in the *Fortnightly* decision just six months earlier, to suppress CATV competition in the very markets in which the most extraordinarily profitable stations are located.[118] It had no intention of giving up the responsibility for

---

facilities. And it might further provide a means for municipal authorities to fulfill any of their communications needs. . . ." *Ibid.*, par. 26. For an intriguing discussion of some of the problems and prospects of CATV systems operating as common carriers, see Johnson, *The Future of Cable Television*, 54–61.

At the same time, properly recognizing the naturally monopolistic character of CATV service, the FCC proposed to limit the number of program originations by the CATV operator himself as well as to consider various possible regulatory controls to prevent concentration of control over alternative communications media, excessive rates, and to assure "reasonable opportunity for the discussion of conflicting views on issues of public importance." Pars. 20 and 19–25, passim.

[115] *In the Matter of Amendment of Part 74, Subpart K, of the Commission's Rules and Regulations Relative to Community Antenna Television Systems, etc.*, Docket No. 18937, First Report and Order, October 24, 1969, 20 FCC 2d 201, Appendix; see also pars. 19–20, 26–28.

[116] "both the CATV system and the broadcast station are . . . competing for audience—yet the one pays for its product and the other, without any payment, brings the same material into the community by simply importing the distant signals. . . ." *Ibid.*, par. 35. But see note 111, above.

[117] It made this proposal for the large markets

only, on the grounds that these were the ones in which new UHF stations were most likely to be able to enter and that the smaller markets have a clear need for the additional signals that CATV brings in. But the Commission promised to keep its eye on the smaller markets as well, and

"to take such action as may be appropriate . . . where there is a substantial public interest showing, e.g., that . . . the cumulative effect of existing and proposed CATV operations . . . would jeopardize the likelihood of [an independent station's] obtaining or retaining a network affiliation or of maintaining audiences large enough to attract needed advertiser support." Par. 55.

[118] That this danger was not purely hypothetical is indicated by the resumption of negotiations between the National Association of Broadcasters and representative of the cable companies. Out of these emerged a tentative agreement to be recommended for FCC approval that would have permitted cable companies to carry up to six commercial channels, including imported signals from distant cities, but would on the other hand have prohibited them from making interconnections such as might eventually produce a new and competitive national network. So once again the FCC seemed ready to deliver into the hands of the broadcasters a weapon that they could use to exact agreements restricting the competitive threat of CATV. The agreement fell apart, however, in mid-1969. *New York Times*, June 21, 1969.

deciding, itself, whether CATV operators were "importing signals from *unnecessarily* distant centers or in such quantity as to *unduly fractionalize* the . . . potential audience of stations in these . . . markets."[119] As Commissioner Bartley pithily summarized the issue in his dissent:

> "The interim procedures, are, I believe, contrary to the public interest because they deny to the people of the United States a communications service for which they have shown a demand in the market place."[120]

But even these protectionist reservations were doomed to continued erosion by the new technology. By October of 1969, persuaded that the CATV systems might not be able to initiate their own programs without additional revenues, the FCC was ready to permit them to sell advertising, provided they presented the messages only at natural breaks and only in connection with their own original programming.[121] And in May of 1970, by a 4 to 3 vote and in an almost complete turnabout, it instructed its staff to bring in proposals that would free CATV systems to import programs into the 100 largest cities as well as all others.[122]

See the attack on the proposed agreement and the implied criticism of the FCC in the *Comments of the U.S. Department of Justice*, FCC Docket 18397, September 5, 1969, processed, 2–3, 10, 13–14, 17–18, and the later repudiation by the Commission of any limitations on the ability of CATV systems to interconnect on a regional or national basis—a development that it recognized could offer new competition with the three major networks. First Report and Order, *op. cit.*, 20 FCC 2d 201, pars. 7 and 17 (1969).

[119] Par. 56. Stress supplied. In this particular statement the Commission is explaining the basis of its continued attention to the impact of CATV operations in the smaller markets.

[120] The Antitrust Division, speaking for the U.S. Department of Justice, endorsed the FCC's proposed liberalizations of the controls on CATV operators but called for giving them even greater opportunity to compete with local stations:

> "We . . . believe that CATVs should not be prevented from . . . accepting advertising. . . . Permitting CATV systems to accept advertising is significant because it provides not only a financial means of supporting program origination, but also provides a new advertising outlet for smaller local firms which may not be able to afford the rates of existing TV stations.
>
> "The Commission . . . should relax its rules on program importation." FCC, Docket No. 18397, *Comments of the U.S. Department of Justice*, April 7, 1969, processed, 13–14, 29.

[121] First Report and Order, *op. cit.*, 20 FCC 2d 201, Appendix and pars. 17, 31–32 (1969):

> "(1) it would permit CATV to derive additional revenue to help defray the costs of origination; (2) it would provide

the public with a new type of service—one where commercials did not interrupt program material . . . (3) it would afford advertisers a new and different type of outlet in terms of size and selectivity of audience . . . and (4) it would be less apt to affect the advertising revenue available to local broadcast services to the same degree that the alternative of unlimited CATV commercials might." *Ibid.*, par. 38.

[122] It proposed also to require the cable operators to carry the commercials of the local UHF stations, without charge, in place of those of the out-of-town broadcaster, at the commercial breaks in the imported programs:

> "The theory here is that most CATV viewers would have been stolen from the UHF stations—but the stations would still be able to sell advertising on the basis of a new combined audience" ("A new FCC tune elates cable-TV," *Business Week*, May 23, 1970, 38)—an interesting confirmation of the argument in note 111, above, to the effect that a CATV system can help a broadcaster when it "steals" his programs and brings them to additional viewers.

In addition, the Commission tentatively decided (1) to ask Congress to enact a tax on the gross revenues of CATV systems, in order to remunerate copyright owners; (2) to require the CATV operators to turn 5 percent of their gross revenues over to the Corporation for Public Broadcasting, as a subsidy to educational television; (3) to require them to carry all local signals, and to set aside channels for the use of city governments and local community groups and for lease to other would-be program originators; and (4) to permit them to use one channel for pay-TV. *Ibid.*; also *Wall Street Journal*, May 19, 1970, 8, and June 26, 1970, 5;

A Few Warning Notes

It would be inaccurate to suggest that regulatory commissions uniformly come down on the side of policies protective of the interests of existing regulated firms, although we shall encounter other illustrations of this tendency as we go along. We have already alluded to the FCC's opposite policy in granting licenses to new radio stations;[123] and to its reversal, in 1968–1970, of most of the earlier rulings that had been so restrictive of CATV competition with licensed broadcasters. In Chapter 4 we shall see several important instances in which the Commission permitted serious competitive encroachments on the theretofore exclusive position of the Bell System in voice and record telephony. The tendencies we have described are real ones; but there are important exceptions. That is the first warning.

The second is that we have made no concerted effort, in this chapter or in those that follow, completely to expunge all pejorative rhetoric in our characterizations of the regulatory process. The economist has certain biases; and the very words that he uses to characterize the inherent tendency of regulation to substitute monopoly for competition and to protect the status quo inevitably disclose that he regards these tendencies at least with suspicion, even if he tries to supply a purely objective account.

In fact we do not pretend to have made a fair or definitive appraisal of the many specific issues that we have described in illustrating these tendencies. The issues are complex; the decision to regulate suggests that uncontrolled competition would not work perfectly in these situations either.

But the objective fact and tendencies remain. When a commission is responsible for the performance of an industry, it is under never completely escapable pressure to protect the health of the companies it regulates, to assure a desirable performance by relying on those monopolistic chosen instruments and its own controls rather than on the unplanned and unplannable forces of competition. And society must take into account this inherent tendency of regulation when it chooses among alternative systems of industrial order.

New York Times, May 18, 1970, 1, and May 20, 1970, 83. The proposals appeared formally in FCC Docket No. 18397-A, *op. cit.* note 80, above, Second Further Notice of Proposed Rule Making, June 24, 1970.

[123] See note 91, p. 37, above. Another example was the decision of the Commission to authorize Mackay Radio and Telegraph to operate a direct radio telegraph circuit between the United States and The Netherlands in direct competition with a similar service offered by RCA and a cable service furnished by Western Union. See *Federal Communications Commission v. RCA Communications, Inc.,* 346 U.S. 86 (1953). The certification policy of the Civil Aeronautics Board has fluctuated from one attitude to the other, reflecting partly its changing membership and partly the fluctuating financial condition of the airlines already certificated. So, in the *Air Freight Case* (10 CAB 572, 1949, affirmed *American Airlines, Inc. v. Civil Aeronautics Board,* 192 F. 2d 417, 1951), the CAB

"certified a number of applicants to engage exclusively in transporting air freight, although existing certified carriers engaging in transporting both passengers and freight showed that their freight capacity was adequate to handle foreseeable traffic and that the air freight business was already being conducted at a loss which would be aggravated by dispersing the business among additional carriers." Louis B. Schwartz, *op. cit., Harvard Law Rev.* (January 1954), LXVII: 441. Copyright 1954 by Harvard Law Review Association.

On the other hand, the Board has reached the opposite conclusion when confronted by arguments precisely the same as those cited by opponents of the certification in the *Air Freight Case.* The discussion in this footnote is based on the description of these cases by Schwartz.

CHAPTER 2

Incentives and Distortions

Regulation has an inherent tendency to place its principal reliance on (1) the decisions of its monopolist chosen instrument and (2) its own controls. In this division of responsibilities, it is also inherent in the institution that management proposes and the commission disposes. It could hardly be otherwise. The decision-making unit is the private corporation itself; it is private management, using private capital, that must initially determine the quality of service, the level of capacity, efficiency, and the rate at which all of these are improved. Typically—but by no means universally, as we shall see—the initiative must be private.

In these circumstances, the central institutional questions have to do with the nature and adequacy of the incentives and pressures that influence private management in making the critical economic decisions. The subsidiary question is: how much scope is there, really, for regulation itself to exert a significant influence? These matters are the subject of this chapter and the next.

Regulation in a private enterprise system almost inevitably operates only at the periphery of the decision-making process. Regulators can presumably exert a considerable influence on the level of profits. They almost certainly can and do control discrimination in rates and service. But for the preponderant portion of the cost of service, they can at most disallow individual components that are flagrantly inflated; and as for quality, they can set minimum standards, and impose limited penalties when service is obviously bad.[1] They are essentially incapable of assuring that performance will be positively good. Probably the most obvious and important manifestation of this weakness has been their inability to force public utility companies to experiment with rate reductions, as long as their overall rates of return were not excessive. The most familiar case is that of electricity rates, where elasticities of demand and economies of scale seem clearly, with the wisdom of hindsight, to have justified bold rate reductions, but the only way in which the government could achieve them was by introducing publicly generated and distributed power.[2] As far as explicit interventions are concerned, regulation itself necessarily operates mainly as a restraining influence.

---

[1] See pp. 22–25, 29–32, Volume 1.   [2] See pp. 105–107, below. Richard A. Posner

This negative character of a regulatory process that concentrates mainly on the rate of return on aggregate company investment entails several inadequacies or adverse consequences. It means that regulation as such contains no built-in mechanism for assuring efficiency. To the extent that it effectively restrains public utility companies from fully exploiting their potential monopoly power, it tends to take away any supernormal returns they might earn as a result of improvements in efficiency, thereby diminishing their incentive to try. And if it permits them to earn only the cost of capital, it creates a situation in which any inefficiencies can simply be passed on in higher rates without injury to existing stockholders.[3] Indeed, it creates strong incentives on the part of the companies to pad their expenses—with management voting itself higher salaries and other emoluments at no cost to stockholders, and stockholders as well benefiting to the extent that the company can succeed in buying its services, raw materials, and other inputs at inflated prices from financially affiliated suppliers.

But, in practice, regulation can never be completely or instantaneously "effective," in the foregoing sense. Indeed, if effectiveness were defined, as it obviously ought to be, with an eye to the institutional requirements for efficiency and innovation, public utility commissions ought not even to *try* continuously and instantaneously to adjust rate levels in such a way as to hold companies continually to some fixed rate of return; and they probably ought not to try either to hold the rate of return down to the bare cost of capital. The *regulatory lag*—the inevitable delay that regulation imposes in the downward adjustment of rate levels that produce excessive rates of return and in the upward adjustments ordinarily called for if profits are too low[4] —is thus to be regarded not as a deplorable imperfection of regulation but as a positive advantage. Freezing rates for the period of the lag imposes penalties for inefficiency, excessive conservatism, and wrong guesses, and offers rewards for their opposites: companies can for a time keep the higher profits they reap from a superior performance and have to suffer the losses from a poor one. A similar function is served by the Commission's following the explicit policy of holding permitted profits not to a fixed percentage, but within a range or "zone of reasonableness," with adjustments in rates permitted or imposed only when returns fall outside that range.

---

cites another interesting example:

"The outcome of the FCC's investigation of Western Union is revealing in this connection. The investigation resulted in a staff report that advised the company to reduce telegram prices selectively in order to recapture business from the telephone companies. Western Union's management disagreed with the staff's diagnosis. They claimed, and still claim, that to reduce telegram rates would be to throw good money after bad. They have not implemented the staff's recommendation—but they have persuaded the Commission to authorize further rate increases." "Natural Monopoly and Its Regulation," *Stanford Law Rev.* (February 1969), XXI: 618. Copyright 1969 by the Board of Trustees of Leland Stanford Junior University.

[3] This will not be so to the extent that the permitted return exceeds the marginal cost of capital. If demand has any elasticity, higher costs and prices will mean lower total sales and a smaller total investment on which the permitted rate of return may be earned, hence lower aggregate profits. And if the permitted return exceeds the cost of attracting new capital, stockholders will be better off with a larger investment than a smaller one. See notes 64 and 69, in Chapter 2, Volume 1, and pp. 49–59, below.

[4] The required rate adjustments for excessive or inadequate returns are stated as they are on the assumption, almost certainly justified, that demand for a sufficient portion of the company's services is inelastic, so that rate changes will ordinarily produce profit changes in the same direction.

Permitting a rate of return above the bare cost of capital, while by no means free of danger, as we shall see, offers similar possible advantages. It causes the interest of a vigorous, growth-oriented management in aggressive expansion of sales and investment to coincide with that of the stockholder: existing stockholders pocket the difference between the cost of raising additional capital and the return they are permitted to earn on it. It is therefore an offset to public utility monopoly itself—to the familiar discrepancy between marginal revenue and average revenue under monopoly, which counsels higher than optimal prices and lower than optimal levels of output and investment. Combined with the presence of incompletely exploited monopoly power, which means that any losses resulting from mistaken or excessive investments or rate reductions may be recouped from existing customers, it encourages the undertaking of risky investments, expenditures on research and development, or efforts at sales promotion that monopoly might otherwise unduly restrict. Considering also the inevitable uncertainties in commission efforts to estimate the cost of capital, it minimizes the danger that an unduly restrictive policy will make management reluctant to raise new capital, for fear of causing a dilution of stockholders' equity.[5]

THE A–J–W EFFECT

As we have already pointed out, the combination of incompletely exploited monopoly power and a rate of return in excess of the marginal cost of capital, both of which regulation is likely to entail, also involves certain dangers.[6] The very incentives to expansion of investment and output to which they give rise may instead be regarded as distortions, tending to produce inefficient results. As Averch, Johnson, and Wellisz, among others, have pointed out, this combination of circumstances may induce public utility companies to make investments the social benefits of which fall short of their social costs, because (1) such investments will expand the rate base on which the companies are entitled to a rate of return in excess of the cost of capital and (2) to the extent that the net revenues directly generated by such incremental investments fall short of yielding the allowed rate of return, they can recoup the revenue deficiencies by raising their rates in markets in which they have thitherto been prevented from pricing at profit-maximizing levels. These considerations could induce them (1) to adopt an excessively capital-intensive technology and (2) to take on additional business, if necessary, at unremunerative rates.[7]

---

[5] See note 64, Chapter 2 of Volume 1; James C. Bonbright, *Principles of Public Utility Rates* (New York: Columbia University Press, 1961), 254–256, and pp. 106–108, below.

[6] See p. 147, Volume 1.

[7] Harvey Averch and Leland L. Johnson, "Behavior of the Firm under Regulatory Constraint," *Amer. Econ. Rev.* (December 1962), LII: 1052–1069; Stanislaw H. Wellisz, "Regulation of Natural Gas Pipeline Companies: An Economic Analysis," *Jour. Pol. Econ.* (February 1963), LXXI: 30–43. See the development of the hypothesis by Arnold F. Parr, *Theory of the Capital Decision in the Regulated Firm*, Ph.D. Dissertation, University of Oklahoma, University Microfilms, 1967, and Eugene P. Coyle, *The Theory of Investment of the Regulated Firm in the Special Context of Electric Power*, Ph.D. Dissertation, Boston College, University Microfilms, 1969. See the review of the literature and important modifications of the hypothesis by William J. Baumol and Alvin K. Klevorick, "Input choices and rate-of-return regulation: an overview of the discussion," *Bell Jour. Econ. and Mgt. Science* (Autumn 1970), I: 162–190.

The "A–J–W effect" (after Averch, Johnson, and Wellisz) undoubtedly describes a real tendency, although demonstrating that it has in fact prevailed over offsetting forces and produced inefficient investments in specific instances or determining whether it has on balance done more harm than good (I incline to the latter view)[8] would take more intensive research than has so far been done. It might be reflected in[9]

1. The resistance of many public utility companies to full peak-responsibility pricing, which would tend to hold down the expansion of demand at the peak and the consequent justification for capacity.[10]
2. A willingness to maintain a large amount of standby capacity, in excess of peak requirements.[11]
3. Some considerable resistance by electric utility companies to the thorough-going regional planning of investment that represents the most highly integrated form of power pooling.[12] The more usual practice, in which the various members of the pool take turns in installing capacity, and the corresponding typical requirement that over the long run each member possess capacity of its own sufficient to meet its peak requirements doubtless have numerous explanations;[13] but, like the resistance to

---

[8] See pp. 106–108, below.

[9] On some of these, see Harold H. Wein, "Fair Rate of Return and Incentives—Some General Considerations," in Trebing (ed.), *Performance under Regulation*, 42–53; and for a careful and critical appraisal, see the "Comment" of William R. Hughes, *ibid.*, 73–87.

[10] See note 34, p. 99, Volume 1. Shepherd characterizes the failure of gas and electric rates to follow this principle as "the most glaring instance" of inefficient pricing. William G. Shepherd and Thomas G. Gies, *Utility Regulation: New Directions in Theory and Practice* (New York: Random House, 1966), 265 n. Also his "Marginal-Cost Pricing in American Utilities," *South. Econ. Jour.* (July 1966), XXXIII: 61–64; Ralph K. Davidson, *Price Discrimination in Selling Gas and Electricity* (Baltimore: Johns Hopkins Press, 1955), 150–151; and Wellisz, *op. cit.*, *Jour. Pol. Econ.* (February 1963), LXXI: 35–36. This contention is not necessarily refuted by the tendency of natural gas pipeline companies to press for peak responsibility cost allocations in opposition to the FPC's *Atlantic Seaboard* formula. They have done so primarily because loading capacity costs on the commodity charge often made it impossible for them to quote off-peak rates for industrial customers low enough to get that business. They have also had the special incentive to do so arising from the fact that the more of the costs that they can get incorporated in the demand charge, the greater is their jurisdictional cost of service. See pp. 98–100, Volume 1.

[11] See, in addition to the citation of this example by Wein and the criticism by Hughes (note 9, above), the partial rebuttal by Irwin M. Stelzer,

"Rate Base Regulation and Some Alternatives: An Appraisal," a paper delivered at a Brookings Institution Symposium on the Rate-Base Approach to Regulation, June 7, 1968, and in *Public Utilities Fortnightly*, September 25, 1969, 3–11. The decline in the late 1960's in this margin of safety in the country at large for electricity—which produced a near-crisis in New York City during the summer of 1969—is apparently attributable to unexpectedly long delays in the delivery of nuclear generating plants and successful opposition by conservationist groups to various proposed installations. Similar congestion in local telephone service clearly reflects gross underestimation of the rate of demand increase. See also note 12.

[12] On both of these, see Shepherd, *op. cit.*, *South. Econ. Jour.* (July 1966), XXXIII: 61, and pp. 64–65, this chapter, below. The FPC's Bureau of Power has clearly implied that the power shortages in New York City, alluded to in the preceding note, would have been less severe had the local supplier been prompter in following the Commission's earlier recommendation that it substantially expand its interconnections with neighboring utilities. *A Review of Consolidated Edison Company 1969 Power Supply Problems and Ten-Year Expansion Plans*, Washington, December 1969, 73–76. See esp. note 57, below.

[13] Among these may be the desire to exclude from membership in the pools smaller, especially municipally owned distribution companies; see pp. 316–323, Chapter 6, below. Other factors explaining the unwillingness of electric companies continuously to purchase their power from others, even when this would produce the lowest cost, are the desire to escape federal juris-

completely integrated pooling itself, they probably reflect the fact also that when a distribution company purchases power from one of its partners, it receives nothing more than reimbursement for those actual expenses, whereas if it generates the power itself it has an expanded rate base on which it is entitled to a return.

4. A resistance to the introduction of capital-saving technology. One public utility engineer has insisted to this writer that the natural gas transmission companies have insufficiently developed underground storage in the Northeast, preferring instead to expand the more capital-intensive pipeline capacity as the principal means of meeting peak winter demands.[14] This same problem has been posed with particular urgency in recent years in the field of communications, where satellites seem to promise very great capital savings over ordinary terrestrial (and underwater cable) facilities.[15]

5. A reluctance to lease facilities from others. The Communications Satellite

---

diction, which extends to interstate sales, and the fear that they would have lesser assurance of continued availability of supply in time of shortage than if they were more nearly self-sufficient. See Hughes, in Trebing (ed.), *op. cit.*, 84–87. Some of these obstacles to the truly integrated planning of investment could be offset by joint ownership of pooled facilities, no matter where located; but some states do not permit their companies to include facilities outside their service areas in their rate bases; and the companies may be reluctant to participate in such joint ventures for fear of coming under the jurisdiction of the Securities and Exchange Commission as holding companies (see pp. 72–73, below).

[14] The winter heating demand creates an extreme seasonal peak in this part of the country. The larger the available storage capacity near the points of consumption, the less the needed pipeline capacity: smaller pipelines could approach capacity operations the entire year-around, bringing up much more gas than was being consumed in the summer months and placing it in storage, and drawing on those stocks to supplement their reduced carrying capacity during the winter peaks. Alternatively, they could serve the same end with a larger pipeline capacity, sufficient to meet the peak requirements with currently flowing gas, and attempting to fill in the summer troughs by developing large off-peak markets at rates relatively unburdened by capacity charges. The charge is that pipeline companies have been influenced, in making their choice between these two alternatives, by a preference for the larger rate base entailed by the second—the inflated costs of which can be passed on to the ultimate consumer while yielding larger aggregate profits. See also p. 100, Volume 1.

[15] See Merton J. Peck, "The Single-Entity

Proposal for International Telecommunications," *Amer. Econ. Rev., Papers and Proceedings* (May 1970), LX: 199–201. This contention is not uncontroverted. When in 1968 the Federal Communications Commission responded favorably to a request by AT&T that it be permitted to apply for authorization to lay a submarine cable between the United States and Spain, it did so because, among other considerations, a majority of the commissioners believed that, at least for the next several years, submarine cable would be the more economical means of providing the international communications service. See note 89, this Chapter, below. Whichever of these views is correct, it is nonetheless instructive that it was the Bell System that wanted to construct the cable—the cost of which would go into its rate base—while representatives of Comsat argued that the demand should be met by an expanded communications satellite system. For indications that similar motives have influenced the (negative) attitude of not only the terrestrial carriers but Comsat as well toward the possibility of direct broadcasting from satellites to receiving sets, see Lawrence Lessing, "Cinderella in the Sky," *Fortune* (October 1967), LXXVI: 131–208. It quotes the President of Comsat as contending that

"Retransmission through established ground channels and TV stations . . . is 'more natural, logical, and economical,' because it allows greater channel capacity and flexibility, and is *less disruptive of the vast investment in ground facilities.*" (Stress supplied)

Lessing observes that

"Comsat is predisposed for its domestic system toward the higher capital-cost distributive system, for it would add more to its rate base than the direct-broadcasting system. . . ." *Ibid.*, 198.

Corporation (Comsat), which was set up in 1962 as the United States' chosen instrument for installing and operating an international satellite communications network in cooperation with other countries, is essentially a carriers' carrier: the only ultimate consumer authorized thus far to deal directly with it is the National Aeronautics and Space Agency (NASA).[16] The possibility of its taking over an increasing share of the communications business is therefore dependent on the patronage and decisions of the common carriers, who would have to lease channels from it and use them in turn to take care of their customers' demands. But the carriers, it seems generally conceded, have less incentive to use the Comsat facilities than to construct their own, the cost of which would go into their rate bases: to the extent that they took the former course, they would make no profit on that portion of the communications operations; all they could do would be to include the rental charges in their own cost of service and get them back dollar for dollar. The latter course, in contrast, would mean greater aggregate profits. This lack of incentive to use leased facilities[17] would seem to be a clear manifestation of the A–J–W distortion and could well, given the peculiar institutional arrangements of the satellite part of the industry, result in overinvestment in economically less efficient facilities and a serious retardation in the development of satellite technology.[18]

---

[16] See the discussion of its constitution and the FCC's decision with respect to its authorized users at pp. 136–139, Chapter 4, below.

[17] For another illuminating example, see "Utilities' Embrace of Nuclear Fuel Stalled by its Classification as a Current Asset," *Wall Street Journal*, November 12, 1968, 4:

"The biggest decision facing the electric companies is whether to purchase their fuel cores or lease them from a supplier or third party. . . .

"There are some unquestioned advantages to leasing. . . . [It] could relieve utility executives of a host of technical problems. . . .

"Many utilities, however, contend that the benefits of leasing are questionable. . . .

"More important . . . many utilities fear that leasing fuel could force them to reduce electric rates at the same time they are undertaking heavy expenditures to switch to nuclear fuel. The reason is that in determining electric rates, state utility commissions allow the generating companies sufficient revenues to recover their operating costs and earn a return . . . on their invested capital.

"By leasing their fuel, however, a utility wouldn't be able to include this substantial investment in its rate base." But see note 29, below.

The FPC in 1970 proposed that electric and gas companies be permitted to capitalize a portion of their research expenditures, in hope that including these in their rate bases would encourage the companies to mount a greater

research effort. *Wall Street Journal*, January 28, 1970.

[18] See the interesting paper by A. Bruce Matthews, Vice President of Comsat, "Problems Posed by Current Regulatory Practices to the Rapid Introduction of Communications Satellite Technology," presented at the Brookings Symposium on the Rate-Base Approach to Regulation, June 7, 1968. A vice-president of AT&T indirectly conceded these possibilities when he posed the question:

"Does it [that is, rate base regulation] make the ownership of property so important that a utility has little or no incentive to lease or make other arrangements for the use of facilities it does not own (e.g., satellite circuits), even if this will result in savings to the users of service?"

"there are . . . situations in the telecommunications field where investment should play only a minor role in regulation. This might well be so where large volumes of business can be carried on with only a small investment being involved. Moreover, it is possible that over the coming years, because of leased plant or other factors, there may well be an increasing number of such situations. In all such situations a method, or methods, of regulation might be used, giving primary weight to the nature and quality of the service performed and little weight to the investment involved." John J. Scanlon, "Is Rate Base-Rate of Return Regulation Obsolete?" presented at the same conference, mimeo., 1, 17.

6. A tendency for public utility companies to adhere to excessively high (because excessively costly) standards of reliability and uninterruptibility of service, with correspondingly high and costly specifications for the equipment they employ. The alleged tendency described briefly under point 2, above, is clearly a special case of this one. It is, of course, extraordinarily difficult to demonstrate. Conceivably, the costs of interruptions in service to users of electricity are so extraordinarily great that the demand for continuity is completely inelastic;[19] or, conceivably, telephone subscribers are so annoyed by any delay whatever in completing their calls or by wrong numbers or misconnections that they, too, would pay whatever is necessary to obtain the very maximum of service that it is physically possible to provide. But the need for an economic calculus in matters such as these is inescapable: electric and gas companies sell services of varying degrees of interruptibility, at correspondingly varying discounts below the price for firm energy; and telephone companies do not place all calls instantaneously and correctly, nor do they devote unlimited resources to research into methods of improving their performance in these respects. It is entirely conceivable, therefore, that the economic calculations they do make are, consciously or unconsciously, influenced by the A–J–W consideration, particularly since it would have a tendency to reinforce their other motivations to do the best possible job—pride, an instinct of workmanship, a desire to minimize public complaint, and so on.[20]

7. A tendency to bargain less hard than they otherwise would in purchasing equipment from outside suppliers. Fred M. Westfield has cited complaints that the electric utility companies were insufficiently perceptive of the electric equipment manufacturers' price conspiracy of the late 1950s and insufficiently vigorous in pressing suits for damages as the basis for his theoretical demonstration that the A–J–W effect could have made these companies not only susceptible to such exploitation but eager for it.[21] It is perhaps significant that that famous conspiracy was broken by the

---

On the general problem that he raises, see also note 25, below.

The FCC has, in certain decisions, recognized the desire of common carriers to participate in the ownership of facilities they use and the possible disincentive to such use if they do not—for example, in requiring AT&T to share ownership of authorized new cable facilities with competing carriers [*In the Matter of American Telephone & Telegraph Co., et al.*, Memorandum Opinion and Order, 37 FCC 1151 (1964)], and in requiring Comsat to share ownership in its various ground stations (for the transmission, receipt and retransmission of signals from satellites) with the other international carriers. *In the Matter of Amendment of Part 25 of the Commission's Rules and Regulations With Respect to Ownership and Operation of Initial Earth Stations in the United States etc.*, Second Report and Order, 5 FCC 2d 812 (1966). See also Herman Schwartz,

"Comsat, the Carriers, and the Earth Stations: Some Problems with 'Melding Variegated Interests,'" *Yale Law Jour.* (January 1967), LXXVI: 443–453, 457–458.

[19] So the Federal Power Commission observed at the outset of its report on the great Northeast power failure of 1965:

"The prime lesson of the blackout . . . was that 'the electric utility industry must strive not merely for good but for virtually perfect service.'"

Major Power Failure Investigation, an Interim Report, as quoted in FPC, *1966 Annual Report*, 42.

[20] For an observation that the Bell System may err in this direction, see John B. Sheahan, *Competition Versus Regulation as a Policy Aim for the Telephone Equipment Industry*, unpublished Ph.D. dissertation, Harvard University, 1951, 90–91.

[21] "Regulation and Conspiracy," *Amer. Econ. Rev.* (June 1965), LV: 424–443.

complaints not of a private company but of the Tennessee Valley Authority.[22]

"the analysis suggests that the capital-goods suppliers of other rate-of-return regulated industries may turn out to be fertile hunting grounds for antitrust law violations."[23]

8. A tendency to reach out for additional business, inside or outside the sphere of their franchised public-utility operations, if need be at rates below incremental costs. As we have already observed, this kind of behavior is most likely to be encountered in competitive situations, because it is there that the elasticity of demand may require unremunerative rates if the regulated company is to obtain the business and in this manner to increase its rate base [24]

It has been suggested that dangers such as these—in particular the reluctance of regulated companies to lease facilities from others—could be forestalled by using some method of determining permissible profits other than one based on allowing a maximum rate of return on a rate base. For example, the ICC makes some use of an operating ratio method for regulated motor carriers; under this method, overall revenue requirements are set at some percentage markup above operating expenses. If this method were applied more generally, a regulated company would be permitted a profit margin on its leasing or labor expenses rather than or in addition to a return on investment in its own facilities. The quick answer, as far as the A–J–W problem is concerned, is that the operating ratio method would substitute a new distortion, or add it to the other: since profits would be a fixed percentage markup over expenses, the regulated companies would now have an incentive to inflate those expenses, rather than (or in addition to) their capital investment.[25]

---

[22] Clarence C. Walton and Frederick W. Cleveland, Jr., *Corporations on Trial: The Electric Cases* (Belmont, California: Wadsworth Publishing Company Inc., 1964), 29–32.

[23] Westfield, *op. cit.*, 442.

[24] See p. 159, Volume 1.

[25] Actually, the operating ratio method is usually advocated only for industries or operations where capital–sales ratios are low. And the major justification proffered is that, in such situations, profits that are held to some fixed percentage of capital investment will involve only a small percentage of sales and can therefore quickly be wiped out by even slight unfavorable developments. Consider the following example offered by Charles Alan Wright of a "typical utility" and a "typical bus company," with the same level of revenues but widely divergent capital requirements, and both permitted a 6 percent return on investment.

	Typical Utility	Typical Bus Company
Annual income	$10,000,000	$10,000,000
Net investment	25,000,000	4,000,000
Operating expenses	8,500,000	9,760,000
Return (6% of investment)	1,500,000	240,000

A 2.4% decline in sales (operating expenses remaining constant) or a 2.5% increase in costs would reduce the latter's profit to zero. An operating ratio of about 93%, permitting revenues of not quite $10,500,000 and profits of $740,000, would give it a fairer margin of protection. "Operating Ratio—A Regulatory Tool," *Public Utilities Fortnightly* (January 1953), LI:

24–26. Also Lawrence S. Knappen, "Transit Operating Ratio—Another View," *ibid.* (April 1953), LI: 485–497.

But, as Stelzer points out, this is only another way of saying that the investment in bus operations is the more risky of the two and requires a higher rate of return (18½% in the above example) on its investment for this reason. There is still no way of determining the proper operating ratio except by ascertaining the appropriate rate of return on investment, whether measured by cost of capital or comparable earnings. *Op. cit.*, Brookings Institution symposium, June 1968.

True, to paraphrase advocates of this method, when capital–sales ratios are low, "investment is not the primary factor in determining revenue needs." But when they proceed then to say something such as "the principal risk is attached to the substantially greater amount of expense," they are being very imprecise. The risk continues to be borne by the owners, and the risk is that they will lose their invested capital. The ratio of expenses to revenues does have an important influence on that risk, by increasing the likelihood that small percentage changes in costs or sales will result in revenues that do not cover that part of operating expenses that cannot readily be sloughed off, that is, that does not represent variable costs in the very short run. But the size of such expenses relative to the probable range of net revenue fluctuations provides a measure of the risk that earnings on capital will fluctuate; and the proper remuneration must therefore be in the rate of return permitted on that investment. The CAB achieved this result in 1960, directly, without recourse to an operating ratio technique, by setting a maximum allowable return at 12.75% (permitting 21.35% on equity alone) for local service airlines and 10.5% for domestic trunk lines. *Re: Rate of Return, Local-Service Carriers Investigation*, Docket No. 8404, Opinion, 31 CAB 685, 690 (1960) and *Re: General Passenger-Fare Investigation*, Docket No. 8008 et al., Opinion, 32 CAB 291 (1960). See also the recent ICC decision rejecting a request by truckers for a general rate increase based on a purported need for an operating ratio of 93% (that is, roughly a 7% profit markup over operating expenses), on the ground that

"The respondents in this proceeding have not attempted to show by any objective measure what amount of money they need over and above operating expenses. . . .

"Some analysis of the capital costs of the carriers' business must be presented to establish a need for additional revenue, and to measure such need." *General increase, Middle Atlantic and New England Territories*, 332 ICC 820 (1969), 837–838.

The reasoning of the Commission is supported and the limitations and possible usefulness of the operating ratio method further spelled out in the following conclusions of a study by National Economic Research Associates of *Methods for Testing the Reasonableness of Motor Carrier Earnings* (processed, New York, April 17, 1967, 1–2). (We have no opinion about the appropriateness of the particular *level* of return that they tentatively recommend.)

"1. Fair and reasonable rates for motor carriers can be meaningfully defined *only* in terms of return on invested capital.

"2. Whether a given operating ratio will provide adequate return cannot be determined without knowing something about the amount of invested capital.

"3. The allowable return on invested capital should be adequate to (1) attract required capital, and (2) match the return earned in industries of comparable risk. Preliminary analysis indicates that the required rate of return should be in the neighborhood of 15–20 percent on equity and 11–13 percent on total capitalization.

"4. For any given rate of return on invested capital there can be found a corresponding operating ratio. Thus, it is possible to apply an operating-ratio standard as a matter of administrative convenience, although return on invested capital would be the ultimate standard.

"5. Because of the short period over which investment is depreciated, the net investment "rate base" may be subject to short-term fluctuations which make the selection of a "test year" extremely difficult.

"6. Therefore, over short periods of time, fluctuations in the operating ratio may more accurately reflect true changes in the cost-revenue relationship than changes in the rate of return on rate base.

"7. Thus, the Commission should select as its standard an operating ratio which, on average, will yield the desired rate of return on invested capital. The Commission should periodically— every five or seven years—review the cost structure of the industry to see whether any change in the operating-ratio standard is required. But in the interim, the operating-ratio standard should be applied in setting rates which are reasonably responsive to changes in cost. This highly flexible approach is necessary in order to minimize regulatory lag which, when profit margins are narrow, can create extremely serious problems for the regulated industry."

Does this solution apply without limit—that is, no matter how low the capital–output ratio? What if the preponderant contribution of a regulated company is the services of a team of professionals—research chemists, management

There just is no easy way of eradicating these possible distortions of incentives, within the regulatory context; all the commission can do is to supervise, prod, and subject proposed investments, promotional prices and the like to economic tests. If, for example, the communications common carriers are truly reluctant to lease circuits from Comsat, on which they are permitted no profit, preferring instead to add uneconomically large owned facilities to their own rate bases, one remedy is for the FCC to refuse to certificate such uneconomic investments: this would force the carriers to use Comsat.

But, by the same token, these dangers can be drastically attenuated or eliminated to the extent that regulated companies can be exposed to the same incentives and pressures as apply *outside* of the regulatory context—the incentive of higher or lower profits depending on individual performance, and the pressures of competition. An automatically effective solution to any reluctance of the above-mentioned carriers to use lower-cost but less capital-intensive satellite facilities would be direct competition between Comsat and them: this would ensure that the business went to the lowest-cost instrumentality. We reserve consideration of this kind of solution for Chapters 4–6 below,[26] confining our attention here to the tendencies and solutions *under regulation*.

Observe that the A–J–W tendency prevails only to the extent that regulation approaches instantaneous effectiveness in holding realized rates of return to a single, legally prescribed level. Only in these circumstances could regulated companies, without fear of loss, undertake investments the marginal product of which fell short of their cost of capital: only if the rate of return that they were previously earning was already at the legal *minimum* and only if, after these investments were made, rates could instantaneously be raised on the inelastic portions of the business to hold the return to that minimum would there be no losses to offset the benefit of the expanded rate base. Only if, to look at it from the opposite direction, all reductions in cost were instantaneously accompanied by equivalent rate reductions, so as instantaneously to take those cost-savings away from them, could regulated companies afford to have no compunctions about adopting excessively capital-intensive, hence cost-inflating methods of production.

But in fact regulation is far from instantaneously effective. The consequence is that the profits of public utility companies would, for longer or shorter

---

or economic consultants—as in the case of a research or consulting contract with a government agency? Suppose, to take the extreme case, the government needs only a research organization, to put to work on a military problem in a government-owned laboratory? If it is unwilling to conscript the scientists—by no means an unthinkable proposition, as long as it conscripts soldiers—and wants to induce companies to bid on the contract, how is it to compute the required profit inducement? Clearly, no company would bid if the contract provided only for reimbursement of the salaries plus some return on the zero company investment. The answer would presumably have to be some measure of

the opportunity cost to a bidding company like General Electric. And this would clearly be only the salaries only if G.E. could instantaneously replace all the scientists it supplied to the government, with no loss in productivity or contribution to its overall profit. So, to put it positively, the necessary profit component of this regulated price would have to be the estimated contribution that the required team of scientists would otherwise make to company profit over and above their salaries and over and above the contribution G.E. might be expected to obtain by using that salary money for other purposes—an easier concept to describe than to measure!
[26] See in particular pp. 137–138, Chapter 4.

periods of time and with a considerable margin of uncertainty about the speed of recoupment, suffer from the undertaking of investments that do not themselves return the cost of capital. Moreover, regulatory commissions seem, typically and understandably, to be much more generous about the rates of return they are prepared to permit in a context of stable or declining rates than when faced by company requests for rate increases. In these circumstances, regulated companies may have a stronger incentive to reduce costs, which enables them to earn a gently rising return for substantial periods of time on a rate base that grows only to the extent justified by comparisons of marginal returns and marginal cost of capital, than to make uneconomic investments in the expectation of being permitted rate increases on inelastic portions of their business sufficient to increase their total profits.[27]

It is with arguments such as these that public utility executives indignantly deny that there exists any such tendency as suggested by the A–J–W hypothesis. In the planning of new investments, they present their engineers with estimated loads and the other relevant constraints—such as minimum service standards—and ask them to compute various alternative ways of meeting that anticipated demand; and their invariable rule, they assert, is to select the lowest-cost alternatives, applying a uniform cost of capital to the capital component of those cost estimates. As long as the engineers do not apply a discount rate that is too low, that is, that underestimates the true cost of capital, this procedure could not lead systematically to the selection of inefficiently capital-intensive methods of production.[28]

They frequently argue, also, that they have found extremely onerous the necessity they have faced since World War II of going regularly to the capital markets to finance the constant additions to capacity required merely to meet their ever-increasing demands. These circumstances, they assert, have forced them assiduously to economize in their use of capital. This assertion might be translated into a contention that these companies can typically raise capital only at increasing costs—that is to say, that the cost of capital to a given company at any time is higher, the larger the amount to be raised.[29] Such a tendency would not only limit the scope of the A–J–W distortion;

---

[27] By the same token, of course, as the rate of return gently approaches what management thinks is the maximum its commission will allow, the A–J–W incentive should become increasingly powerful. It seems doubtful that companies can consciously turn their attention to cost cutting on and off, depending on where they find themselves with respect to the regulatory lag; but there seems no reason to doubt that the vigor with which management insists on saving paper clips, using the mail instead of the telephone and tourist rather than first-class air service does in fact vary as profits are easy and hard to reap.

[28] See the generally corroborative observations of Hughes, in Trebing, *op. cit.*, 74–80, to the effect that the use of redundant capital or paying excessive prices for equipment are likely to be much less attractive outlets for A–J–W tendencies than expanding service and improving

its quality.

[29] It might mean also that, with the generally rising long term interest rates of the late 1950s and 1960s, the cost of additional capital has *over time* approached the permitted average rate of return; such a development would at the limit eradicate the A–J–W tendency. So, in interesting contrast with the attitude expressed in note 17, above, many electric utility companies were reported in late 1969 as planning to *lease* rather than buy nuclear fuel cores, because "[b]uying the fuel entails a sizeable capital outlay of up to $50 million, in an era of sky-high interest rates." *Business Week*, December 27, 1969, 17. With rates on high-grade bonds running well above 8% and permitted rates of return still reflecting the much lower average embedded cost of debt, this shift in attitude was entirely consistent with the A–J–W hypothesis.

it could conceivably produce a distortion in the *opposite* direction.[30]

Another piece of evidence suggests that the alleged tendency toward overly capital-intensive technology has not, in fact, materialized. According to the estimates by John W. Kendrick the margin of superiority of productivity advances in public utilities over American industries generally, during the period 1899 to 1953, is just as great in capital and total factor productivity as in labor productivity alone.[31] If the industry had a tendency to use excessively capital intensive methods of production (and it would be reasonable to assume that the tendencies would be progressive over the 54-year period studied by Kendrick, particularly since public utility regulation almost certainly became increasingly effective over this period), one would have expected it to show up in a more rapid relative rate of increase in labor productivity than in either capital or total factor productivity.[32]

---

[30] A monopsonist faces a rising supply function of whatever it is he is buying: he will have to pay a higher unit price the more he tries to buy. So a labor market monopsonist, for example, will find that the marginal cost of labor to him exceeds the average cost or wage rate, because in addition to the wage for the added worker he must pay higher wages for all the other workers as well. And because of this he will cut off his hiring at the point at which that marginal cost equals the marginal value product of labor; and this will be short of the socially efficient point—which would be where the (average) wage equalled that marginal value product. So here, the firm that faces a rising capital supply function, because of its monopsonistic position in capital markets, might refuse to undertake socially desirable investments, the (average) capital cost of which was less than their marginal product, because raising the additional capital would increase the average cost of all the capital the firm would otherwise have to raise. See Richard S. Bower, "Rising Capital Cost *Versus* Regulatory Restraint," *Public Utilities Fortnightly*, March 4, 1965, 31–33. Shepherd uses a rising marginal cost of capital function in his exposition of the A–J–W tendency. "Regulatory Constraints and Public Utility Investment," *Land Econ.* (August 1966), XLII: 350.

[31] See his *Productivity Trends in the United States* (Princeton: Princeton Univ. Press, 1961), 136–137, 152–153, 166–167. See some of these and later data at pp. 99–100, Chapter 3, below.

[32] Stelzer supplies several additional considerations and pieces of evidence that would appear to be incompatible with the A–J–W tendency. Among these are the general failure of electric and gas companies to take advantage of the mounting public concern with environmental quality as a justification for rapidly expanding their investment in underground transmission and distribution facilities or for installing air and thermal pollution control equipment; the fact that the extension of telephone, electricity, and gas services to rural areas, at rates that may not even cover long-run marginal cost, is probably explicable more generally by the pressures of regulatory commissions and the threat of government competition than by an avid quest by the reluctant companies for additional rate base; and that, similarly, the publicly owned TVA keeps at least as large a reserve of generating capacity as the private part of the industry. *Op. cit.*, Brookings Institution symposium, June 1968. On the similar, at least equally great reluctance of public power companies and tough regulatory commissions to follow or to permit full peak responsibility pricing, see p. 98, Volume 1, and pp. 107–108, Chapter 3, below.

Also in apparent conflict with the A–J–W hypothesis is what appears to have been the typical practice of regulated companies in recent decades to urge regulatory commissions to permit them to depreciate their investment at more rapid rates. If, in fact, it is in their interest to inflate the rate base, it is difficult to understand why they would generally try so hard to get capital out of the rate base faster than commissions have allowed. The companies usually offer in justification a fear of technological obsolescence and their need for capital funds. See, for example, the strong argument by William J. Crowley, "The Management Factor in Accounting Policy," *AGA Monthly*, February 1968, 24. This kind of argument might be interpreted as involving the proposition that the cost of capital is not constant regardless of the life of the equipment in which it is embodied, but increases with equipment longevity because of the increasing uncertainties of recoupment the longer the planning time horizon. Since the A–J–W distortion applies only to the extent that the cost of capital is less than the rate of return, it would in this event not necessarily conflict with the desire of regulated companies to get their capital rapidly out of long-lived equipment subject to rapid obsolescence. The contention by Crowley that "a company that is allowed a realistic

Finally, it should be recognized that the A–J–W distortion is an entirely static one. Its tendency is to produce an overallocation of capital to regulated industries. But the principal institutional deficiency of regulation is dynamic —the absence of a spur to progressive performance comparable to and as reliable as that of competition. Instead, these industries are subject to the restrictive and conservative influences of monopoly. These influences are likely, if anything, to be reinforced by regulatory surveillance, by the necessity of submitting proposed prices, promotional campaigns, and investments to the possibility of veto by a politically appointed commission. The almost inescapable cumbersomeness of administrative procedures, the expense and delay involved in clearing major policy changes with a governmental commission almost certainly tend to breed conservatism in the companies themselves, and an unwillingness to make changes, to take chances.[33] And it is precisely with respect to the dynamic probing of demand elasticity and to risk-taking innovation that the possibilities of earning a return in excess of the cost of capital and of recouping losses from an incompletely exploited fund of monopoly power would seem a desirable offset to monopoly, as we have already suggested. That is why we suggest (at greater length in Chapter 3, below) that the A–J–W tendency, to the limited extent it exists, could well be a more important influence for good than for poor performance.[34] Still, the dangers remain as well; and they call for continuing attention.[35]

INCENTIVE PLANS

Certainly to some extent commissions can devise explicit incentives for dynamic and efficient performance in an attempt to induce managements to overcome the inertia of monopoly, bureaucracy, and regulation itself. The most promising are simply the aforementioned regulatory lag and "zone of reasonableness" rate of return, both of which tend to offer the same sort of automatic stimuli as operate in the unregulated sectors of the economy. Some observers have proposed that these devices be institutionalized, that is, explicitly adopted as a policy, thus assuring to companies the rewards and penalties they provide.[36] This might create more problems than it solves.

---

depreciation expense provision would be more willing to adopt new methods, new labor-saving and cost-cutting ideas and equipment" (*ibid*) seems to reflect the consideration discussed at pp. 118–119, Volume 1, as well.

The attempt of companies with large annual capital needs to finance a larger proportion of their investment internally might be explicable also in terms of the possibility mentioned at p. 57, above—which would, again, be entirely compatible with the A–J–W analysis, but would diminish its practical importance.

[33] For a brief allusion to some of these political-administrative influences and problems, see pp. 87–88, below.

[34] See p. 49, this chapter above; see also Sidney Weintraub, "Rate Making and an Incentive Rate of Return," *Public Utilities Fortnightly*, April 25, 1968, 30–31. So we have pointed out that the effectiveness of regulatory lag in

stimulating continuing attention to cost cutting presumably diminishes, and the A–J–W danger grows, as the rate of return approaches the legal maximum and/or the next cost-of-service computation (see note 27). But in those same circumstances the power of the A–J–W tendency for good as well as evil would likewise be enhanced—in inducing a greater willingness to take risks, or to cut prices experimentally in hope of increasing sales and justifying a larger investment.

[35] See, for example, our discussion of the need for commissions placing an LRMC floor (or an even higher one) under discriminatory rate reductions, particularly in competitive situations, in Chapters 5 and 6 of Volume 1.

[36] On the regulatory lag, see William J. Baumol, "Reasonable Rules for Rate Regulation: Plausible Policies for an Imperfect World," in Almarin Phillips and Oliver E. Williamson, *Prices: Issues*

After the rate of return reached its ceiling or the period of regulatory lag drew to its preannounced close, the incentive for improved performance would be exhausted and could indeed be reversed: the company would now be tempted to construct a high cost of service for the new test year. Paradoxically, the same would tend to happen when profits approached the floor: the company's attention would shift to constructing the strongest possible case for a rate increase. This has led others to propose that the period of the lag and the limits of the zone of reasonableness be left purposely uncertain—which is not far from where we are now.

Of course, if the regulatory lag is on balance helpful, attempts to make regulation "more efficient" in limiting the rate of return to the prescribed levels not just from one major rate case to another but year to year are likely to be on balance harmful. This is the concern one might have about the FCC's proclaimed practice of "continuous surveillance" over telephone rates, even though this device, involving reliance on continuing informal conferences rather than long, drawn-out major rate investigations, has proved fruitful in forcing a prompter translation of the benefits of tax reductions and technological progress into lower prices than would otherwise have been possible.[37] This possible objection could perhaps be eliminated if the surveillance of realized profit rates were conceived of—as in part the FCC evidently has—as a device for reducing not so much *profits* as *prices*. The latter is obviously the more important part of performance.

Suppose the commission found that a company's realized return exceeded the allowable level by a certain number of dollars. If its primary focus were on those dollars, it would regard its efforts as frustrated if the company responded to the order for rate reductions by cleverly choosing those services whose demand is most elastic and production most subject to decreasing costs—as it would be in its interest to do. Indeed, if they took such a narrow view, the regulators might press the company instead to reduce rates in the markets with inelastic demand or subject to increasing costs, or, indeed, *raise* them in markets of elastic demand, because this would most reliably reduce profits. But this would manifestly not be in the public interest. The proper focus would be on getting the maximum reduction in *rates* consistent with the required profit reduction. This suggests that if there is to be continuing surveillance, the corrective orders should run in terms of eliminating a certain number of dollars of test-year profits, *on the assumption that sales would continue at test-year levels*, leaving it to the company to design the optimum structure of rate reductions from its standpoint (within limits of LRMC). This would give it the opportunity and incentive to experiment by trying to make the cuts in areas of the greatest demand elasticity and cost reducibility.

---

in Theory, Practice, and Public Policy (Philadelphia: University of Pennsylvania Press, 1967), 108–123. On the zone of reasonableness:

"I would favor ratemaking based on a relatively wide range of permissible rate of return as providing efficiency incentives which would better serve the public interest in securing efficient service at minimum charges." Commissioner Loevinger, concurring opinion in FCC, *In the Matter of American Telephone & Telegraph Co. et al.*, Docket No. 16258, Interim Decision and Order, 9 FCC 2d 30, 121 (July 1967).

The Commission explicitly adopted the same principle, for the same reason, *ibid.*, Memorandum Opinion and Order on Reconsideration, 9 FCC 2d 960, 963 (September 1967).

[37] William Haber, "Forward: An Introductory Note," and Gies, "The Need for New Concepts in Public Utility Regulation," in Shepherd and Gies, *op. cit.*, vii and 107–111.

True, such cuts in the rate level would be most likely to "fail" by the standard of holding down total profits. But it would have the maximum likelihood of success in terms of the ultimately important standard—cutting rates and extending service within the limits of LRMC.[38]

Of the more specific incentive plans employed or proposed, most involve varying the permissible rate of return (r) according to some indicator of ultimate performance. Most familiar are the various sliding scale plans, in which r is inversely related to comparative rate levels or to changes in rates over time.[39] These plans have typically been short-lived, being usually modified or abandoned when rates of return under them became unacceptably high. Under the famous Washington (D.C.) plan, which was in effect continuously from 1925 to 1955, if earnings rose above $7\frac{1}{2}$ percent, rates were to be reduced in subsequent years in such a way as to eliminate half of the remaining excess; if the return fell below the minimum, the commission was supposed to raise rates sufficiently to restore the deficiency entirely. Since demand grew rapidly in this period and may also have been elastic, returns kept rising during the first two decades; what broke down the plan was the inflation after World War II. It also had the defect of providing no penalty for inefficiency.[39a] A similar device by which corporations would be permitted to retain some percentage of incremental profits while sharing their gains with the rate payers was proposed by Irston R. Barnes. While retaining the feature of the Washington plan that involved rate reductions in a succeeding year by a percentage sufficient to eliminate 50 percent of any excess of earnings actually realized over r, it added the provision that any excesses actually earned be divided, with half of them going into the accumulation (up to 20 percent of the rate base) of an earnings-equalization reserve and the other half going into trust for rate payers. The former reserve could be used by the utility to make good any future deficiencies in earnings; and once the equalization reserve came to exceed 20 percent of the rate base, the company could use the excess for whatever corporate purpose it chose—"an extra dividend to stockholders, a bonus to management, or a profit-sharing agreement for the benefit of the workers." The other half, held in trust for the consuming public, would be used in effect to reduce the rate base; or, if used, for example, for capital expansion, the property thus acquired would not be included in the rate base. In effect, thus, consumers would obtain an equity interest in the company, a share in ownership of the assets, income from which they would receive in the form of an exclusion from the rates charged them of a return on that capital sum.[40]

---

[38] See pp. 142–145, Volume 1. If, then, the cuts proved the following year to have "failed" by the first test, the commission could come back and order another reduction—set, once again, in terms of the number of dollars by which net revenues would have been reduced if sales remained at base-year volumes.

[39] See the extensive survey of these plans in Charles Stillman Morgan, *Regulation and the Management of Public Utilities* (Boston: Houghton Mifflin Company, 1923), 154–187.

[39a] See Harry M. Trebing, "Toward An Incentive System of Regulation," *Public Utilities Fortnightly*

(July 18, 1963), LXXII: 22. Trebing points out that the price of utility services in the District of Columbia fell compared with the United States average in this period and that during the 1925–1940 period rates of return were well above average: the overall rate never fell below 8.8 percent and the return on equity averaged 14.4 percent. For a survey and analysis of such plans see Irvin Bussing, *Public Utility Regulation and the So-Called Sliding Scale* (New York: Columbia Univ. Press, 1936).

[40] *The Economics of Public Utility Regulation* (New York: F. S. Croft & Co., 1942), 529–599.

In his classic study Charles Morgan emphasized above all the necessity of providing incentives for efficient performance directly to management, rather than in the corporate rate of return.

"The principal conclusions reached as a result of this study are that public necessity requires, in the case of public utilities, the establishment of conditions which will specifically conduce to the maximum utilization of the agencies or means of production, and that these conditions shall be such as to stimulate and reward management, rather than capital as such, for superior efficiency."

". . . to reward capital as such through allowing added returns for a show of increased efficiency of operation is both gratuitous and impracticable. So to reward capital would be gratuitous, for capital would thereby receive a return for a contribution which it itself did not make. It is to management and not to capital that we must look for increased efficiency, and it is to management, the human, personal force and that which alone is able to respond to the offer of a special reward for especially meritorious effort, that the appeal of a reward for efficiency should be directed."[41]

His point is well-taken, though probably exaggerated. While higher corporate profits do of course accrue to the current stockholders, they almost certainly benefit managers as well—giving them higher returns on the stock they hold, permitting and justifying the payment of higher salaries and bonuses, increasing the demand for their services by other public utility companies, making it easier for the company in question to justify raising new capital,[42] hence to grow, and in this way as well giving successful managers additional satisfaction and approbation.

In either event, the difficulty with plans such as these or with unplanned regulatory lag is that the levels and trends of rates and earnings reflect a vast complexity of factors in addition to management efficiency and enterprise. Merely permitting companies to earn higher rates of return does not necessarily reward good performance; it may unnecessarily reward good luck and other favorable external developments. Similarly, other companies may be penalized for unfavorable developments in costs and demand that are no fault of their own; and, whatever the cause, commissions will be loath to penalize them if the consequence is to diminish their ability to attract the capital that may be necessary to improve their service. Still, it remains true that sliding-scale rates of return or rewards to management *do* provide one useful and, at least in many circumstances, promising incentive. Regulatory commissions need not be incompetent to identify situations in which the rewards prove to be unnecessarily high and to make the necessary downward adjustments. Or to provide the opposite kind of correction when profits turn out persistently undeservedly and harmfully low.

A fully effective incentive system would require that commissions be able to make direct assessments of the performance of the companies under their supervision, as a basis for rewarding good management and penalizing bad. In view of the diverse and ever-changing factors determining the costs and profits of each, and in view of the numerous, partially conflicting criteria of good performance—low costs, intensive promotion, expanding sales, the

[41] *Op. cit.*, vii–viii, 315–316. Morgan's proposals, set forth in his Chapter 7, include various non-pecuniary devices as well as pecuniary rewards.
[42] See note 64, Chapter 2, Volume 1.

taking of market and technological risks—devising rating scales capable of general acceptance is an extremely difficult task. The fact remains that commissions can and do make such judgments and could do more—if need be with the help of management consultants. For example,

"the Commission has found the reasonable rate of return to which utilities should be entitled to be from 7 to 8 percent of the fair value of the property and business. We believe that in the present case . . . the latter rate of return is fully justified. . . . We cannot escape notice of the fact that the Milwaukee exchange of the Wisconsin Telephone Company has been and is managed with an exceedingly high degree of efficiency. . . . the investment in Milwaukee is very low for an exchange of its size and nature, and . . . the operating expenses appear to be very conservative. . . . As far as we can determine, the officials of the Milwaukee exchange and of the company have been continually on the alert to discover means of conducting the business economically and maintaining desirable relations with the public."[43]

In the most ambitious effort of this kind to date, William Iulo has attempted, by the use of multiple regression analysis, to determine quantitatively the major objective factors determining the individual costs of a sample of approximately 170 electric companies. Selecting his independent variables to exclude those that might themselves be heavily influenced by managerial efforts, he assumes further that any remaining significant differences in costs, unexplained by these external factors, can be attributed in significant measure to managerial efficiency or inefficiency.[44] Obviously if such identifications could be made with confidence, they would permit introduction of a system of direct rewards and penalties for superior or inferior management.[45] At the least, they could identify situations calling for more detailed regulatory scrutiny.[46]

---

[43] From a decision of the Wisconsin Railroad Commission, quoted in Charles S. Morgan, *op. cit.*, 292–293. For examples and for a discussion of the need, the difficulties, and the possibilities, see *ibid.*, 293–300, 323–327, and pp. 30–31, 53–54, in Volume 1. Shepherd is a leading proponent of commissions conducting management audits—making direct appraisals of the efficiency and innovation performance of regulated companies. See his "Regulation, Efficiency and Innovation," a paper presented at the Brookings Institution Symposium on The Rate Base Approach to Regulation, June 1968, unpublished. Also p. 85 and note 119, below.

[44] His analysis enables him to estimate the influence on cost of each of his independent variables (for the most important of these see note 45). Using these data, he is able to derive an estimated cost for each company, depending on the values of these external determinants in each case. He then assumes

"that an efficient utility is one that operates within the historical, operating, and market conditions reflected by the independent factors in such a way that its actual unit electric costs

are substantially less than its unit costs estimated on the basis of the factors included in the regression analysis. Conversely, an inefficient utility will operate, subject to these conditions, in such a manner that its actual unit costs are substantially higher than its unit costs estimated on this basis. . . .

"a utility whose actual unit electric costs are either substantially higher or substantially lower than its estimated unit costs can tentatively be characterized as being relatively inefficient or relatively efficient." *Electric Utilities—Costs and Performance* (Pullman: Washington State Univ. School of Econ. and Business, 1961), 140, 142.

[45] As my student John William Wilson has demonstrated, Iulo's analysis is seriously undermined by the fact that his selected independent cost-determining variables are not truly independent of managerial efficiency or enterprise. Surely, his two most important determinants, consumption per residential customer and the distribution of sales among different classes of customers, could be importantly influenced by rate levels and structures and promotional efforts, as could such other "independent" variables as capacity utilization, consumption per industrial

THE PROBLEM OF INTERCOMPANY COORDINATION

Technology does not necessarily respect the ownership patterns and boundaries that happen to prevail in industry. This is particularly true among the public utilities, where those patterns and boundaries are rigidly prescribed by the government, and businesses are not always free to adapt to the requirements and opportunities presented by a constantly changing technology.

In these circumstances, there are often important cost savings that can be achieved by intercompany coordination. If local entrepreneurs develop community antenna television services, it is likely to be most efficient for them to string their wires from the receiving tower to subscribers' homes along the poles belonging to telephone or electric companies. The most efficient method of making a particular shipment of freight will often require that it make use of the facilities of several carriers—several railroads, or some combination of truck, rail, barge, and ship for different parts of the trip, either consecutively or simultaneously, as in the carriage of truck trailers ("piggyback") on railroad flat cars, or railway freight cars on barges. This calls for intercarrier agreements to fix joint rates, to coordinate their schedules, and to divide the joint revenues. Similarly, because of the prohibitive costs of unloading and reloading boxcars, railroads have to make cooperative agreements for accepting and using each other's cars on shipments going over more than one line—agreements for returning boxcars to their owners and compensating them in the interim.[46a] Electric companies can take fullest advantage of the economies of scale and of diversification—opportunities for both of which have grown enormously in recent decades[47]—only by interconnecting their transmission networks and entering into elaborate power pooling and interchange agreements. These arrangements enable them (1) to build much larger generating units (staggering their separate construction programs over time, taking turns in building very large increments to capacity and selling the surplus among themselves), and to

---

and commercial customer, and the typical size of the steam-electric generating stations. The implication of such interrelationships on Iulo's proposed measurement of managerial efficiency may be best illustrated by an example. Suppose an enterprising management succeeds, by vigorous promotional efforts, in increasing average residential consumption. The latter factor would be included among the (cost-reducing) variables that are assumed to be independent of managerial efficiency; so management would get no credit for its own efforts that produced this result. Indeed it would show up as inefficient, because the promotional expenses would cause actual costs to exceed those estimated by application of the independent variables. See *Residential and Industrial Demand for Electricity*, unpublished Ph.D. dissertation, Cornell University, 1969, 231–246.

[46] On the general problem of direct incentives see Wein in Trebing (ed.), *op. cit.*, 54–67.

[46a] And when the carriers cannot agree on the

division of revenues or transfer prices, the regulatory commission has to decide. See, for example, the Civil Aeronautic Board's threat to rescind a 6.35 percent airline fare increase approved in the fall of 1969 if the carriers could not agree on a new plan for the division of joint fares giving a disproportionate share to the local service airlines, on the ground that their costs per mile are higher than for the trunk carriers. *Wall Street Journal*, December 19, 1969, 4, and February 2, 1970, 3; also note 69, p. 153 of Volume 1. And see the tortured history of the ICC's efforts to find a formula for freight car rental fees that would strike an acceptable balance between the interests of the Western roads, which own most of the cars, and the Eastern, which are car-borrowers. *Boston & Maine Railroad et al. v. U.S. et al.*, 297 F. Supp. 615 (1969), and *Union Pacific Railroad et al. v. U.S. et al.*, 300 F. Supp. 318 (1969), affirmed 396 U.S. 27 (1969).

[47] See page 128, Volume 1.

achieve also (2) lower operating costs (by taking power continuously, as total demand fluctuates from instant to instant, from the lowest-cost sources in the entire, interconnected system)[48] and (3) higher load factors, that is, a higher average utilization of capacity, by virtue of interregional diversities of demand,[49] than any of them could do individually.[50] There may prove to analogous advantages in setting up a more nearly national grid system interconnecting long-distance natural gas pipelines.[51]

The beauty of the free market is that it achieves collaborations of this kind by private contracts freely entered on, wherever they are economically beneficial. If there is a demand to be served, and if A refuses to cooperate with B in serving it, it is reasonable to infer that A feels it can do the entire job itself at lower incremental cost than in collaboration; in this event, it is socially efficient to permit A to do so.[52] If, instead, the collaborative device is the more efficient alternative, one would think that A or B would find it financially possible to offer the other a large enough bribe or participation in the joint benefits to enlist its cooperation.[53] For example:

---

[48] The economist will appreciate the rule that the engineers follow in order to achieve this purpose: with the help of computers, the system operator adjusts output from each source in such a way as to equalize their respective marginal costs of delivered power. See Wallace E. Brand, "Northeast Electric Bulk Power Supply," *Public Utilities Fortnightly* (June 9, 1966), LXXVII: 68, 74–78; Fred M. Westfield, "Marginal Analysis, Multi-plant Firms and Business Practice: An Example," *Q. Jour. Econ.* (May 1965), LXIX: 253–268. See the more formal demonstration of the economics of this at pp. 264–266, Chapter 6, below. As Brand points out, under the most advanced coordination, the location of each investment project will be similarly planned, to minimize system-wide costs; as a result some partners might never build a plant but always purchase from others. *Op. cit.*, 79 and 65–88, *passim*.

[49] If the daily or seasonal peaks of the various interconnected members of the pool do not coincide—that is, if their coincident (or combined, simultaneous) peak is smaller than the sum of their individual noncoincident peaks—clearly they can meet their respective peak demands with a smaller aggregate capacity if they can exchange power than if each must supply its own at all times. (If system A's and B's peaks do not coincide, A can make fuller use of its capacity by meeting some of B's demands at the time of the latter's peak and conversely; in consequence neither has to have the full capacity necessary to supply its own peak requirements. See page 96 of Volume 1, where this principle is shown to justify levying demand charges on the basis of purchases at the time of the coincident, system peak.)

Similarly, pooling permits reduction in the total amount of reserve capacity that has to be carried against the possibility of power failure; if, for example, the worst possible contingency is the loss of the single largest generating unit, one reserve unit of this size will provide full protection against power failure for two interconnected systems, whereas if the two were not connected each would have to have a reserve unit of this size to protect itself. Another way of describing the latter saving is that the chances of simultaneous outages at two or more plants are obviously less than a single outage at any one plant; as a result the same spare capacity can serve to back up many plants, if they are interconnected.

[50] U. S. Federal Power Commission, *National Power Survey, 1964*, I, Washington, October 1964, Chapters 11–16 and *passim*. Closer coordination over wider geographic areas is an important precondition for the $11 billion of savings in annual electricity costs (involving a reduction in average unit costs from the 1962 level of 1.68 cents to 1.23 cents per kwh) that the Commission estimated were achievable by 1980. *Ibid.*, Chapter 17.

[51] See Harry Thomas Koplin, *Natural Gas Certification Policy of the Federal Power Commission*, unpublished Ph.D. dissertation, Cornell University, 1952, 403–417; and Resources for the Future, *U. S. Energy Policies, An Agenda for Research*, RFF Staff Report (Baltimore: Johns Hopkins Press, 1968), 62.

[52] A might, of course, be mistaken. The defense of the free market would be a defense of letting individuals make mistakes and suffer the consequences, as they will in competitive markets.

[53] Suppose, for example, the service could sell at a price of 10, the marginal cost to A of doing the entire job itself were 7, the MC to A of permitting B to use its facilities for this purpose instead were 3 and the separate MC to B for

BARGE LINES PUSH JOINT RATE PLEA
Initiate a New Approach in Courtship
of Railroads

The love-hate relationship between those two arch rivals for hauling bulk cargoes, the barge lines and the railroads, goes back well over a century. . . .

The water carriers have for many years courted the cooperation of the railroads in setting joint water-rail rates, pointing to the better deal this would mean for shippers. . . . Every branch of the Federal Government has looked with favor on such arrangements. . . .

The Water Transport Association has now begun a new approach. . . . it has started offering examples of freight savings that could bring new profits to railroads as well as barge companies.

Floyd H. Blaske, chairman of American Commercial Lines. . . . underlined that these figures of savings were not necessarily entirely for the benefit of the shippers, hinting that "It may well be, on some of these movements, that the right economic decision is to share these savings between the shipper and the connecting railroad."[54]

Or, where even greater efficiency advantages can be achieved if the coordination is effected under the management of a single company, one would expect such companies to emerge or existing companies to consolidate.

So one would think that separate public utility companies could be relied on to see their mutual interest in working out joint rates, or the use of one another's facilities, or pooling arrangements, if and to the extent that coordination were economic. And to a large extent they can and they do.[55] And one might expect public utility companies to combine various operations under the management of a single, integrated enterprise, whether by an individual company taking on additional functions or by merger, where financial consolidation promises additional efficiencies. And, of course, they have.[56]

But voluntary coordination is likely to be incomplete, and has in fact been so, as we shall see. So an important task of regulation is to compel cooperation. The problem illustrates many of the limitations of the institution of regulated monopoly—the inadequate or distorted incentives of regulated companies and the inadequacy of the results when regulation plays only a passive or negative role. It illustrates also certain important problems of preserving the competitive opportunities of individual firms and prescribing the proper mix of intercompany cooperation and rivalry. Our discussion here will therefore overlap to some extent with the consideration of competitive issues in Chapter 6.

It is difficult to be certain of all the reasons for the failure of regulated companies to cooperate to the fullest extent required for optimum performance. The following must be the among the most important:

1. Pressed only sporadically or partially by competition, public utility companies are all too often simply excessively relaxed about seeking out

performing the service, using A's facilities, were 3. If the two collaborated, their total MC would be only 6, leaving a profit of 4, whereas if A did the entire job itself its profit would be only 3. In these circumstances, it would certainly seem that a bargain could be struck, with B giving A something between 6 and 7 and keeping for itself something between 3 and 4, thus leaving both of them better off than if A did the entire job alone.
[54] *The New York Times*, June 9, 1968, Sec. 5, 25. Copyright 1968 by the New York Times

Company. Reprinted by permission.
[55] See, for example, William R. Hughes, "Short-Run Efficiency and the Organization of the Electric Power Industry," *Q. Jour. Econ.* (November 1962), LXXVI: 592–612; Curtis A. Cramer, "Interconnection and Peak Responsibility in the Natural Gas Industry," *Land Econ.* (May 1968), XLIV: 229–234.
[56] See pp. 70–75 and 79–80, this Chapter, and Chapter 6, below.

and availing themselves of all possible opportunities for cost reduction or service improvement.[57]

2. This is particularly likely to be the case when the cost savings can be achieved only by sharing revenues with others, and the alternative is for the company to do the business entirely by itself, at rates that exceed its own incremental costs. In purely static terms, this kind of consideration would be irrational for an unregulated, profit-maximizing firm: as we have already suggested, if a joint operation would either reduce costs or increase revenues, both firms can be better off if they share the business. But this would not necessarily be the case for a public utility company, for A–J–W reasons: if one company's handling all the business itself means a larger rate base, it can earn greater total profits (over and above the cost of capital) by keeping it all to itself.[58]

3. This last obstacle might be removed by financial integration. If the two potential collaborators were to merge, it would be a matter of indifference whose rate base were expanded. Or, if individual regulated companies could integrate freely, performing the various functions under one financial umbrella, then each would find it more nearly in its interest to perform each function with the least-cost combination of media. But, as we shall more fully discuss in Chapter 6, below, financial integration might in some circumstances conflict with the preservation of competition; in consequence this route to coordination is often closed. Nor would it completely eliminate the possibility of an A–J–W distortion: if the Bell System were permitted to operate both communications satellites and underwater cable, it might still have the same irrational (from a social standpoint) preference for the more capital-intensive communications medium, though in less extreme form than when, as at present, it can use the former method only by leasing circuits from Comsat, with no contribution whatever to its own rate base.

4. Obstacles of these kinds are likely to be reinforced by dynamic considerations. When a company feels that it is in a position to hold or to take over a growing market, it may on this account forego the reductions in cost or short-term increases in revenue it might achieve by cooperating with others, if it feels that it might in this way lessen their ability to compete for that business. Telephone companies have apparently been unwilling at times to rent use of their poles at reasonable rates to other

[57] For an analysis attributing the recent difficulties of the electric power industry in large measure to its failure to set up regional grids as urged by the FPC and blaming that failure on the ineptitude, conservatism, and lack of imagination of managements "grown complacent on private monopoly and regulated profits," see Jeremy Main, "A Peak Load of Troubles for the Utilities," *Fortune*, November 1969, 116–119 and ff. For similar explanations of noncooperation on the part of the railroads, see pp. 81–82, this chapter and pp. 271 and 310, Chapter 6, below. [58] See in particular the discussion of the resistance to thoroughly integrated power pooling and lack of incentive to lease facilities at pp. 50–51 and 51–52 (points 3 and 5), above, and the numerical illustration involving joint railroad carriage of traffic, at note 101, p. 81, below. On the need for electric power pooling over wider geographic areas and particularly single-area planning of additions to capacity (locating them always on the basis of cost considerations alone, rather than having the partners simply take turns), see also FPC, *National Power Survey*, I, 3, 5, 14, 30, 169–171, 199–200, and 273; Hughes, *op. cit.*, *Q. Jour. Econ.* (November 1962), LXXVI: 608 note 8; Twentieth Century Fund, *Electric Power and Government Policy* (New York: Twentieth Century Fund, 1948), 33; and notes 48 and 50, above.

communications media, such as CATV companies;[59] and electric companies have been reluctant to exchange power nondiscriminately with, or to deliver power to, cooperatives or municipal electric systems.[60] Railroad companies have often been unwilling to make their facilities available to other kinds of common carriers on reasonable and non-discriminatory terms—for example, to offer joint rates with barge or shipping companies that did not discriminate against the latter in favor of all-rail shipment; or to develop joint rates with truckers for piggyback service fully reflecting the cost and service advantages of that integrated operation as compared with the use of all-rail facilities.[61] The possibility of hampering a competitor and taking over more of the business oneself could outweigh the attraction of a temporarily mutually profitable collaboration.

5. In circumstances such as these, companies are likely to be selective in deciding with which other firms they are prepared to cooperate; and the basis of selection need not coincide with criteria of social efficiency. Railroads, for example, have notoriously been more willing to publish attractive joint rates for all-rail shipments—involving two or more rail carriers—than for trips involving a combination of rail and water, as we shall see. One explanation would seem to be the greater mutuality of interest in the first case than in the second. Railroads are more likely to run end-to-end; and if one railroad is willing to collaborate in this fashion with another, it may expect a return of the favor for shipments in the opposite direction. Water carriers are more likely to be directly competitive. They are more likely also to be at the mercy of the railroad initiating the shipment, to let them have a share of the joint trip, and

---

[59] For example, the TeleCable Corp. complained to the FCC in 1969 that the General Telephone Co. of Illinois had refused to negotiate pole attachment contracts with it, in order to favor a CATV subsidiary of its own, and the Commission, in ordering a hearing, recognized the possibility that the phone company might be trying to monopolize the CATV business. *Telecommunications Reports*, May 12, 1969, 33. See also pp. 308–309, Chapter 6, below. In consequence, the FCC in 1970 prohibited telephone companies offering CATV service themselves within their (telephone) operating territories and required them to offer pole line attachment rights to others at reasonable rates and non-discriminatorily, where space could be offered without injury to the telephone service. *In the Matter of Applications of Telephone Companies, etc.*, Docket 18509, Final Report and Order, January 28, 1970.

[60] This reluctance to cooperate has been accentuated by ideological conflicts between proponents of private and public, subsidized and unsubsidized power. See, for example, the FPC, *National Power Survey*, I, 273, 275. But the ideological rift would surely have less influence on business policy were it not that the two systems are in competition (see pp. 105–106, Chapter 3,

below); and it may be a questionable business practice to help your competitor, even if he is prepared to pay a price for your services that covers your long-run marginal costs. See, on these controversies, pp. 316–323, Chapter 6, below. On July 14, 1969, the Department of Justice filed an antitrust suit against the Otter Tail Power Co., an integrated power system in Minnesota and the Dakotas, accusing it of monopolizing the sale of electric power to more than 400 towns in that area. It allegedly did so by refusing and threatening to refuse to sell power at wholesale to towns that proposed to substitute another local distribution system—privately or municipally owned—for Otter Tail, and by refusing and threatening to refuse to carry power from other wholesale suppliers (including the Bureau of Reclamation) over its transmission lines to such towns. *U. S. v. Otter Tail Power Company*, Civil Action No. 6–69 Civil 139, U. S. District Court, District of Minnesota, 6th Division. The President of the company admitted it had established a policy of refusing to transmit federally generated power from the Missouri Basin development over its lines. *Wall Street Journal*, July 15, 1969, 6.

[61] See pp. 271–272 and 310–311, below.

less able to deny the railroad its share in the traffic they originate, for the inland part of the journey. Similarly, large, vertically integrated electric utility companies are more likely to be willing to pool power with each other, because each has something important to contribute to the pool, than to let in on equal terms small, nonintegrated distribution companies that have very little to contribute except their patronage, which they are in any event not free to take elsewhere (either because they are themselves prohibited from engaging in generation of power, or because their requirements are so small that any plant they could themselves construct would be uneconomically small in scale). In such cases, it has taken regulatory intervention to control what might otherwise be a form of predatory or unfair intermedia competition, and to impose the requirement of coordination on nondiscriminatory terms, in the interest of efficiency or of the preservation of competition. We consider some of these interventions in Chapter 6, below.

There is another, quite different kind of reason for regulatory intervention that is, however, closely related to the last: the regulated companies may "coordinate" their activities with excessive enthusiasm. The institution and division of joint rates, the arrangement of power pooling, or joint use of facilities requires constant communication between firms that are in important respects also competitors or potential competitors. It is very difficult to encourage companies to cooperate in such delicate matters as setting joint rates, the sharing of business, and the planning of investment while insisting that they compete vigorously in other respects, especially where there is a strong, general consensus among their managers that unrestricted competition tends to become destructive. So there is a strong tendency for these collaborative efforts to turn into instruments for the collusive suppression of competition among the participants and the collective exclusion of nonparticipating competitors. In consequence, regulatory commissions and antitrust agencies must try to see to it that railroad rate bureaus do not interfere with the right of individual railroads to set their own rates as they choose;[62] or that shipping conferences—associations of shipping companies that fix rates to which the members agree to adhere—are prevented from employing predatory or exclusionary practices with respect to nonmembers.[63] It will not be surprising, in light of our discussion in Chapter 1, that the

---

[62] See *U. S. v. Ass'n of American Railroads*, Civil Action 246, U. S. District Court, District of Nebraska, Complaint filed August 23, 1944, 4 F.R.D. 510, CCH 1944–45 Trade Cases par. 57,417; *Georgia v. Pennsylvania R. R. Co. et al.*, 324 U.S. 439 (1945); and the ensuing Reed–Bulwinkle Act, which exempted ICC-supervised, common-carrier rate bureaus from the antitrust laws, though still nominally insisting that the right of carriers to act independently be preserved. 49 U.S. Code 5b, 1964 ed. Also Locklin, *op. cit.*, 254, 305–306; note 1, Chapter 4, and pp. 255–307, below.

[63] See note 15, Chapter 1, above. In 1959, 63 of the 113 shipping conferences in the foreign trade of the United States employed a dual rate system, charging preferentially lower rates to shippers giving their patronage exclusively to conference members. Daniel Marx, Jr., "Group or Conference Rate-Making and National Transportation Policy in the United States," *Law and Contemporary Problems* (Autumn 1959), XXIV: 600. See *Federal Maritime Board v. Isbrandtsen Co. Inc., et al.*, 356 U.S. 481 (1958), outlawing the practice, and the 1961 amendment to the Shipping Act of 1916, in which Congress legalized dual rates if approved by the FMC and subject to other restrictions. 46 U.S.C. 813a, 1964 ed. See also *Federal Maritime Commission et al. v. Swedish American Line et al.*, 390 U.S. 238 (1968), and Charles Peter Raynor, "Ocean Shipping Conferences and the Federal Maritime Commission," *Cornell Law Rev.* (July 1968), LIII: 1070–1093.

enthusiasm of the commissions for this kind of effort is not typically great, that the antitrust agencies try harder—since preserving competition is *their* responsibility—and that neither is outstandingly successful.

The Imperfect Adaptation of Business Structure: Electric Power

The problem of intercompany coordination among public utilities, then, springs basically from disparities between the requirements and opportunities of technology, on the one hand, and the ways in which these industries are organized, on the other; and from limitations imposed on the ability of the latter to adapt to the former. It is compounded by the deficiencies of the institution of regulated monopoly—the lesser exposure of such companies to the test and pressure of competition; the possible conflict between letting them pursue their own interests and preserving competition; the A–J–W tendency; and by the limited capacity of regulation itself to require the necessary modifications of business policy—conceiving capacity in the sense both of its ability to envisage all the opportunities and its political power or legal authority to force regulated companies to grasp them.[64]

This inhibiting influence of the institutional structure that the industry has inherited from its past is well illustrated in the failure of the electric industry to take full advantage of the opportunities for power pooling. We have already enumerated both the potential advantages and the obstacles.[65] On the other hand, changing technology has been a powerful influence forcing modifications of business organization and practice over time; it would be highly misleading to imply that the latter have been utterly unresponsive.

In the early days of the industry, economies of scale in generation were slight and transmission of power over long distances uneconomic. It therefore consisted in its first decades of a very large number of self-sufficient, local operators: before 1900, indeed, it was not uncommon to have several competing distribution companies in each locality. By 1900, the pattern had emerged of local, franchised monopolists—to what extent as a result of a recognition of the superior economy of distribution monopoly, to what extent of a quest for monopoly privilege is unimportant to the present argument.[66] Rather than rely on private monopolists, many municipalities set up their own generating and distributing systems: there were 700 to 800 of these at the turn of the century.

With increasing opportunities for economies of scale in generation and the feasibility of transmission over greater distances, a growing national concentration of generating plants was, in any event, inevitable; and this alone would have required some financial consolidation and cooperation among previously separate companies. The rise of the public utility holding company, extending financial control over increasing numbers of operating

---

[64] Some of these deficiencies are peculiar to the public utility arena, others more marked there but by no means absent in unregulated industry generally. It would be an interesting exercise for the reader to consider to what extent they apply outside of the regulated industries.

[65] See pp. 50–51, 64–65, and 66–69 above. On

the inadequately integrated planning in the New England region, see *Municipal Electric Ass'n of Massachusetts et al. v. F.P.C.*, 414 F. 2d 1206, 1208 (1969).

[66] See pp. 2–3, Chapter 1 and pp. 117–119, Chapter 4, below.

companies, was undoubtedly motivated in part by the quest for such economies, including also providing the member companies with more efficient management than they could muster on their own and the advantages of technical assistance, and of centralized, large-scale purchasing of supplies and equipment and raising of capital.

To these inducements the booming stock market of the 1920s added immense opportunities for promotional profits and financial manipulation. The organizers could vote themselves large blocks of stock as compensation for their promotional efforts. By vesting in the holding companies the voting common stock of the operating companies, by raising the preponderant portion of the required capital by sale of bonds, preferred stock and non-voting common, and by pyramiding holding companies on top of holding companies, the promoters could with comparatively small investments control vast empires of subsidiary companies.[67] Exercising this control, they could then exploit the operating companies and through them the ultimate customers, by selling equipment and technical, managerial and financial services to them at inflated prices. They could bid up the prices of operating company assets by exchanging them for securities of the acquiring company —securities that the investing public gobbled up at inflated prices; and they could then write up the book value of the assets acquired in this fashion. With *Smyth v. Ames* still controlling, the result could be a higher rate base for purposes of rate level determination. And by trading so heavily on equity, they could enormously increase the returns on the relatively small amount of invested capital represented by their own investment in common stock and thus also increase its saleability to the avid, investing public—as long as the industry prospered.[68] As a result, the frenzied building of holding

---

[67] Suppose the operating companies that are to be acquired have a total capitalization of $1 billion, $\frac{3}{4}$ financed by sale of senior securities— bonds and preferred stock—and $\frac{1}{4}$ by common stock. Assume for the moment all of the common stock carries voting privileges and that it takes ownership of $\frac{1}{2}$ of it for effective control. In this event, it would take an investment of only $125 million to acquire control over the $1 billion system. But suppose, instead, the acquisition of the required $125 million of operating company stock is made by one or a number of first-level holding companies—perhaps by exchange of holding company securities for operating company stock—themselves financed in the same proportions. These companies—whose assets will consist entirely of the $125 million of operating company common stock—can themselves be controlled, similarly, by a purchase of only $\frac{1}{8}$ of their securities, or only $15,625,000. Assume, finally, that this stock is to represent the total assets of a single, peak holding company, financed in the same proportions, and add the other device: assume that only $\frac{1}{2}$ of *its* common stock carries voting privileges. Then it can be controlled by an investment only $\frac{1}{16}$ as large, or just under $1,000,000. So by a minimal, three-layered pyramid total assets of $1 billion

come to be controlled with an investment of only $\frac{1}{16}$ of $\frac{1}{8}$ of $\frac{1}{8}$, or $1/1024$ of that total. And to the extent that the promoters take any of the voting stock at one or another level for themselves as their promotional fees, the required investment on their part drops to an even smaller fraction.

The $1/1000$ is not at all fanciful. See James C. Bonbright and Gardner C. Means, *The Holding Company* (New York: McGraw–Hill Book Company Inc., 1932), 113–116. The Standard Gas and Electric Co. system, with a total investment of $1.2 billion, was controlled by $23,000 of common stock. Twentieth Century Fund, *op. cit.*, 36.

[68] Suppose the senior securities of all the companies in the example in the preceding footnote carry an interest of 4% and the operating companies earn 5% on their invested capital. Of their total earnings of $50 million, thus, $30 million go to the senior securities' holders (4% of $750 million) and $20 million belongs to the common stock, $\frac{1}{2}$ of which is owned by the first level holding companies. This represents an 8% return on their total invested capital ($10 million on $125 million). Of this $10 million, $3,750,000 goes to the bond and preferred stock holders (4% on the $\frac{3}{4}$ of the $125 million financed in this way), leaving $6,250,000 for the $31,250,000 of

company empires and the resulting consolidation of financial control of the industry went far beyond the dictates of economy or efficiency.

The state regulatory agencies were in large measure powerless to prevent this exploitation of their customers—to disallow the inflated service charges, to write down the inflated rate bases of the operating companies. They were powerless because they lacked the competence to make the necessary evaluations, the financial resources and the political strength to stand up to the powerful holding companies, and the authority to do so unless they could prove "bad faith" or "abuse of discretion" before the courts, to which they were certain to be dragged. Least of all could they strike at the heart of the problem by blocking the spread or requiring the dissolution of these vast and intricate holding company systems that created virtually unlimited opportunities for financial manipulation, overcapitalization, cost of service padding, and concealment—for "prestidigitation, double shuffling, honeyfugling, hornswoggling, and skullduggery," in the words of William Z Ripley.[69] By 1929, seven such systems controlled some 60 percent of the electricity generated in the United States.

Recognition and dissatisfaction with the emergent state of affairs grew during the 1920s. But it was the financial collapse of the major systems after the 1929 crash that set the stage for the ultimate reform. The assets of the holding companies consisted, after all, of little more than the common stock of the operating companies at the base of the pyramid. And since at each layer a very large portion of their capital was raised by debt-financing, it took only a comparatively slight deterioration in the fortunes of the operating companies to convert the enormous rates of profit higher up in the pyramids to equally enormous losses; leverage works downward as well as upward.[70] Widespread defaults on debt and the subsequent revelation of the rich record of financial manipulation and exploitative practices[71] led to the passage of the Public Utility Holding Company Act of 1935.

---

their common stock—a return of 20%. Since the peak holding company owns $\frac{1}{4}$ of that common stock, its total earnings on this account are $3,125,000. Of this amount only $468,750 is needed to pay the holders of its senior securities (4% of the $11,718,750 they have contributed to the entire $15,625,000 investment), leaving $2,656,250 for the common stockholders—a return on their $3,906,250 investment of approximately 68%. If, in this example, the operating companies' return on investment were not 5% but 6%, this would produce a return to their common stockholders of 12% and a return to stockholders of the peak holding company of over 130%. Further pyramiding, such as did in fact occur, would provide even more striking examples of leverage, and these too would not be fanciful. See the clear illustrations of both pyramiding of control and leverage of earnings in Eli W. Clemens, *Economics and Public Utilities* (New York: Appleton–Century–Crofts, Inc., 1950), 491–493.

[69] *Main Street and Wall Street* (Boston: Little, Brown & Co., 1927), 303, as quoted in Clemens,

op. cit., 499.

[70] Let the return of all the operating companies in the example in note 68, above, fall from 5% to 4% and the return on all the common stock, up and down the pyramid, drops to 4% too. Let the former return decline only to $3\frac{1}{2}$% and the common stockholders in the peak holding company suffer a loss—after paying the $468,750 they owe on their senior securities, if they can— of $1,093,750, or about 28% of their total investment in that single year. A drop in operating company return to 3% gives their common stockholders a return of precisely zero and common stock of the peak company earnings of minus 60% on investment.

[71] Notably in the *Final Report* of the Federal Trade Commission's investigation of electric and gas utilities, undertaken in 1928 at the direction of Congress and summarizing some 70 volumes of testimony and exhibits. *Utility Corporations*, 70th Cong., 1st Sess., Senate Document 92, Part 72A (1935). See also Bonbright and Means, *op. cit.*, especially Chapters 5–7.

The Act decreed a "death sentence" for the third and higher levels of holding company pyramids. It directed the Securities and Exchange Commission to effect a simplification and reorganization of the entire structure, to refashion the industry into a number of geographically compact systems each composed of functionally interrelated operating companies, with holding companies being permitted to retain control of more than one such integrated system only on demonstration that dissolution would involve "the loss of substantial economies."[72] In addition, it empowered the SEC to institute pervasive controls over the operations of holding companies and their relationships with subsidiaries.

"By 1951 the Commission had undertaken the reformation of corporate structures including more than 200 holding companies and nearly 2,000 other companies. In 1952 it reported that 85 percent of the job was done."[73]

By 1964, the proportion of electricity generation controlled by holding companies had been cut to 21%.[74]

There seems to be little dissent from the conclusion that the job the SEC did in dismantling the jerry-built holding company structures needed doing and was well done.[75]

But it began to appear, 25–35 years after the passage of the enabling act, that the SEC's discouragement of new holding company systems was increasingly incompatible with the dramatic technological developments that became manifest in the decade after World War II.[76] The sharply increasing economies of scale in generation and long-distance transmission at high voltages counselled integration of the industry over wider and wider areas. Largely because of the traditional, localized structure of the industry, a tradition intensified by the unhappy experience with the holding companies and by the 1935 Act, the necessary coordination was achieved principally by voluntary collaboration among operating companies. The collaboration typically fell considerably short of achieving the full possible advantages of complete integration, and particularly the integrated planning of investment.[77] So, paradoxically, Lister and Homan observe:

"The problems to which the Holding Company Act was directed have almost entirely disappeared, a tribute to the Act and its administration. The great problem of the future for the electrical utilities is that of integration and interconnection of systems."[78]

---

[72] Even in this event, continued affiliation was to be permitted only for geographically contiguous systems and only if "the continued combination . . . is not so large . . . as to impair the advantages of localized management, efficient operation, or the effectiveness of regulation." 15 U.S. Code 79k (b) (1), 1964 ed.

[73] Wilcox, op. cit., 368; see 362–369. For a more detailed discussion of the Act's enforcement, see Robert F. Ritchie, *Integration of Public Utility Holding Companies* (Ann Arbor: Univ. of Michigan Press, 1954).

[74] Lister and Homan, op. cit., IV, Chap. 2, 41; see 30–48.

[75] See, in addition to the others already cited, A. J. G. Priest, op. cit., II, 515. "[P]erhaps," writes Priest, "in Victor Hugo's phrase, God was bored with non-integrated holding companies. He could have been forgiven for that sentiment." *Ibid.*, 520. It is a mildly amusing footnote to a footnote that Professor Priest had not included the qualifying adjective "non-integrated" in an earlier published version of this remark, "The Public Utility Holding Company Act Revisited," *Public Utilities Fortnightly* (August 1, 1968), LXXXII: 31.

[76] See p. 128, Volume 1.

[77] See pp. 50–51 and 66–69, above, and the sources cited there.

[78] *Op. cit.*, IV, Chap. 2, 48.

And so they pose some challenging questions:

"Might a fundamentally different organization of the electric power industry best serve the interests of efficiency? . . . The ways of achieving an efficient production structure are no longer bound to local distribution systems.[79] The existing integrated corporate structures, however, still reflect the local origins; and so far as the corporate entities operate in a self-contained way, they tend to nullify the results of advancing technology. When the advantages of inter-corporate collaboration are recognized, it becomes a matter of public interest that the advantages should materialize; and the question arises, whether this should happen solely at the discretion and convenience of separate corporate managements. This poses a new type of regulatory problem.

"Like the corporate structure of the industry, the authority and procedures of state regulatory commissions also reflect the local origins of the industry. As the generating and transmission systems progressively transcend local and intrastate limits, state authority is not only curtailed, but becomes increasingly ill-defined. If generation and transmission were organized in regional networks separate from distribution functions, the lines of regulatory authority would be clear-cut as between state and federal agencies. With the present corporate structure, they can hardly fail to become confusingly intermingled and overlapping.

"These problems of structure and regulation, it must be recognized, are relative. They have not prevented much of the industry from making striking technical progress. But they do define a fundamental difficulty or anomaly: a striking lack of compatibility between the corporate structure of the industry, its emerging technical imperatives, and the procedures by which it is regulated."[80]

The electric utility industry consisted in 1965 of 3,614 companies in all. Some 3,000 of these were local distribution systems owned by municipalities or rural cooperatives, the majority of which did not generate their own power, but purchased it from the 42 federal projects and from the 243 privately owned systems, preponderantly fully integrated (in generation, transmission, and distribution).[81] The central issue today is whether those 243 are not too many or too incompletely coordinated to take full advantage of the potential economies of scale. The answer seems definitely in the affirmative—as far as the bulk supply of power (in contrast with its local distribution) is concerned. William R. Hughes has concluded that if the private sector of the industry were organized into a maximum of twenty to thirty major systems of roughly equal size it could not only more fully achieve the

[79] See the suggestion by Leland Olds, ten years earlier, that planning for mass production of electric power at minimum cost required the separation of local distribution from generation and vesting the latter in huge regional grids, jointly owned by the distribution companies served. "The Economic Planning Function under Public Regulation," *Amer. Econ. Rev., Papers and Proceedings* (May 1958), XLVIII: 553–561.

[80] *Op. cit.*, IV, Chap. 6, 6–8.

[81] The 243 private companies generated 75% of the power sold for public use, the federal projects an additional 14%. The publicly but not federally owned companies and cooperatives accounted for another 11% of the power generated but served perhaps 20% of the retail customers. Figures from the U. S. Department of Commerce, *Statistical Abstract of the United States, 1967*, 526, with more detailed breakdowns, for 1962, in the FPC, *National Power Survey*, I, 17.

available economies of scale—he estimates the efficiency loss from the actual, suboptimal system at four to ten percent of the total cost of power—but it could also pioneer more effectively in extending the "scale frontiers," that is, in promoting technological progress along lines that would further increase the advantages of size. Others have argued that an even greater consolidation of the industry is desirable.[82]

The industry's response has been a renewed merger movement, which, together with an increased resort by smaller distributors to wholesale purchases of power, has resulted in a sharp decline in the population of small companies, public and private, with their own generating facilities.[83]

As the Lister–Homan observation suggests, it was not just the structure of the private industry that had become outmoded by technological progress; the same was true of its regulatory apparatus. The deficiency to which they refer resides in the federal system, with its division of responsibility between the state and federal governments. One consequence of this has been to increase the reluctance of local electric companies to interconnect and pool with others across state lines, because it would bring them under the jurisdiction of the federal agency.[84] Another has been the imposition of restrictions on such coordination by the various state laws and commissions, for fear that it would make the local companies dependent on outside sources of supply, the reliability of which the individual states are less capable of guaranteeing. From the opposite standpoint, there is the problem that the authority of the responsible agencies to compel companies to take full advantage of the opportunities for integration is frequently inadequate.

The Federal Power Commission has only limited powers along these lines. It lacks authority to license construction of interstate transmission facilities; it can compel interconnection of systems only on the petition of others and it cannot in any case do so if this requires one of the parties to enlarge its generating facilities;[85] and it cannot force the separate systems to adopt a

---

[82] Hughes, "Technological Change, Scale Frontiers, and the Organization of the Bulk Power Industry," to be published in a volume of papers delivered at the Brookings Institution Conference on Technological Change in the Regulated Industries, 1969, processed, Charles River Associates, 15, 42, 52–53. See also p. 281, below.

[83] Between 1955 and 1965, the number of private electric supply systems with generating plants declined from 315 to 243 while the total number of such systems dropped from 581 to 472. In the same period the total of publicly but nonfederally owned systems increased from 2,060 to 2,114, but those with generating plants declined from 913 to 813. *Statistical Abstract of the U.S., 1968*, 513.

[84] See p. 30, above.

[85] "Whenever the Commission, upon application of any state commission or of any person engaged in the transmission or sale of electric energy . . . finds such action necessary or appropriate in the public interest it may by order direct a public utility (if the Commission finds

that no undue burden will be placed upon such public utility thereby) to establish physical connection of its transmission facilities with the facilities of one or more other persons engaged in the transmission or sale of electric energy, to sell energy to or to exchange energy with such persons: *Provided*, That the Commission shall have no authority to compel the enlargement of generating facilities for such purposes, nor to compel such public utility to sell or exchange energy when to do so would impair its ability to render adequate service to its customers. The Commission may prescribe the terms and conditions of the arrangement to be made between the persons affected by any such order, including the apportionment of cost between them and the compensation . . . reasonably due any of them." 16 U.S. Code 824 (b), 1964 ed.

The Commission's authority is similarly limited with respect to natural gas pipelines. 15 U.S. Code 717f (a), 1964 ed.

In any event, the FPC availed itself of the above authority in the landmark *City of Shrewsbury*

completely integrated planning of the construction and utilization of their facilities. In consequence, as we have already observed, the degree of coordination actually achieved falls considerably short of the optimum. The efforts of the FPC to obtain such powers[86] and the development of pooling on a voluntary basis, as well, are both complicated by continuing controversies over the Commission's authority over the wholesale rates charged by pool members[87] and the terms, if any, on which publicly owned generating or distribution companies are to be admitted to such pools. Since these issues concern the appropriate role and definition of competition in the industry, we reserve consideration of them for Chapter 6, below.

There is another potentially effective way in which regulatory commissions can force coordination on reluctant companies: to the extent that they have the authority to certificate (or refuse to certificate) proposed new investments, or to decide what investments they are prepared to permit a company to include in its rate base, they can disallow those commitments of capital that reflect insufficient integration. Thus, as we have already suggested,[88] the Federal Communications Commission has it within its power to overcome any possible reluctance of established common carrier companies to lease facilities from the Communications Satellite Corporation, and any corresponding bias in the direction of constructing their own terrestrial (or submarine) facilities, by refusing to certificate the latter investments. This very issue was presented in the application of AT&T in 1968 to lay additional submarine cable (the TAT–5) between New York and Southern Europe, a request strongly contested by Comsat. The Commission may or may not have made the correct decision in giving the applicants a green light,[89] but there was no question that it had the opportunity here of

---

case, in which it ordered the New England Power Company to interconnect with the facilities of that city's municipal distribution company and in this way to give the city the opportunity of getting its power at a lower rate. *Shrewsbury Municipal Light Department v. New England Power Co.*, 32 FPC 373 (1964), upheld in *New England Power Co. v. F.P.C.*, 349 F. 2d 258 (1965). A number of other small systems responded to that decision by filing similar complaints with the Commission. Charles R. Ross, "An Alternative to Small-Scale Generation and Transmission," an address before the Legal Seminar of the American Public Power Association, Atlanta, Georgia, November 14, 1966 (mimeo), 10–11. For a later example, see the FPC's Opinion 550, November 5, 1968, *Gainesville Utilities Department et al. v. Florida Power*, E–7257, ordering the latter company to interconnect with and to serve the former on terms prescribed by the Commission. The order was sustained by the Circuit Court of Appeals, 5th Circuit, in *Florida Power Corp. v. F.P.C.*, May 1, 1970. See, similarly, *Otter Tail Power Co. v. F.P.C.*, 429 F. 2d 232, (1970).

[86] It has recommended passage of the Electric Power Reliability Act of 1967 (S. 1934, H.R. 10727), which would, among other things, authorize establishment of regional planning

councils, including all segments of the industry, "to review, test and coordinate plans for bulk power facilities throughout a region"; would give it power to review the construction of extrahigh-voltage transmission lines "to insure their consistency with high standards of reliability, usefulness, efficient utilization of land and conservation of historic sites and other limited resources"; and to "authorize the Commission to require interconnections between bulk power suppliers. . . ." FPC, *Annual Report, Fiscal Year 1967*, Washington, 1968, 5. This Report also summarizes the several cases in which the Commission ordered integrated private utility companies to interconnect with publicly owned distribution systems, and to supply them with wholesale power at reduced rates. *Ibid.*, 19–20; see also note 85, immediately preceding.

[87] See the discussion of the FPC's successful assertion of expanded authority along these lines, at note 71, Chapter 1, above, and of the industry's attempt to reverse it, pp. 322–323, Chapter 6.

[88] See pp. 51–52 and 56, this chapter, above.

[89] Its decision has the flavor of an effort to keep both contending parties happy by assuring them "fair shares" in the expanding international communications business. In granting the application of AT&T, IT&T, RCA, and Western

correcting for any possible biases in the investment decisions of the companies subject to its jurisdiction. The burden of the argument of this chapter is that regulatory commissions have too seldom had either the competence, the willingness, or sufficient authority to substitute their judgments for those of private management in this fashion.[90]

REGULATORY PLANNING

As the preceding discussion has demonstrated, regulatory intervention neither need be nor should be confined to the passive offer of inducements to private management. On the contrary, the more competent the commission and its staff and the broader and more clear-cut its legislative mandate, the greater are the possibilities of its assuming the initiative in influencing the performance of the companies under its jurisdiction.

An appropriate place to begin is with the Federal Power Commission

---

Union to participate in the project, it attached a condition that the parties

"use satellite circuits . . . in numbers sufficient to insure that the unfilled portion of the TAT–5 cable and of new satellite facilities (i.e. Intelsat III–1/2 or IV) provided within the 1970–72 time frame . . . will each be filled at the same proportionate rate. . . ." *In the Matter of American Telephone and Telegraph Company et al. Applications for authorization to participate in the construction and operation of an integrated submarine cable and radio system etc.*, Memorandum Opinion, Order and Authorization, 13 FCC 2d 235, at par. 10 (iii) (May 1968).

It is difficult to decide whether this sort of compromise—uncomfortably reminiscent of ICC policy in regulating the competition between different transportation media (see pp. 21–22, Chapter 1, above)—was likely to result in as seriously an inefficient distribution of the business as it has in the field of transportation. The majority of the Commission seemed to feel that there was an immediate prospective need for additional capacity that only the cable could supply, that for that need the cable was the lowest-cost alternative, and that the uncertainty about the future state of the art in both cable and satellite technology justified giving both media an opportunity to grow together and probe the possibilities of improving their respective technologies. On Commissioner Johnson's dissent concerning the relative economy of the two alternatives, see p. 122 of Volume 1 and especially note 98. As he remarked at one point in the proceedings,

"If ATT wants to invest in an uneconomic cable why not let them? If a manufacturer invests in uneconomic plant he will suffer competitive disadvantage, may lose money, and may even go out of business. ATT, however,

suffers no such risk. ATT's investments, once approved by the Commission, go into its 'rate base.' Forever after its charges for telephone service will be fixed by the Commission at levels adequately high to provide a 'rate of return' on that investment. Thus, unless uneconomic capital investments are challenged by the Commission they will be unchecked. . . ." FCC, Letter of February 16, 1968 to Richard R. Hough, Vice President, AT&T, FCC 68–212 12514, Dissenting Opinion.

[90] This is the conclusion, also, of Clemens, *op. cit.*, 127–131. One would have thought that the comparative costs of cable and satellite would have played a major role in the FCC's TAT–5 decision. And, in fact, in its earlier invitation to AT&T to submit that application, the Commission did conclude that the cable would be the more economical expedient for the near future (see note 89, above). Perhaps because of the vigorous dissent on this question by Commissioner Johnson, it is instructive that in its final decision the Commission simply retreated from cost comparisons.

"[W]e do not believe that any useful purpose would be served by going over relative costs. . . .

"[W]e do not feel it necessary to make definitive findings on the relative merits of TAT–5 and present . . . satellites.

"[T]here are difficulties in making comparisons between cable and satellite costs. . . ." As cited by Posner, *op. cit.*, *Stanford Law Rev.* (February 1969), XXI: 617 note.

For another example of a regulatory commission passing up the opportunity to take a strong initiative at the investment planning stage, an initiative strongly proposed by its own staff and presiding examiner, see the discussion in Chapter 4, pp. 154–155, below.

itself, since we have just been commenting on the inadequacy of its powers
to impose true integration on the electric industry. Given these limitations,
the Commission did take an important and creative step forward, in 1964,
under its statutory mandate to:

"divide the country into regional districts for the *voluntary* interconnection
and coordination of facilities for the generation, transmission, and sale of
electric energy. . . . It shall be the duty of the Commission to promote and
encourage such interconnection and coordination. . . ."[91]

Its *National Power Survey*, published in that year, represented the first effort
to carry out that mandate on a national level. As the statutory language
indicates, the Commission has no power to enforce its recommendations, and
there remain difficult problems in securing the necessary cooperation from
the industry. Still, this initiative—involving in its preparation the cooperation
of all portions of the industry, and serving as a stimulus to industry-conducted
efforts, as a goal, and a model—was a laudible and successful effort to overcome the inherent limitations of the regulatory process.[92]

Regulatory commissions may be able to play a creative role of this kind
mainly indirectly—by actively refashioning the structure of the industry—or
directly, by framing comprehensive rules for the conduct of the regulated
companies and specifying the results they are to achieve. The outstanding
example of regulatory intervention along both these lines was the one we have
already briefly described—the complete reconstitution of the financial
superstructure of the electric power industry and pervasive regulation of
dealings between parent companies and subsidiaries, carried out by the SEC
under the Public Utility Holding Act of 1935.

In contrast, the comprehensive and systematic reorganization of the railroads called for in the Transportation Act of 1920 never took place. (A comprehensive restructuring did take place in the 1960s, but as we shall see in
Chapter 6, it was hardly systematic and hardly a reflection of active regulatory planning.) The roads emerged from World War I, during which
period they were actually under government ownership, amid widespread
concern about their financial strength, credit worthiness, and ability to
provide adequate service. In consequence, whereas regulation before 1920
had been essentially restrictive and negative, designed essentially to prevent
abuses, the revision of 1920 directed itself primarily to the promotion of a
strong railroad industry. To this end it specifically instructed the Interstate
Commerce Commission to make valuations of railroad property and adjust
rates to permit a fair return. It conferred on the ICC for the first time the
power to fix minimum as well as maximum rates, reflecting the further
shift in emphasis from the prevention of exploitation to the curtailment of
competition.[93] More directly relevant, it directed the Commission to take a
more active role both in influencing the industry's structure and controlling
its performance. The ICC was, for the first time, given authority to establish

---

[91] 16 U.S. Code 824 (a), 1964 ed., stress supplied.
[92] See Hughes, "Regulation and Technological
Destiny: The National Power Survey," *Amer.
Econ. Rev., Papers and Proceedings* (May 1966),
LVI: 330–338. Also Leland Olds, *op. cit.*, whose
proposals of eight years earlier the FPC was in
part following in making its survey.

[93] This is not at all to disavow the Kolko, Hilton,
or Boies thesis that this had always been an
essential purpose and inherent tendency of the
Interstate Commerce Act. But the novel provisions of the 1920 Act do support our own
qualification of that thesis. See note 64, Chapter
1, above.

rules for the exchange of freight cars (this one happened in 1917), to require joint use of terminals, to control the building of new lines and abandonments of service, to compel a railroad to extend its lines where required "by the public convenience and necessity," and to permit or disallow pooling (which had previously been forbidden) and mergers (which had previously been systematically and successfully attacked under the antitrust laws).[94]

Most dramatically emphasizing the shift intended by the framers of the 1920 Act from negative controls to positive planning, from a primary reliance on competition and antitrust to coordination and consolidation, was the directive to the ICC to prepare a plan for the consolidation of the nation's railroads into a limited number of systems of roughly comparable efficiency, financial strength, and profitability. The primary intention here, as in the rest of the Act, was to improve the financial position of the railroads as a group, while avoiding conferring unnecessarily high returns on the strong companies. The conception was, accordingly, that the reorganization of the industry would involve the joining of strong and weak roads, with the effect of equalizing profitability, permitting such rate increases as were required to improve the financial health and credit attractiveness of the entire system, forestalling abandonment of service by unprofitable lines, and permitting improvement and extension of service generally.[95]

This ambitious legislative effort was an almost total failure. As early as 1921, the Commission boldly published the comprehensive reorganization plan prepared for it by Professor William Z. Ripley of Harvard; but the plan came under such bitter attack, from such a variety of sources within and without the industry, that it lost heart, concluded by the mid-1920s that the task was infeasible, and asked Congress to relieve it of the responsibility. Only after Congress had failed several times to act did the ICC, finally, publish its own plan, in 1929.[96] Partly because of this delay and partly because of the long depression that followed, no consolidations were carried out by plan between 1920 and 1940, in which year the provision was abolished. As a matter of fact, numerous railroad acquisitions and consolidations took place, notably by long-term lease and by the use of holding companies—the latter being uncovered by the Commission's new authority over mergers—but

[94] This account of the Act of 1920 and the experience under it draws heavily on Stuart Daggett, *Principles of Inland Transportation*, rev. ed. (New York: Harper & Brothers Publishers, 1934), 584–606 and Chapter 39, and Locklin, *op. cit.*, 226–252, 296–304, 392–404.

[95] It was hoped that the same purpose could be achieved, in the interim, by the Act's so-called recapture clause, which provided that if in any year a carrier earned in excess of 6 percent on the value of its property, it was to turn over one-half of the excess to the ICC, which could use the proceeds to make loans to needy carriers, or to acquire equipment which it would in turn lease to them. (The other half was to be retained by the successful roads and accumulated in a reserve fund that would enable them to maintain dividends, interest, and rental payments in poor years.) This provision was almost totally in-

effective, because of the inability of the Commission to work out a system of railroad property valuation (on which the 6 percent cutoff rate of return was to be computed) acceptable to the Supreme Court [see *St. Louis & O'Fallon Ry. Co. v. United States*, 279 U.S. 461 (1929), overturning the Commission's valuation for failure to give consideration to reproduction cost]. It was destroyed by the great depression of the 1930s, and was given a decent burial in the Emergency Railroad Transportation Act of 1933. See Locklin, *op. cit.*, 231–232, 248–249, 392–395, 400–401; Sharfman, *op. cit.*, Part III, Vol. B, 221–255.

[96] See the comprehensive account by William Norris Leonard, *Railroad Consolidation Under the Transportation Act of 1920* (New York: Columbia Univ. Press, 1946), Chapters 4 and 5.

"judged in the light of the major object which Congress sought to accomplish when it enacted the consolidation laws, that is, the combination of weak and strong roads into a limited number of systems balanced as to size, competitive strength and earning power. . . . the results were negligible."[97]

We cannot here appraise the purposes of the consolidation clause of the 1920 Transportation Act. Its basic approach of having profitable roads acquire unprofitable ones was economically questionable[98]—involving as it did an implicit intention of fostering internal subsidization, of protecting some companies from deserved extinction and uneconomic services from abandonment. This was not the way to increase the efficiency of the entire system or to equip it to meet the only-just-beginning competition of the motor carrier. On the other hand, there seem to have been significant economies that could have been achieved by a well-designed system of consolidation, including important economies of compulsory coordination;[99] and to a considerable extent all three goals—efficiency, protecting weaker roads, and the preservation of competition—were entirely compatible.

The point is that some of the disadvantages of the smaller roads were purely strategic, rather than a reflection of either inefficiency on their part or an inability of the territories they served to support continued service. And these disadvantages could have been eliminated by an appropriate program of mergers, with the consequence not only of strengthening the smaller roads but also cutting transportation costs. As Daggett stated:

"Some strategically located systems use their exclusive control over certain terminal facilities or their ability to divert traffic from one to another of their connections to extort a species of monopoly profit, which enriches them while keeping other railroads poor. This practice has a two fold result upon the

---

[97] *Ibid.*, 261; see Chapters 6 and 7 and pp. 257–267.

[98] Daggett pointed out it was impossible to achieve the asserted purpose of permitting such rate increases as might be required to raise profits of the railroads, taken together, to reasonable levels, while avoiding the injustice of conferring excessive returns on the already profitable roads—except by concealment. The reason is that the terms of the consolidation would presumably involve the stockholders of the separate companies obtaining participations in the new, merged company more or less in proportion to the earning power of the predecessor railroads. Stockholders of the profitable roads could be expected to acquire stock in the successor company in disproportionately large amounts, and the stockholders of previously unprofitable companies in disproportionately small amounts, compared with their original investments. Raising or holding the return of the successor company to reasonable levels would still have the effect of conferring supernormal returns on the former and subnormal on the latter. *Op. cit.*, 596–597.

[99] Leonard concluded:

"It is safe to say that the failure of the railroads

to consolidate has meant a financial loss to them and the nation running into billions of dollars." *Op. cit.*, 267.

And he criticizes both the Transportation Act and the ICC for their failure sufficiently to have emphasized this purpose, rather than the mere support of weak roads by the strong. *Ibid.*, 281–283. (We will have occasion in Chapter 6 to consider these possibilities and whether the ICC did a more successful job of planning the substantial restructuring of the industry that took place in the 1960s.) These advantages could conceivably have been achieved by coordination alone, without need for financial consolidation. This was the major purpose of the Emergency Railroad Transportation Act of 1933 (Public Law No. 68, 73rd Cong.), creating the office of the Federal Coordinator of Transportation:

"Congress apparently contemplated such things as pooling of equipment, joint use of tracks and terminals, and cooperative effort of many sorts." Locklin, *op. cit.*, 246.

This hope, too, was disappointed: the initiative in working out these plans was to be taken by committees of the railroads themselves, and managements simply could not agree. *Ibid.*

public. That is to say, it tends to hamper railroad development in the territory of the less favorably situated carriers, and it causes deflections of traffic and consequent wastes of transportation that are disadvantageous to shippers and consumers as a whole. The underlying purpose of the Ripley plan was to minimize these practices by giving to each of the great systems of the country easy access both to sources of traffic and to destination points in large selected territories, a result which would be of undoubted advantage to railroad transportation as a whole."[100]

That is to say, consolidation plans could have overcome the handicap of small lines stemming from their lack of direct access to points of traffic interchange or origination. Under unregulated competition this meant their competitors had the first shot at such traffic, even in situations in which the disadvantaged lines might conceivably have been the more efficient carrier for their portion of the journey.

"Too often this factor is overlooked, and consolidation is considered as contributing to the solution of the weak-and-strong-road problem only through saddling weak and unprosperous lines upon the stronger."[101]

In any event, the call for bold Commission planning brought no effective response, mainly because the Act gave the ICC no power to compel such reorganizations as it felt were required. Its only authority was to reject mergers submitted for its consideration that did not, in its judgment, conform to the overall plan. Leaving the initiative entirely to the railroads, the plan failed because railroad managements did not respond to the opportunity—partly because no executive was willing to "consolidate himself out of a job,"[102] and partly because of their ingrained hostility to collaborating in so

---

[100] *Op. cit.*, 601–602. See also 597 ff.

[101] Locklin, *op. cit.*, 396.

The reader will recognize here another illustration of the problem of intercompany coordination, discussed earlier in this chapter: two roads may perform the transportation function more efficiently in combination, but one of them, in a position to do the entire job itself, chooses not to take on the other as a partner. The question may, again, be asked: if B (the weaker line) could do its portion of the haul at lower marginal costs than A, why would it not pay A to turn to B for that portion of the task? It would seem there ought to be a price for the service, somewhere between the incremental costs of A and B, respectively, at which both would profit from such an arrangement—B would make money and A would save money (see note 53, above). Suppose, for example, A originates some X to Z traffic at point X, but for the second part of the trip, between points Y and Z, it could be carried either by A's circuitous route, at an MC of 3, or B's more direct route, at an MC of 2. Clearly both A and B would be better off if A let B do the carrying in exchange for a share of the joint rate anywhere between 2 and 3. But what if the published rate for the YZ trip is 5? If that is the price B charges on traffic

originating at Y and if it would be illegally discriminatory for it to take any less as its share of any joint X to Z rate that it sets in collaboration with A, A would be better off keeping all the traffic and pocketing the difference between its MC (3) and the fare for the Y to Z portion of the trip (5). If, that is, the quoted tariff for the business in question (Y to Z) exceeds the marginal cost of both high- and low-cost carriers, and they are not in a position to negotiate a lower price *between* their marginal costs, it will pay the higher-cost carrier to keep the business rather than share it. A's incentive to do so might be increased, too, by the possibility that, denied the opportunity to participate in such collaborative arrangements, B might eventually have to go out of business, or might be induced to sell out to A at a favorable price. A financial consolidation of the two would eliminate such obstacles to having each portion of the business handled by the physical facility with the lowest incremental cost.

But compulsory coordination, imposed by the regulatory agency, could produce the same result and preserve the competition between A and B. See 273–275, 285–287, below.

[102] Leonard, *op. cit.*, 269 note, quoting the president of the Baltimore and Ohio Railroad.

thoroughgoing a fashion.[103] Finally, some of the blame must go to the ICC itself: it was not to be expected that a commission, with some 40 years behind it of passive and negative regulatory experience, would be prepared to undertake so bold and controversial an initiative.[104]

Interestingly, it was an ICC examiner, John S. Messer, who, 40 years later, tried unsuccessfully to induce the Commission to take a bold new initiative, this time by directly prescribing certain aspects of railroad performance. Messer's radical suggestion was that the ICC for the first time assert the authority to impose on all railroads in interstate commerce certain minimum (and improved) standards for passenger service.[105] The recommendations issued from the first investigation of the adequacy of passenger service in the Commission's 81-year history: it had been generally assumed previously that the ICC had no authority in this area—an assumption that the Commission reaffirmed in 1969 when it overturned the Messer decision.[106]

---

[103] The economist is naturally reluctant to accept explanations of business behavior that run in terms of suspicion and "irrational" attachment to independence. It is conceivable that the proponents of consolidation exaggerated the opportunities for cost reduction; and that the principal reason for the failure of strong lines to merge with weak was that there were no mutually acceptable terms on which the former could have been expected to take on the burdens of the latter. But the institutionalist will recognize that men are motivated by considerations other than maximizing the profitability of the companies they manage; and that they cannot necessarily be counted on to seize all opportunities for pursuing their own goals, whatever they may be.

[104] See *ibid.*, 271–281; Sharfman, *op. cit.*, Vol. 3A, 482–483; Williams, *op. cit.*, 199 ff.; and for a general appraisal, the *Doyle Report*, *op. cit.*, 249–272.

[105] He proposed, among other things, that:

"Trains operating over a line of railroad in excess of 250 miles must include in their consist facilities for meal service of no less a standard than that provided by an automat car as previously described.

"Every train engaged in transporting passengers . . . between the hours of 10 P.M. and 8 A.M. must include in its consist adequate sleeping-car accommodations.

"Trains whose transit-time is 12 hours or more must include in their consist adequate sleeping-car accommodations and a diner-lounge car as well as additional meal service when required.

"All cars used for the transportation of passengers must be equipped with air conditioning and heating facilities, lighting, rest rooms, and drinking water, all in good operational order. These cars must be maintained in clean and sanitary condition, both interior and exterior.

"The average speed of passenger trains must not be less than that of the carrier's most expedited freight train." *Adequacies—Passenger Service—Southern Pacific Company Between California and Louisiana*, Report and Recommended Order, Interstate Commerce Commission, No. 34733, served April 22, 1968, mimeo (hereinafter, Messer, *op. cit.*), 44.

[106] *Adequacies—Passenger Service—Southern Pacific Co. between California and Louisiana*, Report of the Commission, 335 ICC 415 (1969). It was generally accepted that before passage of the Transportation Act of 1958 authority over passenger train service had been left entirely to the states. The 1958 Act gave the ICC authority only with respect to proposed discontinuations of passenger service and only where the operations in question were subject to state regulation: (1) with respect to interstate service, to suspend any proposed discontinuations for one year if it found the continued operation "required by public convenience and necessity" and not unduly burdensome on interstate or foreign commerce and (2) with respect to intrastate service, to *overrule* any state agency's order *prohibiting* discontinuation, on petition by the carrier and on a finding that "the present and future public convenience and necessity permit of such discontinuance . . . and . . . the continued operation or service . . . will constitute an unjust and undue burden upon the interstate operations of such carrier or carriers. . . ." 49 U.S. Code 13a, 1964 ed. See also note 107 immediately following and Locklin, *op. cit.*, 256–257, 578–580.

The Hearing Examiner concluded that the ICC did have the power to regulate the quality of passenger service, on the basis of the provision of the Interstate Commerce Act that imposed on common carriers the duty "to provide and furnish transportation upon reasonable request therefor" and "to provide reasonable facilities." 49 U.S. Code 1 (4), 1964 ed. He justified the

Equally striking is the fact that the recommended decision came ten years after enactment of the Transportation Act of 1958, which made it much easier for railroads to discontinue unremunerative passenger service;[107] during the decade, they had availed themselves of the opportunity in increasing measure, and passenger service had, in fact, been severely constricted in quantity and deteriorated in quality.

The Examiner's proposal reflected a widespread conviction that the railroads were abusing the privilege—pursuing a deliberate policy of downgrading passenger service, in order then to justify its discontinuation. The Commission itself had on this basis refused a few years earlier to permit a requested discontinuation.

"The evidence in this proceeding makes it abundantly clear that Southern Pacific has continued to discourage use of these trains by passengers. In fact, it has intensified its efforts in that direction. Whenever it appears, as it does in this proceeding, that a carrier has deliberately downgraded its service in order to justify discontinuance of a train irrespective of the actual or potential needs of the travelling public, the Commission will order the service to be continued. See *Pennsylvania R. Co. Discontinuance of Passenger Service*, 320 ICC 319, 323 (1963). The Commission will not find burdens on interstate commerce within the meaning of Section 13a of the act to be 'undue' if those burdens are voluntarily created by carriers for the purpose of obtaining a favorable decision from the Commission."[108]

So, in this later *Southern Pacific* case, on the basis of similar findings—

"The evidence . . . justifies the conclusion that the S.P., and other railroads, has downgraded its passenger-train service and that this has contributed materially to the decline in patronage"[109]

Examiner Messer took the next logical step, requiring that the quality of service be positively improved.

---

novel assertion of authority on the ground, first, that the Commission had in the past abstained in deference to the wish of state commissions to control passenger service themselves, whereas in the Southern Pacific proceeding it was five states that had petitioned it to intervene, and second, that it had not been as necessary in the past for the ICC to step in to protect passengers in this way:

"Humans were certainly not excluded from such humanitarian considerations out of callousness or indifference, but rather because the human creature was being treated with deference and accorded every consideration. . . . Today, we are confronted with an entirely different situation. While we still have laws to protect the treatment of dumb animals, the human beings riding the involved passenger trains are provided marginal eating and no sleeping facilities on a 2,033 mile run which takes 45 hours and 15 minutes to complete, if the train is on schedule." Messer, *op. cit.*, 8; see 3–11.

[107] See note 106, immediately preceding. Congress passed the law because it believed that state regulatory commissions had unduly obstructed abandonments, with the consequence that the freight business was forced to subsidize passenger traffic. For other provisions of the Act, see note 12, Chapter 6, Volume 1, and pp. 23–24, Chapter 1, above. As far as interstate service is concerned, the Act gives carriers the right to discontinue any portion thereof, entirely on their own volition, merely by giving 30 days advance notice, subject only to the above-mentioned authority of the ICC to suspend the proposed discontinuation for a year. On intrastate service, the carriers must, as before, apply to the state authorities for permission to discontinue, but the Act for the first time permits them an appeal to the ICC. The latter agency may then overrule any state restraining order under the conditions cited above—that is, where it finds that continued provision of the service does in fact impose a financial burden on the interstate operations of the carriers.

[108] As quoted by Messer, *op. cit.*, 31.

[109] *Ibid.*, 41.

To some extent he was probably trying to force the railroad company to do something that was not to its advantage—that is, to carry on a non-compensatory passenger operation at the expense of its stockholders and other classes of customers. This purpose is betrayed by his references to the public service obligations of the railroads and to the past favors conferred on them by society, giving rise in turn to an obligation to serve that, the Supreme Court had earlier declared, "cannot be avoided merely because it will be attended by some pecuniary loss."[110] This explicit intention to preserve a system of internal subsidization is suggested also by the Examiner's recognition that the increases in freight rates that had been permitted in the past "would not have been as large as they were if there had been no passenger deficit," and by his observation that decisions to abandon certain passenger services were "motivated on the principle that profitability was the only criterion, with total disregard of the social and economic needs of the public."[111]

But in other respects the proposed decision both recommended and reflected a more active assumption of responsibility by the ICC for producing a more efficient performance of the railroad industry in strictly economic terms. First, following the lead of the Commission's own comprehensive 1959 report on the *Railroad Passenger Train Deficit*,[112] as well as the various Congressional and Presidential reports on national transportation policy (alluded to in Chapter 1), it pointed out the numerous ways in which the passenger revenues and costs *of the railroads* understate the total benefits and exaggerate the economic costs of travel by rail relative to other media. Among the externalities and distortions listed were the benefits to local communities at large of continued availability of passenger service, the congestion of roads and airways, the flagrantly discriminatory burden of state property taxation, and the inflation of railway labor costs by unreasonable union contract provisions.[113] So, Messer made wide-ranging recommendations for corrective action by local and state governments, Congress, and the railroads themselves. He recommended, for example, that local governments purchase the railroad depots (thereby removing the property from the tax rolls), maintain them at public expense and rent them back to the roads at reasonable rents; he suggested, further, that carriers be authorized to abandon service to communities refusing to enter into such arrangements.[114] The failure of legislatures to eliminate or correct these many market

---

[110] *Alabama Public Service Commission et al. v. Southern R. Co.*, 341 U.S. 341, 353 (1951).

[111] *Op. cit.*, 39, 29, respectively.

[112] 306 ICC 417 (1959).

[113] On some of these distortions see pp. 130, 161 note 2, 165–166 note 12, and 199, all in Volume 1, and notes 199 and 200, Chapter 5, below.

[114] Messer, *op. cit.*, 45. He summarizes the recommendations of the ICC report on the *Railroad Passenger Train Deficit*:

1. Repeal of the 10 percent federal excise tax on passenger fares;
2. Reduction of federal taxes;
3. Reduction of state and local taxes;
4. Provision of state and local subsidies;
5. Greater use of passenger-trains by various government agencies. All these involve government-imposed distortions or corrections of market imperfections. The remainder call for corrective action by the railroads themselves:
6. Elimination of duplicate services by railroad management;
7. Experimentation with new types of equipment;
8. Improvement in the attractiveness of passenger service, as a means of stimulating more traffic;
9. The undertaking of management studies of possible fare adjustments, schedule

distortions cannot fairly be cited as evidence of the defects of regulation by administrative commission.

Second, and even more challenging, the Examiner did not hesitate to substitute his own judgment for that of the railroad's management in deciding whether passenger service was or could be made to be financially remunerative. He revised the company's proffered revenue and cost figures, which produced a purported operating deficit of over $4 million in the test year (1966)—primarily by excluding from allegedly "out-of-pocket" costs expenditures for such things as maintenance of equipment and of right-of-way and structures on the ground that these would not be "eliminated as a result of discontinuance. These are fully allocated costs and are not of a savable nature."[115] These revisions converted the loss into an estimated $700,000 annual profit. This profit, he asserted, would more than offset the expenses of the sleeping-car and diner-lounge car that he wanted to require the railroad to restore. As for the future, he rejected the company's projections of continued decline in demand for passenger train travel, asserting, instead, that

"If the defeatist attitude of the rail carriers could be overcome and reasonable efforts be made to improve the passenger service, a considerable portion of the lost patronage could be recovered."[116]

Setting aside, for the moment, the fact that it was eventually aborted, what are we to make of this attempt on the part of a regulatory commission to tell private management how to pursue its own interest? To the extent that this last interpretation of the recommended decision is appropriate, a regulator was not here proposing quality standards in order to prevent a monopolist from exploiting consumers by poor service; rather, he was arguing that improvement in service would be in the interest of both company and customers. If the passenger service in question either did or could be made to cover its incremental costs, why would not a profit-maximizing company, monopolist or otherwise, see and pursue its own interest in cultivating it? The question is obviously an institutional one, and cannot be answered within the framework of an assumption of perfectly rational, profit-maximizing behavior by regulated companies.[117] In view precisely of the institutional deficiencies of regulation, an important one of which is the danger that a conservative management may respond to competition by retrenchment rather than by risk-taking innovation, the economist probably should applaud this kind of initiative on the part of regulators. The possible benefits of a more dynamic, competitive performance probably outweigh the economic waste that would occur if the commission's appraisal of the market prospects proved to be incorrect.[118]

---

changes and improved promotional activities. *Ibid.*, 41–42.

These suggestions are more fully discussed also in the *Doyle Report*, 445–491. In the fall of 1969 the Department of Transportation announced that it would shortly propose legislation for upgrading the nation's railroad passenger service. *Wall Street Journal*, September 26, 1969, 3.
[115] *Op. cit.*, 17–18, 37–38, and Appendixes D

and E. On the governing economic principles and the nature of the ICC's measurements, see pp. 150–155, Volume 1.
[116] *Ibid.*, 41.
[117] See the similar observation in note 103, above.
[118] Since the full Commission's rejection of the trial examiner's recommended decision turned on the legal question of its authority to require railroads to improve passenger service, it is not of substantial economic interest. In fact, the ICC

Perhaps the greatest opportunity for regulatory commissions assuming a more active role in the direct planning of industrial performance is offered by the general and growing discontent with traditional rate-base, rate-of-return regulation among regulated companies and public alike. We have already detailed its limitations: its concern with the minor portion of total costs and with a comparatively unimportant aspect of total performance. The question inescapably presents itself: could not commissions instead focus directly on, and specify standards with respect to the major aspects of performance—the level and trend of prices, the extent, quality, variety and reliability of service? These could, most of them, be formulated in quantitative terms; and it could only be helpful to all parties for commissions to monitor and publish their measurements of performance in these various dimensions. Conceivably, commission and companies might concentrate their efforts on striking a bargain specifying what would constitute a reasonable performance in some predetermined period of time, with the former agreeing to permit the latter a rate of return that would vary in proportion to achievement of the agreed-upon goals. Both parties might work toward translating the bargain into an estimate of the company's total financial requirements, and the proportion that it would be allowed to recover in its rates. The emphasis would in this way be shifted from the costs of existing levels of service in some past year to the estimated costs of producing *desired* or *projected* levels of service in the future.

There are obvious problems in designing an acceptable list of performance goals properly related to what is economically achievable and in devising a system of rewards neither too great nor too small to elicit the desired results, and to be payable only upon delivery. But the effort would be in the right direction.

THE ADJUDICATORY ROLE AND ITS CONSEQUENCES

But such examples of Commission initiative—apart from the more informal and continuous advice and prodding, whose intensity, frequency, and effectiveness are difficult to characterize[119]—remain the exception rather than the rule. And, apart from the SEC's enforcement of the Public Utility Holding Company Act, their accomplishments have been limited. Pre-

---

had earlier supported Messer's substantial conclusions, when it refused to let the Southern Pacific drop the service in question on the ground that the company had "deliberately downgraded the service" in order to discourage passengers. See p. 83, above. When, therefore, in overturning the Messer decision, the Commission later decided it lacked authority to regulate the quality of service, it recognized that the petitioning states were powerless, too, and therefore specifically asked Congress to give it that power:

"What we have in mind are requirements for the restoration of reasonable standards of service, equipment, and facilities, giving due regard to the carrier's resources and the willingness of the public to provide its support and patronage. . . .

"Within the framework of these standards . . . we believe the quality of service offered by the Nation's railroads can be significantly improved." 335 ICC 415, 433, 435 (1969).

For another striking example of regulatory initiative, in which an examiner proposed that his Commission rise above the mere choice between competing applicants or mere approval or disapproval of applications before it, see the discussion of the *El Paso* gas case at pp. 154–157, Chapter 4, below.

[119] See Morgan's reference to the "endless cases" in which active commissions have given engineering advice and assistance, *op. cit.*, 242–247, and insistence that much more could be done along these lines, *ibid.*, Chapter 7, "Elements of a Constructive Program."

ponderantly, regulation has been a negative process, with the initiative coming from the companies themselves; private parties act, and commissions react. From this fact follows most of the other severely criticized characteristics of the regulatory process: it proceeds on a case-by-case basis, on issues usually framed and a record made up by contesting parties, rather than on occasions and issues formulated by the government itself in terms of its own, independent judgment of the public concern.[120]

The function of the regulator therefore becomes primarily adjudicatory rather than executive or legislative. Commissions come to be set up as courts, constrained by elaborate rules of evidence designed, principally, to protect the interests of the private litigants rather than for the formulation of general policy by expert bodies. This leads in turn to vexatious restrictions that deny commissioners the right to consult informally with industry representatives or with their own staff, who are treated in the same way as other litigants, when such *ex parte* contacts would be conceived of as prejudicial infringements on the impartiality of the commissioner-judges. Another consequence of this "overjudicialization of procedures"[121] is that Commission decisions typically must be confined to rulings on written records developed by litigants in adversary proceedings; outside evidence may not be considered.

This case-by-case adjudication tends often to degenerate into pragmatic, timid compromises between the contending private interests. The result is all too often a decision to keep existing competitors alive and to permit each to enjoy its "fair share" of the business, rather than one embodying well-formulated general considerations of the public interest.[122] And this of course

---

[120] So, for example, the Circuit Court of Appeals overturned a Federal Power Commission decision licensing the Consolidated Electric Company to install pumped storage facilities on the Hudson River over objections raised by conservationists that the project would destroy scenic values, in the following terms:

"In this case as in many others, the Commission has claimed to be the representative of the public interest. This role does not permit it to act as an umpire blandly calling balls and strikes for adversaries appearing before it; the right of the public must receive active and affirmative protection at the hands of the Commission." *Scenic Hudson Preservation Conference v. Federal Power Commission*, 354 F. 2d 608, CA2d (1965).

As Commissioner Ross interpreted this instruction, the Court was telling the Commission that it

"had a duty to independently advance its own position and not just rely on the position advanced by the utilities, to put on a case that it considered in the public interest." Richard Hellman, *Government Competition in the Electric Utility Industry of the United States*, processed, unpublished Ph.D. dissertation, Columbia University, 1967, 99/12 note.

[121] Harry M. Trebing, "A Critique of the Planning Function in Regulation," *Public*

Utilities Fortnightly (March 16, 1967), LXXIX: 24. See this article, 21–30 and his "Toward Improved Regulatory Planning," in the same journal, March 30, 1967, 15–24, for an excellent summary and survey of these criticisms of regulatory procedures and functions.

[122] "The inability of social organization to adapt quickly and with foresight is illustrated well by the FCC. Despite the vast changes in both technology and the market circumstances of those using the spectrum, the Commission retains the criteria for spectrum allocation developed at the outset of regulation. There is no evidence that it has ever seriously considered revision of its methods of assigning uses of the spectrum in any way which would take directly into account alternative social benefits, though this consideration must implicitly enter into many of its decisions. . . .

"The most disturbing evidence that the Commission is unlikely to lead in the establishment of a new regulatory scheme for communications is its continued practice of separating rather than joining inseparable problems. The Commission has separate inquiries and issues separate rules with respect to STV [subscription television], CATV, telephone rates and earnings, domestic satellite communication, international satellite communication, telegraphy, UHF frequency

reinforces the tendencies to restriction of competition and protectionism already discussed in Chapter 1.[123]

allocation, multiple station ownership, broadcast advertising, computer time-shared operations, etc. As is true of many other organizations, it appears to do little in studying broad aspects of its own *raison d'être* and the public interest therein." Almarin Phillips, "Television and New Communications Technologies: An Overview of Problems of Public Policy," address at the annual meeting of the Southern Economic Association, Nov. 16, 1967, unpublished ms, 26–27.

The criticism of the FCC must surely be tempered by a recognition of the extraordinary difficulty of planning for spectrum allocation in the face of so rapidly changing a technology— and of the limitations of relying on a free market to achieve a more efficient result. But it is instructive that President Johnson felt it necessary to set up a special Task Force on Communications Policy to attack all these interrelated issues in coordinated fashion; the regulatory commission was really not suited for providing this kind of overview. See *Global Communications System, Message from the President of the United States Transmitting Recommendations Relative to World Communications*, House of Representatives, 90th Cong. 1st Sess., Document No. 157, August 14, 1967. See also note 135, below.

According to W. N. Leonard, the deficiencies of this kind of quasi-judicial, case-by-case proceeding have been particularly glaring in the ICC's supervision of the mammoth merger movement among American railroads during the 1960s (see also pp. 288–290, Chapter 6, below).

"The ICC sits as a quasi-judicial body considering each application brought before it by rail managements, limiting its judgment to a determination of issues present in the record. This procedure has numerous drawbacks, namely:

"1. Certain self-interested corporate and financial groups may set the pattern of mergers rather than have it come about as a deliberate expression of public interest.

"2. The ICC cannot go outside the record to promote mergers which might be more in the public interest.

"3. It fails to take into account the fact that one important merger in one section of the country affects all competitive relations in this area, and that where several mergers are pending in one area, the cases inexorably shade into each other requiring a rearrangement of competition on a regional basis.

"4. The ICC can be entrapped into approving merger No. 2 because it has approved merger No. 1, and so on. . . .

"5. It leaves the raising of basic issues to the opponents of the merger, and if the opposition withdraws, as in the case of the Norfolk & Western-Nickel Plate-Wabash merger, there may be an inadequate record." "Issues of Competition and Monopoly in Railroad Mergers," *Transportation Journal* (Summer 1964), III : 8.

"It has been a stereotype of political wisdom that the bureaucrat is ever ready to exercise authority arbitrarily. But there is the far greater danger that the second-rate, insecure personality who often finds his way into bureaucracy will become uncomfortable at having to exercise authority and will anxiously seek to placate as many interests as possible. This fear to offend, complaisance, and readiness to listen and be 'fair' and 'reasonable' clog the muscles of the will, and what begins in amiability can end in corruption." Louis L. Jaffe, "The Scandal in TV Licensing." Copyright 1957, by Harper's Magazine, Inc. Reprinted from September 1957 issue of Harper's Magazine by permission of the author (CCXV: 77).

[123] A logical corollary of "fair-shares" is "don't rock the boat," a particularly inappropriate policy in the face of the rapid technological changes that have occurred in many of these industries.

"They now act more as arbiters of disputes between the modes than as the instigators of industry practices which are designed to keep pace with rapidly changing conditions and techniques. Very much like industry leaders, they subscribe to the principle of: 'Don't rock the boat.' . . . The only trouble with this philosophy of Government is that technical advances and rapid changes in industry do not likewise subscribe to a philosophy of gradualism. 'Fair and impartial regulation of all modes of transportation,' as provided in our national transportation policy, does not mean the disallowance of new methods and business practices based upon technical advances because it is believed one mode will benefit rather than another if permission is granted. There is every reason to believe that the Interstate Commerce Commission's early views upon piggyback, for instance, may have been based upon such apprehensions. This 'Don't rock the boat' philosophy leads to pusillanimity in the regulatory agencies. . . . For instance, in 1958, when

Another result of the case-by-case approach—along with their usual solicitude for the interests of the regulated companies—is the failure of commissions to lay down and enforce clear guidelines of permissible performance. An outstanding example has been the failure of the FCC to make its grant to private broadcasters of exclusive franchises for portions of the precious radio spectrum conditional on adherence to strict standards of quality—with respect, for example, to the length, frequency, and intensity of sound of their commercials or their allocation of time to educational or other public service programming. The Commission does purport to take into account proposed programming, in choosing between applicants for broadcasting licenses, but it has not typically seen to it that successful licensees kept their promises. Except in a few cases of flagrant abuse, involving, for example, continuous attacks on minority groups, or taking of extreme political positions, or the purveying of misleading advertising, the Commission has almost universally and automatically renewed licenses of existing broadcasters.

"The actual programming bears no reasonable similitude to the programming proposed. The Commission knows this but ignores these differentiations at the time when renewal of licenses of the station is before them."[124]

Under strong internal and external pressures (see notes 124 and 126), the FCC began to make threatening gestures during the course of 1969, suggesting it might not renew the licenses of particularly glaring offenders. Although the major cases turned mainly on allegedly excessive concentration of control over communications media in the locality (notably the ownership of TV and radio stations by local newspapers),[125] there were some in which the Commission reluctantly[126] entertained competing applications from parties

---

the rail carriers were urging Congress to permit them to engage in motor and water operations, the position of the expert body, the Interstate Commerce Commission, upon this crucial question was:

'This proposal involves extremely broad policy questions which only the Congress can resolve. . . . Whether this policy should be reversed or modified is a most important question on which the Commission is not prepared to express an opinion at this time.'

"If the expert body was not in a position to express an informed opinion upon this grave question, no one was. As a matter of fact, the members of the Commission could not help but have a strong opinion upon the matter; they simply did not choose to express that opinion individually or as a commission." The *Doyle Report, op. cit.*, 218–219.

[124] Landis, *op. cit.*, 54. For a more thorough survey and indictment see especially the devastating *Broadcasting in America and the FCC's License Renewal Process: An Oklahoma Case Study*, a statement by Commissioners Kenneth A. Cox and Nicholas Johnson on the occasion of the FCC's renewal of the licenses of Oklahoma broadcasters, released June 1968. This study

prompted the *New York Times* to remark, editorially:

"Of all the regulatory agencies in Washington, the Federal Communications Commission is the one with the biggest rubber stamp." June 11, 1968, 42M.

See also a strong earlier dissent by FCC Chairman E. William Henry, joined by Commissioner Cox, on the renewal of licenses of eight stations in Mississippi, Louisana, and Arkansas on July 22, 1964. FCC, Public Notice—B, July 24, 1964, Report No. 5173.

[125] See note 9, p. 254, Chapter 6, below, on these developments.

[126] See the case involving its withdrawal of an earlier renewal of the license of WPIX–TV, in New York—a renewal granted without investigation of charges that the station had been distorting news broadcasts and without considering the competing application by a group of community leaders. *New York Times*, June 19, 1969, 1 and Daniel Zwerdling, "FCC Impropriety," *The New Republic* (June 21, 1969), CLX: 10–11. Also, the opinion of the Circuit Court of Appeals excoriating the Commission for its hostility to intervenor witnesses represent-

who complained that the programming of the incumbent licensees were unusually poor or objectionable—advocating racial segregation, or inadequately representing the interests of minority group viewers, or featuring excessive violence or insufficient public service programming.[127] In one case, involving KHJ–TV in Los Angeles, its examiner, in a 111-page report, recommended stripping the license from a particularly offensive licensee on the ground that it had "miserably failed to serve the public interest," dedicating most of its air time "to the service of the young, the congenitally gullible and those not very bright." He cited surveys that ranked the station first only in showing movies and another that found in one week it had depicted 181 murders, 98 attempted murders, 55 "justifiable killings," 18 shootings, and eight kidnappings.[128] It was generally expected that President Nixon's 1969 appointees to the FCC could be counted on to restore the Commission to its former sanity.[129]

---

ing the United Church of Christ and the National Association for the Advancement of Colored People, who opposed the renewal of a license for WLBT–TV in Jackson, Mississippi on the ground of allegedly racially biased programming. So angered was the Court by the FCC's handling of the case that it voided the licenses itself and ordered the Commission to invite competing applications. *United Church of Christ v. FCC*, CCA for the District of Columbia, June 20, 1969.

[127] See the survey of pending cases in the *New York Times*, April 27, 1969, 72.

[128] *New York Times*, August 18, 1969, 71.

[129] One hopeful sign was that it was the new President's appointee as Chief Justice of the Supreme Court, Judge Warren E. Burger, who had written the condemnation of the Commission's handling of the WLBT–TV, Jackson, Mississippi, license renewal (see note 126, above).

One favorite argument used by broadcasters to resist any kind of consideration or control of their program content has been the statutory prohibition of censorship and the protections of the First Amendment. Holders of these valuable public franchises, which enable them to exclude others from the right to speak over the limited airways, professed to see a violation of the rights of free speech and press in FCC requirements that, for example, they provide fair coverage of opposing political viewpoints and opportunities for reply to persons subjected to personal attacks in their broadcasts. The Supreme Court has unanimously rejected such self-serving defenses, holding that requirements such as these enhance rather than abridge freedom of speech. Significantly, the American Civil Liberties Union intervened on the side of the Commission, not of the broadcasters. Since the argument of the broadcasters has at least superficial plausibility, it is worth reproducing the Court's reasoning.

"Where there are substantially more indivi-

duals who want to broadcast than there are frequencies to allocate, it is idle to posit an unabridgeable First Amendment right to broadcast comparable to the right of every individual to speak, write, or publish. . . .

"as far as the First Amendment is concerned those who are licensed stand no better than those to whom licenses are refused. . . . There is nothing in the First Amendment which prevents the Government from requiring a licensee to share his frequency with others and to conduct himself as a proxy or fiduciary with obligations to present those views and voices which . . . would otherwise, by necessity, be barred from the airwaves. . . .

"It is the purpose of the First Amendment to preserve an uninhibited market place of ideas in which truth will ultimately prevail, rather than to countenance monopolization of that market, whether it be by the Government itself or a private licensee." *Red Lion Broadcasting Co., Inc. et al. v. Federal Communications Commission et al.*, 395 U. S. 367, 388–390 (1969).

See, along similar lines, the decision of a Circuit Court of Appeals upholding against a similar defense, and equally convincingly, an FCC requirement that broadcasters carrying cigarette advertising "devote a significant amount of broadcast time to presenting the case against cigarette smoking":

"The cigarette ruling does not ban any speech. . . .

"Even if some valued speech is inhibited by the ruling, the First Amendment gain is greater than the loss. A primary First Amendment policy has been to foster the widest possible debate and dissemination of information on matters of public importance. . . .

"where, as here, one party to a debate has a financial clout and compelling economic interest in the presentation of one side unmatched by its

The virtual absence of regulatory guidelines of acceptable performance extends also to certification policies. The FCC and the CAB often choose among competing applicants on the basis of informal considerations inadequately disclosed, leaving it to their staffs to write the supporting decisions developing the requisite rationalizations. As a result, certification decisions of these two agencies are said to defy all efforts to trace out a consistent policy.[130]

For these weaknesses, the legislatures must themselves bear a large share of blame. First, they typically lay down only the vaguest policy guidelines, enjoining the commissions to make "reasonable" decisions, to serve "the public interest," or to be guided by the "public convenience and necessity." Second, even more reprehensibly, any commission that decides to take a bold stand in the public interest can be certain that it will be called to account and threatened with reversal by a Congress—or, even worse, by the influential chairman of a congressional committee—that has been aroused to action by complaints of interested parties, including, all too often, the legislators themselves. It would be impossible here to cite more than a fraction of the examples. But this is what happened to the Federal Trade Commission in 1965, when it moved, under its mandate to stop false or misleading advertising, to require cigarette advertisements to carry clear warnings of the hazards to health involved in smoking;[131] to the FCC when it undertook its

---

opponent, and where the public stake in the argument is no less than life itself—we think the purpose of rugged debate is served, not hindered, by an attempt to redress the balance. . . .

"We do not think the principle of free speech stands as a barrier to required broadcasting of facts and information vital to an informed decision to smoke or not to smoke." *John F. Banzhaf, III* (the private party who was almost singlehandedly responsible for the FCC ruling) *v. Federal Communications Commission and U. S. v. WTRF–TV, Inc. and National Association of Broadcasters*, 405 F. 2d 1082, 1101–1103 (1968).

[130] Such procedures give rise also to the suspicion that political connections are more important than economic merit in the awarding process. For a recent example, see the major decisions involving the Trans–Pacific air route awards, in which White House favoritism was widely rumored to have played a role. Since the final decision on international route awards rests with the President, Mr. Nixon stayed the enforcement of these portions of the decision by his predecessor and instituted a reexamination shortly after taking office. *New York Times*, February 27, 1969, 81. For further reference to these inherent dangers of licensing see note 15, p. 177, below.

For a survey of the policies of the FCC and CAB, see especially Henry J. Friendly, *The Federal Administrative Agencies, The Need for Better Definition of Standards* (Cambridge: Harvard Univ. Press, 1962), Chapters 4 and 5.

"In broadcast license cases no criteria for decision have evolved. True, criteria of various

different kinds are articulated but they are patently not the grounds motivating decision. No firm decisional policy has evolved from these case-by-case dispositions. Instead the anonymous opinion writers for the Commission pick from a collection of standards those that will support whatever decision the Commission chooses to make." Landis, *op. cit.*, 53.

See also William K. Jones, *Licensing of Major Broadcast Facilities by the Federal Communications Commission*, a study done for the Administrative Conference of the United States, reprinted in U. S. House of Representatives, Subcommittee No. 6, Select Committee on Small Business, 89th Cong. 2d Sess., *Activities of Regulatory and Enforcement Agencies Relating to Small Business, Hearings*, Part 1, A103–A112, A165–A174; Jaffe, *op. cit.*, *Harper's Magazine* (September 1957), CCXV: 77–84; Harvey J. Levin, "Regulatory Efficiency, Reform and the FCC," *Georgetown Law Jour.* (Fall 1961), L: 1–45.

[131] Congress stepped in to preempt the field for four years, with its Cigarette Labelling and Advertising Act, which vetoed the FTC's proposed action and itself imposed only the very modest requirement that a mild health warning be printed on the cigarette packages. 79 *U. S. Statutes at Large*, P. L. 89–92 (July 27, 1965). In 1969, when the foregoing Act neared expiration, the House of Representatives once again passed a bill that would prohibit any agency requiring a health warning in cigarette advertising and itself proposed a reworded warning on the package. *New York Times*, June 19, 1969, 1.

first limited venture of authorizing a local test of pay-television,[132] again in 1963 when it proposed to set rules covering the length or frequency of broadcast commercials[133] and, later, in response to its timid steps, described above, to examine critically applications for renewal of broadcast licenses.[134]

Finally, Congress must bear principal responsibility for the vast diffusion of regulatory authority in many of these areas. The outstanding illustration of divided, conflicting, and overlapping jurisdiction is provided by transportation, where responsibility is distributed among the ICC, the CAB, the Federal Maritime Commission, the FPC (for natural gas pipelines), the Bureau of Public Roads, the Military Transportation Service, the Army Corps of Engineers, and the Department of Commerce, a defect only very partially and imperfectly eliminated by the constitution of the new Department of Transportation.[135]

---

[132] Wilcox, *op. cit.*, 461.

[133] This example and many others are described in William L. Cary, *Politics and the Regulatory Agencies* (New York: McGraw–Hill Book Co., 1967), 35–59. The FCC effort to limit commercials is a particularly apt illustration because it represents an obviously justified and laudatory effort on the part of a regulatory agency to move away from ad hoc determinations and to set forth general guidelines under its responsibility to issue or renew licenses on the basis of the "public convenience, interest or necessity"; and because it produced the following Congressional gem of rationalization for obstructing more effective regulation.

"In the final analysis, it is the judgment of the community which determines whether a broadcaster meets community needs. . . .

"Self-regulation by industry is an accepted and valuable supplemental regulatory tool, the effective use of which should be encouraged rather than discouraged.

"The adoption by rule of compulsory standards, on the other hand . . . would substitute Commission judgment for individual licensee judgment regarding the licensee's day-to-day responsibility of serving the community which he is licensed to serve. . . .

"Therefore . . . it is necessary for the Congress to limit explicitly the scope of the Commission's powers in this respect. . . .

"The instant rulemaking proceeding constitutes an outstanding example of a regulatory agency arrogating to itself the right to legislate." From U. S. House of Representatives, Committee on Interstate and Foreign Commerce, 88th Cong. 1st Sess., *Lack of Authority of Federal Communications Commission to Make Rules Relating to the Length or Frequency of Broadcast Commercials*, House Report No. 1054, 5–7, as cited in Cary, *op. cit.*, 46–47. The Commission did, however, warn radio stations in 1970 that it would expose them to license renewal hearings if they carried more than 18 minutes of commercials in more than 10% of their weekly broadcast hours. *Wall Street Journal*, March 13, 1970, 28.

[134] In this case Senator Pastore introduced a bill in 1969 that would prohibit the FCC from considering competing applications for broadcast licenses up for renewal unless it had first determined that renewal of the existing licensee "would not be in the public interest." S. 2004, 91st Cong. 1st Sess., April 29, 1969. In this instance the Commission evidently satisfied its Congressional critics without giving up the fight entirely. It issued a *Policy Statement on Comparative Hearings Involving Regular Renewal Applicants* declaring that in confronting competitive applications at renewal time it would give preference to existing licensees who could demonstrate that their programming had "substantially" served the needs and interests of its area. In so doing, it emphasized that by "substantially" it meant a "solid" or "strong" performance, not one "minimally" serving those interests. Commissioner Johnson asserted he could not go along with this compromise solution because it limited the possibilities of competition and denied the public the opportunity of being served by the *best possible* station, as long as the existing licensees' performance was "substantially" in the public interest. But he conceded that the Policy Statement promised a genuine improvement over the previous practice of renewing licenses in cases of all but the most outrageously bad performance.

"I have considerable sympathy and respect for my colleagues' commendable and good faith effort to resolve this conflict between formidable political power and virtually unrepresented public interest. . . . And it is not at all clear to me that more than they have done would have been politically possible, or could have withstood political appeal. It is not even clear that today's effort is secure." *Public Notice*, FCC 70–62 40869, January 15, 1970—B.

[135] See, for example, the *Doyle Report*, 94–97. For similar problems in the field of communi-

Conclusion: The Inherent Limitations of Regulation

There is an enormous body of literature, in the general area of administrative law, addressing itself to these many inadequacies of the regulatory process and proposing procedural, organizational, and substantive reforms. The question is raised, for example, whether the administrative commissions ought to retain as much of their traditional formal independence or whether they ought not, instead, be more closely integrated into the executive branch of the government and subjected more directly to the control and responsibility of the presidency. Some observers have called instead for greater control by the legislature, whether by fuller and more precise declarations of intent in the controlling legislation or by more competent scrutiny and surveillance of commission policies as they evolve. Others have recommended constitution of an ombudsman or a consumers' counsel office in the administrative commissions, to serve as a forum for consumer complaints and as an active and aggressive representative of consumer interests—an ironic suggestion considering that one might naively have assumed that this was the function of the commissions themselves, but perhaps a good one nonetheless.[136]

The extent to which the substantive, policy determinations of regulatory commissions ought to be subject to judicial review is a historic theme in American constitutional law. The courts at certain times in effect have substituted their judgment for that of the regulators in reviewing the compatibility of their decisions with the Fourteenth Amendment or with the legislative intent, and, at others, deferred almost without question to the commission's presumed "expertise." There has been much consideration of the appropriate degree of separation between the administrative, policy-making function, on the one hand, and the judicial functions, on the other, involving a great variety of correlative questions about commission organization, procedures, rules of evidence, and standards of ethical conduct. An inescapable subject has been the problem of reconciling and synchronizing the policies of the various agencies of government exercising responsibility in such fields as transportation, communications, and energy. One pervasive set of interrelated issues concerns the extent to which legislatures should be presumed to have called for a continued reliance on competition except where they have explicitly decreed otherwise; and the corresponding distribution of authority in these fields between the antitrust agencies, operating through the courts, and the regulatory agencies.

We offer no pretense even of adequately characterizing these political, administrative, and legal issues, let alone resolving them, although they

---

cations and energy see Landis, *op. cit.*, 24–30 and note 122, above. The President's Task Force on Communications Policy concluded that as a result of the fragmentation of governmental authority in that field, "policy has evolved as a patchwork of limited, largely *ad hoc* responses to specific issues, rather than a cohesive framework for planning," (*op. cit.*, Chapter 9), and, partly following its recommendations, President Nixon in 1970 established an Office of Telecommunications Policy to help make for a more coherent administration policy. *Telecommunications Reports*

(September 14, 1970), XXXVI: 1–4.

[136] See, for example, the *Utility Consumers' Counsel Act of 1969*, S. 607, sponsored by Senator Lee Metcalf. Also, the responses of the administrative commissions and especially by members of the FCC in the U. S. Senate, Committee on the Judiciary, Subcommittee on Administrative Practice and Procedure, 91st Cong. 1st Sess., *Responses to Questionnaire on Citizen Involvement and Responsive Agency Decision-Making*, Committee Print, September 9, 1969.

obviously have a close bearing on the economic substance of regulation. Nor do we underestimate their importance when we observe that whatever the administrative or statutory arrangements, the tendencies and problems we have described in these two chapters are inherent in the institution of regulated monopoly and inescapable as long as we retain that as our instrument for the governance of industry. Obviously, divided authority and conflicting or unclear statutory mandates must make for an inefficient performance of the regulatory function; but attempts to centralize the responsibility and clarify the mandate cannot in themselves resolve the diverse and often-conflicting purposes that these various public interventions attempt to serve. Making commissions more independent or less, more closely tied to the executive or the legislature, more or less subject to judicial review, will serve the public interest better or worse depending on how one defines that interest, the identity and composition of these various agencies, and what kinds of influences are brought to bear on the decisions of each. There is no way a priori to determine the proper mix of regulation and competition valid for all times and places: that is why regulation is introduced here and not there. But the decision to introduce it cannot be made intelligently except with a full recognition of the inherent tendencies and limitations suggested in these chapters.

CHAPTER 3

Positive Influences on Public Utility Performance

Chapters 1 and 2 consisted, essentially, in a description of the limitations of regulation in the presence of monopoly as an institutional device for assuring good economic performance Were the performance of the public utility industries in fact unrelievedly bad and incapable of improvement under regulation, we could stop at this point and go on to happier matters. But, in fact, neither of these two conclusions would be justified. What, then, have been the positive influences? It is important to ask this question not only if we are fully to understand the objective, historical record but also if we are to find ways of improving it—because, presumably, the way to do so would be first to identify the positive influences, then to strengthen them or give them fuller play.

Evidence of Good Performance

The question of whether the performance of American public utility industries has been good or bad is almost meaningless. For one thing, the category is too broad and embraces far too heterogeneous a group of companies and industries, places and times for successful generalization. But even if we were to break the question down into separate investigations of more nearly homogeneous groups of companies, in single industries, at some particular place and time, certain major difficulties would remain. Presumably, the main relevant aspects of performance would be the following:

1. Efficiency—the level of cost.
2. The relationship of prices individually and collectively to cost—to marginal cost in the short run, to average total cost in the long run.[1]
3. Improvements in efficiency over time and the passing on of the benefits to consumers, as reflected in cost and price trends.
4. The quality of service.
5. Service improvement and innovation over time.

What objective yardsticks could we use for these five criteria, against which to measure the performance of individual companies or industries?

---

[1] The latter on the assumption that private utilities must cover ATC over time, though MC may be less.

There would seem to be only two possibilities: the record in each of these respects of *other* industries in the same area, and the record of the *same* industries in other regions or countries. As far as the first possibility is concerned, interindustry comparisons could meaningfully be made only with respect to criteria (2) and (3) above. One could compare, for example, patterns of price discrimination or rates of return or cost-price trends over time in, say, gas distribution with other industries. But such comparisons would be meaningless with respect to criteria (1), (4), and (5); it would make no sense to compare the cost of producing a ton of steel with the cost of delivering a thousand cubic feet of natural gas, or to compare the quality of the former with that of the latter. And even where arithmetic comparisons can be made, the result can be only vaguely illuminating at best and positively misleading at worst. Suppose we find, for example (as in fact we would), that the price of a day's stay in a general hospital or of a 15-minute appointment in a doctor's office (or even of an economically more meaningful service, such as the cure for a case of influenza, of a given variety and intensity) has increased sharply in the last three decades while the cost and price of a long-distance telephone call between two particular cities has gone down dramatically. This does not permit us to conclude that the performance of the health industry has been poor and that of the telephone industry good, or even that the one has been worse than the other. Obviously, the behavior and composition of the respective demands and, even more important, the character of their respective technologies and potentialities for improvement are utterly different. These same results could therefore have been compatible with the former industry doing an extremely good job and the latter an extremely bad one, considering the character of their problems and the means available to each for meeting them.

To some extent, the same kind of observations would apply to inter-country performance comparisons of the same industries. Any differences in these records might be attributable more to differences in the general conditioning circumstances of the two countries—the character and education of their labor forces, the motivations of their managers, their natural resource endowments, and so on—than to the organization and policies of the specific companies and industries in question. One way of eliminating this problem would be to develop indices of performance for particular public utility industries in, for example, the United States *relative* to that of all other American industries, and compare those ratios with corresponding indices for foreign countries. A little reflection will convince the reader of the immensity of any such task, although it could be worth trying.[2]

In any event, efforts like these could at best produce only rough approxi-

---

[2] Setting aside the question of whether it were, in fact, statistically feasible, such a comparison would presumably eliminate the effect of national differences, insofar as they operated to produce differences in the *average* performance of all industries in the two countries. It would still not eliminate national differences—for example, in the endowment of particular, required raw materials or technological resources—that operated specifically to alter the *relative* performance in each country of the particular industry in question. Yet these industry-specific differences too would have to be eliminated if one were to be left only with differences in performance attributable solely to differences in the controlling institutions, which it would be the purpose of these comparisons to measure. And, of course, the institutions would have to be substantially different among the countries being compared: otherwise the whole comparison would not shed much light on which institutions work well, which badly.

mations of answers to the only relevant question about the performance of any particular industry at any particular time and place: how does its record compare with what *might have been achieved*—by that *same* industry, at that *same* time and place—under some alternative system of control.[3] Since only one of these two records has objective existence, the task must, in the last analysis, always be one of judgment: objective, statistical comparisons can never do any more than help to inform that judgment [4] So, the few pieces of evidence that we proceed now to offer suggesting that the performance of the public utility industries in the United States along the five dimensions listed above has been "good"—or at least, obviously, not all "bad"—cannot be definitive.

It is probably fair to say that the quality of service provided by the U. S. telephone industry and in communications generally, and by the electric and gas utility companies has been good, in terms both of reliability, uniformity of quality, and the speed and courtesy with which they are provided and maintained.[5] In transportation, the verdict on this score would undoubtedly have to be more mixed. But in all these fields, it must be conceded, service is generally good, also, in terms of the variety of alternatives available to customers. In transportation and communications, particularly, there have also occurred commendable service innovations, to which we have from time to time referred—though it is questionable that the rate of innovation has in all cases been the best achievable.

As for the relationship of price to marginal cost: the elaborate value-of-service freight schedules developed by the railroads and imitated by the trucks certainly represented an effort, in principle sound, to reconcile an approach to marginal cost pricing for large-volume, low-value commodities with the coverage of joint and common costs. On the other hand, as we have already seen, the clinging by the railroads to long-outmoded, excessively discriminatory rate structures made it possible for competing carriers to take over great chunks of the business that should on grounds of efficiency have stayed on the rails, with a high resultant cost to society.[6] Although we have

---

[3] See Jesse W. Markham, "An Alternative Approach to the Concept of Workable Competition," *Amer. Econ. Rev.* (June 1950), XL: 349–361, reprinted in American Economic Association, *Readings in Industrial Organization and Public Policy* (Homewood: Richard D. Irwin, 1958), especially 94–95.

[4] See, for example, Corwin D. Edwards, "Public Policy and Business Size," *Jour. of Bus.* (October 1951), XXIV: 280–292, and Alfred E. Kahn, "Standards for Antitrust Policy," *Harv. Law Rev.* (November 1953), LXVII: 28–54, both reprinted in Amer. Econ. Association, *Readings in Industrial Organization and Public Policy*, especially 343–344 and 363–364, respectively.

[5] This verdict is offered in full recognition of the lamentable power failures, shortages, and congestions that have from time to time appeared in these industries. It seems, once again, fair to recognize that the inconvenience and indignation occasioned by these breakdowns reflects in major part the high level and rapidly increasing

volume of service to which we have become accustomed—and addicted.

[6] See John R. Meyer, Merton J. Peck, John Stenason and Charles Zwick, *The Economics of Competition in the Transportation Industries* (Cambridge: Harvard Univ. Press, 1959), 187–195, 243; and pp. 14–15, Chapter 1, above. Some of these discussions are couched in terms of opposition to all value-of-service pricing. But, apart from the possibility of distorting effects at the buyer level, such price discrimination is, as we have seen in Chapters 5 and 6 of Volume 1, not objectionable in principle. The error lay not so much in the principle itself as in its misapplication, and specifically in the assumption that the value of the commodity shipped was an accurate measure of the elasticity of demand for the transportation service. See George W. Wilson, "The Effect of Rate Regulation on Resource Allocation in Transportation," *Amer. Econ. Rev., Papers and Proceedings* (May 1964), LIV: 165–166; Baumol *et al.*, "The Role of Cost in the Minimum

pointed to serious inadequacies in the rate design of the typical electric and gas utility,[7] it could still be true, as Bonbright states, that

"Along with improved engineering technology and with the development and promotion of electrical appliances, it shares the credit for the amazing success of the industry in reducing rates or keeping them from rising materially during a prolonged period of price inflation."[8]

The simplest reflection of the generally satisfactory long-run relationship between price and cost in the public utility industries is to be seen in the comparative profit rates set forth in note 76, page 52 of Volume 1. As these comparisons show, rates of return on stockholder equity have run somewhat below the levels in industry generally during the comparatively prosperous years since World War II—only slightly lower in the case of electric and gas utilities, and markedly below in the case of the telephone companies. Significantly, the profit rate of Western Electric, the manufacturing subsidiary of the Bell System, runs much lower than those of manufacturing companies generally and other electrical equipment manufacturers in particular.[9] Since public utility companies rely disproportionately heavily on debt financing, their returns on total invested capital have run even more markedly below those in manufacturing than profit rates alone.

Whether these rates of return may nonetheless still be too high is very hard to say. That they considerably exceeded the cost of capital during most of these years is suggested by the fact that the common stocks of these companies sold during the 1960s at prices markedly above their book value.[10] Still, they suggest at least a moderately satisfactory long-run relationship of prices to cost.

The much lower returns of the railroads are a good deal more difficult to cite as evidence of satisfactory economic performance. On the contrary, they reflect a combination of intensified competition, on the positive side, and, on the negative, a sluggish response by the rails and by the ICC and an

---

Pricing of Railroad Services," *Jour. of Bus.* (July 1963), XXXVI: 348–351.

It is, of course, possible that neither the rails nor the common carrier truckers were entirely irrational, from their own point of view, in clinging to value-of-service pricing, even though the former lost a large share of the business to the latter and both were forced in consequence to share their markets with unregulated motor carriers. Following the familiar monopolistic calculus, they might conceivably have been better off with high rates on the high-value freight, at the cost of a considerable loss of volume, than with lower rates and a larger share of the business. On the other hand, the recent awakening by the railroads to the deleterious consequences of their value-of-service pricing and their intensified efforts, after careful study, to reduce rates in order to regain a larger share of the traffic suggests that the previous practice was irrational from a private as well as from a social point of view. See also, on the same point, note 103 of Chapter 2 and p. 85, above.

[7] See pp. 96–100, Volume 1.

[8] *Principles of Public Utility Rates,* 315–316. See these pages also for a favorable comparison of the electric utilities in this respect with transportation companies and a quotation from a gas-company executive to the effect that "perhaps no other one factor has contributed so much to the success of the electrical business as the study of the rate problem." *Ibid.,* note 22. The success of the natural gas pipeline companies in wearing down the FPC's *Atlantic Seaboard* formula (see p. 99 and especially note 35, Volume 1) and the profusion of promotional campaigns by both electric and gas companies (see pp. 177–180, Volume 1), whatever their imperfections, similarly contrast favorably with the sluggishness of the railroads until the mid-1950s. On similar improvements by the airlines see pp. 75–76, 149–150, and 153, note 69, Volume 1.

[9] See pp. 291–292, Chapter 6, below. The profit rates of the non-Bell companies have been generally lower than of the Bell System. See Shepherd, in Shepherd and Gies, *op. cit.,* 42–43.

[10] See p. 48, note 69, Volume 1.

unhealthy financial situation that probably impairs the ability of the former to render service for which they would be the most efficient carriers.

Profit rates are, of course, only the minor indication of the appropriateness of the level of price. The major one is the level of the costs to which the profits are added (and against which the allowable rate of return is applied). As we have already suggested, there is no easy way of comparing the costs of public utility with other companies. It is worth noting, however, that the comparatively modest returns on total invested capital are not offset by unusually high rates of executive compensation. On the contrary, an analysis of 1965 data found that the great majority of electric and gas companies paid their chief executives less than companies of the same size in unregulated industries generally, and the discrepancy was even slightly greater in the case of the second and third-highest-paid executives.[11]

table 1 Average Annual Rates of Increase in Total Factor Productivity (Percent)

	1899–1953	1948–1966
Communications and Public Utilities	3.6%	...
Telephone	2.0	
Telegraph	1.8	3.8
Electric utilities	5.5	
Manufactured gas	4.7	3.7
Natural gas	2.0	
Transportation	3.2	...[a]
Railroads	2.6	...[a]
Local transit	2.5	...
Residual transport	4.0	...
Manufacturing	2.0	3.0[a]
Private domestic economy	1.7	2.4

Source. Comparisons of 1899–1953 from John W. Kendrick, *Productivity Trends in the United States*, National Bureau of Economic Research (Princeton: Princeton Univ. Press, 1961), 136–137. Comparisons of 1948–1966 from Kendrick, "Productivity Trends in the U. S. Private Economy and in the Public Utilities, 1948–1966," *Public Utility Valuation and the Rate Making Process Conference, Conference Proceedings*, April 24–26, 1968, Ames, Iowa, C–12, C–14.

[a] For comparisons of labor productivity trends alone, see note 24, this chapter, below.

The most striking indicators of good public utility performance are the long-run comparative trends in their costs and (since there have been no substantially offsetting trends in profits) their rates as well. The data in Tables 1 and 2 show this very dramatically. According to the estimates of Kendrick, the average annual rate of increase in total factor productivity (output per unit of labor and capital, combined) in communications and public utilities was more than twice as great as in the private economy

---

[11] "Executive Compensation in the Utility Industry" (New York: National Economic Research Associates, 1967). Of course, the public utility executives might still be relatively overpaid, in terms of merit!

generally, and 80 percent higher than in manufacturing alone, during the period 1899–1953. Their margin of superiority in the shorter period 1948–1966 was less, but still notable. The performance of the railroads in this respect was, likewise, markedly better than in industry generally and in the economy at large.[12] Roughly reflecting these favorable relative cost trends, though for a more recent time period, are the price changes set forth in Table 2. The most dramatic reductions have been in long-distance communications; but the rates for local telephone service, for electricity, gas and passenger air transportation (but not railroad freight rates) have all risen far less than the general price level. The comparative stability in these prices in a period of general inflation reflects rapid improvement in efficiency, both in absolute terms and relative to the economy at large.

table 2 Percent Change in Price, 1940–1968

Telephone rate, 3 minutes, daytime, station-to-station, New York to San Francisco	− 58
Cable and radio-telegraph, New York to Tokyo	− 53
Cable and radio-telegraph, New York to London	+ 5
Index, interstate telephone rates	− 24
Index, local telephone rates	+51
Index, total telephone rates	+10
Revenue per passenger-mile, domestic trunk airlines	+ 8
Railroad freight rates	…[a]
BLS indexes (% increases)	
Retail price of electricity	+ 5
Retail price, gas	+42
Consumer price index	+ 148
Wholesale price index	+ 153

Source. Telephone rate index numbers from AT&T statement on S. 607, to U. S. Senate, Subcomm. on Intergovernmental Relations, *Consumers' Counsel Act of 1969*, April 30, 1969; airline per mile revenues from CAB, *Handbook of Airline Statistics*, updated figures supplied by courtesy of the Board; railroad freight rates from ICC, Bureau of Economics, *Transport Economics*, June 19, 1969, 9. All others from *Statistical Abstract of the United States, 1969*.

[a] These were increased 36 percent, 1947–1968. The comparable percentage increase in the BLS wholesale price index was 34.

It bears repeating that these impressive accomplishments must reflect, above all, the enormous potentialities of the technology with which these industries work—potentialities for technological progress and for the economies of scale described in Chapter 5 of Volume 1. Whether the public utility industries took the best possible advantage of these opportunities cannot be disclosed by interindustry comparisons.

[12] See also Edwin Mansfield, "Innovation and Technical Change in the Railroad Industry," in *Transportation Economics, op. cit.*, 169–197. It must be recognized that in many of these industries the innovations that made the dramatic improvements in productivity possible were developed not by themselves but by their equipment suppliers. See, for example, Richard J. Barber, "Technological Change in American Transportation: The Role of Government Action," *Virginia Law Rev.* (June 1964), L: 845–852. For calculations producing a much lower estimated rate of advance of total factor productivity in communications than the Kendrick data, see Shepherd, "Communications: Regulation, Innovation and the Changing Margin of Competition," a chapter to appear in a Brookings Institution symposium on *Technological Change in the Regulated Industries*, ms. pp. 42–43.

The fact remains that technology does not develop unassisted by human hands, nor do the benefits of long-run decreasing costs fall as rain from heaven. The data presented do inescapably support a judgment that there have been favorable institutional factors operating in these areas of the economy. What would these be?[13]

Internal Motivations

The Profit Motive. Profit maximizers, even if monopolists, have an incentive to reduce costs, to cut rates if they think demand is sufficiently elastic, to engage in product or service innovation whenever the prospective incremental returns exceed the costs. And, we have suggested in Chapter 2, regulation is sufficiently loose to offer regulated companies an opportunity to retain any additional profits generated in this fashion—all of them for a considerable period of time, some of them (if added rate base is justified) permanently.

Managerialism. To the extent that the interests of managers and stockholders diverge, the divorce of ownership and control can produce worse results rather than better.[14] But tending in the latter direction are the exposure of public utility executives to public scrutiny and criticism, their desire to be associated with growing and progressive companies,[15] to enjoy the approbation that comes from giving good service, and to avoid unpopular rate increases—motives that are reinforced by the presence of regulation.[16]

---

[13] The following discussion draws heavily on my chapter "Inducements to Superior Performance: Price," in Trebing, *Performance under Regulation*, 88–102. Reprinted by permission of the publisher, the Bureau of Business and Economic Research, Division of Research, Graduate School of Business Administration, Michigan State University.

[14] See, for example, pp. 28–29, Volume 1, and 71–72 of this Volume.

[15] On the possible conflict between the interest of stockholders in profits and of managers in sales maximization, and the likelihood of the latter producing a more nearly competitive performance, see Baumol, *Business Behavior, Value and Growth* rev. ed. (New York: Harcourt, Brace & World, Inc., 1967), 73–75 and *passim*.

For demonstrations of the ways in which the performance of regulated companies may be expected to differ depending on the various possible motives of managers, see Milton Z. Kafoglis, "Output of the Restrained Firm," *Amer. Econ. Rev.* (September 1969), LIX: 583–589, and E. E. Zajac, "A Geometric Treatment of Averch-Johnson's Behavior of the Firm Model," *ibid.* (March 1970), LX: 117–125.

The substitution of sales for profit maximization is not unqualifiedly desirable in economic terms. In particular, it might, like the A–J–W tendency, lead to overinvestment and overproduction, with companies undertaking price reductions or promotional campaigns to produce additional sales the value of which to buyers is less than the additional costs that they entail. That is to say, it could cause production to be carried beyond the optimal point, where $MC = AR$; as long as MR is still positive at this point, total revenues could in this way be maximized. On the other hand, this tendency could merely offset undesirable monopolistic restriction of output (since of course producing only up to the point where $MR = MC$ falls short of the optimum when $MR < AR$) and, in dynamic terms, a closer approximation to competitive performance in expanding output, developing new services, and so on.

[16] Here, for example, are some of the observations made in private correspondence by a perceptive executive of a public utility company.

"I think the whole trouble is with the concept of economic man, and especially the assumed characteristics of this construct: perfect intelligence and thorough venality (at least within the limits of the law).

"An instance of the distance between economic man and real man is to be found in the fact that utility people work like mad cutting costs and benefiting consumers despite the fact that the industry is essentially a cost plus industry. . . .

"Despite what I see around me every day, and have seen for decades, some economists 'prove' that since regulation is a cost plus system the management has no incentive to cut costs. . . .

"A second example of the error of the intelligence-cum-venality hypothesis is in the article

Technological Factors

Long-run decreasing costs, in the static sense, and the dynamic *potentialities of their technologies* have already been suggested by the comparisons in Tables 1 and 2, above, and documented in Volume 1 (pp. 124–130). As we pointed out in that latter discussion, these two factors are intertwined in practice: rapidly growing demand both permits suppliers to move down along static, decreasing cost functions and impels them to more rapid technological progress. These conditions create unusually attractive opportunities for both profit and other managerial satisfactions from a progressive and efficient performance.

Market Factors

Elasticity of Demand. The more elastic industry demand, the greater is the incentive for even a profit-maximizing monopolist to set his price at the purely competitive level. The decision to regulate the public utilities undoubtedly reflects the assumption that at least large portions of the demand for their services are inelastic, and that is why consumers need protection; and the assumption is almost certainly more correct than incorrect. The demand for electricity for lighting, the basic residential and commercial demand for telephone service[17] are almost certainly quite inelastic. But in view of the fact that an estimated 47.8 percent of residential usage for electricity in 1966 was for water heating, house heating, clothes drying, and cooking—for all of which there is keen competition with other fuels[18]—there is room for considerable skepticism about the showing of econometric studies that total residential demand is inelastic.[19]

---

by Averch and Johnson. . . .

"when you look at the actual behavior of the utility companies you will quickly see that they go to great lengths to avoid capital investments. For example, the resistance to the undergrounding of electric lines; the resistance to the construction of cooling towers at generating plants . . . the vigor with which we try to buy our land as cheaply as possible despite the 'adverse' effect on our rate bases. We fight zoning cases in order to have a lower capital investment. We try hard to place our gas mains in the locations where the required capital will be less, rather than more. We risk the charge of ugliness in order to save capital by not enclosing our generating stations. . . . In example after example I can demonstrate that the management of an electric and gas utility company is positively stinky stingy in the making of capital investments despite the fact that in almost all situations r [the allowed rate of return] exceeds k [cost of capital].

"I believe it is because the real joy in this industry comes from rendering good service at low rates. . . ."

It is probably not a sufficient answer to the foregoing protestations that the behavior described is fully compatible with profit-maximization, given a sufficient regulatory lag.

There seems to be no reason whatever to doubt that managerial pride and an "instinct of workmanship" represent a separate and additional force operating in the same direction. By the same token, managerial inertia, a common attribute of public utility monopoly, operates in the other direction. See, for example, note 57, Chapter 2, and p. 81, above.

[17] See Carl Stern, "Price Elasticity of Local Telephone Service Demand," *Public Utilities Fortnightly* (Feb. 4, 1965), LXXV: 24–34.

[18] Stelzer, "Impact of Competition on Regulation: Utility Rate-Making," paper presented at a Conference on Public Utility Valuation and the Rate-Making Process, University of Iowa, April 25, 1968 (New York: National Economic Research Associates, 1968), 1–6, 18–20. One electric company reports that the average annual consumption of its customers using electricity for home heating was 22,000 kwh, compared with 5,800 for its other customers. In view of the sharp competition with other fuels for this market, this suggests a high elasticity of total residential demand. Stelzer and Bruce C. Netschert, "Hot War in the Energy Industry," *Harv. Bus. Rev.* (November–December 1967), XLV: 15.

[19] Franklin M. Fisher and Carl Kaysen, *A Study in Econometrics: Demand for Electricity in the United*

The Tennessee Valley Authority was constituted and run on the opposite premise—that sharply reduced retail rates would tap an enormous potential market. The conclusion of most students is that those optimistic predictions were proved correct, at least for that time and that area;[20] and that private power companies were moved in part by that lesson to reduce their own rates on the basis of the same expectation.[21] It is impossible not to be impressed, similarly, by the apparently enormous response of the use of long-distance telephoning to reduced rates in general and particularly to reduced night-time rates in recent years; and the sharp increase in air travel that has attended fare reductions.

"The main reasons for rapid growth in this market . . . have been lower fares and improved service resulting from intensified competition. . . . Traffic on this route appears to be elastic with respect to fares, and the staff study shows that declines in average fares bring more than proportional increases in traffic."[22]

Of course, to the extent that public utility services compete with one another, or with services supplied by outsiders, the elasticity of demand for each and the consequent likelihood of low-price policies is enhanced. This suggests the next market influence—competition.

Competition. We have already alluded at some length to the pervasive and growing competition to which the public utility companies have been subject in recent decades and to the probability that the rapid and ever more diversified progress of technology has increased its variety and intensity.[23] The effectiveness of that competition has, of course, been uneven and the results would, in the absence of regulation, be highly discriminatory. But it has been a powerful influence on at least important segments of these industries in enforcing attention to reducing rates and otherwise promoting

States (Amsterdam: North-Holland Publishing Co., 1962), 2–9, 134–135; H. S. Houthakker and Lester D. Taylor, *Consumer Demand in the United States, 1929–1970* (Cambridge: Harvard Univ. Press, 1966), 88, 153–154. See also Damodar Gujarati, "Demand for Electricity and Natural Gas," *Public Utilities Fortnightly* (January 1969), LXXXIII: 3–6. The Fisher-Kaysen study estimates elasticity by relating price (and other variables) to estimated stocks of various electrical appliances in users' hands. They identify electric ranges and water heaters as "two striking exceptions" to their findings. For these appliances, they assert, "the price of electricity may have a definite influence." *Op. cit.*, 5. My former graduate student, John W. Wilson's own cross-sectional studies show residential demand with an elasticity of around −1.5, and very high responsiveness of the percentage of homes with electric water heaters, furnaces, and ranges to the price of electricity. *Op. cit.*, 11–73. Compare John R. Felton, "Competition in the Energy Market between Gas and Electricity," *Nebraska Jour. Econ. and Bus.* (Autumn 1965), IV: 3–12.

[20] The Fisher-Kaysen and Houthakker-Taylor studies do suggest a considerably higher elasticity

of demand in low-income areas, both within the United States and abroad. Of course, the elasticity of *industrial* demand for TVA power would be expected to be greater than that of total national demand for electricity, because, as Wilson also shows, the location of heavy electricity-using industries is highly responsive to relative price. *Op. cit.*, 172–174, 184.

[21] See, among others, Ben W. Lewis, in Leverett S. Lyon and Victor Abramson, *Government and Economic Life* (Washington: The Brookings Institution, 1940), II: 733–743; Joseph S. Ransmeier, *The Tennessee Valley Authority, A Case Study in the Economics of Multiple Purpose Stream Planning* (Nashville: Vanderbilt Univ. Press, 1942), 167–168; Gordon R. Clapp, *The TVA, An Approach to the Development of a Region* (Chicago: Univ. of Chicago Press, 1955), 93–95; Bonbright, *Public Utilities and the National Power Policies* (New York: Columbia Univ. Press, 1940), 45–47.

[22] From a CAB press release describing a staff report, *Traffic, Fares and Competition, Los Angeles–San Francisco Air Travel Corridor*, September 20, 1965.

[23] See pp. 64–65, Volume 1, and note 17 of Chapter 1, this volume.

sales, cutting costs, improving old services and offering new and more attractive ones—as our discussions in Chapter 6 of Volume 1 will partially attest.[24]

The Threat of Government Enterprise

Governments conduct an enormous variety of businesslike activities even in the United States; and the motives and circumstances have been almost equally diverse.[25]

We do not consider here whether public enterprise is superior or inferior to private enterprise as an instrument for getting the world's work done —although we allude to this question in our concluding chapter: in our judgment the question is too broad and too vague to have any meaning at least in purely economic terms. But there is strong evidence in the public utility arena that *competition between* the two systems of organization, like competition among private businesses, is highly conducive to improved performance. It may take the form of direct rivalry (for the patronage of the same customers in the same market); or of competition-by-example (where comparisons may be drawn between the performances of private and public enterprises in serving their respective customers, in different markets); or by threat of total displacement (where the management of each is aware that voters are examining its performance with the possibility of substituting one system of control for the other). When governments are willing to say to private insurance companies, for example: "if you will not design—and find low-cost ways of selling—simple, reliable, cheap, and nondiscriminatory policies, we shall," the probability of improved performance is surely enhanced[26]—either because the private companies may rise to the challenge or because, if they do not, the government may make good its threat.[27]

---

[24] It would be superfluous to add illustrations at this point. We shall also see, in Chapters 4 and 5, how unregulated competition has contributed to reduced rates and costs in trucking, air transport, and communication and provided large investors with an escape from the discriminatorily high brokerage commissions set collectively by the organized security exchanges.

It is difficult to doubt that intense intermodal competition has made an important contribution to the good record of technological progress in railroads compared with industry generally, demonstrated by the Kendrick estimates in Table 1, p. 99, above. Kendrick presents no estimates of changes in total factor productivity between 1948 and 1966 for transportation, but his figures show railroad output per unit of *labor* input rising no less than 5.1% a year in that period compared with 3.7% in transportation generally and 3.0% in manufacturing. (The source is indicated in Table 1.) This especially favorable showing is no doubt partly the accidental consequence of technological developments elsewhere—notably the introduction of the diesel locomotive and of the computer, which railroads have adopted for operations control. But along with the price and service experi-

mentation, which we have already described, it probably reflects also a delayed competitive response to the long shrinkage in their share of the total freight business. See also Barber, *op. cit.*, 824–895 and especially 836–853.

[25] See, for example, Wilcox, *op. cit.*, Chapter 20.

[26] In response to a series of insurance abuses uncovered in 1905, Louis D. Brandeis initiated a plan for mutual savings banks to sell life insurance policies at favorable rates in competition with private companies. This competition is said eventually to have forced the private carriers to reduce their rates. See Alpheus Thomas Mason, *Brandeis: Lawyer and Judge in the Modern State* (Princeton: Princeton Univ. Press, 1933), 28–30.

[27] Sometimes, of course, private companies fail to provide the service demanded because it is uneconomical, and the government can do "better" only because it subsidizes it. In that event, the government "yardstick" is inaccurate and produces a poorer rather than a better performance. The fact remains that where, as is almost inevitable, the private performance falls short of the ideal, this kind of actual or potential competition between the two systems can play an important role in improving it.

The most familiar illustration of this kind of competition in the United States has been in the field of electric power. There has been endless controversy over whether the numerous municipally owned and operated distribution companies (many of which do their own generation of power as well)[28] or the cooperatives that have been organized to supply power in rural areas, with the aid and encouragement of the Rural Electrification Administration, or the various Federal power projects like those in the Tennessee Valley are really fair "yardsticks" for determining whether private power rates are as low as they might be. Direct comparisons of rates do not, in fact, provide a fair test of relative economic efficiency: the taxes and costs of capital for public and private companies differ in material respects.[29]

The fact remains that there is intense rivalry between these public and private systems, far less in the form of direct competition in the market for the same customers than at the political level, along the lines already suggested.[30] It is clear that the public power companies—most notably TVA— were able to take the risks of setting rates low and thereby to test their assumptions about the high elasticity of demand on the one hand and the downward slope of their long-run cost curves on the other—risks that private companies either could not take or, at any rate, could not be forced by regulatory commissions to take.[31] To what extent it was the example of TVA's experience, demonstrating that it was in their private interest in any event to reduce rates, and to what extent the fear that if they did not do so there would be other TVA's set up to take over their business, is not important. The fact is that the competition-by-example or by threat of displacement

---

[28] See the statistics at p. 74, above.

[29] See, for example, Twentieth Century Fund, *op. cit.*, 436–437, 650–651, 718–720, and Ransmeier, *op. cit.*, 154–169.

[30] For a comprehensive survey and analysis, see Hellman, *Government Competition, op. cit.* There were, as of 1966, 62 cities in the United States with populations over 2,500 served by both publicly and privately owned electric utilities; and in 38 of these there was actually some degree of direct competition, some paralleling of lines, offering some customers a choice of suppliers. The residential customers served by these 38 city plants were only 0.4 percent of the national total; and even in these 38 instances the direct, competitive overlap was minor, frequently limited to some part, usually the oldest part, of the city. In contrast, there were some 1,900 municipalities, with 13 percent of the nation's total residential customers, served by municipally owned monopolies. *Ibid.*, 70–72, 76–77, 102–103.

The Federal Public Works Administration (PWA), which contributed greatly during the 1930s to the expansion of municipally owned electric power plants and distribution systems, gave most of its financial and other assistance to city plants already enjoying a monopoly. Eighty-three of its 319 allotments of funds to such companies did go to entirely new municipal systems, where a private monopoly already existed; but in the great majority of these cases, as well as in an even larger number in which the municipalities had merely made applications for PWA assistance, the application or the grant served the purpose of inducing the private companies to reduce their rates to levels satisfactory to the cities or to sell out to them—in either event avoiding an overlapping of private and public systems. The larger proportion of PWA power allotments went to Federal and State generating and transmission projects. The major contribution that projects such as these made to competition was by offering a supply of cheap, reliable power to cooperatives and municipals; but the latter distributors did not for the most part engage in direct, duplicative competition with private companies. *Ibid.*, 42–51. It has been the deliberate policy of the TVA, similarly, to avoid direct, duplicative competition in its service area; and as far as rural areas are concerned, the TVA Act directed the Authority to bring cheap electricity to rural areas not already served (at the time, only 11 percent of the farms in the country were served by electricity and in the TVA states the percentage was lower), and the Rural Electrification Act of 1935 has a similar restriction. *Ibid.*, 36–40.

[31] See note 36, below.

by public enterprise has greatly improved the performance of this industry.[32] The competition of public with private power has probably been a much more powerful influence than regulation in this respect, and particularly in bringing about dynamic price reduction, sales promotion, and extension of service.[33]

The A–J–W Effect

We have already alluded in various contexts to the tendency of regulation to encourage an uneconomic expansion of company investments, in order to inflate the rate base. As we have already pointed out, regulatory lag greatly diminishes the danger of this distortion. To the extent that it remains, it would seem to manifest itself mainly in the possible tendency for public utility companies to charge less than full marginal cost on some business in order to justify expanded investments. But, it is important to observe, the monopoly power that most public utility companies possess tends to produce the opposite result. Given the unwillingness of any profit-maximizing firm to expand output beyond the point where MR and MC are equated, the gap between MR and AR under monopoly results in a failure to produce up to the optimum level, where MC and P would be equated.

In other words, the circumstances of incompletely exploited monopoly power, regulation, and a return in excess of the cost of capital—all necessary for the A–J–W tendency—make the marginal private return on investment greater than the marginal social return, because to the net revenues directly generated by incremental investments, if they fall short of yielding the allowed rate of return, can be added the revenues the company can recoup by raising rates on other parts of its business. So it tends to produce over-investment. Monopoly has the opposite tendency; it makes marginal private return on output-expanding investments *less* than marginal social return, because it makes marginal revenue less than average revenue; so it tends to result in underinvestment.[34]

If regulation were instantaneously effective, it would eliminate this restrictive effect of monopoly; and that is precisely what it is supposed to do. The economic purpose of holding price to average total cost, including only a competitive return on investment, is to produce the competitive level of investment and output. In principle, regulated companies do not have the choice of restricted output with higher-than-competitive rates of return, on the one hand, and competitive levels of output with competitive rates of return on the other. If they expand investment and output from the monopoly to the competitive level, this will not, in contrast with the unregulated monopoly situation, reduce their *rates* of profit; instead they can only benefit by undertaking the expansion, as long as the price at which they sell the additional output covers marginal cost.[35]

---

[32] Twentieth Century Fund, *op. cit.*, 404, 431–437, 718–720, and *passim*; also the references in note 21, p. 103, above. For an example of the fear that "they might propose another TVA over in the Southwest" inducing a private company to keep its rates low, see Aaron Wildavsky, *Dixon-Yates: A Study in Power Politics* (New Haven: Yale Univ. Press, 1962), 9.

[33] The most thorough exposition and docu-

mentation of this thesis is by Hellman, *op. cit.*

[34] This discussion draws heavily on my "The Graduated Fair Return: Comment," *Amer. Econ. Rev.* (March 1968), LVIII: 170–173.

[35] Or, to put it another way, effective regulation makes the *marginal* revenue product of the utility company's investments (the added output multiplied by MR) the same as the *average* revenue product (the added output multiplied

But the fact is, as we have seen, that regulation is not instantaneously effective. Public utility companies therefore do have some opportunity to choose between higher and lower rates of profit, at correspondingly lower and higher respective rates of output. More important, merely holding the overall rate of return to competitive levels does not suffice to assure competitive levels of capacity and output. The reason for this is that regulators can never be certain about the elasticity of demand and the behavior of unit costs with increased sales. In the face of these inescapable uncertainties, commissions are powerless to order rate reductions as long as the regulated companies are earning no more than the permissible return on their rate bases, even though the reductions could well prove justified after the fact, if only there were some means of putting them into effect.[36] Competition automatically probes the elasticity of demand and the long-run behavior of costs; regulation cannot.[37]

As an offset to monopoly, the A–J–W distortion probably does more good than harm. It encourages risk-taking and output-expanding investment. We have earlier suggested that one possible manifestation of the A–J–W effect is some reluctance of public utilities to adopt thoroughgoing peak-responsibility pricing:[38] if peak users can be charged less than the full capacity costs for which they are (marginally) responsible, this "justifies" a greater capacity and a larger rate base, the costs of which can then be recouped partially from off-peak users. But it is precisely with respect to such investments that monopoly has heretofore been accused of producing excessive conservatism.[39]

It is significant that the main agencies whose purpose is to offset this conservatism, public power authorities and "tough" regulatory commissions, have been, according to Shepherd's survey, as a group, markedly worse than

---

by AR or price), thus eliminating the tendency to monopolistic restriction that exists when the former is less than the latter.

[36] This is graphically illustrated by William Vickrey, "Some Objections to Marginal-Cost Pricing," *Jour. Pol. Econ.* (June 1948), LVI: 228. Suppose, he suggests, demand and *LRAC* have

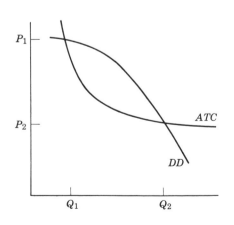

the slopes shown in the accompanying figure, but there is no way of being sure, and price is at P_1. Since the company is earning only ATC there is no way of forcing rate reductions to P_2, which would be the optimum level if revenues had to cover total costs and no discrimination were possible. Competition provides a means of getting from P_1 to P_2; regulation may not.

[37] It is this circumstance that lends attractiveness to government yardstick competition. TVA was able to do what regulatory commissions could not require private companies to do: to set low rates and see what happened to demand and cost. See, for example, Lewis, in Lyon and Abramson, *op. cit.*, II: 733–743; Twentieth Century Fund, *op. cit.*, 493–494, 651–652.

[38] See p. 50, above.

[39] H. M. Gray, "Transportation and Public Utilities, Discussion," *Amer. Econ. Rev., Papers and Proceedings* (May 1958), XXXVIII: 485–487; John Bauer and Peter Costello, *Public Organization of Electric Power, Conditions, Policies and Program* (New York: Harper & Bros. Publishers, 1949), Chapter 2; Robert F. Bryan and Ben W. Lewis, "The 'Earning Base' as a 'Rate Base,'" *Q. Jour. Econ.* (February 1938), LII: 339, 342–345; and M. G. de Chazeau, "Reply," *ibid.*, 346 359.

average offenders against such marginalist principles as peak-responsibility pricing.[40] These agencies have regarded it as their function to promote an expanded use of electricity: this was TVA's explicit purpose and, according to Shepherd, it practices no marginalist pricing at all.

The Role of Regulation

This is a formidable list of favorable influences. But it is the assumption of most economists that they are is not adequate, in the presence of monopoly; and this view probably accords with the political preferences of Western societies as well. We are generally unwilling to rely solely on the benevolence or even the enlightened self-interest of profit-maximizing monopolists or of their managers. We tend to prefer good results that are forced on industries by objective, external constraints such as regulation or competition. So the foregoing influences are not necessarily sufficient to elicit optimum performance—though, obviously, the more powerful they are, the less the need for government intervention. We still have to face the difficult question: what has been the impact of regulation itself? And what light does the foregoing list of favorable circumstances cast on the appropriate emphasis and direction of regulatory policy?

No healthy-minded person would devote large amounts of his time to the study of some institution that he thought had no importance. By this limited, double-negative test, the present writer is healthy-minded. I believe that regulation *does* make some difference. And that by thinking and trying, it can be made to make more of a difference—or, more importantly, a *better* difference.

The assumption that regulation does or can have an important effect is widely shared by practitioners in the field. They, better than anyone else, can observe the tremendous amounts of time, energy, and money devoted to the effort, and can clearly feel the heat with which issues in particular cases are contested. It is their function to argue the cataclysmic effects of legislators or commissions neglecting to follow their advice.

The result can be an occupational myopia. All this tumult and emotion does not prove that regulation does really make a difference, other than the difference of enriching lawyers and economists and using large quantities of resources. Economists have directed astoundingly little attention to this question,[41] and there is little convincing evidence that the performance of regulated industries differs significantly from what it would be in the absence of regulation. Or, even more important, that the benefits of regulation outweigh the costs.[42] Or, to state the proper test precisely, that regulation is carried on only to the point where marginal costs equal marginal benefits.

It may astound the reader to learn that many economists question whether regulation makes any major difference at all; others, that it makes

[40] See p. 98, Volume 1; see also the other references there in note 30, and the description thereafter of the similar effects of tough FPC regulation of natural gas pipelines.

[41] See, for example, any of the standard textbooks on utility regulation.

[42] Richard E. Caves, "Direct Regulation and Market Performance in the American Economy,"

Amer. Econ. Rev., *Papers and Proceedings* (May 1964), LIV: 172–181. See also Paul W. MacAvoy, *The Effectiveness of the Federal Power Commission*, Working Paper, Alfred P. Sloan School of Management, Massachusetts Institute of Technology, undated; a revised version appears in *Bell Jour. Econ. and Mgt. Sciences*; (Autumn 1970) also note 1, Chapter 7, below.

performance better. As one of them summarized a symposium on the subject:

"The views expressed in the papers presented in this session seem, where they overlap, to be broadly in agreement. What the regulatory commissions are trying to do is difficult to discover; what effect these commissions actually have is, to a large extent unknown; when it can be discovered, it is often absurd."[43]

Probably the most influential examination of this question has been the study of electricity rates through 1937 by Stigler and Friedland.[44] They found that interstate differences in average rate levels were explained principally by such factors as the size and density of the respective markets, per capita income and the proportion of power from hydroelectric sources. Introducing the additional consideration of the effectiveness of regulation in each state—as measured by the presence or absence of a special state commission with power to regulate rates—added nothing significant to the explanation of interstate differences. The results were likewise negative when they introduced the effectiveness of regulation, measured in the same way, into equations attempting to explain the relative treatment of small (relative to large) and domestic (relative to industrial) customers in the several states. They surmise:

"The ineffectiveness of regulation lies in two circumstances. The first circumstance is that the individual utility system is not possessed of any large amount of long-run monopoly power. It faces the competition of other energy sources in a large proportion of its product's uses, and it faces the competition of other utility systems. . . . The second circumstance is that the regulatory body is incapable of forcing the utility to operate at a specified combination of output, price, and cost. . . . [R]ecognize that the cost curve falls through time, and recognize also the inevitable time-lags of a regulatory process, and the possibility becomes large that the Commission will proudly win each battlefield that its protagonist has abandoned—except for a squad of lawyers."[45]

The results of the Stigler–Friedland study are sufficiently striking to suggest, at the very least, that the question with which they begin is a meaningful one. Whether their answer will prove to be definitive is still subject to various doubts. First of all, the interstate comparisons are undoubtedly weakened by spillover effects from state to state: it could be, for example, that effective regulation in one state influences rates in adjoining states, by competition or imitation. Second, it is almost certainly true that the statistical indicator they use for the effectiveness of regulation is insufficiently precise; the presence of

[43] Coase, "The Regulated Industries—Discussion," *ibid.*, 194.

[44] George J. Stigler and Claire Friedland, "What Can Regulators Regulate? The Case of Electricity," reprinted from the *Jour. Law and Econ.* (1962), V: 1–16, in Shepherd and Gies, *op. cit.*, 187–211.

[45] *Ibid.*, 200–203. A more recent study, using entirely different techniques, reached a tentative conclusion not far different. On the basis of direct estimates of marginal costs, on the one hand, and elasticity of demand, on the other, Thomas G. Moore concluded that the actual rates of the Detroit Edison Company were approximately the rates one would have expected an unregulated, profit-maximizing monopolist to charge. "The Effect of Regulation on Electrical Power Prices," unpublished paper delivered at North American Regional Conference of the Econometric Society, San Francisco, December, 1966.

commissions has been no guarantor of effective regulation;[46] and several of the states that lack commissions to this day leave regulation to their municipalities and to the control of government enterprise.[47] Moreover, regulation was hamstrung during most or all of the period their investigation covers by the holding company and by the restrictions imposed by the Supreme Court. But finally, it could well be that the impact on electricity rates of such alternative "regulatory" devices as municipal distribution companies and public enterprises for the generation and transmission of power is greater than that of regulation of the traditional type. These possibilities are suggestive only.[48]

It is difficult to read the record of the regular and only partially successful requests of Bell System companies for rate increases in the decade after World War II; or their regular and only partially successful requests for rates of return on equity more nearly comparable with those allowed other regulated companies; or their continuous and largely unsuccessful argument that Western Electric ought to be allowed rates of profit comparable with unregulated electrical equipment manufacturers;[49] or the succession of reductions in long-distance telephone rates introduced in considerable measure under the pressure of the Federal Communications Commission— which in the summer of 1967 required AT&T to put into effect some $120 million of rate reductions after explicitly denying the company's plea for higher earnings than $7\frac{1}{2}$ percent on total invested capital[50]—without concluding that regulation has had some significant influence here in the direction of holding rates down.[51] It is impossible to emerge from discussions of rate making with electric company executives without the very strong impression that most of them *think* major portions of their demands are highly inelastic; and without a great deal of skepticism, therefore, about the Stigler–Friedland hypothesis that "the individual utility system is not possessed of any large amount of long-run monopoly power." The history of

[46] On the wide variation from state to state and from one time to the next in the efficacy of state commissions, see Lewis, in Lyon and Abramson, *op. cit.*, II: 642–643.

[47] See note 36, p. 10, Volume 1.

[48] Richard Hellman contends that the authors' use of gross revenue per kilowatt-hour as their measure is likewise defective. Where electricity is sold under block rate schedules, with the applicable rate varying from one bloc of purchases to the next, the average rate in each state will be determined preponderantly by the composition of the market—that is, by the relative importance of customers using power in different quantities. The influence of this factor could well conceal much of the effect of regulation in determining the level of the entire rate schedule. Review of Shepherd and Gies, *op. cit.*, in *Amer. Econ. Rev.* (March 1967), LVII: 308–309.

[49] See pp. 291–292, Chapter 6, below.

[50] *In the Matter of American Telephone and Telegraph Co. et al.*, Memorandum Opinion and Order on Reconsideration, 9 FCC 2d 960, 971, 979 (September 1967). This followed cuts of $100 million in 1965. As a result of continuing surveillance, the company agreed in the fall of 1969 to further reductions totaling $150 million annually in long-distance rates. *New York Times*, November 6, 1969, 1.

[51] See the careful study of the rate increase requests by the Michigan Bell Telephone Company during the period 1948 through 1961 by Troxel, with the conclusion:

"No one can look at these facts, I think, and deny that the Michigan Commission puts strong constraints on telephone prices and revenues."

"Telephone Regulation in Michigan," in Shepherd and Gies, *op. cit.*, 154; see 151–162 and *passim*. Troxel rejects the possibility that the rate increase requests were inflated, so that in the end the company got pretty much what it wanted. But that possibility is by no means entirely eliminated: he recognizes that the company "has been quick to return to the Commission when it did not get all that it requested in a current decision." (157)

the railroads contradicts the notion that grossly discriminatory exploitation of these inelastic demands would represent no significant danger in the absence of regulation.[52]

Transportation offers a quite convincing demonstration that regulation makes a difference: consider the significance of the single fact that a taxi medallion—symbolizing the license to run a taxicab in New York City— sells for approximately $25,000. Here is market proof that licensing cuts down the number of taxis and increases the profitability of the business, either by raising rates or by keeping the cabs more fully occupied, hence harder to find when needed.[53]

As this last example suggests, if the first proper question is whether regulation has any effect at all, the second is: does it do more good than harm? The second question is inescapably posed by the record in transportation, to which we have already alluded many times.[54] Many students would answer it in the negative, agreeing with the very first sentence of Walter Adams and Horace N. Gray's chapter on "Regulation and Public Utilities" in their book, *Monopoly in America, The Government as Promoter*:

"Among all the devices used by government to promote monopoly, public utility, or public interest, regulation is in some respects perhaps the worst."[55]

In my judgment, regulation does do a great deal of good—notably in providing a public forum for continuing scrutiny of the performance of companies that do still have too much monopoly power, in too large a proportion of the markets in which they sell, to be left unregulated; in providing a check and a goad; in preventing unacceptable discrimination between customers.[55a] The FCC's ruling requiring television stations to give "equal time" to agencies that wished to warn viewers of the dangers of cigarette smoking was a major step in the direction of wiping out a stain on the good name of a market economy.

Regulation also does a great deal of harm—mainly because of its association with restraints on competition. It is this fact, rather than corruption, senility, or "industry-mindedness," as we have suggested, that is fundamental to the many complaints about the regulatory process that we have detailed in Chapters 1 and 2. To take one specific example: we have alluded to the complaints that the FCC and CAB have developed no general guidelines for

[52] On the question of whether regulation makes a difference in transportation, see the thoughtful appraisal by Wilson, *op. cit.*, *Amer. Econ. Rev.*, *Papers and Proceedings* (May 1964), LIV: 160–171.

[53] The equilibrium price for the privilege of operating a taxicab is the price that will just ration the number of available licenses among the people who would like to enter the field. Taxicab rates and revenues must be sufficient to provide an acceptable livelihood for the driver plus a return on the $25,000 investment. Such rates and returns would therefore be excessive if it were not necessary to make that investment; or, to look at the matter from the other end, manifestly many more drivers would wish to enter the field if they could do so without paying so high an entrance fee.

[54] See, for example, pp. 161–166, Volume 1, 14–28, above, and 178–193, Chapter 5, below. See, for a specific illustration, Paul W. MacAvoy and James Sloss, *Regulation of Transport Innovation, The ICC and Unit Coal Trains to the East Coast* (New York: Random House, 1967).

[55] The Macmillan Co., New York, 1955, 39. "In terms of economic efficiency alone, a policy that ended all rate regulation and common carrier obligations [in transportation] would create benefits far in excess of costs." Friedlaender, *op. cit.*, 164. For further consideration of whether regulation is worth what it costs, see p. 326, below.

[55a] For similar views in the field of transportation, see the recommendations cited in note 63, Chapter 1, and note 216, Chapter 5.

certification policy to which their decisions may in any sense be said to conform. Economic logic would suggest that by far the more fundamental determinant of the performance of these industries is the fact that entry is certificated in the first place. Any defects in their subsequent performance would flow more from the fact of entry restriction and fewness of sellers than from remediable deficiencies in the way in which the licensees are selected. If private parties are to have exclusive access to particular radio frequencies for the transmission of radio and television programs, it may be predicted that they will use the privilege to make the most money possible for themselves; and this suggests in turn that it makes relatively little difference whether applicant A is preferred to applicant B or the other way around:

"If there are going to be only three airlines operating between New York and Atlanta, does it really matter to the public whether the third service is rendered by Braniff or Delta?"[56]

None of this is to deprecate the importance of making regulation more intelligent and more effective in those circumstances in which competition is simply infeasible. If, in fact, technical conditions require the restriction of entry into broadcasting, it does become important that the FCC take into account opportunity costs in devising its allocation of the spectrum, set forth intelligent guidelines for certification policy, and make vigorous attempts to define and assert the public interest in the character of programming. More thoroughgoing policy formulation by regulatory commissions, more active planning in the public interest, a more direct scrutiny of industrial performance—efficiency, progressiveness, quality of service, rate structures—are surely necessary, to the extent that motivations of company managers and competition are inevitably inadequate.[57] Improvement of the stimuli and incentives offered regulated companies must also, clearly, be high on the agenda of regulatory improvement.

But, when all is said and done, the critical decisions have to do with the proper role and definition of competition. If we consult our list of favorable factors operating on public utility performance, we cannot help noting that the profit motive, managerialism, decreasing costs, and elasticity of demand are all strengthened by the force of competition. Competition is far more powerful than regulation in forcing businesses to explore the slope of their cost functions and elasticity of their demands, and to push down costs, if they are to prosper. In those situations in which competition is feasible, regulatory commissions clearly should welcome it rather than rush to restrict it.[58]

So we find ourselves face to face with the complex and omnipresent problem that constitutes the subject of the next three chapters.

[56] Roger C. Cramton, "The Effectiveness of Economic Regulation: A Legal View," *Amer. Econ. Rev., Papers and Proceedings* (May 1964), LIV: 185.

[57] See, for example, Trebing, *op. cit., Public Utilities Fortnightly* (July 18, 1963), LXXII:

22–35; Morgan, *Regulation and The Management of Public Utilities*, 242–269; and Chapter 2, above.

[58] For a fuller development of this argument, particularly with respect to public utility pricing, see my paper in Trebing, ed., *op. cit.*, 88–102.

CHAPTER 4

The Role and Definition of Competition : Natural Monopoly

The decision to regulate never represents a clean break with competition. No regulatory statute to the author's knowledge completely abandons reliance on competition as one guarantor of good performance.[1] The determination of the proper mixture of competitive rivalry and government orders in the

---

[1] The following examples are taken mainly from the important article by Louis B. Schwartz, *op. cit.*, *Harvard Law Rev.* (January 1954), LXVII: 436–475.

With respect to the certification of natural gas pipelines, the Natural Gas Act provides that

"a certificate shall be issued to any qualified applicant . . . if it is found that the applicant is able and willing properly to . . . perform the service proposed . . . and that the proposed service . . . is or will be required by the present or future public convenience and necessity. . . ." 15 U.S. Code 717 f (e), 1964 ed.

"Nothing contained in this section shall be construed as a limitation upon the power of the Commission to grant certificates of public convenience and necessity for service of an area already being served by another natural-gas company." 15 U.S. Code 717 f (g), 1964 ed.

The Civil Aeronautics Act of 1938 directs the CAB to

"consider the following among other things as being in the public interest. . . .

"Competition to the extent necessary to assure the sound development of an air-transportation system properly adapted to the needs of the foreign and domestic commerce of the United States, of the Postal Service, and of the national defense. . . ." 49 U.S. Code 1302d, 1964 ed.

Section 7 of the Clayton Act, which prohibits intercorporate stock and asset acquisitions and mergers "where . . . the effect . . . may be

substantially to lessen competition, or to tend to create a monopoly" (15 U.S. Code 18, 1964 ed.), applies to the regulated industries as well as the unregulated, with enforcement authority vested in the ICC, the FCC, the CAB, and the Federal Reserve Board for the industries within their respective jurisdictions. 15 U.S. Code 21a, 1964 ed. And, correspondingly, the Interstate Commerce, Federal Communications, and Federal Power Acts all require that proposed mergers of the regulated companies be subject to approval or disapproval by the corresponding regulatory commissions, and the Federal Aviation Act specifically prohibits mergers

"which would result in creating a monopoly . . . and thereby restrain competition or jeopardize another air carrier. . . ." 49 U.S. Code 1378b, 1964 ed.

The Reed-Bulwinkle Act of 1948, which authorized the Interstate Commerce Commission to approve agreements among carriers for the joint consideration and establishment of rates and gave such approved agreements exemption from the antitrust laws, specifically required that they accord

"to each party the free and unrestrained right to take independent action either before or after any determination arrived at through such procedure. . . ." 49 U.S. Code 5 b (b), 1964 ed. See also pp. 161–165, below.

Of course, such competition as the regulatory statutes permit with or among locally franchised

formula for social control is or ought to be the central, continuing responsibility of legislatures and regulatory commissions.[2]

The question is not simply one of *how much* competition to allow—how much freedom of entry or independence of decision making with respect to price, investment, output, service, promotional effort, financing, and the like. It is a question also of what, in the particular circumstances of each regulated industry, is the proper *definition*, what are the *prerequisites*, of effective competition. The effectiveness of competition cannot be simply measured along a single linear scale running from pure monopoly at one end to pure competition at the other—the latter characterized by an infinite number of sellers, complete independence of action, perfect standardization of products, zero governmental intervention, and zero monopoly power. (Or to "perfect" competition, which includes all the attributes of pure competition and requires, in addition, perfect mobility of factors and perfect knowledge and foresight.) The main reasons why pure competition is in fact not ideal are familiar: (1) economies of scale in production and distribution will typically require that sellers (and buyers) be larger in size and fewer in number than would be consistent with an utter absence of monopoly (or monopsony) power; (2) consumers want variety in product and service qualities and characteristics, which means that there cannot always be a large number of sellers of the same (standardized or undifferentiated) product; (3) effective innovation may, similarly, require firms too large and, hence, too few in number for monopoly power to be completely absent, and may require monopoly profits to finance the necessary innovative effort and to reward the successful innovator; (4) competitive structure may, in the presence of serious imperfections of competition, be too pure in other respects—entry too free and rivalry too intense—for optimum performance. All of these considerations make the determination of what kinds of policy will produce the most effective competition difficult enough in unregulated industry generally;[3] they make it even more difficult in the public utility arena, which has been subjected to more direct regulation precisely because of the presence there of unusually strong circumstances making unrestrained competition both infeasible and undesirable.

In making complex judgments like these, the anticompetitive bias of the regulatory mentality has ample opportunity to manifest itself. The essence of the regulatory approach, we have observed in Chapter 1, is the acceptance of a single company (or selected group of existing companies) as society's *chosen instrument* for performing the service in question. It vests in that chosen

---

telephone, or electric and gas distribution companies is typically only peripheral in character—in wholesale markets only, or only among competing fuels or communications media, or, by example, between public and private or Bell and non-Bell companies.

[2] "regulation as a general systematic alternative to competition is literally inconceivable. We do not have the conceptual foundation to construct or operate a completely regulated economic system. . . . At most, regulation is a supplement or partial alternative to competition, resorted to on a largely *ad hoc* basis to secure particular

objectives which it is thought cannot be obtained by competition." Lee Loevinger, "Regulation and Competition as Alternatives," Reproduced with permission of *The Antitrust Bulletin*, from Volume XI (January–April 1966), 139, © 1965 by Federal Legal Publications, Inc.

[3] For a survey of these problems and of the rich literature on the subject, see Dirlam and Kahn, *Fair Competition, the Law and Economics of Antitrust Policy* (Ithaca: Cornell Univ. Press, 1954), especially Chapter 1. See also the brief reference to some of these problems at page 44 of our Volume 1 and the introduction to this volume.

instrument, by license, explicit responsibility for providing good and economical service to all comers; it imposes obligations on it that go far beyond obligations imposed on private companies in the economy generally; and it subjects it to all sorts of controls. In return, it protects it from competition. In brief, it places society's principal reliance on conscious and explicit planning, by monopolists or a limited number of selected companies on the one hand and regulatory commissions on the other, under cover of a complicated pattern of privileges, public duties, and responsibilities.

The competitive approach, in, contrast, places reliance on the market mechanism itself. Good results are expected to flow from the interplay of independent companies, under conditions of unrestricted entry, independent competitive endeavor, and free contract. Neither government agencies nor any particular private companies need assume explicit overall responsibility for the results that issue—the price and quality of service and so on. The only government planning required is of the antitrust kind—directed at preserving the competitive market *mechanism*—and related efforts to make that mechanism work as well as possible. The only privilege conferred on private companies is the opportunity to compete; and their only responsibility is for each to look to its own interests.

The marriage (perhaps the better term would be miscegenation) of these two approaches in the public utility context is inevitably an uneasy one. But the almost universal conception is that the mixed marriage is better than none: that such competition as can be permitted, consistent with efficiency, can contribute to improved performance; yet unregulated competition is infeasible—provided, that is, that the industry is properly treated as a public utility in the first place!

As we have already suggested in our Introduction, the proper institutional structure for the regulated industries—in particular, the economically optimum mix of competition and regulation and the definition of optimum competition itself—will clearly vary from one to the other: each is in important degree *sui generis*. There are no simple, scientific rules; in each context the formulation of good policy calls for informed judgment—a judicious balancing and appraisal of often conflicting considerations and predictions. But if that last sentence is to mean anything at all—if by "judicious balancing" we are to mean something more than utter pragmatism, or simple compromises of all conflicting views and interests—the judgment must be informed by *something*. That something is presumably experience, from which emerges an ability to discriminate between correct and incorrect, relevant and irrelevant, logical and illogical arguments and considerations—an understanding of whatever generalizations can be drawn from the regulatory experience generally. Chapters 4–6 are an attempt to contribute to that understanding, by defining and analyzing the major aspects of this central institutional question and by describing a few illustrative cases in detail.

The three chapters correspond respectively to the three major facets of the problem. The first and simplest rationalization of the public utility institution is the concept of natural monopoly. Its corollary is the need for restriction of entry—the most decisive limitation of competition. Chapter 4 is devoted to an examination of this concept, of the entry control that it purports to justify, and of the extent to which even natural monopoly may properly be subjected to competition.

Chapter 5 examines the other major justification:[4] the alleged threat of excessive competition and consequent deterioration of service, giving rise to the necessity for restricting competition from both the outside (via entry) and inside. This rationalization is quite different from the first. Although competition among "natural monopolists" will likewise have some tendency to be destructive, the remedy there is to prohibit entry, rely on a single chosen instrument and impose upper limits on his price and minimum standards of service. Here, instead, there is no suggestion that monopoly is technologically desirable. Reliance is placed, rather, on competition, constrained partly by restrictions on entry, partly by price *floors*, and partly by the setting of *ceilings* on service rivalry. (To be sure, maximum prices and minimum specifications of service may likewise be imposed.)

Chapter 6 considers the main aspects of the problem of integration in the public utility industrics—the question of the extent to which regulated companies should either be permitted or required to integrate horizontally, geographically, vertically, or conglomerately, by financial consolidation or by collaboration among themselves. Whereas Chapters 4 and 5 are concerned with the two major rationalizations for limiting competition, this Chapter is basically concerned with its proper definition. The question is, in part: to what extent will integration make for more or less effective *competition* in the public utility context? But the question is not limited to the bearing of integration on competition; the fundamental question is what combination of integration, interfirm collaboration and rivalry will make for the best possible performance in these industries.

ECONOMIES OF SCALE

The possibility of competitive entry is the principal limitation on monopoly power in a market economy. Etymologically, the prime characteristic of monopoly is the presence of a single ("mono") seller of a differentiated product; and economists have demonstrated that joint monopoly power may be exercised also when sellers are few ("oligo") or act in concert. But how badly a monopoly can in the long run perform (relative to the performance that could be achieved under competition) depends on the height of the barriers to entry into its market.[5]

No barrier to entry is more absolute than one imposed or enforced by the sovereign power of the state. All others are potentially subject to hurdling, erosion, or circumvention. So our study of the proper role of competition in the regulated industries properly begins with a consideration of the fact and

---

[4] We have, in Chapter 1, pp. 1–11, above, identified a longer list of reasons for the association of regulation with restraint of competition. There is no need for us to engage in a systematic effort at this point to reconcile the two lists. A perceptive reader will see, however, that all the other reasons except possibly the promotional one reduce in one way or another to the two broad categories set forth here; and even the promotional one can, as we shall see, be regarded as a special variant of the destructive competition case—the belief being that excessively intense rivalry will retard or abort the development of a desired service.

[5] See Joe S. Bain, *Barriers to New Competition* (Cambridge: Harvard Univ. Press, 1956). The United Supreme Court has defined monopoly power under the Sherman Act as the power "to raise prices or to exclude competition when it is desired to do so." *American Tobacco Co. et al. v. United States*, 328 U.S. 781, 811 (1946). But these two conditions are not alternatives, as the Court implied; the first is in the long run dependent on the second.

major rationalization of governmental restriction of entry, the concept of natural monopoly. Whatever its validity as a historical explanation of how these monopolies in fact emerged, this remains the most generally accepted justification for confining at least some aspects of the supply of communications, electricity, gas, water, and perhaps urban transportation to single, chosen instruments.

The essence of the natural monopoly concept can be illustrated by a recent example. In 1968, the President's Task Force on Communications Policy recommended that all United States international communications media be placed under the operating control of a single company.[6] One important basis for this recommendation of monopoly, which we shall elaborate in Chapter 6 (see pp. 264–267, below), is the advantage of permitting a communications company to operate all the available media, so that it can select whatever combination—cable, satellite, radio—will most efficiently perform the function. But these advantages of conglomerate integration do not themselves justify closing the field to *all but one* such conglomerate enterprise. This additional step requires a demonstration that monopoly is the most efficient mechanism for providing international communications services. And this must mean that the potential economies of firm size are so great that only a single firm, capable of supplying the entire market, can take the fullest possible advantage of them.

Evolution of the Natural Monopoly Concept

Until around the turn of the twentieth century, the typical public policy toward the public utility industries was one of local competition rather than monopoly—not of completely unrestricted entry, to be sure, but one of chartering numerous suppliers in the various localities. (This statement is insufficiently precise, since individual cities might themselves be composed of separate marketing areas, for each of which a separate company might be the sole supplier. But, in fact, overlapping franchises were likewise frequent.) Between 1882, when Edison opened his Pearl Street station in New York, and 1907, nonexclusive, competitive electric franchises were granted freely, often as a means of forcing down rates that cities considered too high.[7]

Burton N. Behling cites several reasons for this practice. First, there were technical factors: the use of direct current at low voltages made it impossible to distribute electricity over an area greater than one square mile. Second, it was difficult, at the early stages of the industry, for small, local companies to raise large quantities of capital such as would have been required to serve entire areas exclusively. Electrical equipment manufacturers, competing with one another, would each set up its own generating and distributing company. But the most important explanations were institutional. Competition, or at least laissez-faire, represented the general national policy and there had not yet emerged a general acceptance of the notion that in certain industries regulated monopoly might produce a better performance. And regulatory

---

[6] *Final Report*, Chapter 2.

[7] "The haphazardness of franchise-giving is illustrated by Chicago. During 1882–1905, it granted 29 franchises. Towns it absorbed gave 18. The grants were for such small areas as 'one block each way', or 'a few blocks on the north-

west side', or 'old twelfth ward.' Sixteen were competitive, only one was exclusive. Three covered the entire city: one of these in 1897 was hawked about the streets until in self-defense the Chicago Edison Company bought it up." Hellman, *Government Competition*, 9.

institutions themselves were still in an embryonic state: so, municipalities tended instead to charter competitive companies when they were dissatisfied with the rates being charged by existing suppliers. The experience was similar in the supply of gas and in local telephone service, after the original Bell patent expired, in 1893.[8]

It is not surprising, therefore, that there is no trace of the concept of natural monopoly in the landmark constitutional cases delineating the category of businesses "affected with a public interest."[9] Although *Munn v. Illinois* cited the alleged monopoly power of grain elevators in Illinois in partially justifying regulation of their rates, there was no conception that monopoly in these industries was positively desirable, on grounds of efficiency. Nor was it; grain storage is simply not a natural monopoly.[10]

But competition in the public utility industries typically proved ephemeral and ineffective. While it lasted, it

"favored the public for a time with low rates, but invariably at the expense of a deteriorated service. Financial exhaustion of one or more of the companies eventually brought about a complete consolidation, or an agreement as to rates or territory."[11]

The issuance of competitive franchises was, with discouraging regularity, followed by combination among the franchisees, despite the efforts of legislatures to prevent it. Some promoters took out these licenses merely to sell them to other companies, for whom they might be expected to have at least a nuisance value. In city after city, as a result, one company would emerge with almost all the franchises issued. The policy of competition, it seems generally conceded, was a failure.[12]

It was out of this experience that the concept of "natural monopoly" gradually emerged, as an attempt on the one hand to explain the persistent tendency of competition to produce inferior results and to disappear and, on the other, to justify its abandonment.[13] The logical corollary was the

---

[8] Behling summarizes a special census report of 1902, covering the 1,002 incorporated cities in the United States with population in excess of 4,000 that had telephone facilities: independent companies had a monopoly in 137 and Bell companies in 414 of these; 451 had duplicated service. *Competition and Monopoly in Public Utility Industries* (Urbana: Univ. of Illinois Press, 1938), 20; see also 18–19. In most states, Behling points out, granting of exclusive franchises was either unconstitutional or contrary to statutory law on into the twentieth century. *Ibid.*, 23. See also Martin Glaeser, *Public Utilities in American Capitalism* (New York: The MacMillan Co., 1957), Chapters 4–5.

[9] See pp. 3–8, Volume 1.

[10] "On *political* grounds, grain elevators were particularly vulnerable in the Granger era. They sufficed to raise the essentially ideological issue of the warrant for *any* government price regulation of *any* industry. Yet, in a transportation center the size of Chicago, there is no technical or economic reason why numerous companies

should not operate grain elevators. In short, *Munn v. Illinois* involved a representative industry from the standpoint of establishing the *right to regulate*, but its industrial background was singularly inappropriate as a source of answers to questions about *types of regulation*." James R. Nelson, *op. cit.*, *The Antitrust Bulletin* (January–April 1966), XI: 8.

[11] Behling, *op. cit.*, 20.

[12] See *ibid.*, 21–22; Glaeser, *op. cit.*, 16; Hellman, *Government Competition*, 9–11.

[13] The reference here is to direct, duplicative competition between private companies. As Hellman is at pains to point out and document at length, the advocacy and practice of government enterprise as an alternative device, directly competitive with private enterprise in only a small minority of the cases, but providing competition-by-example and by threat of displacement remained very much alive. See pp. 104–106, above. In 1913, for example, Cleveland undertook direct competition with a private company for the residential market, at the same

constitution of independent regulatory commissions; the first were set up in New York and Wisconsin, in 1907. There remains to this day a widespread consensus that at least some part of these businesses is, in truth, a natural monopoly, in the sense that direct competition is likely in most instances to involve unbearably great inefficiencies. This agreement does not, however, exclude the possibility that the *potentially* superior efficiency of monopoly might in fact not be achieved, whether because of monopolistic inertia or because of the inadequacies of regulation; and, as a corollary, that the inefficiencies introduced by even direct, duplicative competition could, in principle, be less important than its positive stimulus, particularly to a dynamically superior performance.[14]

The Essential Prerequisite of Natural Monopoly

The critical and—if properly defined—all-embracing characteristic of natural monopoly is an inherent tendency to decreasing unit costs over the entire extent of the market. This is so only when the economies achievable by a larger output are internal to the individual firm—if, that is to say, it is only as more output is concentrated in a single supplier that unit costs will decline.[15]

The principal source of this tendency is the necessity of making a large investment merely in order to be in a position to serve customers on demand.[16]

---

time specifying that the 10-cent per kwh company rate be reduced to a flat 3 cents; the eventual compromise was 5:

"Thereafter, both systems prospered under duplicative competition. The company had one of the lowest rates in the country. The competition received wide publicity, and was a thorn in the side of the private industry." *Op. cit.*, 26; see also 11–27 and *passim*.

[14] The following summary statement by the distinguished staff of economists that prepared the 20th Century Fund's factual findings, *Electric Power and Governmental Policy*, back in 1948, may be taken as still summarizing the consensus (p. 29):

"It is well known that in the power industry local monopoly is more economical than competition. If a number of systems compete for a single group of customers, there is duplication of investment. Each system can carry an additional load without a proportionate increase in costs. If they compete, each will take additional business so long as it can be obtained at a price exceeding the added costs; prices will then tend to cover output costs but not capacity costs. Sooner or later they are likely to agree to eliminate competition, or one will drive out the other. While costs *can* be lower under local monopoly than under competition, they may not be. The monopolist, protected from competition, may not operate efficiently, and his waste may be as great as that of competition. Hence prices may be

lower under competition than under monopoly."

Hellman minimizes the purported inefficiencies of competition in the local distribution of electric power, surveys the experience of several cities with direct duplication of municipally owned and private systems, and praises the results. But for the most part his argument is based on the fact that actual duplication is typically slight. The government competition that he strongly supports is far more side-by-side competition by example or by threat than of the direct variety. See *op. cit.*, 70–77, 83–98, and the various city case studies in his Chapter 2; also note 30, Chapter 3, above.

[15] Economies of scale might instead be *external* to the individual firm. It could be, for example, that as an entire industry grows it can acquire some of its inputs at decreasing average costs, because its growth enables the suppliers of those inputs to take advantage of potential economies of scale internal to *their* industry. Increasing returns of this kind are compatible with a competitive organization of the first industry: all firms in it could benefit equally from these emergent external economies, no matter what the scale of their individual outputs. See Howard S. Ellis and William Fellner, "External Economies and Diseconomies," in Amer. Econ. Ass'n, *Readings in Price Theory* (Chicago: Richard D. Irwin, 1952), 242–263.

[16] On the question of whether this fact makes for only short-run rather than long-run decreasing costs, see p. 126, Volume 1.)

The railroad has to construct a roadbed and lay a track before it is in a position to carry any passengers or freight at all; water, gas, electricity, and telephone companies have to dig up the streets and lay down pipes or build poles and string wires from the point of production to every single point of potential consumption and install meters before a single drop, cubic foot, or kilowatt hour can be sold or a single call placed. Those costs may be absolutely fixed and unchanging no matter how many units are sold; to the extent that this is true, average costs per unit decline in inverse proportion to the number of units sold. This tendency is created or accentuated by certain common and interrelated characteristics of many public utility services: that they involve a *fixed* and essentially immovable *connection* between supplier and customer or locality (true even of trains, but not of trucks); that the services are largely nonstorable (true of transportation, electricity, and communications, not of gas and water); that the company is under an obligation to supply instantaneously, on demand—at the flick of a switch, the click of a thermostat, the lifting of a telephone instrument; and that the demands, both of individual customers and on the system as a whole, fluctuate widely from one point in time to the next: for urban and commuter transportation it is concentrated in the rush hours; for almost all of these services it is much larger during the day and possibly early evening than during the night; for gas it is concentrated in the winter; for electricity in the northeast, where the heavier usage is for airconditioning, in the summer. For all these reasons, there has to be a heavy investment in capacity sufficient to meet the peak demands; and it is most efficiently provided by a single supplier, with a single fixed connection to the customer.[17]

Even where the investment in capacity is not totally predetermined and fixed—where, that is, a larger investment will be required if demand is large rather than small, or as demand grows over time—technological economies of scale may still make monopoly the most efficient form of organization. This will be true as long as plants constructed for higher levels of output will have lower average costs than smaller plants, or where it will cost less for an existing supplier to add a given amount of capacity to its existing plant than for a new supplier to provide it. The railroad may have to lay down a second track; gas, electricity, and telephone companies may have to build larger or additional transmission, generating, or exchange capacities; but they will typically be able to do so at lower incremental costs than a competitor starting afresh.[18]

---

[17] The wide divergence between peak and off-peak demand does not in itself contribute to economies of scale or natural monopoly. As far as this factor alone is concerned, the requisite capacity could be provided just as efficiently by a large number of suppliers, with an average load factor corresponding to that of the single one. Nor is the consequent prevalence of excess capacity off-peak a sign of short-run decreasing costs. Peak and off-peak service are two distinct, joint products. As our discussion at pp. 79–83 and 90–95 of Volume 1 demonstrates, the sum of their marginal costs need not on this account be less than their combined average total costs—and it will not be, unless the joint production is itself subject to increasing returns. Compare C. F. Phillips' assumption to the contrary, when he contends that the prevalence of excess capacity off-peak makes competition inherently unstable. *The Economics of Regulation*, rev. ed. (Homewood: Richard D. Irwin, 1969), 24–26.

[18] Paul J. Garfield and Wallace F. Lovejoy's discussion of the possibility that a monopoly may be able to "take full advantage of the economies of large-scale production" has mixed in with this factor another whose relevance is not nearly so clear:

"Once public utilities were able to serve an entire market under the protection of monopoly,

Clearly, these tendencies are related to the fact that fixed or capacity costs bulk unusually large among total costs in most public utility industries.[19] And it is these fixed costs that might be wastefully duplicated if two companies tried to serve the same markets. But heavy fixed costs do not themselves necessarily make for natural monopoly.[20] An industry's technology might be such that all of its costs were fixed—its output produced in fully automatic plants, drawing their energy from the sun and their raw materials from the air—yet in the absence of internal economies of scale over a sufficient range of supply, it might be equally efficient to have that production carried on by a large number of separate firms, each with its own wholly automatic, completely fixed-cost plant. The tendency of agriculture to suffer wide fluctuations in prices is correctly attributed in part to the importance of fixed costs in that industry, a large proportion of a farmer's costs being the return on his own investment in the land and its improvements, in his equipment, and on his own labor. This has the effect of making supply highly inelastic, so that even slight changes in demand result in sharp fluctuations in price.[20a] But since economies of scale in agriculture are very limited relative to the size of the market, the industry is clearly not a natural monopoly.

Obviously, then, the phenomenon of natural monopoly is in some way related to the wastes that would arise if, in the presence of competition, certain facilities would have to be duplicated. But here, as with the phenomenon of heavy fixed costs, it is not the fact of duplication alone that makes for a natural monopoly, but the presence of economies of scale or decreasing costs in the provision and utilization of these facilities.[21] We may have

---

it became feasible for many utilities to concentrate their production in the larger and more efficient plant and equipment units made possible by technological advancement." *Public Utility Economics* (Englewood Cliffs, N.J.: Prentice-Hall, 1964), 18.

But competition, too, has the effect of concentrating production in the "more efficient plants" —that is, in those with the lowest short-run marginal costs (see pp. 264–266, Chapter 6, below). Nor is competition incompatible with firms taking the fullest advantage of technological progress, to the extent that it is economical to do so, on the basis of a comparison of the average variable costs of existing plant and average total costs of new (see p. 118, Volume 1, above). Technological progress contributes to natural monopoly only to the extent that it is of a type that increases the importance of economies of scale relative to the size of the market. For evidence that developments in electricity generation and transmission have been of this character, see p. 128, Volume 1, and 74, Chapter 2, above. For a similar confusion see note 39, p. 12 of Volume 1.

[19] See pp. 35–36, Volume 1.

[20] Compare Garfield and Lovejoy:

"Part of the explanation of this decreasing-cost tendency is found in the fact that public utilities require a relatively greater investment in plant

and equipment than other principal industries. . . . Because public utilities must have greater investment in plant and equipment than other industries, their cost structure is dominated by the costs related to that fixed investment. It is most important to note that plant-related costs are constant in amount and do not fluctuate with variations in production, assuming constant plant size." *Op. cit.*, 17. © 1964. Reprinted by permission of Prentice-Hall, Inc., Englewood Cliffs, N.J.

Fixed costs do, of course, make for a condition of decreasing costs within the limits of the capacity of a given plant; but they do not in themselves give rise to the long-run decreasing costs—that is, the economies of scale—that are the essential condition of natural monopoly.

[20a] See pp. 173–174, below.

[21] Compare Behling's statement to the contrary:

"Even when it is observed that decreasing cost does not extend without limit in public utility enterprise, the conclusion does not follow that monopolistic organization should be abandoned. . . . Whether increasing or decreasing cost applies, a given area can be served more economically by a single enterprise than by rival companies operating in the same territory. Competitive duplication results in a larger total investment and a higher cost per unit. Combined capacity is greater than the market requires, and neither

"competitive duplication" in the form of thousands of farms all producing the same product, scores of doctors practicing in the same locality, and great numbers of salesmen, representing competing manufacturers of the same product, combing the same market territory. None of these "duplications" is necessarily inefficient, as long as the market has need of all these suppliers and none of them is too small to take full advantage of the available economies of scale. It is only when the entire demand can most efficiently be supplied via a single set of telephone poles and gas mains that it becomes inefficient to duplicate them, to have two companies digging up the streets at various times rather than one. So, duplication is inefficient—indeed, one might prefer to say that only in this event does it in fact constitute duplication —only in the presence of the economies of scale that make for natural monopoly.[22]

An additional source of these potential economies of scale is to be found not on the supply but on the demand side. We have mentioned the effect of variability in demand in imposing on a public utility company the burden of maintaining capacity sufficient to supply however much service is demanded at the peak. This variability tends, other things being equal, to make it more efficient to supply many customers and regions than few; that is to say, it gives rise to economies of scale when the dimension along which output is measured is not the quantities taken by some given number of customers but the number and diversity of customers and markets served. The greater the latter, the greater is the likelihood that the variations in their separate demands will tend to cancel one another out; the more diverse the markets, the greater the possibility that the maximum requirements of some will fall at times different from the maximum requirements of others. In consequence, the firm that covers the entire market is likely to have a better relationship (that is, a lower ratio) between total investment costs (which are determined

---

competitor is likely to reach maximum efficiency in terms of cost and economical use of capital resources. Public convenience also dictates the minimum of pipes, poles, and other distribution equipment necessary for service." *Op. cit.*, 36.

[22] The argument here is not merely semantic. If one chooses to characterize the provision of the same services by competitors as duplicative only in the presence of decreasing costs, it remains true that it is the presence of such economies of scale that is the necessary and sufficient condition for converting mere replication into (wasteful) duplication.

Garfield and Lovejoy are guilty of some fuzziness on this score as well:

"Electric and telephone company poles and underground conduits and cables occupy choice and strategic land sites in metropolitan areas and along our highways. Gas and water mains run under our streets. It is not hard to imagine the obstructions which would be presented by a duplication of utility company facilities. . . . The same, of course, holds true for gas and water companies, which occasionally dig up city streets to repair or enlarge their mains. In light of the

automobile traffic situation, it is apparent that more than one bus or streetcar line on a street is disadvantageous." *Op. cit.*, 16.

These considerations sound conclusive; in fact, they are not. The critical question is: *how many* holes, conduits, mains, and buses, how many diggings up of the streets are necessary to serve a city? And are these most efficiently supplied by one company or by many? Suppose, for example, that the provision of water required two separate underground pipes, each of maximum efficient size, in some portion of the city: it would not necessarily require more digging up of the streets, in order, for example, to repair a leak, if each pipe were owned by a separate company rather than both by one. The monopoly is natural only when one pipe, or common ownership of numerous pipes, with a correspondingly mini- mized number of diggings, is the most efficient method of supply. Similarly with buses and street congestion: the presence of competing bus *companies* does not necessarily mean an excessive total number of *buses*. It is only if one company can supply the same aggregate service with fewer buses than two that monopoly becomes natural.

by the total demand placed on it at the system peak) and total dollar sales over the year, hence lower average costs, than two or more separate firms, each supplying some portion of the total market.[23]

Cases of Apparently Increasing Costs

There are cases of natural monopoly that would seem at first blush not explicable in terms of long-run decreasing costs. We have already observed, for example, that as the number of telephone subscribers goes up, the number of possible connections among them grows more rapidly; local exchange service is therefore generally believed to be subject to increasing, not decreasing unit costs, when the unit of output is the number of subscribers.[24] And yet, it seems clear that this service is a natural monopoly: if there were two telephone systems serving a community, each subscriber would have to have two instruments, two lines into his home, two bills if he wanted to be able to call everyone else.[25] Despite the apparent presence of increasing costs, in short, monopoly is still natural because one company can serve any *given* number of subscribers (for example, all in a community) at lower cost than two.[26]

In fact, however, this example is not necessarily an exception to the general principle that long-run decreasing costs are an indispensable condition for natural monopoly. The rise in the exchange cost *per subscriber* as their number

---

[23] We have already seen that this is one possible advantage of power-pooling. See note 49, p. 65, Chapter 2, above. The diversity factor is the ratio of the sum of the (noncoincident) maximum demands of the various subdivisions of a firm's customers to the maximum (coincident) system demand. The higher that ratio, the greater is the total quantity of services that can be supplied over some period of time with a given capacity. A single supplier need have capacity only sufficient to meet the sum total of demands at the time of the system's peak. If, instead, there were separate companies supplying each of these subdivisions of the market, each would have to have a total capacity equal to the peak requirement of its own class of customers; and the sum of those noncoincident peak demands calls for a greater total capacity than if they were supplied by a single monopolist.

Economies of diversity of demand do not, however, necessarily require monopoly. An airline whose peak winter demand is on the New York to Miami route may find it economical to operate also New York to Europe, in order to use its equipment on the transatlantic route during the summer. But this fact does not mean it would be most economical to have only such company. The economies of scale might be equally fully exploited by several such companies, each with a similar diversity of routes with noncoincident peaks. Diversity of demand is thus an argument for geographic integration of operations—not necessarily for monopoly.

[24] See note 4, Chapter 5 of Volume 1; also

Garfield and Lovejoy, *op. cit.*, 198–200.

[25] It is possible to imagine alternative arrangements that would avoid these duplications while having more than one company serve a community, but all would in effect involve monopoly. Each company could serve a separate geographical portion of the community, while interconnecting with the other: in their respective territories all would be monopolists. If their market territories overlapped, each could have its own exclusive set of subscribers (once again with interconnections); but this would obviously involve higher cost unless they used common poles and cables—that is, joined together in a single operation for the naturally monopolistic part of the business.

[26] So, for example, Bonbright takes great pains to refute

"what seems to be a widespread assumption that a public utility *must* be producing on the declining-cost segment of a unit-cost curve in order to justify its claim to acceptance as a natural monopoly. This assumption is quite unwarranted. It ignores the point that, even if the unit cost of supplying a given area with a given type of public utility service must increase with an enhanced rate of output, *any specified* required rate of output can be supplied most economically by a single plant or a single system." *Principles of Public Utility Rates*, 14–15. The point is not one of great urgency, but I believe he is mistaken, for reasons that I proceed to develop in the text immediately following.

increases is the counterpart of an improvement in the quality of service rendered: each telephone is thereby enabled to reach more and more customers. The fact that the dollar cost of a unit of service rises as its quality improves is not a proof of decreasing returns. Increasing or decreasing returns can be measured only by the behavior of costs when there is an increased *quantity* of service of an *unchanging* quality. By that test local exchange service, too, is subject to increasing returns: the same subscriber plant (the phone instrument and the drop-line into the house) can handle additional calls at zero additional costs; and the cost of increasing the capacity of the exchange for this purpose is likewise less than the average.[27]

A different kind of apparent concomitance of long-run increasing costs and natural monopoly is illustrated by the case of an electric utility able to generate most of its power in hydroelectric plants at a low cost, but forced then, if it is to meet the additional demand, to shift to higher-cost steam plants. In this event, its marginal cost will exceed the average. But it might still be a natural monopoly, Bonbright observes,

"For, on the one hand, the single company can secure the maximum advantages of economies of scale and of density, while on the other hand it is no more subject to the diseconomies of enhanced output resulting from scarcity of water power and of other natural resources than would two or more companies if called upon to supply the region with the same total output."[28]

But all this example shows is that certain portions of an industry—those subject to decreasing costs—may be natural monopolies while other portions may not. The point is that the *generation* of electric power is not necessarily a natural monopoly at all—that, to turn Bonbright's observation around, two or more companies in this part of the business might have no higher costs than a single one.

Moreover, as we have already emphasized, the critical factor in the naturalness of monopoly is the presence or absence of economies of scale *internal* to the firm. As Bonbright points out, the rising average costs that are attributable to the exhaustion of choice hydroelectric sites would be a reflection of *external* diseconomies to which the entire industry would be subject, whether composed of one firm or many. In itself, therefore, this upward slope of the industry's LRAC function tells us nothing about whether it is a natural monopoly. The same observation would apply to the apparent tendency for municipal water supply to exhibit long-run increasing costs, evidently because, among other factors, a city has to go farther and farther away—both extensively (geographically) and intensively (for example by resorting to increasingly costly water treatment)—to get additional supplies.[29] And yet water supply, too, is evidently a natural monopoly, because of tendencies to long-run decreasing cost *internal* to the firm.

Moreover, the divergence between marginal cost (of the steam plants for

---

[27] The same observation applies to the apparent tendency to increasing unit cost (that is, per subscriber) as electricity or gas distribution are extended to additional, less sparsely populated areas (see p. 125, Volume 1, above). The reason is that the unit of service is changing in these cases: it is not just the number of kwh or Mcf that is being increased but also the average mileage of transmission service (that is, of "place utility") accompanying each unit of current or gas.

[28] *Ibid.*, 15–16.

[29] See Priest, *Principles of Public Utility Regulation*, II: 751–761.

electricity or desalination plants for water) and average cost is in fact apparent only, and would disappear in perfectly functioning markets. Once the available hydroelectric sites (and nearby fresh water supplies) are exhausted and it becomes necessary to turn to more costly sources of supply, the rental value of the former scarce resources rises sharply. If those scarce inputs (falling and fresh water, respectively) were not owned by the public utility company but were purchased by it in the open market, those rising rents would be incorporated in their purchase prices, and (to confine ourselves to the first illustration) the average unit costs of hydroelectric generation would be increased to those of steam generation. It is the scarcity of certain strategic inputs that is responsible for the external increasing cost tendencies. Payment of their economic rents, reflective of their (growing) scarcity value, would raise the average total costs of all intramarginal output to the long-run cost of the marginal output. And whether, in these circumstances, marginal costs were higher or lower than average total cost would reflect only the presence or absence of internal economies of scale.[30]

In summary, as long as the tendency prevails for unit costs to decline with an increasing volume of business, because of economies of scale internal to the firm, it is more efficient, other things being equal, to have one supplier than several. This does not exclude the possibility that the gains introduced by competition would outweigh the inefficiencies that it entails. But competition in these circumstances has at least a tendency to become (1) destructive: marginal costs are below average cost, and since wholehearted price rivalry means that firms will push prices down to the former level (and even below, if there is hope of driving out a rival), total costs may not be covered for long periods of time, with possible consequent deterioration in the quality of service; and (2) rankly discriminatory—with prices cut to marginal costs in those markets where competitors meet and held at monopolistic levels where they do not.

The first task of public policy, then, is to ascertain for each of these industries the proper scope of natural monopoly, that is, to define the parts of the business where internal economies of scale constitute a strong case on efficiency grounds for permitting only a single supplier. The decision need not be an all-or-nothing one for the entire industry. It may be feasible to permit competition in those branches that are not naturally monopolistic along with, for example, joint ownership or joint utilization of the facilities that are—as when the several railroads crossing the Mississippi River into and out of St. Louis organized themselves into an association to operate bridges and terminal facilities, while yet (at least in principle) continuing to compete in other aspects of their business.[31] In the same way, separate electric distribution companies may take fullest possible advantage of the economies of scale in generation and transmission by participating jointly in the construction of large new generating plants,[32] and private communi-

---

[30] See the references in note 25 on p. 74 of Volume 1.

[31] *U. S. v. Terminal Railroad Association of St. Louis et al.*, 224 U.S. 383 (1912) and 236 U.S. 194 (1915).

[32] See pp. 64–65 and 73–76, in Chapter 2, above. This case is a complicated one, involving natural monopolies of differing geographical scope at the two levels—the locality in distribution and the multistate region in generation. That joint participation in the latter ventures can be conducive to certain important kinds of competition at the distribution level is indicated in our further discussion of power pooling at pp. 316–323, Chapter 6, below.

cations systems may hook up with the Bell interstate switched network monopoly in order to have access to every telephone in the United States (see note 60, p. 133, below).

There is, of course, no general definition of these respective areas valid for all public utility industries or even for any one of them at all times and in all places. The clearest case of natural monopoly is in local distribution, where a single investment in distribution network and plant, a single hook-up with the ultimate user, a single periodic reading of meters and billing can handle an expansion of sales within all foreseeable limits at incremental costs far below average and in important respects at zero cost. A familiar illustration of the way in which the proper definition changes over time is provided by the technological changes of recent decades in electricity generation and transmission, which, by vastly extending the economies of scale, have correspondingly extended the geographic scope of natural monopoly in that part of the business.

COMPETITIVE CERTIFICATION VERSUS CENTRALIZED PLANNING AND RESPONSIBILITY

The most intriguing and actively contested issues involving the proper definition of natural monopoly center not on the desirability of single local distribution systems but on the proper regional, national, and even international structures of the public utility industries. Particularly in communications and the generation and transmission of electricity, but also in the long-distance carriage of natural gas, in the devising of airline schedules and in the operation of railroads, the difficult questions of the 1960s and 1970s have to do with the economies achievable by integration of investment planning and scheduling of operations over wide regions and the proper residual role of competition.

An economist might wonder what it can possibly mean to attempt to preserve competition if the relevant markets are local and in those markets monopoly is natural. Whether a series of local monopolists are linked together financially or retain their separate existence, it would seem, could have no effect on the degree of monopoly power each of them possessed at its point of contact with the ultimate purchaser. The answer will vary from industry to industry; but the general answer is that the relevant markets are not solely local. True, the individual purchaser of electricity, telephone service, and gas will ordinarily have only one local source of supply, and will receive no direct benefit from the presence of separate companies providing the same services in other markets. But there are also wholesale and bulk-sale retail markets, in which the separate local distributor-monopolists and large business customers frequently have the opportunity of choosing among alternative suppliers. In electricity and gas there is also competition-by-example and by threat of takeover, between public and private companies. And in communications, as in transportation, there are possibilities of competition for different parts of various journeys between separate companies, and in almost all the regulated industries large users have the alternative of serving their own needs, as well.

The National Telecommunications Network

It has been the accelerated technological progress of recent decades that has brought these issues to the fore; and nowhere have they been more intense than in the field of communications. We have already alluded to the technological explosion in communications after World War II and discussed some of the numerous competitive issues that it has generated—most prominently the proper role of private microwave relay systems, of communications satellites and transoceanic cable,[33] of community antenna television systems,[34] and the proper pricing of communications services in these circumstances.[35] In the presence of such rapid change, the natural monopoly of yesterday may be transformed into a natural arena of competition today; and vice versa.

That the provision of local telephone service is a natural monopoly is generally conceded. The Bell System makes a powerful argument that the same is true of the entire national telecommunications network. The argument, as all others for natural monopoly, can be embraced under the familiar rubric of decreasing costs over the entire relevant range of production. But it has so many facets in addition to the familiar one of progressive economies of scale in the production of a standardized service that it is worth examining in detail.

The case for a national telecommunications network monopoly has the following interrelated aspects:

1. Simple economies of scale in the provision of a standardized service. The cost per circuit-mile of capacity seems to have a tendency indefinitely to decline, the larger the number of circuit-miles provided for.[36]

2. Aggregate investment costs can be minimized, it is argued, if the planning for the installation and expansion of capacity is done with an eye to the requirements of the entire system. The essence of the service is the provision of physical connections and interconnections—300 million to 400 million calls daily—between the 102 million telephones in the country. Since any of the 5 million billion possible connections that the system must stand ready to make at any point in time may be performed over an almost infinite variety of routes, ranging from the most direct to the most indirect, and since the demand placed on any single portion of a route will fluctuate widely from one moment and one season to the next, the clue to providing instantaneous connections with any given probability of delay, at minimum total investment cost, is the provision for automatic rerouting of calls from one circuit to another in the event that the preceding one is occupied. This means, ideally, that the addition of any individual links of capacity can most efficiently be accomplished only in consideration of the extent to which the particular link will provide backup capacity for all other parts of the system, on the one hand, and, on the other, the extent to which the particular connection being provided for may, in case of need, be provided instead by existing capacity along alternative routes. The principle is the same one as justifies interconnection of electric power companies, because, in the

---

[33] See pp. 65, 122 note 98, Volume 1, and pp. 51–52, Chapter 2, above.
[34] See pp. 32–45, Chapter 1, above.

[35] See pp. 121–122, 134, 156–158, 173–174, Volume 1.
[36] See pp. 125–129, Volume 1.

presence of diversities of demand for the services of each, they can jointly provide for their markets with a smaller total investment than if each were at all times completely dependent on its own resources alone.[37]

3. The higher the standards of service demanded, the greater, it is maintained, is the need for centralized responsibility and control. Specifically, to provide virtually instantaneous connections, automatic switching and high standards of intelligibility of the signals, one company has to be responsible for all the parts whose interaction determines the level of performance.[38] This contention has traditionally provided the support for the Bell System's historic insistence that it alone provide, install, and continue to own and service all equipment hooked up in any way with the telephone network:

"At any one time, during the busy hours, there may be five or ten million simultaneous conversations going on over the network, and thousands of them may be going through a single cable or radio relay system.

"This concentrated use of switching and transmission facilities means that, in order to avoid mutual interference, there must be careful control of the character of the signals used to activate the switching system, and of the level of signals which carry speech or other forms of intelligence."[39]

These high standards of performance, on the one hand, and the inescapable interdependence of all parts of the system, on the other, it is contended, impose extraordinary requirements of compatibility among all parts of the plant, of reliability in the functioning of the millions of its separate components, in the planned availability of repair, maintenance, and backup capacity. And all of these require that a single company have the full and sole responsibility.[40]

4. If the network is to be truly national, if (almost) everyone is to be able at any moment to reach (almost) everyone else, then service must be extended to (almost) everyone, rich and poor, over routes extending to the most isolated parts of the country. It is burdensome to stand ready to serve all users, on demand, on routes that are rarely used, with backup capacity sufficient for almost any emergency (consider the demand on the telephone system imposed when the President was assassinated). No company is likely to assume such responsibilities unless it is given a

---

[37] See note 23, this Chapter, above. To what extent the investment process for the entire Bell System is in fact systematically planned in this fashion, the writer is unable to say; he has heard skepticism expressed on this score.

[38] AT&T describes its network as

"A web of millions of intricate and complicated mechanisms, all of which must work reliably and compatibly at a moment's notice to make any of five million billion possible connections. It is an ever-changing and delicately balanced machine, designed and nurtured to meet the System's responsibility to the public to provide a first class nationwide service—and it

does just that." "Vertical Integration in the Bell System: A Systems Approach to Technological and Economic Imperatives of the Telephone Network," President's Task Force on Communications Policy, Staff Paper 5, Part 2, Appendix C, PB 184 418, June 1969, 2.

[39] "Competition Situations Faced by the Bell System," Company Memorandum, mimeo., December 26, 1968, 6.

[40] These various arguments for a single integrated operation extend also to the necessity for vertical integration: manufacturing, installation, and service functions are all held to be part of the natural monopoly. See pp. 297–302, Chapter 6, below.

monopoly on the lucrative routes as a quid pro quo and as a means of assuring it the ability to cover all the costs of its readiness to serve. The reader will recognize here the argument against competitive cream-skimming (see pp. 7–10, in Chapter 1, above). Since this argument applies not only to the protection of natural monopoly but also to the more general case against competition in regulated industries, we reserve its further consideration for Chapter 5.

This position has been subjected to increasingly intense challenge in recent years, especially in the market for private or bulk communications, which provides large users with circuits of their own for continuous point-to-point communication.

The Above-890 Decisions. The occasion for the first major challenge was the development of microwave radio transmission, which made it possible for such users to set up their own facilities—provided the Federal Communications Commission would allocate to them the required portions of the radio spectrum.[41]

Because the costs of microwave for such purposes promised to be much lower than the common carrier rates, numerous large commercial, industrial, and governmental entities applied to the FCC for the necessary authorizations. Supporting their petitions were various manufacturers of electronic equipment, who were anxious to get into and develop that rich market, from which they would have remained essentially excluded if the field were left entirely to the common carriers and their own, financially affiliated, virtually exclusive manufacturing subsidiaries such as Western Electric. Prominent among the former were representatives of utility companies, the oil industry, railroads, truckers, the National Association of Manufacturers— speaking, among others, for the automobile, air frame manufacturing, chemical and steel industries—state highway officials, state turnpike authorities, municipalities, chiefs of police, and newspaper publishers. The common carriers intervened to oppose the applications.[42] Arguing that (1) the limited capacities of the radio spectrum and (2) the naturally monopolistic character of communications both required that the spectrum be reserved for themselves, they contended that if large users were permitted to build their own facilities the result could only be congestion in the airwaves and higher cost and poorer service for all. The fact remained, the private applicants pointed out, that if permitted to construct their own facilities, they could provide for their needs at much lower costs than the carriers' tariffs.[43]

For a time, the Commission accepted the natural monopoly philosophy, issuing licenses for private systems only on an interim basis, when the

[41] On much of the following see Manley R. Irwin, "The Communication Industry and the Policy of Competition," *Buffalo Law Rev.* (Fall 1964), XIV: 256–273.

[42] They raised no objection to the applications for public safety organizations (police and fire protection) and right-of-way companies—railroads, oil and gas pipelines, and power companies—which need communications facilities along routes generally not served by common-carrier systems. *In the Matter of Allocation of Frequencies in the Bands Above 890 Mc.*, Report and

Order, 27 FCC 359, 367–379, 386 (July 1959).

[43] On the reasons for this discrepancy, see pp. 146–149, below. On the record of this controversy as it developed in the area of television network interconnection services, see FCC, *Network Broadcasting*, Report of the Network Study Staff to the Network Study Committee, published by the U.S. House of Representatives, Committee on Interstate and Foreign Commerce, 85th Cong. 2d Sess., House Report No. 1297, 1958, 542–549.

applicants could demonstrate that common-carrier facilities were not yet available to them, and only until such facilities did become available. But the pressures by private users for a liberalization of this policy continued to mount during the 1950s[44] and finally, in its famous "above 890" decisions of 1959 and 1960, the Commission capitulated. Pointing to the demonstrated need for private point-to-point communications systems, and concluding that there were adequate frequencies above 890 megacycles to take care of present and reasonably foreseeable future needs of both the common carriers and private users, it deprecated the threat to the common carriers and emphasized the advantages of competition in spurring the development of communications technology.[45]

All the major issues confronted by the FCC in these proceedings involved in one form or another the question of whether the public would be better served by free competitive entry, on the one hand, or by a common-carrier monopoly on the other. In response to the carriers' contention that the highest quality and minimum cost would be assured by vesting the responsibility exclusively in them, the Commission instead accepted the views of the applicants that private systems could provide service of a quality and at a cost better tailored to their individual requirements:

"In many cases, the operation of the private users is such that it is not convenient or practicable for common carriers to provide such service (e.g., remote or isolated business operations). . . . Even in areas where common carrier facilities and personnel are readily available, there appears to be a need for private systems. In the first place, the private users do not require, in all cases, the high quality of service provided by the carriers to meet the varied needs of the public. Also, such private systems would provide for better control and flexibility for meeting their own hour-by-hour operational and administrative needs."[46]

The Commission recognized, too, the possibility that the availability of this competitive alternative could contribute to a superior dynamic performance:

"it may be observed that certain of the private users now licensed endeavored to get the common carriers to provide such service initially and constructed their private systems only when the carriers refused to do so."[47]

"There is yet another consideration which impels us to our determination. We feel that the expanded eligibility will afford a competitive spur in the

---

[44] The reader can imagine, from our earlier discussion of the FCC's solicitude for the viability of small television broadcasters, how difficult it must have been for it to resist the claim of these companies that they could not afford AT&T's charges. *Ibid.*, 547–549.

[45] "We stated that the liberalized licensing policies would provide an impetus in the manufacturing of microwave equipment, which, in turn, would result in improvements in the communications art. The evidence in the record shows that the manufacturers of microwave equipment for private users have been reluctant in the past to develop microwave equipment to any substantial extent due to the fact that the licensing of private microwave systems has been on a developmental basis except in the aviation services. With the opening of a new market for microwave equipment, it seems quite clear that the resultant competitive situation among manufacturers will provide the incentive for developing better equipment for meeting the needs of private users and a concomitant improvement in the communications art." *In the Matter of Allocation of Frequencies in the Bands Above 890 Mc.,* Memorandum Opinion and Order, 29 FCC 825, 854 (1960).

[46] 27 FCC 359, 413 (1959).

[47] *Ibid.*

manufacturing of equipment and in the development of the communications art."[48]

It made its endorsement of the freely competitive approach even more complete when it rejected the position of the common carriers that it should not license private users if common-carrier facilities were available or would be made available "within a reasonable length of time," and that any licenses it grant be subject to the condition that the private system be "amortized when common carrier service becomes available."[49]

"we are of the opinion that the public interest would not be served by a policy of restricting or denying the licensing of private point-to-point systems solely because common carrier facilities are available or may become available in the reasonable future. It follows that the Commission should not consider the availability of common carrier facilities as a condition of eligibility for private users."[50]

This attitude contrasts interestingly with the policy followed by the ICC in deciding whether the public convenience and necessity justify its authorizing additional motor carrier service.[51]

On the other hand, the Commission was by no means prepared to authorize additional competition in the common-carrier communications business itself, or to commit itself to a policy of unrestricted competitive entry without regard to the possibility of an unfavorable impact on the carriers and their other customers. On the first point, it refused to permit the private users to share frequencies on a cooperative basis, thus making it clear that it was opening the door only to individual users who wished to supply their own individual needs:

"While it is recognized that such [cooperative] use may, in some cases, result in a better and more effective utilization of frequencies, this argument is, at least, equally persuasive in support of a conclusion that service should be afforded by communication common carriers. Further, although such an arrangement may make it economically feasible for smaller firms and organizations to utilize microwave for their operations, it must be observed that such shared usage is inconsistent with one of the principal justifications urged by private users for their own systems; viz., exclusive control of their own facilities because of special communications problems. Finally, we have some concern with the fact that creation of extensive point-to-point cooperative facilities may lead to undesirable situations where the cooperatives have many of the attributes of communication common carriers without assuming the responsibilities of service and the burdens of regulation which apply to common carriers."[52]

On the latter point, the Commission rejected the objections of the common carriers that a free licensing of private systems would amount to creamskimming, but only on the ground that no showing of such an adverse effect had yet been made:

"Of course, this matter requires continued surveillance, and, if future

---

[48] *Ibid.*, 414. See also note 45, above.
[49] *Ibid.*, 387.
[50] *Ibid.*, 412.

[51] See pp. 15–18, Chapter 1, above.
[52] *Ibid.*, 407–408.

conditions warrant, appropriate consideration will then be given to the problem."[53]

When, then, in the *Comsat Authorized Users* litigation, the Commission determined that there would be such an adverse effect on the general users, it reached a decision that greatly restricted the possibilities of genuine competition, as we shall shortly see.[54]

Any account of the competitive impact of microwave would have to describe AT&T's vigorous reaction to the threat of competitive entry sanctioned by the *above-890* decision. To hold its large customers it offered a new set of private line services at much more favorable rates—several classes of Telpak, Wide Area Telephone, Wide Area Data (WATS and WADS), and Dataphone services.[55] Western Union and Motorola (a leading manufacturer of microwave equipment) promptly charged that the Telpak rates were unduly discriminatory, and the FCC eventually held that they were.[56] The Commission has been almost continuously engaged since 1956 in investigating rates charged by AT&T and Western Union for private line and other business services, examining the possibility that they were (1) injurious to competition and (2) a burden on—that is, subsidized by— the users of ordinary long-distance (message toll telephone—MTT) service.[57] Obviously, these two aspects of the proper role and nature of competition in public utilities—how much freedom of entry and how much freedom to price competitively—are closely interrelated; we consider them together presently. The shift in AT&T strategy in this instance, from an attempt first to exclude competition spawned by technological progress or to subject it to tight licensing, to a demand for greater freedom to engage in selective competitive price cutting is clearly the story of the railroads revisited.

The MCI Cases. The *above-890* decisions opened the door only to private communications systems. An even more direct competitive threat to the common carriers appeared several years later, when a tiny newcomer, Microwave Communications, Inc. (MCI), applied for FCC certification for public, common-carrier, point-to-point microwave radio communications service between Chicago, St. Louis, and intermediate points, with a direct duplication of Bell and Western Union services and facilities.[58] The service MCI proposed to offer was barebone in character: it would simply operate the radio path between its specified points;[59] subscribers would have to

---

[53] *Ibid.*, 412.

[54] See pp. 137–139, below.

[55] See C. F. Phillips, Jr., *op. cit.*, 677–678.

[56] *In the Matter of AT&T Co. Tariff FCC No. 250, TELPAK Service and Channels*, Memorandum Opinion and Order, 37 FCC 1111 (1964). For a later negative decision, see FCC, *In the Matter of TELPAK Tariff Sharing Provisions of American Telephone and Telegraph Company and the Western Union Telegraph Co.*, Docket No. 17457, Decision, June 10, 1970.

[57] *AT&T and Western Union Private Line Cases*, 34 FCC 217 (1963). This was the principal issue in phase 1B of Docket 16258; see pp. 156–158, and 173–174, Volume 1, and pp. 227–233, Chapter 5, below. Pursuant to the stipulated settlement that terminated Phase 1B, AT&T

undertook long-run incremental cost studies to determine whether its various business service rates were compensatory. On the basis of those studies, in 1969 it put into effect increased rates for television program transmission, and filed new tariffs also for TELPAK and TWX service, all of which it estimated would bring in $87,000,000 of added revenue at 1969 volumes; and indicated its intention to introduce corresponding reductions in MTT and WATS rates. *Telecommunications Reports* (October 6, 1969), XXXV:1–7.

[58] FCC, *In re Applications of Microwave Communications, Inc.* Docket No. 16509, Initial Decision of the Hearing Examiner, mimeo., October 17, 1967. See also note 60, below.

[59] The principal use, it was anticipated, would

acquire and maintain their own terminal equipment and build their own connections with the MCI stations—something they were evidently not expected to be willing to do. It hoped to be able to negotiate for interconnection with the common carriers; but in view of the hostility and scorn the latter showed for its proposed operation in their interventions before the FCC, the prospects for this were hardly rosy until the Commission indicated in 1969 it was virtually prepared to order them to interconnect.[60] Its construction quality would be minimal, as were its proposed provisions for service, maintenance, for protection and guarantee against all conceivable types of interference, outage, failure, and other acts of man and God.

And yet MCI offered two things that the Bell companies and Western did not: first, low rates—its proposed charges were less than half those of the established carriers—and second, far greater freedom and flexibility in use of the service: customers could attach such equipment as they saw fit and up to five of them could share the use of a single channel, thus further reducing the cost of each. And it was this proposed contribution that, in the last analysis, induced the FCC to approve the application.[61] MCI had, the Examiner concluded, given sufficient demonstration of a market for its services:

"The specific 'need' which on this record it can be concluded that MCI

---

be for simple interoffice and interplant communications, for voice, teleprinter, facsimile, data transmission, and time-shared computer facilities.

[60] "The Hearing Examiner does not go as far as the Common Carrier Bureau in assuming 'that MCI will be able to negotiate appropriate interconnection arrangements with existing carriers. . . .' The carriers' intransigence, manifested in this case, can hardly be expected to abate. . . . But there is no need to anticipate at this stage. . . . It may be that on full consideration the Commission will refuse to compel interconnection. After the hearing and pleadings, it should come as no surprise to MCI that it will in all likelihood be faced with another round of litigation to enable it to complete its system." *Ibid.*, at par. 107.

"Since they [the common carriers] have indicated that they will not voluntarily provide loop service we shall retain jurisdiction of this proceeding in order to enable MCI to obtain . . . a prompt determination on the matter of interconnection. Thus, at such time as MCI has customers and the facts and details of the customers' requirements are known, MCI may come directly to the Commission with a request for an order of interconnection. We have already concluded that a grant of MCI's proposal is in the public interest. We likewise conclude that, absent a significant showing that interconnection is not technically feasible, the issuance of an order requiring the existing carriers to provide loop service is in the public interest." FCC, *In re Applications of Microwave Communications, Inc.*,

Docket No. 16509, Decision, August 13, 1969, par. 36.

By 1970, compulsory interconnection of common carriers with any and all competitors on reasonable and nondiscriminatory terms had become a general, clearly enunciated FCC policy:

"If access to local facilities is requested and needed by the applicants, we would expect the local carrier—Bell or other carrier—to permit interconnection or leased channel arrangements on reasonable terms and conditions to be negotiated with the new carriers. In other words, where a carrier has monopoly control over essential facilities we shall not condone any policy or practice whereby such carrier would discriminate in favor of an affiliated carrier or show favoritism among competitors. Customers of any new carrier should also be afforded the option by the local carrier to obtain local distribution facilities under reasonable terms set forth in the tariff schedules of the latter." *In the Matter of Establishment of Policies and Procedures for Consideration of Applications to Provide Specialized Common Carrier Services in the Domestic Public Point-to-Point Microwave Radio Service* etc., Docket No. 18920, Notice of Inquiry to Formulate Policy, etc., July 15, 1970, par. 67. On the general principle, and for similar examples in other regulatory situations, see pp. 307–323, Chapter 6, below.

[61] A sharply divided Commission upheld the Examiner's recommended decision in all substantial respects, by a 4 to 3 vote, on August 13, 1969. See the note immediately preceding.

has established that it will fulfill is for a cheaper communications service."
(par. 109)

"It may be found that there is a market for common carrier service of
acceptable quality at a cost substantially lower than results from rates in
filed tariffs." [62]

Conceding "no pretense . . . that MCI . . . is other than a shoestring operation," the Examiner found it had "sufficient money in hand and reasonable
expectation of procuring more to stamp it financially qualified." [63] Recognizing that "from the lofty viewpoint of the carriers, MCI's system is jerry-
built," that "the sites are small; the architecture of the huts is late Sears
Roebuck toolshed," he concluded nonetheless that "there is no reason to
believe that the system will not work." [64]

In endorsing these conclusions, the Commission did not really confront the
critical economic question: would MCI's entry and others like it result in
injury to the common carriers and hence a higher-cost, lower quality
communications service to all other users? Its decision makes the clear case
for competitive entry: a new firm, seeing a market not thus far tapped, is
willing to risk its capital to bring in a new, lower price-quality combination.
But if the telecommunications network is really a natural monopoly, the
indirect costs and inefficiencies imposed on the entire system by such entry
could outweigh its direct benefits. This was the real burden of the carriers'
opposition: they claimed that MCI proposed to engage in mere cream-
skimming, throwing on them and their other customers the costs thereof.
We consider the merits of this objection in our general discussion of the
cream-skimming problem, in Chapter 5.

It is nonetheless difficult for an economist to find fault with the Examiner's
and the Commission majority's general disposition to adopt a "wait and see"
attitude with regard to those possible injuries and to incline on the side of
letting a small, would-be competitor probe the possible existence of a market
for lower-cost service:

"Any such grant [of certification] should not be construed as indicating
that the Commission would favorably regard similar proposals between other
major markets by MCI or others. The instant proposal should be given a
reasonable opportunity to become established and thereby afford the
Commission an opportunity to observe the results and consequences of its
operations in terms of the demand generated for its services, its ability to
operate efficiently and profitably, and its effect upon petitioners' [that is,
AT&T and Western Union's] operations." [65]

Nor can the economist but applaud the Examiner's suggestion that the effect
of this experiment, because of the price-elasticity of demand, could well be
beneficial rather than injurious to the regular carriers as well:

"The record may not be sufficient to warrant a definite conclusion that . . .

---

[62] *Op. cit.*, par. 66. The Examiner did qualify
this finding by recognizing that persons expressing an interest in MCI service had assumed it
would be interconnected with the facilities of the
admittedly hostile common carriers; but decided
it was not his function, in this proceeding, to
decide whether MCI would indeed succeed in
obtaining interconnection. See *ibid.*, par. 67, 69,
and note 60, above.

[63] *Ibid.*, par. 94.

[64] *Ibid.*, pars. 96, 97.

[65] *Ibid.*, par. 103. The Commission's opinion
makes essentially the same observation (par. 37).

there is a 'sub-market' of potential users not able to afford existing service but who could be exploited by MCI. Nevertheless, one can speculate, with justification equal to that underlying the carriers' assumptions about their vulnerability, that there would be an addition to their revenues through interconnection for MCI customers expanding communications usage."[66]

Probing the elasticity of demand is another thing competition can do much more reliably than monopoly, natural or otherwise.

The promise of microwave radio and a burgeoning demand soon proved too powerful to permit the FCC the luxury of following the cautious and tentative policy it had adopted in accepting the modest initial MCI proposal. Within a year it was confronted with no fewer than thirty-seven applications by companies (ten of them associated with MCI), proposing to establish themselves as specialized common carriers. The proposals involved construction of 1713 microwave stations, more than one-third the number in the entire Bell system. The most dramatic of these, submitted by Data Transmission Co. (Datran), was for a $350,000,000 nation-wide switched network solely for the transmission of data, providing end-to-end service in direct competition with the Bell System.[66a] And so, also, within the year, the FCC staff was calling for a radical generalization of the *above-890* and *MCI* decisions into a bold policy of free entry into the field of specialized communications services, within the limits of radio spectrum availability. The logic of its argument was simply that competition could far more effectively than monopoly develop and exploit the varied potentialities of the new technology, particularly in satisfying the specialized requirements of business users:

"In proposing a policy favoring the entry of new specialized common carriers, we look toward a degree of competition oriented toward the development of new communications services and markets and the application of improvements in technology to changing and diverse demands. Thus, we are not faced with the question of whether we should increase the number of carriers which are to serve a fixed market with the same services. . . . Rather we anticipate that the new carriers would be developing new services and would thereby expand the size of the total communications market."[66b]

---

[66] *Op. cit.*, par. 113. The FCC had suggested exactly the same possibility in its *above-890* decision, 27 FCC 359, 388 (1959).

[66a] FCC, *In the Matter of Establishment of Policies*, etc., Docket No. 18920, *op. cit.*, note 60, above, pars. 6, 10–11 and Appendix; and information from AT&T. All the other proposals (besides Datran) were for specialized, private line service from one geographic point to another; none would offer switched, message service, end-to-end (i.e., directly interconnecting subscribers).

[66b] *Ibid.*, par. 29. According to Datran,

"Full realization of the public interest in computer technology requires achievement of appropriate specialized communications services. The users of computer technology are not obtaining adequate service from communications facilities constructed for, and dedicated to, meeting voice and record transmission needs. Effective utilization of existing data processing technology is constrained by present common carrier communications services and facilities, and the design and development of new computer applications requiring data transmission is constrained by high cost as well as unreliable and inflexible service." *Ibid.*, par. 9.

According to the FCC staff,

"In order to realize large scale economies, a single supplier must conglomerate diverse functions and provide general standardized services, thereby foregoing potential economies of specialization that could be derived by serving a specialized portion of the market . . . .

"The sheer size of the AT&T organizational structure, its enormous financing requirements, its vertical integration, and near monopoly

As the foregoing comment indicates, the Staff deprecated the threatened diversion of business from the Bell System and consequent loss of the benefits of scale economies, arguing that only 2 to 4 percent of Bell's existing business would be subject to the competition, that the entrants would mainly be developing new, specialized markets rather than competing for existing business, and that the expanded total sales of communications services to which they could be expected to contribute could well produce a net increase in demand for Bell services, for interconnection and local distribution.[66c]

The Commission itself split 3 to 3 on the question of openly endorsing the Staff's proposals, but its notice scheduling hearings left the strong impression that it was highly receptive to them.[66d]

The Communications Satellite. From the very outset, the intense political struggle over who would be authorized to put up and operate the satellite system was clearly envisaged as determining whether this new communications medium would develop as an integral part of the operations of the existing common carriers or whether, instead, it might develop independently of, and in direct competition with them. Proponents of the latter position argued strenuously that if the carriers, and preponderantly AT&T,[67] controlled the satellite system, they would restrain its development in order to protect their huge investments in existing facilities. They also made much of the Bell System's expressed skepticism about the commercial feasibility of the new techniques and of its preference for the low-level, random, moving satellites, which would (and in fact did) prove to be much more expensive than the 22,300-mile high synchronous satellites now being used.[68] The result was a compromise: in 1962 Congress entrusted the

position . . . may make it slower to perceive and respond to individual, specialized requirements and to initiate market and technical innovations. Competition in the specialized communications field would enlarge the equipment market for manufacturers other than Western Electric, and may stimulate . . . the introduction of new techniques." *Ibid.*, pars. 33, 34.

[66c] *Ibid.*, pars. 39–40.

[66d] For example, some of the applicants claimed that their proposals were mutually exclusive on economic grounds. The FCC nevertheless declined to hold comparative hearings on such claims, asserting that the market potential seemed great enough to support more than one applicant in the same area, and that users ought to have the benefit of a choice of competing services:

"We are not confronted here with applications which seek to duplicate all or even a major portion of the services provided by the existing carriers or to enter a static market. Instead, the applicants seek to develop a relatively new and potentially very large market . . . .

"Various systems may develop along different lines, each offering something of value to the public which would attract sufficient customers for viable operations. The number of successful operations may well depend on the ingenuity, enterprise and initiative of applicants and equipment manufacturers over a period of years in taking advantage of changing circumstances and in coming up with the types of services and equipment that will attract sufficient business to support the particular system." *Ibid.*, pars. 48–49; see also 50–50b.

[67] In the international field, AT&T has the monopoly on message telephone and voice-grade channel service. ITT World Communications, RCA Communications and Western Union International operate in the transmission of recorded messages.

[68] Because the synchronous satellites remain in a fixed position in the sky, they can be fewer in number and can be served by far more simple ground (receiving and transmitting) stations. The stations required for tracking moving satellites across the horizon and shifting automatically from one to the next would have been much more costly. See U.S. Senate, Committee on Foreign Relations, 87th Cong., 2d Sess., *The Communications Satellite Act of 1962, Hearings*, 1962, and the debates in the *Congressional Record*, 87th Cong., 2d Sess., CVIII (1962), particularly the speeches of Senators Morse, Long, Yarborough, and Kefauver.

international field to the Communications Satellite Corporation, a separate, newly established company whose ownership was to be divided equally between the common carriers on the one hand and the investing public on the other, with only six members of its Board of Directors to represent each of these two constituencies and another three to be appointed by the President, and with the further provision that no stockholder could elect more than three directors.[69] The issue of who would be authorized to set up a domestic system was not resolved at that time.[70]

The mere constitution of a quasi-independent corporation did not, however, resolve the question of the extent to which Comsat was to be permitted to compete directly with the established carriers, or whether it was, instead, to serve entirely as their own instrument. The issue was most dramatically posed when, during 1965, the Federal Communications Commission received requests from several companies—including press wire services, a newspaper, a television network, and an airline—about the possibility of their obtaining satellite telecommunication services directly from Comsat. When the Commission set this question down for hearing, a great number of private companies and trade associations (for example, the American Petroleum Institute, the American Trucking Association, the Associated Press, the American Newspaper Publishers Association, Dow Jones) and the United States government intervened to press their interest in being able to deal directly with the satellite corporation, rather than through the common carriers alone. The latter intervened to press the case for confining Comsat to the role of a "carriers' carrier," thus forcing all ultimate customers to depend on them for any communications services using the satellite. While the FCC rejected the latter view, it nevertheless handed down a decision that restricted very severely the circumstances under which noncommon-carrier companies might be authorized to deal directly with Comsat—rejecting even the the contention of the General Services Administration that the United States Government, at least, had the right of unrestricted direct dealings. As for nongovernmental users, the Commission concluded:

"Comsat would be authorized to deal directly with the users in only those instances where the requirement for satellite service is of such an exceptional or unique nature that the service must be tailored to the peculiar needs of the customer and therefore cannot be provided within the terms and conditions of a general public tariff offering."[71]

---

[69] 47 U.S. Code 701–744, 1964 ed. These arrangements were slightly amended in 1969. Public Law 91–3, 91st Cong. 1st Sess., 83 Stat. 4. See also John McDonald, "The Comsat Compromise Starts a Revolution," *Fortune* (October 1965), LXXII: 128–131; Harvey J. Levin, "Organization and Control of Communications Satellites," *Univ. of Penn. Law Rev.* (January 1965), CXIII: 315–357; and Herman Schwartz, "Governmentally Appointed Directors in a Private Corporation—the Communications Satellite Act of 1962," *Harvard Law Rev.* (December 1965), LXXIX: 350–364.

[70] This question was raised in 1965, when the American Broadcasting Company asked FCC

permission to do so. The Commission thereupon invited suggestions from other interested parties. FCC, *In the Matter of the Establishment of Domestic Non-Common Carrier Communications Satellite Facilities by Non-Governmental Entities*, Docket No. 16495. While the matter has not been decisively resolved as of this writing, it appears that development of the domestic system is likely to be more highly competitive. See note 77a, below.

[71] *In the Matter of Authorized Entities and Authorized Users Under the Communications Satellite Act of 1962*, Memorandum Opinion and Statement of Policy, 4 FCC 2d 421, 431 (1966); Memorandum Opinion and Order, 6 FCC 2d 593 (1967).

What was at issue here, clearly, was the right of Comsat to enter the communications market on its own behalf. As long as it remains almost exclusively a carriers' carrier, those companies control the flow of business to it; it is they, therefore, who will determine to what extent this alternative communications medium will in fact be developed—except to the extent that the FCC limits their discretion.[72] And, as we have already pointed out (p. 52, Chapter 2, above), the carriers would presumably not have the same incentive as a competitive Comsat to push the development of this far less capital-intensive technology, when the alternative is to use their own facilities, and thereby justify their own rate bases. The one sure remedy for any A–J–W distortion is of course competition; and the FCC decision on authorized users severely limited the potential scope of that competition— unfortunately in the very situation in which, because of the widely divergent capital intensities of the alternative technologies available, the A–J–W danger seems particularly serious.[73]

On the other hand, as the FCC pointed out, unrestricted competition between Comsat and the other carriers is infeasible. The governing statute limits the former company to the international satellite portion of the service; and it would presumably be intolerably inefficient for it to attempt to duplicate the domestic facilities of the common carriers. Therefore even if the Commission permitted any and all customers to deal directly with Comsat, it would be only the large users that could hook up directly with its ground stations and lease circuits from it. So the only feasible competition would be for these customers alone; only they would receive the full cost savings of satellite transmission.[74] Whether this would produce optimal results

[72] On the condition the FCC attached when it authorized the common carriers to lay another transatlantic cable (the TAT–5) in 1968, see note 89, pp. 76–77, above.

[73] Considerations such as these were clearly relevant, also, in the disputed issue of who would be permitted to own the ground stations serving and served by the satellite, which the FCC resolved in 1966 by conferring joint ownership on the Communications Satellite Corporation on the one hand and the common carriers on the other, at least as far as the six initial earth stations in the United States were concerned. *In the Matter of Amendment to Part 25 of the Commission's Rules and Regulations with respect to Ownership and Operation of Initial Earth Stations* etc., Second Report and Order, 5 FCC 2d 812 (1966). Herman Schwartz has an interesting criticism of this decision: while recognizing that participation in the ground station investment will make the common carriers more inclined than they otherwise would be to make use of the satellite facilities, he points out that this investment would be very slight compared with their stake in cable and conventional radio facilities, and criticizes the decision on the ground that it increases the likelihood of common-carrier control over the development of the satellite system. It seems difficult to reconcile his position here, however, with his approval of the *Authorized*

Users decision, which, he feels, properly forestalled the threat of cream-skimming. (On this point, see our Chapter 5, pp. 227–233, below.) *Op. cit., Yale Law Jour.* (January 1967), LXXVI: 444–453, 457–459, 471–473. As long as few users can deal directly with Comsat, it would seem that the common carriers are in any event in a position to control the rate of its development, which is precisely what Schwartz fears.

[74] The FCC argues that the possibility of unrestricted competition is similarly limited by the inability of the *other* carriers to go into Comsat's exclusive field of operations: if Comsat could deal unrestrictedly with all ultimate customers, it could use its statutory monopoly on the space segment of international communications to deny the other carriers a fair opportunity to compete. *Op. cit.*, 4 FCC 2d 421 (1966), pars. 20, 26. The Commission's reasoning here is somewhat cryptic. What it seems to mean is that Comsat might deny the other carriers access to its international satellite facilities on fair terms, or might divert to its own facilities exclusively whatever traffic it originated. The FCC's opinion does not consider whether such dangers could be forestalled, as in transportation, by requiring Comsat to serve all carriers fairly and nondiscriminatorily and to set joint rates with them. See pp. 273–275, 307–323, below.

is a question we consider once again in our separate discussion of cream-skimming.[75]

The satellite does not eradicate the case for natural monopoly in communications: like microwave radio, it merely redefines its proper scope. There is no question of the specialized microwave systems or whatever carrier operates the satellite directly duplicating the intricate exchange-switching service of the Bell System, although Datran proposes to do exactly this for one specialized market. The question is mainly one of the extent to which the System's transmission facilities are properly subjected to competition where that is commercially feasible. The ideal arrangement would seem to be for the maximum feasible competition among alternative media for those portions of the service for which they do represent viable coexisting alternatives.[76] The satellite is one such; microwave apparently another.[77] Any attempt to deny these competitive media a full and fair opportunity to compete ought properly to bear a substantial burden of proof that their entry would be truly injurious to the common carrier service, causing its quality to deteriorate unjustifiably or its real costs to increase.[77a]

---

[75] See pp. 227–233, Chapter 5, below.

[76] There is another possible "ideal": that "competition" between the alternative communications media be achieved not by market rivalry between companies utilizing only one or the other exclusively but by diversified companies free to use *either*, choosing among them on the basis of which medium or combination of media would do the job best. On the general principle, see pp. 264–267, Chapter 6, below. The choice becomes a difficult one, when the economies of scale are so great, relative to the extent of the market, as to leave room for only one such company, as the President's Task Force on Communications Policy concluded was the case in the international arena (see p. 117, above; note 102 of this chapter; and note 32 of Chapter 6, below).

[77] Direct satellite-to-receiver radio and television broadcasting could bypass the existing communications network entirely (see note 15, p. 51, Chapter 2, above) just as long-distance telephoning completely bypasses the Post Office and the electronic transmission of written messages would do even more effectively. But for most services, the competition would be partial only; for those portions in which a continued Bell monopoly remained "natural," that monopoly could remain inviolate.

[77a] One factor limiting the competitive impact of the satellite is that Comsat was given exclusive jurisdiction in this field, as far as international communications are concerned. This was done evidently on the assumption that a single chosen instrument was required by the economies of scale and that it would be most conducive to the exploitation and development of this as yet unexplored technology. (See our discussion of the promotional case for restricting competition on

pp. 3–4, above). Therefore, it was natural to think of Comsat as essentially a carriers' carrier, rather than, primarily, as their direct competitor.

But since the potential domestic U.S. market for satellite service is so much greater, relative to the available economies of scale, competition is believed to be feasible domestically. Leland L. Johnson, "Technological Advance and Market Structure in Domestic Telecommunications," *Amer. Econ. Rev., Papers and Proceedings* (May 1970), LX: 208. Possibly this is also so because the commercial feasibility of the new technology has now been much more clearly demonstrated. In these circumstances, the possibility is opened up of far more direct and pervasive competition between satellite and terrestrial facilities.

So the FCC appeared ready, in 1970, to consider initiating a test of free entry and competition in the domestic satellite field. The lead was provided by a policy statement by the White House, proposing a three- to five-year test of such a policy:

"In the absence of clear economies of scale and overriding public interest considerations to the contrary, the American economy has relied on competitive private enterprise rather than regulated monopoly to assure technical and market innovation. . . .

"At this stage of domestic satellite planning, it is not possible to identify major economies of scale. Rather, it appears that a diversity of multiple satellite systems as well as multiple earth stations will be required to provide a full range of domestic services.

"Further, we find no public interest grounds for establishing a monopoly in domestic satellite communications. . . .

"Subject to appropriate conditions to preclude

Alien Attachments. The process of defining and redefining the area of natural monopoly is nowhere more clearly illustrated than in the evolving policies of the Bell System with respect to the kinds of equipment it permits customers to attach to the telephone receiver or to hook on to the network and the circumstances, if any, under which it permits interconnection between other communications systems and its own. The original rule was one of complete noncooperation, a rule implying the widest possible definition of the natural monopoly. Until 1913, for example, AT&T refused to interconnect in any way with the numerous independent local telephone companies that had sprung into existence on expiration of the Bell patent; in that year, however, following on the threat of an antitrust suit, it agreed thenceforth to connect its system for toll service purposes with the lines of independent companies whose equipment satisfied its quality specifications.[78] Similarly whereas the independent telephone companies generally have permitted unrestricted interconnection between their facilities and private microwave systems, the Bell companies have historically done so only in very special circumstances.[79]

As far as customer-owned and supplied equipment or attachments were concerned, the Bell rule was unequivocal:

"No equipment, apparatus, circuit or device not furnished by the Telephone Company shall be attached to or connected with the facilities furnished by the Telephone Company, whether physically, by induction or otherwise. . . . In case any such authorized attachment or connection is made, the Telephone Company shall have the right to remove or disconnect

---

harmful interference and anti-competitive practices, any financially qualified public or private entity . . . should be permitted to establish and operate domestic satellite facilities for its own needs; join with related entities in common-user, cooperative facilities; establish facilities for lease to prospective users; or establish facilities to be used in providing specialized carrier services on a competitive basis. . . . Common carriers should be free to establish facilities for either switched public message or specialized services, or both.

"The number of classes of potential offerers of satellite services should not be limited arbitrarily." The White House, *Memorandum for the Honorable Dean Burch, Chairman of the Federal Communications Commission*, mimeo., January 23, 1970.

The FCC is not, as of the time of writing, prepared to go quite so far. It did, in March 1970, invite applications from any and all interested parties, but reserved judgment on whether it would permit any financially qualified applicant to set up and operate a domestic satellite system. Still, its announcement was widely acclaimed, and it elicited statements from AT&T, the broadcast networks, and the University Computing Company's subsidiary, Data Transmission Co. (see p. 135, above) that

they were studying the possibility of applying. *Wall Street Journal*, March 18, 1970, 6, and March 25, 1970, 11.

[78] This agreement was provided in the Kingsbury Commitment, so called because it was contained in a letter to the Attorney General from a company vice-president. On the consequences of this kind of mandatory interconnection, see note 149, p. 308, Chapter 6, below. In that same letter, AT&T agreed also to dispose of a large interest that it had acquired in Western Union in 1909 and also not to acquire control of any additional competing independent phone companies. The controlling legislation now permits telephone companies to merge with the approval of the relevant regulatory agency. 47 U.S. Code 221 (a), 1964 ed.

[79] "where, according to Bell System witnesses, considerations of safety of life and property are involved, and, under certain circumstances, with right-of-way companies." *Above-890*, 27 FCC 359, 409 (1959).

Both of these exceptions, it should be noted, are for private systems that are essentially non-competitive with those of the Bell System itself. *Ibid.*, 396.

As of Jan. 1, 1969, AT&T's general tariff permits interconnection service with private microwave systems generally. See p. 144, below.

the same; or to suspend the service during the continuance of said attachment or connection; or to terminate the service."[80]

So, for example, the Bell companies have consistently refused to connect up with switchboards and associated facilities manufactured by others and furnished by the private users themselves. An extreme example of this policy was its application against the Hush-A-Phone, a purely mechanical attachment to the telephone itself manufactured by an independent company of that name—a cuplike device that could be simply snapped on to the instrument and that, by confining the speaker's voice within its enclosure, provided some privacy for his conversations and quiet in the room and kept room noises out of the transmitter. The Bell companies justified their insistence that this innocent device be removed in familiar terms—it is they who are responsible for the quality and price of their service; if they are to bear and exercise that responsibility, they must have reasonable discretionary control over the kind of equipment used:

"it would be extremely difficult to furnish 'good' telephone service if telephone users were free to attach to the equipment, or use with it, all the numerous kinds of foreign attachments which are marketed by persons who have no responsibility for the quality of telephone service but are primarily interested in exploiting their products."[81]

The rationalization is a powerful one. But there are offsetting considerations. Regulated monopoly is not necessarily the ideal device for ensuring a zealous, continuous quest for improved quality and variety of service. At a very elementary level, the Hush-A-Phone demonstrated this. From 1921, when it was introduced, through 1949, 126,000 of them had been sold; and there was no lack of evidence that many subscribers felt it met a need. The Bell companies contended, in the face of this objective market evidence, that there was "no appreciable public demand for a voice silencer such as the Hush-A-Phone"; they pointed out that they supplied certain devices that fulfilled a similar function (notably the addition of "push-to-talk" and "push-to-listen" switches) and that, if users wanted privacy, "it may be obtained without the use of any attachment to the telephone, as by cupping a hand around the transmitter and talking in a low tone of voice." Finally, it added, "if a general public demand for a handset type voice silencer were encountered, the defendants would undertake to meet that demand!"[82] Big Brother said he would provide best—even in the face of clear evidence that 100,000 people thought he did not.

The FCC sustained the position of the Bell companies in this case, on the ground that the Hush-A-Phone had been shown to "impair telephone service":

"when the device is used for maximum privacy, there is a noticeable loss of intelligibility . . . which means that the person to whom the Hush-A-Phone user is speaking hears a lower and somewhat distorted sound."[83]

[80] FCC, *In the Matter of Use of the Carterfone Device in Message Toll Telephone Service*, Decision, 13 FCC 2d 420, 427 (1968).
[81] *In the Matter of Hush-A-Phone Corporation et al.*, Decision, 20 FCC 391, 415 (1955).
[82] *Ibid.*, 397.
[83] *Hush-A-Phone Corporation et al. v. United States of America and Federal Communications Commission, et al.*, 238 F. 2d 266, 268 (1956). See the FCC decision, *op. cit.*, 405.

Who should decide whether an improvement in product quality in one respect is worth the cost of some possible deterioration in another? The question is not an economic one. But the only answer consistent with the efficiency criteria of a private enterprise economy is the buyer—unless he is illinformed, *or* his independent purchase decisions impose costs on others. But, as the Circuit Court of Appeals pointed out in overturning the FCC in this case, the only parties affected were the two parties to the conversation:[84]

"The question, in the final analysis, is whether the Commission possesses enough control over the subscriber's use of his telephone to authorize the telephone company to prevent him from conversing in comparatively low and distorted tones. . . . [I]ntervenors do not challenge the subscriber's right to seek privacy. They say only that he should achieve it by cupping his hand between the transmitter and his mouth and speaking in a low voice into this makeshift muffler. This substitute, we note, is not less likely to impair intelligibility than the Hush-A-Phone itself. . . . In both instances, the party at the other end of the line hears a comparatively muted and distorted tone because the subscriber has chosen to use his telephone in a way that minimizes the risk of being overheard. . . . The intervenor's tariffs, under the Commission's decision, are in unwarranted interference with the telephone subscriber's right reasonably to use his telephone in ways which are privately beneficial without being publicly detrimental."[85]

The upshot of the Hush-A-Phone decision was a softening of the flat prohibition of alien attachments:

"The provisions . . . shall not be construed or applied to bar a customer from using devices which serve his convenience in his use of the facilities of the Telephone Company . . . provided any such device so used would not endanger the safety of Telephone Company employees or the public; damage, require change in or alteration of, or involve direct electrical connection to the equipment or other facilities of the Telephone Company; or interfere with the proper functioning of such equipment or facilities; or impair the operation of the telephone system or otherwise injure the public in its use of the Telephone Company's services."[86]

But the Bell companies continued to interpret this exception as narrowly as possible and continued their general refusal to interconnect. The next major complainant-victim was the Carter Electronics Corporation, which had, from 1959 through 1966, marketed some 3,500 of its Carterfones, devices which make it possible to conduct two-way conversations between ordinary telephones and the individual units of private mobile radio systems. The device involves no wire-to-wire connection with the telephone network, but only placing a telephone handset, at the office of the mobile radio system's

---

[84] The FCC attempted to stretch the possible annoyance to the party *without* the attachment to his telephone into a threatened impairment of the entire telephone service:

"the use of the Hush-A-Phone affects the quality of telephone service not only to the Hush-A-Phone users but also to all other subscribers who are connected with the same nation-wide telephone system and who may call or be called by Hush-A-Phone users." *Ibid.*, 424.

Surely a grotesque extension of the concept of externalities; all the aggrieved party has to do is say "what"?

[85] *Op. cit.*, 238 F. 2d 266, 269 (1956).

[86] FCC, *Carterfone* decision, *op. cit.*, 13 FCC 2d 420, 427 (1968).

base station operator, in a cradle specially designed to receive it; this device transmits the telephone signals automatically via radio to the private mobile units and amplifies the sounds coming in from the radio field units so that the telephoner can hear them.[87]

The telephone companies had by now elaborated the justification of their policy on foreign attachments into what they termed the "systems concept":

"the network as a whole is regarded as a single system with the effect of every part on each of the other billions of parts being calculated before it is introduced into the system. If this is not done, so goes the theory, the introduction of a single disruptive piece could have an ever widening effect on every other piece in the system and ultimately impair or even destroy the efficacy of the whole. For this reason the telephone companies contend that they must control every element of the system if they are to accept responsibility for its operation."[88]

The Commission found no fault with this basic principle: the common carrier must, indeed, be able to exercise responsibility for the quality of the service and all equipment affecting it:

"This argument is reasonable, plausible and persuasive. If the issue in this proceeding was whether users should have a right to attach anything they choose to the system at any time without restriction or consideration of the consequences the record would not sustain a favorable finding. However, that is not the issue here."[89]

But the Examiner found

"no reason to anticipate that the Carterphone will have an adverse effect on the telephone system or any part thereof. It takes nothing from the system other than the inductive force of the electrical field in the earpiece of the handset, which force is dissipated into the atmosphere in any event. It puts nothing into the system except the sound of a human voice into the mouthpiece of the handset, and that is the precise purpose for which that portion of the system is engineered."[90]

In the circumstances, the FCC found that the tariff provision itself was unreasonable, as well as discriminatorily applied against the Carterfone:

"our conclusion here is that a customer desiring to use an interconnecting device to improve the utility to him of both the telephone system and a private radio system should be able to do so, so long as the interconnection does not adversely affect the telephone company's operations or the telephone system's utility for others. A tariff which prevents this is unreasonable; it is

---

[87] The conversations can be initiated from either end, and must be connected through the radio system's central operator. The operator then contacts the called party, using either the radio system or a telephone connection, depending on where the call was initiated. When both parties are ready, the operator places his own telephone handset into the cradle. The Carterfone cradle essentially merely amplifies the signals—the telephone signal that is then broadcast over the radio transmitter and the radio signal coming in. The description taken from FCC, *In the Matter of*

the Use of the Carterphone Device in Message Toll Telephone Service, Initial Decision of the Hearing Examiner, 13 FCC 2d 430, 432–433 (1967).

[88] *Ibid.*, 434.

[89] *Ibid.* (This statement was by the Hearing Examiner but its purport was endorsed by the FCC.)

[90] *Ibid.*, 434–435. The Examiner's decision also convincingly discusses and dismisses other possible dangers asserted by the telephone companies, 435–437.

also unduly discriminatory when, as here, the telephone company's own interconnecting equipment is approved for use. The vice of the present tariff, here as in *Hush-A-Phone*, is that it prohibits the use of harmless as well as harmful devices."[91]

Far more than *Hush-A-Phone*, *Carterfone* forced the Bell System into a fundamental reexamination of its interconnection and alien attachment policies. In December of 1968 the FCC permitted AT&T to put into effect greatly liberalized tariffs for its business customers (the liberalization does not apply to the residential subscriber). These permit the direct connection of a wide variety of customer-provided terminal devices and communications systems, for the transmission and reception of data and voice signals from computers, facsimile machines, teletypewriters, and so on, subject only to the reservation that the telephone company is to provide protective devices at the "interface" between the private equipment and the telephone network in order to control the quality of the signal. The latter proviso was not acceptable to various independent equipment manufacturers and customers, who complained that they could provide such protective and transmitting devices equally capable of preserving quality and at lower cost; in this they were supported by the Antitrust Division of the Department of Justice. In permitting the tariffs to go into effect, the FCC left open the question of whether customers should be permitted access to the public system through their own network control signalling equipment.[92]

In any event, it was widely anticipated that this liberalization of the tariffs would open up a greatly expanded market for independent equipment manufacturers. Business users of communications facilities, it was widely predicted, would soon have available to them an increasingly rich variety of services, at reduced cost; among such possible attachments now available are fire or burglar alarms that automatically dial police or fire departments and transmit prerecorded calls for help; devices that automatically transfer calls to another number; and so on.

---

[91] 13 FCC 2d 420, 424 (1968). Similarly, although in its *above-890* decisions the Commission did not issue any orders to interconnect with the private systems, it did point out the discrepancy between the Bell companies' policies of refusal to interconnect with private communications systems and the policies of the independent telephone companies and Western Union, concluding

"It is clear from the record that, from a technical standpoint, interconnection of private systems with the common carrier systems is feasible where compatible and adequate transmission standards are maintained." *Op. cit.*, 27 FCC 359, 397 (1959).

Another incident in the controversy over the Carterfone was a $1.35 million antitrust suit that its manufacturer brought against AT&T and the General Telephone Company of the Southwest; the suit was settled out of court in 1969 with the plaintiff accepting $375,000 in damages. *The New York Times*, April 4, 1969.

[92] The Bell companies maintain that the instruments (like the ordinary dial telephone) that control the setting up, disconnecting, and charging for calls "are not mere attachments . . . [but] an integral and essential part of the service," which must, if quality of service is to be guaranteed, be supplied, installed, and maintained by the telephone companies themselves. AT&T, "Network Control Signalling," a statement submitted to the FCC, November 15, 1968. They therefore retained in the revised tariffs a requirement that "network control signalling in the furnishing of long distance message telecommunications service shall be performed by equipment furnished, installed and maintained by the Telephone Company." The Commission permitted retention of this provision pending the institution of technical conferences to assess its merits. *In the Matter of American Telephone and Telegraph Company "Foreign Attachment" Tariff Revisions etc.*, Memorandum Opinion and Order, 15 FCC 2d 605 (1968) and August 13, 1969 (the latter rejecting petitions for reconsideration).

So ended one phase in the continuous process of defining the natural communications monopoly. The enthusiasm expressed by the Chairman of AT&T's Board toward the much more modest definition implicit in the new tariffs contrasts amusingly and hearteningly with the company's attitude in *Hush-A-Phone*, some 10 to 15 years earlier:

"We believe that new regulations will open up new communications potentialities for our customers and afford new opportunities for the many fine companies that are making and marketing information-handling devices. . . .

"First, we welcome the use of our switched network for communications between customer-owned information generating and using equipment. The more the merrier.

"Second, we want to make the connection of such equipment as easy as possible, and the rules and regulations as few as possible. . . .

"We want to find more ways to say, 'Yes' to our customers—to approach these things imaginatively and flexibly."[93]

---

[93] H. I. Romnes, *195 Magazine*, September 16, 1968, as supplied in an internal company memorandum. Mr. Romnes also asserted the continuing responsibility of the Telephone Company for the overall quality of the service, its continued insistence therefore on treating "the network control device as an integral part of the switched network," and its opinion that it could best assure that "energy is not put into the network at such levels and frequencies as to interfere with other users" by "providing for the connection of customer-provided equipment to the network through an inexpensive protective device." *Ibid.*

For a good, general statement of the position of the Department of Justice on the side of maximizing the opportunities for competition in the redefinition of the network monopoly, see Lionel Kestenbaum, "The Limits of a Regulated Monopoly—Telephone Attachments, Interconnection and Use of Circuits," *The Antitrust Bulletin* (Fall 1968), XIII: 979–989.

Another closely related and rapidly developing aspect of this problem has to do with the proper relationship of the communications industry to the burgeoning computer service industry—in particular, the shared use of remote access computers, with the access achieved by wire or radio communications. The complicating factors are that, on the one hand, this use of the computer depends on the provision of communications facilities and, on the other, that the computer itself can perform many of the services now performed by communications common carriers—receiving, storing, and forwarding messages.

So, on the one hand, computer service bureaus are attempting in effect to go into the communications business, providing their customers with message switching services. See, for example,

the description of the Datran application at p. 135, above, and the Bunker-Ramo Corporation's Telequote IV service offering, which permitted stock brokers to place, execute, and confirm stock orders between their offices. Manley R. Irwin, "The Computer Utility: Market Entry in Search of Public Policy," *Jour. Ind. Econ.* (July 1969), XVII: 240–243. And the question has been raised of whether these computer-communications services have sufficiently monopolistic characteristics to justify subjecting them to regulation: the consensus is that they do not. See, e.g., the President's Task Force on Communications Policy, *op. cit.*, Chapter 6, 29–30, and the other sources cited in this note.

On the other hand, it follows equally that the communications companies have the facilities and the talents to move into the entire computer field. Western Union has begun to offer data-processing services, in direct competition with computer service bureaus. The Bell System is prohibited from doing so by the terms of the 1956 Antitrust Consent Decree, which limits its operation to regulated industries; but it is in any event the principal source of the communications services on which this new industry depends, and can by its tariff provisions and rates exert a powerful influence on the nature and speed of its development. The FCC in 1966 scheduled hearings on these complex interrelationships (*In the Matter of Regulatory and Policy Problems Presented by the Interdependence of Computer and Communications Services and Facilities*, Docket No. 16979, Tentative Decision and Notice of Proposed Rate-Making, April 1, 1970) in order to determine, among other things, to what extent such computer operations should be subject to regulation (which step, incidentally, would open the field to the Bell companies, under the 1956 decree) and to what extent the provision of data-

If Competitors Want to Enter, How Natural Can Monopoly Be?

The assertion of natural monopoly is that a single, chosen instrument can achieve lower costs and better service than can a number of competing suppliers. Yet competitors are successfully challenging the telephone company and customers are choosing to serve themselves. These numerous competitive challenges obviously raise serious doubts about the validity of treating the communications industry as a natural monopoly. These doubts might be dismissed if the various attempts at entry were simply mistakes from the standpoint of the interests of the entrants themselves; but their great number and rapid expansion bely any such explanation as a general proposition.[94] Could it be that the Bell natural-emperor really has no clothes on? The answer to this question seems to have at least the following parts:

1. The most important explanation of the increased competitive challenges of recent years must be progress in communications technology. The attraction of microwave or of dealing directly with Comsat is that it promises service at costs lower than current AT&T rates. Since the Bell System has itself pioneered in the development of microwave, that technology is available to it as well as to its competitors. The problem is that its rates have to carry a very heavy and incompletely depreciated investment in a wide variety of communications technologies, new and old. We have, in short, the situation described in Chapter 4 of Volume 1: because traditional depreciation rates have been outrun by technological progress, the average total cost of service, including gross return on historic or book investment, exceeds average total costs under new technology. The emperor has a very heavy and expensive old wardrobe; his challengers are wearing light new clothing.

We have already discussed the knotty problems of efficient rate making

---

processing services by common carriers would involve them in unfair competition with the independent firms now providing these services. The reason for the latter concern is that the independent firms would, on the one hand, be competing with the common carriers and, on the other hand, be dependent on them for an essential part of their services; they might therefore be subjected to a "squeeze" in the margin they could earn between the competitive price they could charge and the prices they would have to pay for those services—a familiar problem in the competition between vertically integrated and nonintegrated companies. On the other hand, since the telephone company's electronic switching system is in effect a giant computer that can be programmed to provide data processing, storage, and retrieval services, it could well be inefficient to confine the company to the transmission and switching of voice messages.

And, once again, the foreign attachments rule must inescapably come under scrutiny, with the computer manufacturers and users demanding the right to furnish their own devices for attaching the computers to the telephone circuits. For a

general survey of these problems, see the Response of the U. S. Department of Justice in the above-mentioned Docket No. 16979, submitted March 5, 1968; Bernard Strassburg, "Competition and Monopoly in the Computer and Data Transmission Industries," *The Antitrust Bulletin* (Fall 1968), XIII: 991–997; Manley R. Irwin, "The Computer Utility: Competition or Regulation?" *Yale Law Jour.* (June 1967), LXXVI: 1299–1320; also Delbert D. Smith, "The Interdependence of Computer and Communications Services and Facilities: A Question of Federal Regulation," *Univ. of Penn. Law Rev.* (April 1969), CXVII: 829–859.

[94] Another possible explanation consistent with the natural monopoly hypothesis is that the incumbent companies were charging such extortionately monopolistic prices as to enable the entrants to profit in spite of their higher costs. While the relatively modest profit rate of the Bell System makes this explanation unconvincing too, as a general proposition, it comes much closer to the mark when the Bell System prices to particular users are compared with the costs of supplying those particular users with systems embodying the latest technology—as we shall see.

in these circumstances.[95] It may be argued, on the one hand, that this discrepancy between ATC_o and ATC_n should come out of the pockets of the stockholders, thus enabling all rates to be set at the latter, more nearly efficient level. As we have seen, a plausible case can be made, instead, for permitting a regulated company to recoup its average historic cost of service from current and future customers—in which case, since marginal costs are less than average total costs, price discrimination may be a justifiable means of doing so.[96]

In any event, to the extent that it is circumstances such as these that have made independent competitive entry profitable, that entry does not necessarily justify rejection of the natural monopoly hypothesis.

2. A second explanation of some of these instances of successful competition, again in principle consistent with the presence of natural monopoly, is AT&T's policy of pricing its communications services uniformly on the basis of national average or system-wide per mile costs rather than, differentially, on the basis of the varying average costs of different portions of the service.[97] As is suggested by our earlier discussion, the tendency to decreasing costs results most markedly from the increasingly intensive utilization of particular route capacities. This apparently means that AT&T's costs of service are far less than its system-wide average on the intensively utilized, heavy traffic routes and correspondingly far above that average on the thin routes. Yet, to take an example that the company itself cited in resisting the MCI application, its rates are the same between Booneville, Indiana, and Big Stone Gap, Virginia, as between Chicago and St. Louis, because the distances are the same. The consequence is that smaller competitors like MCI, confining themselves to the thickly traveled routes,[98] may enjoy lower average total costs than AT&T as a whole and may therefore be able to undercut the Bell rates on those routes.

3. Another way of saying this is that the Bell System has a very different product mix from that of its more specialized competitors. One of the FCC's witnesses in Docket 16258 has deprecated AT&T's demonstration of economies of scale by pointing to the entry of much smaller suppliers

---

[95] See pp. 120–122, 173–174, 176–177, in Volume 1.

[96] The case for price discrimination is admittedly weaker where the gap between LRMC and ATC results from inadequate past depreciation than when it reflects genuine economies of scale. In the short-run, a regulated company finding itself in this situation would probably have no choice but to argue for the right to engage in price discrimination, subject to the various limitations set forth in Chapter 6 of Volume 1. In the longer run, it presumably would be better off directing its efforts toward enhancing its ability to meet competition generated by new technology, by insisting on a more rapid amortization of inadequately depreciated assets, to the point where ATC_o came into line with ATC_n. At that point the artificial competitive handicap would be eliminated and value-of-service pricing would no longer be needed or justified. Such a policy

would, for a time, aggravate the competitive handicap: cost of service would in the short run be inflated by these higher depreciation allowances. But, in the longer run, the company would be in a far better position to justify its claim of natural monopoly in the marketplace, being better able to meet or forestall such competition as new technology spawned without the need for price discrimination.

[97] See the Hearing Examiner's Initial Decision in the *MCI* case, pars. 31–32.

[98] The numerous MCI-like applications to the FCC during the 1968–1970 period (see note 66a, above) all proposed service between major population centers—Chicago and New York City; Boston, New York, and Washington; Minneapolis-St. Paul and Chicago; San Diego and Seattle; Los Angeles, San Francisco, New Orleans and Houston; and so on.

and to the former company's insistence that it has to reduce rates discriminatorily down toward long-run incremental costs to retain the competitive business. Surely, he suggests, if the economies of scale are as great as AT&T says, that gigantic company ought to be able to hold its market against the entry of much smaller rivals even at rates uniformly equal to its average total costs:

"If more than one firm can exist in a market, this would tend to indicate that available economies of scale can be exhausted at a small level of output relative to the size of the market. . . .

"The conditions of extensive economies of scale and a competitive market are incompatible. If the market conditions permit competition, economies of scale should be readily exhausted, and the rate levels for *all* services should approximate long-run incremental cost as well as fully distributed costs. . . . On the other hand, the cost conditions that are prerequisite to the possibility of significant rate reductions in response to competitive necessity, i.e., economies of scale beyond the existing output level, should foreclose the market to competitors."[99] (Stress supplied.)

This is a telling argument and it may be borne out by the facts in this case. But it is not necessarily conclusive. It would be so if the competitors, large and small, were producing a single, homogenous product. But where the companies have widely divergent product mixes and cost structures, there may exist simultaneously both great economies of scale and very strenuous competition for some portions of the business. And, as we have particularly illustrated in discussing the competition between railroads on the one hand and trucking companies and barges on the other, or between electric and oil companies, one of the competitors, enjoying very considerable economies of scale, may have fully distributed costs on all its business that are much higher but marginal costs much lower than the others.[100] In the present context, it could well be that AT&T, serving all areas of the country, might have a lower *average* traffic *density*, and consequently a higher average cost, than its specialized competitors, concentrating on the high-density routes.

4. This leads to a dynamic explanation of the rash of entrants in recent years: these companies have in considerable measure been introducing different services from the ones offered by the Bell System. This has obviously been true of the suppliers of auxiliary equipment, from Hush-A-Phone through Carterfone (Bell companies offer the latter in certain parts of the country but not in others). One of the arguments used by the applicants in the *above-890* case was that private systems, directly integrated with their own operations, could provide them with a service better adapted to their own particular needs. We have already summarized the distinctive features of the proposed MCI service. To some extent these services are of lower quality than Bell's; this could explain their lower cost. These instances, as we have already noted, suggest the need for redefining the area of Bell's natural monopoly. Where the monopolist is not providing the full range and variety of services that customers desire

---

[99] Testimony of William H. Melody, FCC Docket No. 16258, November 25, 1968, mimeo., 22, 25–26.

[100] See, for example, pp. 156–157, and 161–163, Volume 1, and pp. 23–24 of this Volume.

and are willing to pay for, the implication could be that monopoly is not "natural" in these areas, even in the static sense. Or it could mean that monopoly would still be, statically, the most efficient mechanism for providing this range of services, but that it has in practice proved to be inferior to competition in the *dynamic* sense—that is to say, in actively developing and offering to customers the fullest possible range of services and quality-price combinations.

5. Finally, it is possible that the provision of these inferior services is commercially acceptable only on the basis of the assumption that the Bell System stands ready to make good any deficiencies that emerge, by providing backup facilities to which the customers may turn in the event that the competitive service breaks down or proves insufficient to their needs.

For all these reasons, competitive entry does not necessarily justify rejection of the natural monopoly hypothesis. But—and this is the relevant question for us—what kind of regulatory policy do they suggest? Does the possible survival of the natural monopoly thesis suggest, then, that entry ought in fact to be barred? Let the reader remember our admonition at the outset of this volume that there is no scientific or demonstrably correct answer to these essentially institutional questions. The following suggestions are inevitably based on the author's subjective interpretation of the lessons of regulatory experience; their value, if any, lies less in their substance than in the demonstration they afford of the interrelationships between the various facets of regulatory policy.

Above all, if this experience demonstrates anything, it demonstrates the virtue of freedom of entry and competition as a device for innovation—for encouraging the development of new and different services and for assuring the optimal development and exploitation of new technology.[101] The single-firm monopolist, even if a highly effective and energetic innovator, is unlikely to be able to perceive or vigorously to exploit all the possible unsatisfied kinds of demands or fruitful lines of innovation. As for the application of new technology, the way to get microwave radio or communications satellite put into use at the optimum rate is to see to it that prices charged *to the customers of the service that embodies or could embody them* reflect their respective lower costs. To insist, instead, that the lower ATC of the new mode be commingled with the higher ATC of the old, with all users of communication service paying at the resultant average cost, runs the serious risk of uneconomically retarding exploitation of the new. A company specializing in the application of the new technology, with a demand rendered elastic by virtue of its ability to take customers away from the established supplier, will have the maximum incentive to charge rates fully reflecting cost advantages over that competitor.

This is not to deny that even a monopolist supplier of communications

---

[101] For an exposition and partial documentation of the hypothesis that the Bell monopoly has discouraged innovation in areas where entry of competitors is foreclosed and led the company itself to put disproportionately great effort into innovation in areas where competitive entry threatens see Shepherd, *op. cit.*, in the Brookings Institution symposium on *Technological Change in the Regulated Industries.* For a documentation of the latter tendency in the case of another famous monopoly see Carl Kaysen, *United States v. United Shoe Machinery Company* (Cambridge: Harvard Univ. Press, 1956), 175, 200, 260, 264.

services would have an incentive to make the most economical use of the lowest-cost technology, regardless of the pattern of rates that it charged its customers. But, as we have suggested, the motivations of a regulated monopolist with a heavy investment in the old are inevitably mixed, and particularly when (1) the new is less capital-intensive than the old (see pp. 51–52, Chapter 2, above) or (2) the investment in the old has been depreciated at an uneconomically low rate (see pp. 118–119, Volume 1). Moreover, like any monopolist, it has a less elastic demand than one of a number of competitors, and therefore less of an incentive to reduce its rates to (the new) LRMC.[102]

On the other hand, to the extent that the competitive handicap of AT&T is attributable to inadequate past rates of depreciation on its historic investment, it is entitled to point out to the regulatory commissions that they cannot escape responsibility for its difficulties, since it has typically been they that have resisted requests for more rapid amortization. It would be particularly anomalous for the FCC to emerge from its deliberations with a decision that (1) ordered AT&T to put into effect large rate reductions, based on cost-of-service determinations containing unrealistically low, Commission-dictated depreciation allowances, (2) used the willingness of independent firms to enter the market because their ATC_n are below AT&T rates, based on ATC_0, as evidence of the desirability and feasibility of competition, while (3) refusing to permit AT&T the right to meet such competition by reducing rates selectively toward LRMC, on the ground that the company's demonstrated justification for such discrimination—the disparity between LRMC and ATC—is a reflection not of the economies of scale but only of inadequate past depreciation rates![103] To put it another way, it would clearly be inconsistent for the FCC (1) to continue to adhere to the old, unrealistically low depreciation rates, while then (2) permitting free competitive entry by companies able to take full advantage of the new technology while AT&T remains burdened with the cost of old, inadequately depreciated assets, and (3) refusing to permit the latter company to engage in competitive pricing down to full additional costs on competitive business, where this would permit an increased contribution to its remaining burden of overheads, with consequent benefit to all its customers.[104]

The fact that competitive entry has apparently been made possible in part by the Bell System's use of national average cost as the basis for its prices on

---

[102] Whether this last tendency produces only a statically higher price and correspondingly lower output or, additionally, a lower *rate* of introduction of new, cost-saving technology over time is a question too complex to consider here. See especially William Fellner, "The Influence of Market Structure on Technological Progress," in Amer. Econ. Ass'n, *Readings in Industrial Organization and Public Policy*, 277–296. I can only record my conclusion that a tendency of the latter kind as well can be demonstrated.

It is considerations like these that should make one skeptical about the recommendations of the President's Task Force on Communications Policy that the international communications business be turned over to a single chosen

instrument. See on this also note 76, p. 139, above and note 32, Chapter 6; also Peck, *op. cit.*, *Amer. Econ. Rev. Papers and Proceedings* (May 1970), LX: 199–203, and the comments by Kahn, *ibid.*, 219–220.

[103] Yet there is testimony in its Docket 16258—notably by Wein and Melody—that either specifically takes or is wholly consistent with all these positions.

[104] This discussion does not explicitly consider the possibly injurious effect of such discriminatory pricing on competition at the primary level—that is, between AT&T and its competitors. See on this point pp. 175–177, Volume 1, and pp. 247–250, below.

different routes, or by its providing the necessary backup in the event of breakdown, raises the issue of cream-skimming, which we discuss more fully in Chapter 6. Cream-skimming or not, however, the entry affords another example of the beneficial contribution of competition. The prices to different users *should*, on efficiency grounds, reflect differences in the respective cost of serving them;[105] and if users are willing, with full knowledge of what they are getting, to take an inferior or less reliable service, at lower prices, it is the function of the market to provide it to them. AT&T's failure to do so was remedied by competition.

Of course, economic efficiency is not the only socially appropriate goal of pricing. Perhaps there are good, noneconomic reasons for preferring uniform per mile rates regardless of differences in costs, tending as they do to treat all users equally regardless of their location.[106] It may indeed be that such rates are also economically efficient, taking into account externalities: the same (per mile) rates between rural as between urban areas, where the former are below and the latter above their respective *private* marginal costs, are a way of subsidizing living in the less populous areas of the country. To the extent that this slows down the movement of population into the cities, it reduces the congestion costs that would otherwise be imposed on the people already there. If on the other hand society places a high priority on the rehabilitation of its cities, it might well oppose a practice that involves urban subscribers subsidizing the communications rates charged companies that move out of city centers.

But it is not the function of AT&T as such to take these social or external costs into consideration. It is up to Congress or the regulatory commission to make up its mind which it prefers—either (1) enabling the chosen instrument to continue its internal subsidization, by prohibiting entry into the subsidizing markets, or (2) permitting it instead to relate its own rates for individual services more closely to their respective costs. Competitive entry has served a purpose if it forces the FCC to confront this question.

It seems unlikely that any of these considerations eradicates the case for natural monopoly at the core of the telephonic network. The provision of that network and the assumption of centralized responsibility for its planning and for the quality of the service it provides is still, it would seem, best left to a chosen instrument. But that a monopoly works best in certain aspects of the operation is not an argument for retaining its exclusive control over those aspects in which it has demonstrably not worked best. The economic ideal would clearly be for the area of natural monopoly to be defined as narrowly

---

[105] The case is actually more complicated: relative prices should be equated to relative *marginal* costs; and it is conceivable that the marginal costs on more and less densely used routes are equal even if their average costs are markedly different. On the other hand, if (as seems to be the case) it is only on the denser routes that employment of the newest, lowest-cost technology is economically feasible, this suggests that their marginal costs are lowest too and that uniform rates force them to subsidize users in less populous locations.

[106] The FCC members who dissented from the

MCI decision (Docket 16509, *Decision*, August 13, 1969) did so explicitly because they felt it was inconsistent with national-average cost pricing. But they offered no reasoned explanation of why they regarded that system as sacrosanct, except that under it "the small user in the hinterlands is afforded the same rates as the large users in the major cities." Dissent of Chairman Hyde. See also the dissents of Commissioners Lee and Wadsworth. But what, one might ask, about the discrimination against the small user in the center city, in favor of the wealthy company in the suburbs?

as possible, and for the chosen instrument to exercise its responsibility, to the greatest extent possible, by (1) efficient pricing, (2) vigorously anticipating all possible demands on it—thereby subjecting its claim of natural monopoly to the market test—and (3) setting rigorous quality specifications at the critical points—and not before—at which uncontrolled competition demonstrably poses a threat to the quality and efficiency of service.[107]

Natural Gas Transmission

The design of an efficient natural gas pipeline system involves many of the same considerations as the communications network. The local distribution of gas is generally recognized as a natural monopoly of the familiar type, with the same justification: economies of scale with increasing intensity of use of given distribution facilities. But with respect to the pipeline network that carries natural gas from the field to the city gate of the local distribution system, the question of the proper role of competition has come into increasingly intense contention in recent years. For at least a decade after World War II, the energies of the industry and of the Federal Power Commission were directed principally toward extending supply to areas of the country not as yet fully served. With the completion of something like a nation-wide network and with major pipelines crossing each other's paths with increasing frequency, the opportunities for growth in noncompetitive directions have declined and the possibilities of competition expanded cor-

---

[107] The intrusion of competition into the domain of what was previously a "natural monopoly" opens up another kind of intriguing possibility: why not remove the competitive areas entirely from regulation? Harold H. Wein, testifying on behalf of Western Union, and William H. Melody, testifying for the FCC staff, both in Docket 16258, have suggested that this separation be made. They would leave AT&T to make whatever returns it can on the competitive operation, subject only to the restraints of competition, and permit it to recover from its message toll telephone (MTT) customers only the separate costs of that service, determined on the basis of a full cost distribution. Their purpose is to protect the latter from exploitation: they contend that the company has been charging excessive rates on MTT in order to subsidize competitive rates on the business services.

It is impossible without more information to evaluate their proposal. The danger they describe cannot be assumed to be negligible, in view of the uncertainty, so far, that long-run incremental costs of the competitive operation can in fact be readily determined and fixed as a floor below which those rates may not be dropped. Indeed, it would appear at first that their suggestion of separating out the competitive from the non-competitive operations could be only beneficial to the purchasers of the monopoly (MTT) service, since they have been contributing well in excess of the Company's average return on that portion of the total rate base that would be

allocated to them on a fully distributed basis (see p. 157, Volume 1).

But suppose, as it argues is indeed the case, AT&T can profitably obtain the competitive business at rates that more than cover long-run incremental costs but not at rates covering fully distributed costs. If the operations were "separated" in the manner here suggested, it would pay AT&T in the long run to get out and stay out of those competitive markets. The reason is that every sale there has the effect of reducing the MTT rate base—determined on the basis of relative use—and therefore justifying, under regulation, a reduction in the latter rates. The competitive business, that is to say, could be fully remunerative on a long-run incremental cost basis but unremunerative if to those incremental costs must be allocated a share of the total rate base determined on the basis of relative use. In the long run, therefore, AT&T would, under the above assumptions, find it in its interest to serve only the MTT customers. This outcome might be highly satisfactory to its competitor, Western Union, but it would not be in the interest of the purchasers of the monopoly service.

So the Wein–Melody proposal could have the effect of denying to all buyers the benefits of the great economies of scale in AT&T's Long Lines business. The MTT users, in particular, could lose the contribution to common costs made by the competitive business. Whether this possibility of loss outweighs the possible benefits of separation cannot be determined on an a priori basis.

respondingly. Pipeline companies may compete not only for the privilege of serving the incremental demand of existing markets but also for the patronage of existing customers, as contracts between distributors and pipelines come up for renewal.[108]

The analytical issues are familiar. To what extent do economies of scale call for a single chosen instrument to serve particular routes and markets? Are there cost savings that can be achieved only by a coordinated planning of investment and operations? Can the latter economies be achieved, while still leaving the field open to competition? Does competition raise the danger of cream-skimming or of excessive discrimination between those customers in a position to benefit from it and those who are not? To what extent, correspondingly, may customers properly be left free to shop around among competing suppliers? In contrast with oil pipelines and railroads, natural gas pipelines are not typically common carriers; to what extent might it be appropriate to make them so—requiring them to interconnect with others or to carry gas for them?

Economies of Scale. As far as the actual carriage of gas is concerned, economies of scale could not possibly require a single chosen instrument for the entire national market. Pipelines travel from one point to another; in consequence there is ample room for a large number of criss-crossing lines, with ample resultant possibilities of competition both in areas between lines and near their points of junction. The main potential economies of scale are to be found in employing pipe of the maximum diameter available and, to a lesser extent, of further increasing its capacity, within limits, by increasing pressure and by "looping," that is, by constructing parallel lines running through the same compressor stations.[109] But these economies taper off sharply once the largest possible pipe available is used and even more sharply when the limits of further expanding capacity in the manner indicated are reached.[110] Once the market has expanded to sufficient size, as a result, there

---

[108] Carl E. Bagge, "Regulated Competition: An Alternative to Antitrust," Address before the Independent Natural Gas Association of America, San Francisco, September 4, 1967, mimeo., 5. See the prediction of this development back in 1952:

"The Commission has had relatively few cases of these types [requests for competitive certification or competing requests for certification], possibly because so many areas of the country were, until recently, without any natural gas service that natural gas companies did not have to compete for territories. Intensification of the competition between companies to serve given areas may be expected in the future, for natural gas service has now been extended to all but one major area of the country." Koplin, *op. cit.*, 351–352.

[109] The *physical* principle is that whereas the cost of a pipeline, like its perimeter, is (roughly) proportional to its diameter, its capacity is proportionate to the square of the diameter. Whether it is *economical* to use the widest available pipe depends of course on the size and expected growth of demand. Against the lower potential costs of wider-diameter lines must be weighed the cost of building too far ahead of demand.

[110] Koplin computed costs per square inch of cross section per mile for pipelines of various diameters: these decline sharply from $436 for 4-inch line to $124 for a 16-inch and $105, $90, and $83.50, respectively, for 20-, 24- and 26-inch lines. He also found that pipeline and compressor station operating expenses, and supervision and engineering costs all tended to increase proportionately less than pipeline capacity. For later estimates, showing average total costs for a 1,000 mile carriage declining from 10.1¢ per mcf for a 16-inch to 6.0¢ for a 36-inch line, see Paul W. MacAvoy, *Price Formation in Natural Gas Fields* (New Haven: Yale University Press, 1962), 41. Koplin notes also the limitations of these economies to which we have referred. At the time of his writing, 1952, the maximum diameter pipe available was 36 inches, although no line of that size had as yet been constructed. *Op. cit.*, 352–357. The largest line under active discussion in this country today is 42 inches.

is often room, consistent with maximum efficiency, for more than one transmission line traversing roughly the same territory.

But for any particular project, designed to meet given increments in market demand, economies of scale can be extremely important. The possibility that they might counsel one large certification rather than a series of medium-sized and small ones played a central role in the FPC's decision in 1968 involving three separate applications to bring additional gas to the California market. The applications were not, strictly, competitive. The Pacific Gas Transmission Company (PGT) sought permission to import gas from Canada, for ultimate distribution in Northern California; the El Paso Natural Gas Company's application, like that of the Transwestern Pipeline Company, involved bringing additional West Texas gas into the southern part of the state, with each of the two supplying only a portion of the anticipated additional requirements. The Presiding Examiner, Seymour Wenner, made it clear at the outset that the important issue was whether the separate, piecemeal proposals represented the most efficient method of meeting the need:

"Viewed routinely, these applications are steps in a minuet whereby El Paso and Transwestern provide medium scale successive increments to the California market."

"The Transwestern proposal should be considered along with the instant El Paso proposal as a method of supplying California with additional gas over the years through piece-meal medium and small sized additions. Under these proposals the load will be split between the two companies; it will be split again within some four or five years when another round of looping is needed to carry the increased supply. The El Paso 36″ loop is not small. But in combination with the 30″ loops it would deny the market the economies of large diameter—42″—pipe."

"Viewed constructively, the underlying issue in this case is whether the Commission should take the opportunity to find out whether the use of large diameter—42″—pipe for additional supplies can substantially reduce the cost of California's future gas supply."[111]

The FPC staff proposed the substitution, for all three of the proposed projects, of a single, new 42-inch pipeline from West Texas to the California border, pointing out, additionally, that such a line would take the place also of future planned expansions of the El Paso and Transwestern lines through additional looping. The Examiner agreed with the basic intent of this "bold and constructive proposal . . . based on a sound engineering and economic concept" (p. 1182) but mainly because of inadequately resolved uncertainties about the need and adequacy of gas supplies for so large an addition to capacity at so early a time, proposed instead what he called a "minimax solution"—a compromise designed to minimize the risks attendant upon the Staff's proposal while taking maximum advantage of the potential economies of scale. This involved immediate certification of the PGT proposal and postponement of action on the other two (technically, the Transwestern application was not involved in this particular proceeding), in order to permit consideration of the 42-inch alternative.

---

[111] FPC, *Pacific Gas Transmission Company, El Paso Natural Gas Company*, Docket Nos. CP67–187 et al., Presiding Examiner's Initial Decision Upon Applications for Certificates of Public Convenience and Necessity, 40 FPC 1147, 1179–1182 (1968).

Wenner's conclusion contained an eloquent statement of the limitations of the regulatory device as traditionally employed and the case for stronger commission initiatives of the kind that he and the Staff had proposed here:[112]

"The major objection to the immediate approval of the El Paso proposal is that it forever forfeits the opportunity to evaluate and adopt a plan that is reasonably likely to reduce the cost of California's gas. In favor of giving up this chance is the consideration that immediate approval of the El Paso proposal is the easiest way. . . .

"A neglected field of administrative law is the relationship between licensing and rate making. The big opportunities for cost savings to consumers do not lie in the disallowing of particular costs in a rate case. Underlying costs are determined in the certificate case where the project is licensed.

"What is proposed here is that the opportunity be taken to find out—and adopt if the findings be favorable—whether the economies of large scale operation can be secured at minimum risk—economies that will benefit producers through greater sales of gas, pipelines through larger revenues over the long run, and consumers through price reductions." (p. 1189)

The FPC itself rejected the Wenner proposal, on the ground that the need for additional gas was too urgent to permit postponement, and therefore issued the certificates to PGT and El Paso as requested. Its chairman, Lee White, dissented from the latter part of the decision. He would have had the Commission force El Paso to put in a continuous 36-inch line, instead of one involving sections of smaller diameter; its failure to do so, he argued,

"saddles California consumers with a project which is considerably less desirable than an alternative project which would be far cheaper in the long run . . . and which could be certificated on the present record."[113]

It is unnecessary for us to attempt to judge whether the FPC majority was correct in declining to take up these initiatives.[114] The important lessons of the case for us have to do with, first, the limited possibilities of genuine competition between two or three pipelines serving a particular area and the possibility that they may, in such instances, merely take turns in capacity expansion with each retaining a tacitly accepted share of the market; second, the possible superiority of single-firm certification or coordinated planning of additions to capacity, as a means of more fully exploiting the potential economies of scale; and, third, the question of how, in such circumstances, competition can be preserved.[115]

---

[112] On this general problem, see pp. 47–48, 75–77, 86–88 and passim, Chapter 2, above.

[113] *Pacific Gas Transmission Company, El Paso Natural Gas Company*, Opinion and Order, 40 FPC 1147, 1167 (1968). The Commission majority rejected this alternative as well, on the ground that it had not been adequately considered in the record.

[114] It did, however, applaud the Staff's initiative and, in effect, promised to try to profit by its lesson:

"We wish to make clear that our rejection of the Staff's 42-inch line and the Examiner's minimax alternative does not indicate our approval of any practice by El Paso and Transwestern of seeking to meet the growing needs of the California market through relatively small scale facility increments to meet immediate market needs, which though initially less costly cannot hope to achieve available long range economies of scale. To the extent that any such tendency may reflect past actions of this Commission, the Staff's actions herein have forcefully brought to our attention the limitations of such a policy in providing optimum service to the growing California market." *Ibid.*, 1160–1161.

[115] In these circumstances it is possible to ask whether competition serves any social purpose at

On the third point, the dissenting Commissioner White offered an interesting suggestion: he would have certificated the single, more efficient project, but attached a condition that would permit the FPC, if it saw fit in the future, to require the favored applicant to carry gas at cost (perhaps even incremental cost) for its competitors:

"Transwestern, at present the only competitor of El Paso in the rich Permian Basin to California market, is afflicted with all of the ills which face any comparatively small company competing with a giant in an industry where economies of scale are important. The market in California . . . is controlled in effect, by very few buyers. While it is in the interest of those buyers to maintain some competition by keeping Transwestern alive, it is not in their interest to give Transwestern large contracts until it can sell gas as cheaply as El Paso, something it is presently not able to do. But this results in a vicious circle, for low unit gas transportation costs cannot be achieved without large pipelines, and large pipelines cannot be economically built or utilized without large contracts. The action of the majority today condemns Transwestern, or any new competitor, to a repetition of the same dreary cycle—a compromise by building a pipeline which, while too small for eventual use in reducing unit costs low enough really to compete, is initially too large for the small amounts of gas Transwestern will furnish. . . .

"The dilemma facing the Commission is a real one. On the one hand, any rational decision in this proceeding . . . must provide for expansibility at the lowest cost; on the other hand, provision of such expansibility can act to the detriment of El Paso's competitors. Stated differently, the problem is whether there is a way to preserve the fruits of competition and at the same time optimize the construction of pipeline facilities so as to achieve the benefits of scale. I am convinced there is.

---

all. One additional element in the equation, illustrated with particular force in the present instance, is the effect of interpipeline rivalry on the field price of natural gas. Transwestern was organized by gas producers, previously dependent almost exclusively on El Paso for their interstate sales, in hope of getting a better price. And, not surprisingly, Transwestern sharply increased its buying prices for gas in the field compared with the level theretofore paid by El Paso. The question of whether the resulting price increase was justified in terms of economic efficiency raises the whole complex question of whether the field market is or was effectively competitive. On the one hand, there can be little doubt that El Paso was using its monopsony power to hold the price below competitive levels and that the entry of competition on the buying side of the market was a salutary influence from the standpoint of economic efficiency. On the other hand, it is not clear that rivalry among pipelines, each attempting to sew up the large blocs of natural gas reserves that are prerequisite to their obtaining quasi-monopolistic certification to serve a particular market area, produces competitive equilibrium prices for those reserves either. This would be true even if the

pipelines were independent of producer interests: they would be unlikely to bargain hard over the contract price for the natural gas when their getting or not getting the certification was at stake, especially considering that, once certificated, they could confidently expect to incorporate that purchase price in their regulated cost of service. The social desirability of their competition was even more questionable where, as here, they were producers as well as buyers of the gas they proposed to carry. Their vertical integration could be expected to generate a strong incentive to pay above-competitive prices, which they could then incorporate in their cost of service and recover from consumers. For statements of these opposing points of view see MacAvoy, *Price Formation in Natural Gas Fields*, 101–145 and Kahn, "Economic Issues in Regulating the Field Price of Natural Gas," *Amer. Econ. Rev., Papers and Proceedings* (May 1960), L: 508–509, and for a fuller discussion Kahn, testimony before the FPC, *In the matter of Champlin Oil & Refining Co. et al.*, Docket Nos. G–9277 et al. (*Omnibus*), Vol. 38-LC, 4872-LC–5030-LC, and especially 4990-LC–5011-LC. See also the references in note 75, Chapter 1, above.

"While competition in the California market in the past has been less than perfect, it has been beneficial on occasion . . . and may be beneficial in the future. Therefore, considering El Paso's already dominant position in the market, its further expansion at this time must be conditioned to preserve competition and keep its competitors viable. Such a condition should, I believe, make it clear that should it develop in some future proceeding that utilization by some other person of the excess capacity or expansibility of the facilities which are the subject of this proceeding is required to ensure that optimum service is not at the expense of competition, such facilities will be available. This can be accomplished by a condition providing that, if the public interest is found to so require[,] any other person certificated to transport gas . . . will be able to utilize El Paso's cheap expansibility, and that any additional looping or other construction on the El Paso facilities necessary to transport such gas as we may certificate will be installed."[116]

Coordinated Investment Planning. As with the telephone network, the economies of scale that might make monopoly natural could flow not so much from the sheer size of individual production operations as from the centralized planning of investment. An apparently dramatic demonstration of these possibilities was provided by the application of a technique of "network analysis," developed by mathematicians at the United States Office of Emergency Planning, to the hypothetical problem of describing what would have been the optimal natural gas pipeline transmission system for the existing distribution of gas fields in the Gulf of Mexico.[117] The solution produced a system that could have cost less than half the cost of the network actually constructed.

It is not clear how much of this estimated savings reflected the mere advantage of hindsight—that is, of knowing more about the location of the various gas fields, ex post, than the people who designed the existing network knew when they had to make their plans—and how much the superiority of a coordinated application of the new technique. But the report of this exercise emphasizes the latter. It professes to demonstrate that "significant savings in network cost can be achieved even when only partial information is available," (p. 15) specifically considers the problem of designing networks when

---

[116] 40 FPC 1147, 1173–1175 (1968). This obligation would have had to be imposed in advance, as a condition of certification, because the FPC does not have the authority to require lines to serve others when this would necessitate expansion of their facilities (see note 85, Chapter 2, above; also pp. 166–177, Chapter 6, below). The Commission majority rejected this suggestion for several reasons, among them the fact that Transwestern itself had not expressed opposition to the El Paso proposal or requested any such condition. The fact that Transwestern had indeed "vigorously supported" the El Paso application is not necessarily conclusive, as any student of the antitrust literature will recognize; if, as Examiner Wenner suggested, each company was taking its turn in "a minuet" it was no more in the interest of any one of them to object

to the application of the other than it was for the competitors of U.S. Steel to complain of that company's alleged illegal monopolization of steel, since they too profited from the price umbrella that it held over the market. The FPC's citation of the absence of complaint from a competitor in this case could have been just as irrational as the similar contention by the U. S. Supreme Courts' controlling opinion in exonerating the steel company of an antitrust violation back in 1920. *U. S. v. United States Steel Corp. et al.*, 251 U.S. 417, 447–449 (1920).

[117] National Resource Analysis Center, Systems Evaluation Division, *Report R–1, Design of Economical Offshore Natural Gas Pipeline Systems* (A Study Prepared for the Federal Power Commission), Office of Emergency Preparedness, November 1968.

projections of future discoveries are taken into account and identifies as one important inefficiency of the present system the fact that

"separate portions of the gathering system were designed by different pipeline companies working independently. This independence often stems from the conflicting contractual arrangements between various pipeline companies and gas producers which make neighboring pipelines incompatible. Furthermore, pipeline routes from gas fields to onshore separation plants are often selected on the basis of constraints other than minimum network costs, such as interlocking interests between separation plants and pipeline companies." (p. 13)

"The results of this study indicate that increased cooperation among pipeline companies, including coordinated planning and integrated facilities, could yield great economic benefits." (p. 31)

The question is whether these economies of coordinated planning can be achieved under competition. And the solution, once again, would seem to be one of insisting on a chosen instrument approach for conducting the natural monopoly part of the operation—for example, by encouraging or requiring the several parties to organize themselves into a joint venture to perform these functions—while permitting or insisting on independent action in other parts. And the way to preserve the opportunities for competition where that is consistent with efficiency is, as Commissioner White urged in the *El Paso* proceeding, to force the chosen instruments in the naturally monopolistic area to behave like common carriers. For example, when confronted in 1969 with three separate applications by transmission companies to build individual pipeline facilities for bringing offshore Louisiana gas into land, the FPC was reportedly considering one of two alternatives: either to propose that the three companies combine to build one giant project, or to invite competing applications from new and entirely separate companies to build a single system that would serve the onshore facilities of the three applicants:

"These transport concerns ('they'd be like toll bridges,' one planner says) wouldn't be affiliated with either producers or transmission companies, and, in effect, would be a new industry."[118]

The Role of Competitive Considerations. That economies of scale need not preclude certification of competing pipelines seems clearly to have been demonstrated by the case involving the application of the Great Lakes Gas Transmission Company for permission to bring Canadian gas into the north-central portions of the United States.

In 1961, Trans-Canada Pipe Lines Limited decided that the increasing demand for gas in the eastern part of that country could best be served by construction of a new pipeline that would enter the United States in northern Minnesota and, running through northern Wisconsin and Michigan, reenter Canada at Sarnia, Ontario. The project would have the additional advantage, from its standpoint, of making possible expanded sales of Canadian gas in those states. Since this would involve selling gas to American distributors, Trans-Canada entered into discussions with several American companies to see whether any of them might be interested in a joint project. Unable to reach such an agreement, it applied for certification on its own, through

---

[118] *Wall Street Journal*, February 27, 1969, 8.

Great Lakes, its wholly owned subsidiary. Thereupon, the American companies most directly affected, the American Natural Gas and Midwestern Gas Transmission Companies, entered an alternative proposal to accomplish the same purposes. Before the FPC was able to act, the parties resumed negotiations, withdrew their separate, mutually exclusive applications and presented a proposal instead to have the project handled by Great Lakes, in which Trans-Canada would give American Natural a one-half interest. It was this joint venture that the FPC certificated in 1967, in preference to a competing application by the Northern Natural Gas Company. Northern appealed this decision in the courts, contending that the Commission had inadequately taken into account the deleterious effects of the joint venture on competition.[119]

The Court agreed with Northern, and therefore remanded the case to the FPC for further consideration.[120] Its reasoning was simple and convincing. American Natural supplies over 50 percent of all the gas consumed in Michigan and Wisconsin. Had Trans-Canada come in alone (via Great Lakes) it would have been a direct competitor. It obviously had intended to do so. Economies of scale made it sensible for any line planning to carry gas to eastern Canada to build capacity sufficient also to sell in Michigan. There were no economies of scale involved in American's participation in the project: all it did was buy a half-interest. To obtain this interest in a threatening competitor, American was willing to commit itself to take the Canadian gas, even though this would otherwise not have been in its interest or that of its customers:

"these sales were agreed to, not because the Canadian gas was cheaper . . . but rather because American Natural, the parent of the buying subsidiaries, seemed willing to sacrifice the interests of its consumers in order to protect its markets and enhance economically the joint venture in which it owned a half interest. . . .

"American Natural flatly stated that if the joint venture were not certificated it would have no desire to take this Canadian gas. . . ."[121]

---

[119] *Northern Natural Gas Company et al. v. Federal Power Commission*, 399 F. 2d 953 (1968). Northern contended that

"the joint venture resulted in an illegal division of the consumer market between Trans-Canada and American Natural, substantially lessened competition between United States distributors for the supply of Canadian gas, and illegally eliminated competition between independent applicants (Trans-Canada *versus* American Natural and Midwestern) in a Commission comparative proceeding." (*Ibid.*, 958).

[120] It did not agree specifically with Northern's charge (see the note immediately preceding) that the agreements were in violation of the antitrust laws and that the finding of such a violation would suffice to prevent the Commission from certifying the project. As the Court put it

"Although the Commission is not bound by the dictates of the antitrust laws, it is clear that antitrust concepts are intimately involved in a determination of what action is in the public interest, and therefore the Commission is obliged to weigh antitrust policy." *Ibid.*

[121] *Ibid.*, 970–971. On this motivation and consequence the Court accepts the comment of the FPC staff:

"American Natural's agreement to purchase this gas through its subsidiaries was part of the bargaining price it had to pay in order to obtain a half interest in the joint venture. This had an effect not only on those who market United States gas at its source, but ultimately on the consumers in the American Natural system. The staff of the Commission detected this and commented:

"'Thus the consumers . . . to whom service could be rendered more readily and more economically through the combined American Natural System, are the sacrificial pawns by which American Natural received (1) half ownership in Great Lakes and (2) Midwestern's quiet acquiescence in the withdrawal of their joint competitive proposal.'" *Ibid.*, 971.

For Trans-Canada, the quid pro quo was an insured market for their gas, without the need to compete with American-originating gas for that market: they made it clear that they would not have entered into the joint venture without the commitment on the part of American Natural's subsidiaries to take its gas. So the Court concluded:

"From the above it is clear that Trans-Canada will be able to market an additional 170,000 Mcf of gas per day in the United States without having to meet or beat the competition provided by United States source gas, and that American Natural's agreement to purchase this gas through its subsidiaries was part of the bargaining price it had to pay in order to obtain a half interest in the joint venture. . . .

"we believe that the joint venture substantially lessened competition among suppliers in the Michigan–Wisconsin consumer market and between Trans-Canada and suppliers of gas from United States sources. Unless the Commission finds that other important considerations militate in favor of the joint venture and that these considerations are more beneficial to the public than additional competition, the antitrust policies should be respected and the joint venture set aside." (p. 971)

Among the forms of competition that the Court was intent to preserve, and that it regarded as having been unreasonably eliminated in this instance, was the presentation of competing applications before the Commission itself.

"Petitioners have aptly noted that comparative proceedings before regulatory agencies are 'sensitive mechanism[s] for weighing the relative merits of . . . rival . . . projects' and one of the 'main competitive arenas' of the natural gas industry since it is there that the sellers challenge one another for the favor of the Commission. This process could easily be distorted if the Commission permitted potential applicants to get together to decide how a market would be divided before submitting their proposals to the Commission, for then private parties rather than the Commission would be determining what means of meeting a market demand is most closely in accord with the public interest. We cannot permit such an abrogation of administrative responsibility.

"The danger of allowing parties to agree among themselves prior to submitting their proposals to the Commission becomes all the more apparent when it is remembered that the Commission's power is largely a negative one; it must rely heavily on private initiative to propose projects to meet consumer needs. . . .

"There are few opportunities for consumers of natural gas to choose among the several suppliers offering a variety of services and prices. It is therefore extremely important that a competitive edge be maintained in Commission proceedings. This will increase the chance that the public will be given better service at a lower price. If the Commission determines, after reviewing individual proposals, that a joint project would be more advantageous, it can at that time refuse to certify the individual plans and itself suggest a joint application."[122]

---

[122] *Ibid.*, 971–972. It seems unlikely that it would always be practicable for the Commission to follow the Court's advice in this respect. It would seem unnecessarily wasteful, in those instances in which the private parties concerned saw the possibility of large economies achievable by joint operations, to require that they first prepare separate, uneconomic proposals, leaving it

The *Great Lakes* case is additionally interesting because of the excellent discussion it evoked from Judge J. Skelly Wright of the role of competition in this industry and in the regulated industries generally, and of the closely related question of the relationship between the antitrust laws and the regulatory statutes. These are worth quoting at length:

"The nature of the natural gas market was accurately described by Mr. Justice Douglas in *El Paso*:

'This is not a field where merchants are in a continuous daily struggle to hold old customers and to win new ones over from their rivals. In this regulated industry a natural gas company (unless it has excess capacity) must compete for, enter into, and then obtain Commission approval of sale contracts in advance of constructing the pipeline facilities. In the natural gas industry pipelines are very expensive; and to be justified they need long-term contracts for sale of the gas that will travel them. . . . Once the Commission grants authorization to construct facilities or to transport gas in interstate commerce, once the distributing contracts are made, a particular market is withdrawn from competition. *The competition then is for the new increments of demand that may emerge with an expanding population and with an expanding industrial or household use of gas.*' 376 U.S. at 659–660. . . .

"In this case the additional demand in the eastern Canadian market made a new pipeline feasible. . . .

"If a wholly-owned subsidiary of Trans-Canada would have become an actual competitor of suppliers in Michigan and Wisconsin, we believe that the effect would have been substantial and that the northern Wisconsin and Michigan markets could have expected significant benefits. This is so, in large part, because competition, even in a regulated industry, secures benefits which might otherwise be unattainable. Admittedly the Commission possesses a rate-making power and this power is designed to protect the consumers of natural gas. But it is clear that this power is largely a negative one. Thus the Commission may set a selling rate for a supplier only after it has been demonstrated that the present charge is unjust, unreasonable, unduly discriminatory or preferential, a heavy burden even for specialists as intimately familiar with the natural gas industry as is the Commission. On the other hand, if competition exists, albeit in a limited area, there would be

entirely to the Commission to see the advantages of joint action and to require it. At the same time, in the present instance, in which the collaboration apparently had nothing to do with cost savings, the Court's findings are persuasive.

On November 21, 1968, the FPC remanded the case to its Presiding Examiner, for hearings limited to the question of the appropriate ownership and operation of Great Lakes. The Examiner recommended that American Natural be required to divest itself of its interest in Great Lakes, unless Northern Natural was permitted to build the pipeline for which it was seeking authorization to bring Canadian gas into the Midwest. The Commission rejected this advice, concluding that the benefits flowing from American Natural's participation in the joint venture outweighed its anticompetitive effects. The record on remand, it found, showed no substantial possibility of competition between the two companies: Great Lakes was unsuited to sell gas directly to distributors, but would have to depend on pipelines like American, in an essentially symbiotic rather than competitive relationship. Its judgment was influenced by the condition of gas shortage that emerged in the United States during the late 1960's, which, it argued, meant that increasing imports of Canadian gas were required to supplement domestic supplies, rather than to supplant them. *Ibid.*, Opinion and Order on Remand Confirming Issuance of Certificates with Conditions, Opinion No. 580, July 10, 1970.

incentives for innovation by the regulated companies themselves and for their coming forward with proposals for better services, lower prices, or both. And once innovations or proposals are forthcoming by a supplier, the Commission could more easily act to universalize these benefits than it could have acted to extract them initially.

"Consider the types of natural gas markets which exist. There are some markets which are natural monopolies—that is, where the most efficient allocation of resources results in a single supplier. In such markets, competition is sacrificed to avoid wasteful duplication of services and investment, and hence regulation by the Commission is the only protection a consumer has. In virtually all other natural gas markets, there is a tight oligopoly or partial monopoly. In these markets the fortunes of the few sellers are highly dependent, and therefore there is an incentive for the sellers to arrive at a price which will offer the highest return to all of them. Such a uniform price, whether arrived at by formal agreements or merely through price leadership, is in essence a monopoly price and yields monopoly profits. . . .

"But in practice it appears that firms selling in such a market do not always seek a uniform monopoly price and, if sought, do not always attain it. Among the reasons why uniform monopoly prices are not sought or attained is that one seller may believe he can maximize his profits by expanding his total sales rather than taking a maximum profit on each sale. Also, even the mere addition of one seller to an oligopoly market makes the market more complex and less predictable. Therefore, there may be competitive actions and reactions in an oligopoly market.

"One instance of such activity in a tight oligopoly market within the natural gas industry was noted by the Supreme Court in *United States* v. *El Paso Natural Gas Co.*, *supra*, 376 U.S. at 654–655. There Pacific Northwest Pipeline Corporation, a potential supplier to the California natural gas market, sought, in an attempt to gain entrance to that market, to attract a major customer from El Paso. Pacific Northwest offered lower prices and an uninterruptible supply to this customer whose El Paso supply was then subject to interruption during peak demands. Although El Paso was able to hold this customer and thereby prevent Pacific Northwest from entering the California market, it was able to do so only by giving the customer a firm supply and by dropping its selling price 25 percent. It is significant that these benefits were initially the result, not of Commission regulation to which El Paso had always been subjected, but rather of the competition of a single potential entrant to the market. Thereafter, since Section 4(a) of the Natural Gas Act, 15 U.S.C. § 717c(b) (1964 ed.), prohibits suppliers of natural gas from maintaining preferential and unreasonable rates and Section 5(a), 15 U.S.C. § 717d(a) (1964 ed.), empowers the Commission to set reasonable rates after it has established that the prior rates were unjust, it is probable that at least a portion of the 25 percent drop in selling price enjoyed by this single customer who was the subject of the competition was subsequently extended to other customers of El Paso as well. Thus it appears that the competition and direct regulation would complement each other to the benefit of consumers generally.

"This example demonstrates the important role competition can play as a complementary force in regulated industries. . . .

"In sum, Congress, the Supreme Court, and this Court have concurred in the belief that competition has a role to play in the natural gas industry. Both courts have recognized specific instances where the goals of direct regulation and the antitrust laws have coalesced. This would seem to be increasingly true as the natural gas markets grow, often demanding new facilities because existing pipelines have reached their ultimate capacity. And when new facilities must be built, the competitive advantages afforded by a new entrant might often be more meaningful than any economies of scale which could be attained by permitting the present monopolist, or dominant market force, to construct the new facilities and fulfill the increased demand. Even limited competition would seem to encourage suppliers of natural gas to become more aggressive in proposing new rates and services, and thereby increase the effectiveness of regulation by the Commission."[123]

Here is Judge Wright's lucid, capsule account of the relationship of the antitrust to the regulatory statutes:

"Despite a continuing debate, it appears that the basic goal of direct governmental regulation through administrative bodies and the goal of indirect governmental regulation in the form of antitrust law is the same—to achieve the most efficient allocation of resources possible. For instance, whether a regulatory body is dictating the selling price or that price is determined by a market free from unreasonable restraints of trade, the desired result is to establish a selling price which covers costs plus a reasonable rate of return on capital, thereby avoiding monopoly profits. Another example of their common purpose is that both types of regulation seek to establish an atmosphere which will stimulate innovations for better service at a lower cost. This analysis suggests that the two forms of economic regulation complement each other.

"This theory of complementary regulation appears to be borne out by the Supreme Court cases holding that regulated industries must, to some degree at least, accommodate the antitrust laws. *F.M.C.* v. *Aktiebolaget Svenska Amerika Linien*, 390 U.S. 238 (1968) (ocean carriers); *United Mine Workers* v. *Pennington*, 381 U.S. 657 (1965) (labor union); *United States* v. *El Paso Natural Gas Co.*, 376 U.S. 651 (1964) (natural gas distributors); *United States* v. *Philadelphia National Bank*, 374 U.S. 321 (1963) (banking); *Silver* v. *New York Stock Exchange*, 373 U.S. 341 (1963) (stock exchange); *United States* v. *Radio Corporation of America*, 358 U.S. 334 (1959) (television communication); *Georgia* v. *Pennsylvania R. Co.*, 324 U.S. 439 (1945) (railroads); *United States* v. *South-Eastern Underwriters Ass'n*, 322 U.S. 533 (1944) (insurance); *McLean Trucking Co.* v. *United States*, 321 U.S. 67 (1944) (trucking); *United States* v. *Borden Co.*, 308 U.S. 188 (1939) (agricultural cooperatives). Moreover, the Court has held that even where there are specific statutory exemptions for regulated industries from the antitrust laws, such exemptions are to be very narrowly construed. *See, e.g., California* v. *F.P.C., supra*, 369 U.S. at 485–486; *Maryland & Virginia Milk Producers Ass'n* v. *United States*, 362 U.S. 458 (1960).

"The complementary regulation theory is also supported by congressional directives requiring certain regulatory agencies to enforce portions of the antitrust laws.* The Federal Power Commission, while not included on the

---

[123] 399 F. 2d 953, 963–966, 969–970 (1968). In these selections and in those that follow we have eliminated almost all the footnotes.

* "Section 11 of the Clayton Act, 15 U.S.C. § 21(a) (1964 ed.), vests authority to enforce compliance with § 7 by the persons subject thereto

list of enforcement agencies, has been instructed to 'transmit . . . evidence . . . concerning apparent violations of the Federal antitrust laws to the Attorney General.'** Congress has also explicitly advised certain agencies to consider basic issues of competition while regulating the industries within their jurisdiction.† For other agencies the obligation to act in favor of 'public convenience and necessity' has been construed as implying a duty to recognize and weigh traditional antitrust concepts.‡ For example, the Federal Maritime Commission has formulated a rule that acts of shipping conferences interfering with the policies of antitrust laws will be approved only if the conferences can '"bring forth such facts as would demonstrate that the . . . [act] was required by a serious transportation need, necessary to secure important public benefits or in furtherance of a valid regulatory purpose of the Shipping Act."' *F.M.C.* v. *Aktiebolaget Svenska Amerika Linien, supra,* 390 U.S. at 243. In approving this standard the Supreme Court noted that '[b]y its very nature an illegal restraint of trade is in some ways "contrary to the public interest."' *Id.* at 244. And while the Supreme Court did not say that the F.M.C. was obliged to display the degree of deference for antitrust laws suggested by its rule, the Court did conclude that 'the antitrust test formulated by the Commission is an appropriate refinement of the statutory "public interest" standard.' *Id.* at 246.

"This is not to suggest, however, that regulatory agencies have jurisdiction to determine violations of the antitrust laws. *See California* v. *F.P.C., supra,* 369 U.S. at 490; *United States* v. *Radio Corporation of America, supra,* 358 U.S. at 350 n.18; *National Broadcasting Co.* v. *United States,* 319 U.S. 190, 223–224 (1943); *Mansfield Journal Co.* v. *F.C.C.,* 86 U.S.App.D.C. 102, 107, 180 F.2d 28, 33 (1950). Nor are the agencies strictly bound by the dictates of these laws, for they can and do approve actions which violate antitrust policies where other economic, social and political considerations are found to be of overriding importance.* In short, the antitrust laws are merely another tool which a regulatory agency employs to a greater or lesser degree to give 'understandable content to the broad statutory concept of the "public interest."' *F.M.C.* v. *Aktiebolaget Svenska Amerika Linien, supra,* 390 U.S. at 244. But because competitive considerations are an important element of the 'public interest,' we believe that in a case such as this the Commission was obliged to make findings related to the pertinent antitrust policies, draw

"'in the Interstate Commerce Commission where applicable to common carriers subject to the Interstate Commerce Act, as amended; in the Federal Communications Commission where applicable to common carriers engaged in wire or radio communication or radio transmission of energy; in the Civil Aeronautics Board where applicable to air carriers and foreign air carriers subject to the Civil Aeronautics Act of 1938; in the Federal Reserve Board where applicable to banks, banking associations, and trust companies; and in the Federal Trade Commission where applicable to all other character of commerce . . .'."
** Section 20(a) of the Natural Gas Act, 15 U.S.C. § 717s(a) (1964 ed.).
† Savings and Loan Holding Company Amend-

ments, *supra* Note 4; Bank Merger Act, 12 U.S.C. § 1828(c) (1964 ed.); Civil Aeronautics Act, 49 U.S.C. § 488(b) (1964 ed.); Interstate Commerce Act, 49 U.S.C. § 5(2)(c) (1964 ed.).
‡ *F.M.C.* v. *Aktiebolaget Svenska Amerika Linien,* 390 U.S. 238, 243–246 (1968); *California* v. *F.P.C.,* 369 U.S. 482, 484–485 (1962); *United States* v. *Radio Corporation of America,* 358 U.S. 334, 351–352 (1959); *National Broadcasting Co.* v. *United States,* 319 U.S. 190, 222–224 (1943).
* *See Seaboard Air Line R. Co.* v. *United States,* 382 U.S. 154 (1965); *Pan American World Airways, Inc.* v. *United States,* 371 U.S. 296 (1963); *McLean Trucking Co.* v. *United States,* 321 U.S. 67 (1944). Also note the exceptions mentioned above which the F.M.C. has written into its policy.

conclusions from the findings, and weigh these considerations along with other important public interest considerations. *Johnston Broadcasting Co.* v. *F.C.C.*, 85 U.S.App.D.C. 40, 46, 175 F.2d 351, 357 (1949). *See also Baltimore & Ohio R. Co.* v. *United States*, 386 U.S. 372, 402–403, 436–437 (1967) (Mr. Justice Brennan concurring); *Scenic Hudson Preservation Conference* v. *F.P.C.*, 2 Cir., 354 F.2d 608 (1965), *cert. denied*, 384 U.S. 941 (1966)."[124]

Competition for Existing Business versus Protectionism. In the pipeline cases discussed so far, the question at issue concerned the proper role of competition in meeting the incremental needs of growing markets. A series of recent cases, involving attempts by one pipeline to take particular customers away from another and by distribution companies or industrial customers to shift from one supplier to another, has posed with even greater clarity the question of whether the FPC ought to protect its chosen instruments from direct invasions of their thitherto exclusive domains. In general, the Commission has in recent years been increasingly sympathetic to such applications, emphasizing that it recognizes no right of pipelines to protection against competition in their geographic markets.[125]

For example, in 1966 the Commission certificated the Southern Natural Gas Company to supply additional requirements of the Chattanooga Gas Company, over the objections of its existing supplier, the East Tennessee Natural Gas Company, on the ground that East Tennessee's competing proposal would have been insufficient to meet the customer's requirements and Southern's rates were the lowest of the several applicants. In so doing, it also invalidated an exclusive-patronage provision in the Chattanooga-East Tennessee contract, to the effect that

"buyer agrees that it will not purchase gas, natural or manufactured, from any source other than Seller, and also that it will not manufacture gas for use or sale, except as expressly authorized by this contract."[126]

Some years earlier, in the *Lynchburg Gas Company* case, the Commission had taken the opposite position, when it upheld the Atlantic Seaboard Corporation's "partial requirements" (PR) rates, imposing a penalty on customers that did not buy exclusively from it. The FPC had justified that policy on the ground that when customers desert their historic suppliers they leave a heavier burden of fixed charges to be recovered from the ones that remain. The Circuit Court of Appeals overturned that decision, pointing out that there was no evidence in the record of the extent to which the full requirements customers of the Columbia Gas System (of which Atlantic Seaboard is a part) lacked access themselves to second sources of supply; and that the Commission had not considered to what extent any loss of sales to partial requirements customers might be made up by additional sales to others, thus rendering higher rates to the residual patrons unnecessary.[127]

---

[124] 399 F. 2d 953, 959–961 (1968). See also Sections 7(e) and 7(g) of the Natural Gas Act, p. 113, note 1, above.

[125] For earlier illustrations of a similar attitude, see Koplin, *op. cit.*, 359, 361–403; Nelson Lee Smith, "Federal Power Commission and Pipeline Markets: How much Competition?" *Columbia Law Rev.* (April 1968), LXVIII: 667–676.

[126] *Chattanooga Gas Company* v. *East Tennessee Natural Gas Company*, Opinion No. 494, 35 FPC 917 (1966). See also *Transcontinental Gas Pipeline Corporation et al.*, Opinion No. 493, 35 FPC 902 (1966) and Smith, *op. cit.*, 678–679.

[127] *Lynchburg Gas Co.* v. *F.P.C.*, 336 F. 2d 942 (1964).

On remand, the Commission took its newer, more clearly procompetitive line, holding that Columbia had not provided substantial evidence of its need for such a rate.[128] In upholding this later decision, the Circuit Court emphasized the appropriateness of the effort to obtain some of the benefits of competition "as an important and effective tool in increasing economic efficiency and quality of service."[129] Judge Harold Leventhal's judicious decision recognized the possibility of offsetting considerations—"a cross-current appears when cheap gas to one group of consumers results in higher prices to another" (*Ibid.*)—but pointed out that it was the function of the Commission to consider

"the nature and extent of economic consequences that may warrant protection of a historical supplier, and full requirements customers dependent on it, from the impact of competition, from a second source of supply—from competition that the Commission must determine serves the public interest. . . .

"The point is, however, that a policy favoring effective competition necessarily brings with it the reality of economic pinch, present or threatened. The presence of a second seller means that the historic supplier loses out on sales it would have otherwise had—assuming the same ardor in promoting sales in a non-competitive setting. It is through the enhanced efforts made by the supplier in response to such pressure that competition reaps its benefits. The hard problem then is not whether competition may hurt but rather where and how to draw the lines of acceptable range of competition and hurt, in response to the economic characteristics and interrelationships of the industry that require regulation in the first place." *Ibid.*

Similarly, in 1967 and 1968, the FPC certificated a second pipeline to serve distribution companies in the District of Columbia, Maryland and Virginia, which had turned to the new entrant in order to take advantage of its lower commodity rates;[130] permitted the City of Hamilton, Ohio, Municipal Gas Distribution System to shift its purchases to a new supplier, at a markedly lower price;[131] and acceded to the request of the Municipal Distribution System of the City of Corinth, Mississippi, that it order a reluctant Tennessee Gas Pipeline Company to establish a direct physical connection with the City's facilities and supply it with gas at rates more favorable than the ones charged by its previous supplier.[132] All of these decisions were upheld in the Courts.

---

[128] One factor making it easier for the Commission to justify its new determination was that the Columbia companies had in the interim filed restructured tariffs, drastically tilting rates from the old Atlantic Seaboard formula in such a way as to impose the preponderant portion of the System's fixed costs on the demand charge. This meant that the losses of revenues from *commodity* charges when partial requirements customers shifted their patronage would no longer force the pipeline to increase its rates to the remaining customers in order to recover all of its fixed costs. See the discussion of the Atlantic Seaboard formula at pp. 98–100, Volume 1.

[129] *Atlantic Seaboard Corporation et al. v. Federal Power Commission, et al.*, 404 F. 2d 1268, 1272 (1968).

[130] *Atlantic Seaboard Corporation v. Federal Power Commission et al.*, 397 F. 2d 753 (1968).

[131] The *Cincinnati Gas & Electric Company et al. v. Federal Power Commission, et al.*, 389 F. 2d 272 (1968). Cert. was denied by the U. S. Supreme Court, October 14, 1968.

[132] *Alabama–Tennessee Natural Gas Company et al.*, Opinion No. 534, 38 FPC 1069 (1967), sustained in *Alabama–Tennessee Natural Gas Company v. Federal Power Commission*, 417 F. 2d 511 (1969). Certiorari denied February 24, 1970. This case had the interesting feature that the customer's application was opposed by the new supplier as

In view of our repeated emphasis on the importance of competition as a supplement to regulation, it might appear churlish to express some dissatisfaction with the foregoing series of decisions. And yet it is difficult to emerge from reading them with full confidence that they have adequately appraised the limited ways in which competition can function in this industry and the secondary consequences of permitting it to do so in the selective manner that they authorize. Its benefits are almost invariably identified with the fact that particular customers—the Washington Gas Light Company or the Cities of Hamilton, Corinth or Lynchburg—will be able to obtain gas at lower rates. (It should be pointed out, however, that the competition between Atlantic Seaboard on the one hand and Transco on the other for the patronage of the first of these apparently produced another important benefit: "As a result of Transco's proposals, Seaboard reduced its rate and introduced a winter service that afforded pipeline storage."[133]) These savings to the successful customers have been great: they presumably would have to have been, to justify the effort of finding another supplier, investing, as was required in some instances, in additional facilities to connect up with him and contesting their right to shift before the Power Commission and in the Courts.[134]

But the FPC has not typically set forth convincing general economic rationalizations of its decisions, taking into account all their relevant effects, direct and indirect. To be sure, it was required in each case to weigh the injuries that the aggrieved pipelines claimed they would suffer from the loss of business and the possibility that this would force higher rates on their remaining customers. But in most instances, it rather lightly dismissed these countervailing considerations by pointing out that only a small percentage

---

well as the supplanted one. The City's previous exclusive supplier, Alabama–Tennessee, had been buying the gas in question from Tennessee Gas. So the City was asking the FPC to force the latter company thereafter to supply it directly rather than indirectly, so as it give it substantially more favorable rates. The Commission acceded, ordering Tennessee to supply the City's incremental requirements until January 31, 1970, when its contract with Alabama–Tennessee was to expire, and all its requirements thereafter. The basic issue here was the same as in the historic *Shrewsbury* decision (see note 85, Chapter 2, above). In both instances, the FPC ordered a private supplier to render service to a municipal distribution company directly rather than, as previously, through an intermediary.
[133] *Atlantic Seaboard Corporation v. FPC, et al.*, 397 F. 2d 753, 757 (1968). Both the Washington Gas Light Company and Commonwealth Natural Gas contended before the Commission that, because of the extremity of the seasonal fluctuation in demand for their gas and their inability to sell large quantities of interruptible gas because of the absence of heavy industrial users in their market area, they had urgent need for storage service, which Seaboard had been unwilling to supply. *Columbia Gulf Transmission*

Company, et al., Opinion No. 512, 37 FPC 118, 128–130 (1967). An important inducement for Washington to turn to Transco was that the latter company offered it winter sales of gas from its storage capacity. Competition seems to have played an important role here in overcoming the alleged reluctance of pipelines to substitute storage for pipeline capacity. See pp. 99–100, Volume 1 and p. 51, Chapter 2, above.
[134] The demand charge from Alabama–Tennessee to the City of Corinth was $2.69; the corresponding rate at which the Commission directed Tennessee to provide the city service was $1.95; the respective commodity charges were 24.29¢ and 20.44¢ per Mcf. 38 FPC 1069, 1073 note 2 (1967). In the case of the City of Hamilton, Texas Gas Transmission, the successful applicant, had offered the city a commodity charge of 22.22¢ per Mcf; the best counter offer by Cincinnati Gas & Electric, from whom Hamilton proposed to cease purchasing, was 30.5¢ In consequence, the City demonstrated that it would be able to generate substantial additional industrial sales, attracting new industry into the community, and raise its load factor from 33 to an estimated 57 percent. 389 F. 2d 272, 273–274 (1968).

of the pipelines' total sales would be lost and that loss would readily be made good by growth in other sales. But this was hardly a sufficient appraisal of the total consequences: as the Commission itself recognized in the *City of Corinth* case, for example,

"We are not unmindful of the fact that A–T's growth would be even greater were it allowed to keep the Corinth load and that, as a result, its customers might enjoy some additional economies. But we would be derelict in our duty if we were to ignore the immediate and measurable benefits to Corinth on such a theoretical and speculative loss to other A–T customers. Such a rationale would inevitably bind a customer to its existing supplier, thus effectively preclude the realization of the fruits of competition."[135]

This reasoning is not necessarily incorrect. But a satisfying economic appraisal would clearly attempt to answer such questions as: how did it happen that one supplier was able to offer rates on this particular business so much more favorable than its competitors? To what extent was it because one line happened to traverse market territories that gave it a much more favorable load factor than the other?[136] Or because a large customer (like the cities of Corinth and Hamilton) was simply circumventing an intermediary supplier? In these events, what was the net, ultimate effect of the loss of this particular business likely to be on all remaining customers of the deserted supplier—not just absolutely (would their rates have to be raised?) but relatively (how would their rates behave over time relative to those secured by the customers that succeeded in shifting)? What are the merits of permitting certain customers, who happen to be in a position to shift their patronage, to receive the benefits of competitively reduced rates and not others? Do we have here an illustration of the inescapably, and perhaps undesirably, discriminatory character of the kind of limited price competition that alone is possible among public utilities? If not, what will be the

---

[135] 38 FPC 1069, 1076 (1967).

[136] This is the explanation offered by the Trial Examiner of Transco's ability to offer the lower rates that seduced Washington Gas Light and Commonwealth Natural away from Atlantic Seaboard. Apparently the difference was attributable principally to differences in (1) company policy—

"whereas Seaboard had traditionally restricted boiler fuel sales in order to protect its firm service (particularly for domestic use), the newer Transco system had promoted large interruptible loads, including boiler fuel gas for electric generation"—

and (2) rate structure, reflecting once again the historic Atlantic Seaboard formula, which arbitrarily inflated the commodity charge. Smith, *op. cit.*, 685. The Examiner would have denied the Transco application on this account, as would have Smith himself. See the note immediately following. But, as we shall conclude, these facts would not necessarily justify this conclusion. On the contrary, whatever the reasons for the difference in costs of pipelines A and B,

the economic presumption would be in favor of having the business go to the lower-cost supplier. See pp. 170–171, below.

In a private communication Mr. J. David Mann has argued eloquently the infeasibility and irrelevance of the Commission's investigating the causes of the higher rates of the pipeline losing the business:

"I shudder to think what kind of record an imaginative and obstructive lawyer or group of lawyers might compile on that subject. . . . I would hate to undertake the task of proving any pipeline to be inefficient and unreasonably 'high-cost' in its operation and then also prove that its present plight was not of its own doing before I could get a less expensive supply of gas from some other pipeline. . . . If his rates are high and apt to remain so, what real weight should the reason for their being high have in a case involving someone's efforts to obtain gas at the lowest reasonable rates? I should think little or none."

I am much indebted to Mr. Mann for his criticisms of this section.

position of the Commission when the other large customers come around whenever their long-term supply contracts expire, and insist on being accorded the same privilege of shifting?[137] The Commission seems to have given little formal consideration to these possibilities, at least as far as its written opinions show.[138] On the other hand, the position of the critics of these decisions seems also lacking in clarity. Smith points to the estimate that Atlantic Seaboard's loss of some of the business of its Maryland, District of Columbia, and Virginia distribution companies would cut its projected growth rate from 7 percent to 2 percent a year; but this would impose a burden on the remaining customers only if it could be demonstrated that it would result inescapably in a sacrifice of economies of scale in future capacity expansions by the entire Columbia System of which it is a part. As we have already suggested, economies of scale in pipeline transmission taper off sharply after a point; and against any loss of future potential economies, if the increments to one system's capacity are smaller rather than larger, would have to be weighed the corresponding benefit accruing to the successful competitors. Smith also emphasizes Atlantic's competitive handicaps stemming from its poorer load factor; but he recognizes that this was at least in part because the commodity rate in the company's pre-1965 rate schedules contained a substantial contribution to fixed charges. Not surprisingly, therefore, it was base-load sales that the pipeline lost to Transco; it was to take advantage of that supplier's much lower commodity charges that the distribution companies proposed to transfer their patronage. They planned

---

[137] The one strong objection, along these lines, was formulated by the Presiding Examiner in the *Columbia Gulf Transmission* (and Atlantic Seaboard) case (*op. cit.*, note 133, above). Here is the way his views are seen by former Commissioner Smith, who agrees strongly with them:

"He characterized Transco's position as an 'attempted foray directly into Atlantic Seaboard's market with a lower unit cost of service due primarily to its relatively high load factor operations, with which Atlantic Seaboard, which necessarily carries on substantially lower load factor business, cannot compete'. . . . He continued:

"'Although there still may be room in the natural gas business for competition, the rates of pipelines must continue to be based on cost of service tied to a depreciated original cost base, not competition. This means the greater the loss of business by one pipeline to another, the higher will be the unit cost of service of the pipeline having its business syphoned away.'

"The Examiner saw this as resulting in a vicious circle, with the customers playing off one pipeline against another, to their immediate advantage but to the detriment of Seaboard and its other customers. Looking to the future, he noted (i) that since 'Transco can now undersell Atlantic Seaboard, there is every reason to believe that it will always be able to do so' and (ii) that '[t]he Commission would, to be consistent, have to let other customers of Atlantic Seaboard, able and desiring to do so, also obtain their future requirements from Transco'. . . ." *Op. cit.*, 684–685. See also the Concurring Opinion in this case of Commissioner Carver and his concurrence also in the *City of Corinth* case, *op. cit.*, raising similar questions.

[138] "As to long-term effects, Seaboard contends that the loss of sales in view of its lack of storage will result in converting Columbia Gulf to a winter design system with idle capacity and higher costs. As costs increase, it argues, a vicious circle will develop by which Seaboard's customers will try to obtain an increasing proportion of their requirements from Transco. There is nothing in the record to support these speculations. We have already noted how Seaboard's lower rates make sales expansions likely. In any case, however, these problems are not before us. We shall consider any future proposals to divert load from the Columbia system on the basis of the record then before us. Such a record will show the proposed diversion in the light of the most recent information on Columbia's markets. Here the possible losses of market, which are subject to our control, should not prevent us from approving Transco's present proposal with immediate benefits accruing to Washington, Commonwealth and their customers." *Columbia Gulf Transmission Company*, 37 FPC 118, 128 (1967).

no reduction in their purchases from Atlantic Seaboard under its demand charges. As long, therefore, as that charge was framed to follow peak-responsibility principles, this loss of business would involve no loss in the contribution to the pipeline's fixed, capacity costs that would have to be recouped from its other customers. There seems no economic justification for protecting an economically inefficient rate structure against the competitive inroads that it itself invited. On the contrary, it was the prospect of competition itself that forced Seaboard to introduce the above mentioned corrections in its rates.[139]

If a regulated company loses some business that has been bringing in revenues greater than its directly avoidable costs, it is important to bear in mind, that the burden falls, at least in the first instance, on its own profits, not on its other customers. Under what circumstances will or should that burden be passed on to the remaining customers? It would be necessary, first, that the pipeline fail to make good the deficiency in contribution to its fixed charges before its next general rate investigation—that it fall so far short of earning a minimum necessary return on equity as to make a persuasive case for rate increases that would not otherwise be justified. In view of the fact that the return on equity of natural gas pipelines has been running above 11 percent recently,[140] in view of the obstacles posed by long-term supply contracts to quick departures of other customers, and in view of the FPC policy of certificating competitive applications only when it appears existing suppliers would suffer no absolute decline in sales, this danger would seem to be remote. The second possibility would be that the line losing the business would on that account be less able to take advantage of scale economies in its subsequent expansions of capacity. We have already offered some reasons for deprecating this possibility, while recognizing, as in the El Paso–Pacific Gas Transmission Company case, that the Commission might well, in such cases, require competing pipelines to plan their capacity expansions jointly, in order to permit them most fully to achieve the available savings.

In view of the danger that competing pipelines may take on business at unremunerative rates in order to expand their rate bases, it is of course necessary for the FPC to satisfy itself that proposed competitive extensions of service are in fact remunerative. But once it has done so and satisfied itself, additionally, that the additions to capacity are taking the fullest possible advantage of potential economies of scale, it would seem it has sufficiently fulfilled its responsibilities. It is of course possible that captive customers will then pay a higher price for their gas than others in a position to take advantage of competitive offers—perhaps because their pipeline suppliers are paying a higher price for their gas, perhaps because they are using higher-cost, inadequately depreciated plant. But as long as they are not additionally injured by the competitive certifications, it would seem that these can have only desirable effects on balance.

---

[139] *Ibid.*, 126.

[140] The median return of 11 leading natural gas pipeline companies sampled by the author was 13.5 percent in 1966 and 13.3 percent in 1967; since some of these companies were diversified, the return on the pipeline business alone could have been somewhat lower. According to the National City Bank, the return of the 233 companies in its general category of electric power, gas, and others was 11.5 and 11.6 percent in these years (see note 76, p. 52, Volume 1, above).

If pipeline A has higher costs than pipeline B, even if for reasons beyond its control, that is surely not a reason for protecting A against B's competition. On the contrary. The efficient price is the marginal cost of the lowest-cost available alternative. Where competition is feasible it is the most effective device for producing that result. And even if it fails to reduce A's rates, it serves the social function of transferring as much as possible of the business to the company that can do it at the lowest social cost. True, problems are created when competition is feasible only in some markets and not in others. But that may merely reflect the fact that it is, truly, more costly to serve the captive customers of A than those to whom B's services are available.[141] Even in unregulated markets, competition is typically selective and discriminatory. But the dissatisfactions to which it gives rise among customers who are not immediate beneficiaries, raising the possibility that others of them, as well, will try to shift to other suppliers and creating opportunities for competitive entry are the instrument by which its benefits are generalized.

In short, the FPC's instincts have probably been sound in opening up gas wholesale markets to a greater measure of competition in these cases. It would seem appropriate to place on the objectors the burden of proof that the remaining captive customers, rather than merely the stockholders of the pipelines that lose business, will in fact be unjustifiably injured. We have seen reason to doubt that this is the usual case.

---

[141] Consider, for example, the case on efficiency grounds for permitting lower rail rates to shippers who can also be served by lower-cost water carriers than to others lacking this alternative, pp. 166–168, Volume 1.

CHAPTER 5

Destructive Competition and the Quality of Service

All economic regulation involves a limitation or suppression of competition, whether by control of entry or of price rivalry or both. This is true of the natural monopolies, as we have seen,[1] as well as of industries where monopoly is far from natural. And in principle all such regulation has the avowed purpose, among others, of assuring a satisfactory quality of service.

But the economic logic and consequences among the industries that were the subject of Chapter 4 are fundamentally different from those that are the subject of the present chapter. The overwhelming consideration among the natural monopolies is the presence of economies of scale and the omnipresent threat of monopolistic exploitation. Among the industries we propose now to examine, it is competition that is the natural state. Economies of scale are sufficiently limited relative to the extent of the market and entry sufficiently easy in the absence of governmental restraints as to make competition entirely feasible. And the preponderant case for regulation is that such competition tends to be excessively intense and it is for *that* reason, rather than the presence of excessive monopoly power, that the quality of service has to be protected by the imposition of governmental restraints.

In this discussion, as throughout our study, the focus is on avowedly *economic* regulation—that explicitly seeks to supplant competition at the core of the market process. We are not directly concerned, that is, with the mere specifications of product standards or the occupational licensure that purport only to set objective or physical standards of performance or qualification for practice, without determining how many suppliers there ought to be or who they should be or at what price they should sell.[2]

---

[1] See especially pp. 116–119, Chapter 4, above.
[2] We have already referred to the widespread use of occupational licensing as a means of protecting unwary buyers; and we have also described its perversion into an instrument for raising barriers to entry and protecting practitioners of a wide variety of trades from unwanted competition. And we have distinguished that kind of regulation in principle—however close they may come in practice—from the economic regulation that is the subject of these volumes. See pp. 1–2, 8–9, Volume 1, and 5–6, above. On the other hand, we shall draw on that experience as well as that of the regulated industries proper, where it helps illuminate the applicable economic principles and tendencies.

THE THEORY AND PREREQUISITES OF DESTRUCTIVE COMPETITION

What is the theory here? Why might competition prove to be excessive *from the standpoint of the consumer*?[3]

The major prerequisites are fixed or sunk costs that bulk large as a percentage of total cost; and long-sustained and recurrent periods of excess capacity. These two circumstances describe a condition in which marginal costs may for long periods of time be far below average total costs.[4] If in these circumstances the structure of the industry is unconcentrated—that is, its sellers are too small in relation to the total size of the market to perceive and to act on the basis of their joint interest in avoiding competition that drives price down to marginal cost—the possibility arises that the industry as a whole, or at least the majority of its firms, may find themselves operating at a loss for extended periods of time.

Actually, the history of the industries that are generally believed to be subject to destructive competition in the absence of government intervention has not been one of continuous depression. On the contrary, it has been a record of unusually great instability of prices and producer incomes, in both the long and the short-run. And the fundamental cause of this instability is the inelasticity of supply of most of these products.[5] As demand has increased —for example, in wartime or in the upswing of a business cycle—supply has been unresponsive in the short run: it takes several years to develop a coal mine; expanded exploratory effort for crude oil does not instantly produce

---

[3] It is obvious that it could be—indeed typically is—excessive from the standpoint of the seller. This distinction, while obvious, is worth emphasizing in the present context. All competition is "destructive" of the equity of the individual businessman who is subjected to it. That is why businessmen who will rarely (at least in the United States) declare opposition to competition as a general practice will ordinarily hasten to express their objection to competition that is "destructive," "excessive," or "cutthroat," and it is ordinarily difficult to see what price competition they would not so characterize.

[4] As J. M. Clark has pointed out, the feasibility and stability of pure competition depend on the circumstance of increasing marginal costs, both short- and long-run. The latter means that the presence of numerous firms is consistent with efficiency. And the former, that industry demand will ordinarily be intersecting a rising industry marginal cost curve at a point that will for most, or for a sufficiently large number of firms be at or above their average total costs as well (see Figure 1, p. 74 of Volume 1.) But if, as he argues is typically the case in manufacturing, the average variable cost curve (hence the marginal cost) is horizontal up to 90 or even 100 percent of capacity operations and demand fluctuates widely over the cycle, pure competition would drive price below average total cost for most producers most of the time. Moreover, as we

pointed out in Chapters 3 and 4 of Volume 1, it would subject price to wide fluctuations as demand alternatively reached and fell short of the limits of capacity—which would tend to be restricted sufficiently to insure such a result, in order that minimum necessary profits were earned over the cycle. This entire discussion draws heavily on the writings of Clark, notably his *Studies in the Economics of Overhead Cost* (Chicago: Univ. of Chicago Press, 1923), Chapter 21; "Toward a Concept of Workable Competition," in Amer. Econ. Ass'n., *Readings in the Social Control of Industry*, 452–475; and *Competition as a Dynamic Process* (Washington: The Brookings Institution, 1961), 32–34, 58–60, and 120–123.

[5] The demand for some of them has been subject to unusually great fluctuation as well, in transitions from peace to war and back again, or over the business cycle. This has been true of copper, tin, and perhaps bituminous coal. But the demand for these products has been no more unstable than for steel, automobiles, or the services of the construction industry; and the demand for cotton textiles, sugar, coffee, tea, milk, and agricultural products generally—all of which have been subject to violent price fluctuations over time—has surely been more stable than the average, not less. The fundamental cause of price instability in all these cases, therefore, must be sought on the supply side.

additional production capacity; several years must elapse before newly planted rubber trees begin to add to supply; and there is no way of speeding up the biological processes on which expansion of milk supplies depends. In consequence, output of most of these products tends to expand far less than the average in periods of increasing demand—for example, during wartime—and their prices tend therefore to rise much more, as demand rises along a sharply upwardly sloping short-term supply curve. But entry into most of these industries is easy and capacity does finally respond to the incentive created by sharply increasing prices, though with a long delay reflecting the long incubation period between the decision to expand capacity and its emergence.

The "problem" of bituminous coal, agriculture, natural rubber, sugar, oil, milk, coffee, copper, and tin then emerges when the additional capacity becomes available and demand either ceases to grow as rapidly as before or declines; and the industries find themselves with excess capacity. This excess has been inflated, in many cases, by unusually great technological progress, as in the case of agriculture; by the rapid expansion of output in new, lower-cost areas, as in the case of rubber and sugar in the 1920s and 1930s; by the emergence of substitutes—oil for coal, synthetic fibers, plastics, and rubbers for the products of agriculture and plantations; by the growth of output in lower-income areas—textiles and coal in the U. S. South, textiles in the underdeveloped countries of the world. All of these make it possible for entry to continue and the supply curve to move to the right even in the presence of substantial excess capacity and declining incomes experienced by existing firms.

It is the long-delayed expansion of capacity, accentuated by the factors just described, that makes for a "sick industry." The other necessary ingredient is independent competitive behavior. If producers were few or were made to act in concert by government regulation, they would cut back their utilization of capacity (as well as refrain from adding to it), in order to avoid "spoiling the market"—unless, that is, they thought total industry demand was sufficiently price-elastic to make lower prices more profitable than sustained prices for all of them. That is to say, it is competition and a steeply inclined marginal cost function that makes supply inelastic down to the level of each individual firm's out-of-pocket costs, in the face of declining prices and shrinking profit margins; and it is this inelasticity of supply, in the presence of excess capacity, that makes the industry "sick"—in the sense that all or the preponderant proportion of firms in it are failing to cover their total costs, including a "normal" return on investment.[6]

Since a reduction of price below ATC of a sufficient number of firms is

---

[6] Thus, interestingly, aggregate capacity in a "sick industry" is typically not *idle*, and it is the failure to keep it idle that makes it sick. In what sense, then, is it excessive? In the sense that it is more capacity than can be supported at "normal" rates of return. See Lloyd G. Reynolds, "Cutthroat Competition," *Amer. Econ. Rev.* (December 1940), XXX: 736–738. It should be obvious that there is no clear, objective boundary line between a sick and a well industry. Even in the most prosperous of times, there will be firms in competitive industries that earn far less than "normal" returns; and even in the depths of an industry's depression, there will be efficient operators earning entirely acceptable profits. Indeed, as we have already suggested, one of the continuing sources of the "agricultural problem" in the United States (as it was of the textile or bituminous coal industry problems in the 1920s and 1930s) has been the continued expansion of investment and capacity by new and highly successful firms, using the most modern technology.

precisely the way in which a competitive market is supposed to operate in the presence of excess capacity,[7] why might such a circumstance, admittedly injurious to the profits of the sellers in the industry, also pose any threat to the welfare of its customers?

One possible reason is that the pressures of declining or inadequate revenues might force the curtailment of many postponable expenditures that the consumer would in the long run be better off having continued. This might be true of the repair, maintenance, and keeping-in-being of capacity that the market will in the long run wish to have retained and that can be retained at lower cost than it can be resurrected when demand justifies it;[8] research;[9] and the continued offer of temporarily unremunerative services. The economist would entertain some skepticism about this general argument. If, in fact, the capacity will eventually be required and can be maintained more cheaply than eventually resurrected, on proper discounting of the future costs of following the latter course, then, it might be anticipated, it would pay the businessmen to make these investments, for that is what they would be—present outlays in anticipation of the future income. The same should be true of research activities; if the anticipated future benefits, properly discounted, exceed the current outlays, it will pay the business to continue making those outlays, no matter how bad his current income statement looks. And if he lacks the necessary funds, it ought to pay him to turn to the capital markets to obtain them. This danger reduces, then, to the possibility either that, because of imperfect foresight, the producer might not see the desirability of maintaining the temporarily unprofitable operations or, because of imperfections of the capital market, he may not be able to raise the funds necessary to sustain the socially desirable investments. But these possibilities are not necessarily to be dismissed. Managers are likely to be much more willing to use internally generated funds for purposes like these than to go to the capital markets, and investors less reluctant to provide funds—or see them provided—in the first way than in the second.[10]

Indeed, destructive competition would be inconceivable except for the presence of market imperfections. In particular, it is the inability of capital

---

[7] Economic efficiency requires that price be set at short-run marginal cost, not average total cost, not only because this gives buyers the correct signals about the marginal opportunity costs of what they are buying, but also because it will tend automatically to restore the proper balance between capacity and demand. It will do so, first, because only as price falls below the variable costs of the higher-cost producers will they be induced to shut down their inefficient plants; and, second, because a reduction in price below the average total cost of new plants will discourage the entry of new capital—except where it *should* enter because its average total costs are less than the average variable costs of plants required to meet the market demand.

[8] For example, the temporary closing of coal mines may result in flooding if pumping is not continued. Simon N. Whitney, *Antitrust Policies* (New York: Twentieth Century Fund, 1958), I: 395. And the abandonment of pumping on marginal or stripper oil wells may result in permanent loss of their reserves. See, for example, Erich W. Zimmermann, *Conservation in the Production of Petroleum* (New Haven: Yale Univ. Press, 1957), 73–76.

[9] *The Wall Street Journal* periodically has survey articles describing how business firms react to a period in which their profits are being squeezed. These reactions include such diverse remedies as use of the mail in place of the long-distance telephone, travel by tourist instead of first-class, and curtailment of research and development activities. Just like other production, dismantling and later reassembling a research operation may in the long run be more costly than continuing it.

[10] See Dennis C. Mueller, "A Theory of Conglomerate Mergers," *Q. Jour. Econ.* (Nov. 1969), LXXXIII: 644–645, drawing on James S. Duesenberry, *Business Cycles and Economic Growth* (New York: McGraw-Hill, 1958), 87–97.

readily (that is, in the short run) to move out of a situation of excessive capacity, once it has become embodied in that capacity, that creates the possibility of gross returns on investment remaining for extended periods of time below the minimum required in the long run to maintain it.[11]

Another reason why unregulated competition might not in these circumstances be desirable is that, as we have pointed out earlier in considering the ideal behavior of public utility rates, wide fluctuations in price may be no more in the interest of consumers than sellers; they make long-range planning difficult and force a shift in attention from productive efficiency to buying and selling, to speculating and avoiding speculating on price. Price fluctuations are a product of market imperfections and they, in turn, promote uncertainty and inefficiency.

The other prominent imperfection that may make unrestricted competition particularly injurious to consumers is their own limited ability to judge the quality of products and hence to keep it at acceptable levels even when they have a wide range of competitive suppliers to choose from. The quality of service in public utility industries has many dimensions: not just its physical specifications but its reliability, safety, regularity, frequency, and the financial responsibility of its purveyors. A good deal of the case for regulation is the importance of assuring that these services meet acceptable standards in these various respects in the presence of monopoly: consider the extreme importance of having an assured and regular supply of electricity meeting fairly precise voltage requirements, of gas during the heating season, of regular, reliable, and safe telephone and transportation service and honest security brokers and stock exchanges protected against manipulation by insiders at the expense of outside investors. This kind of consumer protection can be equally necessary when price competition is very intense. The decline in price to average variable costs can lead to a skimping on safety, reliability, and frequency of service that consumers may have difficulty in detecting promptly.[12] The greater that difficulty, the greater the temptation of competitors to cut corners, since the competitor that skimps does not at once lose all his customers, while the one that scrupulously maintains quality may be inadequately rewarded for the higher costs of doing so.[13]

---

[11] As we shall see, the same role may be played by the immobility of labor. In fact, the most familiar historic instances of destructive competition for extended periods of time were situations in which it was the inelasticity in the supply of labor to the industry in question, consequent on labor immobility, that made the depression of the industries so deep, so extended and so injurious to the people dependent on it.

[12] That is, the consumer may be deceived when he turns to what looks like a cheaper source of supply: a discount house may turn out to give inadequate service on the appliance he buys from it; the tramp freighter or motor carrier turns out after the fact to be unreliable, to carry inadequate insurance against loss of cargo, and so on. For justifications of restrictions of competition essentially on the ground that uncontrolled rivalry would be highly imperfect, see Marx, *International Shipping Cartels*, Chapters 2, 12, 14;

and P. W. S. Andrews and Frank A. Friday, *Fair Trade, Resale Price Maintenance Re-examined* (London: Macmillan, 1960), 17–22.

[13] It might appear that, if consumers cannot indeed detect deteriorations in quality, it would pay even a monopolist, not just an unethical competitor, to try to cut costs in this manner. But monopolists who expect to be in that line of business for a long time and whose long-run profitability is dependent on the industry's general reputation with consumers will have greater means and incentive to maintain quality than individual smaller competitors, with a shorter time perspective and less of a concern about the industry's continuing reputation with consumers. What we have here, in the competitive case, is the possibility of a deterioration of performance because of (1) imperfections of the capital market—that is the real meaning of the "shorter time perspective" of smaller firms—and

Even if there is a danger of unregulated competition producing an unwanted deterioration in the quality of service, it does not necessarily follow that direct restraints on entry and price competition are the proper remedy. Legally prescribed quality standards could conceivably give consumers sufficient protection without the necessity for suppressing competition in other respects as well. Still, the suppression of competition may make it easier to enforce these other standards, for a number of reasons. First, the fewer the number of sellers, the easier it is to inspect them and to enforce whatever rules are set. Second, if entry is curtailed, the license itself is a valuable privilege, as we shall see. The firms permitted to operate will therefore have a sufficient financial stake in keeping their licenses to make them hesitant about risking cancellation for failure to perform adequately.[14] Third, because the license is valuable, regulatory commissions can require the favored licensees to assume financially burdensome service obligations that would otherwise be unprofitable for them. The protected franchisee becomes a chosen instrument for serving public purposes—maintaining regular schedules in the off-season, or serving unprofitable routes, or assuming the risks of maintaining an orderly market.[15] Finally the mere limitation in the number of firms and reduction in their turnover will itself give each of

---

(2) externalities: since the monopolist *is* the industry, any consumer discontent that results from an adulteration in the quality of service will eventually reflect injuriously on himself; individual competitors, in contrast, may in effect be passing some of those costs of consumer dissatisfaction off to the other firms in the industry.

Another way in which destructive competition may produce deterioration of service is by promoting labor unrest, as the pressures of declining prices and shrinking profits force companies to try to cut corners on wages, safety precautions, and other conditions of employment.

[14] Obviously, the more perfunctory and routine the renewal of licenses, the less effective this particular incentive will be. See the discussion of the policies of the Federal Communications Commission respecting the renewal of broadcast licenses, pp. 89–91, above.

[15] The fixing of minimum commission rates by the membership of organized security exchanges is defended on this last ground. See pp. 199–200, below. We consider at various points elsewhere the question of whether imposition of these unprofitable service obligations is economically justified.

One ironic illustration of this kind of rationalization is provided by New York State's former alcoholic beverage control law, which was supposed, it asserted, "to promote both temperance in the consumption of alcoholic beverages and respect for and obedience to law," by limiting the number of retail outlets and imposing compulsory retail price maintenance. [Quotation from the statute by Anthony M. Radice, "The New York State Liquor Market: The Rocky Road to Competition," *Cornell Law Rev.* (November 1968), LIV: 113–114.] Between 1950 and 1958, a period of sharply increasing state income and population, the State Liquor Authority issued no new licenses. In consequence, the median purchase price of transferred stores rose from $19,490 to $39,503: the store carried the license with it, provided the SLA approved the transfer. Harvey J. Levin, *Some Economic and Regulatory Aspects of Liquor Store Licensing in New York State: A Summary of Research*, (New York: State Moreland Commission on the Alcoholic Beverage Control Law, 1963), 17. It is probably true that the penalty of losing such valuable franchises made licensees hesitant about violating such regulations as the prohibition of sales to minors. But giving government employees the privilege of issuing them was a strange way of promoting "respect for and obedience to law": the predictable result was that some officials accepted bribes for issuing licenses or approving transfers. See *New York Times*, April 19, 1963, 1, and *ibid.*, May 24, 1963, 1. As for the compulsory resale price maintenance, it would probably occur only to an uncouth economist that the effectiveness of a prohibition of retail price competition in promoting temperance would depend on the elasticity of demand and that there was something questionable about using a device that would probably be much more effective for the poor than for the rich.

them a stronger incentive to take the long view of its profit-increasing activities and cultivate the consumer goodwill that would be jeopardized by skimping on service quality.[16]

THE THEORY APPLIED

The possibility must be conceded, then, that competition may in certain circumstances be excessively strong and that restrictions on it can produce an improved performance. The questions that must be asked in each regulatory situation are (1) to what extent those circumstances actually prevail or would prevail if controls were removed, (2) to what extent deterioration of service could instead be prevented merely by imposing standards of quality, safety, financial responsibility, and the like, and (3) whether such additional benefits as might be secured by limitations on entry and price rivalry are greater than the benefits that freer competition brings.

The Case of Trucking

The reader will recognize that arguments like the ones just summarized were used to justify passage of the Motor Carriers Act of 1935.[17] There seems no reason to doubt that the results of unregulated competition had not been satisfactory up to that time. The following is a representative appraisal:

"there was then a surplus of transportation of all kinds. Competition became destructive. Large numbers of small operators were engaging in motor transportation. Their rates were not published. Many of the smaller operators were not aware of the costs of doing business and they made such rates as seemed required to secure traffic. Many of them failed and went out of business, but others promptly took their places. There was no rate structure, variations in individual rates were wide, rates were constantly changing, charges to various shippers using the same carrier were often different, and the service was neither stable nor reliable. Shippers found it increasingly difficult to do business with motor carriers because of the unreliability of service and the financial irresponsibility of many of the carriers, and they were distressed at fluctuating rates and differential treatment."[18]

Does Trucking Pass the Tests? But—following our outline of the proper questions to ask—does trucking have the economic attributes of an industry subject to destructive competition? It would be difficult to find one less qualified. The first requirement is a low ratio of variable to total costs for extended periods of time (recall that in the indefinitely long run all costs are variable): since it is variable costs that fix the floor below which price cannot go (at least not for very long), a low ratio of variable to total costs

---

[16] See note 13, this chapter, above.
[17] See pp. 5–6, 14, Chapter 1, above. He will recall that there were other motives as well, notably the desire to protect the railroads and their value-of-service freight rate structure from increasingly intense motor competition, and the desire of the truckers themselves, backed by the Teamsters' Union, for protection against the competition that had become increasingly intense during the Great Depression.

[18] Marvin L. Fair and Ernest W. Williams, Jr., *Economics of Transportation*, rev. ed. (New York: Harper & Bros., 1959), 488. For a similar view, see Donald V. Harper, *Economic Regulation of the Motor Trucking Industry by the States* (Urbana: Univ. of Illinois Press, 1959), 27–28, 39, 40. For a contemporary view, see the report of the Federal Coordinator of Transportation, op. cit., note 8, Chapter 1, above.

means that price can for extended periods of time fall far enough below average total costs for a large enough proportion of firms in the industry to threaten its ability to provide continued service. In the case of railroads, costs that vary over even as long as five years with the volume of traffic are probably less than half of the total; and even over the much longer run, a period long enough to permit changes in the physical plant, they amount perhaps to 70 to 75 percent of the total.[19] For the motor-carrier industry, in contrast, variable costs amount to at least 90 percent of total costs in the very short run and close to 100 percent over a very short span of years. This same sharp contrast is reflected also in the respective operating ratios of the two industries—the ratio of operating expenses to total revenues: these have since World War II run between 75 and 80 percent for the railroads and between 95 and 97.5 percent for trucks.[20]

These differences are attributable, primarily, to the fact that the railroads have had to construct and maintain their own roadbeds, bridges, and rights-of-way, as well as their elaborate and expensive terminal facilities. The trucks, in contrast, pay for the roads they travel only as they use them—in excise taxes for motor fuel, annual license fees, tolls, and the like. They pay for them also in excises on their vehicles and tires, but these costs, too, vary largely with the rate at which they are used: the depreciation of trucks and tires is essentially a variable cost. Moreover, the trucks that constitute their principal investment thave three other characteristics that tend to reduce the fixed and increase the variable costs associated with them and diminish the possibilities of persistent excess capacity, which constitute the second major prerequisite of destructive competition. They are short-lived. This makes their depreciation far less subject to obsolescence, which is a function only of time and a fixed cost, and far more a function of the rate of their use, hence a variable cost. It also means that motor-carrier companies are within very short periods of time constantly facing the decision of whether to replace their capital equipment and are in a position therefore to do so only if prices cover average total cost (including, as always, a necessary return on investment). Second, the investment involved in each is comparatively small. The consequence is that truckers can increase their capacity in small increments, thereby greatly diminishing the pervasiveness of excessive capacity. Contrast their situation with that of industries where producers are few and the economies of scale are such that they must build capacity ahead of demand in large lumps.[21] Third, they are mobile. The capacity can, without any

---

[19] These are the authoritative estimates of Ford K. Edwards, and include a 4 percent return on investment as part of the capital costs. For references, see the next footnote. As Locklin points out, the earlier, generally accepted estimate, placing variable costs at only about one-third of the total, was much shorter run in perspective and assumed lower rates of capacity utilization than became common in the World War II and postwar periods. These various ratios of variable to total costs are in some measure arbitrary, since obviously, by definition, the ratio of fixed or variable costs to the total will change with different levels of operation.

[20] This last comparison tends to minimize the difference between the two kinds of carriers. Not all operating expenses are truly variable costs; and total rail revenues have not typically provided a return on the industry's extremely heavy fixed investment even remotely comparable to the return enjoyed by the motor carriers. These various cost data are summarized in Locklin, *op. cit.*, 131–135, 154–156, 318–319, 646–648; Dudley F. Pegrum, *Transportation: Economics and Public Policy* (Homewood: Richard D. Irwin, 1968), 138–142.

[21] See note 25, pp. 135–137, Volume 1.

difficulty at all, be transferred from one market to another; there is no reason, therefore, for excess capacity to hang over any one part of the market for extended periods of time, as long as demand in other markets is growing.

It is difficult to disagree with Pegrum, when he says, flatly: "Competition among motor carriers cannot be ruinous."[22] How, then, could it have been so in 1935? There are at least two ways of explaining. First, the mere fact that variable costs are a high proportion of the total does not necessarily protect an industry against the severe compression of prices and incomes characteristic of destructive competition. Variable costs put a stable floor under prices only if that floor is itself immobile. Suppose, however, that the principal component of those variable costs is the industry's wage bill; and suppose that the workers hired by the industry have no possibility of alternative employment, so that the supply of labor to the industry is completely inelastic on the downside within a wide range. The result will be that the burden of competition will be transmitted directly to wage rates: decreases in final product demand will result in the derived demand for labor moving vertically downward along the rigid labor supply curve, with the industry's depression in this case being transmitted directly into declining wages.[23] The long-extended downward wage-price spiral, with its accompanying labor

---

[22] *Public Regulation of Business* (Homewood: Richard D. Irwin, 1959), 531. An even more striking example is provided by the freight forwarders. The forwarder is a common carrier that contracts with shippers for transporting freight between two points and itself handles the shipment by making its own arrangements with the other common carriers. Generally, forwarders handle small shipments, which they pick up, consolidate, and ship at carload or truckload rates, then break down and distribute to their several destinations. Forwarders utilizing the services of common carriers that are regulated by the ICC are themselves subject to this regulation: in particular, they must be licensed by the Commission. Until 1958, these licenses were freely granted. But in 1957, Congress deleted from the original Enabling Act a provision that prohibited the ICC from denying permits on the sole ground that the applicant would compete with other forwarders. Thereafter, the ICC has subjected such applications to the same kind of stringent tests as it applies to would-be common-carrier truckers (see pp. 14–18, Chapter 1, above). The purported justification for such stringent regulation is the belief that free entry would result in "improvident and wasteful duplication of transportation services and facilities." See Comment, "Intermodal Transportation and the Freight Forwarder," *Yale Law Jour.* (June 1967), LXXVI: 1374, quoting from both the Senate and the House Reports on the 1957 Amendment. As this Comment makes quite clear, the alleged

danger of destructive competition is extremely difficult to credit: it points out, for example, that the capital-output ratio of the ICC-regulated forwarders is less than $\frac{1}{200}$ of that of the railroads. (*Ibid.*, 1375; see also pp. 1367–1368.) The CAB, in contrast, imposes no economic restrictions on entry into the air freight forwarding business, possibly because of its strong statutory commitment to the promotion of air transport. (*Ibid.*, 1369–1371, 1376.) But see note 50, Chapter 6, below.

[23] This was in large measure the way in which the "sickness" of the United States bituminous coal industry in the 1920s and 1930s manifested itself. Even though the variable wage costs accounted for over 60 percent of the total (James B. Hendry, "The Bituminous Coal Industry," in Walter Adams, ed., *The Structure of American Industry, Some Case Studies*, 3rd ed., New York: The Macmillan Co., 1961, 86), it was possible for the average value of bituminous coal at the mine to decline from $3.75 a ton in 1920 to $1.78 in 1929 (U. S. Bureau of the Census, *Historical Statistics of the United States, Colonial Times to 1957*, Washington, 1960, 356), because these variable costs themselves proved to be compressible: between 1923 and 1929, a generally prosperous period in the economy at large, the average hourly wage of coal miners declined from 84.54 to 68.14 cents. *Ibid.*, 93.

To the extent that the labor supply is equally inelastic on the upside, increases in final product demand will of course be similarly converted into corresponding increases in wages.

unrest, a typical feature of destructive competition, thus finds its explanation in the inelasticity of the industry's labor supply.[24]

A similar role was played in the motor-carrier industry during the Depression by the large stock of used trucks overhanging the market. The supply of used machinery (as of scrap metal) tends to be highly inelastic above the cost of reclaiming it or its scrap value. As the Depression wore on, the price of used trucks declined sharply, with the result that anyone who could drive could enter the business in the early 1930s with a minimal investment.[25] Part of the brunt of the destructive competition was therefore borne by the used truck market.

Second, a very large percentage of the economic cost of providing trucking service in those early days of the industry consisted in the return for the labor of the owner-operator, exactly as in the case of the family farm. The return on that labor, like the return on the investment in the truck itself, was a residual; it could be high if the industry was prosperous and could be compressed indefinitely, as long as the owners had no alternative employment, if the industry were depressed. During the Depression, these men had no alternative employment to which to turn; so the supply of their labor to this industry was, once again, completely inelastic. Indeed, with the sharp reductions in industrial employment, large numbers of workers moved into the owner-operation of service stations, farms, trucks, and small grocery stores, so that the supply of labor in these industries actually expanded in the face of declining remuneration.[26]

So the supply of the major inputs into the trucking industry was during the early 1930s either inelastic or even negatively elastic—with decreases in demand being either accompanied by or actually inducing an expansion in the quantity of service offered. This tended to produce the same inelasticity of supply as is imparted in other industries subject to destructive competition by a heavy investment in fixed capital.

There was probably another contributing factor—the overly optimistic anticipations that typically induce excessive entry into a young industry. There is every reason to believe that this condition would have been temporary. As G. Shorey Peterson wisely observed in 1929:

"The unusual intensity and irresponsibility of competition, upon which the whole argument rests, is more the outgrowth of the youth of the industry

---

[24] See Reynolds, *op. cit.*, *Amer. Econ. Rev.* (December 1940), XXX: 744–745. Reynolds explains this downward movement in terms of a failure of these industries fully to exploit their monopsonistic power in labor markets in times of comparative prosperity and their progressive exploitation of that power under the downward pressure of competition on their selling prices in periods of excess capacity. Monopsony is not a necessary part of the process, however; the process could have occurred even in purely competitive labor markets, as the simple consequence of declining end-product demand and the inelasticity of labor supply to the industries affected.

[25] See Note, "Federal Regulation of Trucking:

The Emerging Critique," *Columbia Law Rev.* (March 1963), LXIII: 461.

[26] J. M. Clark contrasts interestingly the organization of the major portion of the economy, in which labor is one hired input and its costs are therefore variable, with the self-employment sector, in which its wage, like the return on capital, is a residual. In the latter circumstance, it is possible for the supply of the product to be not merely inelastic but actually backwardly sloping: decreases in price and in remuneration may induce the owners to put in even longer hours, in hope of maintaining their total income, a situation particularly conducive to destructive competition. See his *Competition as a Dynamic Process*, 174–175.

than of any permanent characteristics which it possesses. Competition is not cut-throat in the same sense as in the other public utility fields; it is rather the result of ignorance and of exaggerated ideas of possible profits. Mortality is high in most new industries. Quite obviously it cannot be permanently true that a field of service is unusually seductive in its appeal to new entrants and exceptionally harsh with those who enter it."[27]

These depressing and destabilizing influences have become greatly attenuated since 1935 and would surely have done so without regulation. The capital investment required to enter the industry, while still low, has increased markedly. Although economies of scale in trucking are comparatively slight, still

"the extremely small firm with the owner, his brother-in-law, and son can no longer compete with the twenty-man firm."[28]

Full employment in the economy generally has cut off the large and inelastic supply of labor to the industry. The workers have organized into a powerful union, which has the effect not only of raising wages but of making the labor supply completely elastic at the established wage level, thereby eliminating the downward compressibility of the most important component of the variable cost floor under price.

Yet, it is often asserted, there remains another possible source of destructive competition in trucking. This is the prevalence of joint costs, arising from the fact that the provision of capacity for transportation in one direction inescapably involves the provision of similar capacity, in fixed proportion, for the return haul. The marginal cost of the return haul, if the trucks are going out in the first direction anyway, are virtually zero, since the trucks must come back in any event, loaded or unloaded. This is another way of saying that even if all the costs of motor carriage were variable in the sense that they varied in direct proportion with mileage, the cost of picking up freight for half of the business—the return haul—are really not variable at all but sunk and have to be incurred whether or not transportation service is actually performed. This means that under competition—so the argument goes—rates on "the" back haul will tend to be driven down toward zero. But what, several observers have asked, if the back haul of carrier A is the front haul of carrier B? Competition between the two of them, with each willing to drop rates on *his* back-haul journey rather than return empty, can

---

[27] "Motor Carrier Regulation and Its Economic Bases," *Q. Jour. Econ.* (August 1929), XLIII: 618.
[28] Meyer *et al.*, *op. cit.*, 216. The authors cite the decline in the number of extremely small firms as an indication of this change: in 1935, 81 percent of the intercity trucking firms had annual revenues below $5,000; in 1951, in contrast, only 28 percent had revenues below $25,000. *Ibid.*, 216–217. On the presence or absence of economies of scale, see *ibid.*, 86–88, and for a survey of other studies, see Locklin, *op. cit.*, 644–645. While accepting the assertions of others that there are no marked economies of scale, George Wilson emphasizes the considerable importance of product differentiation in this industry—of speed, dependability, safety, and responsibility—and points out that "many of these qualitative elements tend to correlate positively with carrier size." "The Nature of Competition in the Motor Transport Industry," *Land Econ.* (November 1960), XXXVI: 388–389. Locklin agrees that large firms may have advantages in this respect over smaller ones. Wilson therefore suggests that there may even be a natural tendency to oligopoly in the industry—an additional reason for doubting the likelihood of destructive competition.

have the effect of pushing the rates on the *other's* "front haul" as well down toward unremunerative levels.[29]

This problem can be characterized in terms that we have used earlier in discussing the implications of the joint and common costs that are prevalent among public utilities: that, characteristically, the unit of production in these industries is greater than the unit of sale.[30] In the present context, the unit of production, almost all of whose costs are variable, would be the round trip; the unit of sale, even assuming that a single transaction would suffice to fill the truck, would be the trip in one direction from one point to another. The variable costs associated with the individual sale, assuming that the round trip was in any case going to be made, could be close to zero.

But the implication that the wide gap between the avoidable costs of the individual sale (for example, the return haul) and the average total costs of the unit of production (the round trip) creates a necessary tendency for unregulated competition to be destructive is unjustified. What we have here, in the simple case of trucks moving only from point A to point B and back, is a pure case of joint product. As we have seen in Chapter 3 of Volume 1, there is a determinate, competitive solution to the prices of two joint products; each of them does have a competitive supply price and the sum of those two marginal cost curves will equal the joint marginal production cost. Where the two prices settle—that is, how the joint costs are distributed—will depend on the respective intensities and elasticities of the two demands; and those equilibrium prices will be equal to the respective marginal *opportunity costs* of the two products.[31] Where one of the products, because of the relatively low elasticity and level of its demand, is definitely a by-product (Figure 2, Chapter 3, Volume 1) that marginal opportunity cost will be zero and the other product will cover all the joint costs. But what if C's by-product is D's principal product and vice versa? To this there are two answers. First, what determines for each company which of its hauls is "back" and which "front"? Clearly, it must be the preponderant flow of traffic. But surely that will tend under competition to be the same direction for all competing sellers.[32]

Second, and more fundamentally, if C's trucks are all going out full in a westward direction and either coming back empty or having to charge less than one-half of the round-trip cost in order to return full, while D's trucks are coming eastward full and have to charge less than average total costs in the return direction, and if competition between the two to fill their trucks pushes their aggregate revenues for the round trip below joint costs, it can only mean that their combined capacities are greater than the combined demands for the joint services justify. The critical question, then, is not the presence or absence of joint costs but whether there is sufficient flexibility

---

[29] See Howard W. Nicholson, "Motor Carrier Costs and Minimum Rate Regulation," *Q. Jour. Econ.* (February 1958), LXXII: 150; also Wilson, *op. cit., Land Econ.* (1960), XXXVI: 389.

[30] See p. 77, Volume 1.

[31] See also note 11, pp. 93–94, Volume 1.

[32] If it were not, competition would tend to make it so. If supplier C obtained a greater contribution to joint costs from A to B traffic and supplier D from B to A traffic, obviously it would

pay C to undercut D in order to get more of the B to A customers and D to do the same thing to get more of the shipments going in the opposite direction. Customers would have corresponding incentives to shift to the carrier accepting the lower rates on their particular service. The end result would be that both carriers would end up with the same "front" and "back" hauls—that is, with their peak and off-peak demands falling at the same times or locations.

in the decision of investors to supply capacity for the joint production to assure that capacity will be properly adjusted to the combined demand so as to permit the combined prices for the joint services to cover joint costs over time. The critical question about the feasibility of competition, in short, remains the elasticity of supply.

After all, certain important parts of the "unit of production" always exceed the unit of sale in every production process involving capital investment. A unit of X produced today is, as far as the cost of providing production capacity is concerned, a joint product with the unit of that product produced tomorrow. Yet, they are typically sold separately. The back-haul problem is therefore in no sense unique. Whether those units sold on different days together make a contribution over and above their separate variable costs sufficient to cover their joint cost depends on the adjustment and adjustability of capacity, over time, to their combined demand. Chronic excessive capacity is by no means inevitable.

The ability of truckers to assure a profitable adjustment of capacity to demand is enormously accentuated by the versatility of this mode of transportation—that is, the versatility it would enjoy if it were not for regulation. Not only can the same trucks carry a variety of items; in addition, a truck that moves from point A to point B is of course in no sense constrained to return to A by the same route. The A–B and B–A services are therefore not truly joint; they need not be supplied in fixed proportions. If rates on one leg of the journey fall, the trucker can vary his product mix by moving along alternative routes. It is only, then, if one can demonstrate some reason to expect chronic excessive capacity in the entire industry, over all routes, that the problem of the back haul could create an inherent tendency toward destructive competition.

The ready adjustability of aggregate trucking capacity, because of its comparatively short life and its ability to increase and decrease in small increments, would seem to make far less likely for this industry than most others such chronic overinvestment in "front-haul" capacity as to force joint revenues below total costs.[33]

There is one other characteristic of the industries one thinks of as having tendencies to destructive competition: their products are typically standardized, standardizable, or homogeneous. The reader can satisfy himself on this point by looking over our earlier list of examples.[34] The consequence of this

[33] "a trucker would not undertake a trip unless his expected revenue for the round trip would at least equal expected cost. The revenue from the first leg of the trip is usually known at the start . . . the return trip, however, may yield various amounts. . . . Since a trucker is faced with a probability function of revenue on his return trip, his realized revenue on any particular round trip may not cover his variable (out-of-pocket) costs. Thus, the situation visualized by Nicholson implies a continuing error in estimating return-trip revenue. Although occasional errors will be made, learning is expected to eliminate the source of error which would cause truckers continually to overestimate their return-trip revenues. In the long run, the market

entry and exit of firms has to be relied upon for the movement toward joint-supply equilibrium." W. Miklius and D. B. DeLoch, "A Further Case for Unregulated Truck Transportation," *Jour. Farm Econ.* (November 1965), XLVII: 937. Nicholson recognizes this corrective tendency, but is not convinced of its sufficiency. *Op. cit.*, 148–152.

[34] On the case of coal, however, see Jacob Schmookler, in Walter Adams, ed., *The Structure of American Industry*, rev. ed. (New York: The Macmillan Co., 1954), 79–81.

Another possible exception is gasoline retailing, where there is important product and service differentiation. But the principal source of price wars here is the sale of surplus gasoline, un-

is that competition can center only on price; and, the product of each firm being completely substitutable for those of other firms, any and all price reductions must be met instantaneously by all competitors. Product differentiation, in contrast, has the effect of insulating firms in some degree from immediate loss of all their customers if they do not precisely meet a competitor's price; it gives them the kind of market niche, a partially protected and identifiable position, that Richard B. Heflebower has identified as the source of market stability or balance.[35] And correspondingly, it provides them with a focus for their competitive endeavors other than price.

As Wilson points out, "A truck journey by any particular carrier" is clearly not "equivalent to that of any other."[36] Because of the many important qualitative aspects of the service—dependability, safety, and responsibility—an unregulated industry would almost certainly not be purely competitive; here, again, is a characteristic that diminishes the dangers of destructive competition.[37]

Would Quality Standards Suffice? The second question we said one ought to ask, when confronted with an argument for regulation in order to preserve the quality of service, is whether deterioration can be forestalled instead merely by imposing general quality standards on all suppliers. With respect to safety, for example

"The basic answer to the [Interstate Commerce] Commission's contentions regarding the need for comprehensive regulation to enforce safety standards is that the two underlying assumptions of its position, viz., that exempt or unregulated carriers have worse safety records than regulated carriers and that carriers with low earnings have inferior safety records, have never been proved."[38]

According to the Supreme Court,

"The conclusion that highway safety may be impaired [by permitting trucks exempt from economic regulation to travel the highways] rests . . . on

---

branded, largely by the very refiners that sell the identical products under their own brands. And the tendency to refine more products than they can sell through their own branded distributive channels is explainable by the pressures of truly extremely heavy fixed costs: the modern refinery is almost entirely automatic. The same is true at the service station level: the prime inputs of the service station operation are the labor of the owner-operator himself and the gasoline that comes to him, under price war conditions, at a price adjusted downward to enable him to meet competition.

[35] "Toward a Theory of Industrial Markets and Prices," reprinted from *Amer. Econ. Rev., Papers and Proceedings* (May 1954), XLIV: 121–139, in Amer. Econ. Ass'n, *Readings in Industrial Organization and Public Policy*, 297–315.

[36] *Op. cit., Land Econ.* (November 1960), XXXVI: 388.

[37] See the corroborating evidence of this in the Australian experience after deregulation, p. 191, below. As we have already observed (note 28,

above), Wilson concludes that this creates an inherent tendency toward oligopoly. He raises the question therefore of whether regulation may not have the effect, on balance, of keeping more firms in existence than would otherwise be the case. The much smaller average size of the truckers that are exempt from ICC regulation and the highly competitive character of their markets (as we will see below) casts doubt on this analysis; it seems much more likely that entry control has held down the number of truckers in the regulated part of the business (see James C. Nelson, "The Effects of Entry Control in Surface Transport," in *Transportation Economics, op. cit.*, 399–401). But even if Wilson is right, it would be a dubious defense of regulation that, by imposing artificial restrictions on the operations of motor carriers, it may have kept alive a larger number of firms than would otherwise have survived.

[38] Note, "Federal Regulation of Trucking: The Emerging Critique," *Columbia Law Rev.* (March 1963), LXIII: 505.

informed speculation rather than statistical certainty. A road check examination conducted by the Bureau [of Motor Carriers] did not indicate any significant difference in the number of safety violations [between exempt and regulated vehicles]. . . ."[39]

Further evidence is provided by the experience of Great Britain. Prior to the fall of 1969, Great Britain had a comprehensive licensing system for trucking comparable to the American one. A Report issued in 1965 by a Ministry of Transport committee chaired by Lord Geddes gave considerable attention to the question of whether quantitative or, as we have termed it, economic licensing was in fact a useful device for assuring safety of operations. It concluded that it was not, that the evidence indicated that "the present licensing system . . . has had no appreciable effect, directly or indirectly, on the prevailing safety standards." It specifically rejected the alleged necessity of regulating competition as a device for ensuring safety and concluded that the way to ensure these results was, instead, to issue revocable permits to all carriers, without any quantitative or economic limit, setting only the essential condition that the holder would abide by all safety regulations, and to enforce that condition vigorously by suspending or revoking permits for violations.[40]

The regulations imposed by the ICC with respect to safety, permissible hours of service, and equipment specifications are applied equally to private and exempt for-hire carriers, without subjecting them to the various economic controls that are applied to common and contract carriers generally. Public liability insurance standards could equally be required, as well as fitness and willingness-to-serve tests.

"The convenience of having the same agency administer both safety rules and economic regulation does not make a logical case for economic regulation. Limiting numbers and encouraging the growth of very large carriers may simplify enforcement of safety regulations, but that advantage hardly justifies the resulting market structures. . . .

"Aside from these . . . considerations, it is not at all certain that all regulated services conform to the high standards claimed by advocates of restrictive entry policies. Thus, in its recent annual reports, the Commission has reported about 15,000 informal complaints each year from shippers and receivers of freight, passengers, and others, alleging unsatisfactory service or unlawful practices. Numerous complaints of underestimating charges, slow payments for loss or damage, delayed deliveries, and other service deficiencies have long been levied against household goods carriers and have been the subject of ICC proceedings (during 1960, there were 2,338 shippers making such complaints)."[41]

The Effect on Industry Performance. The final and conclusive question is whether the advantages to the consuming public obtained by limiting competition outweigh the disadvantages. There is no conclusive way of

---

[39] *American Trucking Associations v. U. S.*, 344 U.S. 298, 305 note 7 (1953).
[40] Ministry of Transport, *Carriers' Licensing*, Report of the Committee, London, Her Majesty's Stationery Office, 1965, 44–56. This recommendation was incorporated in the mammoth Transport Act of 1968 (16 and 17 Eliz. 2 Law Reports Statutes, Chapter 73, 1968), although that Act did retain economic regulation of trucks over 16 tons in order to reduce highway congestion. See note 61, below.
[41] James C. Nelson, *op. cit.*, *Transportation Economics*, 416–417.

answering this question, since one cannot be certain how the industry would perform if regulation were completely removed. But there are a number of considerations and pieces of evidence strongly suggesting that the answer, as far as trucking is concerned, is that they do not.[42]

The most convincing is the eagerness of shippers to be served by unregulated companies. As we have already seen, something like two-thirds of all intercity truck traffic is carried in this way.[43] The simple fact of the matter is that most shippers who are in a position to do so "vote with their feet" for a competitive industry.[44]

The purported reason for exempting motor vehicles used to carry agricultural commodities from regulation[45] was that farmers need flexible transportation services, speedy in the case of perishables and adaptable to their seasonally fluctuating and not wholly predictable requirements. These needs of agriculture are special. But many other shippers doubtless have similar ones. It is competition and freedom of entry that provide the flexible adaptation of supply to demand, when and where and in what volume it appears; and it is regulation that, by interfering with the shifting of truckers from one route or product to another as required, introduces the inflexibilities that farmers are anxious to escape.

In this desire they are not alone. How else can one explain the more than 8,000 applications that the ICC receives from truckers each year, typically supported by shippers, requesting permission to enter the industry or to serve new routes?[46] Equally convincing is the phenomenal rise and preponderant role of private carriage. Private carriage recommends itself to companies with special needs that can best be served by their own facilities. But when this objective evidence of the preference of companies doing the major portion of all shipping for avoiding the regulated carriers is considered in conjunction with the evidence, to be mentioned presently, of the ways in which regulation raises costs, decreases flexibility, and holds up rates, it creates a strong presumption that most shippers regard regulation, on balance, as injurious to their interests.

The most important negative effects of regulation are the inefficiencies that it forces on both regulated and unregulated carriers by the detailed and intensive restrictions it places on their operations. A study of the certificates and permits of common and contract carriers as of 1942 by the Board of Investigation and Research (Nelson offers the opinion that "a roughly comparable pattern is in existence today")[47] disclosed that 62 percent of the regulated truckers were limited to special commodities; that 40 percent of these were limited to one commodity or commodity class and 88 percent to six or less; that 70 percent of the regular route common carriers had less than full authority to serve intermediate points, with more than one-tenth of them having no such authority at all; that about one-third of the intercity truckers had restrictions on their ability to carry return hauls and almost 10 percent

---

[42] The following appraisal draws heavily on the analysis of Nelson, *ibid.*, 395–422.

[43] P. 21, Chapter 1, above.

[44] See pp. 19–21, Chapter 1, for some of the efforts of shippers to avoid regulation.

[45] For a history of the agricultural exemption and its interpretation, see Fulda, *op. cit.*, 105–118.

[46] For one illuminating example, see the case study by David Welborn, *op. cit.*, 412–448.

[47] *Op. cit.*, *Transportation Economics*, 393; see pp. 390–393, on which this summary of the BIR report is based. On these restrictions see also pp. 15–18, above.

had no authority to transport any freight on the return trip. The regular-route common carriers must follow specified highways and in case after case have been turned down on applications to use a more direct routing between some of the cities they were authorized to serve. The BIR study found that these restrictions had caused large amounts of avoidable empty hauling, idle truck time, as well as additional mileage over circuitous routes. Among New England truckers surveyed 78 percent believed their operation would be more efficient if certificate restrictions were relaxed.[48] And paradoxically regulation subjects exempt operators to even more onerous restrictions and consequent inefficiencies, by making them confine themselves to exempt carriage. They may not, of course, solicit common- or contract-carrier business when and where they have excess capacity; the Commission has generally denied applications of private carriers for permits to engage in contract carriage on their return trips.[49]

Regulation gives rise to inefficiencies, also, by preventing the flexible response of price to temporary or local discrepancies between demand and supply. The efficient market solution for joint products, we saw in Chapters 3 and 4 of Volume 1, requires that their prices be adjusted to their respective demands, so as to be equated to their marginal opportunity costs. In an industry like trucking, where the geographic pattern of demand is highly complicated and changes from one day to the next, this kind of efficient pricing cannot possibly be prescribed, in advance, in regulatory proceedings. Fixed, regulated rate structures will therefore inevitably make it impossible to achieve the optimum utilization of capacity; and they will do so even more when, as in this instance, the general policy is to base them on average, fully distributed costs.[50]

To these sources of inefficiency must be added the expense and delay of the certification process itself. These costs may be worth incurring in situations of natural monopoly. They are doubly dubious in industries that seem to have all necessary attributes for effective performance without regulation.

The great virtue of the truck and of the competitive industry structure

---

[48] Meyer et al., *op. cit.*, 218–219 and Nelson, *op. cit.*, *Transportation Economics*, 408–409.

[49] See note 38, Chapter 1, p. 19, above, for a discussion of the circumstances under which farm cooperatives can carry nonfarm-related goods on back hauls. Also, ibid., for another illustration of the higher costs imposed by regulation on exempt carriers—the statutory limitations on the number of commodities barges may place on a single tow while retaining their exemption.

Because of these restrictions, it is difficult to interpret the evidence that common carriers tend to have larger average loads and a fuller average utilization of capacity than private or exempt for-hire carriers. That evidence alone might suggest that regulation promotes efficiency, by concentrating the business in the hands of fewer carriers. But to conclude from it that, on balance, regulation makes possible a more efficient utilization of plant in the entire industry, regulated and unregulated alike, would be highly questionable. See James C. Nelson, *op. cit.*,

Transportation Economics, 392, 410–412. For a finding that regulation imposes higher costs on regulated than exempt carriers, see Richard N. Farmer, "The Case for Unregulated Truck Transportation," *Jour. Farm. Econ.* (May 1964), XLVI: 398–409.

[50] See the very clear argument to this effect by Nicholson, *op. cit.*, *Q. Jour. Econ.* (February 1958), LXXII: 148–150. There is, we have already noted, a great deal of price discrimination in the trucking rate structure. But the general policy of the Commission—indeed, as Nicholson points out, the inevitable effect of any system of rate regulation—is to discourage differential contributions to overhead by different parts of the journey, and in particular between main and joint hauls even though in this, the true joint product case, this would *not* be discriminatory! On this last point, see note 11, pp. 93–94, Volume 1. On the evidence of a more flexible adjustment of price under nonregulated conditions, see p. 191, below.

with which its technology is so thoroughly compatible is precisely its flexibility and its versatility, both geographically and functionally—its ability to move on short notice to wherever it is needed and to pick up whatever kind of freight needs shipping. To take the fullest advantage of these attributes, operators must be free to move in these ways and to price flexibly, as market conditions demand. They cannot be free to do so under any regulation— least of all one with a strong protectionist inclination.[51]

There is another way in which regulation has an almost universal tendency to inflate costs. As we have already observed, the essential purpose of cartels is to raise price above the competitive level—that is, above marginal cost. If, as is usually the case, they succeed in holding price also above the average total costs of the most efficient producers and if they do *not* limit entry, the typical result is the entry of newer lower-cost firms, excess capacity, and the necessity for progressive cutbacks of output quotas.[52] If instead, as in trucking, entry is restricted but competition is not completely controlled, the firms within the industry will find it profitable, at the artificially maintained prices, to compete for business in other ways that increase cost. The ICC is not permitted, under the Motor Carriers Act, to place limitations on the amount of equipment and facilities or the schedules put into effect by certificated truckers. Consequently, there is a tendency for trucking companies to compete by offering greater frequency of service, at the cost of lower average utilization of capacity. This does, of course, mean improved service. The only way of testing whether the improvement is worth the higher costs it entails would be to offer shippers the choice between lower rates and less frequent operations, on the one hand, and the higher rates required for the more frequent scheduling, on the other. And it is precisely this choice that regulation prevents. The most convincing evidence that it is not worth the cost is the resort to private carriage by those shippers in a position to take advantage of this alternative.[53]

There is no room for doubt that, at least in the short run, regulation increases the price of transportation. The impact of this on shippers is necessarily very uneven, for two reasons. The first is, of course, that some shippers are in a position to escape by turning to private or exempt carriage. As far as the availability of this one escape-hatch is concerned, regulation would seem to bear most heavily on the small shipper or on the small, outlying community.[54]

---

[51] See especially pp. 14–28, Chapter 1, above.

[52] See pp. 28–29, Chapter 1, above.

[53] See the discussion of this phenomenon in Meyer et al., 219–220; Nelson, *op. cit.*, *Transportation Economics*, 391–392, 411–412.

[54] See, for example, the instance in which the Commission denied the Bee Line Express Company permission to provide direct service between the small town of Boaz and the cities of Birmingham and Chattanooga, even though (1) it was willing to do so and the motor carriers opposing its application were not and (2) shippers expressed dissatisfaction with the circuitous service they were currently getting. The ICC's justification was that the town's existing service was not "so inadequate as to justify a grant of additional authority." U. S. Senate, Select Committee on Small Business, *Competition, Regulation, and the Public Interest in the Motor Carrier Industry, op. cit.*, 6.

In 1956, shippers and carriers of fresh and frozen poultry succeeded in sustaining their position that these were agricultural products, entitled to exemption from ICC regulation; in 1958, the United States Department of Agriculture surveyed the experience in this industry after it became exempt. The results of the questionnaire were by no means unequivocal, but among the results that were consistent were the following: the major alleged disadvantages of regulated trucking included high rates, unwillingness to serve off-line points, slowness of

The second reason is that the restrictions on entry and price competition have helped—and, there is very convincing evidence, were intended to help—to preserve the discriminatory rate structure of the railroads from erosion by truck competition. The Federal Coordinator of Transportation, whose reports to Congress were influential in supporting what became the Motor Carriers Act of 1935, specifically justified this protection on the ground

"that railroad rates had traditionally been based on a formula that favored long hauls and low-value commodities, and that this practice of charging luxury goods relatively higher rates had generally been accepted as socially desirable."[55]

This was not a justification of price discrimination finely tuned, in accordance with the principles set forth in our Chapters 5 and 6 of Volume 1, to serve the interests of all rate payers; the avowed intention, rather, was to permit the continued subsidization of rates to certain shippers, notably farmers, at the expense of others.[56] There can be little doubt that regulation has the tendency to perpetuate these patterns of price discrimination and that the freer competition that is amply possible in truck transportation would go far to eliminate it [57]

These deleterious effects of regulation could well be a small price to pay, if the restraints on competition were necessary to prevent destructive competition and a serious deterioration of the quality of service. But there has been considerable experience with exempt carriage in the United States and with complete deregulation in Australia; and that experience casts considerable doubt on the reality of these dangers under freer competition. In general, it seems to demonstrate not only that competition produces lower rates, a larger number of suppliers, a wider range of alternatives, and more flexible service,[58] but also that it is compatible with efficiency,

---

delivery service, and the difficulties of obtaining service to distant markets. And among the advantages of exempt trucking frequently cited were lower rates and willingness to serve out-of-the-way points and distant markets. U. S. Department of Agriculture, "Interstate Trucking of Fresh and Frozen Poultry Under the Agricultural Exemption," Marketing Research Report No. 224, March 1958, 49, 51. I am indebted to my former students Charles R. Handy and Kenneth E. Kelly for some of these references to the literature describing the experience in the nonregulated sectors of the industry.

It is interesting to note that this evidence is the opposite of what we would expect if we accepted the case against free entry that it would result in cream-skimming and a deterioration of service on thin routes. See pp. 7–10, Chapter 1, above and pp. 220–246, below.

[55] Note, "Federal Regulation of Trucking: The Emerging Critique," op. cit., 462.

[56] See ibid., 462–463, note 17, and the references in note 27, p. 15, Chapter 1, above.

[57] W. Miklius and D. B. DeLoach present a regression analysis of the unregulated rates on

California produce shipped to out-of-state points, which shows a high correlation between rate level and the distance of haul. This suggests little, if any, price discrimination. When rates on frozen poultry were under regulation, distance statistically explained only 56 percent of the rate variation; during 1956–1957, after this commodity was declared exempt (see note 54, above), distance explained 81 percent of the variations. Op. cit., Jour. Farm. Econ. (November 1965), XLVII: 945.

[58] After it had been established that the carriage of poultry was exempt from regulation, the number of firms available for carrying it increased substantially and rates declined 33 to 36 percent in the period of a very few years; and they remained as stable as regulated rates. Of approximately 120 processors responding to the question of how they would react if poultry shipments were to be once again regulated, 46 of them said that they would turn to or increase their utilization of private trucking. U. S. Department of Agriculture, op. cit., note 54, above, 1, 3; Clem C. Linnenberg, Jr., "Agricultural Exemptions in Interstate Trucking—Mend or End Them?", Law and Contemporary Problems

reasonable stability of rates, and continuity of service.[59] Cost comparisons between regulated and unregulated carriers in the United States have produced somewhat conflicting results;[60] but in view of the impediments and inefficiencies that regulation imposes on the exempt carriers, even these inconclusive results suggest that at worst deregulation would be unlikely to result in higher average cost of operation. And if it did, the burden of the higher costs of inefficient companies would be borne by their owners, not by the consuming public.

Australia's experience after it completely removed all regulations from the motor-carriage industry in 1954 has been studied by Stuart Joy; his conclusions are worth quoting at length:

"Immediately regulation was lifted, fierce rate wars ensued on all routes as established operators attempted to fight off intruders. Newcomers entered the industry as fast as new trucks could be purchased or released from other commitments, resulting in the operation of many vehicles which were unsuitable for long-distance haulage, being either too light in construction or having insufficient payload capacity. Overloading and excessive hours of driving were rife. . . . A combination of economic attrition and the stricter enforcement of load limits and driving-hour regulations slowly weeded out the weak, so that by late 1957, a state of uneasy equilibrium had been attained. . . . The rate stability from 1958 onward enabled the larger firms to consolidate their own positions, and by their influence in the industry as a whole, to establish a pattern of operation and administration which exists today. Sporadic attempts have been made to regulate minimum rates through hauliers' associations, but free entry has prevented the enlistment of a large enough proportion of hauliers to have a significant effect on rate levels. . . .

"The flexibility arising from having so many independent units in the market is ideal for a country extending 2,000 miles from the tropics to the cool temperate zone, in which the demand for road haulage varies from area to area throughout the year. Off the inter-capital routes, rates fluctuate freely, ensuring that seasonal demands are met with adequate capacity. This means that in the event of a shortage of work between Melbourne and Sydney, owner-drivers will look elsewhere for traffic rather than 'cut each other's throat' for the remaining inter-capital work. Next in importance are the nation-wide hauliers, a group of about ten firms, each offering comprehensive service, from smalls and parcels to full loads, between all capitals. . . . With their own fleets, and access to a large number of subcontractors, many of whom prefer to work exclusively for them because of their regular work and reliable payment, the larger firms can command higher rates from shippers than can

---

(Winter, 1960), XXV: 169. When frozen fruits and vegetables were added to the exempt list in 1956, according to studies of the U.S. Department of Agriculture, truck rates ranged 11 to 29 percent below their 1955 level; when an amendment to the Act restored them to regulation in 1958, their prices increased. See Ivan W. Ulrey, "Problems and Issues in Transportation Policy and Implications for Agriculture," *Jour. Farm. Econ.*

(December 1964), XLVI: 1284. These experiences are summarized also in James C. Nelson, *op. cit., Transportation Economics*, 414. See also Friedlaender, *op. cit.*, 115–120.

[59] One study of a large sample of exempt carriers found that 75 percent had been in business for more than five years, 60 percent for over ten years. Farmer, *op. cit.*, 403–404.

[60] See p. 188, note 49, above.

owner-drivers or small vehicles having only a limited number of vehicles and customers. Such higher rates include a premium for the larger firms' ability to handle a widely fluctuating volume of traffic from each shipper, after the tradition of railway service. . . .

"The industry is now sufficiently mature to avoid competition at prices below short-run direct costs, largely because traffic gained at such sub-normal rates confers no immediate or future advantage, no good will attaching to panic rates. This was shown in the trade recession in 1960–1, when rates rarely fell below even long-run direct costs. . . .

"Free entry to interstate road haulage has not caused the demise of the railways. In fact, dynamic competition from the roads has been the cause of a vast improvement in the standard and cost of railway operations on competitive routes. But the most important conclusion to be drawn from the Australian experience is that freedom of entry and operation need not necessarily lead to chaotic conditions in the road haulage industry."

"the 'instability' and 'destructive and wasteful' competition so frequently forecast by established road haulage interests as being the inevitable outcome of free entry have not been apparent. Whilst there is an inevitable turnover of hauliers, the road haulage industry in its dealings with users is stable and efficient. It is considered that the availability of regular service at low cost is a more worthy policy objective than that of 'stability', where that term means a quiet life for established interests."[61]

There is no reason to doubt that regulation has produced improvements in the services provided by the motor-carrier industry, especially as compared with the situation before 1935. Dependability of service and the financial responsibility of regulated carriers for loss and damage has undoubtedly increased.[62] The experience with trip leasing did apparently demonstrate that it could be more difficult for the ICC to enforce its various safety regulations—having to do with the avoidance of overloading, equipment safety standards, maximum driving hours, and financial responsibility

---

[61] "Unregulated Road Haulage: The Australian Experience," *Oxford Econ. Papers*, n.s. (July 1964), XVI: 275–285. By permission of Clarendon Press, Oxford.

The British have an elaborate system of licensing controls similar to ours, and similarly introduced during the Great Depression to deal with what was regarded as the evils of excessive competition. The Geddes Committee, set up by the Ministry of Transport to examine these regulations (see note 40, above), concluded that they seriously reduced efficiency, by weakening the spur of competition, by imposing restrictions on the uses to which trucks could be put, and by impairing "the ability of hauliers to adapt quickly to the changing needs of their customers. . . . The haulage services required by trade and industry are ever-changing, often at short notice" (*Carriers' Licensing, op. cit.*, 59), and concluded for this reason, as well as because it conferred monopoly privileges, that economic licensing should be abolished. *Ibid.*, 6, 57–63, and *passim*.

According to the Committee, Sweden was persuaded in 1963 to abolish its comprehensive licensing, for similar reasons. *Ibid.*, 39–40.

The British Parliament did not accept these recommendations. The Transport Act of 1968 retains economic licensing, in an attempt to force the carriage of heavy loads over long distances on to the rails. See "Transport Act: So What is in it?" *The Economist* (November 2, 1968), CCXXIX: 50 and "Who Wants to Kill Transport Bill," *ibid.* (May 4, 1968), CCXXVII: 78.

[62] The survey of shippers of fresh and frozen poultry after carriage of this commodity became exempt (see p. 189, note 54, above) elicited, among the other opinions highly favorable to the new situation, the opinion that the main advantages of regulated carriers included "better service, financial responsibility and greater reliability."

On the other hand, we have already suggested several reasons for believing that the industry performance would have greatly improved in these respects after 1935 without regulation.

—on a large number of essentially unsupervised, uncertificated operators.[63]

Nor is there any reason to believe that a more highly competitive, unregulated motor-carrier industry would function perfectly. The removal of entry barriers would almost certainly lead to a heavy influx of new firms and a resurgence of price competition. Some of the firms would fail. Some of the service provided would be poor. Some rates would probably fall at least temporarily to unremunerative levels.

In the real world, our choices must always be between imperfect systems. The serious imperfections of competition before 1935 could clearly have convinced impartial observers of the necessity for regulation. But the economic conditions of today are vastly different from those of the depressed 1930s and the former conditions seem unlikely to recur. And the motor-carrier industry is a mature one. We now have had ample opportunity to observe the wastes, inefficiencies, and monopolistic consequences of regulation. That such improvements in quality as it may today provide are not deemed sufficient to justify the higher costs is strongly suggested by the general practice of shippers who have alternatives of dealing with nonregulated carriers. It is difficult for an economist to accept the notion that thorough cartelization of an industry is a necessary means of enforcing objective standards of safety and financial responsibility.

What is inconceivable, given the basic economics of this industry, is that deregulation could indeed usher in a long period of chronic sickness. Or that firms capable of providing reliable, efficient, and diversified service would be faced with the choice of either adulterating their product or going bankrupt. The industry simply lacks the essential prerequisites of destructive competition.

What is equally inconceivable is that performance would not improve in vital respects.

Stock Exchange Brokerage Commissions

In the United States all purchases and sales of securities, once they have been issued, are conducted either on the organized exchanges or in the so-called over-the-counter market. The New York Stock Exchange (NYSE) alone in 1962 accounted for 86 percent of the total dollar volume of stocks purchased on the 14 exchanges that are registered with the Securities and Exchange Commission; if one adds the 7 percent share of the American Stock Exchange (Amex) and the shares of the three leading regional exchanges, the Midwest, Pacific Coast, and Philadelphia-Baltimore-Washington, one has covered 99 percent of the total.[64] By 1968, the share of the

---

[63] See William J. Hudson and James A. Constantin, *Motor Transportation, Principles and Practices* (New York: Ronald Press Co., 1958), 553; also the basic Supreme Court decision, *American Trucking Associations v. U. S.*, 344 U. S. 298 (1953), upholding the validity of ICC rules imposing very stringent restrictions on the practice of trip leasing, 304–305. But see pp. 185–186, above.

The hard economic fact remains that trip leasing (see p. 19, Chapter 1, above) arose because it enabled exempt carriers of agricultural products to make use of what would otherwise be empty capacity on return hauls, and certificated carriers, who were willing to lease the equipment, a means of performing the transportation function at lower cost. The ICC rule would simply have ignored the efficiency advantages of trip leasing; from the point of view of the cartelization of the industry, it could be regarded only as a disruptive practice.

[64] Securities and Exchange Commission, *Report of Special Study of the Securities Markets*, Washington, 1963 (hereinafter, SEC, *Special Study*), Part 1, Chapter 1, 11.

New York Exchange had dropped to 74 percent;[65] the reasons for this decline are an important part of the story that follows.

The NYSE was organized in 1792 as a private club and remains largely that, a voluntary association "owned" by its members, who hold "seats" on the exchange. The Securities and Exchange Act of 1934 conferred official recognition and status on it and the other exchanges, however. It required them to register with the SEC and conferred on them, subject to the surveillance of the Commission, the responsibility for regulating the activities of their members, assuring compliance by them and by companies whose securities they listed with the provisions of the Act, and in general serving the purpose of preserving the efficiency and integrity of the securities markets.[66]

From its very origination the NYSE had fixed the minimum commission rates that its members might charge, and the 1934 Act seemed to contemplate a continuation of this practice under the general heading of "self-regulation."[67] Until well into the 1960s this authority went essentially unchallenged and its exercise essentially unsupervised by the SEC.

> "Between 1937 and 1958, the NYSE effected five changes in rate schedules—all increases and generally justified on the ground of rising costs. . . . Except for . . . occasional mildly negative reactions, the Commission, at least until the present [1965], has never interposed any serious objection. . . .
>
> "Despite this history of consistent increases and the obvious importance of an appropriate schedule of rates for the protection of the investor, neither the self-regulatory agencies nor the Commission has formulated a program for determining and evaluating these charges."
>
> "This void is surprising because any immunity from antitrust action in the securities field that may be brought on the grounds of price fixing by member firms presumably rests heavily upon the Commission's jurisdiction in this area. It is to be expected, therefore, that the Commission would have translated the statute's general reference to 'reasonableness' and the Exchange's vague references to such notions as 'fair return' into more meaningful guidelines of action. . . ."[68]

But like other cartel prices, these were at length subjected to a process of competitive erosion that finally forced first the practitioners, then the complaisant SEC and the general public into reexamining the logic and

---

[65] *Statistical Abstract of the U. S., 1969,* 457.

[66] See Sidney Robbins, *The Securities Markets, Operations and Issues* (New York: The Free Press, 1966), Chapter 4, "The Basic Securities Act and Self-Regulation—An Exercise in Government-Industry Cooperation." The recurring themes in the Act are that regulation and self-regulation are supposed to serve the "public interest" and the "protection of investors" by preventing unreasonable price fluctuations and ensuring "the maintenance of fair and honest markets." See *ibid.,* 125 and Chapter 5.

[67] This was generally inferred from the fact that the law gave the SEC the power "to alter or supplement the rules" of the Exchange "in respect of such matters as . . . the fixing of reasonable rates of commission. . . ." Section 19(b)(9) of the Securities Exchange Act, 15 U.S. Code 78s(b), 1964 ed. The authoritative statement of this position is in *Harold Z. Kaplan v. Lehman Brothers,* 250 F. Supp. 562 (1966), affirmed, 371 F. 2d 409 (1967), cert. denied, though with a written dissent by Chief Justice Warren, 389 U. S. 954 (1967).

[68] Robbins, *op. cit.,* 176–177, 70. See the fuller discussion of this problem in the SEC, *Special Study,* Part 2, Chapter V, 294–351.

validity of the price-fixing process.[69] The main reason for their vulnerability

---

[69] Various aspects of the Exchange's self-regulatory activities came also under antitrust attack in the 1960s. The first was launched by one Harold J. Silver, a nonmember over-the-counter broker in Dallas. Silver had enjoyed private wire connections with certain Exchange members, as well as ticker service from the Exchange itself; and then had them cut off, without explanation, by order of the Exchange, under its authority to regulate the dealings of members with nonmembers. The Supreme Court, in upholding the Silver suit against the NYSE for damages and injunction, pointed out that the action complained of would have been illegal *per se* as a group boycott under the antitrust laws but for the self-regulation provisions of the Securities and Exchange Act and the authority of the SEC to disapprove any such rules. But these provisions do not confer a blanket immunity under the antitrust laws. On the contrary, the court held that the failure to provide Silver with either explanation or opportunity for a fair hearing and the lack of SEC authority to review particular applications of its general rules (as in this case) deprived the Exchange of antitrust immunity. *Harold J. Silver v. New York Stock Exchange*, 373 U. S. 341 (1963).

The second attack was brought by one Harold Z. Kaplan and others, on behalf of five mutual fund investment companies of which they were stockholders. The plaintiffs charged that the practice of fixing minimum commission rates was a price-fixing conspiracy in violation of Section 1 of the Sherman Act, and sought treble damages and an injunction against the collective imposition of restraints on the rights of individual Exchange members to set their own commission rates. In this case, the Court held for the defendants, on the ground, already mentioned, that the 1934 Act by implication recognized this authority of the Exchange and immunized its exercise from the antitrust laws. See note 67, above. The New York Stock Exchange would have the SEC interpret the *Kaplan* decision as preventing the Commission ever, on its own discretion, from interfering with the authority of the Exchange to fix minimum rates (other than by approving or disapproving the specific rates set in this manner). The Department of Justice takes the position that *Kaplan* merely declares that such rate fixing is not illegal *per se* but does not preclude the SEC, in the exercise of its supervisory authority, from determining whether the fixing of minimum rates is indeed necessary to carry out the purposes of the 1934 Act. See its *Memorandum on the Fixed Minimum Commission Rate Structure* before the SEC, *In the Matter of Commission Rate Structure of Registered National*

Securities Exchanges, File No. 4–144, January 17, 1969, processed, 32–33.

Although our analysis here concentrates mainly on the fixing of minimum commission rates, it should be emphasized that the unrealistic character of the rates on large transactions and the successful efforts of large investors to circumvent them forced the stock exchanges generally and NYSE in particular to reexamine many of their other rules and practices as well. For example, it has led institutional investors to try to take over brokerage houses, to take out membership on the regional exchanges themselves and to demand a similar privilege of the NYSE as devices for participating in the excessive profits that were being extracted from them—thereby calling into question the NYSE's rules prohibiting public ownership of member firms and denying membership to institutional investors. It led nonmember brokers to demand an explicit sharing in the profits of the business they brought to members, thereby threatening the rules requiring members to charge the same, artificially sustained rates to nonmember brokers and ultimate customers alike.

This last rule, too, has been the subject of a continuing attack under the antitrust laws, by Thill Securities, which claims to act on behalf of 4,000 other nonmember brokers and security dealers. Their assertion that the NYSE's rules barring them from access to the floor for direct trading and prohibiting members' sharing commissions with nonmembers are in violation of the Sherman Act was initially rejected for the reasons set forth in the *Kaplan* decision. *Thill Securities Corp. v. New York Stock Exchange*, U. S. Dist. Ct., E. Wisc., Aug. 21, 1969. But the Circuit Court of Appeals denied "that the mere possibility of SEC review wraps the conduct of the Exchange in an impregnable shield of antitrust immunity." Rather, it held, following the *Silver* precedent, it must be demonstrated, first, that the Commission is in fact "exercising actual and adequate review jurisdiction," and, even so, second, that exemption of this particular rule—which would clearly constitute a group boycott *per se* in violation of the antitrust laws but for the partial exemption in the Securities and Exchange Act—is absolutely necessary for the discharge of the Exchange's responsibilities under the Act. In remanding the case to the District Court for a determination of these two points, the Court permitted itself

"the further observation, without prejudging the issue, that it is difficult to conceive how the Exchange can on remand argue that the anti-rebate rule is 'necessary to make the Act work'

was that the schedule of charges in effect until late in 1968 was grossly discriminatory and, unfortunately for its enforceability, the buyers most seriously discriminated against were those best able to invoke competition to protect their interests. Under that system, the commissions were based on both the value and the number of shares involved in the transaction. To illustrate the first basis, the commission on a purchase of 100 shares at prices of $1, $25, and $100 per share would have been $6.00, $31.50 and $49, respectively. As for the latter basis, the rates were uniform *per 100 shares*, no matter how large the actual transaction; for example, the commission on a purchase of 100 shares of a $25 stock would be $31.50, of 1,000 shares of the same stock, $315.[70] The critical defect was in the latter criterion: it obviously does not cost ten times as much to carry out an order to buy or sell 1,000 as 100 shares; if both purchases are made in a single transaction, the cost is likely to be the same for each. So this schedule of rates embodied a gross discrimination against large orders.

What made this discriminatory structure untenable was the enormous rise of institutional investing between 1958, the date of the last revision of commission rates, and the middle 1960s. Large institutional investors, especially the mutual funds, were able to escape exploitation, at least partially, in two major ways. First, since the schedule of minimum commission rates made their business unusually profitable, they were able to induce member brokers of the Exchange to give up a portion of the inflated commission in one way or another. The Exchange's rules prohibit rebates; so the customers could not demand any kind of direct reimbursement. But before 1969 those rules did permit commissions to be spread among member firms at the direction of the customer. So "give-ups" within the Exchange membership took the form of an order from, say, a mutual fund manager to the executing broker on a large trade to turn over some portion of his commission to another broker, as a reward to the latter for sales of the mutual fund's shares, research, and other services.[71] The extent to which commission rates on large transactions exceeded cost may be gauged from the fact that give-ups apparently ran between 40 and 80 percent of the commission, and some times higher. "Give-ups" to nonmember firms required somewhat more complicated arrangements, because of the NYSE's prohibition of cash payments to outsiders, but accomplished a similar purpose.[72]

---

when its members have gone to imaginative extremes to circumvent the rule when it serves their private economic purposes to do so. It appears from all we can read . . . that the rule is honored much more in its breach than in its observance, as through various devices, member firms routinely share commissions or the equivalent with favored non-member brokers." CCA, Seventh Circuit, August 27, 1970.

[70] SEC, *Special Study*, Part 2, Chapter VI, 296.

[71] It is necessary to distinguish three separate parties in these transactions—the managers of the mutual funds (M), the broker-dealers in their role as retailers of the shares of mutual funds to the investing public (R), and the brokers (B) through whom the funds conducted their own security purchases and sales on the organized exchanges. In the give-up, M would direct B to pay a part of its commission to R, as a reward to R for selling M's shares.

[72] See Carol J. Loomis, "Big Board, Big Volume, Big Trouble," *Fortune* (May 1968), LXXVII: 221; Dept. of Justice, *Memorandum*, January 17, 1969, *op. cit.*, 75, 88–90; "Give-ups kickback on funds," *Business Week*, July 27, 1968, 97–99. The latter article estimates that the amount of give-ups could have been as much as one-half of the $233 million that Mutual Funds paid in broker commissions in 1967:

"Testimony about staggering amounts passing through the hands of individuals has led one

Second, they took their business, in increasing proportion, to the over-the-counter market and to regional exchanges, where they could negotiate commissions more closely related to the cost of serving them.[73]

The SEC itself began in the 1960s to put pressure on the stock exchanges to eliminate these practices, on the one hand by giving volume discounts and on the other by specifically prohibiting certain varieties of the give-up. Its objection to the latter practice was that the benefit of the rebates went not to the holders of mutual fund shares, on whose behalf the securities purchases were made, but to the managers of the funds themselves. The reason was that the typical recipient of the give-up was another broker, to compensate him for selling additional shares of the fund; and the larger the fund, the larger the management fees (typically $\frac{1}{2}$ percent of the net assets of the fund per year). In effect, thus, the give-up provided a means of channeling the cost-savings on commissions away from the funds themselves and their shareholders into additional selling effort, for the benefit not of those shareholders but of management and salesmen.[74]

The SEC therefore in January of 1968 proposed a rule 10b–10 to prohibit give-ups and to see to it that the savings from the excessive commission rates on large purchases would be returned to the benefit of the fund shareholders. During the remainder of 1968, hearings were held on the whole matter of the minimum commission rates; but as an interim measure, the NYSE in December put into effect a volume discount for large transactions and a rule abolishing customer-directed give-ups among its members.[75] It was into this set of hearings that the Department of Justice dropped its bombshell on April 1, 1968, when it argued, flatly, that the SEC ought to consider completely abolishing the collective fixing of minimum commission rates and in so doing set off an intense controversy about the entire future of this concerted restriction on price competition.[76]

SEC staff member to suggest wryly that give-up payments should be registered as securities and traded on exchanges." p. 99.

Robbins describes some of these indirect arrangements. For example, Exchange members would compensate nonmember brokers for their patronage by reciprocity—channeling other transactions through them. Op. cit., 180–184. The American and various regional stock exchanges avoid many of these complications by offering special treatment to nonmember professionals.

[73] In addition, as we have already observed, many of them took out memberships in regional exchanges and did their transacting there. For one interesting example, note the acquisition of Jeffries & Co., a Los Angeles-based firm specializing in institutional brokerage, by Investors Diversified Services. On consummation of the agreement, Jeffries gave up its membership on the New York exchange and proposed to transact its business thereafter in the so-called third market, where the brokerage can be done at negotiated commission rates. *Wall Street Journal*, July 10, 1969, 2.

[74] See Loomis, *op. cit., Fortune*, May 1968, 221; "Give-ups kickback on funds," *Business Week*, July 27, 1968, 97. The typical commission on sales of new mutual fund shares to the investing public is $8\frac{1}{2}$ percent. The competition among mutual fund managers (M—using the schematic representation of note 71, above) to sell additional shares, and in this way to increase the size of their funds, was so intense that they passed almost the entire $8\frac{1}{2}$ percent on to the retail salesmen (R)—themselves typically broker-dealers. The give-ups enabled M to give R an even larger inducement and reward, at no cost to themselves, instead of crediting the savings to the fund itself and hence to its shareholders. On most of the foregoing history, see David L. Ratner, "Regulation of the Compensation of Securities Dealers," *Cornell Law Rev.* (February 1970), LV: 348–389.

[75] *Wall Street Journal*, October 26, 1968, 2. The American Exchange made similar changes. *Ibid.*, November 4, 1968, 6.

[76] "The Commission should promptly take appropriate steps to determine the extent to which commission rate fixing by the NYSE is required by the purposes of the Securities

The NYSE did not respond by defending the existing commission rate structure. On the contrary, it moved to a recognition that rates to large buyers were unrealistic and indefensible and to an acceptance of a genuinely regulated level equated to cost plus a reasonable return and a structure of rates for different transactions more closely in line with their respective costs. To this end it commissioned the consulting firm National Economic Research Associates to analyze its members' costs and revenues and to recommend appropriate changes. In December it took a major step in this direction by introducing quantity discounts on large transactions. In February of 1970 it proposed to the SEC a new schedule, involving further cuts on these transactions, rate increases up to 100 percent on small ones, and a rise in the average sufficient to provide brokerage houses with an average return on invested capital of 15 percent.[77] It also indicated a willingness to consider offering discounts to nonmember brokers, who had theretofore under its rules been required to pay the same rates as the investing public.[78] But the issue remained unresolved as to whether any regulation at all was justified. Why not leave the determination of commissions to the forces of competition?

In October of 1970, the SEC responded with suggestions of its own that came down surprisingly hard on the side of freer competition. It proposed to free commissions on transactions of $100,000 or more (not a high cut-off point, by any means—2500 shares of a $40 security) from all control. In so doing, it in effect proposed to legitimize the actual state of affairs: the ban on give-ups had been subject to all sorts of circumvention—concealed discounts, free services, reciprocal deals—as was inevitable as long as the official rates remained far above cost; so that in fact commissions to institutional investors were already being individually negotiated under pressure of competition.[78a] For smaller transactions, it suggested a scale of rates somewhat lower than had been suggested by the Exchange; and it bade the membership adopt a uniform system of accounting and cost allocation to facilitate cost-based rate-making in the future. And it told the Exchange to bring to it by mid-1971 a plan to permit nonmember brokers some "reasonable access" to its facilities.[78b] This decision may make the issue of minimum rate control

---

Exchange Act. The Commission should then take action (a) to eliminate all rate fixing which is not found to be justified in the public interest; (b) to develop and promulgate standards governing the validity or reasonableness of any commission rates for which rate fixing is permitted to continue; and (c) to determine the proper means for assuring equitable and non-discriminatory access by nonmember broker-dealers to the NYSE market." Before the Securities and Exchange Commission, *Inquiry into Proposals to Modify the Commission Rate Structure of the New York Stock Exchange*, SEC Release No. 8239, *Comments of the United States Department of Justice*, April 1, 1968, mimeo., 6. While expressing the opinion that minimum rate fixing was in fact unjustified, the Department raised the possibility that the setting of *maximum* rates might be warranted; it recognized the possible desirability, also, of the Commission's proposed rule requiring

that any give-ups that institutional investors were able to obtain go to the benefit of their companies.

[77] *New York Times*, February 15, 1970, sec. 3, 1. See the two Reports by National Economic Research Associates, Inc., to the Cost and Revenue Committee of the New York Stock Exchange, *Reasonable Public Rates for Brokerage Commissions*, 2 vols., February 1970, and *Stock Brokerage Commissions: The Development and Application of Standards of Reasonableness for Public Rates*, 2 vols., July 1970.

[78] "Pacific Coast Exchange Accuses Big Board of Trying to Kill Competition by Others," *Wall Street Journal*, June 10, 1969, 4.

[78a] Wayne E. Green, "Brokers and those Minimum-Fee Rules," *Wall Street Journal*, October 29, 1970, 10.

[78b] *New York Times*, October 23, 1970, 1, 69.

versus competition practically moot: since the SEC has the authority to approve or disapprove commission schedules, it is obviously in a position to have its way. But the issue of principle remains important, and by no means definitively resolved.

The major arguments, centering on the question of whether unregulated competition among brokers would be destructive, will have a familiar ring—reflecting either the essential similarity of the economic issues and conflicting interests involved in all proposed restrictions on competition or the fact that the contending parties all read the same economics textbooks. The distinctive aspect of the defense in this instance is attributable to the fact that there are two separate though related markets or industries involved. One is the market for securities, which, it is generally agreed, can be effectively competitive, provided the organized exchanges are regulated—as is the intention of the Securities and Exchange Acts—in order to prevent fraud, the use of information by insiders at the expense of outside investors, to insure financial responsibility of its agents, and so on. The prices here are the prices of the securities. The other market is for the *service of the brokers* who conduct the transactions in the first market. Those agents perform a variety of services for investors, but the essential one in the present context is effectuating purchase and sales orders. The price in question here is the commission rate.

The central defense of suppressing competition in the determination of that second price is that it is essential for the effective functioning of the first market—in the words of the antitrust laws, that the restraint at issue is "reasonably ancillary" or subordinate to the legitimate purpose of promoting the goals of the Securities and Exchange Act. According to this argument, the incentive of brokers to belong to the NYSE and to accept the numerous and costly restrictions imposed on members in order to protect the integrity of the securities markets[79] is dependent in considerable measure on the privileges of membership. One of these is that nonmember brokers must pay the same commission rates as public customers; when members turn to floor brokers to consummate a trade, in contrast, they pay only a fraction of that rate. The other is that the minimum commission rates are insulated from competition. If, instead, minimum rate regulation were removed, nonmember brokers could negotiate the commissions that members would charge them whenever they needed to buy or sell on the Exchange; and the attractions of membership would be correspondingly reduced. Brokerage

---

[79] These include the requirement that they make their trades in stock exchange-listed securities on the exchange floor, where specialists are under obligation to maintain an orderly market and forestall large price fluctuations by trading on their own account to fill temporary imbalances between demand and supply; submitting to pervasive stock exchange rules and surveillance (the NYSE estimates that compliance costs amounted to 15.3 percent on the average of the total costs their members incurred in their securities commission business); contributing to the Exchange's expenses in enforcing the self-policing rules (estimated by the NYSE as costing $6 million in 1968, or one-third of the budget of the SEC itself); and meeting the various qualifications—with respect to the training and background of their personnel, minimum capital requirements, issuance of reports, and the like—imposed by the Exchange. See the New York Stock Exchange, *Economic Effects of Negotiated Commission Rates on the Brokerage Industry, The Market for Corporate Securities, and the Investing Public*, August 1968 (hereinafter, *Economic Effects*, August 1968), 12, 21–22, 26–31, and Appendixes A and B, on which the following account draws heavily. See also its *The Economics of Minimum Commission Rates, Reply to Memorandum of the Antitrust Division of the Department of Justice dated January 17, 1969*, NYSE, May 1, 1969.

houses would be tempted to give up their membership, in order to avoid the onerous restrictions and costs above-mentioned. Where possible, they would avoid paying floor commissions to members by matching buy and sell orders in their own offices, or by trading in third markets wherever profitable, and they would negotiate commission rates for the execution of those orders on which they still needed access to the floor. In consequence, so the argument runs, fewer transactions would be conducted on the organized exchange itself and the result would be an attenuation of the enormous volume and continuity of trading operations that make it so effective a market; this continuity and depth give it a maximum ability to absorb purchase and sale orders with minimal price fluctuations and give investors the ready liquidity that makes them willing to hold securities instead of cash.

The Department of Justice, in contrast, attributes the continuity, depth, and liquidity of the centralized security exchanges not to the artificial incentives to membership provided by noncompetitive commission rates but to the fact that the security exchange—and the NYSE in particular— is a natural monopoly.[80] There is, it asserts, a

> "natural tendency of the securities market to centralize trading which is due to the economies and efficiencies associated with centralized markets. . . .
>
> "The economies and efficiencies of centralized trading are, of course, attested by the development of securities exchanges. To facilitate the bringing together of buy and sell orders, very early in the history of the industry brokers began to congregate in central locations. . . . Even today the chief function of a central securities market is to take advantage of such efficiencies, to provide what has been called space and time utility, to investors. . . .
>
> "In addition to scale economies in operating a market, the greater the number of trades conducted on a single marketplace in a given security the lower would be the per unit cost of trading. As far as stock exchanges are concerned, this evolutionary tendency toward a single marketplace is demonstrated by the near monopoly position now enjoyed by the NYSE in securities listed on the Exchange."[81]

It is undeniable that artificially maintained commission rates have had as at least one of their effects a weakening rather than a strengthening of that monopoly, encouraging the growth of trading in third markets and over the counter, precisely because traders sought in this way to obtain commission rates more closely reflecting the costs of executing their orders. On this ground, at least, competitive commission rates would tend to reverse this dissipation, bringing a greater proportion of the trading back to the stock exchange floor rather than, as the NYSE argument avers, in the opposite direction.[82] (But so would regulated rates more realistically related to costs.)

---

[80] *Memorandum*, January 17, 1969, *op. cit.*

[81] *Ibid.*, 47–49. The Department brief cites in support of this proposition Robert Doede, *The Monopoly Power of the New York Stock Exchange*, unpublished dissertation, University of Chicago, June 1967, and Harold Demsetz, "The Cost of Transacting," *Q. Jour. Econ.* (Feb. 1968), LXXXII: 33–53.

[82] So the Department deprecates the assertedly disincentive effects of competitive commission rates on stock exchange membership, contending that the speed and efficiency with which orders can be executed in the organized exchanges, at the best possible price and the lowest possible cost, would continue to recommend membership, with the advantages it carries of immediate

The Department argues, finally (note the analogy to trucking and occupational licensure generally), that the purposes of investor protection can be served by the direct imposition of rules directed to that end, without the need for suppressing price competition as an indirect inducement to member firms to accept such restrictions.[83]

It is not possible to make an absolute choice between these opposing views on purely a priori grounds. It is certainly arguable that, other things being equal, self-regulation, voluntarily induced by the advantages of membership, is preferable to the imposition of government controls. Conceivably, also, the pressures of price competition would indeed weaken the ties of brokers to the market in some respects—though it would clearly strengthen those of the investors that have fled the organized exchanges for more attractive commission rates. And, in so doing, it could create some incentive to execute orders without recourse to the Exchange; and if this happened small investors particularly might be unable easily to judge whether they had in fact obtained the best possible prices for their transactions. The question then is whether the cost to the public of noncompetitive commission rates is worth the benefits they help secure.

There is one objective and conclusive piece of evidence that the price the public pays is higher than the costs that self-regulation imposes on the members of the Exchange: seats on the New York Stock Exchange sold for around $500,000 in early 1969.[84] If new entrants are willing to pay this price for a ticket of admission, clearly the present value of the monetary benefits of membership exceeds that of the costs by something like this amount. As Harold Demsetz pointed out at the 1968 SEC hearings, the first impact of more competitive commission rates would therefore be not on the number of members in the Exchange but on the price of the seat. That

---

access to the floor and to the entire Exchange community, and of enhancing the reputation and attractiveness of member firms to investors.

"The importance to a firm's business of its reputation and ability to make efficient, timely execution of orders was emphasized by the testimony of a number of NYSE members. . . .

"It is, of course, the strength, 'thickness' and liquidity of the NYSE market which makes membership valuable, and will continue to do so (with or without fixed minimum rates)."

As for the burdens of membership, consequent on the self-regulatory functions of the Exchange:

"This is not to say that NYSE self-regulation is not a positive benefit to the investor. Of course it is. But the recognition of its value is an aspect of the value of NYSE membership. The NYSE in its institutional advertising continually refers to the higher standards of integrity imposed on member firms, and the members must be of the opinion that the public investor will recognize and reward the firm which subjects itself to this stricter form of self-regulation." *Memorandum*, January 17, 1969, 57, 67.

[83] If, for example, companies were moved to surrender their membership in order to escape burdensome regulations, this, it points out, could be counteracted "by raising the standard of regulation applicable to nonmembers" (*ibid.*, 176), something that would be desirable for its own sake in any event. Alternatively, or in addition, brokers might be *required* to become members of the Exchange, so that all would be subject to its discipline (pp. 177–178). Investors might be protected from the effects of the insolvency of brokerage firms by instituting a system of compulsory customer insurance (pp. 178–182). The NYSE instituted a similar plan in December of 1969, when its Board of Governors authorized a year-end transfer of $5 million out of its operating revenues into a special fund established to insure customers against such losses. *New York Times*, December 20, 1969, 45.

[84] It dropped some 50% in the following year. The main reasons for the change were apparently the drop in total trading volume, the reductions in commission rates put into effect the preceding December, and the prospect of a change in Exchange rules that would permit institutional investors to become members of the Exchange, the effect of which would be to take their business away from existing members.

price will fall to whatever extent necessary to make membership as attractive to new entrants after as it was before.[85] And as long as members continue to be required to bring their transactions to the floor of the Exchange, it is difficult to see how the introduction of more competitive rates could truly dilute the continuity or depth of the market. It is only if it can be predicted that the value of a seat will become negative that there is objective reason to anticipate an actual decline in membership.

This leads us to the central question: is the brokerage business inherently subject to destructive or cutthroat competition, in the absence of regulation? The industry model depicted by defenders of minimum rate fixing has these familiar components: a high ratio of fixed to variable costs, particularly in the short run;[86] substantial excess capacity much or most of the time, so that short-run marginal cost is typically below average total cost;[87] a demand for brokerage services that fluctuates sharply over time and is price-

---

[85] This testimony is quoted in the Department of Justice *Memorandum* of January 17, 1969, *op. cit.*, 63, note 25.

[86] It might appear anomalous that an industry with comparatively little investment in fixed capital could have a cost structure susceptible to destructive competition. But capital costs are not the only possible fixed costs. A firm's "capacity" may consist primarily in a pool of skilled personnel the size of which may not be readily responsive to changes in the demand for its services. Defining as variable those expenses that could be readily reduced within a period of a year in response to decreasing output, the NYSE placed in this category commissions and floor brokerage paid to others, clearing charges, commission fees, the compensation of registered representatives (typically a percentage of the volume of transactions), and employee bonuses and profit-sharing plans. It classified as fixed costs clerical and administrative salaries, communications costs, occupancy and equipment costs, and other expenses including promotion, licenses, dues and assessments. This classification produced a computation that 51 percent of total costs of brokerage houses are "overhead" and 49 percent variable; these ratios would shift to 44 percent and 56 percent, respectively, if one-fourth of the clerical and administrative salaries were shifted into the variable category. These fixed-cost ratios of 44 to 51 percent, the Exchange pointed out, are not far below those of electric utilities, are at least as high as those of railroads, and far above airlines and intercity freight motor carriers. *Economic Effects*, August 1968, *op. cit.*, 63–66. Clearly, the computation is highly sensitive to the classification of clerical and administrative salaries and to the use of one year as the relevant time period. It would be interesting to see by what percentage these staffs were in fact cut during the lean years immediately following the

issuance of the 1968 NYSE study. For an estimate that the ranks of job-seeking securities analysts increased 30 to 35% in the year from mid-1969 to mid-1970, see the *Wall Street Journal*, July 21, 1970, 1.

[87] The NYSE study supports this generalization, among other ways, by demonstrating that there was a clear tendency for the unit costs of various firms to move inversely with the number of their transactions between 1965 and 1966. Of the 57 firms, the number of whose transactions declined, one experienced decreased average total costs and 56 increases; among the 94 firms whose transactions rose by more than 25 percent, 62 experienced decreasing costs and 32 increasing. *Ibid.*, 54–58. This limited demonstration is not conclusive. The firms compared have various product- or output-mixes, and the figures for the average cost per "transaction" undoubtedly reflect allocations of common and joint costs the validity of which may be questionable. Also, it is not possible to tell to what extent the improved cost behavior of the firms experiencing an increase in output reflected the previous presence of excess capacity, to what extent economies of scale in the installation of additional capacity to meet the additional demand. At the same time, there is a strong inference here of the presence of excess capacity, at least in 1965, which means that short-run marginal costs were below average total costs in that year. For a criticism of these and other aspects of the NYSE's testimony, see "A Critique of the New York Stock Exchange's Report on the Economic Effects of Negotiated Commission Rates on the Brokerage Industry, the Market for Corporate Securities, and the Investing Public," prepared for the Department of Justice by H. Michael Mann, processed, 1968; and the NYSE's response, *The Economics of Minimum Commission Rates*, May 1, 1969, *op. cit.*, 37–38.

inelastic;[88] and a large number of sellers and low concentration ratios,[89] assuring that if price competition were permitted it would be keen. Such a model would, indeed, produce results of questionable desirability—extreme fluctuations in commission rates, with periods of deeply depressed earnings during which the industry would be reluctant to provide capacity sufficient for peak demands followed by sharp rate increases, as recovering demand pressed hard on the limits of capacity; and an inability of the industry, in the latter period, to provide the kind of instantaneous execution of orders that the public demands.[90]

The NYSE predicts, further, that the introduction of price competition would result in a serious deterioration in the quality of service. Brokerage firms, it asserts, would no longer be able to maintain the research and information-gathering activities in which they now widely engage or to provide this valuable information and advice to their customers, as they now do in large measure, at no extra charge. And this in turn would produce notably poorer investment decisions, particularly by the small investor:

"The discount house concept, which ignores service, would probably become dominant in the securities business. Negotiated rates would force most firms to discontinue or reduce all services other than the execution of orders."[91]

---

[88] On the variability in demand, see the NYSE, *Economic Effects*, August 1968, *op. cit.*, 88–90. The contention that the demand for the services of brokers for executing transactions is price-inelastic is based on the consideration that the commission amounts to less than one percent of the cost of buying and selling securities, so that fluctuations in the former would have only a negligible effect on the decisions of buyers and sellers to engage in such transactions. On the other hand, Henry C. Wallich has pointed out that the commission could well bulk large relative to the prospective capital gains and losses that induce traders to buy and sell, and expressed the opinion that demand could well prove elastic. "Commission Rate Policy for a Large and Growing Auction Market," testimony before the SEC, Oct. 31, 1968, processed, 12–16.

The NYSE study might have recognized that the demand for the services of *NYSE members* had proved to have considerable price-elasticity, with large purchasers going outside the Exchange to consummate their transactions precisely in quest of lower commission rates. But it still could be true that the demand for the services of all brokers, inside and outside the Exchange, is inelastic, so that price competition could still be destructive in its effect on all brokers considered together.

[89] *Economic Effects*, August 1968, *op. cit.*, 70. For the full argument of the NYSE on the danger of destructive competition, see *ibid.*, 43–94.

[90] "Despite these fluctuations in demand, the public expects, and has a right to expect, almost instantaneous executions of its orders. Occasionally, when volume suddenly soars to new peaks

at an unforeseeable rapid pace, the securities industry may fall behind in its back-office work, as has occurred this year. Even at such times of peak volume, explanations and excuses for lack of capacity are unacceptable. . . .

"In some industries . . . it is possible to accumulate unfilled orders for three, six or even twelve months. . . . In the brokerage business, even relatively short delays are inconsistent with the concept of an orderly and efficient securities market. During periods of heavy demand, the industry *must* be prepared to meet peak load requirements.

"In a sense, the securities industry is like the power industry, which must have sufficient reserve capacity to run all air conditioners when temperatures reach an unexpected peak. . . .

"The securities industry must be prepared to handle peak volume, i.e., to carry 'excess' capacity during periods of average volume. In this industry, excess capacity is *not* redundant capacity." *Ibid.*, 89, 91.

One might accept this assertion with a certain amount of irony, coming as it does from an industry that had to close its doors regularly on Wednesdays during half of the year 1968 and was able to keep them open only from 10:00 A.M. to 2:00 P.M. for most of 1969, all in order to enable its back offices to catch up with the flood of paper work. In fairness it must be recognized that the volume of transactions had risen precipitately and unexpectedly in a very few years. On this, see note 93, below.

[91] *Ibid.*, 96.

Finally, it predicts, price competition is likely to be highly selective, centering on the patronage of the large, institutional purchasers, who have alternatives, and discriminating against the small investors, whose demand is more likely to remain exploitable. This is a somewhat ironic defense of a system that has, heretofore, discriminated *against* the large transaction; nevertheless, unless it can confidently be predicted that pure competition would prevail if all controls were removed, it must be taken into account.

The model of the industry that the proponents of greater price competition depict is, naturally, somewhat different. They see a cost structure dominated by the salaries of clerical and administrative personnel, the compensation of salesmen (typically set as a commission on sales), and brokerage and clearing charges related to individual transactions as primarily variable rather than fixed.[92] They see capacity that can be expanded or contracted primarily by hiring or letting go moderately skilled clerical and administrative staff as comparatively readily adaptable to changes in demand, over comparatively short periods of time.[93] Instead of an industry selling a standardized product, and able on this account to compete only in price,[94] they see one whose sellers make a great and successful effort to differentiate their services. The NYSE study itself points to this proliferation of services and the need of many investors for them in defense of noncompetitive rates; it fails to recognize that this differentiability of product

---

[92] See note 86, above. More than half of the costs included by the NYSE study as "overhead" were clerical and administrative salaries. If competition is to be truly destructive, the experience of other industries would seem to suggest, a much larger proportion of (fixed) costs would have to be of a kind that could not be readily adjusted downward in the space of, say, one to three years. There is no explanation in the NYSE study of why most of the clerical and administrative help could not be fired in a considerably shorter space of time than one year, if it seemed that the volume of business in the intermediate-term future did not justify their retention. This consideration does not eliminate the likelihood of firms having large amounts of excess capacity of this type, as demand fluctuates widely from one month or six-month period to the next, however. See also the footnote immediately following.

[93] The NYSE study provides statistics on the number of registered representatives and other personnel of its member firms during each of the years 1960 through 1967, compared with the average daily volume of security transactions. It points out that whereas the volume of trading had by 1964 fully recovered from its decline between 1961 and 1962 and far surpassed the volume of the former year, the number of employees other than registered representatives did not regain its 1961 level until five years later —in purported evidence "that firms respond only sluggishly to rising demand." *Ibid.*, 92. It may well be that they did respond "sluggishly." But their failure during the years 1962 through

1965 to hire as many "other personnel" as they had in 1961 would not seem to reflect any inherent inflexibility of their technology or cost structures. And their ability to increase their registered representatives from 28,000 to 42,000 and other personnel from 54,000 to 78,000 during the period covered by these statistics suggests no difficulty in expanding capacity, if they are willing to do so. True, average daily volume increased even more, from 3 million to 10 million shares; but in view of the NYSE's demonstrations, earlier, of the pervasive presence of excess capacity (note 87, above) and of economies of scale and in view, also, of the abundant opportunities for increasing the productivity of existing personnel by the use of automation, this discrepancy between the expansion in the number of employees on the one hand and the total volume of business on the other was to have been expected. These observations are not intended to suggest that the expansion in capacity was sufficient; there is evidence to the contrary (note 90, above). More directly relevant from the standpoint of the alleged dangers of destructive competition is the fact, demonstrated by these statistics, that between 1961 and 1962, when the average daily volume fell from 4,100,000 to 3,800,000 shares, the member firms reduced their other personnel from 64,000 to 57,500. On these matters, see the Department of Justice, *Memorandum*, January 17, 1969, *op. cit.*, 113–121.

[94] See pp. 184–185, this chapter, above.

is a prime defense against destructive competition. It is difficult to believe that these will not continue to be important methods of competition, that by no means all brokerage firms would find it either desirable or necessary to take the path of the discount appliance house. On the contrary, as in the appliance business itself, the industry would tend to differentiate itself as between firms competing principally on the basis of price and others continuing to emphasize research and other kinds of service, with a wide range of gradations in between.[95]

The counterpart of the NYSE's model of an industry prone to destructive competition is its picture of the industry's performance made possible by minimum rate controls: financially healthy, providing the investor with the benefits of its research and sound advice at no extra charge, encouraging the habit of stock ownership among small, individual investors (possibly subsidizing low commission rates to them by its discrimination against the large transactors), providing brokerage service in small and remote localities where it would otherwise be unprofitable.[96]

---

[95] It is impossible of course to be certain. As Dr. William C. Freund, economist for the NYSE, has reacted to the above in a private communication:

"One person's guess versus another's! One-hundred shares of GM are the same no matter where purchased and represent a highly standardized product. Undoubtedly, some firms could withstand the pressure of destructive price competition on the basis of unique services in a period of contracting volume. But the pressure to cut commission rates would, in general, probably be intense."

Still there is a contradiction between the Exchange's emphasis on the great need and desire of investors for these other services (*Economic Effects*, August 1968, op. cit., 97–100) and its assumption that destructive price competition would be inevitable in the absence of regulation. A similar, at least partial contradiction exists between this prediction and another, to which we have already alluded, that competition would be highly discriminatory, particularly against small investors. This is indeed a possibility; but to the extent that it is, it means it would not be destructive. The more intense the price competition, the less it is possible for any purchaser, no matter how inelastic his demand, to be forced to pay a price higher than any other (in relation, of course, to their respective costs). Interestingly, the Report consistently refers to the rates that would emerge if minimum controls were eliminated as "negotiated," thereby suggesting not a general and uniform decline in prices to unremunerative levels, but a selective, negotiated reduction to some customers and not to others. What seems likely is that commission rates on large orders would, indeed, be negotiated; and that others would be at some published, administered price, relatively

resistant to short-term fluctuations or to pressures down to the level of short-run marginal cost. As we have seen, this is in effect what the SEC proposed in October 1970 to legitimize.

Again, the Report predicts that uncontrolled competition would have a tendency to drive out those firms whose major source of revenue is from commissions, because they will be unable to compete with other, more diversified, brokerage houses that are dependent for only a fraction of their revenues on this business (*ibid.*, 73–83). But this very diversity in the character of brokerage firms could well diminish the likelihood that price competition among them would be destructive. They would not all feel an equal pressure immediately to match all price reductions. And since they undoubtedly vary widely in efficiency, commission rates might not have to fall very far before they would reach the average variable cost of the higher-cost firms, driving them out of business. Differences in the level of marginal cost of different firms impart an elasticity to an industry's supply schedule that is not present if one assumes that all firms are alike in their costs and product mixes and all of them have the *same level* of average variable costs, far below average total costs. On some of these considerations, see the Department of Justice, *Memorandum*, January 1969, op. cit., 96–106. Moreover, the NYSE's solicitude for preserving all the existing firms in business conflicts with its purported evidence elsewhere of economies of scale. Even if its argument were correct that the process by which firms are eliminated would have no relationship whatever to their relative efficiencies, it would still follow, from its reasoning, that concentrating the remaining business in fewer hands would mean that it would be conducted at lower cost.

[96] *Economic Effects*, August 1968, op. cit., 8, 83.

The counterpart of the opposing model, which predicts that competition would be effective and nondestructive, is a much less favorable appraisal of the industry's present performance. According to this model, the prohibition of price competition has been a shelter for inefficiency: the New York Exchange has been extremely sluggish in modernizing its methods, in particular in adopting automation and the computer to handle its geometrically growing volume of paper work.[97] Cartel pricing has driven away large investors, thereby dissipating, rather than reinforcing, the depth and continuity of the market. It has entailed price discrimination and internal subsidization—discrimination against large transactions and against investors (again, typically, the large ones) who wish to purchase only execution of orders and not all the auxiliary services the cost of which is provided in the single price package. These investors have succeeded in escaping this discrimination to some extent, by obtaining give-ups and reciprocal patronage; but these concessions, where mutual funds are involved, have accrued not to the owners but to their managers.[98]

And—to turn directly to one of the main proffered justifications of the present system—regulated, noncompetitive rates have uneconomically encouraged cost-inflating methods of competition. Nicholas Kaldor has pointed out that the inclusion of advertising cost in the price of advertised

---

[97] "In this age of automation, the Street has conspicuously failed to keep pace."

"it is clear that the industry in general, and some brokers in particular, did not get around to putting enough money and effort into the automation of facilities. . . . Besides that, the Street has always thought of sales first and all other things last. . . . [As we will observe presently, this is exactly what one would expect in an industry whose price is held at noncompetitive levels, but whose members are left free to compete in other ways.]

"The Exchange's own record with automation has been very uneven. Any expert studying the floor of the Exchange, and the process by which a trade is executed, would see many possibilities for automation; and indeed some of these are becoming reality. But the plain fact is that beyond a certain point, the members do not really wish to see the stock trade automated. For it is *they* who would be replaced by a computer." Loomis, *op. cit.*, 150–151. Courtesy of *Fortune Magazine*.

"'Characterized as the nerve center of American industry, the Exchange is really a glaring anachronism. . . .

"'The operating procedures of most brokerage houses . . . are in the green eye-shade era where Bob Cratchit would have no trouble fitting in immediately. . . .

"'. . . the technology is available . . . to solve most . . . security industry problems.'" William D. Smith, "Will Market Receive Massage?" *The New York Times*, March 30, 1969, Section 3,

1, 14. See the similar observation by M. J. Rossant, "Warning from S.E.C.," *The New York Times*, October 30, 1966, pp. 67, 73. On some of the respects in which the performance of the smaller exchanges has been superior to that of New York, see also Robbins, *op. cit.*, 266–273.

[98] It is important to recognize that many—but not all—of these defects would be eliminated by the more realistic and cost-related structure that the NYSE now advocates and that effective regulation would help to assure. It would eliminate the price discrimination and internal subsidization, eliminate give-ups, and bring the large institutional investors back to the Exchange. Likewise, contributing to this end would be a relaxation of the rules—currently under scrutiny of the SEC—that now prohibit publicly owned firms holding membership on the Exchange; the institutional investor could partially escape the discrimination against him by buying a seat. The NYSE approved public ownership in September of 1969. But those new regulations would still ban institutional investors from membership: its broker members understandably fear that otherwise the institutions would transfer their immense patronage to their own member subsidiaries. The proposed rules would prohibit any member firm from having as a customer any nonmember that shares in 5 percent or more of its profits—thereby eliminating any incentive of large investors to seek membership in order to share in the profits of handling their own transactions. See "Big Board Heads for a Showdown," *Business Week*, November 8, 1969. 120–125.

products carries an inherent tendency for more advertising to be produced than would be the case if customers had the choice of purchasing or not purchasing it directly. In unregulated markets generally, it is conceivable— although this writer would argue to the contrary—that "information" of this type is not overproduced, or would not be if buyers were well informed and had a fair choice between advertised and nonadvertised products, at prices corresponding to the respective costs of supplying them.[99] But in markets in which price competition is prohibited and consumers have no such choice, there can be no doubt that the Kaldor tendency prevails. As long as the artificially maintained price exceeds the marginal cost of some firms (and if it did not there would be no reason to regulate it), those firms, denied the ability to reach out for additional business by price reductions, will have an incentive to do so by providing "free" services of one kind or another, from salesmanship on the one hand to advice and research on the other. The customer who wants to buy execution of orders plus salesmanship, advice, and research pays the same price as the customer that wants only the first of these. The consequence is an inherent tendency to what might be termed service inflation, in which an equilibrium of cost and price is achieved not by reducing price to marginal cost but raising marginal cost to price.[100]

---

[99] See the references cited in note 103, p. 41, Chapter 1, above; also Telser, "Advertising and Competition," *Jour. Pol. Econ.* (December 1964), LXXII: 537–562.

[100] The NYSE Report offers two intriguing justifications of selling the auxiliary services and the order-execution in a package. The first is that information about securities is in one respect a public good: the marginal cost of making it available to additional customers is zero. Therefore, it contends, economic efficiency requires that its price be zero; and this is in fact accomplished if it is supplied at no additional cost along with the execution of orders. (The resultant higher commission rates, required to cover the cost of providing the services, might discourage the purchase of the joint package; but if the demand for brokerage services taken as a whole is inelastic, there is no offsetting economic inefficiency involved in selling the two together.) *Economic Effects*, August 1968, *op. cit.*, 105.

We have already encountered this reasoning in discussing the economics of free television. And, as we have pointed out there (pp. 40–41, Chapter 1, above) this reasoning is correct, as far as it goes. What it ignores is the fact that in another, equally important respect, the production of information has a marginal cost definitely above zero: the more research in which a company engages, the higher, of course, are the costs. And there is need for some pricing device to determine the proper flow of resources into this productive operation. As against the economic efficiency served by a zero price, of

encouraging the widest possible dissemination where the marginal costs of dissemination itself are practically zero, must be weighed the economic inefficiency of the zero price, in encouraging an excessive production of that information. (One may question, as well, the extent to which the single package price does in fact accomplish free distribution of the information; certainly brokerage houses confine some of it to their own customers.) This kind of calculation is impossible to make in a priori terms. But when one turns to the apparently larger expenditures of brokerage houses on selling expenses, the cost of which is likewise incorporated in the package, the inefficiencies of "service inflation" would seem definitely to outweigh the efficiencies. My student, Barbara Wiget, has in a paper "The Tyranny of the Big Exchange" supplied an amusing and not entirely unfair characterization of the Exchange's defense of the package-selling:

"Salesmanship and information have a way of confusing themselves in . . . [the] presentation. . . . The justification of what some have called a monopoly price on the basis of high selling costs . . . comes close to being a theoretical innovation. J. M. Clark is called on to buttress the argument. . . . Clark did not advocate government support of price fixing to maintain a level of advertising which free competition would reduce."

The other defense offered by the NYSE Report is an interesting adaptation of the present writer's demonstration, in another connection,

The industry provides an even more direct confirmation and illustration of this tendency. In 1969, under pressure of diminishing business and profit margins and in growing recognition of the fact that it was the large transactions that were highly profitable and the small ones that may not even have covered marginal costs, the brokerage firms instituted corresponding adjustments in their selling expenses. They began to cut salesmen's commissions on small transactions and to increase them on the large,[101] thereby once again demonstrating how costs get adjusted to price if price is not free to move.

The elimination of price competition in brokerage rates, then, has had some seriously deleterious effects on the performance of the market. These costs might nonetheless be worth paying—particularly if rates were effectively regulated henceforth, as the NYSE now proposes—if the industry's model of how competition would function in the absence of minimum rate regulation were realistic: as always, the real choice can only be between imperfect systems. There remains a possibility that free price competition would produce undesirable fluctuations in rates with the changing relationship of demand to capacity—fluctuations serving no economic purpose, if, as seems likely, the demand in the aggregate for brokerage services is inelastic. It is certainly possible, too, that price competition would be discriminatory. Product differentiation and an inadequate ability to shop around and obtain concessions could expose smaller customers to charges far in excess of the marginal cost of supplying them, while larger investors, seeking only the bare completion of transactions, could demand rates closely tied to cost.[102] Any such discrimination could produce a distortion in the choice by

---

that the operation of a competitive market can lead to the disappearance of certain, economically justified services, because it has no means of charging buyers what it is worth to them merely to have those services continuously *available*, regardless of whether they actually purchase it. For a fuller statement of the general thesis, see pp. 236–238, this chapter, below.

"individual investors might be unwilling to pay separately for research and advisory services each time they made a small decision to buy or sell stock. But if enough individuals decided against purchasing the information needed for better decision-making, the research and informational facilities of brokers would eventually dwindle, and perhaps disappear. The disappearance of the basic research facilities might constitute a genuine deprivation that customers would willingly have paid a considerable amount *in the aggregate* to avoid." *Economic Effects*, August 1968, *op. cit.*, 102–104.

The difficulty with this particular application of the argument is that there are already a large number of firms selling market information and advice, at a price; and, it must be presumed, there would be even more were it not that consumers already receive such advice "free" from brokerage houses in the commissions that

they pay for the execution of buy and sell orders. If, then, the introduction of competition in the setting of commission rates led some brokers to reduce their supply of these services, it seems almost certain they would not only remain available to customers for separate purchase but be available in greater quantity than theretofore. And even if some of the supply dried up, because buyers were unwilling to pay for it explicitly, there is no reason why it could not be expanded in the future, when and as economically justified.

[101] *Wall Street Journal*, December 9, 1969, 10. After a period in which it explicitly justified the packaging of order-execution and auxiliary services, the New York Exchange indirectly recognized the cogency of the argument against it when it suggested the possibility of a regulated rate structure that would permit separate charging for these services. *The Economics of Minimum Commission Rates*, May 1, 1969, *op. cit.*, 52. But its president later rejected the suggestion as "unrealistic." *Wall Street Journal*, November 24, 1969, 3.

[102] I am indebted to Joel B. Dirlam for emphasizing this side of the coin. And yet it is difficult to reconcile with the Exchange's emphasis on the extreme danger that competition would be destructive. The SEC's proposals of October 1970 would forestall this possibility by making the

small investors between investing on their own account and through the intermediary of mutual funds.

On the other hand, it is extremely difficult for an economist to accept the alternative system—a system of soft, nonprice, cost-inflating competition, grounded in the desire to protect competitors and having the effect of sustaining the capitalized monopoly profits that are reflected in the price of acquiring membership in a stock exchange. Effectively regulated rates—particularly if the auxiliary services were priced separately—could mitigate many of these inefficiencies and, if based on industry-wide cost averages, as is now proposed, could exert heavy pressure on inefficient brokers to mend their ways or to go out of business. But legally prescribed rates based on average industry costs are still not competitive rates; they still protect the relatively inefficient; they deny efficient firms the option of increasing their market shares by price reductions and still give them an incentive to compete by proliferating services.

The Regulation of Nonprice Competition: Air Transport

We have now seen two illustrations of an important economic principle: when limitations are placed on price competition, but market conditions are such as to make continued interfirm rivalry likely, the consequence will be an accentuation of service competition.[103] If the minimum rate regulation is effective, it will almost certainly hold price above the marginal costs of some producers, to which competition would otherwise drive it. (It could conceivably be confined to preventing sales *below* marginal costs, but since producers would not ordinarily make such sales except temporarily, in the hope of holding on to a share of the market in the expectation that prices would shortly improve,[104] it is rarely limited to this modest purpose.) But if competition is sufficiently strong, potentially, to drive price down to that level, it will ordinarily be sufficiently strong to induce these suppliers, confronting a price above their marginal costs, to seek other, nonprice methods of producing additional sales. Specifically, they will be inclined to improve service in one way or another, until their marginal costs, inflated by the service improvements, are equated to price.

Mark the general principle; it is an important one. If price is prevented from falling to marginal cost in the short run or to average total cost in the long run,[105] then, to the extent that competition prevails, it will tend to raise *cost* to the level of *price*. Only when, in this way, marginal cost is once again equated with price will the tendency to service inflation be halted.[106]

---

schedule of commissions on transactions of less than $100,000 maxima as well as minima. The greater danger seems to be that the ceilings on small transactions will not be compensatory.

[103] See pp. 189 and 206–207, this chapter, above.

[104] They might also do so with predatory intention, taking the out-of-pocket losses in order to drive rivals out of the market and in expectation of being able to charge monopoly prices thereafter; or for A–J–W kinds of reasons, in expectation of being permitted to recoup those losses in higher charges to customers with inelastic demand. But neither of these possibilities is typically applicable in minimum rate regula-

tion situations.

[105] To whose MC or ATC? To the costs of supplying just the quantity that customers will demand at the market price—to the marginal cost of producing that quantity (and under pure competition *all* producers will equate their marginal costs to that price) and to the ATC of the highest-cost producer that the market finds it necessary to draw into production in order to meet the demand.

[106] Precisely the same tendency prevails under government or cartel-imposed minimum price controls when entry is free or investment by existing firms is uncontrolled. See our illustration

If, therefore, regulatory commissions have the responsibility of keeping price rivalry from becoming destructive, they cannot escape the responsibility of deciding whether they ought to limit quality competition as well. As we have already pointed out in our discussion of the more traditional public utilities, in which the presumed danger is one of monopolistic exploitation, price regulation alone is meaningless except in terms of some specified unit and quality of service: a baker with a local monopoly can exploit his customers just as effectively by giving them only twelve rolls for some fixed price when in the presence of competition he would be likely to give them thirteen as by continuing to give them a baker's dozen but charging them $8\frac{1}{2}$ percent more than the competitive price. Similarly when regulation is introduced to keep competition from driving a price *down*: it will be futile to affix a minimum price for a dozen rolls if bakers remain free to decide how many rolls constitute a dozen.[107]

Regulation has heretofore shirked this responsibility in trucking and the security brokerage business, with consequences we have already observed. In air transportation, in contrast, the regulators have found it impossible to ignore it, possibly because airline companies, catering much more than the others to the whims of the ultimate consumer, have competed much more intensely in this way. Partly for the same reason, the airline case is more difficult to judge than the others, because there would doubtless be a great deal of service rivalry even in the presence of much sharper price competition than now prevails. Nor is there any reason to doubt that this kind of competition is, within limits that are difficult to define, just as important a contributor to consumer welfare as price rivalry. We return to this difficult problem of evaluation at a later point.

Price competition is discouraged in this industry, first, by the oligopolistic character of airline markets, itself attributable partly to the restrictions on entry imposed by the Civil Aeronautics Board. The oligopolists in this industry show the familiar reluctance to engage in direct price rivalry.[108]

---

of oil production control, pp. 28–29, Chapter 1, above. It is entirely consistent with this principle that when, in 1969–1970, airline profits turned to losses, the companies returned from full meals to sandwiches, stopped handing out macadamia nuts, began to charge for inflight movies, and started pruning their schedules. *New York Times*, October 13, 1970, 18C.

[107] This is not to suggest that the danger of what J. M. Clark has termed product (or service) inflation is confined to highly competitive industries. On the contrary, what Clark was referring to was the possibility that in highly concentrated industries—he referred particularly to American automobiles—competition may take the form principally of cost inflating and largely specious quality improvements. *Competition as a Dynamic Process*, 252–257. The restraint that oligopolists may feel it is in their joint interest to exercise with respect to price rivalry may not extend to improvements in their products or services. This is partly because a successful product variation is not as readily imitated as a price cut, so that the firm that initiates it may feel that the advantages it may bring him, by way of larger sales or the ability to charge a higher price, will last for a while and so be worth the costs of competing in this manner. It may be true, also, because product rivalry—for example, frequent model changes—can move the entire industry demand curve to the right and so be in the interest of all producers; or because it may help cement the power of the oligopoly by raising additional barriers to entry and by being particularly difficult for smaller rivals to emulate. See the fuller discussion of this problem in Joe S. Bain, *Industrial Organization*, rev. ed. (New York: John Wiley & Co., 1968), 223–250, 348–357, 412–418, and this writer's *op. cit.*, *Kyklos* (January 1966), XIX: 39–44. It is cartelization that introduces the danger of service inflation in structurally competitive industries.

[108] See Caves, *Air Transport and its Regulators*, Chapter 1 and 15; Samuel B. Richmond, *Regulation and Competition in Air Transportation*, (New York: Columbia Univ. Press, 1961), 45–47.

Possibly contributing to this same restraint is the fact that they have agreed to notify the Air Transport Association of all proposed rate changes at least 15 days before filing them with the CAB, which undoubtedly gives the other companies an opportunity to put pressure on any one of them proposing to reduce rates.[109] Second, the CAB itself has tended quite consistently to discourage competitive rate reductions.[110] In the international field, price competition has been even more effectively contained by the International Air Transport Association (IATA), which, backed by the authority of governments to deny or withdraw landing privileges to airlines that refuse to adhere to its rate schedules, has imposed a particularly high and non-competitive schedule of rates on international traffic.[111]

In part because the doors to price competition are closed, airline companies compete very strenuously among themselves in the quality of service they offer—most notably in adopting the most modern and attractive equipment and in the frequency with which they schedule flights, but also in providing comfort, attractive hostesses, in-flight entertainment, food and drink.[112] Among these, the one most closely approaching destructiveness in character is scheduling. There is a general belief that the airline with the most flights between any two points is the one to which customers will turn first in making their reservations. The result, where competition is strong and particularly in markets where new entry threatens, is a cumulative tendency to excess capacity, with each company vying with the other by increasing the number of daily flights on its schedule.[113] Ronald E. Miller attributes to

---

[109] Caves, *Air Transport and its Regulators*, 366; Richmond, *op. cit.*, 49–50.

[110] The Board has had to devote a good deal of attention to passing on requests for rate increases as well. See Caves, *Air Transport and its Regulators*, 142–154, 250. On the other hand,

"A red thread running through this narrative has been the Board's fear of any action that might, even indirectly, yield low rates of return for the carriers. There are many other instances of its nervousness about any fare proposals or situations that could lead to substantial general price competition among the carriers."

Ibid., 154; see also pp. 145, 155. The Board has also exercised its authority to prohibit undue or unreasonable rate discrimination generally in order to prohibit selective rate reductions incident to, or that threaten to accentuate, competition. *Ibid.*, 158–163, 167–168. It has imposed tight controls on the smaller, non-scheduled carriers that tend to compete more actively in price. See, for example, *ibid.*, 145, 149; and, on the restrictive policy toward irregular airlines, U.S. Senate, Select Committee on Small Business, *Future of Irregular Airlines*, 83rd Congress, First Session, Report No. 822, July 31, 1953.

[111] See Mahlon R. Straszheim, *The International Airline Industry* (Washington: Brookings Institution, 1969), 131–149, 170–172, 194–196; International Air Transport Association, "How International Airline Fares and Rates Are Made," Vladimir de Boursac, "The Raison d'Être of Traffic Conferences," and Lord Brabazon of Tara, "1962 IATA Paper," (the latter begins: "Coming to your organization, [International Air Transport Association] I must say about it right at the start that my admiration for it has never passed the bounds of moderation"), all reproduced in Stanley C. Hollander, *Passenger Transportation, Readings Selected from a Marketing Viewpoint* (East Lansing: Michigan State University, 1968), 539–560; also U. S. House of Representatives, Committee on the Judiciary, Antitrust Subcommittee, 85th Cong. 1st Sess., *The Airlines Industry*, April 5, 1957, 217–235, 275–276.

[112] The expenses in even the latter category alone are hardly negligible: one airline executive says that his company spends more than $30 for food and liquor for each transatlantic first-class passenger. *New York Times*, March 31, 1969, 39. Also "In Airlines' Battle, Every Inch Counts," *ibid.*, October 28, 1970, 1.

[113] See Caves, *Air Transport and its Regulators*, 333–348; Straszheim, *op. cit.*, 163–164, 168–170, 178–179; and, for example, "Which Cure for TWA?" *Business Week*, September 15, 1962, 48. According to this article, the president of TWA was trying to persuade his counterparts at American and United Airlines to ask the CAB for permission to discuss an agreed-upon reduction in capacity:

this competitive overscheduling the major part of the blame for the excessive capacity in the industry, showing up in load factors (ratios of revenue passenger miles sold to total available seat miles in scheduled service) typically running below 60 percent.[114]

This kind of competition, like persuasive advertising, is in considerable measure self-defeating. It may pay each individual company to advertise, whether aggressively or defensively—A having to advertise in order to keep from losing customers to B and B having to do the same for the same reason—but for all companies together the gain in revenue is probably typically less than the additional selling costs they have incurred. We shall have to take into account, before terminating this discussion, the fact that nonprice competition can mean an improvement in the quality of service: even persuasive advertising is not entirely unproductive, insofar as it provides some information and perhaps provides some assurance to customers of minimal standards of quality. The proliferation of scheduled flights, even more clearly, does mean greater convenience, offering the traveller a greater number of alternative times among which to choose in making any particular trip.[115] But where the scheduling is purely duplicative and the traffic actually generated could be carried in fewer flights, the competition has produced only waste.

The most thorough restrictions on the service competition among airline companies, as on price competition as well—as we have indicated, the latter accentuates the need for the former[116]—have been the ones imposed by the IATA, notably on the tourist flights of its members. Most notorious have been regulations prescribing the maximum allowable knee-room (commodious for midgets), dictating that meals be limited to sandwiches (which unruly competitors persisted in making more and more sumptuous) and requiring a uniform supplementary charge for in-flight motion pictures and other entertainment.[117] But these provide only a sketchy indication of the kinds of rules that are necessary if an agreement on prices is to stick:

> "Even a simple fare structure is meaningless unless a host of other matters is settled. Could this fare be sold by an agent? If so, at what rate of commission? . . .

"The chief drawback to this is that frequency of flight is one of the few competitive weapons that airline management has left. Prices are substantially the same, catering is about the same, speeds are almost identical, and though equipment is vastly different to the experts, it looks pretty much the same to the passenger walking out of the gate. Now Tillinghast is suggesting that numbers of flights be a matter not of management choice but of formula." Reprinted by special permission.

The subsequent sharp recovery in the profitability of the industry evidently took the steam out of the effort, at least temporarily. But sharply diminished profitability and declining load factors in the late 1960's led to a resumption of collective efforts, resulting in a formal request by TWA, United, and American Airlines to the CAB for permission to enter into a joint agree-

ment to reduce flights. *New York Times*, August 29, 1970.

[114] *Domestic Airline Efficiency: An Application of Linear Programming* (Cambridge: M.I.T. Press, 1963), 108–114. Annual load factors can be computed from the CAB's *Annual Reports* to Congress.

[115] See Vickrey, *op. cit., Jour. Pol. Econ.* (June 1948), LVI: note 8 and p. 234. Miller explicitly ignores the welfare loss from diminished frequency of service, in calculating the extent of overscheduling. The objective of his model is to provide the same total amount of passenger trips at "minimum total direct cost." *Op. cit.*, 92 and 94, note 5.

[116] For an observation that the more stringent limitations on price competition internationally have led to more intensive service inflation in those markets, see Straszheim, *op. cit.*, 170–171.

[117] See *ibid.*, 105–107, 143–144.

"Would a stopover be allowed on this fare? If yes, and the stopover took place at night, would the airline be allowed to pay for his hotel accommodation . . .? How long could the stopover be and would he have to have a firm reservation on the next connecting flight? . . .

"How much baggage could he take? If he had his wife with him, could they pool this free baggage allowance? How much baggage could he himself carry over and above his free allowance? . . .

"There are very many more questions like this which have a substantial competitive impact and on which there must be agreement among the airlines to which the fare applies, if the agreement on the fare itself is going to stick. If there is no agreement there can be no fare because obviously if somebody is going to pay 20 percent commission to the agent or give the passenger free hotel accommodation, or let him carry as much luggage as he wants, that airline is going to get more passengers than the others."[118]

The attention paid by the CAB to service competition has been much more sporadic and, indeed, mixed in its intentions and effects.[119] For one thing, just as the Board has from time to time intervened to hold rates *down*, so it has frequently exerted its influence to *improve* the quality of service. Its primary device for doing so has been to grant certificates to competing companies on particular routes, something it has been especially willing to do when it could be demonstrated that the service previously provided was inadequate.[120] This would certainly seem the most efficient way of promoting that goal. It has also attempted to place limitations on overbooking, that is, the practice of accepting more reservations on a flight than there are actual spaces, in expectation that some of the reservations will be cancelled or the passengers will not show up. It has investigated the complaints of particular cities that they were receiving inadequate service and ordered certificated carriers to improve it.

In one important way, these policies have encouraged irrational service inflation. This, as Caves points out, has been the consequence of Board decisions denying carriers with older and less attractive equipment permission to charge correspondingly lower fares:

"the Board . . . . forbids the carrier with older or inferior equipment to set a differential to protect its market position. These policies create an overwhelming incentive for carriers to acquire equipment as modern or as appealing as any used by their direct competitors . . . . The carrier suffering equipment inferiority has all major avenues to protecting its market position blocked except that one."[121]

---

[118] de Boursac, in Hollander, *op. cit.*, 547–548. Reprinted by permission of the publisher, the Bureau of Business and Economic Research, Division of Research, Graduate School of Business Administration, Michigan State University.
[119] See Caves, *Air Transport and its Regulators*, Chapters 9–10, and Aaron J. Gellman, "The Regulation of Service Competition," in Hollander, *op. cit.*, 580–589, on which discussions the following summary draws heavily.
[120] On this policy, see also p. 16, note 29, above.
[121] *Op. cit.*, 241–242; see also 352–355. This is the

conclusion, also, of A. J. Gellman's study, *The Effect of Regulation on Aircraft Choice*, unpublished Ph.D. dissertation, Massachusetts Institute of Technology, 1968, as cited by Almarin Phillips, "Technological Change in the Air Transportation Industry in the United States," a paper presented at the Brookings Institution Conference on Technological Change in the Regulated Industries, February, 1969. For a similar conclusion concerning the international market, see Straszheim, *op. cit.*, 170–171, 180–181.

When, for example, Alaska Airlines sought to introduce a lower fare for flights using DC-4's than Pan American was charging for its DC-6B equipment, the Board denied the request on the ground that, among other things, the latter planes were no more costly to operate than the former.[122] The reason has a superficial plausibility: it sounds as though the CAB was merely following the dictate of marginal-cost pricing. But airline rates are set not at marginal, but at variable costs plus a return on investment. If customers regarded service on the DC-4 as inferior, the consequence of uniform prices could have been to induce all of them to shift to the more attractive and modern Pan American equipment. This would obviously involve society in the necessity for bringing a larger number of these new planes into service, and scrapping more of the older ones, than would have been the case had passengers been presented with a choice between the two at prices reflecting their respective attractiveness. The marginal costs of the Pan American service would therefore have had to include the cost of purchasing additional equipment; the MC of the DC-4's would reflect variable costs alone.[123]

Indeed, the CAB specifically defended its rejection of the Alaska petition on the ground that "a fare differential would lessen the incentive of the carriers to introduce better equipment. . . ."[124] But of course as long as existing, "poorer" equipment can give service at prices in excess of variable costs, there is every economic reason to continue to use it; and to set obstacles in the way of its use in order to give carriers an incentive "to introduce better equipment" is to promote waste.

On the other hand, the Board has at times and in limited ways supplemented its efforts to hold price competition in check by placing collateral restrictions on the quality of service offered. When, after much foot-dragging, it permitted the introduction of coach fares, it took pains to assure that coach flights would be scheduled only at off-peak times and with much denser seating than on first-class trips.[125] So it denied the request of United Airlines that it be permitted to adopt a policy of selling only a portion of the seats available on coach flights, in order to improve passenger comfort, on the ground that this would constitute "an unfair method of competition."[126] Again, when TWA proposed to introduce "Siesta Sleeper Seats" on its transcontinental first-class flights—which would have reduced the number of seats that could be accommodated in the cabin—and United and American Airlines objected that they would have had to do the same if TWA were permitted to go ahead, the Board decided to permit the innovation only if the service was subjected to a 20 percent surcharge:

---

[122] Caves, *Air Transport and its Regulators*, 241, citing the *States-Alaska Fare Case*, Docket No. 6328 *et al.*, 21 CAB 354, 356–358 (1955).

[123] If the total costs of the two kinds of equipment seemed to be equal, it could only have been because the book value of the older equipment—and, consequently, the depreciation and return on investment components of the cost of using it—exceeded its market value. See pp. 117–122, Volume 1, above. This is on the assumption, of course, that Alaska Airlines' proposed lower rates would have covered at least the variable

costs of operating that equipment. If the variable costs of the DC–4's, including a return on the scrap or second hand sale price of the equipment, exceeded the rate necessary for them to get business in competition with the DC–6B's, the equipment should in fact have been withdrawn from service.

[124] Loc. cit., note 122.

[125] See note 110, above.

[126] *United Airlines, Inc.—Petition for Change in Coach Policy and for Exemption*, Docket No. 5884, January 6, 1953, as cited in Gellman, *op. cit.*, 583.

"TWA does not seek to justify the offering of sleeper-seat service at prevailing first-class fares on the ground that such service will promote new air traffic. Rather, it contends that it is offering such service almost exclusively because of competitive considerations. . . . The evidence shows that if all three carriers . . . were to operate a sleeper-seat service, the nonstop transcontinental market would be uneconomical for each."[127]

But these attempts have been comparatively few. One explanation, at least in the case of scheduling, is the limited authority of the Board; according to its enabling act,

"No term, condition, or limitation of a certificate shall restrict the right of an air carrier to add to or change schedules, equipment, accommodations, and facilities for performing the authorized transportation and service as the development of the business and the demands of the public shall require . . ."[128]

Another explanation of this permissiveness is its statutory mandate to promote the growth of air travel, which undoubtedly explains also its own enthusiasm for airlines adopting the most modern equipment. In any event, its controls over service competition have been mainly hortatory.[129] It took the airport congestion emergency of 1968 to induce the Board to authorize consultations among the airlines on the possibility of reducing the number of their scheduled flights during peak hours at the congested airports.[130]

---

[127] *Trans World Airlines Siesta Sleeper-Seat Service*, Docket No. 9063, et. al, Opinion, 27 CAB 788, 790 (November 1958).

[128] 49 U.S. Code 1371(e)(3), 1964 ed. See the similar limitation on the power of the ICC over motor carriers, at p. 189, this chapter, above. The CAB can exert indirect influence on scheduling, equipment purchases, selling, and other expenses of the *subsidized* airlines, because it can disallow costs that it deems excessive in determining the amount of subsidy. See G. E. Hale and Rosemary D. Hale, "Competition or Control IV: Air Carriers," *Univ. of Pennsylvania Law Rev.* (January 1961), CIX: 342. And it can exert similar pressures on the unsubsidized carriers, when they come in for fare increases. See Caves, *op. cit.*, 237–238.

[129] "While competing carriers are expected by the Board and the public to compete with vigor, a measure of scheduling self-discipline by individual carrier management is becoming increasingly imperative in the public interest and in the interest of a healthy industry. Although domestic airlines operate without a rate bureau, we seldom see any trace of what might be regarded as a rate war among competing airlines. Apparently, the industry has been successful in avoiding rate wars through carrier managements acting individually in their own interest. However, it is by no means clear why similar self-interest would not dictate a corresponding restraint against over-scheduling in competitive markets.

"This leads to another area where more and more industry officials have indicated informally that greater restraint by individual carrier managements, in connection with the level of advertising expenditures, may be required. I do not pretend to pass judgment on the proper level of advertising by each carrier in a competitive transportation system, but the questions raised within the industry, as to potential uneconomic advertising expense levels, may suggest an important area of potential economy that would be a worthwhile step towards at least curtailing the cost revenue squeeze." Address by Irving Roth, Director, Bureau of Economics, Civil Aeronautics Board, at the Wings Club Luncheon, New York City, September 18, 1968, processed.

[130] During the course of 1968, the overcrowding of flights during peak hours at several of the country's major airports resulted in delays of several hours in arrivals and departures. In this emergency, the CAB approved agreements between American and foreign air carriers to set up scheduling committees for five airports, for the purpose of instituting voluntary action to bring their combined number of scheduled flights within the safety limitations set up by the Federal Aviation Administration. The CAB, in announcing this approval on December 5, 1968, stated that it recognized that approval of the agreements represented "a departure from our customary policy with respect to so sensitive an area as scheduling."

Clearly, in general, the Board has discouraged price competition far more than service competition, with a strong resultant tendency for the industry to engage in cost-increasing service inflation.

> "While it is undeniably desirable that the level of service afforded the traveling public be raised continually, it is somewhat ludicrous to find virtually unrestricted service competition prevailing in this industry while prices are more or less rigidly controlled."[131]

Rivalry in improving service can obviously be just as productive of benefit to the traveling public as in price. How, then, can an economist presume to judge that it has gone too far? He may not, directly. All he can do is ask whether the service improvements have been subjected to the test of a competitive market. That test requires that customers be provided with a sufficient variety of price-quality combinations—consistent with efficient production—so that each can register a free and tolerably well-informed monetary appraisal of the quality differentials that are offered. By this test product inflation could be said to have occurred only if quality competition had operated in such a way as to eliminate, or to fail to develop, lower quality-price combinations that consumers would willingly have purchased in quantities sufficient to cover the cost of providing them. The reason why it is questionable that the service improvements produced by competition in the airline industry have been worth the cost is that the restrictions on *price* competition have denied consumers the alternative of less sumptuous service at prices reflecting its lower cost. They have therefore not had the opportunity to determine whether the better quality is in their collective judgment worth the higher cost of providing it.[132]

The objection is not necessarily that airlines have been forced by their competition to incur greater costs for denser schedules, advertising, meals, and in-flight entertainment than they would if they were able to get together and restrict such expenditures to the industry profit-maximizing level—although that certainly is what they have done.[133] To adopt any such criterion of industry performance would be to take the results of pure monopoly as the ideal: it is precisely the function of competition to force suppliers to do things that are not in their collective interest. The objection is, rather, that these cost-inflating service improvements have not been subjected to the test of having to compete with lower-cost, lower-price alternatives. The defect, in short, has not been the service competition, as such, but the inadequate play of *price* competition along with it.

The airline industry offers several evidences that price competition can, if it is given a chance, hold service inflation in check. Historically, passenger rates have been geared to first-class Pullman railroad fares, with a corresponding emphasis on luxurious service. "The first real break came when the irregular carriers introduced coach service at rates approximately 65 percent of standard trunk-line fares."[134] These nonscheduled airlines were

---

[131] Gellman, in Hollander, *op. cit.*, 587; see also pp. 585–589.

[132] See, for example, Straszheim, *op. cit.*, 114, 181, and *passim*.

[133] See, for example, the judgment of Caves, *Air Transport and its Regulators*, 347–348, 353.

[134] Horace M. Gray, "The Airlines Industry," in Adams (ed.), *The Structure of American Industry*, 3rd ed., 484. For a description of the similar role played by the irregular airlines in freight operations, driving air cargo down from about 60 to 16 cents per ton-mile, and a description of the efforts of the CAB to hold this competition in check, see *ibid.*, 485, 494–504.

for the most part companies that had come into the business, by the hundreds, after World War II, generally carrying passengers or freight on an irregular basis, when demand justified it, at rates lower than those charged by the regularly certificated trunk-line carriers.[135] For the first several years, coach service was offered only over high-density routes and during off-peak hours, with denser passenger seating than in first-class, and no meals were served. The enormous expansion of coach travel that followed, as the regular carriers introduced similar service of their own, clearly demonstrated that the majority of potential travelers preferred the lower price-quality combination to the one that had previously been available to them.[136] A similar illustration has been provided more recently by the popularity of the group charter flights, at rates substantially below those set by the IATA, and, later, the inclusive tour charters on scheduled North Atlantic flights. These, once again, were pioneered by the nonscheduled (later termed supplemental) air carriers and again subjected to various restrictions by the CAB and the IATA, in order to lessen their impact on the regular rate structures.[137]

Another, even more striking illustration is provided by the extraordinary impact that essentially unregulated price competition has had on the price

---

[135] *Ibid.*, 476.

[136] See the same conclusion of Straszheim, *op. cit.*, 119–120, and, with reference to the similar burgeoning of chartered flights, pp. 50, 181. Between the fiscal years ending June 30, 1952 and June 30, 1968, the share of total certificated revenue passenger miles accounted for by coach traffic rose from 15 to 45 percent. CAB *Annual Reports* for those years, pp. 13 and 4, respectively. Since coach service is not universally available, the statement that the majority of potential travellers prefer it seems reasonable. The emphasis on "potential" passengers is explained by the estimate, cited by Locklin, that as of 1950 about 70 percent of the coach travel was additional traffic to the airlines, and about 30 percent diverted from first class. *Op. cit.*, 777. On the price elasticity of demand for air travel, see also p. 103, above.

[137] The principal restriction is that the groups must have "affinity"—that is, they cannot have been formed merely in order to take advantage of the low group fares. See the CAB *Annual Reports* for 1949 and 1950, 24 and 25, respectively. For a description of CAB efforts to crack down on evasions of this requirement—"You see too many little old ladies getting aboard on the trips offered by the Far West Ski Association"—see *Wall Street Journal*, June 10, 1969, 1. In 1964 the Board for the first time certificated supplemental carriers to engage in the transatlantic charter business, stating that

"Historically, the Board has sought to encourage the development of a large mass international travel market . . . without undue

diversion from the regular route carriers." *Transatlantic Charter Investigation*, Opinion, 40 CAB 233, 253 (1964).

And it liberalized that policy in the subsequent years. See Straszheim, *op. cit.*, 216–220. The number of revenue passenger miles flown by the supplemental lines rose, in consequence, from 1.5 billion in 1963 to 8.7 billion in 1968. *Wall Street Journal*, July 30, 1969, 34.

In addition, travel agents can themselves charter flights and sell tickets to individuals, who need not be members of any cognizable group. But on such charters they may not offer bargain rates for air transportation alone. Instead, they and the airlines themselves can offer only "inclusive tour" packages that include a charge for a minimum of $70 worth of ground services—hotel accommodations, car rentals, and the like; this has the effect of bringing their quoted rates roughly up to the regular tourist fare. The governing U.S. statute requires that the operator of the inclusive tour must sell the package for at least 110 percent of the regular air fare; but the price he pays the airline can be negotiated.

A research report by the CAB's Bureau of Economics concluded there was no evidence that inclusive tour charters would have a materially adverse effect on the regularly scheduled service and recommended that the lower-price service be encouraged because it would open up to the airlines a "great, new, untapped source of potential customers." *Economic Impact of Inclusive Tour Charters on Scheduled North Atlantic Services*, January 1969, 21. See this Study also for a summary of the legal history of these plans.

and volume of air traffic between Los Angeles and San Francisco, Cali-fornia.[138] What made this possible was the fact that wholly intrastate air transport is free of CAB control and that the California Public Utilities Commission has no power to limit entry and has followed the practice, as far as rates are concerned, of approving virtually all changes. The results of this, the closest thing to a "controlled experiment" in public policy, have been summarized by Michael E. Levine as follows:

"Although the Los Angeles-San Francisco market has always been an important one, it was the fifth largest in the United States in 1948 (in terms of passenger miles), and became the largest only in 1961. Today, more revenue passengers travel between Los Angeles and San Francisco than between any pair of cities in the world. . . . The market has grown rapidly . . . and has been characterized by intense competition, a wide variety of marketing strategies, and the lowest overland air fares in the world.

"There are striking contrasts between the performance of this market and the performance of similar markets in the United States regulated by the CAB. For example, although the number of passengers traveling by air in the United States as a whole has increased between the years 1959 and 1964 by approximately 50 per cent, the number of travelers passing between Los Angeles and San Francisco by air has increased almost 300 per cent. Although the average jet coach fare level in the United States is approximately 5.5 cents per mile over stages considerably longer, and hence cheaper to operate, jet coach fare for the 350-mile trip from San Francisco to Los Angeles is approximately 3.9 cents per mile. Although the lowest fare between Boston and Washington, served only by CAB-certificated trunk carriers, is $24.65, Pacific Southwest Airlines, using the same modern turbo-prop equipment, carries passengers between Los Angeles and San Francisco, only 59 miles closer together, for $11.43. The jet fare is only $13.50. In other markets, obsolescent though eco-nomically viable aircraft have been rapidly retired as new aircraft have been introduced prematurely, because the fare structure has emphasized premium service and has not allowed the owner of obsolescent equipment to operate at a fare reflecting his lower capital costs. In Los Angeles-San Francisco, however, it has been common to see obsolescent equipment operated at fares reflecting the lower capital cost until replaced by new equipment so much more efficient that the capital cost charges could be amortized at fares which reflected customer demand for the new equip-ment."[139]

The significance of the 1959 point of comparison is that it was in that year that the Pacific Southwest Airlines (PSA), an intrastate carrier operating without a CAB certificate, first introduced modern turboprop aircraft,

---

[138] The following account is drawn from the very persuasive study of Michael E. Levine, "Is Regulation Necessary? California Air Trans-portation and National Regulatory Policy," *Yale Law Jour.* (July 1965), LXXIV: 1416–1447. See also the CAB, Research and Statistics Division, Bureau of Accounts and Statistics, *Traffic, Fares,* *and Competition, Los Angeles–San Francisco Air Travel Corridor,* Staff Research Report No. 4, Washing-ton, August 1965.

[139] *Op. cit.,* reprinted by permission of the Yale Law Journal Company and Fred B. Rothman & Company from the *Yale Law Journal,* Vol. 74, pp. 1432–1433.

charging rates far below those charged by the three CAB-certificated carriers, United Airlines, TWA, and Western Airlines. In a scant three years, during which its competitors failed to respond, PSA increased its market share from 13 to 43 percent. United and Western eventually reacted by sharply reducing their fares and introducing jet service, beginning around 1962; but PSA likewise introduced jets and retained about 35 percent of the market, as of the early part of 1965. A particularly interesting additional fact is that despite the quintupled scheduling by United, the market leader, in introducing its new jets, load factors remained at a comfortable and profitable two-thirds, far above the national ratio;[140] and despite the drastic reduction in fares, from the $20 to the $11.43–13.50 range, PSA, with no other important source of income, was able to operate profitably:[141]

> "Lack of regulation has not caused chaos in California. Unregulated entry and price competition have not resulted in a multitude of tiny firms scrambling for passengers to the confusion of the general public. As the California market developed, advanced technology and effective marketing became essential to profitable operation; and it became increasingly difficult for a thinly-capitalized fringe operator to survive. Ultimately, no more than three important competitors remained, along with . . . periodically, a fringe operator trying to find a niche in the market. . . .
>
> "the California experience . . . indicates that the public has little to fear from unregulated entry. Participants in a market will be naturally limited to a number which ensures both competition and technical efficiency without chaos. The free-entry California market has and will have for the immediate future approximately the same structure—two to three major carriers—as most regulated routes. The important question is whether these carriers ought to be chosen administratively or by the competitive forces of the market. And the important difference is that transportation by air in the California unregulated market can be purchased for half to seven-tenths as much as it costs elsewhere."[142]

The experience with service inflation in air transportation suggests two possible alternative solutions. One is that if price competition continues to be restrained, service should likewise be subjected to much more consistent and effective controls than have hitherto been imposed on it—thus providing another illustration of the necessity for the regulatory net to be spread wider

---

[140] PSA's load factors ranged between 70 and 80 percent between 1961 and 1964 and were reported to exceed 80 percent on its single Boeing 727 in May of 1965, eight months after United introduced its jet shuttle service. CAB, *Traffic, Fares, and Competition, Los Angeles–San Francisco Air Travel Corridor*, 21.

[141] Except for 1960 and 1961, when it had some temporary difficulties, its return on stockholder equity consistently exceeded 30 percent in the 1959–1964 period. *Ibid.*, 15, 30. Levine describes a few interesting ways in which PSA has been able to hold its operating costs below those of its competitors. The one that is of direct relevance to our discussion of service inflation is:

"PSA has always managed somehow to squeeze a few extra seats into the aircraft it operates. Its 727's have 122 seats, compared to United's 114, because PSA ordered its equipment without full galleys, since meals are not served on this route. United, having ordered its 727's with its system needs in mind, carries the weight and space of the idle equipment." *Op. cit.*, 1439–1440, note 109. Reprinted by permission; see note 139, above.

[142] *Ibid.*, 1440–1441.

"Low fares, intensive advertising and constant innovation in service account for the spectacular growth of the Los Angeles–San Francisco market. This growth indicates that at least here there is elasticity of demand for air transportation." *Ibid.*, 1442.

and wider if it is to be effective.[143] The other would be to free the industry to provide low-price alternatives. Consideration of such a step would require a reexamination of the entire case for restricting competition in this industry. We make no such explicit assessment here, but the reader should by now be able to supply the relevant questions. Suffice it only to point out that many economists have concluded that passenger air transportation does not have the economic attributes of an industry prone to destructive competition, and that the public is entitled to enjoy the enormous potential benefits that freer competition—free entry and pricing—has demonstrated itself capable of providing.[144] One of those benefits would be that it would increase the variety of price-service combinations offered to the public and thereby tend to assure that cost-inflating service improvements were subjected to a fair market test. It would be pleasant if one could omit the "tend to." But how effective the test would in fact be would depend on how free was the competition that resulted from a removal of governmental restrictions. The notion of product inflation was originally developed with unregulated oligopolies in mind; the mere absence of government controls does not assure competition sufficiently keen and perfect to eradicate its possibility.[145]

THE ISSUE OF CREAM-SKIMMING

We have already, in Chapter 1, outlined the case that is frequently made for restrictions on entry or price competition in the interest of preventing cream-skimming; and we have encountered the argument from time to time elsewhere as well.[146] Here is clearly a way in which, allegedly, excessive competition can result in an eventual deterioration of the quality of service.

There are three possible approaches to an issue of this kind, all of which will be familiar to the reader. The first is the approach of the traditional, normative, microeconomic theory that underlies our Chapters 3–6 of Volume 1, and describes the "optimal" economic results that would issue from ideally perfect competition. The second would emphasize the institutional problems and considerations that are the subject matter of the present volume, which is concerned not with describing those "optimal" results but considering how they can be most closely approximated in the imperfect world of reality. This approach has to take into account the limitations of even a perfectly competitive market in serving the very purposes it purports

---

[143] See the judgment of Gellman, p. 216, above.
[144] See, for example, Caves, *Air Transport and its Regulators*, Chapter 18 and *passim*; Keyes, *Federal Control of Entry into Air Transportation*; also her "Reconsideration of Federal Control of Entry into Air Transportation," *Jour. Air Law and Commerce* (Spring 1955), XXII: 192–202; Richmond, *op. cit.*, 254–257; and Straszheim, *op. cit.*, 183–188, and the rest of Chapter 10. These authors recognize that to the extent that we insist on promoting such noneconomic goals as the provision of service on unremunerative routes subsidized by above-cost rates on remunerative routes, the possibilities of introducing more competition must necessarily be limited.

For particularly strong statements of the case for freer competition, see Levine, *op. cit.*, 1416–1447, and Kenneth W. Dam, in an excellent review of the Caves book, *Univ. of Chicago Law Rev.* (Autumn 1964), XXXII: 200–202.
[145] See note 107, p. 210, above. On the other hand, most observers and industry experience as well clearly suggest that freer price competition would in fact ensue and service inflation would, therefore, be held more effectively in check.
[146] Notably in Chapter 4, since the case for restrictions on entry into the market of a "natural monopoly" is often supported on cream-skimming grounds.

to serve—maximum efficiency in the presence of economies of scale, economic progress,[147] and optimum resource allocation in the presence of externalities.[148]

The third approach is to take into account the possibility that noneconomic goals may require qualification of the policy judgments that would flow from considerations of economic efficiency alone.

The Economic Case for Unrestricted Cream-Skimming

The economic case for free, cream-skimming competition is both static and institutional. The former aspect begins with the basic proposition that prices must be equated to marginal cost. Suppose, then, that under unrestricted competition there is a tendency for new firms to enter into particular portions of public utility markets or for existing firms to compete more strenuously for those markets, with the tendency to push down price. Assuming no errors of planning or judgment (we return to this assumption when we consider possible cases *for* restricting competition in circumstances like these), this must mean that prices in those markets are in excess of someone's marginal cost: either (1) existing firms are pricing above their own marginal costs or (2) their own marginal costs are higher than those of the entrants, or (3) price is being held above the marginal cost of some existing firms, but not necessarily of all. In any event, if there is in fact "cream" that some competitors are attempting to "skim," this is the best possible evidence that price in those markets is too high and should come down.

And experience indicates the superiority of competition as an institutional device for achieving this goal. The only forces that can hold price above someone's marginal cost are monopolistic or regulatory restrictions on output or price, conservatism or inertia. The most effective device for overcoming these obstructions is the freedom of individual businessmen to seek out and to exploit the market opportunities that these forces generate.[148a]

But what of the regulated common carriers, who are obliged by law to serve also the less remunerative markets and who may be unable to do so unless they can enjoy the protected profits on the creamy parts of their business? Here we encounter, first, a question of fact: the question is whether the carrying of the less remunerative business is a burden on the regulated company in its competition with allegedly cream-skimming interlopers. If it is not a burden, the cream-skimming case for protection can clearly be rejected. This will be the case as long as the less remunerative business covers its own marginal costs. The telephone company, for example, deserves no artificial protection against the entry of specialist firms seeking to take away its apparently more lucrative, daytime telephone business, in order to ensure

---

[147] See pp. xii and 114, above.

[148] Why do externalities involve "institutional" considerations? The problem of external costs and benefits may be regarded as issuing from defects in our property institutions—such as, for example, permitting one person to impose losses on another, without the latter necessarily being in a position to obtain compensation. A proper system of compensation and assessments would eliminate these distortions. See Morris A. Copeland, "Institutionalism and Welfare

Economics," *Amer. Econ. Rev.* (March 1958), XLVIII: 1–17.

[148a] See the proposal by Milton Friedman for repeal of the law prohibiting private companies from carrying first-class mail:

"The resulting competition would not only improve postal service and reduce its cost. . . . It would also make starkly clear what categories of mail are more than paying their way and what categories are being subsidized." *Wall Street Journal*, March 11, 1970, 18.

its continued provision of nighttime service. Its rates for the former would have to be even higher than they are were it not also in a position, with the same equipment, to supply off-peak, nighttime service at rates in excess of incremental costs. The fact of its integration—it supplies both day and night service—gives it a competitive advantage in both of these markets against specialist competitors. Indeed, in such a situation it is in a sense impossible to say which part of the business is the cream, which part the skimmed milk, because the bulk of the costs are joint.

True, the contribution of the less remunerative business, though positive, may still not be sufficient to overcome other competitive handicaps of the regulated companies. They may be less enterprising or less ably managed than their competitors, or use an outmoded technology; or perhaps the competitors may, by virtue of the character of *their* integration, be able to take on the creamy business at rates covering *their* marginal costs but below those that the regulated company can charge. But none of these circumstances would justify imposing restrictions on that competition. Suppose, for example, that some firm outside the Bell System found a new way to transmit long-distance telephone messages using the rays of the sun—that is, during the daytime only—at total unit costs less than current daytime rates. Should the undermining of those high rates then be prevented on the ground that otherwise night telephone service would disappear? The correct economic answer is that no class of customers should be required to pay more than the total cost of serving it alone. Whether by competition or by regulation, the daytime rates should be brought down at least to the total unit costs under the new technology. If this requires higher nighttime rates for the joint service to continue, the night rate should go up, possibly to the point where that business covers the bulk of the joint costs. The advantages of integration may then still suffice to keep the old established telephone company in the day and night business, perhaps retaining its monopoly in both. Or they may no longer suffice, leaving it only in the latter business; and if that business will not bear the cost of continued service, night telephonic communication is no longer economically feasible and should disappear. In neither case is there economic justification for preventing the competition that brings about the equation of the two prices to their new, respective marginal costs.

But there may be a problem here arising out of the familiar difficulty of equating all prices to marginal cost when marginal costs are less than average. In general, the presumption—on institutional grounds—would still be in favor of competition. The fact that a competitor is willing to enter only the thick markets *suggests* that it is possible to supply them alone at costs lower than the rates previously charged; if his estimate proves wrong, it is he who will bear the costs of his error. On the other hand, we must recognize the possibility that while the rates that the entrant proposes to charge in the creamy market exceed his marginal costs, he may be enabled to take on that business only because he is charging rates in excess of MC on other parts of his business. We return below to this possible conflict between the dictates of economic efficiency (marginal-cost pricing for all) and the covering of total costs, as a possible consideration justifying restriction of cream-skimming competition.

The final possibility, of course, is that the skimmed-milk markets *are* a burden on the regulated company, because they do not cover their own separable, marginal costs. In this event those markets are being internally subsidized—a practice that is inacceptable on purely economic grounds.[149]

To summarize, then, the economic case against prohibitions of cream-skimming is that they are either unnecessary or a means of preserving an inefficient rate structure, and in either case an undesirable interference with the competitive pressures that provide the best possible guarantee of optimum performance, both statically and dynamically.

Possible Cases against Cream-Skimming

The foregoing constitutes a very powerful argument for permitting competition the freest possible play even in public utility industries. It exerts its disciplinary influence where it actually occurs and where it does not. If a natural monopolist is producing and pricing as efficiently as possible, there is no need to bar competitive entry: it is economically unnecessary and will not take place anyhow. The legal barrier is effective only where customers in the creamy markets are being exploited; here competition will spring forth, if it is permitted, precisely because and to the extent that it is required. The burden of proof, and it is a heavy one, must be borne by those who advocate restrictions on competition in order to prevent alleged cream-skimming.

At the same time, it is possible to construct a checklist of possible bases for regulatory intervention on all three grounds suggested at the beginning of this discussion: (1) economic efficiency, (2) institutional inadequacies of competition, and (3) extraeconomic considerations. As we proceed to analyze these cases, we shall at an early point find it necessary to define "cream-skimming" more carefully than is usually done. At times the term is used—typically by those seeking to ban the practice—when "competition" would be just as accurate, the more colorful designation being selected perhaps because it has a more negative connotation. Competition is always more or less selective; naturally it tends to focus on the more lucrative markets and to shun the others. Some items in our checklist will turn out, therefore, simply to be possible cases against competition generally; others will turn out to relate to cream-skimming as a special kind of competition that may indeed produce a special kind of undesirable result.

The Imperfections of Competition Case. Pure competition brings price into equality with short-run marginal cost. It is only under perfect competition that price will be equated continuously and costlessly to SRMC, LRMC and ATC, all at the same time, under conditions of long-run constant or increasing costs.[150] The very case for regulation is, in part, that in the real world competition is highly imperfect. This is really the kernel of the natural monopoly case for limiting entry. Why will not such monopolies arise "naturally" and without governmental assistance or protection—either as a result of the process of competition between existing firms or because no rational firm would choose to enter such an industry in the first place, since it could not hope to be able to survive in competition with that monopolist? The case for regulation must be that an uncontrolled

---

[149] See, for example, pp. 190–191, Volume 1, above.

[150] See note 25, Chapter 3 of Volume 1, p. 74.

On the problem of decreasing costs, see the following subsection of the present discussion.

market would not produce the monopoly result efficiently. Competitors might enter, if permitted to do, in expectation of being able to sell out. Or the several competitors might find it more profitable to live and let live, with rate payers bearing the burden of their excessive costs: there may exist no reliable institutional mechanism for driving out the excessive number of firms, concentrating production in the hands of the natural monopolist, and bringing costs and prices down to the minimum, technologically feasible level.

As we have already observed, the destructive competition argument, similarly, is grounded on alleged imperfections of competition—imperfect knowledge on the part of investors, which may result in excessive investment; immobility of capital and labor, which can produce destructive competition when capacity is excessive; and limited consumer knowledge, which can permit deterioration of service.[151]

So the presence of imperfections weakens the general case we have set forth in the defense of unrestricted cream-skimming. If competitors do enter a market, that case states, the presumption is that the customers were previously paying excessive prices; but this is so only if the entrants have correctly forecast their own costs and market prospects. If customers shift to the new suppliers, the presumption is they are better off with these new alternatives; but this is so only if customers correctly judge their respective qualities. And so on. If these conditions of perfection are not met or approximated, unrestricted cream-skimming can lead to waste, instability of rates, and deterioration of service.

There is no way of laying down general rules, a priori, for deciding whether imperfections of competition justify regulation to prevent cream-skimming. As against the possible imperfections of the competitive process must be weighed the corresponding imperfections of monopoly or regulation, which we have already amply observed. The burden of any mistakes that are made under competition is borne, in large measure, by the businessmen themselves; the burden of the mistakes of monopoly or of its ineffective regulation is borne principally by the consumer. For these reasons, most economists would incline to the competitive solution. The corollary of this rule is that the regulated companies themselves ought ordinarily to be permitted to meet competition by reducing their own rates toward long-run marginal costs. This would tend to forestall unjustified entry into the more lucrative market and give fullest possible recognition to the possible efficiency advantages of natural monopoly.[151a]

The Discrimination Problem. The central problem of cream-skimming is the problem of rate discrimination—of the relative remunerativeness of rates in the rich and the poor markets. If rates for all categories of service were at their respective marginal costs, there would be little purely economic basis for restricting competition. The difficulties arise when MC is below ATC, necessitating—or at least raising the possible desirability of—the kinds of discrimination described in Chapter 5 of our Volume 1.

The fact that most public utility rates must exceed marginal cost if average total costs are to be covered does not in itself constitute a sufficient case against competitive cream-skimming. On the contrary, it is the general

---

[151] See pp. 175–176, this chapter, above.   [151a] See, e.g., pp. 149–152, above.

principle that no class of customers ought to be charged more than the total costs of serving them alone that justifies competition, as a means of preventing exploitation. But serious problems are raised by the fact that such competition is typically highly selective and hence discriminatory.

We have considered at length, in Chapter 6 of Volume 1, the applicable principles in circumstances like these and need only point out here their relationship to the cream-skimming problem. The first rule was that where a particular group of customers could in fact be supplied *alone* at rates lower than those currently charged them, it is appropriate to permit competition to drive rates down to that level, even though the consequent rate structure is discriminatory. The familiar example would be the case that we described of the two towns, A and C, connected by both a river and a rail line that passes through an intermediate town, B, that is not on the river. Here is a case for competitive entry by the water carriers, even if it threatens to "skim the cream" of the railroad's business, and for freedom of the railroad in turn to reduce its A to C rates as far down to marginal costs as necessary to keep the business.[152]

The important thing to notice about this case is that it is not cheaper for the *railroads* to carry the AC than the AB traffic. The "cost justification" for the discrimination is to be found in the fact that (1) AC can be served, by *water*, at an average total cost lower than that of the rail service, (2) its traffic can be retained by the rails at rates in excess of MC, and (3) permitting the discrimination will result in having the transportation function performed at lower total costs to society.

In the case of competition between two roundabout railroads, in contrast, we found no such "cost justification" and therefore no economic justification on grounds of static efficiency for permitting the discrimination.

Here, then, we have two models of competitive and discriminatory price reductions, one of them justifiable, the other not, on grounds of economic efficiency. (The latter is even less justifiable, it seems reasonable to state, on grounds of fairness.) Competition of both these kinds has, as we shall see, been criticized on the ground that it involves cream-skimming. But, strictly speaking, it need not. There is no necessity, in either of these cases, for the AC traffic to be more lucrative than the AB: what we have, merely, is one market in which competition is feasible and another in which it is not. The effect of competition, in these instances, is not to "skim the cream" but to *convert* the competitive market into skimmed milk, and in the proper circumstances to justify price discrimination where none need have prevailed before.

Of course, if one defines as "creamy" whatever business is worth competing for, whether nondiscriminatorily (as by the water carrier) or by the offer of selective rate reductions, then all competition is by definition cream-skimming. But if the latter term is to define an independent phenomenon it must apply to the competition for customers that are making a disproportionately large contribution to overheads.[153] It is for this reason that there is a general

---

[152] See pp. 167–168 and the ensuing pages in Volume 1, on which this discussion draws.

[153] The fact that if entry were free competitors would operate only when and where the traffic is heaviest does not at all demonstrate that these markets represent the "cream." As John Hibbs points out, in assessing the argument for restricting allegedly cream-skimming competition in the passenger bus business,

"This argument fails to take into account that operation through the peak is likely to yield a

presumption in favor of *true* cream-skimming; it tends to *eliminate* unjustified price discrimination. It is *noncream-skimming* competition that should be subjected to special scrutiny, because of the possibility that it may *introduce* unjustified price discrimination. In short, it is precisely because competition of this sort may *not* constitute cream-skimming that it may be economically undesirable.

What we have identified, then, is three distinct cases of what is often called cream-skimming—using that term to characterize any competition that reduces the contribution of some portions of a public utility business to joint or common costs and therefore either endangers the service to other customers or imposes on them a greater share of the burden:

1. True cream-skimming—competition for customers who are being discriminated *against*.[154] This was the case when the motor carriers took away the high value-of-service business of the rails and the nonscheduled airlines moved into the high-volume, peak-season traffic.[155] This competition is presumptively justified as a means of eliminating discrimination *against* the market on which the proposed competition would focus.

2. The rail-water carrier case. This is not a true case of cream-skimming. But competitive entry is justified, because the entrant is able to carry the contested traffic at an ATC below the rates of the existing supplier, and the latter in turn may for this reason be justified in discriminating in *favor* of customers in that market.

3. The rail-rail case, in which the introduction of discrimination in favor of customers in the competitive markets enjoys no such justification.[156]

---

lower net revenue to the monopolist, since that part of his fleet that is needed for peak operation alone and is idle the rest of the day is very costly. . . .

"The 'all day' operator should welcome his appearance [that is, that of the independent or 'pirate'] when traffic is heavy. If he is prepared to carry some of the peak traffic, while in no way reducing the off-peak loadings of the all-day operator, then the latter will find his net revenue increased." *Transport for Passengers*, Hobart Paper 23, Institute of Economic Affairs, London, 1963, 34–35.

[154] They may be the "victims" of discrimination in either of two different ways. (1) Existing suppliers may be practicing internal subsidization—charging rates above *their own* ATC of serving customers A alone in order to charge customers B rates below MC. The railroads have done this to some extent, as we have seen. The practice was economically indefensible even in the absence of the motor-carrier alternative; and one major objection to the Motor Carrier Act of 1935 is that it perpetuated it. (2) The discrimination may be economically justified in accordance with the principles summarized in

Chapter 5 of Volume 1: all customers pay at least their MC; the practice is therefore beneficial even to the customers who are being discriminated against. This was certainly originally true in large measure of rail value-of-service rates (see pp. 155–156, Volume 1, above). But the advent of the truck removed much of the economic justification, because the *new competitors* could serve the disfavored markets at an ATC lower than the rates previously charged them.

[155] See, however, the observation of Hibbs, note 153, above. But when the nonscheduled airlines invaded the New York to Miami market in the winter season and shifted to the transatlantic business in the summer, there was little reason to doubt that they *were* invading the more lucrative markets that had thitherto been subsidizing the low-density and off-season traffic. For evidence that airline costs decrease markedly with route density, so that the most heavily travelled routes are the most profitable, see Straszheim, *op. cit.*, 92–100, 110, 148, and Appendix B.

[156] As we have seen in Volume 1, pp. 168–170, there are instances of rail-rail competition in which such discrimination is justified, for reasons similar to those of the rail-water carrier case.

It will be useful to keep these three separate models in mind as we proceed to examine the three important recent cases in the field of communications in which cream-skimming was allegedly involved.

In the two major microwave cases (*above-890* and *MCI*),[157] one ground on which the common carriers asked the FCC to disallow the applications was that the applicants were would-be cream-skimmers:

"They . . . argued that, if the Commission were to extend microwave eligibility to all those who seek it, the common carriers would stand to lose so much revenue that they would have to compensate for it by increasing their rates to the general public. . . . In this connection, Western Union claimed that . . . the addition of another competitive possibility, namely a private point-to-point communications system . . . might well destroy the ability of the telegraph company to operate at all."[158]

Similarly, in *MCI*:

"possibly their principal complaint . . . is that, as Bell writes . . . 'Grant of the Applications Would Threaten The Integrity of The Nationwide Communications Rate Structure . . .' and Western Union . . . that 'MCI, by its own admission, seeks to enter a specialized and attractive market, with rate based on a particular microwave facility on a particular low cost route.' They assail MCI as a cream-skimmer, lapping up the profits on favorable routes and eschewing high-cost low-return service; accordingly, they say, on losing profitable routes (where expenses were relatively low) to a cream-skimmer, they would be compelled to reexamine their own rate structures, which distribute total costs for their undifferentiated service among customers favorably and unfavorably situated. They would have to saddle high charges then on high-cost users, instead of homogenizing the costs among all."[159]

It was partly for similar reasons that the FCC put tight restrictions on the ability of large users of communications services to deal directly with Comsat:

"Sound policy indicates that . . . they [the terrestrial common carriers] should not be required to depend solely on ComSat for satellite circuits while ComSat is simultaneously allowed to syphon the most profitable part of the business from them. . . .

"we find that revenues from leased circuits provide an important, if not indispensable, part of the carriers' total receipts. . . . Reports to the Commission show that in 1965 these carriers, as a whole, had net operating revenues, before Federal income taxes, of about $20,300,000. Their revenues from leased circuit services for the same year were $20,200,000. . . . Because of the relatively low nonfixed or variable costs associated with this service, the loss of such business could come close to wiping out completely the record carriers' earnings. . . .

"The danger of the loss by the terrestrial carriers of existing or additional leased circuit business to satellite facilities is not merely theoretical. A recent complaint . . . and a press release issued by ComSat . . . indicate

---

[157] See our discussion of the natural monopoly aspects of these cases at pp. 129–136 and 146–152, above.

[158] FCC, *Above 890* Report and Order, 27 FCC

359, 390–391 (1959).

[159] FCC, *MCI* Initial Decision, *op. cit.*, note 58, Chapter 4, par. 93 (1967).

that ComSat would propose to charge both authorized users and carriers approximately the same amount for leased circuits and that the amount is substantially below current or recently proposed charges for leased cable circuits. Accordingly, the terrestrial carriers could reasonably be expected to lose a substantial share of their leased circuit revenues to ComSat. Under these conditions and in light of the data set forth above, it could very well be necessary to permit these carriers to increase rates charged other users in order to enable them to earn a fair return. Certainly such a detriment to the vast majority of users for the apparent benefit of a few large users would be in derogation of the objectives of the Act. The fact is that the Satellite Act requires the opposite result, namely, that the benefits of these lower rates be made available to all users."[160]

In part, genuine (and justified) cream-skimming of our type 1 was involved in these cases. That is, the proposed entry was into high-density, low-cost markets that the common carriers were, by their uniform rate policies, in effect forcing to subsidize the lower-density, high-cost traffic. On purely economic grounds, competitive entry in circumstances such as these should be not merely permitted but applauded.[161] As the Examiner remarked in *MCI:*

"The averaging method is embodied neither in the Decalogue nor in the Constitution. Without danger to the republic, there may be a weighing of the possible public benefits or disadvantages resulting from authorizing competition in selected areas . . .

"Clearly, if the averaging doctrine is sacrosanct (and 'cream-skimming' is an attendant horrific) to the extent the carriers claim, they have insulated themselves against private line competition except from carriers with unlikely initial operations as widespread as theirs. They are like courtiers who deign to accept challenges for duels only from those of equal rank. But the efforts of a relatively impoverished newcomer, proposing a novel if by no means faultless service, to give battle on his chosen ground, should not be impaled by this agency upon a principle devised by his opponents."[162]

There is another respect in which the microwave cases may fall within our first category. MCI proposed to perform no function other than the operation of the radio path, from one geographic point to another; and one reason it was able to do so cheaply was that its system was far less adequately protected against emergencies and outages than the facilities of the common carriers. It conceded that its commercial feasibility depended also on the ability of its customers to interconnect with the facilities of the common

---

[160] FCC, *Authorized Users* decision, 4 FCC 2d 421, 431–433 (1966).

[161] See pp. 147–148, 150–151, above. See, however, the possible externalities consideration mentioned at that point.

[162] *MCI* Initial Decision, pars. 110, 112. Herman Schwartz' defense of the Commission's Comsat *Authorized Users* decision offers support for the view that the users of leased channels who wanted to deal directly with the satellite corporation were victims of a system that forced them to subsidize the general message service:

"Such a policy [that is, that of the FCC] has obvious advantages, especially if Comsat's cost advantages were to be used only for 'cream-skimming' while the far less lucrative general message service, which accounts for most of the traffic, was left to the carriers and forced to support itself." *Op. cit., Yale Law Jour.* (January 1967), LXXVI: 471–472.

carriers, in order to give them end-to-end communications service. The carriers objected, therefore, that customers could subscribe to the MCI service only because they knew they could always call on the backup facilities of the common carriers if it broke down; that, by leaving it to the carriers to bear the financial burdens of providing backup and interconnection, MCI was improperly skimming the cream. It would seem that this problem, like the national average-cost pricing of the common carriers that helped create the opportunity for MCI's entry in the first place, is one of rate structure. If charges for the backup and interconnection services were high enough to cover the capacity costs of the common carriers' fulfilling, or standing ready to fulfill, those obligations, these responsibilities would not limit their ability to compete for the creamy part of the business. To put it another way, if the backup and interconnection services do represent the skimmed milk, the rates for which are subsidized by revenues from the portion of the business that MCI tried to serve, it would appear here as well that the latter's proposed cream-skimming represented a healthy competitive reaction to an improperly discriminatory rate structure.[163]

Apart from these specific instances of genuine cream-skimming in response to internal subsidization, the competition at issue in these cases seems to fall in our category 3. Customers in all three instances were attempting to get direct access to the benefits of new, lower-cost technology. These benefits would have flowed to them not because it was cheaper to serve them than the customers who would have remained dependent on the common carriers, but merely because they were in a position to take direct advantage of this new opportunity, whereas the general users of telephone and telegraph services were not. (It was only the large users of leased circuits who could afford to put in their own private microwave systems or would be served by MCI or could hope to deal directly with Comsat.) The problem was that the marginal costs of service by the most modern and efficient facilities were markedly below the carrier rates, based as they were on the composite costs of old and new facilities.[164]

Ideally, all users should have been charged only the lower ATC_n; but this would not have covered the company's total cost of service. In so far as there was no basis *on the cost side* for singling out some users as deserving that favorable treatment while leaving to others a disproportionate part of the

---

[163] But see also on this the discussion of option demand, pp. 238–240, below, which raises the possibility that adequate backup facilities cannot be provided or properly charged for in a competitive market.

[164] The rates Comsat was charging the common carriers for leased circuits, and that it proposed to offer direct, authorized users, were far below the rates that the carriers were in turn charging their customers. FCC, *Authorized Users* decision, 4 FCC 2d 421, 433 (1966). As one example, Schwartz cites the $4,000 per month per circuit that Comsat charged the Defense Department with the $7,100 per month proposed by the carriers. *Op. cit.*, *Yale Law Jour.* (January 1967), LXXVI: 471, note 143. Claudia Goldin cites others: for example, in the early part of 1967

Comsat's rate to the carriers for a leased half-circuit (from the U.S. earth station to the satellite; the charge for the other half-circuit is set by the foreign agency or government) was $2,700 per month, for communication between New York and Europe, whereas the carriers' rate was $8,000. *The Economic Effects of the Introduction of Satellite Communications in the International Communications Industry*, honors thesis, Department of Economics, Cornell University, May 1967, 29–30. The carriers claimed, in the FCC proceedings, that they "transform . . . a 'raw channel' into a usable circuit." But the non-carrier users argued that they did not require these carrier services and pleaded for the right to deal directly with Comsat. *Ibid.*, 59.

burden of covering total, historic costs, it was indeed the responsibility of the FCC to question whether the selective competition proposed in these cases was economically justified.[165] In short, it appears that the situations fall partly within our category 3. To the extent that there was no inherent reason on the cost side to have the lower rates extended to the big rather than the small users (as in our cases 1 and 2), there is no basis for attributing to the FCC a policy of protecting a system of internal subsidization. (We consider presently whether there may have been a justification on the *demand* side.) The big users were no more subsidizing the small than the reverse.

To the extent that these factual assumptions apply, the FCC's *above-890* and *MCI* decisions were wrong and *Authorized Users* right. The Commission was to this extent justified, in the latter case, in trying to see to it that the benefits of satellite technology were passed on equally to small users and to large, to customers of the common carriers as well as to private users:

> "under unrestricted dealings between ComSat and noncarriers, large users might tend to contract directly with ComSat, while members of the general public are left to deal with the carriers. In such circumstances, it would be clearly impossible for the Commission to carry out its responsibility under Section 201(c)(5) to '. . . insure that any economies made possible by a communications satellite system are appropriately reflected in rates for *public* communications service.'"[166]

> "The foregoing considerations are thus consistent with the general concept pervading the Satellite Act of ComSat as . . . primarily a carrier's carrier, created to provide at least the space segment of international communications as part of an improved global communications network consisting of *all* means of providing such communications services, so that lower rates should be possible to all the using public."[167]

But there remain important reasons for holding to the opposite view: that *above-890* and *MCI* were on balance good decisions and *Authorized Users* questionable. There is the fact, first, that the system-wide average cost pricing by the carriers involves internal subsidization, which increased competition would in all cases have helped correct.

Second, the FCC's cost-averaging policy applies not just geographically but also to facilities embodying new and old technology:

> "rates for communications services are not to depend upon the facility used. Rather, 'composite rates' are to be charged which represent an average of the costs of *all* facilities, new and old, in order to prevent users of the new facility from receiving lower rates than users of the old."[168]

---

[165] It might appear, at first glance, that the situation here would fall into our category 2, the rail-water carrier case, with Comsat (and MCI and private microwave) playing the role of the water carrier—able to serve certain customers at an ATC lower than the ATC of the common carriers previously serving them and therefore properly permitted to do so. But to the extent that this lower ATC was the result not of any inherent advantage of the favored customers corresponding to the location of the AC towns on the river—that is, to the extent that increases in the demand for communications services by large and smaller users equally could have been satisfied by use of the new technology—the large users who happened to have direct access to it had no special claim on efficiency grounds to its lower costs.

[166] Stress supplied. *Authorized Users* Decision, 4 FCC 2d 421, 428 (1966).

[167] *Ibid.*, par. 24.

[168] Schwartz, *op. cit.*, *Yale Law Jour.* (January 1967), LXXVI: 471.

This policy is the correct one where the marginal costs of supplying all users are in fact the same, regardless of which facilities happen to be serving them.[169] But if there are certain groups of customers whose demand is such that it can be satisfied only by the use of the higher-cost facility (and this would be true also if their demand grew and capacity had to be expanded to serve it), and other customers who, regardless of the particular facilities by which they are *actually* being served, could in fact be served by the newer, lower-cost technology, then they constitute two separate markets, with different marginal costs. To charge those two groups uniform rates, representing an average of the high and the low-cost facilities, would be economically inefficient, unduly subsidizing the former customers and discouraging purchases by the latter.

This was apparently the consequence of the FCC's cost-averaging policy. Averaging domestic and international line-haul costs together evidently forced the international users, who alone could benefit by the availability of the satellite, to subsidize domestic communications services. It also must uneconomically have retarded the application of that new technology, since its cost savings were not passed on fully in rates to those customers who alone were in a position to take advantage of it. To the extent that some of those customers could deal directly with Comsat, the latter's cream-skimming entry into competition with the common carriers would have helped eliminate these distortions.

The distortion was accentuated by the fact that the costs and revenues from the international operations of the communications common carriers are a tiny fraction of their system-wide totals. Any cost-savings that they obtain by leasing circuits from Comsat therefore would have been utterly submerged in their aggregate costs of service. The FCC was aware of this danger, however. And so, while it declined to permit Comsat to compete more freely and directly with the carriers, it did order the latter to reflect directly in their international rates the large cost savings made possible by the satellite:

> "Satellite circuits now becoming available should enable the carriers to secure facilities at lower costs in relation to terrestrial facilities and thereby permit them to reduce rates to reflect such cost reductions. We therefore expect the common carriers promptly to give further review to their current rate schedules and file revisions which fully reflect the economies made available through the leasing of circuits in the satellite system. Failure of the carriers to do so promptly and effectively will require the Commission to take such actions as are appropriate. Even though satellite circuits are not now and will not for some time be available to all points to which users presently lease circuits from terrestrial carriers, implementation of this policy by the carriers should also reduce charges to many points to which satellite circuits are not now available."[170]

---

[169] The fact that in a given community certain customers may be supplied electricity from an old plant, while adding the requirements of new customers will call for the construction of a new, lower-cost plant, provides no economic basis for charging the two groups different rates: their marginal costs are the same. See p. 140, Volume 1, above. And so would their average costs be equal, if economically correct depreciation were charged. See p. 121, Volume 1.

[170] *Authorized Users* Decision, 4 FCC 2d 421, 434–435 (1966). AT&T did in fact file substantially reduced rates in the latter part of that year. *Wall Street Journal*, December 29, 1966, 8.

Our analysis of the cream-skimming aspect of these decisions has concentrated thus far on the question of whether the customers who were or would have been favored by the proposed competition "deserved" the lower rates it would have brought, as far as the relative *costs* of serving them were concerned. We must inquire, additionally, whether differential treatment might have been justified because of differences on the demand side. Long-distance communication is, as we have seen, outstandingly characterized by increasing returns, which strongly recommend discriminatory price reductions to markets of elastic demand. And it is, indeed, likely that some portions of the markets that benefited by the microwave decisions and would have benefited by freer access to direct dealing with Comsat are highly elastic: witness the explosive growth in business use of communications services as the lower-cost opportunities have become available to them.[171] For this to justify differential rate reductions to these users, however, it is their total demand that must be relatively elastic and not the demand for the services of one source of supply (private microwave, or MCI, or Comsat) as against another (for example, AT&T). We simply do not know whether this condition obtains—whether, that is, the aggregate demand of these particular users of long-distance communications is any more elastic than the demand of patrons not in a position to set up their own microwave systems or deal directly with MCI or Comsat.

What we do know however is that competition—cream-skimming or not—is usually a more effective institutional mechanism than regulated monopoly for probing the elasticity of demand and encouraging the application of new technology. It is these dynamic, institutional considerations that provide the strongest support for the microwave decisions and the main reason for questioning *Authorized Users*. The principal and compelling demonstration of the numerous applicants in *above-890* was their desire and ability to provide lower-priced communications services than had thitherto been available to them, and what the Examiner proposed to give MCI was an opportunity to demonstrate that it could do the same thing. In *above-890*, the Commission explicitly recognized the potential advantages of the "competitive spur in the manufacturing of equipment and in the development of the communications art."[172] In *MCI*, the Examiner underlined the advantages of permitting the proposed competitive test of the elasticity of demand.[173]

What was disappointingly lacking in the *Authorized Users* decision was any

---

Again, when in its controversial TAT–5 decision, in 1968, the FCC authorized the carriers to lay a new transatlantic cable, it imposed the condition that they reduce charges for message telephone and private line voice-grade channel service by 25 to 30 percent. *TAT–5* Decision, 13 FCC 2d 235, par. 10 (1968).

[171] In the *MCI* case, the Examiner was impressed by the possibility of a large, untapped demand for lower-cost communications services (see his *Initial Decision*, pars. 57, 80, 109, 113). On the other hand, it is of course difficult to ascertain to what extent this growth in business use has been a response to reduced price, to what extent a reflection of expanded demand.

[172] 27 FCC 359, 414 (1959).

"the private users uniformly took the position that, if the Commission were to restrict private microwave where there is available common carrier service, there would be a lessening of competition and a fostering of a monopoly in the manufacture, sale, and use of communications facilities contrary to the public interest. They claimed that such a policy would thwart the improvement and experimentation that accompany competition among manufacturers for the private users' market, and would kill the very incentive for common carriers to improve their service." *Ibid.*, 395.

[173] See pp. 134–135, above.

explicit recognition by the Commission of the similar, dynamic advantages that a less restrictive ruling would have provided. In view of the greater incentive of the established common carriers to use and expand their own terrestrial facilities than to lease additional circuits from Comsat,[174] it would seem particularly important to free the latter company for effective competition with the carriers rather than leave it in a position in which it would be the latter through whom it would have to deal and who would, therefore, be in a position to determine how rapidly use of the satellite would be pressed. That the Commission was not unaware of this danger is indicated by the condition it attached to its approval of the TAT-5, requiring the common carriers to use the new cable and satellite facilities proportionately.[175] It is important to recognize that in markets that are inevitably imperfect, the quest of strong competitors for purely strategic advantages, bearing no necessary relationship to their relative efficiency in serving the public, can be a very powerful force for improved market performance.[176] Even if the large prospective users of private communications systems did not, on efficiency grounds, "deserve" lower rates or costs than other less favorably situated customers, their pressure for such advantages and ability to take advantage of the lower costs promised by the new technology undoubtedly promoted its more rapid development and put corresponding pressures on the common carriers to improve their own service offerings.[177]

The Promotional Case. When a major purpose of regulation is to promote the growth of a new industry, regulators are tempted to prevent cream-skimmers from coming in too early, in order to give the original enterpriser an opportunity to reap the rewards of his pioneering efforts, as well as to hold down the subsidies that the Government may still be paying the industry. If the markets created by costly promotional endeavours can, once those efforts have produced the desired results, immediately be appropriated or invaded by free-loading competitors who have not themselves had to bear the cost of the original promotion, the efforts may never be undertaken in the first place. And if competitive entry is prevented, the monopoly profits that can be earned on the profitable parts of the business can cut down the amount of subsidy that the taxpayer has to contribute.[178] The point is that competition alone does not always necessarily cause an industry to do all the things we want it to do. We have already suggested the analogy to the case for a patent system and for the limitations on competition that it entails.

The purely economic aspect of the promotional argument (we set aside for the moment the possibility that government might wish to promote the development of an industry for such purposes as national defense) is based on alleged externalities: competition would prevent those who incurred the

---

[174] See our discussion of this problem in Chapter 2, pp. 51–52, above.

[175] See note 89, Chapter 2, p. 76, above.

[176] See Dirlam and Kahn, *Fair Competition*, 142–144, 150–152, 173–175, 182–184, 202–205, and *passim*.

[177] For a strong statement of this argument see the testimony of William Vickrey in FCC, *In the Matter of AT&T*, Dockets 16258 and 15011, Networks Exhibit No. 5, July 22, 1968, processed,

65–67. On AT&T's pricing response to the *above-890* decision, see Chapter 4, p. 132, above. In the international sphere, it was apparently only after the direct pressures by the FCC and the threat of direct Comsat competition that the carriers put into effect the substantial rate reductions reflected in Table 2 of our Chapter 3. *Wall Street Journal*, March 7, 1966, 7 and June 29, 1966, 4.

[178] See pp. 3–4, Chapter 1, above.

costs of promoting an industry's expansion from appropriating enough of the benefits to justify the effort. It could well be, for example, that the offering of regular airline service in thin markets and off-season promotes the demand for service generally. If some line runs a feeder service from remote cities in upstate New York to New York City, it will, in so doing, also promote more air travel between New York and Miami. Similarly, if there are regular flights between New York and Miami in the off-peak, summer season, this may help promote travel in the busy winter as well—for example, the summer tourists, by providing additional net revenues to hotels, make possible lower rates during the peak season. If, then, irregular airlines were permitted to enter only the New York to Miami route and only during the winter, they would be reaping where others had sown. This possible market failure would be prevented if one company enjoyed a monopoly in the peak business, in which case it would be the sole beneficiary of its off-peak promotional efforts, or if all airlines participating in the peak traffic were required to set up a joint venture to run the off-peak service, bearing its costs in proportion to their enjoyment of the external benefits.[179] Either arrangement would require denying access to the cream to any firm that did not bear its proper share of the skimmed milk.

Why, however, would any company wish to take on a losing operation merely because it generated additional business for other parts of its operation? There would seem to be only two possibilities, which we can best illustrate with the airlines example. The first and most obvious one is that the second service—the New York to Miami run during the winter—is supernormally profitable. If this is so, it clearly suggests that the purchasers of that service are subsidizing the other—passengers between Ithaca and New York City—in which event the argument against cream-skimming turns, once again, into an argument for the preservation of an economically indefensible internal subsidization.

The second possibility is that the New York to Miami business is not supernormally profitable but is subject to increasing returns. That is, its MC might be less than ATC, because of the presence of either excess capacity or incompletely exploited economies of scale. It could be, then, that the additional New York to Miami traffic generated by the Ithaca to New York run covers its marginal costs (including the losses on the feeder operation), without necessarily bringing in more than its ATC. In this event, the off-peak service would not be a burden on the peak customers, but would make a net contribution to covering some of their joint or overhead costs.

[179] This point is made, briefly, also by James R. Nelson, *op. cit.*, *The Antitrust Bulletin* (January–April 1966), XI: 29. One example of the latter remedy is the joint operation of unprofitable helicopter service between airports by the major airlines benefiting from it. For example, the CAB in 1968 permitted Pan American World Airways and Trans World Airways jointly to purchase the stock of New York Airways, which operates helicopters between Newark, Kennedy, and LaGuardia Airports. CAB Press Release, July 31, 1968. In another proceeding the same year, it issued a certificate for helicopter service between Washington and Baltimore airports to Washington Airways, which had been organized by ten of the 14 scheduled air carriers serving the area. It justified this "departure from our traditional selection of an independent operator to provide a proposed service" on the ground "that the problem of providing economically viable scheduled passenger helicopter service in our metropolitan areas has proven to be exceedingly complex," pointing out that the new service would require considerable financial assistance, which, presumably, only the interested lines would be willing to offer. Press release, November 21, 1968.

This seems a valid, hypothetical economic argument for opposing competitive entry into profitable business, since supply of the off-peak services might cease if the external benefits were skimmed off by competitors.

In fact, the latter case is probably not a good one as applied to the airlines. There is no reason, a priori, to expect that the additional traffic generated by the off-peak service would neatly fit into the airline schedules in such a way as to promote improved load factors; on the contrary, that demand, too, would doubtless have the same peak as the other and require a proportionate expansion in capacity. As for the possibility that it might eventuate in the fuller realization of potential economies of scale, the evidence does not suggest the continuing presence of long-run decreasing costs in airlines within the relevant range.[180] Moreover, if there were significantly increasing returns enjoyed by existing companies operating at the peak, it is difficult to see how new entrants could successfully challenge them.

These considerations do not destroy the promotional case for monopoly, on purely logical grounds. But it is important to emphasize that competition may be a much more effective and powerful promoter than monopoly. Consider, for example, the very important contribution made to the growth of the U.S. airlines industry by the nonscheduled carriers. They received no subsidy and were in varying degrees harassed by the CAB, but persisted in trying by one device or another to get into the lucrative parts of the business. And by their vigorous promotional efforts, not least of them the offer of lower rates, it was they who demonstrated how great and elastic was the potential demand for passenger air service. Moreover, as analyses of the patent system have made abundantly clear, the promotional argument is hardly one for unlimited monopoly, of unlimited duration. Innovation requires the proper combination of protection and competition.[181]

In most situations, external (that is, taxpayer-financed) subsidies are probably a far more efficient method than the protection of monopoly for promoting a more rapid industrial development, because they can directly provide such additional incentives as may be required while taking full advantage of the promotional effects of competition as well. Devising the optimal system of subsidies, whether external or internal, is an extremely difficult task and one that has rarely been done well—on the basis of a careful appraisal of the respective costs and benefits of alternative devices.[182]

---

[180] See Caves, *Air Transport and its Regulators*, 57–61; Locklin, *op. cit.*, 805–806 and the sources cited there; and Straszheim, *op. cit.*, 95–96. See also pp. 149–150 of Volume 1. This summary statement probably does not do justice to this complex question. There is evidence of economies of scale with increasing traffic density on particular routes (see note 155, this chapter, above). But there is evidence also of internal subsidization—that is, of unjustified discrimination against traffic on dense routes; and the question remains: if there are such economies of scale, why is it necessary to restrict entry artificially?

[181] See Kahn, "The Role of Patents," in John Perry Miller, ed., *Competition, Cartels and Their Regulation* (Amsterdam: North-Holland Publishing Company, 1962), 308–346; and Fritz Machlup, *An Economic Review of the Patent System*, U. S. Senate, Committee on the Judiciary, Subcommittee on Patents, Trademarks, and Copyrights, 85th Cong. 1st Sess. (1958).

[182] For a description of the various subsidies provided the United States airlines industry, see Locklin, *op. cit.*, 764–770, 784–787, 817–823. On some of the defects of the system, see Keyes, *Federal Control of Entry Into Air Transportation*, Chapter 8, and *op. cit.*, *Jour. Air Law and Commerce* (Spring 1955), XXII: 192–202; Gray, "The Airlines Industry," in Walter Adams, ed., *op. cit.*, 3rd ed., 487–490, and Caves, *Air Transport and its Regulators*, 403–418.

Externalities, Option Demand and the Tyranny of Small Decisions. Externalities are especially pervasive in the public utility sector, as we have already observed[183]—almost as a matter of definition, since one important reason for singling these industries out for special public supervision and subsidy is the wide spread of their effects. In particular, there exists a wide range of situations in these industries in which the total benefits that society derives, or thinks it derives, from the continued provision of their services exceeds what can be collected from their several customers at prices equated to marginal cost.

This kind of phenomenon is quite easy to see in cases where the provision of a service to some customers confers indirect benefits on others. The quality of life in New York, Chicago, and Los Angeles may be improved by the continued availability of plane, electricity, and telephone service in rural areas, because it helps keep other people happy to live there and so reduces urban congestion. These "external beneficiaries" might be willing, therefore, to pay something to keep rural areas pleasant and comparatively accessible places in which to live. Internal subsidization is one way of accomplishing this.[184] It is, of course, a highly imperfect device: it is not clear why air travelers or telephone subscribers in particular should bear the cost of the benefits of reduced congestion that accrue to entire localities; or why such other beneficiaries as the owners of real estate in the subsidized communities should not also bear part of the costs.[185] But it may be the best device practically available. And it is one that is undermined by cream-skimming entry into the markets that carry the burden of subsidy.

One instance of particular importance among the public utilities derives from the great value of having suppliers at all times ready and able to serve, on demand. Burton A. Weisbrod has described as one external benefit resulting from the actual supply of particular goods or services the mere *availability* of the service to *nonusers*: the service that they enjoy is the *option* to use the facilities whenever they wish. He points out that the competitive market may fail to satisfy this "option demand," when (1) the option is not in fact exercised (or not exercised with sufficient frequency), (2) revenues

---

[183] See pp. 193–195, Volume 1, above.

[184] Once again, the airline example is not a very good one. True, the CAB does to some extent require the certificated, trunk airlines to serve unremunerative markets as the price of their certification for the profitable ones. But once the major airlines stopped receiving governmental subsidies on the basis of financial need (all but one of them after 1957), they lost interest in continuing the unremunerative runs (the revenue deficiencies of which they had been able theretofore to have filled by the subsidy) and dropped them in large numbers. See Caves, *Air Transport and its Regulators*, 403. On the relation of externalities to the case for internal subsidization in communications, see pp. 150–151, Chapter 4, above.

Telephone service provides another interesting example of external economies, though one with little practical relevance to the question of cream-skimming. The value of telephone service to any one subscriber depends on the number of other people who have phones. These benefits are of course mutual: as long, therefore, as each person with whom existing subscribers might conceivably wish to communicate rates the benefits to himself sufficiently high to justify his subscribing, no problem is raised by the fact that his doing so also confers benefits on others. But a case of genuine market failure could arise if any such person was either unable or, after comparing the costs and benefits to himself, unwilling to pay for the service: the resulting loss of benefits to other subscribers would not be reflected in his calculation. This possibility does suggest a valid basis for rate discrimination on the basis of relative elasticities of demand.

[185] This is part of the justification of local communities paying part of the costs of operating airports.

from *actual* purchasers are insufficient to cover the costs of continued operation, and (3) "expansion or recommencement of production at the time [in the future] when occasional purchasers wish to make a purchase . . . [is] difficult or impossible."[186]

I have characterized this possible instance of market failure as arising out of "the tyranny of small decisions"[187] The event that first suggested the phenomenon was the disappearance of passenger railroad service in Ithaca. The service was withdrawn because the individual decisions that travelers made, for each of their projected trips into and out of the various cities served, did not provide the railroad enough revenue to cover incremental costs. What reason was there to question the aggregate effect of those individual choices—withdrawal of the service? The fact is that the railroad provided the one reliable means of getting into and out of Ithaca in all kinds of weather; and I for one would have been willing to pay something to have kept alive this insufficiently exerted option. This suggests an at least hypothetical economic test of whether the service should have disappeared. Suppose each person in the cities served were to ask himself how much he would have been willing to pledge regularly over some time period, say annually, by purchase of prepaid tickets, to keep rail passenger service available to his community. As long as the amount that he would have declared (to himself) would have exceeded what he actually paid on that period—and my own introspective experiment shows that it would—then to that extent the disappearance of the passenger service was an incident of market failure.

The cause of the failure was the discrepancy between the time perspective of the choices that each traveler was given an opportunity to make—deciding, each time he planned a trip, whether to go by train—and that of the railroad, which was a long-run, virtually all-or-nothing and once-and-for-all decision, to retain or abandon passenger service. When each of us chose between the local airline or bus, his own automobile and the railroad, his individual choice had an only negligible effect on the continued availability of the last; it would therefore have been irrational to consider this possible implication of our individual decisions. The fact remains that each selection of x over y constitutes also a vote for eliminating the *possibility thereafter of choosing* y; if enough people vote for x, each time necessarily on the assumption that y will continue to be available, y may in fact disappear. And its disappearance may constitute a genuine deprivation, which customers might willingly have paid something to avoid. The only choice the market offered travelers to influence the longer-run decision of the railroad was thus shorter in its time perspective, and the sum-total of our individual purchases of railroad tickets necessarily added up to a smaller amount, than our actual combined interest in the continued availability of rail service. We were victims of "the tyranny of small decisions."

The railroad running through Ithaca provided service at peak seasons and off-peak, in fair weather and in foul. The airline and the automobiles may be said to have skimmed off the traffic in good weather, leaving to the

---

[186] *Op. cit.*, *Q. Jour. Econ.* (August 1964), LXXVIII: 471–477.
[187] *Op. cit.*, *Kyklos* (January 1966), XIX: 23–47. See the application of the same argument, above,

to the potential disappearances under competition of local television broadcasters (pp. 36–37) and of research services provided by stock exchange brokers (note 100, this Chapter).

trains what they, with characteristic diplomacy, used to refer to as their "foul-weather friends" only. We have suggested earlier, in discussing the *MCI* case, that the problem may have been one merely of improper rate structure: the railroads might, for example, have reduced their rates substantially in good weather and charged much higher passenger fares on rainy or snowy days, when the airplanes were grounded, and in this fashion appropriated a share of the consumer surplus derived from their continued availability for just such emergencies. But this still would not have solved the inherent problem of trying to collect, in a price for individual journeys, the full value to passengers of keeping the service available. At each such time, the individual traveler would still be deciding whether to pay the higher price on the basis of the costs, pains, and benefits facing him in that particular instance. The higher fare might, for example, cause him simply to postpone the trip. He would still have no opportunity to convey to the railroad in cash—on the contrary, he would have an incentive to conceal—his full appraisal of the value to him of having the service available at all times.

It is this problem that is the most troublesome aspect of the *MCI* case and the others like it. If such ventures are economically feasible only on the assumption that when they break down or become congested subscribers may simply shift over to the Bell System for the duration of the emergency, they are indeed supplying an only partial service. If the common carrier is obliged to stand ready to serve and must carry the burden of excess capacity required to meet that obligation, it would seem that its average total costs would necessarily be higher than those of a private shipper or cream-skimming competitor who has no such obligation: the latter can construct capacity merely sufficient for operation at 100 percent load factors, with the expectation that it or its customers can turn to the common carriers in case of need.[188]

The fact that a competitor chooses to supply only service x while the common carrier is required to supply x plus y is not objectionable so long as customers know in each case what they are getting and, as we have already suggested, the separate charges for x and y reflect their respective costs.[189] So the first attempt at a solution to the MCI–AT&T problem (assuming the facts prove to be as we have been hypothesizing here) must be for the latter company to try to recover the costs of the service, the provision of backup capacity, separately from the x. The ideal way would be in the form of a lump-sum demand charge: those who retain the right to use the facilities should pay for the costs of standing by to honor that right, whether or not they actually exercise it. But merely to state this goal is to suggest the difficulties of attaining it. There is no way of determining a subscriber's capacity cost responsibility except in terms of the amount he actually uses it or will probably use it at the system's peak. A system of predetermined charges *per call* at peak hours works reasonably well for regular customers—although even for them it would be preferable to have rates that varied from one moment to the next depending on the degree of actual congestion present.[190] But such a system might not suffice to levy the proper charges on those who have the option but exercise it rarely or never—unless they could

---

[188] See the Doyle Report, 72; and Friedlaender, *op. cit.*, 117–118.

[189] See pp. 206–207, 216, above.

[190] See note 4, p. 88 and pp. 103–109, Volume 1, above.

be made to pay a special, higher charge per call than regular subscribers do, or their services were placed on an interruptible basis.

In short, AT&T might find itself in the position of the passenger railroad, incapable of devising charges for "rainy day" customers sufficient to cover the heavy capacity cost of standing ready to serve them. It is possible, thus, that the competitive market will not cover the costs of an infrequently exercised option that on purely economic grounds ought to be preserved. As in the case of the railroad, if the schedule of charges were high enough to cover the cost of capacity that was infrequently but needed for emergency, it might pay no individual user to make use of it at such times, even though all, together, would obtain sufficient additional satisfaction from its availability to justify the requisite expenditure of society's resources.[191]

It is of course highly unlikely that this new, selective competition could actually destroy the AT&T alternative; unlike the passenger railroad, it is unlikely to disappear in the foreseeable future. But that is only because there are so many customers who do continue to exercise the option of using it. Therefore the more likely development is not that the option will disappear but that AT&T will be incapable of providing it except by levying unjustifiably high charges on its regular customers.

So, paradoxically, MCI's entry might well constitute cream-skimming, but cream-skimming with the effect of *introducing* internal subsidization where none existed before—subsidization of MCI's customers by AT&T's captive customers being forced to carry a disproportionate share of the back-up capacity costs.

This kind of market failure or discriminatory effect of selective entry could be avoided by protecting the public utility from competition. Observe again, however, that this solution would likewise be very imperfect. The customers who prefer the limited competitive service and place little value on the back-up capacity would be denied the former and would be forced to

---

[191] We mention but do not attempt thoroughly to analyze the analogous situation created by the competition of supplemental with regular airlines. The supplemental sells individual *flights* for charter to individuals or groups that can themselves assume the risks of filling them. The scheduled carriers offer the regular *availability* of service and sell individual *seats* on individual flights. The revenues from the latter sales must cover the costs of the former. The unit costs of the charter service *per passenger* per flight are necessarily lower than for scheduled operations— once a flight is scheduled all of its costs are fixed and the cost per passenger will vary in inverse proportion to the percentage of seats sold—and their tickets can therefore sell at a much lower price.

By the kind of service they have chosen to offer, the supplementals skim the cream and their competition has the familiar justification: there are, they have proved, great numbers of travellers who want access only to the chartered flight, who can be served at unit costs much lower than the fares they would previously have had to pay

and who would otherwise have been forced to subsidize the less remunerative portions of the scheduled operations.

But those regular fares cover the costs also of the regular availability of scheduled service and to the extent that unrestricted competition of charter service jeopardizes the ability of the carriers to maintain that service, the travelling public—including the patrons of charter flights— could find itself the victim of the tyranny of small decisions. All travellers value in some measure the mere *availability* of service on a regularly scheduled basis, yet it pays none of them to support those operations when a cheaper charter flight is available. The regular airline might be unable to charge fares high enough for those flights for which competitive charter service is unavailable to cover the cost of standing by to serve for the same reason that railroads could not hope to do so on rainy or snowy days. The result could be the disappearance of an option of genuine value to travellers merely because there was no way of collecting what it was worth to them.

subsidize the continued availability of the latter to those who value it more highly.[192] This might conceivably be justified in the MCI type of situation, where the alternative, competitive policy would evidently involve the opposite distortion we have just described: as we have seen earlier, no system of customer grouping for rate making can avoid being discriminatory among the various members of the group.[192a] But such a "solution" would obviously be unthinkable in the case of railroad passenger service: the economic value of preserving that option between Ithaca and New York City would hardly have justified suppressing the cream-skimming airline, bus, and passenger automobile competition that were responsible for the railroad's financial plight. The preferable method of financing the provision of this back-up capacity, if its provision were economically justified,[193] would be to give it a direct subsidy, financed out of local real-estate taxes, as in the case of the local airports. But this too would be economically imperfect—unless the tax was on the rental value of land alone.[194]

There is one example of the possibly deleterious effect of competitive entry in jeopardizing the continued provision of service with important external benefits that is especially interesting because its relation to the cream-skimming issue has not to my knowledge been observed elsewhere. This is the competition between community antenna television (CATV) companies and the regular broadcasters, a problem we have already discussed at length elsewhere.[195]

Before the advent of CATV, program origination and the transmission of signals from broadcasters to viewers was a single, integrated function.[196] The CATV operators undertook to perform a more limited but important part of this function and for most viewers did it better than it had been done before. This proved to be extremely profitable. Like MCI, thus, they were in a sense cream-skimmers—doing only part of what had previously been a single job and in a sense getting a free ride on services or facilities provided by others. And, as we have seen, this competition did involve some threat to the continued provision of the auxiliary services—broadcasting by local stations and the origination of the programs that CATV operators picked off the air free of charge.

The first of these threats involved another possible external consequence: the loss of broadcasting signals to sparse rural areas, where cable service is uneconomical.[197] It is at least theoretically conceivable that this failure

---

[192] For a similar objection to fair trade laws, even though these too could be justified on the ground that they preserve economically valuable options —keeping in business the diversified book store, the prescription pharmacy, the liquor store that provides delivery service—see Kahn, *op. cit.*, *Kyklos* (January 1966), XIX: 34–39. And see the application of the same argument to the alleged case for fixing minimum brokerage commissions on security transactions, pp. 206–207, this chapter, above.

[192a] See pp. 189–190, Volume 1.

[193] Such an external subsidy would be economically justified only if the total discounted value of benefits to customers from the continued availability of this back-up capacity, though under-

stated by the revenues collectible from them, exceeded the present value of the costs of providing it.

[194] See note 15, pp. 130–131, Volume 1, above.

[195] See pp. 32–45, Chapter 1, above.

[196] The local station originated some of the programs it broadcast and made arrangements with the networks for the others.

[197] Indeed, as we also pointed out, the urban subscribers to the cable might by their individual decisions to subscribe have imposed an external cost on themselves as well, if the consequences were to drive out the local station, on which the FCC, in principle at least, had imposed a requirement that it originate some local programming. It would be difficult to ascribe this

could have been overcome without regulatory intervention. The threatened viewers might have approached the CATV operators and offered to pay them to carry the programs of the local stations and to avoid duplicating them with programs brought in from the outside, so as to diminish the competitive threat to the survival of the local station, on which they were entirely dependent. On the other hand, clearly, such a solution might not have been practical or sufficient. In any event, the FCC chose to intervene to give the local stations some protection against this competition. The intervention was clearly excessively protectionist in character; but in some respects it was, we found, an economically justifiable attempt to correct for possible market failure.

We have offered reasons for questioning the reality of the other possible external consequence of CATV's free ride—the discouragement of programming. But if the danger were a real one, it could presumably have been corrected by imposing charges on the CATV operators for use of the copyrighted material or by requiring them also to originate programs, rather than discouraging it, as was the FCC's original intention.

These external consequences are, in any event, to some extent required for economic efficiency in a dynamic economy. Recall our earlier fanciful hypothesizing that the introduction of sunlight-beamed telephone service might raise the price and threaten the viability of nighttime service. No group of customers has an inalienable right to the continued provision of service that has become uneconomic. If rural families have heretofore been receiving television programs as the free by-product of a system of local broadcasting that has lost its economic justification because small towns are better served by CATV, bringing in numerous signals from the outside, then they no longer have the right on purely economic grounds to that particular free ride. (I say this regretfully, as a rural dweller out of reach of any CATV system.) And there is no economic ground for insisting that they continue to enjoy it at the expense of urban dwellers, by denying the latter the benefits of CATV.

Offsetting Imperfections and the Problem of Second Best. We have already discussed the possible case for regulatory control stemming from the fact that competition in the real world is not perfect. In these circumstances, regulatory intervention may play the role of a kind of 'offsetting imperfection,'' producing a performance more nearly approximating the one that would be achieved by theoretically perfect but practically unachievable competition.[198] By the same token, unrestricted competition in particular markets or industries may produce poorer rather than better results if it is already distorted by the presence of (1) monopoly elements elsewhere in the economy, (2) differential taxes, or (3) subsidies, all of which have the possible

---

result to market failure, however, since if it paid the local station to originate broadcasts, it would presumably equally have paid the cable operators to do so; and if the latter were prevented from doing so by the Commission's rules as originally proposed, the failure would have been one resulting not from the tyranny of small decisions but from the foolishness of the FCC. The same would be true if the FCC had permitted the competition of the cable systems to drive local stations out of business and then failed to impose on the successor companies the same requirements respecting the origination of local programming as they had previously imposed on the local broadcasters.

[198] The case for offsetting imperfections was clearly expressed by J. M. Clark, in his "Toward A Concept of Workable Competition," *loc. cit.*, even though he does not actually use that term.

effect of producing a misallocation of resources between the market in question and all others. What we have, here, is a statement of the practical problem of the second best, to which we have already referred several times. There are some situations in which second-best considerations would seem to argue against unrestricted cream-skimming.

The most obvious illustrations come from the influence of taxes. For the most part, since these typically weigh with unusual severity on the public utilities and, therefore, their customers, they do not usually counsel restraints on competition in these areas. On the contrary, as we have suggested in Chapter 7 of Volume 1, they would seem to counsel the opposite policy, in order to minimize the effect of this distortion. On the other hand, those taxes that are levied only on the public utilities provide a possible case for regulatory restrictions on the operations of their less heavily taxed competitors. For a long time, for example, special excise taxes were levied on transportation and communications common carriers, and they continue to be levied in the latter case. Such taxes clearly distort the competition between common and private carriers—trucks, the private automobile, private microwave systems.

Distortions introduced by differential rates of government subsidy would in principle call for similar regulatory intervention to limit the competition of the favored suppliers. It seems clear, for example, that the large, heavy, diesel-fuel-burning motor trucks fall far short, in the registration fees and excise taxes that they pay, of reimbursing society for the incremental costs that they impose on it by virtue of the additional, wider and heavier-duty roads that they require.[199] Similarly, the usual practice in the United States has been to levy no charges on the carriers using the navigable waterways, on which very large expenditures of public funds are regularly made.[200]

An alternative policy would be to encourage or to permit the common carriers to meet this kind of competition freely by reducing their own rates to long-run incremental costs.[201] This expedient might well suffice, since common carriers do tend to be subject to increasing returns. Freeing the regulated carriers for more effective competition, rather than compounding one distortion issuing from government intervention by instituting yet another, would require loosening the numerous operating restrictions to

---

[199] See Lansing, *op. cit.*, 251–252, summarizing the incremental cost study made by the Bureau of Public Roads (BPR), *The Supplementary Report of the Highway Cost Allocation Study*, 89th Cong. 1st Sess., House Document No. 124 (1965).

[200] *Ibid.*, 60. The "first-best" solution to these distortions would, of course, be to eliminate the original taxes and subsidies. In his *Message on Transportation* to Congress, dated April 4, 1962, President Kennedy called for "consistent policies of taxation and user charges" and specifically for a repeal of the 10 percent passenger transportation tax (which "has undoubtedly discriminated against public transportation in favor of the automobile"), extension of the excise tax on gasoline to cover jet fuel, and adding a 5 percent tax on airline tickets and air freight weigh bills (all "as a minimal step toward recouping the

heavy Federal investment in the airways"), a tax of 2¢ a gallon on all fuels used in transportation on the waterways, legislation "to make the domestic trunk air carriers ineligible for operating subsidies in the future," and "a step-by-step program with specific annual targets, to assure sharp reduction of operating subsidies to all other domestic airlines as well. . . ." *Op. cit.*, Part I(B). And in his 1965 message to Congress calling for the repeal or reduction of various excise taxes, President Johnson recommended additional user taxes on heavy trucks—and specifically an increase in the excise on highway diesel fuel from 4 to 7 cents a gallon. *New York Times*, May 18, 1965, 26.

[201] This was precisely the choice faced by the ICC in the *Southern Railway* grain decision; see note 12, p. 165, Volume 1, and p. 23, above.

which they have been subjected—something that is desirable on its own merits. It would have the crowning virtue, from the point of view of the consuming public, of extending to it the potential benefits of freer competition, rather than making the regulatory withdrawal of those benefits more uniform and complete.

In purely static terms, it is a matter of indifference whether the government corrects for a distortion introduced by a tax or subsidy in one place by introducing offsetting imperfections elsewhere, or by moving to eliminate the original distortion:

> "efficiency would be increased either by increasing the degree of control exercised over the uncontrolled sector or by relaxing the control exercised over the controlled sector. Both of these policies will move the economy in the direction of some second best optimum position."[202]

The preference that we have expressed for the competitive rather than the intensified regulatory correction is based largely on dynamic, institutional grounds.

Noneconomic Considerations. The economist may be betraying his parochialism when he relegates noneconomic considerations to a few summary comments, inserted long after the reader's concentration has begun to flag. It may instead be taken as an expression of the opinion that he has no particular expertise in this area. The reader must not construe the brevity of our treatment here as suggesting that these criteria of policy are unimportant. Such values as fairness, equality of opportunity, or national security are obviously potentially far more important than economic efficiency. Moreover, the criteria of efficiency implied by a market economy are based on highly restrictive assumptions with respect to the distribution of income and the superiority of consumer sovereignty—assumptions that obviously may be rejected by people with other values. The economist may object to internal subsidization on the grounds set forth in Chapter 7 of Volume 1: that it imposes sacrifices on others greater than the benefits to the subsidized customers; and that the poor would get more satisfaction, at less cost to the subsidizers, if they were given direct money grants instead. The noneconomist might well reject such an argument because it takes as its measure of satisfaction or welfare what consumers are willing and able to pay for particular goods and services. He might not only accept as a political fact of life but also approve, on noneconomic grounds, the possibility that society might be willing to help the poor by selling them electricity or telephone service below cost, or by giving their children free lunches, but be unwilling to do so by direct monetary transfers—even though the poor might prefer the latter.

On the other hand, the mere assertion by some interested party that a particular proposed policy is "fair," "just," or required in the interest of national security by no means justifies the accompanying implication that questions of economic efficiency can therefore be disregarded.[203] What the

---

[202] R. G. Lipsey and Kelvin Lancaster, "The General Theory of Second Best," *Rev. Econ. Studies* (1956), XXIV: 15.

[203] See this writer's colloquy with a staff member of the Subcommittee on Antitrust and Monopoly of the Committee on the Judiciary, U.S. Senate, Ninety-First Cong., 1st Session, *Hearings, The Petroleum Industry*, 1969, 147–149, as well as the testimony of other economic witnesses on this same subject.

economist must do is to insist that legislators or regulators (1) satisfy themselves that these other goals cannot equally well be achieved without the
sacrifice of economic efficiency: after all, the economy that makes the most
efficient use of its resources can then afford to make the greater outlays for
national defense or free education; (2) explicitly confront the economic cost
of achieving these other goals, in order to decide whether the benefits do
indeed justify the costs: noneconomic decisions that involve the expenditure
of resources, the sum total of which is limited, must still be made as rationally
as possible, even if they are not made by economists; (3) openly decide who,
appropriately, should bear the financial burden. This last requirement
should conduce to the second as well: an explicit decision to have social
welfare or national security programs paid for openly by taxpayers, rather
than covertly by internal subsidization ought to produce not only a more
just allocation of burdens but also a more rational appraisal of the balance
between purported benefits and cost. On the other hand, democracies do
not necessarily make their decisions rationally. It may well be argued, thus,
that some particular, socially desirable ends would not be pursued if the
costs were openly divulged; and that it is therefore a legitimate political
strategy to have them financed covertly, even at the cost of considerable
economic inefficiency.

The economist does have another kind of expertise to bring to policy
questions like these. He is usually best equipped to trace the indirect consequences of proposed policies, in order to force those in the position to adopt
or reject them to see whether they are in fact required for or do in fact
contribute to the achievement of their avowed goals. Minimum wage laws
are supposed to help the poor: the economist is obliged to ask to what extent
instead they lead to unemployment at the lowest rungs of the labor ladder.
A uniform flat monthly telephone charge for all local calls, or uniform subway
fares within a metropolitan area may both strike the superficial observer as
"fair" and perhaps particularly desirable because they keep down the cost of
telephones or subway travel for the poor. The economist may be able to
demonstrate whether such charges result instead in comparatively wealthy
subscribers or commuters paying less and urban slum dwellers paying more
than the respective marginal costs of serving them. On the other hand, it
hardly requires the skills of an economist to question the national security
justification of the policy that excludes Canadian ships as well as those of
other countries from the United States coastal shipping business or that
lumps petroleum imports from that country together with those that come
from overseas in computing the proportion of total United States oil requirements that can be safely supplied from outside the country.

Considerations such as these obviously carry us well beyond the issue of
cream-skimming alone. But they clearly do bear on that issue. For example,
advocates of entry restrictions in the trunk airline business have justified the
internal subsidization that they protect on the ground that small towns
"deserve air service" as much as large.[204] It is not clear who, exactly, the
people are in those towns who "deserve" such service: presumably, they are
the relatively well-to-do who can afford to travel by air; nor is it immediately
obvious by what morality they deserve to be subsidized in receiving such

---

[204] See p. 9, above.

service, either by general taxpayers or by regular travelers over the routes—like, say, New York to Puerto Rico—that can generate enough traffic to pay their way.[205]

The same questions must be asked about the FCC's attempts to protect local television stations against CATV competition on the ground that each town "ought" wherever feasible to have its own station and that this is the best way of getting diversity of programming. It is clearly worth asking whether such diversity might not be more effectively promoted by permitting CATV systems freely to bring in a maximum number of signals from the outside and to initiate their own programs; and whether cultural quality and diversity are not likely to be better achieved by more public service programming generated in a smaller number of producing centers or by encouraging the growth of educational television.

Again, encroachments by private carriers on common carrier companies in transportation and communications are often resisted on the ground that national security requires the preservation of strong, integrated common carrier systems, available for emergencies. The argument obviously commands respect. At the same time, it is by no means obvious that monopoly and cartelization are the best instruments for serving that purpose. It is the *total* of transportation facilities that is available in the case of military or other emergency, not just the common carrier component. To the extent that restrictions on competition in the interest of protecting the latter succeed in limiting the encroachments on their domain by unregulated carriers, the total national capacity is not necessarily enhanced at all. The argument is sometimes confined to the necessity for keeping in existence a strong railroad network as the backbone of the national communications system in the event of emergencies. But while there is little room for question that our transportation policy has been intended in part to protect the railroads, it is equally clear that minimum rate regulation by the ICC in recent decades has to some considerable extent had the opposite effect—preventing the railroads from regaining the larger share of the total transportation business to which they are entitled on grounds of pure efficiency.[206] There appears to be general agreement that if railroads were freer to compete for traffic, their profits would be larger, not smaller.[207] It is not clear in what way national security is served by preventing this.[208]

Similarly, in communications, national security might be most effectively served by our having the most widespread and diversified networks possible and—a particularly relevant consideration when the major communications companies obtain most of their equipment from their own manufacturing

---

[205] A more difficult case is presented by the increasing financial difficulties encountered in recent years by the Blue Cross hospitalization insurance companies. Blue Cross was founded and granted tax exemption on the expectation that it would offer group insurance at uniform rates, regardless of the age or infirmities of the members. Those uniform rates have naturally encouraged competing carriers to offer cost-related policies, with premiums based on actual hospitalization, to groups with below-average risks. This cream-skimming competition has left Blue Cross with progressively higher average-risk, average-cost subscribers, forcing it in turn to request sharp increases in premium rates. Richard Phalon, "Blue Cross Under Fire," *New York Times*, August 27, 1969, 39.

[206] See Meyer et al., *op. cit.*, 166–167 and *passim*.

[207] See the survey of the evidence by David Boies, Jr., *op. cit.*, 654–663, and in particular Peck, in Almarin Phillips, ed., *op. cit.*, 263–264.

[208] Boies, *op. cit.*, 658–659.

affiliates—by having the manufacturing experience distributed among the greater number of companies that would have the opportunity of acquiring it if the market were more fully open to them.

Conclusion: The Benefits and Dangers of Discriminatory Competition

It is hard to draw conclusions from these two long chapters, covering a wide diversity of situations, without simply rewriting them. What we have done is to identify the various possible cases for imposing regulatory restraint on free entry and unrestricted rivalry in the public utility industries. In the presence of economies of scale and numerous market imperfections, it is clear that competition can produce inefficiency, deterioration in the quality of service, and severe discrimination.

On the other hand, we have observed that regulation, too, has promoted and protected highly discriminatory rate structures, particularly in the industries considered in the present chapter, in which freer competition would otherwise have been feasible. It has also produced or sheltered immense inefficiencies— by interfering with the rational distribution of the public utility function among alternative media, by protecting conservative and inefficient operators from the pressures of competition and by encouraging service inflation—not to mention the costs of administering the regulatory system itself. And competition has made many important contributions to improved performance in these industries.

We have recognized that noneconomic purposes might justify some of these restrictions; but have pointed out how weakly the logical and evidentiary connection is usually made between those purposes and the restraints that are supposed to serve them. Moreover, there are also noneconomic considerations that argue strongly for competition—notably the value of having customers protected from monopolistic exploitation without the need for government intervention, the values of free entry and enterprise, and the values of *not* having businessmen dependent on grants of privilege for the right to enter this or that occupation, with its attendant risks of mutual corruption of both the political and economic processes.[209]

The strongest basis for regulatory limitation of competition is the presence of long-run decreasing costs. On the other hand, the welfare costs of regulation-enforced or protected inefficiency, or monopolistic pricing are particularly great in such situations because they deprive the consumer of the compounded benefit of a lower price that, by giving rise to additional sales and output, brings about a reduction in the average cost of production as well.[210] And this static welfare loss is far less important than the dynamic

---

[209] In a challenging article, Charles A. Reich cites the dispensation of valuable franchises— medallions to taxi companies, route permits to truck, bus, and airline companies, certificates to natural gas pipelines, licenses to liquor stores, allotments to growers of cotton or wheat and concessions in national parks—as one major category of government largesse, the enormous extension of which carries with it, as he very

effectively demonstrates, a corresponding magnification of government power and an erosion of the security, independence and freedoms of the individual. "The New Property," *The Public Interest*, Number 3 (Spring 1966), 57–59.

[210] For an explanation of this same consequence of taxes that bear with unusual severity on public utilities, see p. 197, in Volume 1, above.

one: it seems a fair generalization that regulation has on balance been obstructive both of competition and of the innovation that it helps stimulate and justify. Aaron J. Gellman, Vice President of The Budd Company, argues persuasively, for example, that innovations in railroading have been thwarted not only because of the general discouragement to competition by the ICC, but specifically because of its minimum rate controls. By preventing rate reductions required to generate additional traffic, they have restricted the introduction of innovations that only a greater traffic volume would have justified.[211]

On the other hand, it is precisely in situations of decreasing costs that price competition is most likely to be discriminatory. Price discrimination can introduce serious inefficiencies at the secondary level. It can also *eliminate* competition at the primary level. Along with the possibility of injury to customers discriminated against, the principal rationalization for minimum rate regulation certainly is the alleged threat that large, integrated public utility companies, if free to reduce prices without limit, may drive competitors out of business, leaving only one or a few firms in full possession of the field.[212] The fear of predatory competition, or what Corwin Edwards has referred to as discriminatory sharpshooting, is one widely encountered

---

[211] Gellman cites the Southern Railway case, involving the introduction of "Big John" cars (see p. 23, above) as a classic illustration of this obstruction. "Economic Regulation and Innovative Performance in Surface Transportation," a paper prepared for the Brookings Institution Conference on Technological Change in the Regulated Industries, Washington, February 1969. See also p. 111, note 54, Chapter 3, above. Barber's conclusion, heavily influenced by the historical evidence of striking advances in productivity in transportation, is more equivocal:

"One crucial finding is that government regulation does not appear to have retarded the rate of technological advance in transportation so much as it has affected its composition and exploitation." *Op. cit.*, 883.

But while his own extensive account amply documents the ways in which regulation has frustrated as well as distorted the development and application of new technology, it offers very little persuasive evidence (except with respect to safety) of regulation's positive contributions to that admittedly very favorable record. See *ibid.*, 853–874. The conclusion seems inescapable that the productivity advance has occurred in spite of regulation.

For a view that regulation has had very little effect one way or another on the development of innovation in air transport, see Almarin Phillips, *op. cit.*, at the same Brookings Institution Conference. Phillips recognizes that the oligopolistic structure of passenger air transport and its avoidance of price competition both help explain the carriers' heavy emphasis on com-

petition through differentiation in the selection of aircraft (see our discussion of this point, pp. 211–214, this chapter, above); and that this kind of rivalry has contributed positively to the rapidity with which the industry has adopted the innovations of the aircraft manufacturing industry. But he suggests that the policies of the CAB have made very little independent contribution to this process:

"In a sense . . . the CAB has behaved much as would a reasonably far-sighted trade association operated by a group of oligopolistic carriers with partially overlapping but far from coincident market areas." *Ibid.*, 47.

Our own discussion suggests that the industry would be substantially more competitive in structure and more prone therefore to engage in price competition if it were not regulated. But Phillips' argument is in any event entirely consistent with the view that regulation has helped to implement what "a reasonably far-sighted trade association" would otherwise have wished to do (and would have been less able to do were the industry fully subject to the antitrust laws), and that its effect on the adoption of new equipment has therefore been far from neutral. Whether this influence has been economically sensible is, however, questionable, as we have already suggested.

On the proper regulatory response to technological change, see Adams and Dirlam, in Trebing, ed., *op. cit.*, 131–144.

[212] See, for example, the views of the Supreme Court majority in the *Ingot Molds* case, pp. 162–163, Volume 1.

in competitive industry generally, and was the principal original occasion for passage of Section 2 of the Clayton Act.[213]

Devotees of what they call "hard competition" scoff at the notion that it is necessary to limit price competition in this way in order to preserve it. There is, indeed, a risk of confusing the preservation of competition with the preservation of competitors. But the policy of protecting individual businessmen from the kind of competition that may cause them to fail without regard to their relative efficiency, energy, or assiduity in serving customers is not necessarily paradoxical or inconsistent; and it is at least conceivable that hard competition that is discriminatory and selective might have this effect. And since discriminatory price competition is just about the only kind that is conceivable among public utility companies, the danger must be faced. It is accentuated in the regulatory context by the A-J-W tendency—by the fact that it could be in the long-run interest of a regulated monopolist to take on business at rates below even its SRMC, not merely temporarily, in quest of monopoly, but over longer periods of time—a danger further accentuated by the administrative difficulties of measuring the LRMC floor below which competitive rates ought not to be permitted to fall.

There is no easy solution to this dilemma. It is all very well to say that the only proper test of promotional rates is long-run marginal costs, and if rates that meet this test drive or keep competitors out of business, so be it. But even this principle is not unexceptionally correct: recall the undesirability of permitting rail-rail (or electricity-gas) competition to drive selected rates to marginal cost.[213a] Given the difficulties of measuring LRMC on specific, possibly small parts of a company's business, moreover, the possibility cannot be denied that competition may drive promotional rates too low. There is the additional, institutional consideration, which cannot be rejected out of hand, that even where on grounds of static efficiency only a single firm may "deserve" to survive, there may be dynamic benefits of maintaining a number of sources of initiative—to put it baldly, of keeping some competitors alive in the face of discriminatory competition. If it proved true, for example, that Western Union was incapable of competing with the Bell System in the provision of various business communications services when the latter set rates fully covering LRMC, it remains at least possible that preserving the competitor might in the long run contribute sufficiently to a greater and more varied innovation to outweigh the static welfare loss involved in holding up the Bell rates in order to keep it alive.

The question is not simply one of keeping undeserving competitors alive. The most difficult choices arise when it is the smaller competitor that actually does the pioneering, only to be met with a discriminatory response by the large incumbent firm. For example, in 1957 Sea-Land Service, a water carrier, altered four of its ships so that each could carry 226 truck trailers and announced rates 5 percent to $7\frac{1}{2}$ percent below competing rail rates for this efficient service. A number of railroads responded by cutting their own piggyback rates on competitive traffic to approximately the same level,

---

[213] "it shall be unlawful for any person engaged in commerce, in the course of such commerce, either directly or indirectly to discriminate in price between different purchasers of commodities . . . where the effect of such discrimina-tion may be to substantially lessen competition or tend to create a monopoly in any line of commerce. . . ." 38 U.S. Stat. 730, Sec. 2 (1914).

[213a] See pp. 168–172, Volume 1, above.

which meant, since rail service is faster, that they would retain the lion's share of the business. Although the rail rates were compensatory, one sympathizes with the ICC's decision in 1960—overturned by the Supreme Court in 1963—ordering the railroads to cancel their rate cuts.[214]

On the other hand, the dangers of this kind of protectionism would certainly seem in most instances to outweigh any possible benefits. The foregoing considerations certainly do not justify the rigid limitations on price competition imposed, for example, by the ICC. Section 2 of the Clayton Act at least confines its prohibition to instances in which there is a threat to the continued vitality of competition; the ICC's rate regulation has no such limitation. Given the flexibility and mobility of trucking and water transportation, their ability to shift from one route to another and, therefore, to move back into any market out of which they may have been driven by temporary reductions in rail rates, the possibility of those reductions producing substantial and enduring increases in monopoly power would seem to be far weaker than the opposite one, which has in fact been realized: that minimum rate control will fasten a regime of thoroughgoing cartelization on these industries. We have, in Chapter 3, listed among the inducements to superior performance in public utilities such factors as the profit motive, managerialism, decreasing costs and elasticity of demand. But every one of them is strengthened by competition.

The likelihood of injury to competition at the seller's level would seem to be far more remote in the public utility area than in unregulated industry generally. The greater danger is not ordinarily that one firm may, by predatory pricing, drive out a host of smaller and weaker competitors but that sellers will be too large and too few and their competitive overlap too thin for effective competition. Where there are large numbers of competing sellers, as in the markets for transportation, energy, and private-line communication service, the chances are either (1) that the cost structures of the competitors are so different that it would be socially efficient to permit the firms with lower long-run marginal costs to prevail or (2) that the smaller firms will have large and powerful allies—like petroleum refiners or the producers of electronic equipment for private communications systems—fully capable of competitive survival as long as entry is free of regulatory blockage and is economically desirable.

It seems impossible to deny that in the regulation of competition in transportation we have gone too far in the direction of limiting price rivalry in order to keep competitors alive. If we must err, it would seem best to err in the opposite direction. If this direction of inclination is the correct one, regulatory commissions ought to be very restrained about disallowing promotional rates that do not cover fully distributed historical costs. Where utilities offer substantial reason to believe that particular categories of business can be expanded if offered rates that cover long-run incremental costs, the burden of proof of unremunerativeness ought to be placed on the Commission that would disallow the rates, rather than on the company that proposes them.

There is, of course, the danger that if the estimates prove to be mistaken, other customers may eventually have to pay higher prices in consequence.

---

[214] *ICC v. New York, New Haven & Hartford Railroad Co. et al.*, 372 U.S. 744 (1963). Cf. the brief reference to this decision at p. 23, Chapter 1, above.

But effective regulation can also ensure that they participate in the gains if the estimates are correct. Given regulatory lag, the burden of error will fall first on stockholders and management. In the presence of increasing returns, there are potential gains for all. In these circumstances, it would seem that the balance of public advantage lies on the side of permitting, indeed encouraging, rate experimentation of this kind. The argument in any particular instance that a restriction on competition is necessary in order to preserve competition ought properly to have to sustain a very heavy burden of proof.[215]

Whenever possible, most economists would probably conclude, competition should be permitted to do its job of bringing prices closer to cost, eradicating price discrimination, controlling tendencies to excessive service inflation, weeding out inefficient suppliers, stimulating improvements in efficiency and service. The ideal would be to reduce the scope of regulation, insofar as possible, to applying the LRMC test of remunerativeness, as a floor, and protecting from exploitation those many customers who, inevitably, will continue to lack access to sufficient competitive alternatives.[216] But there is no single best combination of regulation and competition, valid for all industries, in all times and places.

---

[215] This discussion draws heavily on my "Inducements to Superior Performance: Price," in Trebing, ed., *op. cit.*, 96–102.

[216] These are essentially the recommendations of Meyer *et al.* in the field of transportation, *op. cit.*, 196–202, 247–252. See also Wilson, *op. cit.*,

Jour. Pol. Econ. (August 1955), LXIII: 337–344, and Roberts, in *Transportation Economics, op. cit.*, 12, 29–36.

On the other hand, as we have seen, Wilson feels that minimum rate controls are required also in trucking. See note 29, this chapter, above.

CHAPTER 6

The Role and Definition of Competition: Integration

A business firm is said to be integrated when its activities embrace the production or sale of a number of products, or a single product in a number of markets, each of which either is or could conceivably be produced or served by companies that confined themselves to that single activity. It is horizontally integrated if it operates a number of establishments producing or selling the same product or group of products; geographic integration, thus, is one kind of horizontal integration. Obvious examples would be the chain store or the automobile manufacturer that operates a number of assembly plants in various parts of the country. Vertical integration means the carrying on by a single firm of a series of successive functions in the production and distribution process. Outstanding examples are to be found in the petroleum industry, where the largest firms produce crude oil, transport it in their own pipelines, refine it, transport it once again in their own tankers or product pipelines to their own terminals, and distribute it at least in part through service stations that they themselves own or control by long-term lease; the continued presence in the industry of nonintegrated operators, confining their activities to each of these individual strata, meets the second condition for the presence of integration, namely, that these activities are or could be performed by specialists. Conglomerate integration involves the production or sale of a variety of products or services, which may or may not (the term is used in varying ways) be closely interrelated technologically or commercially. Consider, at the two possible extremes of conglomerates, the steel company that produces thousands of varieties of steel products or the petrochemical refiner, the logic of whose product line is determined by the chemistry of petroleum and its derivatives, or the food processing company, that produces and distributes a wide line of merchandise to the grocery store, or the supermarket itself; and, at the other extreme, the textile company that manufactures aerospace equipment (Textron), the electrical equipment manufacturers (IT&T and RCA) that own car-rental agencies; the conglomerate that produces typewriters, nuclear submarines, and owns a restaurant chain and a book publisher (Litton Industries), or the one (Ling-Temco-Vought) with major interests in meat-packing, airlines, sporting goods, jet aircraft, electronics, and steel.[1]

Integration is usually understood as a characteristic of a single business firm or a group of financially affiliated firms. But some of its characteristics and consequences may be achieved by agreement among financially separate companies. Vertical integration is approximated, for example, by one company agreeing to supply the full requirements of another for a particular raw material; by a manufacturer agreeing to distribute his products exclusively through one distributor in each market territory; or by the independent distributor agreeing to handle exclusively the products of one supplier. Power pooling or the similar interchanges among natural gas pipeline companies achieve some of the same results as would the organization of the various participants into one larger, geographically integrated company; and the offer of piggyback rates by railroads for carrying truck trailers on flat cars can lead to the same kind of coordination as would the formation of a conglomerately integrated rail-motor carrier transportation company.

The treatment of integration in the public utility industries exhibits a wide range and variety of policies and attitudes, of which we can hope only to illustrate a few of the more interesting. With respect to financial integration, regulation is in some contexts permissive, even encouraging; in others hostile. Thus, although the link has been subject to almost continuous scrutiny and criticism, the vertical integration between Western Electric and the Bell System has been permitted to continue; railroads, airlines, and banks have been permitted to merge even when there had previously been some competition between them; single companies own a number of radio or television stations; in some states, so-called combination companies have been permitted, in the distribution of both electricity and gas; to a limited extent, railroads have been permitted to conduct auxiliary trucking operations; and producers of natural gas have held financial interests in, and in some cases have been permitted to organize, natural gas pipeline companies.

On the other hand, there is a tradition in the public utility industries that holds integration either obstructive of effective regulation or incompatible with effective competition. We have already described the breaking up of the great holding company empires under the Public Utility Holding

---

[1] As suggested, these terms are not always used in exactly the same way. The antitrust laws subject to particularly sharp scrutiny those instances in which firms integrate by either acquiring other firms or merging with them. Since Section 7 of the Clayton Act (as amended) prohibits such mergers or acquisitions only "where . . . the effect . . . may be substantially to lessen competition, or to tend to create a monopoly" (15 U.S.C. 18, 1964 ed.), in antitrust usage the concept of a horizontal merger is usually confined to a situation in which the two firms joined were previously selling the same product or group of products in the same geographic market—because only in that case could their union eliminate pre-existing competition. According to this usage, market-extension mergers, which join together similar companies operating in geographically separate markets, are generally considered as constituting a separate category of conglomerate, similar to those of the product-extension type, like the acquisition by Procter & Gamble, the leading manufacturer of soaps and detergents, of the Clorox Company, the leading manufacturer of liquid bleaches. See Willard F. Mueller, *Celler-Kefauver Act, 16 Years of Enforcement*, U.S. House of Representatives, 90th Cong. 1st Sess., Committee on the Judiciary, Staff Report to the Antitrust Subcommittee, 1967.

Company Act of 1935,[2] and the compromise embodied in the 1962 Communications Satellite Act between those senators who strongly urged that the development of international satellite communications be turned over to a government corporation and the established common carriers, who wanted to control it themselves.[3] The Panama Canal Act of 1912 amended the Interstate Commerce Act to prohibit railroads from holding "any interest whatsoever" in a water common carrier with which they do or may compete for traffic, though it permits exceptions to be granted by the ICC;[4] the Motor Carrier Act of 1935, as amended by the Transportation Act of 1940, directs the ICC to withhold its approval of railroad acquisition of or merger with a motor carrier,

> "unless it finds that the transaction proposed will be consistent with the public interest and will enable such carrier to use service by motor vehicle to public advantage in its operations and will not unduly restrain competition";[5]

and the ICC applies similar criteria in passing on railroad applications for motor-carrier certificates or permits even though no statute explicitly requires it.[6] Similarly, the consent decree settling the antitrust suit brought against the Bell System, while leaving undisturbed the challenged vertical relationship between AT&T and Western Electric, prohibited the System from engaging, either directly or indirectly, "in any business other than the furnishing of common carrier communications services."[7] The same distrust of integration underlies the Federal Communications Commission's "diversification policy" with respect to its awarding of licenses for radio and television stations:

> "When two or more candidates apply for the same outlet and when 'other things are equal,' the license should go to the non newspaper or to the candidate with no other media affiliations."[8]

The FCC also limits the number of television, AM and FM radio stations

---

[2] See pp. 72–73, Chapter 2, above. On the other hand, as we have seen, the Act does not abolish all holding companies, but directs the SEC to limit their operations "to a single integrated public-utility system, and to such other businesses as are reasonably incidental, or economically necessary or appropriate. . . ." 15 U.S. Code 79k (b) (1), 1964 ed. In a decision that seems certain to be appealed, the SEC in 1970 refused to extend the cover of the latter escape clause to the application of a natural gas company to diversify into financing the construction of low and moderate income housing — even though Congress had, in the National Housing Act, sought to encourage private industry to engage in such ventures. *In the Matter of Michigan Consolidated Gas Company* (70–4778), Administrative Proceeding, File No. 3–2111, Findings and Opinion, June 22, 1970. On this decision, see also note 21a, this chapter, below.

[3] See Chapter 4, pp. 136–137, above.

[4] 49 U.S. Code 5(14)–(16), 1964 ed.

[5] 49 U.S. Code 5(2)(b), 1964 ed.

[6] See Fulda, *op. cit.*, 381–382, and 402, citing the leading case *ICC v. Parker*, 326 U.S. 60 (1945) and his Chapter 12, for a thorough survey of the law; also Locklin, *op. cit.*, 846–853 and the *Doyle Report*, 138–144.

[7] *United States of America v. Western Electric Company Inc., and American Telephone & Telegraph Co.*, Final Judgment, Civil Action No. 17–49, U.S. District Court, District of N.J., January 24, 1956, section V. See also pp. 297, below and 145, note 93, above.

[8] Harvey J. Levin, *Broadcast Regulation and Joint Ownership of Media* (New York: New York Univ. Press, 1960), 173. Since the FCC has more often than not decided that "other things were not equal," Levin concludes that this policy "has exercised only a minor influence on the industry's actual structure," *ibid.*, 193.

Integration and Competition

that any single firm can own to a total of seven of each (no more than five TV stations can be VHF).[9]

---

[9] See Levin, "Competition, Diversity, and the Television Group Ownership Rule," *Columbia Law Rev.* (May 1970), LXX: 791–835.

On March 28, 1968, the Commission issued a Notice of Proposed Rule-Making, proposing in any future applications for new licenses or license transfers to prohibit common ownership of any two stations in the same market, even though in different media (AM radio, FM radio or TV). The Antitrust Division of the Department of Justice, documenting the pervasive multiple-media ownerships in major markets, urged the Commission to extend the prohibitions to license renewal proceedings as well, and to newspaper-broadcasting combinations. *In the Matter of Amendment of Sections 73.35, 73.240 and 73.626 of the Commission Rules*, Docket No. 18110, *Comments of the United States Department of Justice*, August 1, 1968. In early 1969 the Commission responded with a path-breaking decision that spread something close to panic through the industry, when it refused to renew the license of WHDH-TV in Boston on the ground that it was not sufficiently "free from media alliances": the owner of the station was the Boston Herald-Traveler Corporation, a newspaper company that also operated two local radio stations and held a controlling interest in a CATV company. The FCC turned the license over to a citizens group, Boston Broadcasters, Inc., composed of two Harvard professors and the Director of Massachusetts General Hospital. *Newsweek*, February 3, 1969, 65. Later in that year the Commission delayed renewal of the license of Station KRON-TV, in San Francisco, in order to consider whether the fact that it is owned by San Francisco's only morning newspaper constitutes an undue concentration of media control. *The New York Times*, April 27, 1969, 72. In 1970, in the afore-mentioned proceeding (Docket No. 18110), the FCC promulgated the rules it had earlier proposed, limiting ownership of broadcast stations of all kinds (whether AM, FM or TV) to one to each market (though permitting limited AM-FM radio combinations in small towns), so far as future licenses were concerned. It also proposed rules that would require present licensees, within five years, to reduce their holdings to either an AM-FM radio combination, a television station, or a newspaper in the same market. First Report and Order, and Further Notice of Proposed Rule Making, March 25, 1970. See also the submission in this proceeding by James N. Rosse, Bruce M. Owen, and David L. Grey, "Economic Issues in the Joint Ownership of Newspaper and Television Media," including the study by Owen, "Empirical Results on the Price Effects of Joint Ownership in the Mass Media," mimeo., Memorandum No. 97, Research Center in Economic Growth, Stanford University, May, 1970.

For similar indications of the determination of the Department of Justice to attack multi-media companies, see its *Complaint* under Section 7 of the Clayton Act in *U.S. v. Gannett Co., Inc., WREX-TV, Inc. and Rockford Newspapers, Inc.*, Civil Action No. 68 C 48, U.S. District Court, Northern District of Illinois, Western Division, filed December 5, 1968, contesting the acquisition by Gannett, the owner of WREX, of all the common stock of Rockford Newspapers, in 1967; and its submission to the Federal Communications Commission, *In the Matter of Amendment of Part 74, Subpart K, of the Commission's Rules and Regulations Relative to Community Antenna Television Systems et al.*, Docket No. 18397, *Comments of the United States Department of Justice*, April 7, 1969, recommending prohibition of any common ownership between CATV systems and either television stations or newspapers in the same community or market. The FCC complied, partially, in 1970, when it prohibited local cross-ownership of CATV systems by television broadcasters and all ownership of such systems by the TV networks; and it asked for comments on various suggestions for limiting multiple ownership of CATV systems on a regional and national basis, and on cross-ownership of CATV ventures with newspapers, magazines, advertising agencies, and others. *Ibid.*, Docket No. 18397, Second Report and Order, and Docket No. 18891, Notice of Proposed Rule Making and of Inquiry, June 24, 1970.

Separate but related developments, clearly illustrating the political aspects of multimedia ownership, were initiated in 1969, one by a Democrat and one by a Republican. In the first, Milton Shapp, defeated gubernatorial candidate, asked the FCC not to renew the license of WFIL-TV, in Philadelphia, one of the main properties in the publishing and television holdings of Walter Annenburg, whom President Nixon had previously appointed Ambassador to Great Britain. The Annenberg family, Shapp charged, enjoyed a "near news monopoly in the Philadelphia area" and had "conducted a personal vendetta against me," adding that "the news has been censored, omitted, twisted, distorted and used for . . . personal purposes." *New York Times*, July 4, 1969. The other incident was the highly publicized speech by Vice-President Agnew later that year, charging an excessive concentration of control over the news media and specifically singling out the newspaper and

With respect to vertical integration, airplane manufacturers must have the approval of the CAB to hold any ownership interest in airline carriers;[10] the Public Utility Holding Company Act prohibits affiliates from selling services or equipment to operating companies except under terms and conditions set by the SEC;[11] the Clayton Act prohibits common carriers from purchasing supplies without competitive bidding from companies with whom they have interlocking directors;[12] Comsat operates under a mandate to purchase all supplies by competitive bidding.[13]

With regard to the cooperation among unaffiliated companies aimed at achieving some of the benefits of integration, regulatory policies cover the whole range from prohibition to compulsion. As we have already indicated in Chapter 2, these companies have voluntarily sought to achieve the various advantages of collaboration, in which event regulation has been essentially permissive. But where the companies in question have also been actual or potential competitors, their zeal for collaboration has often been excessive rather than inadequate, and directed more to the suppression of competition than reduction in costs or improvement of service. In these circumstances, it has been necessary to police their agreements, in an attempt (though rarely with great assiduity, enthusiasm, or success[14]) to prevent their serving as instruments for the collusive suppression of desirable rivalry among the parties or for the exclusion of outside competitors.

On the other hand, for reasons that we have already examined, private companies do not always cooperate in all the ways that would be socially advantageous.[15] For these reasons, regulatory legislation and administration have from time to time essayed the more positive roles of persuasion, encouragement, and compulsion—though almost certainly far less than would have been desirable. And they have done so in the interest not only of efficiency but of preserving competition.

This combination of considerations and motives illustrates the major problems inherent in policies directed at maintaining competition. Effective competition calls for a balancing-off of considerations of efficiency on the one hand and purity of rivalry on the other. In the presence of economies of integration (as of scale), the balancing has to be between permitting firms large and integrated enough to enjoy these economies and firms numerous enough and with sufficient opportunity for effective rivalry. In the presence of potential economies of interfirm coordination, the balancing is one of cooperation on the one hand and independence of action on the other. At times, these goals coincide rather than conflict—when, for example, coordination is necessary both to save costs and to preserve the competitive opportunities of viable firms that would otherwise be excluded from a fair opportunity to compete. But in other circumstances they may conflict— where, for example, a merger of two competing railroads will reduce costs,

---

broadcasting properties of the (Democratic) *Washington Post* and *New York Times*.

[10] See the CAB proceeding on whether Howard Hughes should be permitted to retain control of Air West, a West Coast feeder line, despite his large interests in aircraft manufacture. *Wall Street Journal*, December 16, 1969, 38.

[11] 15 U.S. Code 79m (b), 1964 ed.

[12] 15 U.S. Code 20, 1964 ed.

[13] See Irwin, "Comment," in Trebing, ed., *op. cit.*, 156–160; but note from our descriptions of the relevant statutory provisions that Irwin's characterizations are not always accurate.

[14] See, for example, Boies, *op. cit.*; also pp. 69–70, above.

[15] See pp. 64–69, Chapter 2, above.

or where the integration of several public utility functions, in the interest of efficiency, gives rise to the danger that independent companies will be denied access to some complementary function on equal terms with their integrated competitors.

Manifestly, we cannot hope here to analyze all the policies we have just summarized, or any one of them thoroughly. The purpose of this chapter is to examine the implications of integration in the regulated industries, the contribution it can make to improved performance, the kinds of problems it raises, and its relationship to the broad yet central question of the proper role and requirements of effective competition in this sector of the economy.

FINANCIAL INTEGRATION

Although the merits of financial integration of public utility companies will differ from one kind of integration to another and from one industry to another, there are certain themes or considerations—both pro and con—that are more or less common to all. It would be efficient, therefore, to lay out the main ones at the outset, to provide a blueprint for the more detailed, individual illustrations that follow. In this way we illustrate, once again, the two parts of the task of devising the best possible institutional structure for any industry: on one side, the development and recognition of common principles and considerations; on the other, striking the best possible balance in the particular, and always in some degree unique, circumstances of each individual case.

The same observations apply equally to the unregulated sectors of the economy as well. What makes their application to the public utility situation in some degree unique is the typically greater degree of monopoly power prevalent in these industries; the greater external restraint on the full exploitation of that power imposed by regulation itself; and the special character of their technology. But these are differences of degree only. It is an open question whether the degree of monopoly power that exists or ought appropriately to be permitted in some of the regulated industries—most notably, transportation—is greater than prevails in such theoretically unregulated sectors of the economy as the production of automobiles or haircuts. It is also an open question how much greater a restraint is imposed on the exercise of monopoly by formal public regulation in these industries than by various informal influences and managerial self-restraint in some of the unregulated sectors of the economy.[16]

The simplest case for integration is that it may be a more efficient way of doing business. In the case of horizontal integration, the extreme situation is the one of natural monopoly. Vertical integration can make possible a closer synchronization of input and output flows, a closer control of quality, a better adjustment of capacity at the several stages of the production process than can be achieved by separate firms dealing with one another at arms length; and it may save enough, additionally, in reduced costs of selling and transferring materials or products from one level to the other to compensate firms for the limitation in their range of choice of suppliers

---

[16] In any event, since the focus of this book is on the formally regulated industries, we make no explicit effort as we go along to demonstrate consistently in which respects the argument applies equally to the unregulated sectors and in which respects it does not.

or customers that it usually involves. The possible efficiency advantages of conglomerate integration may be best conceived as arising from a fuller or better utilization of a firm's capacity, broadly defined—where its management, physical production plant, research laboratories, or distribution facilities can take on an additional product or market with a smaller increase in cost than if those products or markets were supplied by separate firms.

For these reasons alone, integration is potentially promotive of competition, not only because its cost savings may permit firms to compete more effectively, but also by virtue of the act of integration itself: it clearly contributes to competition if firms are free to undertake whatever new functions they choose, whenever they think they can perform them more effectively than they were previously being performed. The mere ability of firms to integrate thus constitutes a kind of potential competition that helps keep other firms on their toes.[17]

As far as vertical and conglomerate integration are concerned, this possible competitive contribution carries as a corollary a defense against the rather widespread supposition that integration is inherently dangerous because it increases business power and creates the threat of monopoly. The defense has two components. First, monopoly power, as the economist defines it, depends principally on the number of sellers of any given commodity or service: it is a horizontal phenomenon. Neither vertical nor conglomerate integration, as such, changes market structure in this respect, at least not for the worse. If accomplished by acquisition, all that changes is the identity of the firm in the market in question; if accomplished by internal expansion—that is, if the integrating firm enters the business by constructing its own facilities—the immediate effect is to increase the number of competitors in the market in question by one. (Clearly this defense does not apply to horizontal integration and particularly when accomplished by merger: in this event the number of competitors in any particular market is reduced by one.)

The second part of the defense is this: if a firm cannot increase its market power by vertical or conglomerate integration, what possible reason would it have to integrate except a belief that it can perform the new function at least as well or better than the firms already doing it? (Of course, if one felt that the possibilities of monopolistic exploitation in any market are increased by the mere fact that firms in it are large and integrated—a view that has adherents among economists[18]—this defense has diminished persuasiveness.)

---

[17] "Large businesses and integration are necessary agencies and inevitable manifestations of a free enterprise system. The firm that competes successfully must be permitted to grow; by the same token, businesses must ordinarily be free to expand if they think they can in this way enhance their ability to serve the customer. Competition requires also that business units be free, ordinarily, to take on new products, new functions, or enter new markets—in short, to integrate." Reprinted from Dirlam and Kahn, *Fair Competition*, 141. Copyright 1954 by Cornell University. Used by permission of Cornell University Press.

"The easiest curb on monopoly power, the most effective cure for poor performance, and the one most consistent with free enterprise, is freedom of entry. And this includes, manifestly, the right of an existing business to extend its operations into any area its managers see fit to enter, i.e., to integrate." *Ibid.*, 151–152.

[18] A leading exponent of this position is Corwin D. Edwards. See, for example, his "Conglomerate Bigness as a Source of Power," *Business Concentration and Price Policy*, A Conference of the Universities–National Bureau Committee for Economic Research (Princeton: Princeton Univ. Press, 1955), 331–361, and his testimony before the Hart Committee, U.S. Senate, Committee on the Judiciary, Subcom-

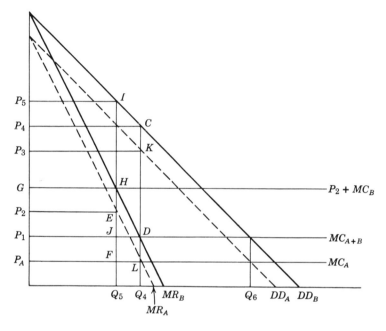

Figure 1. The static effect of vertical integration.

This defense has been developed with particular clarity for the case of vertical integration, but it has also been applied, with modifications, to conglomerate integration and to a host of competitive practices, like exclusive dealing, exclusive territorial distributorships, full-line forcing and tying-in,[19] that achieve some of the benefits of integration and are generally deemed to be at least potentially anticompetitive in effect. While this case must be substantially modified in the public utility context, it is nonetheless important that it be understood. Figure 1 provides the simplest possible explanation of the argument.

Vertical integration raises no problems whatever except in the event of some preexisting monopoly power. If all the horizontal strata of an industry, representing the successive stages of the production process, were purely competitive, there could be no possible effect on competition if some of the firms embraced two or more of these strata within their own spheres of

mittee on Antitrust and Monopoly, the 88th Cong. Second Sess., *Economic Concentration, Hearings*, Part 1, 1964, 36–56; see also the response by Jesse W. Markham, *ibid.*, Part 3,

1269–1281.

[19] See the writings of Bork and Bowman, cited note 21, below.

operation: the integrated firms would still be subject to the uninhibited checks of competition at whatever point they made their final sales. We therefore assume here the ultimate in monopoly—a single firm selling a final product, B, the demand for which is indicated in the figure. And we assume, for simplicity, that the industry has only two strata, one producing the input A and a second that transforms A into B, with respective marginal costs as indicated that we assume for simplicity to be horizontal. If the monopolist is unregulated and able to buy his input A at minimum cost (that is, at MC), he will maximize profit by producing up to the point where MC_{A+B} equals MR_B. His output will be Q_4, his price P_4, and his monopoly profit will be the rectangle P_1P_4CD.[20] As long as he can buy his input A at minimum cost, he has no incentive whatever to integrate vertically; he can extract all the possible monopoly profit there is to be extracted from the market by charging the markup CD over his own marginal costs. Clearly he would integrate backward only if he were paying a higher price for A than (he thinks) it would cost him to produce it himself—because the present suppliers are less efficient than he would be, or because they have monopoly power and are charging him more than MC, or if there were additional efficiencies in the combining of the operations.

Figure 1 illustrates one such possible occasion. Suppose that the suppliers of A do have some monopoly power and are therefore able to charge not P_A but, say, P_2, thus giving them monopoly profits designated by the rectangle P_AP_2EF. In this event, the downstream monopolist would find his own marginal costs elevated to the level P_2+MC_B. In these circumstances, he would maximize his own profit by producing up to the point where this new, artificially elevated marginal cost curve equaled MR_B, or quantity Q_5. He would still be getting some monopoly profits, GP_5IH, but these would clearly be smaller than he had earned before, mainly because he would now have to share some of the potential monopoly profits from the industry with the suppliers of A. In this event, it would obviously pay him to go into the production of A himself, obtaining that input once more at cost, MC_A, increasing his output to Q_4, reducing his price to P_4 and in this way, once more, enjoying the monopoly profits P_1P_4CD. Notice that in this case, in which inputs are transferred from one stratum to another at prices in excess of marginal costs, the price to the ultimate consumer is raised even beyond the level charged by a single, integrated monopolist; and that, therefore, vertical integration is in the interest of the consumer as well as of the monopolist himself.[21]

---

[20] The reader might have some difficulty in accepting the difference between marginal cost and price as a measure of monopoly profits. Pure competition does equate price with marginal cost. But since there is no certainty that short-run marginal cost will in fact cover average total cost, it might be simpler for the reader to interpret the MC lines in the diagram as depicting long-run marginal cost, in an industry which produces under conditions of constant cost. This means that MC may be taken as equal to ATC, when firms operate at the lowest-cost point.

[21] It is in fact in the interest of suppliers at both

levels, jointly. The two back-to-back monopolists do not succeed in maximizing their own aggregate profits when they operate independently in the manner indicated. The total of the profits earned by the suppliers of A and by the B monopolist, P_AP_2EF and GP_5IH, respectively, is less than P_1P_4CD, the profits earned by the latter when he is able to obtain his inputs at MC. The reason for this is quite simple. No matter what the arbitrary price at which A is transferred, the true marginal cost of the entire production process is still MC_{A+B}. The increase in output from Q_5 to Q_4 effected by vertical integration would add more to

So we have a simple illustration of the case for vertical integration on static grounds. Monopoly power is a horizontal, not a vertical phenomenon. It is in the interest of a (horizontal) monopolist to have all the other functions in his industry—the supply of his inputs, the processing, and distribution of his products—performed at minimum cost and charged for at the minimum price. As long as these two conditions prevail, he has no incentive to integrate vertically: he can appropriate the maximum profit available in the industry in the price that he charges for his own service, being assured that that price will be added to and will have added to it the minimum possible charge for all other services upstream and downstream from him. If those conditions do not prevail, it then does pay him to integrate; but in that event (if he made no mistake in doing so) the resultant lowering of the cost or price at which the associated function is performed can only be beneficial to consumers, if it affects them at all.

The possible benefits have a dynamic aspect as well. As we have suggested, the act of integration or the mere threat of entry into a market by this device can contribute the same stimulus as can other forms of direct, horizontal competition to continuing efforts at cost reduction and innovation by companies in that market. In addition, integration can encourage investment and innovation because of the special *incentives* to which it may give rise[21a], the particular *opportunities* it generates, and the additional *ability*

revenues than to costs: the sacrificed profit is represented by the triangle *JHD* (*JH* being the amount by which the cost of *A* to the *B* supplier is inflated by monopoly). The foregoing demonstration is taken essentially from J. J. Spengler, "Vertical Integration and Antitrust Policy," *Jour. Pol. Econ.* (August 1959), LVIII: 347. The argument has been developed at much greater length by Robert H. Bork, notably in his article, "Vertical Integration and the Sherman Act: the Legal History of an Economic Misconception," *Univ. of Chicago Law Rev.* (Autumn 1954), XXII: 157. Bork and Ward S. Bowman Jr. have also applied similar reasoning to conglomerate integration and various allegedly restrictive trade practices in "The Crisis in Antitrust," *Fortune*, reproduced along with exchanges with Harlan M. Blake and William K. Jones as "The Goals of Antitrust: a Dialogue on Policy," *Columbia Law Rev.* (March 1965), LXV: 363–466.

[21a] In refusing to permit the Michigan Consolidated Gas Co. to finance low and moderate income housing projects in the Detroit area (note 2, p. 253, above), the SEC held that the proposed operation lacked the requisite "operating or functional relationship" to the public utility business. The Act did, indeed, seem to envisage continued integration with "other businesses" only in the presence of direct, physical relationships between the several operations such that their integrated operation would result in lower costs of production or distribution. In so doing, it seemed to ignore the

possibility of special *commercial* relationships such as might under integration give rise to an incentive to engage in socially desirable investments that might otherwise not be made. As Commissioner Smith argued, in his dissent:

"The fulcrum of any reasoned analysis of these questions is the term 'business.' Corporate business functions are becoming broader in concept than a strict limitation to operations.... Public utility companies in particular ... have a basic commitment to the areas they serve.... It is not possible for a utility simply to pull up stakes and move to another area.... If large portions of the service area become dilapidated and unfit for habitation, the utility must face not only a possible reduction in revenue but the additional expense and burden of servicing areas that lie beyond....

"In light of the Congressionally recognized relevance of the present investments, I think it can readily be found that those investments are, under Section 11(b)(1), both reasonably incidental and economically necessary or appropriate to the operations of the utility system....

"The proposed housing projects involve modest commitments of capital and provide an economic return on those investments both to investors and consumers. For the same reasons the investments are likewise, under Section 9 (c) (3), 'appropriate in the ordinary course of business' under any construction of that term which takes into account the dynamics of contemporary corporate functions and responsibilities." *Loc. cit.*

that it may confer on a firm to mobilize resources for these purposes. A company will have unusual incentives to develop new equipment or other inputs that it needs in its own operations or better outlets or new uses for its product; it may have unusual opportunities, arising from its own operating experience, to perceive the need and possibilities for such an effort; and it might, by being able to assure successful innovations a market, be best able to justify the application of resources to their development.[22]

---

[22] Whether the superior ability of a large integrated company to raise capital is a reflection of imperfection of the capital market or, instead, a genuine efficiency advantage conferred by integration is a complicated question that cannot be resolved here. Certainly, if company A can raise funds in order to undertake an investment X because investors know that they will be protected by virtue of the wide span of A's operations and sources of income against any possible loss if that particular project proves a failure, whereas company B cannot raise capital for that very same investment, there is an element of imperfection in the capital market; the advantage of integrated company A over nonintegrated company B may be said to be essentially private and strategic. The proper test of whether a particular investment should be made is surely the risk of that investment, not the risk to the *investor*; the latter may be large or small depending on the mere size or diversification of the borrower. See the fuller discussion of this point at note 117, below. Arguing to some extent to the contrary, see George J. Stigler, "Imperfections in the Capital Market," *Jour. Pol. Econ.* (June 1967), LXXV: 287–292.

But where the advantage of A arises from the fact that it is in a better position to perceive the opportunity for the investment or to assure its success, this could be a genuine social, efficiency advantage of integration.

This whole area is one in which economists have not developed entirely satisfactory normative judgments. Because the present writer has grappled with the problem at some length (in collaboration with M. G. de Chazeau) he may be excused for quoting at some length from that earlier study:

"Economic theory has generally found the strongest case for market imperfection in the conditions needed for economic progress. . . . Here, if anywhere, the security of established position, conferred by size and integration, might be needed to balance the hazards of long and costly experimentation, of long-term expenditures on research and development for new products and processes, and of explorations to reveal new sources of crude oil and new ways of developing synthetics to take its

place. A logical case can be made for the proposition that the public benefits from these advantages of the large vertically integrated company—from its greater sensitivity to investment opportunities, ability to marshal funds, and willingness to use them at relatively low anticipated rates of return." *Integration and Competition in the Petroleum Industry* (New Haven: Yale Univ. Press, 1959), 278.

"The possible contributions [of integration to innovation] are varied but the basic one is to be found in the nature of the *incentives* inherent in integration itself—arising out of the mutual reenforcement and support that a company's separate operations lend to one another. The ownership of practically unusable sour crude in large amounts gave Standard Oil an urgent reason to seek a desulfurizing process and to apply it widely once it was found. The low, precarious margins of refiners provided strong incentives to minimize the costs of laying down crude oil at the refinery and distributing its products: they were practically forced to develop pipelines . . . to improve the efficiency of their barge and tanker transport, and to push forward the rationalization of their marketing. Heavy investments in refining and marketing facilities plus declining California output of crude oil undoubtedly spurred Union Oil to acquire oil shale lands and to study methods of using them. . . . One could go on; but the point is simply this: in a closely integrated operation, failure, irritation, need, or surplus at any one level or in any one process of the industry creates an imbalance which stirs up compensatory, socially beneficial activity at other levels. . . .

"The larger the exposure-front of a firm's commercial operations, the greater the probability that experts within its organization will recognize the potentialities of a new idea or product in commercial application; and the wider the firm's commercial interests, the more likely it is to apply its resources for the development of such an idea." Pp. 309–310.

"Imperfect knowledge and imperfect competition are characteristic of all real markets, including capital markets. It is because of these imperfections that the planning and budgeting of capital outlays are such vital management functions, and integration may contribute to

There are offsetting dangers even in unregulated industry, revolving around the possibility that integration may protect, reinforce, or extend preexisting (horizontal) monopoly power. The issue is much disputed and we make no effort further to analyze it here.[23] But these dangers are accentuated by monopoly and regulation. Backward vertical integration is a possible way of circumventing regulation in the exploitation of monopoly power.[24] Consider the situation illustrated in Figure 1, above. The ideal level of output is not Q_4 but Q_6; the efficient price, not P_4 but P_1. And that is the price that an effective regulatory commission would set (assuming, as before, that marginal cost suffices to cover average total cost as well), provided that the regulated company is able to buy input A at the competitive price or produces it itself. If, however, it (or its officers) were able to acquire control over the production of A or some beneficial share in its ownership, and this stratum of the industry were not itself regulated, the regulated company could appropriate all the potential monopoly gains from this industry in the price that it charged for A. That would be P_3—the price which, when there was added to it the marginal cost of performing the B function, would yield the industry profit-maximizing price to the final consumer, P_4. The utility commission would in this event be holding the company to its cost of service, P_4; but the only difference from the unregulated monopoly situation would be that the same total amount of profits, $P_A P_3 KL$, would now flow into the pockets of the affiliated unregulated producer of A rather than, in the form $P_1 P_4 CD$, into the coffers of the public utility company itself.[25]

---

their more effective performance. Firm A, which integrates several levels of production and processing, may know better than firm B, which operates at only one level, what investments will prove profitable for private investment and will meet a continuing public need. Or both A and B may recognize a socially profitable investment opportunity but, because the market for loanable funds is imperfect, only A may be able to effect the necessary financing on acceptable terms. . . . Such an advantage would be A's superior ability to reduce the real risks or realize the full benefits of investment by fitting a particular project into its integrated structure with consequent mutually sustaining or reenforcing advantages at more than one level of operation. For example, it might pay an integrated oil company, but not an outsider, to turn petroleum byproducts into synthetic detergents, carry them to market in its own trucks, and sell them in its own service stations, because the added costs of the project are slight and it already has facilities to do part of the job. . . .

"it seems impossible to doubt that because of the superior access to knowledge, opportunity, incentive, or resources, or because they already have part of the necessary capacity and it takes relatively little added capital to perform the new function, integrated firms

may make investments that would not otherwise be made—investments that may prove economically justifiable in the sense that they add to the social product a sufficient amount of goods and services to justify use of the savings here rather than elsewhere." (*Ibid.*, 260–261.)

For a similar argument, interpreting "Integration as an Adjustment to Risk and Uncertainty," which, by "increasing knowledge and control," promotes efficiency, reduces various insurancelike costs, and in certain circumstances makes commercially feasible the adoption of new cost-reducing technology, see the article by H. R. Jensen, E. W. Kehrberg and D. W. Thomas, *Southern Econ. Jour.* (April 1962), XXVIII: 378–384.

[23] See the Blake & Jones exchange with Bork and Bowman, note 21, above; also Fritz Machlup and Martha Taber, "Bilateral Monopoly, Successive Monopoly and Vertical Integration," *Economica*, n.s. (May 1960), XXVII: 101–119; Dirlam and Kahn, *Fair Competition*, 142–150 and *passim*; and de Chazeau and Kahn, *op. cit.*, 44–50 and *passim*.

[24] See p. 28, esp. note 20, in Volume 1.

[25] This same result can be demonstrated, as we have in the broken lines of Figure 1, by asking what it would be in the interest of a monopoly supplier of input A to charge, if he knew that the downstream function, B, would

A second danger peculiar to the public utilities is the A-J-W tendency: regulated companies might wish to integrate regardless of whether they can perform the added functions more efficiently than others are already doing so, in order to expand their rate bases and their total permitted profits.[26] This is only another way of making the more general point that the defenses of integration set forth above assume not only the absence of a possibility that it may increase monopoly power but also that firms attempt to maximize profits. Where they are prevented from doing so but are permitted to recover all additions to cost including a return on all additional investments, the taking on of losing operations may itself actually conduce to profit maximization. By the same token, these dangers of integration may prevail even in unregulated industries, to the extent that managers are willing to subordinate profit-maximization to the goal of increasing the size or growth of the firms they manage.

The third danger is one that exists also in unregulated industries, but it is accentuated by the greater monopoly power that typically prevails in public utilities: a firm may, by its integration, foreclose competitors from a fair opportunity to compete. This possibility arises, as we shall see, under conglomerate as well as vertical integration, but it can be most easily demonstrated in the latter situation. When a public utility monopolist provides its own input, it forecloses independent suppliers absolutely from selling at all to the entire industry. The typical defense of integration

---

be performed at a price of only MC_B. The derived demand for product A would be DD_A— the demand for the final product minus the marginal cost of performing the B function. In that event, the marginal revenue function for firm A would be MR_A, its profit maximizing point would be at the intersection of that marginal revenue function with its MC_A, its optimum output would be Q_4, its price P_3, to which would be added the MC_B, producing a final price of P_4. As this demonstrates, the possibility that the focus of monopolistic exploitation of the consumer would be simply transferred from the public utility phase, B, to the input-supplying stratum, A, is not itself dependent on vertical integration: it would pay suppliers of A in any event to organize themselves in order to extract such monopoly profits, if they possibly could. But it would not be in the interest of the nonintegrated public utility company to permit them to do so, because the higher price of A would mean lower sales, a smaller rate base, and therefore a smaller permissible total profit. It would therefore have a strong incentive to integrate backward in order to produce the input itself.

[26] An interesting illustration of both the competitive contribution of vertical integration and of its possible dangers is provided by one of the early cases in which the Federal Power Commission certificated a competing natural gas pipeline. The Michigan Consolidated Gas Company was originally almost entirely dependent

for its supplies on the Panhandle Eastern Pipe Line Company. The relationship between the two was a stormy one, particularly during and immediately after World War II, when gas was in short supply and the Michigan company claimed that Panhandle was favoring its industrial users. When Panhandle seemed unwilling to expand its capacity sufficiently to meet the soaring demands of Michigan's market, the latter's parent, American Light and Traction organized a subsidiary, Michigan-Wisconsin Pipe Line Company, which applied to the FPC in 1945 for the right to lay a pipeline from the Southwest into the Michigan and Wisconsin market areas. Panhandle objected, seeking to reserve the market for itself. Since the Commission lacked the authority to require Panhandle to expand its capacity more rapidly, the backward integration by the local distribution companies proved an essential means of giving them the additional supplies that they required and freeing them from complete dependence on their reluctant supplier.

At the same time, the FPC was aware of the danger that those local distribution companies would thereafter give preference to their own affiliated suppliers, whose proposed prices, as it happened, were higher than those charged by Panhandle. It therefore attempted, in certificating the competing line, to protect the rights of Panhandle to share in the market. See Nelson Lee Smith, *op. cit.*, 668–673.

assumes that the integrated companies will continue at critical points to be subject to a market test—vertically integrated firms competing with one another and possibly also with nonintegrated firms at their various levels. In this event, their comparative efficiency is subject always to a test and their incentives to be efficient and progressive remain strong. But the vertically integrated monopolist is subject to no such check. Even, therefore, if it attempts to be as efficient as possible, there is no way of its knowing whether it is in fact succeeding in doing so.

These dangers, it might be argued, are the dangers of simple monopoly. It is monopoly that lacks the competitive spur and test; it is monopoly that is at least potentially subject to managerial stultification or pursuit of goals other than profit. But especially in the presence of regulation, vertical integration can *extend* both the *scope* of that monopoly and the ability to *exploit* it. When a public utility monopolist decides to produce its own equipment, it may (though it need not) by this act eliminate the pressures and tests of competition from the stratum of equipment manufacture as well. In this way it extends the danger of managerial conservatism untested and unspurred by competition to the manufacturing of inputs as well.

So what we have are the possible contributions of integration on the one hand and of competition on the other to efficient and progressive performance, with each institutional device in some ways potentially compatible, in some ways incompatible with the other. No wonder the marriage of competition and regulation is an uneasy one, with the terms of the contract subject to constant redefinition and the parties constantly rushing to their respective lawyers. No wonder, either, that no mere economist is capable of prescribing the ideal contract, ideal for all parties and all circumstances.

Combination Companies

There is one extremely strong case to be made for conglomerately integrated companies in any industry, wherever a service can be provided or performed by a number of alternative media: the company that is in a position to use any or all of the media will find it in its own interest to choose the combination in each case that performs the service at the lowest possible cost.

Figure 2 illustrates the general point. Here we assume an industry composed of three different plants (A, B, and C), with differing marginal cost curves, all capable of supplying a particular product or service. Part D of the figure is simply a (horizontal) summation of parts A, B, and C, representing the marginal cost for the industry as a whole: its horizontal or x-axis scale is smaller, simply in order to keep the size of the figure down. Assume first that the industry is a competitive one (to make this assumption more plausible, assume there are several hundred plants of each type, each separately owned.) Since under pure competition firms will produce up to the point at which marginal cost equals price, these various marginal cost curves will tell how much the various firms will provide at various prices and the horizontal summation of those marginal costs, in part D, is an industry supply curve. Assuming an industry demand curve, AR, the competitive price is P_c and its intersection with the various marginal cost curves for the individual plants specifies their respective outputs, Q_c. Notice, then, that the tendency of each company to produce up to the point at which marginal cost equals a uniform industry price has the effect of equalizing the cost

Production from plants with differing variable costs

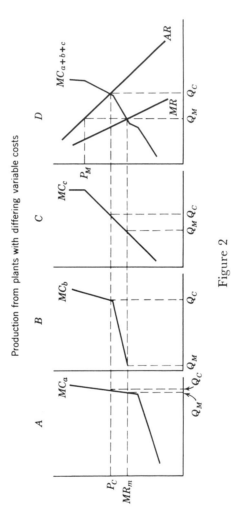

Figure 2

at the margin of each, at P_c. And this results in the aggregate industry output being distributed among the various firms and plants in such a way as to produce it at the minimum cost. Any redistribution of output, for example, an increase in the production of C and a corresponding decrease by B, would involve a greater total utilization of resources, since the cost of the production cut back at B (moving downward to the left along its MC curve) would have been less than the additional cost of producing that quantity in C (moving upward to the right along its MC curve).

The same rule would be followed if all the plants were owned by a rational monopolist. In this event, marginal revenue for that company would be below average revenue, as shown in part D; the monopolist would therefore produce only Q_m, and sell it at the higher price, P_m. But in distributing that lesser output among his various plants, it would obviously be in his interest to do it in such a way as to minimize variable production cost, and that means equalizing the cost at the margin in the respective facilities. Since it is with MR rather than price that the monopolist equates his marginal cost, Figure 2 finds the proper levels of output of the individual plants by drawing the profit-maximizing MR_m leftward through parts A, B, and C of the diagram. The points of intersection between MR and the separate MC's determine the respective Q_m levels of output there indicated. Notice that the cutbacks from the Q_c levels differ greatly from one plant to another: the output of plant A is scarcely curtailed at all, whereas plant B is almost entirely shut down—and correctly so, because to produce any more from B would involve a larger incremental use of resources than would be saved by curtailing the output of plants A or C correspondingly. This is exactly how output would be distributed or redistributed by a cartel, if its several members were willing and able to behave in such a way as to maximize their joint profits;[27] and it is the way in which power pools allocate production from one moment to the next among the various elements in their interconnected network.[28]

It is easy to translate this demonstration into terms appropriate to an integrated transportation or communications company, by interpreting the various types of plants as describing the entire range of alternative media, over all the possible routes, that might be employed to handle a particular shipment. Assuming first, for simplicity, that what customers buy is transportation from one point to another, rather than rail, air, truck, ship, barge, or pipeline transportation over any particular routes as such, then an integrated transportation company would have an interest in supplying that

---

[27] See Don Patinkin, "Multiple-Plant Firms, Cartels, and Imperfect Competition," *Q. Jour. Econ.* (February 1947), LXI: 173–205. Typically, however, cartels have been unable to reach the necessary degree of understanding. Firm B, in our illustration, would be unwilling to curtail production and sales so drastically in the interest of maximizing industry-wide efficiency and profit, unless it obtained compensation from the others; industry profit-maximizing cartel behavior, in short, requires also an acceptable scheme for profit-sharing. More typically, cartels tend to behave in the opposite manner, curtailing output by the usually

larger and lower-cost plants and firms in order to hold price high enough to permit continued production and survival of smaller, higher-cost producers—for the simple reason that the latter, being usually more numerous, have more votes. See Kahn, *op. cit.*, *International Encyclopedia of the Social Sciences*, Vol. II, 320–325 and *op. cit.*, U.S. Senate, Committee on the Judiciary, 137–138, reproduced in *Natural Resources Jour.* (January 1970), X: 58–60. Also Morris A. Adelman, "Efficiency of Resource Use in Crude Petroleum," *South. Econ. Jour.* (October 1964), XXXI: 101–122.

[28] See pp. 64–65, Chapter 2, above.

demand with the lowest-cost combination of media. In this manner, integration would eliminate the conflicts of interest that stand in the way of the wholehearted intermodal coordination required for maximum efficiency.[29] Without significant alteration the same expectations are applicable to companies that distribute both electricity and gas: we have already alluded to the example of a company that especially promoted sales of electricity in the winter and gas in the summer because these were their respective periods of off-peak demand.[30]

It would complicate but not alter this exposition to take into account the fact that the nature and quality of service provided by the various modes of transportation or sources of energy are not homogeneous, differing in such important respects as speed or susceptibility to door-to-door pickup and delivery in one case, cleanliness and cost of associated equipment in the other. It will still pay the integrated company, other things being equal, to provide the particular kind of service demanded by the lowest-cost combination of facilities and to offer higher quality service whenever its added value to customers exceeds the added costs of providing it.[31]

But surely, it will have occurred to the reader, this exposition has failed to take into account the A-J-W effect? Yes, this could well be a danger. Just as regulated companies might be reluctant to coordinate their operations and share some of the business with others, because they would prefer to keep as much of it as possible to justify their own rate bases (see p. 67, Chapter 2, above), so integrated companies, free from that particular constraint, might nonetheless prefer to use the media with the highest capital intensity rather than with the lowest marginal cost.

Whether this danger is important enough to counsel a prohibition of conglomerate integration depends on whether the A-J-W conditions are

---

[29] See pp. 66–69, above.

To be sure, such companies will define the relevant marginal costs in private terms and make no allowance for the possible discrepancies between private and social marginal costs that are so prevalent in transportation because of discriminatory governmental subsidies and taxes. It would be adding one illogicality to another, however, to try to compensate for these latter distortions by prohibiting integration—even though it happens that the railroads, who are the main victims of this discrimination, would presumably be more likely to insist on being permitted to reduce prices to marginal costs in order to win traffic back from their subsidized competitors if ownership of these competing facilities is kept separate than if the railroads too were able to take advantage of the subsidies by conducting their own motor carrier and barge operations.

[30] See note 16, Chapter 4, p. 95 of Volume 1.

[31] One is tempted to surmise, further, that it would be to the interest of such a company to set the price relationships among its various services efficiently—letting customers know exactly how much it would cost to provide them with different kinds of service by equating the rate differentials to the absolute differences in marginal cost, just as would happen under pure competition. (See pp. 174–175, Volume 1, on why this would be ideal.) In that event, the company or a competitive industry would in effect say to a customer: "You may have deliveries in one, two, or three days less time, or door-to-door, but it will cost you so many dollars extra because that is what it will cost me extra (incrementally) to give you this better service." But if the integrated company had monopoly power, it would not necessarily price in this way. If certain customers who required speed of delivery, for example, had inelastic demands *and* inadequate competitive alternatives, the price of the additional speed could be raised far above the incremental cost of supplying it, except to the extent that regulation prohibited it. But, of course, this kind of value-of-service pricing, limited only by the constraints of competition and regulation, prevails in the public utility industries today; conglomerate integration would be objectionable on this count only if it diminished the range of competitive alternatives available to customers with inelastic demand.

present or uncontrolled integration may bring them into being. This is a question that must be examined separately in each specific situation. The single most important condition is monopoly, incompletely exploited: the company has to be in a position in which it is *able* to use higher-cost methods of production when lower-cost methods are available, and to recoup by raising its charges correspondingly. So, to take two polar examples, Congress was obviously well advised to take this danger into consideration in judging whether to give the common carriers exclusive responsibility for developing and exploiting the communications satellite;[32] and, on the other hand, the danger seems a good deal less serious in the field of transportation today.

The efficiency advantages of permitting this kind of conglomerate integration will likewise vary markedly from one industry to another. In the simple model depicted in Figure 2, joining the plants together under common ownership produced no *improvement* in efficiency over the purely competitive outcome; and it resulted in a monopolistic reduction in output and increase in price. Manifestly, the introduction of multiplant or multimedia operations will improve an industry's social performance only if integration itself introduces cost savings or service improvements, or facilitates intermodal coordinations, that are unavailable to nonintegrated firms, or if the competition among nonintegrated companies is or would be seriously imperfect; *and* if the advantages thus achieved are not outweighed by the social disadvantages of increased monopoly power. The balance of social advantage will obviously vary from one industry to another.

Transportation. In the field of transportation the major issue has always been whether the railroad should be permitted to engage in other kinds of transportation. The Panama Canal Act of 1912 (p. 253, above) set the precedent of legislative opposition; and the national policy remains to this day in general one of disapproval except insofar as the proposed motor or water carriage is merely auxiliary and supplementary to the rail service.[33] The historic justification for this policy has been the danger of monopoly if the railroads were permitted to gain control of their major threatening competitors—in the first instance the ships that were about to use the new Panama Canal.

The danger is a real one for the simple reason that the proposed integration is not only conglomerate but at least partly horizontal: it involves joining

---

[32] See pp. 136–138, and note 102, p. 150, Chapter 4, above. On the other hand, as we have observed (note 76, p. 139, above), the President's Task Force on Communications Policy concluded that the possibilities of competition between cable and satellite are so limited in the international field—because the market is so small relative to available economies of scale—that the constitution of a single, multi-media chosen instrument offers the best hope of getting rational investment decisions made. *Op. cit.*, Chapter 2.

[33] According to the ICC interpretations, this means that the truck haul must be for only that portion of the total haul for which rail carriage is uneconomical—typically for picking up less than carload shipments and bringing them to

the rail terminal, breaking up carload shipments and delivery to destination at the other end, and for carriage between points generating very small quantities of traffic. See *Pennsylvania Truck Lines, Inc., Acquisition of Control of Barker Motor Freight, Inc.*, 1 MCC 101 (1936), 5 MCC 9 (1937), and *Rock Island Motor Transit Co.—Purchase—White Line Motor Freight Co., Inc.*, 40 MCC 457 (1946), both as cited and described by Fulda, *op. cit.*, 386–391. The latter decision was sustained in *United States v. Rock Island Motor Transit Co.*, 340 U.S. 419 (1951). On the use of the requirement that the motor carrier handle only shipments that have a prior or subsequent movement by rail, see Fulda, *op. cit.*, 392–393.

together transport media that are not merely complementary (as when a truck picks up less than carload shipments and delivers them to a rail terminal) but also competitive or potentially so. So in its first decision under the Panama Canal Act, in which it demanded that various Eastern railroads give up their financial interests in water carriers on the Great Lakes, the ICC found that the railroads had

"'a complete monopoly . . . over the lake line situation,' used their joint ownership to steadily advance rates and diverted from the lake routes to the all-rail lines some of the tonnage formerly moved by water,"

and concluded that financial separation of the two media would ensure

"'a healthy rivalry and striving between such boat lines themselves and with paralleling railroads for all . . . traffic.'"[34]

Similarly, in its first decision under the corresponding provisions of the Motor Carrier Act of 1935, the Commission asserted:

"we are not convinced that the way to maintain for the future healthful competition between rail and truck service is to give the railroads free opportunity to go into the kind of truck service which is strictly competitive with, rather than auxiliary to, their rail operation. . . . Truck service would not, in our judgment, have developed to the extraordinary extent to which it has developed if it had been under railroad control. . . . The financial and soliciting resources of the railroads could easily be so used in this field that the development of independent service would be greatly hampered and restricted, and with ultimate disadvantage to the public."[35]

But it is precisely the fact that the various media are competing alternatives that constitutes the efficiency argument for permitting companies to sell not just rail or truck or air or water carriage but *transportation*—with freedom to select the least-cost methods of delivery.[36] This kind of diversification carries with it the possibility of dynamic as well as static benefits. Gellman contends that the greater freedom of Canadian than American railroads to operate extensively with other modes of transportation has spurred a great deal more innovation in developing multimodal shipping techniques in that country; it seems generally conceded that the exploitation of these possibilities has been unnecessarily slow in the United States.[37] Certainly the fewer the restrictions of this kind, the greater the possibility that each carrier could develop a range of alternative packages of services

---

[34] *Lake Line Applications Under Panama Canal Act*, 33 ICC 699 (1915) as described in Fulda, *op. cit.*, 378–379.

[35] *Pennsylvania Truck Lines-Barker Motor Freight*, 1 MCC 101 (1936), as quoted in the strong decision by the Supreme Court, *American Trucking Associations, Inc., et al. v. United States, et al.*, 364 U.S. 1, 8n. (1960). The main exception that the Court enunciated in this latter case to the general doctrine of confining trucking operations by railroads to "auxiliary and supplemental service" was in circumstances where the trucking service was not previously being performed adequately by independent companies. *Ibid.*, 11, citing its earlier decision

in *American Trucking Assns. v. United States*, 355 U.S. 141 (1957).

[36] An early enthusiastic advocate was H. G. Moulton. See his "Fundamentals of National Transportation Policy," *Amer. Econ. Rev.*, *Papers and Proceedings* (December 1933), XXIV: 33–46 and *The American Transportation Problem* (Washington: Brookings Institution, 1933), 889–890. For example, railroads have often been able to effect important economies by substituting trucking for more costly rail operations and buses for unprofitable passenger service. Locklin, *op. cit.*, 845.

[37] *Op. cit.*, 35–36, 47–48, and 74–75.

to meet the particular needs of each shipper, thereby relieving the latter of having to put the combinations together himself. The freer the railroads were to proceed along these lines, the freer they would be to compete with other transportation companies, some of them specialized, others as diversified as themselves. The restrictions imposed on the ability of carriers to adopt each other's technologies are at least in part protectionist in character: it is the trucks and water carriers that object to giving greater freedom to the railroads, and airlines that protest against similar efforts by motor carriers. What substance, if any, is there to the argument of these objectors that the public and not merely their own private interest is endangered by integration?

The traditional view has been that if railroads were free to go into water carriage and trucking, they would do so in order to control and suppress intermodal competition. With their preponderant investment in the rails, they would be interested not in promoting but in restricting these competitive media and diverting their traffic to the rails. This would require monopoly control over those rival media; it was feared railroads could achieve this because of their superior financial resources and the profits flowing from the traffic for which they still enjoyed a monopoly; these resources could be used to finance discriminatory sharpshooting, designed to drive their far smaller, nonintegrated rivals out of business.[38] In this unequal competitive combat the railroads would have the strategic advantage also of being able to divert to their own facilities—whether rail, water, or truck—whatever traffic they originated; and they could be expected to refuse to make their rail facilities available to their nonintegrated motor and water competitors on nondiscriminatory terms, so that the latter companies would be unable to offer shippers joint rates for multimedia service.[39]

---

[38] "Railroads, with large investments in fixed equipment . . . necessarily will try to keep as much traffic moving by rail as possible. Control of water or motor carriers would give them the opportunity to engage in destructive competition designed to force the competing water and motor carriers out of business. Once this was accomplished, the railroads could raise the water or motor rates well above the rail rates, thus diverting to the rails traffic normally moved by other modes. Indeed this was the practice of the railroads with respect to shipping on the Great Lakes before the Panama Canal Act." Note, "Coordination of Intermodal Transportation," *Columbia Law Rev.* (February 1969), LXIX: 271.

[39] As the Supreme Court put it, in sustaining ICC limitations on the trucking operations of railroads:

"Such limitation was in furtherance of the National Transportation Policy, for otherwise the resources of railroads might soon make over-the-road truck competition impossible. . . . Motor transportation then would be an adjunct to rail transportation, and hoped-for advancements in land transportation from supervised competition between motors and rails would not materialize. The control of the bulk of rail and motor transportation would be concentrated in one type of operation. Complete rail domination was not envisaged as a way to preserve the inherent advantages of each form of transportation." *United States v. Rock Island Motor Transit Company*, 340 U.S. 419, 432–433 (1951).

The Civil Aeronautics Board uses similar reasoning in barring surface carriers from engaging in air operations except those auxiliary or supplemental to their surface operations:

"the Board would not be justified in closing its eyes to the potential threat which the entry of surface carriers into this field would in many cases offer to independent air carriers or the effect which such participation might have upon the fulfillment of the policies of the Act. Surface carriers engaging in air transportation would at times be under a strong incentive to act for the protection of their investment in surface transportation interests. Again, by reason of their superior resources and extensive facilities for solicitation, such carriers would often be the possessors of powerful competitive weapons which would enable them to crush the competition of independent air carriers." *American President Lines, Ltd., et al.*, Petition, 7 CAB 799, 803 (1947).

The limited American experience with integrated transportation companies has not to my knowledge been analyzed with sufficient incisiveness for us to be able to judge to what extent the foregoing picture represents either an accurate historical diagnosis or a correct prognosis as of 1912 or 1935. It has some, at least, indirect, historical support. In truth, the railroads have shown little interest in collaborating with nonintegrated truck and water carriers, in order to permit shipments to be made with the lowest combination of media; instead, their typical posture has been one of obstruction and discrimination.[40] Of course this does not answer the case for integration—which is, precisely, that their attitude would be very different if the trucks and barges in question were their own. But their interest in the efficient allocation of the transport business has largely been confined, historically, to pressing for the intensification of regulatory protectionism rather than freeing them to compete more vigorously. As the *Doyle Report*, which is basically sympathetic to integration, points out, they have devoted all too little energy to determining the costs of handling different kinds of traffic on different media;[41] their past lethargy in this regard justifies little confidence

---

[40] It is always difficult to be certain whether the cases that have come to light are "typical": controversies arise only when one of the carriers is dissatisfied. But the frequency of these cases involving discrimination, exclusion, and refusal to cooperate with other carriers strongly suggests that this would be their typical behavior in the absence of regulation. See, for example, the section on piggybacking, later on in this chapter.

"Proponents of diversification make much of the possibility of offering a more complete service through that approach to coordination. It is claimed that, as a result of diversification, joint rates and through routes will be offered to shippers desiring service involving more than one mode. No attempt has been made by these proponents to explain why such joint rates and through routes have not been more generally established under present authority to do so but, rather, have been consistently avoided by many of these same proponents of diversification. Although the Interstate Commerce Act makes it the 'duty of rail carriers to establish reasonable through routes with common carriers by water and reasonable rates applicable thereto,' and equitable divisions, and reasonable facilities for the interchange of traffic, the rail carriers have not distinguished themselves for their zeal in fulfilling this duty." *Doyle Report*, 224–225; see also pp. 218 and 225, note 13.

For some examples of flagrant discrimination by the railroads against water carriers, with the rails setting much higher rates for a given portion of a journey when the shipment either originated with or continued by water carrier than if it were all-rail, see Fulda, *op. cit.*, 348–

350 and especially the leading case, *ICC v. Mechling*, 330 U.S. 567 (1947); also *Dixie Carriers, Inc. et al. v. United States*, 351 U.S. 56 (1956). In many of these cases, the ICC refused to eliminate the discrimination. See for example *Seatrain Lines, Inc. v. U.S.*, 233 F. Supp. 199 (1964). Despite its legal victory over the railroads and the Commission in this case, Seatrain went out of the coastal shipping business shortly thereafter; in part, it asserts, because it decided it was "hopeless to try to do business with people who were unwilling to do business with it." (Private communication.)

[41] "The truck is undoubtedly performing services which, in the interests of the best utilization of the economic resources of the country, the railroad should be performing, and the railroad is undoubtedly performing services which can be performed with greater economy by other means of transportation. . . . The arranging of through services, with each mode performing that part which it is best equipped to do, should also be easier if there is more than a vague notion of their respective economic capabilities." Jervis Langdon, Vice President and General Counsel, Baltimore and Ohio Railroad, as quoted in the *Doyle Report*, 214–215.

As the *Report* itself puts it,

"The rail carriers, and all carriers for that matter, have to get down to the business of finding out what their actual costs are on freight hauled in order to determine the proper role which each mode should play in the transportation economy of the country. To a large extent, this is a job which the transportation industry must do for itself." *Ibid.*, 217.

in the rationality with which they would distribute the traffic if permitted to integrate more freely.[42]

There is no reason to doubt the frequent allegations that the rails have at times used their affiliated carriers as "fighting ships" to drive competitors out of business.[43] Or, in view of their history of noncooperation in the development of joint rates and through routes, that they would divert such traffic as they could to their own trucking or barge affiliates and give them preferential access to their facilities—for such purposes as piggybacking—to the extent that the ICC permitted them to do so; and that the Commission has certainly been far from satisfactorily assiduous or effective in correcting such discriminations in the past.[44] This record suggests that any relaxation of the existing restrictions on integration must be accompanied by a broadening of the authority of the ICC to proscribe discriminations of this kind, and in particular to require the institution of intermodal joint rates, through routings and equipment interchanges by railroads with all other common carriers, on reasonable demand.[45]

On the other hand, any assessment of the alleged dangers of giving the railroads greater freedom to integrate conglomerately must center on the two questions of their *ability* and *incentive* to behave in the predicted fashion. As for the first, it seems unlikely that the integration would in fact produce the requisite monopoly power. In view of the ease of entry into trucking and water transport and the ability of existing carriers in these fields to move from one route to another, it is difficult to believe that the railroads would be able to gain control over these alternative media in such a way as to be able to retard their growth (any more than they are able to retard it now, by the discriminations and refusals to collaborate described above), or to raise their rates substantially above competitive levels. Of course, ICC regulation at

---

[42] "No evidence has been uncovered to show that the more powerful rail carriers are willing to abandon their identities to transportation companies; unless they do so there is no possibility of implementing the concept. . . .

"Even when allowed to do so, rail carriers are notorious for not diversifying. . . .

"It is because of this attitude which exists among many carriers that we have ventured the prediction that true transportation companies, as we view their role in the public interest, are still a far way off and that we do not anticipate a rash of grants of applications at a regulatory agency in the event our recommendation for dropping the special restrictions in this respect are enacted into law." *Ibid.*, 221, 224, 226.

For other references to the irrational conservatism of railroad managements, see pp. 14, 21, note 40, and 81–82, above. In fairness, much of the blame must be assessed, also, against the self-defeating obstructionism of the unions. For a specific illustration, see "A derailment at Last Chance Junction?" *Business Week*, March 28, 1970, 68–75.

[43] See for example, Fulda, *op. cit.*, 378–379;

Arne Wiprud, *Justice in Transportation: An Exposé of Monopoly Control* (New York: Ziff-Davis Publishing Co., 1945), 34–36.

[44] The ICC has the authority to require rail and water carriers to establish through routes and joint rates, but not rail and motor carriers or motor and water carriers. See Locklin, *op. cit.*, 867–868; the *Doyle Report*, 148–149. On the lack of assiduity on the part of the ICC, see *ibid.*, 218–229, 225, and President Kennedy's *Message on Transportation*:

"For many years some regulatory agencies have been authorized to appoint joint boards to act on proposals for inter-carrier services; but they have taken virtually no initiative to foster these arrangements which could greatly increase service and convenience to the general public and open up new opportunities for all carriers. I recommend, therefore, that Congress declare as a matter of public policy that through routes and joint rates should be vigorously encouraged, and authorize all transportation agencies to participate in joint boards." *N.Y. Times*, April 6, 1962, 18.

[45] See the specific recommendations to this effect by the *Doyle Report*, 228.

present thwarts these potentialities for competition as far as motor carriers are concerned; but the ICC would always have the power to admit new entrants, as needed. Much more important, a policy of freer competition in this industry, of which a removal of restrictions on conglomerate integration would be part, would surely have to embrace a removal of the economic barriers to entry in trucking. On the other hand, minimum rate regulation would probably have to be retained. Given this safeguard, it would be extremely difficult for the railroads even to undertake predatory competition. And the competitive viability of independent truckers and water carriers and the check on monopoly power that they exercise would be strengthened by adoption of the policies of compulsory interconnection, coordination, and nondiscrimination recommended above.

Equally questionable is the common assumption that it would be in the interest of integrated railroad companies discriminatorily to restrict the expansion of their trucking or barge affiliates. The fact that their principal investments are in the rail part of the operation should not give them any incentive to do so.[46] The larger investment in railroad facilities represents a sunk cost. It does not protect that investment, or enhance the return of the company as a whole, to divert to the rails traffic that the company's own affiliates can carry at lower incremental costs. The way to maximize profits would be to use the facilities with the lowest incremental costs; economic efficiency would require the same.

But would it not pay the company to give preference to the more capital-intensive medium, for A-J-W reasons? It would seem this danger could be dismissed in this instance. The 3.0 percent that the Class I railroads in the National City Bank sample earned on equity in 1967 can hardly be as high as the cost of capital.[47] In these circumstances it is inconceivable that it would pay them as a general policy deliberately to make use of higher incremental-cost media, in the expectation of obtaining rate increases sufficient to recoup the consequent losses, plus a return in excess of the cost of capital on the additional rate base thus justified.

The opponents of rail integration point out that the same efficiencies could be achieved by joint arrangements with nonintegrated motor and water

---

[46] See, for example, note 38, above and the *Doyle Report*, 225–226, citing the following testimony by the president of the Illinois Central Railroad as supporting the fear that

"the owned carrier would not be permitted to compete for traffic with parallel service of the owning carrier, this to the detriment of the user. . . .

"Question. Or if the line was not being operated to the best interests of the railroad, you would then interfere, would you not?

"Answer. To the best interests of the railroad, and to the bargeline, and to the public, we would then have to interfere. . . .

"Question. And the railroad interests would necessarily come first?

"Answer. Certainly, because that is where

our first interest is—

"Question. Your first responsibility, insofar as protecting investments, is the railroads' investment?

"Answer. That is right."

[47] The return is not high enough to justify them financing their capital needs to any appreciable extent by the sale of common stock. Although it is somewhat out of date, the picture of rail earnings and capital requirements in James C. Nelson, *Railroad Transportation and Public Policy*, Chapter 7, is still generally applicable. Of their gross capital expenditures for transportation property, totaling almost $11 billion in the period 1946–1955, the Class I railroads financed not quite $10 million, or less than one-tenth of one percent, by the sale of stock. *Ibid.*, 220.

carriers. There is no shortage of such companies who would be happy to carry the traffic that they are best equipped to do.[48]

The contention is basically correct. Intercompany cooperation can secure many of the same benefits as financial integration. Common ownership has the advantage that it eliminates the necessity for interfirm negotiations and profit-splitting, the obstruction created by the reluctance of one firm's management to give business to another and hence the need for external compulsion. Railroad companies would clearly have a greater incentive to distribute such business as they control most efficiently among alternative methods of carriage if they were integrated.[49] Financial integration, on the other hand, carries with it accentuated dangers of placing competitors at an unfair disadvantage vis-à-vis the affiliates of the integrated company, reducing the intensity of competition and, to the extent that monopoly is achieved, suppressing less capital-intensive alternatives.[50] The first of these

---

[48] So, in a case in which the ICC certificated a subsidiary of the Pennsylvania Railroad to extend the scope of its motor carriage, in order to permit a demonstrated cost-saving, the intervening independent trucking companies argued strenuously that the same cost savings could be achieved by requiring the railroad to coordinate with them, instead. The Supreme Court sustained the ICC action, partly on the ground that the Commission did not have the authority to compel the railroad to enter into such an arrangement with the truckers. *ICC v. Parker*, 326 U.S. 60 (1945).

[49] Their failure to do so sufficiently with non-affiliated carriers obviously does not demonstrate that they would be similarly backward with their own affiliates. Nor do the sordid episodes in which railroads have jointly mounted propaganda and political campaigns to harass their truck competitors. For an outstanding example of the latter, see *Noerr Motor Freight, Inc. v. Eastern Railroad Presidents Conference*, 155 F. Supp. 768 (1957), 166 F. Supp. 163 (1958), 365 U.S. 127 (1961).

Fulda observes

"the admitted policy of the railroads to eliminate the truckers from long-haul transportation appears to be irreconcilable with the recent efforts of the railroads to gain *for themselves* the right to engage in transportation diversification, that is to own or control truck lines, airlines and water carriers, and to operate them without restrictions. Putting it differently, the desire to recapture traffic from motor and water carriers shows confidence in the competitive strength of rail freight traffic; but the desire to expand into other fields seems to indicate the opposite." *Op. cit.*, 377.

Not at all. The efforts disclosed by the Noerr case, however reprehensible, were directed against competitors. They in no sense justify

the inference that the railroads would not make efficient use of those alternative media if they controlled them themselves. What should qualify any confident predictions of major changes if the railroads are given greater freedom to integrate is the demonstrated short-sightedness and conservatism of much railroad management.

[50] The problem is that if the carrier is not permitted to integrate it will often be reluctant to collaborate with other media and will instead try to divert traffic from them. If permitted to integrate, it is likely to be more willing to make use of those other media, through its own affiliates, but it also has a greater incentive to divert the business from competitors to those affiliates.

An interesting illustration of the problem of assessing these respective dangers is provided by the Civil Aeronautics Board's *Motor Carrier-Air Freight Forwarders Investigation* (Docket 16857, decided September 22, 1967). The question presented to the Board was whether long-haul motor carriers should be permitted entry into the air-freight forwarding business. The forwarder is a common carrier who operates no transportation equipment, as we have seen (p. 180, note 22); his major source of revenue is the usual spread in common-carrier schedules between less than carload and carload or truckload rates.

Historically, the CAB had prohibited entry by surface carriers into the air-freight forwarding field where it appeared that this would enable them to divert traffic to surface transportation. In the present case, the CAB majority voted to grant the authorization, largely on the ground that the truckers already had access to much of the potential air traffic "either along the applicants' own extensive motor carrier routes or along the routes of hundreds of regional motor carriers with whom

threats can be reduced by a much more forceful policy than has heretofore been followed of requiring intermedia coordination on equal and non-discriminatory terms, as well as by application of the antitrust laws. The latter dangers would seem to be minimal in this industry. In these altered circumstances of the last forty years or so, in which the scope of the railroads' monopoly has been enormously diminished and the greater need is to free them for more effective competition, it is not surprising that most economists now lean to a loosening of the restrictions on their conglomerate integration.[51]

But the balance of public advantage may have already been shifted away from freer intermodal integration by the railroad mergers of the 1960s.[52]

---

the applicants regularly interline traffic," and that the problem was one of giving them an incentive, in the spread between air-freight rates for small and large shipments, to turn it over to the airlines. The Commission recognized that the price it was paying to induce motor carriers to turn over for air carriage "shipments which are *already* being delivered into the hands of the truckers" was the enhanced danger that they might divert traffic away from the air:

"It is true that the competition of these applicants as air freight forwarders may divert some air freight gathering and consolidating activities from other air freight forwarders and from the direct air carriers themselves." (Stress supplied.)

But they evidently believed that the benefits from the former incentives would outweigh the additional dangers of diversion, and recognized that the latter threat could be diminished by expanding the authority of the nonintegrated air-freight forwarders to provide pickup and delivery services in connection with air transportation beyond their previously limited zones of operation.

The dissenting Commissioner Murphy emphasized the danger—that the interest of the motor carriers would lie in promoting their surface transportation business rather than air freight:

"Whether motor carrier-air freight forwarders would eventually dominate the air freight forwarding industry through their superior economic strength remains to be seen . . . . [I]n any event, I share an apprehension that through such entry by these and other surface carriers our direct air carriers would be made dependent upon their competitors for a major portion of their freight and cargo business."

He noted, in this connection, that no direct air carrier supported the truckers' entry as potential salesmen for their services and many opposed the applications.

The two opinions supply a nice summary of the two possible diversions that had to be weighed, the one in the presence, the other in the absence of integration. Commissioner Murphy was impressed with the former: "There is a great deal of wisdom in the old adage that one does not send a rabbit to market for lettuce." The majority responded,

"the rabbit is already getting the lettuce from the market. This decision will give him a reward for bringing it home instead of eating it himself along the way."

The majority considered its decision

"a real breakthrough in opening up the most hopeful avenue for increasing intermodal transportation of freight by surface and air. . . . [P]roviding this incentive for the truckers to utilize air carriage will make air transportation a stronger competitor for the movement of freight."

The president of the Emery Air Freight Corporation commented, instead, that

"successful coordination is possible only when it is accomplished by a forwarder who has no primary interest in either of the modes to be coordinated."

It may be, however, that he gave the game away when he went on to predict that the result of the decision would be "an excess of competition which will be difficult for all and ruinous for some." *The New York Times*, September 26, 1967.

Emery is a large, nonintegrated air-freight forwarder. Some of these companies tried to have the CAB's decision overturned in the courts, but were unsuccessful; see *Air Freight Forwarders et al.* v. *CAB*, 419 F.2d 154, *cert.* denied, 397 U.S. 1006 (1970).

[51] See, for example, Meyer et al., *op. cit.*, 261–263; Locklin, *op. cit.*, 853; and Friedlaender, *op. cit.*, 155–159. See, especially, the measured and cautious proposals of the *Doyle Report, op. cit.*, 222–229.

[52] See pp. 281–290, below.

As we have already observed, any threat that integration poses to the survival of competition or the welfare of customers diminishes the more integrated firms there are in competition with one another. The more railroad companies there are along major routes, the less is the possibility that any one of them will be in a position to suppress or rely inadequately on lowest-cost media; and the safer it is, therefore, to permit each to integrate freely. As the industry now approaches a structure in which only one or two giant railroads serve entire regions of the country, the greater is the threat of monopoly, the greater the power of a transportation company to deny nonintegrated carriers fair access to the market, to control the development of competing methods of carriage, and to exploit the consumer.[53]

In any event, it is well not to exaggerate the probable consequences, beneficial or harmful, of a greater freedom of railroads to integrate conglomerately. The possibilities of cost savings from a more rational distribution of the transportation business are enormous; but they can in principle be achieved by interfirm coordination and by more competitive pricing, along the lines outlined in our Chapter 6 of Volume 1. On the other hand, the alleged dangers of such a development—the danger that truckers, for example, will be driven out of business in great numbers and freight rates increased in consequence—are at least equally exaggerated.[54]

Electric and Gas. Trucking and water carriage are not easy industries to monopolize. It is this reason, above all others, that makes it difficult to see any menace in permitting railroad companies to extend their operations to competing media, *provided* the competitive opportunities of nonintegrated firms could be adequately protected. It is difficult to see, in those circumstances, that integrated railroad companies could possibly retard or discourage the utilization of trucks or water carriers, even if it were in their interest to do so; and the effect of financial integration would be to make any such retardation less in their interest, not more.

The distribution of electricity and gas, in contrast, are franchised, local monopolies. There is no room for doubt that an integrated company performing both of these services does have the power intentionally or unintentionally to restrict the sales of one product or the other product or both, by high pricing and sluggish promotion. Electricity and gas are substitutes or potential substitutes in large and important uses.[55] To this extent, the integration of the two is not really conglomerate but horizontal: it substitutes monopoly for duopoly.[56]

---

[53] "Thus the final Supreme Court approval of the Penn-Central merger has probably foreclosed the option of deregulation in conjunction with the formation of transportation companies. Now that a company with the potential monopoly power of the Penn Central has been formed, it is inconceivable that it would be permitted to acquire competing trucking and water lines to ensure a virtual transportation monopoly." Friedlaender, *op. cit.*, 168; see also pp. 157–159 and 166–167.

[54] This is also the general conclusion of Lansing, *op. cit.*, 217–218. For an interesting suggestion that the benefits of greater intercarrier coordination might be achieved, without inte-

gration, by "giving the wholesalers of the transportation industry, the freight forwarders, full freedom to operate in all modes of transportation," see Comment, "Intermodal Transportation and the Freight Forwarder," *Yale Law Jour.* (June 1967), LXXVI: 1360–1396.

[55] See pp. 102–104, Chapter 3, above.

[56] It does not remove all competition. Gas or electricity compete also with oil, for example in the home heating market or for use as boiler fuel. But the range of uses in which oil is competitive with the others would seem to be less than the range in which they compete with one another. In 1968, for example, 77 percent of all new homes sold were equipped to be heated

If the competition between financially separate gas and electric companies were in fact fruitful, it would seem that its effects could be measured by comparing their performance with that of the combination companies. Most of the evidence does point in that direction. Franklin H. Cook found that the total operating and maintenance costs per kilowatt hour for a sample of 48 to 51 straight electric companies averaged 0.76 cents in the period 1957–1961; the corresponding figure for 17 to 21 electric and gas combinations was 1.03 cents. He found, correspondingly, that their average revenues per kilowatt hour were 1.85 cents and 2.176 cents respectively.[57] A later comparison by National Economic Research Associates of the 47 straight electric companies with the 40 combination companies on Standard & Poor's Compustat tapes, for 1966, shows a similar result: the former had an average revenue in 1966 of 2.31 cents per kilowatt hour from residential electric sales as compared with 2.58 cents for the latter. Electricity consumption per residential customer averaged 5,744 kwh for the former and only 4,731 for the latter.[58]

Cook draws from these comparisons a presumption against combination companies.[59] But these apparent inferiorities in their performance could be reflective of extraneous factors having nothing to do with their integration. The lower rates and costs and larger average residential sales of the non-integrated companies could, for example, have reflected the benefits of superior location—if, for instance, they happened on the average to have been located closer to coal mines or to sources of hydroelectric or publicly generated power, or in regions of the country where, because of the relatively mild climate, electric heating is more likely to be feasible.[59a] And their greater average sales per residential consumer could well, in view of the economies of increasing consumption per customer, have explained their lower unit costs and prices. The question would remain unanswered whether or to what extent their superior record could have been attributable also to their greater vigor in promoting the sale of electricity in competition with gas. More recently, however, Bruce M. Owen has done a more sophisticated statistical analysis, which attempts to take into account the independent effect of these other variables. And he finds that combination has a marked and statistically significant independent effect in producing a higher price of electricity and lower sales.[59b]

However, if combination itself tends to produce monopolistic retardation, the performance of the combination companies should compare unfavorably also with that of straight gas distribution companies. But the limited evidence available on this point is inconclusive.[60] It might be that there is some-

with gas, 16 percent with electricity and only 6 percent with oil. U.S. Department of Commerce, Bureau of the Census, *Construction Report: Characteristics of New One-Family Homes, 1968*, Table 24B. And the competition for the domestic cooking and clothes drying market is almost entirely between the first two.

[57] "Comparative Price Economies of Combination Utilities," *Public Utilities Fortnightly*, (January 19, 1967), LXXIX: 34–36.

[58] *Combination Companies: A Comparative Study*, processed, New York, November 1968. According to the NERA computations, the straight electric companies also showed greater average

growth rates from 1960 onward in both electricity consumption per residential customer and in the number of residential customers.

[59] *Op. cit.*, 38.

[59a] See note 69, below.

[59b] "Monopoly Pricing in Combined Gas and Electric Utilities," May 1970, to be published in the *Antitrust Bulletin*. See his similar demonstration of the effect of multi-media ownership on advertising rates, *op. cit.*, note 9, above.

[60] According to the NERA study, the same 40 combination companies realized an average revenue of 11.3 cents per therm of residential gas sales in 1966; for a sample of 13 straight

thing in the nature of combination that tends discriminatorily to restrict the sales of electricity alone; and we supply one possible reason for this below. But that is a plausible hypothesis only, nothing more; the objective evidence is still incomplete.

Combination undoubtedly produces some cost savings.[61] Customer expenses—meter reading and billing—are obvious possibilities.[62] The SEC, which, in enforcing the Public Utility Holding Company Act, has followed the general policy of requiring dissolution where there is common ownership of electric and gas properties, has in some instances found economies so significant as to require exceptions to that general policy.[63] But for the most part, these two operations must be essentially distinct. Their technologies, production, transmission, and distribution facilities are entirely separate. The few statistical comparisons that have been made show no evidences other than in customer expenses that the combination companies have lower unit costs than their rivals.[64]

Of course, a combination company would have an incentive, wherever there was a choice, to supply particular demands with the service involving the lower marginal cost. So, for example, we have earlier cited the case of one such company that promoted gas for summer sales (for example, for air conditioning) and electricity in the winter, in recognition of the fact that their respective peaks were at the opposite times. But such an efficient distribution of the business could be achieved also by aggressive competitive promotion and pricing, with a marginal cost floor. The question is whether the competition between duopolists would be sufficiently vigorous to produce

---

gas distribution companies the corresponding figure was 12.0 cents. Average sales per residential customer were 121 mcf for the former and only 108 for the latter. And while the average annual rate of growth in gas consumption per residential customer was the same for the two groups in the period 1961–1966, the number of residential gas customers served by the combination companies increased 27.2 percent in the 1960–1966 period as compared with 23.3 percent for the straight gas companies. Owen's analyses (note 59b, above) failed to discover a statistically significant relationship between combination and the price and volume of gas sales. See, however, note 70, below.

[61] See Emery Troxel, *Economics of Public Utilities* (New York: Rinehart and Company, 1947), 204–206.

[62] According to the NERA study, the customer costs per residential consumer of the combination companies were below those of both the straight electric and the straight gas companies. Either one of these comparisons alone might be suspect, since there must be some arbitrariness in the way in which combination companies allocate these expenses between their electric and gas divisions. But since they come out ahead in comparison with both of their non-integrated rivals, the finding is persuasive.

This cost superiority of the combinations over the straight electric companies disappears when the customer expenses are compared on a per kwh basis, because of the greater average consumption per customer of the latter than of the former. The significance of this alteration of the comparison depends on whether the larger sales per customer by the straight electric companies is in some way attributable to their independence. If it is merely the fortuitous result of some of the other factors suggested above, then it surely remains true that the combination companies have an efficiency advantage with respect to customer costs, even though that advantage is offset by the impact on costs *per unit of sales* of the electrics' greater sales per customer.

[63] For examples, see Ritchie, *op. cit.*, 135–191.

[64] In the NERA study, the straight electric companies showed slightly lower administrative, general, and sales expenses and markedly lower operating and maintenance expenses, per kwh, than the combination companies, but the latter in turn were markedly superior to the straight gas companies in both respects. On the other hand, Fred A. Tarpley is reported to have found "significant cost savings" enjoyed by a multiservice utility firm in *The Economics of Combined Utility and Transit Operations*, a dissertation submitted to Tulane University, 1967, as reported in *The American Economist*, Fall 1967 117–118.

this result in as full a measure as an integrated company, with an interest in minimizing cost. The likelihood of aggressive promotion of each product, it would seem, would be enhanced by financial separation—when there exists, side by side, rival companies, each of whose profit comes only from the successful promotion of its own product. But the recognition by both of their interdependence and mutual interest in not "spoiling the market" could lead them instead into a passive coexistence and market sharing. The evidence that straight electric companies do in fact spend more heavily on sales promotion than the combination companies (see note 68, below) tends to support the former rather than the latter hypothesis.

Furthermore, the incentive of the combination company to minimize costs surely must be reduced by the absence of competition and subject to modification by the A-J-W effect. The latter danger must be increased when the regulated monopolist is in a position to control the rate of exploitation of his major potential substitute; he then has both the incentive and the power to retard promotion of the less capital-intensive service.[65] So, it would seem, a combination company would be less likely than a straight electric company to offer promotional rates sufficiently attractive to induce builders to construct all-electric homes. The latter has the incentive of vastly increased sales, under circumstances of long-run decreasing costs. For the former, any increased sales of electricity are at the expense of sales of gas. Since all homes will be wired for electricity anyhow, it would seem not in its interest to try to cut gas out of the market entirely, thereby removing any justification for construction of the gas distribution facilities that would otherwise go into its rate base. On *a priori* grounds, it seems more likely that it would be straight gas and straight electricity companies that would make major efforts to promote total energy on the one hand or the all-electric home on the other, by the offer of discounts or other concessions that can only be at the expense (as *all* competition is indirectly at the expense) of their combined net revenues.[65a]

It is of course possible that the competition between separate electric and gas duopolists will have more of a cost-inflating than a price-reducing character.[66] Indeed, it seems likely that the separate companies would spend more on advertising, for example, than a single monopolist.[67] But these industries are not overly subject to this kind of rivalry. While selling expenses do seem to constitute a larger percentage of sales revenues for straight electric than for combination companies, the ratio for the former is still apparently below the economy average. Moreover, many of the sales promotional expenses incurred by public utilities really represent a form of price competition—for example, the losses they may take on sales of appliances, or the various cash and cash-equivalent allowances to builders described in

[65] See our earlier expression of concern on these grounds at the recommendation of the President's Task Force on Communications Policy for a single chosen instrument to control all media of international communications—both cable and satellite, p. 150, note 102, above.

[65a] See the much fuller analysis of these and other possibilities in John H. Landon and John W. Wilson, "An Economic Analysis of Combination Utilities," 1970, unpublished as of this writing.

[66] On the tendency of sellers in concentrated markets to compete in this way see note 107 Chapter 5, above.

[67] This is the view of Troxel, who considers the cost-saving possibilities of common ownership of greater promise than duopolistic competition. *Economics of Public Utilities*, 207.

Chapter 6 of Volume 1.[68] And, as we have already suggested, it seems much more likely that separate gas and electric than combination companies would engage in this kind of genuine, though imperfect, price competition—though here again, it would be good to see the hard evidence.[69]

Our tentative conclusion, based still on rather incomplete evidence, is that the efficiency advantages of combination are in this case outweighed by the advantages of preserving the only kind of competition that is feasible in these markets—competition between the two local, natural monopolists.[70]

---

[68] P. 177, Volume 1. According to computations by my former student, John H. Landon, the 122 electric companies listed in the FPC's *Statistics of Electric Utilities in the United States* spent an (unweighted) average of 1.96 percent of sales on selling expenses, whereas the 79 combination companies in the group spent 1.46 percent in their electric operations. These ratios may be compared with the 2.04 median ratio for the 44 consumer goods producers surveyed by Telser, *op. cit., Jour. Pol. Econ.* (Dec. 1964), LXXII: 543. These comparisons must be very rough. Consumer goods producers typically spend a larger percentage of their sales revenues on advertising than others; and only slightly more than 40 percent of the total revenues of electric companies represent sales to residential consumers. Edison Electrical Institute, *Statistical Year Book of the Electric Utility Industry for 1967*, September 1968, 2. On the other hand, it is possible that the selling expenses listed by the FPC, which include "demonstration, advertising, and other sales expenses," are more inclusive than those measured by Telser for the other industries. According to a survey, taken by the Dingell Committee, of utility company promotional payments, for example, only 25 percent of the total represented advertising allowances—payments to dealers, builders, or owners for advertising appliances, homes, or apartments; another 17.4 percent represented contributions to trade associations, for a variety of promotional activities, among other things; the remainder were direct payments to dealers, builders, or owners for the installation or conversion of equipment or appliances, installation of underground wiring, or assistance in financing. U.S. House of Representatives, Select Committee on Small Business, Subcommittee No. 5, 90th Congress, 2nd Session, *Promotional Practices by Public Utilities and Their Effect Upon Small Business*, House Report No. 1984, December 31, 1968, pp. 103–109.

[69] Abraham Gerber, of National Economic Research Associates, made a count for me of the relative use of special residential electric space heating rates by straight electric and combination companies in 1967. Again the evidence, culled from the Edison Electrical Institute rate book, is inconclusive. Of the 95 straight electrics,

only 78 (or 82 percent) had such a rate, as compared with 51 of the 59 (86 percent) of the combination companies. On the other hand, he points out, of the companies in the first group with no such special rates, three had commercial space heating rates, one did not provide residential service at all (suggesting the desirability of a recalculation to omit *all* companies not in the residential market), and five are located in warm climates where electrical heating is in any event more feasible than in the country as a whole—more so than for any of the combination companies. A comparison adjusted for such factors, he surmises, would make the record of the straight electric companies look relatively better.

[70] This has been the general attitude of the SEC, as well, in enforcing the Public Utility Holding Company Act of 1935 (see p. 73, Chapter 2 and note 2, this chapter, above). The Commission has tended to interpret the proviso exempting holding companies from dissolution where this would result in "loss of substantial economies" as requiring the even more stringent showing that the "additional system cannot be operated under separate ownership without the loss of economies so important as to cause a serious impairment of that system." *Securities and Exchange Commission v. New England Electric System et al.*, 390 U.S. 207, 209 (1968).

In this last case, the SEC required the New England holding company to divest itself of a gas distribution system, in the face of an estimate by a management consulting firm that separation would result in a loss of economies amounting to 4.8 percent of the entire system's annual operating revenues. It did so partly because it concluded that the estimate was inadequately supported. But, it also asserted, even if that estimate were substantiated,

"it would not lead us to conclude that such a loss is so substantial, when compared with the loss of economies involved in prior divestment cases and viewed in the light of the objectives of the Act, as to warrant retention of the gas properties. . . ."

It pointed out additionally:

"that other nonaffiliated Massachusetts gas companies, all but one of them smaller than the

Horizontal and Geographic Integration

The electric power industry and the railroads have in recent years engaged in very intensive merger activities of a rather special kind. The merging partners have been essentially similar firms—as much as any such companies can be so characterized. The combinations have not been principally vertical, although the merging of any two railroads could hardly avoid involving some end to end operations. Nor have they been conglomerate, except again that in the nature of the case every railroad and every electric company offers a geographically distinct set of services. The integration can best be described as principally geographic and horizontal; the mergers have tended to produce more nearly integrated regional systems; they have also brought under unified control companies that had to some extent, at some geographic points, been in actual or potential direct competition.[71]

We have already alluded to the mergers in the electric power field, which during the decades of the 1950s and 1960s reduced the number of private systems from about 1,000 to less than 500 and which, according to the prediction of Donald C. Cook, president of American Electric Power Company, will continue until the number reaches something like 15.[72]

In terms of the results already accomplished, the consequent transformation of the railroad industry since the late 1950s—after almost four decades of virtual inactivity under the provisions of the Transportation Act of 1920[73]—has been even more dramatic:

"Even if no more mergers were to be proposed or approved, the effect

---

NEES gas system, are apparently able to operate successfully without electric utility affiliations; [and] . . . NEES did not establish that independent management devoted solely to promoting gas sales would not result in benefits to offset some of the projected losses." *Ibid.*, 213.

On the last point, the Commission was impressed by the fact that all seven of the independent Massachusetts gas distribution companies showed substantially higher gas sales per customer than NEES (83.7 mcf and 51.5 mcf. respectively), higher revenues per customer ($142.10 as compared with $104.49) and lower average prices ($1.70 and $2.03 per mcf).

[71] The same was true of the 1957 acquisition by El Paso Natural Gas Company of the Pacific Northwest Pipeline Corporation, both of which gathered gas in the San Juan Basin and had been involved in direct rivalry for the business of the largest industrial customer in California, in consequence of which the price had been driven down from 40 cents to 30 cents per mcf for a firm supply of gas—in contrast with El Paso's previous price of 32.5 cents for *interruptible* service. This merger was approved by the FPC, then, on the initiation of suit by the Antitrust Division of the Department of Justice, ordered dissolved by the United States Supreme Court,

in a series of landmark decisions concerning the applicability of the antitrust laws to the regulated industries. *California v. F.P.C.*, 369 U.S. 482 (1962); *U.S. v. El Paso Natural Gas Co.*, 376 U.S. 651 (1964); *Cascade Natural Gas Corp. v. El Paso Natural Gas Co.*, 386 U.S. 129 (1967); and *Utah Public Service Comm. v. El Paso Natural Gas Co.*, 395 U.S. 464 (1969). On some of these issues, see the opinion of Judge Wright in the *Northern Natural Gas* case, quoted at length in Chapter 4, pp. 161–165, above. On the competition between El Paso and Pacific Northwest in purchasing gas see also MacAvoy, *Price Formation in Natural Gas Fields*, Chapter 5 and esp. pp. 107–128.

[72] *Wall Street Journal*, January 30, 1969. See pp. 73–75, Chapter 2, above. Mr. Cook's company has sought permission of the SEC (under the Public Utility Holding Company Act of 1935) to acquire the Columbus & Southern Ohio Electric Co. The SEC's Division of Corporate Regulation filed a brief on March 17, 1969 opposing the application on the ground of adverse competitive effects, and the company made application on April 17, 1969 for a reopening of the Hearings for fuller consideration of the competitive issue. The case was still pending in mid 1970.

[73] See pp. 78–82, Chapter 2, above; also the *Doyle Report*, 247–257.

of the railroad merger wave on the nation's transportation network would be profound."[74]

"The current railroad merger wave amounts to the most complete, and the most significant, reorganization of any American industry since the turn of the century."[75]

For example, the series of mergers and acquisitions, beginning in 1959, that moved first the Virginian Railway Company,[76] then the Nickel Plate, the Erie-Lackawanna (itself the product of a merger of the Erie and the Delaware, Lackawanna & Western Railroads, approved in 1960),[77] and the Delaware & Hudson into the Norfolk & Western Railway Company;[78] that joined the Chesapeake & Ohio and the Baltimore & Ohio;[79] and, finally, that permitted the merger of the Pennsylvania and New York Central Railroads, on condition that they also include the New Haven[80]—reduced the provision of service to the entire Northeast and Middle Atlantic region of the country to three major railway systems; and the application of the Norfolk & Western to merge with the Chesapeake & Ohio group[81] would cut it to two. And while the experience of the 1920s justified a good deal of skepticism in assessing the prospects that grandiose nationwide consolidation plans would in fact be put into effect, the manifestly altered climate of the 1960s and the enormous steps that have already been taken lend immediate credibility to proposals of a decade or so ago to reduce the 500 operating railroads in the country to less than ten consolidated systems.[82]

In a sense, the issues in all these cases are the same and are basically simple. The preponderant case for the mergers is the expectation that they will improve efficiency. The preponderant case against them is their possible impairment of competition, for two reasons: first, the merging companies are typically actual or potential competitors in some parts of their business, and, second, they may be enabled by joining together to deny outside firms a fair opportunity to compete. The threshold question in all cases, therefore, is: how realistic are the expectations of important cost-savings? And the corollary question is to what extent the benefits can be achieved without full financial consolidation and with a lesser menace to competition, or to what extent, if the consolidation is permitted, the competitive opportunities of outsiders can be safeguarded.

---

[74] U.S. Department of Transportation, *Western Railroad Mergers*, a Staff Study by the Office of the Assistant Secretary for Policy Development and the Federal Railroad Administration, Washington, January 1969, 2.

[75] *Ibid.*, 1.

[76] 307 ICC 401 (1959).

[77] 312 ICC 185 (1960).

[78] 324 ICC 1 (1964), 330 ICC 780 (1967), 331 ICC 22 (1967), and *Penn Central Merger and N & W Inclusion Cases*, 389 U.S. 486 (1968).

[79] 317 ICC 261 (1962).

[80] 327 ICC 475 (1966), 328 ICC 304 (1966), finally affirmed by the U.S. Supreme Court, 389 U.S. 486 (1968).

[81] *Norfolk & Western Ry. Co.-Merger, etc.-Chesapeake & O. Ry. Co.*, ICC Finance Docket No. 23832. The ICC Hearing Examiner recommended approval of this last merger in a Report and Order served March 20, 1969. These cases are summarized in Carl Helmetag, Jr., "Railroad Mergers: The Accommodation of the Interstate Commerce Act and Antitrust Policies," *Virginia Law Rev.* (December 1968), LIV: 1505–1530.

[82] See the *Doyle Report*, 242; the influential article by Gilbert Burck, "A Plan to Save the Railroads," *Fortune*, August 1958, 82, proposing to consolidate all the railroads in the country into four noncompetitive regional systems; and the thoughtful Staff Study of the Department of Transportation, suggesting a number of hypothetical groupings for consolidating the Western railroads into four or five systems, *op. cit.*, 34–49.

We have already described the technological case for the regional integration of power company investments and operations.[83] The efficiency benefits are unquestionably great. The only question is how much more fully they are achieved by complete financial integration as compared with pooling and interconnection between financially separate systems. The related consideration is the possible impact of *either* device on competition. On this point, there are two opposing considerations. On the one hand, at the point of ultimate sale the "industry" is in any event a collection of regulated, local franchised monopolies. To the extent that this is the case, there can be no objection to regional or national groupings that reduce their several costs. On the other hand, there is nonetheless competition among its members, both actual and potential: the impact of various proposed integrations on this rivalry must therefore also be considered. Since these very questions arise with respect to power pooling as well, we reserve further consideration of these issues for pp. 314–323, below.

The cost savings that the railroad mergers are supposed to achieve are of a different character.[84] Here the overriding fact is the prevalence of excess capacity and duplication of facilities. Michael Conant, a strong proponent, estimated in the early 1960s that the capacity of the railroads was something like 2.8 to 3.5 times the actual amount of traffic they carried.[85] With the total freight ton-miles of the Class I railroads failing to regain their 1947 levels for the next sixteen years while technological changes were tending to increase capacity rather than reduce it; with passenger traffic continuing its dreary, long-run decline throughout the 1960s as well; with competition incapable of eliminating the excess capacity and with continuously low overall earnings, it is not surprising that there finally emerged among railroad executives as well as others the conviction that drastic rationalization was essential; and the only way to achieve it was through mergers.[86]

---

[83] See pp. 64–65, Chapter 2, above.

[84] They are similar in this one basic respect: that they come from concentrating traffic and investment on the lowest-cost routes or sources of supply—that is, from equalizing costs both short- and long-run continuously at the margin.

[85] *Railroad Mergers and Abandonments* (Berkeley: Univ. of California Press, 1964), 8, 11, 16. For a more selective estimate, identifying the very large year-round excess as being mainly in line, to a considerably lesser extent in terminal and passenger carrying and even less than that in freight car and motive power capacity, but concluding that

"It seems likely that the railroads could take on significant accretions of freight and passenger traffic without having to make proportionate additions of fixed capital facilities in all areas of railroading,"

see Nelson, *Railroad Transportation and Public Policy*, 148–171. Of course, freight cars and locomotives could be added readily if demand justified it. See pp. 184–185.

[86] See the *Doyle Report*, 229–230, 266; Conant,

op. cit., passim; Burck, *op. cit.* Burck later offered a similar proposal as "A New Flight Plan for the Airlines," *Fortune*, April 1969, pp. 98–101 and ff. We cannot appraise the latter proposals here. It is important to note, however, that the sentiment for large-scale mergers of airlines, rapidly mounting in 1969 and 1970, should be regarded with skepticism. As we have already suggested, economies of scale do not recommend them. And the advantages of better route patterns and a fuller utilization of equipment can be achieved also by permitting existing companies to diversify their own route structures and inducing them to pool equipment and equipment maintenance. See pp. 122–123 and 235, above.

There was no such general conviction about the essentiality of railroad mergers in the 1920s. The focus of the proposals for consolidation at that time was on the equalization of the profitability of weak and strong roads and the difficulty of authorizing rate increases such as were needed to provide adequate returns to the former without conferring supernormal profits on the latter. See pp. 79–81, Chapter 2, above.

The most important cost savings, it appeared, could be achieved by merger of parallel roads. This would permit the combining of terminal and repair operations, abandonment of parallel, underutilized track, consolidation of schedules and management, improved routing and utilization of equipment.[87] Gilbert Burck estimated, back in 1958, that annual savings of $1 billion, out of total operating expenses of $8 billion, were ultimately possible.[88] It was widely anticipated, also, that with costs reduced in this way, railroads would be in a better position to raise the large amounts of capital required for renovation and modernization of their facilities. The result of this, as well as of the merger itself, would be not only further reductions in cost, but, perhaps even more important, improvements in service because of the reduction of delays, utilization of modern equipment as well as selection of the most rapid routes and elimination of excessive freight interchanges.

It is probably too early to be certain whether estimates like those of Burck were realistic or wildly naive. The merging parties have had a strong incentive, naturally, to exaggerate the estimated savings. The limited experience since some of these major consolidations have gone into effect demonstrates a wide variation in the extent to which the promised savings were realized and most of the variations have been on the disappointing side:

"The conclusion of the economic evidence is that the cost savings arguments for large railroad mergers have to be very largely discounted, and must be applied to individual cases with very great circumspection."[89]

---

[87] See Conant, *op. cit.*, 87–88, summarizing the estimated annual cost savings of nine major mergers; also Department of Transportation Staff Study, *op. cit.*, 5. This generalization is supported by the opinion of most experts and the conclusion of most empirical studies that the economies of sheer scale in railroading are limited; that, for example, as far as sheer size is concerned, railroads like the Pennsylvania and New York Central were already large enough for maximum efficiency, and perhaps too large. The important economies of scale as yet incompletely achieved, if any, are economies of greater density of traffic. See note 6, Chapter 5, pp. 126–127, Volume 1. For example, the Department of Transportation Staff Study found a simple correlation of about 0.62 between the profit to sales ratios and the traffic density (net ton-miles per mile) in 1967 for 23 Western railroads. *Ibid.*, 20. Healy has even expressed skepticism about the remaining available economies of traffic density as well. "The Merger Movement in Transportation," *Amer. Econ. Rev., Papers and Proceedings* (May 1962), LII: 438–439; but see the comments of Merrill J. Roberts, *ibid.*, 445. Meyer et al. likewise tend to deprecate the evidence of unlimited economies of density but concede that the physical plant of railroads generally was excessive for current volumes of traffic:

"the rationalization of investment requires only management vigorous enough to pursue abandonment and sufficient funds to replace existing 'white elephants' with smaller and more efficient facilities." *Op. cit.*, 259–260.

Whether the available economies of rationalization are great or small, it would seem that they are not true economies of scale but manifestations of short-run decreasing costs, arising out of an admitted state of excess capacity. In this sense, it seems unquestionable, large portions of the American railroad system have chronically suffered from inadequate traffic density. Under whatever rubric the projected economies are best classified, it is difficult to escape the conclusion that railroad mergers have offered the opportunity for important savings in cost from rationalization; what remains subject to great uncertainty is the extent to which the management of the consolidated companies will in fact take advantage of it.

[88] *Op. cit.*, Fortune, August 1958, 178. See also the *Doyle Report*, 244–246.

[89] U.S. Department of Transportation Staff Study, *op. cit.*, 13. The study nevertheless strongly supported mergers as an instrument for cutting costs:

"Nearly every transportation expert who has addressed himself to the subject has remarked on the critical need for rationalization of redundant rail facilities in this part of the country. Thus, the cost savings argument retains

There seems no reason to doubt that very important economies and improvements of service *can* be achieved or facilitated by mergers: this is not to say, however, that they *will*. The critical variable is the quality of management; the chief case for mergers seems at times to come down to the hope that the opportunities they create may impel some shaking up of unprogressive managements—an institutional consideration that is very difficult for an economist to evaluate.[90]

The dilemma from the point of view of public policy arises from the fact that these promised cost savings are greatest where the consolidation involves parallel, and therefore substantially competing, roads. In these circumstances, it is important to consider whether the benefits of coordination may be achieved by some other device more consistent with the preservation of competition. In principle, there are such alternatives here. One of the claimed advantages of the Pennsylvania-New York Central Railroad merger was that some traffic, originating with the former, could most efficiently be routed over the water level route of the latter, producing a considerable saving in mileage and cost and an improvement in speed.[91] As we have already suggested in Chapter 2, in principle there must have been a price, lying between the respective marginal costs of the two carriers, that it would have paid the Pennsylvania to offer the Central and the latter to accept to permit the one to use the other's tracks. Separate railroads have been known to enter into pooling agreements, limiting the number of trains

---

its appeal and its cogency for this portion of the Western merger problem." *Ibid.*, 5.

Its negative summary of the experience to date drew on Robert E. Gallamore, *Railroad Mergers: Costs, Competition, and the Future Organization of the American Railroad Industry*, unpublished Ph.D. dissertation, Harvard University, Cambridge, May 1968. The Staff Study quotes Gallamore:

"in most circumstances there have been difficulties in achieving merger savings. . . . [T]he overwhelming evidence is that size and complexity of a merger plan are the qualities that can lead to extra costs, rather than savings, in the wake of consolidation."

And, it points out, "Non-accomplishment of intentions and managerial diseconomies of scale are the biggest dangers." *Ibid.*, 10, 12.

An amusing consequence was that representatives of the Norfolk & Western and Chesapeake and Ohio railroads, in attempting to justify their proposed merger, felt it necessary to explain how their own situation differed from that of the Pennsylvania and New York Central companies, so as to justify their own expectations of cost saving and service improvement in the face of the failure of the latter's merger to have produced those promised results. "New York State Cites Pennsy in Opposing N. & W.— C. & O. Plan," *New York Times*, November 6, 1969, 67. The subsequent financial collapse of the Penn-Central further emphasized the almost

ludicrous gap between the merging parties' promises and their performance. See *Wall Street Journal*, June 12, 1970, 1, and the floor remarks of Senator Philip A. Hart, August 10, 1970.

[90] See, for example, Lansing, *op. cit.*, 213–214, and Meyer et al., who state and concede some validity to the

"subtler and more meritorious argument for the creation of four regional railroads . . . an application of the well-tested proposition of business administration—when in doubt, reorganize,"

although they conclude that these gains will be transitory. *Op. cit.*, 260. Still, there remains the probability that if new opportunities for gain are offered some response will on the average be forthcoming.

"The past decade has seen a continuous stream of innovations, but the quantum jump to containerization, new rolling stock, the avoidance of classification yards, and computerized traffic movement control systems that most experts visualize as essential to railroads achieving their full potential has not been realized. A new innovative spirit on the part of the industry's top management is a much hoped for result of the current merger wave." U.S. Department of Transportation Staff Study, *op. cit.*, 3–4.

[91] See *Pennsylvania Railroad Company-Merger-New York Central Railroad Company*, 327 ICC 475, 490–493 (1966).

or services offered by each, in order to save costs—the freight cars are a prime example of this kind of pool, used by all the roads in common, with each compensating the owner at a fixed rate. If two parallel roads have excess line or terminal capacity, they could enter into agreements to use some of the facilities jointly and abandon others.[92] And there is no doubt that these looser coordinations could fruitfully be much more widely used; Conant proposes that the ICC be given much broader authority than it now has to compel such arrangements.

But, as we have also suggested, these possible collaborations will always inevitably be limited by the continued divergences of interest between the potentially collaborating companies,[93] and, in consequence, such agreements have been comparatively few. As Conant points out,

"such agreements are extremely difficult to negotiate. A railroad with a monopoly franchise on the most efficient route through an area is reluctant to share this route even though rentals would include a monopoly gain. A carrier is especially concerned not to lose its monopoly of the smaller towns solely on its route. . . . The carrier acquiring trackage rights and abandoning its own less-efficient route, runs the risk that the owner will refuse to renew the trackage agreement after the initial term expires. There is also the possibility that in times of heavy traffic, the owning carrier will give the right of way to its own trains and make the leasing carrier suffer all delays. Such uncertainties, when added to the barriers to abandonment of less-efficient routes, make carriers reluctant even to start negotiations for trackage rights on parallel lines."[94]

It must be conceded that mergers remove some of the obstacles and increase the likelihood of wholehearted collaboration.[95]

It is impossible to generalize about whether, or in which cases, the additional benefits of merger will offset the disadvantages of suppressed competition.[96] The general predisposition of the economist would be toward suspicion of mergers that reduce such competition as still prevails in industries like public utilities, where numbers of sellers are typically already few and entry is restricted.[97] This predisposition is intensified when mergers

[92] This discussion draws primarily on Conant, op. cit., 91–112.

[93] See pp. 67–69, Chapter 2, above.

[94] Op. cit., 100–101.

[95] Once again, appraising this likelihood must involve appraising the maddeningly elusive institutional consideration of whether the typically old management of the new company will in fact be moved to take advantage of the opportunities. See notes 87, 89, and 90, above.

[96] Incidentally, some of the interfirm collaborations short of merger would similarly suppress competition—for example, service pooling agreements.

[97] See, for example, Caves, Air Transport and Its Regulators, 444–445. The opposite view is, of course, that since it is not competition but regulation that is relied on to protect the public in the public utility industries, the presumption

is the other way. For example, in dismissing a suit brought by customers of one of two merging companies, challenging an FPC order permitting a merger, the U.S. Circuit Court of Appeals for the 7th Circuit stated:

"Petitioners have shown, in general terms, that the merger will increase Edison's economic power and contribute to economic concentration in the electrical energy industry. They have not shown how such growth and concentration will aggrieve them. In a market characterized by competition a merger or other acquisition necessarily injures the consumer if it substantially lessens competition. In the electric utility industry, where restraints on competition are not only tolerated, but encouraged . . . and where rates are subject to federal or state regulation . . . injury to the consumer cannot be inferred from a merger, but must be demon-

are purportedly justified in order to eliminate the very deficiencies of industrial performance that have been accentuated by insulation from competition:

"economic theory holds that competition will bring about good service to customers, and will stimulate technological improvements, efficient management, and appropriately aggressive marketing. One need not look very deeply into the railroad problem today in order to catalog its most outstanding deficiencies as precisely these: poor service, lack of technological progress, ineffective management, and poor marketing."[98]

It is intensified, similarly, when the mergers are of companies already evidently too large to be managed well.[98a] The fact remains that competition has fallen considerably short of achieving the economies that are apparently available, eliminating excess capacity, and concentrating traffic on remaining low-cost routes and terminals. The oligopolistic character of the intramodal rail market would even in the absence of regulation almost certainly have precluded the driving of rates down below the out-of-pocket costs of the higher cost carriers that would have been required to achieve this result. Nor would it be desirable, in view of the fact that interrailroad competition could only be highly discriminatory, and also given the very wide spread between out-of-pocket and average total costs, in situations of extensive excess capacity. The resultant impact of such destructive competition on the revenues of the surviving roads could on balance be to reduce rather than enhance the efficiency of the system as a whole. In such circumstances, merger is the obvious solution—offering benefits to both partners and promising to improve, rather than weaken, their ability to raise capital and hence to realize the promise of new technology.

It is at least conceivable that well-chosen mergers can invigorate excessively weak competitors and enhance the effectiveness even of intramodal rivalry. This is not the same as merely requiring that the merging partners

---

strated." *Utility Users League v. FPC*, 394 F. 2d 16, 19, 20 (1968).

It is the latter philosophy that is embodied in the Interstate Commerce Act. It sets up as the controlling standard of whether the ICC is to approve mergers merely that they be "consistent with the public interest." In this determination, it provides that,

"the Commission shall give weight to the following considerations, among others: (1) the effect of the proposed transaction upon adequate transportation service to the public; (2) the effect upon the public interest of the inclusion, or failure to include, other railroads in the territory involved in the proposed transaction; (3) the total fixed charges resulting from the proposed transaction; and (4) the interest of the carrier employees affected." 49 U.S. Code 5(2) (c), 1964 ed.

The desirability of preserving competition is not even mentioned, although the Supreme Court has insisted that the Commission explicitly take possible anticompetitive effects into account:

"In short, the Commission must estimate the scope and appraise the effects of the curtailment of competition which will result from the proposed consolidation and consider them along with the advantages of improved service, safer operation, lower costs, etc., to determine whether the consolidation will assist in effectuating the over-all transportation policy." *McLean Trucking Co. v. United States*, 321 U.S. 67, 87 (1944).

For a survey of the law of recent railroad merger cases, demonstrating that the Court has (under the Interstate Commerce Act) permitted mergers that would clearly have been held in violation of the antitrust laws, see Helmetag, *op. cit.*, *Virginia Law Rev.* (December 1968), LIV: 1493–1530.

[98] Department of Transportation, Staff Study, *op. cit.*, 6.

[98a] See the references in note 89, above, especially to Senator Hart, and the evidence of diseconomies of sheer size cited in note 6, p. 126 of Volume 1.

agree, as a condition of ICC approval, to assume the burden of taking into their union weak roads that may be incapable even of covering their variable costs, as has happened in some cases[99]—a policy of enforced internal subsidization. But it is a consideration that argues strongly in favor of the regulatory agency itself proposing combinations

"which bring the unique advantages of given weak roads into a situation in which these advantages can be used to their greatest potential. . . . It is not as important assiduously to pair rich lines with poor (as was thought necessary under the 1920 Act) as it is carefully to consider linkages and rationalization of excess capacity."

"This process can be accomplished more efficiently in the context of an overall restructuring . . . since a decision can be made on the relative merits of merger with each other road, taking into consideration possibilities of abandonment, consolidation of duplicative facilities, extensions of territory, or short-cut routes."[100]

To recognize these possibilities in a well-planned merger program is of course not necessarily to approve of the particular programs of consolidation that have in fact been put into effect. The current merger movement suffers from the same defects as the efforts of the 1920s—notably the fact that the initiative continues to rest with the proposing lines, that the ICC is essentially confined to a quasi-judicial role of approving or disapproving proposals generated by private parties, in consideration of their own interests,[101] and that no one has assumed the responsibility for proposing integrated plans. Each individual merger has inevitable repercussions on other railroads and on the structure of the entire industry. Considering the need for a careful balancing off in each case of the benefits of cost-reduction and the dangers— the elimination of direct competition and diversion of traffic from excluded lines,[102] which gives rise, in turn, to the likelihood that they will then look

---

[99] The New Haven Railroad in the case of the Pennsylvania and New York Central. The ICC conditioned its approval of the Norfolk & Western-Nickel Plate acquisition on offering the Erie-Lackawanna, Delaware & Hudson and Boston & Maine Railroads the opportunity to be included. Helmetag, op. cit., 1514, 1519 note 149. These roads were in financial trouble; I do not know whether they were in fact incapable of covering variable costs.

[100] Department of Transportation, Staff Study, op. cit., 33, 8.

[101] The ICC can and does, however, impose conditions to protect outside parties. It has, for example, required the parties to take in railroads that were financially weaker or that might otherwise have suffered serious traffic diversion; it has inserted provisions to preclude such diversion (see, for example, Helmetag, op. cit., 1511)—requiring, for instance, that merging lines maintain certain existing routes and continue to solicit freight along them, in order to assure that traffic would continue to be available for interchange with excluded parties; it has

forced the merging parties to indemnify outside lines against losses of traffic (this was a condition imposed on the Penn Central merger, with respect to the Erie-Lackawanna, Delaware & Hudson and Boston & Maine Railroads, ibid., 1518); and it has compelled the consolidated carriers to cooperate with outsiders (for example, in the same case, it required the Penn Central to make certain trackage rights available to the Delaware & Hudson, in order to afford the latter a gateway to the New England line, ibid.). In the Pennsylvania-New York Central hearings, the management of the Erie-Lackawanna Railroad claimed that 80 percent of its traffic was subject to diversion if the merger were permitted to go into effect. W. N. Leonard, op. cit., Transportation Journal (Summer 1964), III: 13.

[102] This is not to suggest that all diversion of traffic resulting from mergers is necessarily inefficient. On the contrary, rationalization necessarily involves a considerable rerouting of traffic, which carries with it the high probability that excluded carriers will lose some of the business that they had previously inter-

for similar protection in other consolidations—most observers seem to agree, the proper approach has to be in terms of an integrated regional or national plan.[103]

It does not suffice, in taking account of these possible dangers, that the ICC merely satisfy itself that all railroads that might possibly be injured by any particular merger withdraw their opposition. They would presumably do so once their own interests had been taken care of—whether by promises of incorporation into the system under consideration, or of protections against diversion, indemnification for losses of business, or a promise that they in turn would be incorporated into some other system.[104] There remains the separate question of whether the interest of the consuming public, too, would be best served by the proposed combination.[105]

Ensuring this result requires a greater degree of regulatory planning than the ICC has heretofore been willing to undertake. In the words of the Department of Transportation's Staff Study:

> "The current railroad merger wave amounts to the most complete, and the most significant, reorganization of any American industry since the turn of the century. This reorganization is progressing through the Interstate Commerce Commission and the courts even though a rational and coherent Federal policy toward rail mergers has never been developed and implemented by the ICC and the Executive Branch. Except in cases of conflicting applications, the ICC has been prone to approve each merger application largely as submitted to it, subject, however, to various conditions and to considerable delays—depending on the amount of opposition raised. The results of the rather random manner in which recent mergers have been proposed and approved are twofold. First, there has been no real overview of the public interest in rail mergers. Stated somewhat differently, the mergers proposed and approved were simply not the best of possible and more efficient alternatives. Second, the

---

changed with one or the other of the merging parties. It is to say, rather, that not all diversions that are in the interest of the merging parties are likely to contribute to efficiency in the national transportation system considered as a whole; and it is the function of the regulatory agency to attempt to devise solutions that contribute best to the latter goal. See, for example, Department of Transportation, Staff Study, op. cit., 7–8, 27–31; also pp. 80–81, above.

[103] See, for instance, the *Doyle Report*, 269.

[104] The ICC at first disapproved the proposed mammoth merger of the Great Northern, the Northern Pacific, the Pacific Coast, and the Chicago, Burlington & Quincy Railroad Companies, largely on the ground that it would produce "a drastic lessening of competition," but also because it would adversely affect the Chicago, Milwaukee, St. Paul & Pacific and the Chicago & North Western Railway. 328 ICC 460 (1966). Between 1966 and 1967, the

Northern Lines reached an accommodation with those competitors, accepting certain conditions with respect to traffic diversions and agreeing, also, that it would not oppose their proposed merger if the Northern Lines merger were approved. The resulting withdrawal of opposition on the part of the competing roads was said to be largely responsible for the ICC's reversing its position and approving the merger just a year and a half later. *Great Northern Pacific & Burlington Lines, Inc.,-Merger, etc.-Great Northern Railway Company, et al.*, 331 ICC 228, 231 (1967); see also *Wall Street Journal*, November 15, 1967, 34. The ICC's decision was upheld by the U.S. Supreme Court in *United States v. Interstate Commerce Commission et al.*, 396 U.S. 491 (1970).

[105] It should be pointed out that there has been comparatively little shipper opposition to these proposed mergers, and in some cases substantial shipper support for them. See, for example, Helmetag, op. cit., 1516, 1523–1524.

adversary process, far from resolving the merger issue in each case, has, if anything, created additional intra-industry conflict. Such conflict is especially notable in the phenomenon of 'defensive' mergers."[106]

Vertical Integration in Communications

The issue of the appropriateness of vertical integration has arisen in virtually all the regulated industries. In none has it been so long and intensely contested as in communications. The most famous and important case is the integration between the Western Electric Company and the Bell System. But the same issue is importantly involved in the question of how satellite communication, international and domestic, is to be organized. We have alluded also to the litigation over which companies should be permitted to own the ground stations that send signals to the satellites and receive signals from them. The proper role of independent manufacturers of communications equipment was central to the *Carterfone* case and an important consideration in *above-890* and *MCI* as well. Again, the International Telephone & Telegraph Corporation in 1967 filed an antitrust suit against the General Telephone & Electronics Corporation, contending that the latter's acquisition of a number of independent (that is, non-Bell) telephone companies in preceding years had excluded IT&T from the business of manufacturing and selling telephonic equipment to them.[107] In contrast, there seems to be no major push by the electric utility or railroad or airplane companies to be permitted to manufacture their own equipment, or by the natural gas pipelines, who are in any event not prohibited from doing so, to produce a substantially larger proportion of the gas that they transport.[108]

---

[106] *Op. cit.*, 1. The Staff Study is itself an exploratory effort to develop more satisfactory overall plans for the western part of the country, which would

"further the process of rationalizing uneconomic parallelism without depriving major shipping points of the inherent benefits of competition." *Ibid.*, 36.

For a similar strong and persuasive statement see W. N. Leonard, *op. cit.*, *Transportation Jour.* (Summer 1964), III: 5–15 and see pp. 81–82, Chapter 2, above.

[107] *Wall Street Journal*, October 19, 1967, 2.

[108] Questions about vertical integration have, however, arisen in these industries as well. For example, there remains an important problem of reconciling the integration of electric power generation and transmission by large private companies with protecting the access of small municipal and cooperative distributors to the cheapest possible sources of energy—the very same problem that led to the imposition of common-carrier status on oil company pipelines. The pressure in electric power, similarly, is in the direction of requiring the integrated private companies' transmission systems to "wheel" (that is, transmit) power purchased by the nonintegrated distributors from third parties.

See pp. 316–317, below; also note 60, p. 68, above.

In the heated controversies all through the 1950s and 1960s over the propriety of regulating the field price of natural gas, proponents of regulation pointed out that some of the large jumps in the field price were posted by pipeline purchasers largely owned by producing interests, thus raising the familiar specter of cost-of-service regulation (in this case of the transmission lines) giving rise to an incentive to pay inflated prices for inputs purchased from financially affiliated companies. See note 115, p. 156, Chapter 4, above. And for even longer, pipeline companies have been insisting that their own gas-producing operations ought not to be regulated at all on an individual company cost-of-service basis or ought to receive the same treatment as (that is, the same area prices as are allowed) independent producers rather than being confined to the typically lower prices and rates of return typically permitted the transmission companies themselves. See, for example, *F.P.C. v. Hope Natural Gas Co.*, 320 U.S. 591 (1944); *City of Detroit v. F.P.C.*, 230 F. 2d 810 (1955), *cert.* denied 352 U.S. 829 (1956). See also the FPC's *Pipeline Production Rate Proceeding*, RP 66–24. A trial examiner's initial decision, issued March 3,

The ownership of Western Electric by AT&T raises two kinds of issues of public policy. The first and more fundamental is whether the manufacturer should be financially separated from the Bell companies. The other, raised in numerous rate cases since 1930,[109] concerns the propriety of the prices charged by the manufacturing company, since these enter the cost of service of the operating companies. The most prominent aspect of this controversy concerns the proper rate of return to be allowed Western Electric, in computing its allowable prices: should it be the same, low public utility type of rate allowed the operating companies, or should it be some higher figure reflecting the allegedly greater risks and demonstrably higher comparable earnings of capital goods manufacturing?

In practice these two issues are not easily separated; arguments about them overlap, coincide, and conflict in complicated and curious ways. Western has presented extensive and persuasive testimony, in various forums, defending both the level of its charges and its vertical integration with the operating companies as essential to the excellence of their collaborative performance.

The former demonstrations have been of two kinds. First, Western's prices to the Bell companies have run between 50 and 75 percent of the lowest prices available from all other manufacturers of similar products and, incidentally, far below the average price paid for such equipment by non-Bell telephone companies.[110] Second, its profits have consistently been markedly below those of comparable unregulated companies; and this clearly reflects restraint in pricing, a deliberate practice of charging less than the traffic would bear. According to Western's calculations, its return on the Bell investment in the period 1946 through 1967 averaged 9.3 percent compared with 12.3 percent for the 50 largest manufacturers; its profit per

---

1969, recommended that this production continue to be priced on a company-by-company cost of service basis but with one modification: that the tax-reduction benefits of the allowances for percentage depletion and the expensing of intangible well-drilling costs on newly acquired leases be divided equally between the pipeline-producer and its customers, rather than as theretofore, passed on 100 percent in correspondingly reduced rates. The FPC decision, Opinion 568, instead extended the general area rates to pipeline-produced gas from leases acquired in the future; the appeal from this decision was pending in the Circuit Court of Appeals for the District of Columbia as of November 1970.

[109] See *Smith v. Illinois Bell Telephone Co.*, 282 U.S. 133 (1930) and note 20, p. 29 of Volume 1. The same question is being examined in Phase 2 of the FCC's *In the Matter of AT&T*, Docket 16258.

[110] The Bell companies have been making systematic price comparisons of this kind on their own for several decades. More recently, Western commissioned a comprehensive investigation by McKinsey & Company, *A Study of Western Electric's Performance*, American Telephone and Telegraph Co., New York, 1969. This study compared Western's prices in 1966 with the lowest prices available from other manufacturers, and found ratios of 63 percent for central office, transmissions, and P.B.X. equipment, 48 per cent for telephone apparatus, 52 percent for exchange and toll cable and 74 percent for outside plant equipment (p. 93). This demonstration has in general been corroborated by studies of the FCC and the investigations by John Sheahan using much older data, "Integration and Exclusion in the Telephone Equipment Industry," *Q. Jour. Econ.* (May 1956), LXX: 255–260. On the other hand, Sheahan concludes that Western's costs and prices were not invariably the lowest available. *Ibid.*, 258. One familiar and striking comparison, frequently offered by the Bell companies, is the cost of the basic black telephone handset, for which Pacific Telephone and Telegraph Company paid Western $10.51 in the early 1960s, while the cost of a practically identical instrument from other manufacturers ranged from $23.16 to $27.90. *Pacific Telephone and Telegraph Company v. Public Utilities Commission of the State of California*, 401 P. 2d 353, 369 (1965), Supreme Court of California.

dollar of sales averaged 4.7 cents compared with 6.1 cents for the same 50 companies.[111]

Most states have accepted these demonstrations and approved the Western Electric charges.[112] But some have disallowed part of them. The strictest of these, California (before 1970), shrugged off the proffered evidence as inadequate and irrelevant, precisely because of Western's integration with the operating companies. Its view (before 1970) was that Western enjoys such enormous advantages from the guaranteed access to the huge market of the operating companies, advantages of economies of scale in manufacture and diminution of risk, as to render invalid all price and profit comparisons with other companies enjoying no such advantages.[113] On the same grounds, it rejected Western's contention that the capital goods manufacturing operation justifies a higher rate of return incorporated in the prices it charges to the operating companies than the commissions typically permit the operating companies themselves.[114]

---

[111] AT&T, "Vertical Integration in the Bell System," *op. cit.*, 49. Comparisons with a more representative sample of manufacturing companies show a larger discrepancy: Western's return on beginning of year equity was 11.6 percent in 1966 and 9.7 percent in 1967 (*Annual Reports*, 1966 and 1967); returns for the sample of electrical equipment and electronics corporations surveyed by the First National City Bank of New York were 16.7 and 14.9 percent respectively. *Monthly Economic Letter*, April 1968, 46.

"When Western's returns are compared either to those of other electrical equipment producers, or to what it could earn with the objective a maximum short-run exploitation of its strong position, it seems clear that restraint is being exercised." Sheahan, *op. cit.*, *Q. Jour. Econ.* (May 1956), LXX: 257.

[112] According to information from the Company, Western's charges were sustained in 13 of the 14 cases that went to the highest State courts in the period 1945 to 1966.

[113] "The commission states in its decision that Pacific, after establishing the inherent advantages of a single large market supplied by a single large supplier of telephone material and services, compared Western's prices with those of the 'much smaller non-Bell market of more than 90 manufacturers and suppliers for some similar equipment. Comparability of manufacturers and suppliers was not established and the reasonableness of other company prices, even assuming comparability, was not demonstrated. Moreover, the massive and unique market enjoyed by the nonoperating segments of American in the purchases by operating segments provides an advantage so great in volume alone in each of the fields of manufacturing, installation, purchasing and distribution that competition is effectively eliminated.

Western has a stable, assured and captive market. . . . We find [continues the commission] that little, if any, weight can be accorded such price comparisons in judging the reasonableness of Western's prices. *It is the cost to Western that is significant'*

"Further, according to the decision of the commission, Pacific 'attempted to justify the earnings of Western . . . by a comparison . . . of various financial ratios . . . for Western and for 47 selected utility suppliers. . . .' However, states the commission, Pacific's 'showing in this respect completely disregards the affiliation of Western with the Bell System and the unique conditions under which Western operates . . . and, even assuming comparability, does not demonstrate the reasonableness of earnings of the other companies. The advantage that the Bell System has in its integrated position . . . makes it impossible to compare one phase of its operations, that of Western Electric, with outside companies who have none of the same spread of operations and control. . . .'" *The Pacific Telephone and Telegraph Company v. Public Utility Commission of the State of California*, 401 P. 2d 353, 369 (1965). Stress supplied.

[114] In consequence,

"The [California] commission found and determined that Western's profit on sales to Pacific 'for rate-making purposes, should be adjusted' so as to result in a rate of return to Western not greater than the rate allowed Pacific. Accordingly, in arriving at Pacific's rate base the commission deducted $22,759,000 from payments made to Western which Pacific had included as original cost of plant, and in determining test-year expenses deducted the sum of $3,085,000 from payments by Pacific to Western. It is without question that 'for the purpose of fixing rates' the commission may

There is an element of plausibility in the California position—that is to say its former position, since it reversed itself in 1970.[115] To the extent that Western's evidently extremely efficient operation[116] is attributable to vertical integration, whether because of the economies of scale made possible by its preferential access to the huge Bell market or because of the intimate collaboration between manufacturing and operating companies, its superior performance constitutes a defense of the integration, lending support to the view that manufacturing is part of the "natural monopoly" of telephonic communications. The more "natural" and complete the integration, the less it would seem to make sense to claim that one part of the unit requires a higher rate of return than another. The more natural the monopoly, the more valid is the California Commission's conclusion that in judging the reasonableness of Western's prices, it is not the prices of its competitors but "the cost to Western that is significant."

The question remains: what is the proper measure of those costs? In particular, what is the proper measure of Western's cost of capital (k)? The company has presented extensive testimony documenting the greater variability of its sales than those of the operating companies, as an evidence of its greater risks, more nearly comparable with those of other suppliers of capital goods. The problem, once again, is one of reconciling this demonstration with the company's convictions about the essentiality and intimacy of its integration with the operating companies. It is unclear, in these circumstances, that its commercial risks or cost of capital can in any meaningful sense be said to be any different from those of the entire organization of which it is an integral part.

We make no effort to resolve the issue here. But even if one were persuaded on a priori grounds that it makes no sense to conceive of the Western part of the Bell System as having a k any different from that of the operating companies, it would still seem prudent, in attempting to *measure* it, to do so for the entire Bell System, *including* Western itself. This is not what the California Commission did. It simply assumed that Western's k was the same as that of the Pacific Telephone Co. and incorporated in the former's computed cost of service the same rate of return as it allowed the latter. Integration suggests the desirability of treating the entire enterprise as a unit

---

disallow excessive and unreasonable payments between affiliated corporations." *Ibid.*, p. 368.

For reference to an analogous but not identical practice in Michigan, see note 20, p. 29 of Volume 1.

[115] "The present record establishes that . . . the risks of the manufacturer, Western, are different and significantly greater than the utility, Pacific; that Western has risks of competition; that Western's prices are the lowest available; that . . . Western's cost savings have been passed on to its customer, Pacific; and that Western's financial characteristics are those of a manufacturer."

"Western's prices to Pacific and its earnings on its sales of manufactured products to Pacific have been fair and reasonable. . . ." Public Utilities Commission of the State of California,

Investigation on the Commission's own motion into the practices, contracts, service and facilities of The Pacific Telephone and Telegraph Co., Case No. 8858, Decision No. 76726, January 27, 1970, mimeo., 13a, 17.

[116] The McKinsey & Company study made some efforts to adjust the price comparisons between Western and independent manufacturers of telephone equipment for the differences in the size of their operations, attempting in this way to eliminate the advantages of the former of economies of scale made possible by its integration. Western Electric's costs, thus adjusted, still remained substantially below those of its competitors. *Op. cit.*, 21–25, 94–95. For a stern criticism of the entire McKinsey report, see Shepherd, *op. cit.*, in *Technological Change in the Regulated Industries*, mimeo, p. 45n.

in making cost computations; it does not justify doing so for only one part of the unit and then imputing the cost thus calculated to another part of the unit.[117]

---

[117] This procedure had the interesting consequence of imputing a return on Western Electric *equity* of only 7.05%, as compared with the 8.4% allowed Pacific Bell itself. The reason for this anomalous result is that the 6.9% return that the California Commission allowed the latter company on its *total* investment (and then imputed to Western) was based on its financing 35% of the total with debt, at an embedded cost of only 4.38% (and another 5% with preferred stock and advances). Western's capital structure, in contrast, had only 20% debt, with an embedded cost of 6.3%. (Information supplied by the company.)

The Bell System at one time argued for an enterprise-wide rate of return. It abandoned that position in favor of one arguing for a higher return for Western when it found commissions basing their findings of permissible rates of return solely on the needs of the operating companies and even at times justifying low returns on the ground that integration enabled those companies to shift many of the risks of the business *to* Western Electric!

There is also a reason of economic principle for considering Western's cost of capital separately. Risk, representing the degree of probability that individual expenditures of society's resources in capital investment will fail, in greater or lesser degree, to earn their opportunity costs, is a real, economic cost. And, as we have earlier contended (see note 22, this chapter, above), its proper measure is to be found in the spread of probable results of *particular investments*—not in the danger that the individual *investor* may fail to obtain a sufficient return on the *money* that he puts up to finance the project. The United States government, for example, can reduce the risk to the *lender* almost to zero, because, possessing sovereign power, it can always raise the funds necessary to service its debt by resort to taxation. It is not this minimal risk to the purchaser of government bonds that ought to determine the cost of capital, against which all government investment projects should be tested; rather, it is the opportunity cost of that capital—what it would add to national product in other uses— and the prospective returns of particular, proposed government investment projects, properly adjusted for the *risks of those individual projects*.

So it could well be that the economically proper k against which Western's own investments should be measured and that ought to be reflected in Western's prices is higher than the systemwide average—if indeed the real economic

risks of the *projects* in which Western invests are greater than those of the operating companies.

What remains uncertain is the sufficiency of Western's proffered demonstration of those higher risks. True, fluctuations in sales over time are one commonly accepted indicator of risk, presumably because the more extreme the fluctuations in the success of particular categories of investments, the greater is the likelihood that any one of them will prove, ex post, to have been mistaken. This inference seems particularly justified in competitive markets, where fluctuations in sales may be construed as a reflection, among other things, of the special risks arising from competition itself. What is uncertain is whether a similar inference is justified, in the absence of competition, from the mere fact that the sales of Western Electric fluctuate more than those of the operating companies. If the latter could reliably be counted on to purchase all their requirements from the former, it seems doubtful that the mere fact that they purchase large quantities in some years and small quantities in others makes investment in one sector of the integrated operation any more risky than in the other.

"Western's . . . risk of failure is not distinctly of a different order than that of the Bell System as a whole. Cyclical fluctuations in earnings are more violent for Western than for the operating companies, but this is hardly a reason for a long-run average return significantly in excess of the range considered acceptable for the latter." Sheahan, *op. cit.*, Q. Jour. Econ. (May 1956), LXX: 257.

The foregoing discussion by no means exhausts the merits of this issue. The risks of Western's investments could still be greater than those of the operating companies in these circumstances *because* of regulation—if its profits fluctuate more than theirs but regulatory commissions do not permit it to earn the high profits in good years sufficient to compensate for the deeper decline of its earnings in bad ones. Again, its risks could be greater if the capital to output ratio of the operating companies—specifically, the arithmetic relationship between their purchases of inputs of the type supplied by Western Electric and their output—were subject to important fluctuation or change in the *long run*. This could take place if there occurred any marked secular change in the *rate* of growth of Bell output, since Bell's purchases from Western

In 1949, the United States Department of Justice filed a 73-page complaint against Western Electric and AT&T, the essence of which charge was that the two companies had monopolized

"the production, manufacture, distribution, sale, and installation of telephones, telephone apparatus, telephone equipment, telephone materials, and telephone supplies,"

in violation of the Sherman Act.[118] The two essential instrumentalities of this alleged monopolization were said to be the patent policies of the Bell System and the vertically integrated relationship between the defendants, to both of which the government attributed Western's dominant position in the telephone equipment business.[119]

Note that what the government claimed was being illegally monopolized was the field in which Western Electric operates—the manufacture, distribution, sale, and installation of telephones, and telephone supplies and apparatus; and this was allegedly accomplished

"(1) by vesting in Western the exclusive right to manufacture and sell such equipment to such operating companies and to the Long Lines Department of AT&T;

---

are a function not of its absolute *level* of sales but of their rate of expansion. Again, any decline in the automaticity with which the operating companies or their customers turn to Western for their equipment would have the same effect. Decisions like *Carterfone* weaken that link, hence increase Western's real risk. The rise of competition in communications in recent years has increased the risk of both the operating companies and Western, but not always equivalently.

[118] *United States of America v. Western Electric Company, Inc. and American Telephone & Telegraph Company*, Complaint, U.S. District Court, New Jersey, Civil Action No. 17–49, filed January 14, 1949, par. 59. This document and the Answer of the two defendants, as well as the Final Judgment, dated January 24, 1956, representing a consent settlement of the suit, are all reproduced in U.S. House of Representatives, Committee on the Judiciary, Antitrust Subcommittee, 85th Cong. 2d Sess., *Consent Decree Program of the Department of Justice*, Hearings, Part II—Volume I, Washington, 1958, pp. 1719–1795, 1800–1844, and 1845–1863. References to the paragraphs of the Complaint and Answer will be made directly in the text that follows.

[119] The defendants agreed with the government's charge (Complaint, Par. 45) that

"virtually all of the Bell System requirements for telephones, telephone apparatus, equipment, materials, and supplies are purchased from Western, the only notable excep-

tion being building materials." (Answer, Par. 29)

And since both parties agreed also that the Bell companies owned approximately 85 percent of all the facilities used for rendering local telephone service in the country (Complaint, par. 42, Answer, par. 26), there was no essential dispute about the preponderant position of Western in the industry, thus defined. The government asserted, in addition, that AT&T owned and operated more than 98 percent of the facilities used in providing long-distance telephone service; the defendants responded that virtually all telephone facilities in the country are used from time to time for this purpose. (*Ibid.*) According to testimony by the U.S. General Services Administration, Western supplied about 90 percent of the equipment needs of the Bell companies and almost 80 percent of the U.S. market for telephone and telegraph apparatus in the early 1960s. (Irwin and McKee, "Vertical Integration and the Communication Equipment Industry: Alternatives for Public Policy," *Cornell Law Rev.* (February 1968), LIII: 447.) According to information supplied by the company and prepared for it by J. Fred Weston, it accounted in 1965 for 72.7 percent of total national value of shipments of such apparatus but, of the other products in its line, only 12.7 percent of the nonferrous wire drawing, 3.7 percent of microwave communication equipment, 3 to 7 percent of electron tubes, and 2 to 4 percent of various other instruments, hardware and types of equipment.

"(2) by requiring such operating companies and the Long Lines Department of AT&T to purchase their required equipment exclusively from Western. . . ." (Complaint, par. 60.)[120]

Two evils in particular, the government charged, flowed from this monopolization: excessive charges to the operating companies, on the one hand,[121] and delays in the introduction of cost-reducing innovations, on the other.[122]

---

[120] There are, however, interspersed throughout the Complaint various contentions also that the two defendants collaborated in such a way as to enhance and protect the monopoly positions of the Bell companies in *their* part of the business as well—the provision of telephone service. Under this heading would come the provision of the original contract between AT&T and Western Electric, covering the period 1882–1908, which prohibited the latter from selling telephone equipment to non-Bell companies (Complaint, Par. 56; Answer, Par. 54); the contention that

'Many types of equipment, particularly those essential to the successful operation of toll and long-distance lines, and all types of automatic switching equipment manufactured by Western have been consistently withheld from independent telephone companies" (Complaint, par. 56; see also Complaint, par. 74);

and that in those instances in which Western products are sold to non-Bell companies (through the Graybar Electric Company) the prices are 10 to 25 percent higher than those charged by Western to the Bell companies (Complaint, par. 120; the Answer admits the price differentials, but denies that Western fixes Graybar's prices or—"until recently"—controlled its management, par. 100).

So there are elements of a contention of mutual subsidization: that the operating companies use their monopoly to confer a monopoly in the manufacturing field on Western; and that Western to some extent uses its monopoly power to protect that of the operating companies. This double thesis is explicitly stated in Par. 74 of the Complaint. We make no effort to assess these allegations. There is some room for skepticism about the possibility of this kind of mutual magnification of monopoly. To the extent that Western is prevented by its Bell connections from making outside sales, its own market position and profits are contracted, not extended. To the extent that it either charges the operating companies lower prices or outside companies higher prices than it otherwise would choose to do, it is being forced to limit its monopoly and exploit it less than it otherwise would. (In unregulated markets one should be similarly skeptical about the other half of the model: to

the extent that companies downstream make purchases from affiliates upstream that they would not otherwise make, in order to enhance the monopoly position of those affiliates, they do so at the expense of their own profits. But in regulated industries this kind of behavior could be a means of increasing the profits permitted on the combined operation.) And yet, though the obligations of each party to its partners may in some way restrict its own freedom of action, mutual support and benefit are clearly possible. Clearly, the Bell companies, with their overwhelming share of the telephone business, are in a position to confer on Western benefits large enough to outweigh the costs of its foregoing outside sales. And clearly also a policy of mutual exclusivity of patronage could well have seemed the most profitable one for the entire system.

[121] This contention really had several more or less separate aspects. One was, simply, that the absence of effective competition in the supply of equipment and materials to the operating companies resulted inescapably in the incorporation in the latters' cost of service of excessively high charges (Complaint, par. 124). Second was the contention that the prices of individual items of equipment were only remotely related to their respective costs (Complaint, par. 101). This was apparently a reference to the finding by the FCC, later corroborated by the careful investigations of Sheahan, that Western's computations of standard costs had been permitted to get seriously out of date in the 1930s—an understandable reflection of its comparative freedom from price competition. Sheahan, *op. cit.*, *Q. Jour. Econ.* (May 1956), LXX: 260–261. Third, the Department charged that higher profit margins were charged on items manufactured exclusively for the Bell companies than on items sold outside the system (Complaint, par. 101). This charge conflicts curiously with the opposite one, to which we have already referred, although the company's policy might of course have varied from one item of equipment to another. Sheahan concludes that it is the latter charge that has by far the greater validity: that the prices charged for Western equipment to non-Bell companies are substantially higher than to the Bell companies. See his *Competition*

For remedy, the Department of Justice asked for a long list of injunctions against continuation of the various alleged practices and agreements that it described. But the heart of its request was for two major remedies corresponding to the two major alleged instrumentalities for the illegal monopolization: compulsory licensing of all applicants under Bell System patents at reasonable royalties, and a dissolution of the tie between Western and the Bell System, with the requirement thereafter that the Bell companies be required to employ competitive bidding in all purchases of equipment, materials, and supplies.[123]

The case never went to trial. After seven years, during which considerable pressure was exerted on the Department of Justice to accept less drastic remedies,[124] a consent settlement was entered, the main relevant aspect of which for our present discussion is that it left the relationship between Western Electric and the Bell System essentially intact. The remedies in this part of the case were directed toward making regulation rather than competition more effective.[125]

The Bell System has, over many decades, developed a formidable defense of its vertical integration, the burden of which is that the financial link with manufacturing is essential to the provision of a low-cost, high-quality and ever-improving communications service. Central to this defense is the

---

Versus Regulation as a Policy Aim For the Telephone Equipment Industry, op. cit., 234–244. The final element is that

"Western's prices to Bell Operating Companies have been increased during periods of depression when prices in competitive markets have been reduced in an effort to retain business." (Complaint, par. 101.)

This charge was true, at least of the 1930s. Western's prices are based on anticipated full costs, which typically move inversely with volume. As a result it has at times reduced prices in boom periods after World War II; and it instituted a series of price increases in the early 1930s. Sheahan, *op. cit., Q. Jour. Econ.* (May 1956), LXX: 251, 255–256. The latter increases caused considerable difficulties with various State regulatory commissions, at least ten of which were moved to disallow some of them in computing operating company costs of service. The company is unlikely to repeat that venture; it has adopted the general policy of permitting its rates of return to fluctuate from year to year, rather than to resort to countercyclical pricing.

[122] "The purpose of such delayed introductions was to prevent existing plants from becoming obsolete." (Complaint, par. 102.) The Complaint goes on to document at some length six alleged instances of such retardation in the introduction of major equipment innovations. (Complaint, pars. 102–119.) The defendants answered at length (Answer, pars. 82–99); as we shall point out below, the evidence on this score is

not very strong.

[123] The government asked, in addition, that Western Electric itself be broken up into three separate companies. (Complaint, Part VII, par. 11.)

[124] See the politically charged hearings by the Antitrust Subcommittee of the House of Representatives, covering almost 3,000 pages, in three volumes (note 118, p. 295 above) and the report subsequently issued by the same Subcommittee, 86th Cong., 1st Sess., *Consent Decree Program of the Department of Justice,* January 30, 1959, 29–120 and 290–323.

[125] See Kenneth E. Madsden, "Consent Decree: The History and Effect of Western Electric Co. v. United States," *Cornell Law Q.* (Fall 1959), XLV: 88–96.

Some eight years later, the Department of Justice brought suit to enjoin the acquisition of various independent telephone companies by General Telephone & Electronics Corporation, holding that these would violate Section 7 of the Clayton Act because they would tend to foreclose manufacturers of telephone equipment competitive with General from selling to the acquired operating companies. On November 15, 1966, the Department dropped this suit in consideration of the fact that it had earlier agreed to permit the "vastly greater" vertical integration of Western and Bell. See Manley R. Irwin and Robert E. McKee, *op. cit.,* 460–461. On the other hand, it was these and subsequent acquisitions by General that triggered the treble-damage suit by IT&T, referred to above (p. 290).

conception, already sketched in Chapter 4, of the integrated telecommunications network, "a web of millions of intricate and complicated mechanisms .... an ever-changing and delicately balanced machine," as a natural monopoly. Manufacturing, it adds, is an integral part of that monopoly.[126] This complex web of switching and transmission media, designed for an extremely high level of performance, necessitates, it is claimed, a continuous, intimate collaboration among all contributors to the service—research, development, manufacturing, installation, maintenance, and operations, a collaboration unconstrained by any divergencies of financial and managerial interests. The rapidity of technological change, it is asserted, calls for a similarly intimate collaboration both in the adaptation to it—the System is constantly offering new services, installing new equipment, adopting new technology, all of which must be integrated into the existing network—and, even more important, in fostering it. From a very early point, the scientists and engineers in Bell Laboratories, which does the fundamental research, collaborate continuously with their counterparts in Western and in the operating companies in the development process. Only in the presence of complete financial integration among the various parties, it is asserted, can collaboration be so intimate, continuous, and efficient—unhampered by conflict of financial interest or by the necessity of devising and perpetually redevising new collaborative relationships with financially separate companies, in arms-length negotiations. The role of vertical integration, in short, is to create a community of interest, making possible a free and open exchange of information and wholehearted collaboration in pursuit of the best interests of the telephone system as a whole.

More specifically, this means that the interest of the manufacturing organization is not separately pursued, but is subordinated to the efficient service of the ultimate customer; Western stands ready to meet the operating companies' needs, whatever they are: that is its function.[127] And this joining of manufacture and operations results in minimization of cost,

---

[126] AT&T, "Vertical Integration in the Bell System," 2.
[127] See *ibid.*, 19–20.

Other asserted aspects of this subordination of the interests of the manufacturer, as such, are the willingness of Western to invest promptly in the capacity needed to meet both normal and unanticipated increases in demand,

"even though conditions are not such as to induce the requisite expansion of capacity by an outside manufacturer of telephone equipment. . . .

"Western has knowledge of estimated Operating Company requirements, organizes and tools up accordingly and begins production far in advance of actual orders and without assurance that the estimated requirements will materialize. Outside competing suppliers could not foretell the demand on them unless contractually assured of definite business, and would be reluctant to invest money to meet even predicted demands for the specialized equipment required for telephony without contractual protection." (*Ibid.*, 32–33.)

In consequence, it is said, Western can typically promise a one-year interval between the receipt of an order and the delivery of even its most complex equipment:

"Unaffiliated manufacturers, as for example in the electrical equipment industry, often wait for hard orders to materialize, and back orders of six years are now the general rule for generating equipment. As a result, the electric utilities must wait to have current needs met and must make hazardous estimates of their needs six years from now to be sure of the generating capacity adequate for customer demand," (*Ibid.*,35).

If this comparison is a fair one, it would seem to illustrate the tendency to which we have already referred for vertical integration, and particularly integration with a regulated monopolist who possesses some reserve of incompletely exploited monopoly power, to minimize risk (see pp. 260–262, this chapter and pp. 106–108, Chapter 3 [on the positive effect of A-J-W], above). Western, with its preferential access to the Bell market, and itself pricing like a public utility,

maintenance of the highest possible standards of service, and the most rapid possible improvement in both over time.

The argument is not merely hypothetical. It is buttressed with impressive evidence of good economic performance:

1. Although no definitive, objective comparisons have evidently been made, no one who has had occasion to use the telephone in a fair number of foreign countries would be likely to quarrel with the observation that the United States has a very good telephone system.[128]

2. Long distance telephone rates have dropped sharply in recent decades; the cost of intrastate telephone service has risen far less than the general price level. Correspondingly, the growth of productivity in communications has been markedly higher than in the economy generally, as we have already seen.[129]

3. The comparative performance of Western Electric alone in these respects is even more impressive. In the period 1950–1967, Western's prices for apparatus and equipment declined 16 percent; the Bureau of Labor Statistics price index for electrical equipment generally increased 53 percent in the same period. Again, during these same years, Western's prices for cable and wire rose 14 percent, compared with 95 percent in the BLS Index. Between 1948 and 1967, total factor productivity of Western Electric increased at an average 5.4 percent annually, compared with 3.5 for the entire electrical machinery and supplies industry and 2.5 for all manufacturing in the United States.[130]

---

may be able to afford to make investments in anticipation of demands that nonintegrated suppliers could not afford to make:

"If several manufacturers were competing for the business, and no one of them could be assured of any specified quantity of business over an extended period, they would be unwilling to risk major capital expenditures to meet peak demands." (*Ibid.*, 54.)

The McKinsey & Company study of Western Electric, cited above, repeats and documents many of these same arguments.

It is surely an overstatement to suggest that the nonintegrated manufacturers "would be unwilling" to do so: they do in fact do so, in industry after industry. But they would, presumably, require at least the prospect of a higher average rate of return, corresponding to their higher competitive risks. See our discussion of the ability of vertical integration to overcome the effects of market imperfections and the case of the reluctant nonintegrated supplier in notes 22 and 26 above. Here is another illustration of the possible conflict between the strong case that the Bell companies make for vertical integration and Western's asserted need for a rate of return comparable to that earned by nonintegrated equipment manufacturers. But the contradiction

is not inevitable: the integration, *per se*, reduces risk; but if because of the integration Western does indeed undertake commitments *more* risky than do unaffiliated manufacturers, it could still be that its prices should reflect a rate of discount of the probable returns on its projected investments, or a cost of capital, comparable with theirs.

[128] It ought in principle to be possible to be more precise about this—to compare the average time it takes to complete a call, the percentage of busy circuits encountered, the record of breakdowns and the like. The Bell System regularly compiles such data for its own operations. An international comparison would provide some perspective on such obvious failures as the grossly inadequate capacity that turned up in New York City in 1969–1970 and the one to two years that company officials proclaimed at the time would be required to restore service of normal quality.

[129] See pp. 99–100, Chapter 3, above.

[130] McKinsey & Company, *op. cit.*, 14 and 92. These very substantial improvements in the pricing record after World War II may be regarded in some degree as a correction of what the FCC earlier found were overcharges in one form or another, after its comprehensive investigation of the industry. *Investigation of the Telephone*

This impressive improvement in Western's productivity no doubt reflects a correspondingly above-average research and developmental effort. According to figures supplied by the company, its R & D expenditures in the period 1960–1966 amounted to 5.2 percent of its Bell sales, a ratio that may be compared with less than 2 percent for all manufacturing and 3.5 percent for the communications and electronic equipment industry, excluding Western.[131]

4. As we have already seen, Western's prices are dramatically below those of other manufacturers of comparable supplies and equipment, reflecting a combination of managerial efficiency, the advantages of integration, and a policy of charging less than the traffic will bear.

It is extremely difficult for an economist or anyone else to make a decisive appraisal of the case just summarized. And yet a judgment has to be made by someone—a legislature, a court, or a regulatory commission—though, fortunately, not necessarily by us, here and now.

The factual evidence just summarized would certainly seem to reflect a "good"—perhaps an "excellent"—economic performance; and that must be our tentative verdict. The difficulty is that there is no objective yardstick against which to compare all these results. Comparisons with other companies and other industries must, of course, carry weight—indeed, heavy weight when the evidence shows much lower Western prices for the very products produced by the others and a much more progressive performance by Western than by other companies employing a similar technology. But these are decisive indicators only of a superior performance by Western Electric itself. The question before us is, rather, what the performance of the communications industry might have been if Western were not linked to Bell. And this is the comparison for which the objective facts are, in the very nature of the case, unavailable.

It is difficult, similarly, for an outsider to sift out the poetry from the objective facts in the Bell companies' defense of the financial linkage. On the one hand, it is difficult to credit to mere coincidence the fact that the company whose price and productivity record is so much superior to others with which it may reasonably be compared happens also to be integrated into the Bell System. It should be emphasized, also, that the defense of vertical integration in this industry is almost unique in its assertion of genuine managerial and technological benefits flowing from it.[132] Not in petroleum, steel, cement, aluminum, motion pictures, or grocery distribution, in all of which integration has been both widely prevalent and strenuously debated, have its protagonists based their arguments so directly on technological grounds. The financial union of crude oil production and refining, iron ore mining and steel-making, the production of ingot steel and the fabrication of steel products, electric power generation and aluminum reduction, the production, distribution, and exhibition of motion pictures,

---

Industry in the United States, Washington, 1939. This is the interpretation of Wilcox, *op. cit.*, 381–384. See also C. F. Phillips, *op. cit.*, 658–667. In any event, the improvements were real and very impressive.

[131] AT&T, "Vertical Integration in the Bell System," *op. cit.*, 46–47.

[132] "the case for a carrier-manufacturer tie is at its strongest in telecommunications." President's Task Force on Communications Policy, *The Domestic Telecommunications Carrier Industry*, Staff Paper 5, Part 1, Washington, June 1969, 193.

the manufacture of cement and of ready-mixed concrete, the synthesis of nitrogen compounds and the preparation of mixed fertilizers, coffee-roasting and food distribution have all been defended on such grounds as the necessity for assuring a sufficient and regular supply of vital inputs, more effective marketing, the circumvention of monopoly, the saving of selling costs and—it should be conceded—the possibilities it afforded for a closer specification and control of quality, but rarely or never on the ground that the technological interdependencies were so close that each operation had to be done by the same engineers and managers working in close collaboration.[133]

On the other hand, it is simply unclear how much would be lost if the responsibility for the management, development, and improvement of the communications network were vested exclusively in the operating companies, AT&T and the Bell Laboratories, the financial ties between which have not been subjected to serious question. It is surely they who must in any event bear it, ultimately. It is the Bell Telephone Laboratories that conduct the extensive as well as apparently first-class basic research,[134] systems engineering, and fundamental development work. It is AT&T, not Western Electric, that in the first instance foots the bill for these parts of the operation[135]: the ultimate payer is of course the user of telephone services. It is Bell Labs, AT&T, and the operating companies that play the preponderant role in the initiation and selection of new development projects;[136] it is they that must set the standards and assume the ultimate responsibility for both innovation and operations.

But these speculations do not address themselves to the most difficult and pertinent question. Most of the work of Bell Labs is in development, not research, in highly applied, not pure research. And it is here that the most intimate collaboration is with the manufacturing, not the operating company. The Bell System claims that without this intimate link, the Laboratories would be crippled in the preponderant part of their operations; that Western could similarly not survive without that collaboration; and that, hence, if Western were separated from the System most of the Labs would have to come away with it, thereby severing the vital tie with operations.[137] Once again, the impartial judge encounters the vexing problem of comparing the observable virtues of what is with the uncertain benefits of what might be.

---

[133] One limited exception—there may, of course, be others—apart from the case for closer quality control (which is, however, in none of these industries asserted with anything like the vigor shown in communications) would be the direct saving in fuel costs made possible by the transfer of pig iron in molten form from the blast furnace directly into the steel converter.

[134] Francis Bello "The World's Greatest Industrial Laboratory," *Fortune*, November 1958, pp. 148–150 and ff. An index of the quality of BTL that will appeal to university department chairmen and deans is provided by a count that the Bell System made of 2,703 papers published in 1967 in *The Physical Review*, in terms of the contributors' institutions. The University of California at Berkeley was first, with 150; Bell Labs tied for second with 101; the next industrial company

on the list was General Electric, in 26th place, with 33 papers. "Technological Innovation in the Bell System," Company Memorandum, undated, mimeo., 46–47.

[135] AT&T receives a flat percentage of the operating companies' annual revenues, in return for the various services it provides for them—research, planning, financial, and legal.

[136] McKinsey & Company, *op. cit.*, 243–246.

[137] "The most serious problem would be the disposition of Bell Laboratories . . . [T]he sections of Bell Labs concerned with development could become a part of Western Electric. This would help to eliminate Western's inside track to Bell orders, but it would also destroy the unity of Bell Laboratories." The Presidents' Task Force on Communications Policy, Staff Paper 5, Part 1, *op. cit.*, 191–192.

Clearly Western would, if separated, have to develop (or take with it) its own research and development operation. This could well expand the aggregate R & D effort, in the industry as a whole. What is unclear is how much would be lost if the operating companies abandoned this chosen and exclusive manufacturing instrument and were instead free to work with Western on some parts of the manufacturing and development process, and with companies like General Electric, International Business Machines or Radio Corporation of America on others, when and as it seemed in their interest to do so.

That there would be losses, it seems impossible to deny. The introduction of separate and to some extent conflicting financial interests means the introduction of bargaining, of divergent goals, divisions of loyalty; the substitution of possibly shifting contractual for financially integrated relationships must to some extent diminish the likelihood of continuous and completely open exchanges of information and collaboration.[138] There would be another important loss—the loss of one of the most important weapons a large user of purchased inputs has when confronting suppliers which do not give it good service: the threat to manufacture for itself. In light of the possibility that a nonintegrated telephonic equipment industry might be tightly oligopolistic, this defense ought not lightly to be surrendered.

The fundamental question is whether there would not be offsetting advantages. The fact that Western stands between the needs of the operating companies and other potential suppliers of equipment—even when they use non-Western equipment and materials, the Bell companies purchase them through that company—must severely discourage companies that might otherwise be interested and able to enter into competition for Bell patronage. There would be little point in their offering lower prices to get the business or making the investments that might put them in a position to do so, when the offer would in fact have to be made to Western itself, as purchasing agent for the operating companies. In these circumstances, the fact that Western's prices are consistently lower than those quoted for similar equipment by the much smaller manufacturing companies that must survive on sales to the independent telephone company market becomes considerably less than conclusive demonstration of the superior efficiency of the integrated relationship.[139]

---

[138] The case is not mainly one of a company buying standardized components, which can readily be let out for competitive bids. It is rather one of continuously developing new components for a total system whose design is never firmly set but subject to perpetual alteration, comparable in many ways to the procurement of complex new weapons or aerospace systems. The efforts of the Department of Defence to purchase such systems, to find means of cutting costs, preventing overruns, devising incentives for their efficient development and production are not encouraging in this regard. *Ibid.*, 182–185, 187–189.

[139] It should be recognized, however, that Western's prices are markedly lower also on such items as cable and switchboard lamps, of which it is not at all the largest producer. Its lower

prices are not explainable solely in terms of economies of scale made possible by integration. See notes 110 and 116, above. While agreeing that Western's prices "are almost always lower than outside market prices," so that "the Bell Companies are in effect nearly always buying in the cheapest market when they buy from Western," Sheahan also found "little indication of any tendency for Bell companies to buy from outside in the minority of cases where Western's individual prices are not lowest." *Op. cit., Q. Jour. Econ.* (May 1956), LXX: 259 and his *Competition versus Regulation as a Policy Aim*, 362. See also *ibid.*, 74—93.

"Savings might become more significant if there were an effective rule requiring Western

Most important of all is the likelihood that opening the market to a large number of other, technologically progressive companies, by offering them the opportunity of competing on equal terms for Bell company custom, would contribute powerfully to innovation. The result could well be even more rapid reduction in cost and proliferation of new services than has been accomplished thus far.[140]

"The benefits of freer entry could be considerable. The telephone equipment industry, with its high degree of automation and requirements for systematic design, once stood apart from the rest of the economy. But today those characteristics describe many industries. With the convergence of communications and computer technology, a number of the most progressive and dynamic manufacturers in American industry—firms like IBM, ITT, General Electric, Raytheon, and RCA—have significant potential as innovators and manufacturers of new communications equipment. So do the aerospace manufacturers, with their experience in electronics, materials, system design, and other relevant technologies and skills. . . . In an age where satellites, lasers, computers and other products of space-age industries are becoming increasingly important elements of communications technology, it would be parochial to assume that the carriers' affiliates had a complete monopoly of the ideas and techniques required to fulfill the promise held out to communications users by the course of technological advance."[141]

To a company that has not previously been directly exposed to it, competition represents a plunge into the unknown. It is not unreasonable for AT&T to argue that such a plunge represents a gamble for the ultimate consumer as well as for itself, and that it seems folly to give up a system that is producing efficiently, progressively and well, with demonstrable benefits, on the mere hypothesis that another kind of regime could do better. As Sheahan poignantly concluded:

"The telephone equipment industry could conceivably be termed workably competitive except for the semantical difficulty that its dominant Bell market exhibits practically no competition at all."[142]

On the other hand, the case for competition is not merely semantic or hypothetical. First of all, there is some historical evidence, though far from

---

to turn to outside suppliers in all such cases; a newly created possibility of selling to this gigantic market might lead to more favorable price quotations by outside companies hoping to build a market within the Bell System. As it stands, outside firms can have little reasonable hope of getting much Bell business, and no incentive to try through lower prices to expand their sales in this market." *Op. cit., Q. Jour. Econ.*, 259.

[140] This is the main conclusion of Sheahan's investigation: once the principle was established that the Bell companies were prepared to buy freely from the outside,

"production and research facilities in a good

many alert electrical equipment firms would become active supplements to those now in the Bell System.

"The difficulty now is not that Western is an inferior choice in the usual case; it is that Western is the best of an artificially restricted range of possibilities. Other firms realize quite correctly that they cannot break into this market on any significant scale, and therefore do not choose to invest money and skill in any actual attempt." *Ibid.*, 268.

[141] The President's Task Force on Communications Policy, Staff Paper 5, Part 1, *op. cit.*, 178–179.

[142] *Competition Versus Regulation as a Policy Aim*, 360.

overwhelming, that the Bell companies have at times been slow in adopting innovations originating outside of Western Electric, at least to the extent of waiting first to see whether Western might succeed in coming up with at least as good an alternative.[143]

Second, there are concrete evidences of the contribution competitive innovation can make in communications where it has had an opportunity to work—around the edges of the communications monopoly, as it has doubtless appeared to the independent manufacturers of equipment; uncomfortably close to the heart, in the view of the Bell System. The revolutionary development in the last decade of microwave and satellite communications, the burgeoning of user-owned attachments and in particular those associated with the use of shared computer facilities, the rapid introduction of CATV have, all of them, been vigorously pressed not only by large users and independent entrepreneurs in communications but also, at least with equal vigor, by competing manufacturers of equipment.[144]

---

[143] See the reference, note 122, above, to the much stronger statement in the 1949 antitrust complaint. Wilcox accepts some of these contentions without serious question:

"The company postponed the introduction of improvements such as the hand set and the dial system for many years so that its old equipment might wear out before it was junked." *Op. cit.*, 260.

Of course, this sort of retardation could be in the interest of a monopolist, regardless of whether it was vertically integrated. Sheahan's conclusions, based on a much more thorough appraisal, are much more moderate and qualified. See *Competition versus Regulation as a Policy Aim*, 148–170, and *op. cit.*, Q. Jour. Econ. (May 1956), LXX: 264–265.

[144] See especially pp. 129–131, Chapter 4, above. According to Manley R. Irwin, the main impulse for adopting the microwave radio relay technique came from independent equipment suppliers; the preponderant portion of the private systems, sanctioned by the *above-890* decision, were manufactured by Motorola, Collins Radio, RCA, and General Electric. The Bell System itself made a major contribution to the development of this innovation with a crash program in the 1946–1950 period that produced the TD-2. That intensive effort was evidently inspired in part by the fact that several competitors had entered or threatened to enter the field, it having become clear that microwave would be the logical technique for serving the rapidly growing needs of television. See Shepherd, *op. cit.*, in *Technological Change in the Regulated Industries*, mimeo., 56–58, drawing on, among other sources, F. M. Scherer, *The Development of the TD-X and TD-2 Microwave Radio Relay Systems in Bell Telephone Laboratories*, Weapons Acquisition Research Project, Harvard Univ. Graduate School of Business Administra-

tion, mimeo., October 1960.

In communications satellites, the proposals of the Bell System were for a global network of low- or medium-orbit satellites, approximately 50 in total, the large number required because each individual satellite, as it moved across the horizon, would be within radio range for only some 20 minutes; this required also very large capital outlays for the necessary ground stations. It was the aerospace industry and, in particular, Hughes Aircraft and Lockheed that pressed for and developed the synchronous satellites, which, orbiting at approximately 22,300 miles above the earth's surface, remain in a fixed position relative to that surface, thus vastly reducing the number and complexity of required satellites and ground stations.

Again, according to Irwin, it has been non-integrated firms that have taken the lead in introducing new switching techniques for message communications using computers and in devising a wide variety of "modems," devices that enable computers to transmit data via the telephone network. Not surprisingly, independent innovative activity was far more intense and productive in the 1965–1969 period in developing these and other devices for attachment to the private leased line network—where AT&T has permitted non-Bell attachments since 1965–1966—than for the dialed network, where until *Carterfone* the highly restrictive foreign attachment tariff prevailed. "Innovation and the Communications Industry," a paper presented at a Conference of the President's Task Force on Communications Policy, mimeo., 7; see pp. 5–8 and *passim*; also Irwin and McKee, *op. cit.*, 452–457; and Shepherd, *op. cit.*, in *Technological Change in the Regulated Industries*, mimeo., 50–51. On the role of independents in modems, see "A profitable way to translate computer talk," *Business Week*, May 16, 1970, 124. On the divergent assess-

But, in the last analysis, the plunge into competition is inescapably a plunge into the unknown. The essence of the case for competition is that the potential performance of an industry is unknowable; it is the rivalry of independent suppliers that offers the greatest possible assurance that all economically feasible avenues for cost reduction and service innovation will in fact be explored and their results subjected to the impartial test of the marketplace.

This is not, however, a sufficient guide to public policy in all times and places, as the institution of regulated public utility monopoly itself indicates. It remains possible that the manufacture of equipment for the central core of the natural monopoly, the communications network, is a "natural" part of that monopoly. This writer would find it extremely difficult himself, in the face of the objective record of good performance and the qualitative arguments that provide at least a highly plausible basis for attributing those results in important measure to vertical integration, to recommend the plunge into the unknown.

What does seem clear, as a matter not only of economic logic but of experience, is that the retention of such a vertical tie becomes less objectionable, the more it is possible to introduce competition into the communications business itself; or the more narrowly the area of natural monopoly is defined. What makes vertical integration possibly objectionable is its attachment to a regulated horizontal monopoly. What created the opportunity for independent entry into some portions of the business of manufacturing communications *equipment*, and therefore exposed Western Electric itself to indirect competition, was the entry of new purveyors of communications *service*. If the Bell System had from the outset been given complete control over communications satellites, if it had succeeded in persuading the FCC to deny large business users the right to set up private microwave facilities, and if its restrictive policies with respect to interconnection and alien attachments had been sustained, it seems most probable that the industry's performance would have been much less dynamic than it has been in the last decade. The defect would have been the defect of monopoly. But in those markets where the monopoly is and remains natural, the question must continue to be asked whether the foreclosure of competitive innovation in the supply of its major inputs that vertical integration entails may not be an excessive price to pay for the undoubted benefits flowing from it.[145]

---

ments of and contributions to the potentialities of satellite technology, see also Charles E. Silberman, "The Little Bird that Casts a Big Shadow," *Fortune*, February 1967, 108–111 and ff; also Lawrence Lessing, "Cinderella in the Sky," *Fortune*, October 1967, 131–133 and ff, both of these likewise clearly underlining the same conflict of interest between the common carriers and their affiliated manufacturing units, on the one hand, and nonaffiliated manufacturing innovators like Hughes Aircraft, on the other.

[145] There is a related issue that must be mentioned, even though we cannot pursue it at length here. If there is a strong case for permitting nonintegrated manufacturers fuller access to the communications market, is there not also a strong case for Western Electric competing more forcefully in making sales outside the Bell System? The question is intended to be essentially rhetorical. Partly as a result of historic company policy, partly as a result of the antitrust consent decree, which imposed various restrictions on the right of Western to sell in the open market and restricted AT&T and its operating companies from engaging in any business other than the furnishing of common-carrier communications services and related operations, Western has confined its sales almost exclusively to the Bell System and to the government. The large price differentials that it and the Bell companies proudly cite between Western and competitive equipment could not possibly be sustained if

Integration and Competition

Financial Integration: The Problem of Judgment

The reader may have observed how much more tentative our policy judgments have been so far in this chapter than in Chapter 5. It could be merely that the confidence shown in the previous chapter was misplaced and that only equally tentative conclusions should have been drawn there. But the difference between the two is instructive—illuminating not only the nature and limitations of economics but the important differences between the two situations under examination.

Chapter 5 was concerned with industries both structurally and behaviorally capable of much more effective competition than regulation has permitted. The institution of competition makes prediction possible: the competition of large numbers automatically enforces certain kinds of behavior and guarantees certain kinds of results from an *industry* no matter what the motivations and capabilities of individual members of the group.[146]

In this chapter, in contrast, we deal with small numbers in individual markets, and prediction becomes much more difficult. The economic performance of oligopoly is capable of much wider variation. It can be identical to that of monopoly, at one extreme; it can be intensely competitive; and it can be sometimes one and sometimes the other, in the same industry. When a proposal is under consideration to transform an industry from duopoly to monopoly and the latter offers certain efficiency advantages, as for example in the case of electric and gas distribution, it is very difficult to know how much of genuine competition would actually be surrendered. And one can no longer reliably predict, on the other hand, to what extent the opportunities for greater efficiency will in fact be grasped. The possible inhibiting influence of encrusted bureaucracy and its probable reactions to the new situation must be assessed.

Moreover, when numbers are few, some or all of those few are likely to have substantial monopoly power. And they may on that account be in a position to deny others access to the market on fair and equal terms. One must therefore assess the impact of financial integration on those opportunities for competition and try to determine to what extent can regulation *in practice* actually protect those opportunities.

Economists are understandably uneasy in prescribing policy for industries of small numbers.

Western competed freely in the open market.

No doubt, that company is restrained from doing so by a fear that it would be subject to antitrust attack, particularly if, as seems likely, some smaller telephone equipment suppliers would in consequence be put out of business; and no doubt, also, the consent decree itself reflects this same kind of ambivalance toward genuine competition. Finally, there would always be a danger, if Western and the Bell companies were free to compete in nonutility operations, that they might do so at non-remunerative prices, recouping any such losses in higher rates to their captive, utility customers; and it was to guard against any such possibility that some of the restrictions in the consent settlement were imposed. But even if the vertical tie between manufacturing and operating companies were retained, it would seem that sufficient protections could be devised against any such policy by requiring a strict separation of the accounts for Western's regulated and nonregulated activities; this additional impediment to regulation would, it would seem, be a small price to pay for the benefits that would be expected to flow—most obviously, lower costs for equipment and supplies purchased by independent telephone companies —from the entry of Western itself into direct competition in the electrical and telephonic equipment industries.

[146] See Arman A. Alchian, "Uncertainty, Evolution, and Economic Theory," Amer. Econ. Ass'n, *Readings in Industrial Organization and Public Policy*, 207–219.

INTERCOMPANY COORDINATION

We have alluded in many places to the great economies that can be achieved when public utility companies coordinate their activities in one way or another and have described numerous instances of such collaboration voluntarily undertaken. We have also described the obstacles to complete coordination. Regulatory compulsion has been required not only to ensure that the potential cost savings are more fully achieved but also because intercompany cooperation raises problems with respect to the preservation of competition. The dangers are either that the companies will cooperate not too little but too much—for example, to suppress competition among themselves—or that they will, either individually or collectively, use such power as they have or as they may achieve by cooperation to exclude independent firms from a fair opportunity to compete with them.

We shall consider only two cases in detail in this chapter. It might be useful therefore, in order to convey a fuller sense of the range and pervasiveness of these phenomena, to list a few examples, most of which we have already mentioned:

1. The establishment of joint rates and through routes by separate transportation companies. One problem is that railroads, in particular, have used their rate bureaus or conferences, whose ostensible justification is the need to plan such collaborations, as instruments also for the discouragement or suppression of price competition among themselves. Another is that they have often refused to coordinate on nondiscriminatory terms with water or motor carriers.[147]

2. The exchange of railroad freight cars, avoiding the necessity of transferring freight from the cars of one road to those of another on journeys requiring the facilities of both.[148] One problem has been the necessity of setting compensation rates high enough to induce the borrowing railroads to return cars promptly to their owners in time of shortage.[148a]

3. The requirement that the Bell companies interconnect with independent telephone companies[149], and then with any and all competitors.[149a]

---

[147] See pp. 271–272, above. There is an exellent survey of the railroad rate bureau phenomenon in Fulda, *op. cit.*, Chapter 9; his Chapter 10 is devoted to rate agreements in international shipping.

[148] The airlines similarly interchange equipment, subject to the approval of the Civil Aeronautics Board. For example, in February 1969, the CAB approved an interchange agreement between Northwest Airlines and Pan American World Airways, which will permit through-plane service between Minneapolis on the one hand and various points in Europe on the other. National Airlines has been able to justify purchase of several huge (350-seat) jet airplanes only because it plans to lease the planes to Pan American in its off-season. Gilbert Burck, "A New Flight Plan for the Airlines," *Fortune*, April 1969, 98–101 and ff.

[148a] See note 46a, p. 64, above.

[149] See p. 140, above. Section 766 of the California Public Utilities Code provides that:

"Whenever the Commission . . . finds that a physical connection can reasonably be made between the lines of two or more telephone corporations . . . whose lines can be made to form a continuous line of communication . . . and that public convenience and necessity will be served thereby, or finds that two or more telegraph or telephone corporations have failed to establish joint rates . . . for service by or over their lines, and that joint rates . . . ought to be established, the Commission may . . . require that such connection be made on the payment of such compensation . . . as it finds to be just and reasonable. . . ." As quoted in Public Utilities Commission of the State of California, *In the Matter*

4. The problems of independent manufacturers of communications equipment arising out of the historic Bell System policy of refusing to permit non-Bell equipment to be hooked up with the telephone network and the erosion of that policy by the FCC's *Hush-A-Phone* and *Carterfone* decisions.[150]

5. Voluntary purchases and sales of gas between pipeline companies.[151]

6. The FPC's periodic orders requiring particular natural gas pipeline or electric companies to interconnect with and provide service to municipal distributors at Commission-fixed prices.[152]

7. The attempt of the FPC staff to require competing applicants for certification to pool their plans in order to take fuller advantage of the economies of scale and the attempt of a dissenting Commissioner to attach to the certificate of the successful applicant a condition reserving the Commission's right at a later point to require him, if it saw fit, to carry gas for others.[153]

8. The running of a feeder helicopter service by a number of airline companies cooperatively, as a means of internalizing what would otherwise be the external benefits of that service.[154]

9. The requirement by the FCC that CATV companies carry the programs of local stations, and the problems created for those operators by the reluctance of the Bell Companies to let them use telephone company poles or ducts to carry their cables to subscribers.[155]

---

of the Application of the Pacific Telephone & Telegraph Company et al., Decision No. 74917, November 6, 1968 (mimeo.), p. 40.

The Commission points out that this statute was passed 55 years earlier when the Pacific Telephone Company refused to interconnect with the other companies.

"The Section has well served such purpose, as is evidenced by the fact that since its passage and early enforcement . . . the facilities of telephone companies in this State have become so interconnected that for many years the people of this State have had the public benefit of a wholly integrated toll network." *Ibid.*, 40–41.

"in fact every California independent company is a physical part of the nationwide toll network. The standards of quality for every part of such network, as a practical matter, are set by Bell System requirements. Both the statewide portion and the nationwide toll network have been developed as an integrated whole to allow full compatibility in dialing, signalling and transmission regardless of whether a call originates or terminates at a Bell System or an independent telephone station." *Ibid.*, 35–36.

Section 201 (a) of the Communication Act confers similar authority on the FCC:

"It shall be the duty of every common carrier engaged in interstate or foreign communication by wire or radio to furnish such communication service upon reasonable request therefor; and . . . where the Commission . . . finds such action necessary or desirable in the public interest, to establish physical connections with other carriers, to establish through routes and charges applicable thereto and the divisions of such charges, and to establish and provide facilities and regulations for operating such through routes." 47 U.S. Code 201 (a), 1964 ed.

[149a] See note 60, p. 133, above.

[150] See pp. 140–145, Chapter 4, above.

[151] See p. 66, note 55, above.

[152] See note 85, pp. 75–76, above.

[153] See pp. 154–157, Chapter 4, above.

[154] See note 179 p. 234, above.

[155] See pp. 33–34, Chapter 1 and pp. 67–68, Chapter 2, above. In New York City, the problems of the cable operators are complicated by the fact that while the city has franchised some of them to lay cables under the streets, the duct space beneath Manhattan is controlled by the Empire City Subway Company, which is owned by the New York Telephone Company.

"Empire, the CATV people say, has not been too eager to furnish ducts—even at a rental of $1,350 a mile per year.

"Lack of cooperation from the Bell System is an increasing problem across the country, CATV men assert. The reason? CATV is highly profit-

Piggyback Service

The most important form of intermodal collaboration in the transportation field, in fact and in potential, is the use of truck trailers on railway flatcars (TOFC), popularly known as piggybacking. Piggybacking has the great attraction of combining the flexibility, the door-to-door pickup and delivery capacity of truck service with the far lower line haul costs of the rails (or water carriers) over long distances, while avoiding the often prohibitive costs of transferring freight from one medium to the other.[156] (These same observations apply to containerization generally, of which the use of the truck trailer itself as the container is only one form.) It offers the prospect of savings in cost and improvement in service if the companies operating the different modes can find one way or another of cooperating to offer it.

Piggybacking also greatly increases the likelihood that the rates for different kinds of freight will be based exclusively on costs. The elaborate system of price discrimination involved in the prevailing commodity rate structure requires identification of the commodities in order to assess what each will bear. Containerization lends itself instead to flat all-commodity rates per container or trailer (with appropriate modifications for weight, for example), regardless of its contents.[157] It was for this reason that the ICC in 1931 first rejected proposed piggyback rates: they would have undermined the commodity rate structure—the very structure that encouraged the inefficient transfer of so much traffic to higher-cost modes[158]—

---

able, and many phone companies think they should be in it." "CATV comes down from the hills," *Business Week*, September 16, 1967, 66. Reprinted by special permission.

In July 1969 the Department of Justice filed comments with the FCC, in connection with an inquiry involving certification of CATV systems, in which it maintained there was

"a serious danger that the existing local monopoly positions of the telephone companies as communications common carriers may prevent the development of an independent community antenna television industry."

It therefore recommended that the Commission require telephone companies to offer pole space or conduit space to all applicants on equal and nondiscriminatory terms and to forbid them offering CATV service in areas in which they themselves provide telephone service. *Telecommunications Reports* (July 28, 1969), XXXV: 9–10. The Commission adopted the recommendation (note 59, p. 68, above). Obviously there are possible efficiency advantages in permitting phone companies to offer CATV service integrated with their own; and they might have had superior incentives to innovate in this closely related field. The FCC therefore announced that its rule could be waived when, for example in sparsely populated areas, "CATV service would not exist without the affiliation of the telephone company." *Ibid.* But the historical fact is that CATV was pioneered by independent business-

men; and that the telephone companies had it in their power to hamper that competition and take over the business themselves. In these circumstances compulsory coordination may represent the optimum means of achieving the joint goals of efficiency, innovation, and competition.

[156] See Meyer *et al.*, *op. cit.*, 150–155, also 101–110 and Friedlaender, *op. cit.*, 38–43.

[157] The pioneering venture, the "ferry truck" service introduced in 1926 by the Chicago, North Shore & Milwaukee Railroad Company, at first used the traditional commodity rates; but in 1928 it shifted, with some exceptions, to a flat all-merchandise rate. ICC, *Ex Parte No. 230, Substituted Service—Charges and Practices of For-Hire Carriers and Freight Forwarders (Piggyback Service)* (hereinafter, *Ex Parte No. 230*), 322 ICC 301, 305 (1964). Under the so-called Plan I, in which the trucker merely substitutes rail haul on some part of the trip for traffic that he originates and controls, and Plan II, in which the railroad performs the entire service, door-to-door, freight continues to move under the regular tariffs. Under Plans III and IV, in which the rails' open tariffs impose a flat charge, regardless of the contents of the trailers or containers, those flat rates may apply only to mixed carloads; the ordinary rule is that not more than 60 percent of the weight of a total, two-trailer shipment may consist of any one commodity or article. *Ibid.*, 304–305, 311–312, 319, and 379–380.

[158] See pp. 14, 18–24, Chapter 1, above.

and discriminated against the shippers who would still have been subject to the value-of-service pricing that it embodied.[159]

But the 1931 decision could not indefinitely stave off a development that offered such great mutual benefits to the various carriers, not to mention the ultimate customers. In 1954 the ICC liberalized its rules. Thereafter, in the words of the Commission, the growth of piggybacking was "explosive" and its future appeared "almost unlimited."[160]

But the adoption of this extraordinarily promising device was, nevertheless, far too slow, simply because many railroads were unwilling to undertake the necessary cooperation and division of revenues with truckers. The Interstate Commerce Act requires railroads to establish joint rates and through routes with water carriers, but it imposes no such obligation with respect to motor carriers. The ICC therefore took the position that it lacked authority to compel piggybacking. Until 1964, and for the same reason, it took the position, also, that even if a railroad offered piggybacking service under its own open tariffs, it had the right to withhold it from contract or common-carrier truckers.[161]

So the ICC left the development of this promising innovation to the initiative of the railroads and insisted that their concurrence was necessary if truckers were to participate. In these circumstances, the lack of imagination and "intransigence of some railroad management" and the persistence of value of service rates, which failed to pass on to the shipper the cost savings of piggybacking, seriously retarded its utilization.[162] Most of the

---

[159] See the *Doyle Report, op. cit.*, 653–654, which also describes the first liberalization of that rule in 1936, in the case involving *Trucks on Flatcars Between Chicago and Twin Cities*, 216 ICC 435.

[160] In 1955, 32 railroads reported a total of 168,150 TOFC carloadings; in 1963, it was 63 reporting railroads and 797,500 such loadings. ICC, *Ex Parte No. 230*, 322 ICC 301, 309 (1964). By 1966, while the number of participating railroads had dropped to 56, the number of loadings had risen to 1,162,731. Note, "Piggyback Transportation and the ICC," *Southern Cal. Law Rev.* (1968), XLI: 391.

[161] These flat open-tariff rates were offered to private shippers and freight forwarders, who might supply their own trailers or loaded flatcars (under the so-called Plan IV) or use those of the railroads (Plan III), but not to common or contract-carrier truckers. See note 157, above. The Commission felt it could not require that such service be made available to the latter companies, as well, not only because it lacked the requisite authority but also because such arrangements would violate the principle that no person should be both a carrier and a shipper with respect to any given service: the trucking companies would be carriers *vis-à-vis* their shipper-customers and shippers vis-à-vis the railroads. See *American Trucking Associations, Inc., et al. v. Atchison, Topeka & Santa Fe Railway Co. et al.*, 387 U.S. 397, 403, 415 (1967).

[162] The *Doyle Report*, 659, 662–663.

"The end result of all this is that, although coordination has been regarded as vital for well over half a century, most joint rates are still the result of voluntary agreements between carriers and very little coordination exists except between railroad carriers." *Ibid.*, 653.

On the continued use of the traditional rate structures under Plans I and II, see note 157, above. In a sense, the excluded motor carriers also took an obstructionist position. They favored the use of substituted rail for truck service on traffic that they initiated and controlled (Plan I), a procedure that passed none of the cost savings on to shippers; and they opposed giving freight forwarders access to piggyback service, under Plans III and IV. *Ibid.*, 664–665. But this latter position was understandable, in view of the fact that they themselves were excluded from taking advantage of these open rates. More important, the unwillingness of individual truckers to cooperate could not in any event seriously have impeded the development of piggybacking, in view of the large numbers of truckers and the extreme likelihood that, if the option were open to them, at least some would take advantage of it. In contrast, the obstruction of the railroads, which continued to enjoy very substantial monopoly power over the development of the device over their own routes, ensured

growth of this kind of carriage until 1964 was therefore under all-rail rates and rail billings, with the railroads either picking up and delivering in their own trucks (Plan II) or doing the hauling under open tariffs for the account of private shippers or freight forwarders (Plans III and IV). Only in a minority of the cases were they willing to offer the service to contract or common-motor carriers who initiated the traffic and would in this way have shared in the revenues.[163] Without this kind of collaboration the development of piggybacking would always be impeded.

In 1964, finally, the ICC promulgated two important new rules, whose purpose it was to terminate the discriminatory exclusion of for-hire truckers and thereby also to encourage the more widespread utilization of this technique. Its Rule 2 required any railroad offering piggyback service under an open tariff to make it available at the same rate, without discrimination, to all parties, including competing carriers:

"2 *Availability to all of TOFC service*—TOFC service, if offered by a rail carrier through its open-tariff publications, shall be made available to any person at a charge no greater and no less than that received from any other person or persons for doing for him or them a like and contemporaneous service in the transportation of a like kind of traffic under substantially similar circumstances and conditions."

And its Rule 3 authorized regulated carriers to take advantage of this opportunity, that is, to substitute piggybacking for all or any part of whatever transportation service they were authorized to perform:

"3 *Use of open-tariff TOFC service by motor and water carriers in the performance of economically regulated transportation.*

(a) Except as otherwise may be prohibited by these rules, motor common and contract carriers, water common and contract carriers, and freight forwarders may utilize TOFC service in the performance of all or any portion of their authorized service through the use of open-tariff TOFC rates published by a rail carrier."[164]

The Supreme Court, by a 6–3 vote, sustained these rules over the strenuous objections of railroads and freight forwarders and an adverse District Court decision.[165] It upheld Rule 2 on the basis of the fundamental, common-carrier obligation of the railroads to serve all customers ("any person") nondiscriminatorily:

---

its inadequate exploitation. In the mid-1960's, eighty percent of the railroads offering piggyback service offered Plan I. Friedlaender, *op. cit.*, 121 note 37, citing Merrill J. Roberts and Associates, *Intermodal Freight Transportation Coordination: Problems and Potential* (Univ. of Pittsburgh, Graduate School of Business, 1966), 62. Thus, the preponderant system still embodied value of service rate-making, and thereby discouraged the fullest development of piggybacking. It is Plans III and IV that offer the fullest promise of a rational redistribution of the transportation business, and they too continue to be hampered by ICC restrictions (see note 157, above). Friedlaender, *op. cit.*, 120–125.

[163] Ibid., 657; *American Trucking Associations v.* *Atchison, Topeka & Santa Fe Railway Co.*, 387 U.S. 397, 403–404 (1967).

[164] *Ex Parte No. 230*, 322 ICC 301, 336–337 (1964). These rules followed the recommendations of the *Doyle Report*, 667 and also of Meyer, *et al.*:

"the maintenance of equal access for all to the rail piggyback facilities should take precedence over almost all other regulatory objectives." *Op. cit.*, 262–263.

On the other hand, as we shall see, the 1964 rules did not go as far as these authors recommended.

[165] *American Trucking Associations v. Atchison, Topeka & Santa Fe*, 387 U.S. 397 (1967), reversing 244 F. Supp. 955 (1965).

"The fact that the person tendering traffic is a competitor does not permit the railroad to discriminate against him or in his favor."[166]

As for Rule 3, it simply sustained the authority of the Commission, including its right to change its mind:

"in any event, we agree that the Commission, faced with new developments or in light of reconsideration of the relevant facts and its mandate, may alter its past interpretation. ... In fact ... this kind of flexibility and adaptability to changing needs and patterns of transportation is an essential part of the office of a regulatory agency. Regulatory agencies do not establish rules of conduct to last forever; they are supposed, within the limits of the law and of fair and prudent administration, to adapt their rules and practices to the Nation's needs in a volatile, changing economy."[167]

To which the economist can only say amen. As we have amply observed, regulatory commissions do not always justify the broad deference that courts usually accord to their "administrative expertise."

There are at least three reasons why one's rapture over these laudable decisions must be qualified. First, the ICC still lacks the authority to compel railroads to offer piggyback service to truckers; all it has done has been to require them to do so *if* they offer it also to private shippers and freight forwarders, under open tariffs. The rails might presumably respond by withdrawing their TOFC tariffs, in hope of keeping all use of the piggyback device to themselves.[168]

But this danger is probably remote. Practically all of the reporting railroads were offering TOFC service under open tariffs (under Plan III) at the time of the ICC decision[169] and had by this means attracted a very large amount of business from both for-hire truckers and private carriage.[170] It is unlikely that they could do as well if confined to their own limited abilities to perform door-to-door service (under Plan II). Nor is it clear that they would be permitted to discontinue their previous offerings of piggyback services, under the general regulation of abandonments in the Interstate Commerce Act:

"no carrier by railroad subject to this chapter shall abandon all or any portion of a line of railroad, or the operation thereof, unless and until there shall first have been obtained from the Commission a certificate that the present or future public convenience and necessity permit of such abandonment."[171]

---

[166] *Ibid.*, 407. The three dissenting judges "found it impossible," as Justice Harlan put it "to escape the impact" of the following proviso to the statutory prohibition of discrimination:

"*Provided, however*, that this paragraph shall not be construed to apply to discrimination, prejudice, or disadvantage to the traffic of any other carrier of whatever description." *Ibid.*, 422 and 411, quoting from 49 U.S. Code 3 (1).

[167] *Ibid.*, 416.

[168] This is on the assumption that they would still be permitted to offer Plan II, under which the railroad performs the entire service, door-to-door, using its own trucks and trailers, and charging shippers under its ordinary rate schedules. In any event, there is nothing in those rules to require any railroad to offer piggybacking at all, if it chooses not to do so.

[169] 387 U.S. 397, 404 (1967).

[170] *Ex Parte No.* 230, 322 ICC 301, 307–308 (1964).

[171] 49 U.S. Code 18, 1964 ed. This is the judgment of the author of the Note, "Piggyback Transportation and the I.C.C.," *Southern Cal. Law Rev.* (1968), XLI: 400.

The second reservation about the new rules is that they are silent about the level of TOFC rates, on which the rapidity with which this device is adopted heavily depends. It would of course be in the interest of the railroads to fix the rates somewhere between their own marginal costs and the line-haul costs of the motor carriers: if they were any higher, the latter would have no incentive to use the service. But within that range the railroads will have a strong temptation to exploit the monopoly power that they must inevitably continue to possess on this particular mode of transport, because of their cost advantage; any such tendency will necessarily mean that its exploitation will be uneconomically retarded. It is for this reason that Meyer *et al.* qualify their recommendations for substantial deregulation of transportation by calling for retention of regulatory control over maximum TOFC rates, with the strong recommendation that they be held closely to cost.[172]

Finally, the ability of truckers to take full advantage of this new opportunity continues to be restricted by the numerous limitations that the ICC imposes on their routes. In its 1964 decision, thus, the ICC adopted the following rule:

"5 *Circuity limitations.*

(a) Motor and water common carriers shall not participate in joint intermodal TOFC service which is to be provided in lieu of their authorized line-haul transportation . . . where the distance from origin to destination over the route including the TOFC movement is less than 85 percent of the distance between such points over the motor or water carrier's authorized service route; *provided, however,* that the Interstate Commerce Commission may grant relief from the provisions of this paragraph upon consideration of an appropriate petition."[173]

The fear was that without such a restriction motor carriers authorized to operate between two points by a circuitous route might now choose to substitute piggyback service over a more direct route, thus escaping the limitations in their certifications. The rule permits them to cut no more than 15 percent off the distance that their cargoes travel. The restriction is in itself, of course, a ridiculous prohibition of improved efficiency; but it is entirely consistent with, indeed required by, the routing restrictions in the carriers' certificates and the restrictions on competition that it is their purpose to impose.[174] A similar purpose underlay the Commission's rule that

---

172 *Op. cit.,* 247.

173 *Ex Parte No. 230,* 322 ICC 301, 364 (1964).

174 An intriguing illustration of this kind of upside-down economics is provided by the Commission's description of its earlier decision, *Substituted Rail Service by Red Ball Transfer Co.,* 52 MCC 75 (1950) and 303 ICC 421 (1958), in which it had permitted Red Ball to substitute TOFC service on a particular route even though the rail route was somewhat shorter than its authorized highway route between Chicago and Kansas City, because

"it was found that using TOFC service would not enable Red Ball to provide an improved service and would not affect its competitive situation vis-à-vis motor carriers authorized to operate

directly between Chicago and Kansas City." *Ex Parte No. 230,* 322 ICC 301, 361–362 (1964).

The ICC explains this restriction in terms of its general policies in enforcing the Motor Carriers Act of 1935:

"To allow carriers to ignore the routing and gateway limitations in their operating authorities and to provide service between any points they serve, no matter how indirect their authorized operations, would be to allow them to provide totally new services for which no public need had been established, and would largely negate the certificate and permit requirements of the act. . . . It is obvious that this result would obtain from the indiscriminate substitution of direct TOFC service for indirect all-motor service." *Ibid.*

truckers and water carriers could put their trailers on rail flat cars and take them off only at geographic points that they were actually certificated to serve, thereby overriding the sensible suggestion of the Eastern railroads that it would suffice merely to require that motor carriers possess the authority for the entire freight movement from origin to destination:

> "4(d) Carriers participating in joint intermodal TOFC service shall interchange traffic only at a common point of service."

> "3(e) Motor and water common and contract carriers utilizing open-tariff TOFC service in the performance of authorized transportation shall tender traffic to and receive traffic from rail carriers only at points which the motor and water carriers are authorized to serve."[175]

Despite these reservations, the new ICC rules governing piggybacking should provide an important stimulus to intermodal cooperation consistent with the preservation of competition.

Power Pooling

The numerous power pooling and interconnection arrangements in which the majority of the country's electrical systems now participate likewise provide illustrations of the twin dangers of intercompany coordination: that the parties will cooperate too well and that they will do so too little, or with excessive selectivity.

In the typical power pool—in contrast with the simple purchase agreements by which the majority of the country's small distribution systems obtain their energy requirements—the collaborators are large, integrated private companies; they engage in the generation and transmission as well as local distribution of electricity. This is understandable, in view of the fact that very few of the pools involve complete integration of all the systems in an area: since most of them involve simpler *interchanges* of power between the partners, the participants tend to be companies that have something to exchange with one another, with a rough equivalence of contributions and benefits. There is no published study of the extent to which agreements have attached to them explicit provisions restricting competition among the partners. They could be rare: these companies for the most part stay within their respective service areas anyhow.[176]

On the other hand where there is competition, actual or potential, between participants in pools—or in simple purchase and sales agreements—there is a strong temptation for the participants to attach conditions that limit it.

> "When systems from different segments of the industry attempt to organize

---

[175] *Ibid.*, 355.

[176] "Unquestionably the development of rate-making standards has tended to suppress competition for new service areas between investor-owned companies. The identity of cost characteristics, plus such rate-making, cast a serious damper on reaching for load by seeking to extend its service area boundaries. There is also greater recognition of the higher costs and the chaos which would be involved in the unlimited duplication of facilities. . . . [M]utual respect by investor-owned companies of their respective service area boundaries—even where ill-defined or where one company is large and the other small—is the rule, rather than the exception." Federal Power Commission, Report of the Legal Advisory Committee, *National Power Survey*, 1964, II: 366.

The Carva pool (which covers Virginia and the Carolinas) is, however, reported to have some such provision, to the effect that each member will refrain from using the joint facilities in a way adverse to the interests of any of the others.

a pool . . . all such systems may want to reach one or more formal agreements which have the effect of eliminating competition for loads. This is particularly the case wherever there is the possibility that a participant who is also a competitor may use the advantages derived from a pooling arrangement to undercut and take over the present or potential customers of one or more other participants. In such circumstances, there will necessarily be a hesitancy to enter into such a pooling arrangement unless there is assurance that it will not worsen established competitive positions."[177]

Restrictions cf this kind are, thus, said to be prevalent in the very numerous contracts for the wholesale supply of power to municipal (that is, municipally owned) and cooperative distributors.[178] In such cases the seller, typically a large, integrated private company, imposes some such condition as that the buyer will confine its sales to a particular geographic area, or will not solicit the business of other wholesale customers of the supplying company, or simply will not resell any of the power at wholesale.[179]

The extent to which restrictions such as these are subject to the antitrust laws is still in large measure an open question that we cannot fully explore here. They certainly could be. In the *Pennsylvania Water* case, a Circuit Court of Appeals invalidated under the antitrust laws a division of markets agreement between integrated private utility companies incident to a power pooling arrangement.[180] In 1968, the Department of Justice filed a civil antitrust suit against two members of the Florida Power Interchange Pool, the Tampa Electric Company and the Florida Power Corporation, charging that they had conspired to divide up their respective geographic markets and consequently refrained from soliciting wholesale customers in each other's territory, in violation of the Sherman Act.[181] Representatives of the industry and the Federal Power Commission itself have in recent years supported bills introduced in Congress to give the Commission the power, which it does not now have, to exempt such restrictive arrangements from the antitrust laws.[182] In the absence of an explicit exemption, the legality of these restrictions would hinge on whether they might be found reasonably ancillary to (subsidiary to and necessary for the effectuation of) the power pooling arrangement, which is not itself illegal. The Department of Justice has been skeptical that they are: Donald Turner, the Assistant Attorney General in charge of the Antitrust Division, testified in opposition to the

---

[177] *Ibid.*, 367.

[178] This is felt to be particularly necessary in the case of the rural cooperatives, since these distributors are not typically confined to a specified service area.

[179] See, for example, the proceeding in which the Federal Power Commission disallowed a provision in the wholesale power supply contracts of the Georgia Power Company with its municipal customers, setting a limit to the amount of power that the latter could sell to any industrial companies within their franchised areas. *Georgia Power Company v. Federal Power Commission*, 373 F. 2d 485 (1967). See also *U.S. v. Northern Natural Gas Co.*, Civil No. 5–70–20, U.S. District Ct., District of Minnesota, Fifth Division, Stipulation,

March 31, 1970.

[180] *Pennsylvania Water & Power Company v. Consolidated Gas, Electric Light & Power Company*, 184 F. 2d 552 (1950). See, however, the subsequent history of that arrangement in *Pennsylvania Water & Power Co. v. Federal Power Commission*, 343 U.S. 414 (1952).

[181] Civil Action No. 68–297 CIV.-T., U.S. District Court, Middle Dist. of Florida, Complaint, July 8, 1968.

[182] See, for example, U.S. Senate, Committee on Commerce, *Amendment to Federal Power Act (Antitrust Review)*, *Hearing* on S3136, Serial No. 89–71, July 12–13, 1966. The same bill was reintroduced in the subsequent, 88th Congress (S683).

bill in question, pointing to the widespread adoption of pooling in preceding years without need for explicit exemption from the antitrust laws.[183] And so, apparently, is the FPC itself, at least as far as some of the more flagrant restrictions on competition are concerned.[184] In the absence of any such justification, it would seem that any agreement among pooling partners to stay out of each other's markets would be *per se* illegal under the antitrust laws. Moreover, recent decisions by the United States Supreme Court cast considerable doubt on the legality of restrictions on resale of wholesale power, even when not adopted collusively but imposed by a single supplying company.[185]

The other, and even more controversial, competitive issue has to do with the general tendency of the major pools to exclude from membership smaller, generally less fully integrated distribution companies—and particularly cooperative (coops) and municipally owned distributors ("munis"). As pooling has made possible the construction of larger and larger generating plants, with progressively lower unit costs, access to their supplies on terms not markedly inferior to those enjoyed by the pool participants themselves has become a matter of life or death to these distribution companies, who either lack generating facilities of their own entirely or whose facilities, smaller in scale, are at a progressive cost disadvantage. What is really at stake is the availability of supplies from the pooled facilities to these firms— their ability to purchase them and to have them transmitted ("wheeled") over the lines of the pool members—and the price they have to pay. The excluded companies have generally argued that only membership in the pool gives them the kind of assurance of equal and nondiscriminatory treatment that they require.[186]

The same kind of problem can arise even in the absence of pooling. A large integrated company could conceivably refuse to supply the needs of a local distributor or to "wheel" for it power purchased from some third party. Unless these transactions are effectively regulated, the big private systems that control transmission facilities adjacent to the coops and munis have power over the latter's very survival. Except in those areas in which federally generated electricity, to which they have statutorily preferential access, is available, the small distribution companies can typically hope to obtain economical supplies only from the big private companies. And since such a

---

[183] *Ibid.*, 57–71.

[184] See the reference to the *Georgia Power* case, note 179, above.

[185] See *U.S. v. Arnold, Schwinn & Co. et al.*, 388 U.S. 365 (1967).

[186] See, for example, Joseph A. Ruskay, "Power Play in the Electric Industry: Breaking the 'Birch Rod,'" *The New Leader*, Oct. 9, 1967, 16, describing "the ruthlessness displayed by the private utility combine trying to freeze out the municipal electric companies from access to low-cost, bulk . . . energy. . . ." Also Alex Radin, "The Role of Public Power in a Modern National Power Policy," paper presented at Fall Conference, Federal Bar Ass'n, Committee on Federal Utility and Power Law, October 16, 1967 (mimeo.). Radin emphasizes the advantages conferred by active participation in planning the installation of new facilities. The member

"is in a better position to know what opportunities are available to it and to propose a course of action which will serve its needs. . . . [A] utility which is privy to regional planning will usually have a better knowledge of where power might be bought and . . . sold. . . . [I]t will be able to propose changes in the design and location of the lines to its advantage, and it can more efficiently develop its own transmission system and schedule the installation of generation." *Ibid.*, 32.

company will usually refuse to wheel power from competing sources to whole-sale purchasers within its area, the latter will typically have only one large supplier from whom they can buy. It is this kind of situation that gives point to the authority asserted by the FPC to force the large private companies to interconnect and supply power to smaller distributors, and to fix the prices on these sales.[187] The great economies of scale in generation and transmission, and the control of transmission systems in each area by one or a few large private companies, together confer the same sort of power over the survival of nonintegrated competitors as did control over crude-oil pipelines by large, vertically integrated petroleum refining companies. In the latter case the remedy was amendment of the Interstate Commerce Act to make crude-oil pipelines common carriers and—after a long delay—effective ICC regulation of their rates and conditions of access.[188] As the oil experience suggests, one possible approach to protecting the competitive survival of the nonintegrated electricity distribution companies is to impose common-carrier status on the privately owned transmission lines.[189] The same result would in effect be accomplished in cases of pooling by seeing to it that the smaller companies were admitted to full membership.

The related issues of compulsory interconnection, wheeling, and the membership in power pools illustrate with great clarity the numerous facets of the question of the appropriate role of competition in the regulated in-dustries, and the differences between the competitive and the regulated chosen instrument approach to the organization and control of industry. Consider the following composite outline of the responses that integrated private companies make to the foregoing statement of problems, along with our commentary on those responses:

1. Competition between electric systems is of minor importance and

---

[187] The antitrust laws too may be applicable in such situations. See the summary of the Depart-ment of Justice 1969 complaint against the Otter Tail Power Co., note 60, p. 68, above.
[188] See Roy A. Prewitt, "The Operation and Regulation of Crude Oil and Gasoline Pipe-lines," *Q. Jour. Econ.* (February 1942), LVI: 177–211; Eugene V. Rostow, *A National Policy for the Oil Industry* (New Haven: Yale Univ. Press, 1948), 57–66; de Chazeau and Kahn, *op. cit.*, 116–117, 332–341, 512–515; and George S. Wolbert, *American Pipelines* (Norman: Univ. of Oklahoma Press, 1952).
[189] See also note 192, below. The FPC has concluded that it has no such authority at present under its limited powers to require interconnection and service under Section 202(b) of the Federal Power Act (see pp. 75–76, Chapter 2, above). Following the instruc-tion of *City of Paris, Kentucky v. Federal Power Commission*, 399 F. 2d 983 (1968), it concluded:

"If wheeling means the obligation of one public utility to make its transmission facilities available to 'facilitate' a power supply contract between two other unconnected electric companies, and nothing more, we think the Commission *lacks*

the power to order it. . . ." *City of Paris, Kentucky v. Kentucky Utilities Company*, Opinion and Order on Remand, 41 FPC 45, 49 (1969).

The case arose out of a supply contract between the City of Paris and the East Kentucky Rural Electric Cooperative Corporation, in conse-quence of which the City asked the FPC to require the Kentucky Utilities Company to transmit the power for it. Instead, the Commis-sion approved a rate filing under which Ken-tucky Utilities would supply Paris directly.

Another possible solution to this particular problem—even farther beyond the FPC's statutory mandate—would be to divorce electri-city generation and distribution, and to require the generating company or companies to serve all distributors nondiscriminatorily at cost-related rates. See the discussion at p. 74, Chapter 2, above. The proposals of the Department of Justice and FCC to force common carrier status on CATV systems are based on the same reasoning. See note 114, pp. 43–44, and note 122, p. 45, above; and *Comments of the United States Department of Justice* in FCC Docket No. 18397, September 5, 1969 (mimeo.), 5–6.

should in any event not be encouraged because it leads to wasteful duplication of facilities.[190]

It must be conceded that direct competition among electric companies is, indeed, quite limited; states rarely license more than one company to serve a particular locality or area. At the same time, as the restrictive provisions themselves suggest, there are certain areas and kinds of competition that could be significantly affected.

a. While most distribution companies typically stay within their own exclusive areas, this is not true of coops in most states. With the expansion of suburbs into previously rural areas, in consequence, the coops and the private companies frequently come into competition for new customers.[191] Is this kind of competition socially desirable? Large-scale duplication of distribution facilities would be inefficient. But rivalry at the edges of service areas, to determine which company is to take over a particular overlapping or adjacent market, could avoid serious inefficiency and at the same time, provided regulatory commissions were careful to prevent its taking the form of highly selective and local price cutting, could usefully exert considerable pressure on the affected companies to perform well for all their customers.

b. There is competition between separate utility systems to induce large industrial customers to locate in their respective territories, although its prevalence is disputed.

c. The very technological advances that have made wider and wider pooling desirable have also increased the likelihood of competition in wholesale power markets—by making it economical for distribution systems and companies with surplus generating capacity to reach out farther and farther, the one for supplies, the other for customers. The conception that freer competition should be permitted to prevail in wholesale markets clashes with the reliance on regulated chosen instruments: the latter model would emphasize the greater efficiency and opportunity for long-term investment planning if distributors obtain their wholesale energy under long-term contracts from a neighboring major integrated company, protected not by competition but by commission regulation of the wholesale price. Clearly, if the former conception is to prevail, compulsory wheeling or a common-carrier transmission system is a necessary part of the arrangement.[192] The issue is clearly joined,

---

[190] It is a possible defense to an antitrust proceeding against restrictive agreements that there was no competition for them to have suppressed. But where that was the clear purpose of the agreement, as in the case of simple price fixing or division of markets, the courts are likely to infer the necessary anticompetitive effect from the nature of the agreement itself: why would the parties take the trouble to enter into covenants like these if they did not fear that competition might otherwise break out between them?

[191] See "Competition for Loads between neighboring utility systems," FPC, *National Power Survey*, 1964, Vol. II, 366–367.

[192] The more efficient alternative might be the one already mentioned (note 189, above)—divestiture of distribution and transmission, leaving the latter function to be performed, nondiscriminatorily for all comers, by nonintegrated common carriers. If the duplication of transmission facilities that would otherwise be necessary to create a competitive wholesale power market, in which power could be drawn from a variety of suppliers in various locations, would be inefficient, the obvious answer is that transmission is a natural monopoly and should be performed by regulated common carriers.

therefore, with respect to the sufficiency of regulated monopoly as a device for insuring optimum performance.

d. Yardstick competition. This is of course the principal kind of rivalry between the government–owned, cooperative, and privately owned utility system. It is a competition by example: each company is concerned that the way in which it treats its own customers compares favorably with the corresponding performance of its rivals, in the hope of a favorable political decision whenever the question arises of which kind of utility system is to be certificated for future service areas, or to serve the expanding needs or indeed the present requirements of existing ones. The competition is, in a sense, unfair; the public and coop "yardstick" is not a true measure of the achievable performance of private companies because the former pay less taxes and obtain their capital on more favorable terms; on the other hand, many of them suffer offsetting disadvantages from the smaller scale of their generating operations and their dependence on private companies for much of their energy. The rivalry is nevertheless real and has made an important positive contribution—Richard Hellman would say, far greater than regulation—to the improved performance of the electric industries.[193]

2. It is unfair to force private companies to share the benefits of their efficiency with competitors, and particularly with competitors that enjoy the unfair tax and capital cost advantages referred to above.

This is not an economic argument and will therefore not detain us long. The companies are franchised monopolists, enjoying valuable governmentally conferred privileges. Society has the right and duty to impose such corresponding obligations as it sees fit, as long as investors are then free to refuse the entire bargain. One economically justified obligation, in the presence of monopoly, is the acceptance of common-carrier obligations. Where, moreover, the companies achieve lower costs by collaboration in a pool, the issue is no longer one of depriving *individual* competitors of whatever advantages they may have achieved by their own prudence and efficiency but one of preventing a group of firms, by *combination*, from achieving decisive advantage over excluded rivals. It is an established antitrust principle that such combinations may not deny disadvantaged competitors access to those same opportunities on nondiscriminatory terms.[194] The only relevant question would be whether the imposition of such requirements and the prohibition of anticompetitive covenants would seriously diminish the incentive of the private companies to enter pools and avail themselves of these important economies.

3. It makes no sense to admit customers to membership in pools. This is, indeed, a puzzling and complex aspect of the issue. Power exchanges and pools are arrangements in which two or more similar companies, each with something to contribute, enter into a joint venture. In varying degrees they "pool" their generating facilities as well as their

---

[193] See pp. 104–106, Chapter 3, above.
[194] *U.S. v. The Terminal Railroad Ass'n*, 224 U.S.
383 (1912); *Associated Press v. United States*, 326 U.S. 1 (1945).

requirements; they integrate their capital investments in generation and transmission as well as distribution. Each supplies reserve capacity that becomes available to the other in case of need; and both benefit from the resultant reduction in their combined reserve requirement. And they distribute the benefits to members in rough proportionality to their respective contributions. They provide for money payments only to the extent that there is a "balance of trade" in one direction or another—that is, when an individual member's flows of benefits and costs are unequal.[195]

Most municipalities, in contrast, have no generating capacity at all. Many or most of the remaining ones have only very high-cost generation facilities, access to which is of little or no benefit to the other members. Their interests and contributions are those only of buyers or customers, not of full participants in the pool.[196]

On the other hand, it must be recognized that as pools become more and more intensely integrated, and cover wider and wider areas, these same observations apply in increasing measure to all of their members. The contribution of each becomes decreasingly important relative to the size required to take full advantage of the available economies of scale; that is the reason for pooling in the first place. And—particularly when pools begin to make joint investments in additional facilities—all of the members may properly be regarded as contributors of capital on the one hand and customers on the other; possession of one's own generating facilities becomes a less and less relevant qualification for membership. Where excluded distribution companies have the legal authority to invest in generating facilities (and many do not), it is not clear why each dollar that they contribute to the joint investments represents any less of a contribution to the total benefits of scale economies than each dollar put in by their larger rivals.[197]

---

[195] See Abraham Gerber, "Power Pools and Joint Plant Ownership," *Public Utilities Fortnightly*, September 12, 1968, especially pp. 6–7.

[196] *Ibid.*, 7–10.

[197] See Roland W. Donnem, "Antitrust Aspects of Establishing Nuclear and Other Large-Scale Electricity Generation Facilities," an address before the Atomic Energy Committee, Federal Bar Ass'n, processed, Washington, October 15, 1969, 17 and, for a good survey of the subject, *passim*. In pools in which the members take turns in constructing plants, it would seem possible for the municipal companies to form a group to build a facility of economical size when their turn comes around. These considerations do not exclude the desirability of taking into account the varying contributions of the members of the pool in the apportionment of charges and joint benefits. Charles R. Ross, a former Federal Power Commissioner and a strong proponent of "the absolute necessity for small municipal systems to join the parade and become participants of the newly forming bulk power supply pools" and of "the requirement that membership to all pools be non-discriminatory," nevertheless concedes that non-discriminatory rules might provide for differential sharing of benefits in reflection of different contributions.

"I would be remiss, however, if I failed to point out that the basic principles of economics will have to be recognized in setting the ground rules of the pool agreements. In other words, some of the more well-endowed participants may be able to do better because of their contributions to the pool, such as lower-cost units, better types of load, etc. While this may be the case and a free ride is prohibited, nevertheless, the same general rules should apply to everyone." "Bulk Power Supply for Small Systems," an address before the 24th American Public Power Ass'n Conference, May 9, 1967 (mimeo.), 3–4.

In addition, the larger members typically provide back-up capacity for emergencies; smaller participants that made no such contribution ought clearly to bear their proper share of the costs. See note 200, below.

What then of municipal distributors who are not permitted to own their own generation capacity; if they too must be permitted equal access to membership in pools, why might not large private customers also request the privilege? The answer would seem to be that the distributors, even if nonintegrated, are also competitors or potential competitors of the pool members. If we would rely partly on their competition as a guarantor of good public utility performance, it may be necessary, in recognition of the ambivalent role they play, to treat them differently from other, possibly equally large customers.

4. The issue is really only one of proper public utility rate structures. What the small distribution companies want is to get their power at rates comparable with the costs borne by the pool members. The new pooled facilities may be expected to have lower average total costs than the entire systems of the separate integrated companies on whom the distributors depend for supplies.[198] Presumably the members of the pool obtain this incremental power at those lower costs; but they must recoup the higher average costs of their entire systems from their customers. If the small distributors were to obtain membership and then take all their power from the pool, they might end up getting their entire power supply at average costs lower than their competitors and former suppliers. It makes no economic sense to permit customers who happen to obtain all their supplies from a new facility lower rates than customers that happen to be served by a mixture of new and old facilities.[199] And it would constitute an inacceptable form of cream-skimming, subsidized competition for such customers—or pool members—who did not supply reserve, back-up generating and transmission capacity to obtain the same favorable rates as other members who bore those additional costs.[200] If, then, membership in the pool does not solve the question of the appropriate cost of power to the municipal companies, relative to the total costs borne by their private integrated competitors, it remains unclear why membership is so important, and why the problem could not equally be solved by effective FPC regulation of the wholesale rates charged by pool members to nonmember distribution companies. Even if the latter were members, they would in effect have to be charged rates that covered the costs of providing some of the benefits contributed by the other members and not by them.

[198] This is indeed the common assumption. None of the commentators seems to have explicitly raised the question of why this should normally be so—why ATC_o should be higher than ATC_n —unless the old plant is chronically under-depreciated. See pp. 118–121, Volume 1, above. One possibility is the necessity of keeping older capacity available in reserve, against the possibility of outages. These plants could well have average variable costs in excess of the ATC of new plants *when fully utilized*, but still have value for occasional use, at times of peak demand (see pp. 97–98, Volume 1) or in emergencies when the marginal opportunity cost of current rises sharply.

[199] Donnem suggests that the small distribution companies are entitled simply to the same oppor-

tunities to get the low-cost power as the larger participants—for existing requirements or only for additional needs, for example, depending on how the latter are served. *Op. cit.,* 13.

[200] See the discussion of this problem in the case of alleged cream-skimming at pp. 238–239, Chapter 5, above. Differential charges for reasons of this kind would be entirely compatible with the recommendations of both Donnem and Ross (notes 197 and 199, above). See also Gerber, *op. cit.,* 10 and *passim.* This is one major outstanding issue in the *Gainesville* case (note 85, p. 76, above), which the Supreme Court agreed in October of 1970 to hear: is the Florida Power Co. entitled to charge Gainesville a portion of the fixed costs of maintaining reserve generating capacity?

5. In the last analysis, then, the issue is one of the effectiveness and adequacy of regulation. In principle, it would appear that there is nothing that membership in pools could contribute to giving munis and coops a fair competitive opportunity that could not be ensured also by effective FPC regulation.[201] The fact remains that it has been only in the last several years that the Commission has been vigorously asserting its authority over wholesale rates generally and compelling private integrated companies to interconnect with and supply smaller distributor-competitors. And as it has done so the private sector of the industry has importuned Congress to stop it.[202] It is obviously disingenuous for the private companies to argue on the one hand for the exclusion of the distributors from pools on the ground that they can receive all the reliability of service and protection with respect to price that they need from effective FPC regulation of wholesale sales, and at the same time to press for diminution of the Commission's authority over those sales.

In the last analysis, the issue is an institutional one and cannot be resolved in terms of economic principles. In fact such competition as exists—including the peculiar, essentially political competition of publicly owned "yardsticks" —does play an important role in exerting pressures on regulated monopolists to improve their performance; thus it becomes an important part of the task of public policy to keep it as effective as possible. This is the case for insisting on pool membership on reasonable and nondiscriminatory terms for companies now excluded, rather than relying completely on the regulated chosen-instrument device as the sole means of assuring efficient public service.[203]

But at a minimum it is the case for retaining in the FPC effective authority over wholesale power sales and rates. This is the real significance of the *City of Colton* and *Shrewsbury* decisions (notes 71, p. 30, and 85, p.75, above)— not so much that they make regulation of monopoly itself more effective, but that they make it possible to employ *regulation* to preserve the most effective *competition* possible in this industry—by guaranteeing municipal distributors and coops access to low-cost, pooled power at minimum rates.[204]

---

[201] See, however, note 186, above.

[202] See note 71, p. 30, Chapter 1 and pp. 75–76, Chapter 2, above. So Commissioner Ross urged the municipal power systems to support FPC authority to control the terms of wholesale power contracts,

"We won't be able to make that promise, however, if certain proposals to limit our jurisdiction are successful. Here again, we need your help." *Op. cit.*, 8–9.

On the resistance of the private companies to the extension of FPC authority, see Lister and Homan, *op. cit.*, IV, 2/23–2/25. On the Holland-Smathers Bill, to reduce the Commission's authority on primarily intrastate electric operations see U.S. Senate, Committee on Commerce, *Exemption of Certain Public Utilities from Federal Power Commission Jurisdiction, Hearings* on S. 218,

89th Cong. 1st Sess., Serial No. 89–38, May–June, 1965.

[203] See the similar reasoning of the Circuit Court of Appeals in *Municipal Electric Association of Massachusetts, et. al. v. Securities and Exchange Commission, Respondent, Vermont Yankee Nuclear Power Corporation, et. al, Intervenors*, March 26, 1969.

[204] This point is made forcefully by Hellman, who, as we have seen in Chapter 3, is a leading exponent of the view that government competition is the instrument on which we must place major reliance for assuring the best possible economic performance in this industry. He quotes Alex Radin, general manager of the American Public Power Association, on the ways in which the Association has taken advantage of these decisions, by showing their members when the price they pay for power is excessive and

The clearest summary of the case for this use of regulation to protect and promote competition is provided by the following two representative selections from the testimony, the first in opposition, the second in favor, on the Smathers-Holland bill, which would have at least partially reversed *City of Colton* and *Shrewsbury* by shifting jurisdiction partially to the States. They provide a fitting summary of these last three chapters, whose concern has been the proper role and definition of competition—and therefore also of regulation—in the regulated industries:

> "the Sterling Municipal Electric Light Department testified that the Shrewsbury case in which the FPC ordered a lower wholesale rate to a municipality 'was the first price breakthrough that municipal plants in Massachusetts have ever had. Immediately following ... practically every municipal plant was approached by their supplier and offered a lower rate. ... We firmly believe that FPC is the best court of appeals that wholesale purchasers of electricity like ourselves have available.' "

And

> "Edwin L. Mason, chairman of the Florida commission and a ... [supporter of] S.218: 'The best regulation is very little regulation. This has been proven throughout the history of our country—the best regulation is little or no regulation.' ... Asked by Sen. Bass how cost to the consumer could be regulated when the Florida commission had no jurisdiction over sales to municipality or REC, Mr. Mason replied: 'This is as I say an arm's length transaction between the municipality and the company.' Sen. Bass: 'That is a long arm. ... What you are saying is that you have no jurisdiction and you don't want the FPC to have any jurisdiction?' Mr. Mason: 'That is correct.' "[205]

---

urging them to lodge complaints with the FPC. *Government Competition*, 59–60. His summary of the arguments for and against the Smathers-Holland Bill (note 202, above) is worth reproducing:

"Those for S.218 argued that the State commissions are effective . . . . *Colton* is said to produce duplication between Federal and State jurisdictions, and confusion. It is characterized as an FPC power grab. It was predicted that *Colton* will lead to public ownership.

"The key issue presented by S.218 according to Chairman Swidler of the FPC, is the survival of small and medium-sized municipal and REC [Rural Electric Coop] power systems. They depend on rate regulation under the Federal Power Act which he said the bill would 'destroy.' The companies for the bill, he declared, 'believe they have acquired a vested interest in non-regulation, and they want to preserve it.' Witnesses from the 'grass roots' characterized the State commissions as being ineffective usually and often friendly to companies. The only recourses of municipal and REC systems from company monopoly of wholesale power supply they testified, have been government competition,

and now the FPC. *Colton*, it was said, did not create regulatory duplication, and the jurisdiction to be removed from FPC by S.218 could not be exercised by the States.

"In the final analysis, what were the companies fighting through S.218? It was not regulation as such, for they have fully subscribed to the theory of the regulated natural monopoly. Why are they against FPC regulation of wholesale power rates, particularly after 1961? The answer . . . is that the companies are against regulation that is effective. Conversely, they favor the State commissions because they are inadequate. This is consistent with their actions and attitudes since 1905." *Ibid.*, 61–62.

The reference to 1961 is to the appointment that year of Joseph C. Swidler as the new Chairman of the FPC; thereafter the Commission began aggressively to assert its jurisdiction over wholesale rates.

Hellman cites the hearings on the Bill as having established that it was drafted by representatives of the private power companies.
[205] As reproduced *ibid.*, 99/10–99/12, notes 91b, 91i.

CHAPTER 7

The Institution of Regulated Monopoly: Reprise

Such are the major issues involved in trying to fashion institutional mechanisms for controlling the performance of industries for which competition seems an inappropriate regulator.

Integration, Coordination, and Competition as Partial Alternatives

Manifestly, financial integration, cooperation between separate companies, and freer competition are in large measure alternatives to one another. The first, by eliminating most of the obstacles to wholehearted collaboration between the parties joined together, offers the possibility of important gains in efficiency and innovation. Like interfirm cooperation, therefore, it may make for more effective competition. On the other hand, where associated with substantial monopoly power, it can in other ways seriously weaken the competitive regulator, first, by suppressing potential competition between the functions or modes it joins together and, second, by creating obstacles to the rivalry of outside parties. And competition itself can achieve many of the same benefits as integration without involving those dangers: if it is able to operate, it can produce the socially most efficient distribution of business among the various alternative media as well as supply powerful stimuli to dynamic improvements in efficiency and service.

But the three devices are far from perfect substitutes; and they are not mutually exclusive. The problem of social engineering is to devise the optimum combination of all three, as well as of direct regulation. And of course there are all kinds of regulation possible—of entry but not price (as in broadcasting and most instances of occupational licensure), or of price but not entry (as in oil and other cartels), private price-fixing but not public (as in maritime shipping or, until recently, stock brokerage commission rates), with or without the power to compel intercompany connection and coordination, and so on.

There is no single optimum pattern or combination for all situations. In the case of transportation, we tentatively concluded that the benefits of conglomerate integration outweighed the dangers—provided those dangers are also forestalled, as much as possible, by compelling integrated companies to coordinate their facilities and operations, on nondiscriminatory and closely regulated terms, with their nonintegrated competitors. But we recognized that the massive horizontal and geographic merger movement in railroading might already have tipped the balance the other way. In power pooling, too, it could well be that closer financial integration is once again appropriate, because of the new technology of electric generation and transmission. But it, too, must be subject to regulatory safeguards, not only against the abuses that led to the downfall of the public utility holding company but also in order to protect the competitive opportunities of nonintegrated companies. Conceivably, only vertical separation of electricity generation and transmission on the one hand from distribution on the other can provide the optimum balance. In communications, the case for unified control and centralized responsibility for the operation of the national switched network seems still secure. But it, too, is subject to the qualification of the need for freer entry in some markets, for a more fully guaranteed direct access to the ultimate consumer by the revolutionary new devices of the satellite, microwave transmission and CATV, and by a requirement that the monopolist operator of the switched network interconnect with other communications systems and with customer-purchased equipment, subject to proper safeguards. Here, as in transportation, freer price competition seems both possible and desirable—but must be subject to regulatory safeguards.

And many of the direct benefits promised by integration can in fact be achieved by freer competition. Airline companies can make fuller use of expensive equipment, in season and out, by merging or by interchange of equipment. But they can achieve it also by greater freedom of entry into different routes, with different seasonal patterns: if the carrier with a heavy investment in large, jet airplanes to serve the New York to Miami route in the winter were free to shift to the transatlantic routes in the summer, it would have far less need of joining with other companies in order to make the most efficient use of its equipment. Nothing could better promote a more efficient distribution of the transportation business than freer price competition.

But there is no point in attempting further summary. Two conclusions seem clearly to emerge. First, that competition has a vital role to play in the public utility industries. And, second, the proper balance between competition and monopoly, financial integration and intercompany coordination, voluntary and compulsory, will vary from one regulatory situation to the next and from one moment to the next—and must be the subject of constant regulatory attention and concern.

The Imperfections of Regulated Monopoly

Regulated monopoly is a very imperfect instrument for doing the world's work. It suffers from the evils of monopoly itself—the danger of exploitation, aggressively or by inertia, the absence of pervasive external restraints and stimuli to aggressive, efficient and innovative performance. Regulation itself tends inherently to be protective of monopoly, passive, negative, and unimaginative. The concentration by commissions on the rate base and rate of return has been far disproportionate to their importance compared with other dimensions of performance, has weakened incentive, and introduced distortions. Regulation is ill-equipped to treat the more important aspects of performance—efficiency, service innovation, risk taking, and probing the elasticity of demand. Herein lies the great attraction of competition: it supplies the direct spur and the market test of performance.

The possibility is by no means excluded that on balance regulation does more harm than good, or that such good as it does is not worth the cost. Against the limited gains from a control directed primarily at cutting a few points off the profit rate must be weighed the restrictions on competition with which it is typically associated—not to mention the direct costs of the regulatory process itself, which may run on the order of $1 billion annually.[1]

One inherent weakness of regulation is its inescapable involvement with the political process. It is an interesting exercise to try to discern the ways in which regulatory policy at the national level may be changed by the entry of the Nixon Administration. What will become of the new activism of the FPC, as demonstrated in its *Shrewsbury* decision, *National Power Survey*, or new-found energy in regulating the field price of natural gas? Will the spurt of initiative shown by the FCC in 1969 with respect to radio and television[2] subside, or give way to a more careful scrutiny of the way in which the networks permit commentary on the President's speeches? Again, the basic evil in transportation is not the policy of the ICC but the even balance of powerful interest groups that perpetually defeats effective reform.

This suggests in a way that the imperfections of regulation are inherent defects not of the institution itself but of the political process. Consider, for example, the mundane question of the salaries, prestige, and competence of the regulatory personnel and the adequacy of their budgetary support. Manifestly, elaboration of all the "correct" regulatory principles is of little avail if their interpretation and application are to be entrusted to incompetent and inadequately financed commissioners.[3] It should be clear from these volumes that the principles are far from clear-cut or self-enforcing, but require instead the exercise of the most complex judgments, both of economic analysis and in the reconciliation of economic and noneconomic objectives.

How well the regulation is actually performed, in practice, will depend, in the last analysis, on the fundamental factors that determine the distribution of political power in modern capitalism. This may seem a long jump in

---

[1] For a full—some will feel overly so—and powerful elaboration of this entire argument see Posner, *op. cit.* See also the discussion at pp. 108–112, Chapter 3, above.

[2] See pp. 89–90, Chapter 2, above.

[3] In February of 1969, the Subcommittee on Intergovernmental Relations of the Committee on Government Operations of the U.S. Senate began hearings on the "Utility Consumers' Counsel Act of 1969" (S.607), sponsored by Senator Metcalf. Information gathered by the Subcommittee showed that more than half of the state regulatory agencies had between zero and two lawyers and rate analysts; that 20 had only one or two accountants; that 26 did not have a

securities analyst. A witness from Massachusetts described the responsibilities, staff and compensation of that state's Department of Public Utilities chief accountant, who is also a lawyer and who supervises the examination and audit of the accounting returns filed by 14 electric, 26 gas, 6 phone, 63 water companies, 88 bus and streetcar lines, 816 securities brokers, 2,599 moving firms and 15,055 truck carriers. For this work, he has a staff consisting of one other accountant and a clerk, and his own salary, after 22 years with the department, was $11,752 a year. "Senators Probe Power Rates," *The Washington Post*, April 13, 1969, F 1, 3.

logic—from the salaries of commission staff to the fundamental characteristics of modern capitalism—but it is a direct one. For what we are dealing with is a peculiar institution of American society, the private ownership and management of monopoly in essential industries—a combination of circumstances that leads typically to socialization abroad—subject to governmental regulation. The regulatory power is in principle virtually unlimited. How vigorously and intelligently it will be exercised (and the rate of pay, financial support, and quality of administrative personnel is obviously one aspect of this same phenomenon) will depend on the basically political question of how power is distributed between producer and consumer interests, between public officials and private managers, and how aggressive are the interventions of public officials in asserting their conception of the public interest. These determining conditions will clearly vary from time to time and place to place: contrast, in the United States, the 1920s with the 1930s, the 1950s with the 1960s. Whether one regards these shifts in the balance of political power and of public versus private initiative as large or small, important or unimportant, is a matter, fundamentally, of ideology. The liberal or conservative will be inclined to feel that there was an important difference between the New Deal of the 1930s and the "new era" of the 1920s, and possibly, even, between the administrations of Lyndon Johnson and Dwight Eisenhower; and will regard the accession to power of Richard Nixon with strong emotion. The radical—whether of the right or left—will tend to regard them all as minor variations on the same theme. The same will be true of their respective attitudes toward the efficacy and improvability of the institution of regulation.

The Choice among Imperfect Systems

One's assessment of regulation, then, is closely determined by one's attitude toward American capitalism itself. At one extreme there will be the Marxist critics, who regard it, when they give it any thought at all, as a logical development of monopoly capitalism itself—involving the accumulation of economic power in private hands, subject to nominal control by a government that is itself the servant of that same economic power. Regulation, like political democracy itself, is for them a sham because it leaves undisturbed the locus of power. It serves the purpose of creating and protecting monopoly, not of controlling it. The vagueness of the governing statutes, the "political" character of the administrative commissions, the ever-present threat of legislative intervention if regulation becomes too effective in serving the public interest, the tendency of agencies to become the captive agents of their industries—all are symptoms of that fundamental concentration of power in private hands.[4]

At another extreme are the representatives of what the economist would most readily recognize as "the Chicago school." For these eighteenth century liberals, regulation is unnecessary as far as doing good is concerned but very effective when it comes to doing harm. It is unnecessary because private monopoly power is always limited in size, scope, and duration: the self-interest of even monopolists, the possibilities of competitive entry into all industries if only the government would permit it, the presence of actual

[4] See, for example, Paul A. Baran and Paul M. Sweezy, *Monopoly Capitalism* (New York: Monthly   Review Press, 1966), 65–66.

competition even among the traditional public utilities all make regulation incapable of much improving matters and not worth its costs.[5] But in its association with the use of government power to protect monopoly, especially by restricting entry, regulation is, according to this view, productive of much more harm than good. Monopoly is enduringly dangerous only when conferred and protected by government.[6]

The fact that "right" and "left" converge in their dismissal of regulation does not mean that the truth necessarily lies in splitting the difference between them (a weak metaphor because on this particular point there is in a sense no difference.) It is of considerable interest that some of the intellectual predecessors of the present "Chicago school," equally dedicated to eighteenth century liberalism and the regime of competition and equally condemnatory of regulated monopoly, concluded that the proper solution instead was to socialize the natural monopolies. Their point was that the present institution embodies the worst of both possible worlds—monopoly without effective control, private enterprise without effective incentive or stimulus, governmental supervision without the possibility of effective initiative in the public interest.[7]

The virtual disappearance of this last proposal in the past twenty years is instructive. The experience with selective socialization during this period has demonstrated more clearly than could any *a priori* argument that there is no easy solution in changing the institutional form. The choice remains inescapably one between imperfect institutions. It is difficult to detect any significant improvement or even change in the functioning of the monopolistic industries that Western European governments have socialized. The comparison of American experience with TVA and, for instance, Consolidated Edison or the Pennsylvania Railroad, suggests the possible desirability of going in one direction; comparison of the Post Office with, say, AT&T suggests the opposite.[8] Socialization obviously does not eliminate the problems of monopoly, bureaucracy, inadequate incentives, and political interference.

In between are the great majority who regard the market economy much as they regard democracy—as a manifestly inefficient system that is better than any of the alternatives. To them there is available neither the comforting alternative of simple laissez-faire on the one hand or comprehensive socialization on the other. A politically free society will insist on exercising some control over its economic destiny. It is unwilling to rely on the beneficence or even long-run interest of private monopoly, particularly in the face of abundant historical evidence that the power is real and can be abused. To the pragmatist and twentieth-century liberal, competition is the preferred method for both restraining and prodding private management. To the

---

[5] See Stigler and Friedland, in Shepherd and Gies, *op. cit.*; and Posner, *op. cit.*

[6] See, for example, Friedman, *op. cit.*, Chapter 8; see also the echo of the same view in some of the early constitutional decisions concerning the power of government to regulate—notably the varying assessments of "monopoly of fact" and "monopoly of law," note 21, Chapter 1 of Vol. 1.

[7] See especially Henry Simons, *Economic Policy for A Free Society* (Chicago: Univ. of Chicago

Press, 1948), Chapter 2; Frank D. Graham, *Social Goals and Economic Institutions* (Princeton: Princeton Univ. Press, 1944), Chapter 10; and Friedrich A. Hayek, *The Road to Serfdom* (Chicago: Univ. of Chicago Press, 1944), 36–42.

[8] See the widely applauded and persuasive recommendations of the Report of the President's Commission on Postal Organization, *Towards Postal Excellence*, Washington, D.C., June 1968, which were in large measure enacted in 1970.

extent that it can be relied on, the institution itself, rather than either political or managerial *policy*, takes over responsibility for the public interest. All competition is imperfect; the preferred remedy is to try to diminish the imperfections. Even when highly imperfect, it can often be a valuable supplement to regulation. But to the extent that it is intolerably imperfect, the only acceptable alternative is regulation. And for the inescapable imperfections of regulation, the only available remedy is to try to make it work better. That is the modest underlying assumption of these volumes.

Selected Bibliography

Acton, Jan Paul, "An Evaluation of Economists' Influence on Electric Utility Rate Reforms," *American Economic Review, Papers and Proceedings* (May 1982), LXXII:114–119.

Acton, Jan Paul, Mitchell, Bridger, M., and Manning, Willard G., Jr., "Peak-Load Pricing of Electricity," in Peter N. Nemetz, ed., *Energy Policy: The Global Challenge*, Institute for Research on Public Policy, 1979, pp. 349–362.

Adams, Walter, ed., *The Structure of American Industry*, 7th ed., New York: The Macmillan Co., 1985.

Aigner, Dennis J., and Hirschberg, Joseph G., "Commercial/Industrial Customer Response to Time-of-Use Electricity Prices: Some Experimental Results," *Rand Journal of Economics* (Autumn 1985), XVI:341–355.

Albon, Robert P., and Kirby, Michael G., "Cost-Padding in Profit-Regulated Firms," *Economic Record* (March 1983), LIX:16–27.

Alexis, Marcus, "The Applied Theory of Regulation: Political Economy at the Interstate Commerce Commission," *Public Choice* (1982), XXXIX:5–27.

Amacher, Ryan, Higgins, Richard, Shughart, William, II, and Tollison, Robert, "The Behavior of Regulatory Activity over the Business Cycle: An Empirical Test," *Economic Inquiry* (January 1985), XXIII:7–19.

American Economic Association, *Readings in the Social Control of Industry*, Philadelphia: The Blakiston Co., 1942.

American Economic Association, *Readings in Price Theory*, Chicago: Richard D. Irwin, 1952.

American Economic Association, *Readings in Industrial Organization and Public Policy*, Homewood, IL: Richard D. Irwin, 1958.

American Telephone & Telegraph Co., *Vertical Integration in the Bell System: A Systems Approach to Technological and Economic Imperatives of the Telephone Network*, President's Task Force on Communications Policy, Staff Paper 5, Part 2, Appendix C, PB 184 418, June 1969.

Amit, Eilon, "On Quality and Price Regulation under Competition and under Monopoly," *Southern Economic Journal* (April 1981), XLVII:1056–1062.

Anderson, Douglas D., *Regulatory Policies and Electric Utilities*, Boston: Auburn House, 1981.

Atkinson, Scott E., and Halvorsen, Robert, "A Test of Relative and Absolute Price Efficiency in Regulated Utilities," *Review of Economics and Statistics* (Februrary 1980), LXII:81–88.

Atkinson, Scott E., and Halvorsen, Robert, "The Relative Efficiency of Public and Private Firms in a Regulated Environment: The Case of U.S. Electric Utilities," *Journal of Public Economics* (April 1986), XXIX:281–294.

Averch, Harvey, and Johnson, Leland, "Behavior of the Firm under Regulatory Constraint," *American Economic Review* (December 1962), LII:1052–1069.

Bailey, Elizabeth E., *Economic Theory of Regulatory Constraint*, Lexington, MA: Lexington Books, 1973.

Bailey, Elizabeth E., "Contestability and the Design of Regulatory and Antitrust Policy," *Amer-*

ican Economic Review, Papers and Proceedings (May 1981), LXXI:178–183.

Bailey, Elizabeth E., "Airline Deregulation in the United States: The Benefits Provided and the Lessons Learned," *International Journal of Transport Economics* (June 1985), XII:119–144.

Bailey, Elizabeth E., "Price and Productivity Change Following Deregulation: The U.S. Experience," *Economic Journal* (March 1986), XCVI:1–17.

Bailey, Elizabeth E., and Baumol, William J., "Deregulation and the Theory of Contestable Markets," *Yale Journal on Regulation* (1984), I:111–137.

Bailey, Elizabeth E., and Friedlaender, Ann F., "Market Structure and Multiproduct Industries," *Journal of Economic Literature* (September 1982), XX:1024–1048.

Bailey, Elizabeth E., and Panzar, John C., "The Contestability of Airline Markets During the Transition to Deregulation," *Law and Contemporary Problems* (Winter 1981), XLIV:125–145.

Bailey, Elizabeth E., Graham, David R., and Kaplan, David P., *Deregulating the Airlines*, Cambridge, MA: MIT Press, 1985.

Barber, Richard J., "Technological Change in American Transportation: The Role of Government Action," *Virginia Law Review* (June 1964), L:824–895.

Barnes, Irston Robert, *The Economics of Public Utility Regulation*, New York: F. S. Crofts & Co., 1942.

Bauer, John, and Gold, Nathaniel, *Public Utility Valuation for Purposes of Rate Control*, New York: The Macmillan Co., 1934.

Baumol, William J., "On the Proper Cost Tests for Natural Monopoly in a Multiproduct Industry," *American Economic Review* (December 1977), LXVII:809–822.

Baumol, William J., and Bradford, David F., "Optimal Departures from Marginal Cost Pricing," *American Economic Review* (June 1970), LX:265–283.

Baumol, William J., and Klevorick, Alvin K., "Input Choices and Rate-of-Return Regulation: An Overview of the Discussion," *Bell Journal of Economics and Management Science* (Autumn 1970), I:162–190.

Baumol, William J., and Willig, Robert D., "Fixed Costs, Sunk Costs, Entry Barriers, and Sustainability of Monopoly," *Quarterly Journal of Economics* (August 1981), XCVI:405–431.

Baumol, William J., Panzar, John C., and Willig, Robert D., *Contestable Markets and the Theory of Industry Structure*, San Diego: Harcourt Brace Jovanovich, 1982.

Baumol, William J., et al., "The Role of Cost in the Minimum Pricing of Railroad Services," *Journal of Business* (October 1962), XXXV:357–366.

Becker, Gilbert, "The Public Interest Hypothesis Revisited: A New Test of Peltzman's Theory of Regulation," *Public Choice* (1986), XLIX:223–234.

Behling, Burton Neubert, *Competition and Monopoly in Public Utility Industries*, Urbana: University of Illinois Press, 1938.

Beilock, Richard P., "Is Regulation Necessary for Value-of-Service Pricing?" *Rand Journal of Economics* (Spring 1985), XVI:93–102.

Beilock, Richard P., and Freeman, Jeffrey L., "Deregulated Motor Carrier Service to Small Communities," *Transportation Journal* (Summer 1984), XXIII:71–82.

Berg, Sanford V., and Tschirhart, John, *Natural Monopoly Regulation: Principles and Practice*, New York: Cambridge University Press, forthcoming.

Besen, Stanley M., and Crandall, Robert W., "The Deregulation of Cable Television," *Law and Contemporary Problems* (Winter 1981), XLIV:77–124.

Besen, Stanley M., and Woodbury, John R., "Regulation, Deregulation, and Antitrust in the Telecommunications Industry," *Antitrust Bulletin* (Spring 1983), XXVIII:39–68.

Binder, John J., "Measuring the Effects of Regulation with Stock Price Data," *Rand Journal of Economics* (Summer 1985), XVI:167–183.

Blair, Roger D., Kaserman, David L., and McClave, James T., "Motor Carrier Deregulation: The Florida Experiment," *Review of Economics and Statistics* (February 1986), LXVIII:159–164.

Boies, David, Jr., "Experiment in Mercantilism: Minimum Rate Regulation by the Interstate Commerce Commission," *Columbia Law Review* (April 1968), LXVIII:599–663.

Bonbright, James Cummings, *Principles of Public Utility Rates*, New York: Columbia University Press, 1961.

Bonbright, James Cummings, and Means, Gardiner C., *The Holding Company: Its Public Significance and Its Regulation*, 1st ed., New York and London: McGraw-Hill Book Co., 1932.

Boyer, Kenneth D., "Equalizing Discrimination and Cartel Pricing in Transport Rate Regulation," *Journal of Political Economy* (April 1981), LXXXIX:270–286.

Braeutigam, Ronald R., "Optimal Pricing with Intermodal Competition," *American Economic Review* (March 1979), LXIX:38–49.

Braeutigam, Ronald R., "An Analysis of Fully Distributed Cost Pricing in Regulated Industries," *Bell Journal of Economics* (Spring 1980), XI:182–196.

Braeutigam, Ronald R., and Hubbard, Robert G., "Natural Gas: The Regulatory Transition," in Leonard Weiss and M. Klass, eds., *Regulatory Reform: What Actually Happened*, Boston: Little, Brown and Co., 1986.

Braeutigam, Ronald R., and Noll, Roger G., "The Regulation of Surface Freight Transportation: The Welfare Effects Revisited," *Review of Economics and Statistics* (February 1984), LXVI:80–87.

Brennan, Michael J., and Schwartz, Eduardo S., "Regulation and Corporate Investment Policy," *Journal of Finance* (May 1982), XXXVII:289–300.

Brenner, Melvin A., Leet, James O., and Schott, Elihu, *Airline Deregulation*, Westport: Eno Foundation for Transportation, 1985.

Breyer, Stephen, *Regulation and Its Reform*, Cambridge, MA: Harvard University Press, 1982.

Brigham, Eugene F., "The Effects of Alternative Tax Depreciation Policies on Public Utility Rate Structures," *National Tax Journal* (June 1967), XX:204–218.

Broadman, Harry G., "Natural Gas Deregulation: The Need for Further Reform," *Journal of Policy Analysis and Management* (Spring 1986), V:496–516.

Brock, Gerard W., *The Telecommunications Industry: The Dynamics of Market Structure*, Cambridge, MA: Harvard University Press, 1981.

Brown, Harry Gunnison, *Principles of Commerce, A Study of the Mechanism, the Advantages, and the Transportation Costs of Foreign and Domestic Trade*, New York: The Macmillan Co., 1916.

Brown, Harry Gunnison, "Railroad Valuation and Rate Regulation," *Journal of Political Economy* (October 1925), XXXIII:505–530.

Brown, Harry Gunnison, "Railroad Valuation Again: A Reply," *Journal of Political Economy* (August 1926), XXXIV:500–508.

Brown, Stephen J., and Sibley, David S., *The Theory of Public Utility Pricing*, New York: Cambridge University Press, 1986.

Bryan, Robert F., and Lewis, Ben W., "The 'Earning Base' as a 'Rate Base,'" *Quarterly Journal of Economics* (February 1938), LII:335–345.

Burck, Gilbert, "A Plan to Save the Railroads," *Fortune* (August 1958), LVIII:82–86ff.

Call, Gregory D., and Keeler, Theodore E., "Airline Deregulation, Fares, and Market Behavior: Some Empirical Evidence," in Andrew F. Daugherty, ed., *Analytical Studies in Transport Economics*, New York: Cambridge University Press, 1985.

Callen, Jeffrey, Mathewson, Frank, G., and Mohring, Herbert, "The Benefits and Costs of Rate of Return Regulation," *American Economic Review* (June 1976), LXVI:290–297.

Capelli, Peter, "Competitive Pressures and Labor Relations in the Airline Industry," *Industrial Relations* (1985), XXIV:316–338.

Capron, William M., ed., *Technological Change in Regulated Industries*, Washington, DC: Brookings Institution, 1971.

Carron, Andrew S., and MacAvoy, Paul W., *The Decline of Service in the Regulated Industries*, Washington, DC: American Enterprise Institute, 1981.

Caves, Richard E., *Air Transport and Its Regulators: An Industry Study*, Cambridge, MA: Harvard University Press, 1962.

Chao, Hung-Po, "Peak Load Pricing and Capacity Planning with Demand and Supply Uncertainty," *Bell Journal of Economics* (Spring 1983), XIV:179–190.

Chapman, R., and Waverman, L., "Risk Aversion, Uncertain Demand and the Effects of a Regulatory Constraint," *Journal of Public Economics* (February 1979), XI:107–121.

Clark, John Maurice, *Studies in the Economics of Overhead Costs*, Chicago: The University of Chicago Press, 1923.

Clark, John Maurice, "Toward a Concept of Workable Competition," in American Economic Association, *Readings in the Social Control of Industry*, Philadelphia: The Blakiston Co., 1942.

Clark, John Maurice, *Competition as a Dynamic Process*, Washington, DC: The Brookings Institution, 1961.

Clemens, Eli Winston, "Price Discrimination in Decreasing Cost Industries," *American Economic Review* (December 1941), XXXI:794–802.

Clemens, Eli Winston, *Economics and Public Utilities*, New York: Appleton-Century-Crofts, Inc., 1950.

Coase, Ronald H., "The Federal Communications Commission," *Journal of Law and Economics* (October 1959), II:1–40.

Cole, Lawrence P., "A Note on Fully Distributed Cost Prices: An Analysis of Fully Distributed Cost Pricing in Regulated Industries," *Bell Journal of Economics* (Spring 1981), XII:329–334.

Conant, Michael, *Railroad Mergers and Abandon-ments*, Berkeley: University of California Press, 1964.

Costello, Kenneth W., "Electing Regulators: The Case of Public Utility Commissioners," *Yale Journal on Regulation* (1984), II:83–105.

Courville, Leon, "Regulation and Efficiency in the Electric Utility Industry," *Bell Journal of Economics* (Spring 1974), V:53–74.

Cramer, Curtis A., "The Rate Structure of the Natural Gas Pipeline Industry," *Applied Economics* (March 1975), VII:1–8.

Crew, Michael A., ed., *Problems in Public Utility Economics and Regulation*, Lexington, MA, and Toronto: Heath, Lexington Books, 1979.

Crew, Michael A., ed., *Issues in Public Utility Pricing and Regulation*, Lexington, MA: Lexington Books, 1980.

Crew, Michael A., ed., *Regulatory Reform and Public Utilities*, Lexington, MA: Lexington Books, 1982.

Crew, Michael A., and Kleindorfer, Paul R., *Public Utility Economics*, New York: St. Martin's Press, 1979.

Daggett, Stuart, *Principles of Inland Transportation*, rev. ed., New York: Harper & Bros., 1934.

Damus, Sylvester, "Ramsey Pricing by U.S. Railroads: Can It Exist?" *Journal of Transport Economics and Policy* (January 1984), XVIII:51–61.

Danielsen, Albert L., and Kamerschen, David R., eds., *Current Issues in Public Utility Economics: Essays in Honor of James C. Bonbright*, Lexington, MA: Lexington Books, 1983.

Danielsen, Albert L., and Kamerschen, David R., *Telecommunications in the Post-Divestiture Era*, Lexington, MA: Heath, 1986.

Daughety, Andrew F., "Regulation and Industrial Organization," *Journal of Political Economy* (October 1984), XCII:932–953.

Daughety, Andrew F., ed., *Analytical Studies in Transport Economics*, New York: Cambridge University Press, 1985.

Davidson, Ralph K., *Price Discrimination in Selling Gas and Electricity*, Baltimore: Johns Hopkins Press, 1955.

Dayan, David, "Behavior of the Firm under Regulatory Constraint: A Reexamination," *Industrial Organization Review* (1975), III(2):61–76.

de Chazeau, Melvin G., "The Nature of the 'Rate Base' in the Regulation of Public Utilities," *Quarterly Journal of Economics* (February 1937), LI:298–316.

de Chazeau, Melvin G., "Reply," *Quarterly Journal of Economics* (February 1938), LII:346–359.

de Chazeau, Melvin G., and Kahn, Alfred E., *Integration and Competition in the Petroleum Industry*, New Haven: Yale University Press, 1959.

Demsetz, Harold, "Why Regulate Utilities?" *Journal of Law and Economics* (April 1968), XI:55–65.

Derthick, Martha, and Quirk, Paul J., *The Politics of Deregulation*, Washington, DC: Brookings Institution, 1985.

Dirlam, Joel B., and Kahn, Alfred E., *Fair Competition: The Law and Economics of Antitrust Policy*, Ithaca, NY: Cornell University Press, 1954.

Dirlam, Joel B., and Kahn, Alfred E., "The Merits of Reserving the Cost-Savings from Domestic Communications Satellites for Support of Educational Television," *Yale Law Journal* (January 1968), LXXVII:494–519.

Douglas, George W., and Miller, James C., III, *Economic Regulation of Domestic Air Transport: Theory and Policy*, Washington, DC: Brookings Institution, 1974.

Doyle Report. See U. S. Senate, Committee on Interstate and Foreign Commerce.

Dym, Herbert, and Sussman, Robert M., "Antitrust and Electric Utility Regulation," *Antitrust Bulletin* (Spring 1983), XXVIII:69–99.

Eads, George C., "Competition in the Domestic Trunk Airline Industry: Too Much or Too Little?" in Almarin Phillips, ed., *Promoting Competition in Regulated Markets*, Washington, DC: Brookings Institution, 1975.

Eads, George C., "Airline Competitive Conduct in a Less Regulated Environment: Implications for Antitrust," *Antitrust Bulletin* (Spring 1983), XXVIII:159–184.

Ebrill, Liam P., and Slutsky, Steven M., "Production Efficiency and Optimal Pricing in Intermediate Good Regulated Industries," unpublished manuscript, Department of Economics, University of Florida, Gainesville, 1986.

Ebrill, Liam P., and Slutsky, Steven M., "Joint Pricing Rules for Intermediate and Final Good Regulated Industries," unpublished manuscript, Department of Economics, University of Florida, Gainesville, 1986.

Ebrill, Liam P., and Slutsky, Steven M., "Decentralized Decision-Making with Common Goals: The Altruist's Dilemma and Regulatory Pricing," unpublished manuscript, Department of Economics, University of Florida, Gainesville, 1987.

Evans, David S., ed., *Breaking Up Bell: Essays on Industrial Organization and Regulation*, New York: North-Holland, 1983.

Farmer, Richard N., "The Case for Unregulated Truck Transportation," *Journal of Farm Economics* (May 1964), XLVI:398–409.

Farris, Martin T., "Transportation Regulation and Economic Efficiency," *American Economic Review, Papers and Proceedings* (May 1969), LIX:244–250.

Faulhaber, Gerald R., "Cross-Subsidization: Pricing in Public Enterprises," *American Economic Review* (December 1975), LXV:966–977.

Federal Coordinator of Transportation. See U.S. House of Representatives, Committee on Interstate and Foreign Commerce.

Federal Energy Regulatory Commission, *Regulation of Natural Gas Pipelines after Partial Wellhead Decontrol*, FERC Order No. 436 [50F.R. 424087] (*issued October 9, 1985*), Final Rule and Statement of Policy, Dkt. No. RM85-1-000.

Feldstein, Martin S., "Equity and Efficiency in Public Sector Pricing: The Optimal Two-Part Tariff," *Quarterly Journal of Economics* (May 1972), LXXVI:175–187.

Fellner, William, "The Influence of Market Structure on Technological Progress," in American Economic Association, *Readings in Industrial Organization and Public Policy*, Homewood, IL: Richard D. Irwin, 1958, pp. 277–296.

Fowler, Mark S., Halprin, Albert, and Schlichting, James D., "Back to the Future: A Model for Telecommunications," *Federal Communications Law Journal* (August 1986), XXXVIII:145–200.

Frew, James R., "The Existence of Monopoly Profits in the Motor Carrier Industry," *Journal of Law and Economics* (October 1981), XXIV:289–315.

Friedlaender, Ann F., *The Dilemma of Freight Transport Regulation*, Washington, DC: Brookings Institution, 1969.

Friedlaender, Ann F., "The Social Costs of Regulating the Railroads," *American Economic Review, Papers and Proceedings* (May 1971), LXI:226–234.

Friedlaender, Ann F., and Spady, Richard H., *Freight Transport Regulation: Equity, Efficiency, and Competition in the Rail and Trucking Industries*, Cambridge, MA: MIT Press, 1981.

Friedman, Milton, *Capitalism and Freedom*, Chicago: University of Chicago Press, 1962.

Fromm, Gary, ed., *Studies in Public Regulation*, Cambridge, MA: MIT Press, 1981.

Fulda, Carl F., *Competition in the Regulated Industries: Transportation*, Boston: Little, Brown and Company, 1961.

Garfield, Paul J., and Lovejoy, Wallace F., *Public Utility Economics*, Englewood Cliffs, NJ: Prentice-Hall, Inc., 1964.

Gaskins, Darius W., Jr., and Voytko, James M., "Managing the Transition to Deregulation," *Law and Contemporary Problems* (Winter 1981), XLIV:9–32.

Gellman, Aaron J., "Surface Freight Transportation," in William M. Capron, ed., *Technological Change in Regulated Industries*, Washington, DC: Brookings Institution, 1971, pp. 166–196.

Gerber, Abraham, "Power Pools and Joint Plant Ownership," *Public Utilities Fortnightly* (September 12, 1969), LXXXII:23–31.

Gies, Thomas G., and Sichel, Werner, eds., *Deregulation: Appraisal before the Fact*, Division of Research, Graduate School of Business Administration, The University of Michigan, 1982.

Glaeser, Martin Gustav, *Public Utilities in American Capitalism*, New York: The Macmillan Co., 1957.

Goldberg, Victor P., "Regulation and Administered Contracts," *Bell Journal of Economics* (1976), VII:426–448.

Goldman, M. Barry, Leland, Hayne E., and Sibley, David S., "Optimal Nonuniform Pricing," *Review of Economic Studies* (April 1984), LI:305–319.

Gordon, Myron J., "Comparison of Historical Cost and General Price Level Adjusted Cost Rate Base Regulation," *Journal of Finance* (December 1977), XXXII:1501–1512.

Graham, David R., Kaplan, Daniel P., and Sibley, David S., "Efficiency and Competition in the Airline Industry," *Bell Journal of Economics* (Spring 1983), XIV:118–138.

Gray, Horace M., "The Passing of the Public Utility Concept," reprinted from *The Journal of Land and Public Utility Economics*, February 1940, in American Economic Association, *Readings in the Social Control of Industry*, Philadelphia: Blakiston, 1942, pp. 280–303.

Green, Mark J., and Nader, Ralph, "Economic Regulation vs. Competition: Uncle Sam the Monopoly Man," *Yale Law Journal* (April 1973), LXXXII:871–889.

Greenberg, Edward, "Wire Television and the FCC's Second Report and Order on CATV Systems," *Journal of Law and Economics* (October 1967), X:181–192.

Greenberg, Edward, "Television Station Profitability and FCC Regulatory Policy," *Journal of Industrial Economics* (July 1969), XVII:210–238.

Greenwald, Bruce C., "Rate Base Selection and the Structure of Regulation," *Rand Journal of Economics* (Spring 1984), XV:85–95.

Griffin, James M., "The Welfare Implications of Externalities and Price Elasticities for Telecommunications Pricing," *Review of Economics and Statistics* (February 1982), LXIV:59–66.

Grimm, Curtis M., and Smith, Ken G., "The Impact of Rail Regulatory Reform on Rates, Service Quality, and Management Performance: A Shipper Perspective," *Logistics and Transportation Review* (March 1986), XXII:57–68.

Harper, Donald V., "Consequences of Reform of Federal Economic Regulation of the Motor Trucking Industry," *Transportation Journal* (Summer 1985), XXIV:35–58.

Hayashi, Paul M., and Trapani, John M., "Rate of Return Regulation and the Regulated Firm's Choice of Capital-Labor Ratio: Further Empirical Evidence on the Averch-Johnson Model," *Southern Economic Journal* (January 1976), XLII:384–398.

Hayashi, Paul M., Sevier, Melanie, and Trapani, John M., "Pricing Efficiency under Rate-of-Return Regulation: Some Empirical Evidence for the Electric Utility Industry," *Southern Economic Journal* (January 1985), LI:776–792.

Hellman, Richard, *Government Competition in the Electric Utility Industry: A Theoretical and Empirical Study*, New York: Praeger Publishers, 1972.

Helmetag, Carl, Jr., "Railroad Mergers: The Accommodation of the Interstate Commerce Act and Antitrust Policies," *Virginia Law Review* (December 1968), LIV:1505–1530.

Hilton, George W., "The Basic Behavior of Regulatory Commissions," *American Economic Review, Papers and Proceedings* (May 1972), LXII:47–54.

Hilton, George W., "The Costs to the Economy of the Interstate Commerce Commission," Compendium of Papers Submitted to the Subcommittee on Priorities and Economy in Government of the Joint Economic Committee, *The Economics of Federal Subsidy Programs, Part 6—Transportation Studies*, 93rd Congress, 1 Sess., Washington, DC: Government Printing Office, 1973, pp. 707–733.

Hirschey, Mark, and Pappas, James L., "Regulatory and Life Cycle Influences on Managerial Incentives," *Southern Economic Journal* (October 1981), XLVIII:327–334.

Hirshleifer, Jack, "Peak Loads and Efficient Pricing: Comment," *Quarterly Journal of Economics* (August 1958), LXXII:451–462.

Hoover, Harwood, Jr., "Pricing Behavior of Deregulated Motor Common Carriers," *Transportation Journal* (Winter 1985), XXV:55–61.

Huber, Peter W., *The Geodesic Network*, Report on Competition in the Telephone Industry, Antitrust Division, U.S. Department of Justice, January 1987.

Hughes, William R., "Short-Run Efficiency and the Organization of the Electric Power Industry," *Quarterly Journal of Economics* (November 1962), LXXVI:592–612.

Ippolito, Richard A., and Masson, Robert T., "The Social Cost of Government Regulation of Milk," *Journal of Law and Economics* (April 1978), XXI:33–65.

Irwin, Manley R., and McKee, Robert E., "Vertical Integration and the Communication Equipment Industry: Alternatives for Public Policy," *Cornell Law Review* (February 1968), LII:446–472.

Jarrell, Gregg A., "The Demand for State Regulation of the Electric Utility Industry," *Journal of Law and Economics* (October 1978), XXI:269–295.

Johnson, Leland L., *The Future of Cable Television: Some Problems of Federal Regulation*, Santa Monica: The Rand Corporation, Memorandum RM-6199-FF, January 1970.

Johnson, Leland L., *Incentives to Improve Electric Utility Performance*, Santa Monica: The Rand Corporation, 1985.

Jones, William K., *Cases and Materials on Regulated Industries*, Brooklyn: Foundation Press, 1967.

Jordan, William A., *Airline Regulation in America: Effects and Imperfections*, Baltimore: Johns Hopkins University Press, 1970.

Jorgenson, Dale W., and Slesnick, Daniel T., "Efficiency versus Equity in Natural Gas Price Regulation," *Journal of Econometrics* (Oct./Nov. 1985), 301–316.

Joskow, Paul L., "Pricing Decisions of Regulated Firms: A Behavioral Approach," *Bell Journal of Economics* (Spring 1973), IV:118–140.

Joskow, Paul L., "Inflation and Environmental Concern: Structural Change in the Process of Public Utility Price Regulation," *Journal of Law and Economics* (October 1974), XVII:291–327.

Joskow, Paul L., "Contributions to the Theory of Marginal Cost Pricing," *Bell Journal of Economics* (Spring 1976), VII:197–206.

Joskow, Paul L., and Noll, Roger G., "Regulation in Theory and Practice: An Overview," in Gary Fromm, ed., *Studies in Public Regulation*, Cambridge, MA: MIT Press, 1981, pp. 1–65.

Joskow, Paul L., and Rose, Nancy L., "The Effects of Economic Regulation," MIT Working Paper #447, April 1987 (to be published in Richard Schmalensee and Robert Willig, eds., *The Handbook of Industrial Organization*, North Holland Press).

Joskow, Paul L., and Schmalensee, Richard L., *Markets for Power*, Cambridge, MA: MIT Press, 1983.

Joskow, Paul L., and Schmalensee, Richard L., "Incentive Regulation for Electric Utilities," *Yale Journal on Regulation* (Fall 1986), IV:1–49.

Kahn, Alfred E., "Economic Issues in Regulating the Field Price of Natural Gas," *American Economic Review, Papers and Proceedings* (May 1960), L:507–516.

Kahn, Alfred E., "The Tyranny of Small Decisions: Market Failures, Imperfections, and the Limits of Economics," *Kyklos* (January 1966), XIX:23–47.

Kahn, Alfred E., "Cartels and Trade Associations," *International Encyclopedia of the Social Sciences*, New York: The Macmillan Co. and the Free Press, 1968, II:320–325.

Kahn, Alfred E., "Deregulation of Air Transportation—Getting from Here to There," in *Regulating Business: The Search for an Optimum*, San Francisco: Institute for Contemporary Studies, 1978, pp. 37–63.

Kahn, Alfred E., "Applying Economics to an Imperfect World," the Richard T. Ely Lecture, *American Economic Review, Papers and Proceedings* (May 1979), LXIX:1–13.

Kahn, Alfred E., "The Passing of the Public Utility Concept: A Reprise," in Eli Noam, ed., *Telecommunications Today and Tomorrow*, New York: Harcourt Brace Jovanovich, 1983, pp. 3–37.

Kahn, Alfred E., "The Road to More Intelligent Telephone Pricing," *Yale Journal on Regulation* (1984), I:139–157.

Kahn, Alfred E., "The Macroeconomic Consequences of Sensible Microeconomic Policies," the First Distinguished Lecture on Economics in Government, Annual Meeting of the American Economic Association and Society of Government Economists, Dallas, December 28, 1984, White Plains, NY: National Economic Research Associates, 1985.

Kahn, Alfred E., and Shew, William B., "Current Issues in Telecommunications Regulation: Pricing," *Yale Journal on Regulation* (Spring 1987), IV:191–256.

Kaserman, David L., Kavanaugh, L. Roy, and Tepel, Richard C., "To Which Fiddle Does the Regulator Dance? Some Empirical Evidence," *Review of Industrial Organization* (Winter 1984), I:246–258.

Katz, Michael L., "Nonuniform Pricing, Output and Welfare under Monopoly," *Review of Economic Studies* (January 1983), L:37–56.

Keeler, James P., "Effects of Cost-Based Regulation of Prices," *International Journal of Transport Economics* (February 1985), XII:51–61.

Keeler, Theodore, "Airline Regulation and Market Performance," *Bell Journal of Economics* (Autumn 1972), III:399–424.

Keeler, Theodore, *Railroads, Freight and Public Policy*, Washington, DC: Brookings Institution, 1983.

Keeler, Theodore, "Theories of Regulation and the Deregulation Movement," *Public Choice* (1984), XLIV:103–145.

Kelman, Steven, "Regulation and Paternalism," *Public Policy* (Spring 1981), XXIX:219–254.

Keyes, Lucile Shepherd, *Federal Control of Entry into Air Transportation*, Cambridge, MA: Harvard University Press, 1951.

Keyes, Lucile Shepherd, "Reconsideration of Federal Control of Entry into Air Transportation," *Journal of Air Law and Commerce* (Spring 1955), XXII:192–202.

Kihlstrom, Richard E., and Levhari, David, "Quality, Regulation and Efficiency," *Kyklos* (1977), II:214–234.

Kolbe, A. Lawrence, and Read, James A., Jr., with Hall, George R., *The Cost of Capital: Estimating the Rate of Return for Public Utilities*, Cambridge, MA: MIT Press, 1984.

Koplin, Harry Thomas, "Natural Gas Act Certification Policy of the Federal Power Commission," unpublished Ph.D. dissertation, Cornell University, September 1952.

Landis, James M., *Report on Regulatory Agencies to the President-Elect*, U.S. Senate, Committee on the Judiciary, 86th Cong., 2d Sess., Committee Print, 1960.

Lansing, John B., *Transportation and Economic Policy*, New York: The Free Press, 1966.

Leland, Hayne E., "Regulation of Natural Monopolies and the Fair Rate of Return," *Bell Journal of Economics* (Spring 1974), V:3–15.

Leland, Hayne E., "Quacks, Lemons, and Licensing: A Theory of Minimum Quality Standards," *Journal of Political Economy* (December 1979), LXXXVII:1328–1346.

Leonard, William Norris, *Railroad Consolidation under the Transportation Act of 1920*, New York: Columbia University Press, 1946.

Leonard, William Norris, "Issues of Competition and Monopoly in Railroad Mergers," *Transportation Journal* (Summer 1964), III:5–15.

Levin, Richard C., "Railroad Rates, Profitability and Welfare under Deregulation," *Bell Journal of Economics* (Spring 1981), XII:1–62.

Levine, Michael E., "Is Regulation Necessary? California Air Transportation and National Regulatory Policy," *Yale Law Journal* (July 1965), LXXIV:1416–1447.

Levine, Michael E., "Landing Fees and the Airport Congestion Problem," *Journal of Law and Economics* (April 1969), XII:79–108.

Levine, Michael E., "Airline Competition in Deregulated Markets: Theory, Firm Strategy, and Public Policy," *Yale Journal on Regulation* (Spring 1987), IV:393–494.

Lewis, Lucinda M., and Reynolds, Robert J., "Appraising Alternatives to Regulation for Natural Monopolies," in Edward J. Mitchell, ed., *Oil Pipelines and Public Policy: Analysis of Proposals for Industry Reform and Reorganization*, AEI Symposia, No. 79E, Washington, DC: American Enterprise Institute 1979, pp. 135–140.

Lewis, William Arthur, *Overhead Costs: Some Essays in Economic Analysis*, New York: Rinehart, 1949.

Lipsey, R. G., and Lancaster, Kelvin, "The General Theory of Second Best," *Review of Economic Studies* (1956), XXIV:11–32.

Little, I. M. D., *A Critique of Welfare Economics*, 2nd ed., Oxford: Clarendon Press, 1957.

Little, I. M. D., *The Price of Fuel*, Oxford: Clarendon Press, 1957.

Littlechild, Stephen C., "Marginal Cost Pricing with Joint Costs," *Economic Journal* (June 1970), LXXX:323–335.

Littlechild, Stephen C., "Two-Part Tariffs and Consumption Externalities," *Bell Journal of Economics* (Autumn 1975), VI:661–670.

Littlechild, Stephen C., "The Structure of Telephone Tariffs," *International Journal of Industrial Organization* (December 1983), I:365–377.

Locklin, D. Philip, *Economics of Transportation*, 6th ed., Homewood, IL: Richard D. Irwin, 1966.

Lyon, Leverett S., and Abramson, Victor, *Government and Economic Life, Development and Current Issues of American Public Policy*, Washington, DC: The Brookings Institution, 1940.

MacAvoy, Paul W., *Price Formation in Natural Gas Fields: A Study of Competition, Monopsony, and Regulation*, New Haven: Yale University Press, 1962.

MacAvoy, Paul W., "The Regulation-Induced Shortage of Natural Gas," *Journal of Law and Economics* (April 1971), XIV:167–199.

MacAvoy, Paul W., and Robinson, Kenneth, "Winning By Losing: The AT&T Settlement," *Yale Journal on Regulation* (1983), I:1–42.

MacAvoy, Paul W., and Robinson, Kenneth, "Losing by Judicial Policymaking: The First Year of the AT&T Divestiture," *Yale Journal on Regulation* (1985), II:225–262.

MacAvoy, Paul W., and Sloss, James, *Regulation of Transport Innovation*, New York: Random House, 1967.

MacAvoy, Paul W., and Snow, John W., eds., *Regulation of Entry and Pricing in Truck Transportation*, Washington, DC: American Enterprise Institute, 1977.

Marshall, William J., Yawitz, Jess B., and Greenberg, Edward, "Optimal Regulation under Uncertainty," *Journal of Finance* (September 1981), XXXVI:909–921.

Mayo, John W., "Multiproduct Monopoly, Regulation, and Firm Costs," *Southern Economic Journal* (July 1984), LI:208–218.

McCraw, Thomas K., "Regulation in America: A Review Article," *Business History Review* (Summer 1975), XLIX:159–183.

McCraw, Thomas K., *Prophets of Regulation*, Cambridge, MA: Harvard University Press, 1984.

McFarland, Henry, "Ramsey Pricing of Inputs with Downstream Monopoly Power and Regulation: Implications for Railroad Rate Setting," *Journal of Transport Economics and Policy* (January 1986), 81–90.

Meek, Ronald L., "An Application of Marginal Cost Pricing: The 'Green Tariff' in Theory and Practice," *Journal of Industrial Economics* (July 1963), XI:217–236, and (November 1963), XII:45–63.

Meyer, John R., and Oster, Clinton V., Jr., et al., *Deregulation and the New Airline Entrepreneurs*, Cambridge, MA: MIT Press, 1984.

Meyer, John R., and Tye, William B., "The Regulatory Transition," *American Economic Review, Papers and Proceedings* (May 1985), LXXV:46–51.

Meyer, John R., Peck, Merton J., Stenason, John, and Zwick, Charles, *The Economics of Competition in the Transportation Industries*, Cambridge, MA: Harvard University Press, 1959.

Meyer John R., Wilson, Robert W., Baughcum, Marshall A., Burton, Ellen, and Caouette, L., *The Economics of Competition in the Telecommunications Industry*, Boston: Charles River, 1979.

Meyer, John R., Oster, Clinton, V., Jr., et al., *Deregulation and the Future of Intercity Passenger Travel*, Cambridge, MA: MIT Press, 1987.

Miklius, W., and DeLoch, D. B., "A Further Case for Unregulated Truck Transportation," *Journal of Farm Economics* (November 1965), XLVII:933–942.

Miller, Edythe S., "Rate Structure Reform: A Review of the Current Debate," *Journal of Economic Issues* (September 1978), XII:609–626.

Miller, Edythe S., "Back to the Future: A Comment," *Telematics* (March 1987), XL:1–2, 14–16.

Miller, Merton H., "Decreasing Average Cost and the Theory of Railroad Rates," *Southern Economic Journal* (April 1955), XXI:390–404.

Mirman, Leonard J., Tauman, Yair, and Zang, Israel, "Supportability, Sustainability, and Subsidy-Free Prices," *Rand Journal of Economics* (Spring 1985), XVI:114–126.

Mitchell, Bridger M., "Optimal Pricing of Local Telephone Service," *American Economic Review* (September 1978), LXVIII:517–537.

Mitchell, Edward J., ed., *Oil Pipelines and Public Policy: Analysis of Proposals for Industry Reform and Reorganization*, AEI Symposia, No. 79E, Washington, DC: American Enterprise Institute, 1979.

Moore, Thomas G., "The Effectiveness of Regulation of Electric Utility Prices," *Southern Economic Journal* (April 1970), XXXVI:365–375.

Moore, Thomas G., "Deregulating Surface Freight Transportation," in Almarin Phillips, ed., *Promoting Competition in Regulated Markets*, Washington, DC: Brookings Institution, 1975.

Moore, Thomas G., "Rail and Trucking Regulation," in Leonard Weiss and M. Klass, eds., *Regulatory Reform: What Actually Happened*, Boston: Little, Brown and Co., 1986.

Moore, Thomas G., "U.S. Airline Deregulation: Its Effects on Passengers, Capital, and Labor," *Journal of Law and Economics* (April 1986), XXIX:1–28.

Morgan, Charles Stillman, *Regulation and the Management of Public Utilities*, Boston and New York: Houghton Mifflin Co., 1923.

Morrison, Steven, and Winston, Clifford, *The Economic Effects of Airline Deregulation*, Washington, DC: Brookings Institution, 1986.

Morton, Walter A., "Rate of Return and the Value of Money in the Public Utilities," *Land Economics* (May 1952), XXVIII:91–131.

Myers, Stewart C., Kolbe, A. Lawrence, and Tye, William B., "Inflation and Rate of Return Regulation," *Research in Transportation Economics* (1985), II:83–119.

Navarro, Peter, "Public Utility Commission Regulation: Performance, Determinants, and Energy Policy Impacts," *Energy Journal* (April 1982), III:119–139.

Nelson, James C., *Railroad Transportation and Public Policy*, Washington: Brookings Institution, 1959.

Nelson, James R., *Marginal Cost Pricing in Practice*, Englewood Cliffs, NJ: Prentice-Hall, Inc., 1964.

Nelson, James R., "The Role of Competition in the Regulated Industries," *Antitrust Bulletin* (January–April 1966), XI:1–36.

Nelson, Randy A., "An Empirical Test of the Ramsey Theory and Stigler-Peltzman Theory of Public Utility Pricing," *Economic Inquiry* (April 1982), II:277–290.

Nicholson, Howard W., "Motor Carrier Costs and Minimum Rate Regulation," *Quarterly Journal of Economics* (February 1958), LXXII:139–152.

Noam, Eli M., ed., *Telecommunications Regulation Today and Tomorrow*, New York: Harcourt Brace Jovanovich, 1983.

Noll, Roger G., "'Let Them Make Toll Calls': A State Regulator's Lament," *American Economic Review, Papers and Proceedings* (May 1985), LXXV:52–56.

Noll, Roger G., *Regulatory Policy and the Social Sciences*, Berkeley: University of California Press, 1985.

Noll, Roger G., and Owen, Bruce M., *The Political Economy of Deregulation*, Washington, DC: American Enterprise Institute, 1983.

Noll, Roger G., Peck, Merton J., and McGowan, John J., *Economic Aspects of Television Regulation*, Washington, DC: Brookings Institution, 1973.

Note, "Federal Regulation of Trucking: The Emerging Critique," *Columbia Law Review* (March 1963), LXIII:460–514.

Olds, Leland, "The Economic Planning Function under Public Regulation," *American Economic Review, Papers and Proceedings* (May 1958), XLVIII:553–567.

Oster, Sharon, "Product Regulations: A Measure of the Benefits," *Journal of Industrial Economics* (June 1981), XXIX:395–411.

Owen, Bruce M., and Braeutigam, Ronald R., *The Regulation Game: Strategic Use of the Administrative Process*, Cambridge, MA: Ballinger, 1978.

Panzar, John C., "Regulation, Deregulation, and Economic Efficiency: The Case of the CAB," *American Economic Review, Papers and Proceedings* (May 1980), LXX:311–315.

Panzar, John C., and Willig, Robert D., "Free Entry and the Sustainability of Natural Monopoly," *Bell Journal of Economics* (Spring 1977), VIII:1–22.

Panzar, John C., and Willig, Robert D., "Economies of Scale in Multi-Output Production," *Quarterly Journal of Economics* (May 1981), XCI:481–493.

Panzar, John C., and Willig, Robert D., "Economies of Scope," *American Economic Review, Papers and Proceedings* (May 1981), LXXI:268–272.

Park, Rolla Edward, and Mitchell, Bridger M., *Optimal Peak-Load Pricing for Local Telephone Calls*, Santa Monica: The Rand Corporation, revised 1987.

Parmesano, Hethie, Bridgman, William, and Perry-Failor, Virginia, "The Role and Nature of Marginal and Avoided Costs in Ratemaking: A Survey," White Plains, NY: National Economic Research Associates, November 25, 1987.

Peck, Merton J., "Competitive Policy for Transportation?" in Almarin Phillips, ed., *Perspectives on Antitrust Policy*, Princeton: Princeton University Press, 1965, pp. 244–272.

Peltzman, Sam, "Toward a More General Theory of Regulation," *Journal of Law and Economics* (August 1976), XIX:211–240.

Perry, Charles F., *Deregulation and the Decline of the Unionized Trucking Industry*, Philadelphia: Industrial Research Unit, The Wharton School, University of Pennsylvania, 1986.

Pertschuk, Michael, *Revolt against Regulation: The Rise & Pause of the Consumer Movement*, Berkeley: University of California Press, 1987.

Petersen, H. Craig, "An Empirical Test of Regulatory Effects," *Bell Journal of Economics* (Spring 1975), VI:111–126.

Phillips, Almarin, "Air Transportation in the United States," in William M. Capron, ed., *Technological Change in Regulated Industries*, Washington, DC: Brookings Institution, 1971.

Phillips, Almarin, ed., *Promoting Competition in Regulated Markets*, Washington, DC: Brookings Institution, 1975.

Phillips, Almarin, and Williamson, Oliver E., eds., *Prices: Issues in Theory, Practice, and Public Policy*, Philadelphia: University of Pennsylvania Press, 1967.

Phillips, Charles F., Jr., *The Regulation of Public Utilities: Theory and Practice*, Arlington, VA: Public Utility Reports, Inc., 1984.

Posner, Richard A., "Natural Monopoly and Its Regulation," *Stanford Law Review* (February 1969), XXI:548–643.

Posner, Richard A., "Theories of Economic Regulation," *Bell Journal of Economics* (Autumn 1974), V:335–358.

Posner, Richard A., "The Social Costs of Monopoly and Regulation," *Journal of Political Economy* (August 1975), LXXXIII:807–827.

Posonby, G. T., "The Problem of the Peak, with Special Reference to Road Passenger Transport," *Economic Journal* (March 1958), LXVIII:74–88.

Presidential Advisory Committee on Transport Policy and Organization. See U.S. Presidential Advisory Committee on Transport Policy and Organization.

President's Task Force on Communications Policy. See U.S. President's Task Force on Communications Policy.

Priest, A. J. G., *Principles of Public Utility Regulation: Theory and Application*, Charlottesville, VA: Michie Co., 1969.

Pustay, Michael W., "Industry Inefficiency under Regulatory Surveillance," *Journal of Industrial Economics* (September 1978), XXVII:49–68.

Pustay, Michael W., "The Social Costs of Monopoly and Regulation: An Empirical Evaluation," *Southern Economic Journal* (October 1978), XLV:583–591.

Ramsey, Frank P., "A Contribution to the Theory of Taxation," *Economic Journal* (1927), XXXVII:47–61.

Ransmeier, Joseph Sirera, *The Tennessee Valley Authority, A Case Study in the Economics of Multiple Purpose Stream Planning*, Nashville: Vanderbilt University Press, 1942.

Rassenti, S. J., and Smith, Vernon L., "Electric Utility Deregulation," University of Arizona Department of Economics Working Paper 86-3, 1986.

Reynolds, Lloyd G., "Cutthroat Competition," *American Economic Review* (December 1940), XXX:736–747.

Richmond, Samuel B., *Regulation and Competition in Air Transportation*, New York: Columbia University Press, 1961.

Ritchie, Robert F., *Integration of Public Utility Holding Companies*, Ann Arbor: University of Michigan Press, 1954.

Robbins, Sidney, *The Securities Markets, Operations and Issues*, New York: The Free Press, 1966.

Rose, Joseph R., "Regulation of Intermodal Rate Competition in Transportation," *Michigan Law Review* (May 1971), LXIX:1011–1032.

Rose, Nancy L., "The Incidence of Regulatory Rents in the Motor Carrier Industry," *Rand Journal of Economics* (Autumn 1985), XVI:299–318.

Rozek, Richard P., "Competition as a Complement to Regulation," *Energy Journal* (July 1985), VI:79–90.

Ruggles, Nancy, "Recent Developments in the Theory of Marginal Cost Pricing," *Review of Economic Studies* (1949–50), XVII:107–126.

Scheidell, John M., "The Relevance of Demand Elasticity for Rate-of-Return Regulation," *Southern Economic Journal* (October 1976), XLIII:1088–1095.

Schmalensee, Richard, *The Control of Natural Monopolies*, Lexington, MA: Lexington Books, 1979.

Schmalensee, Richard, and Golub, Bennett W., "Estimating Effective Concentration in Deregulated Wholesale Electricity Markets," *Rand Journal of Economics* (Spring 1984), XV:12–26.

Schwartz, Herman, "Comsat, the Carriers, and the Earth Stations: Some Problems with 'Melding Variegated Interests,'" *Yale Law Journal* (January 1967), LXXVI:441–484.

Schwartz, Louis B., "Legal Restriction of Competition in the Regulated Industries: An Abdication of Judicial Responsibility," *Harvard Law Review* (January 1954), LXVII:436–475.

Scott, Frank A., Jr., "Assessing USA Postal Ratemaking: An Application of Ramsey Prices," *Journal of Industrial Economics* (March 1986), XXXIV:279–290.

Sharfman, I. L., *The Interstate Commerce Commission*, 4 vols., New York: The Commonwealth Fund, 1931–1937.

Sharkey, William W., *The Theory of Natural Monopoly*, New York: Cambridge University Press, 1982.

Sheahan, John B., "Competition versus Regulation as a Policy Aim for the Telephone Equipment Industry," unpublished Ph.D. dissertation, Harvard University, 1951.

Sheahan, John B., "Integration and Exclusion in the Telephone Equipment Industry," *Quarterly Journal of Economics* (May 1956), LXX:249–269.

Shepherd, William G., "Marginal-Cost Pricing in American Utilities," *Southern Economic Journal* (July 1966), XXXIII:58–70.

Shepherd, William G., "Regulatory Constraints and Public Utility Investment," *Land Economics* (August 1966), XLII:348–354.

Shepherd, William G., "The Competitive Margin in Communications," in William M. Capron, ed., *Technological Change in Regulated Industries*, Washington, DC: Brookings Institution, 1971, pp. 86–122.

Shepherd, William G., "Entry as a Substitute for Regulation," *American Economic Review, Papers and Proceedings* (May 1973), LXIII:98–105.

Shepherd, William G., *The Treatment of Market Power—Antitrust, Regulation, and Public Enterprise*, New York: Columbia University Press, 1975.

Shepherd, William G., "Competition and Sustainability," in Thomas G. Gies and Werner Sichel, eds., *Deregulation: Appraisal before the Fact*, Ann Arbor: Division of Research, Graduate School of Business Administration, The University of Michigan, 1982, pp. 13–34.

Shepherd, William G., and Gies, Thomas G., *Utility Regulation, New Directions in Theory and Policy*, New York: Random House, 1966.

Sherman, Roger, "Curing Regulatory Bias in U.S. Public Utilities," *Journal of Economics and Business* (Fall 1976), XXIX:1–9.

Sherman, Roger, "Ex Ante Rates of Return for Regulated Utilities," *Land Economics* (May 1977), LIII:172–184.

Sherman, Roger, "Financial Aspects of Rate-of-Return Regulation," *Southern Economic Journal* (October 1977), XLIV:240–248.

Sherman, Roger, "The Averch and Johnson Analysis of Public Utility Regulation Twenty Years Later," *Review of Industrial Organization* (1985), II:178–193.

Siegan, Bernard H., ed., *Regulation, Economics, and the Law*, Lexington, MA, and Toronto: Heath, Lexington Books, 1979.

Smidt, Seymour, "Flexible Pricing of Computer Services," *Management Science* (June 1968), XIV:B581–600.

Smith, Nelson Lee, "Federal Power Commission and Pipeline Markets: How Much Competition?" *Columbia Law Review* (April 1968), LXVIII:667–676.

Smith, V. Kerry, "The Implications of Regulation for Induced Technical Change," *Bell Journal of Economics* (Autumn 1974), V:623–632.

Spann, Robert M., "Rate of Return Regulation and Efficiency in Production: An Empirical Test of the Averch-Johnson Thesis," *Bell Journal of Economics* (Spring 1974), V:38–52.

Spann, Robert M., "The Regulatory Cobweb: Inflation, Deflation, Regulatory Lags and the Effects of Alternative Administrative Rules in Public Utilities," *Southern Economic Journal* (July 1976), XLIII:827–839.

Stalon, Charles G., "The Diminishing Role of Regulation in the Natural Gas Industry," *Energy Journal* (April 1986), VII:1–12.

Stein, Jerome L., and Borts, George H., "Behavior of the Firm under Regulatory Constraint," *American Economic Review* (December 1972), LXII:964–970.

Steiner, Peter O., "Peak Loads and Efficient Pricing," *Quarterly Journal of Economics* (November 1957), LXXI:585–610.

Steiner, Peter O., "The Legalization of American Society: Economic Regulation," *Michigan Law Review* (April 1983), LXXXI:1285–1306.

Stelzer, Irwin M., "Rate Base Regulation and Some Alternatives: An Appraisal," a paper presented at a Brookings Institution *Symposium on the Rate Base Approach to Regulation*, mimeo, June 1968, reproduced in *Public Utilities Fortnightly* (September 25, 1969), pp. 3–11.

Stelzer, Irwin M., "Electric Utilities in the Near-Term Future: A Hard Look," White Plains: National Economic Research Associates, August 7, 1985.

Stelzer, Irwin M., "The Electric Utility Industry circa 1985: A Quest for Managers," Keynote Address, 1985 Policy Issues Forum, The Aspen Institute, New York: Irwin M. Stelzer Associates, 1985.

Stevenson, Rodney E., "Institutional Objectives, Structural Barriers, and Deregulation in the Electric Utility Industry," *Journal of Economic Issues* (June 1983), XVII:443–452.

Stigler, George J., "The Process of Economic Regulation," *Antitrust Bulletin* (Spring 1972), XVII:207–235.

Stigler, George J., "The Theory of Economic Regulation," *Bell Journal of Economics and Management Science* (Spring 1971), II:3–21.

Stoll, Hans R., "Revolution in the Regulation of Securities Markets: An Examination of the Effects of Increased Competition," in Leonard W. Weiss and Michael W. Klass, eds., *Case Studies in Regulation: Revolution and Reform*, Boston: Little, Brown and Co., 1981.

Straszheim, Mahlon R., *The International Airline Industry*, Washington, DC: Brookings Institution, 1969.

Streiter, Sally Hunt, "Trending the Rate Base," *Public Utilities Fortnightly* (May 13, 1982), CIV (No. 12):40–47.

Streiter, Sally Hunt, "Indexed Bonds and Other Issues," *Public Utilities Fortnightly* (June 10, 1982), CIV (No. 12):40–47.

Streiter, Sally Hunt, "Avoiding the 'Money-Saving' Rate Increase," *Public Utilities Fortnightly* (June 24, 1982), CIV (No. 13):18–22.

Sweeney, George, "Adoption of Cost-Saving Innovations by a Regulated Firm," *American Economic Review* (June 1981), LXXI:437–447.

Sweeney, George, "Welfare Implications of Fully Distributed Cost Pricing Applied to Partially Regulated Firms," *Bell Journal of Economics* (Autumn 1982), XIII:525–533.

Swidler, Joseph C., "The Challenge to State Regulation Agencies: The Experience of New York State," *Annals of the American Academy of Political and Social Science* (November 1973), CDX:106–119.

Taggart, Robert A., Jr., "Effects of Regulation on Utility Financing: Theory and Evidence," *Journal of Industrial Economics* (March 1985), XXXIII:257–276.

Takayama, Akira, "Behavior of the Firm under Regulatory Constraint," *American Economic Review* (June 1969), LIX:255–260.

Transportation Economics. See Universities-National Bureau Committee for Economic Research.

Trebing, Harry M., "Toward an Incentive System of Regulation," *Public Utilities Fortnightly* (July 18, 1963), LXXII:22–37.

Trebing, Harry M., ed., *Performance under Regulation*, East Lansing: Institute of Public Utilities, Michigan State University, 1968.

Trebing, Harry M., ed., *Issues in Public Utility Regulation: Proceedings of the Institute of Public Utilities Tenth Annual Conference*, MSU Public Utilities Papers, East Lansing: Michigan State University, Graduate School of Business Administration, Division of Research, 1979.

Trebing, Harry M., "Public Utility Regulation: A Case Study in the Debate over Effectiveness of Economic Regulation," *Journal of Economic Issues* (March 1984), XVIII:223–250.

Trebing, Harry M., "Apologetics of Deregulation in Energy and Telecommunications: An Institutionalist Assessment," *Journal of Economic Issues* (September 1986), XX:613–632.

Trebing, Harry M., and Howard, R. Hayden, *Rate of Return under Regulation, New Directions and Perspectives*, East Lansing: Institute of Public Utilities, Michigan State University, 1969.

Troxel, Emery, *Economics of Public Utilities*, New York: Rinehart and Co., 1947.

Turvey, Ralph, *Optimal Pricing and Investment in Electricity Supply, An Essay in Applied Welfare Economics*, London: George Allen and Unwin, Ltd., 1968.

Turvey, Ralph, "Peak-Load Pricing," *Journal of Political Economy* (February 1968), LXXVI:101–113.

Tussing, Arlon R., and Barlow, Connie C., "The Decline and Fall of Regulation in the Natural Gas Industry," *Energy Journal* (October 1982), III:103–122.

Twentieth Century Fund, *Electric Power and Government Policy*, New York: Twentieth Century Fund, 1948.

Tye, William B., "Ironies to the Application of the Inverse Elasticity Rule to the Pricing of U.S.

Postal Services," *Logistics and Transportation Review* (October 1983), XIX:245–260.

Tye, William B., and Leonard, Herman, "On the Problems of Applying Ramsey Pricing to the Railroad Industry with Uncertain Demand Elasticities," *Transportation Research* (1983), XVII(A)(6):439–450.

Tye, William B., "Problems of Applying Stand-Alone Costs as an Indicator of Market Dominance and Rail Rate Reasonableness," *International Journal of Transport Economics* (February 1985), XII:7–30.

Tye, William B., "Stand-Alone Costs as an Indicatior of Market Dominance and Rate Reasonableness under the Staggers Rail Act," *International Journal of Transport Economics* (February 1986), XIII:21–40.

Tye, William B., *Encouraging Cooperation among Competitors: The Case of Motor Carrier Deregulation and Collective Ratemaking*, Westport: Quorum Books, 1987.

Tye, William B., "Pricing Rail Competitive Access in the Transition to Deregulation with the Revenue/Variable Cost Test," *The Antitrust Bulletin* (Spring 1987), XXXII:101–135.

Tyndall, David G., "The Relative Merits of Average Cost Pricing, Marginal Cost Pricing and Price Discrimination," *Quarterly Journal of Economics* (August 1951), LXV:342–372.

Universities-National Bureau Committee for Economic Research, *Transportation Economics*, a Conference of the Universities-National Bureau Committee for Economic Research, New York: National Bureau of Economic Research, 1965.

U.S. Federal Coordinator of Transportation. See U.S. House of Representatives, Committee on Interstate and Foreign Commerce.

U.S. Federal Power Commission, *National Power Survey*, Washington, 1964.

U.S. House of Representatives, Committee on Interstate and Foreign Commerce, 74th Cong., 1st Sess., *Report of the Federal Coordinator of Transportation, 1934*, House Document No. 89, Washington, January 30, 1935.

U.S. Interstate Commerce Commission, *Investigation of Costs of Intercity Rail Passenger Service*, Washington, July 1969.

U.S. Presidential Advisory Committee on Transport Policy and Organization, *Revision of Federal Transportation Policy*, reproduced in U.S. Department of Commerce, *Modern Transportation Policy*, documents relating to the report of the Presidential Advisory Committee on Transport Policy and Organization and Implementing Legislation, Washington, 1956.

U.S. President's Task Force on Communications Policy, *Final Report*, Washington, December 7, 1968.

U.S. President's Task Force on Communications Policy, *The Domestic Telecommunications Carrier Industry*, Staff Paper 5, Part 1, Washington, June 1969.

U.S. Senate, Committee on Interstate and Foreign Commerce, 87th Cong., 1st Sess., *National Transportation Policy*, Preliminary Draft of a Report prepared by the Special Study Group on Transportation Policies in the United States (John P. Doyle, Staff Director), Washington, January 1961.

U.S. Senate, Select Committee on Small Business, 84th Cong., 2nd Sess., *Competition, Regulation and the Public Interest in the Motor Carrier Industry*, Senate Report No. 1693, Washington, March 19, 1956.

Vickrey, William S., "Some Objections to Marginal Cost-Pricing," *Journal of Political Economy* (June 1948), LVI:218–238.

Vickrey, William S., "Some Implications of Marginal Cost Pricing for Public Utilities," *American Economic Review, Papers and Proceedings* (May 1955), XLV:605–620.

Vickrey, William S., "Pricing in Urban and Suburban Transport," *American Economic Review, Papers and Proceedings* (May 1963), LIII:452–465.

Vickrey, William S., "Pricing Policies," in *International Encyclopedia of the Social Sciences*, New York: The Macmillan Co. and The Free Press, 1968, XII:457–463.

Wallace, Donald A., "Joint and Overhead Cost and Railway Rate Policy," *Quarterly Journal of Economics* (August 1934), XLVIII:583–619.

Waverman, Leonard, "Peak-Load Pricing under Regulatory Constraint: A Proof of Inefficiency," *Journal of Political Economy* (June 1975), LXXXIII:645–654.

Waverman, Leonard, "The Regulation of Intercity Telecommunications," in Almarin Phillips, ed., *Promoting Competition in Regulated Markets*, Washington, DC: Brookings Institution, 1975.

Weisbrod, Burton A., "Collective-Consumption Services of Individual-Consumption Goods," *Quarterly Journal of Economics* (August 1964), LXXVIII:471–477.

Weiss, Leonard W., and Klass, Michael W., eds., *Regulatory Reform: What Actually Happened*, Boston: Little, Brown and Co., 1986.

Wellisz, Stanislaw H., "Regulation of Natural Gas Pipeline Companies: An Economic Analysis," *Journal of Political Economy* (February 1963), LXXI:30–43.

Wenders, John, *The Economics of Telecommunications*, Cambridge, MA: Ballinger, 1987.

Westfield, Fred M., "Regulation and Conspiracy," *American Economic Review* (1965), LV:424–443.

Westfield, Fred M., "Methodology of Evaluating Economic Regulation," *American Economic Review, Papers and Proceedings* (May 1971), LXI:211–217.

Wilcox, Clair, *Public Policies Toward Business*, 3rd ed., Homewood, IL: Richard D. Irwin, 1966.

Williams, Ernest, Jr., *The Regulation of Rail-Motor Rate Competition*, New York: Harper & Bros., 1958.

Williamson, Oliver E., "Franchise Bidding for Natural Monopolies: In General and with Respect to CATV," *Bell Journal of Economics* (Spring 1976), VII:73–104.

Willig, Robert D., "Pareto-Superior Nonlinear Outlay Schedules," *Bell Journal of Economics* (Spring 1978), IX:56–69.

Wilson, George W., "Effects of Value-of-Service Pricing upon Motor Common Carriers," *Journal of Political Economy* (August 1955), LXIII:337–344.

Wilson, George W., "The Nature of Competition in the Motor Transport Industry," *Land Economics* (November 1960), XXXVI:387–391.

Wilson, George W., *Essays on Some Unsettled Questions in the Economics of Transportation*, Bloomington: Graduate School of Business, Indiana University, 1962.

Wilson, George W., "The Effect of Rate Regulation on Resource Allocation in Transportation," *American Economic Review, Papers and Proceedings* (May 1964), LIV:160–171.

Wilson, George W., *Economic Analysis of Intercity Freight Transportation*, Bloomington: Indiana University Press, 1980.

Wilson, James Q., ed., *The Politics of Regulation*, New York: Basic Books, 1980.

Wilson, John William, "Residential and Industrial Demand for Electricity," unpublished Ph.D. dissertation, Cornell University, 1969.

Winter, Ralph K., Jr., "Economic Regulation vs. Competition: Ralph Nader and Creeping Capitalism," *Yale Law Journal* (April 1973), LXXXII:890–902.

Woodbury, John R., Besen, Stanley M., and Fournier, Gary M., "The Determinants of Network Television Program Prices: Implicit Contracts, Regulation, and Bargaining Power," *Bell Journal of Economics* (Autumn 1983), XIV:351–365.

Zajac, Edward E., *Fairness or Efficiency: An Introduction to Public Utility Pricing*, Cambridge, MA: Ballinger, 1979.

Index

VOLUMES I and II